Make the Grade.
Your Atomic Dog Online Edition.

The Atomic Dog Online Edition includes proven study tools that expand and enhance key concepts in your text. Reinforce and review the information you absolutely 'need to know' with features like:

- **Review Quizzes**
- Key term Assessments
- Interactive Animations and Simulations
- Notes and Information from Your Instructor
- Pop-up Glossary Terms
- A Full Text Search Engine

Ensure that you 'make the grade'. Follow your lectures, complete assignments, and take advantage of all your available study resources like the Atomic Dog Online Edition.

How to Access Your Online Edition

- **If you purchased this text directly from Atomic Dog ....**
  Visit atomicdog.com and enter your email address and password in the login box at the top-right corner of the page.

- **If you purchased this text NEW from another source....**
  Visit our Students' Page on atomicdog.com and enter the **activation key located below** to register and access your Online Edition.

- **If you purchased this text USED from another source....**
  Using the Book Activation key below you can access the Online Edition at a discounted rate. Visit our Students' Page on atomicdog.com and enter the **Book Activation Key in** the field provided to register and gain access to the Online Edition.

Be sure to download our ***How to Use Your Online Edition*** guide located on atomicdog.com to learn about additional features!

This key activates your online edition. Visit atomicdog.com to enter your Book Activation Key and start accessing your online resources. For more information, give us a call at (800) 310-5661 or send us an email at support@atomicdog.com

200Q7NPLU

PKG

*Some online Editions do not contain all features.

MODERN MARKETING RESEARCH

Concepts, Methods and Cases

FRED M. FEINBERG, THOMAS C. KINNEAR &
JAMES R. TAYLOR

Concepts, Methods and Cases

FRED M. FEINBERG, THOMAS C. KINNEAR &
JAMES R. TAYLOR

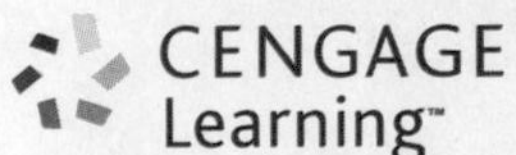

Modern Marketing Research: Concepts, Methods and Cases

Fred M. Feinberg, Thomas C. Kinnear and James R. Taylor

Developmental Editor: Sarah Blasco

Custom Production Editorial Manager: Kim Fry

Technology Project Manager: David Sterkin

Permissions Specialist: Todd Osborne

Custom Production Editor: K.A. Espy

Manufacturing Manager: Donna M. Brown

Production Manager: Robin Richie

Project Coordinator: Katie Nussbaum

Compositor: Cadmus/KGL

Library of Congress Control Number: 2007926708

BOOK ISBN-13: 978-0-759-39171-8
BOOK ISBN-10: 0-759-39171-8

PKG ISBN 13: 978-1-426-62560-2
PKG ISBN 10: 1-426-62560-X

Cengage Learning
5191 Natorp Blvd.
Mason, OH 45040
USA

Cengage Learning products are represented in Canada by Nelson Education, Ltd.

Printed in the United States of America
1 2 3 4 5 6 7 12 11 10 09

BRIEF CONTENTS

CONTENTS

PREFACE

To live, we consume. Every human being, especially those of us living in complex, market economies, is faced daily with a bewildering variety of choices. We live in a vastly interdependent, constructed environment, filled with objects and fueled by services that were deliberately produced and then selected over other available options. To get by, we continually reassess our preferences, examine opportunities, predict what the future may hold, and pick from arrays of possibilities. In other words, we are each performing research—specifically, marketing research—on our own behalf, more or less constantly.

In this book, we will introduce and study the major *formal* methods of marketing research. The book's chief "official" purpose is to acquaint budding managers with the vast array of useful techniques built up by marketing research professionals and academic researchers over the past 50 or more years. This knowledge is indispensable in a world that is rapidly diversifying, globalizing, customizing, and relentlessly evolving. But the book has a secondary purpose: to convince you that you already have a great deal of personal knowledge of marketing research, because you have been doing it yourself all your life in one form or another. Learning to harness your own experiences and supplement them with the rigorous, codified methods of marketing research produces a hybrid far more powerful than either taken on its own. In a real sense, facilitating that synthesis is our prime objective.

Persuading business students that marketing research is important is a fine example of preaching to the choir. Yet it bears repeating that *all* major business organizations utilize marketing research methods; for some, it is all they do. Vanishingly rare is the firm that makes just one product, never changes it, and keeps selling it to the same clientele. Because business practices, technologies, distribution methods, global trends, local economies, and whole societies are always progressing (or at least changing), firms must *plan*. And planning requires not only data—raw numbers—but bankable information. The chief activity of marketing researchers is discerning what information is truly needed, then devising an unbiased, cost-effective method to collect and analyze the data that will reveal that information. The process of carrying out marketing research is complex and task-dependent, but can be mastered through principles, examples, and practice. And this is precisely the process you will encounter, and hopefully even learn to love, as you make your way through this book.

We presume that the reader has a good working knowledge of general marketing principles. And so we can meaningfully discuss the *competitive positioning* of this book itself. There are dozens of marketing research texts vying for your attention, and you may wonder why you should select this one (even if it was chosen for you by your instructor) as your guide. The title of the book, "Modern Marketing Research: Concepts, Methods and Cases," is not merely an ad slogan, but an accurate descriptor of the book's pedagogical approach. Take the first word, "modern." Like the world they hope to illuminate, marketing research methods are always evolving, and the book emphasizes not only the timeless, Platonic principles of the discipline, but also those that have emerged only recently yet are quickly becoming mainstays of managerial practice. The breakdown into "concepts, methods and cases" is also deliberate: throughout, we have attempted to provide clear, detailed *conceptual* explanations of how various techniques perform their magic, the *why* behind the *what*, preceding and alongside the methods themselves. The many cases in the book highlight how these techniques were put into play by actual organizations, with you the reader as arbiter of their appropriateness and utility.

There may have been a time when managers said, metaphorically, "build it and they will come," or envisioned a world beating a path to their better mousetrap. That day, if it existed, is long gone, and is receding ever further into a mythical past. Modern organizations need to do their homework, know their customer, adopt the latest technology, and get the lay of the competitive landscape. All these informational goals require a deep appreciation of the power and flexibility of marketing research, a trend that will only expand over the coming decades.

Organization of the Book

Modern Marketing Research: Concepts, Methods and Cases is organized into three major parts, comprising 12 chapters, that track the steps managers would follow in a typical project. Broadly speaking, the parts correspond to these topics: What Marketing Research Is All About, Procuring Data, and Making Your Data Speak. The first of these explains why we conduct marketing research at all, the processes by which we do so, and research designs that work well. The second discusses all the ways one can obtain data, and best practices for carrying out experiments, field research, and interacting with commercial data providers. The third part is a detailed tour of all the major statistical methods used to illuminate the underlying structure of, and important managerial messages embedded in, complex modern marketing data.

Each chapter was written to serve as a rung in an integrated approach to designing effective marketing research projects and analyzing the data they generate. There are many byways and alleys off this grand road, collectively allowing a fuller understanding of various aspects of marketing research practice, and we hope the student will take the time to explore them. Chapters 1 and 2 provide an overview of marketing research and the sorts of problems it can fruitfully address. Chapters 3 and 4 introduce some of the data sources and types with which researchers need to gain familiarity, while Chapters 5 and 6 discuss how to set up designs or experiments to collect useful data. Chapter 7 delves deeply into what many people believe (erroneously!) is *all* marketing researchers do: design questions and surveys. Chapter 8 begins our full treatment of statistical methods for marketing research with the elements of sampling, and Chapter 9 surveys the most common univariate and bivariate (one- and two-variable) methods. The last three chapters form one of the unique advantages of this text: comprehensive, comprehensible coverage of all the "many-variable" (multivariate) methods that form the core of modern marketing research practice. A number of these were developed only recently, and Chapter 12 covers several truly cutting-edge methods, like Bayesian estimation and sample selection models, that help overcome limitations of standard methods like regression and that are finding wide application in industry.

Supplementing every aspect of the book's core material is the full suite of cases that showcase marketing research in action: real companies, real data, real decisions. They cover a broad gamut of classic and uniquely contemporary facets of marketing practice and allow students to gain a feel for how various techniques are put to use, for better or worse, by actual firms. The cases offer a rare opportunity to engage in Monday-morning quarterbacking: what would *you* have done differently if you were in the managers' shoes, and why do you think it would have worked out better? Many of the cases invite the use of analytical tools to supplement decision making, including the sophisticated methods introduced in the final part of the book.

Features of the Book

There are certain attributes of this book that distinguish it from others covering the same ground. These include:

Writing Style and Design

- This text is designed to be easily read and digested. Great care has been taken to explain technical issues in a step-by-step fashion. Copious graphs and illustrations lend a visual guide to developing marketing research projects and running complex analyses on one's own.
- Marketing research is presented as a managerially and decision-making-oriented subject, and in a pragmatic, "here's how to do it" fashion.
- Advanced quantitative procedures are dealt with in great detail. Although not a text on quantitative techniques in marketing research per se, it provides broad coverage of the most common research methods, as well as a number of truly state-of-the-art techniques.

Modular Construction

This text has been designed for flexibility of use; the more complex chapters and appendixes may be sidestepped without disrupting the flow of the book.

Special Boxed Features

- **Marketing Research Focus:** Numerous "real-world" marketing research issues and their resolutions are presented, along with applications in areas with wider social impact, such as political polling and judicial decision-making.

- **Research Innovations and Technologies:** Discusses recent advances in marketing research practice, driven by technical breakthroughs and advances in methodology.
- **International Issues:** Provides substantial insights and examples on international marketing research.
- **Special Sections and Special Expert Features:** Timely articles, written by guest authors especially for this text, on the areas they helped pioneer.

End-of-Chapter Material

- Each chapter concludes with a Summary, which highlights and reinforces key chapter concepts.
- Questions and/or problems are provided for student discussion, plus a minicase.
- Ten multiple-choice questions are provided at the end of each chapter and act as quizzes in the Online Edition. The student can take the quiz as many times as he or she likes, with only the initial results being reported to the instructor.
- Key terms are identified throughout the text in bold, with definitions in the margins in the print version, pop-up definitions for the online version, and full glossaries for both.
- The student is provided with a Web Exercise for every chapter, which can be found in the chapter Study Guide for the Online Edition of the text. The Web exercises direct the student to a Web site, applicable to chapter content, and guide them through activities or questions developed around chapter material and the respective web page.

Cases

Throughout the book, the thrust is pragmatic, showing what it is like to actually *do* a marketing research project, and consistently focusing on providing the decision maker with relevant information. This approach is aided by over three dozen full-length real-world cases, many accompanied by data, actual questionnaires, and detailed analyses. These cases allow the student to apply knowledge gained in the part in which they appear, and they extend well beyond the scope of the basic material.

Data Sets

The "raw" data (in nicely processed form, suitable for SPSS and Excel) are provided for all basic statistical analyses in the book proper, for complex techniques like choice-based conjoint, as well as for several cases that illustrate the use of advanced methods.

Special Expert Features

An exciting and unique feature of the text lies in its many expert features, written especially to complement the chapter material that they accompany. These include features by:

- Barbara Everitt Bryant, Director of the U.S. Census, on "The U.S. Census Bureau: Census of Population and Housing, Economic Census and Indicators, and Household Surveys," covering the history, methodology, accuracy, and future of the largest and most complex data-gathering activity in the world.
- Norbert Schwarz, one of the world's premier researchers on survey design methodology, and Andy Peytchev on "Self-Reports in Marketing Research: How the Questions Shape the Answers," a distillation of his multidecade research into how phrasing and placement of survey questions and suggested answers can strongly bias responses, as well as "best practices."
- GM Marketing Research on how they run their extensive conjoint analysis project.
- Ray Pettit, author of *Market Research in the Internet Age* and *Learning From Winners*, on "The Current State of Online Market Research: An Applied Perspective."
- The Survey Research Team at Qualtrics.com, on a tour of their state-of-the-art online survey system and the future evolution of the practice.

Other features include those by industry and academic leaders on such topics as neuromarketing, industrial marketing research, the future of marketing research and engineering, controlling total survey error, and more.

Applied Approach

- The text is deeply concerned with the *use* of marketing research techniques and with the role of managers and researchers in the research process.
- It deals with the technical aspects of marketing research in a manner that allows the reader to apply these procedures to real applications.
- It presents extensive materials on techniques from a user-oriented perspective, including regression (linear, binary, ordinal, multinomial logistic), factor analysis, multidimensional scaling, cluster and latent class analyses, conjoint analysis, and powerful, recently-developed topics such as sample selection bias, heterogeneity, Bayesian estimation, and hierarchical models.
- It conveys numerous examples of marketing research "in action," including special features from those on the leading edge of research technique development and deployment.

Online and in Print

Modern Marketing Research: Concepts, Methods and Cases is available online as well as in print. The online version demonstrates how the interactive media components of the text enhance presentation and understanding. For example:

- Animated illustrations help clarify concepts and bring them to life.
- Clickable glossary terms provide immediate definitions of key concepts.
- References and footnotes "pop up" with a click.
- Highlighting capabilities allow students to emphasize main ideas. They can also add personal notes in the margin.
- The search function allows students to quickly locate discussions of specific topics throughout the text.
- An interactive study guide at the end of each chapter provides tools for learning, such as interactive key-term matching and the ability to review customized content in one place.

Students may choose to use just the online version of the text or both the online and print versions together. This gives them the flexibility to choose which combination or resources works best for them. To assist those who use the online and print version together, the primary heads and subheads in each chapter are numbered the same. For example, the first primary head in Chapter 1 is labeled 1-1, the second primary head in this chapter is labeled 1-2, and so on. The subheads build from the designation of their corresponding primary head: 1-1a, 1-1b, etc. This numbering system is designed to make moving between the online and print versions as seamless as possible.

Finally, next to a number of figures and exhibits in the print version of the text, you will see an icon similar to the icon in the margin. This icon indicates that this figure in the online edition is interactive in a way that applies, illustrates, or reinforces the concept.

Supplemental Materials

Atomic Dog is pleased to offer a robust suite of supplemental materials for instructors using its textbooks. These ancillaries include a Test Bank, PowerPoint® slides, and Instructor's Manual.

PowerPoint® Presentations

A full set of PowerPoint® slides is available for this text. This is designed to provide instructors with comprehensive visual aids for each chapter in the book. These slides include outlines of each chapter, highlighting important terms, concepts, and discussion points.

ExamView

The Test Bank for this book includes hundreds of questions in a wide range of difficulty levels for each chapter. The Test Bank offers not only the correct answer for each question, but also a rationale or explanation for the correct answer and a reference—the location in the chapter where the materials addressing the question can be found. This Test Bank comes with ExamViewPro® software for easily creating customized or multiple versions of a test, and includes the option of editing or adding to the existing question bank.

Instructor's Manual

The Instructor's Manual for this book offers sample lesson plans, chapter outlines/important topics, key terms, teaching ideas and suggestions, suggested answers to the case discussion questions, and essay questions with suggested answers.

Lumenaut Software

As a service to our students, all users of *Modern Marketing Research* are provided with a complimentary student license for Lumenaut: a powerful, intuitive, and elegant statistical package that works right within your Excel spreadsheet. Lumenaut was used to generate much of the statistical output in this text, and makes running regressions and other analyses a breeze. To access the software, please go to http://www.lumenaut.com/FKT.htm

About Atomic Dog

Atomic Dog is faithfully dedicated to meeting the needs of today's faculty and students, offering a unique and clear alternative to the traditional textbook. Breaking down textbooks and study tools into their basic "atomic parts," we then recombine them and utilize rich digital media to create a new breed of textbook.

This blend of online content, interactive multimedia, and print creates unprecedented adaptability to meet different educational settings and individual learning styles. As part of Cengage Custom Solutions, we offer even greater flexibility and resources in creating a learning solution tailor-fit to your course.

Atomic Dog is loyally dedicated to our customers and our environment, adhering to three key tenets:

- **Focus on essential and quality content:** We are proud to work with our authors to deliver a high-quality textbook at a lower cost. We focus on the essential information and resources students need and present them in an efficient but student-friendly format.
- **Value and choice for students:** Our products are a great value and provide students with more choices in "what and how" they buy—often at savings of 30 to 40 percent. Students who choose the Online Edition may see even greater savings compared with a print textbook. Faculty play an important and willing roll, working with us to keep costs low for their students by evaluating texts and supplementary materials online.
- **Reducing our environmental "paw-print":** Atomic Dog is working to reduce its impact on our environment in several ways. Our textbooks and marketing materials are all printed on recycled paper. We encourage faculty to review text materials online instead of requesting a print review copy. Students who buy the Online Edition do their part by going "paperless" and eliminating the need for additional packaging or shipping. Atomic Dog will continue to explore new ways that we can reduce our "paw-print" in the environment and hope you will join us in these efforts.

Atomic Dog is dedicated to faithfully serving the needs of faculty and students—providing a learning tool that helps make the connection. We hope that after you try our texts, Atomic Dog—like other great dogs—will become your faithful companion.

Acknowledgments

Authors can delude themselves into thinking their work is wholly their own. In our case, that is so off the mark that it's pointless even to try. We're happy to have this opportunity to acknowledge the scores of people who helped this book come to be and improved it beyond measure.

Despite the copious verbiage in the text, words fail us when trying to describe Cat Woods's influence on the final product. She started out as "tech editor," but wound up serving in about a hundred other roles. Anything good in this book would have been less so without her clarity, vision, and ferocious organizational efficiency. Laureen Ranz of Cengage also provided the sort of nurturing, constructive support and painstaking attention to quality one is scared even to hope for in Editors, never once chiding us for tardiness or missing Excel files, but nonetheless keeping the project humming along. Maria Angelidou is owed a huge debt of gratitude for her superb research on the Cases and Features, ably complemented by both Nick Gonzales and Michael Mathai.

Many people gave freely of their time and knowledge to make the book's cutting-edge material live up to that name. Expert Features and "deep help" with special sections were offered by Mark Beltramo, Barbara Bowen, Barbara Everitt Bryant, Jim Christian, Elea Feit, Nancy Karp, Jeremy Michalek, Tom Novak, Sean Otto, Stanton Peele, Ray Pettit, Andy Peytchev, Norbert Schwarz, and Dan Snider. Never has the phrase "it takes a village" been more decisively illustrated. Thanks also to Aura Ahuvia, Arri Bachrach, Andrys Basten, Ruy Cardoso, Chu Chang, Gerrie Collins, Marta Dapena-Baron, Anne Doerner, Connie Fearnside, Erica Gould, Hillary Kelleher, Lisa Kieda, Ann Littlewood, Tali Makell, Eric Mitchell, Sheryl Manning, Steve Math, Patrice Mathews, Chee Kong Mok, Bob Novick, Ed Pollak, Lizz Restuccia, David Rosenfeld, Mustafa Sakarya, Susan Schiro, Richard Sherman, CJ Yoon, Sunny Yoon, and above all Varda Ullman Novick for passing along articles, anecdotes, and sage advice that permeate the text. Special notes of appreciation go to Dave Sanderson, whose powerful-yet-friendly Excel add-in, Lumenaut, was used to generate ziggurats of statistical analyses and graphics, and to Craig Matteson, for enabling extensive use of the powerful human resource assessment and survey system HRGems.com.

We also gratefully acknowledge the professors who gave of their time to review portions of the manuscript and provide invaluable feedback for improvement: Arun K. Jain (SUNY Buffalo), Daniel Rutledge (Purdue University, North Central) and Cynthia Webster (Mississippi State University).

We owe a more diffuse, but no less deep, debt to our many colleagues and students here at the Ross School of Business, University of Michigan. The Deans, Marketing Group, and Faculty have been especially generous in sharing resources, "war stories," case materials, and other tools of the trade. Particularly big thanks go to Professors Anocha Aribarg, Rick Bagozzi, Rajeev Batra, Christie Brown, Katherine Burson, Jerry Davis, Claes Fornell, Andy Gershoff, Mrinal Ghosh, Aradhna Krishna, Fiona Lee, Peter Lenk, Claude Martin, Christie Nordhielm, Venkat Ramaswamy, Mike Ryan, David Wooten, Frank Yates, Carolyn Yoon, and Kathy Yuan, and to Deans Bob Dolan, Gene Anderson, Kathie Sutcliffe. You are all, collectively and individually, The Best.

Colleagues throughout the University of Michigan were also immensely helpful, including Professors Aaron Ahuvia, Jan-Henrik Andersen, Bob Barsky, Rich Gonzalez, Ben Hansen, John Jackson, Jag Jagadish, Helen Levy, Susan Murphy, Daphna Oyserman, Emre Ozendoren, Panos Papalambros, Chris Peterson, Colleen Seifert, Steve Skerlos, Mike Wellman, and Yu Xie. And those in the profession-at-large were no less generous, especially so Professors Feray Adigüzel, Eric Bradlow, Pierre Desmet, Peter Ebbes, Pete Fader, David Goldstein, Zeynep Gurhan-Canli, Angela Gutchess, Lynn Hasher, John Hauser, Scott Hawkins, Donna Hoffman, Joel Huber, Barbara Kahn, Jin Gyo Kim, Amna Kirmani, Angela Lee, Marcus Lee, Michelle Lee, John D. C. Little, Leigh McAlister, Uli Menzefricke, Joan Meyers-Levy, Denise Park, Bob Pollak, Vivian Pollak, Debu Purohit, Ambar Rao, Steve Raudenbush, Gary Russell, Linda Salisbury, Suresh Sethi, Ale Smidts, Kathy Stecke, Philip Stern, Michel Wedel, Jia Lin Xie, Yuanping Ying, and John Zhang. The Michael R. and Mary Kay Hallman Fellowship and the Eugene Applebaum, Bank One Corporation, and S. S. Kresge Chairs helped support the authors' academic research throughout the writing process.

We are surely in a weird business, one in which our students teach us as much or more than vice versa. Every line of this book has been honed over the years by their incisive commentary and unwillingness to settle for slipshod thinking. It is our fondest hope that they will render what we've taught them obsolete by personally surpassing it.

Fred M. Feinberg
Thomas C. Kinnear
James R. Taylor

Dedication

Fred Feinberg:

for Carolyn, Betty, Eddie, Kangro, Kyunghee, Ben and Grazzi

Tom Kinnear:

for Connie, Maggie, Jamie, Nina, and Ethan Kinnear

Jim Taylor:

for my wife Linda R. Powell and daughters, Pamela T. Stone and Sandra T. Paulsen

About the Authors

FRED M. FEINBERG is Professor of Marketing at the Ross School of Business, University of Michigan. He holds undergraduate degrees in Mathematics and Philosophy from the Massachusetts Institute of Technology, did graduate work in Mathematics at Cornell University, and received a Ph.D. in Management from the MIT Sloan School of Management. He was previously on the faculties of Duke University's Fuqua School of Business and the University of Toronto's Rotman School of Management.

For the past twenty years, he has taught project-oriented Marketing Research courses, on which much of this text is based, as well as Marketing Models and Statistical Methods for Management. His research concerns how people make choices in uncertain environments, particularly involving sequential choices among related items (such as brands in the same category), as well as models of advertising and consumer variety-seeking. He is Senior Editor for Marketing at *Production and Operations Management* and on the editorial boards of *Marketing Science, Review of Marketing Science,* and *Marketing Letters.* In his spare time, he attempts to play classical piano music that will remain forever beyond his capabilities.

THOMAS C. KINNEAR is Eugene Applebaum Professor of Entrepreneurial Studies and Professor of Marketing, Ross School of Business, University of Michigan, where he is also Executive Director of the Samuel Zell and Robert H. Lurie Institute for Entrepreneurial Studies. He holds an undergraduate and honorary LL.D. degree from Queen's University, Kingston, Ontario; an M.B.A. from Harvard University; and a Ph.D. in Business Administration from the University of Michigan.

He previously held a faculty appointment at the University of Western Ontario and visiting appointments at Harvard University, Stanford University, and the European Management Institute (INSEAD) at Fontainebleau, France. His teaching and research interests are in the areas of marketing planning and marketing research. His research activity has resulted in publications in numerous scholarly journals, including the *Journal of Marketing, Journal of Marketing Research, the Journal of Consumer Research, the Journal of Public Policy and Marketing*, and *the Journal of Business Research*. He is former editor of the *Journal of Marketing* and founding editor of the *Journal of Public Policy and Marketing.*

He is coauthor of *Principles of Marketing* (4th edition, Scott Foresman, 1995), *Marketing Research: An Applied Approach* (5th edition, McGraw-Hill, 1996), *Promotional Strategy* (9th edition, Pinnaflex, 2000), *Cases in Marketing Management* (6th edition, McGraw Hill-Irwin, 1994), and simulations *StratSimMarketing* and *PharmaSim* (Interpretive Simulations, 2006).

Professor Kinnear has worked in the field of marketing management education and consulting. His major consulting relationships are in the telecommunications, automotive, petroleum, heating and air conditioning, and beverage industries. His clients have included Aetna, AT&T, Daimler-Chrysler, General Motors, General Electric, Kodak, and Machine Vision International. He has served as a director of the American Marketing Association and the Association for Consumer Research, and he currently serves as a member of the board of directors in several companies and nonprofit organizations.

JAMES R. TAYLOR is S. S. Kresge Professor Emeritus of Marketing at the Ross School of Business, University of Michigan. He received his Ph.D. from the University of Minnesota with a specialization in marketing, psychology, and statistics. His dissertation, "An Empirical Evaluation of Coombs' Unfolding Theory," won the American Marketing Association Dissertation Award.

Professor Taylor's teaching and research interests are in the areas of strategic marketing planning, market segmentation, marketing research, and marketing management. During his academic career, he has been area chair for marketing and the chair of 15 Ph.D. dissertations and a member of 16 additional dissertations.

Dr. Taylor has published over 40 articles in academic journals, including *The Journal of Marketing, Journal of Marketing Research,* and *Journal of Consumer Research.* He has authored 10 books and monographs, including *Emerging Markets Simulation* (Interpretive Simulations, 2006), *Marketing Research: An Applied Approach* and *Exercises in Marketing Research* (5th edition, McGraw-Hill, 1995) and *Introduction to Marketing Management, Text and Cases* (5th edition, Irwin, 1985).

His professional activity includes membership in the American Marketing Association and Association for Consumer Research. He has been Vice President of the Detroit Chapter of the American Marketing Association, Executive Secretary of the Association of Consumer Research, and on the editorial board of the *Journal of Marketing, Journal of Marketing Research* and *The Journal of Consumer Research.*

Dr. Taylor's business experience includes seven years with General Mills, Inc., in marketing and new product development. In addition, he has been a project director for Accenture Consulting and Booz Allen Hamilton. Over his career, Dr. Taylor has served as consultant to numerous business organizations such as General Electric, Ford, DuPont, G.T.E., Johnson & Johnson, General Foods, and Procter & Gamble. He actively participates in company management education programs and has lectured in Brazil, Singapore, Hungary, France, Taiwan, Poland, Russia, Malaysia, Switzerland, and the United Kingdom.

PART 1

INTRODUCTION, RESEARCH PROCESS, AND DATA SOURCES

CHAPTER ONE
THE PURPOSE OF MARKETING RESEARCH

Marketing research is a set of formal practices for doing what people do all the time: gathering **information** and using it to make better decisions.

marketing research
The systematic process of using formal research and consistent data gathering to improve the Marketing function within an organization. Information from marketing research is used to identify opportunities and problems, to monitor performance, and to link marketing inputs with outputs of interest, such as awareness, satisfaction, sales, share and profitability.

information
The specific data required by decision-makers to reduce uncertainty in a known decision situation.

systematic
The requirements that a research project be planned and well-organized, the strategic and tactical aspects of the research designed in advance, the nature of the data gathered and the mode of analysis pre-determined.

In any society, products will be produced, and products will be consumed. If those doing the production fail to take into account those doing the consumption—literally, the "producers" ignoring the activities and desires of the "consumers"—the result will be poor decisions and a waste of resources. For example, if a factory produces an equal number of garments in every possible size, many will go unwanted, while potential customers may complain that the most commonly needed sizes are out of stock. Making better decisions requires information flow between needs and the attempts to fill those needs. The methodology of marketing research facilitates that flow of information in a **systematic** and rigorous way. Its theory and practices apply beyond the scope of traditional markets, to any field where the preferences and probable behavior of groups of people need to be monitored scientifically.

1.1 Managerial Decision-Making

Decisions related to markets demand some ability to track and predict the behavior of large groups of people. Predicting even one person's decisions can be enormously difficult. How can a decision-maker hope to predict the behavior of *many* people? The answer lies in gathering data intelligently, with an eye toward rigorous, often statistical, future analysis. The procedures and methodology of marketing research make it feasible to gather usable information regarding such group behavior, to quantify related data, and to assess them in an unbiased manner.

Broadly stated, the purpose of marketing research is to gather information that will improve managerial decisions, including those related to markets, as well as those related to the economy and society as a whole. Although the methods of marketing research are statistical, the underlying idea of gathering information to improve our decisions is something most of us do in our lives all the time, even if we do so informally. For example, if we are planning a party, we try to find out how many people are expected, what sort of food and music they might like, how long they might stay, and so on, to ensure a good overall outcome. The distinguishing features of marketing research are its rigor and its specific focus on marketing decisions, although its methods apply well beyond the traditional issues faced by marketers.

1.1a Research Methodologies for Decision-Making

The field of marketing research amounts to a set of methodologies designed to aid managerial decision-making. The essential steps of this approach to research are:

1. Determine what information is needed;
2. Design a method for collecting this information;
3. Manage the data collection;
4. Analyze and interpret the results;
5. Communicate the findings in a way that clarifies the implications for managerial decision-making.

market research
The collection, storage, and analysis of data for a specific marketing and/or consumer group; often contrasted with *marketing research* by its limitation to a particular market or segment.

Before discussing how research is conducted, we should have a good working definition of what research *is*, and that is the topic of *Marketing Research Focus 1.1*.

1.1b What Is Marketing Research?

marketing mix
The set of variables that a manager or firm can use to influence a marketing outcome of interest, usually sales or market share. Marketing mix variables usually comprise the "Four Ps"—price, product (characteristics, packaging), place (distribution channels), and promotion (consumer and trade)—as well as ad expenditures.

Information from marketing research is used to identify both opportunities and problems in marketing and to choose more effective actions in the marketplace. Its methodologies provide a way to monitor the effects of these actions and to build understanding of marketing processes. This is the classic definition of marketing research. It differs from what is often referred to as "**market research**" in that its scope is not limited to information about markets or consumers. Marketing research provides information for decision-making from all sources related to marketing (the firm, competitors, channel structure, "**marketing mix**," and both the social and technological environment) and has applications beyond the field of marketing. We will examine all of these roles in detail later in this chapter and throughout the text.

Marketing Research Focus 1.1

What Is Research?

We all like to believe we know what "research" means, and probably we all do. "Research" refers to finding out new information—the search for what is **objective**; useful; and, ordinarily, quantifiable. In common parlance, we often say we're "doing research" when we go about gathering informal information on any topic; say, purchasing a new computer or automobile. And this is indeed one form of "research": goal-directed, carried out only once, using whatever information comes up most readily. Throughout our discussions, we will also take note of another sort of research—carried out systematically over time, and seeking to construct an ongoing, decision-focused database of many interrelated variables. Common to all forms of research, however, is a *rigorous* method of collecting timely, relevant information and subsequently *processing* it to arrive at an informed, superior set of decisions.

objective
A key criterion of marketing research that involves careful screening of possible biases, as well as impartial application of quantifiable empirical methods during the design, implementation, interpretation, and presentation of a research project.

The methodology of objective empirical research seeks to formalize statistical reasoning in the analysis and interpretation of data. Many people consider the field of statistics very dry—an arcane discipline reserved for professional mathematicians. In actuality, most people use statistical reasoning all the time without realizing it. For example, consider applying to college. One must decide how many applications to submit and to which schools. This would require knowledge of tuition, possible majors, the time it takes to prepare each application, and many other pieces of information, which would then be weighed against the likelihood of being admitted. Precisely the same logic underlies job-seeking and many other decisions one makes in life. Although one seldom thinks of it as such, this entire process is an example of statistical reasoning: How do you gather appropriate data and draw conclusions? How do you decide that you will apply to, say, 10 schools, including two "dream schools" and one "safety"? Or say a friend asks you to play a dice game. The dice come up exactly the same way 10 times in a row. You think this person must be cheating, but how certain are you of this? If you are going to accuse your friend of dishonesty, you would want to be *very* sure. (And, in fact, this is precisely the key issue we will address in *all* statistical analyses.) Suppose the dice come up the same way 7 times out of 10; how certain are you then that the game has been meddled with? Every day, we ask ourselves questions involving data-collection and statistical reasoning: What are the chances? How great of a consensus has been built? Is it worthwhile to take this course of action? What if we are wrong? And how likely is that?

Research formalizes the process of collecting information. Statistics formalizes the reasoning that we use every day and attempts to assign firm numbers to these ideas based on data—to *scientifically* draw conclusions from the data. What distinguishes this from the kind of intuitive use of statistical reasoning mentioned earlier is that research has to be dispassionate, repeatable, and reason-based. Its conclusions have to be reliable and unbiased. Human beings in their ordinary reasoning have proven themselves to be easily fooled by features of data that seem important but are not. In Chapter 7, we will discuss some of the situations in which data tend to fool even seasoned researchers. Beyond a certain level of complexity or sheer volume of data, ordinary human reasoning is hopeless. Given vast quantities of interrelated numbers, we need help to pick out the important patterns from the formal methodology of statistics and computer calculations.

The purpose of research is to build a library of empirically based knowledge, which is continually being improved by further experimentation and analysis. It is a way to formally supplement human reasoning, not to supplant it, but to enhance and empower it.

Marketing research currently plays a role in four main settings:

1. *Role in Marketing*

   The primary setting in which marketing research methodologies are employed is, unsurprisingly, that of marketing. In this role, marketing research informs the various classic marketing functions, such as "the four P's" (pricing, product design, place/distribution channels, promotion), advertising, and "the three C's" (the company, consumer behavior, competition). The range of applications and practices related directly to marketing is extraordinarily vast and will be the major subject of this text. Examples of effective actions in this case include predicting the proportion of customers who will respond to a sale, determining a reasonable price for a new product, choosing among three possible ad campaigns, or deciding which features a new appliance has to offer to be successful in an already crowded marketplace.

   Just as we needed to understand what "research" meant before learning to carry it out, we also need a strong working definition of "market," the topic of *Marketing Research Focus 1.2*.

2. *Role in the Firm*

   The next level of application is the relevance of marketing research information to the firm in general. This involves assessing things beyond the traditional marketing function, such as finance, cost accounting, internal firm dynamics, logistics/operations, and other business practices. An example of

Marketing Research Focus 1.2

What Is a Market?

We often hear references in the media to "the market," as in "the wisdom of the market," "the market is heading downward," or, said with great flourish, "we must enter new markets to survive!" Implicit in such utterances is a notion of what a market really is, and to this question there are several plausible answers. A fairly generic one is that the market is everyone who could possibly participate in buying, leasing, subscribing, or trading for a specific product or service of interest and everything that could plausibly be involved in these activities. Underlying this idea is that there is a base of potential customers or consumers that needs to be identified and eventually "targeted." One of the main issues in marketing research is figuring out who these potential customers are, what they want, how they behave, and how to communicate effectively with them. One might call this entire undertaking "marketing" to one's "market."

There is another, distinct meaning of "market," and this is more akin to market*place*, an arena in which various similar products or firms compete with one another. Marketing research comprises this aspect of the "market" as well, and it seeks useful information about the marketplace in general, so that firms can create and position their products more effectively, as well as plan for the future.

effective action on this level would be estimating long-term sales of a currently successful product in order to decide how much to re-invest in research and development or in the building of a new plant. This role includes any informational needs of the firm outside of the classic marketing functions.

3. *Role in the Marketing Research Industry*
   The marketing research industry also conducts the sorts of general information-gathering that firms will not, or cannot, carry out themselves. One example of the syndicated research services these companies provide is maintaining large-scale consumer panels and tracking what its participants do, buy, and think. A single company interested in its own specific markets is unlikely to be able to invest in such a broad research undertaking, yet many companies can benefit from the information provided by such research. The marketing research industry is discussed in much greater detail later in this chapter, and specific aspects of the industry, such as e-panels and web-based surveys, will be considered in Chapter 6.
4. *Role in Society*
   The research and analysis techniques of marketing research have applications beyond the ordinary concept of a market or even the world of business in general. The essential steps and statistical reasoning of marketing research apply not only to people buying products but also to any group behaviors that anyone wishes to track, understand, or affect scientifically. If one stretches the concept of a "market" to mean a group of people whose behavior a "marketer" wishes to understand or influence in a specific way, it becomes apparent that techniques to improve market performance are also applicable to educational, public service, and political campaigns, in designing strategies to persuade people to vote a certain way, recycle, or engage in desirable behaviors (e.g., reading to their children, quitting smoking). In every case, there will be variables that can be controlled and variables that cannot (but can usually be measured), a plan for achieving the goal, and a means of assessing the success of the overall plan.

   Marketing research techniques apply to all sorts of information-gathering common in the public sphere. Governments use these same methods, for example, to collect census data, as well as to gauge life satisfaction, labor patterns, demographic trends, and other indicators regarding the economy. Journalists and politicians apply these techniques to enable more accurate political polling. Marketing Research Focus 7.6 describes an application of these methods to evaluate how well voting methods represent voter preferences.

1.1c Marketing Research Criteria

The four main criteria for marketing research are that it be systematic, objective, informational, and targeted for decision-making. *Systematic* refers to the requirement that a research project be planned and well-organized: researchers must detail the strategic and tactical aspects of the research design in advance, and they must anticipate the nature of the data they will gather and the mode of analysis they will employ.

Objective means that marketing researchers strive to be unbiased and impartial in conducting their research. A prevailing and oft-quoted conception of marketing research is that it is "the application of the scientific method to marketing." A hallmark of the scientific method is the objective gathering, analysis, and interpretation of data. Marketing research may operate in settings different from those of the physical, social, and medical sciences, but it shares with them the standard of objectivity.

The remaining two criteria differentiate marketing research from research in other fields. The primary purpose of marketing research is to provide *information* specifically related to aiding the management decision-making process.

decision-making process
A series of steps undertaken in the course of making a marketing-related decision. These can be conceptualized as: (1) recognizing a problem or opportunity, (2) clarifying the decision, (3) identifying alternative courses of action, (4) evaluating alternatives, and (5) selecting a specific course of action.

Data consist of observations and evidence. Information refers to data that reduce uncertainty in a decision situation. This definition makes use of the term "information" dependent on the decision-maker and the situation. For example, a ship's captain pilots the ship into a treacherous harbor at night. To aid the decision-making process, the captain is radioed the following data: (1) channel depth, (2) wind speed and direction, (3) the score of the local baseball game, and (4) tide speed and direction. Given the captain's problem, most readers will find it fairly easy to make the distinction between information relevant to the captain's decision (1, 2, and 4) and data irrelevant to the decision (the baseball score, despite its being of potential personal interest). Even though the baseball score is explicit, numerical, and objective, in this context we would not deem it "information." With typical marketing decisions, distinguishing between data and information can be substantially more challenging.

1.2 What Is Marketing?

Marketing research grew out of the needs and demands of the marketing system. Figure 1.1 depicts a conceptual scheme of the marketing system from the perspective of the selling organization. This model is predicated on an idea called "the marketing concept," which refers to a shift in emphasis from optimizing production processes to improving all aspects of marketing practice. The marketing concept stresses the role of everything other than "the stuff inside the package"—pricing, advertising, promotion, distribution, even packaging—in generating successful products and consumer experiences. One of the tacit assumptions in

marketing system
A conceptual model viewing the marketing mix (what managers can control: price, product, and so forth) and situational variables (what managers cannot: competition, legal factors, and so forth) as independent variables ("inputs") that give rise to consumers' behavioral responses, which in turn determine performance measures ("output variables"), such as sales, share, and profit levels.

marketing concept
A focus on the role of marketing mix variables (e.g., price, distribution, promotion) and not merely what's "inside the box" in driving the success of a product.

Figure 1.1 Model of the Marketing System

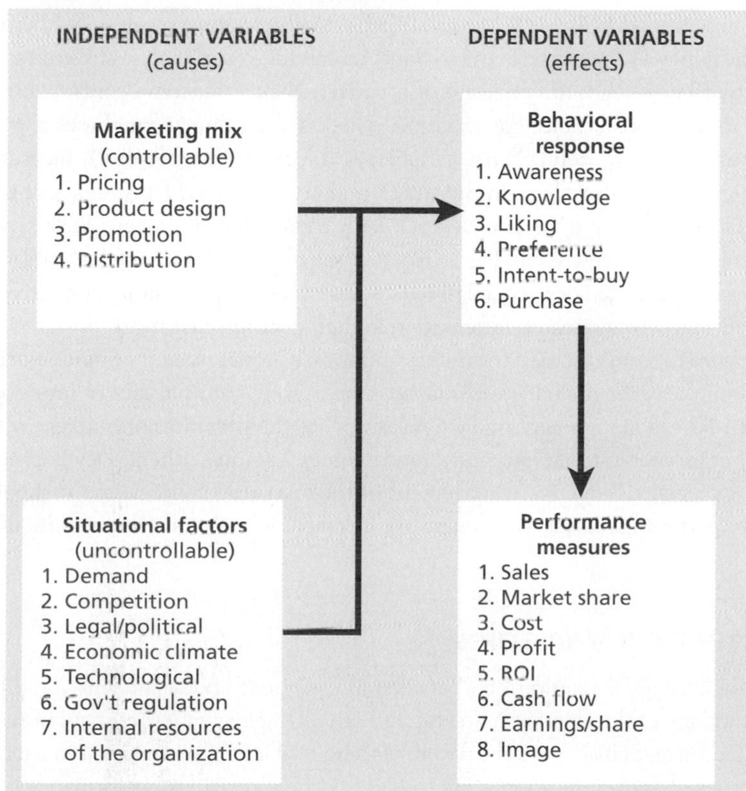

this book and throughout marketing management is that, except for commodities and highly undifferentiated products, such activities are essential to marketplace success and revenue creation.

variable
Anything that can take on different (usually numerical) values. In marketing, age, gender, price, package size, sales, and share are commonly used variables.

Variables are, as one might guess, quantities which can and do vary. The chief goal of statistical analysis is understanding why variables vary in the way they do and to use the values of other variables to fashion a *model* to aid in this understanding. We will consistently refer to two sorts of variables: dependent variables, which are phenomena one seeks to explain or "effects," and independent variables (also called predictors, inputs, covariates, or 'causes') used to explain them. The manner in which we use them forms the basis of all statistical inference and will be discussed thoroughly in Chapters 9–12.

dependent variable
The variable whose value is related to or determined by the values of a number of independent variables; often called the "outcome variable."

independent variables
Variables that can be controlled or measured, which one hopes to relate to the dependent variable, ordinarily via a statistical model.

inputs
Independent variables, such as the marketing mix, that feed into marketing systems and help managers to exert some degree of control over them.

1.2a Independent Variables

Independent variables in marketing research are separated into situational factors, which cannot be readily controlled, and various (usually marketing-related) decisions made by the organization. Situational variables represent the environment to which the selling organization must adapt in formulating and implementing its marketing program. These factors include availability of resources, actions of competitors, economic climate, market trends, government regulation, and even geography. Although these cannot be controlled, they *can* be measured, and so they are available for use in statistical analyses. By contrast, there are numerous variables that are difficult or impossible to measure, such as consumers' moods while they are shopping or the precise time the last can of a specific brand of coffee was taken off a store's shelves, and which must be treated as *unobservable*.

There are numerous decisions and choices under the control of the organization. Among the most important of these is the marketing mix, which includes pricing, manufacturer and retail promotion, point-of-purchase displays, ad spending, and such aspects of distribution as trade deals. Combinations of different levels of these variables form alternative marketing programs or courses of action. It is customary, when trying to understand market dynamics and consumer behavior, to view these as inputs or decision variables that the firm uses to help steer the market.

decision variables
The quantities that must be determined, as in a particular marketing research project, typically including pricing, distribution, promotion levels, and sales goals.

1.2b Dependent Variables

Both sets of independent variables—marketing mix and situational factors—combine to influence behavioral response such as purchases, buying intentions, preferences, and attitudes. It would be foolish, both statistically and procedurally, to believe that behavioral responses result *only* from (independent) variables under the control of marketers, and we must be careful in our analyses to strenuously avoid this presumption. Actual behavior is an amalgam of a variety of effects—some controllable, some merely measurable, and some unobservable. For example, whether a consumer purchases a particular brand results from a combination of controllable variables (e.g., the marketing mix), measurable variables (e.g., purchases made of other products in the store), and unobservables (how much of the product the consumer has at home or other stores shopped at). This complicates the question of how to develop a marketing program that effectively handles a dynamic set of variables and behavioral responses, only some of which can be controlled or even measured. Skilled managers can offer perspective on past experience as they apply marketing research information in their decision-making.

behavioral response
Any of a number of actions or mental states triggered by marketing actions. These can include actual purchases, intentions to purchase, feelings, attitudes or beliefs.

Behavioral responses form the basis for the organization's monetary and nonmonetary performance measures. Monetary measures include sales, market share, profit, internal rate of return, and return on investment (ROI). Nonmonetary performance measures are the organization's image, attitudes toward the organization, consumer satisfaction, and brand "equity," among others. Developing valid performance measures is crucial to effective management of the marketing system, and it should be borne in mind that many important barometers of a brand's or a company's performance are difficult to place on a numerical scale.

performance measures
The output variables of the marketing system, including brand equity, consumer satisfaction or loyalty, sales, share, and profit levels.

1.2c Connecting Variables

Uncovering and analyzing the relationships between independent and dependent variables in the marketing system is fundamental to marketing research. Formally identifying these functional relationships can be time-consuming and elusive, yet the nature of these relationships is implicit in a manager's choice of alternative courses of action. In attempting to identify these relationships, a manager must consider the cost of gathering the information relative to the level of confidence gained in selecting the optimal course of action.

In practice, decision-making rarely relies wholly on an input–output framework and formal statistical models but combines them with managers' experience, judgment, and intuition. Of course, managers also can and do make decisions without undertaking explicit marketing research. These decisions may be sound if the manager has relevant experience; good judgment; and timely, accurate information. It is important to realize that the overarching goal is always to make an effective decision, not to decide on what is the best marketing research to sponsor. Just as in everyday life, when we sometimes "just make up our mind" about what to do, there are situations where is it unwise to expend resources—time, funds, thinking—on carrying out formal research when it is unlikely to substantially improve the quality of a decision. Indeed, one might go so far as to say that the first step in the marketing research process is deciding whether it is worthwhile to undertake research at all.

1.3 Marketing Management Decisions

Among marketing managers' key roles is making decisions regarding marketing mix elements. The decision-making process so permeates the management process that the two terms are often considered synonymous.

An organization's well-being is dependent on the wisdom of the decisions made by its managers. The majority of decisions made by managers involve recurring situations that are familiar to the management. These ordinary decisions involve little uncertainty and have a low potential for surprise. Managers rely heavily, if not exclusively, on their experience and judgment in making such decisions. Sometimes, these decisions aren't even viewed as such, like the "decision" to keep a particular brand on a supermarket's shelves or to continue to employ a regional distribution manager. If such issues needed to be decided and optimized on a moment-by-moment basis, business would grind quickly to a halt. Thus, it is crucial for managers to recognize such nondescisions before attempting to improve their marketing practices.

A second type of decision involves situations in which past experience and judgment are less relevant. With unfamiliar decisions, some aspect of the situation is unique enough that the manager's usual decision-making approach does not fit neatly into the new setting. Because all firms operate in a dynamic environment punctuated by the evolution of new products, practices, and services, managers will often need to follow a more formal approach, which we will call the decision-making process.

1.3a Steps of the Decision-Making Process

The decision-making process may be conceived as a series of steps, as illustrated in Figure 1.2. The first step is *recognizing a unique marketing problem or opportunity*. Performance measures may signal the

Figure 1.2 The Decision-Making Process

1. Recognize a unique marketing problem or opportunity.
2. Clarify the decision.
3. Identify alternative courses of action.
4. Evaluate alternatives.
5. Select a course of action.
6. Implement the selected course of action and monitor results.

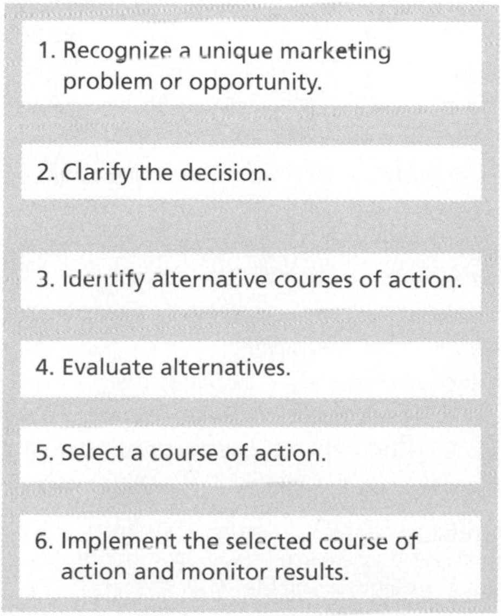

presence of problems, whereas the monitoring of situational factors may indicate both problems and opportunities. For example, a manager may learn that a product's market share has declined, that a competitor intends to introduce a new product, that demand for a product has risen faster than anticipated, or that government action has negatively influenced the sale of a competitor's product. Managers consequently make decisions to solve problems or to capitalize on opportunities. Note that problems and opportunities are not opposites, but may be two faces of the same situation: when a performance measure such as sales goes down, it may be doing so for an entire industry, signaling an opportunity to create a new product or product line extension to draw back previous customers or increase the usage rate of loyal ones. How one major company distinguished problems from opportunities is illustrated in *Marketing Research Focus 1.3*.

The second step in the formalized decision-making process is *clarifying the decision*. The manager needs to define and clarify the main issues and causal factors operating in the decision situation. It is not always easy to identify which fundamental variables are creating trouble and what needs correcting. By involving marketing research personnel and techniques in this early phase of the decision-making process, a marketing manager can better assess the problems and opportunities, while at the same time laying the groundwork for effective marketing research in later stages of the process.

The third step is *identifying alternative courses of action*. In marketing, a course of action means a specific combination of marketing mix variables. "Doing nothing new" or "maintaining the status quo" is just as much a course of action as planning new marketing activities. The quality of the alternatives considered determines the potential effectiveness of management decisions. It is therefore critical that the best alternatives be identified and *not* be artificially limited to what has been tried before, what competitors are already doing, and the like. This is a *creative* process. The manager and the marketing researcher need to brainstorm new ideas, accessing their imaginations and employing techniques designed to stimulate the creative process, increase innovative thinking, and broaden the domain of alternatives.

The fourth and fifth steps are *evaluating alternatives* and *selecting a course of action*. To make a decision, at least two courses of action must be identified. For the formal decision-making process to apply, there must also be uncertainty about which course of action will best achieve management objectives. If the

Marketing Research Focus 1.3

Performance Measures Reveal an Opportunity, Not a Problem

Although the old showbiz adage "There's no such thing as bad publicity" isn't the wisest marketing advice, Smucker's found it can sometimes apply. In 1999, Smucker's was granted a patent for "sealed crusted sandwiches," the basis for the Uncrustables frozen peanut butter and jelly sandwiches the company introduced in 2003. Smucker's attempted to use its patent to force a small Michigan company, Albie's Foods, to cease its production of peanut butter and jelly sandwiches for a school district. Albie's instead took the case to federal court in 2001 and then asked the patent office to invalidate Smucker's original patent. Albie's claimed that a crustless sandwich with crimped edges had been popular in the area for decades as a "pasty," albeit in a form typically containing meat or other savory filling.

Kevin Heinl, a lawyer for Albie's, said that the company was caught off guard because "they didn't think you could patent a peanut butter and jelly sandwich." Both the headlines and patent office spokespeople confirmed that patenting peanut butter and jelly sandwiches tested the limits of federal patents. The companies eventually settled out of court, leaving the validity of Smucker's original patent untested.

Smucker's sought to expand their original patent in 2004, claiming that the crimping method used on the edges of the sandwiches was one-of-a-kind and deserved a separate patent. This new patent was denied by the U.S. Patent and Trademark Office, which ruled that the crimping method was similar to that used for ravioli or pie crusts. Smucker's appealed this to the Board of Patent Appeals, which upheld the decision.

After Patent Appeals rejected Smucker's' claims, Smucker's took the case to the U.S. Court of Appeals for the Federal Circuit. This court also upheld the decision to deny the patent.

Did Smucker's consider the negative court decisions and the outraged headlines a problem? No. Its performance measures showed that during the period that the patent situation received a great deal of free press, sales of Uncrustables continued to rise, with a 20% increase from 2004 to 2005. The "bad press" around the patent filing proved to be an opportunity to increase brand awareness.

Sources: "Smuckers Frozen Out of Sandwich Patent"; *Quick Frozen Foods International News*, April 14, 2005.
"This Headline Is Patented" David Streitfeld. *LA Times*. February 7, 2003. J. M. Smucker Company Fourth Quarter 2005 Earnings Conference Call, FD (Fair Disclosure) Wire, Voxant Inc. June 16, 2005.

decision-maker is faced with a situation in which there is only one realistic course of action and that is to "do nothing," then this manager is not making a decision, even though the problem or opportunity confronting management may have significant consequences for the organization.

It is also crucial to take into account uncertainty and risk. Some courses of action have far more predictable outcomes than others; for example, raising price by 5% vs. by 50%, even though neither can be forecast perfectly. Decisions relating to unfamiliar situations can never be as informed as managers would like. This is partly due to uncertainty about the future state of situational factors; partly to natural limits on the ability to gather precise, unambiguous information about the outcomes of the alternatives; and partly to human factors involved in all decision-making. A common error in evaluating options is to merely associate them with their most likely outcome, ignoring differences in risk. Generally speaking, higher risk should accord with higher expected return, and a key element of decision-making in business and life in general is "managing" risk by trading it off against potential reward. Formal marketing research techniques help quantify and process all these variables in a manner consistent with a firm's stated objectives.

The final step in the decision-making process is *implementing the selected course of action and monitoring its effects*. Marketing research supplies the means for monitoring the effectiveness of this program of action and the situational variables that influence the program's performance. The timespan between making decisions and receiving definite feedback plus the uncertainty regarding the cause-and-effect relations in the marketing system increase the difficulty of reaching definitive conclusions. It is also frequently the case that not all metrics of success will agree about a decision's effectiveness. When a product is promoted (that is, its price is temporarily reduced), sales volume and share of the market will typically go up, but unit profit and even sometimes total profit will decrease. It is unrealistic to expect that a marketing decision will look equally good on every valid criterion. Managers must learn to weigh these criteria against one another to determine whether the decision was, in fact, a sound one.

Just because the end of the decision-making process has been reached does not mean the decision is set in stone. It is crucial that implementation be followed by explicit monitoring and some degree of ongoing vigilance. For example, if the result of the decision-making process is to introduce a new size of an existing product, a wise manager would ensure that it is marketed appropriately and that it does not unduly cannibalize sales of existing products and perhaps determine whether its success signals that additional new sizes might be successful as well.

1.3b The Marketing Management Process

The chief task of marketing management is to comprehend the marketing system well enough to make decisions that affect that system in accordance with the organization's goals. This role of informational feedback between the marketing system and the decision-making process, called the **marketing management process**, is diagrammed in Figure 1.3. Managers make decisions aiming to influence the performance measure in a predictable manner, based on their information about the marketing system. They are informed by their past experience and marketing research, and they plan future actions by comparing performance against objectives.

marketing management process
A process formally relating three ongoing, interactive elements: information inputs (from marketing research and managerial judgment), the decision-making process within the marketing organization, and the marketing system itself (marketing mix, situational factors, performance measures, and behavioral responses).

1.3c Information Needs

For the purpose of planning, marketing researchers seek to answer questions regarding three essential sets of information, corresponding to the measurable types of variables in the marketing system: situational variables, marketing mix variables, and performance measures. Figure 1.4 presents an outline of sample questions regarding these informational needs.

A **situational analysis** collects information to answer questions regarding "**situational factors**" in the system. A typical situational analysis includes an analysis of demand, as evidenced by market characteristics and buyer behavior; an understanding of the competition; an evaluation of surrounding trends, such as economics, government regulation, cultural factors, and technological innovations; and an assessment of the internal resources available in the organization. Examples of specific questions for detailing the situational analysis are included in Section I of the outline of information needs.

Section II of the outline refers to the marketing mix. Marketing research projects are typically designed to determine such elements as desired product features, attractive pricing policies, appropriate distribution, and promotional options. Taken together, these form the new marketing plan.

situational analysis
The use of present and/or historical data to determine which variables and factors affect business performance; often aided by SWOT (strengths, weaknesses, opportunities, and treats) analysis to identify both internal and external factors.

situational factors
Independent variables that feed into the marketing system from the general business environment and which are therefore less affected or controlled by the choices of any single firm. These include demand; competition; the legal, political, and economic climates; technological innovations; and governmental regulation.

Figure 1.3 The Marketing Management Process

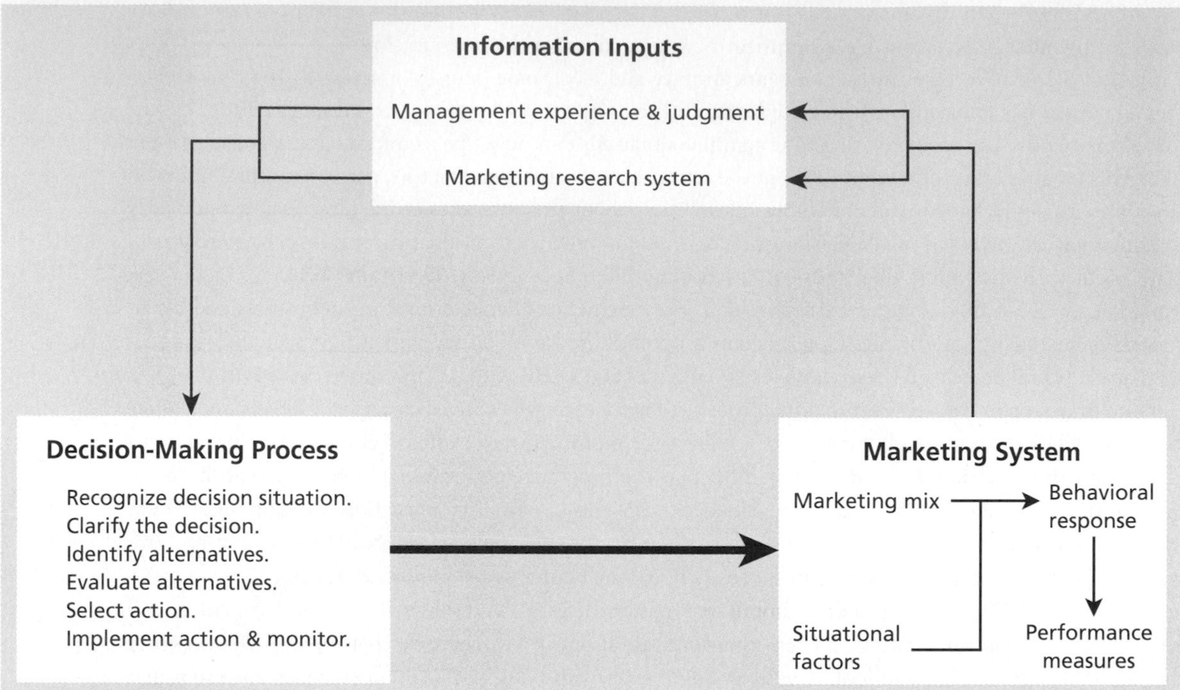

Collecting data on performance measures is necessary, both for informing decisions regarding the marketing mix and for monitoring the results of the marketing plan, once implemented. Section III of Figure 1.4 presents specific, typical questions regarding this sort of information.

1.3d Good Planning through Marketing Research

A systematic approach to researching the information needs of marketing management facilitates good organizational planning in developing objectives, allocating marketing resources, and auditing performance. The marketing manager uses knowledge of the marketing system and the kind of informational questions presented in Figure 1.4 to design a program of the controllable marketing mix variables that will accomplish the desired level of performance measures. Further ad hoc research may also be needed as problems and opportunities develop in the course of implementing the marketing plan.

Given the need to make effective marketing decisions in the face of uncertainty, the potential for marketing research to provide both strategic and tactical insight is tremendous. A marketing researcher with the competence to provide managerial insights from technically competent research is invaluable to many companies and at times makes the critical difference in a company's successful turnaround. Let us see how one service-oriented firm was able to use marketing research with just such a purpose in *Marketing Research Focus 1.4*.

1.3e The Marketing Research System

Marketing research has become increasingly more important since the shift from the focus on production to the much greater emphasis on consumption and consumer choices after World War II. Increased focus on the quality of products and services has accentuated the emphasis on marketing research in identifying consumer needs and in measuring consumer satisfaction. The increasingly global nature of markets and competition has enhanced and underscored the need to carry out marketing research in nondomestic environments. Improved data technology, due to both hardware and software innovations, has vastly expanded the potential scope and reach of research.

Organizations tend to operate on one of two main concepts of the role assigned to marketing research. The first views research as mainly an ad hoc data-gathering and analysis function; the other

Figure 1.4 Information Needed for Organizational Planning

I. Situational analysis
  A. Demand analysis
    1. Buyers' behavior and characteristics:
      a. What do they buy? [e.g., product classes, brands, sizes, UPCs]
      b. Who buys? [e.g., age, income, education, location, which family members]
      c. Where do they buy? [e.g., type of store, urban vs. rural, on-line vs. brick-and-mortar]
      d. Why do they buy? [e.g., planned purchase, item on sale, gift, etc.]
      e. How do they buy? [e.g., credit, cash, promotional purchase]
      f. When do they buy? [e.g., time of day, holidays, season of the year]
      g. How much do they buy? [e.g., product size, number of units, total quantity, heavy vs. light user]
      h. How will buyers' behavior and characteristics change in the future?
      i. Are customers satisfied? At what level?
      j. Are customers retained? At what level?
    2. Market characteristics:
      a. Market size potential: forecast of attainable market as function of marketing expenditures
      b. Segments: broken down by demographics (e.g., "college-educated women with children") or by overall pattern of response to a variety of questions ("latent segmentation," see Chapters 11 and 12.)
      c. Selective demand: high-knowledge, purchase-ready consumers aware of competition
      d. Future market trends
  B. Competition
    1. Who are our competitors?
    2. Competitor characteristics:
      a. Marketing programs: how does competitive marketing mix and product portfolio compare?
      b. Competitive behavior: how does competition *react* to your marketing efforts and actions?
      c. Resources (e.g., salesforce, brand 'equity', distribution channels, high awareness, monetary reserves)
    3. Major strengths and weaknesses
    4. Future competitive environment
  C. General Environment
    1. Economic conditions and trends
    2. Government regulation and trends
    3. Pollution, safety, consumer-based concerns
    4. Technological trends
    5. Political climate
  D. Internal Environment: how do your firm's 'core competencies' compare to those of competitors'?
    1. Marketing resources/skills
    2. Production resources/skills
    3. Financial resources/skills
    4. Technological resources/skills
    5. Future trends in internal environment

II. Marketing mix
  A. Product
    1. What product attributes/benefits are important?
    2. How should the product be differentiated?
    3. What segments will be attracted? Are consumers *heterogeneous* in their needs?
    4. How important are service, warranty, and other risk-reducing, intangible aspects of the purchase?
    5. Is there a need for product variants or an entire product line?
    6. How important is packaging?
    7. How is the product perceived relative to competitive offerings?
  B. Place (Distribution Channels)
    1. What types of distributors should handle the product?
    2. What are the distributors' attitudes and motivations?
    3. What intensity of wholesale/retail coverage is needed?
    4. What margins are appropriate for each channel partner?
    5. What forms of physical distribution are needed?
  C. Price
    1. What is the elasticity of demand? How can we calculate it?
    2. What pricing *policies* are appropriate? [e.g., enter with a low price 'penetration' strategy]
    3. How should the product line be priced? Will one product unduly cannibalize the others?
    4. How do we establish price variations for a product?
    5. How should we react to a competitive price threat?
    6. How important is price to the buyer? Do they view price as a signal of quality?
  D. Promotion and Advertising
    1. What is the optimal promotional budget?
    2. How important are sales promotion, advertising, and personal selling in stimulating demand?
    3. What is the proper promotion mix? Should more be devoted to the trade or directly to consumers?
    4. How do you measure the effectiveness of the promotion tools?
    5. What ad copy is most effective?
    6. What media are most effective? How can we determine the best *media mix*?

III. Performance measures
  1. What are current sales by product line?
  2. What are current market shares by product line?
  3. What are current sales/market share by customer types, sales region, and across other relevant dimensions?
  4. What is our product/company image among customers, distributors, and the public?
  5. What is the awareness level of various promotional offers and ad messages?
  6. What is the recall level – aided and unaided – of our brand name?
  7. What percentage distributorship do we have in large, medium and small retailers? By geography? Customer type?
  8. What percentage of the channel is selling below suggested retail price? What is the average retail price of our product?
  9. What percentage of customers are satisfied? Is this trending downward?
  10. What percentage of current customers are likely to repeat? Will they require a promotional incentive or loyalty program?

defines the role of research more broadly, viewing the marketing research department as an information center for decision-making. This concept, referred to as the *marketing research system*, implies a deeply involved role for research in the marketing management process. This includes the active participation of research in the decision-making process, with particular emphasis on providing meaningful information for planning and achieving predictable influence on performance measures. The purpose of this information input is to reduce error and broaden perspective during decision-making. In short, better decisions should result from better information inputs.

Marketing Research Focus 1.4

Marketing Research Aids Company Turnaround

Harrah's Entertainment had a bumpy ride during the latter part of the 1990s. In 1993, Harrah's was taking advantage of relaxed regulations on casinos in the United States and grabbing new customers and revenues by expanding their casinos into the Midwest and East Coast. This quick growth came to an abrupt halt in 1998. In addition to tighter government regulations on casinos limiting Harrah's growth opportunities, many competitors had also expanded eastward and moved into the Midwest and East Coast states, eroding and in some cases even eliminating Harrah's profits by offering customers fancier hotels, casinos, and amenities.

With increased competition and decreasing profits, Harrah's back was against the wall. To make matters worse, Harrah's could not follow the typical industry strategy for revamping growth. With little available capital following their expansion of 1993, then–CEO Gary Loveman stated, "We couldn't do the typical thing of investing more money in 'more gaming,' building bigger and better casinos." Instead, the firm had to find ways to modify consumer behavior.

In response, Harrah's launched an extensive customer loyalty program, Total Rewards. Harrah's customers registered free for the program and in turn received a Total Rewards membership card they could use at every Harrah's casino. Customers used their membership cards when they entered and exited the casino, and each time they sat down at a slot machine or gambling table. The more customers gambled and used their Total Rewards cards, the more benefits and discounts they received. Customers quickly responded to this program, as they were provided with the extra incentive to make frequent trips to Harrah's.

Increasing customer loyalty was not the only benefit of the Total Rewards program. Through the membership cards, Harrah's gained a great source of customer information. Each card not only contained information on a gambler's age, gender, and home address, it also revealed a great deal about gambling behavior because gamblers swiped their card every time they entered, exited, or gambled at a Harrah's casino. Harrah's "winner's information network" (WINet) collects information from all of Harrah's transactional, slot machine, hotel management, and reservation systems. Each time a player inserts his or her Total Rewards card into a slot machine or hands it to a floor manager, the amounts of time played and money gambled are recorded in a data warehouse. Harrah's has been able to gain comprehensive insight on a number of different characteristics, including what kind of games customers gamble on, how long they gamble, how much they typically spend, and the amount of time they spend at the casino.

Harrah's uses this information to design individualized marketing for each Harrah's gambler, based on gambling behavior, preferences, and an index of the projected customer value. Meanwhile, customer loyalty has skyrocketed. Between 2000 and 2001, Harrah's saw an increase in cardholder revenue from 86% of their cardholders, with 40% of these customers tripling their overall expenditures Over a five-year period, Harrah's customer database grew steadily, from 13.8 million in 1998 to 26.6 million, while its revenues jumped from $1.9 billion to $4.1 billion. This shows not only the financial value that can be unlocked from performing market research, but also the potential competitive advantage that results from getting in touch with one's customers.

Sources: "Dare to Be Different"; John R Brandt. *Chief Executive Magazine*. May 1, 2003.
"Double Down CRM Is the Cornerstone of IT at Harrah's Entertainment"; Brad Barth. *Executive Technology*. March 1, 2004.

marketing research system
The series of steps involved in a research project from inception to completion, including definition of a problem or opportunity, exploratory research, design of sample, survey and data collection method, data collection, data analysis, interpretation, and presentation of results.

intelligence system
An integrated computer system/database that collects and stores recurring marketing data, interprets it for managers via statistical models, and provides a user interface for accessing the resulting information.

marketing information systems
Large-scale databases and explicit procedures for the collection, storage, and analysis of data useful in making ongoing marketing decisions.

decision support system (DSS)
A dedicated system—usually comprising both hardware (e.g., computer systems and the databases they house) and software (e.g., custom-coded programs for collecting, managing, and analyzing data)—useful for making marketing decisions and analyzing the expected outcomes of specific marketing actions (also known as "what if?" or sensitivity analyses).

The **marketing research system** comprises components often referred to as **intelligence systems**. These can be what are known as **marketing information systems** (MIS)—or, alternately, marketing research information systems (MRIS) to distinguish the term from "management information systems" often used in corporations—or **decision support systems** (DSS). Both kinds of intelligence systems involve the modeling of recurring information based on ongoing data collection. These are discussed in more detail in Chapter 3.

1.4 The Marketing Research Industry

The themes and objectives of marketing research have developed into a complex, multifaceted, and dynamic industry.

The development of marketing research in the early twentieth century paralleled the rise of the marketing concept. During the period 1900–1930, management concern was focused primarily on the problems and opportunities associated with production; between 1930 and the late 1940s, this orientation shifted to the problems and opportunities associated with distribution; since the late 1940s, increased attention has been focused on consumer needs and desires. The nature and role of marketing activity reflect this shift in management philosophy.

1.4a History of Marketing Research

Although marketing research was used occasionally before 1910, the period from 1910–1920 is recognized as the formal beginning of marketing research. In 1911, J. George Frederick established a research firm called The Business Bourse. Charles Coolidge Parlin was appointed manager of the Commercial Research Division of the Curtis Publishing Company that same year, one of the early examples of the term "research" being applied to a business service. The success of Parlin's work soon inspired several industrial firms (such as the United States Rubber Company and Swift and Company) to establish commercial research departments of their own.

In 1919, Professor C. S. Duncan of the University of Chicago published the first major book on marketing research, *Commercial Research: An Outline of Working Principle*. Percival White's *Market Analysis*, published in 1921, was the first research book to gain a large readership. *Market Research and Analysis* by Lyndon O. Brown, published in 1937, became one of the most popular college textbooks of the period, reflecting the growing interest in marketing research on college campuses. After 1940, numerous research textbooks were introduced, and the number of business schools offering research courses rapidly expanded.

After World War II, the growth of marketing research activity dramatically increased with the growing acceptance of the marketing concept. By 1948, more than 200 marketing research organizations had been formed in the United States alone. Over the next four decades, expenditures on marketing research activities increased more than twentyfold. This was accompanied by a shift in emphasis from "market research," which implied a focus solely on analyzing markets, to "marketing research," which emphasized a broader role of research, including contact between researchers and the marketing management process.

1.4b Methodological Development

Advances in marketing research methodology parallel the development of research methodology in the social sciences, of which marketing is properly a part. The methodological advances made by psychologists, economists, sociologists, and political scientists had a pronounced influence on marketing research methodology.

From 1910 to 1920, questionnaires and surveys became popular modes of data collection. With the growth of survey research came improvements in questionnaire design and question construction, along with an awareness of biases resulting from the questioning and the interviewing process. Several social scientists who entered the field were interested in working on these applied methodological problems. This established a methodological communication link between marketing and the other social sciences that exists to this day.

During the 1930s, sampling became a serious methodological issue. As statistical training developed beyond descriptive statistics (calculation of means, variances, simple correlation, and construction of index numbers) to an emphasis on inferential statistics, nonprobability sampling procedures came under heavy attack. Modern probability sampling approaches (described in detail in Chapter 8) slowly gained acceptance during this period.

Methodological innovation occurred at a fairly steady pace from 1950 through the early 1960s. At this time, the commercialization of the computer rapidly increased the pace of methodological innovation, especially in the area of quantitative marketing research. Subsequent technological innovations, such as checkout scanners in supermarkets, computer-assisted telephone interviewing, data analysis by personal computer, and the advent of web surveys, e-mail, and e-commerce have greatly impacted the marketing research profession.

1.4c Marketing Research Institutions

The institutional structure of the marketing research business is complex, encompassing many thousands of different types of organizations. The main distinction is between the organizations that *use* marketing research (e.g., manufacturers, wholesalers, retailers, service organizations, trade associations, and government agencies); those that *do* marketing research for the use of other organizations (e.g. research firms for ad hoc studies, syndicated data sources, universities, and research institutes); and those organizations that fill both roles, undertaking research studies for their own planning purposes, as well as doing research on behalf of clients (e.g., advertising agencies and advertising media).

research suppliers
Marketing research institutions that perform research for client organizations.

Marketing research providers can be further divided into full-service and limited-service research suppliers. Full-service suppliers will undertake complete research studies for client organizations, including problem definition, questionnaire design, sampling, interviewing, coding, editing, and data analysis and interpretation. Limited-service suppliers perform only some of these activities—for example, firms that do only field interviewing or data analysis, firms specializing in advertising research or product testing, or firms concentrating on one geographic region of the country.

Research firms may provide ad hoc studies designed to solve *client-specific* problems or syndicated data sources that are not client-specific. Syndicated data sources collect certain types of data and then sell these data on a subscription basis to any organization that will buy them. Common types of syndicated data measure retail sales, wholesale product shipments, activities of consumer panels, advertising media audiences, advertising effectiveness, and consumer attitudes. A detailed description of the types of syndicated data available and some of the better-known organizations providing it are presented in Chapter 3.

Business research departments of universities also engage in some aspects of marketing research. Research may be undertaken for specific client organizations, but usually it is made public because of university regulations. The major analytic tools and methods of marketing research covered at length later in this text were developed over many decades primarily by university researchers, with the results freely published for unrestricted use. Government agencies make the greatest use of this sort of research, particularly large-scale field studies. In addition, individual faculty undertaking marketing research on a consulting basis can be considered suppliers of ad hoc studies. Research institutes, such as Survey Research Center of the University of Michigan (www.isr.umich.edu/src/), can be embedded within a university structure or operate independently, providing both ad hoc and syndicated information, usually for government agencies.

1.4d Marketing Research Careers

research director
A marketing research position that involves the management of a research department.

analyst
A marketing research position involving the general design and supervision of marketing research studies.

technical specialist
A marketing research position that involves providing expertise in solving a specialized aspect of marketing research, such as questionnaire design or sampling.

Within most corporations and marketing research suppliers, there are four main categories of marketing research jobs: research director, analyst, technical specialist, and clerical staff. Research directors are responsible for all activities in a research department. The majority hold at least a bachelor's degree; a significant number hold a master's degree, and a few hold a doctoral degree. Analysts, sometimes referred to as *research generalists*, do the bulk of the design and supervision of marketing research studies. Responsibilities of a research generalist include developing understanding and good judgment regarding various industries, as well as the research process; identifying and evaluating problems, opportunities, and management alternatives; balancing decision risks and research costs in the effort to close information gaps; and providing perspective on long-range research needs. Analysts are usually required to have a master's or bachelor's degree, with an interdisciplinary degree involving marketing, statistics, economics, general business, or psychology often preferred. Most managers also look for overall ability, analytic training, imagination/creativity, interpersonal skills, curiosity, writing proficiency, and drive/ambition. Technical specialists generally address narrow aspects of marketing research problems, including, for example, questionnaire design, sampling, data analysis, and computers.

Table 1.1 presents a more detailed description of the jobs that one would expect to find in a larger marketing research organization. Research generalists and specialists are discussed further in Chapter 2.

1.4e Consumer versus **Industrial Research**

industrial research
Marketing research aimed not at individual consumers, but at interactions between firms and their representatives; for example, in so-called "B2B" contexts.

secondary data
Data collected, usually by an outside firm, for some purpose other than the study at hand (e.g., The U.S. Census). Secondary data are the appropriate starting point for almost all marketing research projects.

Another major distinction among types of marketing research is that between consumer and industrial marketing research. Table 1.2 details some of the differences involved.

Despite these differences, the underlying methods and skills are nearly identical for consumer and industrial marketing research. Both are concerned with problem definition, research design, use of secondary data, sampling, measurement, field work, data processing and analysis, and presentation of results. Whether one conducts a consumer or industrial marketing research study:

- The overall administration, design, execution, and analysis of research tend to follow the same basic rules and procedures;
- The research study design should address the problem and the information needed in a valid and reliable manner;

Table 1.1 Description of Typical Marketing Research Jobs

1. *Research Director/Vice President of Marketing Research*. This is the senior position in research, responsible for the entire research program of the company. Accepts assignments from other company entities or from clients, and may develop and propose research undertakings to company executives. Employs personnel and executes general supervision of research department. Presents research findings to clients or to company executives.
2. *Assistant Director of Research*. This position usually represents a defined "second in command," a senior staff member having responsibilities superseding those of other staff members.
3. *Statistician/Data Processing Specialist*. Duties are usually those of an expert consultant on theory and application of statistical techniques to specific research problems. Usually responsible for experimental design and data processing.
4. *Qualitative Specialist*. Monitors the quality of interviews in work with focus groups.
5. *Senior Analyst*. Ordinarily works in larger research departments. Participates with directors and executives in initial planning of research projects, and oversees execution of projects assigned, operating with minimal supervision. Prepares, or works with analysts in preparing, questionnaires. Selects research techniques, conducts analyses, and writes final report. Has budgetary control over projects and primary responsibility for meeting time schedules. Usually supervises other analysts who do the majority of project work.
6. *Analyst*. The analyst usually handles the bulk of the work required for execution of research projects. Often works under senior analyst supervision. The analyst assists in questionnaire preparation, pretests questionnaires, and makes preliminary analyses of results. Most of the library research or work with company data is handled by the analyst.
7. *Junior Analyst*. Working under rather close supervision, junior analysts handle routine assignments: for example, editing and coding of questionnaires, statistical calculations above the clerical level, and simpler forms of library research. A large portion of the junior analyst's time is spent on tasks assigned by more experienced members of the research team.
8. *Librarian*. The librarian builds and maintains a database or cache of reference sources adequate to the needs of the research department.
9. *Clerical Supervisor*. In larger departments, the central handling and processing of statistical data are the responsibilities of one or more clerical supervisors. Duties include work scheduling and responsibility for accuracy.
10. *Field Work Director*. Usually only larger departments have a field work director who hires, trains, and supervises field interviewers.
11. *Full-Time Interviewer*. The interviewer conducts personal interviews and works under direct supervision of the field work director. Few companies employ full-time interviewers, typically subcontracting or hiring on an as-needed basis.
12. *Tabulating and Clerical Help*. The routine, day-to-day work of the department is performed by these individuals.

Source: Reprinted with permission from Survey of Marketing Research, published by the American Marketing Association, Thomas C. Kinnear and Ann R. Root, 1995.

- The data processing procedures—coding, editing, and weighting—are consistent;
- The analysis of data requires the same types of skill and knowledge;
- The marketing researcher in a business environment is a problem-solver and marketing consultant, and
- The researcher's "tools of the trade" are the application of valid and reliable research techniques to uncover information that helps make a better decision.[1]

consumer research
Marketing research into consumer characteristics, attitudes, beliefs, opinions, and behavior.

Table 1.2 Consumer Versus Industrial Marketing Research

	Consumer	Industrial
Population	Large. More than 100 million households in the United States alone.	Small. Fairly limited in total population, and even more so if within a defined industry or category.
Respondent accessibility	Fairly easy. Can interview at home, on the telephone, by mail, or on the Internet.	Difficult. Usually only during working hours at plant, office, or on the road. Respondent is usually preoccupied with other priorities.
Respondent cooperation	Has become increasingly more difficult to obtain, given hectic lives and prohibitive time constraints.	A major concern. Due to the small population, the industrial respondent is being over-researched.
Sample size	Can usually be drawn as large as needed for a target level of statistical confidence.	Usually much smaller than a consumer sample to achieve similar statistical confidence, given the ratio of the sample to the total population.
Respondent definitions	Usually fairly simple. Those aware of a category or brand, users of a category or brand, demographic criteria, and the like.	Somewhat more difficult. The user and the purchasing decision-maker in most cases are not the same. The users are best able to evaluate products and services, but in many cases have little or no influence on the decision-making process.
Interviewers	Can be readily trained, as they are also consumers and tend to be somewhat familiar with the area under investigation for most categories.	Difficult to find good executive interviewers. A strong working knowledge of the product class or subject being surveyed is essential, as are exceptional interpersonal skills and professionalism.
Study costs	Key dictators of cost are sample size and incidence. Lower-incidence usage categories or demographic or behavioral screening criteria can raise costs considerably.	Relative to consumer research, the critical elements resulting in significantly higher per-interview costs are lower incidence levels, difficulties in locating the "right" respondent (that is, the purchase decision-maker), and securing cooperation (time and concentration of effort) for the interview itself.

1.4f Organizational Structures

The organizational contexts in which analysts work have different structural and organizational forms. Because every organization differs in the relative importance attached to marketing research and the scale and complexity of research methods employed, the marketing research department should be custom-tailored to fit the firm's informational requirements. This discussion applies most directly to large organizations.

The primary structural choice is that between a centralized and de-centralized organization. Completely centralizing the research function of a company by, for example, locating it at corporate headquarters, means that all research is under the control of a single individual, ordinarily the vice president of marketing. Completely decentralizing the department along divisional lines means that the marketing researcher is responsible to the division manager and not to a top corporate executive. Table 1.3 compares the advantages and disadvantages of a **centralized** or **de-centralized structure**. The effects of organizational structure on management, research, and effective articulation between the two are discussed further in Chapter 2.

centralized structure
A form of organization in which the marketing research function is brought together into a single unit, ordinarily overseen by corporate management.

de-centralized structure
A form of organization in which the marketing research function is spread out across different corporate departments or divisions, with decision-making authority delegated accordingly.

Divisions of companies may be organized by products, by customers, or by geographic regions. De-centralized marketing research structures often exactly parallel this divisional assignment of the company. Thus, research personnel are expected to become expert in the research-based problems of particular products, customer markets, or geographic regions.

The "integrated" structure has proved to be a viable alternative form of organization. This increasingly popular research structure makes use of a central staff (which includes a highly qualified marketing research function) available as needed to counsel with and reinforce individual research departments within each division. Such a hybrid relationship is intended to combine the best features of centralization and de-centralization into one system capable of more coordinated and effective research. The central research staff arranges for the exchange of pertinent marketing data to the various divisions, acts as a central purchasing agent for all services common to the needs of the research teams, carries out research projects with company-wide implications, undertakes projects for departments too small to have their own research staffs, and assists divisional research staffs when they become overloaded. In addition, the company can set research standards to be maintained at all levels. By having additional research teams located at the divisional level, a company achieves its goal of making the research function part of the firm's marketing team, allowing researchers to become experts in their fields and placing their information-gathering techniques closer to the "consumer" of research.

The main disadvantage to the integrated system is potential control conflicts over the research staffs and their projects, particularly when the lines of authority in a company are not clearly delineated. Theoretically, the central research staff is organized solely as an advisory branch. But all too often, divisional researchers look to corporate staffers as their ultimate bosses, instead of to their divisional heads. Other drawbacks to the integrated system include disadvantages attributed to de-centralized research departments, such as high cost, duplication of efforts, and lack of an adequate number of competent specialists.

Table 1.3 **Relative Merits of Centralized and De-Centralized Structures**

	Centralized	De-centralized
Advantages	1. Effective coordination and control of the research activity 2. More economical and flexible use of facilities and personnel 3. Increased usefulness and objectivity of research results to corporate executives 4. Greater institutional prestige and credibility to marketing research 5. Greater likelihood of attracting top-notch researchers and securing an adequate budget 6. Cross-fertilization of ideas	1. Researchers are "close to the action" of marketing problems and implementation of their recommendations. 2. More specialization is available on product, customers, or markets. 3. Greater attention paid by divisional managers, who can directly interact with to marketing research personnel 4. More likely breakdown of corporate/divisional barriers
Disadvantages	1. Isolates researchers from day-to-day activities and problems 2. Corporate problems receive time and attention at the expense of divisions. 3. Separates researchers from the action programs based on the research; takes no responsibility for their implemented recommendations	1. Tendency to bias results in favor of the marketing group for which the researcher works 2. Inadequate research controls, standards, and procedures 3. Difficulty in finding qualified people 4. High cost 5. Duplication of effort 6. Central management needs not attended to

In addition to divisional organization, marketing research departments can also be organized according to marketing activity (product design, e-commerce, demand analysis, and so forth) or research method (experimental design, modeling, questionnaire design, interviewing, statistical analysis, and so forth). Many large companies employ some combination of these in their organizational structure because there are no handy "cookbook" methods to determine the optimal structure. There are, however, a number of criteria which can be followed to help narrow the selection alternatives. The first criterion, and perhaps the most important, is that the marketing research function should be situated near the location where the marketing decisions are made and the information is consequently needed most and with the greatest frequency. For example, if a firm makes one or two products for a few customers, a research staff located at the corporate level might suffice. However, for a firm of the sheer breadth of Procter and Gamble, which produces myriad products for a host of different customers, it would likely be better to de-centralize or integrate the research function to put market information closest to those who use it.

demand analysis
A formal model that will help forecast demand (either unit or volume sales) for a product. Such an analysis consists of determining the variables giving rise to demand as well as tying them in statistically to a demand forecast, usually via regression and time-series techniques.

The second criterion to consider is that researchers should be free from undue influence or manipulation by those areas or staff for whom they conduct research projects. Although it is tempting to allow project sponsors to have intermittent input, such input more often biases a project's outcome than aids in its expedient completion. A third criterion is that the marketing research function should be organized so that the firm can satisfy the demand for research projects quickly and efficiently. If the firm's divisions exhibit a steady volume of requests for research projects, it would be advisable to de-centralize the research function. On the other hand, if the demand for research within a firm is sparse or fluctuates widely, it may be more effective to centralize all research activities in a corporate office. The final criterion is a matter of practicality that can often be overlooked: the research department should report to an executive who has a genuine interest in marketing research, understands how it operates, knows its potential, and possesses sufficient authority to ensure that the actions called for by the research are undertaken.

In the final analysis, there is no completely right or wrong organizational structure for marketing research in a firm. Moreover, organizational structure needs to be responsive to changes in a firm's core business practice and adjust accordingly.

1.4g Buyer–Supplier Relationships

One decision that confronts all marketing research directors and a great many analysts is whether and how best to use research suppliers. These suppliers may be involved with a few aspects of a research study, or they may be given total responsibility for the study in its entirety.

The primary advantages of using research suppliers include: the overall cost may be lower than that of hiring additional personnel and other expenditures of an internal project; outside suppliers can be used as needed, as opposed to the fixed cost of a personnel hire; suppliers offer special skills not available internally; managers have greater flexibility in selecting the best supplier available for a specific type of problem; outside suppliers have greater objectivity and are usually not involved in the politics of the company; and the sponsoring company can remain anonymous, if it wishes to.

There are a number of disadvantages of using research suppliers that must be weighed as well; among them: the supplier may be less familiar with the objectives and problems of the company and/or industry; there is a risk, especially in the first purchase from a supplier, that the research will not be done well or on time; there is a greater risk that results of studies or company activities will become known to competitors, despite nondisclosure agreements and other protective arrangements; and overall costs can be higher, as nonsuppliers must earn a profit that allows for slack periods, start-up/learning costs, and for studies that generate net losses.

Ensuring the highest quality end-product from outside marketing research suppliers is of great concern to marketing research directors and analysts. The first step in selecting a specific supplier for a project is to seek recommendations—from associates within the firm, other research suppliers, advertising agencies, trade associations, or private consultants. Impersonal sources such as trade publications, professional directories, journals, and promotional material of suppliers may also provide potential supply firms. Evaluating prospective suppliers usually involves discussions with other people for whom they have done work and the examination of some piece of research they have done.

Criteria for choosing a supplier may include the capabilities of key personnel (technical competence, education, specialization, communication skills, timeliness, responsiveness and other personal characteristics);

facilities for field work, data processing, and analysis; quality of design for research, questionnaires, and data presentation; quality of reports (well-written and insightful, putting forth conclusions and recommendations that are responsible and accurate); orientation toward marketing management; ethics; location; delivery schedule; and cost. Buyers of research may request several proposals for a project. They may also use more than one supplier, to compare their performance. Maintaining continual evaluation and individual assessment of suppliers is another way to improve the quality of outside research: get involved in the specifications of the tabulation (data analysis), and ask the supplier's views on the research findings' implications.

Most experienced buyers of research develop a short list of suppliers with whom they deal on a regular basis. It is often difficult for a new firm to be included on the preapproved list if there is no formal vetting process, as is often the case.

In the interaction between the buyers of research and the suppliers, certain ground rules should apply. The supplier must be able to satisfy specific requirements of the buyer and provide information on the list of criteria the buyer is using in making the selection. The supplier should also be able to expect a number of things from the buyer, among them:

- general background and description of the management problem at hand
- explanation of the research problem and objectives
- opportunity to discuss these problems and their background
- budget range for the project
- timing and deadlines
- assurance that the supplier will be approached only when there is a reasonable expectation that the buyer will select the product

1.4h Proposal Guidelines

research proposal
A document submitted by a marketing research firm to a potential client, detailing the problem, objectives, possible courses of action, information needs, personnel qualifications of the research team, budget, and timeline of deliverables for the research project.

Most clients desiring marketing research require that all interested research firms submit a proposal for research. The topics in the following list sketch guidelines for writing such a **research proposal**. The number of topics covered in the proposal will depend on the size of the project. Obviously, the proposal for a multimillion-dollar research project will cover more topics and go into much greater depth than the proposal for a $10,000 project. Topics to consider include:

1. *Problem*. The problem (or opportunity) must be clearly defined. Does it affect only one area of the firm or is it company-wide? What are the underlying causes of the decision situation?
2. *Objectives*. What are the decision objectives? What does management expect to gain from research, both tangibly and in terms of underlying "intelligence"? Objectives should be stated clearly and concisely.
3. *Alternatives*. What are the alternative courses of action? What are their anticipated consequences?
4. *Information needs*. What information is needed? How, specifically and in detail, will it be gathered? State the initial plan and organization, search of literature, interviews, questionnaires, experiments, and so forth.
5. *Personnel qualifications*. Cite your experience and success with problems of a similar nature. Include dates and references (with permission, of course) to allow verification. Also, list job descriptions, names, and one-page resumes of key personnel who will be working on the project.
6. *Evaluation*. State how the data will be handled and stored. Specify whether the project can be duplicated in other branches of the company or other areas of the country. Show how you will evaluate the project while it is under way, and how you will determine whether to continue, change, or terminate it. What criteria will be used to recommend the best alternative? What is the likelihood of success? Be realistic—don't promise more than you can deliver.
7. *Budget*. Do not over-budget: a padded budget is quickly rejected. Show clients where their money will go—list the salaries, equipment and supplies, travel requirements, miscellaneous expenses and indirect costs, and allowances for the unexpected. Provide concise justification for each budget item.
8. *Timetable*. Provide an accurate timetable for the completion of work and any milestones or deliverables.

After the appropriate topics have been covered in rough-draft form, assemble these answers in a logical, coherent format, such as the one presented in Figure 1.5.

Figure 1.5 Proposal Form

1. **Prefatory parts**
   - Letter of transmittal (a short note explaining documents being transmitted)
   - Title page
   - Table of contents
   - List of tables (if any)
   - List of figures (if any)
2. **Body of proposal**
   - Introduction
     - Problem
     - Need
     - Background
   - Objectives/purpose
   - Procedures
     - Methods and sources
     - Plan of attack
     - Sequence of activities
     - Equipment and facilities available
     - Personnel qualifications
   - Evaluation
   - Budget
3. **Supplementary parts**
   - Agency forms
     - Budget justification (if any)
     - References
   - Tables or figures (if any)

1.5 Global Themes in Marketing Research

It has become a truism close to cliché that, due in part to the emergence of the Internet, most marketing must be considered global. Marketing managers need to consider their place within open, worldwide markets and a global economy as they formulate their plans. As businesses become more global in the markets they serve, marketing research is becoming ever more valuable because managers with useful experience and insights in one country or region often find these assets only partly applicable in unfamiliar and foreign contexts. One large-scale study of multinational marketing firms found that insufficient research was a critical factor in determining the failure of global marketing activity. The study concluded that roughly two thirds of global programs that did not undertake formal marketing research programs before launch failed to meet expectations, whereas two thirds of those that did do marketing research achieved their expectations. Although it is difficult to extrapolate from a general study of this nature, the underlying message is clear: foreign contexts require additional research resources to verify and contextualize research carried out domestically.

Even when researchers have been diligent in carrying out international marketing studies, mistakes, even large or comical ones, are possible. *International Issues 1.1* takes a closer look at a few such blunders.

Some of the challenges involved in conducting effective marketing research internationally include:

- Researchers must often deal with multiple languages and cultural differences that complicate data collection and interpretation.
- Markets in countries or industries that are still actively developing are less likely to have as much secondary data (data already collected and published in some form) available as those in more developed countries or industries.
- Secondary data that are available on these markets are sometimes of questionable quality relative to the standards of data in more developed countries and industries.
- The marketing research industry in countries that have less of a history of industrial and entrepreneurial activity has less of the institutional infrastructure necessary to provide syndicated data, select samples, and do interviews than that in countries with more of this economic history.
- In some countries, cultural dynamics or concerns about government surveillance may negatively impact the willingness of consumers and distributors to participate in research projects or may bias the responses obtained.
- The logistical dimensions of implementing marketing research internationally are complex, and international costs can be far higher than domestic costs.
- There are a great many "external" considerations—those on which a firm can have little direct influence—including: structure of local competition; government-mandated regulations, trade incentives and barriers; widespread prejudice against imports; the availability of mass media and electronic commerce infrastructure, distribution/transportation; warehousing and storage; and the nature and operation of local retailing institutions. Generally speaking, *none* of these can be assumed to be constant across borders, and many would need to be an explicit part of the research design, affecting the very viability of domestically successful operations abroad.

International Issues 1.1

Global Marketing Blunders

The lesson on the value of marketing research in international operations has often been learned the hard way. Following are a few classic examples of international marketing failures that likely would have been avoided with competent marketing research, some merely by involving culturally native personnel to vet plans early on.

- A large, U.S.-based carbonated soft-drink firm set up large bottling facilities in Indonesia in an attempt to break into a huge new potential market. The judgment of management proved wrong, and sales fell substantially below expectations. Later marketing research suggested the reasons. First, demographic data revealed that Indonesians had little disposable income to support the purchase of the product. Second, the consumption of the product was mainly by tourists and expatriates in the major cities. Third, most Indonesians preferred noncarbonated, coconut-based drinks. In this case, fairly basic research would have uncovered that core preferences would have to be changed for the product to be successful, a difficult, time-consuming undertaking.
- Vic Tanny's franchised health club tried to implement its U.S.-based marketing strategy in Singapore. Its U.S.-style facilities and exercise equipment drew few customers. Again, basically only expatriates were interested. Later, marketing research revealed that to be successful the club would need to appeal to Singapore residents' preference for Western-style competitive sports, Chinese calisthenics, and traditional Asian exercise.
- Lego A/S, the Danish toy company, implemented a Western-style consumer promotion in Japan. Consisting of bonus packs of Legos and gift promotions, the promotion had caused sales increases in the United States and Europe when implemented there. It seemed to have no impact in the Japanese market. Subsequent marketing research revealed that Japanese consumers considered the promotion to be wasteful, expensive, and not very appealing.*
- There are endless examples of ad copy not being appropriately tested, causing harm to the brand that can, with hindsight, seem humorous. An Internet phenomenon is the so-called "Chevy Nova Award," given in honor of the infamous campaign to market that automobile in Mexico, where the name of the model translated as "It doesn't go." Some highlights of the "award" include:
  1. The "Mist Stick," a curling iron, was introduced into Germany, where "mist" is slang for manure. It failed to capture much share.
  2. When "Cue" toothpaste was introduced in France, sharing a name with a notorious pornographic magazine, it hardly inspired confidence.
  3. When prepared baby food was first sold in some African countries, the same packaging was used as in the United States, with a smiling baby on the label, to avoid problems with multilingual translation. It turns out that, for the same reason, local food-producing firms often use photos of *what is inside the package*.
  4. The American Dairy Association had huge success with their "Got Milk?" campaign, and so sought to extend it to Latin America. Unfortunately, the translation came out roughly as "Are you lactating?"

Almost all multi-national firms have experienced some degree of shock when seemingly sound campaigns and strategies are unleashed in places where they are novel to the point of offensiveness or simply out of cultural bounds. There is no substitute for careful, small-scale testing of marketing campaigns using an appropriate local sample.

***Sources:** Charles F. Valentine, "Blunders Abroad," *Nation's Business*, pp. 54, 56, March 1989; Kamran Kashani, "Beware the Pitfalls of Global Marketing," *Harvard Business Review*, pp. 91–98, September–October 1989.

1.6 Ethical Themes in Market Research

Marketing research is limited in its ability to inform decision-making. The effects or dependent variables considered usually fall within a narrowly defined scope and are relatively short-term. The formal edifice of marketing research practice neither speaks to nor replaces the need for ethical criteria in decision-making. An ethical dimension must be overlaid and constantly considered by the decision-making team over and above the desire for useful information and a sound research design.

1.6a Ethics of Performing Research

The first order of these ethical themes comes up during research itself. The collection, processing, and evaluation of information entails responsibilities—some explicit, many unspoken. Not all information is value-neutral, and some has the potential to adversely affect people and public institutions. In the process of collecting marketing research information, ethical issues frequently arise regarding the integrity of the research (for example, withholding, altering, or misinterpreting data) and the treatment of

Marketing Research Focus 1.5

American Marketing Association's Marketing Research Code of Ethics

For Research Users, Practitioners, and Interviewers

1. No individual or organization will undertake any activity that is directly or indirectly represented to be marketing research, but that has as its real purpose the attempted sale of merchandise or services to some or all of the respondents interviewed in the course of the research.
2. If a respondent has been led to believe, directly or indirectly, that he is participating in a marketing research survey and that his anonymity will be protected, his name shall not be made known to anyone outside the research organization or research department or used for other than research purposes.

For Research Practitioners

1. There will be no intentional or deliberate misrepresentation of research methods or results. An adequate description of methods employed will be made available on request to the sponsor of the research. Evidence that field work has been completed according to specifications will, on request, be made available to buyers of research.
2. The identity of the survey sponsor and/or the ultimate client for whom a survey is being done will be held in confidence at all times, unless this identity is to be revealed as part of the research design. Research information shall be held in confidence by the research organization or department and not used for personal gain or made available to any outside party unless the client specifically authorizes such release.
3. A research organization shall not undertake marketing studies for competitive clients when such studies would jeopardize the confidential nature of client–agency relationships.

For Users of Marketing Research

1. A user of research shall not knowingly disseminate conclusions from a given research project or service that are inconsistent with or not warranted by the data.
2. To the extent that there is involved in a research project a unique design involving techniques, approaches, or concepts not commonly available to research practitioners, the prospective user of research shall not solicit such a design from one practitioner and deliver it to another for execution without the approval of the design originator.

For Field Interviewers

1. Research assignments and materials received, as well as information obtained from respondents, shall be held in confidence by the interviewer and revealed to no one except the research organization conducting the marketing study.
2. No information gained through a marketing research activity shall be used, directly or indirectly, for the personal gain or advantage of the interviewer.
3. Interviews shall be conducted in strict accordance with specifications and instructions received.
4. An interviewer shall not carry out two or more interviewing assignments simultaneously unless authorized by all contractors or employees concerned. Members of the American Marketing Association will be expected to conduct themselves in accordance with the provisions of this code in all of their marketing research activities.

Source: Paper developed by The Market Research Council's Ethics Committee. Reprinted with permission from Leo Bogart.

participants and clients. Are subjects' rights to privacy respected during surveys? Are data shared between subsidiaries, with sales staff, or between research projects? Has the firm resorted to espionage to gather information on competitors? Has the research been designed to support a particular viewpoint? Have respondents been misled as to the purpose of the study? Have subcontractors been allowed to violate research requirements? Did study design errors come to light after a report was written? Have the data been stored and secured in a manner that truly protects the individuals who supplied it?

Universities, medical establishments, and government agencies all have **Institutional Review Boards** (IRBs) to ensure, under any reasonable circumstances, that participants in research are unlikely to be physically, economically, or psychologically harmed. But the private sphere is, by and large, a different story. Protections of research participants involve a constantly changing legal and technological landscape.

Because of actual and potential abuses, a number of codes of ethics have been developed to guide researchers. The American Marketing Association publishes a ***code of ethics*** (*See Marketing Research Focus 1.5: American Marketing Association's Marketing Research Code of Ethics*) for marketing research

Institutional Review Boards (IRBs)
A panel charged with reviewing research proposals in regard to their potential for psychological or physical harm and to safeguard the rights of potential participants.

code of ethics
A system of rules, standards, and guidelines defining ethical behavior within professional organizations and in relation to the general public.

regarding issues of misrepresentation, confidentiality, conflicting interests of competitors as clients, integrity of conclusions, and use of data. Various other associations have published codes of ethics for marketing research, including the Marketing Research Association.

1.6b Ethics of Using Research

Users of marketing research also encounter ethical issues. Has the company deceived research suppliers by asking for detailed research proposals only to use the proposed design for their own research? Are managers pressuring researchers to come up with research that favors their viewpoint of what should be done? Have statistics been misused to support claims based on data that are not statistically meaningful? Have details been withheld to make a pet project look better?

A further order of ethical implications relates to the impact of marketing choices beyond measurable performance criteria or beyond the timeframe of standard marketing research. For example, a marketing research project may be able to predict whether a particular type of plastic packaging will increase a company's market share for its product; it cannot speak to the rate of injury to sea life or even the longer-term effects of environmental pollution on the health of the industry or consumer attitudes toward the company. Such larger concerns have to be brought in from sources other than the marketing research system during the decision-making process.

Marketing research can be considered a study of a specific subset of measurable phenomena, a kind of microcosm. It serves as a good source of information for decision-making, so long as its scope and limitations are kept in mind, and so long as other sources of information relevant to the decision are also considered. The human conscience cannot be replaced by science, and the ethical implications of marketing decisions cannot be avoided or nullified by marketing research. In many of the case studies in this book, possible ethical questions or implications of marketing choices will be brought explicitly to the attention of the reader, although it should be borne in mind that *all* research and data-gathering have ethical implications and the consequent potential for misuse.

Special Expert Feature

Industrial Marketing Research

Daniel J. Snider

"Market assessment"; "Benchmarking"; "Competitive analysis"; "Voice of the customer"; "Product optimization"; "Market entry strategy"; "Sourcing"—these terms may immediately conjure thoughts of some cutting-edge consumer product, a new sports drink or cosmetic line, for example. Although indeed ubiquitous in the design, production, and marketing of consumer goods, these market research tools are just as important for the industrial sector: introducing a new type of synthetic brick to the home-building industry, more bandwidth into an urban utility market, or gaining market share for a fleet of commercial trucks. It is often bandied about that more than half of marketing graduates will be employed in the business-to-business (B2B) sector. Although the tools that marketing research offers are every bit as applicable in the B2B universe as when businesses sell to consumers (B2C), they are seldom recognized as such, perhaps because so much of this marketing activity is "hidden" from consumers, taking place before products ever hit retail shelves, as well as for products never intended for retail distribution (e.g., products sold to contractors or components sold to other manufacturers).

Industrial marketing can range from automotive components to building materials to medical devices to hundreds of other applications and settings. The companies that produce these products (or supply the industries that do) have, if anything, an even greater stake than consumer products producers in detailed market research. With consumer products, there is a vast pool of potential consumers to target; many market segments can be sizeable, offering strong profit potential, even if a relatively rarefied niche is chosen, as for luxury goods. In the industrial realm, the customer base is made up of far fewer companies or individuals with whom business can be done. Consequently, the failure to meet the needs of *any* segment of the industry is a looming possibility. This makes tools like data validation, to take but one example, especially critical because firms lack the large pools of primary consumer data typical in B2C customer satisfaction studies, and each "data point" (i.e., potential business client) can represent millions, or even billions, in revenue.

Another challenge that arises in industrial market research is that the consumer's is rarely the critical opinion to capture: there may be multiple industrial decision-makers, or even formal committees, whose

continued

opinions and value systems need to be sampled. For example, the manufacturing engineers might feel the need to incorporate a new polypropylene material into the door panel of the vehicle their team is working on; the design engineers may feel this degrades perceptions of aerodynamic efficiency but are not sure how; however, it is the purchasing manager who will make the final decision, taking into account the cost factor involved in using this new material as well as other nonengineering issues. As marketing researchers, would we need to survey each of these "players," or merely the ultimate decision-maker? How might we reasonably measure all their perceptions and subsequently integrate them? In fact, simply mapping the decision-making process can be dramatically more challenging in an industrial setting than in a consumer-oriented setting, and this must be completed *before* data collection begins.

Each of the essential skill-sets typically gained in market research courses are as broadly applicable in the industrial sphere as in the consumer arena. At Ducker Research, we conduct conjoint analyses, regression analyses, and attitude measurement, using a wide variety of scale types, as well as other tools, to assess market sizing and segmentation; profitability analysis, pricing studies, and purchase decision analysis; detailed customer satisfaction inventories; and many other mainstays of modern marketing research methodology. What emerges as most important is primary research: direct contact with those in the industry who can offer the right information and opinions about the product (or, occasionally, service) in question. This involves making contact with purchasing departments, engineers, salespeople, and often even other "internal" marketing personnel. Focus groups are difficult in the industrial sector (it is tough, for example, to bring manufacturing people together), so face-to-face interviews, online chat forums, phone conversations, and online surveys become important ways to conduct research. The amount of secondary data available about the marketability of the product that you're researching, even given the ubiquity of the Internet, is minute when compared with that available for a consumer goods product (e.g., Nielsen or IRI reports, the census, scanner data, or other panel-based sources).

A Senior Market Analyst's responsibilities include developing interview outlines comprising both quantitative and qualitative questions, conducting the actual primary and secondary research, performing detailed data analysis, writing the report, and presenting findings to the client. A solid grasp of spreadsheet and report presentation software and a thorough grounding in statistical methods and how to present their conclusions in "human language," are required workaday skills.

At Ducker, the range of industrial market research encompasses *construction* (interior and exterior wall cladding, windows and glass, doors, insulation, flooring, cabinets and countertops, and hardware and fixtures), *engineered and industrial products* (chemicals, electronics, HVAC, lighting, machine tools, robotics, telecommunications, and motors and drives), and *transportation* (automotive, aerospace, aftermarket, components and systems, electronics and audio, finishes, interiors, materials, medium and heavy truck, and off-highway vehicles). Even this abbreviated list amply conveys that industrial marketing—and the research it depends on—covers an array of products underlying the backbone of our economy. Ducker carries out global research in conjunction with its offices in Europe, Asia, and India, in addition to subcontract work for other European research companies requiring research conducted domestically in the United States.

Case Study

To convey the flavor of what a typical industrial marketing research project encompasses, let us consider a real case study. A private equity firm wished to purchase a growing company (Company X) that manufactured a certain type of machine tool for the global manufacturing economy. Ducker's tasks were to evaluate and assess the following: the direction in which the market was heading for this type of machinery (substitute products?); identification and size of competitors; competition from overseas (Asian) markets; strengths and weaknesses of Company X vs. the competition; how Company X is perceived in the market as compared with competitors; unmet needs of industrial customers; purchase drivers; and other issues (which it is often the job of the researcher to fill in as the project progresses). Research outlines were developed for discussions with end-users, both present customers of Company X and noncustomers, and with competitors. As an example of the analysis that was performed on the research data, quantitative rating scales were used to determine relative performance and perception of Company X compared with its direct competitors, and Gap Analysis was presented to show potential improvements for Company X, should the private equity firm decide in the end to go ahead with the acquisition.

Each new project in industrial marketing brings with it the opportunity to utilize a different combination of research skills, so there is, as the saying goes, never a dull moment. Industrial marketing research may not carry the cachet of consumer-packaged goods (CPGs), but the challenge of working with such a diversity of industries, applications, and internal decision-makers makes the job an exciting, rewarding, never-ending learning experience.

Dan Snider is Senior Market Analyst, Ducker Research Company, Troy, MI. Courtesy of Daniel J. Snider.

Summary

The primary purpose of marketing research is to provide information to facilitate all stages of the decision-making process, from recognizing a decision to selecting a course of action. Marketing research must be systematic and without bias in providing information relevant to decision-making.

Most marketing decisions are repetitive and familiar, requiring little marketing research input; but in unfamiliar situations, marketing research information is typically the primary guide for decisions.

Marketing research is even more crucial to marketing managers when considering the global aspects of their markets. Useful experience and insights from one country or region are not always applicable in unfamiliar and foreign contexts.

Marketing research projects should be designed to provide a more systematic and continuous flow of information, in accord with the organization's overall planning process. This fits with the concept of a marketing research system, in which management views marketing research as an information center for decision-making, as opposed to the mere gathering and analysis of data.

The methodology and statistical rigor of marketing research make it feasible to obtain information regarding behavior of groups of people and institutions, providing a means to quantify related data and assess them in an unbiased manner. Marketing research methodology plays a key role in how internal marketing and business activities are conducted, how the general marketing research industry operates, and a wide variety of applications in society at large.

The model of the marketing system includes situational factors, marketing mix factors controllable through the marketing plan, the behavioral response of the market, and performance measures used to assess that response. Marketing research provides information regarding each of these aspects of the marketing system, which helps to keep the model up to date and builds understanding of how components of the marketing system interrelate and jointly function.

Marketing research has developed into a complex, global, multifaceted industry encompassing a variety of emphases, organizational contexts, and possible careers.

Marketing research is limited in scope of measurable information and time frame. Managers must consider ethical implications separately from other criteria informing their decisions. Information provided by marketing research does not eliminate personal responsibility for decisions based on it.

Key Terms

analyst (p. 16)
behavioral response (p. 8)
centralized structure (p. 18)
code of ethics (p. 23)
consumer research (p. 17)
de-centralized structure (p. 18)
decision support system (DSS) (p. 14)
decision variables (p. 8)
decision-making process (p. 7)
demand analysis (p. 19)
dependent variable (p. 8)
independent variables (p. 8)
industrial research (p. 16)
information (p. 4)
inputs (p. 8)
institutional review boards (p. 23)
intelligence system (p. 14)
market research (p. 4)
marketing concept (p. 7)
marketing information systems (p. 14)
marketing management process (p. 11)
marketing mix (p. 4)
marketing research (p. 4)
marketing research system (p. 14)
marketing system (p. 7)
objective (p. 5)
performance measures (p. 8)
research director (p. 16)
research proposal (p. 20)
research suppliers (p. 16)
secondary data (p. 16)
situational analysis (p. 11)
situational factors (p. 11)
systematic (p. 4)
technical specialist (p. 16)
variable (p. 8)

Discussion Questions

1 Outline the steps in the marketing decision-making process for marketing managers considering introducing a new formulation of a laundry detergent.

2 What factors determine the relative importance of managerial experience versus marketing research in a given situation?

3 A marketing manager responsible for video games has received a copy of 10 new books on this industry and five new industry reports prepared by industry consultants. These items total more than 3000 pages. "All this data will be a great help with the new games we are planning," noted the analyst who delivered the documents. Comment on this quote, and describe how the manager should proceed.

4 How might the following organizations effectively employ marketing research?
   - a National Museum of Art
   - b American Airlines
   - c the census
   - d American Consumer Satisfaction Index
   - e a senatorial campaign
   - f Dell Computer
   - g a public campaign against cigarette smoking

5 If you were to undertake a research project involving a country with which you had no familiarity, what sorts of issues would you study before starting to design the project? What special considerations would you need to remain aware of after the project was underway?

Review Questions

1 Which role of marketing research is involved in opinion polling?
   - a role in marketing
   - b role in firm
   - c role in marketing research industry
   - d role in society

2 Which of the following is not an example of statistical reasoning?
   - a What are the chances of that happening?
   - b candidate B
   - c received 16 votes out of 19
   - d We're more likely to get what we want if we don't compromise up front.
   - e Is there enough interest in this idea to be worth going ahead with it?

3 Over which independent variables does a company exert control?
   - a marketing mix
   - b performance measures
   - c situational variables
   - d all independent variables

4 A ______________ may include an assessment of the competition and the internal resources of the company.
   - a demand analysis
   - b performance measure
   - c distribution assessment
   - d situational analysis

5 Which of the following did not contribute to the historical development of the marketing research industry?
   - a the availability of personal computers
   - b the emphasis on production
   - c the rise of the marketing concept
   - d formal research in psychology
   - e the development of probabilistic sampling methods

6 What distinguishes marketing research from what is usually referred to as market research, as well as other sorts of social science research?
   - a the application of rigorous methodology
   - b focus on managerial decision making, broader than markets and consumers
   - c the systematic collection of multiple, different types of data
   - d the overall approach to data processing and statistical analysis

7 Which of the following data are most likely to be considered information for someone anticipating voting in an upcoming election?
   a the number of people voting, according to recent polls
   b the prior occupations of the candidates' staff
   c the candidates' stated platforms
   d the countries that candidates have visited recently

8 Examples of inputs (independent variables) and outputs (dependent variables) studied in marketing research are, respectively:
   a marketing mix; profits.
   b performance measures; pricing.
   c behavioral responses; situational factors.
   d government regulation; economic climate.

9 Which is an advantage of a centralized research structure?
   a It allows one to provide greater customer specialization.
   b It avoids distraction by ever-changing activities, problems, and organizational imperatives.
   c It allows company resources to be allocated and deployed more economically in most cases.
   d Corporate issues will take precedence over those at divisional and lower levels.

10 For what purposes should a company seeking to enter a new market in a foreign country undergo marketing research?
   a to help avoid linguistic (e.g., translation) and cultural blunders
   b to design products and services that fit local markets better than those already being sold elsewhere
   c to assess whether a market-entry decision is prudent
   d all of the above

Web Exercise

Log in to the Online Edition of your textbook at www.atomicdog.com to participate in this Web Exercise, which can be found in your Online Study Guide for this chapter.

Further Reading

"Essentials of Marketing," Dana-Nicoleta Lascu, Ph.D., Kenneth E. Clow, Ph.D.
"Marketing 9e: Marketing in the 21st Century," Joel R. Evans, Ph.D., Barry Berman, Ph.D.
"Marketing Management," Michael Czinkota, Masaaki Kotabe
"Strategic Marketing," Syed Akhter
http://www.marketingpower.com/ [American Marketing Association]
http://www.knowthis.com/
http://www.mra-net.org/ [Marketing Research Association]
http://www.quirks.com/

Note

1 Reprinted with permission from *Marketing News*, published by the American Marketing Association, Marvin Katz, "Use Same Theory, Skills for Consumer, Industrial Research," January 12, 1979, p. 16.

CHAPTER TWO
THE MARKETING RESEARCH PROCESS

"Advertising people who ignore research are as dangerous as generals who ignore decodes of enemy signals."

DAVID OGILVY

The steps of the overall marketing research process are briefly described in the Overview section. The initial steps of that process, establishing the need for information and defining research objectives and information needs, are presented in much greater detail in subsequent sections of this chapter. (Later chapters detail the remaining steps.) In the *Special Section* at the end of the chapter, a real-world example provides a concrete illustration of how the steps of the marketing research process apply to a large-scale project.

2.1 Overview of the Research Process

The essential steps of the research process are diagrammed in Figure 2.1.

2.1a Establish Need for Information

Rarely does an initial request for help adequately establish the need for research information. Managers often react to hunches and symptoms rather than to clearly identified decision situations. Yet the need for research information must be precisely defined if the research project is to provide information pertinent to the necessary decisions. Too often, the importance of this initial step is overlooked in the excitement of undertaking a research project, resulting in research findings that do not adequately inform decisions.

symptoms
Marketing measures, often those of particular concern (e.g., decreasing sales or loyalty), which in themselves lack meaningful information for improving management decisions, but that signal that corrective action may need to be undertaken.

Figure 2.1 The Marketing Research Process

Manager decides whether to request research.

1. Establish Need For Information
   - Recognition of a Decision Situation
   - Defining the Decision ↔ *possible exploratory research*
     - Decision Objectives
     - Statement of Problems and Opportunities
   - Identifying Alternative Courses of Action ↔ *possible exploratory research*
   - Evaluating Courses of Action

Marketing researcher has received request for research help.

1. Establish Need For Information
   - Identify Decision Maker
   - Objectives of the Decision Maker
   - Effective Statement of Problems and Opportunities ↔ *possible exploratory research*
   - Identify Courses of Action ↔ *possible exploratory research*
2. Detail Research Objectives and Information Needs
   - Visualize Research Findings
   - Develop Decision Criteria
   - Determine the Cost & Value of the Research
   - Present the Proposal for Research
3. Set Research Design and Data Sources
4. Design Data Collection Procedure
5. Design Sample
6. Collect Data
7. Process and Code Data
8. Analyze Data
9. Presentation of Results

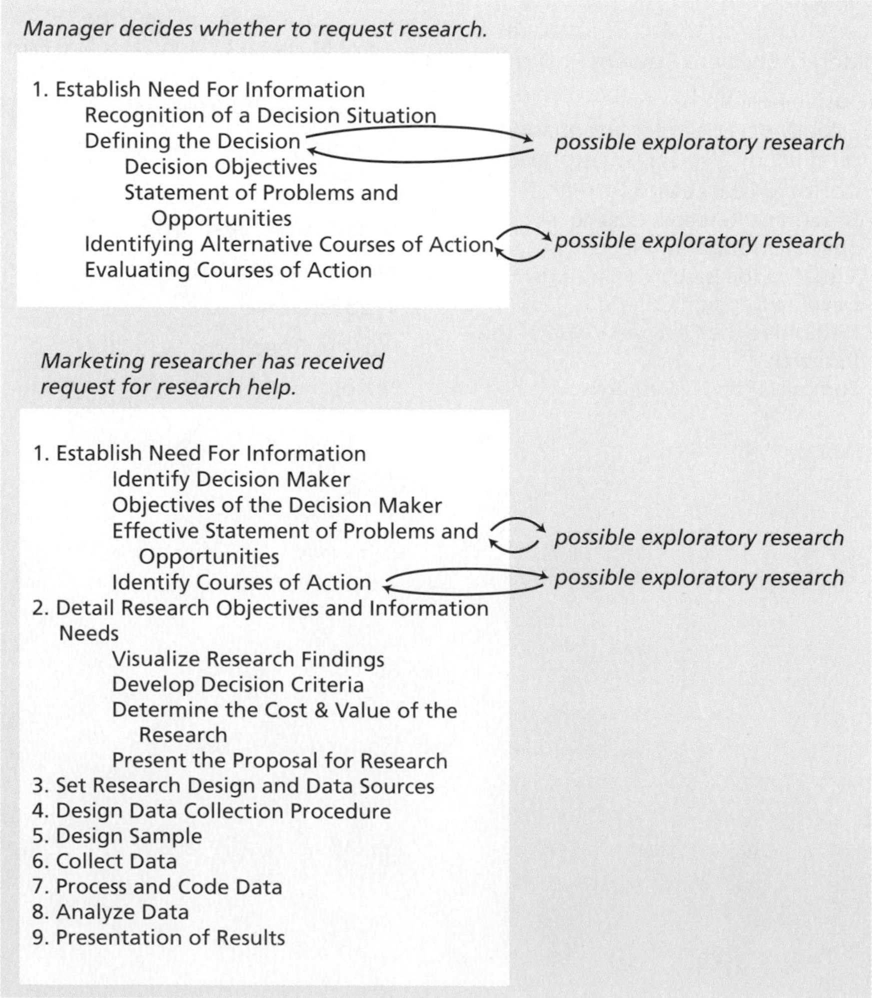

2.1b Detail Research Objectives and Information Needs

After the general need for information is clearly established, researchers must list, specifically and in detail, the objectives and information needs of the proposed research. Research objectives answer the question, "Why is this project being conducted?" and are typically put in writing before the project is undertaken. Information needs answer the question, "What specific information is required to attain the objectives?"

information needs
The specific information required to attain the stated objectives of a marketing research project.

2.1c Design Research and Data Sources

Once the study objectives are determined, researchers design the formal research project, including the appropriate sources of data for the study. A research design is the general plan guiding the data collection and analysis phases of the research. It is the framework that specifies the type of information to be collected, the sources of data, and the data-collection procedures and analysis.

Data sources include internal sources, such as previous research studies and company records, and external sources, such as commercial research reports and trade magazine, industry, or government reports. If data are found that fit the information needs, the researcher must examine the research design to determine the data's appropriateness, timeliness and, to the extent this is possible in advance, accuracy and reliability. The reputation of the organization that collected and analyzed the data is often a guide to reliability.

If the data are not available from internal or external sources, researchers will need to collect new data by means of interviews, observation, experimentation, or, if an explicit mathematical or statistical model has been built, via simulation.

research design
The general plan guiding the data collection and analysis phases of the research: a framework that specifies the type of information to be collected, the sources of data, and all data collection procedures and analysis.

data sources
Any of a number of commercial vendors or internal repositories of information used to improve marketing research decisions. Typically include prior primary research, internal firm records, various trade publications and both industry and government reports.

2.1d Design Data-Collection Procedure

Researchers must develop a data-collection procedure that establishes an effective link between the information needs and the questions to be asked or the observations to be recorded. The success of the study is dependent on the researchers' skill and creativity in establishing this link.

2.1e Design Sample

Researchers need to clearly define who or what is to be included in the sample, the population from which the sample is to be drawn, the methods used to select the sample, and the sample size. Sample selection methods can be classified as to whether they involve a probability or a non-probability procedure. (These methods will be discussed in Chapter 8.)

2.1f Collect Data

Collecting data typically involves a large proportion of the research budget and a sizeable proportion of the "total error" in the research results. Consequently, selection, training, and control of interviewers are essential to effective marketing research studies.

2.1g Process and Code Data

Data processing includes the functions of editing and coding. Editing involves reviewing the data forms as to legibility, consistency, and completeness. Coding involves establishing categories for responses or groups of responses so that numerals can be used to represent the categories. The data are then ready for computer analysis.

2.1h Analyze Data

Data analysis must be consistent with the requirements of the detailed information needs identified at the beginning of the project. Analysis is usually performed by using appropriate statistical software packages.

2.1i Presentation of Results

The research results are typically communicated to the manager through a written report and an oral presentation. Research findings should be presented in a simple format and addressed to the information needs of the decision situation. No matter how proficiently all previous steps have been dispatched, the project will be no more successful than the research report.

2.2 Is Research Needed?

The decision to undertake marketing research is critical to the research process. This is the aspect of research that requires that the questions being asked are the right ones for determining an appropriate strategy or effective course of action. Indeed, if this aspect is not done well, then all the other steps in the process will be wasted.

In the excitement of doing a research study, the analysis leading to the decision to undertake research is frequently passed over superficially or is poorly executed. The consequences are inadequate information for decision-making, wasted research funds, and management dissatisfaction with the marketing research system.

Unfamiliar decision situations call for a formal decision-making process, as described in Chapter 1. The following sections cover the steps of the decision-making process in greater detail regarding the decision to undertake research.

2.2a Recognition of a Decision Situation

problems
Conditions resulting in decreased performance (assessed by standard output measures) that may be rectified through alternate courses of action.

opportunities
Situations in which a company can improve its performance by adopting a new course of action, usually stated in terms of changes in its marketing mix.

Performance measures signal symptoms of underlying **problems** and **opportunities** produced by the marketing mix and situational factors. The decision-maker's task is to respond to symptoms by analyzing the underlying problems and opportunities to determine whether the situation calls for a decision.

Noticing Symptoms

Symptoms are performance measures, metrics, and diagnostics that signal the presence of a problem or an opportunity. For example, a product's share of market could be below forecasted share; the effectiveness of a new advertising campaign could be below desired awareness levels; the expenses associated with the introduction of a new product could be over budget. In general, the existence of a problem is detected when actual performance does not match expected performance. Assessing whether such a problem exists therefore requires managers to monitor ongoing performance along a variety of dimensions and to continually measure them against well-established metrics.

Symptoms themselves rarely contain information regarding their cause. For example, a decline in sales volume (from historical, forecasted, or recent levels) is a symptom indicating the existence of a problem; it does not identify what the problem is. One task of marketing research is to provide measures of symptoms, such as a decline in customer satisfaction; another task is to help identify root causes of symptoms, such as poor training of customer representatives. Symptoms play a critical position in recognizing the need for management decision by triggering the analysis process designed to identify and define the problems or opportunities.

Identifying Problems

Decisions must aim at solving problems or taking advantage of opportunities, not at treating symptoms. Researchers need to carefully distinguish the symptoms that allow a problem to be detected from the actual underlying problem. In marketing research, the word "problem" refers to those variables—particularly variables under direct managerial control—that lead the organization's performance measures to fall short of objectives. Problems can result from an ineffective marketing program (e.g., product, price, place/distribution, promotion) or changes in situational factors, or from some combination of the two.

During the analysis process, the variables initially identified as causing the symptom may themselves be revealed as the consequences of more fundamental variables. Investigation may uncover a complicated sequence of influences that interact to produce the symptom. For example, say a restaurant suddenly experiences a decrease in sales. Defining the underlying problem may not be unambiguous. At one level of analysis, the problem could be defined as a competing restaurant opening on the same block. At another level, the underlying problem could be that the new establishment's marquee overshadows that of the first restaurant, that the new restaurant has more effective advertising, or that the first restaurant's star chef has left to work for the new one. Identifying the true, underlying problem is crucial, and it is fundamental to generating a range of appropriate solutions. The problem isn't merely the decline in sales. The problem, in short, is not the symptom, as researchers must constantly remind themselves.

Identifying Opportunities

"Opportunity" refers to a situation where performance can be improved by a change in activities. Opportunities often go unrecognized, because they rarely force themselves on managers in the same way that problems do. Most firms have formal methods for detecting the presence of problems via their performance measures but less formal methods for monitoring potential opportunities, just as individual workers may be more attuned to the possibility of being laid off than to avenues for advancement.

As an example of an opportunity, changes in consumer tastes toward snack products with less fat content created an opportunity. The introduction of various snacks in Snackwell's low-fat cookie line throughout the mid-1990s was a successful actualization of this opportunity. The opportunity would have existed even if the firm had not made an effort to actualize it. Most of Snackwell's competitors were slow to market similar products. A similar scenario played itself out a decade later with the introduction and rapid growth of low-carbohydrate product lines, an opportunity kindled by the renewed popularity of the Atkins Diet. In the case of low-carb products, however, the opportunity was highlighted by the cannibalization of traditional food products and brands and was therefore noticed, and capitalized on, more quickly than for low-fat products a decade before.

Note that problems can themselves present opportunities. Consider a smoker of cigarettes: The smoker has symptoms of reduced lung capacity and decreased performance in exercise due to the underlying problem of a smoking habit. The smoker also has an opportunity for better health by quitting. In marketing, opportunities arising from problems most often come about from general situational factors to which a company can respond uniquely well. For example, if customer loyalty appears to be waning in general, a company with the capability to do a better job than its competitors in responding to this problem can, by taking steps to increase its own customer loyalty, differentially avail itself of this opportunity relative to other firms in its market.

2.2b Defining the Decision

Once the manager recognizes the need for a decision, the next step is to clearly define the nature of that decision. This requires achieving a thorough understanding of the objectives surrounding the decision situation and delineating the problems and opportunities.

The decision-maker may choose to formulate the decision problem based on an analysis of existing information. This approach relies upon the manager's experience, judgment, and skills in analyzing data relevant to the decision situation. Another option is to use **exploratory research** to aid in defining the decision. This initiates a process of interaction between hypotheses previously formulated based on existing information and hypotheses developed from the exploratory research findings.

exploratory research
Research less focused on quantification than on generating qualitative insights. Such research helps to generate hypotheses rather than systematically investigate them, and it is useful in breaking down broad, complex problems into smaller, more tractable ones.

Decision Objectives

Decision objectives include organizational goals, such as increasing earnings per share by 10 percent next year, and the personal objectives of the decision-makers and those who influence those individuals. For example, a marketing manager may have the personal objective of becoming the vice president of marketing or of acquiring more prestige among his or her peers.

When both organizational and personal objectives coincide, the decision-making process flows more smoothly than when there is conflict between them. The question of how to resolve a conflict in favor of organizational objectives is obviously a complex one. One approach is to have explicitly stated organizational objectives. (This can be aided through the process of concept mapping, described in *Research Innovations and Technologies 2.1: Concept Mapping to Aid Innovative Thinking*.) In addition, the development of formal decision criteria for the selection among alternative courses of action can often ensure that organizational objectives will prevail in the decision.

decision objectives
The goals of the company (and decision-makers) that the marketing research project will help to achieve. These goals must be explicitly recognized when identifying the project's information needs.

In situations where two or more people must make decisions as a group, not only is there potential for conflict between organizational and personal objectives, but also there can be conflict among the personal objectives of the individuals involved in the decision process. Formulating an explicit statement of organizational objectives can persuade, or even pressure, decision-makers to suppress personal objectives. Those involved in this part of the research process should be prepared for possible resistance. Although clarifying organizational objectives may be better for the organization and the quality of the needed research, some individuals may feel that making certain aspects of the decision process explicit threatens their status and position as decision-makers.

Statement of Problems and Opportunities

In Chapter 1, a situational analysis was described as an analysis identifying the information needs regarding situational factors of the marketing system. In this section, we use a slightly broader definition, to include analysis of the marketing mix variables as well. With either usage, the purpose of a situational analysis is the same: to identify problems and opportunities in the marketing system.

The process of identifying problems and opportunities involves analyzing past, present, and possible future situations facing an organization to uncover those variables that either cause poor performance or represent opportunities for future growth. Specifically, this means that a diagnosis and a prognosis of the marketing program and situational variables in the marketing system must be made.

The situational analysis is a creative process attempting to isolate and understand the "causal" variables influencing the marketing system. (The term "causal" is used cautiously because such a relationship can only be hypothesized and provisionally supported by data but never established definitively by statistical means.) This often requires a diversity of information sources and flexibility in thinking to develop insight and hypotheses regarding the causal factors.

2.2c Identifying Alternative Courses of Action

Recall from Chapter 1 that a decision opportunity exists only when there are two or more actions to be taken and uncertainty as to which is the best one to take. Given a clear statement of the decision problem, the next step is to identify alternative courses of action.

course of action
One of the specific possible sets of actions to be evaluated via conclusive research.

A **course of action** specifies how the organization's resources are to be deployed in a given time period. Maintaining the status quo or "doing nothing new" is a course of action just as much as is designating a change in the status quo.

The ultimate management decision can be no better than the best alternative under evaluation. Identifying mediocre courses of action, which partially solve a problem, is often an easy task. The real challenge is to identify the course of action that will result in high performance and give the organization a competitive edge. Creativity and innovative thinking can make a decisive difference at this stage of the process (and ultimately, therefore, in overall management success).

Merely identifying new and different courses of action is hard work, involving "thinking outside the box" and considering various techniques to jumpstart the process. *Research Innovations and Technologies 2.1* takes a close look at one such method, called "Concept Mapping."

Exploratory research can be especially helpful in identifying innovative courses of action. For example, firms intending to introduce a new product into a well-established category first study closely the products presently available to best "position" themselves relative to the existing competition. In the course of carrying out this exploratory research, the firm may learn that the younger, convenience-oriented, urban segment of the market is not well served by existing alternatives. Introducing a product variant (flavor, packaging, ad message, or the like) to appeal to that segment may now become a potential action, to be formally studied in depth. One problem with this approach is that it is not systematic: there is no foolproof way to know in advance that exploratory research will turn up innovative approaches or courses of action. Human insight, "holistic" understanding, hunches, and creativity will always play a large role in any such endeavor.

2.2d Evaluating Courses of Action

At the point of evaluation, the manager faces the question, "What information is needed to properly choose among the courses of action?" This may be answered with the help of information inputs from

Research Innovations and Technologies 2.1

Concept Mapping to Aid Innovative Thinking by Barbara Bowen, PhD

Within any organization, people possess disparate collections of knowledge that can be hard to tap into, or formally represent, to fruitfully address complex, team-based projects. Concept maps—graphical, hierarchical, and interactive representations of the knowledge of a person or group—can offer order and transparency in such situations. The hierarchically arranged nodes or cells each contain a concept, item, or question and can be linked to related documents or URLs. Directional arrows indicate the direction of relationships between the nodes.

The technique of concept mapping can facilitate such conceptual processes as making organizational goals explicit or, as illustrated in the example Figure 2.2, aid decision-making by sketching out the givens of a particular decision-focused situation. Concept mapping is especially useful as a way to elicit and represent tacit knowledge—the internal mental models and intuitions that influence much of how we think and the meaning we give to new information but that often remain invisible.

The concept map in Figure 2.2 shows the (formerly) tacit knowledge of an expert in the field of structured settlements. As a result of his expert knowledge of new rules and regulations, he saw opportunities for new products, services, and strategic alliances. This concept map shows the hierarchy of, and interconnections among, key concepts defining the competitive landscape for the structured settlement industry; it reveals that "IRC 5891," a new internal revenue code put into effect in January 2002, is the source of new business opportunities.

The designer of this concept map used the map in a marketing presentation to one of his key clients (here called "ABC") and another company ("XYZ"), with whom ABC wanted to create a strategic partnership. He framed his PowerPoint presentation with the concept map—using it to provide an introductory overview, as well as the final summary. The presentation resulted in XYZ's understanding how the proposed partnership would create new business opportunities for them—something they had not taken away from previous discussions. The position of "IRC 5891" at the top of the concept map, and the visual interconnections it showed among concepts, provided the clear, direct framework needed for a new understanding to be created.

This concept map was used by its designer subsequently in other presentations to communicate the nature of the changed business landscape for structured settlements after the events of September 11, 2001.

Figure 2.2 Example of Concept Map (new business opportunities for a company)

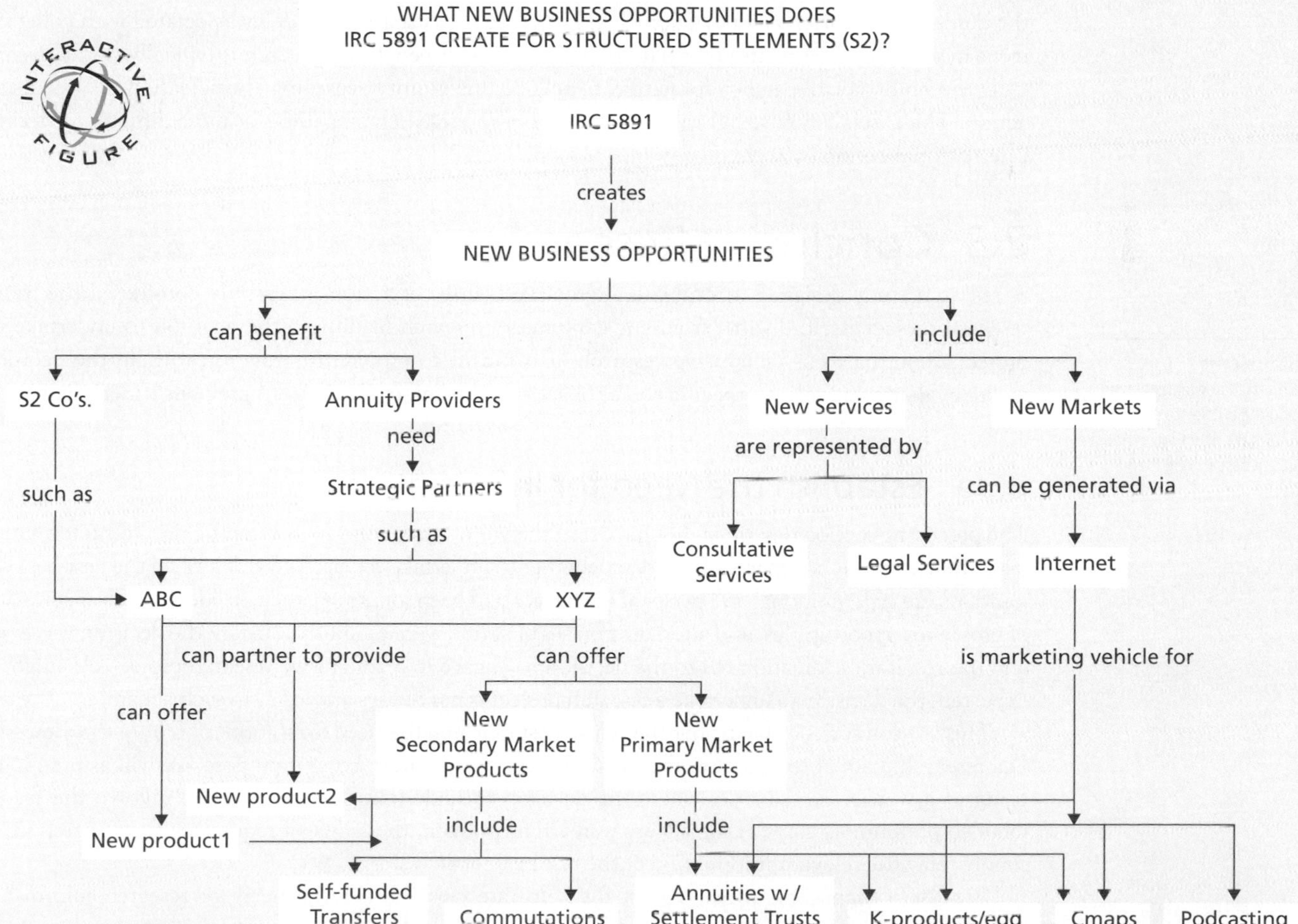

The tacit knowledge of experts and company executives is especially valuable for decision-making. A good concept map makes this informal—and formerly invisible—knowledge visible, shareable, and improvable, transforming it into an asset for the whole organization. The resulting shared conceptual framework aids sense-making, innovation, and insights.

Concept mapping was developed by Prof. Joseph Novak of Cornell University as a way to enhance meaningful learning of scientific knowledge. It has proved useful in a wide variety of educational domains.[1]

In an organizational context, concept maps can help communicate organizational objectives. The ability to link digital documents to any concept node makes it possible to organize all relevant materials through the central access point of the concept map, rather than merely diagramming them. In a decision-making situation, this enables new information to be incorporated and understood in its proper context much more quickly and easily.

Concept maps support local and global collaboration. With the ongoing addition of digital text, audio and video documents such as budget forecasts, sales reports, engineering diagrams, and marketing strategy memos, concept maps become resource-rich organizational knowledge assets.

In addition to their knowledge-creation function, the context-rich maps also facilitate knowledge retention and help preserve the knowledge of a team or organization as it goes through inevitable changes in leadership and personnel over time.

Concept mapping tools can be downloaded at no cost from CmapTools. Click on the icon attached to the "Downloaded" concept node to begin.

Barbara Bowen, Ph.D, managing director, Sound Knowledge Strategies, helps her clients enhance productivity and innovation through the creation and effective use of strategic knowledge. Bowen has extensive experience in applying cognitive research and cognitive tools to increase effectiveness. During her 10 years at Apple Computer, Inc., Dr. Bowen directed the Apple Education Fund and created Apple's External Research Program. External Research accelerated innovation in key technologies including human interface, systems software, and manufacturing. She graduated from Oberlin College and earned a Ph.D. from Cornell University. Reprinted by permission of Dr. Bowen.

the manager's experience and judgment, plus information currently available through the marketing research system. Alternatively, the manager may decide that new information is needed and request that a formal marketing research study be conducted.

Before making the decision to formally commission research, the manager must consider whether the desired information can be obtained and whether the cost and time delay associated with collecting it are more than offset by its potential value. The value or benefit of research is typically commensurate with the ability of research information to reduce uncertainty regarding the selection of a course of action. The costs, benefits, and value of commissioning research can all be far more difficult to assess in international contexts, as detailed in *International Issues 2.1*.

2.3 Conclusive Research

A research study designed to evaluate alternative courses of action is typically considered the formal research project itself, distinct from any exploratory research leading to the decision to undertake the project. Referred to as **conclusive research**, it is meant to provide information to help the decision-maker evaluate and select a specific course of action from among the options previously identified.

conclusive research
Research aimed at evaluating and predicting the outcomes of several possible courses of action, ordinarily to select the best among them.

2.3a Establish the Need for Information

The preceding section described in some detail the various steps of establishing the need for information, from the viewpoint of a manager deciding whether to undertake research. We described the best-case scenario, where organizational and personal objectives had been identified and considered; a clear statement of problems, opportunities, and alternate courses of action were established before the decision was made; and the resultant evaluation led to the decision to engage in a conclusive research project. As might be expected, the decision to undertake a research project is not always arrived at in such a manner.

This section starts by laying out the steps of establishing the need for information from the viewpoint of a research team at the point of the initial request for research. For our purpose, we will assume something of a worst-case scenario, where the decision to undertake research did not involve the recommended preliminary steps. If these steps were, in fact, taken, the manager requesting the research would simply relay the relevant information to the research team.

Because a manager's initial request for help rarely establishes the need for research information adequately, the researcher usually has an important role to play in ensuring that information is actually needed and that the research study will provide useful information for decision-making. The researcher must recognize who the decision-maker is; consider the decision-maker's objectives; and ensure that the problems, opportunities, and courses of action are clearly delineated.

International Issues 2.1

Commissioning International Marketing Research

The approach to commissioning marketing research outlined in this chapter is applicable to both the domestic and the international context. However, there are some special issues that are unique to the international arena.

First, the level of uncertainty pervading the entire enterprise will be greater in the international than in the domestic context because the managers' (and firms') experiences and insights are typically less developed for the international situation, unless there is an ongoing history of operation for the other countries and cultures in question. Unfortunately, some marketing managers believe that domestic-based research findings and experience apply directly to the international situation, and they actually perceive *less* uncertainty than in the domestic context prior to the completion of the domestic research. The successful application of marketing research information domestically can sometimes convey the mistaken belief that one now "really" understands the marketing of a product or service in all parts of the world. (Some examples of the dire consequences of this lowered uncertainty level appeared in the *International Issues 1.1*)

Second, the cost of doing marketing research is often much higher outside areas in which there is a highly developed research infrastructure, such as presently exists throughout most of North America, the European Union, and urban centers in Asia. Samples are harder to select; interviewing is more complicated; the research capabilities of marketing research firms are often less developed or available; and communications facilities cannot be so universally relied on. Third, markets in developing areas are often not as large, so potential revenue and profit are more modest than in the well-established consumer markets where marketing research has long been practiced.

The commissioning of international marketing research is therefore often restricted, relative to that of domestic marketing research: the managers' perceived uncertainty may (erroneously) be less; the cost is often higher; and possible profit increases from the decision are often lower, reducing the perceived value of the marketing research to the manager. Decisions must be correspondingly judicious and should rarely aim for a similar degree of coverage to what would be typical in one's home country.

The marketing research department can take several steps to improve managers' perceptions of the value of marketing research. There is a great need to educate managers to the level of uncertainty that they actually should hold in foreign environments. Research studies designed to combine several countries on the basis of relevant similar characteristics, such as geography and economic conditions, will increase the market size and the potential profit outcome of the marketing decisions. Great care must be taken not to combine so many countries such that meaningful marketing differences are lost.

One common error is to combine data from different regions for reasons unrelated to marketing, such as a linguistic basis, as is sometimes done, for example, in discussions of the "Hispanic market" in the United States. So doing ignores core differences in culture and outlook among groups that, although they can intercommunicate, may have lived thousands of miles apart—buying different products and consuming different media in vastly different geodemographic climates—before emigrating. Decisions to aggregate across different countries need to be based on the type of consumer behavior directly relevant to the decision context, which in practice can be quite difficult conceptually and statistically.*

Compared with marketing research carried out in one's home country or region, international marketing research has generally been found to be less formal and less quantitative. Managers seem to rely more on their subjective assessments than on systematic, objective analyses in assessing foreign market potentials and in evaluating foreign distributors. Reasons for this more casual and subjective approach include the difficulty involved in gathering relevant and reliable information and time and budgetary constraints, as well as simple lack of familiarity.

The nature and complexity of international marketing research are also found to be functions of a company's international involvement and the risks it encounters. When the amount at stake is not substantial, managers often prefer to make decisions on the basis of limited research, aided by judgment calls.

The stage of a company's internationalization is another determinant of the nature and complexity of research. Many multinational companies with high degrees of internationalization have developed fairly formalized and sophisticated procedures for international marketing research. They have also accumulated large bases of relevant information and expertise concerning foreign markets. This is almost always the case with large multi-national firms, whose core competence—the essence of their business plan—is to operate seamlessly across geographical boundaries and borders. The advent of the Internet and e-business in general has greatly heightened this tendency, even for businesses firmly rooted in one country yet selling abroad.

*Academic marketing researchers have tackled this problem via advanced statistical methods, scientifically determining which countries should be aggregated, based on a variety of factors. More information on such approaches can be found in "International Market Segmentation Based on Consumer Product Relations," *Journal of Marketing Research*, 36, February, 1999, by Frenkel ter Hofsted, Jan-Benedict Steenkamp and Michel Wedel.

Identify Decision-Maker

The researcher must distinguish between the decision-maker and those who represent, or claim to represent, the decision-maker. Often, the person who first requests assistance from the marketing research system is not the decision-maker. This individual may or may not know how the decision-maker views the specifics of the decision situation. Valuable time and effort can be saved if the researcher insists on meeting directly with the individual who has major responsibility for making the decision.

Meeting with the decision-maker may be difficult in practice. Many organizations have complicated formal and informal command structures; the organizational status of the researcher or the research department may make it difficult to reach the ultimate decision-maker; and, in many decision situations, a number of individuals may influence the decision or make the decision collectively. Meeting with decision-makers as a group or individually may be difficult, and the coordination of a clear statement regarding the decision situation may be even more so. Despite these potential problems, it is essential that the researcher understand the problem situation from the perspective of the decision-maker.

Identify Objectives of Decision-Maker

Decisions are made to accomplish objectives. So, the success of a research study depends on a clear understanding of what those decision objectives are; consequently, a major task of the marketing researcher is to identify the organizational objectives and to be sensitive to the personal objectives lurking in the background of the decision process. A successful researcher may be one who can design research to serve the needs of the organization effectively while at the same time enhancing the personal objectives of the decision-maker.

Not only are objectives rarely relayed to the researcher at the outset, decision-makers seldom formulate objectives accurately. They are more likely to state the objectives in the form of platitudes lacking operational significance. Consequently, objectives usually have to be extracted, sometimes in a pointed manner, by the researcher. This may indeed prove to be the most useful service provided by the researcher to the decision-maker. Decision-makers will often state objectives that mix in various symptoms, problems, and other arcana, such as "We need to hold off the competition," a reasonable overarching business practice but hopeless as a point of research. The researcher, through interviews, exploratory analysis, and incisive questioning, should be able to translate such loosely stated goals into focused objectives on which a formal research study can be built.

Direct questioning of the decision-maker seldom reveals all relevant objectives at play. One effective technique for uncovering these objectives is to present each of the possible solutions to a problem and ask whether the decision-maker would follow that course of action. Where the answer is "no," further probing will usually reveal objectives that are not served by the course of action.

Identify Problems and Opportunities

There is probably no activity more critical to the success of the formal research process than a clear and concise statement of problems and opportunities. Far too often, this task is neglected when a research project is initiated. Improper definition of a problem can easily lead astray all subsequent efforts to provide useful information for decision-making.

The researcher must be sensitive to managers who are reacting to symptoms or vague feelings. The researcher's task is to pose a series of questions to the manager to determine the existing degree of knowledge regarding the underlying causes of the decision situation. Exploratory research is often needed to facilitate the development of the statement of problems and opportunities.

Identify Courses of Action

The researcher must be satisfied that the relevant courses of action have been identified and approved by management. Nothing can destroy an otherwise successful research study more decisively than finding that a key alternative was not evaluated.

2.3b Determine Research Objectives

The remaining steps of this section are all parts of Step 2, "Detail Research Objectives and Information Needs," described in the Overview section. Subsequent steps of the research process will be explored in much greater detail in later chapters.

Research objectives answer the question, "What is the purpose of the research project?" The research objectives should be put in writing and communicated to the decision-maker, explaining why the project is being conducted. It is important that the researcher and decision-maker be in agreement on this point.

Research objectives can be stated so broadly that they fail to communicate the specifics of why the study is being conducted. For example, the following statement lacks the detail needed for a research objective: *To study consumer reactions to cartoon characters in advertising.* A more precise and useful formulation would be:

1. to determine which breakfast cereal markets have the most positive consumer (purchaser and user) response to the use of cartoon characters in TV and print advertising;
2. to determine the characteristics of cartoon characters that most, and most broadly, appeal to consumers (purchasers and users) of breakfast cereal.

The original statement does not indicate what type of market is to be studied, what is to be measured, or how the information might be used. Importantly, it is also entirely open-ended, with no sense of what it would mean to have definitively completed the project. For example, it states its objectives as "to study"; but something might be studied forever. The object of study is "consumer reactions"; but consumers react in many ways, both in laboratory and retail settings. It fails to specify which consumers will be studied, where they will be studied, or even what sort of advertising they will be exposed to. All this information is critical, and it must be explicitly conceptualized and codified *before* research begins, not as a consequence of its having been started and gone awry. Although the degree of detail in the research objectives depends on the nature of the decision situation, generally speaking, the more specific the statement of objectives, the lower the risk that management will misperceive the purpose of the study.

2.3c Specify Information Needs

The next question to be answered is, "What specific information is needed by the decision-maker?" Research objectives that are specified in great detail often coincide with a more general listing of information needs. That is, the list of information needs can be conceived as a finer degree of detail regarding the research objectives, just as questions on data collection forms can be considered finer detail relative to information needs. Consequently, research objectives serve to guide the research project by giving direction to the specific information to be gathered, which in turn guides the specific questions developed for the questionnaire. Each question on the questionnaire should have a direct correspondence to an information need, and each information need should have a direct correspondence to at least one research objective; otherwise, unneeded data will be collected. A common error in designing data-collection devices is including questions that "would be nice to know," that "may lead somewhere," that might be suggestive of future research, or that are aimed at giving a sense of unspecified intangibles. Such questions are prime evidence that the researcher has not done appropriate homework in the form of exploratory research, subsequently funneled down to concrete research objectives.

Only the decision-maker has a clear perspective on the specific information needed to reduce the uncertainty surrounding the decision situation, so the decision-maker should be actively involved in formulating the information needs. Failure to involve the decision-maker at this stage can severely hamper the success of the research project.

When developing the list of information needs, both the manager and the researcher should ask, for each item, "*Realistically*, can this information be obtained?" The data-collection process imposes many limitations on the types of information that can be collected. In surveys, buyers or distributors may refuse to disclose certain types of information, or they may not have the knowledge to answer the questions accurately or objectively. Distributors or wholesalers are understandably reluctant to disclose their cost structures, for example, and may refuse to complete a survey instrument on which even one question along those lines appears. Legal and cultural restrictions may interfere with the collection of data. Consumers in many countries consider it bad form to be asked to disclose their salaries, addresses, or even seemingly mundane details about their purchases. Consequently, many excellent information needs may be developed, but if it is not realistic to expect to be able to collect the information, time and effort will be wasted.

2.3d Visualize the Research Findings

Assuming that the information can be gathered, the researcher must concretely conceptualize, even visualize, the potential research findings and ask the question, "Of what *use* are these data to the decision situation?" Many managers and researchers find that mocking up the potential research findings is a valuable way to ensure that the data to be collected will fit the information needs specified by the decision-maker. Often, the decision-maker can identify gaps in the original list of needs, which can be easily corrected at this preliminary stage of the research project.

It is often worthwhile to go so far as to generate a full statistical analysis and final report based on the generated or "guesstimated" data to ensure that, once the required information is collected, there are no conceptual bottlenecks preventing the project from being swiftly and professionally completed. In essence, the research process and presentation are simulated before conducting the project. (Doing so, however, puts the cart before the horse in one crucial way: specific survey questions would need to be concocted for such an exercise, well before a formal survey would normally be developed. As such, presenting research sponsors with a mocked-up report of this nature runs the risk that, in terms of information presented, it will differ substantially from the final research report.)

The data chosen for presentation in the mock-up may represent a range of optimistic, most likely, and pessimistic results. From this simulation of findings, the manager and researcher may be able to determine whether the data intended to be collected will serve to reduce the uncertainty surrounding the decision situation. If not, the wisdom of collecting the data should be challenged. A danger in using such mocked-up data is that, when researchers generate data on their own, the data tend to be unusually "nice" and lack uncooperative features present in almost all real-world data, such as missing fields, high multi-collinearity, miscodes, and **self-selection bias**, among other problems. This being the case, even the "pessimistic" projection can often be unduly rosy, and researchers should try to stack their generated data up against historical or competitive benchmarks, if available.

self-selection bias
Sample selection arises when some respondents, firms, or other entities decide not to supply data for reasons related to the study itself or to any variable germane to the research study. The resulting data will not only fail to be a random sample of the underlying population, but will typically lead to biased results.

Often, the manager can more clearly specify how the data should be analyzed and presented after seeing a mock-up of the potential findings, requesting, for example, additional cross tabulations or multi-variate analysis approaches. Certain data analysis approaches require that the questionnaire be developed in a certain format, that specific questions be asked, or that the data be tabulated in a certain manner. If these issues are not addressed before implementation, the project may incur costs and delays at later stages, may fail to obtain needed data, or may be perceived as not meeting the organization's core needs. Directions received from the manager before starting can be invaluable to the project's success and the eventual implementation of its suggestions.

2.3e Develop Decision Criteria

decision criteria
A set of if-then guidelines that help managers select among predetermined courses of action; for example, that a product will be introduced nationally if its share at test market is above a certain threshold value.

Decision criteria are rules for selecting among courses of action, given various data outcomes. Researchers work with the decision-maker to develop a series of "if–then" statements, which become the decision criteria. For example:

1. If the research finds a 5 percent potential market share or larger for our new product, then we will proceed to test market.
2. If the research finds a 3–5 percent potential market share, then we will reformulate the new product.
3. If the research finds less than a 3 percent potential market share, then we will abandon the project.

It is *crucial* that decision criteria be developed before anyone involved learns the actual results. Having clear decision rules before revealing the research results ensures that organizational objectives take priority over personal objectives and assist the data analysis and reporting stages. This is akin to there being concrete grievance procedures in a corporation or clearly formulated grading policies in a course. Absence of decision criteria can also result in inappropriate weight being assigned to the research findings or to doubts being cast on their accuracy. Managers who will praise a report suggesting that a pet project be terminated are uncommon, unless the criteria for doing so were explicitly delineated in advance.

2.3f Determine the Cost and Value of the Research

Managers evaluate most activities in an organization on a cost-benefit basis. Quantifying the costs associated with a research project is fairly straightforward, but it is difficult to quantify the benefits. Benefits are often subjective in nature, and as a consequence, evaluation of research is inherently subjective. Costs, being tangible, may weigh more heavily in cost-benefit analyses than intrinsically hazy benefits.

Given the cost of research, it is possible to determine the number of units of a product that need to be sold to break even on the cost of the research project. For example, if the research project costs $10,000 and the amount of profit per unit, or **contribution margin**, was $0.10 per unit (e.g., selling price = $1; variable cost = $0.90), the information gathered by the research project will have to result in the sale of 100,000 additional units before the cost of the project is paid off. However, if the contribution margin was $0.80 per unit (e.g., selling price = $1; variable cost $0.20), the breakeven point is reduced to 12,500 units. Given a large market size (e.g., 1 million units), these breakeven points represent a relatively small share of market (i.e., 1 percent and 0.125 percent). For a much smaller market (e.g., 10,000 units), the breakeven points for the same products would be substantially higher (i.e., 100 percent and 12.5 percent), and the research would be correspondingly more difficult to justify.

contribution margin
Sales revenue minus variable costs. When calculated for a single product (unit), often called "unit contribution," and represents the pure profit made by selling one additional unit.

A contribution margin of $200 in a market of 500,000 units—not uncommon for automobiles—implies a total contribution of $100 million. This level of contribution can easily support even a relatively large research project, and one of only $10,000 would be negligible. However, a contribution margin of $0.20 (as is common for hardware items, paper products, and other small commodity-type items) in a market of even 100,000 units translates to only $20,000. Spending half of this contribution on a $10,000 research project is obviously a very major decision. It is a sobering fact that the cost of carrying out a research project isn't strongly affected by the contribution margin or market size of the product being studied. Low-margin products with limited markets therefore find most professionally conducted market research studies to be prohibitively costly. Table 2.1 provides a simple breakdown for examples of real markets and the amount of marketing research they can support based on market size and contribution margin.

Simple arithmetic suggests that it is easier to justify the cost of research as the market size increases and as the ratio of variable cost to selling price decreases. Therefore, the benefits resulting from a (say, $10,000) research project designed to evaluate alternative advertising campaigns to stimulate demand is easier to justify for long-distance phone calls than for a new hobby kit glue. Although this type of calculation does not determine the actual benefit derived from such a study, it does indicate the level of benefit needed to cover the cost of research. Although attempting an explicit typology based on Table 2.1 is premature, some generalities are justified. High-cost durable goods, such as cars and appliances, require huge capital investments to produce new market entries, and large budgets to convey their advantages; consequently, they are among the types of products for which research is most common. By contrast, frequently purchased consumer goods, particularly those which are largely undifferentiated (e.g., trash bags) or which have niche markets (e.g., "ethnic" food condiments), tend to be supported by little formal research. This describes in part why we are inundated with print, television, and Internet advertising for new cars, but rarely if ever for any of the products in the "Small Market/Small Contribution" section.

How a manager evaluates the benefits of marketing research directly relates to his or her degree of certainty about particular outcomes of the organization's courses of action. A manager who says, "I am 95 percent sure that this advertising theme will be a success" is much less likely to undertake research on the new advertising theme than a manager who says, "I am about 50 percent sure that this advertising theme will be a success," or, in the most extreme case, "I have no idea whatsoever whether this advertising theme will be a success." The purpose of marketing research is to reduce the uncertainty about outcomes, so the value of research to a manager increases as the degree of certainty decreases.

Table 2.1 Research Value as Function of Contribution Margin and Market Size

	Contribution Margin	
Market Size	**Small**	**Large**
Small	Unlikely that research will be supported, *e.g., hobby glue (Elmer's), nail clippers (Trim), screwdriver (Stanley), some "niche"over-the-counter drugs (Zicam)*	Can support limited research, *e.g., specialty tape (3M), pharmaceuticals (GlaxoSmithKline), executive aircraft (Lear)*
Large	Can support a substantial amount of research, particularly ongoing maintenance-type research, *e.g., razor blades (Gillette), laundry detergent (P&G), soft drinks (Coca-Cola), snacks (Frito-Lay)*	Large-scale research feasible throughout the organization, *e.g., automobiles (Ford), large appliances (General Electric), information services (AT&T), insurance (State Farm)*

2.3g Formally Propose Research

Most organizations require that the decision to undertake research be in writing and approved by upper management and the director of marketing research. This formal request typically involves a standard form that is completed by the decision-maker and/or the marketing researcher. Figure 2.3 illustrates the type of information ordinarily requested on such a form.

The research request form reminds the decision-makers and researchers of all the points to be covered and imposes a contractual degree of commitment that rarely exists with informal agreements.

For projects conducted predominantly within the organization, a research request form usually serves as the research proposal. In practice, outside contractors will often conduct some phase of the study. It is standard procedure in many organizations, when choosing to rely entirely on an outside contractor to conduct the research study, to request several outside contractors to submit proposals for research, as described in Chapter 1.

2.4 The Management–Research Relationship

The success of a research project and the effectiveness of the research system depend on the ability of the managers and researchers to work together to ensure that research is used effectively in the decision-making process. The researcher must develop an effective working relationship with the decision-maker and be sensitive to the decision-maker's individual management style. Many factors influence the success of this interpersonal contact, such as differences in job responsibilities, career objectives, and educational backgrounds.

2.4a Organizational Design

The various organizational designs discussed in Chapter 1 affect the contacts between decision-makers and researchers. One design assigns management responsibility for the initial and final stages of the research process; here, the responsibility for the effectiveness of the research rests predominantly in the management camp. The researcher's responsibility is that of adviser regarding the initial and final stages, with primary responsibility for the middle stages of data collection and processing. Typically, a researcher has the right to refuse to conduct a study that the researcher views as inappropriate.

An alternative organizational design keeps the responsibility for the research process within the research camp while giving the researcher a more powerful organizational role in dealing with management. For example, the researcher may be required to participate in the majority of management meetings, regardless of whether the use of research is an issue. Here, the researcher is viewed as part of the management team and is assigned responsibility for identifying decision situations in which research is appropriate.

A compromise between these two organizational designs involves creating the position of research generalist, someone who serves as an intermediary between the research and management camps.

Figure 2.3 Research Request Form

Title:	Date prepared:
Requested by:	Start of project:
Approved by:	Report due:
Date approved:	Budget:
Project number:	Supplier:

1. *Background.* What led to the recognition that research was needed? Were there specific metrics which suggested research be conducted?
2. *Objectives.* What, specifically, are the decision objectives?
3. *Problem / Opportunity.* What are the 'causal factors' underlying the decision situation?
4. *Decision alternatives.* What, specifically, are the alternative courses of action?
5. *Research objectives.* What is the overall purpose of the research? How will one know if that purpose has been satisfied?
6. *Information needs.* What types of information are needed? By what means can each be attained?
7. *Example of questions.* What sorts of representative questions might be asked?
8. *Decision criteria.* What concrete criteria should be used to select the best alternative?
9. *Value of research.* Why is the research useful? Can the usefulness be measured against hard figures such as sales, share or profit?

The generalist's main responsibility is to promote effective contacts between decision-makers and researchers.

2.4b Research Specialists

The research system requires specialized skills and knowledge. A research department may include individuals specializing in various steps of the research process—for example, questionnaire design, field supervision, data processing, data analysis, and report preparation. Specialization involving the marketing mix decision areas is common; individuals or groups may specialize in advertising research, distribution research, product development research, and so on. People with special training in statistics, mathematics, psychology, computer science, and economics often qualify for such specialized positions. Frequently, these individuals have limited training and perspective regarding the role of applied research in the management decision-making process.

A research specialist who is not management-oriented will often accept a request for research help without clearly establishing the need for research. This person may fail to ask perceptive or appropriate questions regarding the decision situation and may not examine whether research will facilitate the decision-making process. In addition, many specialists are more concerned with the technical sophistication of the research design and methodology than with the information needs of management. This focus can lead researchers to actively seek out decision situations where they can apply the latest research techniques. Due to this tendency, some managers view researchers as more concerned with finding an application for their techniques than with supplying information for decision-making, a criticism which, if unheeded, can lead to costly, untested, and difficult-to-interpret techniques being brought to bear. Such an emphasis on technique can also result in overuse of technical jargon and arcane ways of presenting research findings, rather than making comprehensible communication with management a priority in the presentation of the research report.

2.4c Role of Researchers

Some researchers fail to recognize that their role is advisory; they are *not* being asked to make the decision for management. The researcher can play a very active and supportive role in the decision-making process, but the responsibility for making the decision rests with management. The researcher may become frustrated by the constraints of this advisory role and develop the feeling that "I can make better decisions than management," rather like an interior designer unwilling to take the client's tastes suitably into account.

Why shouldn't the researcher participate in making the decision? First, the objectivity of the research process could be influenced. The researcher's personal biases and vested interests associated with various decision outcomes could decrease the objectivity of the research design and the analysis of the findings. Second, the researcher would weigh the research findings heavily in selecting a course of action. In contrast, the manager can evaluate and weigh the significance of the research findings in the context of experience and knowledge plus the broader policy considerations associated with the decision. Finally, researchers seldom have organizational depth of experience comparable to the managers vested with decision-making authority. Although the researcher may be an expert within the narrow domain of the study carried out, final decisions need to weigh organizational factors of which the researcher is unaware.

2.4d Role of Managers

Although some researchers are not sufficiently management-oriented, some managers are not sufficiently research-oriented. Far too many managers have little or no training in marketing research and a limited perspective on the nature and role of research in the decision-making process, inhibiting their active involvement in research projects. This lack of participation can diminish the usefulness of the research findings. If the manager does not view research as a natural aspect of the decision-making process, the researcher is forced to solicit research studies from the manager. This results in myopic and fragmented studies, which rarely make a valuable contribution to the decision-making process. The effectiveness of marketing research is dependent on the skills and perspective of the manager in using the research to appropriately inform decision-making.

Some managers operate as if the researcher were clairvoyant regarding the nature of the decision situation, the courses of action that appear reasonable, the objective to be accomplished, and the information needed to reduce the decision uncertainty. Few managers explain these areas clearly to the researcher. In some cases, the manager may be unwilling or unable to communicate this type of information. Often, managers are so familiar with core processes or basic facts about the organization that they presume the researcher is similarly conversant with them. Research projects may consequently fail to inform necessary decisions due to the manager's presumptions or poor communication skills.

2.4e Other Motives

pseudo-research
Projects presented as true marketing research that are aimed toward goals unrelated to reducing uncertainty in a decision situation or to meeting the stated information needs of the research.

The manager may view research as a way to satisfy needs other than those related to decision-making, resulting in a phenomenon that is sometimes called "**pseudo-research**." Some typical motives in this category:

- *using marketing research as a way to gain visibility and power in the organization*
  Example: Organizational units with large research budgets seem more vital than others and can often leverage additional resources and personnel.
- *justifying decisions already made*
  Example: If the research results contradict the decision, the manager can declare the research invalid or simply ignore it altogether. This is often called the "file drawer effect": research that fails to support a preferred outcome gets tucked away forever within one's files.
- *establishing a scapegoat for marketing decisions that do not accomplish objectives*
  Example: If the decision is successful, the manager can take full credit; if it is not successful, "inadequate" marketing research is to blame.
- *promoting service organizations such as advertising agencies and media to attract new business and impress current clients*
  Example: A new product can be highly touted and generate "spin" on the basis of marketing research studies showing great demand for it.
- *soothing an anxious manager with the knowledge that "something is being done" or allowing an overwhelmed staff to "buy time"*
  Example: If a product prototype is not yet ready near deadline, a months-long research study could be commissioned to ensure that the prototype is what consumers actually want.
- *following or supporting marketing research studies and new research methodology as a current trend or fad in management practice*
  Example: A manager who wishes to appear *au courant* within the organization might read about "hierarchical Bayes conjoint analysis" (see Chapter 12) and decide it should be used, even if it is not relevant to the decision situation.

To be of ongoing use and to retain credibility, research studies need to be undertaken and used to support marketing decision-making, not for ceremonial reasons, to try out the latest methodology, to bolster pre-existing decisions, or to aid internal power struggles. Many of these goals occur with regularity in real-world decision contexts, and researchers need to be astute about circumventing them and not allowing them to influence the goals and outcome of commissioned studies. *Marketing Research Focus 2.1* illustrates some of the reasonable, and not-so-reasonable, motivations for commissioning and carrying out research.

2.4f Obstacles to Effective Use of Research

Barriers to the effective use of marketing research by management include:

- *viewing research as a threat to their personal status as decision makers*
  Some managers fear that marketing research information may conflict with or invalidate the value of their experience and judgment, calling into question their status and position. Particularly troubling is research that concludes that prior actions or decisions were misguided.
- *absence of systematic planning procedures and common organizational objectives*
  In the absence of clear organizational objectives, managers will sometimes substitute their own objectives, which can result in internal conflict among managers. Research may be seen as a way to support one's view in this internal struggle for power. Managers who believe that marketing research will enhance their position will favor it, whereas others will oppose it.
- *inability to work with researchers or use their knowledge and skills*
  The interdisciplinary training of specialists can make communication difficult. A persistent difficulty is a proper understanding of statistical methods, terminology, and results, particularly among upper management unused to and often distrustful of "managing by numbers alone."

Marketing Research Focus 2.1

Reasons Marketing Research Is Used

In one major consumer food company, the vice president of marketing research hired an outside consulting firm to survey the attitudes of marketing managers within the company to assess the impact of marketing research on the organization. The consulting firm specialized in employee attitude studies, and it had a strong reputation for providing valid results in that domain. The consultants' report contained many positive remarks concerning how marketing research personnel were perceived by the managers. However, four of the question areas were of concern. These questions and the percentage of managers either agreeing or strongly agreeing with the question statement were as shown in the following table.

Question	Percent in agreement
Managers often request marketing research to have power and knowledge over other managers.	45
Managers often request marketing research to support a decision that has already been made.	53
Managers often request marketing research reports to appease their superiors.	30
Managers often request marketing research studies because it is a policy requirement.	37

The VP wanted marketing managers to use marketing research as an aid to real decision-making, not for the politics of office power, to pay lip service to a policy requirement, or to keep superiors off their backs. She was most disturbed to see that more than half of the managers were sanctioning studies related to decisions that had already been made. She said, "Clearly, we've won some battles here in the effective use of marketing research, but I'm afraid that the war is still in doubt. We need an approach in this marketing department to assure that these types of abuses of marketing research do not continue."

(See the discussion of questionnaire design under Section 2-5c, Types of Non-Sampling Errors, later in this chapter, for further discussion of the appropriateness of these questions and the results based on them.)

- *isolation of marketing research personnel from managers*
  The theory underpinning marketing research assumes that research personnel will have a close and continuous relationship with decision-makers. Marketing research departments are sometimes handicapped in this regard by low organizational status. The weakness of this organizational arrangement is that effective use of marketing research depends on the initiative of the manager. Managers who are unfamiliar with the nature and role of research may be unable to identify problems well enough to ask for the help they need. Research departments that operate on management requests tend to be occupied with routine, short-range operating problems.
- *differences in emphasis and temperament*
  Researchers and marketers often come from different worlds: their training, motivation, timescale, and areas of expertise are all different. It is no surprise that they don't always see eye-to-eye throughout a research project. *Marketing Research Focus 2.2* discusses how to anticipate and handle such cultural and motivational differences.

Conflict between researchers and managers can become a formidable barrier to the appreciation and successful deployment of marketing research. Conflicts can arise around research responsibility, research personnel, budget, assignments, **problem definition**, research reporting, and the proper organizational uses of research. Table 2.2 presents the typical positions of top management and marketing research staff on these areas of conflict.

problem definition
A crucial step in the marketing research process that precisely identifies the problem to be studied and solved via the acquisition and analysis of data.

2.5 Errors in Marketing Research

Although the results of a study may appear accurate, managers and researchers need to recognize that every marketing research study contains errors. On occasion, these errors can result in serious misinformation being communicated to managers. A professionally designed and managed research study must recognize the potential sources of error, make no attempt to obscure their presence, and manage the size of those errors in a way consistent with the accuracy required by the decision situation.

Every step in the marketing research process can produce substantial errors, and much of the rest of this text is concerned with measuring, understanding, and controlling them. There are two main types of errors:

Marketing Research Focus 2.2

Handling Common Differences between Researchers and Marketers

Although stereotyping is unfair and rarely helpful, knowing the preferences and outlooks of people with whom you have to work can aid communication. Following are generalizations common in the industry regarding the differences between researchers and managers and advice for improving the manager–researcher interface.

- Researchers love a surprise. Managers do not like surprises; when they are surprised, they tend to reject the research.
- Researchers like to explore. Managers prefer to confirm. Researchers should be sensitive to managerial "comfort zones."
- Technical quality does not speak for itself. Working together influences perceptions of technical quality and creates trust in the research results.
- Political acceptability of research results is perceived by researchers as a major consideration for use. An effective working relationship between researcher and manager can enhance political acceptability.
- Manager–researcher interaction, of all variables studied, has the highest total influence on research use. Open and frequent communication between researchers and managers is vital to marketing research effectiveness.
- Good horizontal relationships (teaming of researchers with product managers) are more important than vertical ones (e.g., reporting to the senior marketing executive).
- Involvement in the strategic planning process separates more effective marketing research departments from less effective ones. Managers expect research to come up with innovative solutions or courses of action, but they perceive research as failing to do so. Meanwhile, researchers feel excluded from strategy formulation and sometimes believe that managers' use of research is either largely tactical or "misses the point" the research implied.
- Smooth planning and delivery of marketing research services have a strong influence on management satisfaction. On the other hand, researchers perceive managers as making sudden changes in data needs, priorities, or deadlines unrelated to the intrinsic needs of the research process.

Table 2.2 Common Areas of Top Management–Marketing Research Conflict

Area	Top Management Position	Marketing Research Position
Research responsibility	Marketing research (MR) lacks a sense of accountability or organizational reality. Sole MR function is as an information provider.	Responsibility should be explicitly defined and consistently followed. MR deserves decision-making involvement with top management (TM).
Research personnel	Researchers are poor communicators. They lack enthusiasm; sales expertise; and, ultimately, imagination.	TM is anti-intellectual. Researchers should be judged and compensated based on research capabilities, not on whether a particular implementation was successful.
Budget	Research costs too much. Because MR contribution is difficult to measure, budget cuts are relatively defensible.	"You get what you pay for." There needs to be a continuing, long-range TM commitment to research.
Assignments	Assignments tend to be over-engineered. They are not executed with a proper sense of urgency. MR exhibits ritualized, staid approach.	There are too many non-researchable, "fire-fighting," and proof-of-concept requests. Insufficient time and money are allocated.
Problem definition	MR is best equipped to do this. General direction is sufficient. MR must appreciate and respond when circumstances change.	TM is generally unsympathetic to this widespread problem. MR is not given all the relevant facts. Problems are often re-defined after research is under way.
Research reporting	Reports are characterized as dull, with too much "researchese" and too many qualifiers. Reporting is not decision-oriented. Too often, reports come after the fact.	TM treats reports superficially. Good research demands thorough reporting and documentation, with degree of certainty clearly communicated. Insufficient lead time is given.
Use of research	TM is free to use research as it pleases, and MR shouldn't question it. Changes in need and timing of research are sometimes unavoidable. MR is privy to facts and outcomes on a "need to know" basis.	TM uses research to support a predetermined position, which represents misuse. Research isn't used after it has been requested and conducted; it is wasteful. TM uses research to confirm or excuse past actions.

sampling errors and non-sampling errors. The following example illustrates how central the issue of error control is to being able to claim marketing research as credible. Researchers who wish to preserve their professional reputation, and that of their firm, must be vigilant in adhering to standards of error control.

Let us examine such a case in depth, in *Marketing Research Focus 2.3*.

sampling error
The error in any measurement associated only with the randomness intrinsic to sampling itself. Often defined as the difference between the observed value of a variable and the *long-run average* of its repeated measurement.

non-sampling error
Any error that occurs that is not due to the vagaries of sampling itself. Non-sampling errors can introduce biases of unknown direction and magnitude, and they can arise because of faulty or incorrect problem definition, a non-representative sampling frame, non-response or measurement errors, poor questionnaire design, improper causal inferences, or even poor arithmetic.

Marketing Research Focus 2.3

Title IX Fellowships in Peril

One might laugh at the notion that a legal landmark like Title IX, which in 1972 banned sex discrimination in school athletics, could be threatened by something as common and trivial as e-mail. But Donna Lopiano, chief executive officer for the Women's Sports Foundation, is not laughing, as a recent Department of Education proposal could mean fewer girls and women get the opportunity to play organized sports. "It's all laughable because the law has been working well. Women's sport opportunities have grown steadily," says Lopiano, adding, "It's not broken. This is not an attempted fix. This is knocking one of the wheels off."

The source of her concern is a proposal by the Department of Education to let schools use an e-mail–based survey to determine if they are complying with Title IX law, which supporters say is under attack. A common way to assess such compliance is to simply measure interest in sports among female students and follow up to see if schools are providing commensurate opportunities. Some schools attempted to use formal surveys to measure interest, a laudable undertaking. But the Department of Education claims that the surveys haven't worked well. The main issue is unintended bias, of the type commonly discussed by survey researchers. For example, questionnaires were often just left in a public place for students to take of their own volition, so that few were routinely filled out.

To remedy these and other sampling problems, in March 2005 a letter went out to schools across the United States proposing what seemed to be a far more inclusive method: a simple and streamlined e-mail survey. The Department of Education believed this would, for the first time, accurately measure interest in sports, in a way that would allow each school to scientifically determine whether it was complying with the broad provisions of Title IX.

One of the problems with the proposal is that students and parents need to be prepared for receiving the survey. According to Susan Aspey, a spokeswoman for the Department of Education, "The onus is on the schools to show that they have gotten the word out about this survey. They can't just haphazardly send out a mass e-mail to students and, if nobody responds, then say, 'Hey, you know, we've done our part.' That doesn't cut it." Although Ms. Aspey is doubtless correct about the importance of preparation, professional researchers remained dubious. Professor Don Sabo, of the State University of New York at Buffalo, expressed a common concern: "Their intentions may be good, but the methods they've unfurled are flawed." He underscored that e-mail surveys often have low response rates. Moreover, it's possible that those who respond may differ systematically from those who do not; for example, students already active in sports may be more likely to notice and reply, whereas those feeling shut out may ignore the process entirely.

Professor Sabo, echoing other Title IX supporters, was also worried about *inferences* that might be made by the Department of Education about students who did not fill out the survey. Specifically, this may be taken as evidence of lack of interest in sports, instead of a lack of interest in filling out a survey or simply forgetting to. Another researcher expressing concern with the "no response equals no interest" aspect of the proposal was University of Oregon Professor Kim Sheehan, an authority on e-mail surveys, who put it very clearly: "I think right now they're setting up the survey to show results that students are not interested in athletics." Many Title IX proponents share exactly that suspicion— that the department may wish to deliberately skew results toward lower interest in sports among female students. This in turn would allow schools to offer minimal opportunities, exactly the scenario Title IX was meant to prevent.

The Department of Education was hardly sympathetic to this criticism. Spokesperson Aspey insisted there is no anti-Title IX plot in the federal government, and the e-mail surveys can work if schools follow the detailed instructions laid out in the 177-page letter of guidance. "We've developed a scientifically sound survey that schools don't even have to use if they don't want to and yet, you know, we have an outcry," adding that "one could make a good argument this is pretty much special interest hyperbole."

The Department of Education was apparently unwilling to rule out multiple types of *non-sampling error*, those that are commonly referred to as biases. In this case, students would self-select into replying to the survey, and those who did would face the "reward" of greater opportunities for women students, suggesting at the very least a gender bias in participation. This type of allegation of bias in field work has the potential to damage the reputation of both the sponsoring organization, the research firm carrying out the survey, and even the interests of the ostensive beneficiaries, women athletes in this case. Poor research techniques can often open the door to a host of lawsuits, making the costs of the research far outweigh any potential benefits.

Source: "Education Dept. E-Mail Survey Sparks Title IX Debate"; Tom Goldman. *NPR News: Morning Edition*. May 9, 2005.

2.5a Sampling Errors

Most marketing research projects study samples of people, products, or stores. Based on these sample results, researchers and managers draw conclusions about the whole population from which the sample was selected. For example, the attitudes of all Chevrolet owners are inferred from a sample of a thousand Chevrolet owners. The sample is used to estimate certain key quantities in the population, and its accuracy as an estimate depends on how the sample was selected. The differences between the **sample value** and the true underlying **population value**, called sampling error, is discussed in detail in Chapter 8.

sample value
The value of a statistic within a particular sample drawn from a target population.

population value
The value a statistic would take on if the sample were the entire population.

As a brief working definition helpful for the purposes of this chapter, sampling error can be thought of as *unavoidable inaccuracy* stemming from not having a huge quantity of data, as opposed to any misunderstandings or mistakes. Consider a flawlessly conducted, unbiased poll of the American population that contains only 25 respondents. Such a poll may be free of non-sampling error (as we shall discuss in the following section) but will be rife with sampling error because one would never want to have so few respondents standing in for such a large population, even if the poll is conducted with the highest professional standards.

2.5b Non-Sampling Errors

Non-sampling errors refer to all errors that may occur in the research process over and above the sampling error, including those arising from both inadvertent mistakes and deliberate deceptions. Unfortunately, such mistakes and deceptions occur with enough frequency in the marketing research process that researchers need take account of them. We must therefore be aware of what sorts of non-sampling errors may occur, what effect these errors may have on our results, and what steps we can take to reduce them.

Fortunately for the researcher, sampling error is measurable, and it decreases in a lawlike way as the sample size increases. Unfortunately, neither of these desirable qualities can be ascribed to non-sampling errors. In fact, in all likelihood, non-sampling errors *increase* as sample size increases, simply because there are more possibilities for anomalies and problems to arise. Non-sampling errors introduce biases of unknown direction and magnitude into the study results. One practicing researcher says of the effect of non-sampling errors, "Over the years I have used a simple rule of thumb that the true mean squared error [see Chapter 10] of field studies is at least twice the size of reported theoretical sampling error, though there is evidence to suggest that it is larger in many commercial surveys." Indeed, non-sampling error, if left uncontrolled or treated carelessly, can render the results of a study useless.

2.5c Types of Non-Sampling Errors

Faulty Problem Definition

As discussed earlier, information to solve a condition that is not the actual problem will not be helpful and may even mislead. Say, for example, that a product manager requests a study to test a specific media mix in an effort to stem a recent sales slide. If the true problem is pricing strategy, then any research conducted, no matter how technically correct or illuminating about media effects, will not be helpful in addressing the manager's core problem.

Incorrect **Population Definition**

population definition
Identification of the group to be studied directly by a marketing research project.

The study population must be defined to fit the study objectives. Consider the case of the manager of one of the restaurants in a major metropolitan airport. She would like to know what sort of image the restaurant has among those who have some likelihood of eating in the airport. The population is defined as people older than 18 years who disembark from planes in the week of September 12 to 19. If she selects the sample from this population, she is likely to get misleading results. The sample does not include substantial numbers of potential customers, such as ticket-holders waiting to depart. Also, the sample includes people who have no chance of eating at the restaurant—for example, people who change planes without entering the section of the airport where this particular restaurant is located. Conclusions from the study may be accurate for the target population as (incorrectly) defined, but not for the phenomenon in question.

Sampling Frame Non-Representative of the Population

The sampling frame must match the defined population. Suppose an investment company uses the telephone book (the frame) to select a sample of potential stock buyers. This frame would not cover the defined population well, as a significant number of high-income people—prime potential stock buyers—have unlisted phone numbers. A sampling frame of visitors to a particular Web site will over-represent users of whatever that site provides and demographic groups interested in the site. In either case, conclusions will be suspect.

Non-Response Errors

Errors occur because people asked to participate in the research either refuse to be a part of the sample or are unavailable during the sampling period. The actual sample should be representative of the target population; if some of the targeted elements do not form part of the realized sample, it may not be a truly representative sample. The resulting error is called **non-response error**. (The *only* time it is not problematic occurs when the elements who fail to respond are truly and totally random, as if a coin toss determined which would be discarded. Needless to say, such situations are exceedingly rare.)

non-response error
A form of "non sampling error" that occurs when some elements meant to be included in the sample are either unavailable for measurement or choose not to reply.

As an example of this problem, consider the case of a resort developer who attempts to interview people during the day. The study yields some refusals and a lot of "not at homes." We must wonder whether the refusals as a group hold different attitudes about the development from those who respond. Also, by interviewing only in the day, the developer missed all families in which both the spouses work. This group may be a prime prospect. Such non-response errors are exceedingly common when potential respondents are contacted via electronic means, such as e-mail, but exist in all sampling situations, even when prior commitments have been secured. Frame problems and non-response errors are discussed in Chapter 6 and statistical methods (e.g., sample selection models) to help de-bias results appear in Chapter 12.

Poor Questionnaire Design

Surveys are sometimes constructed for polemical purposes, to elicit specific answers of use to the designer. To take an extreme example, in a survey of his constituents, a member of Congress asked, "Should the Congress challenge the do-nothing administration and take action on unemployment?" This is hardly the way to tease out the true feelings of his constituency on a complex issue. There is little good in measuring sampling error in such situations because other biases are so blatant. Typical survey design problems are more complex and subtle than this, relating to question sequence, length, word usage, and so on, and in many cases the researcher may not be fully aware of them. This important topic is discussed fully in Chapter 7, including the special section on biases in self-reports in that chapter.

Another example is the study mentioned earlier in '*Marketing Research Focus 2.3*' about a consumer food company. Several questions remained from that study regarding terminology and proper questionnaire design. All four questions posed in the survey used the term "often," but it was unclear what respondents took away. Did "often" mean "more than just once or twice ever;" "more than a small fraction of the time;" or its stronger, more colloquial sense of "more than half the time"? It was also unclear whether the behaviors in question appeared *in conjunction* with legitimate goals. For example, it was entirely possible that managers commissioned research both to yield useful information *and* to "appease their superiors." Ironically, one result of the research was that more in-depth research was needed to assess the significance of the managers' responses.

This important topic is discussed fully in Chapter 7 and in the *Special Expert Feature* on biases in self-reports following that chapter.

Measurement Error

measurement error
Any source of error—either systematic or random—on an observed variable. It is often defined as the difference between the measured value of the variable and its true value.

Measurement is the process of assigning numbers to observed phenomena. A researcher may try to develop a scale of interest in a new product, but the scaling may be done improperly. Generally speaking, developing new scales that truly and reliably measure a construct of interest is a complex, time-consuming undertaking, one addressed in more depth in Chapter 4.

Improper Causal Inferences

causal inference
A set of statistical techniques used to suggest likely cause-and-effect relationships among a set of variables.

The search for *causes* bedevils scientists; philosophers; and, of course, market researchers. Vast experience has shown that it is exceedingly difficult to make statements of the form "A caused B," for a variety of reasons taken up at length in Chapter 5. Examples exist throughout marketing research applications. For example, a producer of heavy equipment changes the compensation scheme of its sales force, and the following year sales double. Management infers that the new compensation plan *caused* the sales increase. It is also possible that other factors could have influenced it; for example, the economy might have improved, the product might have improved, salespersons may have become more experienced, or the main competitor could have folded. In such situations, inferring "the cause" can be so fraught with difficulty as to be effectively impossible, even with powerful statistical tools and the experience to apply them judiciously.

SPECIAL SECTION

Example of Industry-Level Marketing Research

The research project described here was conducted for the Rigid Container Division of the Society of the Plastic Industry (SPI), which represents many U.S. manufacturers of rigid plastic containers. Many of these companies are small manufacturing units with limited marketing and marketing research capabilities. A six-member executive board administers the activities of the Rigid Container Division.

Problem Recognition and Definition

Plastic packaging had penetrated substantially into the markets of more conventional packaging materials such as paper, paperboard, glass, and metal. At the time of the study, plastic containers represented less than 20 percent of industry volume, with steady, albeit not rapid, growth.

Several SPI research studies indicated that rigid plastic containers offered the following consumer advantages: light weight, resistance to breakage, toughness, resealability, and potential for reuse. Advantages to producers were low cost, easy storage, and availability in an almost limitless variety of colors and designs.

Much of the growth in plastic container sales had stemmed from the initiative of food manufacturers in seeking new packaging concepts for products being developed. An example of this situation was the development of soft margarine early in the twentieth century, and the proliferation of plastic margarine containers after Parkay's immensely successful "Talking Tub" advertising campaign, which started running in 1973 and is still successful more than 30 years later. The manufacturer had requested the development of a reusable container specifically designed for this new product.

There were several constraints on future growth:

1. growing uncertainty regarding the cost of raw materials, especially petroleum-based products, and the competitive influence this would have on container selection
2. future competitive moves from glass, metal, and paper manufacturers, as well as more exotic hybrid materials using various combinations. Many of these firms were large and had extensive research and development (R&D) and marketing capabilities.
3. growing concern about environmental and safety issues regarding packaging containers, particularly the non-biodegradable property of most plastics and possible health effects for humans and marine animals. (See the conclusion of this section for additional examples and references.)
4. growing concern among SPI members that possibly the high potential markets for plastic containers had been saturated. Expansion of plastics production had resulted in manufacturing capacity in excess of demand for the majority of SPI members.

SPI members wanted to identify new markets and programs developed to achieve the market potential. Consequently, the executive board of the Rigid Container Division of SPI commissioned a marketing research study for that purpose. After an initial meeting of presentations and discussions, the research firm requested a formal statement of objectives and potential courses of action available for reaching the objectives. In response, SPI members agreed to the following statement:

I. *SPI objective:*
To increase the market penetration of plastic containers to at least 30 percent within five years.

II. *Courses of action:*

A. develop and implement a marketing program to maintain or improve the acceptance of plastic containers in markets where plastic now dominates
B. develop and implement a marketing program to expand the acceptance of plastic containers in markets where plastic has a low or moderate penetration
C. develop and implement a marketing program to enter new markets currently dominated by paper, paperboard, glass, metal, and/or hybrid materials
D. develop and implement a marketing program to work actively with manufacturers of new products

continued

The Problem Setting in Perspective

The marketing alternatives of concern to the Rigid Container Division involved broad and extensive information requirements.

One research approach involved studying the reactions of individuals and organizations that influenced the market acceptance of plastic containers. The ultimate consumers can be an influential group in this acceptance process. Consumers may have preferences for packaging characteristics that favor plastic over other packaging materials. Retailers and wholesalers may find packaging characteristics (such as stacking ability, display appeal, and potential for breakage) important in their selection. Manufacturers may consider the preferences and reactions of consumers, retailers, and wholesalers; container costs and related investment; and degree of product protection, promotional features, and ecological issues when deciding on a packaging container for their product. Studying this complex chain of influence for each market under consideration would involve several research projects.

Analyzing current markets was another area of investigation. The task here would be to quantify markets on characteristics such as size, trends in size, current mix of packaging forms, and fit of packaging requirements with existing plastic container manufacturing processes. This research approach would involve the use of published data sources such as research reports, trade association data, and trade periodicals.

Additional studies might prove necessary, including profitability analysis of current lines of plastic containers, customer analysis, competitive analysis, and environmental analysis.

The information needs of this project ranged from small exploratory studies with consumers, retailers, wholesalers, and manufacturers to more formal studies using observation, interrogation, experimentation, and published data sources internal and external to the sponsoring organizations.

The Study Proposal

A research proposal was developed and sent to each of the executive board members for review. At a subsequent meeting with the research firm, the board approved an amended proposal. The final proposal comprised two sections, packaging markets and consumer acceptance, summarized in the following sections.

Study of Packaging Markets

Rationale for the Study

The purpose of this study is to identify and characterize packaging markets and to screen these markets as to their potential for penetration by plastic containers. The high-potential markets identified through this study will be further screened in a study of consumer acceptance.

Research Objectives

1. to compare current and potential packaging markets with regard to dimensions indicative of market potential
2. to categorize packaging markets as to the degree of plastic container penetration
3. to evaluate the high-potential markets in terms of the compatibility of packaging requirements with existing production and material capabilities

Information Needs

1. to rank container markets by number of containers used per year; to illustrate trends over the past five years
2. to classify markets as to the most likely plastic manufacturing process (thermoforming, injection molding, spin welding, or blow molding)
3. to classify markets by proportion of containers that are paper, paperboard, glass, metal, and plastic; to illustrate trends over the past five years
4. to rank container markets by retail price of the product; to illustrate trends over the past five years
5. to rank container markets by proportion of retail price represented by packaging costs; to illustrate trends over the past five years
6. to rank container markets by magnitude of packaging cost increase or decrease resulting from a change to a plastic container
7. to classify markets as to the degree of fit with existing production and material capabilities—high, medium, or low fit
8. to calculate the plastic container manufacturer's break-even volume for each market, determine the proportion of market penetration required to break even for each market, and rank the markets accordingly

Data Sources

The data used to meet the information needs will include internal and external reports, publications, and records. Data that are not available in published form will be gathered by interviews with knowledgeable people in the industry.

The following published and Web-based sources have been identified:

1. SPI, "The Plastic Industry in the Year 2000."
2. Southall, T. (2005). "Size and Impact of the Plastics Industry on the U.S. Economy." SPI. Washington DC.
3. Web sites for SPI (socplas.org), the Canadian Plastics Industry Association (plastics.ca), the Plastics USA portal (plasticsusa.com), The PlasticsNet Digital Marketplace (plasticsnet.com) the Plastics News site (plastics-news.com), the American Plastics Council industry statistics site (americanplasticscouncil.org) and The National Association for PET Container Resources (napcor.com).
4. Brydson, J.A. (1999). *Plastics Materials,* 7th ed., Butterworth-Heinemann, Oxford.
5. Rosato, D.V. (2000). *Concise Encyclopedia of Plastics,* Kluwer, Boston.
6. Harvard Business School, "The Packaging Revolution" from *A Note on the Metal Container Industry.* Watertown, MA.
7. "New Container Push Accents Packaging," *Industrial Marketing,* December 1991.
8. "Packaging Seen as Effective Marketing Tool," *Advertising Age,* September 1990.
9. Census of Manufactures and 2002 Economic Census for Food Sales (SIC 20) and Plastic Sales (SIC 30794).
10. Standard and Poor's Industry Surveys ("Retailing Food" and "Containers").
11. *Modern Plastics and Modern Plastics Encyclopedia.*

continued

12. *Plastics, Additives and Compounding* (journal).
13. *Society of Petroleum Engineers* (journal).
14. *Modern Packaging and Modern Packaging Encyclopedia.*
15. Brody, A.L., and Marsh, K. S. (1997). *Marsh Encyclopedia of Packaging Technology*, 2nd ed., Wiley, Hoboken, New Jersey.
16. Midwest Research Institute, Resource and Environmental Profile Analysis of Plastic and Non-Plastic Containers.
17. United Nations Report, World Demand for Plastic.

Study of Consumer Acceptance

Rationale for the Study

It is the opinion of this research firm that demonstrating consumer acceptance or preference is the critical factor in influencing a manufacturer to use a plastic container, in the absence of an unfavorable cost differential or excessive distribution problems. Establishing consumer preference for a plastic container over existing packaging would provide evidence for a potential sales increase resulting from a change to a plastic container. Understanding the characteristics of plastic containers underlying consumer preference for them would also aid in developing a promotional program.

Research Objectives

1. to determine which container markets have the greatest consumer acceptance of plastic containers
2. to determine the characteristics of plastic containers that represent advantages compared with paper, paperboard, glass, metal, and hybrid containers

Information Needs

1. to identify the characteristics or attributes that differentiate alternative packaging materials
2. to determine the importance of packaging attributes in container markets
3. to determine consumer preference for alternative packaging materials in container markets
4. to identify the characteristics of packaging containers that influence consumer preference
5. to determine which attributes of plastic containers represent important selling points
6. to determine the characteristics of the "ideal" packaging container
7. to determine the likes and dislikes of consumers regarding current packaging containers
8. to determine what suggestions consumers have for packaging improvement in container market
9. to determine which markets have the most inadequate packaging, and whether plastic containers represent an improvement
10. to determine consumer attitudes toward ecological aspects of packaging materials, specifically plastic
11. to determine consumers' perceptions regarding the cost of alternative packaging materials; do some containers have a "high-price/high-quality" image?
12. to determine the nature of the tradeoffs consumers will make in selecting a brand or package. How large a price increase will be accepted for a superior packaging form? How much will a lower price offset packaging deficiencies?
13. to determine the characteristics (demographic, life cycle, usage rates) of consumers who are most receptive to plastic containers.

Data Sources

Acquiring data to meet the information needs will involve the questioning of consumers, starting with a series of focus-group interviews. The purpose is to explore consumer attitudes, feelings, and motives concerning the information-need areas. Based on these findings, specific questions can be developed for more systematic data collection. The second phase will involve a consumer questionnaire administered by personal interview.

The Research Project

SPI started this phase of the research project by furnishing an extensive list of packaging markets that seemed to hold good potential for rigid plastic containers. SPI developed the list through continuous monitoring of the packaging industry and further screened it to include only those markets where rigid plastic containers were judged to be feasible from the standpoint of both technology and cost. By researching secondary data sources, they were then able to trim from the list those markets with obviously undesirable demand characteristics and categorize the remaining markets according to the current penetration of plastic containers, as follows:

Potential Markets for Rigid Plastic Containers

Major Plastics Markets (already high penetration)	
Cultured dairy (cottage cheese, yogurt, etc.)	
Butter and margarine	
Portion packs (e.g., meat cold cuts)	
Pantyhose	
Minor Plastics Markets	
Shortening	Cosmetic creams and gels
Ice cream	Auto oil and grease
Spreads and dips	Food sauces
Frozen juice	Meat trays
Minimal or Non-Plastics Markets	
Jelly and preserves	Pet foods
Salad dressing	Auto parts and kits
Baby food	Cheese
Coffee	Household cleaners, wax, car care
Drink powders (e.g., Kool-Aid)	

At least two types of markets had high potential for rigid plastic containers: rapidly growing markets, where plastic already has significant penetration; and large or growing markets, where the penetration of plastic could be increased. High-penetration markets with stable or declining primary demand afforded little opportunity and therefore did not appear on the list.

This study of packaging markets can be viewed as exploratory research identifying alternative courses of action to reach the SPI objectives previously discussed. In this case, "alternative courses of action" would be the different container markets at which promotional efforts might be directed.

The study of consumer acceptance involved not only the exploratory research to identify these specific container market alternatives, but also conclusive research to evaluate and select a course of action as well.

continued

Group Studies

This stage of the project involved a series of group discussions exploring consumer attitudes on the advantages and disadvantages of different types of containers. The qualitative information derived from these sessions served to guide the quantitative research conducted later.

Design and Procedure

Eight to twelve paid participants attended each of the sessions held at a special facility run by the research firm, where participants were made as comfortable as possible in a family livingroom environment. The sessions were videotaped for later analysis, but the equipment was as unobtrusive as possible to minimize anxiety.

Each possible use of plastic containers was discussed in more than one session, usually in the context of a different set of other possible uses. When uses such as baby food and pet food containers were discussed, it was necessary to screen for panel members who were all purchasers of these products.

Sample Selection

Each session used a panel of consumers who were largely homogeneous in terms of their position in the family life cycle, so that there would be lifestyle commonalities within any particular session and thus common points of discussion. To help identify the most probable users of certain sets of products, family lifestyle position was varied *across* panel sessions. Using a screening questionnaire that identified marital status, number and ages of children living at home, occupational status, and usage rates of those products defined as markets for plastic containers, interviewers selected a convenient sample at a nearby shopping center. Those who agreed to participate were given a time and place to appear.

Moderator and Guide Questions

The group discussions were led by trained moderators, whose function was to channel the conversation along particular lines. They in turn were directed by a "moderator's guide," which specified the set of topics that the group was to cover and suggested questions for broaching the topics, such as:

- When was the last time you found yourself extremely dissatisfied with the container used for a product you had purchased?
- Certain types of containers are best suited for certain types of products. Describe for me the kind of product you would expect to find in a glass jar. How about a metal can? Paper or cardboard? Plastic? Hybrids?
- In general, what do you consider to be the advantages and disadvantages of glass, metal, paper, hybrid, and plastic containers?
- Let's discuss the kinds of experiences you have had with the containers used for ice cream, jelly, coffee, meat.
- Do you think it usually costs more to package a product in plastic rather than glass? Metal? Paper?
- Assume that the brand of ice cream you buy was available in the standard paper carton, a plastic container, or a sturdy cardboard container (the cylindrical kind with the separate top). If the price were the same for the three versions, which would you buy? What sort of person can you visualize buying the other two versions?

The moderators applied various techniques to help keep the conversation lively and uninhibited without allowing it to stray too far from the assigned topics or letting a few panel members dominate. One such technique was to identify panel members holding widely divergent points of view and then to guide them into a debate; another was to call on shy or retiring members directly for their opinions.

Analysis

After the tapes of the completed sessions were transcribed, the content was summarized into reports. The summary reports categorized and listed comments in such a way as to define the domain of the problem. The individual tapes were also edited into a summary tape that included the most significant dialogue from each session.

Results

What emerged from these sessions was:

1. a better understanding of how consumers think about containers, the terms they use, and the attributes and characteristics they consider relevant
2. a more thorough list of the advantages and disadvantages associated with different types, depending on how they are used
3. some new ideas on the kinds of products that might be contained in rigid plastic

For example, ice cream, especially the "super premium" segment, represented a market with relatively modest plastic penetration and would therefore seem to offer good potential for the future. A large proportion of half-gallon–sized ice cream containers, particularly at the lower-price end of the market, were paper cartons, which according to the panel members, had these deficiencies:

1. When the ice cream melts, they leak;
2. They are flimsy and tear easily;
3. Children don't know which end is the top, and they open both;
4. They are susceptible to freezer burn; and
5. They tend to absorb moisture.

By comparison, the participants saw these advantages to plastic containers for ice cream:

1. They are re-usable;
2. They are re-sealable;
3. They are strong;
4. They are less messy, because they don't leak;
5. They help prevent freezer burn;
6. Sherbet, gelato, and other iced desserts often come like this, and experiences with them have been good;
7. Plastic often has a higher price/quality image;
8. They are easy to use and have a wide mouth; and
9. There is an incentive value in seeing the ice cream, if a clear material is used.

This qualitative research did not provide sufficient evidence in itself to say that ice cream in rigid plastic containers would definitely enhance consumer perceptions. The sample was small and not representative, so there were no statistics projectable to the general population. All nine positive

continued

aspects on the list could also easily have been outweighed by a single important disadvantage not uncovered for some reason. Further conclusive research was needed.

Survey of Consumers

The survey of consumers followed a fairly standard series of steps for this type of research: questionnaire design and pre-testing; sample selection and field work; editing, coding, and data processing; and analysis and reporting. The methodology employed some error-reducing techniques that are not always used in marketing research due to cost.

Questionnaire Design and Pre-Testing

One principle in the design of a questionnaire is that the questions should proceed from the general to the specific. In this study, for example, respondents were asked to recall some products they had seen contained in plastic before being asked questions that specifically mentioned product names. Similar questions were also phrased with alternate wordings to avoid an acquiescence bias; and the order of items on lists was rotated to avoid an order bias. The response categories were pre-coded for computer processing and subsequent statistical analysis. Examples of questions on the questionnaire:

1. Of the packages you currently purchase, which do you feel could be improved? Why?
2. What products do you currently purchase that come packaged in a plastic container?
3. What are the advantages of a plastic container?
4. What are the disadvantages of a plastic container?
5. Would you please evaluate [packaging container] in regard to the degree it possesses the characteristic of [attribute]? [*rating scale*]
6. How important is the packaging characteristic of [attribute] for a [packaging container]? [*rating scale*]
7. (Interviewer checks "male" or "female.")
8. What is your marital status?
9. How many people are there in your household?
10. How many children do you have at home?
11. What are their ages?
12. What is the highest grade of school or college that you have completed?

The questionnaire was pre-tested on a convenience sample of about 75 consumers to make sure that it flowed well and that the questions were understandable to ordinary individuals. The pre-testing also provided the opportunity to analyze the items for redundancy by subjecting the data to Factor Analysis (see Chapter 11). This technique revealed that several of the attributes actually measured the same underlying characteristic, so the researchers were able to eliminate a few of them.

Sample Selection and Field Work

Telephone numbers for interviews were selected using the method of random-digit dialing. The advantage of random-digit dialing is that there is no bias against newly listed or unlisted numbers, as occurs when samples are selected from telephone directories. However, households without telephones were excluded from the target population; there is some inefficiency in connections made to business numbers; and households with two or more phone listings have a higher probability of being included in the sample. The interviews were conducted at various times of the day, and a number of callbacks were made when there was no answer or the line was busy. About 500 interviews were completed over the course of several weeks.

Editing, Coding, and Data Processing

Completed interviews were edited to make sure that they were legible, complete, and the pattern of answers in each was self-consistent and seemingly accurate. In cases where data were missing, estimates were made of what the responses would have been based on other information in the questionnaire, using a statistical technique called imputation, a form of multivariate regression (see Chapters 9 and 10). Open-ended questions were coded to make the data machine-readable. The coded interviews were then entered into an online queryable database, verified by standard data-processing software, and set up for statistical analysis.

Analysis and Reporting

The sample's demographics were compared with U.S. census data to determine whether it was broadly representative of the population. Except for minor sampling variations, the sample and population distributions were very similar.

Descriptive statistics, including measures of central tendency and dispersion, were obtained on the response to every item in the questionnaire. This helped to identify a number of "wild codes" that needed to be corrected. Some of these univariate statistics were used to make interval estimates of the proportion of consumers in the general population who felt a particular way on a certain issue. For example, it was of interest to the SPI to know that, at the 95 percent confidence level, somewhere between 43 percent and 51 percent of the population would prefer that their ice cream come in a rigid plastic container.

There were other cases where a univariate analysis was not revealing enough. For instance, 25 percent of the respondents said they would switch brands of ice cream to obtain a plastic container. A cross tabulation revealed that the result varied, depending on the level of educational attainment, as evidenced in Table 1. Only 17 percent of those who had graduated from high school said they would switch brands for plastic packaging, compared with 37 percent of those who had not graduated.

Table 1 Intention to Switch Brands by Level of Educational Attainment

	Total, %	Did not graduate, %	Graduated from high school, %
Would switch	25	37	17
Would not	75	63	83
Total	100	100	100

Note in Table 2 that, regardless of the level of educational attainment, only 20 percent of those who were aware that plastic is non-biodegradable said they

continued

Table 2 Intention to Switch Brands by Level of Educational Attainment and Bio-Awareness

	Did not graduate from high school			Graduated from high school		
	Total, %	Aware, %	Not aware, %	Total, %	Aware, %	Not aware, %
Would switch	37	20	43	17	20	43
Would not	63	80	57	83	80	57
Total	100	100	100	100	100	100

would switch brands, compared with 43 percent of those who were not aware. This suggests that the influence of education was that more people with a high school education were aware that plastic is non-biodegradable (50 percent compared with 25 percent).

In addition, many other two-way and higher-order multivariate relationships were studied to discern key drivers of consumer acceptance of rigid plastic containers. But these analyses were only as good as the data collected, and the researchers recognized that much more remained to be done to gain any longer-term sense of market evolution with respect to plastic food packaging. For example, there are clearly grounds for further study as awareness grows around other issues associated with plastics, particularly environmental and health-related ones. In recent years, there has been a rise in advocacy by individuals and organizations such as the Campaign Against the Plastic Plague and Plastic Debris River to Sea, with the purpose of educating consumers on the safety and environmental hazards posed by plastic products and packaging. These include harmful health effects of plastic-related chemicals,[2] the leaching of certain compounds into food,[3] damage to marine life due to plastic (even so called "biodegradable plastic") debris,[4] and other impacts. SPI currently participates in an advisory board with environmental groups and government agencies to discuss the problem of plastic debris in the marine environment, indicating industry interest in finding new solutions to these concerns.[5,6]

Stephanie Barger, Executive Director of Earth Resource Foundation, suggested the following for the future of the plastics industry: "If biodegradable plastics were accompanied by efforts to increase the infrastructure for composting the debris and raise consumer awareness of the need to do so, the plastics industry could take the lead in turning a liability into a substantial public relations and marketing gain." Clearly, this represents both potential problems and opportunities for the future of plastic food packaging, as well as for the marketers and researchers responsible for its deployment in the marketplace.

Summary

The *marketing research process* refers to the systematic assemblage, processing, and interpretation of market-related information to enhance managerial decision-making. It includes a series of basic steps: establishing the need for information; detailing research objectives; designing the research, data collection procedure, and sample; collecting, coding, and analyzing the data; and presenting the results.

The first question the researcher must answer is whether research is needed at all. In the course of this decision-making process, some of the preliminary steps of the research process may be fulfilled. Exploratory research may be helpful to define the decision or to identify alternative courses of action.

If research is deemed necessary, conclusive research seeks to evaluate the possible courses of action. If the preliminary steps of the research process (establishing the need for information, determining research objectives, and specifying information needs) have not already been accomplished, this should happen first. The research findings also need to be envisioned and even mocked up, with specific feedback from the decision-maker regarding the usefulness of the mocked-up data to the decision.

Through interviewing and simulated data reports, the researcher then works with the decision-maker to come up with decision criteria involving if–then statements about the conditions justifying particular courses of action. The final hurdle is to weigh the cost of the research against the perceived benefit, and if deemed worthwhile, formally propose the research.

Management–research relationships are key to the success of research. Various factors, motives, and organizational obstacles can affect these relationships.

Error in marketing research is of two main types: errors associated with the particular sample that happened to have been selected, called sampling errors; and all other errors, called non-sampling errors. Non-sampling errors include flaws in defining the problem or population, choosing a selection frame, measurement, questionnaire design, and inference of causes, as well as non-response errors.

Key Terms

causal inference (p. 49)
conclusive research (p. 36)
contribution margin (p. 41)
course of action (p. 34)
data sources (p. 31)
decision criteria (p. 40)
decision objectives (p. 33)
exploratory research (p. 33)
information needs (p. 31)
measurement error (p. 49)
non-response error (p. 49)
non-sampling error (p. 47)
opportunities (p. 32)
population definition (p. 48)
population value (p. 48)
problem definition (p. 45)
problems (p. 32)
pseudo-research (p. 44)
research design (p. 31)
sample value (p. 48)
sampling error (p. 47)
self-selection bias (p. 40)
symptoms (p. 30)

Discussion Questions

1 Why is the analysis preceding the decision to undertake research so crucial to the success of the project?

2 What are the implications for the marketing researcher of a decision situation characterized by primary (organizational) and secondary (personal) objectives?

3 Procter & Gamble is considering the simultaneous launch of a liquid detergent in 10 European countries. This product is based on a successful product introduction in the United States. What marketing research program would you recommend that P&G undertake?

4 The Wool Producers Board of New Zealand wants to stimulate the primary demand for wool in the world. What marketing research could the board do to facilitate the development of such a primary demand stimulation campaign? Describe a program of marketing research in detail. Explain how potential errors in marketing research will be controlled in this program.

5 Suppose that your role in a research project were to perform statistical analyses and help explain them for the research report. You realize later that, of the many dozens of analyses run, only those explicitly supporting a costly departmental expansion—and not those that either failed to support it or called it directly into question—were included in the final report put together by other members of the research team to be read by upper management. What might you do, and how would it affect how you carried out future analyses?

6 How might one go about mocking up research report data if questions themselves have not even been generated? How detailed can, and should, statistical analyses be in such a report? How, practically speaking, would one go about generating data in this situation if the goal is to ensure that the analysis plan and sequence of calculations are viable and potentially useful?

Review Questions

1 The variable cost of a new anti-depressant is $0.50 per pill. The market size is 600,000 pills, and a bottle of 20 pills sells for $35. If the firm decides that marketing research is justified up to 5%, what is the maximum available for marketing research?

a $1,050,000
b $51,750
c $37,500
d $17,143

2 Survey questions are to information needs as information needs are to ______________.

a population sampling
b research objectives
c data collection
d research protocols

3 Which of the following is a problem? In the past 6 months:
   a Sales revenue has increased half as quickly as projected.
   b Sales revenue has decreased 20% overall.
   c Customer satisfaction with the company has decreased 5%.
   d A new competitor is charging a lower price on quality-matched items.

4 A situational analysis is also known as ______________________.
   a a data analysis
   b an evaluation of courses of action
   c a statement of problems and opportunities
   d exploratory research

5 The value of research to a manager increases as:
   a the market size increases.
   b the contribution margin increases.
   c uncertainty about outcomes increases.
   d all of the above.

6 The outcome of the manager's final decision is limited by:
   a the overall cost of the marketing research.
   b the quality of courses of action considered.
   c the nature of the performance measures leading to the research.
   d all of the above.

7 An evaluation of various courses of action is called:
   a exploratory research.
   b a situational analysis.
   c a multi-variate analysis approach.
   d conclusive research.

8 A mock-up of research findings using simulated data is valuable because:
   a It prepares managers for the experience.
   b It reduces the expense of collecting actual data.
   c It helps managers to notice omissions and develop decision criteria.
   d Marketing researchers tend to be better at visualization than managers.

9 Which is a valid reason for undertaking a marketing research project?
   a The contribution margin and the market size are large.
   b A major decision has been made, and managers wish to be able to justify the decision.
   c A top manager is anxious and needs assurance about courses of action.
   d A manager is uncertain about a decision and wishes to decrease this uncertainty

10 "The reduction of customer service was responsible for a 15% increase in revenues over the past year." This is an example of which non-sampling error:
   a improper causal inference.
   b faulty problem definition.
   c sampling frame non-representative of the population.
   d poor questionnaire design.

Web Exercise

Log in to the Online Edition of your textbook at www.atomicdog.com to participate in this Web Exercise, which can be found in your Online Study Guide for this chapter.

Further Reading

Survey Nonresponse (Wiley Series in Survey Methodology), by Robert M. Groves, Don A. Dillman, John L. Eltinge, Roderick J. A. Little. Wiley-Interscience. October 25, 2001.

Real World Research: A Resource for Social Scientists and Practitioner-Researchers, 2nd Edition by Colin Robson. Malden, MA: Blackwell Publishing, Incorporated. February 1, 2002.

Research Proposals: A Guide to Success, 3rd Edition by Thomas E. Ogden, Israel A. Goldberg. Burlington, MA: Academic Press, Elsevier. June 2002.

Measurement Error and Research Design, by Madhu Viswanathan. Thousand Oaks, CA: Sage Publications. February 10, 2005.

The Market Research Toolbox: A Concise Guide for Beginners, 2nd Edition by Edward F. McQuarrie. Thousand Oaks, CA: Sage Publications. June 15, 2005.

Notes

1 "Perspectives on Concept Mapping"; J. D. Novak, J. H. Wandersee. Special issue of the *Journal of Research in Science Teaching*, 27(10): 921–1075. 1990.

2 Sources: Report: Widely Used Chemical Could Harm Humans; Joan Lowy. *Scripps Howard News Service*: April 13, 2005.

3 Estrogen Imitator in Womb May Lead to Cancer in Men, Study Finds; Marla Cone. *Los Angeles Times*. Los Angeles, California: May 3, 2005.

4 Scientists Raise Spectre Of Cancer-Causing Packaging; *Food Navigator Europe:* April 20, 2005.

5 Study Cites Risk of Compound in Plastic Bottles; Marla Cone. Los Angeles, California: Los Angeles Times. April 13, 2005.

6 Plastic Trash Washes into Oceans, Endangering Marine Life; Heherson T. Alvarez. Manila, Philippines: Manila Times. March 29, 2005.

CHAPTER THREE
RESEARCH DESIGN AND DATA SOURCES

"Somewhere, something incredible is waiting to be known."
CARL SAGAN

This chapter discusses step 3 in the marketing research process: the nature of research design, potential sources of data, and how researchers go about using them together. Once researchers have adequately addressed the preliminary issues of planning and analysis involved in the decision to undertake research, their attention turns to designing the formal research project and identifying appropriate sources of data. The primary task will be to supply the decision-maker with conclusive research: information that increases the level of confidence regarding the best course of action to accomplish explicitly stated objectives.

In this chapter, we discuss three types of research design, their relationship to the stages of the manager's decision-making process, and the nature and role of research design in the research process. This includes a detailed discussion of the basic sources of marketing data: surveys of respondents, observation, studies of analogous situations, experimentation, and secondary data. The chapter concludes with a more comprehensive discussion of marketing-decision support systems, which was touched on briefly in Chapter 1.

3.1 Research Design: Delineating What Data to Collect and How to Collect Them

A research design is the basic plan that guides the data collection and analysis phases of the research project. It can be thought of as a framework that specifies, at minimum, the type of information to be collected, possible data sources, and the collection procedure. A good design will ensure that any information gathered is consistent with the study objectives and that the data are collected accurately, economically, and within a specified time period. Unlike formal statistical procedures, there is no standard or idealized design to guide the researcher because many different designs can be used to accomplish the same objective. In this sense, designing good research is part art, part science; it benefits from close study of best practices and prior efforts.

The overall objectives of the project logically suggest characteristics of the research design, and designs tend to be classified according to the type and objective of research they comprise. This system is not always a perfect means of classification because research designs can serve many objectives and include numerous types of research; but it does serve as a structure for discussion.

3.1a Types of Research

Marketing research can be broadly classified into three sometimes overlapping streams, according to the stage in the decision-making process for which the information is needed: (1) exploratory research, (2) conclusive research, and (3) performance-monitoring (routine feedback) research. Exploratory research aids the early stages of the decision-making process and investigates how to hold down cost and time expenditure. Conclusive research provides information that helps the manager evaluate and select a course of action. Performance monitoring is essential to ensure that marketing programs are proceeding in accordance with preset plans. Figure 3.1 illustrates the interdependence of these types of research, and *Marketing Research Focus 3.1* illustrates how some major packaged goods firms relied on research to help better position their products.

3.1b Exploratory Research: Determining the "Space" of Possible Marketing Actions

The purpose of exploratory research is to facilitate problem recognition and definition and to narrow down the manifold possibilities. It is appropriate when the research objectives include (1) identifying, or developing a more precise formulation of, problems or opportunities; (2) gaining perspective regarding the breadth of variables operating in a situation; (3) establishing priorities regarding the potential significance of various problems or opportunities; (4) gaining management and researcher perspective concerning the character of the problem; (5) formulating possible courses of action; and (6) gathering information on the possible pitfalls associated with doing conclusive research.

When identifying possible courses of action, the manager seeks clues to innovative marketing approaches. The objective is to broaden the domain of possibilities to consider, with the hope, obviously,

Figure 3.1 Types of Research

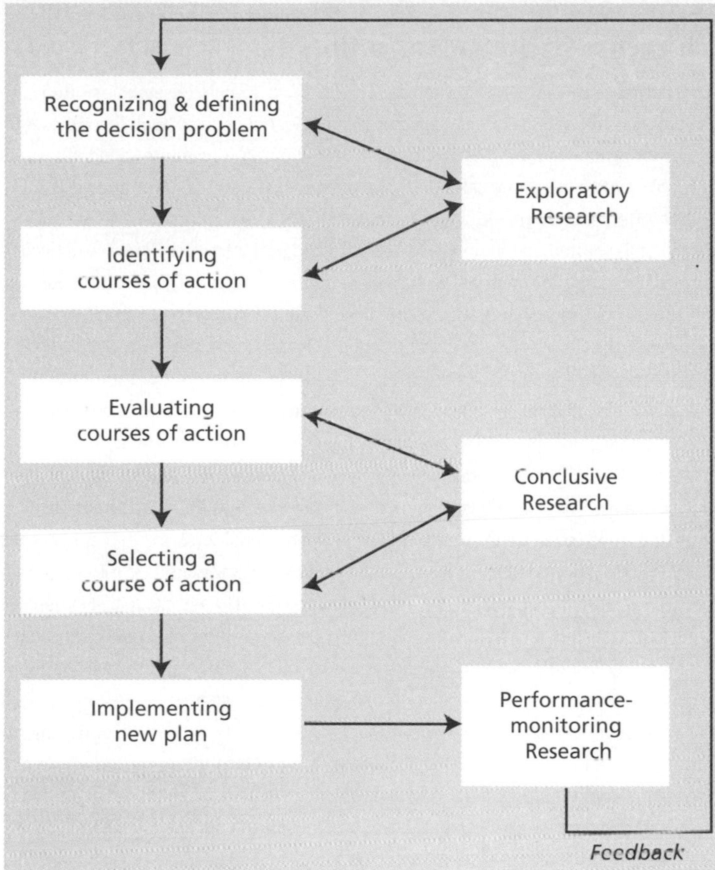

of including the "best" alternative in the set to be formally evaluated. Exploratory research generally aims to identify a set of reasonable plans; eventually, the decision-maker will rely on conclusive research to choose from among this set.

The design of exploratory research is characterized by flexibility—changing course midstream, if necessary, to respond to the unexpected and to discover insights not previously recognized. A common error in carrying out early stage research is specifying what is sought in too rigid a fashion so that unanticipated relationships are never explored. Exploratory research therefore relies on wide-ranging and versatile approaches, including secondary data sources, observation, interviews with experts, focus groups with knowledgeable persons and "insiders," internet-based data gathering, and case histories.

Exploratory research aims to generate formal, testable hypotheses regarding potential problems or opportunities, or both. We use the term **hypothesis** to refer to a conjectural statement about the relationship between two or more variables. This statement should carry clear implications for measuring the variables and for testing the stated relationship.

hypothesis
A specific statement about a set of measurable quantities, usually assessed by collecting data.

For example, consider a situation in which management responds to the symptom of declining share of market by asking, "What is the problem?" but no suggestions or hunches are put forth as likely culprits. The task of exploratory research would be to identify tentative, plausible hypotheses about what variables and drivers may be behind this decline. Potential hypotheses may be narrowed by further conclusive research, to the point where a definitive statement of problems and opportunities can be developed.

Some examples of hypotheses developed from exploratory research:

1. An advertising theme emphasizing the "nutritional value" of food product X will increase brand awareness more than a theme emphasizing "good flavor."
2. A change in the ingredients of product X from artificial chocolate to real chocolate will increase the preference for product X compared with its competition.
3. A 10 percent cut in the retail price of product X will result in a 1 percent market share gain within 6 months.

Marketing Research Focus 3.1

Research Facilitates Product Positioning

Marketing research can facilitate problem-solving when a product's sales decline. Researchers often use focus groups (see Chapter 6) to diagnose problems related to market positioning and to identify and evaluate hypotheses regarding improved positioning. Following are some real-life examples of successful repositioning in response to marketing research.

When Campbell Soup sought to invigorate sales of its line of condensed soups, it conducted focus groups of children, on the theory that children often have input into which soups their families will purchase. The interviews corroborated that parents and children often collaborated on the purchase decisions and that Campbell Soup could become a "kid brand" in addition to a "mom brand" if it communicated well with children on their own terms. Campbell Soup repositioned some of its products to appeal to children, recruiting youth sports celebrities like soccer star Freddy Adu as "spokes-kids" and launching new pasta shapes for its Chicken Noodle Soup, SpaghettiOs, and Sports Pastas based on Nickelodeon characters. The result has been a marked increase in sales for these lines, attributed to kid-focused promotions.

Kellogg's focus groups revealed that many adults feel a need for their breakfast cereal to be sweet-tasting. When asked, a high percentage of adults said they appreciated the health benefits of shredded wheat cereal but wanted something sweeter. Armed with this bit of insight, Kellogg decided to reposition Frosted Mini-Wheats via campaigns aimed at 35- to 49-year-olds who sought out a high-fiber breakfast cereal but also don't want to forsake a sweet taste.

Dial Corporation was perturbed by declining sales for its line of antibacterial soaps in what appeared to be a strong market. To stem this erosion in sales, they conducted focus groups, hoping to glean insights into consumer perceptions that might account for the decline. Results suggested that consumers perceived Dial's product as intended for older people (whereas much of the market consisted of families with young children) and as masculine (whereas purchase decisions in this category were made primarily by women). Accordingly, Dial repositioned its soap to appeal to a specific segment—women, aged 25 to 49 with families—using a campaign promoting Dial soap as a provider of a safe and comfortable haven where women, free of germs, could feel clean and positive about themselves. The ads invoked childhood memories of innocence and purity through nostalgic black and white television ads featuring Judy Garland's voice and a little girl in a bathtub. This campaign marked a sharp break with Dial's former image and succeeded in increasing its market among women.

When Sears purchased the name and several locations of Eaton's, a Canadian department retailer, it hoped to reposition the flagging Eaton's brand to revitalize the purchased stores. Based on surveys of Canadian attitudes toward shopping, Sears developed new concepts for the Eaton's chain and tested these concepts in focus groups of female Eaton's customers, between the ages of 25 and 50, who had spent more than $1000 a year on clothing. Sears learned from the focus groups that Eaton's, although perceived as middle-aged, middle-class, and comfortable, was still associated with prestige and grandeur, and that these consumers were eager to embrace a modern, active Eaton's with hip and sophisticated store "sensory stations" and event areas. Sears implemented these conclusions and re-opened the Eaton's stores with successfully repositioned branding.

Successful repositioning involves a variety of research forms in addition to focus groups, including performance monitoring and attitudinal surveys. The examples of focus groups presented here demonstrate, at the most visible level, how research can enable companies to both measure and respond successfully to shifting market conditions.

Sources: "Campbell Aims Squarely at Kids with Push for Pastas and Soups"; Stephanie Thompson. *Advertising Age*. May 31, 2004.
"Companies Sweeten Sales of Adult Cereal with Sugar"; Janet Adamy, *Wall Street Journal*. March 11, 2005.
"Dial Soap Campaign Aims to Calm Fears of a Germ-Ridden World"; Tara Parker-Pope. *Wall Street Journal*. January 20, 1998.
"Second Time Friendly: Seven Eaton's Stores in Choice Downtown Locations Across Canada are About to be Reborn as, Wait for it, a Retail Chain for Urban Hipsters"; Sean Silcoff. *Canadian Business*. May 29, 2000.

Note that each of these admits a firm "Either/Or" or "Yes/No" answer, rather than allowing a range of possibilities to be further winnowed down. The formulation of hypotheses rarely comes to the mind of the manager or researcher through the application of fixed and rigid procedures. Of all the stages of the decision-making process, identification of problems and opportunities eludes formal description. Although the ability to formulate the decision problem requires input from the realm of inspiration, various procedures can assist this creative process: (1) searching secondary sources, (2) interviewing knowledgeable parties, and (3) compiling case histories.

3.1c Conclusive Research: Narrowing Down Strategic Alternatives

The purpose of conclusive research is to narrow the field of strategic alternatives down to one. The design of conclusive research is characterized by formal research procedures and clearly defined research objectives and information needs. Typically, one draws up a detailed questionnaire; a formal sampling plan; and, eventually, a planned set of (statistical) analyses. It should be clear how the information to be collected relates to the alternatives under evaluation. Possible research approaches include surveys; experiments; observations; and, when appropriate information can allow for it, simulation.

Conclusive research can be sub-classified into **descriptive research** and **causal research**.

3.1d Descriptive Research

The vast majority of marketing research studies involve the type of conclusive research called *descriptive research.* Most of these studies rely heavily on an amalgam of respondent interviews and data available from secondary data sources. Descriptive research is appropriate when the research objectives include (1) portraying the characteristics of marketing phenomena and determining the frequency of occurrence, (2) determining the degree to which marketing variables are associated, and (3) making predictions regarding the occurrence of marketing phenomena.

A substantial proportion of research falls under the first of these objectives, portraying the characteristics of marketing phenomena and determining the frequency of occurrence. **Consumer profile** studies are conducted by firms like General Motors and Procter & Gamble to describe the user characteristics for particular products or services. Such profiles can be set up in terms of demographic, socioeconomic, geographic, and **psychographic** characteristics, as well as consumption rates; usually a situation-specific combination of these works best.

Firms typically run a wide variety of other types of descriptive studies for this same general purpose, either as needed or on an ongoing basis. Descriptive studies determine buyer perceptions of product characteristics and **audience profiles** for media such as television and magazines. **Market potential** describes the size of the market, the buying power of consumers, the availability of distributors, and buyer profiles for a product. Product usage studies describe consumption patterns for various members of a household or as aggregated into specific **geodemographic** groups. **Market-share studies** determine the proportion of total sales received by both a company and its competitors, in terms of units, volume, and total dollar sales. **Sales analysis** describes sales patterns by geographic region, type, size of account, and product line characteristics. **Distribution research** determines the number and location of distributors, as well as various aspects of their business practice and such crucial mix variables as trade deal support. **Pricing research** describes the range and frequency of (regular or "de-promoted") prices charged for both a company's products and those of its competitors. These represent only a sample of the numerous studies conducted in this area because descriptive research is pervasive and a major activity in large-scale firms.

The second category of descriptive research involves determining the degree to which marketing variables are associated with output measures of interest, such as sales, profit, ad awareness, or share. For example, a company may study the degree of association between sales of a product and such buyer characteristics as income and age to best target its ad and promotional spending.

The final category of descriptive research provides information used to make predictions about the occurrence—the timing, likelihood, and frequency—of various marketing phenomena. Although data regarding a possible association among variables can be used for predictive purposes, these data are not adequate to establish a causal relationship. On the other hand, it is not always necessary to understand causal relations to make accurate predictive statements. For example, if your friend tends to visit you on Tuesday, it may be because she has that day off from work; if her work schedule changes, so will her availability for visits, so "Tuesday-ness" itself has no causal relation to your friend's availability. Similarly, a company may establish an association between the sales of a product and seasons of the year, and a sales forecast based on this association may have a high probability of success regarding future sales volume, even though the causal relationship has not been established. Of course, if conditions change, the quality of this prediction can degrade wildly if the correct causal model has not been established. The concept is to identify variables that are associated with the variable to be predicted and that can be accurately measured at the time the prediction is needed.

Although descriptive research may characterize marketing phenomena and demonstrate an association among variables, statements regarding cause-and-effect relationships are not possible with descriptive research, although the error of doing so is tempting and all too commonly made. The decision-maker may predict that certain actions will result in specific performance outcomes *based on* the evidence provided from a descriptive study, but this evidence in itself does *not* demonstrate a cause-and-effect relationship.

descriptive research
Research whose emphasis is not causal, but on providing a rich descriptive portrait; for example, determining the frequency with which a marketing action or outcome occurs or the degree to which two marketing variables co-occur.

causal research
A formal research design whose purpose is to determine cause-and-effect relationships among a set of marketing variables.

consumer profile
Comprehensive description of the characteristics of consumers of a particular product or service, typically including geodemographic, psychographic, and purchase data.

psychographic
A variable that accounts for the ways in which people live their lives, comprising such concepts as lifestyle, social classification, and personality type. Psychographic variables transcend mere demographic categories (e.g., whereas young, urban, and professional are geodemographic descriptors, "yuppie" is psychographic and connotes far more).

audience profiles
Geodemographic and psychographic characteristics of the consumers exposed to a particular media or advertising vehicle.

market potential
An estimate of the maximum possible sales of a product or service in a specific industry over a stated time period.

geodemographic
A *geodemographic* variable gives information about the basic facts of someone's life, such as age, income level, education, gender, ethnic background, location, and many other such (typically categorical) variables. They are almost always collected on consumer surveys, and they allow for useful breakdowns of market behavior; for example, to men vs. women or urban vs. rural. Note that geodemographic variables do *not* include descriptions of attitudes, intentions, or behavior

Generally speaking, causality is frightfully difficult to determine, even in well-controlled experimental research, and should be considered off-limits based only on uncontrolled "field data." (See Chapter 5 for a detailed discussion of causal designs.)

The character and purpose of descriptive research are substantially different from that of exploratory research. Effective descriptive research is marked by a clear statement of the decision problem, specific research objectives, and detailed information needs. It is characterized by a carefully planned and structured research design. Because the overarching purpose is to provide information regarding specific questions or hypotheses, the research must be designed to ensure accuracy of the eventual findings. Here "**accuracy**" refers to a design that minimizes systematic error and maximizes the reliability of collected evidence. **Systematic error** refers to a constant bias in the measurement process, whereas **reliability** refers to the extent to which the measurement process is free from random errors. In simple terms, systematic error incorrectly influences conclusions in one direction, whereas random error does so in any number of ways. (In-depth discussions of both types of error can be found in Chapter 4.)

3.1e Cross-Sectional Design

Descriptive research typically makes use of a cross-sectional research design; that is, taking a **sample** of population elements at one point in time. Frequently termed a **survey research design**, this is the most popular and familiar type of research design. The survey design is useful in describing the characteristics of consumers and in determining the frequency of marketing phenomena, although it is often expensive and requires skillful and competent research personnel to conduct it effectively. The distinguishing features of a **cross-sectional design** are that it is intended to be done just once, and participants cannot typically be matched up to specific participants in other studies; that is, there is no *individual-level* identification from one study to another. This makes comparing successive cross-sectional samples difficult because relevant distinctions can be driven by demographic (and other) differences across the samples themselves. In practice, it is exceptionally important to collect detailed sample information to attempt to control for such sample-to-sample differences.

3.1f Implicit Causal Models

The evidence provided by descriptive research can be very useful when combined with the decision-maker's implicit model of how the marketing system functions in regard to the specific area under investigation. This **causal model** is typically based on the experience and judgment of the decision-maker and represents key assumptions underlying supposed cause-and-effect relationships in the marketing system. A descriptive study can help resolve specific questions and hypotheses about the current state of variables in the causal model. Given this descriptive evidence, the decision-maker can draw conclusions about the effects of various courses of action and reach a decision about which course of action will best accomplish the stated objectives. Consequently, descriptive research in itself may not provide evidence directly related to selecting a course of action; it must instead be incorporated into the decision-maker's personal model of the marketing system.

To illustrate, suppose that a marketing manager wishes to test the following hypothesis: "The reason for the decline in share for our aspirin-free analgesic product is the consumer's misperception that the product contains aspirin." We will presume that this hypothesis is sound enough to warrant being formally tested, having been developed from several exploratory group interviews with former users of the product in question. Descriptive research is then conducted, and an extensive survey of several hundred former and potential consumers supports the hypothesis. Note that the outcome of the study does not directly suggest any specific course of action. Rather, the marketing manager combines this descriptive evidence with a causal model of how the analgesic market functions to determine what to do next, and she eventually decides to develop an advertising campaign stressing the product's absence of aspirin and the benefits associated with aspirin-free products.

As this example points out, descriptive research presupposes that a sound causal model of the marketing system exists, either organizationally or in the mind of the decision-maker. Although it may appear obvious, it is worth stressing that the lower the decision-maker's confidence in the wisdom of the causal model, the lower the value of descriptive research in the decision-making process. For example,

market-share studies
Research undertaken to determine potential demand estimates as a function of the marketing mix, particular various pricing levels. Can be accomplished readily in test markets, but is typically approached more affordably via various pre-marketing forecasting methods, for example, ASSESSOR.

sales analysis
A large-scale study of a firm's sales data, across business units, products, over time or with competitive figures.

distribution research
Marketing studies focused on the movement and dissemination of products, from the manufacturer to the wholesaler and retailer up through the point of purchase.

pricing research
Research undertaken to determine viable pricing levels for a product or service, especially the expected sales and share levels associated with each.

accuracy
Reducing both systematic (i.e., in a definite direction, a bias) and random (in any direction at all; noise) errors increases the *accuracy* of research results.

systematic error
An error in measurement attributable to a consistent bias, one not attributable merely to the randomness of the sampling process.

reliability
The degree to which a variable is consistent in repeated measurements taken under identical conditions.

sample
The units selected by the researcher, usually at random from some target population, to participate in the research study.

survey research design
A common marketing research design that involves a (cross-sectional) sample of various population subgroups at a particular moment in time.

cross-sectional design
Research involving a sample of units (people, firms, products, etc.) selected from the population of interest and measured at only a single specific time.

descriptive research for brand positioning is of little value if one has no idea how brand positioning relates to the success of the brand. In short, one should not commission descriptive research without a clear plan for how to put the results to use. Descriptive research is all too easy to conduct when the decision-maker gives the researcher free rein to collect what are believed to be interesting facts, often referred to derisively as a "fishing expedition." This can encourage vague research objectives, loosely formulated research questions or hypotheses, and insufficient attention to how the evidence can be used to aid decision-making. In such cases, the bulk of the data typically turn out to be useless, and management has wasted both funds and time. An exploratory research study might have provided better information, faster and at a lower cost, than a fact-finding descriptive study.

Although descriptive research designs frequently draw on newly collected, proprietary information, they may also use data from direct questioning of respondents (e.g., surveys, focus groups), secondary data (commercially provided, or from government and academic databases), and even simulation. In all cases, however, the main issue is that the research be aimed at reaching a conclusion, not to open up more options for study, as exploratory research does.

causal model
A formal system laying out which marketing variables result in specific outcomes; the causal model can be supported or refuted by empirical data.

3.1g Causal Research

Causal research is a type of conclusive research designed to gather evidence regarding the cause-and-effect relationships operating in the marketing system. It requires a planned and structured design that will not only minimize systematic error and maximize reliability, but will also permit reasonably unambiguous conclusions regarding causality, with an eye toward choosing among potential courses of action.

Before describing such research and its uses, we must mention that "causal" is something of a taboo term in statistical and methodological circles. Even though causality is a mainstay of everyday speech—"I did it on account of you," "I passed because I studied so hard"—many statisticians are philosophically opposed to causal statements. For example, "I did it on account of you" presumes the speaker would not have done it otherwise, and to verify "I passed because I studied so hard" would require re-playing history with various lesser levels of study and observing these alternate results. Although there are some cases of clear-cut causality (e.g., "the pitcher broke because I knocked it over"), real-world examples, where dozens of variables operate and interact in complex ways, are exceedingly rare.

Causal research is appropriate, given the following research objectives: (1) to understand which variables combine to give rise to the effect, focusing on "why the effect happens"; and (2) to understand the nature of the functional relationship between the causal factors and the effect. With both of these elements in hand, it may be possible to fashion a useful statistical model to predict the effect based on its identified causes.

In practice, marketing managers and executives conceptualize and make decisions based on their implicit causal model of the marketing system. If prices are reduced on a product or the promotion budget is increased, and subsequent unit sales of the product show an upward surge, one might infer that this sales increase was caused by the changes in price level or the promotion budget. However, can we truly conclude that the change in unit sales was caused by the change in price and promotion levels? Certainly not with a high degree of confidence. Many other variables could be involved. Even if we can rule out most other potential causes, we may still be left with two or more variables affecting sales or various interactions among them. Consequently, causal research must be designed such that the evidence regarding causality is clear, and research designs vary substantially in the degree of causal ambiguity at the conclusion of the study.

The main sources of data for causal research are (1) questioning respondents through surveys and (2) conducting experiments. Although surveys can test hypotheses and determine the degree of association among variables, they are far less adept at determining causality than experiments. A skillfully designed experiment can ensure that evidence regarding causality is reasonably unambiguous in interpretation, because experiments *manipulate* key causal quantities, whereas surveys merely *measure* them as they are. As we will see, the ability to control and (independently) set variables to values of interest is invaluable in being able to assess causal hypotheses. Because of the complexity of the research designs appropriate for experimental research, a separate section of this book has been devoted to their explanation. Chapter 5 discusses the principles of experimentation and alternative research designs in a unified framework, including causal designs.

3.1h Performance-Monitoring Research: Relating Inputs to Outputs

Once a course of action is selected and the marketing program is implemented, performance-monitoring research is needed to answer the question, "What is really going on?" Managers and researcher should never presume that a marketing plan has been flawlessly implemented in the field. Deviation from pre-set plans and improper execution of the marketing program can come about in a bewildering variety of ways: from targets not being met, lack of efficiency in implementation, unanticipated delays, and unanticipated changes in situational and economic factors (such as interest rate changes, supplier hold-ups, or the cost of transportation). That is, to determine whether and how a marketing program affects key performance measures (e.g., sales, profit), it is crucial to ensure that it is actually being carried out as planned—that ads are placed on time, products actually appear on store shelves, and so forth. Effective performance monitoring therefore involves tracking both marketing mix and situational variables, in addition to traditional performance measures such as sales, share of market, profit, and return on investment.

The purpose of performance-monitoring research is to track and report relevant changes along several marketing-related dimensions: (1) in performance measures, such as sales and market share, to determine whether plans are "on the right vector" to achieve stated objectives; (2) in sub-objectives, such as awareness and knowledge levels, distribution penetration, and price levels, to determine whether the marketing program is being implemented as planned; and (3) in situational variables, such as competitive activity, economic conditions, and demand trends, to determine whether the business environment is as anticipated when plans were formulated. Data sources appropriate for performance-monitoring research include questioning of respondents, secondary data, and observation, as gathered by special (ad hoc) studies or a continuous research program.

continuous performance measures
Measures of marketing performance (e.g., weekly sales) taken at regular intervals on an ongoing basis.

Ad hoc performance monitoring tracks new or special marketing programs of the organization or competitor. Although traditionally this was limited to test markets for new products, these days it is common to also monitor such situational variables as government regulation, availability of resources, changing lifestyles of buyers, and concerns of consumer groups. Ad hoc performance monitoring is usually carried out using a survey-based, cross-sectional design.

longitudinal research design
Research involving a sample of units (people, firms, products, etc.) selected from the population of interest and measured at multiple points in time, yielding a time-series for each.

Continuous performance measures are, in general, formal systems designed to monitor the dependent variables in the marketing system. In recent years, increased effort has been directed to monitoring the independent variables as well. The most common performance measures involve "product movement" data, such as units sold, sales volume, and market share. Many organizations have formal systems to monitor the performance of the distribution system, promotional programs, and sales force, the latter via the routine submission of formal reports concerning market and competitive conditions.

panel
A group of respondents who have agreed in advance to offer data to a specific researcher. Panels are common in supermarket purchases (so-called scanner panels), media assessment (e.g., Nielsen households), and online. They allow researchers to have a stable set of respondents whose core characteristics are already known, and so do not need to be measured afresh each time data are collected. They also provide individual-level response histories, allowing changes to be accurately assessed over time.

3.1i Longitudinal Design and Panel-Based Research

Continuous performance monitoring typically requires a **longitudinal research design;** that is, one in which a *fixed* sample of population elements is measured repeatedly. A **"panel,"** often used synonymously with "longitudinal design," repeatedly measures a *fixed* sample over time. Panels come in two main types: the traditional panel and the omnibus panel. With a **traditional panel,** the same variables are repeatedly measured over time for the same sample. For example, Information Resources' BehaviorScan Ad Testing tracks more than 100,000 households in four cities to quantify the impact of new creative and media strategies.

traditional panel
A group of respondents whose measurements are taken repeatedly over time, using the same variables.

With an **omnibus panel,** different variables are measured over time for the same sample of respondents. Packaged goods companies frequently use omnibus household panels, asking members to evaluate different food products at different times. Although it is therefore possible to build up a longitudinal, within-household profile of food preferences, contrasting preference measures from one time to another can literally be comparing apples to oranges.

omnibus panel
A group of respondents whose measurements are taken repeatedly over time, such as in a longitudinal study, but with the important proviso that the *variables* on which they are measured can change from one time to the next.

The motivation for obtaining longitudinal data is to measure the effect of marketing variables over time. It is difficult to overstate the importance of such longitudinal data. Statistical methods are dramatically more relevant when they can call on a longitudinal (time-wise) association across data points.

The following examples illustrate a range of situations where panel data are particularly useful.

1. *Measuring the effect of a soft drink offer*: The "steady state" purchasing pattern is established for a sample of households by monitoring purchases using grocery store scanner data. A special soft drink

promotion is introduced to the families through split-cable television, online advertising, or special inserts in magazines and newspapers every week for 4 weeks. The researchers continue to monitor purchase patterns to measure the short- and long-term effects of the promotional deal.

2. *Tracking brand purchases of frozen food*: Detailed data are collected every week for several years regarding family purchases of frozen food. Estimates are derived regarding the extent to which purchasers remain loyal to different brands and how market shares shift over time among different groups of consumers.
3. *Monitoring the acceptance of a new toy line*: Information is obtained every month on the toy purchases of families with children. Such information allows marketers to determine the types of families that are buying new toys and how soon after market introduction they make their purchases.

Companies use such panel data for a seemingly boundless variety of marketing ends: monitoring trends, constructing demographic profiles, conducting brand-switching analyses, examining new try-er and repeat buyer patterns, checking purchase combinations, predicting product success in test markets, evaluating special promotions, among many others. This diversity of panel studies means that they involve disparate design demands, time intervals, and data collection methods. Panels need not be limited to individuals or to individual households, but can also consist of stores, business firms, or other types of entities. The key issue is that the **units of analysis** are kept constant across the study, and they are tracked individually over time.

units of analysis
The main entity being analyzed in the course of a research project; usually the "lowest level" of data available, with other comparisons based on aggregation. In marketing applications, the unit of analysis may be consumers, groups/segments, locations, salespeople, stores, or channel members.

A major advantage of longitudinal data versus cross-sectional data is their ability to reflect the true extent of change taking place in a population. Cross-sectional data can be very misleading because surveys at two points in time, conducted with different respondents in the sample, can mask even dramatic changes taking place in the population or indicate great changes when none are taking place. A classic example is that of a supermarket which offers a deep discount (i.e., a large price percentage) on a particular item, say canned tuna. Naturally, supermarkets wish to know whether their promotions are successful. Suppose the discount (say, 25%) on canned tuna increases sales fivefold. If the unit margin is still healthy, this seems like an extremely successful promotion, considered cross-sectionally. However, *we don't know which households have purchased the tuna*. If the purchasers of the discounted tuna consisted of households who rarely shop in the store, but who did for the discount, that is good for the store; even if it consisted of households who seldom purchase tuna, the store benefited. BUT, if the purchasers consisted of households who typically bought tuna anyway, at full price, it could be that the store lost revenue and profit on every can of that fivefold increase. Without monitoring the longitudinal purchase histories of individual households, we cannot even assess whether a promotion was profitable. A purely cross-sectional analysis in such a case could be grossly misleading.

Table 3.1 provides an example to illustrate the contrast between longitudinal and cross-sectional comparisons. (Note that there are three dimensions of data to be accounted for: purchase vs. no purchase, period 1 vs. period 2, and brand A vs. brand B. For the cross-sectional data, there is no information to connect the purchasers of period 1 to the purchasers of period 2, so one dimension of the data collapses. For the longitudinal data, four categories of purchasers—those who purchased in both periods, those who purchased only in period 1, those who purchased only in period 2, and those who purchased in neither period—have to be represented for two brands.)

Cross-sectional reported purchases of brands A and B remain the same in time periods 1 and 2 but show dramatic differences when reported longitudinally. In the cross-sectional surveys, the purchases of brands A and B both represent 20 percent of purchases in each time period. In the longitudinal data, we see that the total purchases within a time period reflect the cross-sectional data in that 20 percent of purchases are brands A and B. However, substantial variation exists when we observe the repeat purchase patterns. In particular, none of the individuals who purchase brand B in time period 1 repeat their purchase in time period 2, whereas all individuals who purchase brand A in time period 1 repurchase brand A in time period 2. These dramatic differences in the repurchase patterns for brands A and B are not reflected in the cross-sectional data and have important implications for the marketing strategies of the two brands. Although this example is contrived, it amply illustrates how crucial aspects of actual behavior can be entirely obscured by ignoring the longitudinal nature of purchase and other such data.

A number of powerful statistical approaches—addressed thoroughly in Chapters 10–12—have been developed to analyze this type of data set. These methods allow the study of changes in attitudes, knowledge, and behavior for the *same* respondents or households at different points in time. Such effects can be related to changes in marketing program variables (price, promotion, distribution, and product), as well as to changes in situational variables (e.g., competition and economic conditions). Decades of

Table 3.1 Cross-Sectional Data May Not Reflect Longitudinal Data

CROSS-SECTIONAL DATA

Brand A	Period 1 Survey	Period 2 Survey
Purchase	200	200
No purchase	800	800
Total	1000	1000
Brand B		
Purchase	200	200
No purchase	800	800
Total	1000	1000

LONGITUDINAL DATA

Brand A

	No purchase in Period 1	Purchase in Period 1	Total
No purchase in Period 2	800	0	800
Purchase in Period 2	0	200	200
Total	800	200	1000

Brand B

	No purchase in Period 1	Purchase in Period 1	Total
No purchase in Period 2	600	200	800
Purchase in Period 2	200	0	200
Total	800	200	1000

intensive statistical research have shown that analogous analyses of cross-sectional data fail to offer similar insights or predictive accuracy. In short, the depth of managerial insight afforded by longitudinal panels can simply never be wrung from the associated cross-sectional data.

Another advantage of the panel design relates to the amount of information that can be collected. Because panel members are often compensated for their participation, they are more cooperative regarding longer and more demanding interviews and recording detailed purchase histories. Consequently, panels are able to gather extensive background and geodemographic information on all household members in addition to more detailed data regarding the primary variables of interest.

Panel data are generally more accurate than those gained via typical cross-sectional surveys. Surveys require the respondent to recall past purchases that can be biased by forgetfulness, mis-association, and wishful thinking. Bias is reduced in the panel design because there is a period-by-period recording of purchases in written diaries, in-store scanners, or in-home UPC readers. Historically, panel members have been paid to maintain accurate records. Even small payments tend to produce very accurate data, and variations in workloads among panel members have been found to have at most modest effects on accuracy.

The per–data-point cost of panel data can also be lower than the cost of comparable data collected through a survey. The fixed costs associated with developing and maintaining a panel can be spread over the many clients who use it and across the relatively long collection period of its use, whereas a comparable survey ordinarily requires that the incurred fixed cost be charged directly to a single client, and that each wave of data collection start afresh with new, uninitiated—and often unremunerated—respondents.

3.1j Unrepresentative Sampling and Response Bias

The main disadvantages of panels stem from a defect they can share with cross-sectional survey research: lack of representativeness. This lack can manifest as two separate major problems: unrepresentative sampling and response bias.

The problem of **unrepresentative sampling** arises from the need to have panel members serve for a long period. As an inducement, they are offered gifts and a modest ongoing stipend (if the inducement were too great, it might affect purchasing patterns). Individuals who are highly mobile, are uninterested in panel activities or inducements, are unable to perform the tasks required, or are unwilling to have their activities recorded (a growing phenomenon) tend not to serve on the panel in the first place. Despite attempts to match the sample to selected population characteristics such as age, education, occupation, and so on, it is enormously difficult to have the sample perfectly reflect a target population, even along a restricted set of criteria or measured variables. In particular, it is especially hard to induce those in high-income professions to participate, which can affect the tracking of luxury goods and high-end services. Another issue relates to the "mortality" rates of existing panel members and the representativeness of the new members chosen to replace them. Mortality rates (resulting from members moving, losing interest, passing away, or other forms of attrition) can range as high as 20 percent per year for some panels, particularly long-term ones.

unrepresentative sampling
A frequent problem in panels, where those likely to take part do not represent the general population due, for example, to a greater sensitivity to inducements or a general willingness to have their purchases and behavior recorded.

Despite these potential biases in sample representativeness, extensive research suggests that this problem is not a serious issue for professionally administered panels. Nor is **response bias** particularly serious for well-managed panels. The response biases that need to be controlled result from the panel members believing they are "experts," wanting to look good or give the "right" answer, becoming biased from boredom and fatigue, and not routinely completing diary entries. Some research does suggest that new panel members are often biased in their initial responses. For example, new members tend to increase or over-report the behavior being measured, for example, television viewing and food purchasing. Often, this merely involves semi-conscious emphasis on the part of panel members, who are aware of being "monitored," but not aware of it overtly influencing their behavior. Professionally managed panels minimize this type of bias by initially excluding or under-weighting data of new members from panel results, at least until an initialization or trial period has been completed. After the novelty of being on the panel declines, data accuracy and representativeness increase, while various biases naturally decline. Researchers working with panels need to be careful when posing questions, as the very act of being asked can influence not only perceptions or recollections of behavior, but behavior itself. Asking about visits to a Mexican restaurant might reveal zero frequency for a particular individual (i.e., no visits), but merely being asked may spur such a visit in the near future, which will then be recorded and turn up as a biased measurement. (This kind of effect is discussed in more detail in *Marketing Research Focus* 4.5.)

response bias
A tendency on the part of a respondent, either conscious or unconscious, to mis-report the quantity the researcher is attempting to measure.

3.2 Data Sources for Marketing Research Applications

Although there are countless sources of marketing data, they can all be categorized into at least one of four basic groups: respondents, analogous situations, experimentation, and secondary data. Each is so common that even seasoned researchers seldom reflect on their basic differences and relative strengths or how they can work synergistically in concert. In practice, it is rare for a major research project to rely on just one of these data source types and not at all uncommon for all four to be brought to bear. *Marketing Research Focus 3.2* illustrates how various data sources can be brought to bear in one of the most critical of all marketing activities: **segmentation**.

segmentation
The ability to break a market, consumers or sets of objects into groups; these groups should be relatively homogeneous in terms of the criteria chosen by the researcher—e.g., demographics, behavior, prior experience—and differ substantively across the groups.

3.2a Communication with Respondents

Respondents are a major source of marketing data, in some ways *the* major source. In the popular imagination, in fact, gathering data from respondents—either people, firms, or social institutions—is what marketing research literally is. There are two principal methods of obtaining data from respondents: communication and observation. Communication requires the respondent to actively provide data through verbal response, whereas observation requires the recording of the respondent's (often passive) behavior.

The most common source of marketing data is communication; that is, asking questions. In our daily activities, we gather information by making inquiries of persons whom we consider knowledgeable. As we emphasized in Chapter 1, marketing research is really just a more formal and scientific way of gathering such information: choosing the right people to ask; choosing enough people to ask; and processing their answers into reliable, decision-oriented information.

Marketing Research Focus 3.2

Data Sources Aid Marketing Segmentation

Customer segmentation is among the most vital and important activities in all of marketing research. It recognizes something each of us already knows: people are different. The trick in segmentation is to precisely quantify this difference and to be able to act on the knowledge gained from doing so. Practically speaking, segmentation involves identifying subdivisions of a market that share specific traits, attitudes, or behavioral tendencies. The ability to target clearly defined market segments is essential to effective product development, value propositions, pricing, and distribution. Although segmentation has been traditionally carried out "by hand"—that is, having managers seek out commonalities across customer profiles—modern information systems can systematically analyze enormous amounts of data across numerous variables to facilitate more precise identification of marketing sub-segments.

As might be expected, the quality and precision of segmentation vary with the accuracy and dimensions of the consumer data. With traditional methods, data often only supported higher level aggregation of wants or needs, without the finer detail about variations *within* the segments themselves. That is, everyone within a segment was considered, for all intents and purposes, interchangeable. A company with six identified segments, for example, would probably find more precise segmentation helpful, particularly if each segment accounted for millions of customers. (To see this, try to sort everyone you have ever met into just six "groups," so that people in each group seem exactly like one another, or nearly so.)

As one of the management information systems described in more detail in Section 3-4c, Customer Relationship Management (CRM) applications have substantially increased the amount of customer data available and the options for processing and interpreting that data quickly, allowing nearly real-time responsiveness to multiple data sources, including those on purchases, market variables, and competition. In this way, they are very much in line with the management information systems described in more detail in Section 3-4c and present similar benefits and challenges. The warehousing of data allows the incorporation of centralized information into detailed analysis of customer segmentation.

In 2004, RBC Royal Bank set out to evaluate the hypothesis that bank customers aged 18–35, who were generally considered relatively unprofitable, could prove to be a profit source in the near future. RBC turned to its data warehouse of strategic customer models—including customer profitability, life stage, potential, defection risk, and loyalty—and tactical models of propensity to buy, likelihood of cancellation, and degree of usage. Analysis identified a subsegment of 18- to 35-year-olds likely to become profitable customers: medical and dental school students and interns. RBC targeted this group with a new program providing loans for tuition and new practices. By the following year, RBC had increased its market share in this subsegment from 2 percent to 18 percent, and increased its per-client revenues by a factor of four.

This trend in segmentation analysis is still in its infancy; the ultimate goal would be to target products and offerings to individuals, a prospect that internet-based marketing may shortly allow. Cathy Hotka, a marketing consultant, elaborated, "Retailers are trying to get to where they were in 1903. In 1903, the person who runs the store knows the customers, can put things on credit, knows what will sell and when, and knows what not to buy. When they went to mass markets, that granularity was lost. Regaining that intimacy with the audience is very difficult."

Road Runner Sports, the largest retailer of running shoes in the United States, has already moved in this direction. Its CRM system includes tracking of every color, size, and model of shoe purchased since 1989, and analyses of this information to develop precise marketing campaigns. For instance, because individual runners often have a favorite model of running shoe, Road Runner sends "close-out" notices to all users of a particular model if it is discontinued. Customers appreciate the opportunity to stock up on their favorite model at low prices before the model is terminated.

Although modern information systems have made more precise sub-segmentation possible, the expense and scale involved render these beyond the reach of many companies. Current applications still require enormous quantities of data and a great deal of customization to generate meaningful results. There are few guidelines for smaller companies to use pre-packaged applications effectively. Yet as the technology develops and spreads, costs come down, usability increases, and best practices become more commonplace because, as Larry Selden of Columbia Business School put it, "Subsegmenting is where the gold is."

Sources: "How To Do Customer Segmentation Right"; Alice Dragoon. *CIO*. October 1, 2005.
"Turning Data Into Dollars; Retail CRM finds the payoff in reams of consumer data"; Stacy Collett. *Computerworld*. September 20, 2004.
"Unleashing the Power of Customer Data"; David Jacoby. *Economist Intelligence Unit*. January 6, 2006.

When the information needs of a study require data about respondents' attitudes, perceptions, motivations, knowledge, and intended behavior, asking questions is essential. The respondents can be consumers, industrial buyers, wholesalers, retailers, or any knowledgeable persons who can provide data useful to a decision situation. Effective communication with respondents requires special training and skill if the data are to be useful. Questions that are biased or require respondents to provide data that they will not or cannot disclose can result in misleading data.

The research design can range from questioning a few knowledgeable respondents individually or in small groups (for exploratory research) to surveying hundreds of respondents (for conclusive research) to surveying an entire population (i.e., a census), although the last is, for obvious reasons, only undertaken every 10 years.

Focus group interviews provide free-flowing unstructured situations designed to stimulate ideas and insights into a problem situation through group interaction. This typically involves posing probing, open-ended, questions over a relatively long time span (usually 1 to 2 hours). In-depth interviews use extensive questioning of respondents individually to explore their attitudes and behavior, and what might underlie them, with a focus of developing hypotheses and insights as to the "why" of past and future behavior. In contrast, conclusive research is designed to explain what is happening *now* (along with accompanying frequencies of occurrence) and typically poses just a few simple, closed-ended questions to a large sample of respondents in a brief time span (i.e., 5 to 20 minutes, depending on format). As always, exploratory research is conducted first, to gain a general portrait of "what is going on," after which conclusive research obtains precise, targeted information to settle specific hypotheses. Focus groups will be covered in depth in Chapter 6.

focus group
An exploratory research technique consisting of a group discussion led by a moderator, and used to gauge consumer attitudes, beliefs and preferences towards a (perhaps novel) product or service. It is particularly useful in the early stages of a complex marketing research project, and helps avoid biases intrinsic to closed-form survey questions.

The data collection methods used in communicating with respondents include personal interviews, telephone interviews, mail questionnaires, and electronically mediated surveys, the last either in dedicated facilities used for formal, complex experiments or, increasingly, via the Internet. Questions are asked and answered verbally in personal and telephone interviews, via handwriting with mail questionnaires, and by typing and clicking in electronic settings. The popularity of the various interview methods is influenced primarily by unit cost, with Internet-based surveys not only taking a huge bite out of the share of the other methods, but dramatically expanding the entire market for survey-based research overall. Generally speaking, Internet-based surveys cost the least, followed by telephone interviews, then mail, and finally personal interviews. Of course, one must weigh these costs against the disadvantages each of the methods can entail, such as self-selection bias, lack of observation ability, the use of dedicated personnel, time lags, and a host of others.

3.2b Observation of Respondents

Observation is the process of recognizing and recording relevant objects and events, and important and commonplace activities in our daily routines. Just as no one would say you can understand human interactions and psychology simply by asking people questions and recording their verbal responses, market researchers know that one cannot rely solely on surveys to understand consumers' reactions. Valuable information pertaining to a decision situation can be obtained by observing either present behavior or the results of past behavior.

Observational methods allow the recording of behavior when it occurs, eliminating errors associated with the recall of behavior. This is often less costly and more accurate than asking the respondent to recall the same behavior at another point in time. Although observation can accurately record what people do and how it is done, it cannot be used to determine the motivations, attitudes, and knowledge that underlie behavior.

The many issues involved in obtaining data from respondents through communication and observation are discussed in Chapters 6 and 7.

3.2c Case Histories

In everyday reasoning, when presented with a seemingly new situation, one asks, "Have I come across anything like this before?" Similarly, a logical way to approach any decision situation is to examine analogous or similar ones, including one's past, others' case histories, and simulations.

The case history approach is an old and established method in the behavioral sciences and has been used successfully in marketing research for decades. The study "design" involves intense investigation of prior situations that are analogous or appear relevant to the current one. Typically, one selects several target cases for which a thorough analysis will (1) identify relevant variables, (2) indicate the nature of the relationship among those variables and, by doing so, (3) identify the nature of the problem or opportunity present in the original decision situation. For example, the research might involve searching for analogous cases in data from selected retail stores, sales territories, markets, salespeople, or industrial buyers, to better understand which variables are relevant and operational.

The case history method is especially useful in situations in which a complicated set of variables interact to produce the problem or opportunity. For example, cases that can be studied are those reflecting: contrasting performance levels, as in good and poor markets; rapid changes in performance, such as entry of a competitor into a market; or the order in which events occurred, such as sales regions that are in various stages of transition from indirect to direct selling efforts. Data can be obtained by a search through records and reports (usually via electronic databases), observation of key variables, and discussions with experts and lay users.

3.2d Marketing Simulation

The creation of an analogous version of a real-world phenomenon, through a likeness or formal (mathematical or statistical) model, is known as *simulation*. It is by nature an incomplete representation of reality, one which tries to capture the essential features of the phenomenon without replicating every possible detail. Common examples of simulation are weather forecasts, model airplanes, road maps, and planetariums. Although no one would confuse these with actual weather, trains, roads or heavenly bodies, they exist because of their illustrative vividness; accuracy; and, above all, ability to help with forecasting, even though their nature is obviously fundamentally different from what they seek to explain.

What, then, is a marketing simulation? It can be somewhat stiffly defined as an incomplete representation of the marketing system or some salient aspects of that system. With the advent of Moore's "Law"—that computational power doubles roughly every 18 months—the computer has emerged as the tool of choice in the overwhelming variety of simulations. Simulation can be used to gain insight into the dynamics of the marketing system by manipulation of the independent variables (marketing mix and situational factors) and by observation of their influence on the dependent variable(s). A marketing simulation requires data inputs regarding the characteristics of the phenomenon to be represented and the relationships present. More often than not, the relationships between these are taken to be statistical in nature, incorporating some degree of uncertainty, rather than purely deterministic, which would assume we have captured all relevant variables and represented their interrelations perfectly.

To develop a marketing simulation, the builder must conceptualize and document the structural components of the system and establish probabilities corresponding to various behaviors of the components. The components or units of the simulation represent objects in the marketing system. For example, depending on the phenomenon under study, the units can be buyers, households, retailers, advertisers, manufacturers, and so forth. The variables in the system specify how the units behave and the allowed latitude and levers of their behavior. There is a staggering number of variables that can come into play in any real-world marketing situation. Some obvious candidates are price levels, advertising expenditures, product quality, competitive strategy, sales force compensation, and deals to both the consumer and the trade.

Once the formal system is built up from complete knowledge of the operant variables, their interrelationships, and their (perhaps interactive) effect on the dependent variable(s) under study, the simulation can be used to generate probabilities for outcomes of interest. The over-riding objective is to observe how the simulation units imitate the behavior of the marketing system units that they represent, just as a weather forecasting system should mimic the actual weather. For example, the numerical output could be share of market, sales, profitability, consumer awareness, or other metric of managerial interest. The parameters of the simulation encode constraints and sensitivities that can be changed by the user on the basis of measurements or experience. These might be competitive advertising levels, price elasticity, proportion of children in the market, and other quantities that are vital in understanding market dynamics. Parameters allow the user to experiment with the simulation, explore alternative marketing strategies, and determine the influence of changes in situational factors. One should be able to ask, for example, whether and how a recession, new product introduction, or competitive promotional campaign will affect output measures like sales and profit. To do so requires the input of such measures as competitive promotional effectiveness to better gauge sensitivity to these environmental parameters, often using a formal **sensitivity analysis**.

sensitivity analysis
An analysis performed to gauge the effects of *assumed parameter values or assumptions* on a final answer, policy, or other dependent variable. For example, if we have assumed that 10 percent of people will reply to a survey, to calculate total costs, a sensitivity analysis would ask how much costs might change for each 1 percent difference in response rates in the range 5 percent–15 percent.

What are the advantages of simulation compared with other data sources? One of the chief advantages can be cost: it is ordinarily less expensive to simulate reactions than to conduct a survey or test market, given the time and effort involved with collecting and analyzing respondent data. (However, even exceptionally good simulations should not be considered substitutes for large, well-designed test markets.) Simulation can be conducted with complete non-disclosure within an organization; other data sources may not assure this degree of security, because the information is especially vital for new product launches. Simulation allows the evaluation of alternative marketing strategies and provides "proof" regarding the superiority of one strategy over another, in terms of underlying market drivers and forces that might be difficult to control or alter in the field. In addition, the consequences of changes in the marketing system can be evaluated without the risk of making changes in the *real* system, which could not only be disastrous, but difficult to recover from, even if the old marketing mix were reinstated. This allows the evaluation of multiple strategies and encourages creativity, in that radical strategy changes can be evaluated. Of course, the more radical the strategy, the less likely one can simulate it strictly using extant data and prior experience. Finally, simulation can be used as a training device for members of the organization, as is common for pilots training on flight simulators. Individuals not directly involved in marketing activities may develop an appreciation of how the marketing system operates and how it affects decisions in their areas, for example, R&D or manufacturing.

The limitations of simulation are the difficulty of developing a valid simulation model and the time and cost of updating the model as conditions change. In situations where the organization has limited background and experience regarding the marketing phenomenon under investigation (e.g., new markets), simulation may not be a feasible data source. Widely deployed simulations require extensive consultation with experts on the phenomena in question, with statisticians who literally build the model, and with systems programmers who develop an interface so that non-specialists can interact with it. Finally, often some of the key quantities necessary for simulation are not readily available, such as competitors' outlays for advertising and future plans, subtle cultural shifts, or pending legislation. A particularly thorny quantity is often called endogeneity—the idea that what a firm does affects consumers, whose decisions also affect the firm and its competition, all of whom are making multiple decisions over time. For example, are prices going down because more people are entering the market, or are more people entering the market because prices are going down? The answer is typically a bit of both, and simulations are especially hard-pressed to capture such subtly dynamic decision-making.

endogeneity
As opposed to an *exogenous* variable, which can be completely controlled to understand its effects on a system, an *endogenous* variable is itself at least partially affected by the system it is part of. One's decision to apply to college is affected by tuition rates, but tuition rates are also affected by the number of students applying to college. One might say, therefore, that tuition rates are determined *endogenously*.

3.2e Experimentation

Experimentation is a relatively new source of marketing data. Because experiments allow key variables to be directly manipulated—rather than simply "coming about"—relatively unambiguous statements can be made regarding cause-and-effect relationships.

An experiment consists of one or more independent variables, which are consciously controlled, and measurements of their effects on the dependent variable(s). The objective is twofold: to measure the effects of the independent variables on a dependent variable and to simultaneously control for other variables that might confuse one's ability to make valid causal inferences. Various experimental designs have been developed to reduce or eliminate the possible influence of extraneous variables on the dependent variable, some of them quite subtle and sophisticated. Chapter 5 deals extensively with the concept of experimentation and associated research designs.

3.3 Secondary Data

There are two general types of marketing data—primary and secondary. Primary data are collected specifically for the research needs at hand. Secondary data are already collected and often published, typically for some other purpose. Secondary data can be further classified as internal or external, the former being generated and made available within the organization, the latter originating outside it. External data come from an array of sources, such as government publications, trade association data, books, bulletins, reports, and periodicals. Data from these sources are often available at minimal or no cost in libraries or through the Internet, although commercial sources available via university libraries can entail large annual subscription fees. Later in the chapter, we will examine such data in detail. (See the Appendices at the conclusion of this chapter as well, which cover syndicated and library sources of marketing data.) External data sources that are not available publicly can be expensive to acquire. Usually referred to as syndicated sources, they are predominantly collected by for-profit organizations that provide standardized data to an array of clients, spreading the large cost of maintaining panels and databases across multiple subscribing firms.

3.3a Internal Data

As stated already, internal data originate within a target organization. Internal data collected for purposes other than specifically for the research being conducted are internal secondary data.

All organizations collect internal data as part of their normal operations. Sales and cost data are recorded, sales reports submitted, advertising and promotion activities recorded, and research and development and manufacturing reports made. Sales and cost data collected for accounting purposes represent particularly promising sources for many research projects. For example, if the research objectives of a project are to evaluate previous marketing activity or to determine the organization's competitive position, sales and cost data collected over time can be very helpful.

Many organizations do not collect and maintain sales and cost data in sufficient detail to be used for many research purposes, especially smaller "brick and mortar" firms for whom extensive database operations are not part of normal business activities. Sales records should allow for classification by type of customer, payment procedure (in-full or credit), product line, sales territory, time period, and so on. By simple analysis of this type of data, the researcher can determine the level and trend in sales, costs, and profitability by customer, territory, and product. More sophisticated analyses could attempt to measure the effect of changes in the marketing program or situational variables on sales, costs, and profitability. One must be careful not to confuse such data with that of an experiment, which manipulates some variables while controlling others. Sales and costs are typically determined by a wide array of consumer, internal, and environmental variables, few of which are under direct managerial control. As such, statistical analyses based on even very complete longitudinal sales and cost data must be interpreted with great care.

Three often-cited advantages of internal secondary data are their low cost, their accuracy, and their easy availability. Unfortunately, many organizations fail to recognize that they have or could have useful internal data available at low cost. These organizations could benefit from specially designed programs to organize and maintain secondary internal data for marketing research purposes. Often, marketing decision support systems allow for maintaining and integrating just this sort of data on an ongoing basis.

3.3b External Data—Syndicated

The growing demand for marketing data has given rise to an increasing number of companies whose core business is collecting and selling standardized data to other firms. The data collected are selected to serve information needs shared by client firms, the most common of which are those associated with performance-monitoring research. This section presents an overview of the main types of syndicated data sources. Although some examples appear throughout this section, a far more comprehensive listing and discussion of syndicated data sources is provided in Appendix A at the end of this chapter.

Consumer Data

Several services collect data from consumers regarding purchases and the circumstances surrounding them, such as the retail environment and marketing mix. For example, the National Purchase Diary (NPD) Group, Inc. (www.npd.com) maintains the NPD Houseworld® panel, with more than 600,000 online core panelists who provide information in several consumer good categories, from food to automotive supplies to home improvement. Such panels operate cross-nationally as well; MDP (www.maildiarypanel.com) runs a large-scale panel operating in the United States, Australia, New Zealand, and Indonesia, allowing cross-market comparisons of numerous variables, among them lifestyle and attitude measures, media habits, brand and product usage, purchase intentions, retail activity, service preferences, and recreational activities.

Various services survey large groups of consumers regarding purchases and the purchase environment. For example, Mediamark, Inc. (www.mediamark.com), the leading U.S. supplier of multimedia audience research, conducts more than 25,000 personal interviews with consumers and offers comprehensive demographic, lifestyle, product usage, and exposure profiles to all forms of advertising media—magazines, television, radio, Internet, leading national advertisers—collected from a single sample.

Numerous other surveys are designed to measure other attitudes and opinions that may be relevant to marketing. The Roper Poll (www.gfk.com), often called the "gold standard" of public opinion research, conducts monthly surveys with several thousand adults on a wide variety of social and political topics, as well as on opinions of various consumer products and services, both in the United States and across the world. Yankelovich Partners' (www.yankelovich.com) MONITOR service has, since 1971, conducted a nationally representative annual study of 2,500 adult men and women, via 90-minute in-home interviews and one-hour leave-behind questionnaires probing a variety of social trends and consumer lifestyle characteristics, designed to aid marketing managers in their strategic decision-making. The Survey Research Center at the University of Michigan (www.isr.umich.edu/src/) monitors consumer consumption patterns, attitudes, and intentions on financial issues and the purchase of durable goods, among a wide variety of other studies on economic, demographic, and social activities. The American Consumer Satisfaction Index (ACSI), produced by the University of Michigan's Ross School of Business, measures satisfaction with 200 major consumer companies and a large number of federal government agencies. Index scores are publicly available at www.theacsi.org, and subscribers can access a wide variety of additional information.

Retail Data

Numerous services rely on retailing establishments for their data. The data collected focus on the products or services sold through the outlets or on characteristics of the outlets themselves. Such services conduct store audits of supermarkets, drugstores, mass merchandisers, and other retail outlets. The data reported to a client include total sales by product class, sales by brand, sales of competing brands, and a variety of other dimensions. Two of the better-known services are A. C. Nielsen's Retail Index and Audits and Surveys' National Total-Market Audit. (Extensive details appear on their Web sites, referenced in Appendix A.)

Wholesale Data

Many businesses rely on warehouse shipment data to estimate sales at retail. Clients who buy reports covering such wholesale data can receive information on the movement of each brand in a specified set of product categories, including estimates of brand-level sales and competitive brands in the market. Such data allow the client to analyze trends in sales or package size and the impact of promotions and competitive actions. Wholesale reports become available more quickly than, say, Nielsen data, but the latter represent actual retail purchases, whereas wholesale data represent retail orders from the warehouse. At present, there are substantially more syndicated data services available to consumer goods manufacturers than to industrial goods suppliers, although this may change with the advent of such technologies as Radio Frequency Identification (RFID) tags.

Advertising Evaluation Data

Billions of advertising dollars are spent each year on media such as magazines and television, with the expectation that these expenditures will result in sales. Consequently, advertisers are interested in data that measure the effectiveness of these expenditures. (See Appendix B for a listing and discussion of specific firms and their information services.)

Evaluating different types of advertising—print, radio, television, and Internet—requires different approaches. For print media, one often classifies readership of a newspaper or magazine into groups; for example, those who remember seeing a particular advertisement ("Noted"), those who associated the sponsor's name with the advertisement ("Seen-Associated"), and those who read half or more of its copy ("Read Most"). These sorts of evaluations can be performed both "closed book" and "open book"; that is, when consumers are either allowed or denied access to the media in question to help discern recognition or aided recall ("open") from unaided recall ("closed"). Evaluations can be provided for consumer magazines and industrial publications alike, and they allow the assessment of individual advertisement effectiveness and the tracking of successive campaigns over time.

Services that evaluate television commercials use two basic approaches—the recruited audience method and the normal viewing environment method. With the **recruited audience method**,

recruited audience method
A form of advertising research that measures audience reactions in a controlled environment outside their homes.

respondents are recruited and brought to a viewing center (a theater or mobile viewing laboratory) for purposes of pre-testing television commercials. Researchers gather data regarding the viewers' attitudes, knowledge, preference, and selection of products. With the second approach, the **normal viewing environment method**, participants evaluate commercials at home. New commercials are pre-tested by substituting the test commercial for a regular commercial on established programming. This can be done at the network level or in local markets. A sample of viewers is then interviewed to determine the new advertisement's effectiveness.

normal viewing environment method A form of advertising research that measures audience reactions as in their own homes, rather than in an unfamiliar environment.

Media and Audience Data

The task of a media planner is to identify media that possess audience characteristics similar to those of the target market to be reached. The types of data used in matching markets and media typically include demographics, psychographics, and product usage rates. For example, A. C. Nielsen provides audience data for television programs, and a number of other syndicated audience measurement services specialize in providing audience measurement data for a particular medium. The Simmons Market Research Bureau allows the media planner to compare audience characteristics over an array of media and describes the audiences of magazines and newspapers, as well as network television programs, geodemographically and in terms of product usage profiles. Mediamark Research offers demographic, psychographic, product usage, and advertising media (magazines, television, radio, Internet) exposure data collected from a single sample, augmented with tens of thousands of annual interviews with consumers.

Media planners need data regarding the advertising effects of competitors. It is important to know how much competitors are spending, where they are spending their advertising dollars, and in what media mix. Several syndicated services provide this type of data, among them A. C. Nielsen and the Advertising Checking Bureau.

3.4 Data Technology and Information Systems

Innovations in the data gathering and processing techniques used in marketing research keep pace with the breakneck developments in hardware and software technologies since the introduction of the computer.

3.4a Technology Changes

As technology improves, all the data types covered in this chapter are increasingly gathered by electronic methods. Whereas panel consumers used to record their purchases by laboriously writing them out, costs have come down to the point where panel members today can easily be provided with in-home UPC scanner pens and Internet-enabled information gathering systems. In the United States, all but the smallest mom-and-pop stores are equipped with UPC scanners. Split-cable TV allows the accurate assessment of new ads and promotional incentives; Web browsers and server logs catalog individual-level Internet shopping and viewing histories; and "people meters" (TV set-top boxes that automatically record what individual family members are watching) ever more accurately measure television viewership. *Research Innovations and Technologies 3.1* takes a closer look at people meters and possible biases they may entail.

It is no exaggeration to say that the supermarket checkout scanner led to a revolution in marketing research for consumer goods. The panel of consumers who manually maintain a diary of purchases has been entirely supplanted by panels whose purchases are recorded and compiled by checkout scanners (with in-home additions for such items as soft drink cans, candy, and other convenience goods often bought from machines). Panel members present an ID card when checking out, and each item of the panel member's purchases is captured, compiled, and entered into a large longitudinal database.

A study performed by J. Walter Thompson Inc. listed a number of significant changes spurred by the proliferation of scanner data, an up-to-date version of which would include the following:

- Significantly better data in areas such as volume/share tracking, promotion tracking, and consumer purchase dynamics, compared with traditional, hand-counted store audits;
- The proliferation of high-quality, user-friendly analysis packages, including data, software, and hardware to handle the huge quantity of data—often more than a gigabyte per store per week—generated by scanning services;

Research Innovations and Technologies 3.1

Are Nielsen's "People Meters" Biased against Certain Population Groups?

Nielsen Media Research, which has performed virtually all of the audience measurement done in the United States since the 1950s, found itself having to defend its measurement techniques regarding the $60 billion market of television. At issue were electronic "people meters" installed in a trial sample of Nielsen homes in New York for local ratings.

Nielsen's traditional diary system compiles local ratings from 500 families ("Nielsen families") who record what they watch in a diary and send this to the company on a weekly basis. The new methodology involves the installation of electronic boxes on the television sets that automatically record what people watch—including which members of each family watch specific shows. The meters connect directly to the central Nielsen office and transfer the data.

Critics claim that the electronic meters appear to be flawed or unreliable. For example, people-meter data indicated a substantial decrease—as much as 62 percent relative to the diary method—in viewership for television shows that feature minorities, causing an understandable outcry: so drastic a drop for shows with predominantly minority casts was unprecedented in previous measurements through diary reports. Community activists are concerned that programming and advertising toward African American, Hispanic, and Asian viewers will be cut. Paul Williams, president of 100 Black Men of New York, explained, "A drop in ratings translates to a drop in advertising, which translates to a drop in programming, which translates to a drop in opportunities for the black community." His organization is one of several calling on Nielsen to review its metering technology.

Nielsen counters that reliability was precisely the reason it implemented the people meters. Anne Elliot, a vice president at Nielsen, said of the technology, "This is 24-hour-a-day, seven-day-a-week, electronic measurement. It's totally passive. It's installed on every television set, every VCR, every video game set. So we know that when the TV's on, we can identify what's going on."

There is no question that Nielsen's monopoly on commercial measurement of broadcast media audiences gives it tremendous influence on the direction of the industry. Nielsen ratings are the basis of how advertisers spend money, whether television series continue for 10 years or disappear abruptly before the end of the first season, and how programming executives succeed or fail in the business.

The question is whether the electronic technology incorporates some kind of bias in its implementation or whether it is more accurate than traditional diaries. The diary method itself has known flaws. With diaries, Nielsen can only do local-level measurements four times a year, during what is known as "sweeps week." Consequently, TV producers often use exceptional, sensationalistic ploys to boost their ratings during sweeps week. This, of course, makes the measurements less applicable to normal programming and viewing. Nielsen viewers also often wait until the end of the week to fill out their viewing diaries, causing the entries to be less accurate. Elliot points out, "There may be a tendency in a diary for people to forget to write down what they were watching until a couple days later. With people meters you don't have to go back and remember what you watched a week ago."

Could there be unforeseen bias in people meters or are they correcting over-reporting that happens through the diary method? Although it may be possible that the meters are flawed or the sample assigned the meters was less than representative, other explanations are also possible. People may be watching less of certain shows because of racial bias, or the shows themselves may be less appealing and people are over reporting their viewing to *counteract* presumed bias. In the opinion of one (non-Nielsen) viewer, "We're not talking about *The Jeffersons* here, or Cosby or other quality minority-themed TV; we're talking about really mediocre TV." In this view, the higher accuracy of people meters may help minority communities by demanding a higher quality of minority-themed programming.

While Elliot defended the people meters, "We do absolutely stand by them as being accurate," Nielsen also delayed fuller implementation of its people meters in New York to hold discussions about the ratings variances with minority groups and television networks.

If there is a problem with the metering technology, no one has yet identified the cause. Nielsen said that an internal audit of the local people meters revealed no apparent problems. The meters have been used for Nielsen's national ratings since 1987 without any problem.

Nielsen installed 800 of the meters in New York City in households that were not previously on the diary system. Due to differences in how much data are collected from each household and variation across them, this larger number of metered households is necessary to maintain the same level of statistical relevance as the 500 diary households. Nielsen continued to roll out the local people meters in Boston, Los Angeles, Chicago, San Francisco, Philadelphia, Washington, D.C., Dallas, Detroit, and Atlanta.

Source: Nielsen "People Meters" Draw Fire; Amit Asaravala. *Wired News*. April 16, 2004. http://www.wired.com/news/business/0,1367,63080,00.html.

- Shortening of reaction time by advertisers to their competitors because store-specific data can be made available on an ongoing basis;
- Availability of timely data, which, if analyzed quickly and appropriately, can lead to more preemptive and reactive marketing strategies;
- Ability to quickly determine short-term effects of pricing differentials and trade dealing, which may lead businesses to favor certain types of promotions over others or over advertising in general;
- Greater emphasis by marketers on consumer attitudes and awareness tracking to account for the "why" behind the data;
- Accurate and effortless tracking of consumer panel members' data, allowing new insights into how both marketing stimuli and environmental/economic influences lead to purchase dynamics, through statistical analysis of *household-level, longitudinal purchase histories*; and
- Shortage of trained professionals who can analyze and interpret the data provided by scanner systems.

selection bias
Any of a number of possible factors that result in a non-random sample being selected from the target population, thereby causing an inaccurate measurement in a desired output.

The scanner system also provides dramatically more accurate data than a traditional (hand-recorded) diary panel or store audit. The data are available more quickly; there is less **selection bias** and price sensitivity bias; and the effects of simple forgetting and carelessness are greatly mitigated. Because the scanner method requires little effort, panel members are much less conscious of their roles as members of the panel, and how their purchases may reflect on them. Scanner data also eliminate recall bias; because information is captured instantly, the data are generally more complete and more accurate. Yet another advantage is that in-store data, such as different pricing or promotional offers, are built into the data-recording procedure; the laborious process of matching up in-store audits with home-recorded purchase panel data is automatically done away with.

The shift toward scanner data did more than change the physical collection of data; scanner data changed the way the data are interpreted. The extensive detail afforded by the computer data allows marketers to review detailed product data on a geographic (national, regional, city, neighborhood) or store-by-store basis. Furthermore, the sheer number of purchases automatically recorded allows analysis of narrower product categories than is practical with diary panels.

The system gives stores detailed information on their sales, which makes it easier for them to make business decisions. Indeed, scanner data services from Information Resources, Inc. or A. C. Nielsen include the ability to "slice and dice" purchase data along any of dozens of dimensions, such as heavy vs. light users, day of the week, product sizes, product categories, depth of promotion, sales and dollar volume by store, and so forth. Any of these variables can be broken out to fine detail and cross-tabulated with others. Classic examples include the store chains that realized sales of candy bars nearly doubled when they were displayed near the checkout counter, and sauce mixes sold much better when displayed near their companion products (e.g., spaghetti sauce located near the spaghetti). Thus, scanner data should not be construed as a glorified method of accounting, but a mainstay of packaged goods marketing research that helps both manufacturers and retailers optimize and streamline their operations.

One of the "last frontiers" of scanner-based research is to assess the effects of advertising; this is enormously more difficult than with, say, pricing, which is recorded for each brand in the store on a continual basis. In ISI's BehaviorScan, diary panel households receive all their at-home television programming through the local cable company. This allows researchers to split the panel by feeding an experimental commercial to one segment of the test group and the standard commercial to a control group. The effects of the ad are tested by tracking the purchases of the test group with detailed scanner data. Not just ads themselves, but entire ad strategies (part of the "media mix") can be evaluated, including new copy rotation strategies, "day part mixes" (which ads are run when, and how intensively), ad dollar allocation to cable vs. network outlets, and various expenditure plans (i.e., whether ad spending should be reduced or "pulsed" occasionally).

single source
A type of data stemming from one research provider alone, who has either collected comprehensive data directly or skillfully aggregated it from multiple sources.

3.4b Single Sourcing

Single sourcing is a syndicated marketing research concept that has gained credibility as technology has allowed the gathering of more resources and data under one roof. A **single source** is a marketing research provider having a single, comprehensive, and integrated database that essentially contains everything the client needs to conduct its marketing research program. Such services nearly always provide sales tracking and household-level purchase behavior, but can include any data collected via UPC scanners, people meters (for media measurement), split-cable advertising, and longitudinal customer databases. For example, the same family could have its product consumption, media consumption, and demographic characteristics monitored to provide integrated data over a period of months or years.

One of the goals of single-source information is to allow for real-time decision-making; that is, to respond to market opportunities as they appear. The quicker a supplier can provide data to identify an opportunity—and the more comprehensive and integrated the data—the greater the decision-making value to the client, as cause-and-effect relationships become easier to identify and extraneous effects are conclusively ruled out.

The marketing researcher, however, must not lose sight of the fact that, while these technologies can capture consumer activities and transactions, *interpretation* of the huge amounts of data will still be the key to success in the marketplace. Analysis of such rich, voluminous data is non-trivial, and it amounts to more than running a few regressions or cross-tabulations. Specialized statistical techniques to account for the intrinsically categorical nature of brand purchase data—where each household buys a specific brand from among a large, fixed set of possibilities—have been developed, but still require some training to deploy well. Over the past decade, user-friendly statistical and decision-based analysis systems have kept pace with this information explosion, and they allow even casual users the opportunity to rigorously analyze scanner data, once the underlying methods are understood. (The main such method, logistic regression, is covered in Chapter 10.) Despite the insight afforded by the timeliness, accuracy, and completeness of single-source marketing data, it will never completely displace custom research.

3.4c Marketing Intelligence Systems

Marketing decision support systems (DSSs or MDSSs) and marketing research information systems (MISs or MRISs) were introduced in Chapter 1 as examples of marketing intelligence systems that are components of the overall marketing research system. The key features of an intelligence system are a system for the collection and storage of recurring data, a model for interpreting the data, and a presentation or interface for accessing this information. The models employed range from assumptions regarding the customer base and economic activities to complex statistical analyses of interrelated variables. Data inputs range from a narrow focus on, say, one supermarket's cash register scanners to a wide variety of data and forecasts regarding consumer attitudes, general demographics, market shares of competitors, interest rates, and new industry trends and technologies, all incorporated into a sophisticated DSS.

MISs can involve any ongoing collection of marketing information, usually resulting in the generation of regular reports according to the needs of managers. These reports vary greatly in the scope of data included, how much emphasis is placed on programming a model to translate the data into information for decision-making, and how much this programming has been catered to the specific situation or needs.

DSSs are typically computer-based systems to which data are continually input and in turn analyzed by software specifically geared to aid decision-making. An interactive user interface allows managers to, for example, input distributors' current prices to find out how many stock-keeping units (SKUs) of milk at what selling price are optimum under current conditions. By formal definition, a DSS could also involve processes such as consumer interviews, but in practice it generally refers to software and accompanying hardware. A good DSS should give multiple options for displaying data and facilitating the recognition of trends. Managers need a way of considering various "what if" questions and simulating their effects, and a full-featured DSS will allow for such a **scenario analysis**.

scenario analysis
Assessing how results change when input quantities are assumed to take on a variety of different values (e.g., how a product's sales projections change at various price levels).

MDSS Requirements

The integrated system of data, statistical analysis, modeling, and display formats of an MDSS is diagrammed in Figure 3.2. An MDSS must be designed to respond quickly and easily to managerial questions such as:

- What is the change in the cost per unit if we drop one optional feature and add a new one?
- What are the sales for product X each month? For the year to date? How would these change if we offered wholesalers specific new incentives?
- How do our year-to-date expenditures on magazine advertising compare with our budget? What would happen to sales and profits if we put more money into magazine advertising?

Figure 3.2 Marketing Decision Support System

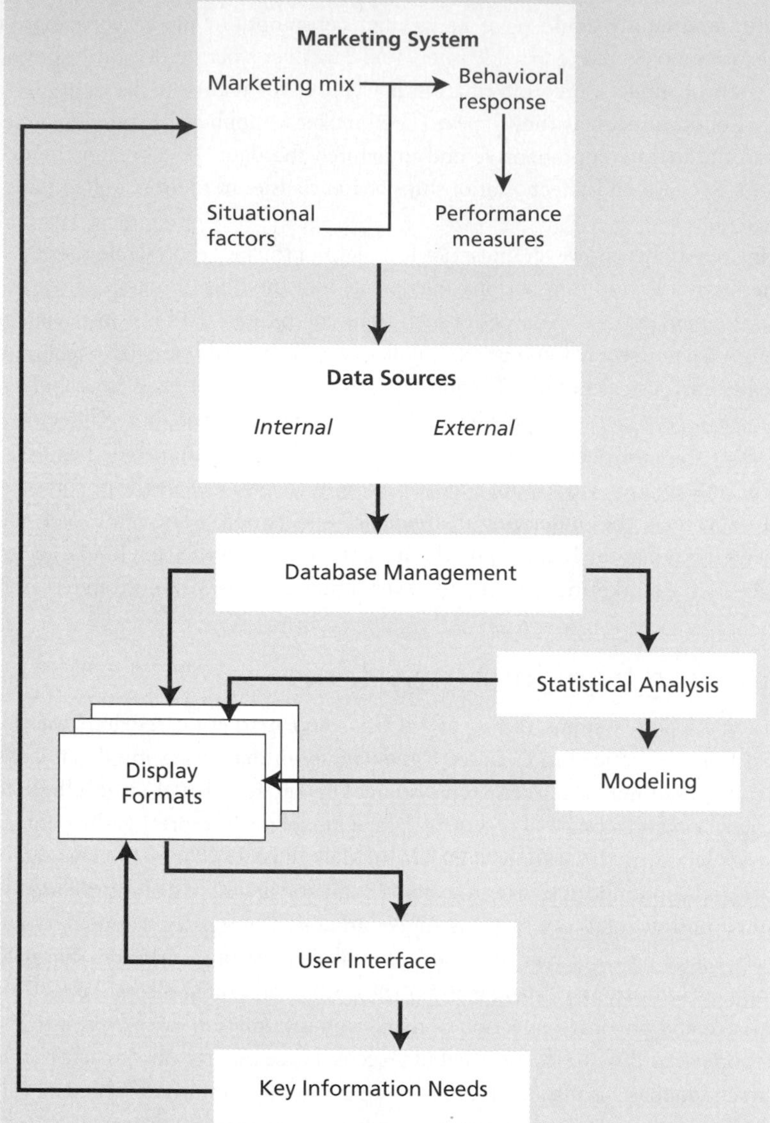

To meet such managerial needs, a good MDSS should allow for user-friendly interaction and provide on-the-spot results. Since the manager must make changes in control variables in real time, delays can be costly and can render the MDSS obsolete. It should be flexible, so that the manager can sort, average, total, or otherwise manipulate the data to look at them from a unique perspective, revealing both expected and unsuspected relationships; and it needs to be oriented toward discovery, so that the manager can search for trends, identify problems, and ask new questions on the basis of information provided.

Before developing an MDSS, an organization must review and overhaul its relevant data sources, identifying and organizing them into systematic structures. Important internal data sources for a marketing intelligence system are the organization's sales personnel, who can provide information relevant to many aspects of the marketing system, especially so its accounting system, which contains data on sales, inventory levels, cost allocations, and accounts receivable. Such information is important in monitoring the performance of marketing programs and in signaling problems and opportunities. Syndicated services and library sources represent key external data sources (see Appendix B).

Current Status of MDSS Concept

The widespread deployment of information technology in the business community and throughout the developed world and its stunning acceleration of data processing and analysis capabilities created a movement that advocated an idealized MDSS concept: a total system that encompasses the lion's share of the decision-maker's information requirements. This excitement, which lasted nearly to the end of the past century, was soon dampened by the practical difficulties of implementing such a concept. As with the promise of chatty robots who would tirelessly anticipate and satisfy our whims, all-purpose MDSSs capable of seamlessly integrating firms' overall marketing activities remain a glimmer in the eye of the future.

A weakness of the idealized MDSS concept relates to the fact that information needs of decision-makers are varied, often complicated, and specific to their individual skills, knowledge, experience, and personalities. No simple combination of data inputs and information outputs is likely to meet a given decision-maker's requirements for information. Although the sophistication of statistical models has grown on pace with that of computer technology, models that can account for the bewildering variety of real-world economic, supply-driven, consumer, and marketing-related circumstances and reliably relate them to sales and profit resist easy formulation.

The objective of the marketing research system is to create an information center of diverse data sources for marketing decision-making through use of a combination of research approaches, philosophies, and technologies that fit the special needs of the organization and the individual decision-makers. The structure and interactive people-machine concepts found in the MDSS concept are tools serving this larger goal, and implementations of this tool continue to be developed to better match the needs of decision-makers.

3.5 Role of Secondary Data

Once research objectives and information needs have been specified, the researcher turns to the task of formulating the research design and determining the appropriate sources of marketing data. This discussion focuses on secondary data and their role in the research process.

All too frequently, the beginning researcher assumes that surveying respondents is the only way to collect data for a research project. Actually, survey research should be used *only* if the data cannot be collected via more efficient data sources; that is, using secondary data. Consequently, the first step in the data collection stage is to determine whether the data have already been collected.

Secondary data are ubiquitous, and the majority of businesses use them in their day-to-day activities. As discussed earlier, internal secondary data are those available within the organization (e.g., accounting records and sales reports), whereas external secondary data are those provided by sources outside the organization (e.g., syndicated services, periodicals, and online resources). Primary data, by contrast, are those collected afresh specifically for purposes of the research needs at hand. For example, if a retailer collects data from shoppers regarding store image, the resulting data are primary.

Internal secondary data sources should be searched thoroughly before turning to external sources; they are less costly, tend to be more accurate or company-specific, and can often reveal synergies within a company, for example, between accounting, finance, and marketing. As discussed previously, the two main sources of external secondary data are syndicated and library sources. Syndicated sources, which collect standardized data to serve the needs of an array of clients, tend to be costly, and their availability may be contractually restricted to certain clients or industries. Library sources, outlined in more detail in this section, include a wide range of publicly circulated publications.

3.5a Advantages of Secondary Data

The advantage of secondary data is savings in cost and time in comparison with primary data. Consider the research objective of estimating the market potential for a product. If secondary data are available, the researcher may be able to visit a library or Web site, identify the appropriate source, and collect the desired data relating to market potential, often electronically in database or spreadsheet format. This may take a few hours of the researcher's time and involve minimal cost; even if the database is a subscription service, time, effort, and costs will be far less than attempting any sort of primary data collection. Contrast this situation with collecting similar data via a survey. Several weeks or months may be required to design and pre-test a questionnaire, train the interviewers, devise a sampling plan, and collect and process the data. In addition, the cost of such a project would be non-trivial. Consequently, it is important to search secondary data sources before proceeding to primary sources. Although it is rare that secondary data completely fulfill the data requirements of a research project, typically they can aid in the formulation of the decision problem, suggest methods and types of data for meeting the information needs, and serve as a source of comparative data by which primary data can be interpreted and evaluated. Even when such data are not directly usable to enact a decision, they can still be helpful; for example, seeing how a professional service has structured and formulated its surveys and research plan can often help guide additional primary research, as well as allow the resulting data (e.g., demographic) to be checked against it.

Another advantage of secondary data is that they may be so wide-ranging or so sophisticated that collecting them would be beyond the means of the typical organization. For example, this would be true of the data available from the Bureau of the Census, or indeed many government-sponsored databases.

3.5b Disadvantages of Secondary Data

The major disadvantages of secondary data relate to the extent that the data fit the information needs of the project and to the level of aggregation, accuracy, and timeliness of the data.

Data Fit Problem

The degree of fit between secondary data and the information needs of the project can range from completely inadequate to quite close. This degree of fit is influenced by units of measurement and definition of classes.

It is common for a researcher to discover that the secondary data are expressed in units different from those required by the project. For example, a project may require data regarding household income. The researcher may find that income is measured by individual, family, spending unit, or tax return, rather than by household. Extreme caution should be exercised in estimating the desired data from measurements in other units. For example, suppose one found that the average household in a particular country had a total annual income of 200,000 francs and that the average family size was four. It would be wrong to conclude that the average salary was 50,000 francs because not all members of a family work. We would need data on the number of adults in the household, the distribution of how many adults work based on the number and ages of children in the home, and other quantities. Even if one has asked a question carefully, by requesting the "total income of all adults (18+) living more than half the year in your household," there are still questions involving taxation, expenses (tuition, mortgage, medical), investments, assets, and other financial details that can make assessing something like "income" complicated. In using secondary data for such a task, it is crucial to understand how the data were collected, how questions were phrased, and what sorts of assumptions were made.

Another problem relates to the class boundaries used to summarize the data. Assuming the unit of measurement is correct, a researcher could find that data on household income are cited with $15,000 boundaries ($0–14,999, $15,000–29,999, and so on), when the project's information needs require $5000 boundaries. In such cases, researchers can make simple, but probably poor, assumptions—in our example, perhaps that each $15,000 class is equally divided into three $5000 classes. Another approach is to use some sort of statistical model, one which attempts to come up with "best guesses" for each of the $5000 classes, which can be treated like missing data, based on the entire *distribution* of income data (a process sometimes called "imputation"). An even more sophisticated analysis would be to *predict* the distribution of the $5000 income classes, based on other variables collected, using a statistical model like regression. Of course, the reverse problem is no problem at all: data on smaller classes (i.e., $5000) can be easily summed up for wider ones (i.e., $15,000).

Level of Aggregation

A common problem with secondary data is that they are highly aggregated; that is, they are not broken down or cross-tabulated in a way consistent with the project's information needs. Consider a company that wishes to market a video game to college-aged women. Much to their delight, they find extensive data on the video game habits of (1) men vs. women and (2) different age groups, containing exactly the 18–22 year group they desire. Their relief at not having to collect primary data would be short-lived, as they realize that they seek the behavior of "women aged 18–22," and this *cannot* be "backed out" of quantities relating the behavior of "women" and "persons aged 18–22." For example, it is possible that many women play video games, and many people aged 18–22 play video games, but that "women aged 18–22" have no interest in them at all. When one realized that target segments typically involve a host of geodemographic descriptors, such as "college-educated men, aged 30–45, who have at least one child in the home," the likelihood of finding secondary data at exactly the right level of aggregation seems remote. Generally speaking, for purchased data from a commercial provider, costs will rise as level of aggregation falls ("highly disaggregate data"): the more variables and levels of each, the more costly the data will be.

Accuracy Problem

A serious limitation of secondary data is the difficulty of evaluating their accuracy. Error in the sampling, data collection, analysis, and reporting stages of the research process influences the accuracy of the data. These sources of error can be more easily evaluated when the researcher directly participates in the research process, as is the situation with primary research. The lack of participation in the research process in no way reduces the responsibility of the researcher to evaluate the accuracy of the data used. The following criteria can be used in the difficult task of assessing the accuracy of secondary data: source, purpose of the publication, and evidence concerning quality.

The *source* of data is important in evaluating their accuracy. Secondary data may be secured from an original source or an acquired source. An original source is the source that originated the data, whereas an acquired source is the source that procured the data from the original source. The Statistical Abstract of the United States, published annually by the Bureau of the Census, is an example of an acquired source. All the data in the Statistical Abstract are taken from other government and trade sources. A fundamental rule in using secondary data is to secure data directly from the original source, rather than using acquired sources, whenever possible. There are two reasons for this guideline. First, the original source is in most cases the only place where the details of the data collection and analysis process are described in full; knowledge of the research process is essential in evaluating the accuracy of the data. Second, the original source is generally more detailed, more accurate, and more complete than the acquired source. Errors in transcription and failure to reproduce footnotes and other textual comments can seriously influence the accuracy of the data.

Evaluation of the *purpose* of a publication is the second criterion for determining the accuracy of secondary data. The researcher needs to be sensitive to the purpose of the publication and cautious in evaluating the data, to detect those who would misrepresent and distort statistics to support a position or belief. This is particularly true for data made available on Web sites, where the bar for accuracy and dissemination can be low, and polemical organizations can easily ape the appearance of trusted data sources.

The third criterion for evaluating the accuracy of secondary data is to assess the general evidence regarding the *quality* of the data. If the primary source does not disclose details of the research design, the researcher should exercise caution, as the supplying organization may have something it wishes to conceal. When the details of the research design are disclosed, the researcher should evaluate areas such as the sampling plan, data collection procedure, quality of field training, questionnaire technique, data analysis procedures, and discussion of the limitations of the research design and data. When limited information is available regarding the research design, the researcher can still evaluate the quality of the reporting of the data. Important here are items such as the labeling of tables and figures, the internal consistency of the data, and whether the data support the conclusions drawn in the report.

Timeliness Problem

Secondary data present a set of facts about the world at the particular point in time that the data were collected. Between data collection and the use of the data by a marketing researcher, a substantial amount of time may pass because the data need to be analyzed and then published in a variety of sources available to the researcher. It is not uncommon for a marketing researcher to be using secondary data that is several years old, and one should keep in mind that that best-conceived and -conducted of all data collection efforts, the U.S. Census of Population and Housing, up through the 2000 Census was only updated once per decade. That changed in 2005 (see the *Special Expert Feature* on The U.S. Census Bureau later in this chapter) with the introduction of the American Community Survey. All data are perishable with the passage of time. Therefore, the data may not be relevant to the time that the marketer is researching, particularly if the data are to be used for forecasts.

3.5c Library Sources of Secondary Data

Library sources of marketing data include an array of publicly circulated material—for example, government documents, periodicals, books, research reports, and trade association publications. What types of research objectives and information needs might call for secondary data? Some examples would be:

- to estimate the total market potential for paper-based storage materials in a given area;
- to develop a method for establishing sales quotas for flat panel TV sets by state;
- to establish national, state, and county sales projections for auto battery replacements;
- to determine the market potential for industrial lubricants in all counties in a particular state;
- to estimate the market for major appliances (clothes washers and dryers, dishwashers, refrigerators, and the like) sets in the Chicago, Illinois, metropolitan statistical area (MSA);
- to estimate national demand for portable music players (tape, CD, MP3, and other formats) by U.S. region for the next 3–5 years;
- to select two counties in the Seattle, Washington, MSA in which to locate new supermarkets; or
- to disperse an advertising budget in proportion to the potential markets, by state, in the South Atlantic region.

The information needs represented by these research objectives could be met, partially or fully, by secondary data available from library sources, such as employment data, population data, television sales, family median income, aggregate income of the population, occupied housing units, automobile registration, music purchases, grocery store sales, value of box shipments by end use, employment by industry group, and many others. Although one must stop short of claiming each of these research objectives could be entirely met via extant databases, the quantity of primary research needed would be cut by an extraordinary degree by first combing secondary sources and judiciously collecting additional data to fill information gaps.

3.5d Government Data Sources

Since 1790, when the first census was taken, the largest single source of statistical data has been the U.S. government. For years, marketing researchers have relied on this source of data for developing market potential and sales forecasts; determining sales territories and sales quotas; and locating retail, wholesale, and manufacturing establishments. As the breadth and depth of government data have increased over the years, the relevance of this source of data to marketing information needs has increased dramatically, all the more so as the data have been made Web-accessible in database format. Consequently, effective marketing research requires a thorough knowledge of government data.

Census Data

Within the federal government, the Bureau of the Census is the leading source of data relevant to marketing. Its vast resources and years of experience combine to give census data a high reputation for quality. The data are generally detailed enough for most marketing information needs and are available in a variety of formats through the Web, in printed form, or archived on optical media.

The census breaks its reports into three main headings, each comprising many sub-units; among those of particular interest to marketers, demographers, and other social science researchers:

People: Estimates, American Community Survey, Projections, Housing, Income, Poverty, International
Business: Economic Census, NAICS, Survey of Business Owners, Government, E-Stats, Foreign Trade, Export Codes, Local Employment Dynamics
Geography: Maps, TIGER, Gazetteer

A *Special Expert Feature* on the 2000 Census is included at this chapter. Data stemming from the 2000 census on population and housing are summarized in Table 3.2. Note that some census items are collected through the use of samples, as opposed to the entire population.

The census data are available at many levels, ranging all the way from the nation as a whole down to city blocks. Figure 3.3 shows the hierarchical relationships among the geographic units used by the Bureau of the Census. Most census data are published only down to the "tract" level. Some of the levels are governmental units—states, counties, and so on—whereas others are just statistical units used by the Bureau of the Census—divisions, MSAs, and so forth. Table 3.3 presents definitions of the geographic units shown in Figure 3.3.

Figure 3.4 further illustrates the types of geographic units used. It presents the geographic subdivision of an MSA all the way down to a city block. Clearly, many detailed data of relevance to marketers are available in the census reports.

Table 3.2 **Subjects in the 2000 Census Classified as Complete-Count (Short Form) or Sample Items (Long Form)**

Items collected at every household via Short Form ("complete-count items")	
Household relationship	Race
Sex	Tenure (home is owned/rented)
Age	Vacancy characteristics
Hispanic or Latino origin	
Additional items collected at sample households via Long Form	
Population	*Housing*
Marital status	Value of home or monthly rent paid
Place of birth, citizenship, and year of entry	Units in structure
School enrollment/educational attainment	Year structure built
Ancestry	Number of rooms and number of bedrooms
Migration (residence in 1995)	Year moved into residence
Language spoken at home/ability to speak English	Plumbing and kitchen facilities
Veteran status	Telephone service
Disability	Vehicles available
Grandparents as caregivers	Heating fuel
Labor force status	Farm residence
Place of work and journey to work	Utilities, mortgage, taxes, insurance, and fuel costs
Occupation, industry, and class of worker	
Work status in 1999	
Income in 1999	

Source: The 2000 Census. Page: 69 http://www.census.gov/main/www/cen2000.htmlhttp://www.census.gov/prod/2001pubs/mso-01icdp.pdf

Census data are not without defects. Like all secondary data, they have the limitation of not being collected for the specific information needs of a marketing research project. Some definitions have been changed from census to census. Even within a census, definitions can have different meanings. For the researcher who is not familiar with the details of census data, it can be very useful to seek the advice of a professional in this area regarding the specifics of how the data are to be used. Numerous publications, workshops, and conferences sponsored by the Bureau of the Census and its parent agency, the U.S. Department of Commerce, are designed to aid the user of census data. In addition, the accuracy of the census before 2000 has been questioned because of potential under-counts of minority groups and those without fixed addresses, especially in urban areas; the 2000 census took great care to accurately represent these and other difficult-to-reach segments of the population. *Marketing Research Focus 3.3* takes a closer look at the census and marketing to specific ethnic groups.

North American Industry Classification System

Many sources of marketing data were classified according to the Standard Industrial Classification, or SIC, code, which has been replaced by the North American Industry Classification System (NAICS). Whereas SIC was developed by the federal government in connection with its Census of Manufactures, NAICS was developed jointly by the United States, Canada, and Mexico to provide broad statistical comparability regarding business activity across North America. The classification system is based on the products produced or operations performed. The NAICS code classifies all businesses into 20 major industry groups (Agriculture; Mining; Utilities; Construction; Manufacturing; Wholesale Trade; Retail Trade; Transportation and Warehousing; Information; Finance and Insurance; Real Estate; Professional, Scientific, and Technical Services; Management of Companies and Enterprises; Administrative, Support, Waste Management and Remediation Services; Educational Services; Health Care; Arts, Entertainment, and Recreation; Accommodation and Food Services; Other Services; and Public Administration), each further classified into more than 1100 product categories designated by a six-digit code. The entire classification system is available electronically (www.census.gov/epcd/naics02/). A new North American Product Classification System (NAPCS) is presently under development, with initial focus on service industries.

Additional Data Sources

In addition to government sources, a large number of other publications contain data applicable to a wide number of research objectives. The task of identifying relevant sources of data can be a difficult one for researchers who are not familiar with the area under investigation. Fortunately, there are many published

Figure 3.3 Bureau of the Census Geographic Units and Their Hierarchical Relationships

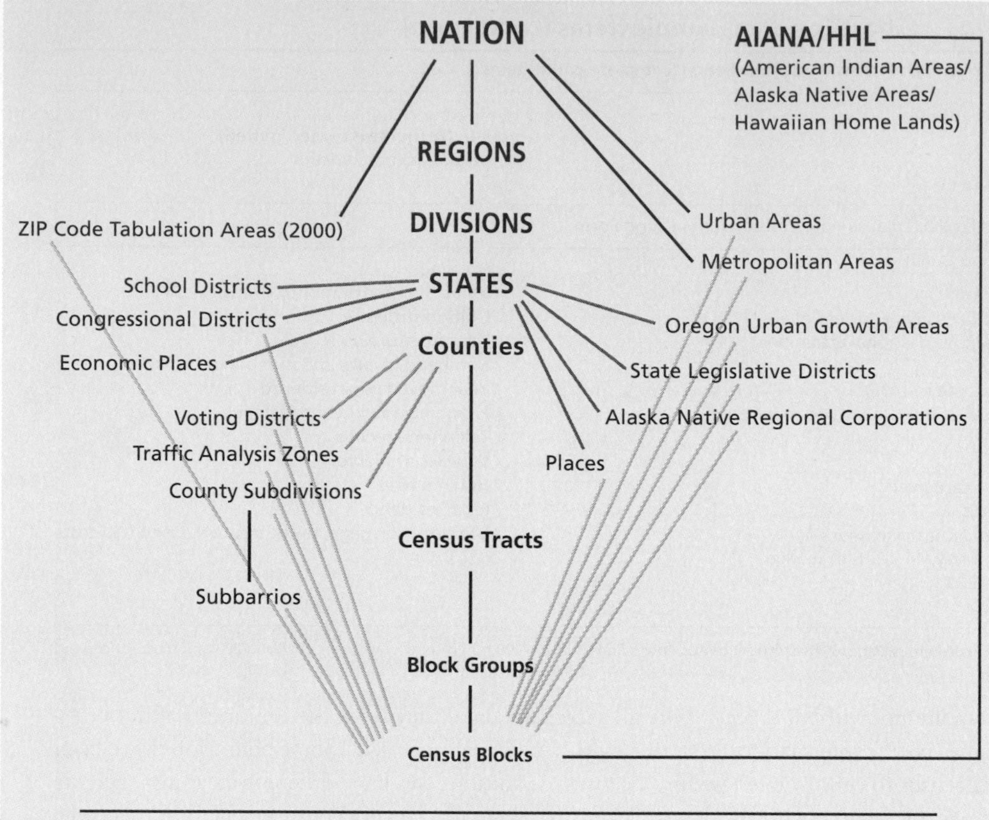

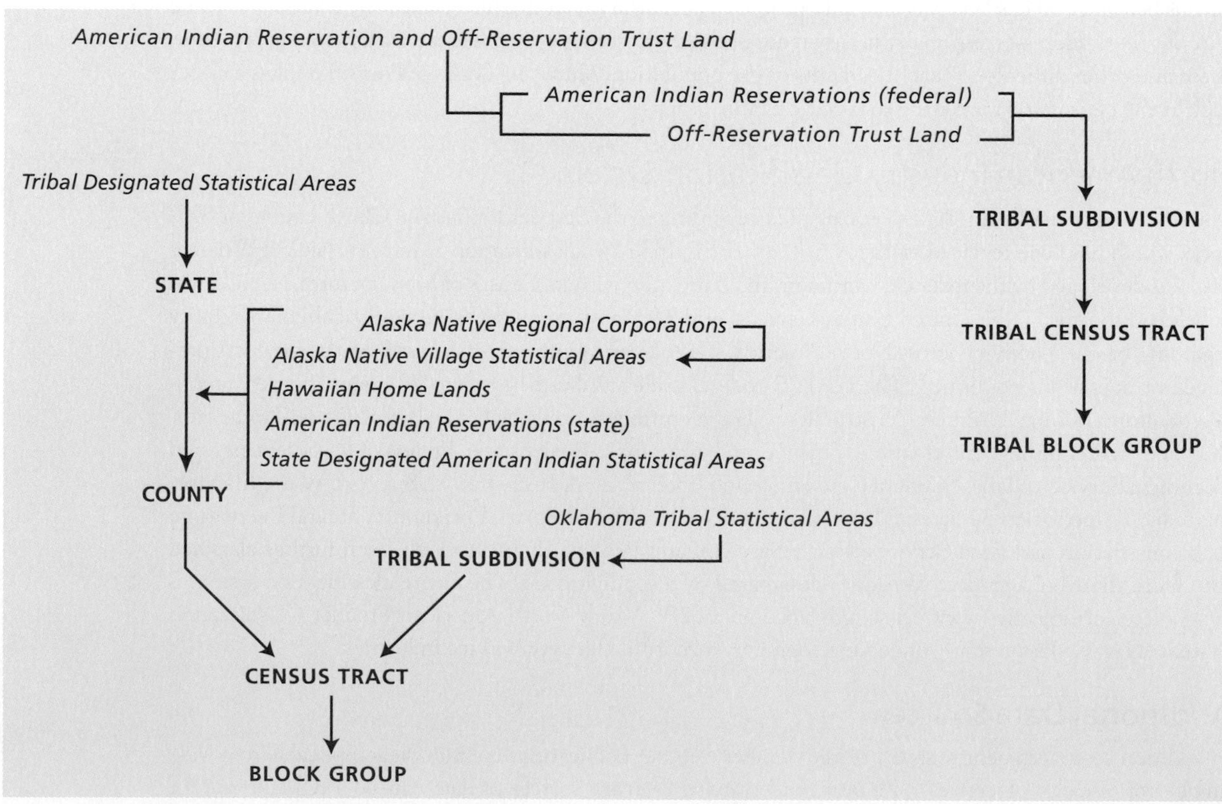

Table 3.3 Definitions of Geographic Units Used by the Bureau of the Census

Nation	The United States as a whole
Region	The United States is divided into four regions: West, South, Northeast, and North Central
Division	The regions are divided into a total of nine geographic divisions, each of which is composed of a specific group of contiguous states: Pacific, Mountain, West South Central, East South Central, South Atlantic, Middle Atlantic, New England, East North Central, and West North Central
State	A state of the union
MSA	A metropolitan statistical area (MSA) is a city or a Census Bureau–defined urbanized area with 50,000 or more inhabitants. There are 362 MSAs in the United States.
County	A primary division of a state, as defined by state law (called a parish in Louisiana; there are none in Alaska)
Urban	The part of a county containing cities and towns of 2500 population or more
Rural	The complement of the urban population, containing farm and non-farm components
Urbanized area	A central city of 50,000 or more, or twin cities of 50,000 or more, with the smallest having 15,000 people or more, plus the surrounding urban buildup or fringe (suburbs)
Other urban places	An urban area not qualifying as an urbanized area (i.e., a place of over 2500 but less than 50,000)
Central city	The area designated by the title of an urbanized area
Urban fringe	A suburb of a central city
MCD	A minor civil division (MCD) is a component part of a county. MCDs represent political or administrative subdivisions called townships, districts, precincts, and so forth.
CCD	Census county divisions (CCD) are small county divisions in 21 states where MCDs are not adequate for reporting sub-county statistics.
Tract	One of the small areas, averaging about 4,000 people, into which large cities and their adjacent areas have been divided for statistical purposes
BG	A block group (BG) is a subdivision of a tract made up of a number of city blocks.
Block	Generally a well-defined piece of land bounded by roads, legal boundaries, and other features; a block is the smallest area for which data are available.
Non-metro area	A part of a state not included in an MSA
Unincorporated place	A concentration of population of at least 1000 which is not legally a city

Figure 3.4 Geographic Subdivisions of an MSA

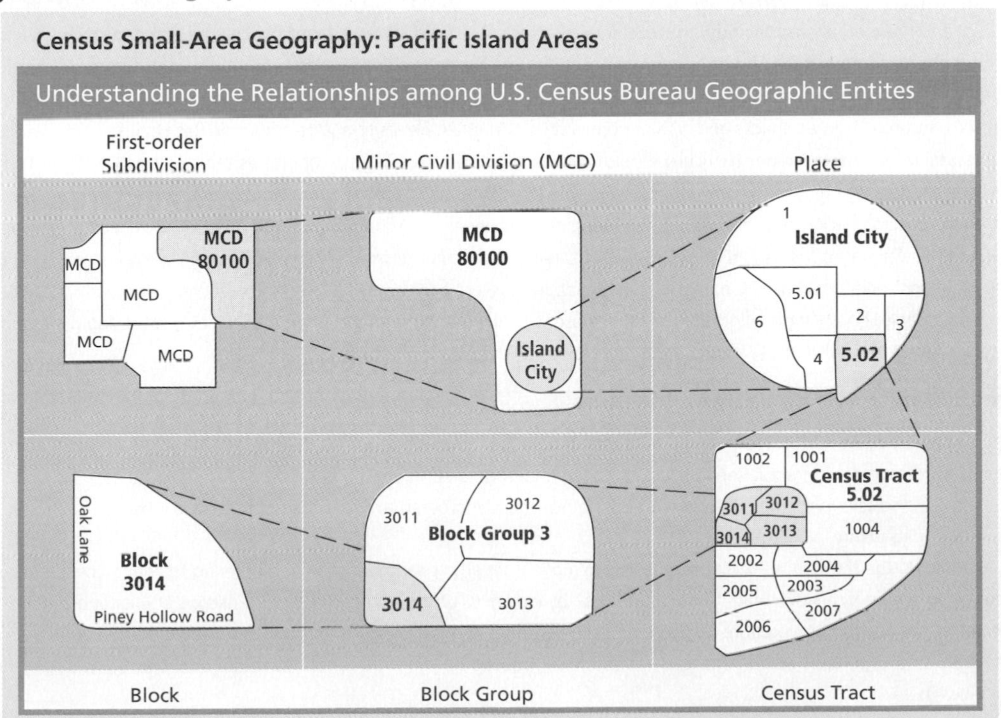

Source: http://www.census.gov/

Marketing Research Focus 3.3

Effect of Census on Ethnic Marketing

When the figures from the 1990 and 2000 censuses were released in 1991 and 2001, American marketers took notice of the large and rapidly growing immigrant and ethnic populations and their corresponding purchasing power. In New Jersey, for example, 2000 data showed that the Asian population had doubled since the previous census of a decade before to 6 percent of the state population.

Census data indicated a particular boost in Hispanic markets. In the summer of 2005, the Bureau of the Census reported that the Hispanic population in the United States is growing at a rate three times faster than the general population, owing largely to an influx from Mexico and the rest of Latin America. At 41.3 million (almost 14 percent of the population), Hispanics are now are the largest ethnic minority in the United States, outnumbering African-American population of 39 million.

Although some companies had targeted ethnic markets long before this, especially those offering services more obviously needed by immigrants (e.g., long-distance telephone, air travel, money transfer), the new demographic data justified this practice and triggered the launch of many more marketing strategies geared toward the needs and tastes of ethnic communities. Bill Duggan, senior vice president at the Advertising Club of New York, said of the effect of the 2000 census on multicultural marketing, "If somebody wasn't on board already, it really opened their eyes."

Although this advertising trend includes voiceovers in Spanish, Chinese, or other languages, the most effective multicultural commercials also appeal to characteristics within a culture with which the target community identifies. Commercials increasingly include cultural features to appeal to specific ethnic markets, such as salsa music, Spanish colloquialisms, or traditional Indian music, and spokespeople for products increasingly include ethnic celebrities considered representative or even iconic to their communities. For example, in a prize-winning Doritos commercial, the message "El reventon de sabor" (loosely, "It's a huge party of flavor") was accompanied by Latin singer Chayanne dancing to merengue-salsa music.

State Farm insurance company appealed to the Asian market by incorporating into its Chinese language ads a play on its traditional branding of "like a good neighbor," using an old Chinese saying, "A neighbor close by is better than a close family far away" while showing images of several generations of Chinese-Americans. Bank of America ran an ad campaign emphasizing the value in Asian communities of their skill as entrepreneurs, with one ad presenting the story of an immigrant who rose from a seller of vegetables grown in his home garden to become the biggest supplier of vegetables in the Texan Asian market.

Marketing research into cultural trends of ethnic groups goes deeper than translating slogans, identifying popular spokespeople, or constructing campaigns with cultural appeal. The different needs and preferences of ethnic communities also affect products themselves. Many companies are marketing new lines of products that are traditional in ethnic markets or products specifically targeted at the ethnic populations. Hispanic consumers, for example, tend to prefer sweeter, fruit-flavored drinks to regular colas or lower-sugar drinks and are the most likely of any ethnic group to purchase sports drinks. As a consequence, Pepsi began marketing Gatorade Xtremo and two of its top flavors from Mexico, apple-flavored Manzanita Sol and orange-flavored Mirinda, to Hispanic markets in the United States; Coca-Cola launched Coca-Cola with Lime with print advertising in both English and Spanish; and Minute Maid developed its Mifruta line of aguas frescas beverages using flavors based on popular Mexican fruits, with names in the original Spanish. African-American preferences have led to more barbecue-flavored snacks and greater popularity of Mountain Dew's Live Wire and Code Red drinks.

Presuming that people in any particular ethnic group share preferences in tastes or brands can be a costly error, as there can be great heterogeneity within any ethnic group. The term "Hispanic," for example, denotes a linguistic category, and is not a reference to geography, culture, or commonality of experience. As Jorge Goldsmit Gerson, president of Eat Inc., which makes Canita Aguas Frescas drinks, puts it, "It's really hard to lump Hispanics into one category. You have Hispanics who were born here; you have Hispanics whose grandparents were born here; and Hispanics who were born abroad. They don't necessarily like the same things for the same reasons." Hibiscus, for example, is the Canita flavor most popular among Mexican-Americans, whereas Tamarind flavor is preferred by most Hispanics from Latin America.

Youth Market as Inherently Multicultural

Companies, of course, prefer to achieve cross-over success, if possible, rather than to appeal only to a small demographic or to each demographic separately with different products. Although aguas frescas are traditional Mexican drinks, Canita's line also sells in the health food segment not specifically targeted to Hispanics, such as Whole Foods supermarket chain, due to its being "all natural."

In addition, the trend in marketing to youth is to move from ethnic segmentation to marketing to young consumers as tribes more bound by a new multiethnic culture than by individual ethnicity. According to Giuseppe D'Alessandro, Pepsi's director of multicultural marketing, 40 percent of the Pepsi world is multicultural—20 percent Latino, 15 percent African-American, and 6 percent Asian-American—with concentrations of youthful minorities in major urban centers forming majorities there.

Such diversity is widely embraced in youth culture. "Race is not the unifier," says D'Alessandro. "The multicultural mind-set is more about your interests, like music, than whether you're African-American or Latino." Pepsi does not limit its multicultural campaigns to Black Entertainment Television and Hispanic Univision broadcasts, as was standard practice even in the 1990s. Singers Beyonce Knowles and Shakira, for example, were featured in Pepsi's multicultural ads that emphasized imagination and passion while selling "the joy of Pepsi." D'Alessandro points out that ethnic minorities now "see their reflection in the popular culture, almost to the point of exaggeration. We call it the multicultural heart."

In targeting youth, he says that it is difficult to discern what percentage of Pepsi's advertising budget is targeted to any particular ethnic group. Because much of Pepsi's youth market are bicultural Hispanics who are as familiar with mainstream American culture and English-speaking media as they are with their ancestral or local culture and Spanish-speaking media, advertisers also need to keep this hybrid culture in mind as a new milieu. "That can be hard for marketers to understand. They always thought Spanish was the main thing, when in reality it's not [about] the language."

As the ethnic composition of the U.S. changes and ethnic identities continue to evolve and cross-pollinate, marketers face new challenges in reaching this new cultural "melting pot" and catering to the wide buffet of its sub-cultures and preferences.

Sources: As Demographics Change, Advertisements Target Ethnic Groups; Hugh R. Morley. *Hackensack Record*. Hackensack, NJ: February 11, 2002.
Pepsi Puts Interests Before Ethnicity; Laurel Wentz. *Advertising Age*. July 7, 2003.
Latin Flair In Bebidas For The Masses; Elizabeth Fuhrman. *Beverage Industry*. August 1, 2005.

guides and indexes to assist them in this pursuit. (See the appendices to this chapter for a listing of the main guides and indexes to, as well as the more predominant sources of, marketing-related data.) In addition, researchers will find that a competent reference librarian can identify relevant sources of data.

In evaluating the quality of the data identified, the researcher must be sensitive to the origin of the data and the research design. At times, this may be difficult to determine. Library data originate from an array of sources such as federal, state, and local governments; colleges and universities; trade associations; chambers of commerce; commercial organizations; foundations; and publishing companies. Some publications present the results of original research; some summarize the research findings of others; and some present interpretations and conclusions regarding the research findings of others.

One development in the provision of demographic data to marketers is the growth of private companies that market census-related products. These companies provide the fastest way to get census data tailored to one's needs. In addition, they offer updates on census data at the tract level and above and between census years, and they provide clients with a range of services designed to assist in using demographics in planning, marketing, and forecasting.

One of the most sophisticated systems that uses census data is PRIZM (Potential Rating Index for Zip Markets), developed by Claritas Corp. PRIZM uses census data combined with national surveys, individual interviews, other marketing data, and the U.S. Postal Service's ZIP+4 Code System to group America's population into 66 colorfully named ("blueblood estates," "pools and patios," "Norma Rae-ville," and others) lifestyle clusters, based on shared socioeconomic characteristics.

SPECIAL EXPERT FEATURE

The U.S. Census Bureau: Census of Population and Housing, Economic Census and Indicators, Household Surveys

By Barbara Everitt Bryant

The Web site for the Bureau of the Census (www.census.gov) is the candy store for data. It's a candy store at which all of the products are both free and accessible—and particularly accessible on its easy-to-use site www.factfinder.census.gov. Census

continued

Bureau–produced data became available on the Internet in 1994. However, since 1790—whether on paper, computer tape (beginning with the 1950 decennial census), or CD-ROMs (1987 economic census and 1990 population census), the U.S. census has been the source of what marketers, politicians, government officials, policy-makers, media, and ordinary people know about the population and businesses of the nation, and their characteristics.

Establishment of the Census

Taking a census was written into the Constitution of the United States (Article I, Section 2) as part of the compromise between the large and small colonies about what form of legislature the new nation would have. The compromise divided power by setting up a two-house legislature, in which each state would have equal representation in the Senate, whereas seats in the House of Representatives would be apportioned according to population. If the House were to be divided according to population, then a mechanism needed to be set up to measure the population as the nation grew. Thus, it was written: "Representatives and direct Taxes shall be apportioned among the several States which may be included within this Union, according to their respective Numbers. . . . The actual Enumeration shall be made within three Years after the first Meeting of the Congress of the United States, and within every subsequent Term of ten Years in such manner as they shall by Law direct." The first enumeration started on August 1, 1790, the 22nd was conducted in the spring of 2000, and the 2010 census started in 2005 in a totally new form with data from the American Community Survey.

The founding fathers did not have marketing in mind when they compromised on dividing power in the legislature and set up a census. However, cementing the taking of a census into the Constitution means that the United States has the longest-running periodic census in the world. Other countries have older ones—China counted 57.6 million in its first recorded census in 2 A.D.—but no other country has kept up the taking of a census periodically as long as the United States has. Censuses that are not embedded in a constitution are often aborted for political and economic reasons. The duration of the U.S. census means that marketers have trend data on population growth, distribution, migration, changing household patterns, and demographic characteristics as well as the slice-in-time data provided by each census and by the many surveys conducted by the Bureau of the Census.

Every question in both the Census of Population and Housing and the Economic Census has either a federal agency use or is required by law.

The Census of Population and Housing and Its History

The decennial Census of Population and Housing asks no marketing questions nor does it ask any attitudinal, opinion, or religious questions. However, what it does ask provides marketers with a wealth of information useful for market decision-making, location analyses, and other marketing activities. The data also serve city planners, policy makers, Congress, and a host of others. A major reason the population census is such a powerful tool is that each individual and household is enumerated and the statistics are attached to a small geographic area, most recently to one of the 8,205,582 blocks into which the nation is divided. Thus, block data can be aggregated to larger areas of interest—a block group (600 to 3000 individuals), a census tract (about 4000 individuals), a city, a ZIP code, a school district, an Indian community, a metropolitan area, a county, a state, and finally to the nation (see Figure 3.3). The fine geographic detail makes census data useful for identifying groups with specific demographic characteristics that can be used for target marketing of products, services, political candidates, or issues; for providing social service programs; for transportation planning; or for projecting growth or decline in a school district or city.

Every-Ten-Year Data: 1790–2000

Federal marshals went out on horseback to call on every residence in 1790. They had no census forms or questionnaires, only plain paper, and they asked only six questions regarding the identity of the head of family, the number of free persons and slaves, and the number of free persons distinguished by gender and race. The population count came in at 3.9 million in the 13 original states plus Kentucky, Maine, Vermont, and the Southwest Territory (mostly Tennessee). The next several censuses were much the same. In 1810, a question was added about agriculture, and in subsequent censuses questions were added on agriculture, mining, governments, religious bodies (discontinued after 1936), business, housing, and transportation. Thus, the population census also became an economic census. An economic census on manufactures was separated from the population and housing census in 1905.

The census grew as new states were added to the union.

The Census Act of 1830 authorized establishment of a centralized census office during each enumeration, rather than simply appointing a Superintendent of the Census to supervise the marshals who collected the data. Printed schedules, rather than plain paper, were introduced for 1830. Through 1840, the unit of enumeration was the household. In 1850, enumeration of individuals within households began, with questions that provided social statistics at the individual level.

The 1870 census marked the beginning of rudimentary tallying of results, beyond simple counts, and publication of maps and charts. It was not until 1880 that the federal marshals were replaced by specially appointed agents. It took until nearly 1890 to complete all the tabulations of the 1880 census because the population had grown to 50.2 million.

The year 1890 marked the use of separate census schedules for each household—before that time, responses were marked on charts with a line for each household. 1890 also marked the start of electric tabulation, not just for the U.S. census, but for the world. Herman Hollerith, who had been one of the special agents for the 1880 census, developed punch cards and electric tabulation machines that dropped needles through the holes in the cards to complete electric circuits and record results. The machines he designed eventually became part of the

continued

startup of IBM. 1890 was also memorable because the Superintendent of the Census announced that there was no longer a frontier—the nation was populated from the Atlantic to the Pacific Oceans. (Note that, in keeping with the mindset of the time, this discounted the American Indians—who had populated the country for centuries.)

In 1902, a permanent Bureau of the Census was established in the Department of the Interior. A year later, it moved to the newly created Department of Commerce and Labor—later made two departments. It remains part of the Department of Commerce today.

Statistical sampling, with known margins of error, was developed during the 1930s. The year 1940 marked the start of sampling a small (5 percent) sample of households enumerated in the census to ask more questions than were asked of every household. In more recent censuses, the sample has been enlarged to 17 percent who are asked questions on what is called the long form, and 100 percent of households are asked questions on the short form. The long-form responses from the sample are then projected to the entire population. Short-form results are used for re-apportioning the House of Representatives. The contents of the short-form and long-form questions used in the 2000 census are shown in Table 3.2.

The first non-military, federal government computer, UNIVAC I, was delivered to the Census Bureau in 1951 and used for tabulations of the 1950 census. The year 1960 saw the Bureau's introduction of optical scanning to replace punched cards. From 1960 through 1990, respondents marked question responses by filling in circles next to answers; the schedules were photographed onto microfilm; and the films were fed to a machine (Film Optical Sensing Device for Input to Computers [FOSDIC]) that read the blackened circles. FOSDIC was a Census Bureau invention before commercial optical scanning machines. Commercial optical scanners were used in 2000 to capture data.

1960 also marked the first use of the mail, rather than in-person interviews, for self-enumeration. In 1960, a sample of households had their questionnaires delivered by enumerators, who asked that they be mailed back. From then on, mail became the vehicle for delivering and returning the majority of questionnaires: 60 percent in 1970, 90 perecent in 1980, and 94 percent in 1990 and 2000. Households that did not return their questionnaires (typically about one third) were followed up by in-person calls by census enumerators, as were the small proportion with non-geographic addresses (such as a post office box). Much of the cost of recent decennial censuses has been in following up on non-responders. The last several percent of households enumerated are a disproportionate cost of census-taking.

The 1990 census marked another pioneering technological breakthrough for the Census Bureau, in concert with the U.S. Geological Survey. That was the development of a computerized geographic information system with the mapping of every block in the nation. Called TIGER (Typologically Integrated Geographic Encoding and Referencing System), this became the basis for development of an entire new geographic information systems (GIS) industry that today delivers widely used, detailed maps of any location in the United States via the Internet. TIGER was a gift to the nation because the Census Bureau is not allowed to patent its developments.

Also in 1990, the Census Bureau for the first time developed a computerized household address list, the Master Address File (MAF). Both TIGER and MAF are updated continuously.

The questions asked in the census have varied greatly in content and number through the years, reflecting changes in households, racial terminology, and living patterns. However, the questions have been fairly stable for the past 40 years. A question identifying those of Hispanic/Latino ethnicity was added in 1980 to reflect growing immigration from Latin America; one on condominiums was added in 1990; one on whether a grandparent was raising children in the household was added in 2000, required by a law passed by Congress in 1996.

Through 210 years (1790–2000), the nation only had population census data every 10 years. In rapidly changing areas—and there are many in the nation—there was a rising clamor for more frequent updates, a demand that the Census Bureau has filled with its population estimates program, which began in 1940. Population estimates, however, provide only counts for a few demographic groups. Beginning in the 1980s, the Census Bureau began considering the possibility of doing a "rolling census" to collect sample data every year on the population characteristics in the long-form questions, with a total census with only the short-form questions to obtain an accurate count for re-apportionment every 10 years. Serious research on this possibility started in the 1990s.

How Accurate is the U.S. Census?

Given that the United States has no mandatory population register—as many other countries have—and that it is a very mobile country, census counts in recent years have been very close to the best estimates of the population from two types of research: (1) demographic analysis (births – deaths + immigration – emigration), and (2) post-enumeration surveys (1980–2000) in which questionnaires from a large household survey are matched to those from the actual census, and capture/recapture estimation is used. Although demographic estimates are limited, post-enumeration survey estimates can be carried down to many demographic groups and to small geographic areas and thus, if sufficiently accurate, could be used to adjust a census statistically.

Table 3.4 Percent Estimated Undercount by Race in the Censuses of 1940–2000 According to Demographic Analysis

	1940	1950	1960	1970	1980	1990	2000
Total population	5.4	4.1	3.1	2.7	1.2	1.8	0.1
Non-blacks	5.0	3.8	2.7	2.2	0.8	1.3	–0.3*
Blacks	8.4	7.5	6.6	6.5	4.5	5.7	2.8

*Over-count

continued

The fact that there was a measurable under-count came to light in 1940 when more black males registered for the draft in the fall than had been counted in the April census. Although George Washington had complained of an under-count when the 1790 count came in at 3.9 million—he had hoped for 4 million to impress Europe—nobody knew how to measure it.

In 1980 and 1990, with post-enumeration survey results available, the under-count was the subject of much controversy and lawsuits to adjust the numbers—a debate made hot because the under-count was shown to be disproportionately among those in rental housing and, therefore, disproportionately in large cities; areas with recent immigration; and among African-Americans/Blacks and Hispanics/Latinos. Surprisingly, it also included children who move around, living with mothers, fathers, grandmothers, and extended family, none of whom list them on their census forms. There was also some over-count among those with two homes and among college students who were counted at their college addresses while their families listed them at the home address. No readjustment was ever ordered by the courts, although the 1990 post-enumeration survey was debatably accurate enough to have been used for adjustment.

The 2000 census count came in accurate enough that it could not have been statistically adjusted. Improvements over the 1990 census included an extensive advertising campaign; better designed, more user-friendly questionnaires; and an outreach campaign, expanded over the one in 1990, directed to hard-to-count groups. However, while the 1990 census cost $2.6 billion (or about $10.40 for each of the 249.8 million persons counted), the 2000 census cost $6.4 billion (or about $23 for each of the 281.4 million counted).

The 2010 Census: A Re-Engineered Census for the Twenty-First Century

The 2010 census will be the first to combine survey (long-form) data taken over the decade with a complete enumeration using the short form in the census year. The "rolling census" envisioned for years has finally come to pass.

After a number of test runs begun in 1996, census-taking in the United States changed dramatically in 2005. The first year's data from the American Community Survey (ACS) became the first portion released of a re-engineered 2010 census. In ACS, data are collected every month from a sample of approximately 250,000 households. By 2009, ACS will have sampled 15 million households, slightly short of the number that received the long form in 2000 (18.3 million). No address will receive the ACS more than once in a 5-year period. Communities of 250,000 or more residents had estimated data on their populations and characteristics of those populations available from 2001 to 2004 from ACS testing and in 2005 from official ACS data collected (by mail and enumerator follow-up) in the 12 months of 2004. The ACS schedule—and thus the 2010 census—starts with long-form data available for communities of different sizes over a several-year period. Data are then available on an annual basis for communities of all sizes beginning in 2010.

The 5-year accumulations of data include detail down to the census-tract (about 4000 individuals) and block-group (about 600–3000 individuals) levels from 2010 on.

Some questions will be different from those used in past censuses. For example, the place of residence will be the surveyed address of the housing unit where each individual is interviewed. In past censuses, it was the place where the individual resided the largest part of the census year. Income figures will be those from the past 12 months, rather than for the calendar year ending in "9."

What happens to the complete count census? There will still be a census in 2010, but one which asks only the questions on the short form—the ones needed for the constitutionally mandated re-apportionment of the Congress by states. Taking of the actual census (that is, obtaining information from every household) is the means for calibrating the population and housing-unit counts. The housing-unit count is the basis (or frame) from which samples are selected for the subsequent decade for the American Community Survey and for the numerous other surveys the Census Bureau conducts. The decennial base count of housing units is supplemented throughout the decade by the addition of new construction data, also collected by the Census Bureau.

The American Community Survey is taken via long-form–type questionnaires mailed to a random sample of addresses each month. The Census Bureau mails a pre-notice letter to these households, informing them that they will shortly receive a questionnaire, which they are asked to mail back. If no response is received, a reminder card is mailed, followed by a replacement questionnaire. Addresses that do not respond within 6 weeks of the first mailing will be contacted by telephone. After 4 more weeks, the remaining non-responding addresses are sampled, and Census Bureau field representatives make personal visits to conduct an interview in the home.

Table 3.5 **American Community Survey Estimate Intervals by Size of Resident Population**

Resident Population	ACS Estimate Interval	Year of First Estimate
250,000 or more*	Annual	2001**
65, 000 or more	Annual	2006**
20,000 or more	3-year average	2008
Less than 20,000	5-year average	2010
All size populations	Annual from 2010 on	2010

*Areas of population of 250,000 or more received data from ACS testing between 2000 and 2004.

**Household data only. For funding reasons, no data were collected on those in group quarters (dormitories, prisons, and so forth). It is hoped that budget will allow adding group quarters enumeration in future years.

continued

The complete-count census in 2010 will be conducted in much the same way—by mailed short-form questionnaires with replacement questionnaires and then intensive personal interview follow-up to all non-responders.

The American Community Survey has two great advantages over collecting the data on the long form every 10 years: (1) obviously, it will provide more timely information on population and housing characteristics for communities and geographic areas; (2) it should also provide more accurate data. Response rates have always been higher from households mailed only the short form. Additionally, those who follow up on non-responding households will be permanent Census Bureau employees in its corps of highly trained field representatives. In the time frame of past recent censuses, follow-ups on non-respondents (May to August of census years), the Census Bureau has had to hire and quickly train more than a half a million temporary enumerators, whose ranges of competence varied.

Although the primary aim of the actual census is coverage (that is, getting every housing unit and individual enumerated), the primary aim of the ACS is to provide demographic, social, housing, and economic content. Together, they form a new type census.

The Economic Census and Economic Indicators

Economic Census

The Economic Census provides a detailed portrait of the U.S. economy every 5 years from the national to the local level for the years ending in "2" and "7." The 2002 Economic Census covered 18 NAICS (North American Industrial Classification System) sectors, 651 industries, and reported on 833 geographic areas. The NAICS was developed jointly by the U.S., Mexico, and Canada and introduced in 1997.

For the Economic Census, questionnaires are mailed to every business establishment in the United States that has a payroll, asking questions on sales, payroll, and number of employees. The Economic Census is a mother lode for those considering establishing a business, choosing a location, looking at competition, or understanding the scope of an industry.

When the United States was largely an agricultural economy, economic and business data could be collected as part of the population census. Starting with questions on agriculture in 1810, questions were added in subsequent censuses covering manufacturing, mining, and some commercial activities. The 1905 Manufacturers' Census was the first taken separately from the decennial population census. Censuses covering retail and wholesale trade and construction industries were added in 1930, as were some service industries in 1933. The 1954 Economic Census was the first time the various economic censuses were integrated into a single census. Starting in 1967, these have continued at 5-year intervals. The Economic Census has never covered the entire economy, but the program expanded until1992, when it covered 98 percent of economic activity.

The once-every-5-year census also provides the business address list, statistical controls, and sampling frames used for surveys that provide many of the nation's economic indicators.

Economic Census data are available for the United States, metropolitan areas, counties, places of 2500+ population, and ZIP codes. There is increasingly less detail at small area levels, however, as no information is released that would identify an individual establishment or company. Employers are promised confidentiality.

The Economic Census uses approximately 500 questionnaire versions customized to specific industries. Questionnaires are not sent to businesses without payroll ("mom-and-pops," individual sales persons, and so forth). Data for these are gathered from administrative records of other federal agencies.

Data are collected on the basis of a business establishment at a specific geographic location. Some census results are classified by company or firm. A third classification is by products produced or sold. However, most of the census statistics reflect the classification of establishments, rather than companies or products. Each establishment is classified into only one NAICS code on the basis of its primary activity.

Economic Indicators

Besides the economic census, the Census Bureau is the source for a number of the nation's economic indicators. Its role often goes unrecognized because many of the indicators are released with the Department of Commerce shown as the source. Many do not realize that the Census Bureau is part of that Department. Other indicators are released by federal agencies for which the Census Bureau collects the data. Some of the major indicators produced at the Census Bureau using surveys are:

- Construction Spending
- Durable Goods New Orders
- Home Ownership
- Household Income
- Housing Starts
- Housing Vacancies
- Manufacturers' New Orders
- Manufacturers' Profits
- Monthly Retail Sales
- Monthly Wholesale Trade
- New Home Sales
- Poverty
- Quarterly Services
- Retail Profits
- Total Business Sales
- Trade Balance

Data for other economic indicators such as employment, unemployment, and the Consumer Price Index (CPI) are collected through surveys conducted for other federal agencies (see next section).

Household Surveys Conducted by the Bureau of the Census

Use of statistical sampling allows data collection through surveys. Surveys use smaller numbers of interviews than a census and, therefore, are much less costly. Surveys have known sampling errors and provide sufficient information, unless data are needed for very small areas. Because the Census Bureau has access to the MAF from the previous census—updated with new construction information it collects—the Census Bureau has the most accurate sampling frame in the nation from which to select a survey sample of addresses. For this reason, many federal agencies contract for surveys conducted by the Census Bureau.

continued

Table 3.6 Major Household Surveys Conducted by the Bureau of the Census

Survey Name	Sample Size and Frequency	Purpose and Sponsor
American Housing Survey (AHS)	National—54,000 addresses/biennially in odd years Metropolitan—75,000 addresses/biennially in even years	Inform housing policy and housing program design and evaluation—Department of Housing and Urban Development (HUD)
Consumer Expenditure Survey (CE)	15,000 addresses/quarterly 12,400 addresses/annually—diaries with 2-week reference periods throughout the year	Update Consumer Price Index and analyze consumer expenditures—Bureau of Labor Statistics (BLS)
Current Population Survey (CPS)	59,500 addresses/monthly	Provide monthly estimates of employment, unemployment, labor force characteristics, annual estimate of income, poverty, work experience, and periodic estimates of other topics—Bureau of Labor Statistics and Census Bureau
National Crime Victimization Survey (NCVS)	56,000 addresses, 104,000 people age 12+/semi-annually 56,000 addresses, 96,000 people age 16+/triennially 10,000 households 14,000 students/ biennially	Provide estimates of crime victimization Provide estimates of interaction with police and police use of excessive force Provide information on school-related victimization—Bureau of Justice Statistics
National Health Interview Survey (NHIS)	41,000 completed interviews/annually	Provide estimates of the amount and distribution of illness and utilization of health care services—National Center for Health Statistics
Survey of Women (SW) Component of the National Longitudinal Surveys (NLS)	5700 women/biennially	Provide estimates of the work experience and characteristics of cohorts of women ages 30–44 in 1968 and ages 14–24 in 1967—Bureau of Labor Statistics
National Survey of College Graduates (NSCG)	42,500 adults	Estimate size and characteristics of U.S. scientists and engineers—National Science Foundation
New York City Housing Vacancy Study (NYCHVS)	18,000 housing units/triennially	Estimate the vacancy rate for New York City's rental stock and the characteristics of housing and residents in the city—New York City Department of Housing Preservation and Development

The Census Bureau is the major survey research agency of the federal government.

The Census Bureau also collects data for the Social Security Administration, the Bureau of Transportation Statistics (including the journey-to-work information from questions formerly in the census long form and now in the American Community Survey). The National Center for Education Statistics uses census data at the school district level; the Department of Housing and Urban Development gets a complete profile of the nation's housing stock from the census.

Confidentiality of Census and Survey Information

Individual and household information from both the short and long forms of the Census of Population and Housing, from the Economic Census, and from surveys conducted by the Census Bureau are confidential. Both individuals and employers are promised confidentiality when they respond. In 1880, when federal marshals were replaced as enumerators by specially appointed agents, these agents were forbidden to disclose census data. Until then, such data were public, even posted on trees in the communities for the first censuses. There have been census laws through the years, but in 1954, the confidentiality provisions that apply today were cemented into the law as Title 13, U.S. Code. That law says that information provided by respondents can be used only for statistical purposes (that is, in aggregated form), and that no one other than sworn officers or employees can see individual reports. There are severe penalties for Census Bureau employees—large fines and up to 5 years in prison—who violate confidentiality of respondent information. Data are not available that would identify an individual, a housing unit, or a business establishment. Title 13 also makes it mandatory for households and employers to respond to censuses (but not to surveys other than the American Community Survey). Other federal agencies or local or state governments do not have access to individual or establishment census data, but federal agencies are required to share their data with the Census Bureau.

Addresses are also confidential, with an exception in the Census Address List Improvement Act of 1994, which states that the Census Bureau can share its address list with the U.S. Postal Service and state and local officials, solely for the purpose of updating the census address list. Otherwise, the MAF and the business establishment list are not publicly available—much as marketing, survey research, and direct mailing organizations would like to have access to these.

There is an exception to access to household and individual information (not business information)—but only after 72 years. In 1952, the director of the Census Bureau

continued

and the National Archives agreed that records from the population and housing census are made publicly available after 72 years. Records of the 1930 census were released in 2002. These are the records genealogists use to research family trees.

Barbara Everitt Bryant was Director of the U.S. Bureau of the Census from 1989 until 1993. She is presently Adjunct Research Scientist at Stephen M. Ross School of Business, University of Michigan.

References

Anderson, Margo J., *The American Census: A Social History* (New Haven: Yale University Press, 1988).

"American Community Survey: A Handbook for State and Local Officials," (Washington, D.C.: U.S. Department of Commerce, Bureau of the Census, December 2004).

Bryant, Barbara Everitt and William Dunn, *Moving Power and Money: The Politics of Census Taking* (Ithaca, N.Y.: New Strategist Publications, Inc., 1995).

Encyclopedia of the Census, Margo J. Anderson, editor-in-chief (Washington, D.C.: Congressional Quarterly Press, 2000) particularly articles on the American Community Survey, Census Law, Decennial Censuses 1790–1990, Economic Census, Confidentiality.

Mathers, Mark, Kerri L. Rivers, and Linda A. Jacobsen, "The American Community Survey," (Washington, D.C.: Population Reference Bureau, Population Bulletin 60, 3, September 2005).

200 Years of Census Taking: Population and Housing Questions, 1790–1990, (Washington, D.C.: U.S. Department of Commerce, Bureau of the Census, November 1989).

TIGER: The Coast-to-Coast Digital Map Data Base, (Washington, D.C: U. S. Department of Commerce, Bureau of the Census, November 1990).

Courtesy of Barbara Everitt Bryant.

3.6 International Research Design and Data Sources

All the types of research designs described earlier in this chapter are applicable to both domestic and international situations. Though the fundamentals of marketing research apply universally, there are differences in the implementation of research designs required by the variations in available technology, research institutions, and culture across countries. There are a great many differences in the data sources available to marketing researchers across countries.

3.6a International Data Sources

International research data—both marketing-specific and relating to more general economic trends—can be obtained from a variety of sources, including the U.S. Department of Commerce (U.S. DOC) and other governmental agencies; international organizations such as the Organization for Economic Cooperation and Development (OECD), the Food and Agriculture Organization (FAO) of the United Nations (UN), and the United Nations Conference on Trade and Development (UNCTAD); service organizations such as banks, export trading companies, trade associations, and world trade clubs; and numerous private research organizations and their respective publications (e.g., Research and Markets, Datamonitor, Economist Intelligence Unit, International Business Strategies). The majority of these data are available online; and from the mind-boggling array of available data, researchers must sort out the information that is most relevant, timely, and useful for the current information needs. When searching online, it is often useful to add the word "international" and/or the name of the country or region to the topic (e.g., consumer panels or market segmentation) and to try both the singular and plural forms of the terms.

While sorting the results of their searches, researchers must evaluate each source of information with an eye to its overall ongoing performance, using the data to identify trends and to process, filter, and analyze the data accordingly. When selecting sources of international marketing research data, among the key determinants are the company's size and the degree to which it carries out its business operations cross-nationally. Larger and more internationally involved firms, especially multinational corporations, often have sophisticated internal databases, which they supplement, using data from private sector suppliers. *International Issues 3.1* presents a summary of data sources for specific stages of foreign market opportunity analysis.

3.6b International Secondary Data Sources

Secondary data sources are helpful in providing general information, such as economic indicators, political stability, and the exchange-rate fluctuations. Virtually every country in the world has available

International Issues 3.1

Specific Techniques for Foreign Market Opportunity Analysis

Preliminary Screening for Attractive Markets

- Scrutiny of news media, trade publications, and automated Web feeds
- Examination of favorable and unfavorable aspects of markets in country
- Analysis of secondary statistics (syndicated and government-generated)
- Participation in international trade fairs and shows
- Queries directed to and interaction with prospective distributors and end users
- Country clustering (e.g., by demographic, political, and cultural characteristics)

Industry Market Potential Assessment

- Trend analysis—domestic production, plus imports minus exports
- Econometric forecasting (time series, regression)
- Analysis of key indicators of demand
- Noting activities of major international contractors and providers
- Other top-down estimates (multiple-factor indices, income elasticity measures, input–output analysis, etc.)

Company Sales Potential and Profitability Analysis

- Surveys of end-users, distributors, and e-commerce channels
- Trade audits
- Competitive intelligence gathering
- Customized market research

secondary data from both government and private sources. In addition, international organizations such as the United Nations, the World Bank and the International Monetary Fund collect extensive secondary data that are made available to public institutions and private citizens alike.

Great care must be taken in using international secondary data. Data are often not comparable across countries, as the definitions used for variables are sometimes different (particularly so for socioeconomic categories), and the timeframes in which the data are collected may be different. In addition, the accuracy of the data even from some government sources is suspect because of lack of careful procedures or even outright propaganda. However, almost every nation conducts it own census. (A complete listing is available at www.census.gov/main/www/stat_int.html.) Although few of these are as extensive or complete as the U.S. Census, they are carried out according to widely accepted methodologies, and in most cases the actual protocols and analysis methods can be freely accessed for scrutiny by outside researchers. Two hundred and one (201) of 230 countries conducted a census during the 2000 round (1995–2004), according to Paul Cheung, Director, United Nations Statistics Division. These covered 91 percent of the world's population, but only 57 percent of the African population. (Questionnaires are available at http://unstats.un.org/unsd/demographic/sources/census/censusquest.htm.) *International Issues 3.2* lists some commonly used international, non-census, secondary data sources.

International Issues 3.2

Sources of International Secondary Data

With the advent of electronic media, one can learn a great deal about international business opportunities and marketing tactics without leaving the office. Although armchair research techniques are no substitute for a trip to the region in question, they can yield valuable strategic and tactical information about your international competitors quickly, usually at minimal cost. The vast majority of newspapers and magazines now have online editions, typically searchable through major library databases or such private-party services as Google News.

In addition to newspapers and magazines, there are numerous other published research sources and techniques for conducting secondary research on foreign competitors. These include:

- *Corporate information databases.* Hundreds of foreign-produced databases are available online, either without cost or via subscription.

- *FAX, phone, e-mail, and Web chats.* Direct contact generates fast and accurate information. Foreign telephone directories are increasingly being made available online, although text searching in non-alphabetic languages (e.g., Mandarin) remains a stumbling block.
- *Foreign brokerage houses.* These firms specialize in specific regions of the world and produce analytical reports on companies in their home countries.
- *International ministries of commerce.* Foreign chambers of commerce often act as public relations offices for their mother countries, dispensing large quantities of company data.
- *The Library of Congress.* The section head for the country in question regularly tracks new sources of information, including those that are privately published, government-produced, or issued on a database.
- *Foreign trade organizations.* Organizations such as the Japanese External Trade Organization (JETRO) are engaged by both foreign corporations and their governments to promote their industries throughout the world, staffing local offices, publishing books, directories, and lists of companies with offices in the United States and around the globe. The Foreign Trade Information System offers a vast compendium of data and documents for firms operating internationally. The International Chamber of Commerce (ICC), the "voice of world business," promotes the global economy in general, assertively championing free global trade to world governments and providing a wide array of related information

The list of foreign intelligence-gathering sources and techniques is extensive, and the great majority can be accessed online. Some additional useful sources include:

- *MarketSearch, the International Directory of Published Market Research.* This continually updated searchable database provides more than 20,000 multiclient study references throughout the world.
- *Marketing Surveys Index (MSI).* This index includes virtually all international multiclient studies, from more than 1000 research publishers.
- *International Market Research Information (IMRI).* An online, searchable directory that aims to provide details of all major worldwide sources of market research information and expertise.
- *Quirks.com.* Maintains an updated list of international research organizations.
- *Regional directories.* Electronically available for most of the developed world, including essentially all of Europe and most of Asia and Latin America.

Summary

A research design is the basic plan that guides the data collection and analysis phases of the research project. Its purpose is to ensure that the information gathered is consistent with the research objectives and that the data collection and analysis phases involve accurate and economical procedures.

Exploratory research facilitates the development of hypotheses regarding the decision and problem definitions and identification of possible courses of action. Its design is characterized by its lack of structure and its flexibility; its strategy for data collection and analysis is to search for new or better ideas.

Conclusive research to evaluate possible courses of action can be sub-classified into descriptive and causal research. Descriptive research, which characterizes marketing phenomena, determines the association among variables or predicts future marketing phenomena. Effective descriptive research is marked by a clear statement of the decision problem, specific research objectives, and detailed information needs, and it is characterized by a carefully structured design, usually involving cross-sectional samples or surveys. When combined with the decision-maker's implicit model of how the marketing system functions, descriptive research can aid evaluations of possible courses of action. Appropriate design for research regarding cause-and-effect relationships varies substantially in complexity and in the degree of ambiguity present in the evidence regarding causality.

Performance-monitoring research provides evidence regarding performance measures and situational factors of the marketing system. Continuous performance monitoring requires a longitudinal research design, often called a panel design, in which a fixed sample is measured repeatedly across time.

The main sources of marketing data are respondents, analogous situations, experiments, and secondary data. Researchers obtain data from respondents through direct questioning; during surveys or focus group interviews; or observation of behavior through panels, checkout scanners, and online shopping activities. Analogous situations include case histories; investigations of situations relevant to a particular problem; and simulations, creating an analog or likeness of a real-world phenomenon. Experimentation permits relatively unambiguous statements regarding cause-and-effect relationships (compared with other data sources).

Secondary data are gathered from other research sources than the current project. These include internal data available within the organization and external data that are available through library or syndicated sources. Syndicated data services provide standardized data, including consumer, retail, wholesale, industry, advertising evaluation, media and audience, scanner data, Web server log, and Internet activity data. Library sources include an array of publicly circulated publications.

The first phase of data collection should involve a search of internal and external secondary data sources. Primary data sources should not be employed until after it is determined that appropriate data are not available from secondary data sources. The advantages of secondary data are their lower cost, quick retrieval, and extensive array of variables, compared with primary data. The disadvantages of secondary data are related to the accuracy of the data, which can often not be checked directly, and the degree of fit between the data and the information needs of the project.

Key Terms

accuracy (p. 64)
audience profiles (p. 63)
causal model (p. 64)
causal research (p. 63)
consumer profile (p. 63)
continuous performance measures (p. 66)
cross-sectional design (p. 64)
descriptive research (p. 63)
distribution research (p. 63)
endogeneity (p. 73)
focus group (p. 71)
geodemographic (p. 63)
hypothesis (p. 61)
longitudinal research design (p. 66)
market potential (p. 63)
market-share studies (p. 63)
normal viewing environment method (p. 76)
omnibus panel (p. 66)
panel (p. 66)
pricing research (p. 63)
psychographic (p. 63)
recruited audience method (p. 75)
reliability (p. 64)
response bias (p. 69)
sales analysis (p. 63)
sample (p. 64)
scenario analysis (p. 79)
segmentation (p. 69)
selection bias (p. 78)
sensitivity analysis (p. 72)
single source (p. 78)
survey research design (p. 64)
systematic error (p. 64)
traditional panel (p. 66)
units of analysis (p. 67)
unrepresentative sampling (p. 69)

Discussion Questions

1 Provide an example of a business situation in which a cross-sectional design could provide misleading results compared with a similar individual-level longitudinal study.

2 If you had to design research to examine consumer buying habits regarding various consumer goods and to develop hypotheses regarding the positioning of a particular brand, which syndicated data sources would be useful? Which specific firms might you consult?

3 What is the role of secondary data in the research process? What are the advantages and disadvantages of secondary data relative to primary data? How can they be used in concert to arrive at quicker, more accurate results than relying on either alone?

4 Using the most recent data published by the Bureau of the Census, compare the demographic characteristics of your county, your state, and the United States in general. Include analyses of total population, general level of education, income, and employment in each population unit. Write a short report describing how your county compares with your state and the nation, noting "significant" differences when applicable.

5 Using the U.S. Bureau of the Census's most recent edition of Census Tracts, report for the MSA of your choice. Compare the totals for the MSA with two tracts within the MSA. Select and compare two tracts that will provide significant contrasts in areas that interest you, such as ethnic make-up, age breakdowns, industries employing residents, education levels, income, or others. Provide a short report comparing the two tracts and the MSA for each area you studied, including appropriate graphical evidence.

6 MINICASE: You have been hired by an electronics automobile parts marketer to research the market in Europe for its products. The company has tentatively targeted SAAB and Volvo in Sweden, Fiat in Italy,

Renault in France, and Audi in Germany as its prime prospects. Outline an approach to the use of secondary data to help assist the marketers in the assessment of these markets.

Review Questions

1 Which of the following is an example of a research design?
   a using syndicated secondary data
   b setting up a consumer panel using UPC scanners
   c statistical analysis and modeling through an MDSS
   d identifying a plausible hypothesis regarding a marketing problem by interviewing experts

2 Which of the following is not a formal hypothesis?
   a Improving the quality of the product by using rubber instead of plastic will increase the percentage of repeat buyers by 20 percent.
   b A consumer panel will test how consumers respond to a 25 percent increase in advertising frequency.
   c A television campaign emphasizing the achievements of candidate X will result in an 8 percent boost in the polls.
   d Moving the root beer display nearer to the ice cream freezer will result in a sales increase of both products.

3 Research aimed at making predictions regarding the occurrence of marketing phenomena based on association between marketing variables is a form of:
   a descriptive research.
   b psychographic analysis.
   c causal research.
   d market potential study.

4 Cross-sectional design relates to longitudinal design in what way?
   a Sampling across one dimension of data gives a different result than across an orthogonal (i.e., uncorrelated) dimension.
   b Cross-sectional research cannot avail itself of certain statistical methods, such as clustering or ordinal regression.
   c Longitudinal samples (e.g., panels) provide information about the same group of units over a period of time.
   d Survey research focuses more on attitudinal issues than longitudinal panel research.

5 A causal model does what in marketing research?
   a It allows a cataloguing of sources of systematic response error.
   b It facilitates effective marketing choices by gathering evidence for conclusive research.
   c It provides a basis for hypotheses and a means of incorporating evidence toward arriving at a sound final decision.
   d It is the statistical analysis input into an MDSS.

6 A response bias is:
   a a bias a respondent has about the surveyor.
   b an error caused by people who are too mobile or well-off to be interested in panel inducements not being selected for the study.
   c also called a "mortality rate," resulting from members moving or losing interest or other forms of attrition.
   d a tendency, conscious or not, to mis-report the degree of the behavior being monitored.

7 On omnibus panel:
   a measures the *same* variables over time for a set of respondents.
   b measures *different* variables over time for a set of respondents.
   c provides suggestions for researchers about which questions are facilitating their marketing decision-making, and how to change them if not.
   d surveys the market potential for privately owned marketing firms and their syndicated data services.

8 When pre-testing commercial messages to be aired on television, which of these methods allows for immediate observation of participants' responses?

- **a** public opinion survey
- **b** diary panel
- **c** recruited-audience method
- **d** normal viewing environment method

9 Which of the following is not an advantage of the use of scanner panel data over other methods of consumer data collection?

- **a** accurate longitudinal histories of household purchases
- **b** allowance for shelf usage optimization
- **c** better tracking of consumer awareness and attitudes
- **d** full demographics of panel households

10 Suppose your research objective was to determine the potential market for a dog-themed work organizer. Specifically, you are to determine the probability that dog-owning office workers would purchase such an item. Which of the following pieces of secondary data would enable you to come up with such an estimate?

- **a** income profiles of dog-owning office workers
- **b** probability that a dog owner would buy such a product
- **c** probability that an office worker would buy such a product
- **d** all of the above
- **e** none of the above

Web Exercise

Log in to the Online Edition of your textbook at www.atomicdog.com to participate in this Web Exercise, which can be found in your Online Study Guide for this chapter.

Further Reading

Creswell, John W., 2002. *Research Design: Qualitative, Quantitative, and Mixed Methods Approaches*. Thousand Oaks, CA: SAGE Publications.

Laudon, Kenneth C. and Jane P., 1997. *Management Information Systems: New Approaches to Organization and Technology*. Upper Saddle River, NJ: Prentice-Hall.

Laudon, Kenneth C. and Jane P., 2003. *Management Information Systems*. Upper Saddle River, NJ: Prentice-Hall.

Maxwell, Joseph A., 2004. *Qualitative Research Design: An Interactive Approach (Applied Social Research Methods)*. Thousand Oaks, CA: SAGE Publications.

Patzer, Gordon L., 1995. *Using Secondary Data in Marketing Research*. Westport, CT: Quorum Books. Greenwood Publishing Group, Inc.

Smith, Robert B. *Handbook of Social Science Methods: Volume 3: Focused Survey Research and Causal Modeling*. Westport, CT: Praeger Publishers. Greenwood Publishing Group, Inc.

Social Science Research Methods Database. http://www.socialresearchmethods.net/

APPENDIX 3A: SYNDICATED SOURCES OF MARKETING DATA[1]

This appendix catalogs the leading syndicated sources of marketing data. For each service, a brief abstract is presented, as well as a URL, where available. Because of the fast-moving nature of syndicated services and the rapid evolution of Web-based databases, omissions and inaccuracies are inevitable. More detailed and contemporary information regarding a particular service can be obtained by contacting the organization directly.

The data services listed here are classified under the following headings:

A. Consumer Data: Purchase and Consumption Patterns
B. Consumer Data: Attitudes, Opinions, and Behavior Patterns
C. Retail Data
D. Media and Audience Data
E. Internet Data Collection
F. Do-It-Yourself Data Collection
G. Sites to Learn More

A. Consumer Data: Purchase and Consumption Patterns

GfK AG

GfK is among the largest market research firms in Europe, tracking consumer preferences through continuous surveys, retail sale analysis, and analysis of consumer purchase behavior and purchase decisions.

Company Web site: www.gfk.com

IMS Health

IMS Health is the leading market research company in the pharmaceutical and health care industries. The company collects its data by tracking sales of both prescription and over-the-counter products and surveying physicians and hospitals about which drugs they are prescribing. From this data, IMS Health is able to provide clients with market forecasts, sales territory reports, prescription tracking reports, and even the productivity of individual sales reps.

Company Web site: www.imshealth.com

NFO WorldGroup (A division of Taylor Nelson Sofres)

NFO WorldGroup is a leader in panel-based market research, as it maintains a panel of more than 500,000 households. Through polling this panel with both mail and telephone surveys, NFO is able to collect comprehensive data on consumer behavior, brand performance, and campaign effectiveness. To augment this panel, NFO collects data online, where it polls an additional 1 million homes.

Company Web site: www.tns-global.com/na

The NPD Group

The NPD Group is a marketing information company that measures consumer purchasing in a number of industries. The company is named after their National Purchase Diary (NPD) panel, which tracks consumer purchase behavior, distribution, and sales for a variety of non-packaged goods industries. NPD's research methods also include data collection from consumer panels, manufacturers' shipments, electronic feeds from cash registers, and the NPD Online panel, which has more than 2 million registered users.

Company Web site: www.npd.com

B. Consumer Data: Attitudes, Opinions, and Behavior Patterns

Harris Interactive

This market research and polling firm has moved extensively toward Internet-based surveys, although it still conducts research through traditional methods such as direct mail, telephone surveys, focus groups, and in-person interviews to gather information about the views, experiences, and attitudes of people worldwide. The firm is best known for their Harris Poll, which polls public opinion on various topics each week.

Company Web site: www.harrisinteractive.com

J.D. Power and Associates

J.D. Power and Associates is a marketing services company that conducts independent consumer surveys of product and service quality, customer satisfaction, and buyer behavior. From the results of these independent surveys, J.D. Power is able to award its well-known badges of excellence, which its top performers use in their advertising.

Company Web site: www.jdpower.com

Simmons Market Research Bureau

Simmons conducts market research measuring aspects such as product purchase, shopping, and media usage behavior of consumers. The majority of this data are collected through the company's annual Simmons National Consumer survey, which surveys more than 27,000 people and allows Simmons to produce demographic, psychographic, lifestyle, and attitudinal descriptions of consumers nationwide.

Company Web site: www.smrb.com

Taylor Nelson Sofres (TNS)

As the world's second-largest market research conglomerate, TNS collects market data from a number of sources, including television audience ratings, social and political polling, and surveys. Through this research, TNS provides insight to clients on matters such as market segmentation, advertising and communications, new product development, and brand performance.

Company Web site: www.tns-global.com

C. Retail Data

ACNielsen (Nielsen Rating Index)

ACNielsen's main role is collecting and compiling data from in-store audits and from sale points such as retail store scanners. With this data, ACNielsen is able to provide its clients with information on sales trends, market share, pricing, stock levels, and promotional effectiveness. ACNielsen also collects information on brand loyalty, purchases, and demographics through its consumer panel of more than 125,000 households in close to 20 countries.

Company Web site: www.acnielsen.com

Audits and Surveys Worldwide Inc.

Audits and Surveys Worldwide Inc. offers a specialized audit service called National Total Market. Through the service, Audit and Surveys provides retail sales, retail distribution, and retailer inventory for product categories such as food, tobacco, health, and beauty. Audit and Surveys also can provide clients with data on market size and market shares; sales by outlet type, region, and size of city; inventory levels; and percentage of distribution and out-of-stock situations.

Information Resources (Infoscan)

Information Resources provides census-based sales data for consumer packaged goods gathered from checkout scanners at 32,000 locations. IRI's census-based approach, where information is collected from every store within a particular retail chain rather than a sample of a few representative stores, sets the company apart in the industry. To supplement its scanner data, IRI also gathers data from its consumer panels of more than 50,000 households.

Company Web site: www.infores.com

D. Media and Audience Data

ACNielsen (Nielsen Media Research)

Nielsen Media Research is the top media researcher in the United States. Nielsen is most well-known for its television ratings, which it collects from a random sample of 5,000 U.S. households. These data are collected using a device called a people meter, which continuously monitors and records when a television set is turned on, what channels are being viewed, how much time is spent on each channel, and who is watching.

Company Web site: www.acnielsen.com

Arbitron Inc.

Arbitron is an international marketing research firm serving radio and TV broadcasters, cable companies, and advertising agencies. Arbitron collects data measuring statistics on not only what radio stations people are listening to or what TV channels they are watching, but also demographic information about those people, including income, lifestyles, and shopping habits.

Company Web site: www.arbitron.com

Mediamark Research, Inc.

A unit of the larger marketing research firm NOP World, Mediamark Research collects audience demographic data for media forms such as television, print, radio, and the Internet. Advertisers use this data to increase their ad's potential exposure to its intended audience.

Company Web site: www.mediamark.com

Ipsos

Ipsos conducts marketing research for print, radio, television, and online media. The company's main role is to gain insight into the tastes and behavior of customers. Ipsos gains this insight through syndicated surveys and ad hoc research. Additionally, Ipsos performs advertising pre-testing, brand tracking, and post-testing, and provides advertisers with information on how to best reach a target audience.

Company Web site: www.ipsos.com

Simmons Marketing Research Bureau

Simmons conducts market research measuring aspects such as product purchase, shopping, and media usage behavior of consumers. The majority of Simmons' media data are gathered through their Study of Media and Markets (SMM), which Simmons compiles after a series of interactions with respondents, including personal interviews, a self-administered questionnaire, and a personal viewing diary. From these interactions, Simmons is able to gather data on media exposure, as well as product-usage behavior.

Company Web site: www.smrb.com

E. Internet Data Collection

Greenfield Online

Greenfield Online provides online research and online data collection for some of the largest market research companies in the industry. Through surveys and its online panel of nearly 5 million people, Greenfield Online is able to collect demographic data, track brand awareness, measure consumer interest in products and services, and test new advertising campaigns.

Company Web site: www.greenfieldonline.com

Survey.com

Survey.com primarily focuses on Internet-based primary market research. They offer clients the full range of resources needed to conduct marketing research online: customized online survey programming, in-house data management and analysis, and comprehensive reporting solutions.

Company Web site: www.survey.com

The NPD Group

The NPD Group is a marketing information company that measures consumer purchasing in a number of industries. The company is named after their National Purchase Diary (NPD) panel, which tracks consumer purchase behavior, distribution, and sales for a variety of non-packaged goods industries. NPD's research methods also include data collection from consumer panels, manufacturers' shipments, electronic feeds from cash registers, and the NPD Online panel, which has more than 2 million registered users.

Company Web site: www.npd.com

Westat Inc.

Westat Inc. provides survey and statistical research services for businesses and government agencies. One of the company's most popular services is the development and operation of Internet sites that allow clients to disseminate survey and statistical information, thereby simplifying the data-collection process.

Company Web site: www.westat.com

F. Do-It-Yourself Data Collection

MarketTools Inc.

MarketTools provides online applications that gather and analyze information about customers and business. One of the company's most popular products is its Zoomerang software, which allows customers to create and distribute their own surveys and therefore collect very focused marketing data.

Company Web site: www.markettools.com

WebSurveyor Corporation

WebSurveyor provides clients with software and Internet hosting services. Through these offerings, WebSurveyor's clients gain the ability to administer online surveys and gather important business insights.

Company Web site: www.websurveyor.com

G. Sites to Learn More

American Marketing Association

The American Marketing Association offers tools such as marketing best practices and research studies and job resources to its more than 38,000 members. The site also offers an extremely comprehensive directory of the top marketing research and marketing services companies.

Web site: www.marketingpower.com

Bradford's Directory of Marketing Research Agencies and Management Consultants in the U.S. and the World

This directory of marketing research agencies lists not only some of the top research firms in the world, but also includes a list of officers and scope of activity for each company.

Honomichl List

Also found through the American Marketing Association is the Honomichl List. The Honomichl List, compiled annually by the AMA, lists the 25 largest global marketing research companies, as well as the 50 largest U.S. marketing research firms. Included in each list is an abstract discussing each of the companies' roles in the industry.

Web site: www.marketingpower.com

KnowThis.com

KnowThis.com is one of the leading Web resource and reference sites for all marketers; it provides tools for business professionals, academics, and students. One of the most valuable resources offered by

KnowThis.com is their Marketing Virtual Library, which is a collection of marketing-related Web sites updated frequently and maintained by industry experts.

Web site: www.KnowThis.com

Quirks.com

Quirks.com is a companion to *Quirk's Marketing Research Review* magazine, which is printed monthly. Through an article archive of more than 1000 cases, a comprehensive directory of custom research providers, and a number of other marketing tools, Quirks.com is a top provider of marketing resources online.

Website: www.Quirks.com

APPENDIX 3B: LIBRARY SOURCES OF MARKETING DATA[1]

The purpose of this appendix is to catalog the predominant library sources of marketing data and to identify the main guides to and databases of marketing data. In this text, a syndicated source is defined as one that is specialized information at a deeper level of detail and is often costly. The sources listed in this appendix are library sources; they are generally reasonably priced, are often found in university and larger public libraries, and are sometimes purchased by corporate libraries. Some sources build on government data, whereas others bring together different kinds of information for convenience.

For each listing, the name of the publication, the publisher and Web site if available, and a brief description are presented. Web site links sometimes go directly to the source,* other times to a publisher link to descriptive information about the source. Watch for additional relevant resources available on publisher Web sites. Check your library's catalog or consult a librarian for availability of the actual source if a URL is not included here. Because of the ever-changing nature of information sources, some information and links may have changed. More contemporary information regarding a particular data source, as well as information on additional sources, can be obtained from a reference librarian.

A note on international sources: If a source is devoted to a particular country or region, it is listed in a separate section. Otherwise, international sources are included in various sections where appropriate. Many sources include international as well as domestic information.

Electronic Information Sources

In recent years, business information has become available in a variety of formats in addition to paper. These formats include electronic (online), optical media (CD and DVD ROM), and magnetic tape, although its use is waning. Many libraries of all types now offer access to resources in various formats.

Many sources are available in more than one format. Publisher Web sites listed in this appendix identify formats. Among online resources are those searched through the World Wide Web. Some databases are currently available online but not through the web, but this is subject to change. Web search engines such as Google have become very popular, and they are often a good starting point for any timely information search. It is important to researchers to note that not all pertinent information is available electronically through search engines because a great deal of marketing research is locked into subscription services. Users of search engines must also consider the source when retrieving and evaluating Web

---

*Titles where the Web site link goes to actual data or to full publication text are marked with an asterisk.

information. Is the Web information being issued by an individual who has set up his or her own Web site or by an established database vendor?

A variety of information of interest to business is available in electronic format, including articles; consumer, business, and economic data; industry information; market research; and guides to finding sources. The rise of the availability of international business information has been significant in recent years, and it will develop rapidly as much of the world industrializes.

Many database vendors offer more than one database. One advantage is that search techniques are, where possible, similar across databases, putting the learning curve at the user's advantage. Among the vendors offering access to multiple business-related databases are Dialog Information Services (www.dialog.com), ProQuest Co. (www.proquest.com), and Thomson (www.thomson.com). Vendors usually have customer service departments that offer the user good search support. Search techniques for online databases are getting progressively more user-friendly, but it is often useful for the searcher to take one of the search courses offered by librarians or database vendors to learn how to search files that are not menu-driven. Additional database vendors of note: (Financial): Dun & Bradstreet (www.dnb.com/US/), Mergent (www.mergent.com); (Economic) Economist Intelligence Unit (www.eiu.com); (Company) Hoover's (www.hoovers.com).

Among the useful sources of current information available on databases in all formats is *The Gale Directory of Databases* (Thomson Gale, www.gale.com) and *Fulltext Sources Online* (Information Today, Inc., www.infotoday.com).

Guides to Business Literature Sources

These sources either contain sections or materials on marketing or are devoted to the topic.

Business Information: How to Find It, How to Use It, Michael R. Lavin, ed. (Greenwood Publishing Group, www.greenwood.com, 1992). A still useful, unique source that combines basic concepts of how to use business information sources with detailed descriptions of hundreds of business publications. It includes sections on how to research a company, how to use statistical information, and how to do research on a particular discipline such as consumer research or labor law.

Encyclopedia of Business Information Sources (Thomson Gale, www.gale.com). Arranged by subject (industry, business function, other topics), this source lists a wide variety of sources, including periodicals, statistics sources, directories, bibliographies, general works, research centers, and databases.

Strauss's Handbook of Business Information: A Guide for Librarians, Students and Researchers (Libraries Unlimited, www.lu.com, 2004). Gives descriptive information on a large number of key business publications. The first section covers general titles according to format, such as guides, directories, government documents, and loose-leaf services. The second section focuses on specific fields of business, including marketing. Background discussions on each discipline are included. A source like this would be useful as part of a personal business reference collection.

Washington Researchers (www.washingtonresearchers.com). This group publishes a variety of guides to often hard-to-find information about companies and industries, which are topics of interest to marketers. Both standard and little-known resources are included. Among currently available titles are *Researching Global Firms, Researching Divisions, Subsidiaries and Products, and Researching Private Companies.*

Marketing Information, A Professional Reference Guide. 3d ed. Jack L. Goldstucker and Hiram C. Barksdale, eds. (Georgia State University Business Press, 1995). A still valuable, book-length guide devoted to the marketing field. Material is organized under 27 current subject areas, such as services marketing, health care marketing, and non-profit marketing. Books, periodicals, and other information sources are presented for each category. Lists marketing associations and organizations by subject and location, and details other sources, such as libraries, government agencies, and private research and consulting companies.

International Business Information: How to Find It, How to Use It. Ruth A. Pagell and Michael Halperin. (Greenwood Publishing Group, www.greenwood.com, 1998). The growth of the global economy has prompted the growth of information in the international business area. This source is similar in approach and organization to the Lavin book described previously. Major sources are described in detail.

World Directory of Marketing Information Sources (Euromonitor International, www.euromonitor.com). A list of sources without any background text on the topic. Good for locating possible contacts for specialized as well as more general information in that it lists major business libraries, leading market research publications and companies, and online databases. Detailed information for each listing includes some information on activities and publications.

Databases

See Web sites for information on additional databases of interest to businesses and marketers. Databases contain newspaper, journal, and magazine articles; government publications; research reports; and other types of publications.

ABI/Inform Global (ProQuest, www.proquest.com). This database includes a wide variety of academic and industry-oriented business periodical literature, as well as full-text access to selected newspapers and other resources.

Business & Company Resource Center (Thomson Gale, www.gale.com). This database conveniently brings together company profiles, brand information, rankings, investment reports, company histories, chronologies, and periodicals. Search this database using a company name, ticker symbol, industry code or description, geographic location, or personal name.

Business Source Complete (Ebsco, www.epnet.com/academic/default.asp). This database contains more than 2000 full-text scholarly journals and business periodicals covering management, economics, finance, accounting, and international business. The database also includes country economic reports from the EIU, WEFA, ICON Group, and CountryWatch. This database is similar in scope to ABI/Inform Global, and they are often used together.

Factiva.com (Joint venture of Dow Jones and Reuters, www.proquest.com). This database offers company and industry financial data and news stories, as well as full-text articles in 6000 trade publications, newspapers, newswires, and magazines. This source is of interest to researchers in marketing and economics as well as finance.

LexisNexis Academic (LexisNexis, www.lexisnexis.com). This database contains full-text business and legal articles, legal cases, reports, and documents from numerous sources.

Guides to Finding Statistics

Guides

*Census Catalog** (U.S. Bureau of the Census, www.census.gov; click on Catalog or Publications). A comprehensive annotated guide to U.S. Census Bureau publications, including data files and special tabulations. Publications cover agriculture, foreign trade, governments, population, and the economic censuses, as well as retail trade, wholesale trade, service industries, construction industries, manufacturers, mineral industries, and transportation. Also listed are materials available in non-print formats (such as CD-ROM), as well as special tabulations.

*Guide to Foreign Trade Statistics** (U.S. Bureau of the Census www.census.gov/foreign-trade/guide/). A guide to primarily monthly and annual foreign trade statistics. Includes descriptions of Bureau of the Census publications dealing with foreign trade and sample tables.

Statistics Sources (Thomson Gale, www.gale.com). A worldwide subject guide to business, industrial, financial, social, and other topics. Detailed sub-headings are used under each subject to aid in fast location of sources.

Guides with Statistics

American Statistics Index: A Comprehensive Guide and Index to the Statistical Publications of the U.S. Government (LexisNexis, www.lexisnexis.com). A guide to the statistical publications of federal government agencies, Congress, and other organizations. A typical abstract includes a complete description of the data given. Material is indexed according to subject, author, title, report number, demographic, or other category. Related titles include *Statistical Reference Index* (private publisher and state government data) and *Index to International Statistics* (international data).

Statistical Abstract of the United States* (U.S. Bureau of the Census www.census.gov/statab/www/). This valuable publication is a basic reference for individuals searching for secondary data. Includes more than 1400 tables, presenting social, economic, political, and demographic data. The tables serve as both an abstract and reference for data available in other published sources. For many researchers, this publication is the initial reference in their search for external secondary data.

Market Share Reporter (Thomson Gale, www.gale.com). This source brings hard-to-locate, detailed, market share data together in one source. It is both an information source and a guide, in that each table gives the source of the data for further reference. Often these sources are published on a regular basis, sometimes making older or more recent data easier to find. Covers companies, products, and services.

*Fedstats** (www.fedstats.gov). Links to statistics on a variety of topics available through U.S. government agencies, with links to particular agencies. Links to data on states, counties, cities. Also links to published collections of statistics available online.

International (Country) Information

Sources in this section contain data for countries. Other international sources are listed elsewhere in this appendix.

International Marketing Data and Statistics (Euromonitor International, www.euromonitor.com). Includes current and historical statistical data on countries in Asia, Africa, Oceania, and the Americas. Topics covered include demographic trends and forecasts, economic indicators, trade, consumer expenditures and markets, retailing, and advertising. A companion volume by the same publisher, *European Marketing Data and Statistics*, covers essentially the same topics.

Consumer International (Euromonitor International, www.euromonitor.com). Focuses on product data; gives sales figures for numerous products for various countries. Statistics here are similar to data found in Global Market Information Database. There are other titles in this "Consumer" series, covering Europe, Western Europe, China, Latin America, and the Middle East.

ISI Emerging Market Database (ISI Emerging Markets, www.securities.com). Rapidly growing database of company, industry, macroeconomic, and other information on numerous emerging market countries. Often contains unique information not found elsewhere because of the specialized nature of the resources included.

The following are Census Bureau and United Nations Web sites that provide demographic, social, and economic information and data by country:

*International Database** www.census.gov/ipc/www/idbnew.html
*International Statistical Agencies** www.census.gov/main/www/stat_int.html
*United Nations Statistical Databases** unstats.un.org/unsd/databases.htm

Market Guides and Data

These sources include sales, retail, and other business information, as well as some demographics. For additional demographic sources, see the Consumer Demographics section that follows.

Market Guide (Editor and Publisher, www.editorandpublisher.com). Contains data for 1500 U.S. and Canadian newspaper markets. Data include principal industries, population, transportation facilities, households, banks, and retail outlets. Includes estimates based on government data.

Rand McNally Commercial Atlas and Marketing Guide (Rand McNally Company, www.randmcnally.com). Contains detailed statistics for countries, cities, MSAs, and principal business centers. Covers trade, manufacturing, transportation, population, and related data. Each state section includes maps and some business data for countries and cities.

*Registration Data.** A wide variety of registration data is collected by government. Typically, this information is difficult and inconvenient to locate and acquire. Examples are automobile and boat registrations; licenses for business activities; data on births, deaths, and marriages; income tax returns; and school enrollments. See firstgov.gov for links to federal, state, and local government sites.

Sales and Marketing Management (V N U Business Publications, www.vnubusinessmedia.com). The "Survey of Buying Power" issue of this magazine contains data on population, effective buying income, and retail sales for U.S. markets, as well as comparable data for Canada.

Consumer Demographics

There are numerous publishers of consumer data. Much of this data are reported by geographic area, but there are also more general data. As mentioned earlier, non-government publishers often build on existing census data, adding more recent data and additional data, such as forecasts.

Government Sources

The Census Bureau is a major issuer of consumer related data. Users can access this useful information through the www.census.gov and the easy-to-use *American Factfinder** Web site (factfinder.census.gov). This site covers the decennial census that counts population and housing units, the annual American Community Survey and the Annual Population Estimates series (both in part update the decennial census), and material from the Economic Census. The Census Bureau publishes data in paper form also, such as *County and City Data Book** (www.census.gov/statab/www/ccdb.html).

*Census of Population and Housing** (U.S. Bureau of the Census, www.census.gov/prod/www/abs/decennial/index.htm). This Web site covers detailed demographic population and housing characteristics for census tracts, block numbering areas, and congressional districts. It also includes summary population and housing characteristics and housing unit counts. Updated information is available at these census sites: www.census.gov/population/www/ and www.census.gov/hhes/www/housing.html.

There are also census Web sites that lead quickly to demographic data, such as:

*State and County QuickFacts** quickfacts.census.gov/qfd/index.html
*Population** www.census.gov/prod/www/abs/popula.html

The U.S. Bureau of Labor Statistics issues the Consumer Expenditure Survey* (www.bls.gov/cex/). Conducted for the Bureau of Labor Statistics by the Census Bureau, this source provides detailed data on expenditure and buying habits for families and single consumers.

Non-government Sources

Community Sourcebook of Zip Code Demographics (ESRI Business Information Solutions, www.esribis.com). ZIP codes are arranged first by state, then numerically within each state, with total population, population profile, housing profile, and income and employment statistics for each ZIP code. It also provides the Market Potential Index, which measures the propensity of the residences of a particular ZIP code to purchase goods in one of 13 categories of goods and services. The same publisher also issues *Community Sourcebook of County Demographics*.

Demographics USA, Zip Edition (Trade Dimensions International, www.tradedimensions.com). This publication is similar in scope to the *Community Sourcebook of Zip Code Demographics*. There is also a County Edition.

Lifestyle Market Analyst (Standard Rate & Data Service, www.srds.com). This publication provides lifestyle data for cities not easily found elsewhere. Included are data on such topics as hobbies and interests, travel habits, high-tech activities, sports, and fitness interests. Also included is a profile for each lifestyle activity, such as the demographic and lifestyle characteristics of those who donate to charitable causes.

Business and Industry Data

Government Sources

The Economic Census series from the U.S. Census Bureau profiles the U.S. economy from the national to the local level. This census series is taken every 5 years, in years ending with 2 and 7. Various census publications serve to in part update these reports. For information on and links to the Economic Census, see www.census.gov/prod/www/abs/02index.html. In addition to the Web sites listed here, as mentioned previously, Economic Census data is also available at the Census Bureau's American Factfinder* (factfinder.census.gov).

*Census of Construction Industries** (U.S. Bureau of the Census, www.census.gov/prod/www/abs/construction-ind2002.html). This census outlines number of establishments, receipts, employment, and payments for materials. Area statistics reports cover states. Interim census reports (actual data) that update in part the Census of Construction Industries include such sites as Current Construction Reports: Housing Starts* (www.census.gov/prod/www/abs/c20.html) and Current Construction Reports: Housing Completions* (www.census.gov/prod/www/abs/c22.html).

*Census of Manufactures** (U.S. Bureau of the Census, www.census.gov/prod/www/abs/manu-min.html). Manufacturing establishments are categorized under approximately 450 industries. Statistics are provided on number and size of establishments; capital expenditures; quantity of output; inventories;

employment; payroll; and consumption of fuel, materials, and energy. Additional reports cover special subjects, such as concentration ratios and plant and equipment expenditures. Separate state reports provide a geographic approach to the data. Interim census reports (actual data) that in part update the Census of Manufactures include *Annual Survey of Manufactures** (www.census.gov/mcd/asmhome.html) and the Current Industrial Reports* (www.census.gov/cir/www/).

*Census of Retail Trade** (U.S. Bureau of the Census, www.census.gov/prod/www/abs/retail-a.html and www.census.gov/prod/www/abs/retail-geo.html). This census contains information on about 100 kind-of-business classifications. Statistics are available on number of establishments, total sales, and sales by merchandise lines, size of firm, employment, and payroll for states, MSAs, counties, and cities of 2500 or more. Interim census resources (actual data) that update in part the Census of Retail Trade can be found at www.census.gov/econ/www/retmenu.html.

*Census of Transportation** (U.S. Bureau of the Census, www.census.gov/prod/www/abs/transpor.html). This report provides a summary of establishment-based statistics for selected transportation industries. Additional census publications on transportation (actual data) can be found at www.census.gov/prod/www/abs/transpor.html.

*Census of Wholesale Trade** (U.S. Bureau of the Census, www.census.gov/prod/www/abs/whsale-a.html and www.census.gov/prod/www/abs/whsale-geo.htm). This publication presents data on more than 100 kind-of-business classifications. Statistics are available on the number of establishments, sales, personnel, and payroll for states, MSAs, counties, and cities. Interim census resources (actual data) that update in part the Census of Wholesale Trade can be found at www.census.gov/econ/www/retmenu.html.

*County Business Patterns** (U.S. Bureau of the Census, censtats.census.gov/cbpnaic/cbpnaic.shtml). This report presents a county breakdown of business by type, employment, and payroll. The data can be used to develop industrial market potential studies. There is a separate report for each state as well as one for the United States.

Non-government Sources

CRB Commodity Yearbook (Wiley, www.wiley.com). This publication contains data on production, prices, consumption, and import and export flow for approximately 100 individual commodities.

Manufacturing and Distribution USA: Industry Analyses, Statistics and Leading Companies (Thomson Gale, www.gale.com). This covers almost 500 manufacturing industries for such areas as leading companies, materials consumer, industry data by state, employment, compensation, production, and establishment statistics.

Standard & Poor's Industry Surveys (Standard & Poor's, www.standardandpoors.com). Use this source as an introduction to a major industry. It covers about 70 major domestic industries, arranged into about 40 major industry groups. Text and summary statistics are part of a basic analysis for each group. Regular updates are provided. It includes discussion of current situation, recent trends, and outlook. The basic analysis includes financial data allowing comparison of major companies within an industry.

At this writing, the U.S. Department of Commerce is working on a Web version of their popular publication, *U.S. Industry and Trade Outlook*. A start date for availability of the Web version is uncertain. This source was last published in 2000 (paper form). It is often used along with *Standard & Poor's Industry Surveys* when a researcher seeks some general introductions to industries.

Market Research

Selected Databases

Investext Plus (Thomson Gale, www.gale.com). This database provides thousands of investment, company, and industry analyst reports in full-text format from more than 500 brokers worldwide. In general, reports cover 1982 to present. Content is often unique and can be useful as market research reports.

Global Market Information Database (Euromonitor International, www.euromonitor.com). This database offers extensive industry, demographic, consumer, and economic data for numerous countries worldwide. GMID includes market, demographic, and economic forecast data to 2010, as well as market data for 330 consumer products in 49 countries. The database includes full-text market analysis reports on a wide variety of topics.

MarketResearch.com Academic (www.marketresearch.com). This database provides access to the full text of market research reports. Coverage is international. Topics cover a range of areas, including business services, consumer goods, food and beverages, life sciences, demographics, heavy industry, and technology/media. The 550 full reports are often quite lengthy; these reports are at least 1 year old. The 250 MarketLooks reports are 15–30 page summaries of reports and are more current. Overall, coverage begins with 1994 material.

Market Research Library (www.export.gov/marketresearch.html). This database contains market research reports and country commercial guides from the U.S. Commercial Service, Department of Commerce.

Guides to Locating Reports

Mindbranch (www.mindbranch.com)
Marketsearch Directory (www.marketsearch-dir.com)
ECNext Knowledge Center (www.ecnext.com/commercial/index.shtml)

Trade Associations

Encyclopedia of Associations (Thomson Gale, www.gale.com). This publication covers U.S., international, and U.S. regional/state/local organizations. It lists active trade, business, professional, and other national organizations; each entry briefly describes the organization's activities and lists available publications. These organizations often prove to be sources of hard-to-find data on industries and other topics. If they cannot provide an answer, they are often able to refer the researcher to a more promising source.

Market Research Firms

*Green Book: International Directory of Marketing Research Houses and Services** (New York AMA Communication Services Inc., www.greenbook.org). An alphabetical listing of marketing research houses in the United States and some foreign countries. Each entry describes available services. Firms are also listed by geographic location.

Advertising and Promotion Data

Advertising Age (Crain Communication, Inc., www.crain.com). In addition to serving as a premier advertising industry newspaper, *Ad Age* publishes a number of special issues of interest to marketers. Special issues include "Agency Report Profiles," providing billing figures and information on accounts won and lost; and "Top 100 National Advertisers," giving for each, data on advertising expenditures, sales and profits, rank of leading product line and brands, market share, sales, and advertising personnel. Also publishes "Top 100 Leading Media Companies" with data on U.S. media revenue.

Advertising Red Books (LexisNexis, www.lexisnexis.com/redbooks). This well-known series includes information on U.S. and worldwide advertising agencies: agency officers, accounts, annual billings, area of specialty. It also covers U.S. and foreign advertisers, including data on ad expenditures, media used, ad agency, and other key data.

Standard Rate and Data Service, Inc. (SRDS, www.srds.com). Provides current advertising rates and related data for U.S. radio and TV stations, consumer magazines, business publications, newspapers, and other media. Some market data included in the ratio, TV, and newspaper volumes. The SRDS is considered a standard source of cost estimation for media planning. Company Web sites also often provide advertising rates.

World Advertising Trends (World Advertising Research Center, www.warc.com). After some worldwide summary data, most of this source gives advertising data by medium. Data are arranged by country. Historical data are included to aid in examining growth trends.

Advertising Growth Trends (Schonfeld & Associates Inc., www.saiBooks.com). Search by industry code to find advertising data for selected companies within the industry. This source gives ad spending for each of the past 5 years. It also provides the percent share of advertising the company expended in relation to the total spending by its competitors, plus additional data. There is also some industry summary data.

Note

1 The authors wish to acknowledge the invaluable assistance of Nancy S. Karp, Senior Reference Librarian at the Stephen M. Ross School of Business, University of Michigan, in preparing this chapter and these appendices.

CASES FOR PART ONE

CASE 1.1 FRESH IMPRESSIONS—NUTRITIONAL LABELING

Jose Martinez was the president of Middle America Research (MAR). He was in the process of preparing a marketing research proposal for Fresh Impressions, a large midwestern supermarket chain. Fresh Impressions' market share had been declining steadily for the past year and a half, and the marketing department was determined to turn things around. The senior members in the department had formulated a plan, but they needed marketing research data to verify the plan's validity to other Fresh Impressions departments. MAR was one of three major marketing research firms vying for this research project. The completed research proposal was due in 2 weeks.

Martinez had had a meeting with Fresh Impressions' marketing department earlier in the month to roughly define the purpose of the project. Michelle Stead, vice president in charge of marketing at Fresh Impressions, had not outlined the specific information needs; rather, she had gone over the problems facing Fresh Impressions. She had indicated to Martinez that it would be up to him to formulate research objectives based on his perception of the information needs.

Stead told him that Fresh Impressions' sales had been increasing at a slower pace than its competitors' and that Fresh Impressions wanted to reverse this trend through "goodwill gestures" aimed at consumers. The tentative plan was to provide shoppers with detailed nutritional information about the packaged foods sold in Fresh Impressions stores. But Fresh Impressions executives were not sure exactly how the information should be presented to consumers, how the consumers would react to it, or even whether the consumers would use the information. Because of these concerns, initiation of the program had been delayed until consumers' attitudes could be researched.

Bart Russell, Fresh Impressions' district manager for Illinois and Indiana, foresaw several potential problems with the proposed "solution." First of all, he told Martinez, stores would be reluctant to post information that might cut their profits. Because many of the high-margin items were also the least nutritious, consumers might avoid the nonnutritious—but highly profitable—foods if nutritional information were available. Second, the cost to provide this information would be high unless the stores were subsidized by the Fresh Impressions main office. The majority of Fresh Impressions' stores could not afford to offer additional services to shoppers without boosting prices. But, said Russell, store managers would furnish nutritional information readily if they were shown that the cost of providing this information would be offset by the benefits gained if more people began shopping at Fresh Impressions. The marketing department hoped that presenting favorable marketing research results to the store managers would make them more willing to accept the idea of forgoing some short-term profits for long-range benefits.

The nutritional information had already been gathered by Fresh Impressions, so the only cost to the individual stores would come from disseminating these data to consumers. The information had, for the most part, been obtained from outside sources. For 85 percent of all products, the required nutritional information had been collected from the manufacturers—either directly from the food labels or in response to a written request. For another 9 percent of the products, Fresh Impressions managers had weighed the contents of the packages and combined that data with information from the manufacturers, or from the U.S. Department of Agriculture, to determine the nutrient content of the foods. For the remaining 6 percent, Fresh Impressions could not acquire nutritional information. Most of these foods were "mixed" foods with low sales volume, such as frozen mixed vegetables or multipacks of single-serving breakfast cereals.

Fresh Impressions executives from other (nonmarketing) departments had indicated a willingness to help stores implement the nutrition-information program, but only if marketing research showed that:

1. Shoppers would actually benefit from the information.
2. They would make use of the information.

Even if sales did not increase right away, Fresh Impressions' top management felt that providing this extra service to consumers would benefit Fresh Impressions in the long run by increasing customer loyalty.

Because this project was such a major undertaking, Martinez spent a great deal of time conversing with Stead, as she would be very influential in choosing which company got the research grant. Martinez wanted to be absolutely certain that he had enough information to identify the problem areas Fresh Impressions was most concerned with so that he could define the research objectives correctly. Stead had not set an upper limit on the project's budget, but Martinez wanted to keep it at a reasonable level so as to remain competitive. In the end, though, he knew that the quality of his research proposal would determine whether MAR would be awarded the project.

Case Questions

1 Translate the problems stated by the Fresh Impressions executives into specific project objectives and information needs. What kind of questions should be asked to determine each of these?

2 Is it necessary for the research firm to know who the decision-maker is in the Fresh Impressions organization? Why or why not? Identify the decision-maker in this case.

3 Considering the project objectives and information needs, identify appropriate data sources for this study. State the criteria for your selection, as well as what you anticipate learning from each.

4 Based on your answers to the previous questions, prepare a research proposal for this study.

5 If Martinez is assigned this study, what are the issues he should consider when selecting the research sample? What are your recommendations regarding each of the issues you listed?

6 What research errors should Martinez avoid? How might they be categorized? Finally, what should Martinez do to avoid them? Be specific.

7 What factors should Martinez examine to identify whether this is a "pseudo-research" project? Provide an example of the probable incentives beyond the pseudo-nature of the project. If the project does appear to be pseudo-research, how should Martinez proceed? Should the project be undertaken at all?

8 According to the American Marketing Association's code of ethics for marketing research (see Chapter 1) and given the objectives of the project, what practices should be clearly avoided by Martinez and the decision-maker within the Fresh Impressions company? Are there any practices that seem unadvisable, even though they may not be explicitly prohibited by the ethics codes?

CASE 1.2 OBERON FOOD COMPANY

The following episodes explore the complexities of relationships between research and management. As described in Chapter 2, lack of communication, miscommunications, misunderstandings, conflicts between various personal and organizational goals, and differences in perspective concerning professional roles can affect the day-to-day workings of a research project; these miscues can also go so far as to undermine the success of the project. For each of these episodes, consider what is actually going on in the dynamics between people and roles in the organization. Do the relations between researchers and managers facilitate effective research? What is working, and what is undermining research? What could be done differently to improve the situation? Which of these suggestions can be generalized into principles for establishing effective research-management relationships in an organization?

Episode A

Tom Murphy, director of research for the Oberon Food Company, has been striving to establish a cordial relationship with the advertising department for several months. He feels that the research department can supply very useful information regarding the advertising programs of the Oberon Food Company.

In response to these efforts, Samantha Jones, the advertising manager, called Murphy, asking for help in developing a new advertising program. "We need to know customers' perceptions, attitudes, and preferences toward our new line of diet products."

Murphy initiates and personally directs an extensive research study on the diet product line. Seven weeks later, a thorough report and presentation on current users' attitudes, perceptions, and preference patterns is presented to Jones and her staff. After the presentation, Jones's reaction is: "Certainly a lot of interesting data that we weren't aware of; but how does this help us design a new advertising campaign to switch buyers from competitive diet lines to ours and entice potential dieters to try our line?"

Episode B

Jane Phelps, product manager for Oberon's "Magic" scouring pads, calls on Tom Murphy, director of research, to discuss a problem she has. "Good to see you again, Tom. As you know, sales volume on 'Magic' has not reached the targeted market share. We are seven points off target. I feel it is time to do some research on this problem. It's obvious to me that the culprit is our package design. We just don't catch the eye of the consumer like SOS does. Also, the package does a poor job in conveying the product concept and our point of difference from SOS."

Murphy concurs with Phelps that the packaging is poorly done and that the research department could provide useful information concerning the selection of a new package design.

He goes on to say, "This type of problem lends itself to controlled experimentation very well. As you know, Barbara Kindle is an expert on experimental design and would be delighted to develop a research proposal that would get right at this problem."

Phelps reacts:	Sounds excellent to me. Can you have a proposal put together by Thursday?
Murphy replies:	I'll have to check with Barbara first; but let's plan on a Thursday afternoon meeting in conference room C.
Phelps:	That's great. I know I can always count on the cooperation of the research department.

Episode C

Tom Murphy, director of research, cautious about vaguely stated research study objectives, has been impressing on a senior staff member, Sid Alsen, the need for clearly written research proposals including management objectives, information requirements, and anticipated uses of expected results.

During their conversation, Murphy receives a call from the marketing department asking for a research staff member to participate in a planning meeting where research needs will be discussed. Murphy tells Alsen about the call and suggests that he attend the meeting. Before leaving, Murphy advises Alsen: "Be sure to develop a careful specification of how the information required will be used."

Later in the afternoon, Sid returns from the meeting thoroughly defeated. "They told me it wasn't any of my business what they were going to do with the information. We are just supposed to get it and they will decide what to do with it." Murphy tells Alsen not to give up yet, because he still has some political capital to spend on behalf of the research department. A new vice president was brought on board recently, whom Murphy knows to have an adequate understanding of the nature and role of marketing research. Murphy is uncertain how much pull the VP has in the marketing department at this point, but thinks he may be able to exert some influence. He pauses to ask Alsen how Alsen reacted during the meeting.

Episode D

Ellen Tod, senior research analyst, reviews the marketing plan for the instant potato line and reports to her manager, Tom Murphy: "If they had paid any attention to my research report they wouldn't be doing these things. They must be fools up there; why, I could run that program better!"

Murphy later receives a call from the planning manager, telling him: "If that analyst [Ellen Tod] can't just report the facts and stop trying to make us look silly, we would rather do without her!"

In an attempt to resolve the conflict, Murphy arranges formal interviews with both the analyst and the planning manager to ascertain the facts of what happened. Tod points out that the decision criteria developed before the research results clearly required a different course of action than that currently enacted by the planning manager. She expresses frustration at wasting 6 months on a research project that is being ignored. She is convinced that the research department as a whole will lose credibility in the company this way. The planning manager considers the decision criteria absurd and refuses to consider them. He admits to attending the meeting where the decision criteria were designed, but says that they were just "playing with numbers." On further questioning, he reveals that the current plan was the brainchild of a top executive who was not in attendance at this meeting.

Episode E

The following dialog takes place between a product manager, Jim Phiel, and Ellen Tod, senior research analyst.

Tod: I understand you are interested in a consumer test on product C-11.

Phiel: Yes, we definitely need to get some good market feedback.

Tod: What will you do if the results are favorable?

Phiel: National introduction, of course. This product has a great future.

Tod: What if the results are negative?

Phiel: Don't worry about that. I know C-11 will be accepted with enthusiasm.

Tod: But what happens if your expectations are wrong?

Phiel: Look, if you design a good test, we won't have any problems. There are a lot of hopes riding on the success of this product, and we need some good information behind it.

Tod: You do understand that going into a research project with a predetermined outcome renders the research unnecessary and its results meaningless, don't you?

Phiel: We're just following proper procedures. It's part of our job. Your job is to back us up with good research.

CASE 1.3 FIELD MODULAR OFFICE FURNITURE

Introduction

Jane Donne, product manager for Field Modular Office Furniture, one product line of the office furniture division of Stone Corporation, was discussing ways to expand sales with one of the summer interns. The Field line was currently focused on panel technology for office buildings, but Jane was looking for new markets. The new product intern, Cindy Cole, had recently earned her M.B.A., and was eager to put her newfound knowledge to work in the field.

Jane had long felt that sales of panel technology and modular furniture in office buildings were approaching saturation point. Modular furniture and panels allow construction of cubicles and the division of open spaces, and are easily reconfigured for design changes. Field needed to expand into other markets. Cindy's assignment for the summer had been to conduct preliminary research and identify promising areas for further research. The presentation of her ideas had gone well, and Jane had invited Cindy to her office to discuss the action plan.

"Cindy, this is a great report. I think you've done an excellent job in identifying areas where Field may have an advantage. I was especially interested in this section on day-care centers . . . no, that's not the official name . . . early childhood institutions (ECIs). With the increase in working mothers and working hours, their enrollments must be skyrocketing. I know our corporate center is furnished with the panels, but no one realized that other places might be interested. What do you propose we do to follow up on your report?"

Cindy smiled. "Actually, Jane, I wanted to discuss that with you. You'll note that I listed ECIs as one of my 'hot' prospects. That status comes from their growth, which is very healthy. My research was based on secondary sources, of course, including your department's 'idea' file. What we need now is some primary research in this market. You need to get someone to actually talk to the people running the ECIs and learn what they look for in furnishings, what their budgets are like, and how they respond to the concept."

"In other words, marketing research. I wish you were going to be here to continue on this project. It would really be a blessing for me not to have to supervise another research project. The research department is great technically, but they're corporate. It's not always easy to get them to see the divisional point of view. And you know so much about it by now."

"Jane, if you're serious, I have a suggestion. My marketing research professor just called me to ask if there was any possibility of Field or Stone sponsoring a project for his class in the fall. As I told you in my interviews, my class was taught through the use of one comprehensive project, from design to final report. The student team writes a proposal, prepares a study design, conducts the research and writes a report. Because we have such a clear-cut problem, this project would be ideal for the class. I could serve as your liaison to the class team, advise you on the progress of the project, and prepare recommendations at the end, based on my knowledge of the Field furniture line and the research findings. What do you think?"

"It sounds like a great idea. Why don't you write a memo detailing your involvement and have your professor send me a letter explaining the arrangements?"

Initial Steps

"Cindy, this is Professor Jenkins. There is a small problem with the Stone research project."

Enrollment in Professor Jenkins's marketing research class had been higher than anticipated. He was running out of corporate research projects, and he was now preparing one to be done under his own auspices on the effect of cultural background on food choice at fast-food restaurants. Two student groups had requested to work on the Stone project, and neither one seemed thrilled about fast food. He had a solution to the impasse, but it required Stone's cooperation. His proposal was as follows.

Each group was to submit a well-written, comprehensive proposal to its company for review. The proposal, prepared after several exploratory meetings, was to include the research goals, information needs, and preliminary research design, including details of methodology.

Professor Jenkins's idea was to have Cindy and her manager brief each group separately. Each group would prepare a proposal. Both would be submitted to Field, and Field would select the one it preferred. The other group would then conduct the professor's fast-food study. After consulting Jane, Cindy gave Professor Jenkins the go-ahead and provided the following information to the groups.

Company Background

Field Modular Office Furniture and Panel Technology was one product line of the Sword Group, which was a fully owned subsidiary of the Stone Corporation. Field's product was a high-quality panel system of modular furniture for office buildings. The line was currently selling well, through a sales force of 30 representatives and 120 dealers.

Sword Group manufactured office furniture of all types, including metal work stations. Sword Group's sales in the most recent 12-month period totaled $30 million. The current employment level was 400.

Stone Corporation functioned as a holding company, having diversified into home and office furniture a decade earlier. Other areas of involvement were automobile products and building supplies. Stone Corporation's most recent year-to-date total sales were $1.4 billion.

ECI Preliminary Information

Early childhood institutions included day-care centers, preschools, and kindergartens. One industry source estimated that there were 150,000 ECIs in the United States. This included for-profit (both franchise and independent organizations) and nonprofit institutions, as well as those sponsored by organizations such as military bases, hospitals, and corporations. Approximately 60 percent of the institutions were run on a for-profit basis.

It was estimated that, within 2 years, 15 million children of preschool age would have mothers in the workforce; 8 years earlier, the most recent year for which data were available, 23 percent of these children were in ECIs. The real growth rate of the market was estimated at 5 percent per year.

Field Goals

Cindy's research, based on several previous studies and notes in the "idea" file, suggested that Field might have a line extension opportunity that would enable it to serve the child-care market, which appeared to be growing quickly.

Field's overall goal for the research project was clear. They wanted to determine:

- Whether it was worthwhile to develop a product line for ECIs.
- If so, how to design products that would have an advantage in this market.
- If so, how and to whom the products should be marketed.

With this background, and operating on a tight deadline, the student groups went to work.

Submission of Proposals

Two weeks later, Cindy and Jane met to hear the groups' presentations of the following proposals.

Proposal of Group 1

Research Objectives

To enable the Sword Group to determine whether market pricing and budgetary considerations would support introduction of a high-quality room partition into the day-care market.

Primary research will be conducted to determine price points, interior furnishing budgets, purchase frequency, and desirable product attributes.

Secondary research will be conducted to collect complementary information on the structure of the market, the purchase decision process for interior furnishings, spatial design of centers, competitor identification, and distribution methods.

Primary Research Design

Focus Groups

Two focus groups will be held in small, nearby cities. Participants will be recruited from the administrative level of local day-care centers. Efforts will be made to recruit participants representing a wide variety of centers: corporate- and church-sponsored as well as independent and franchise centers. Participants will be informed of the topics in advance and offered a $35 incentive. Each session will last approximately 2 hours and will be videotaped for client review.

The focus groups will probe a center's current use of space and physical layout, desirable attributes in furniture, and budgeting and purchasing decisions. The Field product line concept will then be expanded. Participants will be shown several drawings of the panels in question. General feedback about the concept will be requested, as will specific benefits, drawbacks, and suggestions. Pricing issues will also be discussed, in the context of what the participants would be willing to pay for such a product.

Survey

The focus group findings will then be incorporated into a survey, which will be administered over the telephone to day-care directors. Respondents will be drawn from a national list in Child Care Information Exchange, a publication targeted at day-care administrators. A sample frame of 100 has been selected. The survey will include a broad array of questions, exploring such areas as:

- the purchase decision process
- competitors
- desired attributes in furniture
- current methods of space division
- pricing
- demographics

The survey will also test the Field product concept, by describing the panel and its uses and asking for an evaluation of the concept, likelihood of use, and willingness to pay.

Detailed statistical analysis will be performed on the results, including cluster analysis specifically, to get some idea of market segmentation, if possible.

Proposal of Group 2

Research Objectives

- Determine the extent of demand for equipment such as furniture among early childhood institutions (ECIs).
- Identify the nature of demand for such products, including product attributes, price, distribution channels, and information sources.
- Suggest which market segments are the most viable for Sword/Field day-care equipment.

Research Design

Preliminary Research

Secondary sources will be used to determine market size, growth, and interior environment needs. These data will then be used as initial input for the primary research.

Primary Research

A two-step primary research approach will be used.

Interviews. The first exploratory stage of research will be achieved by conducting in-depth, one-on-one interviews with local ECI directors. The group will conduct eight interviews. An outline of suggested topics will be followed for each interview to guarantee consistency. The interview will conclude with the display of a drawing of the product to the director, to solicit their feedback. The group members feel that in-depth interviews at the center will allow them to better understand the functioning of the ECIs.

Survey. The data from the interviews will then be used as input for a mail survey. The goal of the written survey is to develop profiles of different segments of the ECI market, primarily through the use of cluster analysis.

The survey will be mailed to 1,000 ECIs throughout the United States. The list used for the survey will be purchased from a mailing list broker whose database includes 152,038 ECIs, excluding family-run or in-home institutions.

The survey is currently expected to cover issues such as:

- distribution
- physical layout
- furniture purchase process
- type of center operated

The group also plans to include a question on the amount spent by the ECIs on adult office furniture to determine whether this could be a new market for Field's traditional panel technology.

Statistical analysis will be performed, including cross-tabulations, cluster analysis, and regression analysis.

Qualifications of the Research Group

Pierre Duchesne is currently earning his M.B.A., with an emphasis on marketing and international business. Before returning to school for this semester, he was a credit analyst at Credit Suisse.

Teresa Tompkins has more than 10 years of experience in industrial marketing communications. The past 7 years of her career have been spent with Mustard & Swerther, Inc., a local business-to-business advertising agency. She is currently the agency's marketing specialist and senior account executive. She is also just completing an M.B.A. along with Mr. Duchesne.

Jonathan Williams is currently earning an M.B.A. along with Mr. Duchesne and Ms. Tompkins, focusing on international finance. He is currently a loan officer with Formidable Bank.

Conclusion

Cindy and Jane adjourned to a local coffeehouse to read the proposals, after thanking the groups for the presentation. Jane looked across the marble table. "Well, Cindy, which proposal do you suggest we go with? And why?"

CASE 1.4 UNITED WAY OF AMERICA

United Way of America Background

United Way of America is a nonprofit membership organization of 1400 community-based United Way organizations across America. Each organization is independent, separately incorporated, and governed by local volunteers. Headquartered in Alexandria, Virginia, it serves as the national service and training center for its members, liaison to national organizations and the federal government, and secretariat for

United Way International affiliates in 42 foreign countries. United Way of America raises several billions of dollars through its annual campaign, government grants, corporate sponsorships, special events and other major gifts, investment income, and fee-for-service activities. These funds are distributed to local and national nonprofit organizations providing health and human service programs. United Way's volunteer forces total more than 1 million on an annual basis. These volunteers serve in the following capacities: board members, loaned executives, day of caring volunteers, campaign coordinators, planned giving volunteers, and other direct service volunteers. The resources at its disposal and the sheer number of volunteers involved in the United Way of America helped make it the largest charitable organization in North America, and among the largest in the world.

United Way of America Customers and Markets

United Way of America (UWA) is a national organization supported primarily by local United Way affiliates through membership dues. Specifically, UWA receives annual membership support through a licensing arrangement with local United Ways, which, in exchange, acquire the right to use the name and various service markings and logos owned by UWA. In this way, local United Way organizations can be easily identified as UWA's prime customers. Other customers include national agencies such as American Red Cross and Girl Scouts of America, national media, national labor organizations, national and international corporations, national associations, and the federal government.

United Way's markets include individual and corporate donors, volunteers, and people in need. The organization interacts through its customers to affect these markets, including the contributions by its donors, the quality and amount of time given by volunteers, and the amelioration of the health and human service problems of people in need.

United Way of America Research

UWA provides multiple support services to local United Ways and its other customers, including training, consultation, mediation, conferencing, and assessment tools. National research is one of the major services used by UWA customers. UWA is considered a leader in research in such areas as philanthropy, the nonprofit sector, and social and economic trends. Public and private sector decision-makers and the general public view UWA research as a leading nonpartisan source of data and analysis.

Among the research services now available to UWA customers are the following:

1. United Way State of Caring Index

The United Way State of Caring Index® is a dynamic approach to measuring the health and well-being of the nation. It creates a summary measure of Americans' capacity to care for one another by analyzing 36 social and economic indicators at the state and national levels in the following areas:

- economic and financial well-being
- education
- health
- voluntarism/charity/civic engagement
- safety
- natural environment and other factors

The index provides critical information on pressing social, economic, and environmental issues in each state and across the country and offers decision makers, as well as other persons interested in the business of caring, a research tool that can be easily used to:

- highlight areas of success in each state and the nation as a whole,
- identify areas that need improvement,
- compare current conditions with past performance, and
- Compare the conditions in any one state with those in other states or the nation.

The index is a valuable tool for United Way member organizations and their partners in education, business, government, and the nonprofit sector, who are working to improve the quality of life in the communities they serve. The index can also serve as an inspiration and a framework for developing or improving indicator efforts at the local level. Use of the United Way State of Caring Index can help identify critical community needs and determine the capacities available to meet them. The index can help focus efforts to maximize the impact of efforts on the community agenda and promote further in-depth analyses of particular issues of local concern.

2. Community Involvement Survey

UWA conducted the Community Involvement Survey to determine the level of community involvement in America since the events of September 11, 2001, and to identify any roadblocks or changes needed to increase community involvement. The survey used a nationally representative sample of more than 2000 American adults and was conducted via telephone. The major findings from this survey include the following key points:

- Active community involvement is regarded as a virtue by almost all Americans. Ninety-seven percent of Americans say that it is either very or somewhat important to volunteer in the community.
- Almost 60 percent of those who volunteer believe that their volunteer activities were very effective. Meanwhile, roughly 70 percent of those who volunteer said it was very easy to find "the right volunteer opportunity."
- Although active community involvement is held to be a virtue by almost all Americans, relatively few are active in making this virtue a reality. Although 97 percent of Americans believe that it is important to volunteer, only 34 percent of Americans have in fact volunteered during the previous 12 months. The same appears to be the case for other forms of community involvement activities.
- Most Americans have the desire to volunteer but are stymied by some obstacle. A "demanding work schedule" was the most frequently mentioned obstacle (37 percent), mentioned four times as often as the next most prominent impediment, a "lack of knowledge of how to begin" (8 percent). Clearly, the demands from the world of work far supersede any other obstacle to active community involvement, at least if self-reports are to be believed.
- Nearly four out of five Americans (79 percent) indicate that they would volunteer during the workday if their employer helped to arrange it and it did not conflict with their work.
- Retirees represent an untapped resource for active community involvement. Although they have more time to spend on volunteer activities and a lifetime of skills and resources to offer, retirees are less likely to volunteer than part-time and full-time employees.
- People who believe in the effectiveness of local charities are more likely to be actively involved in their communities and to give to charities. Moreover, as the general level of involvement with a charity increases, so does the likelihood of giving.

3. Generations X and Y as Potential Philanthropic Investors

UWA provides its customers with information necessary to understand and target Generations X and Y (or so-called "Millennials") as largely untapped philanthropic investors. Although it is not possible to precisely characterize individuals according to their generation cohort, they do share experiences that help shape their attitudes and behaviors. When interacting with Generations X-ers and Millennials, charitable organizations must look to new methods of building and sustaining relationships with this group that acknowledges the differences in their operating styles. As WWII-ers and Boomers leave the workplace, charitable organizations must learn to connect with the independent and adventurous spirit of the Generation X-ers and the energy and entrepreneurial nature of the Millennials and begin focusing efforts to reach this 120-million-strong group early on with messages tailored to their viewpoints.

Some United Ways across America have already started to more actively engage and connect with younger philanthropic investors, but this emerging market still goes widely untapped. Several of the major points that UWA research provides to understand Generations X and Y are the following:

- Younger investors, those between the ages of 18 and 34, often have a more positive response toward charitable messages than the older Baby Boomer generation.
- However, survey results show that 18- to 34-year-olds most often have not participated in charitable campaigns, and 62 percent say they have not even been asked to give or volunteer.
- Generation X does engage in philanthropic activity, but they have a strong demand that they get something out of the experience. To this generation, this could involve the immediate gratification

of mentoring, the adventure of trekking through Africa, or a full accounting of the outcomes of their efforts. Indeed, one of the things X-ers want to "get out" of philanthropy is a feeling of having had an impact.

- As Generation Y begins to enter the workforce, they demand direct involvement, to be treated as peers, access to information, seek mentors, and they have an ability to react quickly, which could run counter to many traditional volunteer and committee structures.

Case Questions

1 Considering the nature of the United Way of America national organization, as well as its customers and markets, what are the challenges and the opportunities of the UWA research department?

2 Identify potential project objectives and information needs for the three research examples provided in the case.

3 Discuss the factors that should be examined to determine whether or not the sample used in the Community Involvement Survey was nationally representative. Evaluate the appropriateness of the research design used in this survey. What are the advantages and the disadvantages of using telephone interviews for this type of survey?

4 How could the customers of the UWA benefit from the surveys described in this case? What specific actions could be designed using each survey to materialize these benefits? UWA has segmented its emerging volunteer base according to age group and affiliation (e.g., Gen-X-ers, Millenials, etc.). Is this appropriate? Are there other meaningful groupings that cut across these lines, and are there important sub-groups within the segments that already exist? What would be the implications for effective communication, recruitment, and targeting?

Source: www.unitedway.org, including source questionnaire. Go to: http://national.unitedway.org/files/pdf/soc/2002/survey_with_final_results.pdf

CASE 1.5 ETHICAL DIMENSIONS IN MARKETING RESEARCH

The following situations and questions have occurred many times in the real world of marketing research. Each raises ethical concerns about the practice of marketing research. For each situation or question, identify what you believe to be the ethical issue and indicate what you would do in place of the decision-maker, manager, or firm in question. Give thought as well to how such situations could have been avoided in the first place with proper planning, as well as to how both the sponsoring organization and future clients might react to your proposed course of action.

1. A research buyer asks for competitive proposals from a number of research suppliers. The buyer takes ideas from several of these proposals without offering payment for the ideas and then awards the contract to one of the research suppliers to conduct the study, using all the ideas.
2. A research organization uses questions developed for one client in designing a questionnaire for another client.
3. While conducting an online survey for a client, a research firm inadvertently omits several questions regarding respondents' demographic data. A researcher discovers this error after the survey is completed and the budget exhausted. She reports this to her superior, who is immediately concerned about possible harm to the firm's reputation. The research firm's upper management decides to impute (i.e., use some method to guess or determine the values of) the missing demographic data through Internet research tracking and linking data. This practice is only partially successful at reconstructing the data, and the client wants to know why some data values are missing.
4. A major error is discovered by a research supplier in a study that has been completed and submitted to the client, an error which does not critically affect the suggested recommendations, but which calls into doubt some of the intermittent findings.
5. A research firm is asked to conduct a study by a firm that is in direct competition with one of the research firm's clients.

6. A research firm is asked to perform a study for a client. After questioning the decision-maker, the researcher discovers that the research objective is to find the most plausible public relations story to excuse and minimize substantial damage to communities and the environment caused by the company's practices.
7. A research firm accepts an assignment with the knowledge that it cannot complete the project in the designated time, hoping to alter the scope or nature of the project as data are collected.
8. A research firm wonders what the ethical issues, if any, are in using entertainment and gifts to help in soliciting business, given that these are often standard practices among its competitors.
9. A research firm conducts a large-scale consumer survey. Survey participants have been assured that their personal information will not be used for any purposes other than research. A sales manager in the company has demanded that the personal information be made available to the company and has the support of top management responsible for this project and the decision to initiate any future projects. One manager in the research firm points out that it would be impossible to prove how the company came across the information.
10. The director of marketing research presents to senior management the results of a study conducted by a member of the marketing research staff. No mention of this staff member is made during the presentation. In a footnote in the written report, the staff member is given credit for the contribution. The director reasons that the staff member accepted the assignment and was compensated for having done it, so no further attribution is necessary.
11. For a launch of a new skin care product for women, a research firm recruits female participants of different age groups to participate in online focus groups. The best moderator available for this project happens to be male. Management has asked him to pretend online to be female. They reason that, as it will only be carried out online, with no video input, the difference will not be detectable, and so participants will behave more naturally and respond more openly to the moderator's questions about a female-oriented product if they believe they are interacting with a female moderator.
12. A project director has proposed using ultraviolet ink on a questionnaire in a mail survey. The letter with the survey promises that the respondent will not be identified, but the director thinks that the ink identification is needed to save money in the mailing of a follow-up questionnaire to those who do not respond to the first mailing. Without the ink marking, the follow-up questionnaire will have to be mailed to all subjects in the sample, including those who responded to the first mailing. Because no identifying information will be recorded subsequently, the director reasons this is only a cost-savings measure and does not compromise anonymity.
13. While in a meeting with an advertising firm a company is considering hiring, a sales manager notices a competitor's artwork for an upcoming ad campaign lying inconspicuously on a counter in the corner of the room. When the advertising agent leaves the room for a moment, the manager peers more closely at the artwork and learns of both the new product line and the advertising strategy. When she returns to her company, she mentions this to the marketing research director.
14. An interviewer tells a respondent that an interview will last only 15 minutes, knowing that few will complete it in that time, and quite a few will require a half-hour or more. Experience has shown that many respondents who will grant a 15-minute interview would refuse one lasting 30 minutes. However, once subjects agree to participate, they usually complete the interview process—even if it runs longer than the originally cited time. Thus, nonresponse error can be reduced and data accuracy increased. Further, because some respondents finish the survey in the promised time, it does not seem particularly egregious to claim 15 minutes as a target completion time.
15. A marketing research firm is hired to provide research to reduce the uncertainty in choosing between two proposed new marketing strategies. Each marketing strategy is backed by a group of managers and a corresponding executive in top management. The marketing research team finds itself lobbied from both sides of an internal power struggle in the company. Each side wants the marketing research project to prove it right and approves or thwarts suggestions by the team based on whether the suggestion is suspected of being helpful to its preferred course of action. The marketing research team gathers privately to discuss what can be done to protect the project and the reputation of their firm. The management of the marketing research firm considers this project too lucrative to consider backing out.
16. As part of a study on family buying processes, a family is videotaped as it examines automobiles in a dealer showroom. Also, conversations within the family are recorded by a "shopper"/researcher.

The family is not aware that it is being monitored. No identifying demographic information is requested.

17. A marketing research firm provides a client firm with statistical information regarding customer preferences in their markets. The client takes statistical data from these reports and makes fallacious, unsupportable advertising claims based on them. In print ads, the fine print cites the marketing research study as a source.
18. A family places its trash in a public alley for pickup. Without asking permission, a researcher sorts through the garbage as part of a brand-preference survey (a process sometimes termed "garbology").
19. After a final presentation on a business-to-business market research study, the client thanks the project leader from the research company and then asks for the list of companies that responded to the survey, along with their survey responses, which could indicate whether they were currently in the market for the client's services. The research supplier has not promised anonymity to those who responded, but did promise that the supplier would not contact respondents based on their answers.
20. In a kick-off meeting for a new research project, the client turns up with a previously commissioned research study from another marketing research provider. The researcher tactfully notes that the research design (a qualitative study) was completely inappropriate for the research purpose, a quantitative estimate of market potential. The potential client nonetheless says that she "really liked" the previous study, and asks if the researcher can replicate it in another product category. The researcher realizes that doing such a study will not supply the information needed by the client, yet it is clear that if the researcher says no, the client will simply return to the original provider.

CASE 1.6 PRIVATE LABEL PRODUCTS AT AMARANTE*

Amarante is a major retailer in the European market, with more than 6000 stores worldwide under various national and regional chain names. Amarante entered the North American market with the grand opening of two mass merchandisers in Illinois and Massachusetts. A year after start of operations in the United States, the company failed to achieve the targeted sales mix of private labels and branded products. On average, 45 percent of products sold in Europe were sold via private labels; however, only 25 percent of the U.S. stores' sales were of private label products.

Private labels were identified as Amarante's key strategic direction for a number of interrelated reasons. It was one of the main differentiating elements from a competitive standpoint, and allowed the retailer to provide extensive product variety to its shoppers, variety which could be easily customized even down to the store level. Improving bargaining leverage over brand manufacturers, creating greater consumer dependence on store services, and obtaining additional latitude in its pricing strategy were some of the major advantages of a product strategy more heavily focused on private labels.

Amarante gradually built up an impressive knowledge base of the private label shopper segment. Unfortunately, the retailer's expertise could not be readily used by its U.S. stores. North American and European consumers' perceptions, attitudes, and purchasing behaviors seemed to differ substantially, a fact also reflected by a 20 percentile point difference in private labels' contribution to the revenues of the two regions. Because understanding the U.S. consumer marker was essential to increasing private label sales in North America, Amarante's management felt some type of primary data collection, most likely in the form of a questionnaire, was a good first step toward this goal.

A closer look at the sales of private labels per product category revealed that the Electronics Division suffered most, with Amarante's private labels contributing only 5 percent to the division's sales. Therefore, the North American management team decided to start by exploring the current and potential consumers of the retailer's Electronics Division private labels. A leading European research group, with offices in New York and Chicago, was selected to conduct the first survey, which would serve as a pilot for future surveys in other product divisions.

Simon Stoner, marketing manager at Amarante North America, was assigned to lead the project. To provide the research firm with a clear understanding of the project deliverables, he developed a detailed

*The name of the company has been altered.

briefing document. The briefing included background information on the company, definition of the current problem, the information needs, and the project's objectives; the document clearly communicated that the retailer was seeking information that would enable its executives to design a marketing plan, one which would achieve a higher contribution from the private label products to the Electronics Division's revenues.

Case Questions

1. Considering the situation in which Amarante finds itself, develop the project's briefing document, to be submitted to the research firm selected to conduct the survey. Be specific when describing Amarante's information needs and project objectives.
2. In view of the information needs and objectives stated in your briefing document, what are the appropriate data sources for this study? Explain your answer. Be sure to consider the relative cost and complexity associated with obtaining such data.
3. Evaluate the management team's decision to start building expertise about the private label shoppers in North America by conducting a consumer survey about the private label shoppers of electronics. Specifically, was it wise to focus on the most under-performing of all the categories as having the greatest eventual profit impact? Was it wise to focus on that category for a first survey, one meant to generalize eventually to other categories?
4. Provide an action plan Amarante can follow to help build a knowledge base of private label consumers in North America, being careful to provide concrete support for each of your decisions. Consider as well whether Amarante should collect additional data on other consumer segments, perhaps even outside the United States.

CASE 1.7 TWIN PINES GOLF AND COUNTRY CLUB

In mid-May, the Capital Planning Committee of the Twin Pines Golf and Country Club met to discuss a research report that they had just received. This report gave the results of a survey of the club members on the issue of which projects the club should begin this fiscal year. Members of the committee intended to use the report as a basis for selecting among alternative capital projects. A biographical description of the committee members is given in Appendix 1.

Background

Twin Pines Golf and Country Club is a private club situated in the southwestern corner of Hinsdale, Illinois, a suburb of Chicago. The club was founded in 1956 with an 18-hole golf course and a dining room. In 1966, an additional nine holes were built; in 1989 three outdoor tennis courts were added to the club; and in 2004 the entire club was enabled for wireless communication to accommodate business collaboration on premises.

The Capital Planning Committee is a permanent committee of the Twin Pines Club. Its task in recent years involved the overseeing of the maintenance of current facilities. However, this particular year the board of directors of the club has given an additional task to the committee: making recommendations on new capital facilities. In a letter to the committee, the president of the club stated, "We must be prepared to add new facilities to serve the current and future interests of our members and to attract new members. It is your task to make recommendations in this matter."

In response to this request, the Capital Planning Committee held a series of meetings to discuss possible projects requiring capital expenditures during the next few years. They identified five potential projects and the associated capital costs and operating costs per year. These projects and their costs are shown in Table C1.7.1.

The committee decided to obtain the opinion of the membership on the five projects before reaching a decision. In December, a research subcommittee was formed to obtain the views of the membership. It was the expressed intention of the whole committee to recommend the capital project or projects that the membership desired.

Table C1.7.1 Projects and Costs

	Capital cost	Operating cost per year
An additional nine golf holes, complete with automatic watering systems on existing lands	$2,800,000	$450,000
Swimming pool and clubhouse with lockers	750,000	150,000
Tennis clubhouse, court lighting, and bubble cover for winter	450,000	80,000
Three new tennis courts	250,000	60,000
Purchase of 150 acres of land adjacent to club as a buffer against city expansion or for club expansion	2,500,000	135,000

The Study

The research subcommittee developed a questionnaire (see Appendix 2) designed to measure the preferences of the membership in relation to the five projects. In March, this questionnaire was mailed to all senior and intermediate members of the club. Table C1.7.2 shows the number of questionnaires mailed to each class of membership and the associated return rate. The report prepared by the research subcommittee consisted of a set of tables giving what the committee members thought were the main findings of the survey. These are presented as Tables C1.7.3 to C1.7.5.

May 15 Meeting

All members of the Capital Planning Committee were present for the meeting held in the Twin Pines boardroom on May 15. John Watts, the committee chairperson, opened the meeting by thanking the

Table C1.7.2 Questionnaire Returns by Class of Membership

	Number mailed	Number returned	Percent returned
Senior male (club shareholders)	710	540	76
Senior female	650	402	62
Intermediate male (ages 21–26)	250	110	44
Intermediate female (ages 21–26)	75	32	43
Total	1685	1084	64

Table C1.7.3 Project Preference Given Knowledge of the Effect on Annual Fees (Question 4 in the Questionnaire)

	Projects					
	Golf	Swimming pool	Tennis clubhouse	Tennis courts	Land	Total responses
Yes	32.5%	37.1%	32.9%	27.4%	23.7%	
	(352)	(402)	(357)	(297)	(257)	1665
No	50.6%	59.6%	51.1%	53.6%	60.4%	
	(549)	(646)	(554)	(581)	(655)	2985
No opinion	16.9%	3.3%	16.0%	19.0%	15.9%	
	(183)	(36)	(173)	(206)	(172)	770
Total respondents	1084	1084	1084	1084	1084	5420

Table C1.7.4 Project Preference by Type of Membership (Yes to Question 4 and Categories of Question 1)

	Projects					
Membership type*	Golf	Swimming pool	Tennis clubhouse	Tennis courts	Land	Total responses
Senior male	30.2%[†]	25.9%	27.6%	23.5%	27.2%	
	(163)	(140)	(149)	(127)	(147)	726
Senior female	36.4%	38.8%	28.1%	28.7%	19.7%	
	(146)	(156)	(113)	(115)	(79)	609
Intermediate male	31.2%	73.6%	67.3%	38.2%	21.4%	
	(34)	(81)	(74)	(42)	(24)	255
Intermediate female	29.7%	78.1%	65.6%	40.1%	20.7%	
	(9)	(25)	(21)	(13)	(7)	75
Total responses	352	402	357	297	257	1665

*Total response per membership type adds up to more than 100 percent of the respondents because of multiple responses. Total number of respondents = 1084.

[†]That is, 30.2 percent of senior male members are in favor of the golf project.

Table C1.7.5 Priority Club Should Attach to Projects (Responses to Question 3b)

	High	Medium	Low	No opinion
Additional nine holes	24.7	21.0	45.1	9.2
Swimming pool	28.5	18.7	45.9	6.9
Tennis clubhouse and lights	16.4	16.9	51.2	15.5
Three tennis courts	17.6	15.9	52.0	14.5
Land	19.7	21.4	46.0	12.9

Note: All numbers are percentages by rows. Total number of respondents = 1084.

research subcommittee for their efforts. He also noted that the board of directors of the club had asked him to be prepared to make a recommendation concerning capital expenditures at the next board meeting. This meeting was to be held on May 21. Because of this time pressure, it would be necessary for the Capital Planning Committee to reach a decision at the May 15 meeting.

Case Questions

1 What action should the committee take?

2 Why?

APPENDIX 1 BIOGRAPHICAL DESCRIPTIONS OF CAPITAL

Planning Committee Members

	Age	Family	Occupation	Club Activities
John B. Watts (Chairman)	62	Married, two sons, ages 29 and 27	President, Exeter Tool Company	Golf
Dr. L. Gary Johnston	45	Married, one daughter, age 20; two sons, ages 17 and 12	Dentist	Golf, tennis
Joseph R. Taylor	35	Married, one son, age 7	Lawyer	Golf
Robert H. Robertson*	59	Married, three daughters, ages 32, 30, and 27	President, Robert Advertising	Golf
Dr. Malcolm R. Richardson	42	Unmarried	Internal medicine specialist	Golf, tennis
Kenneth L. Wecker*	69	Widower, two daughters, ages 42 and 38	Retired, president of Alpha Associates, Management Consultants	Golf
Dr. W. Lloyd Hains	53	Married, no children	General practitioner	Golf
Bruce A. Frederick*	46	Married, one son, age 16	Sales manager, Beta Electronics	Golf

*Member of research subcommittee.

APPENDIX 2 QUESTIONNAIRE

1. Class of membership

   Please indicate your membership class:

Senior	( )
Senior female	( )
Intermediate male	( )
Intermediate female	( )

2. Junior members living at home

Ages of sons	( )	( )	( )	( )	( )
Ages of daughters	( )	( )	( )	( )	( )

3. Proposed capital projects
   Your Capital Planning Committee is presently evaluating a number of possible projects. As part of this evaluation we would like your opinion on the projects listed.

	Capital cost	Operating cost per year
Nine-hole golf course with automatic watering system	$800,000	$90,000
Swimming pool and clubhouse with lockers	160,000	60,000
Tennis clubhouse, court lighting, and bubble cover for winter	240,000	40,000
Three new tennis courts	60,000	20,000
Purchase of land (150 acres) adjacent to the 16th and 17th holes	600,000	55,000

   a. What is your interest in these projects?

	High	Medium	Low
Additional 9 holes	( )	( )	( )
Swimming pool	( )	( )	( )
Tennis clubhouse and lights	( )	( )	( )
Three tennis courts	( )	( )	( )
Land	( )	( )	( )

b. What priority should the club attach to each of these projects?

	High	Medium	Low
Additional 9 holes	( )	( )	( )
Swimming pool	( )	( )	( )
Tennis clubhouse and lights	( )	( )	( )
Three tennis courts	( )	( )	( )
Land	( )	( )	( )

4. Financing
   Your committee has expressed the capital and operating costs for each project. We have stated these costs in terms of the effect these projects will have on the fees of senior members. Would you be in favor of proceeding with the following projects?

	To finance construction over 10 years	Operating costs	Total	In favor	
				Yes	No
Additional 9 holes	$60	$65	$125	( )	( )
Swimming pool	$10	$45	$55	( )	( )
Tennis clubhouse and lights	$18	$30	$48	( )	( )
Three tennis courts	$5	$15	$20	( )	( )
Land	$45	$40	$85	( )	( )

CASE 1.8 HEPWORTH GOLDEN AUTO

Hepworth Golden Auto (HGA) is a large wholesaler located in Valparaiso, Indiana. It supplies auto parts to service stations, department stores, discount houses, and retail parts outlets in and around the Valparaiso area. Bill Douglass, president of HGA, was concerned about his company's declining sales. Between 2001 and 2005, revenues dropped from $16 million to $10 million, and he feared the business would go under unless something was done to improve its sales picture. "It's those foreign imports," lamented Douglass, "they're ruining my parts business." HGA sold only parts for domestic cars, and Douglass did not want to enter the foreign parts market.

In an effort to improve profits, Douglass had asked the Rightway Research firm to submit a proposal for marketing research that would help in formulating a long-range growth strategy for HGA. Limited funds forced Douglass to set a low budget for the research project. Douglass had received Rightway's proposal and was in the process of evaluating it. The proposal follows.

Rightway Research's Proposal

The influx of foreign cars into the American auto market has had an adverse effect on all suppliers of domestic parts. Success in this market is dependent on two things: accurate automobile demand forecasts and a sufficient inventory to meet retailers' needs. Lack of either can result in disaster. HGA's research objective is thus: To obtain the data that would enable HGA to (1) accurately forecast demand for autos and (2) make proper inventory decisions.

A list of the information needs and sources of information to meet those needs follows.

As you can see, most of the information needed is readily available in federal, state, and county publications; trade journals; manufacturers' publications; and syndicated sources. These data can be obtained at low or moderate cost. The following list is by no means complete; rather it represents the minimum sources that HGA should be aware of and carefully monitor.

Information needs	Source(s)
Auto industry	
Total demand	*Wards Automotive Reports*
Demand by make and model	Motor Statistics from R.L. Polk & Co.
Proportion of new versus used sales Diesel car sales	City, county, and state planning commission reports
Projected gasoline prices	Energy Information Administration http://eia.doe.gov
Availability of parts from manufacturers	Manufacturers
Government regulations	U. S. Department of Transportation http://www.dot.gov
Population	
Growth Age and sex composition	*Statistical Abstracts of the United States* http://www.census.gov
Economic	
Number of dual-career households	Local Employment Bureau http://lehd.dsd.census.gov/led
Employment, payroll, and sales of the major industries in market area Labor market	*Statistical Abstracts of the United States* http://www.census.gov
GNP for market area	Bureau of Economic Analysis http://www.bea.gov
Availability of money for loans; status of interest rates Current government position on imports—quotas versus free trade	Federal Reserve System http://www.federalreserve.gov

Case Questions

1. What developments in HGA performance led Bill Douglass to ask for Rightway Research's help? What is the decision-making process that Mr. Douglass expects to be facilitated with the insights provided by the research findings?
2. Evaluate the stated research objective. Does it thoroughly address HGA's core problems?
3. Evaluate the information needs stated in the proposal. Have these been correctly identified? Should any be altered, deleted or added?
4. Consider the data sources listed in the proposal. Are these sources appropriate for the stated information needs and research objective? Why or why not? What other data sources could be used? Consider accessibility, accuracy and cost in making source suggestions.
5. Evaluate the data collection framework.
6. What other possible research design and data sources could be used? How would these fit the information needs relative to the given design?
7. Considering the research proposal, do you think Rightway Research truly understood why the information was needed, and for what eventual purpose? Explain your answers.
8. Building on your previous answers, prepare a new research proposal for the HGA research project.

CASE 1.9 COMPUTER DISCOUNT WAREHOUSE CORPORATION

As the power of traditional brand advertising wanes, new players from Taiwan, Korea, and China are entering the already overheated electronics and computer hardware markets. As a result, both commoditization and price competition intensify. Yet one direct-sales company is taking a radically new value-added approach to marketing. This approach concentrates on establishing consistent dialogue with interested consumers, as opposed to the traditional monologue with the mass market. Computer Discount Warehouse Corporation (CDW) offers a prime example of this new marketing strategy.

Since founder Michael Krasny started the business at his kitchen table 20 years ago, CDW has emerged as a leading provider of technology-based solutions for business, government, and education. Despite competing in a highly volatile industry against thousands of local rivals, CDW has managed to become a high-tech heavyweight. The company, based in Vernon Hills, Illinois, outside Chicago, now sells around $5 billion worth of computer equipment and services a year. CDW serves as a middleman between the primarily government and enterprise businesses and manufacturers such as HP, IBM, Apple, Microsoft, and Sony. The consumer always has the option to buy directly from the manufacturer, but CDW gets its business by knowing its customers and their needs.

Traditionally, brand-building for packaged goods has been likened to a box, with three important dimensions:

1. The "height" of the impressions on consumers: the sheer extent of advertising bombardment achieved by purchase of advertising time and space in various media
2. The "depth" of the brand awareness achieved, based on the power of the image or sales argument in the advertising
3. The "width" of the distribution and the muscle available to push the brand to a prominent place on the shelf at the point of sale

CDW added a fourth dimension by using individualized marketing and moving into the lives and activities of prospects and customers as a genuinely helpful and trusted companion, understanding their individual needs. Although CDW's customers could always shop around hoping for a better price, CDW is typically able to avoid such price-based decisions by offering "three S's": selection, speed, and service. Its inventory breadth and base of operations are impressive, with more than 80,000 products available, same-day shipping on more than 90 percent of its orders, and the ability to function as a de facto IT department for many of its 400,000-plus small-business clients.

CDW operates in an expanding market, but a brutally competitive one: although sales have been growing steadily, IT prices continue to drop, margins become razor-thin, and both enticing new customers and retaining prior ones is key to simply staying afloat. CDW's sales philosophy reflects one of company founder Krasny's core beliefs, that "people do business with people they like"; so embedded is this business mantra that it appears on posters throughout the company to remind the 1,880-member sales force of its primacy. Although many sales organizations preach a similar service philosophy, CDW breathes it as few organizations do, particularly among those close to their imposing size. Customer surveys consistently award CDW high marks, and indicate the desire for a long-term partnership. What drives this uncommon degree of loyalty? Customers say almost with one voice that it is the one-on-one relationships with account managers. As the director of operations for a major bar-code scanner systems firm put it so succinctly, "They're not just selling but getting into people's lives"—and he even cites CDW as a model for his own company's sales staff.

Relationships of such reciprocity and depth do not just happen on their own, and certainly not overnight, but come about via "a methodology," as Harry Harczak, executive vice president of sales, puts it. CDW has an integrated approach, and its customer-management software, compensation, training, and culture were devised from the ground up to help facilitate close and long-lasting client partnerships. The training required of account managers is lengthy, comprehensive, and pervasive; CDW CEO John Edwardson (former head of United Airlines), notes that they receive more training than some pilots: 6 months of orientation, then 6 months of sales training in CDW Academy, then another year of monthly training sessions in the "masters' program."

Although it is tempting to believe that customer relationships depend solely on the likeability quotient of the sales staff, this is off the mark. Rather, the key ingredient is the ability to help customers succeed: to understand their world, anticipate their needs, and offer solutions to their problems. For example, when raging storms battered Florida, several account managers contacted clients there about battery and backup-storage solutions. Key to being able to offer such critical, specialized help is the many customer information databases CDW maintains, primarily to anticipate client needs and offer customized account management.

Customer databases help not only in generating CDW's internal growth, but also in its deployment of external expansion strategies, such as when CDW paid $22 million to acquire Micro Warehouse, in part for access to the regional customer databases gained with the acquisition. When speaking of this deal, CEO Edwardson shared this view: "We believe that more than 75 percent of Micro Warehouse's corporate and public sector revenue is from customers who are new to CDW."

Case Questions

1. Considering CDW's business model, what sort of information should be collected and warehoused in CDW's customer databases? In what ways could this information be used to help their customers succeed by understanding their world, anticipating their needs, or offering solutions to their problems? Provide your reasoning for the information you propose collecting.
2. What types of typical marketing management scenarios/problems can CDW's customer databases help clarify and improve? What types are specific to CDW, and how do they differ from standard ones?
3. What are the technical requirements and costs associated with the development of these types of databases? How often will they need to be updated, and with what sort of additional information over time?
4. Given CDW's business model, in what ways might their cost analyses differ from those under a more typical model for their industry? What would be reasonable criteria for determining whether specific services are cost-effective for CDW?
5. How might a marketing decision support system (MDSS) interface with these types of databases? What kinds of models can one reasonably expect to deploy to help CDW with its business processes?
6. How could Micro Warehouse's regional customer databases be used to CDW's advantage? Give specific examples.
7. Suppose that the internal CDW databases and the newly acquired Micro Warehouse databases not only fail to provide identical information, but that their overlap is not even substantial. As a marketing manager of CDW, how would you deal with this matter? What if the unit of analysis (e.g., customer, account, purchase occasions, household) is different in the two databases?
8. Are there any ethical questions raised by CDW's maintaining such customer databases, and accessing those collected by other organizations for different purposes? If so, what are they, and how should they be dealt with?
9. How would you propose that CDW evaluate information in the new database so as to maximize its ability to provide critical, specialized help to its customers? Would it be best to disregard information evaluated as not crucial to this ability? Why or why not?

Source: www.cdw.com > About Us > Corporate Information > Company Overview "CDW Corporate Overview," www.hoovers.com.

Rezendes, Christoper J. "CDW Acquires Micro Warehouse." Christopher J. Rezendes. Venture Development Corporation Report.

Salter, Chuck (2005), "The Soft Sell." *Fast Company* 90, 72–73

CASE 1.10 SPORTZONE CLEANSING PRODUCTS FOR MEN

SportZone was fast becoming a leading brand in the Antiperspirant and Deodorant category. Several years ago, SportZone's brand management team leveraged the success of this brand among younger (typically younger than 35) deodorant users by launching SportZone Bar Soap and SportZone Body Wash. These new products enjoyed phenomenal success in their first 2 years in the market, exceeding sales goals for both initiatives. Considering the products' superior sales performance, as well as growing demand for male-targeted cleansing products, the brand management team forecasted a 10 percent increase in sales volume for the following fiscal year and was fairly confident this level could be achieved.

Over the past quarter, however, the competitive landscape has changed dramatically. Five competitors, perhaps lured by the success of the SportZone line, extended their product portfolio by launching care products targeted exclusively to men. Additionally, several other competitors announced their intentions to explore the "male care" products market. The traditional market of personal care products targeted to women had reached saturation levels, and was not expected to provide great growth potential. At the same time, one of the key trends in the personal care market was identified as "the blossoming of the 'metrosexual' man." According to ACNielsen, the male population was becoming more focused on improving its image, boosting sales in personal care products in general and for specialized grooming products in particular.

Despite increased competition over the past couple of months, SportZone was continuing on its previous, highly positive, trends in sales and market share. Given this comforting degree of growth, the brand management team decided not to alter the original *total* marketing budget allocated to support the brand. However, little was known about optimal *allocation*. Consequently, it was decided to conduct a study to understand how this fixed budget could be spent most effectively to continue driving SportZone awareness and trial among males ages 18–34 in face of increased competition.

The information needs for the study's purpose included the following:

- What are the most effective drivers of awareness, and what are the barriers that SportZone must overcome to capitalize on the identified drivers?
- What are the most effective drivers of trial, and what are the barriers to trial that the brand must overcome to increase penetration among SportZone nonusers?
- What are the product attributes that seem to most effectively convert nonusers to users after trial? That is, which should be emphasized among potential consumers?
- Who and/or what influences the purchase/repeat purchase decision, both at the time of use and at the point-of-purchase?

The information needs and the study's objective were communicated to the newly formed internal research department. The research executives judged that a "primary consumer" survey would be most appropriate to provide the information sought by the brand management team. The consumer survey was proposed to be conducted at the point-of-sale, in major grocery stores and mass merchandisers of three major metropolitan cities: New York, Chicago, and Los Angeles. Professional interviewers would be recruited to conduct the interviews with 2000 males, ages 18–34, while they approach personal care products shelves within the store.

The draft questionnaire sent to SportZone's brand management team for review is presented in Exhibit A.

Exhibit A: Personal Cleansing Product Survey Questionnaire

For the following two questions please circle the number that most closely represents your perception of personal cleansing products:

1 Please circle the number on the following scale that best describes your perception of bar soap:

Scented	1	2	3	4	5	6	7	Nonscented
Expensive	1	2	3	4	5	6	7	Inexpensive
Traditional	1	2	3	4	5	6	7	Contemporary
Masculine	1	2	3	4	5	6	7	Feminine
Premium	1	2	3	4	5	6	7	Standard
Moisturizing	1	2	3	4	5	6	7	Nonmoisturizing

2 Please circle the number on the following scale that best describes your perception of body wash:

Scented	1	2	3	4	5	6	7	Nonscented
Expensive	1	2	3	4	5	6	7	Inexpensive
Traditional	1	2	3	4	5	6	7	Contemporary
Masculine	1	2	3	4	5	6	7	Feminine
Premium	1	2	3	4	5	6	7	Standard
Moisturizing	1	2	3	4	5	6	7	Nonmoisturizing

3 Please list up to three brands of men's body wash of which you are aware:

________________ ________________ ________________

4 How did you learn about these brands? (Please circle all that apply)

a TV

b Newspaper

c Magazine
d Coupons
e Word-of-mouth
f Online
g E-mail
h Mail promotions
i Posters
j Campus promotional events
k In-store
l Radio
m Other ____________________

5 How effective do you consider the following venues in promoting personal cleansing products to you personally? (1 = very ineffective; 4 = neutral; 7 = very effective)

	(very ineffective)			**(neutral)**			**(very effective)**
Local promotional events	1	2	3	4	5	6	7
Mail promotions	1	2	3	4	5	6	7
Newspaper	1	2	3	4	5	6	7
Online	1	2	3	4	5	6	7
Posters	1	2	3	4	5	6	7
Radio	1	2	3	4	5	6	7
TV	1	2	3	4	5	6	7
Coupons	1	2	3	4	5	6	7
Word-of-mouth	1	2	3	4	5	6	7
E-mail	1	2	3	4	5	6	7

6 In just the past 3 months, which of the following best represented your own personal use of body cleansing products when taking a bath or shower?
Select one response
a bar soap only
b body wash only
c bar soap and body wash, about equally
d both bar soap and body wash, but bar soap more often
e both bar soap and body wash, but body wash more often

7 In just the past 3 months, what ONE brand of bar soap and/or body wash did you, yourself, use most of the time for taking a bath or shower?
Body wash ______________________
Bar soap ______________________

8 Who, in the past month, usually purchased the personal cleansing products that you, personally, use?
a self
b significant other
c roommate
d mother
e father
f other ____________________

9 Of the following descriptors, please rank the top three characteristics in choosing a men's personal cleansing product (1 = most important; 2 = second most important; 3 = third most important):
________ Scent
________ Price
________ Moisturizing level

_______ Packaging appeal
_______ Brand name
_______ Cleansing power
_______ Lather
_______ Other _______________

10 How often, if ever, do you, personally, use body wash in the shower or bath?

a Every time I shower or take a bath
b Once every 2–3 times I shower or take a bath
c Once every 4–6 times I shower or take a bath
d Never

11 If you have tried body wash in the past, what prompted you to do so?

____

12 If you have not tried body wash in the past, why not?

____

13 Are you aware of any of the following SportZone personal products? (please circle all that apply)

a Deodorant
b Body wash
c Bar soap
d I am not aware of any of the products listed above.

14 Have you, personally, ever used any of the following SportZone personal products? (please circle all that apply)

a Deodorant
b Body wash
c Bar soap
d I have never used any of the products listed above.

15 Have you, personally, used any other SportZone products (e.g., deodorant, aftershave, etc.) in the past year?

a Yes
b No

16 Age ___________

17 Please indicate which of the following ethnic groups best describes you.

_____ Asian
_____ Hispanic
_____ Black/African American
_____ White
_____ Other _______________

Please select only one answer for questions 18 through 20:

18 School

_____ Undergraduate _____ Graduate _____ Not Presently Attending

19 Marital status

_____Single _____Married _____Divorced _____Widowed _____Separated

20 Hometown zip code _________

Thank you!

Case Questions

1. Evaluate the appropriateness of the stated information needs in addressing the study's objective. Provide specific advantages and disadvantages. If you were asked to restate the information needs, would you change anything? Explain your answer.
2. List any additional information needs that you would formulate if you were in the SportZone brand manager's position. What if cost and time for the survey and other research were not serious issues?
3. Evaluate the research design that was proposed by the internal research department. Discuss advantages and disadvantages and, for the latter, suggest specific improvements. Was the segmentation of the customer base and product line warranted?
4. If you were asked to develop the research proposal for the SportZone's study, what would you recommend regarding the study's sources and specific design details?
5. Evaluate the appropriateness of the draft questionnaire for usage in the proposed consumer survey. If you were SportZone's brand manager, what specific details would you discuss during the review of the questionnaire, and why?
6. The questionnaire makes use of a variety of scale and question types. Are these well-suited to the design goal? Which will be particularly difficult to analyze? Are the geodemographic and other classification-based questions appropriate? Finally, are there any questions that can be readily improved, in terms of phraseology, directions, specific choices offered, or along other dimensions?

Source: http://www2.acnielsen.com/pubs/documents/2004_q3_ci_personal.pdf

PART 2

PLANNING PROJECTS, DESIGNING SURVEYS, AND SAMPLING

CHAPTER FOUR
MEASUREMENT IN MARKETING RESEARCH

"One accurate measurement is worth a thousand expert opinions."

ADMIRAL GRACE HOPPER

This chapter on measurement, along with Chapters 5 (on causal research and experimentation), 6 (on data collection), and 7 (on design of surveys and data collection instruments), covers the fourth step of the marketing research process: developing the data collection procedure.

Measurement issues are a constant challenge, not only in marketing research, but throughout the social sciences. Although we may be reasonably certain that we have measured well "solid," objective quantities like a consumer's age, income, or purchase frequency, making the same claim about education (is this merely the number of years someone has been in school?), ethnicity, or lifestyle category (psychographics) is certainly more tenuous. And just how do we know whether we have a reliable and valid measure of constructs like loyalty, purchase intention, and consumer satisfaction? None of these things has a clear physical meaning, and even experts can debate them as psychological entities.

The process of measurement is a commonplace occurrence throughout life. Entrance or aptitude examinations are measuring devices designed to assess one's potential for more advanced work. Later, one is confronted with an array of examinations to measure achievement in courses and work skills. Various forms of measurement are involved when students or employees are counted, classified (as male or female, as to their area of residence, as to their department, and so on), or judged (as to performance or even personality). These are only a few examples of the use of measurement in everyday activities; measurement is so common that it is often taken for granted. Rarely do we stop to think about the differences in the type of measurements taken and the accuracy of the conclusions drawn. In this chapter, we systematically examine aspects of measurement, how they are applied, how they might go awry, and "best practice" guidelines for marketing research applications, as well as the pivotal importance of attitudes to marketing theory and practice.

4.1 Basic Concepts in Measurement

The process of measurement is a fundamental component of essentially all marketing research activities. Rare is the marketing situation where *no* quantification is undertaken and decision makers "go by their gut" alone, with no insight gleaned from data. For this reason, the topic of measurement is of critical concern to those in the field of marketing.

Decision makers are interested in measuring many aspects of the marketing system. For example, they may want to measure the market potential for a new product; to group buyers by demographic or psychographic characteristics; to learn buyers' attitudes, perceptions, or preferences toward a new brand; or to determine the effectiveness of a new advertising campaign. Consequently, the measurement of marketing phenomena is essential to the process of providing meaningful information for decision making.

Developing effective measures of marketing phenomena is not an easy task. In Chapter 2, measurement error was highlighted as often constituting a substantial portion of the total error in marketing research information. For many research projects, measurement error can be substantially *greater* than sampling error, particularly when measurements involve subjective consumer information such as attitudes, preferences, and intentions. Having a clear understanding of the measurement problem and how to control this error is an important aspect of designing an effective marketing research project and must be considered before the project gets under way—not after the data have been collected and found wanting.

The marketing manager rarely becomes directly involved in the actual measurement process. The task of selecting and designing measurement techniques is the responsibility of the research specialist. However, the decision maker usually must approve the recommended measurement techniques and needs to be confident that these techniques will effectively control or reduce measurement error.

To control measurement error effectively, the marketing manager needs to take account of three distinct issues: the specification of information needs should recognize the *degree of difficulty* in obtaining accurate measures, the *alternate measurement procedures* for obtaining the information, and the *cost of measurement* relative to the accuracy of measurement.

Look at how a firm that specializes in the provision of information to other firms dealt with allegations that its methods could be put to misleading uses. *Marketing Research Focus 4.1* presents the case of J. D. Power & Associates, whose customer satisfaction surveys and scores have become mainstays of the automotive industry.

Marketing Research Focus 4.1

J. D. Power's Customer Satisfaction Tracking Impacts Automotive Industry

Ford Motor Company was notably upset by Chrysler Corporation ads implying that buyers rank Chrysler first among U.S. automakers. Ford asserted that such claims were false, but it allocated some of the blame to the automobile marketing research firm of J. D. Power & Associates. J. D. Power approved the ads based on one of its customer satisfaction surveys. The survey did, indeed, rank Chrysler first in the domestic market, but the ranking was based more on dealer service than on actual car quality, a fact that failed to come out in the ads.

Chrysler's use of the J. D. Power name in its ads made the claim more egregiously misleading, in Ford's view, because many potential buyers view the Power name as the automobile industry's version of the *Good Housekeeping* Seal of Approval. Power's automotive marketing research and its tracking of consumer satisfaction exert a major influence over customer buying patterns. This ultimately affects all competitors in the $500 billion U.S. automotive industry.

Those who are ill affected are far from happy, and quite possibly for good reason. Most of Power's studies are based on questionnaires sent to car owners. A division general manager at Ford complained that many of Power's opinion samples were not extensive enough to support the broad conclusions the company draws. Speaking anonymously, one former employee said that the company's research fails to meet purist standards: "From a methodological standpoint, there are many automotive manufacturers with better resources" than Power's. Internal researchers often echoed these concerns about research methods, specifically that samples could be larger, questions may sometimes be worded in a way that could influence results, measurement error (in terms of whether the construct of satisfaction is really measured) is not always conclusively ruled out, and there should be greater variance in the times of year that the data are collected.

Power defended its methods publicly, and many clients agreed, dismissing the critics as "jealous snipers" who didn't understand an enterprising firm conducting business in a slightly different way. Nonetheless, these types of allegations of bias and carelessness in sampling, measurement, and fieldwork have the potential to damage both the research firm's and the client's reputation.

4.1a The Measurement Process

In marketing research, the measurement process involves using numbers to represent each of the marketing phenomena under investigation. Carefully distinguishing these concepts—the marketing phenomena themselves from the numerical quantities used to represent them—will help avoid confusion later. We will call the set of marketing phenomena under study the **empirical system**; it will include such concepts and activities as buyer reactions, ad spending, competitive promotions, and sales response. By contrast, the **abstract system** consists of all quantities used to represent these marketing phenomena. This correspondence between the two is depicted in Figure 4.1. In some cases, this correspondence will be fairly obvious and beyond debate, such as using retail volume as a measure of sales activity. But often researchers need to engage in multiple measurements and a good deal of thought to capture and numerically track even common marketing concepts such as competitive reaction or promotional activity.

empirical system
The set of marketing phenomena under study, often including such quantities as consumer behavior, ad expenditure, competitive tactics, and sales.

abstract system
The theoretical constructs used to model marketing phenomena and to make predictions; these can then be compared with empirical data on the phenomena under study.

Figure 4.1 The Measurement Process

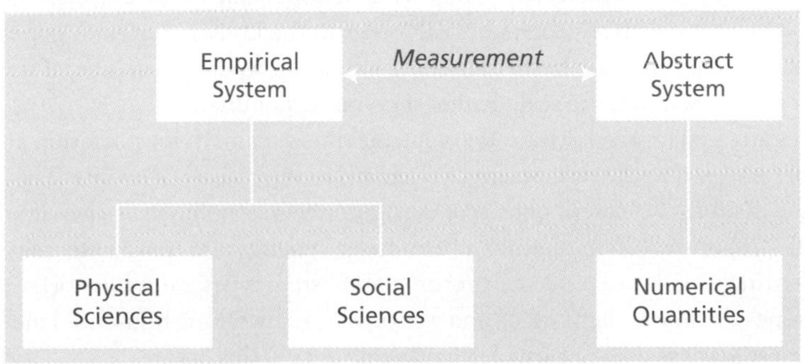

4.1b Definition of Measurement

In keeping with the correspondence between the empirical system (marketing phenomena) and the abstract system (numerical measures), measurement may be defined as assigning numbers to objects, characteristics, or events in the empirical system according to a set of known, specific rules in the abstract system. If the correspondence between the two systems is misrepresented or misconstrued, measurement error can occur, a topic taken up at length later in the chapter.

The term *number* in the definition of measurement imposes certain restrictions on the type of numerical manipulations admissible. Numbers are being used as symbols to model the characteristics of interest in the empirical system. The nature of the relationships existing in the empirical system determines the type of numerical manipulations that are valid in the abstract system. Let us briefly consider characteristics of the number system to provide a better understanding of this often-overlooked issue.

4.1c Number System Characteristics

Early in our educational career, we learned four characteristics of the number system that consists of the numerals 0, 1, 2, 3, 4, 5, 6, 7, 8, and 9. First, each number in the series is *unique*, and there are precisely ten of them. Second, the *ordering* of the numbers is given by convention; for example, $2 > 1 > 0$. Third, we can define *equal differences;* for example, $3 - 2 = 7 - 6$; $7 - 5 = 3 - 1$. Fourth, we can define *equal ratios*, for example, $10/5 = 6/3$. As it turns out, these observations, yawningly common after a lifetime of experience, have major ramifications for the different types of measurement scales prevalent throughout marketing research.

The manipulation of numbers via arithmetic, and by extension, statistical analysis, involves one or more of these four characteristics of the number system. There is temptation to use more of these characteristics in the data analysis than may exist in the empirical system being modeled. The problem is one of focusing on determining how many of these four characteristics are present in the marketing phenomena under investigation and then restricting the data analysis to using only appropriate characteristics in the manipulation of the numbers. Often, this restriction hampers the sophistication of data analysis that can properly be performed. Throughout the text, particularly in the chapters on specific data analysis techniques, we take great care to specify which of these operations are appropriate for various sorts of data.

4.1d Types of Scales

Historically, scales have been classified in terms of the four characteristics of the number system. These scales of measurement are universally referred to as *nominal, ordinal, interval*, and *ratio*, and their characteristics are summarized in Table 4.1. An understanding of these scales is crucial for data collection and analysis.

4.1e Nominal Scale

nominal scale
A measurement scale for which numbers are assigned to objects only as labels.

A **nominal scale** is one on which numbers serve only as labels to identify or categorize objects or events. A familiar example is the use of numbers to identify members of a sports team. Numbers used in this manner serve as labels only to identify the players, not to numerically compare them. For example, player number 44 is not "greater than" player number 11, nor does the player possess "four times" as much of any particular quantity. The same is true when we assign numbers to states, provinces, or nations for the purpose of coding them, such as geographic ZIP codes in the United States. A good informal test for whether a scale is nominal is to ask whether anything important would be affected if two categories simply swapped their numbers; if not, the scale is almost certainly nominal.

Nominal scales are used for the lowest form of measurement, namely, classification and identification. Few restrictions are imposed in the assignment of numerals to the objects or events. The rule is simple: do not assign the same number to different objects or events or different numbers to the same object or event.

A substantial proportion of marketing phenomena require nominal scale measurement. Such nominal-level identification is needed to categorize brands, store types, sales territories, geographic locations, brand awareness, heavy vs. light users, and working vs. nonworking household members. It is a rare marketing research study that does not involve marketing data of this nature.

Table 4.1 Measurement Scale Characteristics

Scale	Number System Properties	Marketing Phenomena	Appropriate Summaries and Statistical Techniques*
Nominal	Unique definition of numerical labels	Brands in a category	Percentages
	(0, 1, 2, ...)	Store types (e.g., supermarket, drug)	Logistic regression
		Sales territories	Mode
		Demographics (e.g., gender, occupation)	Cross-tabulation
			Chi-square test
Ordinal	Order of numerals	Preferences	Percentiles
	(0 < 1 < 2 ...)	Subjective frequencies	Median
		Purchase likelihood	Rank-order correlation
		Demographics (e.g., age group, education)	Ordinal regression
Interval	Equality of differences	Attitudes	Range
	(2 − 1 = 7 − 6)	Opinions	Arithmetic mean
		Index numbers	Standard deviation
			Linear regression
Ratio	Equality of ratios	Objective frequencies	Geometric mean
	(2/4 = 4/8)	Costs	Harmonic mean
		Number of customers	Coefficient of variation
		Sales (units/dollars)	Ratios and products of variables (interactions)

*Statistics appropriate for each scale apply to all those beneath it.

Although we take analysis up at length later in the text, it bears mention that nominal data are easy to use for categorization but notoriously difficult to analyze rigorously. For example, given data on customer gender breakdown by five major U.S. sales regions, it would be simple to form a 2 cell × 5 cell table representing them. However, answering even basic questions like "Are these independent?" or "How can we predict one variable from the other?" can be difficult. The main tools for handling this type of problem go under the name categorical data analysis. Among the more common statistical tests in this area is the chi-square test for contingency tables, like the 2-by-5 one described previously. In Chapters 10–12, we look closely at a more powerful general class of methods, discrete choice models, and among them logistic regression.

categorical data analysis
A branch of statistics concerned with the analysis of nominal data that includes special forms of regression-like models, such as the logit and probit models for the analysis of discrete choices.

4.1f Ordinal Scale

An ordinal scale defines the ordered relationship among objects or events. Ordinal scales measure whether an object or event has more or less of a characteristic than some other object or event. However, this scale does not provide information on *how much* more or less of the characteristic various objects or events possess. That is, it offers only information on the order, not the degree, of differences.

contingency tables
A table containing numerical observations keyed to two or more (usually categorical) variables that is frequently analyzed using a chi-square test for independence.

Let us illustrate ordinal measurement by assuming that a bicycle manufacturer is interested in determining the preference ordering for males among the firm's new "hybrid" bicycle (A) and two leading competitors (B and C) with regard to a particular characteristic, in this case, speed. A survey is conducted of 200 male potential buyers, the results of which are presented in Table 4.2.

discrete choice models
A class of statistical models used to analyze the choices made by consumers, or any dependent variable of the "choose for exactly one from many" type.

An ordinal scale can be developed by assigning numerals to the first-, second-, and third-order preference judgments. This involves the assignment of numerals such that the resulting numerical series properly maintains the ordered relationship of the preference judgments. (Note that this will suffice because there are only three products being compared. A serious practical issue arises in using ordinal scales when there are many, perhaps even hundreds, of items to be compared, such as in lists of favorite films, and respondents cannot possibly order them all. In such cases, researchers often resort to just asking for the "top three" or "top five," although there are no strict guidelines as to how many to request.)

ordinal scale
A measurement scale for which numbers are assigned to objects based on their order (i.e., greater than or less than) or direction.

Table 4.2 Male Preference Ordering of Bicycles A, B, and C with Regard to Speed ($n = 200$)

	Proportion of Preferences			
Preference ordering	A	B	C	Total
First	0.15	0.35	0.50	1.00
Second	0.50	0.25	0.25	1.00
Third	0.35	0.40	0.25	1.00
Total	1.00	1.00	1.00	

Which set of numbers should be assigned? Any set of numbers will do, the only restriction being that the numbers must correspond to the ordinal relationships present in the preference judgments. For example, the number 1 can be used to represent the first-order preferences; number 2, the second-order preferences; and number 3, the third-order preferences. But one could just as well have used {1, 3, 5}, {1, 3, 30}, or {14, 73, 1128}. All these numerical sets form acceptable ordinal scales, and we cannot argue that one set is better than the others. Convention dictates that we use {1, 2, 3} for clarity, but it is imperative that researchers not presume that the "distance" between 1 and 2 is the same as that between 2 and 3. That would require an interval scale, whose properties we consider later in this chapter. Consequently, with an ordinal scale, the only restriction in the assignment of a new series of numbers is that an increasing **monotonic transformation** be used, as illustrated in the graph of ordinal scale in Figure 4.2.

monotonic transformation
Any process that takes one set of numbers and produces another from them so that if values taken from the first set are increasing then the corresponding numbers from the second set will, too; common examples include the logarithm of squaring (for positive numbers) or exponentiating (for any numbers).

Consider results obtained from an ordinal scale relative to two such (supposedly equivalent) scalings: {1, 2, 3} (set 1) and {1, 3, 30} (set 2). The overall ranking of the three bicycles based on the mode—an appropriate measure of **central tendency** for ordinal scales—is presented in Table 4.3. It is important to note that the preference ordering of the three bicycles is identical for both numerical scales (numerical sets 1 and 2). Here, the overall preference ordering is bicycle C first, A second, and B third. Research findings will not be affected by the numerical set selected for data analysis. More formally, we can state that for any increasing monotonic scale transformation, the conclusions drawn from the data analysis using statistics appropriate for ordinal data will not change as a result of the assignment of alternative numerical sets.

central tendency
Any of a number of estimates of the most common of, or the center of, a variable's values; the most common measures of central tendency are the mean, median, and mode.

Recall that some of the statistics appropriate for ordinal data were presented in Table 4.1 (corresponding analyses are taken up later in Chapter 10). Note that the mean is *not* an appropriate statistic for ordinal data. What happens if we calculate the mean? The preference ordering of the three bicycles is different for the two numerical assignments, and this should never happen: for numerical set 1 ({1, 2, 3}), bicycle C is first, B is second, and A is last, but for numerical set 2 ({1, 3, 30}), C is first, A is second, and B is third. Bicycles A and B have *reversed positions because of the scale transformation*. This result is not surprising when we realize that the calculation of a mean involves the equal-interval characteristic of the number system: a unit difference in one direction should balance an identical difference in the other. Because the scale transformation maintained only a monotonic or ranked relationship rather than an equal-interval relationship, the results of a simple "statistical" analysis depend on the number series selected. This is a clear example of *measurement error*. Although it is fairly common to see ordinal data represented by means even in professionally prepared reports, this is not statistically justified and should only be done in those rare cases when there is explicit evidence that the ordinal scale is close to an interval one.

An important segment of marketing data involves ordinal measurement. Most data collected by the process of questionnaires and personal interviews have ordinal properties. For example, the measurement of attitudes, opinions, preference ("strongly," "moderately," or "mildly" agree), subjective frequencies ("rarely," "sometimes," or "often"), and perception often involves a "greater than" or "less than" intrinsically ordinal judgment. One of the most common methods for assessing opinions and attitudes involves an "agree–disagree" scale of the following type:

Please indicate how much you agree with the listed statement by choosing the appropriate point on the scale that follows: "This appliance would make an attractive addition to my kitchen."

Strongly disagree	Disagree	Mildly disagree	Neither agree nor disagree	Mildly agree	Agree	Strongly agree
1	2	3	4	5	6	7

Figure 4.2 Permissible Transformation by Scale Type. Each graph represents two possible transformations for each of the ordinal, interval, and ratio scale types. The *x* axis represents the original numbers assigned by the scale, and the *y* axis shows the new ones assigned by the transformation. In each case, the transformation (*y*) retains the (ordinal, interval, or ratio) information contained in the original (*x*) data.

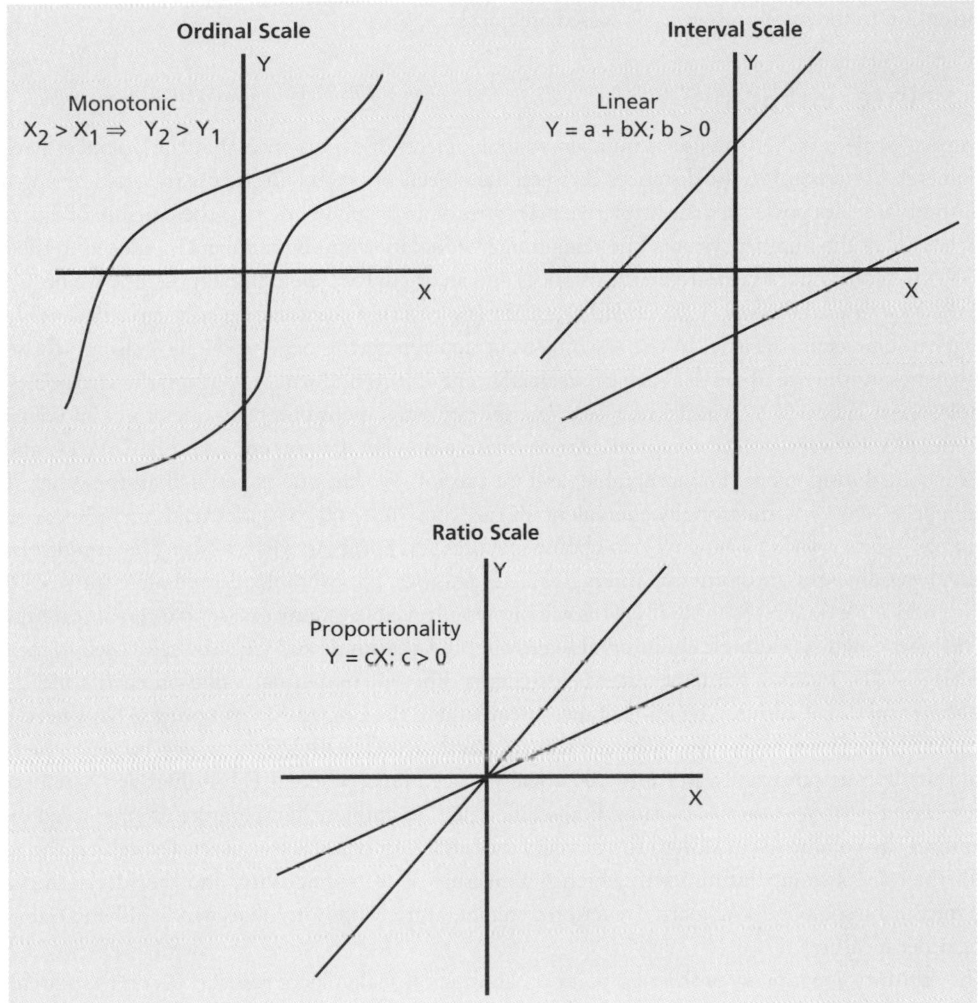

It is important to realize that, although we have what appears to be an evenly spaced scale in the numbers {1, 2, 3, 4, 5, 6, 7}, they are still only *ordinally* related. There could be an enormous subjective difference between "strongly disagreeing" with something and merely "disagreeing" with it—quite likely greater than the difference between "mildly" disagreeing and "neither" agreeing nor disagreeing—yet the

Table 4.3 Overall Ranking of Bicycles A, B, and C

	Ranking		
Descriptive statistic	**First**	**Second**	**Third**
Mode (set 1, {1, 2, 3})	C (1)	A (2)	B (3)
Mode (set 2, {1, 3, 30})	C (1)	A (3)	B (30)
Mean (set 1, {1, 2, 3})	C (1.75)*	B (2.05)	A (2.20)
Mean (set 2, {1, 3, 30})	C (8.75)	A (12.15)	B (13.10)

*Mean = (1) (0.50) + (2) (0.25) + (3) (0.25) + 1 = 1.75.

interval between 1 and 2 is the same as between 3 and 4. One should never assume that the properties of the *numbers assigned* to verbal descriptions mimic the relation of the verbal descriptions themselves, especially with nominal and ordinal scales.

Finally, because many characteristics of buyers or purchasing units can involve a ranked characteristic (e.g., occupation, social class, or image), a substantial proportion of marketing research data involves ordinal judgments. The analysis of these data must be approached using the appropriate statistical tools and attention to the scale properties discussed previously.

4.1g Interval Scale

interval scale
A measurement scale for which differences in consecutive numbers assigned correspond to constant values in the phenomenon under study; e.g., the difference in the strength of a respondent's views between 1 and 2 on a seven-point interval scale should be the same as the difference between 5 and 6.

linear transformation
Any transformation that involves taking variables or a group of numbers and either multiplying them by or adding to them some constant, e.g., $y = a + bx$.

An **interval scale** involves the use of numbers to rank objects or events such that the distances between the numerals correspond to the distances between the objects or events on the characteristic being measured. Interval scales possess all the attractive properties of an ordinal scale plus the equality of difference characteristic of the number system. The remaining freedom in assigning numbers is reduced to the arbitrary selection of a unit of measurement (distance) and an origin (zero point). Suppose that we have measured the four ordered objects A, B, C, and D and determined that the distance between adjacent objects is equal on some characteristic. In the assignment of numbers to the objects, we must arbitrarily decide how to represent the size of the distance between adjacent objects and where to assign the zero points. For example, the numbers 0, 1, 2, and 3 represent an arbitrary assignment of zero to one object and of a one-unit difference between adjacent objects. An alternative number assignment could be 7, 9, 11, and 13. Both numerical assignments are acceptable, and we cannot say that one is better than the other. They are, in a deep sense, informationally equivalent and are often referred to as identical "up to **linear transformation**," a fancy way of saying we can choose spacings and zero points as we like. The key idea is that we can always linearly transform one interval scale to another. For example, if we double the scale {0, 1, 2, 3} and add 7, we obtain {7, 9, 11, 13}. This will always be possible for any two such interval scalings.

The most common examples of interval scales are the Fahrenheit and Celsius scales used to measure temperature. The freezing point of water is assigned a different numerical value on each scale, 32 on Fahrenheit and 0 on Celsius. The units of measurement and the origins (or zero points) have been arbitrarily determined for these scales, although Celsius was designed to divide the region between the freezing and the boiling points of water into 100 equally spaced units whereas Fahrenheit was based on the properties of a particular saline solution. Equal differences in ambient temperature are measured by, for example, equal-volume expansion in the mercury used in a standard thermometer. (Note that the scales are not the same as temperature itself, which is a measure of atomic activity, and they do an imperfect job of measuring someone's subjective reaction to temperature, which involves wind chill and humidity, among other measures.)

The arbitrary assignment of the zero point on an interval scale places restrictions on the statements that can be made regarding comparisons of intervals. For example, it would be considered quite odd to claim that, with either temperature system, a 10-degree day is "half as warm" as a 20-degree day and absurd to say a −40-degree day was "negative two times as warm." The zero point on each scale is arbitrary, so comparison of absolute magnitudes or ratios is meaningless.

This temperature-based example applies to all interval scales. Assume that we have scaled brands A, B, and C on an interval scale regarding buyers' degree of liking of the brands. Brand A receives a 6, the highest liking score; B receives a 3; and C receives a 2. What can we say about these interval-scaled data? First, the liking for brand A is more favorable than that for brand B (order of numerals). Second, the degree of liking between A and B is three times greater than the liking between B and C (equality of differences). What we cannot say is that brand A is liked "twice as much" as brand B. Such a statement assumes that the absolute zero point, or the absence of liking, has been identified and assigned the value zero on the interval scale.

Latitude in assigning new numerical value sets to an interval scale is more restricted than for an ordinal scale. This new numerical assignment involves a linear transformation of the form $y = a + bx$ (where b is positive); therefore, a graph of x, the original scale number, vs. y, the new scale number, is a straight line with a constant slope. The graph of interval scale in Figure 4.2 gives examples of two such transformations. A positive (i.e., $b > 0$) linear scale transformation of an interval scale will not alter research findings when appropriate statistical techniques are used. The majority of such techniques can be used to analyze interval data, as shown in Table 4.1; they include the range, arithmetic mean, standard deviation, and product–moment correlation. Only a few statistical techniques (such as geometric mean, harmonic mean, and coefficient of variation) could lead to misleading results if applied to interval data.

A crucial advantage of interval scales is that they allow the use of **linear regression** techniques, which are, by a wide margin, the dominant analysis methods in all of social science. It is difficult to overstate the importance of linear regression in marketing research applications, and we examine these techniques at length in Chapters 10–12. The appearance of *linear* in both *linear regression* and *linear transformation* is no coincidence. It is this linearity that allows the power of linear regression—so long as we are sure that all variables used in the analysis have the interval property. As we demonstrate, linear regression is insensitive to the scale (b, also called the slope) or location (a, also called the zero point or intercept, sometimes notated as b_0) used in linearly transforming any of the input variables. It will automatically extract the same information content, irrespective of scaling. Such methods are sometimes called *scale free* to emphasize that the researcher cannot affect substantive results merely by rescaling, no more than you can affect your income by counting it in pennies instead of dollars.

linear regression
The most common form of statistical model, in which a dependent variable, Y, is related to a group of independent variables, $\{X_1, X_2, \ldots, X_k\}$, as follows: $Y = b_0 + b_1X_1 + b_2X_2 + \ldots + b_kX_k + \varepsilon$, where ε represents error, usually normally distributed, the coefficients, $\{b_0, b_1, b_2, \ldots, b_k\}$, are estimated based on data from a sample.

In marketing, it is common for attitudinal, opinion, and predisposition judgments to be treated as interval data. To be technically correct, these judgments are ordinal. Researchers disagree as to the amount of measurement error present in the results given by ordinal data treated as interval data. The magnitude of this error must be weighed against the data analysis advantages associated with the more sophisticated statistical techniques applicable to analysis of interval data. It is often argued that although the equality-of-interval characteristic may be violated, the degree of violation is typically small and the results of most statistical techniques are not affected to the point that significant measurement error exists, but often this amounts to little more than guesswork or wishful thinking. In the final analysis, it is the responsibility of the researcher to determine (1) how closely the relationships in the marketing phenomena under study approximate an interval scale and (2) the appropriateness of treating the data as interval-scaled.

4.1h Ratio Scale

A **ratio scale** has all the properties of an interval scale plus an absolute zero point. With ratio measurement, only one number may be assigned arbitrarily, namely, the unit of measurement or distance. Once this is determined, the remaining numerical assignments are determined as well.

ratio scale
A measurement scale in which the values assigned to choices or objects possess an absolute zero point, so that both differences and quotients of scale points make sense; e.g., it makes sense to say someone is twice as old as someone else, or lives half as far away, indicating that age and distance are ratio-scaled variables.

Absolute or *natural zero point* refers to the assignment of the number zero to the absence of the characteristic being measured. For example, in our discussion of the Fahrenheit and Celsius temperature scales, it was stated that the zero points were arbitrarily assigned on both scales. Consequently, the zero points on these scales do not correspond to the total absence of heat. But such a temperature scale does exist: in the Kelvin scale, absolute zero (−273.15°C) truly represents the absence of heat and the cessation of atomic activity. Whenever people mention "absolute zero," they unwittingly reinforce that Kelvin is a ratio scale in that its zero point carries some deep, or absolute, meaning.

A ratio scale requires that equal ratios among the scale values correspond to equal ratios among the marketing phenomena being measured. For example, the statement that the sales of product A are twice as large as the sales of product B is legitimate with ratio scale data because the concept of zero sales is meaningful, not an arbitrarily assigned quantity. The scale transformations for a ratio scale involve a positive proportionate transformation of the form $y = cx$; $c > 0$. This means that the scale before and after transformation have to share the same value of zero; on the graph of ratio scale in Figure 4.2, the transformation therefore must pass through (0,0), the origin.

Many important marketing phenomena possess the properties of a ratio scale. These include sales, market share, costs, ages, number of customers, and other geodemographic quantities. In each case, a natural or absolute zero exists, and descriptors like "half as much," "three times as far," and "25 percent more" make natural, intuitive sense.

The entire bounty of statistical techniques can be applied to the analysis of ratio-scaled data, making it the "best" data to have. It is important, however, to avoid the temptation to treat nonratio data as ratio data. Note that little is gained, in terms of data analysis techniques, in having ratio-scaled as opposed to interval-scaled data. Because linear regression applies to both, researchers usually concern themselves with the interval property, treating ratio scaling as a nice bonus but not crucial. *Marketing Research Focus 4.2* takes a closer look at measurement scales and some of their properties of interest to marketing researchers.

Marketing Research Focus 4.2

An Example Comparing Measurement Scales

Thus far, our discussion of measurement scales has been largely, and deliberately, theoretical. Although we show many examples of these scales when question types are discussed in Chapter 7, we are now in a position to compare them in terms of a concrete example. Because we can "destructure" ratio-scaled information but cannot impose structure on information that is only nominal, let us take a common ratio-scaled construct—age—and see how we can ask a question about it using each of the scale types considered thus far. Note that it would be decidedly odd to ask for age using only nominal categories; we do so purely for illustration. So, suppose a researcher wished to ask for a respondent's age and has at least four ways to do so:

Ratio age: How many years have elapsed *since you were born?*
Interval age: How many years have elapsed *since your 18th birthday?*
Ordinal age, version 1: Which of the following *age groups* do you fall into?
• 18–22 • 23–29 • 30–39 • 40–55 • Over 55
Ordinal age, version 2: Which of the following best describes your *age group?*
• Young adult • Middle-aged • Mature • Old as the hills
Categorical age: If over 70, which of the following *best describes your age?*
• Elderly • Getting up there • No spring chicken • Not what I used to be

Although parts of this example are whimsical, the basic idea is not. The "ratio age" variable is comparable not only *additively* but also *multiplicatively:* you can be 10 years older than someone, or twice their age, and both comparisons make sense. The "interval age" variable is quite similar, with one exception: someone 10 years past an 18th birthday is not twice as old as someone 5 years past; only additive comparisons are sensible. Note that with the ratio and interval question data all statistical methods based on regression apply if used with care. By contrast, analysis is more complex when we deal with categorical variables, because there isn't a neat linear relationship to express their interrelations.

In both versions of the ordinal variable we have been discussing, it is clear that *everyone in a particular category is older than everyone in previous categories* (and younger than everyone in subsequent categories). It is important to realize that it would be incorrect to replace the ordinal categories in the first version with their midpoints; the last group (older than 55) doesn't even have a midpoint. In the second version, it is unclear even what the category cutoffs are; furthermore, *they may be different for different people* (is a 55-year-old "middle-aged" or "mature"?). But different people would still agree that the categories themselves were ordered. The last variable type, nominal (sometimes referred to as *categorical*), is merely a set of labels that cannot be compared with one another numerically. In this case, they must be treated as mere adjectives, and it is anyone's guess as to which of "getting up there" or "elderly" will be judged to sound older.

Note that a ratio and interval variable can easily be made ordinal or nominal by parceling it into "bins" (such as in version 1 of Ordered); of course, doing so sacrifices some structure and is usually called for only when assuming linearity is not really correct (e.g., using age in years to predict calories consumed per day, which rises more-or-less linearly from birth through adolescence, and then plateaus; appropriately fashioned ordered categories would be superior in this case).

Although it is tempting to try to make all questions at least interval, budding researchers should be cautioned against doing so except in cases, like age, that measure a precise physical or chronological construct. Although we can measure the number of years since someone's 18th birthday accurately and unambiguously, we cannot accurately and unambiguously measure the number of times they have gone shopping (even though a precise definition can be imposed on it) or the number of times they have been depressed, much less the number of times they have seriously considered purchasing a particular product.

4.2 Difficulty in Measurement

When the measurement process is discussed, many people's minds drift to their own experiences with weight, height, and distance, "Since I've been jogging two miles each day, my weight has dropped by 5 pounds." The measurement of such physically tangible, ratio-scaled variables as weight, distance, and height is typically an easy task. Natural zero points ("no weight loss," "no distance") and equality of differences ("one mile further every month") are obvious. This type of measurement situation is more characteristic of the physical sciences than of the social sciences, including marketing. Consequently, the measurement task in marketing is typically more difficult and involves "lower" scales of measurement (ordinal and nominal) than those typical in the physical sciences.

Why is measurement so difficult in marketing? Whereas the physical sciences are concerned with inert objects—subatomic particles, geographic strata, galaxies—obeying what appear to be natural laws, marketing studies that most irregular and unruled of entities, human behavior. As the philosopher David Hume put it in 1742, "But what is Man but a heap of contradictions!" The marketing researcher attempts to make sense of this "heap of contradictions" using the decidedly crude yardsticks of surveys, personal interviews, and such aggregated field measurements as sales and promotional activity, all subject to substantial measurement error.

4.2a Concepts and Constructs

The measurement task in marketing is complicated by the many concepts and constructs that pervade marketing thought, the varying definitions that have been proposed for them, and the multitude of settings in which they appear, each with its own particularities.

The terms *concept* and *construct* have similar meanings and are used interchangeably throughout marketing. A **construct** is an abstraction we build in our minds based on perceptions of a phenomenon. Constructs serve as the building blocks of our larger models of interacting forces, such as the field of marketing research provides of the marketing system. In marketing, we refer to constructs such as sales, product positioning, demand, attitudes, and brand loyalty. Constructs simplify and synthesize the complex phenomena present in the marketing system, allowing a common language and conceptual basis for decision-makers to resolve problems.

construct
Any abstraction used by the researcher based on perceptions of a phenomenon, meant to serve as building blocks for more complex marketing; typical examples include sales, product positioning, demand, attitudes, and brand loyalty.

Some constructs are directly related to aspects of physical reality. For example, the constructs of length and weight are closely related to observations regarding heavy or light and tall or short. The measurement of these constructs is commonplace and fairly easy. In marketing, such constructs are less common, although such readily measured quantities as sales or ad spending would qualify.

Far more common in marketing are the many constructs lacking observable physical references. Examples include purchase intent, attitude, preference, and image. These constructs exist in the minds of individuals and are not directly observable, even given a precise operational definition. Effective marketing research requires that constructs be defined unambiguously and precisely. This can be done in two general ways: by a constitutive definition and by an operational definition.

A **constitutive definition** defines a construct with other constructs. Although this may sound circular, this approach is used universally in a dictionary, where words are used to define other words. A constitutive definition should identify the main features of the construct such that it is clearly differentiated from other constructs. For example, how might one define brand loyalty? One common definition is "a consumer's preferential, attitudinal, and behavioral response toward a target brand, expressed over a period of time." In this definition, constructs such as preferential attitude, behavioral response, and consumer are used to define the construct "brand loyalty." Another is "the ability to withstand competitive inducements from other brands." Again, this requires knowledge of competitive inducements and what constitutes withstanding them.

constitutive definition
When a construct is defined in terms of other constructs, often in the form of an equation.

An **operational definition** specifies how a construct is to be measured. An operational definition is a sort of manual of instructions to the investigator. It says, in effect, "Do such-and-such in so-and-so manner." Thus, it defines or gives meaning to a variable by spelling out what the investigator must do to measure it. In practice, important marketing constructs—like brand loyalty, purchase intent, or equity—will have had several operational definitions proposed for them, usually because they are intrinsically multidimensional and difficult to capture in a single numerical summary measure, rather like "personality" or "intelligence" for people.

operational definition
Specifies how a construct is to be measured; defines or gives meaning to a variable by spelling out what the investigator must do to measure it.

A constitutive definition directs the development of an operational definition. Consider the first of our previous constitutive definitions of brand loyalty, which speaks solely about what is going on in a consumer's head rather than tying it into what a consumer purchases. It does not, for example, appeal to consecutive purchases of the brand, as many definitions of loyalty have done. For example, a pattern of consecutive purchases of brand B could result from convenience ("it is what they carry at the nearest store"), lack of availability of substitutes ("it is all you can find in this area"), indifference ("all the brands are the same"), or lower price ("it is been on sale a lot") rather than from an intrinsic preferential attitude toward the brand. Consequently, an operational definition that is consistent with this constitutive definition of brand loyalty must specify how the preferential attitude is to be measured, what type of behavioral response is consistent with this loyalty state, and how the consumer is to be defined.

The second constitutive definition refers to the ability to withstand competitive inducements and would require that we know how to measure them and process brand purchase data accordingly. We could then posit any number of measures that "reward" a brand's loyalty score for full-price purchases and "punish" it for both promotional and full-price purchases of other brands, although this leaves open the question of which other brands to include, how to measure promotional activity, and how much rewarding and punishing should occur. Fashioning a useful and reliable operational measure of brand loyalty has been the subject of a great deal of academic research in marketing, and the matter is by no means settled. The key point is that to engage in meaningful research and analysis, the researcher must state a clear, calculable operational definition before research is carried out.

Marketing has few examples of standardized constitutive and operational definitions of constructs. This has been a serious hindrance to the effectiveness of marketing research projects, largely reflecting the difficulty of the measurement process. With the advent of large-scale, longitudinal (i.e., collected over time) databases from UPC scanners and Web site logs, operational definitions have come a long way, yet they are far from standardized within product categories, let alone across them.

4.2b Validity and Reliability Concepts

Measurement error is minimized when a direct correspondence exists between the number system and the marketing phenomena being measured; in this case, the numbers accurately represent the characteristics being measured and nothing else. This is an idealized situation that rarely exists in practice. More typically, our measurements possess some degree of error in that the numerical scale does not precisely reflect the marketing phenomenon under investigation.

Common potential sources of error can be classified as follows:

1. Respondent characteristics: Personal factors such as mood, fatigue, willingness to participate, and even health at the time of administration
2. Situational factors: Variations in the environment in which the measurements are reached, such as time of day, temperature, presence of family members, and point-of-purchase marketing activities
3. Data collection factors: Variations in how the questions are administered, including the influence of the interviewing method (e.g., phone, personal contact, Web-based, or mail)
4. Measuring instrument factors: The degree of ambiguity and difficulty of the questions and the ability of the respondent to answer them
5. Data analysis factors: Errors made in the coding and tabulation process

The total error of measurement consists of two components. The first is systematic error, which is error that causes a *constant bias* in the measurements. For example, assume we are judging a swim meet using a stopwatch that runs 10 percent faster than it should. To the disappointment of the swimmers, this will cause a consistent upward bias (of 10 percent) in the measured times for all events (and therefore a downward bias in measured speeds). Even though the measurement instrument is consistent, it will introduce a predictable, directional bias into all results. In marketing, one encounters such biases in all sorts of self-reports. For example, people tend to report that they engage more in "virtuous" activities (exercising, reading) and less in other activities (eating, watching television) than they actually do. These measures are not merely inaccurate but nearly always skew in one direction for all respondents.

The second component of the total error of measurement is *random error*, which involves influences that bias measurements but are not systematic. For example, in the swim meet, several stopwatches could be used to time the race. Assuming the absence of systematic error, we would find that the recorded times fall within a range around the true time, with roughly half above and half below. One informal test of whether bias is random or systematic is that the central tendency will tend to reflect true values when error is random but not when it is systematic. No matter how many fast-running stopwatches we average, we will never recover the true race time.

We can think of the stopwatch time or observed measurement, O, as composed of three elements: (1) the true speed or score T, (2) systematic error e_S, and (3) random error e_R. Formally, we can state the relationship as

$$O = T + e_S + e_R$$

It is helpful to keep this little equation in mind in the forthcoming discussions of measurement error regarding the ways an estimate can fail to be valid or reliable.

4.2c Validity and Reliability: Definition and Types

The reliability of a measure refers to the extent to which the measurement process is free from random errors alone. Reliability is thus concerned with the consistency, precision, and predictability of research findings. The measure itself can be a poor one, but it would still be considered reliable if it is measured perfectly. The validity of a measure, by contrast, refers to the extent to which the measurement process is free from both systematic and random error. Validity asks, "Are we measuring what we think we are measuring?" Validity is therefore a broader and more difficult issue than reliability. If we used an atomic scale to record people's weights while they held a 5-kilogram slab of lead, our measure of their weight would be reliable but certainly not valid.

Assume we are conducting a survey of buyers to estimate the market share for brand X. For purposes of illustration, assume the market share is actually 10 percent. Also assume that four potential conditions exist regarding the influence of systematic and random error on the observed measure of market share. Condition A is no systematic error and low random error; condition B is high systematic error and low random error; condition C is no systematic error and high random error; and condition D is high systematic error and high random error. These four conditions, illustrated in Figure 4.3, represent extremes; the more typical situation would lie somewhere in the middle.

The figure also presents the influence of systematic and random error on the distribution of sample means for each of these four conditions. In condition A, the expected value of the distribution of sample means is identical to the true market share of 10 percent. The low random error is reflected in a tight distribution of sample means. Here, repeated samples consistently produce means that are close to the true market share. In this condition, the survey results would be described as both highly valid and reliable.

Figure 4.3 Reliability and Validity

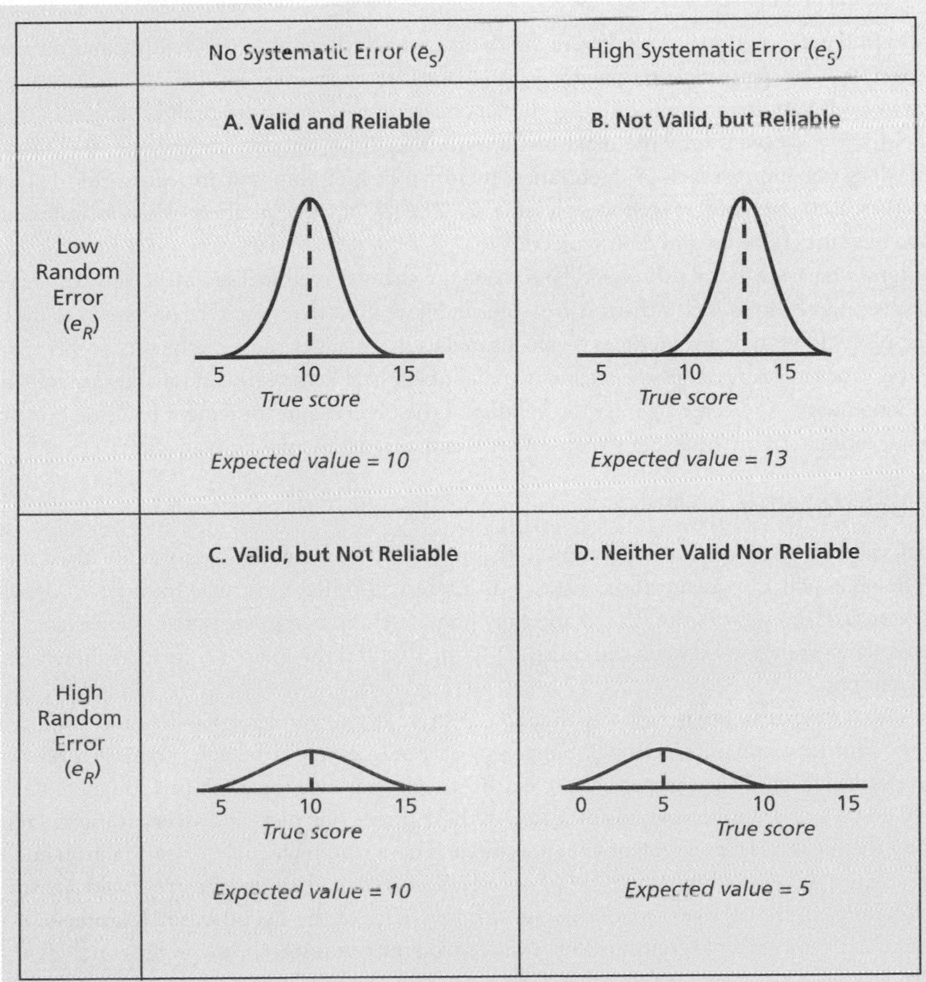

Condition B has the same tight distribution of sample means, but the influence of the high systematic error has biased the expected value three points above the true share of market. Repeated sampling would produce means close to 13 percent, a consistent upward bias. In this situation, the survey results would be reliable but not valid, a "good estimate of the wrong quantity."

In condition C, the expected value of the distribution of sample means is identical to the true market share of 10 percent, but the high random error causes the distribution of sample means to be highly dispersed. Here, repeated sampling would find many sample means dramatically different from the true market share. In this condition, the survey results would be described as neither valid nor reliable. Finally, condition D has the same high random error as condition C, but here the systematic error is also high, causing the expected value of the sampling distribution to be five points less than the true market share. In this situation, the survey results would again be described as neither valid nor reliable. One might object and say that, although conditions C and D portray situations with neither validity nor reliability, D is somehow "worse" because it is also biased, and C still gives an expected value equal to the true value. In a sense, this is true. In real-world applications, however, a measure that is highly dispersed, even if it is right on average, as in situation C, is of little practical use. Validity and reliability are really about the degree of confidence we can place in a measure, and high dispersion destroys any such confidence.

To summarize, for a measure to be valid, it must be reliable. Here, systematic error e_S and random error e_R are small or zero. However, if a measure is not reliable, it cannot be valid; if it is reliable, it may or may not be valid, just as when someone who gives you the same answer every time you ask may or may not be telling the truth. Consequently, the validity of a measure is usually researchers' main concern because it involves both systematic and random error. Reliability, which involves only random error, is more easily measured, which is why research studies report reliability scores more often than validity scores.

4.2d Estimating Validity

It is rare to find a decision maker expending funds and time to determine the validity and reliability of research results. The pressures and practical considerations of the typical decision-making situation leave the issue of validity and reliability to those concerned with basic research or academic projects. Consequently, we overview only the main methods for measuring validity and reliability. This concise treatment does not imply a lack of importance, merely a lack of emphasis in real-world applications. Marketing researchers would do well to at least consider each of these methods when formulating constructs and measures to be used in their projects.

A foolproof measure of validity would be to compare the observed measurement with the true measure. However, rarely do we know the true measure, and if we did, there would be no reason to measure it in the first place. Researchers sometimes conduct simulation studies or run experiments simply to be able to know the "true" measure, but these are rarely useful or applicable in real-world marketing research situations. Consequently, researchers infer the validity of the observed measurement by using one or more of the major estimation methods: construct, content, concurrent, and predictive validity.

Construct Validity

construct validity
Relating a construct of interest to other constructs in order to develop a comprehensive theoretical framework for the (marketing) phenomenon being studied; construct validity is enhanced when the correlation between the construct of interest and the related constructs increases in the predicted manner.

Construct validity involves understanding the theoretical rationale underlying the obtained measurements. The approach is to relate the construct of interest to other constructs in order to develop an entire theoretical framework for the marketing phenomenon being measured. Construct validity increases as the correlation between the construct of interest and the related constructs increases in the predicted manner.

Because construct validity is probably the most abstruse of the various reliability and validity measures, let us consider a concrete example. Suppose that a sales manager believes there is a relationship among job satisfaction, degree of personality extroversion, and sales force job performance. Construct validity could be assessed by developing measures of these three constructs and ascertaining the relationship among the measures for a group of sales personnel. Those who have high job satisfaction and extrovert personalities should exhibit high job performance scores; if they do not, we could question the construct validity of the measures and/or question the validity of the hypothesized relationship. If that relationship had been strongly confirmed by a variety of previous research, we might conclude that the measures do not measure what we think they do.

Construct validity can be evaluated with other approaches. If a construct exists, it should be successfully measured by methods that are different or independent. **Convergent validity** involves the measurement of a construct with independent measurement techniques and the demonstration of a high correlation among the measures. Alternatively, if a construct exists, it should be distinguished from constructs that differ from it. **Discriminant validity** involves demonstrating a lack of correlation among differing constructs. The formal statistical technique of factor analysis (see Chapter 11) can often be helpful in assessing the convergent and discriminant validity across a variety of measures.

convergent validity
Measuring a construct with independent measurement techniques and demonstrating a high degree of correlation among the measures.

discriminant validity
The degree to which concepts or variables that a theory says should not be related differ in reality (often assessed by correlation, when the variables involved are interval-scaled).

Content Validity

Content validity involves subjective judgments by experts as to the appropriateness of the measurement. This is a common method used in marketing research to determine the validity of measurements because experts are typically more plentiful than hard data.

To illustrate content validity, assume we are going to measure the image of retail stores in a grocery chain. Rather than asking a simple question, we develop a multi-item measuring technique. Assume that 20 items or questions are proposed that, when combined in an index, represent the measure of store image. The content validity of these 20 items would be determined by having an expert or experts assess the representativeness of the items used to measure store image. The content validity could be challenged if items such as store cleanliness, friendly atmosphere, or price competitiveness were excluded from the list of items. Content validity is often called **face validity** because of the emphasis on the expert's critical eye in determining the relevance of the measurements to the underlying construct.

content validity
Often called *face validity,* the relation of the appropriateness of the measurement to subjective judgments, typically by experts.

face validity
A method of validating measures, by noting its relationship to another independent measure and whether it accords with a theory's predictions.

Concurrent Validity

Concurrent validity involves correlating two different measurements of the same marketing phenomenon administered at the same point in time. It is primarily used to determine the validity of new measuring techniques by correlating them with established ones, which have presumably performed well in the past.

To illustrate concurrent validity, assume that our previous 20-item measurement technique of store image is valid (i.e., has low systematic and random error). Also, assume that an alternative technique, which is quicker and cheaper, is proposed. Concurrent validation would involve administering both techniques under similar or identical conditions and correlating the two measures of store image. A high correlation would establish the concurrent validity of the new technique. The key issue here is that the validity of the measurement is judged by the existence of another criterion measure taken, as the name implies, concurrently. For example, medical screening tests are often chosen because they correlate well with more costly lab tests, which are only administered to those flagged by the screener.

concurrent validity
Correlating two different measurements of the same (marketing) phenomenon administered at the same point in time, primarily to determine the validity of new measurement techniques by correlating them with established ones.

Predictive Validity

Predictive validity involves the ability of a measured marketing phenomenon at one point in time to predict another marketing phenomenon at a future point. If the correlation between the two measures is high, the initial measure is said to have predictive validity, sometimes also called *pragmatic validity* or *criterion-related validity*. It differs from concurrent validity, wherein the two correlated measures occur at the same point in time.

To illustrate predictive validity, consider the use of the Graduate Management Aptitude Test (GMAT) to predict performance in many master of business administration (MBA) programs. Here, the test supposedly measures the student's aptitude for masters-level study, and this is used as a predictor of future performance in the classroom and workplace. The use of this test as part of the admissions criteria by many MBA programs suggests that program administrators believe in its predictive validity (regarding student performance); however, this does not replace the need to survey and measure student performance to back up such a claim of validity. In the medical testing example, a screening test would be said to have predictive validity if it accurately measured the presence of a disease agent or process, as verified by subsequent tests. For example, when testing for the presence of the human immunodeficiency virus (HIV), it is common to first give patients the enzyme-linked immunosorbent assay (ELISA) screening test; if this test is positive, it is then confirmed with a second, more specific (and costly) test called the Western blot. If the two tests correlate well, the first could be said to have strong predictive validity, even if it is not always perfectly predictive.

predictive validity
A form of construct validity, also called pragmatic or criterion-related validity, that occurs when a measure can accurately predict what theory says it should.

4.2e Estimating Reliability

Let us now turn from validity to reliability. The main methods for measuring reliability are test–retest, alternative-forms, and split-half method reliability.

Test–Retest Reliability

test–retest reliability
Repeatedly measuring the same person or group, using the same scaling device, under similar conditions, and comparing results; the greater the discrepancy, the greater the random error in the measurement process and the lower the reliability.

Test–retest reliability involves repeated measurement of the same person or group using the same scaling device under conditions judged to be similar. The results of these measurements are compared to determine their similarity. This approach assumes that the greater the discrepancy in scores, the greater the random error present in the measurement process and thus the lower the reliability.

Let's return to our multi-item technique for measuring retail store image, discussed in reference to content validity. Test–retest reliability would involve administering our 20-item measuring technique to a group of store shoppers at two points in time. The results of the two measurements would then be correlated to determine the degree of correspondence. The lower the correlation, the lower the reliability.

There are a number of problems with this approach to measuring reliability. First, it may not be logical or possible to administer the measurement twice to the same subject (e.g., shoppers randomly recruited in a mall). Second, the first measurement may change the subject's response to the second measurement (e.g., unaided recall of a brand or ad). Third, situational factors may change, causing the second measurement to differ from the first even if underlying attitudes are the same. These types of problems can bias our measurement of reliability.

Alternative-Forms Reliability

alternative-forms reliability
A method to test the reliability of a measure by giving each subject two distinct forms of the measure believed to be equivalent; the results of the measurements are then compared to determine reliability.

Alternative-forms reliability involves giving the subject two forms judged equivalent (by prior testing or a panel of experts) but not identical. The results of the two measurements are compared to determine the degree of discrepancy in scores, as in the test–retest approach.

Using this approach to determining reliability would require a second set of 20 items to be developed for our retail image-measuring instrument. The two equivalent forms would be administered to the same subjects, and the degree of correspondence would be determined. The problems associated with the alternative-forms approach are the expense and delay associated with developing a second measuring instrument and the difficulty of making the two instruments equivalent. Alternative-forms reliability is what makes such tests as the SAT, GRE, GMAT, and various IQ batteries (Wechsler-Binet, Ravens, Norwegian matrices, Belgian Shapes, and so forth) "standardized," with gargantuan efforts on the part of the administering organizations like the Educational Testing Service (www.ets.org) to keep them so over time. Even so, the so-called Flynn effect has found astonishing gains in IQ, from 9 to 15 depending on the test, from generation to generation throughout the world. Whether this reflects true intelligence gains or is merely an artifact of testing itself is a subject of vigorous debate, calling the criterion of alternative-forms reliability into question.

Split-Half Reliability

split-half reliability
A method of testing reliability where a multi-item measurement device is divided into equivalent groups and the item responses are compared among the groups.

Split-half reliability involves dividing a multi-item measurement device into equivalent groups and correlating the item responses to estimate reliability. This approach is a version of the alternative-forms technique, with the forms being different sections of the device.

For example, if we believed that the retail image was composed of a single characteristic or dimension (e.g., favorable–unfavorable image dimension), we could use split-half reliability to measure the internal consistency or homogeneity of the 20 items forming the retail image-measuring index. Here, each item is assumed to measure this single characteristic independently. The approach would be to randomly divide the 20 items into two groups and determine the degree of correspondence. High correlation coefficients (r) suggest that the items are measuring the same characteristic (although not necessarily the one we would like to measure).

4.2f Measurement Difficulties in International Marketing Research

The difficulties of measurement in marketing, the nature of the number system, the types of scales, and the issues of reliability and validity apply equally well to both domestic and international marketing research. However, there is one major measurement concern that arises uniquely in international marketing research. This is the issue of the reliability and validity of a measurement construct across countries or cultures.

For example, a global consumer financial services company may want to use demographic and lifestyle measures across many countries in its marketing research for a new type of consumer product but may be concerned about whether such measures will be reliable and valid across those countries. Extensive evidence suggests that such measures are quite reliable across countries for "hard" variables like geodemographics (age, gender, location, and so on) but have limited reliability for "soft" variables like lifestyle, product involvement, and attitudes. These must be ascertained uniquely in each country, a costly and time-intensive procedure often involving extensive translation, in addition to other difficulties. *International Issues 4.1* examines some of these measurement difficulties in greater detail.

International Issues 4.1

Measurement Difficulties in International Marketing Research

Marketing Research

Examples of cultural or national differences in the reliability or validity of measures:

- A set of attitude questions about the need for government regulation of business affairs received high scores (indicating the desire for high government involvement) from respondents in Poland and Russia. However, when it was made clear to the respondents that government officials and police would not have access to their answers, the desire for government involvement in business affairs declined substantially.
- A major international marketer of industrial machine tools found different reliability measures for attitude scores related to the use of technology in manufacturing across various nations and regions. Middle Eastern manufacturers had lower reliability measures on these scores than did their U.S. counterparts, for whom they were originally developed. Possible reasons for these underlying differences included the higher cost of technology outside the United States, the lack of appropriate training and infrastructure, and a general distrust of technological solutions to problems solved in some cases for centuries by highly trained human laborers. Whether the differences in the measured *scores* reflected any of these technologically based issues, differences in underlying attitudes, scale usage differences, or just willingness to offer candid opinions could not be easily teased out.
- A study of attitudes toward organ donation in several countries and across ethnic groups in North America found wider variation in donation willingness among U.S. citizens than among residents of Japan and several other Asian countries. A more extensive follow-up study, meant to get at the reasons for this discrepancy, found that perhaps the most important one was Japanese respondents' unwillingness to express strong views, precluding their use of the highest scale categories. This made it difficult to determine who was less than willing to donate as opposed to less than willing to *say* they would.
- The sales manager of a German company used an aptitude test to screen prospective hires for the company's sales force. This instrument had high measures of predictive validity for the success of its German salespeople. However, when the test was applied elsewhere, it had low predictive validity results, particularly so for its French and U.S. subsidiaries. Such outcomes are common and reflect problems in applying any sort of predictive model outside the data environment for which is was developed. Developers of "general aptitude" tests for the American military found something similar when those tests were applied to the general population: that is, a much lower degree of predictive validity for the civilian population.
- A large-scale survey of customer satisfaction, conducted annually over many years in the United States, northern Europe, and East Asia, discovered that older consumers were generally more satisfied, in almost every category of product, than their younger counterparts in the same country. This was true even after (statistically) "correcting" for differences in income, education, and other socioeconomic factors. One hypothesis is that older consumers compare today's products to those they grew up with and remark on the far greater variety available now, as well as dramatic improvements in all technological products, another is that older consumers have simply determined which brands they like best and have stuck with them; and a third is that they are intrinsically more easily satisfied after experiencing so much in their lives. Whatever the reason, it means that countries with a higher proportion of elderly consumers will, perhaps paradoxically, have higher average consumer satisfaction scores than those with more young people. Given the oft-touted "graying of America," companies may see their measured satisfaction levels rise for this reason alone.

4.3 Attitude Measurement

An attitude is an individual's enduring perceptual, knowledge-based, evaluative, and action-oriented processes with respect to an object or phenomenon. Attitudes are generally considered to have three main components: (1) a cognitive component comprising a person's beliefs about the object of concern, such as its speed or durability; (2) an affective component comprising a person's feelings about the object, such as "good" or "bad"; and (3) a behavioral component comprising a person's readiness to respond behaviorally to the object. Although these are interrelated, they are hardly identical. It is possible to think a product is well made but to find "something about its styling" troublesome, leaving the person undecided about whether to purchase a product in the category. Alternatively, someone could be committed to purchase, and have positive feelings about a specific product, yet still find it below par on some level. Simply put, it is possible to have distinctly different cognitive, affective, and behavioral orientations toward a product or service without being contradictory.

Because marketing deals with people—who design, produce, sell, distribute, retail, and purchase products and services—the measurement of attitudes, opinions, and intentions is central to most marketing situations. Breaking the entire universe of consumers into like-minded groups via market **segmentation** is typically based primarily on such attitudinal data. With segments in hand and firm indications of their respective attitudes, marketing managers can confidently develop various positioning strategies by emphasizing features that differentially appeal to each segment.

segmentation
The ability to break a market, consumers or sets of objects into groups; these groups should be relatively homogeneous in terms of the criteria chosen by the researcher—e.g., demographics, behavior, prior experience—and differ substantively across the groups.

Attitude measurement is crucial in evaluating the effectiveness of an advertising campaign because people not only need to recall an ad but also have a favorable reaction to its message. In practice, marketers operate under the presumption of a strong relationship between attitudes and behavior. If attitudes can be swayed or influenced by exposing consumers to pertinent product information, so can purchase behavior through effective marketing programs.

4.3a Difficulty of Measuring Attitude

The marketing manager for a leading shampoo aimed at the adult female market listens to an exploratory research group discussion on women's reactions to the product. The following statements typify the discussion:

"I like the design of the bottle."
"It has lots of suds, more than other shampoos like it."
"I don't care for the rose smell. It's cloying."
"It's overpriced, if you ask me."
"I used to but it all the time, but don't anymore. I don't know why. I just don't."
"I always purchase that product, but I get something else for my kids, too."

After listening to this discussion for more than an hour, the marketing research manager is asked to comment on what this discussion means and why it is important. The manager's job is to extract meaning from this sea of verbal response data and to conclude how prospective users "feel" about the product, or what their underlying attitudes are. It is important to characterize clearly the meaning of the attitudes expressed by the discussion group, to establish why these attitudes are important to the successful marketing of the product, and to point out how their significance can be established by formally measuring them—not an easy or trivial task.

The construct of attitude, because it exists in the minds of individuals and is not directly observable, is difficult to measure and typically involves the "lower" scales of measurement (nominal and ordinal) discussed earlier.

4.3b Linking Attitudes and Behavior

Attitudes are important in marketing decision making because of the readily observed relationship between attitudes and eventual behavior. Models that conceptualize the construct of attitude typically represent an attitude as a sequential series of components that lead to behavior. Research indicates that the link between attitudes and behavior is not simplistic—it is hardly the case that knowing what people think or believe will allow perfect prediction of their behavior—and the decision-maker and researcher should be cautious in assuming that such a relationship is somehow definitive or strongly behaviorally predictive in a particular decision context.

With that said, because statistical methods can help smooth over the vagaries of individual behavior, predictions for an aggregate group will be generally more accurate than those for individuals within the aggregate. For example, knowing which products in a category are on promotion is far more helpful in predicting brand-by-brand volume sales than what any particular household will buy. Because most decision situations are concerned with aggregate behavior rather than individual behavior, the attitude–behavior link offers statistical forecasting power for many marketing decision situations. However, attitudes are but one of many influences on behavior, and in many decision situations, other factors could be more influential than attitudes. An obvious example would be an individual who has a highly favorable attitude toward a new sports car but, because of economic or familial constraints, must purchase something less personally desirable.

The marketing implications of this attitude–behavior link relate to measuring the cognitive and affective components of the buyer's attitude and being able to predict future purchase behavior. Influencing the cognitive and affective components could influence purchase behavior as well. This does not mean that these will be the only components of a predictive model, or even necessarily the most influential ones.

4.3c A Model of Behavioral Response

The purpose of marketing activity is to stimulate response from the targeted market segment, which can be the entire market. The response may be at the cognitive, affective, or behavioral level or some combination of these. Figure 4.4 depicts the three components of behavioral response, detailed further according to the hierarchy-of-effects model. This model hypothesizes that the buyer's response falls along spectrums for each component, from awareness to knowledge, liking to preference, and intention-to-buy

hierarchy of-effects model
A hypothetical model of buyer response, moving from awareness to knowledge, liking to preference, and intention-to-buy to purchase, that is often applied to assess response to advertising.

Figure 4.4 Model of Behavioral Response

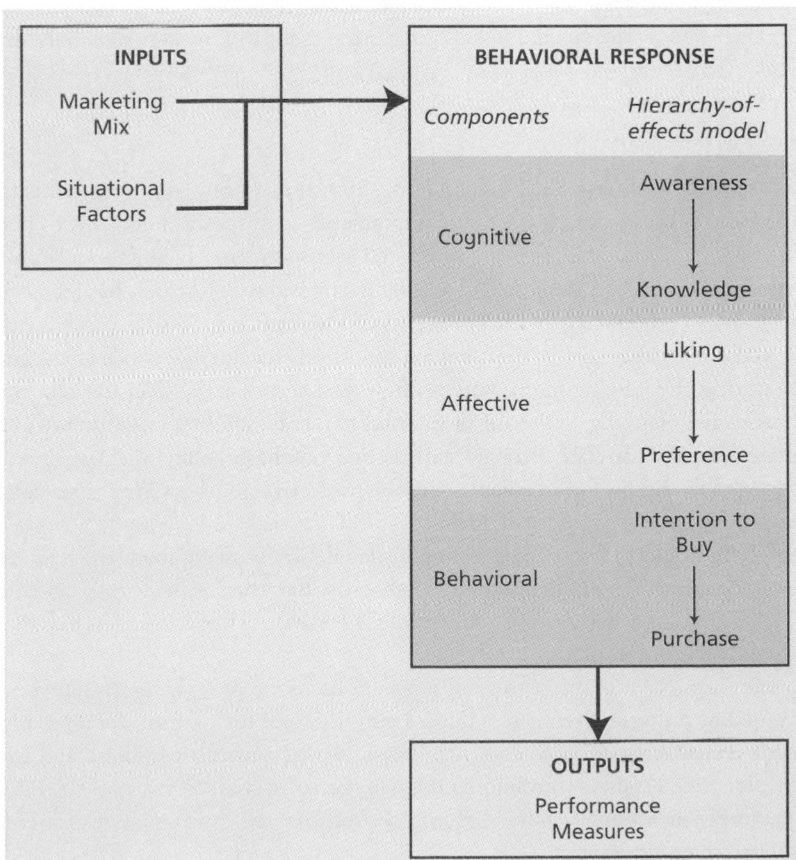

to purchase. These can occur in different sequences, depending on the degree of buyer involvement with the purchase and the degree of differentiation among the alternatives. The degree of influence of each stage, as well as its duration, can also vary dramatically across consumers in the targeted segment.

Cognitive Component

cognitive component
In attitude research, a person's beliefs about the object of concern; typically focuses on the elements that can be deliberately thought about, not on feelings or behaviors.

The **cognitive component** refers to the respondent's awareness of and knowledge about an object or phenomenon. This is sometimes called the belief component. It is expressed by statements such as "I believe product A does..." or "I know that product B will...."

The cognitive component is of considerable importance for many types of information needs. Many decision situations require information regarding the market's awareness of or knowledge about product features, advertising campaigns, pricing, product availability, and so on. A classic example concerns computers and other high-tech products. Many consumers who are ready to purchase and who have otherwise positive feelings toward the category and some of its brands are often hampered by the maze of daunting technical terms and acronyms, like SDRAM, IEEE-1394, and MPEG3. In such cases, there is a large cognitive hurdle, one that would require marketers to focus on educating the consumer and demystifying the product, much as Apple did by rechristening IEEE-1394 as "FireWire."

Affective Component

affective component
In assessing consumer attitudes toward a product, service, or brand, the component related to emotional response and subjective feelings, such as overall liking and preference.

The **affective component** refers to the respondent's liking and preference for an object or phenomenon. Sometimes called the *feeling component*, it is expressed by such statements as "I dislike product A," "Advertisement X is poor," and "I prefer product A to product B."

The affective component is an important aspect of the information needs for many decision situations, such as in determining buyers' feelings and preferences regarding an organization's marketing program relative to its competitors. As opposed to the sort of "high cognitive load" high-tech products discussed previously, luxury products, particularly those used in or on the body, require a fine understanding of consumers' affective reactions. Consumers may believe the "scientific studies" quoted in a face cream's advertising, but such studies alone are unlikely to drive the high retail prices, extreme emphasis on packaging, and point-of-purchase inducements typical of that category. Rather, positive feelings must be generated by the operant beliefs, suggesting the use of imagery over hard information in cosmetic advertising in general.

Behavioral Component

behavioral component
A consumer's intention to take action, particularly toward the purchase of a product or service, as well as their eventual behavior.

The **behavioral component** refers to the respondent's intention to buy and eventual actual purchase behavior. The intention-to-buy stage refers to the respondent's predisposition to act (i.e., purchase) prior to the actual purchase decision. Marketers are interested in respondents' buying intentions as indicators of future purchase behavior, and a great deal of academic and industry research has focused on the connection. One such survey, conducted by the University of Michigan's Survey Research Center (www.isr.umich.edu/src), asked consumers about their buying intentions for durable goods (such as automobiles and appliances) during the coming months. It is often assumed that the decision process for durable goods involves extensive planning, gathering of information, and judicious weighting of evidence; if so, purchase intentions should correlate strongly with actual purchase behavior. Despite this seemingly impeccable logic, humans simply fail to comply, and the predictive ability of intentions data is generally poorer than many, even experts, would anticipate.

Survey researchers would like to believe that consumers, when asked about their intention to purchase a specific good or service, will accurately indicate what they believe they will do. *Marketing Research Focus 4.3* considers whether researchers should bank on what consumers say they will do or whether this is merely wishful thinking.

In common parlance, *behavior* refers to what a person has done or is doing. In marketing, behavior has a more restricted meaning and refers to a buyer's purchase and use patterns for a product or service. Information needs typically focus on what is purchased, in what quantities, where and when the purchase took place, the circumstances surrounding the purchase, the characteristics of the buyer, and associated data. Accurately measuring behavior, therefore, requires the development of a comprehensive description of the purchase situation.

Marketing Research Focus 4.3

Do Intentions Really Predict Behavior?

Research often depends on self-reports of intentions as indicative of expected behavior. Intentions to repurchase, for example, are widely used as a measure of consumer satisfaction, as are purchase intentions to predict the success of a new product. Yet it is a truism familiar to all that people don't always do what they had intended to do. Are reported intentions a valid measure of subsequent purchase behavior?

Studies investigating this question have measured purchase intentions and then analyzed actual purchase behavior of the same consumers. The ACNielsen BASES model uses such data to arrive at conversion rates for predicting purchase rates from purchase intentions (e.g., that 75 percent of those who indicate the highest level of purchase intention will purchase the product).

Can the Act of Measuring Interfere with the Result?

In the physical sciences, the observation or measurement process can create what are called *artifacts*. For example, the act of preparing tissue for electron microscopy can change the tissue in such a way as to significantly alter what the scientist will observe, even creating illusions that did not exist in the tissue before preparation.

Similarly, one problem with the studies used to arrive at conversion rates for forecasting purchase rates from purchase intentions is *self-generated validity;* that is, part of the connection between the consumer's intention and that person's subsequent behavior may be caused by the measurement of intentions itself. If one considers common strategies for dieting or achieving personal goals—formulating and focusing on an intention and then reminding oneself of it—this result is not as surprising as it may sound. Answering survey questions regarding a purchase intention brings this intention to conscious awareness and thus serves as a reminder toward an actual purchase. Without such focus being brought to an intention, a consumer may be more easily influenced by mood, promotions, or other factors. The question for researchers then becomes, "What is the connection between intentions and behavior in consumers whose intentions have *not* been measured?"

To measure this, researchers require a way to estimate intentions for a group of consumers *without asking them*. One study did this by using two groups of consumers sampled from the same population in an identical way—one group to survey regarding purchase intentions and a control group to not survey. Using a series of statistical analyses (i.e., various forms of regression), researchers were able to demonstrate the difference between the purchase behavior of surveyed consumers and that of nonsurveyed consumers.

Measurement Influences How Intentions Affect Behavior

Three large field studies found that the correlation between purchase intentions and actual purchase was 58 percent greater among surveyed consumers than among similar nonsurveyed consumers. For example, a difference of one point on a five-point scale measuring purchase intentions resulted in a 52.71-euro gain in customer profitability when intentions were measured but only a 23.95-euro gain when intentions were not measured. Measuring intentions was also found to *decrease* purchase behavior among consumers who did not intend to purchase, corroborating the hypothesis that measurement effects are due to surveys making consumers more likely to remember and follow their original intentions. The surveys did not simply enhance consumer approval across the board or persuade all participants to inflate their original purchase intentions; either of these cases would have resulted in increased purchase behavior even among consumers with little or no intention to purchase.

Because the predictive validity of measured purchase intentions has been demonstrated to be significantly weaker than formerly thought, common procedures for measuring the relationship between intentions and behavior overestimate this association and exaggerate the actual probability of purchase. Marketers have in turn been led by this to focus too much on consumers with high purchase intentions. The studies suggest that consumers with neutral or even negative purchase intentions are more likely to purchase than they claim and therefore could be considered more worthwhile as a customer target.

In addition, these studies imply that research with the objective of exploring the relationship among concepts (not just measures of intentions but also those of beliefs, attitudes, or satisfaction) need to also test for self-generated validity effects by using a control sample of participants for whom the concept is not measured.

Source: Chandon, Pierre, Vicki G. Morwitz, and Werner J. Reinartz (2005), "Do Intentions Really Predict Behavior? Self-Generated Validity Effects in Survey Research," *Journal of Marketing*, 69(2), 1–14.

Other References: Chandon, Pierre, Vicki G. Morwitz, and Werner J. Reinartz (2004), "The Short- and Long-Term Effects of Measuring Intent to Repurchase," *Journal of Consumer Research*, 31(3), 566–572.

Feldman, Jack M. and John G. Lynch Jr. (1988), "Self-Generated Validity and Other Effects of Measurement on Belief, Attitude, Intention, and Behavior," *Journal of Applied Psychology*, 73(3), 421–435.

Morwitz, Vicki G., Eric Johnson, and David Schmittlein (1993), "Does Measuring Intent Change Behavior?" *Journal of Consumer Research*, 20(1), 46–61.

4.4 Attitude-Scaling Procedures

attitude scaling
Operational definitions made to help measure, using specific scales, consumers' attitudes, beliefs, intentions, and other subjective mental states.

Attitude scaling refers to the various operational definitions developed to measure the construct of attitude and accompanying beliefs, intentions, and other subjective mental states. When measuring attitudes, the researcher must be especially sensitive to the scale-level assumptions and the restrictions these assumptions impose on data analysis. Typically, attitudes are measured at the nominal or ordinal level, although several more complex scaling procedures can sometimes allow measurement at the interval level. There is always the temptation to presume that attitude measurements possess interval scale properties to leverage the power of linear regression methods. The researcher must always be mindful of the characteristics of the construct being measured, and the properties of the number system properly relating to this construct, regardless of the attractiveness of certain methods of analysis.

In marketing, attitude scaling tends to focus on measuring respondents' beliefs about a product's attributes (cognitive component) and feelings about their desirability (affective component). Some amalgam of beliefs and feelings is then presumed to underlie, influence, or directly determine intention to buy (behavioral component). Attitude measurement procedures rely on data culled from respondents, either by communicating with them directly or by observation.

4.4a Communication Techniques

Direct communication with respondents falls into three main categories: self-reports, responses to stimuli, and performance of tasks.

Self-Reports

Respondents are directly asked to report their beliefs or feelings by responding to one or more questions on a questionnaire. A number of scaling techniques have been developed to measure such beliefs and feelings. (An in-depth discussion of self-reporting is included in the *Special Expert Feature* at the end of Chapter 7.)

Responses to Stimuli

Respondents are shown unstructured, partially structured, or pictorial stimuli (such as a picture of a product being purchased, being used, or in some other situation) and are asked to express their reaction. Approaches also include storytelling, word-association tests, and sentence completion.

Performance of Objective Tasks

Respondents are asked to memorize and/or report factual information about products. These responses are analyzed to uncover the nature of the respondent's beliefs and feelings under the assumption that respondents are more likely to recall information consistent with their personal beliefs and feelings. This assumption is not always warranted, however; if a statement presented as a product "fact" is grossly contradictory with one's own views, it could cause it to be especially well *recalled* without being *believed*.

4.4b Observation Techniques

Researchers may observe both the external and the internal behavioral responses of respondents.

Overt Behavior

Individuals are placed in a situation that allows their behavior patterns to be exhibited and recorded, which, *when interpreted appropriately*, should allow inferences about their underlying beliefs and feelings.

Physiological Reactions

Researchers measure physiological reactions as respondents are exposed to products, service descriptions, or advertisements. Common measurement devices are the galvanic skin response (GSR) technique, which measures sweating of the hand, and the eye dilation technique, which measures changes in the diameter of the pupil of the eye. A limitation intrinsic to physiological response measurement is that it records only the intensity of feelings, not their direction (positive or negative) or any sense of what causes or accompanies them. A "strong" reaction can be one of delight, disgust, or whimsy, unbeknownst to the researcher. A new set of techniques goes under the banner of "neuromarketing," involving the use of noninvasive neuroimaging techniques, such as functional magnetic resonance imaging (fMRI), to "peer into the brain" while emotions are experienced, cognitions are pondered, and decisions are made. Significant ethical questions surround the use of such techniques, with watchdog organizations (such as the Center for Cognitive Liberty and Ethics and Ralph Nader's Commercial Alert) monitoring developments closely. See the *Special Section* at the end of this chapter for a more in-depth discussion of this topic.

4.5 Self-Reporting Techniques

Of the general methods for measuring attitudes, self-reporting is by far the most widely used, and the remainder of this chapter focuses on the various scaling procedures suited to it. These procedures are most appropriate for conclusive research studies, which require that attitudes be formally measured and quantified using a large sample of respondents. Attitude measurement methods other than self-reporting are more appropriate for exploratory research designed to elucidate the nature of beliefs and feelings fundamental to a decision situation. These methods are discussed in more detail in Chapter 6, which deal extensively with data collection. Several self-reporting techniques are discussed here, with emphasis on the development of **unidimensional measures**, those that try to capture constructs of interest using a single value on a predefined numerical scale.

unidimensional measures
Measures of some variable that result in a single score on a predefined numerical scale.

4.5a Nominal Scale

The simplest self-reporting scale is a nominal scale, where the respondent's beliefs are classified in two or more categories. For example, a nominal scale can be developed from responses to the question: "Does your automobile have radial tires: yes or no?" Because this scale is binary, it is statistically acceptable to treat it as a so-called **dummy variable** (i.e., a 0 for "no" and a 1 for "yes"), which can be used as-is in a linear regression analysis. However, a third category of "don't know" might be included for those respondents who are not informed concerning this feature of their automobile (and, were this a sensitive topic, a fourth category along the lines of "don't wish to disclose"). The result of this scaling is a three-category classification of respondents with respect to their responses: yes, no, and don't know. This scale is not ordinal; "don't know" does not lie somewhere between "yes" and "no," indicating some intermediate degree of tire possession, but is a genuinely distinct response indicating lack of knowledge. The resulting scale is therefore nominal, with numbers assigned to the categories for data analysis purposes.

dummy variable
A variable that takes on binary values (0 or 1), usually used to indicate whether a condition holds or not.

4.5b Rating Scale

Rating scales refer to measurement situations that involve ordinal, interval, and ratio scales, which allow far greater statistical power in categorizing, prioritizing and rigorously analyzing affective responses. A rating scale requires respondents to indicate the position on a continuum or among ordered categories that best corresponds to their attitude. Numerical values may be part of the scale or be assigned after respondents complete the self-rating task.

An ordinal scale is formed when respondents reply to a question like "When it comes to radial tires, do you like them, dislike them, or are you indifferent to them?" The result of this scaling is a three-category ordinal scale that ranks the respondents according to their feeling about radial tires, that is, dislike–indifferent–like. In practice, a three-category question is uncommon, because it confers little statistical power over a binary "yes"-or-"no"-type question yet substantially complicates statistical analysis. Numbers, typically {1, 2, 3}, are assigned to these ordered categories for purposes of data analysis. These scale points are merely ordinal, not interval, and so should not be correlated or linearly regressed with other interval-scaled variables. Researchers should also keep in mind that respondents can be confused when questions are phrased like the example here, with "like" followed by "dislike" then "indifferent," that is, with verbal labels not appearing in the correct scale order. It is considered better form to ask a question like "Which of the following best indicates your feelings toward radial tires?" followed by a scale consisting of descriptors such as "strongly dislike," "moderately dislike," "indifferent," "moderately like," and "strongly like."

4.5c Graphic Rating Scale

A graphic rating scale requires the respondents to indicate their position on a continuum that ranges from one extreme of the attitude in question to the other extreme. The format of this graphic continuum is as varied as the imaginations of the researchers who devise such a scale.

Figure 4.5 presents two examples of graphic scales, scales A and C. Assume that several respondents have sampled a new formulation of cake mix and we want to measure their feelings about the sweetness of the mix. Scale A relies on a series of facial expressions to represent the varying degrees of like and dislike. The respondents are asked to indicate which of the facial expressions best represents their reaction to the sweetness level. A most favorable response means the sweetness level is "just right" (extreme smile), and a least favorable response (extreme frown) means the cake is either "too sweet" or "not sweet enough." Such an unfavorable response would require additional questioning of the respondent to determine what was wrong with the sweetness level. It is also possible to have such a scale indicate the degree of sweetness, from low to high, rather than a subject's reaction to the sweetness, or any number of other possibilities. Graphic scales of this nature are especially useful when the researcher and the respondents speak different languages or when the respondents are children, elderly, or infirm. As such, they can often spare researchers great time and expense in cross-translation across different cultures and linguistic barriers, so long as the facial expressions in question are fairly universal.

Scale C presents a positive–negative continuum. The respondents are asked to indicate their position by checking a location on this continuum. Once the judgments are recorded, the researcher can subdivide the continuum into an appropriate set of categories and assign numerals to the judgments.

Figure 4.5 Graphic and Verbal Rating Scales

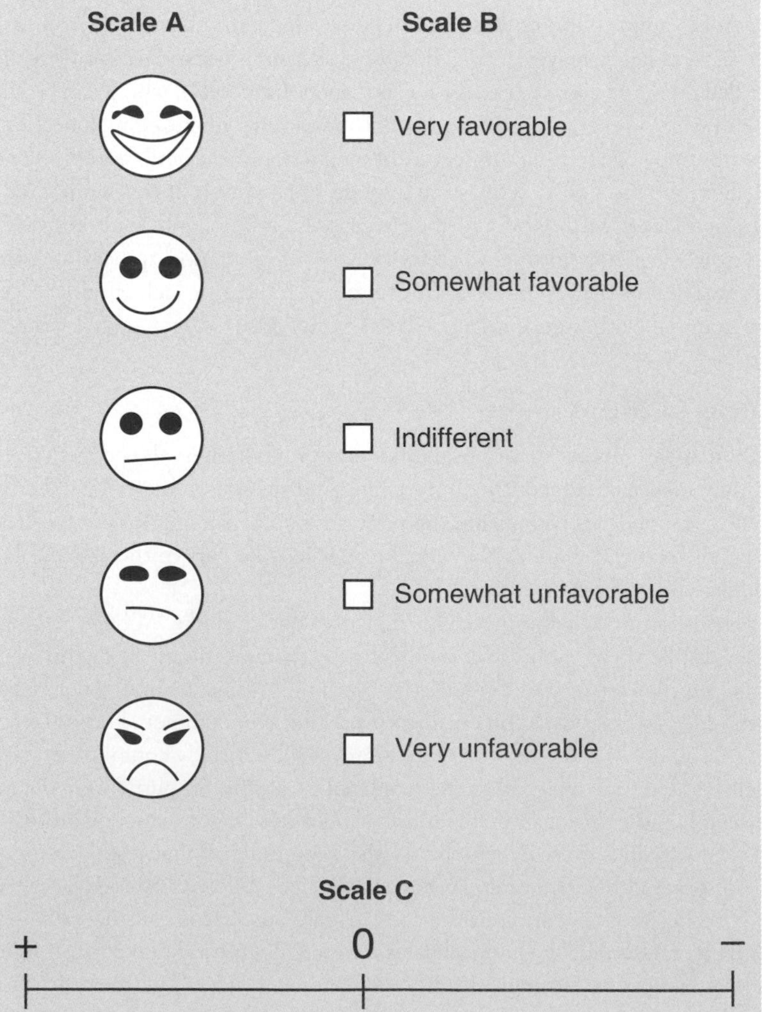

One advantage of this continuous scale is that the respondents are not confronted with a predetermined set of response categories. Rather, the categorization of the scale is left to the respondents, who implicitly determine the number of categories during the judgment process; this is considered a means of reducing bias. A disadvantage of this graphic scale is that it requires respondents to deal with an abstract judgment, without "anchors" to guide their response. In addition, because the researcher does not know how different respondents perceived or subdivided the continuum, comparisons and groupings of responses *across* respondents are difficult to justify. This sort of **heterogeneity** can complicate, and potentially enrich, statistical analyses substantially, as discussed in Chapter 12.

heterogeneity
A general term for when a group of items, people, variables, or statistically estimated quantities differ; often applied to differences in consumers, particularly in their reactions to the same marketing stimulus.

4.5d Verbal Rating Scale

Verbal rating scales are probably the most frequently used scales in all of social science, and certainly in marketing research. These require respondents to indicate their positions by selecting among verbally identified categories. Scale B in Figure 4.5 is an example; here, the respondents are asked to check the box adjacent to the phrase that best corresponds to their individual reactions, ranging from "very" (favorable or unfavorable) at the extremes to "somewhat" and "indifferent." Such scales are ubiquitous on standardized exams and in the media, so researchers seldom need to educate respondents in their use, an important advantage over less familiar scale types.

It is important to understand several issues intrinsic to the construction of useful, appropriate verbal rating scales, among them: (1) the overall number of categories, (2) an odd or an even number of categories, (3) a balanced vs. an unbalanced scale, (4) the extent of verbal description, (5) category numbering, (6) a forced vs. a nonforced scale, (7) a comparative vs. a noncomparative scale, (8) a symmetric vs. an asymmetric scale, (9) scale direction, and (10) choice of endpoints. Other issues arise in specific contexts, and the researcher must use common sense in generating verbal scales. Nevertheless, these end issues rear their heads in the vast majority of research contexts, so we consider them each in detail. Before doing so, we emphasize that we are speaking here not of scale *type*—nominal, ordinal, interval, or ratio—but of "best practices" for creating scales in general. With that said, because the vast majority of verbal scales possess the ordinal property but cannot be claimed to be interval, these discussions are especially relevant to ordinal scales.

Number of Categories

Although there is no established number of categories deemed optimal for a scale, scales of five, six, or seven categories are typical in practice. Some researchers argue that more than seven are needed when small changes in attitude are to be measured. Others argue that it is doubtful that the majority of respondents can distinguish among more than six categories. Beyond this point, additional categories do not increase the precision with which the attitude is being measured but merely confuse respondents and require extensive training to enable them to distinguish, for example, categories like "highly satisfied" from "extremely satisfied." Most researchers find that it is as easy to administer and analyze a scale with five to seven categories as it is to use one with, say, three categories, which not only reduces statistical power but also forces respondents into an "all, half, or none"-type decision, at which many will bristle. Consequently, researchers typically utilize at least a five-category scale unless special circumstances dictate fewer or more. Such decisions are complicated in cross-cultural or cross-age-group research. For example, some cultures, like those in East Asia, frown on publicly expressing strong opinions, compared with the "Express yourself!" ideal that permeates many Western societies; similar attitudes often pervade communities of older adults even in Western cultures. Consequently, respondents in these cultural and age groups often fail to use the extreme ends of scales or avoid the "negative" end. Such *scale usage heterogeneity* makes it difficult to figure out whether a particular group actually likes a product better or is simply less willing to express dissatisfaction. This is a nontrivial practical problem for multinational marketing researchers.

Odd or Even Number of Categories

Should the scale have an odd or even number of categories? There is no general or consensus view on this issue, although each has its adherents. If an odd number of categories is selected, the middle category is typically identified as a neutral position. If an even number is selected, the scale does not have a category precisely in the middle (e.g., "neither agree nor disagree"), so the respondent is requested to express some degree of feeling (e.g., "mildly disagree"). One research study comparing an odd (five- or seven-category) scale with an even (six-category) scale concluded that there was no significant difference in the results between the scales. Still, it is difficult to extend these results to particular situations. Generally, if the subject is one that generates substantial emotional reactions—politics, religion, social practices—an odd-numbered scale, including an explicit neutrality point, runs less risk of offending or upsetting respondents or of skewing their eventual responses.

Balanced or Unbalanced Scale

Should the number of favorable and unfavorable categories be balanced or unbalanced? A balanced scale has the same number of favorable categories as unfavorable categories. The argument for an unbalanced scale relates to the nature of the attitude distribution to be measured. If the distribution is predominantly favorable, an unbalanced scale with more favorable categories than unfavorable categories will be appropriate. The argument for balanced scales emphasizes the potential biasing of responses that can result from limiting the response categories on the favorable or unfavorable side of the scale. It is not uncommon for businesses running their own satisfaction surveys to present respondents with suspiciously unbalanced scales, ranging from "not fully satisfied" to enthusiastic endorsements on the positive side. Serious researchers should attempt to avoid the bias of such lack of balance and labeling. Unless there is a strong rationale for not doing so, scales should strive to be as balanced as possible, at least in pretesting; if responses are naturally strongly skewed based on the pretest, an unbalanced scale could be substituted to reflect the empirical distribution of responses gathered.

Extent of Verbal Description

How extensive should the verbal description of a category be? Some researchers believe that clearly defined response categories increase the reliability of the ensuing measurements and that each category should carry a verbal description using clear wording, differentiating the categories precisely. This view is reasonable in longer surveys with highly motivated respondents and when a scale can be used multiple times in the same survey (generally a good guideline: if respondents are troubled to learn to use a scale, they would do well to use it multiple times).

One of the rationales put forth for using carefully crafted verbal labels is that the researcher could then treat the respondents' judgments as *interval* data. Implicit in this view is the assumption that the respondent perceives the differences between adjacent verbal descriptions to be equally spaced. In practice, this is awesomely difficult to achieve. For example, this would mean that, when using the phrases "very good," "fairly good," and "neutral" as verbal descriptions for an interval scale, the researcher assumes that the distance between "very good" and "neutral" is twice the distance of that between "fairly good" and "neutral." Such assumptions can actually be tested, using appropriate statistical methods (specifically, ordinal regression; see Chapter 10). One study that did so measured the relative size of the adjectival labels "very" and "fairly" and found respective weights of +3.74 and +1.22 rather than the assumed weights of +2.00 and +1.00. In this situation, presuming interval scaling for purposes of data analysis would introduce obvious measurement error into the results. Although it is fairly common even among marketing professionals to treat such intrinsically ordinal rating scales as interval-scaled—to take advantage of simple means, correlations, and the power of linear regression, researchers should be sensitive to this practice and remember the potential for measurement error and biased research findings.

Category Numbering

Should numbers be assigned to the response categories? There are many arguments for doing so and many situations in which they appear. One is, as discussed previously, when the researcher believes the respondent's judgments can be treated as interval data (a belief that should be carefully considered and empirically investigated). Another is when numerical labels can help guide the respondent as to the progression of the categories and demonstrate that the scale is indeed ordinal, not merely a nominal set of labels. And another is when the numbers correspond to some quantity explicitly represented in the question itself, like a frequency. In such cases, researchers must decide whether the scale runs from low to high (e.g., 1, 2, 3, 4, 5) or high to low (the former is generally less confusing for respondents) and, furthermore, whether negative numbers are allowed. For example, one could place numerical labels on the following agree–disagree scale in either of the following ways, with the second of them more faithfully capturing the verbal labels but perhaps confusing respondents and overemphasizing negativity:

Strongly disagree	Moderately disagree	Slightly disagree	Neither agree nor disagree	Slightly agree	Moderately agree	Strongly agree
1	2	3	4	5	6	7
−3	−2	−1	0	1	2	3

Forced vs. Nonforced Scale

Another issue in constructing a rating scale concerns the use of a forced or a nonforced scale. A forced scale requires all respondents (except those who refuse to provide a response) to indicate a position on the attitude scale. The argument for a forced scale is that those who are reluctant to reveal their attitude are encouraged to do so with the forced scale. Respondents who have no opinion or no knowledge typically mark the "neutral" category on the scale. When a substantial proportion of the respondents may literally have no opinion, as opposed to a reluctance to reveal their feelings, it is best to include a category such as "no opinion," "don't know," or "prefer not to answer"—or even more than one of these, because they are distinct—rather than force the respondents to choose the neutral category. A common example occurs in knowledge-intensive surveys, for example, those dealing with technical equipment. When asked a question about computer memory, some respondents may not know, some may not care, and some, perhaps concerned with privacy issues, may not wish to say. Note that each of these is distinct from a scale midpoint like "neutral" or "moderately satisfied" and has different implications for marketing decisions: someone who does not know needs to be educated, someone who does not care needs to be motivated, and someone who is only "moderately satisfied" needs to be queried further about what product attributes are below expectations. Finally, a forced vs. a nonforced scale should be distinguished from an odd vs. an even number of scale points: a nonforced scale can have *any* number of points (5, 6, 7, ...) but must include an explicit option indicating an unwillingness or inability to reply (e.g., "I don't know/can't say"). This is different from merely including a response that is in the middle of a scale, particularly for knowledge questions (e.g., "I don't know").

Comparative vs. Noncomparative Scale

For each question, researchers must decide whether to use a comparative or a noncomparative scale. A comparative scale, as the name implies, provides respondents with an explicit referent or example with which to compare to express their attitudes. For example, one could say, "Compared with the dish soap you're using now, the one portrayed in the ad seems gentler," followed by agree–disagree options. An attractive feature of comparative scales is that the researcher can select the referent or even vary it across respondents to see how the resulting information is affected. Common examples of referents are the current brand used (which the respondent would specify), an "ideal" product (which the respondent would describe), or a specific competitive brand (which the researcher would control).

A comparative scale allows the researcher to report the respondents' attitudes relative to a standard that may be of specific importance in a decision situation, rather than some abstract, unstated example in the respondent's mind. Conversely, an argument for noncomparative scales is that they allow each respondent to choose a reference point, consequently achieving a more accurate measurement of the respondent's attitude. In practice, the selection of comparative and noncomparative scales depends on the specific information needs of the decision situation, and both are often used in the same survey. Note that a **time referent** is nearly always a good idea; that is, rather than asking about behavior or intentions in the abstract, provide a horizon or past time period, like "over the next year" or "in the past 2 weeks."

time referent
An important element in questions referring to past behavior, specifying a time interval (e.g., "in the last year") during which the behavior took place.

Symmetric vs. Asymmetric Scale

A practical issue that arises frequently in scaling is whether a particular question is better suited to a symmetric or an asymmetric scale. Let us consider two renderings of a frequency question:

(A) How frequently do you engage in aerobic exercise?

(1) Never (2) Rarely (3) Sometimes (4) Frequently (5) All the time

(B) Indicate your agreement with the statement "I engage in aerobic exercise":

(1) Strongly disagree (2) Moderately disagree (3) Neither agree nor disagree (4) Moderately agree (5) Strongly agree

Both of these questions attempt to ascertain how much someone engages in aerobic exercise (which should be rigorously defined elsewhere in the survey). Rendering B, however, by phrasing it in terms of agreement with a general statement, can impose a neutrality point, and thereby symmetry; a response of 3 truly is at the center of this scale. By contrast, rendering A has "sometimes" as the central category, and this is not the same as midway between "never" and "all the time." It is not even clear what that might mean; "sometimes" certainly does not equate to "half the time." Rendering A is very much an ordinal question, with no possible interpretation as an equally spaced, interval-scaled question. Rendering B, however, although the scale points may not be equally spaced, is at least clearly symmetric around the central category, "neither agree nor disagree." Therefore, calculating means is far more justified for rendering B than for rendering A. Whether the two renderings measure the same underlying behavioral issue, however, is unclear, requiring experimentation with both in actual research studies.

Scale Direction

valence
Property of a scale that everyone would agree is ordered in some meaningful way; e.g., everyone would agree that a lower price is more attractive than a higher one, all else being equal. However, people might differ as to whether "traditional" or "contemporary" was superior, so this would not be a valenced scale.

Scales must also be designed with attention to their direction and what respondents will infer from it; this is sometimes referred to as valence. For example, should an attitude scale go from "disagree" (on the left) to "agree" (on the right) or in the opposite direction? In most orthographic (writing) systems in use today, one reads from left to right, and there is a consequent convention to place more negative or less voluminous descriptors on the left. In this text, we typically follow this convention, going from smaller to larger, negative to positive, as we move across the page from left to right. Although this is not absolutely standard, it is expedient, and researchers would be well advised to at least be consistent within a survey as to scale direction.

Note, however, that some scales are *not* valenced, and placing them in certain contexts can be unintentionally confusing, humorous, or offensive. Consider, for example, these *semantic differential* scales (which we examine in more detail later in this chapter), frequently used in product positioning:

Unpleasant	−1	−2	0	1	2	Pleasant
Flimsy	−1	−2	0	1	2	Sturdy
Ugly	−1	−2	0	1	2	Beautiful
Male	−1	−2	0	1	2	Female
Hazardous	−1	−2	0	1	2	Safe

By placing all the clearly negative items on the left ("unpleasant," "flimsy," "ugly," and "hazardous")—and reinforcing their negativity with corresponding scale numbers—the researcher would also (hopefully unintentionally) imply the same about the "male–female" dimension. Great care must be expended on not having the scale connote information regarding the underlying comparison other than what the researcher wishes to deliberately impose, if anything.

Choice of Endpoints

A final issue concerns choice of endpoints and, more generally, of points throughout the scale. Even when a scale is intrinsically nonnumerical, researchers can design scales that seemingly allow a range of response but actually restrict permissible answers. For example, consider the following question, meant to measure public opinion regarding television content during prime time:

How do you feel about the quantity of violent content during weeknight, prime time, and publicly broadcast television shows? Do you believe it should be:

(1) Kept as is (2) Slightly reduced (3) Moderately reduced (4) Greatly reduced

This question appears to allow great latitude to respondents, but it makes a strong presumption: that no one could want a *greater* quantity of violent content on television. The most extreme endpoint in the question actually represents neutrality about the overall quantity of violent content: that it should stay the same. Although in rare cases such assumptions are probably empirically justified ("How much would you like your taxes to increase?" or "How much more painful should this medical procedure be?"), in general they are not, and questions should be strenuously scrutinized for appropriateness.

A more serious issue arises in asking about issues in which respondents are likely to take their cues from the question scale itself. Consider a common task for marketing researchers, asking about reasonable price points, and two possible scalings:

What would you expect the retail price of this new kitchen appliance to be?

Set A:	(1) $200	(2) $250	(3) $300	(4) $350	(5) $400
Set B:	(1) $300	(2) $350	(3) $400	(4) $450	(5) $500

A respondent who believes the product will be sold for about $350 will choose a relatively high scale point in set A and a relatively low one in set B. A belief of a $450 price tag will exceed the maximum in set A, whereas one of $250 will fall short of the minimum in set A; in both cases, this will cause respondents to alter their answer, a clear bias. Studies have also established that the presence of an unusually high or low value at the end of a scale can strongly affect reactions to the remainder of the scale, even if no one chooses the unusual value. Such *context* and *framing* effects have been widely studied and are known to occur in many distinct settings. Marketing researchers can best guard against them by extensively pretesting scales, varying labels, spacings, and endpoints, and comparing performance using eventual output measures like forecast accuracy or usefulness for segmentation.

4.5e Rank-Order Scale

The **rank-order technique** involves having the respondent place various objects in strict order with regard to the attitude in question. For example:

rank-order technique
When the respondent is asked to place various objects or items in strict order with regard to the criterion (attitudes, opinions, beliefs, etc.) in question.

Please rank each of the following "classic" movies from 1 to 5, with 1 indicating your favorite among the listed set and 5 indicating your least favorite:

_____ *Gone with the Wind*
_____ *Casablanca*
_____ *Citizen Kane*
_____ *The Godfather*
_____ *Lawrence of Arabia*

This technique is widely used in marketing research and survey research in general. It is intrinsically comparative in nature and forms an ordinal scale of the objects evaluated.

The rank-order technique has important advantages. It is simple in concept, easy to administer, and less time-consuming for respondents to complete than comparative techniques, such as paired comparisons. Instructions for ranking objects are easy to comprehend; consequently, the technique is suited to self-administered questionnaires. In addition, the process of ranking is akin to what each of us does whenever we are confronted with a set of objects from which to choose. Although rating each of a set of objects on some made-up scale is unnatural (how often do we say, "I rate this breakfast cereal a 7.3 on a 10-point scale"?), simply *choosing* one to purchase by "ranking" it highest is an everyday occurrence. When we consider buying an item like cereal, where there are literally hundreds of alternatives, we commonly have a preferred list, called a **consideration set**, of products that rank high on our own personal lists. By providing a simulated consideration set, the rank-order technique imitates the purchase decision process and encourages respondents to discriminate among products in a realistic manner.

consideration set
A group of alternatives that a consumer evaluates, thinks about, or makes implicit references to when making a decision.

One limitation of rank-order techniques is that the forced-choice and comparative nature of the technique results in a ranking of objects, regardless of the attitudinal position of the respondent to the objects as a group. It could be that the respondent dislikes *all* the objects in the set, and the object ranked first is the least disliked, like a "favorite form of dental surgery" or "most preferred type of line to wait in." The researcher must be sensitive to the attitudinal position of the respondent and be confident that a realistic set of objects is being evaluated.

Just as obviously, one can never compare such ranked responses *across* questions so that a second-favorite flavor of ice cream is inferred to be inferior to a favorite flavor of cough syrup. This lack of **cross-scale comparability** is a substantial stumbling block to extracting meaningful, real-world information using ranked questions. One must also bear in mind that there can only be one "best" or "most" in each set of options given. Respondents who see little difference across the offered set—due to lack of experience, knowledge, or interest—will offer the same type of data as an expert with strong opinions. Consequently, the set of items one chooses for ranking must be cohesive, self-explanatory, and relevant for a variety of respondents.

cross-scale comparability
When answers to different questions using the same scale are comparable.

Another limitation of the rank-order technique is that it produces only ordinal data. Although there are scaling and analytic techniques appropriate for ranked input data, they require more than passing familiarity to apply, and they add a degree of complexity that many analysts and managers would do well to avoid (we look more closely at the main such technique, the rank-order or "exploded" logit model, in Chapter 10). Most of this complexity stems from the fact that rank-order data cannot, even in principle, be uncorrelated: if you are ranking two items, as soon as you choose your favorite, the other item is pegged as your second favorite, with no leeway for an alternative opinion. When five items are to be ranked, each must be assigned numerals from among {1, 2, 3, 4, 5}, with no overlaps or reuse (unless the researcher has made an explicit provision for ties; this is rare, given the complexities involved). The vast majority of statistical techniques cannot account for this built-in feature of rank-order data, so the researcher must resort to special methods and apply them with unusual care.

Several studies have found that the ranking and rating-scale techniques, if used well, yield broadly similar results (this alone does not imply that they both always measure a construct *accurately*, just that they tend to agree with each other). Researchers must consider the specific needs of the research project in selecting among rating, ranking, and other scale types.

4.5f Paired-Comparison Scale

On a paired-comparison scale, respondents are presented with two objects from a set and required to pick one as better with regard to the attitude or quality in question. Thus, the respondent is required to make a series of paired judgments between objects regarding preference, amount of some attribute present, and so on.

The data collection procedure typically requires the respondent to compare all possible pairs of the objects. If there are four objects to be evaluated, there will be six paired comparisons required in the judgment task: comparing item 1 to items 2, 3, and 4; item 2 to items 3 and 4; and item 3 to item 4. (For n objects, $[n(n-1)/2]$ comparisons will be required, because the first will be paired with the remaining $(n-1)$, the next with the remaining $(n-2)$, and so on, and these can be shown to add to $[n(n-1)/2)]$). So, the evaluation of $n = 20$ objects requires $[20(19-1)/2] = 190$ paired comparisons, and $n = 50$ requires more than 1200. The rapid expansion in the number of paired comparisons needed as the number of items increases limits the usefulness of this technique for the evaluation of large object sets. If the researcher does not need data at the individual level, however, respondents can be given different subsets of the paired comparisons necessary to evaluate when n is large so that eventually every pair is evaluated by at least one respondent.

In Table 4.4, Matrix I presents paired-comparison data for five brands of cake mix: A, B, C, D, and E. The judgment task was for the respondents to pick the cake mix sample that they personally preferred. Each cell entry in Matrix I represents the proportion of respondents who preferred the column brand over the row brand (so, the two "halves" of the matrix, above and below the diagonal, add to 1; note that researchers will often evenly split the votes of respondents who express no preference). For example, in the brand A vs. brand B comparison, 90 percent of the respondents preferred B to A; correspondingly, 10 percent indicated the reverse, that A was preferred to B. An inspection of the column proportions reveals that brand B dominates the other brands on the attribute being measured (overall preference, although other attributes could be assessed separately).

How can an ordinal scale be developed, given these paired-comparison data? One way is to try to take the data of Matrix I and convert them into something simpler to understand (even though this will discard some information about magnitudes): binary (i.e., 0 or 1) scores, indicating whether the column brand dominates the row brand based on Matrix I; this yields Matrix II in Table 4.4. Here, 1 is assigned to a cell if the column brand dominates the row brand (if the proportion is greater than 0.5), and 0 is assigned otherwise. An ordinal relationship among brands can be determined by simply totaling the columns. Here, the ordinal scaling of the brands appears to be B > C > A > E > D. Thus, brand B can be said, overall, to be liked best, followed by C, A, E, and D. (We could have simply added the scores of Matrix I, although for technical reasons that are beyond our scope, this will not possess the ordinal scale property; note that the order that comes about from doing so, B > C > A > E > D, is the same, although in general this is not guaranteed.)

Note, however, that this analysis ignores two important qualities: *effect size* and *heterogeneity*. When the data in Matrix I were processed into that for Matrix II, all data in column B were translated into 1 because they were all greater than 0.5. But a fairly weak proportion 0.68 (B vs. C)—which may not even be statistically significantly greater than half—became a 1 just as surely as an overwhelmingly high proportion like 0.98 (B vs. D). In a sense, this isn't "fair" to brand C, which is preferred by roughly one-third

Table 4.4 Paired-Comparison Data

Matrix I

Proportion preferring the column brand over the row brand

	A	B	C	D	E
A	—	0.90	0.64	0.14	0.27
B	0.10	—	0.32	0.02	0.21
C	0.36	0.68	—	0.15	0.36
D	0.86	0.98	0.85	—	0.52
E	0.73	0.79	0.64	0.48	—
Total	2.05	3.35	2.45	0.79	1.36

Matrix II

Binary preference of the column brand over the row brand

	A	B	C	D	E
A	—	1	1	0	0
B	0	—	0	0	0
C	0	1	—	0	0
D	1	1	1	—	1
E	1	1	1	0	—
Total	2	4	3	0	1

of the respondents, compared with D, which almost no one liked. In marketing research and data analysis more generally, it is poor form to discard intrinsic structure of data, which we did in this case by asking only whether a number was greater than half. We also took no account of heterogeneity, that different people have different preferences. Some people may have a radically different view of the entire cake mix category, but their views are "smoothed out" by Matrix I, which *aggregates* across all respondents. We look at heterogeneity and how to account for it statistically in Chapter 12.

The arguments in favor of the paired-comparison technique relate to the simplicity of the judgment task, the comparative nature of the task, and the availability of scaling methods that produce interval data. This interval-scaling feature can be important in assessing differences among competitive products and advertisements. One of the major techniques of marketing research, multidimensional scaling (see Chapter 11), affords a powerful way to visualize paired-comparison data and use them to create especially revealing perceptual maps.

perceptual maps
A two- or higher-dimensional visualization of an entire market or category that can be created by working with an explicit set of attributes (e.g., durability and effectiveness) or by implicit or latent scaling techniques (e.g., multidimensional scaling).

As mentioned earlier, the paired-comparison technique is limited in application because the number of paired comparisons increases geometrically as the number of objects (in marketing applications, usually products or brands) to be evaluated increases arithmetically. Consequently, the technique is limited to a small number of objects to control respondent fatigue during the judgment process, or involves breaking up sets of comparisons across respondents. Research also indicates that the order in which the objects are presented can bias the results (although this can be mitigated by counterbalancing); that the paired-comparison task is not typical of the actual choice process present in the marketplace, where people choose among many options, not just two; and that simpler noncomparative rating scales usually provide results similar to those obtained from paired comparisons. So, although paired comparisons are easy to set up and simple for respondents, they should be used sparingly and judiciously, except in anticipation of particular analytic techniques like multidimensional scaling.

counterbalancing
A means of preventing the order of questions or listed alternatives from affecting resulting responses by rotating their order among respondents; counterbalancing well can be difficult, so it is usually handled by computer, using an orthogonal design.

4.5g Semantic Differential Scale

The semantic differential scale is a popular attitude measurement technique in marketing research and is applied widely in corporate and brand image studies. For example, an image can be defined as an

semantic differential scale
A question type in which respondents assess an object in terms of where it falls between two opposed (bipolar) adjectives (e.g., "male–female" or "costly–inexpensive").

amalgam or composite of many separate attitudes toward a company, brand, or concept. As discussed previously, each separate attitude can be thought of as having three interrelated components: cognitive, affective, and behavioral. Consequently, image measurement requires respondents to express their position on many attitudes, using a multiscale questionnaire. The semantic differential typically requires the respondents to evaluate an object on a seven-point rating scale bounded at each end by *bipolar adjectives*, two descriptor terms that anyone would view as nearly opposite so that a spectrum is naturally formed between them. For example:

For each pair of adjectives, please place an X between them to indicate your view of the item listed at the top.

Target retail store:

Reliable			X					Unreliable
Friendly	X							Unfriendly
Modern					X			Old-fashioned
Inexpensive						X		Expensive
Progressive				X				Not progressive

Respondents are instructed to check the blank location that most accurately reflects their view of the listed object (in this case, a retail store) in connection with each of the bipolar adjectives. The technique is typically adapted to fit the needs of the research project at hand, as the following examples demonstrate.

- Descriptive phrases: The single-word adjectives are sometimes replaced with descriptive phrases tailored to a particular company, product, or concept. The following could be used, for example, to measure the brand image of a soft drink:

  Very special drink–Just another drink
  Fun type of drink–Serious sort of drink
  Regular people drink it–Snobs drink it

  Such specially designed comparisons require extensive pretesting; for example, some respondents may not view the opposite of "regular people" to be "snobs" and so skew their answers accordingly, biasing the desired measurement.
- Moderating extremes: The polar opposites can be replaced with phrases that may not include extremes and may eliminate the overtly negative portion of the scale. Potential motivations for doing so are that some respondents are unwilling to check the extremes of a scale; some are simply unwilling to express a negative view; or few have negative views toward the objects under investigation to begin with, so a negative portion of the scale would be "wasted." The following phrases represent this adaptation:

  High-quality product–So-so product
  Modern company–Somewhat old-fashioned company

  One way to mitigate potential biases from lopping off one side of a scale is to counterbalance so that a portion of the respondents see the full scale (e.g., "high-quality product–low-quality product") and others see a mirror image, with mostly negative responses (e.g., "so-so product–low-quality product"). If there is consistent evidence from a pretest that the negative portion of the scale is naturally omitted, it is fine to remove it for the full-sample survey.
- Comparison to ideal: Many researchers have the respondent evaluate an "ideal product" or an "ideal company" in addition to the objects under investigation. This approach allows the objects under investigation to be compared with a norm or standard. If such a comparison appears early in the survey, it will help norm the rest of the responses. However, it may also restrict all subsequent answers to the range of the scale dictated by the comparison to the "ideal." For example, if the "ideal" product receives a five on a seven-point scale, all subsequent responses may receive even lower values.
- Numerical scale: Each position on the scale can be assigned a numerical value, such as {7, 6, 5, 4, 3, 2, 1} or {+3, +2, +1, 0, −1, −2, −3}. The assumption is that the respondents' judgments can be treated as interval data, which makes possible the calculation of the arithmetic mean for an object

on each scale. This approach is common among researchers who use the semantic differential due to its clarity and expedience for analysis. However, treating these measurements as interval data is, strictly speaking, inappropriate, because they only possess the ordinal property. In that case, the median is the appropriate summary measure, and ordinal regression is the analytic method of choice.

Semantic differential data are typically analyzed using the profile analysis approach. This involves calculating the arithmetic mean or median for each set of verbal phrases or polar opposites for each object evaluated. These summary measures are usually plotted on the scales so that the profiles of the objects can be compared. Figure 4.6 provides an illustration of the profiles for three brands of beer. Because all "positive" adjective anchors are placed on the left (with the possible exception of "light feeling" vs. "heavy feeling"), we might conclude that brand X has the most favorable brand image and brand Z the least favorable. Note, however, that all three brand images veer toward the positive side of the scales, so none of them is markedly disliked, even though brand Z is strongly dominated by the competition across all included dimensions. Other approaches to analyzing the sort of multivariate scale data generated by a variety of semantic differential scales include factor analysis (to see whether there is redundancy in the various scales) and cluster analysis (to determine whether different objects that have been rated on the scales fall naturally into groups). Chapter 11 covers both these topics in detail.

The popularity of the semantic differential is attributed to its versatility and simplicity. The technique is easy to develop and administer, respondents uniformly understand it (and often find it stimulating),

Figure 4.6 Profile Analysis of Beer Brand Images

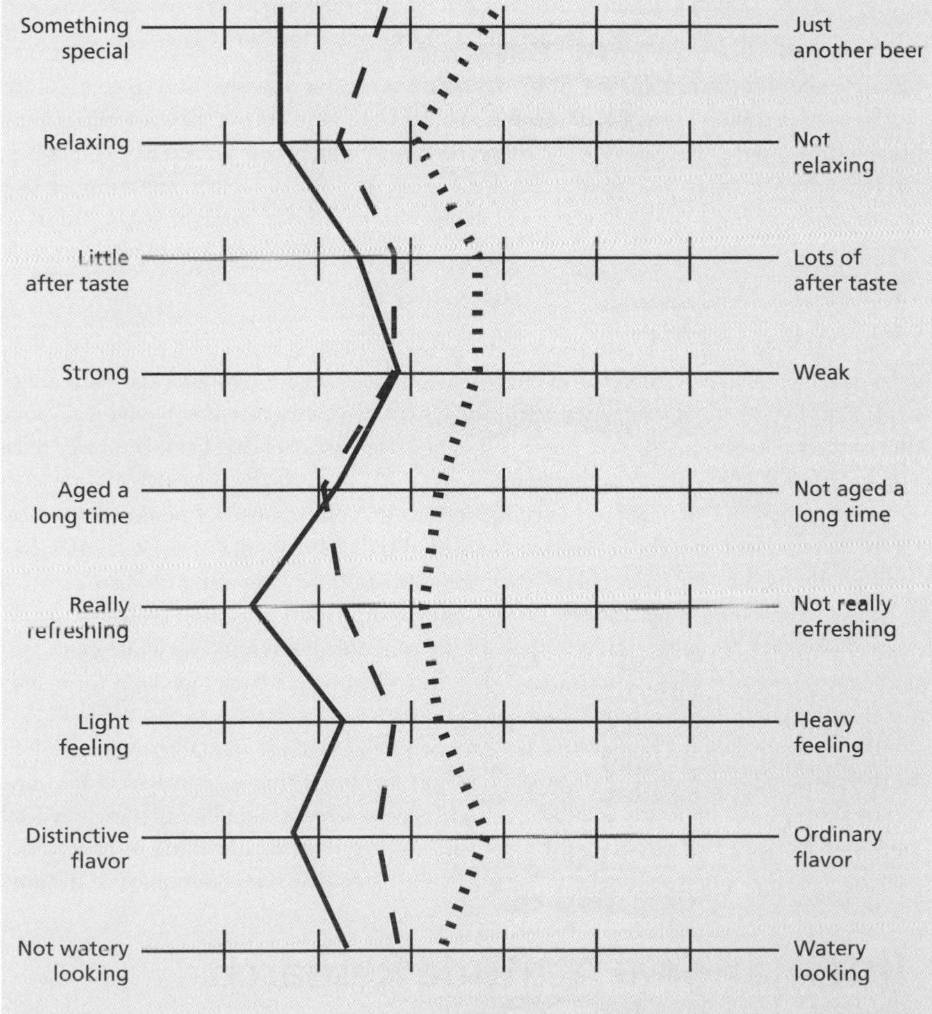

and the results can be readily communicated to management. It allows researchers to measure how items fare along a variety of readily conveyed dimensions of their own choosing, making it ideal for research on marketing positioning. In addition, it has been found to be a discriminating and reliable research tool.

The limitation of the schematic differential relates to the requirement that the scales be composed of true bipolar adjectives or phrases. All too often, scales are presented with endpoint pairs like "undesirable–attractive" or "cheap–luxurious" that are not strictly antonyms (unattractive products like cinder blocks can still be desirable when building something, and expensive items need not be luxurious). Pilot testing can be costly and time-consuming, so in practice it is rarely done; rather, the bipolar adjectives or phrases are developed using the researchers' judgment. Researchers also run the risk of failing to include relevant attribute dimensions because the only attitudes respondents can express are those explicitly set by the researcher. It is possible to safeguard against this somewhat by comparing against the positioning-based results of a multidimensional scaling study.

4.5h Stapel Scale

The Stapel scale is a modification of the semantic differential scale. It is a unipolar, typically 10-point, rating scale with values ranging from +5 to −5 (note that the convention for writing Stapel scales, descending from positive to negative, is different from that for other scales, although it is certainly possible to present the scale values in the opposite direction). The scaling technique is designed to measure the direction and intensity of attitudes simultaneously. It differs from the semantic differential in that the scale values indicate how closely the descriptor or adjective fits the object evaluated.

For a Stapel scale, respondents are instructed to evaluate how accurately the adjective or phrase describes the object to be evaluated. The respondent is instructed as follows:

> Select a *plus* number for words that you think describe brand A accurately. The more accurately you think the word describes it, the larger the plus number you would choose. Select a *minus* number for words you think do not describe it accurately. The less accurately you think a word describes it, the larger the minus number you would choose. Therefore, you can select any number from +5, for words that you think are very accurate, all the way to −5, for words that you think are very inaccurate.

+5 +4 +3 +2 +1	Fast service	−1 −2 −3 −4 −5
+5 +4 +3 +2 +1	Friendly	−1 −2 −3 −4 −5

Unipolar judgments can be analyzed in the same way that semantic differential data are treated. Figure 4.7 presents hypothetical results of a profile analysis of two banks based on Stapel scale data. Note that neither of the banks dominates, and the only sizeable differences are that bank B appears to be more convenient and bank A offers higher savings rates.

The arguments in favor of the Stapel scale relate to its convenience of administration and the absence of the requirement that the scales be composed of truly bipolar adjectives or phrases. Respondents are universally used to situations where they are asked to "rate something on a scale of 1 to 10," which the Stapel scale merely replaces with +5 to −5 (excluding zero). Research indicates that the Stapel scale can produce results quite similar to those of the semantic differential. In addition, the scale has produced satisfactory results when administered over the telephone, a tricky medium for many of the other scales discussed here due to respondent memory limitations.

Despite these advantages, the Stapel scale has experienced limited use in marketing research in comparison to the semantic differential. One possible reason for this is that a Stapel scale measuring, for example, "fast service" can be nearly identically rendered as a semantic differential anchored by "slow service" and "fast service." It is often argued, however, that respondents unwilling to choose negative-sounding anchors like "slow service" are better served by the Stapel-based representation of the question.

4.6 International Attitude Research

The attitude measurement procedures described in this chapter are equally applicable to both domestic and international marketing research. As noted earlier, great care must be taken to assure the reliability and validity of the attitude measures used internationally and to avoid merely assuming their

Figure 4.7 Stapel Scale Comparative Profiles

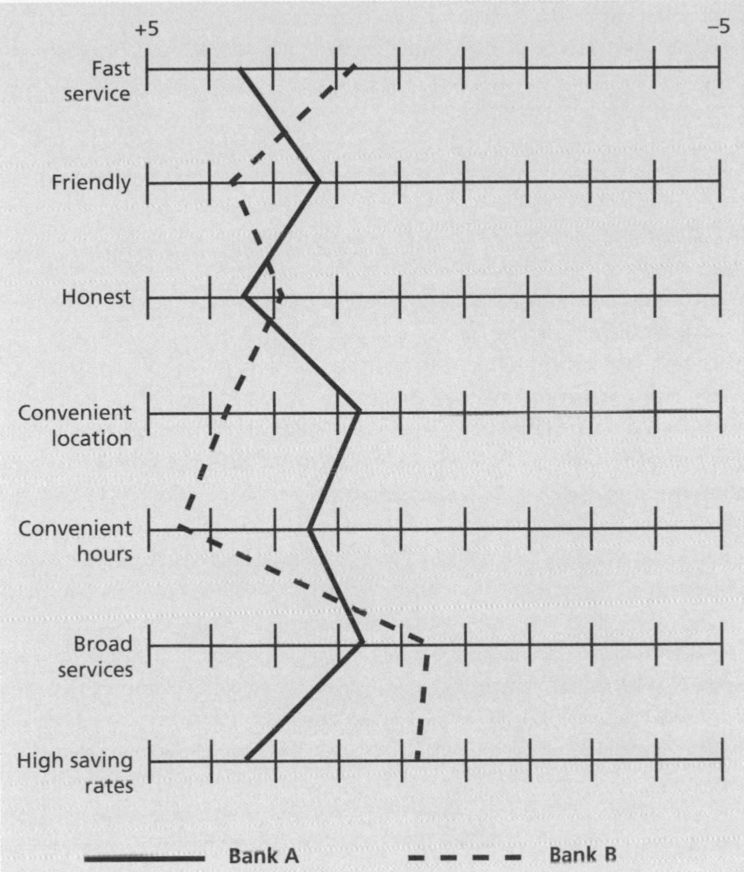

cross-cultural comparability. International marketing research suppliers tend to use lifestyle scales, such as Global Scan, Japan VALS, and Cross Cultural Consumer Characterization, to segment markets according to consumer attitude. These scales, along with segmentation, are discussed in Chapter 11. Often, international firms and research suppliers must enact fairly large changes when conducting business in countries with cultures dissimilar to that of their home base; *International Issues 4.2* focuses on how one of North America's largest retailers needed to do so when attempting to penetrate a distinctly different shopping culture.

International Issues 4.2

Wal-Mart Caters to Local Culture in China

After observing the encouraging results of other chain stores commencing operations in East Asia during the early 1990s, in 1994 Wal-Mart decided to do the same in Hong Kong, potentially as a gateway to the lucrative Chinese market. This entry was accomplished without opening stores that resembled, in any meaningful way, the classic U.S.-based Wal-Mart or Sam's Club stores. Instead, Wal-Mart opened three of what it called Value Clubs, outlets targeted at both individual consumers and small businesses.

A Value Club is somewhat like a small Sam's Club, reflecting local dynamics typical of Hong Kong. The stores tend to be located in malls, amid high-rise apartment buildings; they offer smaller sizes of packages and smaller lots than in the United States and focus mainly on products familiar to Chinese customers.

This strategy was chosen based on attitudes of Hong Kong residents as revealed by surveys. "There was a tremendous need for Wal-Mart to adapt to the unique Hong Kong shopping attitudes and habits," noted one marketing expert. Convenient location is the primary consideration to customers in Hong Kong, for example, because of traffic congestion, lack of parking, and widespread dependence on public transportation. Chinese workers tend to shop every day on the way home from work and to view traveling a great distance to shop as wasteful and counterproductive. "Convenience," according to Hong Kong customers, means within a 10- or 15-minute walk. Because apartments tend to be small with little storage space, compared with typical U.S. living quarters, oversize containers popular in the United States are exceedingly impractical to Chinese customers. Few people have counter or refrigerator space sufficient for gallon jugs, for instance, or cupboards for storing a 6-month's supply of a product. Unlike U.S. customers, they do not consider bargains for bulk purchases worth the trouble of storing the excess product.

Wal-Mart paid attention to these attitudes and adapted to them by locating small stores, reflecting the size of the population within walking or biking distance from each store, near where the consumers lived. These Value Clubs carried small sizes of products sold in small lot sizes. They capitalized on the venerated theme of frugality and cultural practices that stressed arriving at a good deal as one of the chief goals of shopping.

In 1996, Wal-Mart introduced Value Clubs in other parts of China. Because the Chinese would visit a Wal-Mart store only if they could find cheaper prices on products already familiar to them from local markets, Wal-Mart checked their prices against those in local markets three times a day.

Another value Wal-Mart sought to offer Chinese customers was a safer shopping environment than crowded open-air markets, held in narrow alleyways that were often wet and slippery. Wal-Mart attempted to attract customers with spacious, clean interiors; wide aisles; and clear signage, as well as with food that was more convenient and safer to eat than some of that bought in street markets, including ready-made single-serving meals and hygienically wrapped and attractively packaged baked goods, meat, and fish. Because Chinese customers like to buy fresh and shop frequently, Wal-Mart put a strong emphasis on food (food accounts for half the revenue of its Chinese stores, compared with 30 to 40 percent elsewhere). Stores also added attractions such as huge karaoke contests, a Special Olympics, a marathon, and a variety of other contests and events.

Despite these strategies, Wal-Mart encountered obstacles to success in China due to supply chain instabilities, inadequate infrastructure (such as road transportation and private and commercial trucking), customs clearance, and purchasing between provinces. In 1999, regulations were liberalized, increasing the number of approved cities for Chinese-foreign retail joint ventures. Meanwhile, since 1994, Wumart Stores has become China's answer to Wal-Mart, a leading retail chain with 430 hypermarkets, supermarkets, and convenience stores rivaling Wal-Mart in the Beijing area.

Wal-Mart opened its first China Supercenter in Shenzhen in 2000, offering roughly 20,000 products, 95 percent of which were Chinese, with considerable success. Within a few years, China became an important market for Wal-Mart. In 2005, with more than 40 stores in China already, Wal-Mart teamed up with CITIC Pacific Company to open hundreds of stores in China over 5 years. Although increasing oil prices are slowing the U.S. economy, Wal-Mart hopes to take advantage of faster Chinese growth by accelerating store openings and expansion into smaller Chinese cities.

Sources: Herndon, Neil (1994), "Wal-Mart Goes to Hong Kong, Looks at China," *Marketing News*, No.21 November, pp.2.
Herndon, Neil (1995), "Hong Kong Shoppers Cool to Wal-Mart's Value Club," *Marketing News* (November 20) Vol. 29, No. 24, pp. 11–13.
Hoover's (2005), "Wal-Mart Stores, Inc.," *Hoover's Company Profiles* (September 8).
Hoover's (2005), "Wumart Stores, Inc.," *Hoover's Company Profiles* (September 28).
China Daily Information (2005), "Wal-Mart Eyes Smaller Cities," *Industry Updates* (September 8).

SPECIAL SECTION

Neuromarketing and the "Buy Button"

The technology of neuromarketing has opened up a nascent field in marketing research, one that, for some people, calls into question traditional boundaries of privacy—and even the notion of "free will."

It has been roughly estimated that 95 percent of human cognition takes place below the level of consciousness. Marketing has always sought to influence consumer choices through a mix of rational and emotional appeals. Since the late 1950s, critics have raised the issue of whether marketing deliberately bypasses conscious, rational deliberation through emotional manipulation or subliminal or "sub-threshold" messages. Neuromarketing gives the marketer more detailed information on involuntary human responses in the brain, digging toward the "old brain" or "reptilian brain," the seat of the subconscious, as well as other key sites in the brain, where, researchers believe, the process of decision making takes place.

In addition to eye-tracking, which monitors what people look at on a page or screen and for how long, and GSR, which can gauge emotional involvement, neuromarketing researchers use RI and electroencephalographs (EEGs) to measure activity and track cognitive functions in the brain in response to stimuli. The goal is to find out what potential buyers really think and feel without relying on self-reporting, which is considered fundamentally flawed by the truism that people often do not know their own mind.

continued

What "Lights Up" in the Brain

The brain activity registered when a subject first views an image or product often occurs in the visual cortex. Mentally examining the product in the imagination from different angles triggers memory circuits in the left inferotemporal cortex. The parietal lobe shows activity when a subject is integrating visual images. Activity in the left prefrontal cortex can suggest, in many people, attraction to the brand or message, whereas in the right prefrontal cortex it can indicate instinctive revulsion. The medial prefrontal cortex is often activated when people are stimulated by images of things to which they are extremely attached.

In one intriguing study, Pepsi was found to stimulate five times more activity than Coke in the brain's ventral putamen, an area of the brain associated with a sense of reward. When the experiment was repeated, this time announcing which of the samples were Coke, not only did most subjects say they preferred Coke, the subjects also showed more activity in the medial prefrontal cortex, which is associated with higher cognition and sense of self. The Coke *brand* apparently influenced the subjects' brain activity and affected their preference.

Because memory and emotion play a major role in brand recognition and loyalty, much neuromarketing research focuses on the neural activities involved in memory storage and recall. In the words of Michael Brammer, chairman of Neurosense (a "neuromarketing consultancy"), "We can scan people looking at lots of different images, find out afterward which ones they remembered, and then go back to the scan data and find out what was specific about the brain activity that occurred in response to the remembered images." Neuromarketing researchers look for the parts of advertising messages that stimulate electrical activity in areas of the brain indicating long-term memory encoding, which is thought to be associated with a higher likelihood of purchasing a product.

Gregory Berns, a researcher at Emory University in Atlanta, used brain imaging to demonstrate the effects of peer pressure on perception. By comparing activity in the parietal lobe and prefrontal cortex between subjects shown an image and subjects shown the same image after being told how others perceived it, he showed that the majority view of a group tends to change what a subject perceives. "There is probably some reward or kick in conforming to a group," Berns suggested.

Although it is generally agreed that the medial frontal cortex is important to decision making, a quick survey of the rationales of neuromarketing reveals that scientists are far from a consensus on the neural mechanics of making decisions. Some neuromarketing researchers claim that activity in the right parietal cortex, above and behind the right ear, should be the target of advertising, indicating a "strongly preferred choice." Some claim that increased activity in the medial prefrontal cortex occurs whenever a subject identifies with a product strongly, thinking, "That's me!" These researchers present this area as "the magic spot" for advertising, with activity in this area indicating that a consumer is not deliberating but "itching to buy"—in contrast to activity in the somatosensory cortex (associated with sensory imagination), which, they claim, indicates that the consumer is "trying out" rather than instantly identifying with the product.

In a somewhat contradictory theory, some claim that the amygdala in the old brain, the seat of emotional response, especially to threats and sexual imagery, is the key to effective advertising, especially to young children or people older than age 50, whose prefrontal cortex (in this theory presented as the seat of more rational deliberation rather than instant identification) is less active and therefore more susceptible to emotional appeals. Another theory along those lines has been used to explain responses to campaign advertising for political candidates. In this study, subjects tended to show emotional reactions to all candidates in the amygdala or ventromedial prefrontal cortex (associated with reflexive reactions); but in response to advertising for an opposing party's candidate, their brains showed more activity in the rational part of the brain, the dorsolateral prefrontal cortex. One researcher theorized, "It seems as if they're really identifying with their own candidate, whereas when they see the opponent, they're using their rational apparatus to argue against him."

The "Buy Button": Claims, Counterclaims, and Reactions

Purveyors of neuromarketing technology have added to the confusion by exaggerating confidence in their assertions and the power of the technology to influence buying behavior in consumers, even claiming to have discovered the "buy button" inside the human mind. Neuromarketing enthusiasts claimed focus groups and the traditional methodologies of political consultants were "so last century" because "brain waves don't lie." An executive at BrightHouse Institute was quoted as saying "What [neuromarketing] really does is give unprecedented insight into the consumer mind. And it will actually result in higher product sales or in brand preference or in getting customers to behave the way they want them to behave."

In response to such ambitious claims came a corresponding upsurge of consumer alarm and action against the technology due to the potential for exploitation. The idea of a "buy button" brought up the fear that advertisers would be able to bypass consumers' conscious reasoning, making them slaves or automatons programmed by advertisers or politicians. Gary Ruskin, executive director of Commercial Alert, wrote in a letter to the U.S. Office for Human Research Protections, "It sounds like something that could have happened in the former Soviet Union, for purposes of behavior control." Ruskin claimed that aggressive marketing already contributes to "an epidemic of marketing-related diseases," such as obesity, eating disorders, diabetes, alcoholism, and lung disease, and to the promotion of degraded values, such as materialism, addiction, violence, gambling, and other antisocial behavior, and that neuromarketing could increase this effect. He pointed to neuromarketing experiments investigating the effectiveness of political advertising and brought up the dangers of more effective political propaganda in a world environment of dictators,

continued

human rights violations, and totalitarian regimes.

In another letter to Senator John McCain, then chairman of the Senate Commerce Committee, Ruskin wrote, "What would happen in this country if corporate marketers and political consultants could literally peer inside our brains, and chart the neural activity that leads to our selections in the supermarket and the voting booth? What if they then could trigger this neural activity by various means, so as to modify our behavior to serve their own ends? Orwellian is not too strong a term for this prospect."

As Douglas Rushkoff, author of the book *Coercion*, phrased the concerns, "The thought of a once-respected university surrendering its MRI equipment, psychiatrists and addiction experts to an advertising agency in order for them to mine deep into our pre-conscious neural patterns and speak directly to our reptilian brains is disconcerting, to say the least. It represents both the decline of American academic integrity and the rather unlimited reach of marketing into the most private realms of human thought and emotion." He claimed that neuromarketing technology "has a bias to a specific type of abuse. What we have to decide is whether we want to live in a society where our behaviors are for sale to the highest bidder."

Although such alarm may, in the future, prove justified, it is currently premature. Neuroscientists have not yet agreed on a map of the brain or how it functions, never mind how to manipulate it to increase sales or ensure obedience. Since the initial flurry of exaggerated claims and denouncements, the controversy over neuromarketing has subsided. BrightHouse Institute, the subject of much of the controversy, removed neuromarketing from its Web site. Rushkoff eventually suggested that alarmed consumer reaction might serve only as a marketing coup for companies wishing to sell a technology that has not yet proven itself—going so far as to predict, "we'll realize that the only people who ended up being hypnotized by [neuromarketers'] wares were the daft corporate executives who paid for them." Elizabeth Phelps, a professor of psychology at New York University, put it even more colorfully, "I keep joking that I could do this Gucci shoes study, where I'd show people shoes I think are beautiful, and see whether women like them. I'll see activity in the brain. I definitely will. But it's not like I've found 'the shoe center of the brain.'"

Skeptical scientists seem confident that neuromarketing technology is a long way from enslaving the average consumer. In the words of John Van Horn, a professor and researcher at Dartmouth College in New Hampshire, "The human brain is the most complicated thing in the universe. It would be arrogant to say we could stick someone in a machine and understand everything."

Sources: Rushkoff, Douglas (2004), "Reading the Consumer Mind," *NY Press* (February).

Schabner, Douglas (2004), "Playing With Your Mind: Is Neuromarketing Research Giving Advertisers the Keys to Your Decision-Making?" ABC-NEWS.com (January 13).

Thompson, Clive (2003), "There's a Sucker Born in Every Medial Prefrontal Cortex," *New York Times* (October 26).

Tierney, John (2004), "Using M.R.I.s to See Politics on the Brain," *New York Times* (April 20).

Wells, Melanie (2003), "In Search of the Buy Button," *Forbes Magazine* (September 1).

Witchalls, Clint (2004), "Pushing the Buy Button," *Newsweek* (March 22).

Summary

Measurement in marketing research uses numbers to represent the marketing phenomena under investigation. The measurement process assigns values from an abstract numerical system to the characteristics of objects or events in the empirical system, according to specific rules. When the characteristics of the number system do not represent the relationships present in the marketing phenomena being measured, the measurement is in error.

Four possible characteristics of number systems are equality of numerals, order of numerals, equality of differences, and equality of ratios; these correspond to the four scales of measurement, respectively: nominal, ordinal, interval, and ratio. A nominal scale uses numbers to identify and categorize, with no implications of "more or less." An ordinal scale uses numbers to rank or order, implying "more" and "less" but with no indication as to the interval between rankings or the relative "amount" of a characteristic. An interval scale uses numbers to rank with a uniform distance between rankings; a ratio scale also does this, with the additional requirement of defining a zero point consistent between numerical assignments on different scales. Progressing from nominal to ratio measurement, the rules for assigning numerals to marketing phenomena become increasingly more restrictive as the range of statistical techniques available to analyze the data increases.

The total error of measurement consists of systematic and random error. The validity of a measurement is the extent to which the measurement process is free from both systematic and random error. The reliability of a measure refers to the extent to which the measurement process is free from random error. Therefore, reliability is a necessary but not a sufficient condition for validity. As a less rigorous concept, it is easier to measure than validity.

Attitude measurement plays a central role in developing segmentation or positioning strategies, evaluating the effectiveness of advertising, predicting product acceptance, and facilitating the development of marketing programs.

An attitude is a construct that exists in the mind of an individual representing the individual's enduring perceptual, knowledge-based, evaluative, and action-oriented processes with respect to an object or phenomenon. The three components of an attitude are (1) cognitive, relating to beliefs; (2) affective, relating to feelings; and (3) behavioral, relating to action. The hierarchy-of-effects model postulates a cognitive–affective–behavioral sequence resulting from a marketing effort. Measurement of an attitude component early in the sequence may allow predictions regarding the character of subsequent components.

Attitude measurement methods generally rely on communicating with and observing respondents. Communication techniques include self-reports, responses to unstructured or partially structured stimuli, and performance of objective tasks; observation methods include observation of overt behavioral and physiological reactions.

The self-reporting technique, through verbal and graphic rating scales and other scaling approaches, is the most widely used method of attitude measurement in marketing. Rating scales should be constructed after considering the number of categories, whether the scale is balanced, whether it forces a position, whether it is comparative, the extent of verbal description, and other factors that contribute to the scale's usefulness to a particular measurement.

Rank-order and paired-comparison scaling use a ranking or a series of pairwise judgments, respectively, to arrive at an ordinal scaling of the objects. Semantic differential and Stapel scaling measure "image" through a profile analysis of many separate attitudes toward a company, brand, or concept.

Key Terms

Discussion Questions

1 For each of the four scales of measurement, give an example of how it might be appropriate for measuring a particular marketing phenomenon.

2 Discuss what it means for a measurement to be valid, and give a specific example of steps that might be taken to test the validity of a measure.

3 What considerations must a researcher always keep in mind when measuring attitudes?

4 Follow the instructions in each of the following scaling problems:

a Verbal rating scale construction: Construct a set of verbal rating scales to measure high-school students' attitudes toward attending your alma mater. Briefly discuss the issues involved in constructing such verbal scales, and identify the appropriate level of measurement (ordinal, interval, or ratio) for each. What sorts of dimensions would you believe to be relevant regarding the decision as to (1) which colleges or universities to apply to and (2) which one to attend from among those that offer admission? Do these require separate surveys, different questions, and/or different choices on each?

b Image measurement: Construct a set of scales to measure the image high-school students have of your college and its top three competitors (be sure to elicit which these are because that perception will vary across respondents). What sorts of underlying dimensions are relevant to capture this image, and how do you think they are best measured?

c Measuring the hierarchy of effects: Develop questions to measure each level of the hierarchy of effects (awareness, knowledge, liking, preference, intention-to-buy, and purchase) for any among this set of magazines: *Scientific American, National Geographic, Vanity Fair, Newsweek*. Obtain responses to your questions from two respondents, and use them to generate tentative conclusions about the elements of the effects hierarchy.

d Paired-comparison data: In Matrix II, develop an ordinal scale of the five brands using the paired-comparison data in Matrix I. Do any conclusions jump out at you regarding the five brands? Are the conclusions based on any arbitrary choices you made in setting up the ordinal scale, if any? Be specific.

Matrix I

	A	B	C	D	E
A	—	0.60	0.44	0.59	0.25
B	0.40	—	0.42	0.52	0.37
C	0.56	0.58	—	0.52	0.13
D	0.41	0.48	0.48	—	0.43
E	0.75	0.63	0.87	0.57	—

Matrix II

	A	B	C	D	E
A	—				
B		—			
C			—		
D				—	
E					—
Total					

Ordinal scaling: ___>___>___>___>___

5 MINICASE

In its domestic U.S. operations, the Gillette Company (www.gillette.com) makes extensive use of consumer measures about advertisements that it is considering using on television. These measures include awareness, brand association, recall, and believability. Gillette has standard measures of each of these constructs. When the company considers a major new marketing entry into Korea, Japan, Singapore, Indonesia, and other East Asian countries, concern is raised about the appropriateness of these standard measures.

a How could each of these constructs be measured?

b What scale level would these constructs be?

c What steps could Gillette take to determine the appropriateness of these measures in the new markets? Be specific.

d What cultural and translation-based difficulties would you anticipate in translating consumer measures tested in the U.S. to East Asian markets? Which such markets do you believe would require the most extensive additional testing and potential alterations?

6 MINICASE

Prepare a set of attitude measurement questions that Wal-Mart could have used in its research in Hong Kong and China (see *International Issues 4.2*). Consider possible usages of the following types of scales: nominal, verbal rating, numerical rating, graphic rating, rank-order, paired-comparison, semantic differential, and Stapel. Which do you think is most useful in this context, and why? Given that this is cross-cultural research, which of the scales seems to you to be most and least affected by cultural differences and the vagaries of translation?

7 Read the *Special Section* on neuromarketing at the end of this chapter. How would you assess the various claims and counterclaims regarding the effectiveness of neuromarketing? Which claims have been substantiated? Which have been disproven? Do you think this subject warrants careful attention in the future? Why or why not?

Review Questions

1 The term *empirical system* refers to:
  a the symbolic representation of phenomena through numbers.
  b the actual phenomena under investigation.
  c a valid and reliable system of measurement.
  d the mental abstraction of perceived experience.

2 A nominal scale (not ordinal, interval, or ratio) would be appropriate for the representation of:
  a ZIP codes.
  b simple preferences.
  c ambient temperature.
  d age ranges.

3 "Dictionary entry" is to "words" as "constitutive" definition is to
  a "valence."
  b "operational definition."
  c "validity measures."
  d "constructs."

4 Systematic error leads directly to which of the following in resulting measurements?
  a random fluctuations
  b constant bias
  c minor reductions of validity
  d major reductions of reliability

5 According to their definitions, measurements that are valid are also:
  a concurrent.
  b operational.
  c reliable.
  d convergent.

6 Suppose a consumer considers a banking service beneficial in its terms but is reluctant to purchase the service because of the particular bank's reputation for disregarding social responsibility. Which statement accurately reflects the components of attitude involved?
  a The cognitive component is positive, the affective negative, and the behavioral not yet determined.
  b The affective and behavioral components are positive, but the cognitive is negative.
  c None of the components can yet be measured because there is a conflict of belief.
  d The behavioral component counterbalances the affective component due to the consumer's belief in reputation.

7 What can be said about the link between attitudes and behavior?
  a Several sequential components of attitude can lead to eventual behavior.
  b Knowing what people think and believe does not allow perfect prediction of their purchasing behavior.
  c Marketing situations involving groups of consumers allow for the statistical forecasting of aggregate behavior.
  d all of the above

8 Attempting to capture a construct of interest using a value on a predefined numerical scale is known as:
  a a hierarchy-of-effects model.
  b a unidimensional measure.

c an interval scale.
d an observation technique.

9 Consider the following question put to respondents:

How do you rate product B regarding its daily usefulness?

Not useful	Only slightly useful	Somewhat useful	Fairly useful	Very useful

What characteristics does this scale have?
a odd number of categories, forced, noncomparative, unbalanced, asymmetric
b odd number, nonforced, noncomparative, balanced, symmetric
c odd number, nonforced, comparative, unbalanced, asymmetric
d odd number, forced, noncomparative, balanced, symmetric

10 A consumer packaged goods company runs many studies to test the flavor of various products and collects rankings from many people. It then averages the ranks across many people. For product class A, the averaged flavor rankings five brands came out in decreasing preference as follows: A3 > A5 > A2 > A1 > A4. For another product class, five other brands came out as follows: B2 > B5 > B1 > B4 > B3. Based on these averaged rankings, what can you conclude about relative flavor preferences?
a A3 is liked about as well as B2.
b A3 is liked better than B3.
c The overall liking for the five A brands is about the same as for the B brands.
d none of these

Web Exercise

Log in to the Online Edition of your textbook at www.atomicdog.com to participate in this Web exercise, which can be found in your Online Study Guide for this chapter.

Further Reading

Bearden, William O., and Richard G. Netemeyer (1999), *Handbook of Marketing Scales: Multi-Item Measures for Marketing and Consumer Behavior Research*, Sage Publications, 2nd Edition.

Bruner, Gordon C. II, and Paul J. Hensel (1992), *Marketing Scales Handbook: Volume 1: A Compilation of Multi-Item Measures*, South-Western Educational Publishing, 1st Edition.

Fowler, Floyd J. Jr. (1995), *Improving Survey Questions: Design and Evaluation*, Sage Publications.

Richard G. Netemeyer, William O. Bearden, and Subhash Sharma (2003), *Scaling Procedures: Issues and Applications*, Sage Publications.

Robinson, John P. (Editor) (1990), *Measures of Personality and Social Psychological Attitudes: Volume 1: Measures of Social Psychological Attitudes (Measures of Social Psychological Attitudes)*, Academic Press.

www.socialresearchmethods.net/kb/

CHAPTER FIVE
CAUSAL DESIGNS AND MARKETING EXPERIMENTS

"I know quite certainly that I have no special gift. Curiosity, obsession and dogged endurance have brought me my ideas."

ALBERT EINSTEIN

In Chapter 2, improper "causal" inferences were identified as one type of nonsampling error. In this chapter, we discuss this problem in the context of different types of research designs and their ability to distinguish causality. We stress that it is not possible, even in principle, to use statistical methods to determine with certainty whether one variable "causes" another. In practice, however, statistical methods can give a relatively clear indication of which variables tend to give rise to others, in a way clarified throughout this chapter. To that end, we first describe the necessary conditions for causality to be inferred, then the principles of both experimental and quasi experimental design and important managerial aspects of those designs, and finally the basics of designed experiments. *Marketing Research Focus 5.1* examines how one packaged goods firm used rigorous experimental design techniques to better understand the effect of its advertising.

Marketing Research Focus 5.1

Experimental Field Study Reveals Media and Creative Impacts on V8 Juice Sales

V8 is a well-established, tomato-based vegetable juice marketed by the Campbell Soup Company. For decades, it enjoyed enviable growth and a unique market positioning, based on "its blend of eight vegetable juices" providing the nutrition of two servings of vegetables per eight-ounce glass, with a low calorie and carbohydrate content. Management attributed this healthy sales growth and strong market positioning to the brand's advertising campaign, which focused on V8's superior taste relative to tomato juice, in addition to its nutritional benefits. The brand also responded to changing demographics and emphasis on health with the introduction of the V.Fusion and V8 Splash lines, which incorporate fruits and are rich in antioxidants.

Sales growth, although healthy over a multidecade horizon, was not always smooth and steady. During several periods of sales decline, advertising on the brand was reduced or even discontinued in many markets. Management believed these diminishing sales trends were attributable to "advertising wearout," whereby a successful campaign loses effectiveness over time due to consumer overfamiliarity. On two of these occasions, the institution of a new campaign revived declining sales trends.

To evaluate this general approach, the Campbell Soup Company conducted a series of studies for V8 over 5 years. The first of these studies was a controlled experiment to evaluate the effectiveness of a specific new campaign and media mix. The new campaign differed from V8's previous campaign in two important ways. First, the new campaign was primarily based on television, whereas previous campaigns had been weighted heavily toward radio. Second, the new campaign required a significantly larger budget to achieve similar exposure goals.

A controlled experiment was designed to evaluate the advantages, if any, of the new campaign. The study was designed to evaluate both the new and the old campaigns at the proposed higher budget using three different media mixes: television and radio, prime-time television only, and "fringe" television only (i.e., less costly placements outside prime time). The old campaign was also tested using only radio; the new campaign's design precluded a radio-only test. A "control" condition was also created using the old campaign, the old budget level, and the old media mix. The purpose of this control was to discern any start-up effects related to the mere act of advertising after a 6- to 9-month hiatus. Based on the assumption that the start-up effect was independent of the actual campaign, the study allowed marketers to estimate campaign and budget effects by comparing a test cell with the control cell, as presented in the diagram that follows:

Budget level	Media mix	New creative	Old creative
New budget	Television/radio	118.8* (2 markets)	111.2 (2 markets)
	Television, prime time	121.8 (2 markets)	116.6 (2 markets)
	Television, fringe	113.6 (2 markets)	116.2 (2 markets)
	Radio	Not tested	107.2 (4 markets)
Old budget	Primarily radio (old mix)	Not tested	110.0 (15 markets; control)

*Entries are the ratios of cumulative actual sales to cumulative forecast sales in each market after 3 months, averaged over the markets in each cell and multiplied by 100. Under the (null) hypothesis of no treatment effect, the expected value of these entries is 100, assuming unbiased forecasts.

Experimental "markets" within geographic areas received their television signals from a central town or city, facilitating the implementation of a new media mix or advertising budget change. Warehouse withdrawals were also recorded monthly, by market, for each size and brand in a particular product category, allowing marketers to track V8 sales for each market. The experiment used 31 markets: 15 as control cells and 16 as various test cells.

With the same media mix, response to the new campaign was 4 percent higher than that to the old campaign. The new campaign, combined with the television/radio and prime-time television media mixes, corresponded to a 10 percent increase in sales relative to the control group. The study identified a definite relationship between the strong consumer response and the new creative approach, the media mix, and the budget level, underscoring the usefulness of causal designs in marketing research.

Sources: www.v8juice.com

"Campbell Soup at Consumer Analyst Group of New York 2006 Conference—Final," *Voxant FD (Fair Disclosure) Wire* (February 22, 2006).

"Splash! Campbell to Introduce New Fruit and Carrot Juice-Based V8 Splash; Launch Coupled With $20 Million Advertising Campaign For V8 Juice Products," *PR Newswire* (April 21, 1997).

Eastlack, Joseph O., and Ambar G. Rao (1986), "Modeling Response to Advertising and Pricing Changes for V8 Cocktail Vegetable Juice," *Marketing Science* (Summer) Vol. 5, No. 3. (Summer, 1986), pp. 245–259.

5.1 The Quest for Causality

Marketing managers want to be able to make causal statements about the effects of their actions: "The new advertising campaign we developed has resulted in a 10 percent increase in sales." In similar fashion, a sales manager might boast, "The new sales training program has resulted in lower sales force turnover." In both of these examples, the managers are making causal statements. But are these statements valid? We cannot answer, because we do not have enough information about them. The brand manager has observed that sales increased *after* the change in the advertising campaign, and the sales manager has observed lower sales force turnover *after* the change in the sales training program. Events follow other events all the time; moreover, many events take place simultaneously that precede those later events of interest. Surely, precedence alone tells us little about causality. The fundamental question that should be asked in the face of all causal statements has been neither asked nor answered: "Are there *other* possible factors or events that could have led to the observed changes?" Rigorously and honestly answering this one question lies at the heart of all investigations of causality and forms a major part of conclusive marketing research.

Consider the brand manager's increase in sales. A sales spike can be caused by increased product penetration in the distribution channel, a strike at a competitor's plant, a new package design, or a decrease in price, among other activities and events. The decrease in sales force turnover that the sales manager boasted about could have resulted from (i.e., been caused by) a new quota payment system, a change in the type of people hired by the company, poor economic conditions that have made job opportunities at other companies scarce, and so on. Managers and researchers must be able to discern the conditions under which proper causal statements can be formulated and claimed to hold. Unfortunately, it is in the very nature of marketing decision making that not all conditions allowing for the most accurate causal statements are typically present. For example, economic conditions are constantly changing, as are consumer tastes, competitors' tactics, and a host of other quantities difficult to measure and assess in terms of influence. In such circumstances, which one encounters all the time, marketing managers still tend to make causal statements. In doing so, they should clearly understand and account for the risk of error they are taking, not simply ignore it just because "the economy is always changing" and the like.

This chapter provides a framework for understanding the conditions necessary for making causal inferences, a framework used throughout the natural and social sciences. Although this framework will not guarantee that one will be able to make a causal inference in a given situation, it does provide a method so that, once such an inference is made, one can convey its content, rigor, and accuracy in a universally agreed-on manner.

5.1a Necessary Conditions for Causality

Before outlining the conditions that allow causal statements to be made, we must first develop a more formal understanding of the concept of causality. The scientific concept of causality is complex and differs substantially from the one held by the "person on the street." Both natural and social scientists, as well as philosophers, have identified a number of differences between the scientific and the so-called commonsense concepts of causality. The commonsense view holds that a single event (the cause) always results in another event (the effect). In science, we recognize that an event has a number of determining conditions or causes that act together to make the effect probable.

deterministic causation
The ordinary concept of causality that presumes that an effect always follows a cause; differs from the scientific concept of probabilistic causation conceptualizing effects in terms of their statistical probability.

probabilistic causation
The notion, common in philosophy of science, that research can never truly prove causality, only infer it with some degree of confidence.

Note that in the commonsense notion of causality, the effect always follows the cause. We refer to this as **deterministic causation**. In contrast, the scientific notion specifies the effect only as being probable. This is called **probabilistic causation**. The commonsense notion talks of proving that *X* causes *Y*; the scientific notion holds that we can only infer causality and never really prove it. Statisticians have studied the problem of *inference based on data* for many decades. Generally, the chance of an incorrect inference always exists because data are never perfect (e.g., biases, coding errors, missing values, or entire variables), our statistical models can never be proven correct, and variables can interrelate in extremely complex ways. This is true even in the "hard" sciences, where one deals with inert objects assumedly under the sway of physical law. In social sciences, like marketing and economics, the prospect of ascertaining strict causality becomes dramatically more dubious.

In the scientific view, marketing effects are probabilistically caused by multiple factors and we can only *infer* a causal relationship; we can never demonstrate it definitively. It is always possible that we have not identified the true causal relationship. Sales may have gone up just as much without the new advertising campaign; a distributor may have relocated even if another had not entered its region; price competition may have intensified even if a new factory had not come on line. We must always live with this "even if," a phrase that lies at the heart of causal inference in social science applications, with the exception of well-controlled laboratory experiments.

There are three conditions under which researchers can claim to have made causal inferences, and all should be met: (1) concomitant variation, (2) time order of occurrence of variables, and (3) elimination of other possible causal factors.

5.1b Concomitant Variation

hypothesis
A specific statement about a set of measurable quantities, usually assessed by collecting data.

Concomitant variation is the extent to which a cause, *X*, and an effect, *Y*, *occur together or vary together* in the way predicted by a **hypothesis** under consideration. Consider the example of a marketer of small foreign cars. This company has undertaken a new advertising campaign "to improve the attitudes people have toward our cars and therefore to increase sales." Suppose that in testing the results of this campaign the company finds that both aims have been achieved: attitudes have become more positive, and sales have increased. We can then say that there is concomitant variation between attitudes and sales. Note that the implied hypothesis here is that improved attitudes cause sales to increase. We can now conclude that the hypothesis of a causal relationship between attitudes and sales is tenable; that is, it has not been ruled out and there is reason to explore it further.

However, the hypothesis has not yet been proven. There are other possible explanations of the observed relationship—which is only one of *correlation* at this point—that are equally tenable. Several readily come to mind: (1) The increase in sales resulted in people becoming more experienced with these cars, which may have resulted in the observed improvement in attitudes; that is, the increase in sales led to (i.e., caused) the attitude change, not the other way around. (2) Some other variables not included in the study may have caused the observed relationship; for example, the company may have improved the quality of its cars during the period in question. (3) Advertising may have increased the number of people visiting the showroom, which in turn generated more sales, but attitudes themselves may not have increased enough to cause the sales change; so, although attitudes improved, they cannot be claimed to have caused the sales increase. These three types of relationships—respectively, reverse causation, omitted variables, and insufficient variation—are extremely common in empirical marketing research and must always be considered before proclaiming that causation is occurring. Clearly, we must go beyond concomitant variation before making valid causal inferences.

5.1c Time Occurrence of Variables

The hypothesis that improved attitudes cause increases in sales can be examined further by collecting data about attitudes from people at *various times* in their purchase process, specifically before exposure to the advertising campaign, after exposure but before car purchase, and after both exposure and car purchase. If attitudes improved after exposure to the campaign but before car purchase, we would have more evidence that the hypothesis was tenable. If, however, attitudes improved only after car purchase, the hypothesis would be untenable. That sales increases caused improved attitudes would be a more tenable hypothesis in this situation.

The general statement of this intuitive concept is that one event cannot cause another if it occurs *after* the other event. The causing event must occur either before or simultaneously with the effect. There is one complication in this seemingly straightforward concept; namely, that it is possible for each of two events to be both a cause and an effect of the other. In the example, improved attitudes may cause increases in sales, and increased sales may cause improved attitudes. Thus, the relationship between attitudes and sales could be that they alternately or simultaneously "feed into" one other. This type of relationship would be demonstrated in a purchase decision study if attitudes improved both before and after an increase in sales. However, in such cases, the very concepts of "cause" and "effect" are muddled, and it is, in general, difficult to tease them apart without additional, controlled studies or extremely careful sampling for just that purpose.

5.1d Elimination of Other Possible Causal Factors

Consider the case of a befuddled scientist who formulated a hypothesis that soda water causes intoxication. To test this hypothesis, the scientist gave, to a randomly selected group of participants, soda water mixed with one of these substances: scotch, gin, vodka, or pure ethanol. Intoxication was observed in each case. The scientist then reasoned: "I have observed concomitant variation between soda consumption and intoxication. Also, the proper time order of events to infer causality is present. My hypothesis is, therefore, correct." Only the most addled among us would not counter that another factor, the presence of alcohol, was the true cause of what the scientist observed. Other possible causes were not systematically eliminated, and the research design did not allow for the identification of the true causal relationship. One might guess that the scientist only needed to test one other liquid, plain soda water, on the participants, and this certainly would have been prudent. However, to rule out other possible causes, other experimental conditions would have to feature the various alcoholic beverages *without* soda water, different types of test tubes to house the mixtures, different times of day, different researchers doing the administration, and so on. To make airtight causal inferences, almost every element of a study needs to be scrutinized, varied, and statistically analyzed for its potential effects. This is both necessary and laborious in controlled laboratory studies but nearly impossible in real-world field research.

We must note that the brand manager and the sales manager who made the causal statements examined earlier were making exactly the same type of causal inference as our befuddled scientist and were no less befuddled. They failed to test for and systematically exclude other possible explanations. This failure is perhaps the most common and pernicious error in marketing research, and one must be especially diligent in trying to rule it out.

5.2 Experimentation

The fundamental research tool used to help identify causal relationships is the experiment. The objective of an experiment is to measure the effect of explanatory (independent) variables on another (dependent) variable of interest *while controlling for* other variables that might confuse the ability to make causal inferences. It is the second part of this definition that is ordinarily glossed over, and you are cautioned to take note of it. It is never sufficient simply to examine how some (independent) variables affect another (dependent) variable; the researcher must attempt to assess, control for, and rule out the effects of any *other* variables that may reasonably figure into the phenomenon in question.

Experimentation has been used successfully for decades, in thousands of studies, to reach conclusive answers to such questions as the following:

1. Can we increase profits by servicing small accounts by mail rather than from branch stores (i.e., can a change from branch stores to mail *cause* an increase in profits)?
2. Can we increase supermarket sales of our product by obtaining additional shelf space (i.e., will additional shelf space *cause* a sales increase)?
3. Will addition of stannous fluoride to our toothpaste reduce users' cavities (i.e., does stannous fluoride *cause* fewer cavities to form)?

4. Does the number of times that a salesperson calls on a particular account in a given period affect the size of the order obtained from that account (i.e., does each additional call *cause* a change in order size)?
5. Is a given newspaper advertisement more effective in color than in black and white (i.e., does the addition of color *cause* a greater response)?
6. Which of several promotional techniques is most effective in selling a particular product (i.e., does a change in technique *cause* a change in sales)?
7. Is it necessary for an advertisement to change the attitude of subjects to convince them to use more of the product (i.e., can one *cause* increased usage without enhanced attitude)?

This list could be extended indefinitely, because experimental procedures are useful across the domain of marketing decision making.

5.2a Basic Definitions in Experimentation

To understand experimentation properly, one must first become comfortable with some basic definitions and concepts.

Experiments

experiment
A rigorous investigation in which the researcher controls several (independent) variables and measures or observes their effects on one or more dependent variables.

An **experiment** is carried out when one or more independent variables is deliberately manipulated or controlled by the experimenter in a planned fashion and the effects on the dependent variable (or variables) is measured.

In surveys and observational studies, there is no manipulation of independent variables by the researchers. This is the fundamental difference between experimental and nonexperimental research. In searching for causal relationships in nonexperimental situations, the researcher must proceed in reverse: observe the effect and then search for a cause. In these circumstances, one can never be sure of the proper time order of occurrence of variables and the effects of other possible independent variables that have been excluded from consideration. Even if great foresight and exceptional measurement techniques are deployed in an observational study, the superiority of experiments in discerning causality is striking, and many researchers view it as absolute.

Treatments

treatments
In experimental design, treatments are the manipulated alternatives or independent variables whose effects are then measured.

Treatments are the manipulated alternatives or independent variables whose effects are then measured. Examples in marketing are plentiful, including product design, packaging or name, advertising themes, price levels, distribution strategies, and promotional incentives. In terms of measurement, treatments need only form a nominal scale (the lowest level), meaning that ordinal, interval, and ratio treatments are therefore automatically acceptable. For example, if we are interested in sales response, the treatments can range from different ad designs (nominal) to various promotional price-reduction percentages (ratio, because "0 percent" has a specific objective meaning). Whatever data type the treatments themselves form, it is critical that the researcher specify them clearly and definitively in the experimental design, before the experiment is carried out.

Test Units

test units
In experimental design, the entities to whom (or to which) treatments are presented and whose response to the treatments is measured; in practice, these are typically people, products, or firms.

The **test units** are the entities to whom (or to which) the treatments are presented and whose response to the treatments is measured. It is common in marketing for both people and physical entities, such as stores or geographic areas, to be used as test units. For example, people (the test units) may be asked to try a product (the treatment) and then have their attitudes and opinions toward it measured (dependent variables). Alternatively, different end-aisle displays (treatments) may be set up in supermarkets (test units) and sales levels (dependent variables) can be measured. Conceptualizing a marketing experiment in just these terms (test units, treatments, and dependent measures) during the planning phase helps avoid conceptual and analytic complications later.

Dependent Variables

The dependent variables are the measures taken on the test units. Typical marketing examples are sales, preference, awareness, willingness to purchase, attitudes, and a host of related concepts. To allow for ease of analysis, it is helpful if the dependent variable forms an interval scale so that the standard regression methods universally supported in statistical packages can be used. However, more sophisticated methods, such as binary or ordinal regression (see Chapter 10), can be brought to bear when dependent measures cannot be considered interval-scaled.

Extraneous Variables

The extraneous variables are all variables *other than the treatments* that potentially affect the response of the test units to the treatments. These variables can distort the dependent variable measures in such a way as to weaken or entirely invalidate a researcher's ability to make causal inferences, and as such they are often thought of as "nuisance factors," getting in the researcher's way of performing accurate measurements. For example, a book publisher attempting to measure the responses of buyers to two different cover designs would want to keep other aspects of the book the same for each buyer group. If the publisher allowed extraneous variables like price, book dimensions, title, or paper quality to vary between buyer groups, she could not be sure that she was measuring the effect of the cover. These other variables are then said to "confound" the experiment and are often referred to as *confounds*.

extraneous variable
Any variable, other than those specific to the treatment administered to test units, that may affect the response of the test units to the treatments, including the history effect, maturation effect, testing effect, instrumentation effect, statistical regression effect, selection bias, and test unit mortality; also referred to as a *confound*.

The researcher has three possible courses of action with respect to extraneous variables. First, when practicable, an extraneous variable may be controlled. In the book example, the price or dimensions of the book could be held constant. Second, if physical control is not possible, the assignment of treatments to test units may be randomized. The book publisher could randomly assign different prices to all buyers. In experiments with human test units, this usually takes the form of randomly assigning the test units to the different treatments. In this way, it is hoped that extraneous factors that could plausibly affect the outcome (such as education, age, or product experience) are equally represented in each treatment group, or at least have the potential to be. Note that certain characteristics like blood type or length of index finger, lacking a plausible relationship to the dependent measure, do not have to be randomized, although in practice it is often difficult to know which such relationships are plausible and which are not.

We would prefer physical control, but, unfortunately, in marketing applications (or any in which the characteristics of human subjects are pivotal), we must often rely on randomization. Note that the choice between physical control and randomization is not either-or; in many cases, we require both. If we are testing two book covers, one with candy and talking animals and the other with striking modernist design, we cannot have one group consist only of children and the other of their parents. Holding price and other extraneous variables (regarding the book covers themselves) constant across the two groups does not eliminate the need to randomize assignment to treatments. In this case, the lack of randomization would quite likely lead to faulty causal conclusions because the groups differ so obviously in composition and probable reaction to the cover design elements.

The third way to control the effects of extraneous variables is through the use of specific experimental designs that accomplish this purpose. Much of the rest of this chapter discusses how specific designs can accomplish this task.

If physical control, randomization, and design features do not eliminate the differential effects of extraneous variables among treatment groups, the experiment has been confounded, and no causal statements are possible. As mentioned previously, we call such an extraneous variable a confounding variable or simply a confound. For example, suppose we are using two cities as our test units and it rains in one city but not in the other. If rain affects the dependent variable (say, the number of car washes), the experiment has been confounded and rain was the confounding variable.

confounding variable (confound)
Any variable, other than those specific to the treatment, that may affect how test units respond to the treatments; confounds make it difficult to attribute effects to variables controlled or manipulated by the experimenter.

There is one line of defense against the confounding variable: its effects on the dependent variable may be statistically controlled through a technique called *analysis of covariance* (ANCOVA). To make use of ANCOVA, we must be aware of the confounding variable and be able to measure it. Consequently, the kind of extraneous variable that worries us most in experimentation is one that appears or operates differentially among treatment groups and is either unknown to the experimenter or difficult to measure reliably, such as respondent mood or an individual's stock of a certain household good.

Experimental Design

An experimental design involves the specification of treatments to be manipulated, test units to be used, dependent variables to be measured, and procedures for dealing with extraneous variables.

experimental design
A form of investigation in which the researcher can directly control one or more (independent) variables to study their effects on some other (dependent) variables.

Validity in Experimentation

internal validity
A way to evaluate experiments by verifying that changes in the dependent or criterion variable truly arose from changes in the independent or treatment variables alone.

external validity
A method of evaluating the results of experiments; formally, the degree to which conclusions would hold under other, presumably identical circumstances (e.g., for other respondents, places, and times).

Two concepts of validity are relevant in experimentation: internal validity and external validity.

Internal validity is the basic minimum validity that must be present in an experiment before any conclusion about treatment effects can be made. It relates to whether the observed effects on the test units could have been caused by variables other than the treatment, that is, by extraneous variables. Without internal validity, the experiment is confounded and largely useless for the purposes of causal inference.

External validity is concerned with the "generalizability" of experimental results. To what populations, geographic areas, treatment variables, and measurement variables can the measured effect be *projected?* A typical error in conducting research is relying on so-called convenience samples, those test units (usually people or stores) most easily examined. For example, student researchers often rely on other students or stores near campus. Even if their experiments are otherwise flawless, it would be premature to claim that results extend outside the realm of their fellow students (or others with highly similar characteristics) or campus retail environment.

Ideally, an experimental design should be strong on both types of validity; unfortunately, one type must often be traded against the other. To correct for the effects of an extraneous variable, we may create an artificial environment for an experiment. In doing this, we may decrease the generalizability of the results to more realistic environments. For example, an advertiser may ask respondents to view advertisements in a lab or rented space in a mall. Can any effects measured in such environments be generalized to a home viewing environment? Can consumers compensated to participate in a study and tested on their knowledge be claimed equivalent to those sitting at home watching a sitcom? Such questions are of enormous practical importance for the marketing researcher and have been discussed extensively by marketing academics, philosophers of science, and practicing managers.[1]

5.2b Rigorously Defining Experiments

For researchers to collaborate and understand the results of one another's experiments, a common language is required. Such a language has evolved and is used nearly universally throughout experimental science. As with any novel conceptual system or language, learning the rudiments can at first seem dull or pointlessly difficult. Persisting past this initial difficulty to become conversant with the basic details will provide a smoother, easier understanding of subsequent discussions and a logical clarity impossible without having learned them.

X-O-R Syntax

X-O-R syntax
A special shorthand used to convey experimental designs: *X* represents the exposure of a test group to an experimental treatment; *O* refers to processes of observation or measurement of the dependent variable on the test units; *R* indicates that individuals have been assigned at random to separate treatment groups or that groups themselves have been allocated at random to separate treatments.

To facilitate our discussion of specific experimental designs, we use of a set of symbols, referred to as **X-O-R syntax**, that have become standard in marketing research applications, as follows:

- *X* represents the *exposure* of a test group to an experimental treatment, the effects of which are to be determined.
- O refers to processes of *observation* or measurement of the dependent variable on the test units.
- *R* indicates that individuals have been assigned at *random* to separate treatment groups or that groups themselves have been allocated at random to separate treatments.

In addition, the following conventions are widely observed and are always used in this text:

- Movement from left to right indicates passage through time.
- All symbols in any one row (i.e., aligned horizontally) refer to a specific treatment group.
- Symbols that are directly above or below one another (i.e., aligned vertically) refer to activities or events that occur simultaneously.

Simply put, rows represent units and columns represent successive instants of time. A few examples should make this symbolic scheme clear. The symbols

$$O_1 \quad X_1 \quad O_1$$

indicate that the *same* group (because they are in a single row) received the measurement of the *same* dependent variable (because the subscript, 1, is the same) both before (O_1) and after (O_1) the presentation of the treatment (X_1). Further, the symbols

$$R \quad X_1 \quad O_1$$
$$R \quad X_2 \quad O_2$$

indicate that two *different* groups (they appear in different rows) were randomly assigned to two *different* treatment groups at the *same* time (because they are aligned vertically). In addition, the groups received *different* experimental treatments at the *same* time, and the dependent variables were measured in the two groups at the same time. When one grasps that this entire pattern of complex information can be conveyed in a simple form, one comes to appreciate the logic and power of the X-O-R syntax.

5.2c Types of Extraneous Variables

As discussed previously, extraneous variables need to be controlled to ensure that the experiment has not been confounded. That is, we want to be assured that the experiment is internally valid.

history effect
The occurrence of events outside of, but taking place at the same time as, the experiment that can affect the dependent variable.

History

A **history effect** refers to the occurrence of specific events that are external to the experiment but that take place at the same time as the experiment. These events may affect the dependent variable. For example, consider the design

$$O_1 \quad X_1 \quad O_2,$$

where O_1 and O_2 are measures of the dollar sales of sales personnel and X_1 represents a new sales training program. The difference $O_2 - O_1$ is the measurement of the treatment effect (if it is positive, this indicates that dollar sales have increased from before the time of the program). However, the new sales training program is not the only possible explanation of a positive difference $O_2 - O_1$; an improvement in general business conditions between O_1 and O_2 is just as plausible a hypothesis for explaining the observed increase in sales, and there may be many other variables that changed during this period. The greater the length of time between observations, the greater the chance of history confounding an experiment of this type. What is clearly required is a procedure for controlling the effects of history.

maturation effect
An effect similar to the history effect except that it pertains to changes in the experimental units themselves over time (e.g., getting older, developing fatigue, gaining experience, or learning).

Maturation

A **maturation effect** is similar to history except that it is concerned with changes in the experimental units themselves that occur with the passage of time. Examples include getting older, growing hungrier, developing fatigue, and undergoing many types of learning or experience. In the sales training design, sales may have increased because the sales force has become marginally more experienced or their customers have become more loyal. Clearly, people change over time. However, so do stores, geographic regions, and organizations. The longer the time between O_1 and O_2, the greater the chance that maturation effects will occur.

testing effect
An effect that can come about when the pretest itself exerts an influence on how participants perform on the posttest (e.g., when both are tests of the same skill and participants learn from the pretest).

direct testing effect
Same as *main testing effect;* occurs when the first of two observations affects the second.

main testing effect
Same as *direct testing effect;* involves the effect of an earlier observation on the subject's response at a later observation.

Testing

A **testing effect** is concerned with the possible effects on the experiment of taking a measure on the dependent variable *before* presentation of the treatment. There are two kinds of testing effects. The first could be called the **direct** or **main testing effect**, and it occurs when the first observation affects the second observation. For example, consider the case of respondents who have completed a pretreatment questionnaire. If they are asked to complete the *same* questionnaire after exposure to the treatment, they may respond differently just because they are now "experts" with that questionnaire or to express variety of opinion. The internal validity of the experiment is then compromised.

reactive testing effect
When a test unit's pretreatment measurement affects its reaction to the treatment; same as *interactive testing effect.*

interactive testing effect
In an experiment, the effect of the test unit's pretreatment measurement on the reaction to the treatment; same as *reactive testing effect.*

The second testing effect influences external validity but is important enough to mention here. It is called the **reactive** or **interactive testing effect**. This is the situation where the test unit's pretreatment measurement affects the reaction to the treatment. For example, a pretreatment questionnaire that asks questions about shampoo brands may sensitize the respondent to the shampoo market and distort the awareness levels of a new introduction (the treatment). The measured effects are then not generalizable to nonsensitized people. Researchers must be aware of the broad potential for such reactive effects. Subjects' responses are readily swayed even by subtle cues from the researcher, the environment, or the mere act of having their reactions recorded. See the *Special Expert Feature: Self-Reports in Marketing Research: How the Questions Shape the Answers* at the end of Chapter 7 for more detail on this problem.

Instrumentation

instrumentation effect
In statistical models, an effect that arises when instruments, observers, or scorers change over the course of an experiment.

Instrumentation effect refers to changes in the calibration of the measuring instrument used or changes in the observers or scorers. In the sales training study mentioned previously, the dependent variable, sales, was measured in dollars. If sales were measured in a different store or geographic region after the study, or if the accounting calculated net sales differently, the difference $O_2 - O_1$ could be explained by this change in instrumentation. An interviewer presenting the pre- and posttreatment questionnaires in different fashions—one written, one verbal, for example—could also impose an instrumentation effect. Careful studies try to engage the services of a single researcher to administer all test materials, in the same way, at all times; failing that, different research assistants can be intensively trained to ensure minimal presentation differences.

Statistical Regression

statistical-regression effects
When, in an experiment, test units are selected (for exposure to the treatment) based on an extreme pretreatment score; usually considered poor research practice.

Statistical-regression effects occur where test units have been selected for exposure to the treatment on the basis of an extreme pretreatment score. This is almost always bad research practice. Such *outliers* tend naturally to move toward a more average position with the passage of time. For example, suppose that in the sales training example only poorly performing salespeople had been given the new training program. Subsequent sales increases might be attributed to the regression effect, because random occurrences such as weather, family problems, or luck helped define good and poor performance of salespeople in the pretreatment measurement. Subsequent random occurrences will make some of the poor performers do better the following year, thus confounding the experiment. Students can easily examine successive grades in their courses to notice that very poor performances are almost always followed by better ones, and vice versa for stellar ones, just as world-record breakers seldom break their own records the next time out. In addition to multiple measures of the same outlying test unit tending toward average over time, the effect applies to the same measure being taken across populations. If your neighbor is an exceptionally good concert violinist, it is less likely that you and the others living on your street are as proficient at playing violin. The point is, if we did a study on the musical ability of neighbors, we might come to the "shocking" conclusion that, even if musically talented people tend to cluster in neighborhoods, neighbors of great violinists are decidedly less proficient on the violin. Of course, there is nothing shocking about this, because it is practically ensured by how the sample was chosen and the ensuing regression effects. Such regression effects are an expected, natural, and common phenomenon, and they indicate little about other forces under study.

Selection Bias

Selection bias refers to the assigning of test units to treatment groups in such a way that the groups differ on the dependent variable before the presentation of the treatments. If test units self-select their own groups or are assigned to groups on the basis of researcher judgment, the possibility of selection bias exists. Test units should be randomly assigned to treatment groups. In field research, where experimenters have little or no control over group assignment, selection bias is an enormous problem. One cannot simply compare shoppers in two different stores, or students in two different universities, and assume everything else about their respective groups is either identical or unimportant to the intent of the experiment.

Test Unit Mortality

test unit mortality
A serious problem that occurs when test units withdraw from an experiment before their role is completed.

Test unit mortality refers to test units withdrawing from the experiment while it is in progress. What can we conclude if a number of salespeople quit the company between X_1 and O_2? It is possible that those who were not improving quit or that just the opposite happened. A common way to guard against this is to have test units precommit to the full length of the experiment. Of course, doing so may induce selection biases: those unwilling to commit may not participate.

All these types of extraneous variables constitute alternative explanations for what is observed in an experiment. They are the rivals to the hypothesis that the researcher is hoping to definitively test. One objective of our research designs should be to mitigate or even eliminate the possibility that these effects will confound our results. The science of experimental design is concerned with doing exactly that: isolating treatments of interest and rigorously assessing their effects on test units.

5.2d Three Preexperimental Designs

What follows is an examination of three preexperimental designs, considered so because inherent weaknesses in the designs render internal validity highly questionable. This will highlight the threats to validity that can plague any but "true" experiments.

One-Shot Case Study

The **one-shot case study design** is presented symbolically as follows:

$$X \quad O$$

A single group of test units is first exposed to a treatment, X, and then a measurement is taken on the dependent variables (subscripts are often dropped when there is a single subject group, that is, only one treatment). Note that the symbol *R* does not appear in the design, so there was no random assignment of test units to the treatment group. The test units were self-selected or selected by the experimenter using some criterion, hopefully reflecting representativeness and presumably not a convenience sample. An example of this design might be as follows. A manager requests volunteers take part in a new sales training program, and a measure of their sales performance is taken some time after the program is completed. The impossibility of drawing meaningful conclusions from such a design should be apparent. The level of O is the result of many uncontrolled factors, and it cannot be deemed to be good or bad in the absence of a pretreatment observation of sales performance. Thus, history, maturation, selection, and mortality problems all render this design internally invalid. It is unfortunately trotted out with great frequency in informal discussions, where all that is noted is that some phenomenon (O) follows an event (X) to which a causal interpretation is attributed. Researchers must be especially diligent in avoiding this one-shot study sort of reasoning.

one-shot case study design
A simple form of preexperimental design where a single group of test units is first exposed to a treatment and a measurement is then taken on the dependent variables; there is no random assignment of test units to the treatment group.

One-Group Pretest–Posttest Design

The **one-group pretest–posttest design** is presented symbolically as follows:

$$O_1 \quad X \quad O_2$$

Here, for example, we have added a pretest measurement of sales performance to the one-shot case study design. It should be apparent that this is an intrinsically more reasonable procedure, if for no other reason than that it has an additional measure, O_1. If we then took the difference between O_2 and O_1 as the measure of experimental effect, would we have a valid measure of the effect of the sales training program? Clearly, a number of extraneous variables could explain the difference $O_2 - O_1$, rendering this design essentially useless for reaching conclusive answers. Specifically, every problem previously identified could rear its head: the economic situation could have changed (history); the salespeople could have gained more experience (maturation); the premeasure could have affected performance (testing); prices of goods sold could have changed (instrumentation); the test units could have been self-selected (selection bias); some test units could have dropped out before O_2 could be measured (mortality); and test units may have selected due to a particularly bad year so that the next one is almost certainly better by chance alone (regression). Even if this design had been

$$R \quad O_1 \quad X \quad O_2,$$

all sources of invalidity except selection bias (also referred to simply as *selection*) would still apply. Recall that this design was the one used by the befuddled scientist in the soda water experiment, which failed to control for the extraneous variable, alcohol intake (history).

one-group pretest–posttest design
A simple form of preexperimental design, equivalent to a one-shot case study design but where an additional pretest measurement is taken before the treatment.

Static-Group Comparison

The **static-group comparison design** uses two treatment groups, one that has been exposed to the treatment and one that has not. Both groups are observed only after the treatment has been presented, and test units are not randomly assigned to the groups. Symbolically, this design is as follows:

Group 1:	X	O_1
Group 2:		O_2

static-group comparison design
An experimental design in which two treatment groups, one that has been exposed to the treatment and one that has not, are observed after the treatment has been presented.

control group
A group that is comparable to the treatment group in terms of measurable characteristics but did not receive the treatment; effects can thus be attributed to the treatment and not to between-group differences.

Group 2 is called a **control group** because it has not received the treatment and so may serve as the baseline for comparison. In marketing, we often define the control group treatment as the current level of marketing activity. This can be shown symbolically:

Experimental group:	X_1	O_1
Control group:	X_2	O_2

baseline
A figure that can be used to provide context for a comparison with another figure.

Here, X_2 is the baseline marketing program with which we wish to compare X_1. For example, in trying the new sales training program on some salespeople, the sales manager would not be likely to drop all sales training for the other salespeople. The manager is interested in comparing one program with another, so the old program is the control group treatment. (Modified versions of this setup are common in medical testing, albeit with careful screening, subject selection procedures, and many additional measures, including pretest measures when they will not overtly interfere with later ones.)

The overwhelming source of invalidity in this design is selection. Test units have not been randomly assigned to treatment groups; therefore, the groups may differ on the dependent variable before the presentation of the treatment. The experimental result $O_1 - O_2$ could therefore be attributable to this pretest difference, not the treatment. Consider, for example, test marketing a weight loss regimen, with groups assigned by whether subjects believed they needed to lose weight. In such a case, the weight difference $(O_1 - O_2)$ might well be positive (indicating that the group on the weight loss plan weighed *more* afterward), simply because they weighed more to begin with. Differential test unit mortality is also possible because of the nature of the treatment; this is common in many settings where the being in the experimental group requires arduous or uncomfortable procedures or large time sacrifices. In the example, more experimental-group test units may have withdrawn because of the nature of the new sales training program.

5.2e Three True Experimental Designs

A true experimental design is one where the researcher is able to eliminate all extraneous variables as competitive hypotheses to the treatment, at least in theory. Examine three of these in detail. It is helpful to consider the threats to validity underscored in the examples of preexperimental designs discussed previously, and to check whether these true designs really rule them out.

Pretest–Posttest Control Group Design

pretest–posttest control group design
An experimental design in which all extraneous variables operate equally on both the experimental group and the control group; the only difference between the groups is the presentation of the treatment to the experimental group.

The **pretest–posttest control group design** is presented symbolically as follows:

Experimental group:	*R*	O_1	X_1	O_2
Control group:	*R*	O_3		O_4

Here, X_1 is the treatment of interest. (Note that the control group could have a baseline treatment applied to it, in which case X_2 would appear directly below X_1.) The random assignment of test units to the treatment groups eliminates selection bias as a potential confounding variable.

The premise here is that all extraneous variables operate *equally* on both the experimental group and the control group. The *only* difference between the groups is the presentation of the treatment to the experimental group. Therefore, the difference $O_2 - O_1$ is the sum of the treatment effect plus the effects of the extraneous variables, whereas the difference $O_4 - O_3$ is the sum of the extraneous variables only. In symbols,

$$O_2 - O_1 = \text{EXT} + \text{TE}$$
$$O_4 - O_3 = \text{EXT},$$

where TE is the treatment effect and EXT represents the sum of all extraneous effects, that is, EXT = (history + maturation + testing + instrumentation + regression + test unit mortality). Simple arithmetic then shows that

$$(O_2 - O_1) - (O_4 - O_3) = \text{TE},$$

which is the true treatment effect sought. We have thus found a way to identify the effect of an independent (treatment) variable. Because EXT can represent not just the six effects we identified in our discussions but any such effects, all potential destroyers of internal validity are controlled by this design. Note the fundamental principle of experimental design invoked here: the experimenter does not care what extraneous variables are present *so long as they operate equally on all treatment and control groups*. Even with a control group design, the experiment is confounded if an extraneous variable operates differentially among treatment and control groups. The assumption is that they must operate equally. We have also tacitly assumed, in calculating $(O_2 - O_1) - (O_4 - O_3) = TE$, that the treatment effect operates linearly, but in practice this can be relaxed and accounted for using a variety of statistical models (see Chapter 10 for more detail).

A major difficulty with this design is the effect of the pretest measurement on the test units' reaction to the treatment (the interactive testing effect described earlier). Because this is a potential confounder of external validity, in the experimental group we must add another variable to the equation explaining the difference $O_2 - O_1$: IT, the interactive testing effect. If we again define EXT as the sum of all other extraneous variables, then

$$O_2 - O_1 = EXT + TE + IT$$
$$O_4 - O_3 = EXT$$

and, therefore, taking the difference as before,

$$(O_2 - O_1) - (O_4 - O_3) = TE + IT.$$

Unfortunately, this shows that in this design we cannot disentangle the interactive testing effect from the treatment effect. We must therefore always retain some doubt about the generalizability of the treatment.

If the scientist doing the experiment with soda water had used this design, the conclusion would *not* have been that soda water causes intoxication, because the control group would have consumed the alcohol *without* the soda water and the level of intoxication of the control group would have equaled that of the experimental groups. (Here we have not considered another possibility, that there is some strange synergy between the soda water and the alcohol, making them inebriating only if consumed together, or some more complex effect involving temperature, digestive system conditions, or the like.) The possibility of the interactive testing effect occurring here seems quite small: we should be able to gauge pretest levels of intoxication without unduly sensitizing the participants to the coming treatment and thereby affecting their posttest intoxication levels. Other researchers cannot be so presumptuous, however. Consider again a shampoo marketer, who uses this design to measure the effect of a new advertising campaign. An interactive testing effect could clearly arise; specifically, the pretest may sensitize test units in the experimental group to advertisements in the shampoo product category, and the resultant posttest levels of advertising awareness would not be generalizable to a nonsensitized population. In this case, the researcher would need to look to other designs to control for this effect, such as the one we consider next.

Solomon Four-Group Design

The **Solomon four-group design** controls for all extraneous variable effects on internal validity, plus the interactive testing effect. Symbolically, this design is as follows:

Solomon four-group design
An experimental design that controls for extraneous variable effects, as well as interactive testing effects. It involves four groups, two of which receive the treatment; one treatment group and one control group receive a pretest, whereas the others do not.

Experimental group 1:	*R*	O_1	X	O_2
Control group 1:	*R*	O_3		O_4
Experimental group 2:	*R*		X	O_5
Control group 2:	*R*			O_6

What has been done here is that we have added another experimental group and another control group to the previous (pretest–posttest control group) design. This second experimental group receives no pretest but otherwise is identical to the first experimental group; the second control group receives only a posttest measurement. What is the point of using twice as many groups? That is, what effects do the differences among various pre- and postmeasures give us? This can be shown symbolically:

Experimental group 1:	$O_2 - O_1 = TE + EXT + IT$
Control group 1:	$O_4 - O_3 = EXT$
Experimental group 2:	$O_5 - O_1 = TE + EXT$
	$O_5 - O_3 = TE + EXT$
Control group 2:	$O_6 - O_1 = EXT$
	$O_6 - O_3 = EXT$

This may be a bit difficult to follow at first, and you are encouraged to try to work out these relationships directly. It helps to note three things: (1) that all equations contain all extraneous effects (EXT), since they are external and not under experimental control; (2) treatment effects (TE) occur only in the experimental groups, not the controls; and (3) the interactive testing (IT) effect occurs only when a group is tested twice *and* receives the treatment, which happens only for the first experimental group.

The goal is to isolate both the treatment (TE) and interactive testing (IT) effects. There are many ways to do this using the six equations we have previously written to relate TE, EXT, and IT, using simple algebra. For example, it is quite simple to check that an estimate of TE is simply $O_5 - O_6$. However, statistically, we wish to use the results of the four groups *equally* so that no one result affects our estimates more than any other. To do so, the values of $O_1, \ldots, O_6$ are typically fed into a full-featured statistical program, like SPSS or SAS, and analyzed using analysis of variance (ANOVA; see the appendix to Chapter 11). This ensures that the most appropriate statistical estimates are obtained for the effects of interest, TE and IT.

Now we not only have *controlled* all extraneous variables and the interactive testing effect but also have succeeded in *measuring* their effects. Unfortunately, these benefits come at the expense of increases in the time, cost, and effort needed to conduct the experiment; consequently, this design is uncommon in marketing practice except when there is strong reason to believe the pretest will grossly affect the posttest. However, it does serve as a "gold standard" against which to compare other designs. What we would like is a leaner design that controls extraneous variables and the interactive testing effect; we examine such a design next.

Posttest-Only Control Group Design

posttest-only control group design An experimental design in which randomly assigned groups receive only a posttest measurement; equivalent to the last two groups of a Solomon four-group design.

The posttest-only control group design is written as follows:

Experimental group:	*R*	X	O_1
Control group:	*R*		O_2

It is essentially the last two groups of the Solomon four-group design. Here, the O_1 and O_2 measurements are composed of the following parts:

Experimental group:	$O_1 = TE + EXT$
Control group:	$O_2 = EXT$

Therefore, we easily isolate the treatment effect:

$$O_1 - O_2 = TE$$

Because there is no pretest in this design, the interactive testing effect cannot occur. Also, the extraneous variables have been controlled, and we have a nonconfounded measure of the treatment effect. But wait: suppose the pretreatment measures on the dependent variable were different between the experimental group and the control group? Would not this confound the experiment? Indeed, it would. We assume that the random assignment of test units to the groups has resulted in the groups being approximately equal on the dependent variable before the presentation of the treatment to the experimental group (and such an assumption could be backed up by comparing various geodemographic and behavioristic variables across participant groups). In the weight loss regimen example, randomization would have helped assign subjects of various weights nearly equally across groups, ruling out selection biases. Other assumptions are invoked to dispense with pretest measures. For example, we also assume that test unit mortality affects each group in the same way. With large enough samples and proper randomization, these assumptions are not unreasonable—a fact that, when combined with the reactive nature of a great deal of marketing research, helps explain why this design is among the most often used in marketing practice. The soda-testing scientist, the sales manager, and the shampoo manufacturer could all have used this design to obtain a nonconfounded measure of their treatment effect.

5.3 Quasi Experimentation

In designing a true experiment, the researcher often creates artificial environments to have control over independent and extraneous variables and to confer as much internal validity on the study as possible.

As a result, serious questions are raised about the external validity of the experimental findings. One response to this problem has been the development and use of quasi experimental designs.

A **quasi experimental design** is one in which the researcher has control over data collection procedures (i.e., the "when" and "to whom" of *measurement*) but lacks complete control over the scheduling of the treatments (i.e., the "when" and "to whom" of *exposure*) and lacks the ability to randomize test units' exposure to treatments. With loss of control of test unit assignments and treatment manipulations, the possibility of obtaining confounded results is great. The researcher must then be aware of specific variables that are not controlled and attempt to incorporate the possible effects of these uncontrolled variables when interpreting findings. We now turn to an examination of selected quasi experimental designs. Sources for additional information on all aspects of experimental design appear at the end of this chapter.

quasi experimental design
A research design that appears to be true experimentation but that relies on nonrandom assignment: the researcher has control over data collection procedures but neither over the scheduling of treatments nor the assignment of respondents to treatment groups.

5.3a Time-Series Experiment

A **time-series experiment** may be presented symbolically as follows:

time-series experiment
An experiment in which data are collected at various points in time, ordinarily for the same set of variables and multiple test units.

$$O_1 \quad O_2 \quad O_3 \quad O_4 \quad X \quad O_5 \quad O_6 \quad O_7 \quad O_8$$

The essence of this design is the undertaking of a periodic measurement on the dependent variables for some test units. The treatment is then introduced, or occurs naturally, and the periodic measurements are continued on the same test units to monitor the effects of the treatment. (For time-series experiments, even if the same measure is taken every time; subscripts are often used to distinguish different periods, but they are optional notation.)

Note how this design conforms to the definition of a quasi experiment. The researcher does have control over *when* measurements are taken and *on whom* they are taken. However, there is no randomization of test units to treatments, and the timing of treatment presentation, as well as which test units are exposed to the treatment, may not be within the researcher's control. A common example is consumer purchase panels, which provide periodic measures on participants' purchase activity (the Os). A marketer may undertake a new advertising campaign (the X) and examine the panel data to look for effects of interest, such as purchases or coupon usage. Here, the marketer has control over the timing of the advertising campaign but cannot be sure when the panel members were exposed to it or even whether they were exposed. Also, other consumers outside the panel would be exposed to the campaign. Attempting to make causal inferences from this type of situation is common in marketing, and a variety of time-series models have been proposed to do so, some designed specifically for panel data (see Chapter 10 regarding the logit model, in particular).

This design is similar to the preexperimental one-group pretest–posttest design, $O_1 \times O_2$. So, does not the time-series design inherit its many problems? The answer is, for the most part, no; the fact that we have taken *many* pretest and posttest measurements provides a greater degree of control over extraneous variables. To illustrate this increase in control, let us examine some possible results of this type of design (see Figure 5.1). Assume that the X represents a change in advertising campaign, and the Os represent the market share of the product in question.

The following conclusions about the advertising campaign seem reasonable:

1. In situation A, the campaign has had both a short-run and a long-run positive effect.
2. In situation B, the campaign has had a short-run positive effect.
3. In situation C, the campaign may have had a longer-term effect. Because the reaction was delayed for a period, we cannot be as sure as we were in A and B.
4. In situations D, E, and F, the changes that occur after X are consistent with the pattern before X. Therefore, we cannot infer that the advertising campaign had an effect.

Note that the one-group pretest–posttest design would have measured only O_4 and O_5. With these measures only, we could easily infer an effect of the campaign, $O_5 - O_4$, in situations D, E, and F; we could also miss the effect in C and the nature of the effects in A and B.

The multiple observations in this design also provide additional control of extraneous variables. For example, the maturation effect on $O_5 - O_4$ can be ruled out, because this effect would almost certainly also show up in other observations; it would be unlikely to affect the O_4 to O_5 periods alone. By similar reasoning, main testing, instrumentation, and statistical-regression effects can be deemed doubtful. If we then randomly (or with good judgment) choose test units and take strong measures to prevent panel

Figure 5.1 Some Possible Results of a Time-Series Experiment

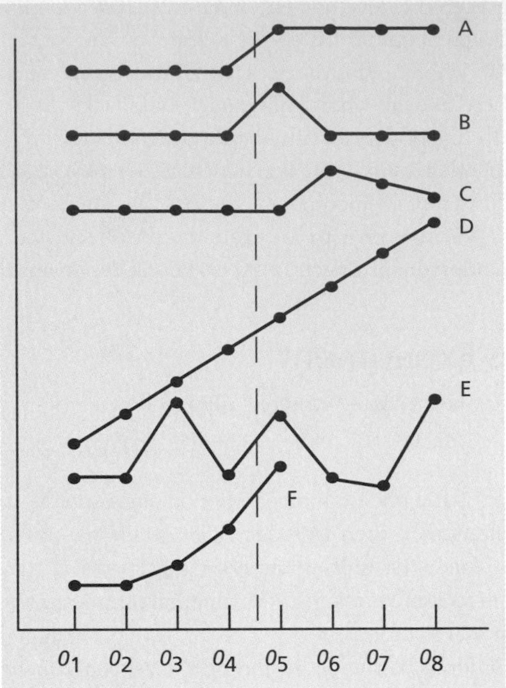

members from dropping out, we can at least partially rule out the effects of selection bias and test unit mortality.

The fundamental weakness of this design is the experimenter's inability to control history. To compensate for this, the experimenter can maintain a careful log of all possible relevant external happenings that could reasonably have an effect. If this process fails to turn up any unusual competitive activity, economic changes, and so on, the experimenter may reasonably conclude that the treatment has had an effect. Of course, "all possible relevant effects" can be difficult to monitor, and firms will always have more data on their own activities than on those of their competitors. By judicious use of external and syndicated data—particularly so for panels—such effects can usually be monitored fairly reliably.

The other weakness of this design is the possibility of an interactive testing effect from the repeated measurements being made on test units. For example, panel members may become "expert" shoppers, thus making generalizations to other populations more difficult, or asking shoppers multiple times whether they "recalled" seeing a particular ad could lead to questionable results, since the shoppers may start to actively seek the ad out. Nevertheless, this design is used a great deal, and it can provide meaningful information if used carefully.

5.3b Multiple Time-Series Design

multiple time-series design
A form of quasi experiment utilizing a time-series design in which the researcher has put together another group of test units to serve as a control group.

In some studies utilizing the time-series design, it may be possible to find another group of test units to act as a control group, thus creating a **multiple time-series design**. For example, an advertiser may try a new campaign in a few cities only. Panel members in these cities would constitute the experimental group, whereas members from other cities would constitute a control group. In symbols, this design is as follows:

Experimental group:	O	O	O	X	O	O	O
Control group:	O	O	O		O	O	O

If the researcher is careful in selecting the control group, this design can add more certainty to the interpretation of the treatment effect than is obtainable with the (single) time-series experiment. This is so because the treatment effect is tested both in its own group *and* against the control group. The main problems with this design lie in the possibility of an interactive effect in the experimental group and in the difficulty of selecting a well-matched control group. For example, suppose an ad has been tested in New York City; it is not obvious that any other city would provide an appropriate control group (for this reason, such testing is almost always done in groups of smaller cities or in carefully selected, demographically matched nearby areas).

5.3c Equivalent Time-Sample Design

An alternative to finding a control group is to use the experimental group itself as its own control in what is called an **equivalent time-sample design**. In symbols, this design might be

$$O \quad X_1 \quad O \quad X_0 \quad OOO \quad X_1 \quad OO \quad X_0 \quad O,$$

where X_1 is the experimental treatment and X_0 is the absence of the treatment. Here, the treatment is repeatedly presented, measurements are repeatedly taken, and periods of treatment absence are spaced between. This design is best utilized when the effect of the treatment is transient or reversible. (The grouping of measurements, such as OOO, indicates variable timings and numbers of observations between periods of treatment and absence of treatment.)

equivalent time-sample design An experimental design where the experimental group is used as its own control. The treatment is presented several times, measurements are repeatedly taken, and periods of treatment absence are spaced between. This design is most appropriate when the effect of the treatment is transient or reversible.

An example of this design is the testing of the effect of in-store conditions, such as music, lighting, color, or temperature, on total purchases per customer. We could use a single store, whose customers make up the test units, and utilize equivalent sets of days with and without various combinations of environmental variables over many months. The effects of each variable could then be discerned via statistical techniques like regression or more complex time-series models.

The biggest problem with this design is, once again, the possibility of the interactive testing effect. Because of all the measurements taken, it is basically a reactive design; therefore, it is best used where the repeated measurements are unobtrusive. In situations like the store example, we are able to measure per-customer sales without sensitizing customers to the treatment unless the music was blaring or temperatures were extreme. If we did repeated *interviewing* of customers about in-store music, for example, sensitization would no doubt be a problem.

5.3d Nonequivalent Control Group Design

In **nonequivalent control group design**, both the experimental group and the control group are given pretest and posttest measurements, but the two groups do *not* have preexperimental test unit selection equivalence; that is, the control group cannot be considered equivalent to the test group. Symbolically, this design is as follows:

Experimental group:	O_1	X	O_2
Control group:	O_3	O_4	

nonequivalent control group design A quasi-experimental design involving a control group that does not have preexperimental test unit selection equivalence to the experimental group (often because the groups were convenience or self-selected, rather than random, samples); both the experimental group and the control group are given pretest and posttest measurements.

This is a quasi experimental design because the groups were not created by the random assignment of test units from a single population but may have arisen by natural means, convenience, or self-selection. However, the existence of even a nonequivalent control group improves the ability of the researcher to interpret results in comparison to the one-group pretest–posttest design discussed previously. In a nonequivalent control group design, the researcher has control over *who* is exposed to the treatment. Clearly, the more similar the experimental and the control groups are in composition, and the closer the pretest measurements, the more useful the control group becomes. If these criteria are met, this design can effectively control the effects of history, maturation, main testing, instrumentation, selection, and test unit mortality. Regression may become a major problem in this design if either group has been selected on the basis of extreme scores, for example, if the experimental group is composed of shoppers reacting to a deep discount or the highest-volume purchasers in a category. In such cases, some of the differences in pretest and posttest measures may result from regression effects, and care must be taken to avoid this problem and account for it in analyses. Because there are multiple measures in each group, an interactive testing effect is also possible.

5.4 Managerial Aspects of Experimentation and Quasi Experimentation

In this section, we discuss issues important to managers when using experimental and quasi experimental designs.

5.4a Comparison with Other Procedures

Of the many procedures for collecting data in marketing research, most are essentially descriptive techniques (e.g., the use of secondary data, observation, surveys, panels, and Web log analysis and simulation) that can only measure correlation. It cannot be stressed often or ardently enough that correlation on its own does not imply causation. The cause and the effect can never be rigorously or reliably separated. Yet all too often, descriptive studies are used to argue causal relationships. Only experimental and quasi experimental designs can identify such causal relationships.

This does not mean that a correct causal relationship cannot be posited in or suggested by descriptive studies; the researcher may be correct with a causal guess. The point is that researchers can never be sure. Descriptive studies are the most frequently used type of study in marketing research practice, and they will no doubt continue to be used to assert causal relationships. Constraints of time, money, and other resources often conspire to make this the only type of study available to a manager. This being the case, managers must be especially aware of the risk of error when using descriptive studies for causal purposes.

5.4b Laboratory vs. Field Environments

field environment
As opposed to a controlled laboratory environment, an actual "real world" market setting under which an experiment is carried out.

There are two types of environments in which an experiment may be conducted. The first is a laboratory environment where the experiment is conducted in an artificial environment designed expressly for that purpose. The alternative is a **field environment** where the experiment is conducted in actual market situations and no attempts are made to change the real-life nature of the environment. An example of a laboratory experiment would be the showing of test commercials to test units in a theater or mall. This same experiment could be conducted in the field by having test commercials run on actual television programs in consumers' homes. There are striking pros and cons to experimental studies and field studies, surrounding issues of validity, accuracy, cost, control variables, and many others. Large-scale research projects will attempt to meld them, tracking, for example, in-store sales for a panel (field environment), as well as simulated purchase test methods like conjoint analysis using specially configured workstations (laboratory environment).

- Validity: Laboratory environments provide the researcher with maximum control over possible confounding variables and thus afford greater internal validity than do field studies. A consequence of the artificial nature of a laboratory, however, is the loss of generalizability to real-world situations. Consequently, laboratory experiments have lower external validity than do field studies. Often a field experiment provides so little control over extraneous variables that we must be content to conduct a quasi experiment.
- Cost: Laboratory experiments are generally less expensive than field experiments. They tend to be smaller in size (i.e., with a smaller number of test units), shorter in duration, more tightly defined geographically, and therefore easier to administer. However, some studies, such as test markets, simply cannot be run in a laboratory at any cost. Generally, the greater the number of interacting variables and entities that must come together to understand a phenomenon, the less likely one will be able to run a feasible, cost-effective lab study.
- Time: The simpler nature of laboratory experiments also means that they often require less time to execute. An exception is when a large number of respondents can be gathered at one time or in a single spot, like in Web-based studies or those undertaken in malls or theaters. E-panels can often provide many thousands of survey replies in an hour, and e-commerce sites' logs allow for the analysis of numerous consumer behavior variables, in real time, for enormous numbers of consumers.

A researcher must trade off these factors—validity, cost, and time—in selecting an environment for an experiment. Overall, lab experiments excel in terms of internal validity, cost, and speed, whereas field experiments offer greater external validity.

5.4c Control of Invalidity

In presenting alternative experimental and quasi experimental designs, we discussed possible sources of invalidity in detail; this section contains a managerial summary of these points. Table 5.1 presents the

Table 5.1 Sources of Invalidity of Preexperimental and Experimental Designs

<table>
<tr><th></th><th colspan="8">Source of invalidity</th></tr>
<tr><th></th><th colspan="7">Internal</th><th>External</th></tr>
<tr><th>Design</th><th>History</th><th>Maturation</th><th>Testing</th><th>Instrumentation</th><th>Regression</th><th>Selection</th><th>Mortality</th><th>Interaction of testing and X</th></tr>
<tr><td>Preexperimental designs:
One-shot case study
X O</td><td>–</td><td>–</td><td></td><td></td><td></td><td>–</td><td>–</td><td></td></tr>
<tr><td>One-group pretest-posttest design
O X O</td><td>–</td><td>–</td><td>–</td><td>–</td><td>?</td><td></td><td></td><td>–</td></tr>
<tr><td>Static-group comparison
X O
O</td><td>+</td><td>?</td><td>+</td><td>|</td><td>|</td><td>–</td><td>–</td><td></td></tr>
<tr><td>True experimental designs:
Pretest-posttest control group design
R O X O
R O O</td><td>+</td><td>+</td><td>|</td><td>+</td><td>+</td><td>+</td><td>+</td><td>–</td></tr>
<tr><td>Solomon four-group design
R O X O
R O O
R X O
R O</td><td>+</td><td>+</td><td>+</td><td>+</td><td>+</td><td>+</td><td>+</td><td>+</td></tr>
<tr><td>Posttest-only control group design
R X O
R O</td><td>+</td><td>+</td><td>+</td><td>+</td><td>+</td><td>+</td><td>+</td><td>+</td></tr>
<tr><td>Quasi experimental designs:
Time series
O O O X O O O</td><td></td><td>+</td><td>+</td><td>?</td><td>+</td><td>+</td><td>+</td><td>–</td></tr>
<tr><td>Multiple time series
O O O X O O O
O O O O O O</td><td>+</td><td>+</td><td>+</td><td>+</td><td>+</td><td>+</td><td>+</td><td>–</td></tr>
<tr><td>Equivalent time sample
O X_1O X_0O X_1O</td><td>+</td><td>+</td><td>+</td><td>+</td><td>+</td><td>+</td><td>+</td><td>–</td></tr>
<tr><td>Nonequivalent control group
O X O
O O</td><td>+</td><td>+</td><td>+</td><td>+</td><td>–?</td><td>+</td><td>+</td><td>–</td></tr>
</table>

sources of invalidity of true, pre-, and quasi experimental designs. In this table, a minus sign indicates a definite weakness in that design in controlling the relevant sources of invalidity; a plus sign indicates that the factor is controlled; a question mark indicates a possible source of concern; and a blank indicates that the factor is not directly relevant. When using this table, it is important to understand why each design is classified as it is.

5.4d Limitations of Experimentation

Managers must learn to recognize that experimentation, as a methodology, has certain built-in limitations:

- It is not always possible to control the effects of extraneous variables. Differential effects created by extraneous variables among treatment groups can easily occur in field experiments.
- In field experiments, lack of cooperation from wholesalers, retailers, consumers, and competitors can limit experimental activity. In particular, channel members may need incentives or remuneration to cooperate in experiments.

- Lack of knowledge about experimental procedures on the part of marketing personnel may limit the use of experimentation; worse, it may lead to experimental conclusions being discarded as not meaningful when they conflict with imperatives or plans elsewhere in the organization.
- Experiments can be costly, can consume time, and can provide vast quantities of data requiring expert analysis.
- In using people as test units, care must be taken that the experimenter does not say and do things that bias responses. Extensive pretesting is ordinarily required, adding to time, cost, and complexity.

5.4e Stages in Conducting an Experiment

Once researchers have acquired a firm understanding of procedures alternative to experimentation, considered what environment might be used, developed a good understanding of how to control sources of invalidity, and recognized the limitations of experimental procedures, they are ready to begin the necessary steps for properly conducting an experiment.

1. State the problem, clearly and in plain language.
2. Formulate a hypothesis or series of hypotheses.
3. Construct an experimental design.
4. Formulate mocked-up data ("results") and use them to check to see that they meet the specifications in the problem statement. In other words, be sure that the design answers the question at hand.
5. Check that the types of experimental results possible can be analyzed by available statistical procedures. This step must be completed *before* actual data are collected.
6. Perform the experiment.
7. Apply statistical analysis procedures to the results to determine whether effects are real (i.e., "significant") or just experimental noise (i.e., "error").
8. Draw conclusions, paying attention to both internal and external validity.

As stressed throughout this text, the emphasis is on a meaningful problem statement and providing information relevant to the problem at hand. Only if these conditions are met will the design and analysis possibly prove useful to the marketer. As in all such undertakings, even a well-planned, perfectly executed, and rigorously analyzed experiment may yield disappointing or inconclusive results. Such a situation is not a failure of the experimenter but simply a state of the world. Generally, experiments can be expected to provide unambiguous results only when the "signal" they attempt to detect is relatively clear and strong. This leads us to the question of what such phrases as "significant," "relatively clear and strong," and "error" really mean in terms of rigorous, statistical analysis, a topic we take up next.

5.5 Four Design Procedures: An Overview

We have just examined the design procedures that allow us to make proper causal inferences. Now we address the issue of statistical significance in experimentation. Specifically, we shall describe procedures that allow us to determine when a measured effect is *greater than that due to sampling error*. That is the key question in the vast majority of statistical procedures: when is the signal—due to what we are attempting to measure—more pronounced than purely random noise? This will be among the core issues examined in depth in Chapters 10–12.

The topic of experimental design procedures is vast and the subject of numerous book-length treatments, several of which are referenced in "Further Reading" at the end of this chapter. In this section, we present a selective overview of four experimental design procedures especially relevant for marketing applications: completely randomized design, randomized block design, Latin square design, and factorial design.

5.5a Completely Randomized Design

completely randomized design (CRD)
An experimental design in which treatments are assigned to test units in an entirely random manner.

A **completely randomized design (CRD)** is the simplest type of designed experiment. It is useful when the researcher is investigating *the effect of only one independent variable*. This independent variable need only be nominally scaled so that it may have many categories. Each category of the nominal independent variable is a treatment. As an example, suppose that the independent variable of interest is "type of sales training program" and that it has the following three categories:

1. No sales training
2. Head office lectures for sales training
3. On-the-job sales training

There is therefore one independent variable (type of sales training program), with three categories, each representing a treatment. Category 1, with no training program, represents the control group treatment.

In a CRD, the experimental treatments are assigned to test units randomly. In the sales training example, salespeople would randomly receive the three treatments without any regard for external factors such as their previous experience, their ages, or the sizes of the sales territories to which they will be assigned. If sales were the dependent variable, we would then compare the average sales level of each of the three treatment groups to determine which treatment was best.

5.5b Randomized Block Design

In the CRD, all extraneous variables were assumed constant over all treatment groups. But what if this were not the case? What if salespeople receiving on-the-job training tended to be assigned to larger territories than those in other treatment groups? Such selective assignment is quite common in the business world. Would the results obtained be misleading? Indeed, they would. The size-of-territory effect would be interfering with and thereby obscuring the measurement of the treatment effect. What we would like to do is "block out" this extraneous size-of-territory effect. One procedure for doing this is the **randomized block design (RBD)**.

randomized block design (RBD) An experimental design where test units are combined into blocks based on an external criterion, with blocks formed so that the test units' scores should vary less within a block than in the group as a whole.

This design is built on the principle of combining test units into blocks based on an external criterion variable. In the example, size of sales territory would be natural criterion variable to choose. These blocks are formed with the anticipation that the test units' scores on the dependent variable within each block will be more homogeneous (i.e., have the same value), in the absence of treatment, than those of test units selected at random from all test units. That is, the dependent variable should vary less within a block than in the group as a whole.

For example, divide the sales territories into three blocks, based on sales potential, as follows:

Block number	Sales potential per year
1	\$1,000,000–\$1,999,999
2	\$2,000,000–\$2,999,999
3	\$3,000,000–\$3,999,999

The key idea is this: sales levels will be more uniform (homogeneous) within these blocks than if we had thrown all the test units together, without blocking, at random. Note that this is true if we assume that the blocking factor, sales potential per year, is correlated with the dependent variable, salesperson sales level. Note also that the blocking is done before the presentation of the treatment.

Once the blocks have been established and the test units have been identified by block, we are ready to assign treatments. In this design, each treatment must appear at least once in each block. Thus, each block must have, at a minimum, a number of test units equal to the number of treatments. In our example, we would therefore need at least three salespeople in each sales potential block, each receiving a different sales training treatment (no sales training, head office lectures, or on-the-job training). The goal is to disperse the treatment types among the blocks as equally as possible, with at least one treatment type in each block.

The fundamental reason for doing blocking is to allow the researcher to obtain a measure of sampling error smaller than the error that would result from a CRD. The potentially lower sampling error in an RBD is possible because *some* variation in the dependent variable is attributable to the blocking factor, leaving a smaller sampling error once this additional part of the variation has been accounted for.

In the RBD, the researcher can use only one blocking factor. However, we can define the blocking factor by using more than one external variable. For example, in the sales training situation, we could have defined the blocking factor using both sales potential in territories and age of salespeople. Assume that the sales potential categories were defined as before and age was categorized as follows:

Category 1	18–30
Category 2	Older than 30

Then, with three sales potential categories and two age categories, we would have a blocking factor composed of $3 \times 2 = 6$ blocks, as follows:

Block number	Description
1	\$1,000,000–\$1,999,999 potential and age 18–30
2	\$2,000,000–\$2,999,999 potential and age 18–30
3	\$3,000,000–\$3,999,999 potential and age 18–30
4	\$1,000,000–\$1,999,999 potential and age older than 30
5	\$2,000,000–\$2,999,999 potential and age older than 30
6	\$3,000,000–\$3,999,999 potential and age older than 30

Note that blocks are nominally scaled and that the number of variables used to create a blocking factor can clearly be extended beyond two. The problem in doing so is that the number of resulting blocks can quickly become enormous; using five variables with just three levels each results in 243 blocks, rendering all but the largest-scale studies impractical. The other problem with blocking by using more than one external variable is that the researcher can account for only the overall effect of the blocking factor; the separate effects of the variables defining the blocking factor cannot be statistically isolated. This is particularly discouraging after going through the process of blocking and assignment, which can be tedious in large designs. A possible partial solution to this problem is the Latin square design.

5.5c Latin Square Design

Latin square (LS) design
A type of experimental design in which the researcher needs to control for the effects of more than one extraneous variable.

When the researcher wishes to control for the effects of two extraneous variables, the **Latin square (LS) design** may be used. Table 5.2 illustrates the layout of an LS design applied to the sales training example. The rows and columns of the table designate the extraneous variables that are to be controlled for. In the example, we have identified three categories for the row variable, age of salesperson, and three categories for the column variable, sales potential per year. The three treatments are identified by the letters *A*, *B*, and *C*, where A = no sales training, B = head office lectures for sales training, and C = on-the-job sales training. *The number of categories of each variable to be controlled exactly equals the number of treatments*. This is a necessary condition for using the LS design, and something of a limitation in real-world applications. (This is the reason we have three age categories in this situation even though there were only two in the RBD, discussed previously; without this condition, we would not have a square design, hence the "square" in "Latin square.") Our example therefore yields a 3×3 LS design; if we had four treatments, we would be forced to designate four categories for the row and column variables, generating a 4×4 LS.

Another necessary condition for the use of the LS design relates to the way in which the treatments are assigned to cells of the square; they are assigned to cells randomly, subject to the restriction that each treatment occurs once with each blocking situation. Because each row and column

Table 5.2 LS Design for Sales Training Experiment

	Sales Potential per Year (in thousands)		
Ages of salespeople	\$1000–\$1999	\$2000–\$2999	\$3000–\$3999
18–25	*A*	*B*	*C*
26–30	*B*	*C*	*A*
Older than 30	*C*	*A*	*B*

A = no sales training, B = head office lectures for sales training, C = on-the-job sales training.

category defines a blocking situation, each treatment must appear once in each row and once in each column. The treatments in Table 5.2 conform to this restriction; statistical programs can be used to generate larger LS designs to assign the treatments to cells randomly but in a way that obeys the "exactly once in each row and column" restriction. LS designs offer a powerful way to not only account for the combined effects of two extraneous variables but also to disentangle them: by assigning treatments to test units grouped according to these extraneous variables, their effects can be controlled for separately; that is, the effects of the independent variable on the dependent variable can be "de-biased" for two extraneous "nuisance" variables simultaneously. LS designs can be extended: Graeco-Latin square designs allow three extraneous variables to be controlled for, and Hyper-Graeco-Latin square designs allow four.

5.5d Factorial Design

In marketing, we are often interested in the simultaneous effects of two or more independent variables. The three design procedures discussed so far allow for the use of only one independent variable (even if they allow more than one extraneous variable to be controlled for in measuring the effect of that one independent variable). If we wish to examine two or more independent variables in an experimental situation, we must use a **factorial design**, among the most common experimental procedures in all of social science.

factorial design
An experimental design technique used to study the effects of two or more variables at the same time, where every level of each variable is presented ("crossed") with every level of all other variables.

Suppose that, in the sales training example, the interest was in measuring the effects of two (independent) variables: sales training procedure and compensation scheme. Also suppose that there were two categories of compensation scheme to be tested, as follows:

Category number	Compensation type
1	Straight salary
2	Straight commission

The two independent variables (sales training and compensation scheme) each form a nominal scale; the first has three categories, the second two. In a factorial design, the categories of the independent variables are called *levels*. In the design, each level of each independent variable appears with each level of all other independent variables. In our example, we would say that we have a 3 × 2 factorial design. This design would yield 3 × 2 = 6 cells in a *design matrix*. Table 5.3 shows the layout of the 3 × 2 factorial experiment. (Note that, if we were conducting an experiment with four independent variables, with 2, 3, 3, and 4 levels, respectively, we would have 2 × 3 × 3 × 4 = 72 cells in the design matrix; obviously, one should add independent variables and levels with great care to avoid this combinatorial explosion in design cells.)

Note again that the individual independent variable categories are no longer called *treatments* but *levels*. The treatments are now the various combinations of levels that occur; in the example, there are six treatments, defined by the combinations of training and compensation, $A_1B_1, \ldots, A_3B_2$. A factorial design allows us to measure the *separate* effects of each variable working on its own. It is helpful to contrast this with a CRD: although the sales training effect calculated from a factorial design would be exactly the same as that from a CRD, the factorial design would also yield the **individual effect** of the

individual effect
In statistical models, when a coefficient (or another such measure) can be calculated for each of the units individually, as opposed to taking a single value for the entire sample.

Table 5.3 3 × 2 Factorial Design for Sales Training and Compensation Experiment

			B	
			B_1	B_2
			Straight salary	Straight commission
A	A_1	No sales training	A_1B_1	A_1B_2
	A_2	Head office lectures	A_2B_1	A_2B_2
	A_3	On-the-job training	A_3B_1	A_3B_2

main effect
In a statistical model, any effect that takes the same value for all levels of a variable, regardless of the values of other variables.

interaction effect
In statistical models, any effect whose values must be summarized based on the levels of more than one variable.

compensation schemes by allowing them to be measured separately. These individual effects, attributable each of the independent variables, are called **main effects**.

There is one other type of effect that is important in factorial designs. This effect is used to recognize that a number of independent variables *working together* often have a total effect greater than the straight sum of their main effects. Such an extra effect is called an **interaction effect**. More formally, interaction occurs when the relationship between an independent variable and the dependent variable is different for different categories of *another* independent variable. In the example, the relationship between sales level (the dependent variable) and type of sales training program (the first independent variable) may vary, depending on which compensation scheme was used (the second independent variable). If this were so, we would say that the two independent variables, type of training and compensation scheme, interacted. We take note of interaction effects all the time in our everyday lives. A common example is that driving is slightly dangerous, and drinking is slightly dangerous, but drinking *and* driving (a combination of the independent variables) is extremely dangerous, not just the sum of slightly dangerous and slightly dangerous. The two levels "driving" and "drunk" interact in an exceedingly negative way, far more than suggested by their individual main effects.

Tables 5.4 and 5.5 illustrate main and interaction effects at work, using simplified versions of the sales experiment. Here, we have just two training programs, A_1 and A_2, and two compensation schemes, B_1 and B_2. The entries in the cells represent average salesperson sales in thousands of dollars during the experiment. We note that, regardless of the compensation scheme used, training program A_1 yields \$10,000 more sales on average than A_2 and, regardless of the sales training program used, compensation scheme B_1 yields \$50,000 more sales on average than B_2. Thus, the main effect of A_1 is \$10,000, the main effect of B_1 is \$50,000, and the total effect of treatment A_1B_1 is \$10,000 + \$50,000 = \$60,000. No *interaction* between sales training and compensation is apparent: the data in the table can be explained by the two main effects[2] in that one can say "there is a base compensation of \$140,000 for A_2B_2; B_1 adds another \$50,000, and A_1 adds \$10,000 more."

Table 5.5 presents the same design matrix with different results. Here, the effect of the training program depends on the compensation scheme used. Specifically, A_1 is \$10,000 better than A_2 when B_1 is used and \$40,000 better than A_2 when B_2 is used. Similarly, B_1 is \$20,000 better than B_2 when A_1 is used and \$50,000 better than B_2 when A_2 is used. Here, the effect of one independent variable on the dependent variable is *different for different levels* of the other independent variable. We have thus identified an interaction. Statistical procedures for factorial experiments can separate both interaction and main effects, regardless of the complexity of the design, and such procedures are built directly into many statistical programs for this purpose.

We should note that the number of interactions rises as the number of independent variables increases. For example, a listing of main and interaction effects for two and three independent variables follows:

Number of Independent Variables and Description	Main Effects	Interaction Effects
2: A and B	A, B	AB
3: A, B, and C	A, B, C	AB
		AC
		BC
		ABC
n: A, B, C, . . .	*n*	$(2)^n - (n + 1)$

In marketing, interaction among marketing variables is the rule rather than the exception. The factorial design is thus an important one, given its ability to identify and measure interactions. It may be

Table 5.4 An Illustration of Main Effects

		Compensation Scheme	
		B_1	B_2
Training program	A_1	\$200,000	\$150,000
	A_2	\$190,000	\$140,000

Table 5.5 An Illustration of Interaction Effects

		Compensation Scheme	
		B_1	B_2
Training program	A_1	$200,000	$180,000
	A_2	$190,000	$140,000

used in a CRD, an RBD, or within an LS design, but these refinements are beyond the scope of this book. (See the "Further Reading" section to explore this topic further.) A final noteworthy aspect of designs and interactions: The RBD presumes that there is no interaction between the blocking factor and the independent variable, and the LS design assumes that there is no interaction between the two blocking factors; only the factorial design allows us to measure the effect of interaction.

5.5e Usage in Practice

Almost all real marketing problems involve the need to control extraneous variables or to simultaneous apply more than one marketing variable. Thus, RBDs, LS designs, and factorial designs are the most used in practice. Commonly used blocking factors in marketing include store size, days of the week, time of the year, and geographic regions, all of which often contribute extraneous variation in the dependent variables that interest marketers. For example, you might be interested in measuring the effects of different prices on coffee sales. Suppose that these sales are measured in food stores on each day of the week and in different regions of the country. The actual sales of coffee that we observe might be affected by the different prices plus the different sizes of stores, the day of the week, and the region of the country. Some days (e.g., weekends) are high volume, and some regions of the country are higher in per capita coffee consumption than others. What we do is control the effects of these extraneous variables—to not allow variation induced in them to contaminate what we wish to measure; that is, to get a clear measure of the price effect.

Even with great care to properly design a field experiment, and even with the provision of blocking for statistical control, it is difficult, sometimes impossible, to have a completely controlled field experiment. There are simply too many events that can take place in the field capable of impacting treatments differentially, and researchers cannot possibly anticipate them all, much less statistically correct for them. Thus, it is common in marketing research to think of these experimental settings as being somewhat quasi experimental, regardless of the design or how well the resulting data are analyzed. *Marketing Research Focus 5.2* illustrates how a factorial experiment carried out in the field can be used to help evaluate the effectiveness of common marketing activities.

Marketing Research Focus 5.2

A Factorial Field Experiment Determines Marketing Effects on Navy Enlistment

Marketing researchers conducted a study to evaluate the marketing effectiveness of the U.S. Navy recruiting program and to quantify the relationship between marketing efforts, primarily advertising, and enlistment achievements. This was done by estimating the impact of changes in the advertising budget and the size of the Navy recruiting force on Navy enlistment contracts for various categories of recruits. The study was based on a 1-year controlled experiment in which levels of Navy recruiters and advertising were systematically varied.

Researchers chose the **area of dominant influence (ADI)** as their analysis unit for the experiment. ADIs are geographic areas that receive their television signals from a central city or town. Electronic media-rating services assign individual counties to ADIs based on media-use patterns of sampled households. ADIs allow researchers to execute and measure changes in electronic advertising throughout the experiment. Of the more than 200 ADIs in the United States, 26 were chosen as experimental markets because of their relative insulation (i.e., the degree of dominance of local broadcasters was especially pronounced). An additional 17 markets were chosen as control cells.

The Wharton Applied Research Center team assigned various treatment conditions to each of the 26 treatment markets. A number of characteristics differed across these markets: demographic, socioeconomic, levels of total military

area of dominant influence (ADI)
A specific geographic area surrounding a town or city; broadcasters operating within that town or city account for a larger share of viewing (television) or listening (radio) households than do other broadcasters operating nearby.

enlistments per capita, and the Navy's share of total military enlistment. Since the Navy Recruiting Command believed the last two variables were major factors in the effectiveness of marketing efforts, the marketing research team ensured that markets exposed to treatment conditions covered a variety of "total enlistment" and "the Navy's share of total enlistment" levels. Markets were classified in terms of these variables and randomly assigned to treatment conditions. Treatment conditions included combinations of increasing or decreasing advertising by 50 or 100 percent, increasing or decreasing the number of recruiters by 20 percent, leaving advertising at prestudy levels, and leaving the number of recruiters at prestudy levels. Control conditions were created in the markets that maintained prestudy levels of both advertising and recruiters.

Detailed data were collected on the 42 chosen markets and divided into four broad categories: enlistment contracts, recruiters, advertising, and environmental variables. Monthly data were compiled for both Navy contracts and total Department of Defense contracts. This information was further sorted into the following categories: high school and non–high school, women, African Americans, and two groups based on aptitude (as determined by IQ and other testing). Navy recruiter data was collected on the basis of both applied worker-months and total recruiters present during each month. This information was divided into two groups: recruiters who were established in the recruiting function, and recruiters who were in the first 4 months or last 6 months of their tour (when researchers hypothesize they are less effective). Advertising deliveries, measured by both gross impressions and dollars, were collected for each ADI and broken down by national print (further divided into magazines, newspapers, and direct mail), national electronic (broken down into television and radio), local, and joint campaigns for all armed services. Four environmental variables were also taken into account: percentage of unemployment, median family income, percentage of the African American population, and urbanization (the percentage of 17- to 21-year-old males who reside in counties with populations of more than 150,000). These variables served as blocking factors in the field experiment.

The experimental markets used, the structure of the assignment of treatment conditions, and the control markets used are noted in Figure 5.2.

Figure 5.2 Navy Experimental Design

	Recruiters –20%	**Recruiters same**	**Recruiters +20%**
ADV + 100%		Davenport-Rock Island	
ADV + 50%	Tulsa Roanoke Syracuse	Washington Indianapolis Richmond	Boston St. Louis Charleston-Huntington
ADV same	Baltimore Cheyenne, WY Laurel, MS	Providence Terre Haute Springfield, IL*	Providence Terre Haute Springfield, IL*
ADV - 50%	Wilkes Barre Phoenix Odessa-Midland	Chicago Pittsburgh Columbus, OH	Chicago Pittsburgh Columbus, OH
ADV - 100%		Johnstown- Altoona	

*Additional control markets:

Nashville	Des Moines	Waco
Los Angeles	Youngstown	Sioux City
Charlotte	West Palm Beach	McAllen
Greenville	Chattanooga	Anniston
Knoxville	Huntsville	

Analysis of the data collected led to a number of conclusions: The number of recruiters did have a significant impact on enlistments. A recruiter's effectiveness was dependent on the recruiter's tenure. Only certain types of advertising expenditures were effective, with a wide variation in the degree of media impact. Socioeconomic factors also had major impacts on enlistment. And in addition to increasing Navy enlistments, the Navy's marketing efforts expanded the total market for military enlistments.

Sources: Carroll, Vincent P., Ambar G. Rao, Hau L. Lee, Arthur Shapiro, and Barry L. Bayus (1985), "The Navy Enlistment Marketing Experiment," *Marketing Science*, 4(4), 352–374.

MacInnis, Deborah J., Ambar G. Rao, and Allen M. Weiss (2002), "Assessing When Increased Media Weight of Real-World Advertisements Helps Sales," *Journal of Marketing Research*, 39(4), 391–407.

International Issues 5.1

Causal Studies in International Marketing Research

Procter & Gamble (P&G) in Europe ran a market test (a quasi experiment) in Berlin before launching its Vizir brand of liquid laundry detergent in several European countries. The market test allowed P&G to better set sales objectives, product positioning against competition, and price point.

An Italian advertising agency tested the effectiveness of alternative advertisements for its car company client in movie theaters in different cities in Italy and Spain. Three different advertising approaches in the ads were tested in different theaters in a total of 10 cities. Only one ad was seen in any one theater on any given day. These theater tests allowed the agency to recommend to the client the ad that best created brand awareness and preference for the client's car.

Swatch Watch ran pricing quasi experiments in the United States, Germany, France, Italy, the United Kingdom (UK), Japan, and other countries before setting a world price for its basic watch. These tests allowed Swatch to reject the pricing policy that its management had originally desired.

Unilever UK ran a full factorial experiment with consumers to test the taste and texture preferences for several formulations of a new baking product. This experiment allowed Unilever to establish the optimal ingredient mix of the product. Although it did not account for consumer *heterogeneity*—for example, coming up with various mixes for different market niches—the data collected from the experiment would allow the company to develop these over time.

International research of a different sort has been carried out for at least three decades across the globe: on racial discrimination in hiring. Many experiments have involved demographically matched samples of job applications that differed in terms of their ethnic background or national origin; for example, having equal numbers of study participants be Britons, West Indians, and Greeks in the United Kingdom or split equally by European or African ancestry in the United States. Other variables often used in these designs were whether the application was made by phone or in person, whether the position required interaction with the public, degree of prior training, salary levels, and ethnic background of those in charge of applicant selection. Results have allowed governments to successfully "de market" practices that have been shown to allow for, and in some cases exacerbate, discriminatory outcomes, finding the practices themselves to differ greatly by job type and region.

5.6 International Marketing Experiments

Unlike much else in marketing research, the principles of causality, the structure of experimental design, and the nature of marketplace quasi experiments all hold equally well for domestic and for international research. *International Issues 5.1* provides examples of international causal studies in marketing.

Summary

Causality may be inferred after ascertaining concomitant variation and the proper time order of occurrence of variables, as well as eliminating other possible causal factors. Experimental and quasi experimental procedures are the only ones that allow proper causal inferences to be made.

An experiment involves consciously manipulating and controlling one or more independent variables and measuring their effect on the dependent variable. Treatments are manipulated alternatives whose effects are measured. Test units are the entities to whom (or to which) the treatments are presented and whose response to the treatments is measured. Dependent variables are the measures taken on the test units.

Extraneous variables are all variables, other than the treatments, that affect the response of the test units to the treatments. Categories of extraneous variables are history, maturation, testing, instrumentation, and statistical regression effects; selection bias; and test unit mortality. Their effects can be separated from the treatment effect through physical control or randomization.

Internal validity is concerned with the question of whether the observed effects could have been caused by variables other than the treatments. External validity is concerned with the generalizability of experimental results outside the experimental environment. Specific experimental designs differ in their ability to control extraneous variables.

In a completely randomized design (CRD), treatments are assigned to test units randomly. In a randomized block design (RBD), test units are combined into blocks based on some external criterion variable to measure and control one blocking factor. Treatments are then randomly assigned within blocks of test units. In a Latin square (LS) design, test units are combined into blocks based on two external criterion variables to measure and control two blocking factors. Treatments are then randomly assigned to blocks subject to the restriction that each treatment occurs once within each blocking situation.

When independent variables interact, the relationship between an independent variable and the dependent variable is different for different categories of another independent variable. A factorial design allows for the analysis of the main effects of more than one independent variable, as well as the effect of the interaction among those independent variables.

Key Terms

area of dominant influence (ADI) (p. 205)
baseline (p. 192)
completely randomized design (CRD) (p. 200)
confounding variable (p. 187)
control group (p. 192)
deterministic causation (p. 184)
direct testing effect (p. 189)
equivalent time-sample design (p. 197)
experiment (p. 186)
experimental design (p. 187)
external validity (p. 188)
extraneous variable (p. 187)
factorial design (p. 203)
field environment (p. 198)
history effect (p. 189)
hypothesis (p. 184)
individual effect (p. 203)
Instrumentation effect (p. 190)
interaction effect (p. 204)
interactive testing effect (p. 189)
internal validity (p. 188)
Latin square (LS) design (p. 202)
main effect (p. 204)
main testing effect (p. 189)
maturation effect (p. 189)
multiple time-series design (p. 196)
nonequivalent control group design (p. 197)
one-group pretest–posttest design (p. 191)
one-shot case study design (p. 191)
posttest-only control group design (p. 194)
pretest–posttest control group design (p. 192)
probabilistic causation (p. 184)
quasi experimental design (p. 195)
randomized block design (RBD) (p. 201)
reactive testing effect (p. 189)
Solomon four-group design (p. 193)
static-group comparison design (p. 191)
statistical-regression effects (p. 190)
test unit mortality (p. 190)
test units (p. 186)
testing effect (p. 189)
time-series experiment (p. 195)
treatments (p. 186)
X-O-R syntax (p. 188)

Discussion Questions

1 What is the fundamental question that should be asked in searching for causality?
2 How can a design described as $R\ O_1 \times O_2$ be confounded? What design could control the confounding variables?
3 Under what circumstances is it extremely difficult or even impossible for even the best design to control an extraneous variable?
4 What are internal and external validity? Can each exist in the absence of the other? Which do you think is more important in typical marketing research applications?
5 How might one choose between laboratory and field environments? What are the distinct advantages of each over the other in the course of an entire marketing research project, and at which stages would each be especially valuable?
6 Why are LS designs so often utilized in marketing field experiments? Despite their wide application, what are their main weaknesses?
7 For the *Marketing Research Focus 5.2* experiment,
   a use X-O-R syntax to describe the experiment.
   b how is control of extraneous variables handled?
   c what factor could confound the experiment?
   d could a LS design be used for this experiment? If so, present your design explicitly.
8 Find an organization's new marketing program or activity described in a newspaper or magazine—*BusinessWeek, Marketing News*, or *Advertising Age*, for example. The program might be a new advertising

theme, distribution plan, or pricing strategy or some other marketing control variable. Your assignment is to design an experiment or a quasi experiment to measure the effectiveness of this new program or activity. Be sure to address the following six items:

a Describe the new marketing program or activity.
b Describe the treatments.
c Describe the dependent variable or variables and how they will be measured.
d What or who are the test units?
e How will extraneous variables be controlled?
f Use X-O-R syntax to describe the experiment.

9 MINICASE

Design an experiment to test the following hypothesis: "Attitudes toward foreign cars are influenced by their price." First, determine the precise meaning of this statement and what is being claimed to influence what, perhaps comparatively (e.g., "foreign," "price," and "attitudes"). Then, record the required experimental components.

a Describe the treatments.
b Describe the dependent variable(s) and how they will be measured.
c What are the test units?
d How will extraneous variables be controlled?
e Use X-O-R syntax to describe the experiment.

Review Questions

1 A researcher wishes to test consumer response to a new jingle for Fruit Roll-Ups. How can the effects of the extraneous variable of age best be controlled?

a Physically control the variable by testing only consumers in the 40- to 50-year-old age bracket.
b Randomize age in the sample groups.
c Design the experiment to avoid the maturation effect on the test units.
d None of the above will work without a time-series experiment.

2 How does a time-series experiment allow for the control of extraneous variables?

a by keeping the extraneous variables uniform over periodic observations
b by randomizing each of the extraneous variables over time
c by making the extraneous variables irrelevant due to the history effect
d by taking multiple measures and statistically correcting for the extraneous variables over time

3 Which of the following is an accurate statement regarding the scientific notion of causation?

a Concomitant variation, time order of occurrence, and elimination of other possible causal factors are required to prove causation.
b Rigorous examination of data under specific conditions is necessary to substantiate scientific statements of deterministic causation.
c An observed effect is never truly caused by one factor.
d Causal inferences demand that the cause and effect be observed to vary together, the effect be observed subsequent to the cause, and other possible causes be ruled out.

4 What is the difference between the main testing effect and the interactive testing effect?

a The main testing effect is the effect of the treatment being measured; the interactive testing effect is the distortion of this by communication among respondents.
b The results of the treatment are the main and interactive testing effects, after they have been separated from distortion by extraneous variables.
c The main testing effect is the effect of one test on a subsequent test; the interactive testing effect is the effect of a test on the subsequent behavior being measured.
d The main testing effect is the effect of instrumentation on the results; the interactive testing effect is the effect of selection bias.

Figure 5.3 **Time-Series Experiment of Panel with Advertising Campaign between O_4 and O_5**

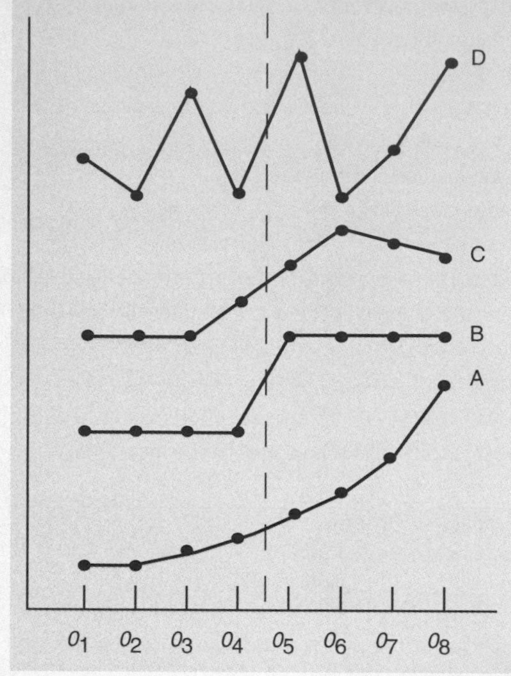

5 Consider the graph of a time-series experiment in Figure 5.3. From which of the graphs can a long-term effect of the treatment most properly be inferred?

a Graph A
b Graph B
c Graph C
d Graph D

6 If a one-group pretest–posttest experiment had been done in the study in Figure 5.3, at O_4 and O_5, what illusions might have resulted?

a Graph C would not show a strong response to the treatment.
b Graph A would not show a strong response to the treatment.
c Graph D would show a stronger response than graph B.
d all of the above

7 In a multiple time-series experiment, larger cities are preferable because

a there is less chance of interactive testing effect.
b people in larger cities interact more anonymously.
c larger cities provide a much larger and more diverse population for sampling.
d actually, larger cities are not preferable.

8 Which experimental or quasi experimental design controls sources of invalidity most completely?

a Solomon four-group design and posttest-only control group design
b one-group pretest–posttest design
c pretest–posttest control group design
d multiple time-series design

9 Assume your firm is considering two separate plans to influence customer spending: instituting a company program to improve customer service and changing to one of three different store layouts. What kind of experimental design would be most appropriate to understand the dependent variable (customer spending) in this situation?

a a CRD with the three store layouts and the customer service program
b a RBD with six blocks for the six combinations
c an LS design with the three store layouts as treatments and three categories of customer service training
d a factorial design with six combinations of levels

10 An interaction effect in the preceding experiment would mean

- **a** an early measurement affected the results of a later measurement.
- **b** the effect of the different store designs was different depending on the level of customer service training.
- **c** measuring both variables at once made it impossible to separate the effects of either.
- **d** all of the above.

Web Exercise

Log in to the Online Edition of your textbook at www.atomicdog.com to participate in this Web Exercise, which can be found in your Online Study Guide for this chapter.

Further Reading

Asher, Herbert B. (1983), *Causal Modeling (Quantitative Applications in the Social Sciences)*, Sage Publications, 2nd Edition.

Campbell, Donald T., and Julian C. Stanley (1969), *Experimental and Quasi-Experimental Designs for Research*. Boston: Houghton Mifflin.

Cook, Thomas D., and Donald T. Campbell (1979), *Quasi-Experimentation: Design and Analysis Issues for Field Settings*. Boston: Houghton Mifflin.

Jones, Russell A. (1996), *Research Methods in the Social and Behavioral Sciences*, 2nd Edition. Sunderland, MA: Sinauer Associates.

Kennedy, Andrew J. (1985), *An Introduction to the Design and Analysis of Experiments in Behavioral Research*. Lanham, MD: University Press of America.

Keppel, Geoffrey, and Thomas D. Wickens. (2004), *Design and Analysis: A Researcher's Handbook, 4th Edition*. Englewood Cliffs, NJ: Prentice Hall.

Pearl, Judea (2000), *Causality: Models, Reasoning, and Inference*, New York, NY: Cambridge University Press.

Smith, Robert B. (1985), *Handbook of Social Science Methods: Volume 3: Focused Survey Research and Causal Modeling*. Westport, CT: Praeger Publishers. Greenwood Publishing Group, Inc.

Spector, Paul E. (1981), *Research Designs*. Thousand Oaks, California: Sage Publications.

Winer, Benjamin J., Donald R. Brown, Kenneth M. Michaels. (1991), *Statistical Principles in Experimental Design*. New York: McGraw-Hill, 3rd Edition.

Notes

1 Brinberg, David L., and J. McGrath (1985), *Validity and the Research Process*, Sage Publications.

Calder, Bobby J., Lynn Phillips, and Alice M. Tybout (1982), "The Concept of External Validity," *Journal of Consumer Research*, 9, 240–244.

Calder, Bobby J., Alice M. Tybout, and Brian Sternthal (1983), "Beyond External Validity," *Journal of Consumer Research*, 10 (June), 112–114.

Cronbach, Lee J. (1975), "Beyond the Two Disciplines of Scientific Psychology," *American Psychologist*, 29, 116–127.

Lynch, John G. Jr. (1982), "On the External Validity of Experiments in Consumer Research," *Journal of Consumer Research*, 9, 225–239.

Lynch, John G. Jr. (1983), "The Role of External Validity in Theoretical Research," *Journal of Consumer Research*, 10, 109–111.

McGrath, Joseph E. and David Brinberg (1983), "External Validity and the Research Process: A Comment on the Calder/Lynch Dialogue," *Journal of Consumer Research*, 10 (June), 115–124.

Sternthal, Brian, Alice M. Tybout, and Bobby J. Calder (1987), "Confirmatory versus Comparative Approaches to Judging Theory Tests," *Journal of Consumer Research*, 14 (June), 114–125.

2 Note that this use of *main effect* and *interaction effect* is not entirely standard, because such effects are typically referred to in terms of entire factors and not specific levels within them and are each assessed via a single statistical test for the entire factor.

CHAPTER SIX
DATA COLLECTION: EXPLORATORY AND CONCLUSIVE RESEARCH

"I attribute the little I know to my not having been ashamed to ask for information."

John Locke

"The formulation of a problem is often more essential than its solution, which may be merely a matter of mathematical or experimental skill. To raise new questions, new possibilities, to regard old problems from a new angle, requires creative imagination and marks real advances."

Albert Einstein

This chapter covers data collection techniques for exploratory and conclusive research in greater depth. We examine focus groups and in-depth interviews, two qualitative methodologies used in exploratory research, and structured data collection techniques used for quantitative evaluation in conclusive research.

6.1 Qualitative Techniques for Exploratory Research

As explained in earlier chapters, exploratory research involves collecting information from primary or secondary sources to provide insight into the management problem and identify courses of action, if necessary, early in the research process. Although secondary sources can provide useful background information or historical perspective, primary sources of information, such as the qualitative techniques used in focus groups and in-depth interviews, provide current data on customer buying behavior, perceptions, attitudes, and motivations.

How much (accurate) information a decision situation requires depends on the uncertainty present and the risk levels acceptable to the decision-maker. Crucial decisions require both more information and more accurate information, just as the decision to buy a house commands more attention than one to buy a pizza. Depending on the situation and the specific context of the management problem, some steps in the research process may be skipped or eliminated. For example, if decision-makers have longitudinal or recent accurate information about a decision situation, they may find that adequate information exists and may proceed to making a decision without taking on the cost, time, and complexity conclusive research typically requires. Exploratory research may also be used to identify decision options that are low in risk and thus do not require the conclusive research phase, such as whether to offer an existing product in a new size rather than an entirely new product.

6.1a Qualitative Techniques

Qualitative research techniques are unstructured: techniques in which no rigid format is followed but the respondent (or group of respondents) is queried directly about the issue at hand and allowed to answer at length. Such techniques are often touted as the only types of research that allow the decision-maker and the researcher to see respondents "in the flesh" and hear them talk about marketing issues "in their own words." For this reason, they are widely used in marketing research and usually to complement conclusive, quantitative, or survey-based research to offer a fuller portrait of the decision environment. These sorts of data differ from the nuts-and-bolts measures derived from panels and store audits, which tend to be accurate and numerical yet to lack the sort of human insight and richness many marketers claim to be the most useful in evaluating new product features, ad campaigns, and promotional options.

Qualitative techniques can usually be identified by the following characteristics:

- Small convenience or quota samples are often used, rather than rigorous, statistically meaningful samples.
- The information sought relates to respondents' motivations, beliefs, feelings, and attitudes, not to facts about their lives and behavior.
- An intuitive, subjective approach is used in gathering the data.
- The data collection format is open ended, allowing respondents to express themselves in their own words at a length they deem appropriate.
- The approach is not intended to provide statistically or scientifically accurate data but often to guide further investigation that will.

By contrast, quantitative data are intended to quantify or precisely measure a problem, often using sophisticated statistical procedures and scientifically drawn samples. Quantitative data are usually associated with conclusive research. According to a study by the Committee on Qualitative Research of the Advertising Research Foundation, the most prevalent reasons for using qualitative research are applicability of results to immediate action, the chance to hear consumers' thoughts in their own words, and the speed of results.

6.1b Focus Groups

The focus group (see Figure 6.1 for a sample session) is one of the most frequently used techniques in marketing research. A **focus group** can be defined as a loosely structured interactive discussion by a trained moderator among a small group of respondents. Although the interview requires a pre-interview organization of topics or an interviewer guide, the setting emphasizes flexibility. The value of the technique lies in the potential to discover the unexpected, which is far more possible in a free-flowing group discussion than in a typical survey setting.

focus group
A type of qualitative research in which a group of people — usually between 4 and 10, selected based on their demographic characteristics — discuss their attitudes, feelings and beliefs towards a product or service under the guidance of a moderator.

Focus groups can be used for a number of purposes. Interviews with researchers suggest the following uses (followed by typical examples):

- To help generate hypotheses that can be further tested quantitatively ("those who claim to like the product are more educated, urban, and professional")
- To generate information helpful in structuring consumer questionnaires ("once we mention the celebrity endorser, people recognize the product")
- To provide overall background information on a product category ("what do you serve with dinner, and how long does it typically take to prepare?")
- To get impressions on new-product concepts for which there is little information available ("what aspect of food shopping do you find most tiresome?")
- To stimulate new ideas about older products ("do you use baking soda for anything other than baking?")
- To generate ideas for new creative concepts ("if you could wish for anything that would make housekeeping easier, what would that be?")
- To interpret previously obtained quantitative results ("people have previously told us that this is too much trouble to use, and we are curious as to why")
- To understand emotional reactions to brands ("if this product were discontinued, what three adjectives would express your reaction?")

Focus groups are so widely used in the marketing research industry that considerable resources exist for design and planning; Qualitative Research Consultants Association (QRCA), Marketing Research Association, and Marketing Navigation offer many articles and sources of information, and QRCA offers directories of moderators and research consultants.

6.1c Group Design Issues

In designing effective focus groups, the researcher must be especially sensitive to management objectives and to the role of qualitative and quantitative research in meeting these objectives. Managers often believe they can use qualitative research as a substitute for quantitative research on the flawed premise that "listening to the voice of the customer" is always superior to numerical results, no matter how rigorous. Although customers' voices are important, they are notoriously difficult to interpret, so qualitative research should be combined with, tempered by, and usually followed by a rigorous quantitative study. Consequently, the researcher must not allow the misuse of research methodology but instead should clearly communicate to management the true role of qualitative research in the decision process. At the same time, in real applications there are often insufficient funds or time to accommodate large-scale conclusive research, particularly for fast-changing opinion settings, as in political polling. As a compromise, often a short "screener" survey is done *before* a focus group to help use group time most effectively; after the focus group, another short survey can be administered. Although this is no substitute for rigorous conclusive research, it is often the best a firm can do with limited temporal and financial resources.

The following guidelines can be helpful in the design of an effective focus group study. See also the detailed guide to focus group implementation in Figure 6.2.

Figure 6.1 Sample Focus Group Session

In this focus group session, 10 people are being asked questions about what they think about a new, health-focused cereal, featuring bran and a variety of real, dried fruits. The participants are white, male, fortyish, and in the lower-middle to upper-middle income classes. Here are sample segments of that session.

Introduction
Moderator: Why don't you go ahead and introduce yourselves...

Ray: My name is Ray. I am a business consultant with three children.

Jim: My name is Jim. I own a trucking company in Chicago. I have three kids.

Kyle: I'm Kyle. I am a paramedic and a fireman.

Probe on what is important in a cereal
Moderator: What kind of cereal do you like?

Ray: I like the bran stuff because of the low cholesterol.

Kyle: I don't like sugar cereals, only healthy cereals.

Jim: I mainly eat Raisin Bran because it is good-tasting and good for you.

Introduction of new health-focused bran cereal with dried fruit
Moderator: How many of you have heard of this cereal?

Jim: Yeah, I have heard of it before and tried it before.

Kyle: Someone mentioned the name once before and said it was overpriced.

Ray: I have never heard of it before.

Moderator gives each participant a sample of the cereal to taste-test.

Getting feedback
Moderator: What do you think of it now?

Jim: You can taste the raisins a lot.

Kyle: It doesn't have a lot of sugar – that's good.

Ray: It's different. I thought it would taste blah.

Probing
Moderator: Ray, what do you mean by saying you thought it would taste blah?

Ray: I mean I expected it would be without any taste since it looked like a health cereal.

End
Moderator: I want to thank all of you for your time.

Figure 6.2 Guide for Implementing a Focus Group

1. Establish objectives
   - *Definition of management problem.* What does management want to achieve?
   - *Definition of marketing research objectives.* What information is needed to meet the needs of management?
2. Determine the research design.
   - *Target market segments.* What areas need exploring?
   - *Size of groups.* How many people are needed for the focus group?
   - *Number of groups.* Is more than one session required?
   - *Length of sessions and timing.* How long should the sessions last? What time of day should they be held?
   - *Location of group sessions.* Where should the sessions be held?
3. Develop a screening profile for the focus group members—a way to select the type of people you need to look at.
   - *Demographic characteristics.* Look at gender, age, and so forth.
   - *Product or service experience.* Is the session going to be dealing with professionals or experienced people in this area?
4. Establish your budget.
   - *Incentive level for participants.* What will motivate people to participate in a focus group?
   - *Costs of analyzing the focus group results.* Once the session is done, how long will it take to review the data? How much will it cost?
   - *Budget expected costs.* Estimate costs of moderator, facilities, participants, incidentals, equipment, rentals, travel expenses, analysis.
5. Find and rent a location for the focus group. The environment may affect participants' answers, and the client may want to observe the sessions. The following are important criteria:
   - *Relaxed, comfortable atmosphere.*
   - *Availability of video/audio equipment as needed.*
   - *Client observation facilities, via mirrors or electronics.*
   - *Accessibility for focus group members.*
6. Screen and select focus group members. Now that the type of person needed is known, eliminate poor choices from the focus group candidate pool.
   - *Disqualify anyone who works in the marketing research business, for a competitor, and so forth.*
   - *Consider the needs of the research project regarding homogeneity of group members.*
   - *Work with the recruiting field service to assure choice of appropriate participants.*
   - *Check the complete screening questionnaires before use to be sure appropriate people are recruited.*
7. Select a moderator. Since a moderator is very important in a focus group, there are many factors to consider.
   - *Previous experience.*
   - *Familiarity with the product and/or the industry.*
   - *Cost.*
   - *Availability.*
   - *Gender of the moderator* (if specifically relevant).
   - *Use of one or more moderators, alternating.*
8. Develop a moderator's guide or agenda to be used to help the moderator achieve the goals of the marketing research.
   - *Research objectives.*
   - *Topics to be covered.*
   - *Time to be allocated.*
9. Meet with the moderator, to further prepare him or her for the session.
   - *Review the discussion guide and the research objectives.*
   - *Educate the moderator on the client's business and products.*
10. Conduct the focus groups.
11. Analyze the results. Compile all the data into meaningful information.
12. Write and present a report to management, explaining the findings and their consequences.

Homogeneity

Among the major decisions in conducting focus groups is whether participants should resemble one another demographically, that is, be relatively homogeneous. One school of thought contends that, when the researcher has little idea about the relevant target group or niche, using a heterogeneous group is reasonable and doing so can generate a variety of opinions. In most marketing research applications, however, knowing little about target consumer segments is rare and often represents a failure of preliminary research. Far more common is the situation where extensive, predevelopment research has indicated a consumer need in a specific group or set of groups. In such cases, the focus group should be composed of respondents with fairly homogenous characteristics. One large firm, which conducts approximately 600 focus groups per year, goes so far as to avoid combining women who have children and who work full time in the home and childless women who work outside the home because their lifestyles and objectives are substantially different. They also avoid grouping men with women, as well as teenagers with younger children, for the same reasons. Except in rare instances (as noted previously), it is useful to maintain as much homogeneity or commonality among group members as possible to avoid interactions and conflicts among group members on issues not relevant to the study objectives. Doing so may be difficult because people may agree on a number of overt demographic characteristics yet differ on ones more difficult to observe or discern before focus group recruitment, such as political outlook or degree of religious conviction.

Size

The size of the group can be as large as 10 or 12 people for consumer goods research. Experience suggests that in a group with fewer than 8 people, the discussion can be dominated by a few respondents and that having more than 12 people tends to diminish the opportunity for some respondents to participate. For nonconsumer goods research (pertaining to architects, doctors, industrial purchasers, engineers, investors, contractors, and so on), a group of 6 or 7 people may be best for maximum interaction among participants because these products and services have longer purchase cycles, are more costly, and have less tangible attributes or the sort that benefit from extended discussion. Although it is rare in marketing applications, large focus groups are sometimes desirable. For example, in legal settings, mock juries are essentially large focus groups, comprising 25 to 50 participants. In such settings, the emphasis is on collecting as many people's views as possible in the shortest span of time, and interaction among them is nonexistent. Larger groups, however, run the risk of attracting the "professional group participant," who can simply fail to contribute without being noticed.

Screening

Careful screening of respondents is essential to the success of the focus group. First, the group members must have had adequate experience with the object or issue being discussed unless valuable group time can be expended on bringing them up to speed. Second, respondents who have participated in a group session in the recent past generally should not be included, although some research organizations do accept respondents who have not participated in a session within the last year. Among the reasons for this restriction are that former participants often play the role of "expert" by dominating the discussion and trying to show off for first-time participants and that prior participants have some idea of the moderator's plans or flow, anticipating and short-circuiting the discussion.

As part of the screening process, the researcher must be sensitive to potential participants' motivations for taking part in the focus group. This is important not only to draw a large pool of respondents, but also to understand whether the participant will be fully interested and involved in the group discussion. One study found that the top three reasons for participation (a respondent was allowed to list more than one) were "money" (more than half the participants listed this first), "focus groups are interesting/the topic was interesting," and "met qualifications/time was convenient."[1] Although being motivated by remuneration is expected, it should not be the sole motivation, and "professional" focus group participants should be strenuously avoided. In practice, however, it is difficult to ferret such participants out because there is nothing resembling a national registry of focus group participants; researchers and moderators must simply be on guard when recruiting.

Another issue in respondent selection relates to allowing people to participate in a group that contains a relative, neighbor, or friend. Because friends often tend to talk mainly to one another, not to the whole group, and may avoid any disagreement, many researchers will not select respondents from organizations where participants have established relationships.

A Manager Observes a Focus Group through a One-Way Mirror

Focus Group Facility with One-Way Mirror and Multiple Monitoring and Recording Capabilities

Duration

A focus group typically lasts 1 to 2 hours. This period is needed to establish rapport with the respondents and explore in depth their beliefs, feelings, ideas, and insights regarding the discussion topic. Longer times are required for truly novel products, those at high price points, those with long interpurchase times, or those with many attributes. For example, an entirely new class of automobile—like those using hybrid engine technology—would require a far longer session than a new size of canned vegetable. When participants and researchers have a good deal of prior experience, the focus group can explore the relevant "space" of responses far more quickly.

Sessions

The number of group sessions to be conducted depends on the nature of the issue at hand, the number of market segments involved, and the time and cost constraints of the project. Typically, the researcher must concentrate the group session on those segments most critical to the topic being considered. It is good practice to replicate the focus group session for each market segment being studied, more than once if redundancy is useful, as in the case of risky products or those entirely new to the market.

Environment

The physical setting is crucial to the effectiveness of the group session. The atmosphere should induce a relaxed feeling so that informal and spontaneous comments will be encouraged, akin to a "bull session." Although living rooms in private homes are often used in rural areas and countries lacking dedicated group facilities, most research organizations have participants come to a central facility, often a specially designed laboratory furnished like a comfortable, but not overly elaborate, living room. Note, however, that participants are there to work, not to socialize; they should not be uncomfortable, nor should they be so comfortable as to drift off or lose touch with the other participants. The main advantage of holding sessions in a laboratory lies in the availability of facilities for recording the session and for indirect observation by the client. Clients frequently choose to observe the focus group session, either remotely via a video feed or behind a one-way mirror; it is not a good idea to place them in the room with participants, even if their identity is not revealed, so as to avoid the danger of disrupting the group session by having the participants observe the client's reactions. If certain areas need more exploration, the client can cue the moderator during short breaks in the session or using an in-ear audio monitor. In specialized situations, it may be appropriate to allow the client to come in at the *end* of the group session, after participant's views can no longer be biased by the presence of the sponsor, so that any complex, last-minute, or purely technical questions can be answered definitively and so that the sponsor can pose any residual questions directly.

Costs

Generally, focus groups are quicker and less expensive than quantitative research efforts, and they can be planned, carried out, and transcribed in a matter of weeks. Although costs will vary depending on the type of participant sought, the sophistication of the moderator, and other factors, a focus group report could end up costing between $5000 and $25,000. This includes such components as room or facility rental, respondent incentives (varying greatly, depending on the specific group required), travel expenses, moderator fees, data preparation and analysis, and final report production.

Moderator

The moderator's role is of prime importance to the success of the focus group technique. Highly skilled moderators can ensure that proper respondent rapport is established, that the discussion is appropriately directed and maintained along study-relevant dimensions, that bias is kept at bay, and that the degree of probing is sufficient to accomplish the research objectives. In addition, the moderator is central to the analysis and interpretation of the data. Great skill, experience, knowledge of the discussion topic, and intuitive insights into the nature of group dynamics are required to accomplish this task. Consequently, the moderator is typically a full-time professional, often a trained psychologist who has developed special moderator skills through intensive study and practice.

The moderator's skill is crucial to maintaining a high degree of interaction among group members. Unskilled moderators typically find themselves conducting individual interviews with each of the participants rather than stimulating interaction among the group participants. Only with sufficient interactivity among the participants will the discussion be appropriately spontaneous, with the kind of give-and-take rapport and emotional involvement that generates in-depth attitudinal and behavioral information.

When choosing a moderator, the following key skills should be checked for explicitly:

- A combination of empathy and firmness: To encourage an appropriate degree of interaction, the moderator must combine disciplined detachment with understanding. This often requires spurring on less knowledgeable participants and gently chiding those who move the discussion in counterproductive directions.
- Permissiveness: An atmosphere of permissiveness is desirable to encourage open communication. The moderator must also be alert for any indications that the group atmosphere of cordiality is disintegrating.
- Ability to encourage involvement: Because a principal reason for the group interview is to expose feelings and to obtain reactions indicative of deeper feelings, the moderator must encourage and stimulate intensive personal involvement. Although the dynamics of the group situation facilitate the participation of all members in the interaction, there may be individuals who resist contributing. It is the moderator's job to draw these people into the discussion.
- Ability to convey incomplete understanding: An extremely useful skill for a group moderator is the ability to convey lack of complete understanding of the information being presented. This allows participants to elaborate, without having to be asked directly, in the spirit of clarification.
- Flexibility: The moderator should be equipped before the session with a topic outline (see the discussion of the moderator's guide later in this chapter) of the subject matter to be covered. He or she should commit the topics to memory before the interview, and should use the outline during the session only as a reminder of content areas omitted or covered incompletely. This allows flexibility in the flow of the discussion while ensuring that key topics and issues are not omitted entirely.
- Sensitivity: The moderator must be able to identify, as the group discussion progresses, the informational level on which it is being conducted and to determine whether this level is appropriate for the subject under review. Sensitive areas will frequently produce superficial responses as participants attempt to avoid deeper areas while appearing to offer some minimal degree of information. Depth is ordinarily achieved when participants become emotionally involved, to some degree, in the discussion. The moderator needs to notice when participants begin to "show how they feel" about the subject, rather than simply telling what they think about it. Experienced moderators know how to engage participants and help them express such feelings, without antagonizing or offending their sensibilities. Research sponsors need to be aware that moderators cannot work miracles in this regard, and there are a number of issues—social status, income, sexuality, religion, and politics—about which it is difficult to elicit reliable information.
- Knowledge of subject matter or willingness to obtain it: Although moderators do not necessarily need to have knowledge specific to the subject of study—they cannot, after all, be experts on everything—it is important that moderators appear well informed and that simple gaffes are avoided. Many focus groups are run with various "expert" participants (doctors, attorneys, computer programmers), and they will quickly notice if a moderator is the least informed person in the room. Even when the target participant is the proverbial "person on the street," the moderator should be able to answer basic questions about the product or service being studied.
- Creativity: Focus groups are, at base, interactions among groups of people—interactions that, by their nature, are unpredictable. Just as a professor can teach the same class twice in one day and have one go superbly and the other be a disaster, the same can and does happen with focus groups. It is therefore crucial that the moderator be creative, willing to spontaneously change course to stimulate a group when the discussion is not productive. Moderators who insist on sticking to a preset script may waste a great deal of group time and client resources in the process.

6.1d Choosing a Moderator

A question often bandied about among researchers is whether the gender of the moderator influences the effectiveness of the group session in any substantively important way. There are two views on this issue. The first holds that the gender of the moderator should be the same as that of the group members (or of the majority of them, if the group is composed of both genders) to ensure proper rapport. Although this was standard throughout much of the 20th century, today is it considered somewhat parochial to assume that people of different genders cannot establish a proper focus group atmosphere. The second view is that the gender of the moderator should be different from that of the group members, under the premise that the participants will be less likely to assume the moderator shares their views and knowledge base and so will be more expansive and explanatory in their responses. Regardless of one's view on this issue, there is no question that overall personality and generated comfort level are more important to running a successful group than social categories like age, gender, or ethnicity, except in rare cases where these are themselves crucial elements of the study (e.g., a new magazine targeted explicitly at women or a pharmaceutical for a condition specific to older people).

Moderators frequently need to avail themselves of special techniques to ensure that the group's limited time is used productively. For example, when one person tries to dominate the discussion, the moderator can stop the proceedings and poll each participant regarding the issue at hand. This technique is also useful to encourage reluctant, reticent, or shy participants to express their views. To obtain closure and tentative conclusions, at the close of the session, each person can be asked to summarize what the group has determined or resolved. Another useful technique involves contacting each participant a day (or up to a week) after the completed session and having them express their viewpoints again. Many times, their viewpoints change with the passage of time, because they have reflected on the issue or they have gathered additional information. Permission to do such follow-up interviews should be secured ahead of time, usually at the conclusion of the group session.

A final issue concerns whether the *same* moderator should directly conduct, or at least oversee, all group sessions on a particular topic. Most researchers believe so—more strongly than in the case of survey or even telephone interview research. There are several reasons for this. First and foremost, the very substance of the focus group hinges critically on the moderator's ability to direct the discussion; more subtle "intangibles" such as tone of voice, likeability, and sincerity; and a host of other qualities impossible to standardize across moderators. Furthermore, with each session the moderator becomes more effective and gains additional insight into the analysis and interpretation of the sessions. Usually, initial sessions will raise as many questions as they settle. An experienced moderator will know how to make a new session "pick up where the last one left off" without confusing participants so that the sessions have maximal cumulative impact in terms of generated behavioral and attitudinal information.

Moderator's Guide

The moderator's guide is a discussion agenda used by the moderator during group sessions. It serves two purposes: It provides a detailed outline of the issues to be addressed in the discussion, including the approach, the types of questions to be raised, the sequence of issues, and any stimuli to be introduced (this is invaluable in situations where multiple moderators must be used). It also serves as a memory aid for the moderator so that all groups follow the same general sequence and no topics of interest are inadvertently omitted.

The moderator's guide requires a thorough understanding of the objectives of the study. It is generally prepared using question or topic areas rather than specific questions. Guides often begin with the most general topics and then move to specific topics, so the researcher must anticipate whether the participants may take positions on a general topic that will prejudice their perception of new ideas, products, or concepts. Moderators will be more effective and insightful if they are involved in drafting the guide; this reduces reliability problems, especially with multiple sessions, and enables a moderator to better understand the research objectives and how the findings will be used. Figure 6.3 is an example of a moderator's guide.

6.1e Analyzing Focus Groups

Figuring out what "people are really saying"—doing so objectively and rigorously—is a dramatically more complex enterprise than working with numerical data stemming from a survey research project. The vast arsenal of analytic techniques available for numerical analysis does not work on words, at least not without substantial processing on the part of the researcher. Consider an extended real example to see how this might go in practice.

Figure 6.3 Guide for Focus Group Sessions on Automobile Insurance

1. Ask, "Do you currently have insurance on the automobile you own (or use most)?"
   a. Ask those who do have it, "Why?" Also ask the following questions.
      - "What are the most important reasons for your having automobile insurance?"
      - "What are some other reasons?"
      - "What reasons have you heard—for instance, through advertising—that you think are *not* important?"
      - "Have you ever driven without insurance?"
      - "What were the circumstances? Have you done this often?"
      - "Would you do it again?"

      Ask the others in the group, "What do you think? Would you drive without insurance?"
   b. Ask those who are not presently carrying insurance the following questions.
      - "Why do you not have automobile insurance?"
      - "Have you ever had it?"
      - "Why did you drop it?"
      - "Do you expect to obtain insurance at some point? When?"
2. Turn the discussion to types of auto insurance coverage.
   a. Say, "We are interested in your experiences with various types of insurance, and how you view them. For example, when you hear the term 'collision insurance,' what do you think that means?" Try to get the group to define it, but make sure they know that it means insurance that pays for damage to the owner's car as a result of an accident, no matter whose fault. Also be sure to follow up with these questions:
      - "Do you presently have collision insurance?"
      - "Why?"
        (Probe.) "Have you ever had it?"
        (If yes.) "Why did you drop it?"
      - "Do you expect to obtain it again at some point?"

      Encourage discussion on the merits of this type of insurance between group members who do have it and those who don't. Focus, if necessary, on such issues as cost, coverage, difficulty of obtaining it, and other inputs into the purchase decision.
   b. Repeat the same questions for the following topics.
      - *Liability insurance* (bodily injury and property damage). Insurance that pays for damage done by a driver to other cars or property or to other people.
      - *Comprehensive insurance* (fire, theft, etc.). Insurance that pays for loss or damage to a car as a result of fire, theft, natural hazards, vandalism, and so forth.
      - *Medical payments insurance*. Insurance that pays medical expenses of guests in the car.
3. When the discussion winds down, ask "Is there anything else pertaining to auto insurance that you would like to tell us about?" If not, thank the participants and instruct them on how to obtain compensation and exit the facility.

Suppose your boss approaches you with a new assignment—to prepare a report on the results of six recently conducted focus groups with business managers regarding the use and purchase of personal computers for their businesses. The six session (video) recordings consist of two focus groups of small businesses (with 1 to 50 employees), two focus groups of medium-sized businesses (with 51 to 500 employees), and two focus groups of large businesses (with more than 500 employees). Each recording contains more than 2 hours of comments, from a total of 48 people. You sit back in your chair and wonder, "How can I analyze more than 12 hours of focus group recordings? Should I just watch them first, then make notes, and watch them again? Should I involve others? Should I have them transcribed first?" Instead of sitting in your chair asking yourself rhetorical questions, you would do well to follow the steps given here.

Step 1. Review the Research Purpose

Although the purpose of focus groups can vary, the primary purpose is to build a foundation for the conclusive research phase of the project. Focus groups provide a wealth of insights regarding *how and why* buyers purchase products. This information can be used to formulate structured questions and to determine the sequence of these questions in the questionnaire, if one is planned.

Step 2. Thoroughly Study the Group Discussions

The raw data of focus groups are the tones, emotions, body movements, and verbatim comments involved in the group interaction. Consequently, the researcher must first deeply study the focus group videos to become familiar with the issues explored in the group sessions. A verbatim transcript of each videotape is a useful reference source for the researcher in this process. If verbatim transcripts are not available, repeated viewing of the tapes is required. At this stage, the researcher should be concerned about developing an understanding of the group dynamics and should begin to form general impressions about the topics discussed. These general impressions will become more formalized in the next stage of the analysis.

Step 3. Create Categories

The first task in categorization is to develop a demographic profile of the respondent base. Figure 6.4 presents such a profile for the Personal Computer focus groups. The demographic information can come

Figure 6.4 Demographic Profile

Number	1	2	3	4	48
Respondent	Eric	Regine	Ashley	Bill	Samir
Firm size	14	20	993	180	330
Number of PCs owned	2	10	48	56	125
Type of business	Wholesale	Insurance	Manufacturing	Retail	Insurance

from the screening questionnaire used to select the focus group participants or from facts collected on a questionnaire administered before the start of the focus group session. It is important that these questions not be seen as invasive or prying, lest that color the subsequent group dynamics.

The second task in categorization is to develop a respondent profile based on what is observed in the focus group sessions. The moderator's guide serves as a useful starting point for developing categories. In the example, the following issues were covered in the moderator's guide and discussed actively by the participants in all six groups:

1. Compatibility
2. Service and support
3. Price
4. Networking

Figure 6.5 presents selected comments by respondents on the important issues explored in the group sessions. Each respondent's comments on particular issues were categorized by the researcher as (1) very important, (2) somewhat important, or (3) not very important, although more or fewer categories could easily have been used. For example, Eric's comments on the "service and support" issue were classified (subjectively, by the researcher) as "very important" (see Figure 6.5). Each of the 48 respondents was

Figure 6.5 Selected Comments by Respondents

	Eric
Service and support	"Fast and expert computer service is critical to our business because we cannot afford to have our computers or networks fail at any time during business hours. If the system goes down, we lose customers."
Classification	Very important
	Regine
Compatibility	"At this early stage of the company's development, price is the number one factor in buying computer equipment. Compatibility just doesn't figure into the purchase decision."
Classification	Not important
	Ashley
Networking	"We just upgraded our network this past month; it was a lot of work, and I'm waiting to see tangible benefits. I'm convinced that the upgrade was the right way to go long-term, but just haven't seen the evidence as of yet."
Classification	Somewhat important

classified on each of the issues discussed in the focus groups. Respondents who did not have opinions, or whose opinions were not observable on the videos, were categorized as such.

Step 4. Identify Potential Relationships

Once the researcher has classified the various comments made by individual respondents, they can be analyzed as nominal (i.e., categorical) variables. Relationships in this "qualitative data matrix" can be explored with simple cross-tabulations of variables. Figure 6.6 presents two such relationships between (1) firm size and compatibility and (2) firm size and service and support. Although it is possible to use sophisticated categorical data analytic methods on this data set, the researcher must remember the limitations of the data collected and the purpose of the analysis. This is not a quantitative data set on which inferences about a larger population can be drawn; the "data" here was generated based on the researcher's *subjective interpretation* of the focus group transcriptions. Also bear in mind that the main purpose of exploratory research is to develop insights and hypotheses that can be tested for validity in the conclusive research phase of the research project. So, although complex statistical analyses are possible, they are unlikely to be useful at this stage of the project and can safely be saved for data resulting from a survey designed with the focus group results as a guide.

Step 5. Add the Finishing Touches

The focus group report combines results from the previous stages into a "deliverable" document. Although this report can be organized in many ways, the following is never far off the mark in terms of client expectations and is usually a fine prototype to follow:

- Executive summary
- Research purpose
- Methodology
- Results and hypothesis identified
- Implications for further study
- Appendix of supplemental materials (raw data summaries, analysis output, research protocols, etc.)

6.1f Variations on Focus Groups

Focus groups, when used extensively and rigorously, can entail substantial costs, time, and team effort, despite being crucial in most research projects. There are, however, a number of variations on the

Figure 6.6 Cross-Tabulation Analysis

Compatibility, frequency (%)

	High	Medium	Low	Total
Large	8(50)	6(38)	2(12)	16(100)
Medium	6(38)	6(38)	4(24)	16(100)
Small	3(19)	5(32)	8(50)	16(100)
Total	17	17	14	48

Hypothesis: Large businesses are more concerned with compatibility than are small and medium businesses.

Service, frequency (%)

	High	Medium	Low	Total
Large	5(32)	4(25)	7(44)	16(100)
Medium	4(25)	8(50)	4(25)	16(100)
Small	9(56)	4(25)	3(19)	16(100)
Total	18	16	14	48

Hypothesis: Small businesses are more concerned with service and support than are large and medium businesses.

standard focus group that could be equally informative, depending on the nature of the overall research project, allotted budget, and prior experience. These include the following:

1. Minigroups: The group consists of a moderator and four to five participants, rather than the usual eight to ten participants. The minigroup may be especially effective for private or sensitive issues or if greater depth of probing is sought and is less costly on a per group basis (although more on a per respondent basis).
2. Two-way focus groups: One target group listens in on a related group to gain an understanding or greater appreciation of an issue. The target group then holds its own discussion. Because this technique requires a good deal of time for the second group and can be tricky to analyze, it is less commonly used than other methods discussed here.
3. Dual-moderator group: Two moderators share or split the responsibilities of moderating the group, with the intention of allowing both to give more attention to the actual group discussion and to probing the selected issues. Often, the moderators will deliberately "tag team" participants, either disagreeing with each other to encourage side-taking or adamantly agreeing to gauge participant reaction.
4. Client–participant groups: Clients attend the focus group itself and are identified to the participants. The clients take part in the discussion and can answer questions or provide clarification. In such cases, clients must be carefully briefed to prevent antagonism, overreaction to negative feedback, and biasing participants toward positive reactions.
5. Online focus groups: The Internet has allowed discussions among participants who are not physically co-located, using high-speed connections and low-cost video conferencing equipment. Although such groups are inexpensive and can be set up quickly, the ability to closely monitor body language and participant interaction is greatly compromised. Because of this, they are typically used when budgets are highly constrained, speedy feedback is paramount, or it is early in the research process so that more formal groups can be conducted afterward. *Marketing Research Focus 6.1* discusses the uses and future potential of online focus groups in greater detail.

6.1g Advantages of Focus Groups

The major advantage of the focus group interview rests on the premise that if you want to understand your consumers, you simply have to listen to them, auditing the so-called voice of the customer. There is much to be gained from listening to consumers describe a product in their own vernacular and from having them portray how they come to buy products and how they perceive product benefits and limitations in language that makes sense to them because they selected it themselves. Data such as these highlight potential problems and opportunities of which the researcher was wholly unaware and can identify possible marketing strategies unlike those used previously.

In comparison to other data collection techniques, the focus group interview has a number of specific, tangible advantages:

1. Synergism: The combined effect of the group will produce a wider range of information, insight, and ideas than will an accumulation of the responses of a number of individuals when these replies are secured privately.
2. Snowballing: A bandwagon effect can operate in a group interview situation, in that a comment by one individual often triggers a chain of responses from the other participants.
3. Stimulation: Usually after a brief introductory period, the respondents get "turned on." They want to express their ideas and expose their feelings as the general level of excitement over the topic increases in the group, presuming the moderator is skillful enough to make this happen.
4. Security: The participants can usually find comfort in the group as they discover that their feelings are not greatly different from those of other participants. With this encouragement, they become more willing to express their ideas and feelings. They will also not feel especially cowed by the presence of the moderator and can choose to be silent when needed without inducing painful lapses in the interview.
5. Spontaneity: Because individuals are not required to answer questions in a group interview, their responses can be more spontaneous and less conventional. This should provide a more accurate picture of their positions on some issues.

Marketing Research Focus 6.1

Online Focus Groups

Online focus groups have been slow to replace face-to-face and telephone focus groups. Although the Internet offers easier access for participation, a greater sense of psychological "safety" for discussing sensitive issues, and the option to choose between real-time chat room environments and asynchronous bulletin board environments (which allow flexibility of time as well as space), the loss of the opportunity to observe cues from facial expressions, body language, and tone of voice continued to weigh heavily in favor of in-person focus group meetings for years after Internet access became commonplace.

As broadband and online video and audio technology catch on and attain ubiquity on par with telephone or cable service, some of these in-person cues can be recouped, although at the risk of biasing participant selection toward those who have easy access to these technologies in their homes. Consequently, online focus groups are more frequently used in high-tech industries, where the potential technology bias favors selection of the desired target population.

As a supplemental tool in the qualitative research toolbox, online focus groups reach markets that are difficult or impossible to recruit by traditional methods: those of especially low incidence (which must be recruited across large geographic regions) and topics that are particularly sensitive. Online groups are also often used in conjunction with traditional qualitative research, particularly as pre- and postphases.

Other disadvantages of online focus groups are greater difficulty in securing the identity of participants and a lack of depth sometimes characteristic of Internet communications. These problems have so far proven to be mostly surmountable. Screening processes are distinct in character for Internet research; rather than a marked contrast between "depth" in person and "lack of depth" online, this, too, is more a difference in character or culture. Participants and moderators need to be comfortable with online sharing and familiar with cues other than sight and sound. As long as this cultural requirement does not introduce a substantial bias to the sample, the process itself is workable. Researchers and moderators need to be especially vigilant to discern such cross-cultural biases because they can be quite subtle.

Because bulletin board groups take place over longer durations of time, at the leisure of the participants, they can sometimes result in depths of involvement and insights *greater* than those possible during an in-person meeting if appropriate care is taken in their analysis. In real-time groups, the depth issue is more of a problem, particularly because participation may be highly affected by typing speed. Despite this, online groups have less of a problem with domination by strong or overbearing personalities because the Internet reduces the impact of intimidating social factors and participants are composing and submitting responses independently of one another. This can sometimes introduce odd asynchronies, where topics appear to change among some participants while others lag, or a splintering of topics among participants scrutinizing the comments only of those in the same conversational subgroup; in some cases, transcripts can resemble a cocktail party in which all conversations in the room are indexed by time but not who addressed what to whom.

For all text-based communication, adequate keyboard skills are essential for both participants and moderator. In addition to the general qualifications for a good focus group moderator, an online moderator needs to be able to establish leadership at the outset, be thoroughly familiar with the software being used, and be able to handle multiple simultaneous inputs. Online moderators cannot avail themselves of subtle auditory or visual cues like altering tone of voice or enacting hand motions, so they must rely on aids built into the system software. As such, technical issues, such as how to reenter the group if a connection is lost, need to be explained carefully and extensively before commencing. When participants review Web sites or complete requested tasks in their home, the moderator should instruct them to indicate when they have completed the task but to withhold all comments until the rest of the group has returned.

Online qualitative research technologies continue to develop rapidly. Although traditional methodologies are unlikely to evaporate overnight, they are increasingly complemented with online counterparts. Some marketing researchers have even found that developing relationships through Internet "blogs" aids their qualitative research phase. As technological capacities increase and become more widespread, and as the corresponding cultural changes develop and become more widely accepted, qualitative research will evolve accordingly.

Sources: Creamer, Matthew (2005), "Slowly, Marketers Learn How to Let Go and Let Blog," *Advertising Age* (October 31). Vol.76 Issue 44, p1–35.

Silverman, George, "A Comparison between Face-to-Face Focus Groups, Telephone Focus Groups and Online Focus Groups," Market Navigation, Inc. http://www.mnav.com/onlinetablesort.htm.

Sweet, Casey (2001), "Designing and Conducting Virtual Focus Groups," *Qualitative Market Research: An International Journal* (June). Volume 4, Number 3, 2001, pp. 130–135(6).

6. Serendipity: It is more often the case in a group rather than in an individual interview that some idea will "drop out of the blue." Moderators can employ various techniques to encourage such thinking "outside the box," techniques that can seem contrived or onerous one-on-one.

7. Specialization: The group interview allows the use of a more highly trained interviewer because a number of individuals are being "interviewed" simultaneously. Although the cost of the interviewer is higher, the per-respondent cost is quite a bit lower.
8. Scientific scrutiny: The group interview allows closer scrutiny of the data collection process in two ways: (1) several observers can witness the session, and (2) it can be recorded for later playback and analysis. Although recording is possible with individual interviews, it can bias the process, because the prospect of being recorded individually often spooks some respondents, sometimes to the point of refusing to participate.
9. Structure: The group interview affords more flexibility than the individual interview with regard to the topics covered and the depth with which they are treated. Deficiencies in knowledge or willingness on the part of some participants can be compensated for through the expertise and openness of others, keeping the discussion flowing even through rough topics.
10. Speed: Because a number of individuals are being interviewed at the same time, the group interview speeds up the data collection and analysis process. With individual interviews, there are often a large number of blind alleys, areas of discussion that turn up nothing useful, but this is rare in group settings.

6.1h Disadvantages of Focus Groups

A major disadvantage of the focus group interview is that the decision maker cannot use the evidence gained, at great time and financial cost, as part of conclusive research. The evidence is not projectable to a target segment for two reasons. First, despite the care used in recruitment, the sample should not be considered representative of the target segment: quantitative statements cannot be made regarding the significance of the research findings, even if many groups are run. Second, the evidence itself is highly dependent on the experience, style, and perception of the moderator, as well as on other observers and participants (if the moderator is superb, this could be advantageous, but it is still something for the researcher to monitor closely). A special danger is that the decision-maker may try to use the exploratory findings as conclusive evidence to support preconceived notions. Sadly, when confronted with a mass of verbal statements from dozens of participants, it is seldom difficult to cherry-pick just those that appear to support a pet conclusion. This must be strenuously avoided.

As in any area of human endeavor, there are those who will compromise proper research procedures for various reasons, including personal gain. With the focus group interview, these improper procedures involve improper or biased recruitment of participants, provision of a poor physical environment, and use of an unskilled moderator. Experienced moderators can offer valuable advice on best practices for conducting focus groups and should be involved in the process to ensure that they can do their job effectively, including the difficult task of post-group analysis.

The focus group is an exploratory research technique that can be extremely valuable in developing hypotheses regarding problems and opportunities, facilitating the development of a clear statement of the decision problem, and stimulating the creative process so as to formulate alternative courses of action. Conclusive research is the next logical step in the testing of these hypotheses and the evaluation of the courses of action. In special circumstances, the decision-maker's experience and judgment may be sufficient to enable selection of a course of action without conclusive research evidence. Typically, however, such evidence is mandatory, and the decision-maker could be making a serious error by assuming that the focus group interview provides evidence of a conclusive nature, a subject treated extensively later in this chapter.

6.1i Depth Interview

The **depth interview** may be defined as an unstructured personal interview that uses extensive probing to get a single respondent to talk freely and to express detailed beliefs and feelings on a topic. The purpose of this technique is to get below the respondent's surface reactions and to discover the more fundamental reasons underlying the respondent's attitudes and behavior.

depth interview
A qualitative technique in which the interviewer conducts a semistructured conversation with a respondent in an effort to accurately gauge attitudes, emotions, beliefs, and feelings.

The depth interview can last an hour or more, and the interviewer typically has committed to memory the outline of topics to be covered. The actual wording and sequencing of questions are left to the discretion of the interviewer, who tries to identify general areas for discussion and then encourages the respondent to discuss the topic of interest freely and in depth. The interviewer probes responses of interest by encouraging elaboration, asking questions such as "That's interesting; can you tell me more?" or "Why do you say that?" until a satisfactory level of detail is elicited.

The interviewer plays a critical role in the success of the depth interview technique. It is the interviewer's responsibility to create an environment where the respondent feels relaxed and free to present beliefs and feelings without fear of being criticized or misunderstood. As in the focus group interview, the interviewer's role is central, crucial to the quality of the eventual outcome. The interviewer must probe into attitudes, beliefs, and feelings behind simple, initially offered answers, avoiding the appearance of superiority; remaining objective; and encouraging extensive, honest responses.

The depth interview, like the focus group interview, is used primarily for exploratory research. The technique is useful in developing hypotheses, defining decision problems, and formulating courses of action. The individual interview can be useful when the marketing problem relates to particularly confidential, sensitive, or potentially embarrassing issues or when group pressure or norms would affect the responses.

experience survey
A type of individual or depth interview with a selective cross section of respondents familiar with the problem.

The **experience survey** is a type of individual (depth) interview. In an experience survey, the researcher is interested in the views of a selective cross section of people associated with the research problem. Participants are sought for their ability to articulate responses, as well as their familiarity with the problem. For example, executives and distributors on different levels in a retail industry may be questioned on the effectiveness of a distribution channel. The research objective is simply to seek insights into the problem at hand, so the survey is usually informal and the questions open-ended.

One advantage of the depth interview over the focus group interview relates to the greater depth of insight that can be uncovered and the ability to associate the response directly with the respondent, and not to that person having been led there by others in the group. In the focus group interview, it can be difficult to determine which respondent made a particular response, that is, who merely hinted at it vs. who articulated it precisely and unambiguously; such are the complexities of having to make rigorous sense of verbal responses. Another advantage of the depth interview is that the interviewer can develop—if the interviewer is suitably skillful—a high level of rapport with the respondent, which results in responses that are given more freely than may be possible in a focus group, where there is the ubiquitous risk of judgment by others. It is often joked that depth interviews are to focus groups as psychoanalysis is to group therapy, and the general comparison is quite apt.

Still, the depth interview is used far less frequently in marketing research than are focus groups. Among the main concerns is that a depth interview's success rests on the skills and experience of the interviewer to a far greater extent than it does with other techniques. That being the case, it is especially problematic to attempt to meld or average results across different interviewers; at the same time, having a single interviewer work with dozens of respondents is enormously demanding and time-consuming. That there are few highly qualified interviewers, and those who are qualified command relatively large salaries, has prevented the technique from gaining wide currency as a regular research tool. The length of the interview, combined with high interviewer cost, dictates that the number of people interviewed in a project be kept manageable. The small sample size and complete reliance on the interviewer for analysis and interpretation are important limitations that restrict use of this technique to special problem situations.

6.2 Exploratory Research Worldwide

As with conclusive research, what constitutes exploratory research is substantively similar in the United States and in the rest of the world. However, there are clear differences in the *implementation* of research methodologies such as focus groups and in-depth interviews. These differences result from variations in cultural and infrastructures characteristics among countries. In the United Kingdom, for example, the majority of focus groups are held in interviewers' homes rather than in specially designed laboratory facilities. Consequently, clients rarely attend group sessions. The typical group size is smaller (six to eight people) in the United Kingdom. In Asia, focus groups are a popular form of exploratory research, reflecting Asian marketers' belief that the focus group offers the best approach to understanding consumers. The implementation of focus groups in Asia is similar to that in the United States, with the exception that moderators cannot presume the sort of familiarity characterizing informal and even professional relationships in the United States. Outside the Western Hemisphere, mixing genders is often less common, and groups can require a moderator who is not only the same gender but also older than the participants to elicit the requisite respect necessary to guiding the group. Generally, it is wise to recruit experienced moderators locally so that prevailing customs are considered in conducting the group.

6.3 Quantitative Techniques for Conclusive Research

Having considered exploratory research in depth, we now look at the next step in the research process: using the findings from the exploratory phase to engage in conclusive research. The qualitative data gathered during exploratory research are used in formulating problems and in stimulating the creative process of identifying alternative courses of action. In short, qualitative data can provide an intuitive understanding of the problem. Using this intuitive understanding as a guide, the decision problem can be clearly stated and alternative courses of action can be specified, after which the conclusive research phase of the research project can be initiated.

Conclusive research involves a systematic and objective process through which a target market is sampled and responses are measured using a structured data collection technique. (Sampling issues are deferred to later chapters, where they are treated in depth.) In conclusive research, we focus on conclusive research data collection techniques: what types of information we are looking for and how we go about getting it. In so doing, we begin to discuss the research design stage, where the market researcher begins the *quantitative* evaluation process for the alternative courses of action. The resulting conclusive research results will be statistically and scientifically valid, legitimizing their use for a variety of marketing research purposes, primarily forecasting the success or failure of various managerial alternatives.

In a fundamental sense, all marketing decision making is concerned with taking action today so that future objectives can be accomplished. In this context, marketing research can be viewed as a forecasting technique designed to facilitate the process of predicting market behavior. With this in mind, we now focus on the process of gathering primary data directly from respondents. The types of data that can be obtained from respondents—for use in forecasting market behavior—include past behavior, attitudes, and respondent characteristics; we look at each in turn.

6.3a Past Behavior

Evidence regarding the respondent's past behavior has wide usage as a predictor of future behavior. In our personal activities, we all use evidence of past behavior to predict the future behavior of our friends, relatives, and co-workers. In similar fashion, a marketing research study can gather evidence on a respondent's behavior regarding purchase and use of a product or brand for the purpose of predicting future behavior. Each of the following constitutes evidence frequently gathered to elucidate individuals' past behavior: What was purchased, used, or both? How much was purchased or used? How was it purchased or used? Where was it purchased or used? When was it purchased or used? Who purchased or used it? And so on. Any circumstance concerning the purchase or use of a product, including substitute (competitive) or complementary products, can be asked about directly. Understanding past behavior involves many dimensions; researchers must be sensitive to the key behavioral dimensions relevant to predicting future behavior when specifying the data required to meet a study's information needs.

6.3b Attitudes

Attitudes are important in marketing because of the presumed relationship between attitudes and behavior. Simply put, we don't just do things but do them for certain reasons, reasons that reflect our underlying attitudes and intentions. Attitudinal data are used to identify market segments, develop "positioning" strategies, and evaluate advertising programs, among other goals. Consequently, they are among the most sought-after respondent data in marketing research.

As discussed in depth in Chapter 4, an attitude is considered to have three main components, a *cognitive* component, an *affective* component, and a *behavioral* component, and attitudinal measurement through self-reports is accomplished via a variety of scaling techniques. Here, we focus on additional specific techniques for identifying the nature of attitudes, measuring them, and connecting attitudes and eventual behavior statistically, with an eye toward prediction.

6.3c Respondent Characteristics

The phrase *respondent characteristics* refers to descriptions of respondents along particular dimensions of interest, including demographic, socioeconomic, and psychological variables. For many products, such variables are known to correlate well with eventual purchase behavior. In addition, variables such as age, gender, marital status, family size, income, occupation, and education level have been found useful in sample stratification (see Section 8.5) and validation.

A popular way of describing a respondent is in terms of *lifestyle*, defined as a distinctive mode of living of a society or of a segment of a society. Lifestyle research focuses on respondents' activities, interests, and opinions (**A-I-O items**) and on demographic characteristics. Examples of A-I-O items are listed in Table 6.1.

A-I-O items
In lifestyle research, the respondents' activities, interests, and opinions.

The term psychographics is closely related to the concept of lifestyle, although it is a broader term that includes the lifestyle concept. It is often formally defined along the following lines:

> *Psychographics* is a quantitative research procedure that attempts to explain why people behave as they do and why they hold their current attitudes. It seeks to take quantitative research beyond demographic, socioeconomic, and user-or-nonuser analysis, employing three additional variables: lifestyle and both psychological and product benefits.

Note that psychographics is a *quantitative* tool, its goal being to help categorize and measure aspects of how people behave, believe, and reason for the explicit purposes of understanding and prediction. Although qualitative techniques (focus groups and interviews) can help generate psychographic categories, they are not the natural environment of psychographic measurement.

6.4 Methods of Collecting Respondent Data

The two basic methods of collecting data from respondents are communication and observation. Both are used widely and offer complementary benefits.

6.4a Communication Method

The communication method of data collection is based on the direct questioning of respondents. It is quite logical, if you want to know what brand of soup they buy, which television programs they view, or why they shop at a particular store, to ask respondents these questions directly because (unlike attitudes,

Table 6.1 Lifestyle Characteristics

Activities	Interests	Opinions
Work	Family	Themselves
Hobbies	Home	Social issues
Social events	Job	Politics
Vacations	Community	Business
Entertainment	Recreation	Economics
Club membership	Fashion	Education
Community	Food	Products
Shopping	Media	Future
Sports	Achievements	Culture

emotions, and intentions) they have "correct" answers. Such questions may be asked verbally or in writing, and the responses may be in either form. The data collection instrument typically used in this process, as we have previously discussed, is a *questionnaire*. The questionnaire has come to be the predominant data collection instrument in marketing research. It is estimated that more than half of the U.S. public has participated in one or more research studies of this nature, and Internet users have overwhelmingly been asked to take part.

Advantages of the Communication Method

The main advantage of the communication method is its *versatility*, the ability of the method to collect data on a range of information needs. The majority of marketing decision problems involve people: what they do, think, plan, and feel. Consequently, information needs overwhelmingly focus on people's past behavior, attitudes, and characteristics. The communication method can be used quite successfully to gather data in all of these areas. Additional advantages relate to the speed and cost of communication, as compared to the observation method. The communication method is faster in that it provides more control over the data collection process; the researcher does not have to predict when and where the behavior will occur nor to wait for it to. For example, it is faster and cheaper to ask a respondent about the purchase of a dishwasher than to try to anticipate and observe the purchase.

Disadvantages of the Communication Method

There are three important limitations to the communication method. The first relates to the respondent's *unwillingness to provide the desired data*. The respondent may refuse to take the time to be interviewed, refuse to respond to particular questions, or provide data that is deliberately vague (a particular problem with open-ended questions). The second limitation concerns the respondent's *inability to provide the data*. The respondent may not recall the facts in question, may never have known them, or may attempt to extrapolate from what is known, often inaccurately. The third limitation involves the *influence of the questioning process on the responses*. For example, respondents may bias their responses in order to give a socially acceptable answer or to please the interviewer; if the study is not carefully designed, information provided in one question may affect responses to a later one (the *Special Expert Feature* in Chapter 7 addressing biases in self-reports covers this problem in detail with specific examples).

Communicating with Respondents

The four types of communication approaches available for obtaining data from respondents are the personal interview, the telephone interview, the mail interview, and the Internet-based interview. The first three of these communication approaches have traditionally been widely used in marketing research. The use of Internet-based methodologies is growing as fast Internet access becomes ubiquitous in homes and offices, particularly so wirelessly.

6.4b Personal Interview

In the personal interview, an interviewer asks questions of one or more respondents in a face-to-face situation. The interviewer's task is to contact the respondent or respondents, ask the questions, and record the responses. The questions must be asked in a clear manner and recorded accurately. The recording of responses can take place either during or after the interview. The face-to-face interviewing process may cause respondents to bias their responses, for example, because of a desire to please or impress the interviewer or to avoid socially undesirable responses. (The potential for introduction of bias into personal interview data because of social motivations will be discussed in more detail in Section 6.4f on criteria for selecting a communication medium.)

6.4c Telephone Interview

In the telephone interview, an interviewer asks questions of one or more respondents, as one might guess, over the phone. Telephone interviewing is the most widely used of the three traditional communication media. It is popular because of its efficient and economical procedures, its application to a range

scalability
The ability for a project or process to be substantially expanded as required by the researcher; some methods, such as conducting one-on-one interviews using the same interviewer, are not easily scalable, whereas others, such as Internet-based surveys, are.

of information needs, and its scalability (i.e., the ability to hire more telephone interviewers if a project expands or needs quicker completion, without requiring dedicated physical facilities, as for a personal interview). With the telephone interview, the lower degree of social interaction—specifically, the lack of visual information and nuance—between the interviewer and the respondent reduces the potential for bias, compared with a personal interview on the same topic. The basic limitations of the telephone interview relate to the limited amount of data that can be obtained, the impossibility of accurately recording nonverbal information, and the potential bias that can result from an incomplete listing of the target population.

6.4d Mail Interview

In the mail interview, a questionnaire is sent by post to the respondent, and the completed questionnaire is returned by mail to the research organization. The mail interview is roughly as popular as the personal interview but less so than the telephone interview. Mail interviews are flexible in their application and relatively low in cost—*if* response rates are suitably high—and they lack the potential for bias resulting from the interviewer–respondent interaction. Their major disadvantage relates to the problem of nonresponse error. In practice, this is a major limitation for two reasons. First, it is difficult to ensure in advance that some specified number of total responses is received. Second, it is impossible to ensure that those who return the questionnaire are representative of the sample that was asked to, much less the population of interest; after all, those who returned the questionnaire differ in one obvious way from those who did not: they are more likely to return questionnaires. Although this may appear a trivial observation, if that subset is more helpful or kind, their responses may also be less critical.

Many approaches to distributing and collecting the questionnaire can be used. The questionnaire can be left and/or retrieved by an individual rather than being sent by mail. It can be distributed in magazines and newspapers. Warranty cards packaged with products provide an opportunity to collect data regarding the characteristics of the purchaser and the purchase decision process. With proper prior permission, they can be left in the workplace, in various business locations, or in public places. Office fax machines have created an opportunity for a "hybrid" mail interview, where the questionnaire is faxed to the respondent and faxed back when complete. Although this is expedient, it is crucial to obtain consent beforehand (e.g., by e-mail), because unsolicited faxing is a strong breach of business etiquette.

6.4e Internet-based Methods

Because of the growing access to the Internet in all corners of commercial and private life, Internet-based interviews are an increasingly popular option. This is especially true in efforts to reach business professionals, who rely on the Internet for communication to a greater degree than any other medium. Web-based interviews can be used to ask for open-ended responses and to assess qualitative issues. The respondent can take time in responding to the questions, resulting in better-quality comments. An advantage of Web-based interviews is their ability to branch and skip questions automatically based on initial responses.

Modern e-survey systems allow researchers enormous flexibility over question rotation (counterbalancing), the use of contingent questions or responses (i.e., prior responses are used to determine future possibilities), branching, and other elements exceptionally difficult to carry out using paper-based surveys; coding and analysis are also substantially simplified because responses are automatically placed in a database, which can be queried for any pattern of responses. In this manner, respondents are not exposed to irrelevant questions, and compiling their responses is automatic, with essentially zero errors other than those made by the respondents themselves. The necessity for access to the Internet limits the available respondent pool and could result in sampling error if convenience samples are used, such as when a request for responses is placed in a particular Internet newsgroup or on Web sites catering to narrow interests. Still, Internet-based interviewing is by far the most rapidly growing methodology in all of marketing research and is poised to supplant other methods in the coming decade.

Internet surveys can be preferable when a convenience sample is adequate, when the target population is a list of people for whom e-mail addresses are known, when the target population is too small of a percentage to efficiently contact by traditional methods, when the sample size is large enough to justify the higher start-up costs, when the survey touches on highly sensitive issues, when the survey includes many open-ended questions where electronic input saves on transcription costs, and when the survey includes digital interactive elements.

6.4f Criteria for Selecting the Communication Approach

In evaluating which communication approach best meets the needs of a research project, several criteria are relevant, namely, versatility, cost, time, sample control, quantity of data, quality of data, and response rate. The importance assigned to these criteria, all of which we now discuss in detail, will vary with the specific needs of the research project.

Versatility

Versatility refers to the ability to adapt the data collection process to the special needs of the study's information needs or the particular respondent. In this regard, the personal interview is the most versatile of the four communication approaches, followed by telephone and Web-based interviews; the mail interview is the least versatile.

The personal interview has high versatility in that the interviewing process involves a face-to-face relationship between the respondent and the interviewer. The latter can explain and clarify complex questions, administer lengthy or tricky questionnaires, utilize unstructured techniques, and present visual cues such as advertisements and product concepts to the respondent, all as part of the questioning process. The telephone interview is markedly less versatile in that the interviewer is not in a face-to-face relationship with the respondent, making it more difficult to use unstructured techniques, complex questions, and open-ended response types. Web-based surveys can allow for complex questions, as well as in-depth answers, if the study is suitably programmed. When the research design involves structured questions with simple instructions that can be answered easily by the respondent, the interviewer's role can often be mitigated or eliminated entirely so that the mail interview may be the most appropriate medium for the study.

Personal and phone interviews are now often conducted with the aid of digital technology. Computer-aided telephone interviewing (CATI) and computer-aided personal interviewing (CAPI) are conducted with software that enables the researcher to include complex questions while skipping over or adding questions as the respondent's answers dictate. These types of computer-aided research increase the versatility of personal and phone interviews tremendously, rendering them faster and thereby less costly. The researcher must determine the degree of versatility required by a research project and select the communication approach that best meets its needs. In practice, most research projects do not require the high versatility that the personal interview affords.

Cost

The number of hours of labor involved tends to determine the relative costs of the four communication approaches. Labor costs include the salaries of the interviewers and the supervisory costs associated with controlling the quality of the data collection process. The personal interview is typically the most expensive approach per completed interview, and telephone interviews are usually more expensive than those conducted by mail. When the questionnaire is short, the cost of a telephone interview is usually comparable to that of a mail interview, particularly if mail response rates are low. Web-based interviews will often cost more up-front because they require extensive programming and pretesting, but will save time, and therefore funds, in interviewing and data input.

Time

Of the four communication approaches, the Web-based interview is by far the speediest way to obtain large quantities of data, particularly if a dedicated online panel is used. It is now possible to obtain thousands of responses to a Web-based survey in an hour using some of the largest online panels, which number in the millions. Mail questionnaires can also provide tremendous quantities of data, using a sufficiently large mail-out, although the earliest responses aren't available for a few days and still trickle in weeks later. Telephone interviews can also provide quick data: with a short questionnaire, an interviewer can complete ten or more interviews per hour. Using the same questionnaire, a personal interviewer would be fortunate to complete two or three interviews per hour; travel time between interviews represents a serious time constraint on the personal interviewer's completion rate. Consequently, personal interview studies typically have greater elapsed time from the beginning of fieldwork to project completion than any of the other methods.

The total project completion time can be shortened by increasing the number of interviewers working on the study when the personal or telephone interview is used. With the telephone interview, it is reasonably easy to train and coordinate the staff of interviewers, particularly if there is a strict script off which all interviewers can work or a computer program generating questions in real time. Because the interviewing staff can phone from a central location, the project supervisor can easily monitor the interviews and control the quality of the interviewing. Consequently, a large interviewing force can be efficiently used with telephone interviewing to meet the time constraints placed on a research project. Although the number of personal interviewers can also be increased to meet such time constraints, the problems associated with training and coordinating a large interviewing staff, and controlling the quality of the interviews, are compounded quickly to a point where it is neither feasible nor economical to increase the number of interviewers on the project.

It is difficult to shorten the elapsed time for completing a mail study. Once the questionnaires are mailed, there is little the researcher can do to speed the replies. A series of follow-up mailings may be required to stimulate the return of the remaining questionnaires. It may be necessary to wait two or more weeks after each follow-up mailing to determine whether an acceptable response rate is going to be achieved. Although it could take several months to complete a mail study, if the number of interviews to be completed is large, the elapsed time may not be as great as that required to conduct a similar study using personal interviews.

Sample Control

sample control
In survey-based research, the ability to reach the designated units in the sampling plan effectively and efficiently.

sampling frame
The list of units from which a sample will be drawn.

Sample control refers to the ability of the communication approach to reach the designated units in the sampling plan effectively and efficiently. The four communication approaches differ significantly in this regard.

The personal interview offers the greatest degree of sample control because it is more possible to verify information and to select people based, for example, on which stores they shop in. As we discuss in Section 8.8, area sampling procedures can overcome the problems created by the absence of a complete listing of the **sampling frame**, the list of population units from which the sample will be drawn. Sampling procedures that do not require a list of the sampling units rely heavily on the personal interviewer in the process of selecting the sample. Working through the personal interviewer, the researcher can control which sampling units are interviewed, who is interviewed, the degree of participation of other members of the unit in the interview, and many other aspects of the data collection process.

The telephone interview is highly dependent on a sampling frame. One or more electronic directories usually serve as the sampling frame, with respondents being selected from directories serving the population of interest through probabilistic selection procedures. Telephone directories are often poor sampling frames in that they offer incomplete listings of people in a given area, because not everyone has a phone, new phones that have been placed in service since the directory was updated are not listed, some people have unlisted phones, and cell phones numbers are not only difficult to find but also have owners who fit a different geodemographic profile than landline users.

Phone ownership is typically not a serious problem for most telephone studies conducted in North America, western Europe, and much of Asia and South America, where almost all households have a phone or access to one. However, in some areas, estimates of the percentage of unlisted numbers run as high as 30 percent. This can be a serious source of bias because research indicates that households with voluntarily unlisted numbers differ from those with listed numbers on a number of important demographic characteristics, such as income, education, age, and family size.

Because of unrepresentative directories and ownership patterns, the telephone interview permits only limited control over the sample. One procedure designed to overcome this problem is *random-digit dialing* (see Section 8.9), a procedure that involves the random generation of at least some of the digits used in the sampling plan. A central interviewing facility can be used to place calls, using the Wide Area Telecommunications Service (WATS), a special service that allows a customer to make calls to specific geographic zones, allowing a widely dispersed sampling plan, if desired. However, even with these improvements, telephone surveys still mainly rely on simple random sampling or systematic sampling; as discussed in the chapters on sampling, alternative sampling procedures exist that are more efficient than either of these sampling types.

The mail interview, like the telephone interview, requires a listing of the population elements. Ideally, this frame is composed of both names and addresses. Typically, street directories are used for a listing of the general population, and these share all the problems of the telephone directories discussed previously, including additional ones based on whether a residence is owned, rented, or shared.

Mailing lists for specialized groups of respondents can be purchased from firms that specialize in the area and trade entities such as the Mailing & Fulfillment Service Association. Organizations like the American List Council sell catalogs containing thousands of lists, many of which can be segmented in various ways. Generally, the more targeted the list, the more costly it will be to obtain on a per respondent basis. Note that even with a mailing list that contains the target population the researcher has the problem of limited control over the person or people at the mailing address who complete the questionnaire, as well as whether the questionnaire will be returned.

Sampling error is a grave concern with Internet surveys, which are more effective when qualitative data are sought, rather than quantitative data for which statistical validity is important. Unless the system used for surveying has built-in security, verification, data checking, and other such measures, the possibility of unauthorized or unqualified people providing data are nontrivial, particularly when incentives are offered for participation. Results stemming from surveys conducted by simply e-mailing a link to vast numbers of random addresses are especially suspect, even if they deal with general topics that anyone can in principle offer information about.

Quantity of Data

Generally, the largest amount of data can be collected using Web-based surveys, followed by personal interviews, mail, then telephone. In situations where the respondents are emotionally involved in the topic, all four approaches can provide substantial amounts of data. Because the Web-based methodology is **disintermediated** (i.e., no interviewer is needed) and nontangible (requiring no materials), in principle it can put millions of potential respondents at the researcher's disposal, instantaneously. In this regard, no other method can come close to matching it.

disintermediated
When a respondent can interact with a test instrument without intervention by a researcher or interviewer.

The main advantage of the personal interview stems from the social relationship between the interviewer and the respondent. This social setting typically motivates the respondent to spend more time in the interview setting. The University of Michigan Survey Research Center finds that a 75-minute interview is feasible with the personal interview, whereas the telephone interview must be limited to 30 to 40 minutes. It is easier for the respondent to terminate the telephone, mail, or Internet interview, because of their impersonal nature, than to terminate the personal interview, where respondents must literally turn their back on a real person.

An advantage that both the personal and the telephone interview have over the mail or Web interview is that less effort is required of the *respondent* in the data collection process, particularly when literacy may be problematic (which it can be in some regions, or when working with younger participants). Here, the interviewer asks the questions, probes the responses, and records the answers. The personal interview has the added advantage of allowing the visual presentation of rating scale categories and other support material that can facilitate the respondent's comprehension of the questions asked. These advantages all contribute to the respondent's willingness to provide a greater quality of data. On the other hand, both mail and Web interviews allow the respondent total flexibility as to how to schedule the process of providing answers, and where it will take place. By contrast, telephone interviewers spend inordinate amounts of time speaking with people who later decline to take part in or to complete a partially answered survey, simply due to scheduling problems.

Quality of Data

Quality of data refers to the degree to which the data are free from potential bias resulting from the use of a particular communication approach. When the subject matter is unemotional and the questionnaire is properly designed and administered, quality data will generally result regardless of which approach is used.

quality of data
The degree to which the data are not explicitly biased by the choice of a particular communication approach (e.g., mail, phone, or Internet survey).

Researchers have found substantial differences among the three traditional approaches—personal, telephone, and mail interviews—when sensitive or embarrassing questions are involved, for example, questions about debt, income, politics, and relationships. There is evidence that mail surveys collect better-quality data on such sensitive topics than do personal interviews, where the respondent must "confess" to a real person. Telephone interviews typically lie somewhere between these two approaches. At present, there is rather little hard data on the relative ability of Web-based surveys to elicit sensitive information, but, given the relative anonymity afforded by the Web, many researchers believe its potential to be somewhat better than even mail in this regard.

Another source of bias can result from confusion by respondents regarding the question asked. Because the respondent cannot seek clarification from the interviewer through the mail or over the Web (unless a Web chat or video system is implemented), these methods offer the greatest chance for inaccurate results resulting from confusion. The telephone interview offers more potential for bias caused by confusion than does the personal interview because the interviewer is not physically present, but at least clarification can be sought verbally when needed.

The mail interview has another potential for bias in that the respondents may read through all the questions before answering them or may change answers in the early parts of the questionnaire as a result of responses given later in the questionnaire, even if they are told not to, often to make their responses appear "consistent." Both the personal and the telephone interview are relatively free from this type of bias, and Web-based survey systems can be designed to prevent the respondent from either looking ahead or going back and changing responses; they offer unprecedented control over such aspects of questionnaire flow. Both telephone and personal interviews have an important advantage over mail and Web interviews in that they can be used to collect data near the time the behavior occurs and can be directly triggered by it, such as if shoppers are asked to complete a survey when they are observed undertaking some action (e.g., looking through a cache of coupons or intently reading a product label). This can help reduce the bias associated with failure to recall events accurately, long after they have occurred.

Response Rate

response rate
The proportion of the anticipated sample (i.e., the sampling frame) for which data are actually collected.

The **response rate** is the percentage of the original sample that is actually interviewed. As mentioned in Chapter 2, the nonresponse error is the difference between those who respond and those who do not respond, with respect to the variables of interest. A low response rate *may* result in a high nonresponse error, which can invalidate the research findings. For example, if a survey is conducted by phone during the day, the interviewer reaches primarily those who are not working outside the home. Such people will, all else being equal, tend to be able to afford to do so, to be taking care of children or the elderly, or to be unemployed. As such, they are a highly skewed sample of all households with phones; any questions pertaining to office work would produce highly biased results due to nonresponse error.

The probability of nonresponse error increases as the survey response rate decreases, because those who do reply become more highly self-selected. However, a low response rate does not in itself imply that a high nonresponse error is present in the data. It is only when there is a difference between respondents and nonrespondents on the variables of interest that nonresponse error occurs. If the reason for nonresponse is independent of the key variables of interest, there should be little difference between respondent and nonrespondent groups. In practice, however, such situations are relatively uncommon, and researchers must be careful not to presume this sort of independence.

Nonresponse can result from people not being at home or accessible or from outright refusals to participate. Nonresponse caused by the respondent not being at home or not answering their phone can seriously affect telephone and personal interviews, but it has much less influence on mail and Web surveys. Access to consumers through the telephone, however, is becoming increasingly difficult. The ubiquitous use of telephone answering machines, special calling services (such as call blocking), and cell phones creates a stumbling block for the telephone interviewer. Consumer reaction to telemarketing is affecting the marketing researcher's ability to gain cooperation, and a large-scale survey on the matter found that two-thirds of respondents believed that research surveys and telemarketing are the same thing or could not distinguish between the two.[2] Telemarketing contact rises with respondents' ages, education levels, and incomes, although high-income households are more likely to use some form of electronic call screening, often making them more difficult to access. Hostility toward telemarketing has increased the refusal rate on telephone research surveys, potentially leading to a less representative pool of cooperative respondents, including those who cannot easily afford call-blocking technology.

Once a potential respondent has informed the interviewer of an unwillingness to be interviewed, there is little that can be done to reverse the respondent's position. Although the offer to call at another time may be favorably received by some respondents, the majority still refuse the interview. Although the mail or Web survey avoids the nonresponse caused by not-at-homes, it is seriously influenced by the refusal to respond, which can be overwhelming because there is no "real person" to disappoint with a refusal. However, failure to complete and return the questionnaire on time does not imply a strong unwillingness to respond. Many respondents may be influenced to respond if reminded.

Reducing nonresponse in personal and telephone interviews centers on establishing contact with the potential respondent. A series of callbacks is required to reduce the proportion of not-at-homes. Most situations require a minimum of three callbacks, which can incur substantial personnel costs. The callback schedule should be varied by time of day and by day of the week. An excellent overview for scheduling telephone and personal interviews is provided by Nonresponse in Federal Household Surveys, a publication of the Bureau of the Census, based on unparalleled experience attempting to gain compliance with a vast number of U.S. households.

Reducing nonresponse in mail and Web surveys means motivating the respondent to answer the questionnaire and, in the case of mail, return it. The response rate of the mail or Web interview is directly related to the respondent's interest in the survey topic, and this interest can be positive or negative (e.g., the desire to complain). Among the more successful ways to increase the response rate of mail and Web surveys are the following:

- Use an advance letter, e-mail, or telephone call to notify the respondent of the study and to request cooperation.
- Provide hand-stamped return envelopes in mailings to respondents.
- Consider the use of a monetary incentive in situations where motivation needs to be stimulated. This can be done via lottery if it is too costly to directly remunerate each respondent.
- Use a postcard or letter in follow-up contacts requesting completion and return of the questionnaire. Other follow-ups include making phone contact, sending an e-mail, mailing a new questionnaire, or even making personal contact.

Mail surveys conducted by experienced researchers can typically achieve response rates of 50 percent or more. A mail survey that achieves an 80 percent return rate is comparable to many personal and telephone interview studies in terms of the proportion of completed interviews. An 80 percent response rate is suggested as the standard for mail surveys by the Advertising Research Foundation. In practice, most fall substantially below this rate, particularly if the survey lacks advance warning or prepaid return or if respondents are not chosen in a way conducive to their being interested in the topic of study.

For all four communication approaches, the decision regarding the number of callbacks involves weighing the benefits of reduced nonresponse error against the additional cost of the callback campaign. The central issue is: how different is the nonrespondent group from the respondent group? Several methods for estimating the degree of nonresponse error have been proposed, among them (see Table 6.2 as well):

1. **Sensitivity analysis**: Determine how different each successive callback group is from the previous respondent group. If the management decision is insensitive to this difference, cease further callbacks.
2. **Trend projection**: On the basis of the results of successive waves of callbacks, if a trend develops on the variables of interest, it can be used to estimate the characteristics of the nonrespondent group.
3. **Subsample measurement**: A specially designed telephone or personal interview is used to estimate the results of the nonrespondent group. This estimate is then incorporated into the data set of those who responded to the survey.
4. **Subjective estimate**: The researcher, given the nature of the survey topic, uses experience and judgment to estimate the degree of nonresponse error. Researchers must have sufficient (historical) experience to use such subjective estimates.

sensitivity analysis
An analysis performed to gauge the effects of *assumed parameter values or assumptions* on a final answer, policy, or other dependent variable. For example, if we have assumed that 10 percent of people will reply to a survey, to calculate total costs, a sensitivity analysis would ask how much costs might change for each 1 percent difference in response rates in the range 5 percent–15 percent.

trend projection
A method for estimating the degree of nonresponse error. If a trend is apparent in the variables of interest in the respondent group, it can be used to estimate the characteristics of the nonrespondent group.

subsample measurement
A method for estimating the degree of nonresponse error, wherein a specially designed telephone or personal interview is used to estimate the results of the nonrespondent group; the resulting estimate is then incorporated into the data set of those who did respond.

subjective estimate
When the researcher uses experience and judgment to estimate the degree of nonresponse error; requires sufficient (historical) experience with the phenomenon under study.

Table 6.2 Summary of Communication Approaches

	Communication Approach			
Criteria	**Personal interview**	**Phone interview**	**Mail**	**Web**
Versatility*	High	Moderate	Very little	Moderate
Cost	Highest	Moderate	Moderate to low	Low to very low
Time	Months	Days	Weeks to months	Weeks to months
Sample control	Highest	High	High	Moderate
Quantity of data	High	Moderate to high	High	Highest
Quality of data	High	High	Moderate	Low to moderate
Response rate†	Moderate	Moderate	Moderate to low	Low

*Varies greatly depending on whether computer-assisted software packages are being used; with the use of software tools, the versatility increases tremendously.

†Varies greatly, particularly for mail surveys, based on length of interview, callbacks (or number of mailings), and selection of respondents; the typical business interview is about 20 minutes, with two callbacks and a random selection of respondents.

6.4g Observation Method

Observation involves the process of recognizing and recording the behavior of people, objects, and events. The techniques used in formal observation are designed to control sampling and nonsampling errors and to provide valid data for decision making. It is rare for a research design to rely entirely on the observation method; in practice, observational techniques are used in conjunction with other data collection techniques. It is important to understand the advantages and disadvantages of the observation method so as to understand its role in the array of data collection tools available to the researcher.

Observational techniques fall into five broad classes: (1) natural or contrived observation, (2) disguised or undisguised observation, (3) structured or unstructured observation, (4) direct or indirect observation, and (5) human or mechanical observation. Consider these, and see how each fits into the scheme of conclusive research.

Natural vs. Contrived Observation

natural observation
Observing behavior as it takes place in its typical environment (e.g., consumers while they are shopping at the grocery store).

contrived observation
Observations of behavior within an artificial environment where most environmental variables can be controlled.

Natural observation involves observing behavior as it takes place normally in the environment, for example, while people are shopping in a grocery store. **Contrived observation** involves creating an artificial environment and observing the behavior patterns exhibited by people put in this environment, for example, having people shop in a simulated grocery store. The advantage of a natural environmental setting is an increased probability that the exhibited behavior will accurately reflect true behavior patterns. Against this must be weighted the added costs of waiting for the behavior to occur and the difficulty of measuring behavior in a natural setting, where few environmental variables are under the researchers' control.

Disguised vs. Undisguised Observation

Disguised vs. undisguised observation refers to whether or not respondents are aware they are being observed. The role of the observer should be disguised in situations in which people would behave differently if they knew they were being observed. Various approaches, such as two-way mirrors, hidden cameras, and observers dressed as salesclerks, can be used to disguise the observation. Researchers disagree about how much the presence of the observer will affect people's behavior patterns. One position is that the observer effect is small and short-term, and the other is that the observer can introduce serious bias into observed behavior patterns. There are many situations—shopping in a supermarket or a mall, for example—where people are aware they are being observed by many others and behavior is unlikely to be influenced. In more reflective, solitary situations, or in those where there is any potential for embarrassment, the overt presence of a researcher is likely to affect observed behavior. It is important to bear in mind that there are serious ethical issues involved with disguised observation, particularly if it is recorded. All universities and government organizations have strict protocols and review boards to ensure that such observation and recording are done with informed consent and cannot be used to harm participants. Researchers in the private sector need to be similarly circumspect about their activities in this regard.

Structured vs. Unstructured Observation

When the decision problem and information needs have been clearly defined, **structured observation** involves observing and measuring the clear set of behavior patterns indicated by the information needs of the project. A checklist of "behaviors of interest" allows researchers to focus attention on a small subset of all possible actions undertaken by participants. In situations in which the decision problem has yet to be formulated, **unstructured observation** involves observing a more open, flexible set of behaviors in order to develop hypotheses useful in defining the problem and in identifying opportunities. For example, in trying to make sense of a focus group video, a researcher can specify the relatively unstructured criterion of recording every time participants "seem annoyed" or the more structured one of every time certain phrases are used, such as "angry," "upset," "stressed," or "mad."

Structured observation is more appropriate in conclusive research studies. When using the structured approach, the research must specify in detail what is to be observed and how the measurements are to be recorded. The structuring of the observation reduces the potential for observer bias and increases the reliability of the data. Unstructured observation is more appropriate in exploratory research studies. Here, the observer is free to monitor the behavior patterns that seem relevant to the decision situation. Because there is great opportunity for observer bias, the research findings should be treated as hypotheses to be tested with a conclusive research design. Recording is especially important in such situations so that multiple "raters" can view the same behavioral data and one idiosyncratic view doesn't automatically prevail.

structured observation
When conducting (or analyzing) focus groups or sets of depth interviews, using predetermined protocols to determine the entire course of the interaction.

unstructured observation
When conducting (or analyzing) focus groups or sets of depth interviews, using no predetermined protocols and allowing questions to be formulated naturally as the interview progresses.

Direct vs. Indirect Observation

Direct observation refers to observing behavior directly, either in real time as it occurs or via a high-fidelity, typically video, recording. **Indirect observation** refers to observing some *indicator* of past behavior. Here, the effects of behavior are observed rather than the behavior itself. This involves the examination of physical traces, a process that may include, to take one particularly invasive example, counting the number of empty liquor containers in trash cans to estimate the liquor consumption of households (a process sometimes referred to as "garbology"). A **pantry audit** is another example of the use of physical traces. Here, the observer asks respondents for permission to inspect their pantries for certain types of products, information that cannot be obtained from scanner records or simply by asking because most respondents cannot estimate this accurately. Success with the indirect observation approach rests on the ability of the researcher to creatively identify the physical traces that can provide useful information for the research problem at hand.

direct observation
A research technique in which an observer attempts to unobtrusively gather as much data as possible without taking part in the activity under study.

indirect observation
Observing some indicator of behavior, as opposed to the behavior itself.

pantry audit
In consumer research, when a researcher or observer asks respondents for permission to inspect their pantries for certain types of products because such information cannot be obtained from scanner records or simply by asking

Human vs. Mechanical Observation

In some situations, it is appropriate to supplement or replace the human observer with some form of mechanical observer. The reason could be increased accuracy, lower costs, or special measurement requirements. The major mechanical devices used in observation include the video camera, the audimeter, the psychogalvanometer, the eye-camera, and the pupilometer. The video camera can be used to record shopping behavior in supermarkets, drugstores, and the like. The researcher evaluates the resulting video and measures the desired behavior. The use of several observers plus repeated viewing allows more accurate measurement of behavior. The **audimeter** is a device developed by the A. C. Nielsen Company to record when radio and television sets are turned on and the station to which they are tuned. The observations made from a sample of households are important in determining which programs are aired and which are canceled.

Several mechanical devices require not only consent from participants but also a good deal of physical preparation to enable their use. The **psychogalvanometer** measures changes in perspiration rate.

audimeter
An electronic device attached to a consumer's television that monitors when it is used and the channel to which it is tuned.

psychogalvanometer
A device used in experimental research to measure perspiration rate.

Inferences are drawn from these measurements regarding the person's emotional reaction to stimuli present at the time of the measurement. The stimuli presented might include brand names, copy slogans, or advertisements. The **eye-camera** or eye-tracker measures the movement of the eye and is used to determine how a person reads a magazine, newspaper, advertisement, package, or other printed material. Both the sequence of what is observed and the time spent looking at various sections are measured, and sophisticated statistical algorithms can assess typical patterns of information acquisition across the consumer pool. The **pupilometer** measures changes in the diameter of the pupil of the eye, where increases tend to reflect a favorable reaction to the stimuli being observed.

eye-camera
Also called an eye-tracker, a device that measures the movement of the eye and helps determine the manner in which a person reads a magazine, newspaper, advertisement, product package, or other printed material.

pupilometer
Used often in advertising research, a device that measures a respondent's pupil dilation, thereby helping to indicate attention and interest in a visual stimulus (e.g., a print or TV ad).

Advantages of the Observation Method

Observation offers several advantages over the communication method. First, the potential bias caused by the interviewer and the interviewing process is reduced or in many cases eliminated, so observational data should be more accurate. Second, certain types of data can be collected only by observation, such as responses to humor or behavior patterns of which the respondent is not aware; for example, one cannot tell from respondents' answers to a five-category question whether they found the question amusing, offensive, or difficult to understand, but one can observe laughter, facial expressions, nonverbal sounds, and tone of voice. Third, it does not rely on the respondent's explicit willingness to engage in the time and bother to provide the desired data, particularly when that data is difficult or undesirable to relate, like evidence of sleepiness or breaks taken from answering a survey.

Disadvantages of the Observation Method

The weaknesses of the observation method significantly limit its use. First, it is not possible to observe such things as awareness, beliefs, feelings, and preferences directly, because these have no obvious physical or verbal manifestations. It can also be arduous to observe a host of personal activities such as applying makeup, eating, playing with the children, and watching television late in the evening. Among the restrictions on the behavior patterns to be observed, if the cost and time requirements are to be competitive with other data collection techniques, are that they be of short duration, occur frequently, or be reasonably predictable. Finally, there are substantial ethical issues in the use of any sort of observation. Professional researchers take care to pretest their observational techniques and fully debrief participants, who can elect to have their data purged.

6.4h Collecting Data from Children

With children today representing a multibillion-dollar personal purchase market, it is no wonder that marketers are anxious to understand their wants and needs. This is no simple task, however. Some children are reluctant to respond to any type of questioning; others do their best to resist giving accurate responses to the interviewer; and still others give what they feel is the "right answer" rather than divulging their true feelings. Researchers have come up with several techniques to help overcome these problems, provided parents have given full consent.

First, marketing information can be collected by observing children's play. Small groups are placed in structured lab settings, where products of possible interest are scattered throughout the lab. The manufacturer or advertisers can then observe the children's reactions to the various products. Other methods of analyzing play include having a researcher play games with the children while a psychologist observes and analyzes their reactions. "Games" can include charades, word associations, pretending to be a trusted adult figure like a family member or teacher, and acting out favorite commercials.

Structured questions have been used successfully with children. The questionnaires are typically short (capable of being administered in 5 to 10 minutes) and are specifically designed for children in a particular age category. Research has found children's questionnaires to be reliable, having both statistically high internal consistency and test–retest reliability. In using depth interviews with children, it often behooves an interviewer to ask for nonverbal, rather than verbal, responses, especially from younger children. Children are more likely to point to a picture or a smiling face to indicate their responses than to say exactly what they feel.

In working with children, it is essential to secure full parental consent and participation. By law, data collection cannot take place on the Web for children under a certain age, currently 13 in the United States and can only be obtained from their parents or guardians.

6.5 Conclusive Research Worldwide

International and domestic marketing research programs are undertaken for the same reasons: to forecast market behavior based on respondents' past behavior, attitudes, and characteristics. What is different in international marketing research is the implementation issues designed to overcome cultural and infrastructure differences across countries and linguistic or cultural barriers.

6.5a Personal Interview

Personal interviews are used extensively in international research. In many countries, cultural and infrastructure constraints preclude telephone, mail, and Web interviews as research options. Interviews in the home are typical in most of the world. In addition, intercept interviews are common in places where the target market gathers, such as shopping areas, sporting events, town squares, and parks.

6.5b Telephone Interview

The use of the telephone interview depends on whether the desired respondents have telephones and are willing to be interviewed over the phone. The availability of phones varies widely across countries. In addition, cultures differ in terms of willingness to grant phone interviews. Attempting a phone interview in much of Latin America, for instance, was considered for many years to be inappropriate, as the telephone was—and in some places still is—viewed more as a communication medium between family members and close friends. This is changing as cell technology proliferates across the globe and becomes the standard for business communication.

6.5c Mail Interview

Mail interviews are used widely in European countries, Canada, and Japan. These countries have high literacy rates, well-developed postal systems, and address listings for target markets. Mail is not a good method in parts of the world that have unreliable postal systems and low literacy rates. Note that these conditions can vary widely even within one country, often with pronounced differences between urban and rural dwellers.

6.5d Observation Method

The observation method depends less on infrastructure and cultural constraints than do interview methods. Consequently, observation is used in worldwide research similarly to the ways in which it is used in the U.S. domestic market. Note, however, that some countries prohibit the recording of disguised observation in public or even private venues, and statutes must be checked in advance of any type of audio or video recording. *International Issues 6.1* takes a closer look at some of the unique issues and challenges presented by cross-cultural research.

We close our discussion of data collection with two comprehensive features from industry leaders. In Special Expert Feature 6.1, Ray Pettit discusses the state-of-the-art of online marketing research, and predicts trends that will shape this important methodology in the coming decade. Special Expert Feature 6.2, by the team at leading online survey solution provider Qualtrics.com, delves into the nitty-gritty of modern online data collection, showcasing what practitioners need to know when doing research via the Web.

International Issues 6.1

Cultural Differences in International Research

Culture can mean many things to different people—ways of looking the world, systems of family and social relations, holidays and celebrations, modes of dress, ethnic affiliations, languages spoken, even foods one tends to eat. Sociologists often refer to these collectively as a knowledge system of cognitive processes and behaviors. For marketers and marketing researchers, understanding the psychological processes of perception, cognition, emotion, and motivation can supplement other cross-cultural data in trying to understand patterns of preference and consumption across the world's many cultures.

When conducting surveys and other forms of research in countries other than their own, researchers must be careful about language and cultural differences. For example, in a comprehensive survey of the banking industry in Malaysia, it was found that it was best to have ethnic Malay interviewers talk with Malay bankers and Chinese interviewers talk with Chinese bankers, even though all interviews were conducted in English; many cultural cues transcend mere language and extend to shared assumptions and ways of conveying nonverbal information. The language situation can also be different when dealing with small shop owners, who work directly with their customers and speak colloquially with them, than it is when dealing, for example, with bankers, who must convey uniform policies in neutral, company-approved language. And it is impossible to overstress the importance of using native speakers conversant with the local culture when choosing interviewers, who frequently must follow up on questions or misunderstandings and cannot rely wholly on a preestablished script.

metric equivalence
In cross-cultural research, when researchers can verify that psychometric properties of the data exhibit the same structure across cultures (e.g., when it can be shown that people in multiple countries use a seven-point agree–disagree scale in the same way).

Culture can affect many aspects of the research design. Researchers must justify the **metric equivalence** of concepts between cultures—that is, that psychometric properties of the data exhibit the same coherence or structure across cultures. This can be extraordinarily difficult to do; imagine trying to ensure the equivalence of "pleasant dining experience" or "roomy dwelling" to both a Wall Street executive and a Mongolian yurt-dweller. A crucial step is defining the marketing research problem itself so that it is nearly conceptually equivalent across the cultures included in the study. Many concepts taken for granted by someone in one culture do not have equivalents or have a different meaning in another culture. For example, temporary price reductions are commonplace throughout North America and Europe but not elsewhere in the world, where posted prices and on-the-side haggling are the rule, and even certain types of promotions, like "two-for-one," are rare outside American markets. Even elements universal to all cultures, such as marriage, can differ dramatically in meaning, ritual, and connotation (e.g., "bridal gown," "veil," and "to death do us part") from one culture to another.

self-reference criteria
In cross-cultural research, any references to one's own cultural values that are ordinarily taken for granted.

To compensate for this problem, researchers would do well to examine **self-reference criteria**, the references to their own cultural values ordinarily taken for granted, in advance of undertaking any study calling on them and to rigorously attempt to minimize their influence on the cross-cultural variables measured in the course of marketing research. Uncovering such self-reference criteria can be an elusive and time-consuming practice, but some general guidelines can help: first, define the marketing research problem as it relates to cultural characteristics (e.g., economics, values, needs, and habits) of the domestic environment; next, do the same thing for the "foreign" environment, with extensive input from those natively familiar with the culture; third, isolate the influence of the self-reference criteria by analyzing the differences between the first definition and the second one; and finally, redefine the marketing research problem with at most minimal influence of the self-reference criteria. Without a formal process of this nature, researchers can never be sure whether their "cross-cultural" conclusions truly reflect cultural differences or merely poor choices of wording or explanation.

An example of this process is Coca-Cola's efforts to increase its penetration of the soft drink market in India. In the United States, soft drinks are widely consumed; therefore, the problem is to entice existing consumers to increase their consumption of soft drinks, for example, at meals. In India, a far lower percentage of households consume soft drinks, and water is consumed with meals. Soft drinks are viewed more as a specialty item and are generally served only to guests and on special occasions. Therefore, the problem is distinctly different. The self-reference criterion would be the American assumption that soft drinks are an all-purpose beverage, and it would be wrong to ask how to convince Indian consumers to simply drink more Coca-Cola at meals because they are seldom consumed in that way (rather like asking how to get Americans to drink more champagne along with their meals). The problem for India should therefore be redefined in more culturally neutral terms, for example, as how to get more Indian consumers to consume soft drinks during a wider set of situations, to consume them more often for themselves, and to increase consumption during the occasions on which they are already being served.

When conducting focus groups, researchers must consider how foundational cultural differences, such as the concept of time and the type of thinking regularly practiced, may affect everything from recruitment results to responses during the session. If a financial incentive is offered for participating in a focus group or a survey, it must be presented in the proper context. In Japan, offering a cash *payment* is considered crude, but a cash *gift,* as a token of appreciation, is quite acceptable. In Singapore, much the same is true, except a contribution to a charitable organization is also acceptable. Once again, the use of local residents in the role of interviewers helps avoid cultural gaffes.

Demographic factors may be substantially more complex relative to the ones familiar to the researchers in their home country, including factors such as religion and tribal membership. The moderator should be familiar with the language, culture, and social mores of the country of study, including the different nonverbal cues of tone and gesture. In cultures where people are hesitant to discuss their feelings in a group, focus groups may be replaced with in-depth interviews. One must be especially sensitive to gender and age issues here, because in some cultures it is considered impertinent for members of certain groups to offer their opinions before others or to contradict them openly.

Cross-cultural research, especially that regarding sensitive issues, often employs observational methods to compensate for cultural reluctance to share truthfully. These methods still encounter difficulties due to the reduced knowledge of a "natural" setting for the culture and the difficulty of inferring attitude and belief from behavior.

At all phases of the research, equivalency can be difficult to establish. A bicycle in one country may be considered recreational, whereas in another country it may be the primary means of transportation, resulting in a different set of beliefs, attitudes, and behaviors regarding bicycles. A promotional sale may be seen as an opportunity for a good deal in one culture, whereas in a different culture it means that the goods are probably poor quality. This applies to measurement devices as well. When using a photo or drawing in measuring responses, it may mean something entirely different in one culture than in another. Care must be taken even with simple verbal labels; one study found that, for Japanese managers, "definitely true," "somewhat true," and "not at all true" were more understandable than "agree" and "disagree." In some countries, the number one is always best, and in some it is always worst. Sometimes, it is easiest to simply allow respondents to set their own anchor points for their cultural norms, describing them to the interviewer, who records them on a pre-established scale that is not presented to respondents directly.

As culture forms the context of thought, attitude, and behavior in myriad ways, researchers must continue to seek better understanding of cultural influences on consumer behavior. Efforts to improve methods for cross-cultural marketing research should incorporate information gathered by the more anthropological approach, as well as a deeper understanding of cultural psychologies.

Sources: Malhotra, Naresh, James Agarwal, and Mark Peterson (1996), "Methodological Issues in Cross-Cultural Marketing Research," *International Marketing Review*, 13(5), Volume 13, Number 5, 1996, pp. 7–43.

Salciuviene, Laura, Vilte Auruskeviciene, and Zigmas Lydeka (2005), "An Assessment of Various Approaches for Cross-Cultural Consumer Research," *Problems and Perspectives in Management*, 3, 147–159.

Steenkamp, Jan-Benedict E. M. (2001), "The Role of National Culture in International Marketing Research," *International Marketing Review*, 18(1), Volume 18, Number 1, 2001, pp. 30–44.

Special Expert Feature 6.1

The Current State of Online Market Research: An Applied Perspective

By Ray Pettit

Traditional marketing—conceived as an art form with a mysterious process of ideation and a more mysterious language to describe its success—is rapidly disappearing. Along with it, the fundamental processes of market research—data collection, data manipulation, data analysis, and reporting—are slowly evolving. Marketing expenditures have become investments, and the tools of the trade—advertising and communications—are now being challenged to demonstrate a satisfactory return to the organization and its shareholders. Part of this "new reality" is focused on driving *greater efficiency*, primarily through the use of technology—while the other is in achieving *greater effectiveness*, which is primarily through the application of improved analytic methods, techniques, and approaches.

This review presents a careful examination of the status quo of online marketing research. The beauty of marketing science is that a broad, rich, and powerful set of analytic, sampling, and survey techniques and methods already exist. As well, highly valuable and essential marketing information is being collected and stored in various operational and business information systems across the corporation. The problem is that it is often lying unconnected to marketing and advertising research data or is unused or misused in relation to it. To make matters worse, the marketing research data that exists is often chopped into separate, distinct pieces of information linked to specific projects or activities that have been defined, developed, and deployed independently. In most cases, this splintered body of marketing knowledge provides an

continued

incomplete picture and insufficient analytic guidance to help marketers work better or do better work.

As a result, the real power of market research is often dissipated and unknown. Slowly, however, this picture is beginning to improve, as the Internet and technology better sustain and support more streamlined and efficient data, analysis, linkage, and reporting systems. This feature offers an applied perspective on the variety of ways this is occurring today.

How Is Online Affecting the Process of Market Research?

Data Collection

A study of the growth of the use of online for research uncovers some parallel dynamics. First, although the initial "promise" was ridiculously oversold, it was quickly brought down to earth by the insistence of established players and associations such as the Council of American Survey Research Organizations (CASRO) to consider the sampling and response implications and realities of online. This is because the sampling frame for online still does not (even today) encompass the total population universe that mail and telephone offer. This is a good thing, as much work has been done to build the necessary procedures to ensure representativeness in panels and/or statistical techniques that can adjust on the back end, if need be, to meet those requirements.

Another, less obvious, hindrance was the fact that most pure data collection firms and those major market research giants who run service bureaus providing sample and/or data collection have invested inordinate amounts of money in telephone banks, consumer panels, and people to service them doing telephone surveys. Products, methods, and approaches, particularly telephone advertising and brand tracking studies, are built on the use of telephone. Thus, much revenue, capital, and human service is at stake. This has to be considered a factor in decisions not to jump wholeheartedly into online research or data collection.

That said, online sample providers sort into a number of categories:

- *Panel majors (pure):* Survey Sampling, Greenfield, Luth, and so on, only do data collection or provide sample but do no research.
- *Panel majors (service bureau):* Harris, Markettools, OTX, TNS, GfK, Ipsos/NPD, Kantar Group, comScore, Synovate, and Global Market Insite (GMI) maintain a separate service bureau to do online research but also have full service companies or firms doing analysis, reporting, or consulting.
- *Panel niche:* Testspin and other firms that provide hard-to-get samples (e.g., very young or old consumers or ethnic markets) or difficult to locate segments (top executives, extremely wealthy individuals, etc.).
- *Qualitative:* Online focus groups, such as GQG, while logically tempting, have not developed the traction that online survey research has because there is still inherent power in face-to-face research. Even with the rise of Web conferencing, and so on, and the worldwide terrorism threat, personal meetings have not diminished. The qualitative component at this point is a second choice add-on—done for less important things or if budget is impossibly tight. That said, there are still loyal adherents, and many attempts to bring technology to the qualitative research sphere through the use of software specifically built for it, as part of a larger system (GMI), or by using such tools as Microsoft Live Meeting.

All online panels, with one exception, are built using traditional recruitment techniques. That is, people are recruited via phone, by mail, and on the Internet to purposefully build a panel that is representative of the population (of the country). Then all panelists complete extensive profile forms that gather additional demographic, psychographic, or lifestyle information for survey purposes. This information is appended to online survey results as a matter of course.

One firm, comScore, recruits exclusively online and has amassed an impressive global panel of 4 million. To ensure representativeness of its online panel, comScore runs a separate telephone/mail panel of more than 20,000 that is precisely matched to the U.S. population census frame. This calibration panel, as it is called, is used to weight responses from the larger online panel, using a proprietary statistical weighting technique developed by comScore. This technique, although not standard, is being studied and verified by the Advertising Research Foundation, but early indications are positive.

In addition, comScore holds the distinction of being the only online panel that tracks the online behavior of its panelists continuously. Panel members sign a waiver to allow comScore to install a piece of code that allows this tracking to occur. This behavioral "surfing" information is used to enhance and extend analyses done by comScore and its clients.

Market Research Process Management

All of the firms just mentioned have some sort of software in place that supports the full lifecycle of market research. These include tools to program surveys online, Internet technology to disseminate surveys and collect results, and program management tools to help track costs and timing.

In addition, a variety of built-in analytic tools and/or the ability to route the raw data to the most common data formats (Excel) or statistical software (SPSS, SAS, etc.) is available. Reporting tools or publishers that can be accessed internally or by clients with necessary permissions are a regular feature. Reports can be real-time updates of survey results to finished report products that are made accessible online.

Analysis

In general, built-in analysis tools try to address the most common things marketers do, such as cross-tabs, called *top lines* by most researchers. They are less successful when they try to imitate the formidable capabilities of SPSS, SAS, or Stata.

Vendors of market research are less apt to want clients to be able to manipulate raw survey data—they do not like being second guessed on analysis or being caught if data is particularly dirty or incomplete. Analysis still requires expertise and knowledge of statistics and numerical methods, as well as experience and understanding of the business problem or objective. Although the

continued

real-time promise is compelling, unless every knowledge worker is adequately educated, the power of insight and data-driven intelligence will not be realized and will continue to be the responsibility and task of an expert analyst or consultant.

Reporting

Real-time reporting has not lived up to its promise because expert analysis facilitates the step of drawing insights from the data. More likely is the further development of ways to package and share interactive reports (as opposed to in-person static presentations) with clients. For example, hierarchical reports could present key performance metrics to top executives, more detailed summaries down the line, and actual access to the raw data by the client or consulting analysts.

Marketing intelligence dashboard vendors have tried to ride this concept, as well as a similar one put forth by customer relationship management (CRM), Six Sigma, and business intelligence software providers (e.g., Cognos and MicroStrategy), but the bottom line is that a dashboard needs high-quality content behind it. That content is the result of a well-trained analyst who derives results and data-driven conclusions and combines this with skills in the synthesis and analysis of information to produce meaningful and helpful business decision support.

The current scene harkens back to the dot-com era, for example, in that it is looking for a "silver bullet" solution. Instead, what is important is a thorough application of market research to produce the results and metrics that can populate the dashboard, not the dashboard itself. The truth is that every online market research vendor has the capabilities of linking to clients and presenting results online. In most cases, a specially designed and configured "dashboard" is not necessary (see Figure 6.7).

Figure 6.7 Dashboards Are Not a "Silver Bullet"

Marketing Intelligence Dashboards are important, but just one element of a purposeful strategic measurement process:

- Understand measurement goals and objectives
- Determine key ROI needs and metrics to be reported and/or tracked
- Deploy a proven research method that delivers both an ROI audit, as well as data driven diagnostics for marketing improvement
- Enable delivery of text insights, data results, and presentational reports that meet the needs of users and objectives of managers on multiple levels
- Develop cost effective dashboard delivery
    - Link to existing client system or portal
    - Use dashboard developed by market research vendor
    - Build customized dashboard
- Pre-establish and pre-plan future goals that involve technology, such as linkage to existing CRM, BI, tracking, forecasting, or financial systems to save money in the future

Linking to Other Data Systems

Less common, but with much potential, is the linking of survey data to other data systems found within the walls of the corporation. Online, this becomes a simple exercise in data manipulation. CRM and business intelligence software systems are all potential partners to online market research because the data stored in data warehouse or marts can be manipulated at a metadata layer. This opens up the possibility of building enhanced databases and using new statistical methods to address the merged data (see Figure 6.8).

What Forms of Analysis Are Most Prevalent?

The types of analysis and the problems they address are independent of the ability to do research online. They have existed for quite some time. Certain forms of analysis, however, have become more prevalent because they meet common and traditional needs of marketers—and because they fit well in the online environment and sometimes are enhanced by it. The danger here is that these relatively simple and familiar procedures, which can be accomplished so well online, will hinder the desire or motivation to continue to push the envelope on more advanced or innovative ways to design research and analyze data.

Online surveys afford the potential to present picture, video, audio, virtual stores or products, and so on, in the context of the survey instrument. As such, this provides a more tangible experience in the survey for the respondent and potentially higher-quality data. Recognition testing, for example, is enhanced over telephone interviewing when doing recall of ads seen—in the online survey instrument, respondents can "see" the television ad in its entirety to prompt recall and/or frequency.

The other form of presenting surveys online is the ability to initiate a game-like aspect to the survey. As much online

Figure 6.8 Enhanced Segmentation

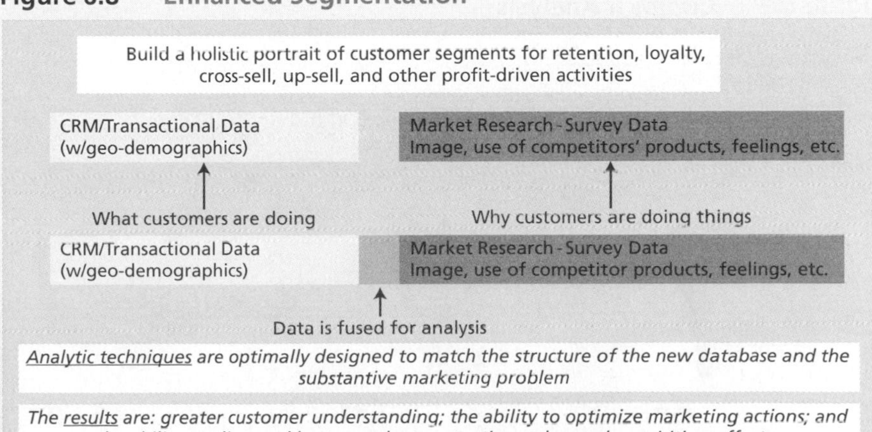

continued

gaming is prevalent and available from children all the way to hard-core gamers, this technique can be used to collect responses in a "fresh" way.

Survey Analysis

By far, the largest application of online marketing research analysis is for standard consumer and customer surveys. Procedures and systems have been built to accommodate the basic processes, and the most common output, cross-tabulations of survey results, are readily available.

Conjoint Analysis

The techniques of conjoint analysis, particularly for product testing and/or evaluation of shopping behavior, have enjoyed much success online. This is due to the ability of the survey respondent to manipulate images and the survey designer to control choice procedures and present virtual environments to the respondent. Notwithstanding the drawbacks of this forced-choice analytic procedure, the innovations of the presentation of conjoint online surveys have been impressive (see Figure 6.9).

Text Analysis (Customer Feedback)

Although not exclusively limited to the analysis of open-ended responses but also applied to chat rooms, buzz or blog Web sites, and so on, text analysis is based on the premise that statistical algorithms can analyze the content and context of text (written) responses. Although online market researchers tend to stick with fairly pedantic methods of analyzing text data, text analysis tools come and go across the landscape. See Island Data for an example.

Loyalty, Satisfaction, and Branding Measurement

The primary application of online surveys is to assess or track customer loyalty, satisfaction, or brand impacts. Note that these are all short of sales measures but remain popular even given the challenge of marketing accountability. Some examples:

- Satmetrix's Net Promoter: Based on Fred Reichheld's Net Promoter score and book called *The Loyalty Effect*, Satmetrix offers its approach online for its clients.
- Walker and customer loyalty: Walker Information has taken what it traditionally has done and put it online.
- CustomerSat and customer satisfaction: CustomerSat offers a naive but standardized approach to customer satisfaction measurement.

All major market research organizations (see the Honomichl Top Ten) have brand and ad tracking models that are essentially the same; not all have moved exclusively to online data collection, given their massive investments in telephone panels, but the trend is there. For example, Millward Brown, a member of the Kantar Group of WPP, purchased Dynamic Logic, an online advertising-effectiveness measurement firm.

Advanced Techniques

A portion of the online market research community is chasing broader or more innovative pathways. Some are focused on bringing advanced or improved techniques to bear on measurement, whereas others are looking at the broader picture of enterprise-wide marketing intelligence.

- CFI Group–ForeSee Results uses an advanced application of path analysis to measure customer satisfaction using online surveys. CFI runs the well-known ASCI survey program, with results that are reported yearly in the *Wall Street Journal* and widely disseminated.
- Accenture—and other major management consultancies—are focused on a large-scale, multidimensional effort to bring database marketing, brand strategy, and marketing science together. A typical engagement will result in a blue print and long-range plan—and it will involve and embed online data collection, advanced analytic, and data fusion techniques into the resulting processes. Online research is a minor, but important, part of all this.
- Marketing mix modeling—Information Resources (IRI), Nielsen, Marketing Management Analytics—is a method fairly limited in its use in an industry that avoids survey research altogether but does use Internet and database technology to bring together disparate collections of data. This data, which requires about 3 years of consistent history, is massaged, transformed, and normalized into one data store that is then modeled by econometric procedures. The results are often streamed via an online reporting system, but typically this analysis is only done once a year and costs in the millions.
- Return on marketing investment (ROMI)—Longwoods International, Communicus, Lenskold Group—uses survey-based methods that tackle the accountability challenge from a different angle. Online survey techniques and the principles of experimental design and sampling are utilized to achieve the single-source dataset the modelers build with historical data, albeit with a large representative sample, as opposed to all consumers in a client's database. Consequently, the results of the surveys can be mapped to CRM systems and lead to enhanced segmentation and profiling

continued

Figure 6.9 Conjoint Analysis

- Growth of techniques using the power of adaptive and complicated interviews online
- Adaptive Conjoint analysis and Conjoint with graphical components
- Price work with realistic products and dynamic pricing

analysis when special techniques are used.

- GMI has built perhaps the most complete online software system available today. The breadth and depth of the system is based on the concept of enterprise marketing intelligence. That is, all primary forms of data collection normally encountered by marketers can be handled in one system. The system provides extensive project management features, intuitive online survey design tools, and the ability to seamlessly link vendor and client via the Internet. The ability to bring all forms of research together in one database (actually maintained on Web-based servers that GMI runs) can contribute to gains in efficiency and organization, as well as the potential to allow cross-comparison studies or "on the fly" tracking analysis.

Online Research: Current Practices and Trends

Simon Chadwick, principal of Cambiar, recently completed an excellent set of studies about current practices and trends in online market research. Chadwick completed two surveys among senior and marketing executives concerning their use and management of online market research.

The first study was conducted among 43 senior market research directors, customer insights directors, and senior marketing managers. Over a quarter of these worked in companies with revenues of $1 billion or more, and a third worked in companies with revenues of between $100 million and $999 million. Sixty-five percent of these companies characterized their activities as global. As may be expected of a sample of this nature, 66 percent of the executives in the survey worked in the United States and a further 19 percent in Europe.

The second study was designed to understand the degree to which online market research has become a tool of marketing in smaller companies in the United States and around the world. As such, 77 percent of the sample of 411 managers worked in companies whose revenues were $99 million or less. Over 33 percent of respondents were owners or senior officers in their companies. Only 31 percent of these companies reported being global in character, the remainder describing themselves as either national or regional in scope. Although 57 percent of respondents worked in North America and 17 percent in Europe, the sample contained substantial representation from Asia and the Asia-Pacific (18 percent), Latin America (3 percent), and Africa and the Middle East (3 percent).

The following key questions were being studied:

- To what degree have established buyers and users of research adopted online? Is there room for growth? And how do they manage this new form of research? How much do they do themselves? How much do they outsource, and to whom?
- Is online research the great leveler that it was touted to be? Has it enabled smaller companies to buy and use research to a greater extent than before? If so, is this a trend that will continue to grow?

In its earliest stages, the promise of online market research mimicked the larger promise of the dot-com revolution. Chadwick's quest was to "take the temperature" of the online market research industry and report to what extent the promise was being fulfilled.

Findings of the Chadwick Studies

Online research appears set to continue growing strongly. Chadwick estimated that the market for this type of research will likely grow from around $1.3 billion today to $4 billion by 2008.

This growth will be driven not only by new users coming into the market (both established research users and smaller companies around the world) but also through a broadening of the *types* of research for which online is used. The research suggests that once a company (of whatever size or origin) adopts online, about 30 percent of its research budget becomes devoted to this method.

Many clients of all sizes show a strong interest in building proprietary panels over the next 3 years. Clients not only are looking for robust features, reliability of the system, and the ability to field studies of any size but also want software that is easy to use and intuitive for their project managers to deploy. The primary concern among all user companies today is the quality of the sample that they will be using and the response rates that may be expected.

Overall, online research continues to show strong prospects for growth, both as a discipline in and of itself and as an area in which possibilities for software and panel providers exist in abundance. But quality of sample, ease of software use, and good customer service will be key to enabling this growth.

Revisiting Five Predictions for Market Research Practice

In my first book, *Market Research in the Internet Age: Leveraging Technology for Market Measurement and Consumer Insight,* I made five predictions about the state of market research practice for the years to come. How close were these forecasts, based on data and information available in 2000-2001? Excerpts from the book will be followed by comments concerning the "reality" of today.

> What will be the state of the market research industry in coming years? Although predictions are always fraught with danger, even when well informed by a study of the past and present, we believe that five reasonable observations—based on the comprehensive frames of reference we have employed—can be advanced. All have to do with structural changes in the way market research is done. Throughout the book we have presented many concepts, ideas, and example of evolving methods, practices, and procedures that are fostered by embracing an integrative and collaborative technology mindset. But to forward these as predictions would be unwise, except to say that the fundamental value that traditional market research brings to the table will most likely still be the same in 5 years as it is today.

Hmm. . . not bad. The value of what research brings to the table *hasn't* really changed.

continued

Our sense is that these structural changes will form the fundamental platform for the practice of market research to evolve into a compelling and vital marketing support and customer intelligence function driving business growth, development, and success. Technology alone is a naive solution. To believe that CRM analytics and the study of behavioral data on consumers will tell you about customer's feelings, perception, motivations, and awareness—all foundational forces driving customer satisfaction, relationships, loyalty, and ultimately return on investment—is not only misguided, it is dangerous. Technology as an enabling force that supports increased communication, information collection, dissemination, and learning, however, is extremely valuable.

Also true—we are still struggling with our ability to bring behavioral and attitudinal insights together in some integrated manner.

Thus, our predictions focus on these aspects:

1. *Internet-Based Market Research* will be the standard for quantitative multi-country consumer research. Research suppliers who have not fully embraced the Internet will have lost out, or sold out, to more Net-savvy competitors. Global 500 firms increasingly adopt a single-source model for selection of research suppliers. Technology is about efficiency and effectiveness. A Net-centric architecture clearly supports this. While most traditional techniques will not disappear, we will see a gradual blending and shifting of processes and methods moved to the online channel. As well, we will see highly effective offline methodologies tied into the Internet-centric system, such as through the use of Net-CAPI and Net-CATI solutions.

   Global 500 corporations are already in the process of developing and deploying CRM, SCM [supply chain management], and enterprise application integration (EAI) solutions for the express purpose of achieving and enhancing global efficiency, enterprise standardization, and corporate collaboration. Market research must be equipped to be part of this solution. The only way to do this will be through exploring, investing, and adopting ways to move the best of what the industry has to offer to a Net-centric platform. The alternative is the dissolution of the industry or the gradual displacement of the market research function by tech-driven solutions that are essentially engaged in re-inventing the wheel.

   For the large global clients of research and business information, a single-source solution will increasingly become the partnership of choice. As the Internet brings consumers and markets together, the ability for research providers—in multiple capacities: primary, secondary, information management/delivery, and syndicated research—to afford research across borders and the enterprise will become a requirement. Further, new "global" consumers and markets will appear that will demand another level of research exploration, understanding, and insight delivery to commence. Internet-centric systems and processes will then be mandatory for any firm expecting to be competitive.

   We were a little ambitious here. The evolution is taking longer than we expected. That said, the direction is certainly correct, although the CRM and business intelligence folks have not moved the needle much on "displacing" market research as a core insight function of the organization.

2. *Multi-Channel* data collection using Internet-based data consolidation will streamline traditional research and enable new market research techniques, methods, and business processes.

   Online marketplaces dealing in perishable commodity services—such as call center hours—emerge. Once a foundational, scaleable architecture is achieved, the real work of taking the extensive expertise and marketing knowledge the industry has accumulated and putting it to work in an efficient, usable, and compelling form can begin. Companies, with the support of sizeable partners and investors, are already attempting to take the combined marketing wisdom, knowledge, and expertise of global corporate leaders and transfer it to online systems capable of driving improved and efficient marketing systems. This is just the beginning of a revolution in the use of enabling technology that will be become even more evident in the next few years.

   Market research must and will join the knowledge management and business information revolution. As data is integrated from multiple channels—and easily accessed via components specifically developed for market research—new techniques, methods, and business processes will naturally appear. In addition, ways to move commodity services—such as call centers, interviewing, and syndicated tracking studies—to forms that improve cost-effectiveness and support measurable ROI [return on investment] will emerge.

   Call centers still operate the way they always have. The Internet has really been applied mostly to survey research, analysis, and reporting and not as much to the cross-channel data collection we were discussing. Again, perhaps, we were too ambitious in anticipating a changeover that embraced online methods.

3. *The Mobile and Wireless Internet* will accelerate the growth of the Internet in emerging markets, enabling increasingly representative research to be conducted, particularly by using pre-profiled panels of respondents. Already this is occurring in countries that exhibit substantial usage of wireless devices and have a strong foundation in doing phone research, such as Scandinavia. Research efforts under way there will form the foundation for future efforts around the world. As mobile and wireless communications become ubiquitous, the data collected will be increasingly concentrated in single-source databases, accessible as an integrated whole, rather than the current silos of data prevalent today. As well, pre-profiled and customized global

continued

respondent panels will appear, as market researchers locate the appropriate and preferred way to contact individuals to carry out research not only in countries or regions but also around the world.

Of primary importance, however, is the ability for the data to be collected and sourced as a data stream, via a single data store enhanced by metadata layers. This will result in the possibility of constructing representative global access panels. Some panelists may respond only via wireless; others, by fixed-line phones, on the Internet, or via iTV. Regardless, the panel will be used as a representative cross-sectional panel or as a source to do targeted surveys or research. The ability of market research firms to leverage their expertise and leadership in this capacity will define a large part of their success in capturing a premier place in the corporate business information industry and in taking control of a vital and unique contribution to global marketing, advertising, and sales success.

What we were anticipating here was a move to doing research accessing people on cell phones and the like. This has not happened. If anything more restrictions and resistance has grown to trying to reach people who are "on the move."

4. *The Analysis of Research Results* will be conducted via Web-based applications accessing centrally stored data, effectively replacing the desktop analyzer using locally stored data. Work on building exploration data warehouses, data stores, and data marts to afford efficient and real-time access to data across the enterprise is already under way. The continuing development of a mediating architecture—based on metadata concepts and solutions—will continue to enhance the development of flexible and powerful systems that can utilize many forms of data. The primary goal, not achieved yet, is to achieve dynamic interaction with customers to provide richer, deeper client relationships across all relationship channels. The role of market research will be to provide powerful insights into consumer and marketing behavior patterns, propensities, preferences, feelings, and attitudes.

To fully integrate market research enterprise solutions into corporate network infrastructures, corporations will present new requirements to market research providers for capacity and connectivity via rules-based processes that enable cross-channel synchronization and real-time customer interaction. This emerging technical architecture includes an EAI solution, in which middleware provides for the sharing of applications and data to ensure data consistency across databases and to support multiple end user devices and interfaces related to the market research function.

In order to provide real-time analysis and dissemination of customer data, technical solutions such as a "customer data store" or a "marketing information database" are being explored. This architecture provides a data storage core dedicated to amassing current customer information that is drawn from real-time data from operational and Net-Centric research systems; historical data from the data warehouse; and stored results from qualitative–quantitative market research. This can then support rich, value-added analysis to leverage improved interactions with customers. The "customer data store" concept, for example, provides for more intelligent, streamlined processing. Scoring, rules, filters, original research results (qualitative and quantitative), and predictive/descriptive data mining techniques are applied to real time data focusing only on information that has been identified as having potential value (vs. batch scoring/batch data feeds of everything). This scalable approach is more flexible, allowing "learning about" learning based on changes in data attributes, business rules, and more qualitative features that provoke and invoke marketer's experience and insight.

This was a far-reaching prediction that has not occurred and may still be a ways off. The hoped for cooperation between technology and marketing has not been evident, which this scenario would require. Tech folks still focus on things that can be done easily relative to architectures they are familiar with—whereas marketing continues to do what it does best in a silo. It appears that data overload is still a factor, making it more of a challenge to integrate and bring together disparate data streams for analysis.

5. *Consumer Data* will be closely integrated into global enterprise computing systems, thereby further blurring the lines between market research, CRM, and business intelligence. A new mega-merger phase will emerge, linking CRM, business intelligence, and market research firms into powerhouse companies that are global and Net-centric. Behavioral data on consumers will continue to accumulate and become part of increasingly complete stores of accessible data. As a result, all facets of information gathered about consumers and customers will be fair game for analysis. The triad of key functions undergirding marketing, sales, and advertising—market research, CRM, and business intelligence tools will blend into one complete system that supports and enhances data collection, data analysis, and data delivery, as well as supporting higher levels of collaborative, insight-generation, decision-guidance, and knowledge management processes. To use the analogy of a fully functioning human system, the digital nervous system (CRM) will have a brain (market research) and a sensory system ([business intelligence] tools)—specialized components each delivering their own unique value while blended into a complex, interrelated structure.

Solutions, such as the ability to map individual customers to densely informed hierarchical segment models, will arise that will enable personalization, customization, and relationships to thrive without infringing on personal individual privacy. Just as today, a successful, in-person, sales/service person can combine observation, a few questions, and intuition (literally, working with generalized internal experience maps to guide decisions and actions) to build a solid customer relationship and

continued

outcome—technology-driven analytics will support front-line service people in the future. This is only possible, however, with all of the elements—network communications, analytics, software linkages, data mining, and market research information—in close harmony.

As a result of the conceptual and functional changes increasingly sought in the race to understand and relate to the customer, mergers involving CRM, [market research], and [business intelligence] companies will appear. Further driving this mega-merger phase will be the adoption of a Net-centric infrastructure that will enable global systems to be effectively deployed and used.

The immense cultural and structural change required to achieve such an integrated picture has not occurred. Megacompanies that combine technology and marketing science firms have not emerged. Instead, technology is slowly infiltrating naturally into the corporation in the form of supporting systems. Viewed with hindsight, this scenario may be quite a ways off—anyone for 2020?

Dr. Pettit is Chief Strategist at MarketShare Partners, a global marketing consultancy, working at the juncture of technology and marketing science to drive improved return on marketing and advertising investments. His new book, entitled "Learning From Winners", is being released in Summer 2007 by LEA/Psychology Press. Ray delivers workshops on advertising effectiveness for Executive MBA programs at the University of Illinois and UCLA, is the author of books on the integration of marketing science techniques with new and enabling technologies, and has been a Quantitative and Market Research Consultant and Executive for a number of U.S. and European firms.

Sources:

Chadwick, Simon (2005), "The Modern Online Research Industry," Cambiar.

Pettit, R. (2002), *Market Research in the Internet Age: Leveraging Technology for Market Measurement and Consumer Insight*, Hoboken, NJ: John Wiley & Sons.

Courtesy of Ray Pettit.

SPECIAL EXPERT FEATURE 6.2

Modern Online Data Collection: The State-of-the-Art at Qualtrics.com

Sean D. Otto

Looking back over the history of research methodology, one sees that marketing organizations took the initial lead in developing online surveys as a convenient method for gathering data. As with any new innovation, survey research has expanded its original boundaries. Online data collection has developed into a burgeoning field all its own, one poised to supplement, and perhaps one day supplant, the kind of survey methodology that has served marketing researchers so well throughout the 20th century.

Qualtrics.com provides online survey building, data collection (via panels or corporate/personal contacts), a real-time view of survey results, and advanced "dashboard reporting tools." Over the past decade, Qualtrics has developed four distinct survey engines that are among the most advanced in the marketing industry. A special attraction to anyone outside an information technology (IT) department is the fact that Qualtrics can be operated without the assistance of a programmer.

Over the past few years, Qualtrics has seen a dramatic upswing in organizations expressing an interest in branded survey software. This trend, which migrates software deployment and development in-house, allows organizations to outsource fewer of their marketing research needs and simultaneously provides many additional functions at a sharply reduced cost. For example, several of our Fortune 500 clients rely on Qualtrics as a corporate-wide survey solution. Contrary to some initial expectations, it turns out that human resource (HR) departments account for more than 60 percent of corporate survey use, and HR applications are hardly the only "nontraditional" use of online data collection. From "360-feedback" to employee pulse surveys to Sarbanes-Oxley Compliance, online surveys are now a necessity in organizations that need rapid data-gathering capabilities. Qualtrics' coupling of a powerful survey engine and a user-friendly interface has helped expand survey research out of specialized niches and into the hands of end users in diverse corporate departments. The software is easy enough for an intern but potent enough for a professional researcher.

Our business model, like that of many in the field, has changed substantially since our inception. Today, the service we perform is known as "enterprise survey software" or "enterprise feedback management" and the new and emergent wave of "enterprise information management" that focuses on data reporting tools.

continued

Previously, designing a survey page for research in a corporation required the dedicated involvement of an IT department. But IT departments are strapped for time, and survey methodology has advanced to the point that few IT departments are adept enough to adequately accommodate effective question choices and state-of-the art modes of survey presentation. In recent years, online survey providers have offered a more efficient and universally deployable pathway to conduct survey research. Corporations large and small have found that using an enterprise-wide survey solution not only frees the IT department to attend to other tasks but also lowers overall costs, allows for more specialized survey methodologies, and decreases turnaround time. This new need for corporations to control their own survey software has also caused the software itself to evolve in terms of its functionality and features. Among the most prominent of these newfound functions are the following:

- Development of business-to-consumer (B2C) and business-to-business (B2B) panels;
- Development of advanced reporting dashboards, keeping employee data safe and secure;
- Branded surveys that match corporate branding guidelines; companies spend vast sums maintaining a corporate brand identity that, ironically, can be compromised by a simple nonbranded survey;
- Advanced functionality that embeds surveys within surveys and keeps track of participant responses across the various survey instruments;
- Integration into corporate CRM tools and other legacy applications;
- Advanced analysis, including conjoint, correspondence, discriminate and cluster analyses, and multidimensional scaling;
- Enhanced "graphicacy," a fancy word for turning numbers into images
- Textual analysis; companies recognize the value locked away in qualitative responses but get bogged down by their analysis;
- Increased confidence in results gained through careful experimental design.

Because our software is designed for corporation-wide usage, and because of the challenge of corporations creating their own surveys, Qualtrics offers three distinct services. The first is a comprehensive set of more than 250 survey templates, organized into an accessible survey library and arranged by area of application: Customer Satisfaction; Employee Surveys; Product Surveys; Service Evaluation; Marketing; Web Site; IT Products/Hardware/Software; Restaurant/Hotel; Retail; Health Care; Travel; Business to Business; Education; Community Affairs; Personal Interest; Demographics/Psychographics. In this way, end users in a variety of product and service industries can readily create professional-quality survey instruments.

The second is the ability to schedule survey reviews with in-house experts, many of whom hold doctorates in survey methodology. Few organizations possess this level of in-house expertise but are rightly concerned that their survey instruments may reflect poorly on them. Offering our clients the ability to talk directly with someone adept at creating online surveys—who can give effective feedback on question types, direction, survey length, and participants—obviates the need for them to contract separately for this level of expertise.

Lastly is the analysis review. Data presented in statistics courses and used to illustrate analysis programs always magically "works," but real-world data can have all sorts of anomalies, even throwing the occasional red herring. Qualtrics wants its clients to be able develop effective surveys but also to understand the resulting data correctly and quickly to enable effective business decision-making. (We have found that turnaround times of 4 weeks or less are often possible, depending on the scope and complexity of the research project; such an outcome was unthinkable in the days of pencil-and-paper surveys and telephone interviews.)

Indeed, understanding data is the objective any survey-based project begins with. There is a common phrase used among programmers: Garbage In, Garbage Out. This is no different with online surveys. The sophistication of a survey's design will determine the sophistication of the data and the subtlety required of their analysis. Qualtrics' survey engine, data management system, and analysis capabilities were built to enable this level of sophistication. For example, Qualtrics specializes in a capability called *branching*. This goes beyond skip logic, where on a piece of paper one might say, "if you answer 'No' to question 7 please go onto question 9." Branching confers the ability to do the following:

- Qualify respondents and send individuals not in the study target group to the end of a survey or to a different survey entirely
- Allow respondents to skip sections or questions that do not apply to them
- Track sample groups and ask questions based on fulfillment of sample quotas
- Conduct different surveys depending on the demographics or corporate profile of the respondent

More advanced features such as text piping (transferring text from a previous question choice or CRM), along with looping or extraction (dynamic branching based on multiple responses to the same question), provide for survey design logic and interviewing capabilities of seemingly limitless levels of complexity. Additional functionality Qualtrics survey software provides includes the use of triggers for sales forces or HR departments: When a customer answers a specific way to a question or set of questions, a customizable e-mail is sent automatically to an individual or group.

This recent and pressing need for enterprise-wide survey solutions has fueled an explosive growth in the industry, and Qualtrics strives to be at the forefront of online survey innovation. Over the next few years, we anticipate that survey software will become an even more popular corporate solution for gathering information.

Sean Otto is director of research and development at Qualtrics.com, an online survey software provider. He received his Ph.D. in business administration (marketing), and psychology (psychometrics and theory and philosophy) from Brigham Young University.

Summary

Focus group interviews and in-depth interviews are qualitative techniques used in implementing exploratory research. These tools involve a high degree of flexibility in how the questions are asked and in the degree of probing used, with focus groups being by far the most popular.

It is important that the qualitative data be thoroughly analyzed to identify potential quantitative relationships and insights that can be validated in the conclusive research phase.

A primary source of marketing data is collecting data from respondents through communication and observation. Communication requires the respondent to provide data actively through verbal or written responses, whereas observation involves the recording of the respondent's behavior. Respondent data falls into the general categories of past behavior, attitudes, and respondent characteristics.

The advantages of the communication method are versatility, speed, and cost. The possible disadvantages are the respondent's unwillingness or inability to provide data and the influence of the questioning process.

The questionnaire is the most common data collection technique. The questions and the possible responses are predetermined, and the objective of the study is obvious to the respondent from the questions asked. This technique is used for conclusive research purposes.

Interviews may be conducted in person or through the telephone, Internet, or mail. The criteria for selecting among these means of communication are versatility, time and cost, sample control, quantity and quality of data, and response rate.

The advantages of the observation method are that it decreases the potential for bias from the interviewer and the interviewing process and that certain types of data can be collected only with this method. The disadvantages are that mental reactions and certain behavior patterns cannot be observed and that cost and time constraints limit observation to behavior patterns that are short in duration, occur frequently, or are predictable.

Observational techniques can be classified as natural or contrived, disguised or undisguised, structured or unstructured, direct or indirect, or human or mechanical.

Gathering data from children is a special case for which both communication and observational techniques must be adapted.

Key Terms

(A-I-O items) (p. 230)
audimeter (p. 239)
contrived observation (p. 238)
depth interview (p. 227)
direct observation (p. 239)
disintermediated (p. 235)
experience survey (p. 228)
eye-camera (p. 240)
focus group (p. 215)
indirect observation (p. 239)
metric equivalence (p. 242)
natural observation (p. 238)
pantry audit (p. 239)
psychogalvanometer (p. 239)
pupilometer (p. 240)
quality of data (p. 235)
response rate (p. 236)
sample control (p. 234)
sampling frame (p. 234)
scalability (p. 232)
self-reference criteria (p. 242)
sensitivity analysis (p. 237)
structured observation (p. 239)
subjective estimate (p. 237)
subsample measurement (p. 237)
trend projection (p. 237)
unstructured observation (p. 239)

Discussion Questions

1 Discuss some of the problems that may arise in the process of designing or conducting a focus group. In particular, to what extent can moderators anticipate the likely directions (and misdirections) the discussion may take?

2 What are some of the desirable characteristics of focus group moderators? How might a researcher go about ensuring that potential moderators are appropriate for a specific project, over and above general qualifications?

3 When would an in-depth interview be more useful than a focus group, and vice versa? Give examples of each, and explain your rationale.

4 What are the issues and steps in the analysis of qualitative data? Are there qualitative data that cannot be "analyzed" in that fashion? What sort of data do you believe would be most difficult to subject to rigorous scrutiny?

5 There are many types of data that can be, and typically are, collected from respondents. Give examples of the main types of such data and, for each, well-posed questions that would provide each type.

6 Identify and explain the techniques used for estimating nonresponse error when communication approaches are used. Which do you think would be the most broadly applicable or the most broadly successful?

7 Discuss the classification of observational techniques. For each technique, give an example for which it would be suited and one for which it may yield misleading results.

8 Discuss the issues involved in determining when and where an automobile tire manufacturer should conduct focus groups to get feedback from customers on its line of winter tires. Would this topic be a good candidate for online recruitment? Why or why not? Give a brief description of customers who would be good candidates for this type of focus group. What kind of questions would you use for screening?

Review Questions

1 How do qualitative techniques aid exploratory research?

a by providing primary sources of data on consumer behavior and attitudes
b by providing background information on a management problem and a historical perspective from which to assess the nature of a problem situation
c by providing longitudinal or recent accurate information about a decision situation
d all of the above

2 In which of the following ways are qualitative techniques distinguished from quantitative techniques used in marketing research?

a Qualitative techniques give more "human" information regarding consumer attitudes and thinking.
b Quantitative techniques are necessary to help achieve the decision-oriented rigor required of conclusive research.
c Qualitative techniques can aid the initial development of hypotheses to be tested later by quantitative methods.
d all of the above

3 Which of the following objectives would be best served by a focus group?

a to assess the likelihood of success of a new marketing (pricing, promotions, distribution) plan
b to test hypotheses regarding the demographics of good target markets for a product
c to gather further information to interpret the results of prior quantitative research
d to decrease uncertainty about the demand forecast before the release of a new product

4 You are screening people for a focus group on the market for ladies' razors among working women. Which of these candidates would make acceptable participants?

a a woman who currently works as a bank teller and who recently emigrated from China
b a woman of European ancestry with three children who works in her own home and has proven herself a competent focus group participant
c a Native American woman who works for Gillette and has never participated in a focus group before
d a woman from the Caribbean who used to work as a store clerk and is currently training to become a dentist

5 Which of the following abilities would be useful for a focus group moderator to convey in the context of running a group?

a the ability to display encyclopedic knowledge of the product, its uses, and market perceptions of it
b the ability to keep groups focused and on topic by providing a disciplined structure for communication

- c the ability to notice when a few people are dominating and others are reserved or silent and to encourage better balance in discreet ways
- d all of the above

6 How can a researcher maintain a scientific approach to the analysis of qualitative data generated from a focus group, one-on-one interview, or other technique generating a great deal of verbal or visual data?
- a create categorical (nominal) variables before the session is conducted, evaluate session feedback accordingly, and apply categorical data analysis methods to the resultant data set
- b have multiple, independent judges apply personal interpretations to the session data and decide on appropriate methods of data analysis accordingly
- c test for validity of hypotheses based on session feedback
- d none of the above

7 Which of these are advantages of depth interviews relative to focus groups?
- a The success of depth interviews depends on the skill of the interviewer, whereas the success of focus groups does not.
- b It is easier to associate a participant's feeling with related beliefs in a depth interview.
- c Depth interviews are more like group therapy and allow participants to connect with their inner values, beliefs, and feelings.
- d Focus groups involve sampling the target segment and therefore give more accurate information on the market.

8 Characteristics of conclusive research are that it
- a is concerned with making explicit predictions.
- b often seeks to objectively quantify and accurately measure attitudes, beliefs, and feelings.
- c involves communication with or observation of respondents and their behavior.
- d all of the above.

9 In selecting a communication method for collecting respondent data, which of the following is not always among the main considerations?
- a ability to reach the target sample
- b potential bias of using specific media
- c interviewer skills
- d response rate

10 How may researchers compensate for nonresponse error?
- a estimate the nonresponse error subjectively, based on experience
- b notice trends in successive callbacks and project these to estimate the characteristics of those who do not respond
- c measure subsamples of the nonrespondent group in order to estimate the results for that group
- d all of the above

Web Exercise

Log in to the Online Edition of your textbook at www.atomicdog.com to participate in this Web exercise, which can be found in your Online Study Guide for this chapter.

Further Reading

Bystedt, Jean, Siri Lynn, Deborah Potts, and Gregg Fraley (2003), *Moderating to the Max: A Full-Tilt Guide to Creative Insightful Focus Groups and Depth Interviews*, Ithaca, NY: Paramount Market Publishing.

Dillman, Don A. (2000), *Mail and Internet Surveys: The Tailored Design Method*, Hoboken, NJ: John Wiley & Sons.

Fern, Edward F. (2001), *Advanced Focus Group Research*, Thousand Oaks, CA: Sage Publications.

Fowler, Floyd J. (2002), *Survey Research Methods*, 3rd Edition. Thousand Oaks, CA: Sage Publications.

Groves, Robert M., Don A. Dillman, John L. Eltinge, and Roderick J. A. Little (2001), *Survey Nonresponse*, Hoboken, NJ: Wiley.

Groves, Robert M., Floyd J. Fowler, Mick P. Couper, James M. Lepkowski, Eleanor Singer, and Roger Tourangeau (2004), *Survey Methodology*, Hoboken, NJ: Wiley.

Krueger, Richard A. (2000), *Focus Groups: A Practical Guide for Applied Research*, 3rd Edition. Thousand Oaks, CA: Sage Publications.

Morgan, David L. (1997), *Focus Groups as Qualitative Research*, 2nd Edition. Thousand Oaks, CA: Sage Publications.

Strauss, Anselm, and Juliet M. Corbin (1998), *Basics of Qualitative Research: Techniques and Procedures for Developing Grounded Theory*, 2nd Edition. Thousand Oaks, CA: Sage Publications.

Notes

1 Peter Tuckel, Elaine Leppo, and Barbara Kaplan (1992), "Focus Groups under Scrutiny," *Marketing Research: A Magazine of Management & Applications* (June).

2 Remington, Todd (1992), "Rising Refusal Rates: The Impact of Telemarketing," *Quirk's Marketing Research Review* (May).

CHAPTER SEVEN
DESIGNING SURVEYS AND DATA COLLECTION INSTRUMENTS

"Everyone takes surveys. Whoever makes a statement about human behavior has engaged in a survey of some sort."

ANDREW GREELEY

"That is the essence of science: Ask an impertinent question, and you are on the way to a pertinent answer."

JACOB BRONOWSKI

In previous chapters we have discussed the types of primary and secondary marketing data. We now consider the issues involved in designing forms for primary data collection. The emphasis is on constructing forms appropriate for conclusive research, where the research design requires a structured data collection method capable of providing valid and relevant data for decision making.

To the lay public, surveys and questionnaires *are* marketing research; such is their ubiquity and influence. Although they represent but a part of the marketing researcher's arsenal of techniques, data collection forms are indeed a central, pivotal component of most research studies. All four major communication media—personal, telephone, computer-based, and mail interviews—rely on questionnaires. Because questionnaire studies are far more prevalent than observational studies, the bulk of this chapter will be devoted to issues involved in questionnaire construction. Much of this discussion will be relevant to the issues involved in developing data collection forms for observation, and the final section will be specifically devoted to observational forms.

7.1 Function and Importance of Questionnaires

A *questionnaire* is a formalized method for collecting data from respondents. The function of the questionnaire is, in a word, measurement. Questionnaires can be used to measure a wide variety of marketing-related quantities, including past purchase and usage behavior, attitudes and opinions, intentions, awareness and knowledge, ownership, and a variety of respondent characteristics.

Measurement error is a serious problem in questionnaire construction (see the Special Expert Feature on survey biases at the end of this chapter for greater detail). For example, the Survey Research Center at the University of Michigan once asked half of respondents on a consumer survey the following question regarding attitudes toward a gasoline price increase: "Are you in favor of the proposed gasoline tax, starting with five cents and rising to 50 cents, which will be imposed if we do not meet conservation goals?" The results were that 27 percent favored the additional taxes, whereas 65 percent opposed them. The other half of the respondents were asked, "If the United States had to choose between becoming dependent on uncertain foreign oil supplies and curbing gasoline use by raising taxes, which would you favor?" In contrast to the previous finding, 71 percent favored the higher tax alternative, with only 13 percent opting for uncertain oil sources. What could cause such a marked difference in responses? The answer, obvious when both questions are put before us, lies in wording and context. The first question does not pose an explicit alternative to the consumer and involves no *trade-off of valued options*. Rather, the consumer is offered the implicit alternative of higher gasoline prices versus lower gasoline prices, that is, the status quo versus a pure loss. It is unsurprising that most consumers would prefer lower prices, particularly given that the higher prices would continue to escalate. The second question poses the trade-off of higher prices now versus greater dependence on foreign oil supplies in the future. Respondents can easily tell the purpose of the higher prices and that they represent a trade-off between their short-term financial gain and longer-term social dependency issues. The lesson here is that when a preference question is asked without posing realistic alternatives or plausible trade-offs, results can be misleading or even meaningless.

Let us consider another example, one with special relevance as women throughout the industrialized world enter the workforce, many in "second careers" after time taken off for additional training, raising families, or higher education. Two outwardly similar ways of posing a question to women not presently in the workforce have been widely used. The first is: "Would you like to be employed outside the home, if this were currently feasible?" The second is: "Would you prefer to be employed outside the home, or would you prefer to continue to work on your current projects and stay within the home?" The second question makes explicit the implied choice in the first question, namely, that there are many activities for which there would be less time if outside employment were sought (and, perhaps, also "legitimizing" work done within the home). When questions of this nature were put to a sample of nonworking women,

Marketing Research Focus 7.1

Questioning the Reliability of Questionnaires

Over the past 2 decades, consumer-oriented studies have proliferated worldwide, as businesses seek to get a handle on consumer opinions and habits. Sometimes such studies degenerate into little more than corporate public relations efforts or product pitches. In fact, a growth area of research is the "promotional" study, conducted solely for its public relations value. A serious problem occurs when a survey purporting to contain unbiased and useful information is conducted in a way that affects the result by deliberately skewing the construction of questions or through poor methodology.

Studies quoted as "independent" are often sponsored by groups with an abiding interest in the study's outcome. Such sponsorship can mean that questions are designed in such a way as to elicit responses desired by the sponsor, which can then be used in ad copy or other promotional contexts. These errors may not be discoverable by the lay public or outside researchers because the original survey text is rarely available. For example, Levi Strauss & Co. questioned students about which fashions would be most popular, and 90 percent of those surveyed chose Levi's 501 jeans. The 501s were the only jeans listed explicitly on the questionnaire. Whether this was merely poor research design or an overt attempt to skew results is difficult to say, although there can be little question of an overall biasing effect.

Although "independent" researchers are never explicitly told by a sponsor what results are desired, an implicit message is rarely difficult to discern; favorable conclusions result in further funding and follow-up studies. Budget constraints, combined with shorter timelines, also lead researchers to use smaller sample sizes. These samples cause problems when researchers attempt to project results onto a larger population, because of the sampling error intrinsic to the undertaking. For example, in a national poll using a healthy sample size of 10,000 people, demographic subsegments of particular interest are far smaller. Among those 10,000, there may be only a few dozen university-educated women with at least two children living in the home, and even fewer men older than 75 years who chose to respond to the survey. Summaries of their views may misestimate those of the groups they are meant to represent, even if the sample size of the entire poll is admirably large.

In one famous case, that of Anita Hill's allegations regarding Clarence Thomas during hearings on his nomination to the Supreme Court, national polls typically included only 500 to 700 people. When broken into segments, margins of error could easily top 10 percent. Therefore, when an ABC–*Washington Post* poll (in which 500 people were polled, of whom 50 percent were women) concluded that more women believed Thomas (38 percent) than Hill (28 percent), the opposite could easily have been true, owing to sampling error alone. (Explicit statistical calculations show $p = \sim.025$, for "more women in the population believe Thomas than Hill," a reasonable level of significance, but not small enough for an ironclad conclusion.)

Other factors can affect a survey's credibility. The sample participants may not be representative of the general population, data analysis may not have been undertaken correctly, and conclusions may be selected so that only the most favorable results are reported. The most famous sampling error in history occurred in the early years of public opinion polling. In the 1936 presidential election, *Literary Digest* magazine declared Republican Alf Landon a landslide victor over Franklin D. Roosevelt. The sample contained only people who had telephones or owned automobiles in the midst of the Great Depression—in other words, affluent respondents. The modern science of sampling helps rule out such obvious errors, but in practice it is tricky to do so definitively.

News media often exacerbate these sorts of problems by seizing on biased studies and passing their conclusions on to consumers without criticism. Journalists are seldom qualified to determine whether a study's methodology was properly carried out. Sometimes this information is not easily obtainable, as technical details are often considered proprietary. Statistics are extensively cited, even when inappropriate sampling renders them little short of meaningless.

The Council of American Survey Research Organizations (www.casro.org), a trade group, has published a code of standards, mandatory for all its members, covering methodology and sponsorship to increase researchers' responsibility to the public. A dual standard of information has been proposed whereby "entertainment" and "informative" studies would be clearly separated. Until such standards are implemented universally, survey readers need to be on their guard.

Source: Crossen, Cynthia, "Margin of Error: Studies and Surveys Proliferate, but Poor Methodology Makes Many Unreliable," *The Wall Street Journal.* November 14, 1991.
www.casro.org/codeofstandards.cfm

the first type resulted in 81 percent stating that they would like to work outside the home, and the second type resulted in a 32 percent figure. This dramatic difference again emphasizes the importance of questionnaire wording. The researcher must ask, "Do the questions truly measure what they are supposed to?" If the answer is no, measurement error is present. Although sampling error rarely results in outcome differences of the magnitude in the example, it is still crucial to control it, as it is often *the* largest source of preventable error in market research, far exceeding errors in sampling plans or administration. *Marketing Research Focus 7.1* examines a number of situations in which survey reliability is in doubt and skepticism on the part of both researchers and ordinary consumers is warranted.

7.2 Questionnaire Components

A questionnaire typically comprises five sections:

- identification data,
- request for cooperation,
- instructions,
- information sought, and
- classification data.

Let us look at each in turn.

Identification data, often placed first (though sometimes last) in the questionnaire, asks for such information as the respondent's name, address, and phone number. Part of all of this information is typically obtained before the interview from sources such as respondent lists or preinterview screening contacts. Any incomplete identification data can be determined at the end of the request for cooperation section or at the end of the questionnaire when more detailed classification data are sought. Additional data would include items such as the time and date of the interview, as well as the interviewer's name or code number. Identification data are typically used only internally and are not reported along with research results, for reasons of confidentiality. Unless such data are needed explicitly, for record-keeping, classification, or otherwise, it is often best to omit them from the research plan, assigning each respondent a numerical code, or to allow respondents to choose which data they wish to provide.

The *request for cooperation* is an opening statement designed to enlist the respondent's help regarding the interview. This statement typically first identifies the interviewer and/or the interviewing organization. Next, the purpose of the study is explained, and the time required to complete the interview is given. Often researchers will elect to include the purpose of the study if disclosing it will not bias respondent outcomes.

The *instructions* are comments to the interviewer or the respondent about how to interact with and eventually complete the questionnaire. The comments appear directly on the questionnaire in a mail or computer survey. With the personal or telephone survey, a separate sheet titled "Interviewer Instructions" explains the purpose of the study, the sampling plan, and other aspects of the data collection process. In addition, the questionnaire may contain special instructions on how to use specific questions—for example, an attitude scaling technique. Researchers should bear in mind that instructions need to be clear and universally comprehensible, free of jargon and requiring that respondents need memorize as little as possible, particularly for phone surveys.

The *information sought* forms the major, and invariably the longest, portion of the questionnaire. The remainder of this chapter deals with designing this aspect of the questionnaire.

The *classification data* section concerns the characteristics of the respondent, primarily "geodemographic" data, which locates respondents and allows one to place them in factual categories. These data are provided directly by the respondent in the case of a mail or computer-based survey; in a personal or telephone interview survey the data are usually collected from the respondent by the interviewer. In some cases the personal interviewer may estimate sensitive types of data (for example, income) based on observation. Classification data are typically collected at the end of the interview, since some respondents may be reluctant to disclose personal data (e.g., income, age, education level, and occupation) until rapport with the interviewing situation has been established through the question-and-answer process. However, some sampling procedures require that classification data be collected at the beginning of the interview, to determine whether the person qualifies as part of the sampling plan. In such cases, it is typical practice to disclose the group being explicitly surveyed so that respondents can simply indicate whether they qualify, without needing to provide extensive personal information at the outset.

7.3 Questionnaire Design

Questionnaire design is more an art form than a scientific undertaking. No steps, principles, or guidelines can absolutely guarantee an effective and efficient questionnaire. In fact, slavishly following fixed steps may lead researchers to devise overly lengthy, uninspired survey instruments that merely avoid making obvious errors. Questionnaire design is a skill that the researcher learns through experience, after some basic principles are assimilated. The only way to develop this skill is to write a questionnaire, use it in a series of interviews, analyze its weaknesses, revise it, and then repeat this process for new surveys.

Figure 7.1 Guidelines for Questionnaire Design

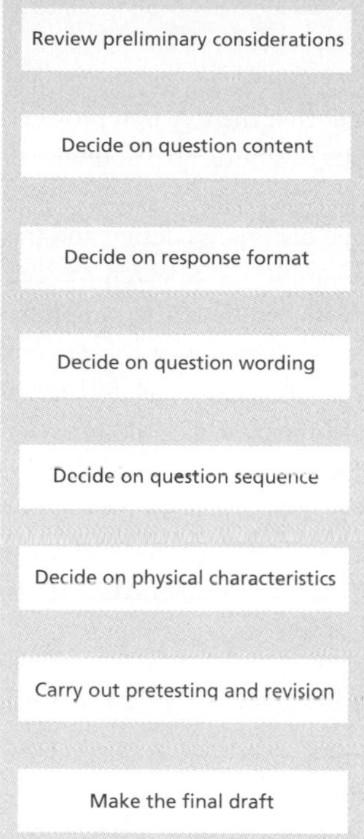

What we do know about questionnaire design comes from the experience of researchers who have specialized in this area. From this accumulated experience have emerged a series of best practices that can be useful to the beginning researcher confronted with the task of designing a questionnaire. These rules are useful in avoiding serious errors; fine-tuning questionnaire design requires the creative inspiration of the skilled researcher. Although the guidelines discussed in this section lay the foundation for questionnaire design, ultimately the quality of the questionnaire depends on the skill and judgment of the researcher, a clear understanding of the information needed, a firm idea of how the data will eventually be analyzed, a sensitivity to the role of the respondent, and extensive pretesting. In our experience, a beginning researcher is likely to undervalue pretesting, which roots out real-world survey problems that no amount of discussion or prelaunch checking can fully catch.

When constructing questionnaires, researchers follow a set of broad, interrelated guidelines. Figure 7.1 presents these guidelines as separate steps:

1. Review preliminary considerations.
2. Decide on question content.
3. Decide on response format.
4. Decide on question wording.
5. Decide on question sequence.
6. Decide on physical characteristics.
7. Carry out pretesting and revision.
8. Make the final draft.

However, no step should be considered fully "stand alone"; decisions made early in the sequence will often influence choices later in the sequence, and vice versa. It is common for researchers to iterate among them until a final research plan emerges.

7.3a Preliminary Considerations: Getting Started

The preliminary considerations for conducting conclusive research were discussed in Chapter 2, which focused on methods of establishing an effective link between the decision-making process and the research process. Central to this process is the development of research objectives and the listing of information needs. The research design must be formulated, the steps in the research process visualized and planned, and many decisions made before the questionnaire can be designed.

Previous Decisions

The questionnaire design stage presumes that the research project is well under way and that many decisions have already been made. Decisions regarding questionnaire design must build on and be consistent with decisions relating to other aspects of the research project.

Previous decisions regarding the type of research design and the sources of data directly influence the character and the role of the questionnaire in the research project. It is essential to have a clear picture of the target population and to know the details of the sampling plan (see Chapter 8). Questionnaire design is critically influenced by the characteristics of the respondent group. The more heterogeneous the respondent group—that is, the more variation in geodemographics, attitudes, and behavior amongst the members of the group—the more difficult it is to design a single questionnaire that is universally appropriate. Typically, the questionnaire must be designed to be comprehensible to the least able respondent, without requiring additional information or intervention. The measurement scales and communication media that will be used must be specified and the nature of the research findings, including the necessary data processing and analysis, visualized. The tactical aspects of questionnaire design are closely related to these final stages of the research process.

Link between Information Needs and Data to Be Collected

From a detailed listing of information needs and a clear definition of the respondent group, the researcher begins to design the questionnaire.

Each question included on the questionnaire should relate to a specific information need. Questions unrelated to specific, explicit information needs can be justified, however, if they help secure the respondent's cooperation or add continuity to the questioning process. In practice, there is a strong tendency to include questions that seem "interesting" but have no specific link to the information needs, on the theory that something intriguing, important, or unexpected might be turned up. However, unnecessary or frivolous questions add expense to the survey and increase the demands placed on the respondent. A general guideline is that any such additional questions should enhance the verifiability or accuracy of the information collected, as opposed to opening up entirely new areas of inquiry not originally part of the research design.

7.3b Decide on Question Content: What, Exactly, Do We Need to Know?

The content of the questions is influenced by the respondent's ability and/or willingness to respond accurately. It is imperative that the researcher envision the various ways in which a respondent might fail to answer a question accurately or at all, leading to thorny problems of response bias or missing data.

Ability to Answer Accurately

Assuming that the desired data are relevant to the decision problem, the researcher must be sensitive to the respondent's ability to provide the data. Many types of data cannot be accurately collected from respondents. Inaccurate data can result from any combination of the respondent being uninformed or forgetful and (unintentionally) misremembering. Note that this holds aside the issue of respondents' knowingly omitting data or providing inaccurate answers.

Respondent Is Uninformed. We are frequently asked questions to which we do not have the answers. (As students, we confront this situation far more often than we would like.) Respondents may confront this situation when they try to fill out questionnaires. They may be asked to provide data about their spouses' monthly gross incomes or about credit card purchases—subjects about which they do not possess accurate information. They may be asked questions about advertisements, products, brands, or retail outlets of which they are unaware. Researchers have discovered that respondents will often answer questions even though they have limited knowledge of the topic, perhaps because they overestimate their own degree of expertise or are unwilling to admit their lack of knowledge. This situation represents a serious source of measurement error, one which is difficult to overcome without careful planning.

Often the phrasing of a question implies that the answer should be known, encouraging the respondent to try to answer it somehow. The question "What is the current interest rate you receive on your savings account?" implies that the respondent should know the answer. An alternative would be "Do you know the current interest rate on your savings account?" This question implies that some holders of savings accounts do not know the interest rate, which makes it easier for the respondent to admit a lack of knowledge. If the respondent answers this question in the affirmative, the first question can then be asked. It is often a good idea to place disclaimers about knowledge in the overall instructions, or in a section header, along the lines of: "Please fill in the following information if you happen to know it offhand. If not, feel free to leave any answer blank." This lets respondents know that omitting information is acceptable and that they should not guess or extrapolate in order to please the researchers. Another possibility, if a rough answer is preferred to none at all, is prefacing questions with qualifiers such as "approximately" or "within [a certain range]." Note that this is risky, and may cause researchers to grossly overstate confidence in the reported information.

Respondent Is Forgetful. People are frequently asked questions the answers to which they once knew but have now forgotten. (Again, as students, we are continually confronted with this situation.) Numerous studies have shown that we forget most events fairly rapidly after we learn about them, unless we make a point of "rehearsing" the information specifically to be able to recall it when needed. The rate of forgetting is quite rapid over the first few days and continues with the passage of time. The probability of forgetting is influenced by the importance of the event and how often it is repeated, as well as by its vividness. It is easier to remember important facts such as the first person on the moon or the first car we purchased, in what psychologists sometimes refer to as "flashbulb memory." In contrast, how many of us remember with equal ease and clarity the second person on the moon or the second car we purchased? It is also easier to remember events that are repeated frequently—for example, products bought on a regular basis or ads that have run for a long time.

When the information needs of a study require questions that ask the respondent to recall events that are unimportant to the respondent or that occur infrequently, the researcher has a potentially serious problem in designing the questionnaire. He or she must not overestimate the ability of the respondent to recall the event and the surrounding circumstances accurately. This is an easy mistake to make when the topic of the questionnaire is particularly important in the eyes of the researcher or decision maker. The mistake can be compounded by providing subtle clues in one part of the survey or worse yet, overt information, which will "cue" respondents to provide data that would ordinarily be difficult for them to recall on their own. For example, mentioning a particular fast-food restaurant early in a survey can severely bias any questions appearing later on about eating habits or food preferences. Avoiding such situations and revealing pertinent information at the appropriate point are among the chief considerations in the design of questionnaires meant to elicit, and measure the degree of, consumer knowledge.

In collecting data about "unimportant" or infrequently occurring events, there are several options available. The researcher can try to interview the respondents who are most likely to remember—for example, recent purchasers. This may provide useful data about those who remember but will grossly overstate the likelihood of a typical consumer remembering in the first place. Alternatively, the questionnaire can include techniques that stimulate respondents' recall of the event, hopefully without biasing the very information the researcher seeks. The three main methods of accomplishing this are *unaided recall*, *aided recall*, and *recognition*.

Several studies suggest that questions that rely on unaided recall—questions that do not give cues about the event—can underestimate the actual occurrence of the event. Many researchers appreciate unaided recall because it is a "strong test": because it does not jog respondent memory or provide any leading information, data provided are never contaminated by other parts of the survey or by information unintentionally revealed by an interviewer. But unaided recall has an enormous disadvantage, in that one must survey many respondents who will, in the end, provide no useful information. Because of the time and costs associated with large-scale consumer research, unaided recall is seldom the method of choice.

An approach relying on aided recall attempts to overcome problems of respondent memory and lack of efficiency in administering questionnaires. Its key feature is that it provides the respondent with cues and partial information regarding the event of interest. Rather than ask respondents to list anything that caught their interest or to recall small details that they would be unlikely to remember on their own, aided recall provides a clear context so that if a respondent does have some memory for the event in

unaided recall
A test of ad effectiveness that does not allow for any form of "prompting" or cueing (i.e., no relevant information is provided that might help jog the memory) when requesting that respondents recall any ad messages they remember being exposed to (seeing or hearing) during a stated time period.

aided recall
A test of ad effectiveness that relies on "prompting" or cueing (i.e., providing some form of relevant information) when requesting that respondents recall any ad messages they remember being exposed to (seeing or hearing) during a stated time period.

recognition
A method of stimulating a respondent's recall of an event (often, seeing an advertisement) that involves direct reference to that event, such as showing the respondent the actual ad, or some part thereof, and asking if the respondent has seen it before.

question, it is dramatically more likely to be elicited than in unaided recall. One can go even further on this spectrum, all the way to recognition, whereby a researcher simply asks whether a respondent has in fact come across or experienced something. Recognition is often considered a potentially misleading method, since there is no cost to a respondent to answer yes, which can come about merely to avoid seeming unknowledgeable. Respondents can also simply misremember or mistakenly believe that a positive response somehow helps the interviewer.

It is easy to compare and contrast unaided recall, aided recall, and recognition; doing so helps one to see their relative merits and weaknesses writ large. For example, consider a research project meant to determine awareness of a new TV commercial (a very common task for market researchers) for a new athletic shoe. An unaided recall question might ask, "What products do you recall having been advertised in the last week?"—perhaps with some details. The aided-recall version might ask instead specifically about advertisements for athletic products on TV, perhaps adding that a celebrity endorser was involved. And a recognition version might simply show the ad in question and ask whether the respondent had seen it before. It is not difficult to see why aided recall is usually the method of choice in marketing research. The unaided recall version will have the virtue of not revealing potentially biasing clues, but it will generate an enormous amount of information about *other* products and perhaps almost none about what researchers are really after, using up enormous and costly respondent samples in the process. By contrast, anyone who has seen a commercial *like* the one shown in the recognition task—using a similar endorser, for a competitive product or even a prior ad for the same product line—may indicate that he or she has seen it before. The "art" in creating good aided recall questions is to provide enough aid to elicit useful information, without offering so much that one skews critical measurements.

A classic illustration of the perils of recognition comes from a study run by the U.S. Army, keen to determine which of 375 food items were most liked and disliked by soldiers. Concerned that some respondents might be answering randomly, misremembering, or simply choosing interesting-sounding foods, the researchers cleverly included several items that the soldiers had never tried and still others that were not even foods, including such fake delicacies as "funistrada" and "braised trake." Much to their surprise, "funistrada" proved highly popular, even more so than such real foods as eggplant, apricot pie, and lima beans. "Braised trake" was notably less popular, although it was hard to tell whether this was because it did not exist. Survey results of this type, where nonexistent items elicit high praise, offer strong caution against the casual use of recognition as a sole criterion.

Respondent Misremembers. When respondents forget something they once knew, we as researchers would like to believe that they will simply omit the information from their responses. In the real world, however, people often remember *that* they knew something without being able to recall the thing itself. We all once knew the address and phone number of houses we lived in, or every teacher we took a class from, and we *know that we knew*, without being able to recall it reliably at will. In such cases, respondents often attempt to reconstruct that knowledge when asked to provide it. The chief problem here is that such remembering is not "unbiased" in the statistical sense, that is, that one is equally likely to overestimate or underestimate a requested quantity or to remember all comparable items with equal likelihood. All of us are familiar with what is sometimes called a "nostalgic bias," the tendency to remember past events in a more positive light. Older consumers, in particular, often have detailed memories of events long past but have greater trouble recalling more recent ones; in such cases, what is easily recalled may be substituted for what was never committed to memory in the first place, often without full respondent awareness. Generally speaking, it is extremely difficult to guard against this sort of biased misremembering. Using appropriate scales, providing relevant time referents (e.g., "in the past month"), asking the question in multiple ways to different respondents (a "split" questionnaire design), and relying on aided recall can all be helpful in keeping such memory biases to a minimum.

Willingness to Respond Accurately

Assuming that respondents *can* accurately answer the question, the next issue is to determine their willingness to do so. Unwillingness to respond accurately can be reflected in refusal to respond to a question or a series of questions, that is, item nonresponse error; or deliberate provision of an incorrect or distorted response to a question, that is, measurement error. Combinations of the two are also possible, where respondents are asked to provide a list of items (e.g., books read, exercise activities undertaken in the past 6 months) but do so selectively.

Respondents may be unwilling to respond accurately for several interrelated reasons. For example, they may consider the situation inappropriate for disclosing the data or too invasive, such as when a department store asks for a home address to include in its database when one has simply made a purchase. It is also possible that disclosing the data would be embarrassing; health researchers seeking to track the spread of certain diseases or to curb the use of street drugs are constantly hampered by such concerns. Or disclosure may pose a potential threat to respondents' social standing or normative views, such as when their education or salary is not commensurate with their current position or when they know that they engaged in certain behavior as youths that they now openly oppose.

It is important to remember that respondents have limited motivation to answer questions *accurately*, even if they are being compensated for participation. In personal or telephone interviews, respondents may be more concerned about how the interviewer may react to their responses than about the accuracy of the responses (this is one reason that interviewers must practice a studied neutrality on hearing verbal responses). This is especially the situation if the questions are embarrassing or threaten respondents' prestige or viewpoints. The result can be item nonresponse or, worse yet, inaccurate responses.

Respondents' willingness to answer questions is conditioned by the interviewing context. A question regarding personal hygiene may be considered appropriate when asked by a nurse or doctor as part of a physical examination but inappropriate when asked by an interviewer conducting a study for a pharmaceutical manufacturer. Respondents' willingness to answer a question is also a function of their understanding of whether the data are needed for a legitimate purpose. The collection of classification data can present a serious problem in this regard. A respondent may be hesitant to provide accurate data when abruptly faced with personal questions regarding age, occupation, and income. A question of the form "Next, I would like to ask some questions about yourself. What is your … ?" fails to offer any motivation for answering or a sense of the purpose of the request. Even a brief explanation can make such a request legitimate for most respondents, as in: "To better understand how the reactions to this new product differ among people with different age, income, and occupational characteristics, we need to know your …" Often it is enough merely to suggest that the data will be used for "classification" or "statistical purposes." If the data will be held confidential, respondents should be told this directly.

Following are some approaches that have been developed to mitigate bias resulting from respondents' unwillingness to respond accurately.

- **Counterbiasing statement.** Begin the question with a statement suggesting that the subject behavior is rather common and then ask the respondent the question. There is a risk, however, that this may overcorrect if not applied with care.
- **Indirect statement.** Phrase the sensitive question so that it refers to "other people," "people you know," or even "people like you." The respondent's own behavior or attitude will likely be reflected in the response.
- **Labeled response categories.** Present the respondent with a card that lists the sensitive response alternatives and has the responses identified by letters or numbers. The respondent uses the letter or number to indicate a response to the sensitive question. In very sensitive situations, answers can be placed in a locked box with no identifying information, dropped off with another researcher, or anonymously e-mailed.
- **Randomized response technique.** Present the respondent with two questions, either of which can be answered yes or no. One question concerns the sensitive issue (e.g., "Have you shoplifted in the past month?"), whereas the other question concerns a nonsensitive (e.g., "Were you born in the same month as your best friend?") about which the researcher can gain no direct knowledge, only a probability (e.g., the chance that the two were born in the same month is approximately 1/12, but this can be estimated using survey data as well). Which question is answered depends on the outcome of a *randomizing device*, usually of a transparent nature, like a coin flip. For example, the respondent flips the coin, notes the outcome (which is *not* disclosed to the researcher), and answers the sensitive question if the outcome is, say, heads. Since the response format of the two questions is identical (i.e., yes or no), *the interviewer never knows for certain which question the respondent has answered.* It may seem impossible to reconstruct information about the question of interest, but this is not so, as long as the proportion of respondents who answer yes to the nonsensitive question can be determined through secondary sources, through another research survey, or through a "mathematical model" (e.g., one that says that approximately 1/12 of people were born in the same month as their best friends). The

counterbiasing statement
A statement made by an interviewer suggesting that the behavior in question is normal or natural, to offset a respondent's reluctance to answer honestly about a sensitive topic.

indirect statement
A method of posing sensitive questions so that they refer explicitly to others, and not to respondents themselves.

labeled response categories
A method, often used to compensate for a respondent's reluctance to answer a sensitive question, that labels response options with letters or numbers and asks the respondent to refer to one of the labels.

randomized response technique
A survey technique in which respondents are presented with pairs of questions, one they may be reluctant to answer (i.e., because of embarrassment or unwillingness to disclose) and one that is innocuous; which they are assigned to answer is determined randomly—for example, by a coin flip.

proportion of people who answer yes to the sensitive issue can be determined through a formula based on conditional probability. For simplicity, let us assume that the randomizing device (e.g., the coin flip) produces two equally likely outcomes, so that the chances of answering the sensitive and nonsensitive questions are the same (that is, the probability is 1/2). We will also know the likelihood of responding yes to the nonsensitive question. So we will observe a yes answer if a respondent is randomly selected for the sensitive question (with probability 1/2) and answers yes, *or* if the respondent is selected for the nonsensitive question and answers yes.
Mathematically:

$$\text{Prob[Yes]} = (1/2)\ \text{Prob[Yes on Sensitive Question]} + (1/2)\ \text{Prob[Yes on Nonsensitive Question]}.$$

(Note that if the randomizing device has a different probability, we can substitute for 1/2 easily in the equation.) Simple algebra reveals that the quantity we are after can be expressed as:

$$\text{Prob[Yes on Sensitive Question]} = 2^{*}\text{Prob[Yes]} - \text{Prob[Yes on Nonsensitive Question]}.$$

In the shoplifting study, if 17 of 248 total respondents answer yes overall, the proportion born in the same month as their best friend is assumed to be 1/12 (or found empirically through a secondary source like a survey), and we have indeed used a coin flip (so that the probability of answering each question is 0.5), the estimate of the proportion of respondents answering yes to the shoplifting question is as follows:

$$\text{Prob[Yes on Sensitive Question]} = 2^{*}(17/248) - 1/12 = 0.054.$$

The randomized response technique shows that approximately 5.4 percent of the respondents have shoplifted. Note, however, that it will not tell you *which* respondents have shoplifted. If it is important to match shoplifting behavior to variables (covariates) like age, income, or other individual-specific data, randomized response should not be the method of choice. Nonetheless, it is a powerful way to allow respondents to keep sensitive information to themselves while allowing researchers to gain useful statistical knowledge. Note as well that the nonsensitive question should never be something easily discernible, such as gender or eye color, but something the respondent has not been asked to disclose, such as birth month.

7.3c Decide on Response Format

Once the content of the questions has been analyzed and associated problems have been ironed out, the next issue concerns the *type* of questions to use. The main issue here is the *degree of structure* imposed on a person's responses. In courtrooms, witnesses are often asked, "Please restrict your responses to yes or no"; in other situations, the instructions are "please describe in your own words. . . ." In survey research, one constantly faces the analogous issue of whether to allow for the complex, lengthy, and complete data enabled by using one's own words, or the easily understood and definitive data obtained by restricting what a respondent can indicate. We next consider three types of questions, ranging from unstructured to structured response formats, and the benefits and deficits of each. Survey researchers need to conceptualize in advance which question type is appropriate to the needs of the project.

Open-Ended Questions

open-ended (or free-response or free-answer) question
A question design that allows respondents to provide answers freely, in their own words, instead of choosing among various options defined by the interviewer.

An open-ended question, also often referred to as a *free-response* (or *free-answer*) *question*, allows respondents to provide their own answers, usually in their own words. In a mail or computer-based interview, space is provided in which the respondent can write or key in the answer. In a personal or telephone interview, the respondent verbally reports the answer to the interviewer, who records it on the questionnaire. Examples of open-ended questions are easy to find, as we use them constantly in daily life, whenever we make a verbal request for information or clarification. For example:

What brand of laundry detergent did you last purchase?
What is the mission statement of your company?
How often to you exercise, and why?

Advantages of Open-Ended Questions. An open-ended question can serve as an excellent first question on a topic, so long as it is not so broad as to require a lengthy answer (e.g., "Tell us about your

Marketing Research Focus 7.2

Verbatims and "Person Who" Arguments

Researchers in social psychology have found that people are often far more swayed by firsthand accounts than by even well-conducted statistical studies. This is sometimes known as a "Person who" argument. The name derives from situations in which one might say, "Well, even though clinical trials show that drug to be safe and effective, I know a *person who* got terribly sick from it." A whimsical example of this arose when a major American university undertook a study of its food services, asking nearly a thousand of its current users what they liked and disliked about it. It emerged that cleanliness was a problem, but not the most pressing one. However, this was completely superseded by a single verbatim comment used in the final presentation: "It would help if you hosed it down every month or so." The image of the food service being "hosed down" pervaded the remaining discussion and caused perceived lack of cleanliness to be taken more seriously than the problems that were being specifically measured as part of the research design. Although the quote used was admirably persuasive, it had the perverse effect of skewing results carefully teased out and thoughtfully presented by the research team.

childhood"). These questions allow general attitudes to be expressed, which can aid in interpreting more structured questions, if any, to follow. In addition, they establish rapport and gain the respondent's cooperation in answering more specific and more structured questions. Open-ended questions exert minimal influence on subsequent responses, because respondents are not biased by a predetermined set of response alternatives and can freely express views divergent from the researcher's expectations. This characteristic makes open-ended questions useful for exploratory research purposes. Finally, open-ended questions can provide the researcher with insights, side comments, and explanations that are useful in developing a "feel" for the research findings. The final report may include quotations from open-ended questions (often called "verbatims") to add a sense of realism and life to the more structured research findings. Indeed, there are certain instances in which such verbatim quotes can be oddly compelling, as detailed in *Marketing Research Focus 7.2*.

Disadvantages of Open-Ended Questions. A major disadvantage of open-ended questions is the high potential for interviewer bias. Interviewers rarely record respondents' answers exactly as they are offered, except on written surveys (where respondents tend to fatigue easily and use their own shorthand). This results in the interviewer summarizing the respondents' answers or deleting the aspects of an answer that he or she deems unimportant. In addition, interviewers who write slowly typically fail to record parts of answers due to time constraints. The more the interviewer summarizes and edits the respondent's answers, the more the recorded responses will vary from the actual responses. A recording device should be used if verbatim responses are required.

A second major disadvantage of open-ended questions lies in the time and cost associated with coding the responses. For a large survey, extensive coding procedures are required to summarize the divergent responses in a format useful for data analysis and presentation. The coding process can contribute significantly to the total cost of the research project *(see Marketing Research Focus 7.3)*.

Sometimes, to gain the advantages of open-ended questions yet avoid some of the time and cost associated with the editing and coding process, precoded questions are used. A precoded question is in multiple-choice format but is presented to the respondent as open ended. The response alternatives are not read to the respondent. Rather, the interviewer selects the appropriate response alternative based on the respondent's reply to the open-ended question. This approach works well when the response is easily formulated in the respondent's mind and the possible answers are limited in variety—for example, when the question concerns the number of household members, the age of the refrigerator, or monthly grocery expenditures. However, questions that are not well formulated in the respondent's mind and that result in a variety of answers have a high probability of interviewer bias. Often one of the main uses of open-ended questions is in pretest surveys run on a small subsample specifically to gain enough verbatim replies in order to formulate meaningful, inclusive categories to use on a final survey. Generally speaking, it is unreasonable for researchers to believe that they can anticipate every possible categorical response likely to emerge in the course of a major research project. Using open ends as part of a preliminary strategy is helpful in avoiding this problem.

Other disadvantages include the implicit extra weight given to respondents who are more articulate and tend to raise more points in their answers. One principal rule in research is that each respondent

Marketing Research Focus 7.3

Coding Verbal Data from Open-Ended Questions

Sometimes researchers simply must rely on open-ended questions, like when certain detailed attitudes or emotional states must be described, or when people's answers are so heterogeneous that no list will do. In such cases, researchers can simply read through verbal data and attempt to make sense of it—a process fraught with potential bias—or to "process" the verbal data into categories amenable to statistical analysis. When the latter course is practicable, one must start with a great deal of words and statements, scientifically and fairly parceling them into a modest number of defensible, and possibly nonoverlapping, categories. The step-by-step process we describe next can help ensure that this occurs but falls into the "excruciatingly correct" category, in that it requires the involvement of six people and a great deal of time. When such resources are not available, two or three people can divide up the tasks, perhaps curtailing or even skipping the last two steps.

- *Step 1:* Have two reviewers (#1 and #2) independently read through all verbal responses (open-ended questions from a survey, transcriptions of a focus group, etc.).
- *Step 2:* Each reviewer should form a comprehensive list of key words and phrases (or behavioral responses/attitudes/types of response) potentially useful for categorization.
- *Step 3:* Together with a third person (#3), who has not taken part thus far, the reviewers should merge their separate lists and standardize terminology so that all responses fit into *at least one* category (and, possibly, *at most* one, although this will be harder). Categories may be assigned titles based on the *types* of responses to be found in them. An imperative here is to have the number of categories be modest, far fewer than the responses on which they were based.
- *Step 4:* Two other people (#4 and #5) should sort the responses into the given categories, making note of those that do not seem to fit.
- *Step 5:* Together with another person (#6), they should come to an agreement on the sorting, possibly altering the original categorization scheme.

count equally. But what if some respondents, when asked for examples, offer 10, whereas others offer one? Researchers must have clear guidelines about how such answers will be processed in order to make eventual inferences. Open-ended questions are less suited for self-administered questionnaires, because respondents tend to write more briefly than they speak; and there is also the problem of illegible handwriting. When using open-ended questions on a printed or computer-based survey, one should avoid placing them on the very first page or screen, as it conveys that the survey is long and effortful, lowering participation rates. Finally, compared with questions that have structured response formats, open ends are approximately five times more costly, owing to the complexity associated with data processing, and much slower for respondents. (*See Marketing Research Focus 7.3*, "Coding Verbal Data from Open-Ended Questions.")

In general, open-ended questions are most appropriate for exploratory research purposes and for research designed to develop more structured questions. Although the up-front cost of developing effective structured questions can be high, the expense must be weighed against the numerous disadvantages of open-ended questions, which should in any case be used sparingly in all but verbally administered questionnaires.

Multiple-Response Questions

multiple-response (or multiple-choice) question A question type requiring the respondent to choose from a fixed list of pre-established answers.

A **multiple-response** (or **multiple-choice**) **question** requires the respondent to choose an answer from an explicit, codified list provided either in the question proper or following the question. The respondent may be asked to choose one or more of the alternatives presented. There is a bewildering variety of question types that fall under the rubric of "multiple response." Let us look at some of the main types to gain familiarity with their typical features.

1. Members of the U.S. Congress should be limited to two terms in office.

Strongly disagree		Neutral		Strongly agree
1	2	3	4	5

2. What is your age?

___ Younger than 18 ___ 18–25 ___ 26–35 ___ 36–45 ___ 46–55 ___ 56–65 ___ Older than 65

3. Choose your country of residence from the dropdown list:

-Choose Country/Region-

-Choose Country/Region-
Afghanistan
Albania
Algeria
America (USA)
American Samoa
Andorra
Angola

4. Indicate which of the following products you have purchased in the past month (check all that apply):

☐ Mayonnaise ☐ Ketchup ☐ Mustard ☐ Salsa ☐ Relish

5. Please rank the following courses in terms of your interest, from 1 (most interest) to 5 (least):

_____ Managerial accounting
_____ Organizational behavior
_____ Statistics
_____ Microeconomics
_____ Finance

Some of these questions rely on scales, whereas others ask for rankings; some require trade-offs, whereas others allow for "all that apply." These differences are not superficial, and we will examine various types of multiple-response questions in detail. The key feature they all share is that the researcher has decided to limit possible responses and prespecify a particular set as especially relevant.

Advantages of Multiple-Response Questions. Multiple-response questions overcome many of the disadvantages associated with open-ended questions. Most important, they reduce interviewer bias (in attempting to interpret verbal responses), the effort respondents must put into replying, and the cost and time associated with data processing. Typically, the interviewer will find multiple-response questionnaires comparatively easy and quick to administer. Note also that with self-administered questionnaires, cooperation by respondents is difficult to maintain unless the bulk of the questions have a structured-response format. One useful aspect of multiple-response questions is that the researcher can limit responses to a particular set that "matter"; for example, there is no point in asking respondents to list all desirable locations for a new restaurant if only certain spots are available for building.

Disadvantages of Multiple-Response Questions. Against these advantages must be weighed several disadvantages. First, the design of effective multiple-response questions requires considerable time and cost. Typically, an exploratory study using open-ended questions is required to formulate the response alternatives. If the latter do not include one or more of the predominant responses, substantial bias can be introduced into the results. Even with an alternative of "other (specify)," there is a tendency for the respondent to choose from among the alternatives specified rather than to use the "other" alternative. Multiple-response questions tend to bias the data by the order in which the response alternatives are listed. When such questions are administered electronically, it is wise to have the computer randomize the order of the answers, an example of the counterbalancing process that is difficult to enact in a paper-and-pencil format.

Issues in Multiple-Response Question Design. The main issues arising in the design of multiple-response questions are the number of alternatives, the alternatives themselves, and position bias.

The *number* of alternatives to include in a question is typically influenced by the following guidelines. First, the response alternatives should be **collectively exhaustive**; that is, they should include all the possible response alternatives. The inclusion of the alternative labeled "other (specify: _______)," always accompanied by a space for recording the answer, is an attempt to comply with this guideline. It

collectively exhaustive
When the response choices for a question include all possible options—for example, a listing of all the days of the week.

is hoped that major response alternatives that were excluded will be identified under "other." Second, when possible, the response alternatives should be **mutually exclusive**; that is, the respondents should be able to identify *one* alternative that clearly represents their response. In some situations, however, allowing two or more choices is appropriate—for example, if the question pertains to which countries one has ever visited, movies one has seen in the past year, and so forth. Researchers should be aware, though, that multiple responses create special data processing and analysis problems because the number of possible answer patterns is very large (consider the number of possible sets of "movies one has seen"). If the list of response alternatives is reasonably short, the alternatives may be included in the question proper. In most cases, there are too many alternatives to be included in that manner, and they are listed at the end of the question. In a personal interview, if there is a long list of alternatives, the choices should be listed on a card and given to the respondent for inspection. This is not possible, of course, in telephone interviews, in which case the interviewer usually asks respondents to listen to the entire potential response list first, which can then be repeated as needed to obtain accurate data.

mutually exclusive
When a variable is such that a respondent cannot assign two values simultaneously—for example, age categories (because one cannot be two ages at once).

Typically the researcher has thought a great deal about the information to be included in *the alternatives* themselves while deciding on their number. The content of the alternatives should be selected so that the verbiage and grammar are standardized across alternatives, to promote universal comprehensibility. A reasonable rule of thumb is that the explicit alternatives listed—those not covered by the "other" category, if any—should cover the selections of approximately 95 percent of respondents. A substantially smaller proportion than that will open up the possibility of too many "missing" pieces of data, as respondents fail to complete the question or merely select "other" without providing additional information. It is often a good idea to do a pilot study to ensure that nearly all respondents can find appropriate answers to the bulk of the questions on the survey and that "other" is selected only rarely.

Another important issue concerns **position bias**. With a list of numbers, such as prices or how many times per week a respondent visits a store, there is a bias toward the central position of the number array. When a respondent has little knowledge about the issue being researched or low motivation to reply, the response scale itself may be viewed as a "suggestion," and the central point chosen without much thought. When ideas are involved, the first alternative on the list has a greater chance of being chosen. To control position bias, the researcher should alternate the order in which alternatives are listed, to average out the response bias. Unfortunately, it is not easy to rotate most numbers because they logically should appear as a sequence (e.g., 5, 6, 7, 8, 9). Even if the numbers are presented out of order, the respondent may mentally sort them into sequence before making a choice. Another possibility involves the use of a "split design," where half of respondents see one scale, and the other half see a different one. If the sorts of answers (especially, the average or **modal answer**) obtained using the two scales differ substantially, there is a strong scale bias, and additional rounds of pretesting are called for. Finally, it is possible in verbally administered (e.g., telephone) surveys for respondents to have trouble recalling items from even a moderately long list; in such cases, they may choose those they heard last, with a so-called **recency bias**, or to ignore anything they heard after the first few replies, with a **primacy bias**.

position bias
When a respondent's answer to some question is affected by the order of the question in the survey or the order of a set of presented answers.

modal answer
The most common of a set of responses.

recency bias
A survey bias that results from a respondent having better memory of, or greater preference for, the response options listed most recently.

primacy bias
A survey bias that results when respondents have better memory of or preference for the response options listed earliest.

Dichotomous Questions

A **dichotomous question** is an extreme form of the multiple-response question that allows the respondent a choice of only yes or no, did or did not, or agree or disagree. Often, the two alternatives of interest are combined with a neutral alternative, such as "no opinion" or "don't know." For example:

Should children in the United States attend school year-round?

- o Yes
- o No
- o No opinion

Have you purchased a new car within the past year?

- o Did
- o Did not

dichotomous question
A question in which respondents are asked to choose one of two possible responses.

Advantages of Dichotomous Questions. The advantages of dichotomous questions are essentially the same as those mentioned for multiple-response questions. Interviewers find the questions quick and easy to administer, and respondents universally understand them. There is little chance of interviewer bias, and the responses are easy to code, process, analyze, and report. Responses are called **binary**, and can be analyzed using powerful methods of discrete choice, such as the binary logit and probit models (see Chapter 10).

binary
A variable having only two possible states, for example, 1 or 0, yes or no, Male or Female, Domestic or Foreign, etc.

Disadvantages of Dichotomous Questions. There is a risk of assuming that the respondent group approaches the topic of interest in dichotomous terms when, in reality, many grades of feeling may be present or indecision may predominate. Forcing respondents to express their views in a dichotomous manner when they are not thus polarized can produce results that contain substantial measurement error. Dichotomous questions are especially susceptible to error resulting from how they are worded. For example, the positive or negative posture of the question can have a strong effect on the nature of the response; compare "Do you think you should give to charity?" with "*Don't* you think you should give to charity?" The second implies that you should, and respondents will be far more likely to agree. Note as well that speakers can be easily put off by complex phrasing of a supposedly yes-no question. For example, "Don't you disagree that the president didn't do a poor job … ?" is likely to elicit confusion rather than usable answers. This is especially the case in cross-cultural research; in some languages, a double-negative, far from becoming a positive, is considered *strongly* negative. It is therefore imperative to phrase dichotomous questions as clearly and transparently as possible, and in the affirmative.

Issues in Dichotomous Question Design. The central issue is whether to include a neutral response alternative in the question. If such an alternative is not included, the respondent is forced to select between the two positions presented. If a neutral alternative is available, and especially if it is shown to the respondent, the latter can avoid taking a position on the topic by selecting the neutral alternative. When the neutral alternative is included, the number of nonresponses should decline and the number of neutral responses should increase. If a significant number of respondents are truly neutral, the inclusion of the neutral alternative should increase the accuracy of the results. However, a source of bias can enter when respondents who are not neutral select the neutral alternative for reasons of convenience, embarrassment, or the like. If the proportion of respondents who are truly neutral is large, it is best to include the neutral alternative. If it is believed that the proportion of neutral respondents is small, it is best to force the respondents to select between the two positions of interest. Note as well that there are large conceptual differences between "neutral," "no opinion," and "do not know," particularly for sensitive questions. It is rare, for example, for people to be literally neutral on topics such as abortion, but they may say they have "no opinion" because they simply do not wish to share it, whereas "do not know" is nearly meaningless in such a context. Generally speaking, introducing "neutral" as the only scale point between yes and no is a poor idea, as it creates a three-point scale that is very difficult to analyze and will attract *all* respondents who merely wish to avoid extreme positions. Generally speaking, dichotomous questions are best suited for *facts* and *past behavior*, which either took place or failed to. If neutrality is offered as an option, it should be as the center of a scale with at least five points, one that unambiguously refers to views, beliefs, attitudes, or opinions.

7.3d Decide on Question Wording

The heart of the questionnaire consists of the questions—the link between the data and the information needs of the study. It is critical that the researcher and the respondent assign the same meaning to the questions asked. Otherwise, serious measurement error will be present in the research results.

You should never be misled into believing that there are "right" and "wrong" ways of asking questions. In a real sense, survey data are created rather than unobtrusively collected. By this we mean that respondents do not possess a preexisting set of responses just sitting there, waiting to be recorded, but rather will construct answers to the questions the interviewer chooses to ask, in the formats allowed by the questions themselves. Researchers must keep in mind that a relatively small proportion of questions refer to purely factual, objective, verifiable data like age or education; a far larger proportion concern issues that respondents must, in essence, ask themselves about in order to reply to accurately. This being the case, the manner in which data are collected determines to a large degree the character of the data. Consequently, researchers must be very sensitive to the effect of the question wording on the character of the results to be obtained.

Following are several simple, general guidelines for appropriate question wording:

- Use simple language.
- Use unambiguous words.

- Avoid leading questions.
- Avoid biasing questions.
- Avoid implicit alternatives.
- Avoid implicit assumptions.
- Avoid estimates.
- Avoid double-barreled questions.
- Consider the frame of reference.

Let us examine each of these guidelines in greater detail.

Use Simple Language

The words used in the questionnaire should be consistent with the vocabulary level of the respondents. If in doubt, it is best to err on the side of simplicity.

Questions designed for children obviously must have a simpler vocabulary than those designed for, say, physicians. When designing a questionnaire for the general public, however, keep in mind the surprising fact that many terms understood by most middle school children (about 12 years of age) are not commonly known by some adults. For example, a substantial proportion of the general population does not understand the words for component parts of a computer ("hard drive," "RAM"), whereas most 12-year-olds do. Of course, the opposite is commonly true, as there are few children fully conversant with the full range of adult vocabulary. Finally, in most countries in the industrialized world, a sizable portion of the population learned the predominant language as adults and cannot be counted on to have mastered vernacular, abbreviations, or all but the most common expressions. Consequently, when designing a questionnaire, be certain that it is comprehensible to nearly all persons likely to be asked to complete it.

Use Unambiguous Words

Words that are "clear" have a single meaning that is known to all respondents. Unfortunately, identifying words that are clear or unambiguous is more difficult than one might expect. Many words that might seem to be clear to everyone can have different meanings among population groups and geographic locations.

Consider the words "dinner" and "lunch." Studies indicate that middle- and upper-class families use "dinner" to refer to the evening meal and "lunch" to refer to the noon meal. In contrast, many working-class families refer to the evening meal as "supper" and the noon meal as "dinner," although this is changing. There are regional variations in these usages as well. In designing a question that refers to mealtime, it would be better to use "noon meal" and "evening meal" rather than "lunch" and "dinner." Because comparable responses cannot be expected from respondents who assign different meanings to a word, serious measurement error would be introduced if the words "lunch" and "dinner" were used in the question.

In a study of soup usage in the home, the question "How often do you serve soup at home?" resulted in responses that suggested that soup usage was lower than believed by the management group sponsoring the survey. Additional research indicated that to many respondents, the word "serve" indicated a special occasion, such as when entertaining. Soup eaten by the family alone was not considered to be "served." Other respondents believed that the question pertained to when they, personally, did the serving. A revised question with better wording is simply, "How often do you eat soup at home?" This isolates the behavior of interest unmistakably.

Researchers have found that words such as "usually," "regularly," "kind," "normally," and "frequently" are ambiguous. It is difficult to be sensitive to all the commonly used words that some respondents interpret one way and others another way. Frequency questions are particularly troublesome; some people can say that they do not exercise "regularly" because they sometimes skip a day, whereas others can believe they do exercise regularly because they take a short walk every weekend. In this regard, it is a good idea for the researcher not only to use common sense, but to consult a standard dictionary or thesaurus and to be particularly sensitive to usage differences across ages, ethnic backgrounds, socioeconomic statuses, and geographic regions. Asking the following questions about each word in a question is also helpful:

1. Does the word truly convey what the researchers intend?
2. Can respondents impose or extrapolate any distinct, alternative meaning?
3. If so, does context help make the intended meaning clear?
4. Is there any word with similar pronunciation or spelling that could be confused with it?

5. Is capitalization important or indicated?
6. Could we use a simpler word, or even a phrase, instead?

Avoid Leading Questions

A *leading question* is one that gives the respondent a cue as to what the answer should be. Leading questions often unknowingly reflect the researcher's or the decision-maker's viewpoint. A leading question causes a consistent measurement error that is difficult to undo after the fact. A question to measure the claim service of automobile insurance companies was preceded by the following statement: "It has been alleged that some low-rate companies are much tougher in adjusting claims than are standard-rate companies and that you are more likely to have to go to court to collect the sum due you." This statement would probably influence responses to the questions on the companies' claim service. Be aware that statements designed to clarify a question can influence the responses, and be sensitive to this source of measurement error when wording questions.

Consider the question "Do you own a Sony television set?" The researcher would find out that this was a leading question if the reported ownership of Sony television sets were higher in response to this question than to the simpler question "What brand of television set do you own?" The use of a brand or company name in a question can cause the respondent to believe that this company is the sponsor of the survey. There is a tendency for the respondent to express positive feelings toward the survey sponsor (or at least to be reluctant to express negative reactions), which can result in measurement error. Worse yet, future questions, particularly open-ended ones that rely on respondent memory, may be grossly affected by information unwittingly revealed in an earlier question.

Avoid Biasing Questions

A *biasing question* includes words or phrases that are emotionally colored and that suggest a feeling of approval or disapproval. Most researchers would recognize the biasing effect of a question that began, "Don't you agree with the Surgeon General that … ?" or "Do you believe that dangerous oil monopolies should be … ?" No reputable researcher would phrase questions in this manner. Unfortunately, the biasing effect of words and phrases is often far more subtle than these examples suggest.

The mere suggestion that an attitude or a position is associated with a prestigious or nonprestigious person or organization can seriously bias the respondent's reply. The question "Do you agree or disagree with the American Dental Association's position that advertising presweetened cereal to children is …?" would have such an effect. The nature of the bias would be increased support reported for the position held by the prestigious person or organization over that reported when the person or organization was not included in the question. The reverse could obtain if the person or organization included is widely held as disreputable.

It is difficult to avoid leading questions because words or phrases that bias one respondent group can seem neutral to another group. In political circles, for example, descriptors like "liberal" and "conservative" not only mean different things to different groups, but are also viewed positively by some and negatively by others. Pretesting the questionnaire is one way to identify which respondent groups find the question biased.

Avoid Implicit Alternatives

Examples presented in the first section of this chapter ("Function and Importance of Questionnaires") indicated marked differences in the answers to questions that pose implicit, as opposed to explicit, alternatives. As a rule, it is best to state clearly all relevant alternatives to a question unless there is a special reason for not doing so. Research indicates that the order in which explicit alternatives are presented can affect the response. When the list of alternatives is long and complex or close in preference, the alternatives presented at the end of the list have a higher chance of being selected, simply because they are "top of mind." As stated earlier, counterbalancing and using "split" designs can help overcome such problems.

Avoid Implicit Assumptions

It is all too easy to design a question for which the answer is dependent on a number of implicit assumptions. Consider the question "Are you in favor of curtailing the amount of sugar allowed in children's cereals?" Implicit in this question is the idea that sugar is detrimental in some way and that the suggested action will result in some favorable outcome—for example, a lower rate of tooth decay. Other ways of probing the underlying issue could involve asking for impressions of sugar levels in cereal or of children's cereals in general, or including several explicit outcomes, as in "Are you in favor of curtailing the amount of sugar allowed in children's cereal if it will result in lower rates of tooth decay, the use of artificial sweeteners, and a 10 percent cost increase?" (Such questions are staples of conjoint analysis; see Chapter 11.) The failure to make explicit the assumption in a question often results in overestimation of respondents' support for the issue at hand. This is an example of the generally well taken practice of providing trade-offs: When a question pits one alternative against another that looks uniformly better—"Would you like the manufacturer to put more in the package?" "Should the government lower your taxes?"—results will be greatly skewed. In such cases, one needs to report the "fine print"—for example, that increasing package sizes will raise the price or that lower taxes will negatively affect social services.

Avoid Estimates

Questions should be designed in such a way that the respondent does not have to answer by giving an estimate or making a generalization. Consider the question "How many boxes of powdered soap do you purchase in a year?" This question asks for a feat of memory few respondents will possess; some will simply call up the number of boxes of powdered soap purchased in a month and multiply by 12, and others may simply take a wild guess. Results would likely be more accurate if the question were phrased, "How many boxes of powdered soap do you purchase in a month?" The yearly figure can then be estimated by multiplying by 12. In formulating such questions, researchers need a good idea of common levels of consumption, or typical answers. It would be foolish, for example, to ask, "How many cars did you buy last month?" because car purchase frequency is much lower than monthly. A good guideline is that the typical respondent should answer somewhere in the range of two to five, and if possible, the time interval should be a "natural" one, like a week, a month, or a year. If answers are expected to be well outside the two to five range, consider altering the time interval (which should *always* be made explicit). In our soap example, 3 months might be a more reasonable interval to suggest answers greater than zero or one box purchased, although this still may require a difficult memory feat for many respondents. Note as well that seasonality can be important. In judging yearly consumption of suntan lotion, one would not ask for monthly consumption in a winter or a summer month and simply multiply by 12.

Avoid Double-Barreled Questions

double-barreled question
A question that requires the respondent to supply two separate bits of information and that therefore has the potential to create conflict or confusion.

A **double-barreled question** is one in which the wording calls for two responses. Consider the question "What is your evaluation of the snowmobile's ride and acceleration?" It is possible that the respondent finds the acceleration exhilarating but the ride jarringly unpleasant. Here, two questions have been melded into one; a single response of, say, "Fine" may obscure differences of opinion on the individual components of the question. As a rule, when the question includes "and," review it to see whether two responses are really required. If so, split the question in two.

Consider the Frame of Reference

frame of reference
The viewpoint of a respondent invoked by the orientation of a question.

Frame of reference refers to the respondent's viewpoint in answering the question. Consider these two questions:

"Are automobile manufacturers making satisfactory progress in controlling automobile emissions?"
"Are you satisfied with the progress automobile manufacturers are making in controlling automobile emissions?"

The viewpoint of the first question is that of an objective evaluation based on how people in general would react. The second question is oriented toward the respondent's personal feelings regarding the issue of automobile emissions and thus is more subjective. The objectives of the research study will determine which frame of reference is more appropriate. There are many occasions in which researchers might wish to leverage "market knowledge." For example, consider the question "What would you, personally, pay for this athletic shoe?" An answer of zero could result because the respondent just purchased similar shoes or never wears such shoes to begin with. Such data would be useless in setting price. By contrast, "How much do you think this athletic shoe would be sold for?" can elicit price expectations even if a particular respondent is personally uninterested. The main point here is to be aware that a question's implied viewpoint can seriously influence the study results.

Professional researchers know that even vast experience will not always produce flawless questions on the first try. Rather, good survey questions *evolve,* through a process of continual scrutiny, usually aided by extensive pretesting. *Marketing Research Focus 7.4* illustrates how a question can change radically, and for the better, in small, measured steps.

Marketing Research Focus 7.4

Metamorphosis of a Question

Stage 1

Shouldn't there be changes in the amount of violence shown on TV?

Yes

No

(Problem: This question begs for an affirmative answer.)

Stage 2

Should there be changes in the amount of violence shown on TV?

Yes

No

(Problem: What kind of changes?)

Stage 3

Should there be less violence shown on TV?

Yes

No

(Problem: Ambiguous, in that "less" can mean fewer violent incidents or that the incidents themselves should be less extreme.)

Stage 4

Should there be stricter control over violent content on TV?

Yes

No

(Problem: Where? Everywhere? At every time?)

Stage 5

Should there be stricter control over violent content on network TV during prime-time hours (8 to 11 p.m., Monday to Thursday)?

Yes

No

(Problem: Hidden assumption; what if the respondent believes that existing controls should be *less* strict?)

Stage 6

Should control over violent content on network TV during prime-time hours (8 to 11 p.m., Monday to Thursday) be more strict, less strict, or stay about the same?

Should be more strict

Should be less strict

Should stay about the same

(Problem: Scale is now ordinal, but the choices go from "more" to "less" to "middle.")

Stage 7

How strictly should violent content on network TV during prime-time hours (8 to 11 p.m., Monday to Thursday) be controlled?

Controlled more strictly

Controlled as they are now

Controlled less strictly

(Problem: What sort of violent content, and what sort of controls?)

Stage 8

How strictly should depictions of shootings and assaults on network TV during prime-time hours (8 to 11 p.m., Monday to Thursday) be controlled?

Controlled more strictly

Controlled as they are now

Controlled less strictly

(Problem: This is a double-barreled question. It asks about shootings and assaults together. Some respondents will react more strongly to one than to the other.)

Stage 9

How strictly should depictions of shootings on network TV during prime-time hours (8 to 11 p.m., Monday to Thursday) be controlled?

Controlled more strictly
Controlled as they are now
Controlled less strictly

(Problem: This is excessively wordy.)

Stage 10

Depictions of shootings on network TV during prime-time hours (8 to 11 p.m., Monday to Thursday) should be:

Controlled more strictly
Controlled as they are now
Controlled less strictly

7.3e Decide on Question Sequence

Once the wording of the questions has been determined, the next step is to establish their sequence, that is, the order or flow of the questions in the questionnaire. The sequencing of questions can influence the nature of the respondents' answers and cause serious error in interpreting the overall survey findings. Although this aspect of questionnaire design draws heavily on the skills of an experienced researcher, we next present several informal guidelines that the beginning researcher should find useful. The overriding concern is that questions are sequenced in a manner that retains respondent interest and attention while not introducing bias in subsequent questions.

Use an Intriguing, Readily Understood Opening Question

The opening question must capture interest and curiosity immediately, or the respondent may simply decide not to proceed. Often, the opening question does not relate to the information needs of the study directly but is geared toward gaining the respondent's cooperation and establishing rapport. In this regard, a simple question that asks the respondent to express an attitude is a good starter because most people like to express their feelings and can do so easily. This approach gives respondents confidence that they can answer the remaining questions in the interview. For example, one company conducting a telephone survey on cookbooks opened with "Do you like to cook?" A financial institution started with the nearly rhetorical "Do you like to save money?" On printed surveys, open-ended questions should be avoided at the outset, as they convey that the survey may be arduous to complete. Rather, the opening page or screen should be uncluttered and simple to fill out.

Ask General Questions First

Within a topic, general questions should precede specific ones. Consider the following two questions:

"What considerations are important to you in buying cereal?"
"When you are buying cereal, is the sugar content important to you?"

If these questions were asked in reverse order, sugar content would be listed more frequently as a consideration in response to the general question. Asking general questions first and specific questions second reduces the chance of **sequence bias**. A broad principle is to avoid using any specific examples until they are absolutely needed. For example, if the research purpose were to study restaurant eating habits, questions involving eating out in general would appear first, followed perhaps by questions involving fast food (both venues and types), and only much later seeking information about specific fast-food restaurants or menu items.

sequence bias
When responses to a questionnaire are affected by the order in which questions or choices appear; often addressed by counterbalancing.

Place Uninteresting and Difficult Questions Late in the Sequence

Sequence any questions that are embarrassing, sensitive, complex, or dull well down in the questionnaire. After rapport has been established through familiarity with the interviewer and the questioning process, the respondent is less apt to object to more demanding questions, as well as to personal questions about income, age, or other sensitive issues. It is rare for a respondent who has completed the bulk of a survey to simply give up shortly before completing it, although this can happen if the survey is excessively lengthy, particularly in online environments where "rapport" is only with a computer screen. Any personal information that is not absolutely required for screening purposes, including demographics, should be placed last in the survey, and respondent confidentiality should be stressed.

Arrange Questions in Logical Order

The flow of the questioning process must be logical from the respondent's perspective. A question sequence designed to facilitate data processing or established from the perspective of the researcher can create confusion, frustration, and indecision among respondents, with serious adverse effects on cooperation and rapport. The question order that is most likely to get good response is (1) interest, (2) information, and (3) classification. First capture the respondent's attention; next, elicit the necessary information; and then approach potentially sensitive demographic or classification questions. At the very end can be potentially lengthy, catchall questions, such as "Please list any other health care you have purchased in the last year" or "If there is anything else you would like to tell us ...," which would greatly interrupt flow if placed earlier on.

When the information needs of a study are extensive and different groups within the sample need to be asked different questions, it is helpful to "flowchart" the question sequence. Figure 7.2 presents a

Figure 7.2 Example of a Flowchart Plan for a Draft Questionnaire

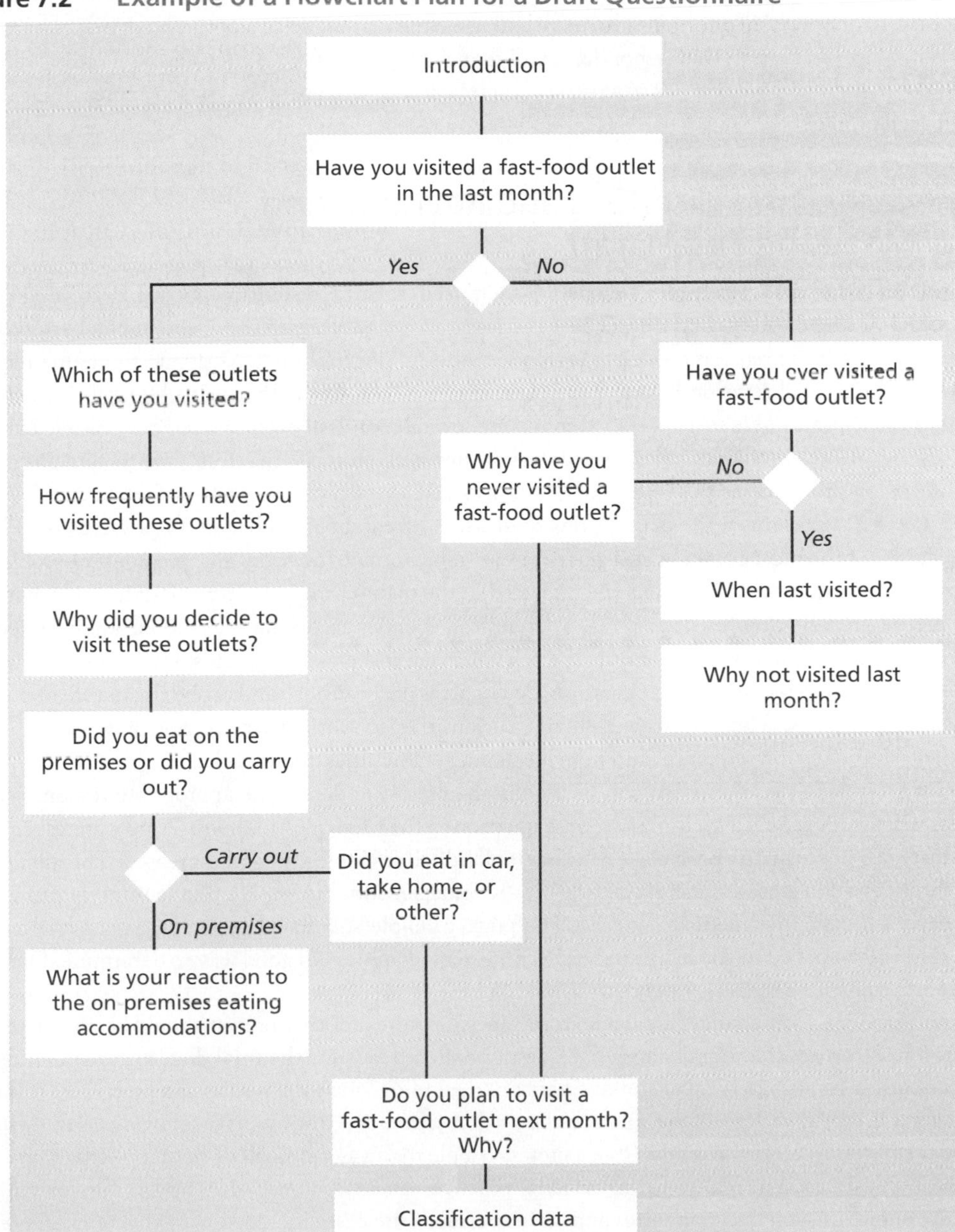

flowchart plan for a questionnaire. Flowcharting can help researchers to visualize the structure of the questionnaire and to ensure that the questions flow logically.

7.3f Decide on Physical Characteristics

The physical appearance of the questionnaire can be influential in securing the cooperation of the respondent. This is particularly the case with mail and computer-based surveys, where there is no face-to-face contact. For the mail surveys, the quality of the paper and printing often determines the respondent's first reaction to the questionnaire; for computer-based surveys, professional formatting and graphics help convey credibility. It is typically important that the name of the organization sponsoring the survey (even though the name is often fictitious, to avoid introducing bias) and the project name appear clearly on the first page, if for no other reason than to allow respondents to refer to it.

With personal and telephone interviews, the questionnaires should be numbered serially. This facilitates control of the questionnaires in field operations and during data processing. Mail questionnaires should not be identified numerically when respondent anonymity has been promised. Finally, the format of a question can influence the degree of response. With both self-administered and interviewer-administered questionnaires, researchers have discovered that the more lines or space left for recording the response to open-ended questions, the more extensive the replies, up to a point. Fledgling researchers should not, however, believe that respondents will reply with paragraphs of information if only given the space to do so; most will quickly tire of writing or typing, unless strongly motivated to express their views on a particular topic.

7.3g Carry Out Pretesting and Revision, and Make the Final Draft

pretesting
Running a smaller experiment run before the main one, so as to quickly and inexpensively perform critical measurements that may affect how the main test is conducted.

Before the questionnaire is ready for field operations, it needs to be pretested and revised. **Pretesting** refers to the initial testing of one or more aspects of the research design. Regardless of the researcher's skill in questionnaire design, a pretest is needed to search out areas for improvement. Most questionnaires require at least one pretest and revision before they are "ready for prime time," that is, to be used in the field. Large, nationally projectable surveys will often require several rounds of each to weed out possible biases.

Pretesting, although crucial, takes a good deal of time and effort. It therefore pays to catch as many potential survey problems as possible *before* extensive rounds of pretesting are undertaken. *Marketing Research Focus 7.5* presents a list of questions that, when asked about each item on a survey, can help weed out some of the most common and readily preventable formatting, wording, and content problems.

In general, the questionnaire should be pretested in the manner intended for the final study, but it is best to pretest an early draft using personal interviewers, even when the survey is to be administered by mail or telephone. It is important that only the best interviewers be used for pretest work. A skilled interviewer can respond to requests for explanation, detect areas of confusion, and probe the nature of potential misunderstandings. The interviewer should be sensitive to words that are not understood by all respondents, test question sequence, and note mechanical difficulties and the like.

The open-ended response format can be used in the pretest to determine appropriate response categories for what will become a multiple-response question in the final questionnaire. A new pretest should be conducted to uncover any problems with the standardized response categories created. The *number* of people interviewed in a pretest can range from 15–30 for a personnel-intensive phone interview to many times that for a computer-mediated survey. The pretest sample should be as similar as possible to the sample that will be tested in the main study; checking demographics is a good way to determine if sample characteristics are close to those intended.

Whenever significant changes are made in the questionnaire, another pretest should be conducted. If the pretest results suggest minor changes, the questionnaire is ready for the final draft and distribution to field operators. It is ultimately up to the researcher to determine when the results of a pretest are suitable to allow for a finalized version of the survey to be used. A common error involves allowing a survey to be finalized prematurely, based on results from a pretest sample that was too small or nonrepresentative.

Questionnaires used in real-world managerial practice vary enormously in length, complexity, and format. Examples of such questionnaires appear in several of the cases included with this text, and readers are encouraged to scrutinize them in light of the material presented in this and prior chapters.

Marketing Research Focus 7.5

Survey Format and Wording Problem Checklist

In designing a questionnaire, it is wise to consider the following issues while the pretest is being prepared.

In terms of physical appearance:

1. Will your questionnaire appeal to respondents and motivate them to cooperate? Is there anything that might cause a certain type of respondent to decline, biasing the sample?
2. Does your questionnaire include brief and precise instructions?
3. Is your format conducive to your chosen method of data entry (e.g., keying, scanning, hand tabulation)?

In terms of content:

1. Does the question use abbreviations, acronyms, jargon, or unconventional phrases? [e.g., FBI, AARP, GPA, PROC-GLM, GARCH model]
2. Is the question biased in favor of a particular response? (e.g., "Don't you agree that people should … ?")
3. Is the question overly vague or open ended? (e.g., "Tell us about your life.")
4. Does the question require too much precision or knowledge? (e.g., "What exact sort of RAM does your computer use?")
5. Will the words be uniformly understood? (e.g., "rarely," "large," "costly")
6. Is the question objectionable? (e.g., references to religion, politics, sexual habits, financial details)
7. Is the question too demanding? (e.g., "List all comedy films you have seen in the past 5 years.")
8. Does each question ask for only one bit of information, or is it a double-barreled question? (e.g., "Do you like to eat eggs for lunch or dinner?")
9. Do any of the question's words have a double meaning? (e.g., "right," "sound," "sweet")
10. Are the answers mutually exclusive? (e.g., "chemist," "engineer," "chemical engineer")
11. Does the question contain a double negative? (e.g., "Don't you think you shouldn't … ?")
12. Is an appropriate time referent provided? (e.g., "How many times have you gone shopping recently?")
13. Can the question be understood when taken out of order or context? (e.g., "For the brand of ice cream you wrote in response to the last question … ")
14. Can responses be compared with existing information? (e.g., demographics, locations, purchase frequencies)
15. Does the question assume things about the world or in the respondent's life? (e.g., "How old is your spouse?")
16. Might information in the question (or a prior one) affect a respondent's ability to give an unbiased answer? (e.g., "How would you like a fast-food restaurant, such as McDonald's, to open in your neighborhood?")

Source: Dillman, D. A. (1978), *Mail and Telephone Surveys: The Total Design Method.* New York: John Wiley & Sons.

Surveys are often used to make real-world decisions, on the theory that they truly represent respondents' feelings and preferences. This is a fine theory, but one that has been challenged both empirically (on the basis of actual survey answers) and, surprisingly, mathematically. Voting, for example, is a form of surveying for which candidate is most suitable. As such, voting and other forms of preference polling have received a great deal of attention from researchers. *Marketing Research Focus 7.6* discusses some of the qualities that good survey and voting systems should possess in order to truly represent the "will of the people," and some of the difficulties of doing so accurately, yet confidentially.

7.4 Computer-Aided Questionnaire Design

Computer-based questionnaires have become ubiquitous, and special design programs have come into substantial use in marketing research. These programs have predefined question formats for many kinds of attitude scales, for paired comparisons, for demographics, and for virtually all other commonly used questions. They allow the designer to specify question switching and skip patterns based on previous answers, to randomize the order of presentation of brand names or other questions, to reverse positive and negative scale directions, and to custom-tailor standard question formats using a full-screen editor, among other felicities. The resulting questionnaire may be generated in a paper-based form or stored electronically for computer-based use. We will take a closer look at computer-based interviewing in Chapters 6 and 7.

Marketing Research Focus 7.6

Representing Respondent Preferences in Social Decision Making

How to most accurately represent respondent preferences is a question that has been studied for several centuries, most often in the field of social decision making. For example, Nicolas Condorcet, a leader of the French Revolution, designed a method of pairwise comparisons of respondent rankings in the 1700s.

In evaluating various systems of voting and interpreting votes in social decision making, several **fairness criteria** come into play. These criteria include principles most people take for granted: For example, a criterion called **anonymity** requires that every respondent's vote be weighted equally; group decisions should therefore have the support of a majority of the group (otherwise the votes of the minority have been given greater weight). By extension, plurality voting systems, which base decisions on which option gets the most votes, but without a requirement that the final decision have majority (greater than 50 percent) support, do not represent respondent preferences as well as do systems that possess the criteria of **universality**. The universality criterion includes the provisions that the voting system rank all possible choices relative to each other and process all possible preferences.

fairness criteria
Criteria for evaluating voting methods in terms of how accurately each allows the voting population's preferences to be represented.

anonymity
A fairness criterion for decision-making systems that requires that all participants be treated equally.

universality
One of the fairness criteria referenced in Arrow's impossibility theorem. It requires that a voting system (1) produce a ranking of all possible choices relative to one another, (2) be capable of processing all possible voter preferences, and (3) always produce the same result for the same set of votes; sometimes called "unrestricted domain."

Several election systems meet this criterion of processing ranked choices. The ballot or survey lists a number of choices, and the respondent ranks all acceptable choices in order: 1, 2, 3, and so on. Leaving a choice blank is equivalent to voting for "no other candidate" or no other choice, meaning that no option after the last ranked choice is acceptable to the respondent.

Condorcet's method compares each possible pair of choices in a matrix that evaluates which choice is most often preferred to other choices. The benefits of this method are its maintenance of each preference between each pair and its ability to produce an overall ranking of the choices as a result.

A method popularly called "instant runoff voting" (IRV) eliminates choices in successive rounds in order to come up with a single winner with majority support. It got its name from the idea that each round in the calculation represents a kind of runoff election. During the first round, only the first-choice votes are counted. At the end of the first round, the choice with the smallest number of votes is eliminated; these votes are then transferred to the respondents' second choice. Exactly the same procedure applies at the end of the second round, and this continues until a candidate has reached a majority (>50 percent). The benefits of IRV are that it is straightforward to follow and blends both strength or height of support (number of higher rankings) with breadth of support (broader approval). To achieve an overall ranking, the IRV calculation itself must be performed successive times, each time withdrawing the winner and using the same ballots to elect the next-ranked candidate.

IRV is a special case of *single transferable voting* (STV, also called "choice voting"), which is used in multiple-seat elections in order to provide proportional representation to legislative bodies. In other words, a choice with 25 percent support should receive one seat out of four. The Borda method gives each choice a number of points based on the reverse order of ranking. For example, if respondents are allowed three rankings, their first choice gets three points, their second choice two points, and their third choice one point.

A number of methods that do not process rankings also have some usefulness in representing respondent preferences, or some aspect of those preferences. The Cardinal Ratings method allows voters to rate each choice on a numeric scale that determines the number of points. On a 1 to 10 scale, 10 would be most preferable, and respondents may assign as many or as few points as they wish to each choice, without regard to the number of points given to other choices. Approval voting is a special case of the Cardinal Ratings method, in which respondents give one vote to all acceptable choices. Approval voting allows respondents to vote for as many choices as they consider acceptable. The choice with the most votes is therefore the choice with the broadest approval in the group.

In evaluating these and other systems for specific situations, the relevant issue is how well the system represents the preferences of the respondents. In a ranked system, respondents are not being given "extra votes"; they are choosing the ranking that best represents their intention. **Gaming** refers to respondents (especially groups of respondents) misrepresenting their true preferences in order to achieve a desired outcome. Susceptibility to gaming is considered a flaw in an election system. An election system is evaluated based on how well it meets various fairness criteria and how susceptible it is to gaming.

gaming
Subverting the fairness of a particular voting method by attempting to manipulate the likelihood of one's own preference winning; also known as "strategic voting."

Is there a perfect way to represent respondent preferences? No. **Arrow's impossibility theorem**, proved by economist Kenneth Arrow, shows that it is impossible for a voting system to obey all five of a certain set of fairness criteria at the same time:

1. Universality: The voting system should rank all possible choices relative to each other, process all possible preferences, and always give the same result for the same set of votes.
2. Citizen sovereignty: Every resultant set of preferences should be achievable by some set of individual preferences.
3. Nondictatorship: The voting system should not give the preferences of a single individual special privilege.
4. Monotonicity: Promoting an option should never be able to hurt its ranking in the resultant preference order.
5. Independence of irrelevant alternatives: Applying a voting system to a subset of the options should yield a result that is consistent with the result from the whole set of options.

Arrow's impossibility theorem
A theorem proven by Kenneth Arrow that demonstrates that no voting system can simultaneously meet all five of a certain set of fairness criteria (universality, citizen sovereignty, nondictatorship, monotonicity, and independence of irrelevant alternatives).

So, rather than defining a perfect voting method, fairness criteria provide a gauge for evaluating voting methods objectively. Marketing researchers should realize that they face similar difficulties whenever they ask respondents for their "favorite" from a predefined list, a very common practice. Although requesting a partial ranking (e.g., "list your top 3") or a point split (e.g., "please divide 100 points among these options ...") will offer a fuller picture of respondent preferences, representation across the entire consumer pool will never be perfect. Fortunately, this is seldom critical when deciding which of a set of products to sell or produce, even though it is highly desirable in a formal voting system.

By Cat Woods

7.5 Observational Forms

Observational forms are generally easier to design than questionnaires because the question-asking process is eliminated and design problems related to controlling nonsampling error are reduced. Even so, there are important issues in the construction of observational forms. The researcher needs to be very explicit about the types of observations to be made and how they are to be measured, whether they be made in real time by a live observer or later by reviewing the output from a mechanical recording device. It is in any case crucial to obtain appropriate legal permissions for any type of clandestine recording *before* engaging in any research.

The design of observational forms should flow logically from the listing of information needs, which must clearly specify the aspects of behavior that are to be observed. It is often useful to characterize the information needs as the "who, what, when, and where" of behavior. Consider the information needs for a study designed to observe shoppers purchasing cereal. The following items should all be specified in detail.

- *Who is to be observed?* Purchasers, "lookers," males, females, couples, couples with children, children alone, (others).
- *What is to be observed?* Brands purchased, size purchased, brands considered, influence of children and adults, price of product package inspected. (Much of this can be done automatically if shoppers are part of a panel or have an ID card linking them to their UPC scanner record.)
- *When is observation to be made?* Days of week, hours, date, and time of purchase.
- *Where should observations be made?* Type of store, location, how selected.

Observational forms should be simple to use and designed so that they logically follow the behavior observed. They should permit the observer to record the behavior in detail, rather than requiring a summary regarding a number of behavior patterns. The physical layout of the form should follow the guidelines just presented for questionnaires. Finally, observational forms need the same degree of pretesting and revision as do questionnaires, as well as training of the observation personnel to allow standardized reportage.

7.6 International Questionnaire Design

This chapter has discussed the complex issues involved in the construction of an effective and efficient questionnaire, given a common language and culture. The difficulty of this task is increased substantially when the questionnaire is to be used across national boundaries, languages, and cultures. For example:

- The questionnaire format may have to be changed to reflect the different interviewing modes of personal, telephone, and mail.
- The questionnaire will have to be translated. (Even if the target audience speaks the same language, often there are large regional variations in usage.) The accuracy of the translation needs to be tested *extensively* in the countries where they will be administered. Typically this is done by having the questionnaire translated into the target language and then translated back into the original, and then comparing the two. Even so, expert opinion from natively bilingual speakers is crucial.
- In many parts of the world, special attention must be given to how answer categories are structured. In some cultures, people are simply reluctant to say "no" to express dislike for a proposed product or to use the lower categories in an attitudinal scale. Questions may have to be asked in several different ways to get accurate answers.

- These sorts of complexities can add a great deal of pre- and postprocessing time to a survey project done abroad, typically on the order of several months. Moreover, marketing research costs more when done offsite or abroad, mostly attributable to translation, coding, training of interviewers, securing facilities, and back-translation. Although it is hard to pin down such costs, they are typically between two and five times those for a survey run domestically, in the research team's native language.

Special Expert Feature

Self-Reports in Marketing Research: How the Questions Shape the Answers

By Norbert Schwarz and Andy Peytchev

Among the main problems in designing and interpreting survey research are unspoken assumptions on the part of researchers themselves. Researchers often assume that respondents understand a question as it was intended, are well aware of their own behaviors and thoughts, and can, in Angus Campbell's phrase, report on it "with candor and accuracy," but may sometimes not wish to do so.

Such a view contradicts the reality of working with actual respondents, who may view questions as ambiguous, have only vague recollections of their own behaviors, or may not hold an articulate opinion on the topic. It is therefore not surprising that most answers are constructed on the spot and are highly context dependent, threads that will run throughout the ensuing discussion.

Respondents face a number of concrete tasks when asked to provide information in a survey context. First, they must understand the question itself. Next, they need to retrieve relevant information from memory to form a judgment. Once they have arrived at a judgment in their own minds, they are rarely able to report it in their own words. Instead, they need to format their answers to fit the response alternatives provided by the researcher. Finally, they may hesitate to report an answer they consider undesirable and may edit their response before communicating it to the interviewer.

Question Comprehension

Researchers are commonly advised to avoid unfamiliar terms and complex question wordings. This is good advice, but not enough. Suppose you were asked, "What have you done today?" Each of the words in the question is admirably clear, but what does the questioner want to know? Should you provide a narrative of every activity from waking up through the present moment? Should you report that you took a shower? When asked in an open-ended format, "What have you done today?" elicits few reports of taking a shower or other mundane, common activities that "go without saying." However, when asked in closed format, many respondents check off "taking a shower" when it is offered among the response alternatives. In general, any answer is more likely to be endorsed when offered as part of the response alternatives than to be volunteered in an open-ended format, mostly because the response alternatives clarify what the researcher is interested in. As this example illustrates, giving a meaningful answer requires more than understanding the words (i.e., the literal meaning of the question)—it requires inferences about what the questioner wants to know (i.e., the pragmatic meaning of the question). To draw these inferences, respondents consult apparently formal features of the questionnaire, such as the response scale, as well as the context in which the question is asked.

Frequency Scales

A particularly problematic area of inquiry is determining how often respondents engage in specific target behaviors. Because the meanings of labels such as "sometimes" or "frequently" can vary dramatically across respondents, researchers have learned to avoid them in favor of absolute or objective scales. Such scales, however, can introduce more subtle problems. Consider the following questions, the first asked with two different scales:

- "How often did you go shopping last month?"

  Low Frequency Scale

  ☐ 0–1 ☐ 2–3 ☐ 4–5 ☐ 6 or more

  High Frequency Scale

  ☐ 5 or less ☐ 6–7 ☐ 8–9 ☐ 10 or more

- "How much did you spend on a typical occasion?"

What does the researcher mean by "shopping"? Does this term refer to major shopping trips, or does it include picking up some cookies at the neighborhood store? Consulting the frequency scale for relevant hints, respondents may infer from the low frequency scale that the researcher has major instances of shopping in mind, but they may infer from the high frequency scale that minor instances of shopping are to be included as well. Confirming this prediction, respondents who received the low frequency scale subsequently reported that they "typically" spent $38.97, whereas those who received the high frequency scale reported that they "typically" spent $10.84.

In a similar study, students were asked about shopping habits on three time scales, "How often did you go shopping last *week* (*month, semester*)?" and then "How much did you spend on a typical occasion?" And, once again, the "typical" shopping occasion set them back, respectively, $8.23,

continued

$32.14, and $53.12. Evidently, the very meaning of a "typical occasion of shopping" is altered by the time period one is asked to consider.

In combination, these findings highlight the ambiguity of familiar terms such as "shopping." To resolve these ambiguities, respondents draw on apparently formal details of the question, such as the frequency scale or the reference period, and report on substantively different instances of shopping. Accordingly, reports pertaining to different reference periods cannot be directly compared because they also involve a shift in question meaning.

Numerical Rating Scales

Many survey researchers and textbooks treat the following rating scales as if they are equivalent:

0	1	2	3	4	5	6	7	8	9	10
–5	–4	–3	–2	–1	0	+1	+2	+3	+4	+5

However, respondents do not necessarily use them the same way. For example, researchers posed the question "How successful would you say you have been in life?" and presented respondents with an 11-point rating scale, ranging from "not at all successful" to "extremely successful." When the numeric values of the rating scale ranged from 0 to 10, as in the first scale describer earlier, 34 percent checked a value below the midpoint (of 5); but when the numeric values ranged from –5 to +5, as in the second scale, only 13 percent checked a numerically equivalent value below the midpoint (of 0). Follow-up experiments showed that the numeric values of the scale clarified the meaning of "not at all successful"—does this term refer to the absence of particular success or to the presence of actual failure? Respondents adopted the former interpretation when "not at all successful" was combined with the numeric value 0, but the latter when it was combined with the numeric value –5. Given this differential interpretation of the question, more respondents reported that they did not do anything great than that they actually failed.

Survey researchers commonly distinguish between *unipolar* scales (e.g., 0 to 10), which can indicate absence or presence of attributes such as success, and *bipolar* scales (e.g., –5 to 5), which can indicate the presence of *opposite* attributes, such as success and failure. In such cases, it is crucial that numeric scale values match researchers' intended meaning and that text, graphics, and layout convey the same meaning.

It is important to realize that standard pretests will *not* catch such phenomena and their associated interpretive problems, because respondents will not have any difficulties using the scales as presented, nor will there be discrepancies over time using standard reliability measures. Similarly, the influence of reference periods or frequency scales will not be apparent, as respondents assume that they understood the question as intended. Instead, researchers need to use "cognitive" pretests, where respondents elaborate on what they are thinking as they digest the question, to catch unintended contextual influences on question interpretation.

Behavioral Reports

It is well known that "autobiographical memory" is rather poor, unless the behavior is of considerable importance. But even for highly vivid and supposedly memorable events, respondents can display surprisingly poor recall. For example, one study found that 3 percent did not recall overnight hospitalization within 10 weeks, and 42 percent forgot within 1 year. This is not necessarily due to forgetting that one visited the hospital at all but can arise from failure to recall staying over, or when the visit took place. These problems are compounded when researchers ask about common or frequent behaviors and experiences, which are not always represented as single episodes but can blur into generic memories of "having headaches," "shopping for groceries," or any of hundreds of daily or weekly activities. Many of these are just the sorts marketing researchers wish to know about. Although people will sometimes be able to recall distinct episodes and count them when the behavior is rare and important, they are unlikely to accomplish this for frequent behaviors. Thus, buying a car or home will produce more reliable recollections than buying a coffee maker, and dramatically better ones than buying a can of vegetables.

Estimation Strategies

When respondents cannot recall specific instances, they resort to a variety of estimation strategies; which strategy they select is highly context dependent. One particular estimation strategy is often suggested by the question itself. This is the case when the question presents a numeric frequency scale. Many respondents assume that researchers know what they are looking for and hence construct meaningful scales. Specifically, they assume that the average or typical frequency is represented by values in the middle range of the scale and that the extremes of the scale correspond to the extremes of the distribution. Based on these assumptions, they use the scale as a frame of reference to estimate their own behavioral frequency. This results in higher frequency reports along high rather than low frequency scales.

As an example, consider the following scales, presented to survey takers in a German study as part of a question regarding their daily TV consumption

Low Frequency	High Frequency
☐ Up to 1/2 hour	☐ Up to 2 1/2 hours
☐ 1/2 to 1 hour	☐ 2 1/2 to 3 hours
☐ 1 to 1 1/2 hours	☐ 3 to 3 1/2 hours
☐ 1 1/2 to 2 hours	☐ 3 1/2 to 4 hours
☐ 2 to 2 1/2 hours	☐ 4 to 4 1/2 hours
☐ More than 2 1/2 hours	☐ More than 4 1/2 hours

When researchers tallied the proportion of responses greater than 2 1/2 hours—approximately the true median value for the population from which the respondents were drawn—37.5 percent of those using the high frequency scale reported watching that much TV, but only 16.2 percent of those using the low frequency scale did. This finding is very robust and has been replicated for many common consumer, health, and social behaviors. Moreover, this effect gets stronger with the need to estimate; that is, hazier and longer-ago behaviors are especially susceptible.

Complicating researchers' tasks even further is that many of these effects vary in intensity across demographic and cultural groups. Sociologists distinguish between "collectivist" cultures, which place a premium on social harmony and fitting in, and "individualist" cultures, which value self-expression and discourage conformity for its own sake. In collectivist cultures, publicly observable behaviors (such as coming late to class) are minutely monitored and are well recalled because social reputation depends on them. This is far less the case in

continued

individualistic cultures. And, indeed, studies have found that survey respondents in Asia, where culture is more collectivist, are far less influenced by scaling effects *for observable behaviors* than are their counterparts in the West. Asian respondents need not estimate when responding about such behaviors, as they are easily recalled and explicitly tracked. For private, *unobservable behaviors* (such as the prevalence of nightmares), respondents in both cultures are equally susceptible to scaling effects. This is hardly limited to Eastern or Western cultures and use of frequency scales. The same logic applies to any other comparisons—in particular those *across groups* for whom a behavior is differentially important and memorable, and those *across behaviors* that are differentially important and memorable within a group. The bottom line for marketing researchers is that they simply cannot presume that using the same scale across cultures or demographic groups will guard against interpretive errors, even with extensive pretesting and faultless translation.

Subsequent Judgments

We would like to believe that respondents "leave behind" the context and presumptions of prior questions when moving on in a survey, but this is not always the case. Subsequent judgments can be affected by the "frame" set in an earlier question, even if that frame arises from a scale. Let us consider again the German respondents asked about TV watching, using the low frequency and high frequency scales shown earlier. A follow-up question concerned how *important* TV was as a component of one's leisure time. Recall that those using the low frequency scale reported watching less TV overall. Yet, the same respondents also reported that TV was *more* important in their leisure time (4.6 on a 1 to 7 scale) than did respondents who received the high frequency scale (3.8). It is not difficult to see why. Recall that respondents assume that the average person is represented in the middle range of the scale. Hence, endorsing a value at the high end of the low frequency scale conveys to respondents that their own TV watching is above average, whereas the high frequency scale conveys that a similar behavior is below average—resulting in different perceptions of the importance of TV in their leisure time.

Note the irony here, in that researchers will observe a higher importance despite a lower frequency report! Again, such problems will not be caught by pretesting alone, and they are hardly limited to frequencies. They can easily occur throughout marketing research. One study found that great service could be coupled with low reported levels of satisfaction, merely as an artifact of scale range. In a study of satisfaction with a university's interlibrary loan system, patrons were asked, "How many days did you have to wait for your book?" The library knew that the true average wait was around 5 days. Two scales were used in the study:

Low:	☐ 1	☐ 2	☐ 3	☐ 4	☐ 5 or more
High:	☐ 5 or less	☐ 6	☐ 7	☐ 8	☐ 9 or more

Patrons were then asked two questions intended to measure customer satisfaction, "How satisfied are you with the service you received?" (i.e., a "personal" reaction) and "How good a job is the interlibrary loan service doing?" (i.e., a "general" reaction); both were asked using a 1 to 9 scale, with 9 being "very satisfied" in the first case and "excellent" in the second. The results paint an interesting portrait of customer satisfaction and the power of scaling.

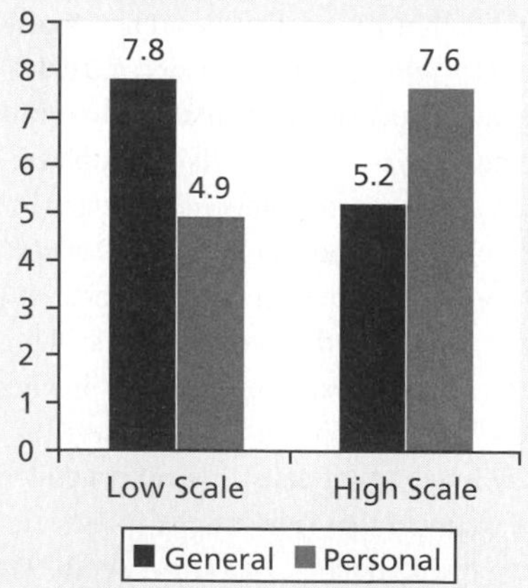

Using the low scale, patrons were not very satisfied—after all, they were waiting 5 days on average, which is at the very top of the scale—but the *library itself* seemed to be doing an impressive job because the scale suggests that it fulfilled most requests quickly. Using the high scale, the library looked to be taking its time, with a minimum category of "5 days or less"; yet patrons were highly satisfied because most of them fell into this category! It is a sobering thought that merely by viewing a scale chosen for them by researchers, respondents will make inferences not only about how a product or service is performing, but about their *own experience* and their feelings about it.

Once again, these context effects—judging one's own experience relative to that of others—can be especially pronounced for frequency scales. Such scales can appear to provide important information about the *absolute* range of a phenomenon (e.g., from 5 days to 9 days) as well as one's *relative* placement. As such, the mere scaling of frequencies can influence a variety of subsequent judgments, of both the comparative and noncomparativetypes. Researchers have documented these sorts of scaling effects for satisfaction with health, relationships, brands, and companies, as well as for the risk of HIV infection, judgments of competence, and many evaluative tasks.

Methodological Implications

Marketers need to keep several caveats in mind when using a variety of scales in their research. First, reports along different scales are not comparable, and neither are *subsequent* judgments, which are often contaminated by inferences arising from the scale itself. Second, scales can attenuate differences between groups; the same reference frame can "pull in" extremes, making disparate groups appear more similar than they are. Third, open response formats—"You had to wait _____ days to receive your book"—can often reduce these systematic biases.

Given these problems with frequency reports, you may wonder if it is not simpler to use so-called vague quantifiers, such as "rarely," "sometimes," and "often." Unfortunately, this is the worst possible solution because vague quantifiers always represent frequencies *relative to norms or expectations*. Someone with occasional heart palpitations may report that he experiences them "often" but that he "rarely" watches TV news because most people never experience heart palpitations but watch TV news all the time. Answers using such quantifiers are not comparable across behaviors, respondents, or time and should be used "rarely" (in this case, meaning almost never).

continued

Attitude Reports

When asking attitude questions, researchers usually hope that respondents know how they feel about the issue under study and simply recall a previously formed opinion from memory. Unfortunately, this is seldom the case, even when the attitude object is as familiar as one's own life. In most cases, respondents retrieve some information about the attitude object and form a judgment on the spot. Worse, they rarely retrieve all information that may be relevant but truncate the search process as soon as "enough" information has come to mind to form a judgment. Hence, their judgment is strongly influenced by the information that comes to mind first, giving rise to pronounced question order effects.

For example, one study asked students about both their life satisfaction and their dating frequency. When asked in that order, the correlation in their answers was negligible, $r = 0.11$, indicating that just more than 1 percent (that is, $(0.11)^2$) of the variation in reported life satisfaction was explained by the variation in dating frequency. Yet, when the order was reversed, and respondents were first asked about their dating frequency, the correlation soared to $r = 0.62$, suggesting a strong relationship between dating frequency and life satisfaction. Findings of this type reflect that we can draw on a myriad of different aspects of our lives to evaluate our life satisfaction—and whichever one comes to mind first will dominate our judgment.

Essentially the same result was obtained in a study of satisfaction with one's job and salary. When asked first about job satisfaction, correlation between the two was a modest $r = 0.22$, but it rose to $r = 0.53$ in the opposite order. Again, the researcher would draw very different inferences about the role of pay satisfaction in overall job satisfaction in the two cases. Interestingly, the $r = 0.53$ correlation essentially disappeared ($r = 0.07$) when respondents were first asked simply to *describe* their jobs, thus bringing a number of different aspects of their jobs to mind. Throughout, any aspect of the attitude object becomes more important and influential when one focuses on it—and loses some of its influence when one considers other aspects.

Such findings highlight that survey answers, like any other judgment, depend on what comes to mind at the time the judgment is formed. In daily life, this is often information that the person is preoccupied with. But in research situations it may simply be the information that was brought to mind by a preceding question. Unfortunately, such question order effects undermine generalizations from the sample, which was exposed to the preceding question, to the population, which was not.

Conclusions and Implications for Marketing Researchers

Among the main tasks of marketing researchers are assessments of attitudes, preferences, intentions, opinions, beliefs, and satisfaction. Marketers have long understood that these are subjective, that each person brings a unique perspective to bear, and that there are no "right answers"—but they have only recently started to realize how elusive and fragile the answers can be. We must always bear in mind that much of what we assess are *evaluative judgments*, constructed "on the spot," based on what happens to spring to mind when respondents are asked. These judgments are highly context dependent and easily swayed by the wording and ordering both of questions and of the presented response alternatives, as well as the manifold properties of common scales and their layouts.

As researchers, we need to always keep in mind that respondents' thought processes are critically shaped by the research instrument we design. They are not black boxes filled with objective information that will be faithfully reported regardless of how questions are worded, formatted, ordered, or perceived. We must also remember that the very purpose of statistics is to generalize from samples to populations; context effects can undermine precisely these sorts of generalizations. Consequently, no statistical magic can compensate for mistakes at the data collection stage. This principle often goes by the evocative phrase "garbage in, garbage out." If we collect biased, inaccurate data, all the regressions in the world will not rescue it. In the end, there is no substitute for thinking deeply about the process of answering questions, and working closely with respondents in pilot studies to weed out problems before large-scale data collection takes place.

Norbert Schwarz is professor of psychology at the University of Michigan, professor of marketing at the Ross School of Business, and research professor at Michigan's Institute for Social Research. His research interests focus on human cognition and judgment, including their implications for social science methodology.

Andy Peytchev is a PhD candidate in survey methodology at the University of Michigan. His research interests include participation decisions and measurement errors in surveys.

Further Reading

Schwarz, Norman (1999), "Self-Reports." *American Psychologist,* 54, 93–105.

Schwarz, Norman, and Daphna Oyserman (2001), "Asking Questions About Behavior." *American Journal of Evaluation,* 22, 127–160.

Sudman, Seymour, Norman M. Bradburn, and Norman Schwarz (1996), *Thinking About Answers.* San Francisco: Jossey-Bass.

Tourangeau, Roger, Lance J. Rips, and Kenneth Rasinski (2000), *The Psychology of Survey Response.* Cambridge, UK: Cambridge University Press.

Courtesy of Norbert Schwarz and Andy Peytchev.

Summary

A questionnaire is a formalized instrument for collecting data from respondents on past behavior, attitudes, and respondent characteristics. The questionnaire is a critical component of the research project; a poorly designed questionnaire can be a major source of error in the research results.

The sections of a questionnaire are: identification data, request for cooperation, instructions, information sought, and classification data. The steps in designing a questionnaire design are: review preliminary considerations; decide on question content, response format, question wording, question sequence, and physical characteristics; carry out pretesting and revision; and make the final draft.

The questionnaire links the information needed with the data to be collected, based on the research design, data sources, target population, sampling plan, communication media, measurement techniques, and data processing and analysis plan.

Question content is influenced by the respondent's ability and willingness to respond accurately. Response formats can be open ended, multiple response, or dichotomous. General guidelines for designing questions include using simple and unambiguous wording; avoiding estimates, implicit alternatives or assumptions, and leading, biasing, or double-barreled questions; and considering the question's frame of reference. Guidelines for determining how to sequence the questions include using a simple and interesting opening question, asking general questions before more specific ones, placing uninteresting and difficult questions later in the sequence, and arranging questions in logical order. The physical characteristics of the questionnaire can influence the degree of respondent cooperation and the character of the responses.

A questionnaire needs to be pretested before it is ready for use in the field. Observational forms are easier to design than questionnaires because some of the design problems associated with the questionnaire are reduced or eliminated in the observational form.

In general, design of data collection forms should flow logically from a clear specification of the types of observations to be made and how they are to be measured.

Key Terms

aided recall (p. 263)
anonymity (p. 280)
Arrow's impossibility theorem (p. 280)
binary (p. 271)
collectively exhaustive (p. 269)
counterbiasing statement (p. 265)
dichotomous question (p. 270)
double-barreled question (p. 274)
fairness criteria (p. 280)
frame of reference (p. 274)
gaming (p. 280)
indirect statement (p. 265)
labeled response categories (p. 265)
modal answer (p. 270)
multiple-response (or multiple-choice) question (p. 268)
mutually exclusive (p. 270)
open-ended (or free-response or free-answer) question (p. 266)
position bias (p. 270)
pretesting (p. 278)
primacy bias (p. 270)
randomized response technique (p. 265)
recency bias (p. 270)
recognition (p. 264)
sequence bias (p. 276)
unaided recall (p. 263)
universality (p. 280)

Discussion Questions

1 What decisions precede the questionnaire design stage? What criteria govern the inclusion of questions in the questionnaire?

2 How does the respondent affect the content of the questions? Can respondents influence the forms of questions as well, or the range and wording of choices? In which ways?

3 How can a researcher overcome the problems associated with collecting data about events that are unimportant to respondents or that occur infrequently?

4 What approaches are available for dealing with the bias resulting from a respondent's unwillingness to respond accurately? Are there some biases that cannot be realistically overcome?

5 What are the advantages and disadvantages of open-ended questions relative to multiple-response questions? How might they be used synergistically so that each helps overcome weaknesses in the other?

6 What does a researcher need to consider when designing multiple-response questions? What general guidelines should be utilized in determining the wording of a question? the range and content of responses? the order of questions and of responses?

7 Under what conditions would dichotomous questions be inappropriate? What sorts of questions would be indicated instead?

8 MINICASE

Suppose you are researching attitudes about computer peripherals among your classmates. Specify the information needs for this project, and then develop a concise questionnaire to measure the target group's perceived needs, attitudes, and purchase intentions. Be sure to consider that knowledge, purchase readiness, and opinions themselves are all likely to be heterogeneous, even in this self-selected group (in fact, what is considered a "peripheral" may be heterogeneous as well). How might you use the resulting data set to determine which peripherals are most likely to be needed, valued, and purchased?

Review Questions

1 Which of the following survey questions is most likely to achieve meaningful research results?

a Do you support using $15 per taxpayer to fund the campaigns of political candidates?
b How long ago did you purchase your refrigerator?
c Have you purchased canned vegetables from the supermarket in the last month?
d When buying ice cream, how do you weigh the caloric content and healthfulness relative to the experiential quality of the flavor?

2 Which of the following is an improvement on this question: "What type of cat food do you prepare for your cat?" (assuming the respondent has a cat)

a What brand of cat food do you prepare for your cat?
b What do you feed your cat?
c What does your cat like to eat?
d none of the above

3 "*Consumer Reports* has ranked this dishwasher as the best in its class. How would you rate it relative to other brands?" The flaw in this question is:

a it is a biasing question.
b it assumes too much knowledge on the part of the respondent.
c it is ambiguous.
d all of the above.

4 Which of the following corrects one of the main problems in the question "Do you favor warning labels on cosmetic products?"

a Have you ever noticed and been disturbed by warning labels on cosmetic products?
b Do you favor warning labels on cosmetics if it means that animals do not need to be tested?
c Do you agree with People for the Ethical Treatment of Animals (PETA) that cosmetic products should have warning labels?
d Are warning labels on cosmetic products a good idea?

5 Which of the following is a well-posed survey question?

a How much do you spend for groceries per year?
b Was the service you experienced at the store friendly and efficient?
c How would you rate the service at this store on friendliness and efficiency (on a scale of 1 to 10)?
d How much did you spend for groceries on your last visit to the grocery store?

6 Which of the following two questions is a better, and why?
"Are the operating hours of your local library adequate to your community's needs, in your opinion?"
"Are you, personally, content with your local library's hours of operation?"

a The first one, because it is more specific to information needed for research.
b The second one, because it gives information on the respondent's attitude.
c Both are fine, for different purposes.
d Neither is good, because they assume too much knowledge on the part of the respondent.

7 Put the following questions in the best order for a survey:
   w Please fill in: male/female ethnic group __________ yearly income __________
   x Would you consider a capital investment in your farm, if it resulted in greater profits?
   y Would you consider converting your egg farm to a factory for chicken pies, if it resulted in greater profits?
   z Are you frustrated by lower profits than you are capable of achieving?
      a x, y, w, z
      b z, x, y, w
      c z, w, y, x
      d w, z, x, y

8 In which of the following ways would initial questions be most likely to bias the sample?
   a if questions are too uninteresting to the respondent
   b if questions are partisan or highly specific
   c if questions are too simplistic or obvious
   d if responses are not mutually exclusive

9 Which of the following voting systems adheres to the fairness criteria of anonymity?
   a secret ballots
   b majority wins
   c two-thirds majority wins
   d plurality wins

10 What problem may be encountered with this question: "Should clients be given a buy-in to incentivize their participation and prevent a run?"
   a "Buy-in" is not defined.
   b Alternatives are not explicit.
   c When you take out the jargon, the question is nearly meaningless.
   d all of the above

Web Exercise

Log in to the Online Edition of your textbook at www.atomicdog.com to participate in this Web exercise, which can be found in your Online Study Guide for this chapter.

Further Reading

Couper, Mick P., Michael W. Traugott, and Mark J. Lamias (2001), "Web Survey Design and Administration." *Public Opinion Quarterly*, 65, 230–253.

Creswell, John W. (2002), *Research Design: Qualitative, Quantitative, and Mixed Methods Approaches*; 2nd edition. Thousand Oaks, CA: Sage Publications.

Dillman, Don A. (1999), *Mail and Internet Surveys: The Tailored Design Method*; 2nd edition. Hoboken, NJ: Wiley.

Fowler, Floyd J. (2001), *Survey Research Methods*, 3rd edition. Thousand Oaks, CA: Sage Publications.

Oppenheim, A. N. (1992), *Questionnaire Design, Interviewing, and Attitude Measurement*. London, United Kingdom: Pinter Publishers.

Reynolds, Nina, Adamantios Diamantopoulos, and Bodo Schlegelmilch (1993), "Pre-testing in Questionnaire Design: A Review of the Literature and Suggestions for Further Research." *Journal of the Market Research Society*, 35, 171–182.

Sudman, Seymour, Norman M. Bradburn, and Norbert Schwarz (1982), *Asking Questions: A Practical Guide to Questionnaire Design*. San Francisco, CA: Jossey-Bass.

CHAPTER EIGHT
SAMPLING

"Errors using inadequate data are much less than those using no data at all."
CHARLES BABBAGE

8.1 Sampling: An Introduction

This chapter discusses both the theory of sampling and the practical application of sampling to real marketing situations. We begin with an overview of sampling terminology and sampling procedures, then consider the many ways in which sampling pervades marketing practice and social science in general.

It is often said that without water, life would be impossible. Similarly, without sampling, marketing research as we know it would be impossible. Virtually every marketing research study requires the selection of some kind of sample: when a new product is placed in households for trial, we must select the households in question; when we want to monitor sales in a geographical area, we must select which stores' sales to record; when we want to conduct a group interview about prices, products, features, social policy, or anything else, we must select the people to take part in the group, and perhaps even a set of such groups.

Sampling is vitally important for one reason: the alternative is gathering data from every person, every household, every store, every firm, every town, and so on—in which case we have a *census*. Although potentially extremely accurate, it is also quite obviously slow, costly, and effortful. If speed, cost, and efficiency of effort are not vitally important in a specific project, neither is sampling. But such situations are exceedingly rare. In the real world, budgets are limited, time horizons are tight, and personnel have much to do, so censuses are limited almost exclusively to governments, and marketing researchers always depend on samples.

For sampling to be useful, it must be done well, and much of this chapter is devoted to that goal. *Marketing Research Focus 8.1* presents several examples of what might ensue if sampling is *not* done appropriately.

8.1a The Benefits of Sampling

Sampling is used frequently in marketing research because it offers some major benefits over taking a census.

1. *A sample saves money*. The cost of an hour-long in-person interview can be prohibitive, once the respondent and interviewer are compensated and setup time, missed calls, transcription services, call center rental, phone charges, and other items are accounted for. Clearly, interviewing a thousand people rather than, say, the million who may make up the relevant population would involve a huge cost savings. This is true for in-person, mail, telephone, and even Internet-based surveys.
2. *A sample saves time*. In the previous example, we would have 1000 hours of interviewing with a sample versus one million hours with a census. To this we must add the time for, say, printing questionnaires, training field interviewers, and preparing the completed questionnaires for data analysis.
3. *A sample may be more accurate*. Surprising as it may seem, this is indeed true. This results from several sources of inaccuracy through nonsampling errors that can occur in the marketing research process (as discussed in Chapter 2). In a census study, we will need more interviewers, more supervisors of interviewers, more people to convert the raw questionnaires to computer input, etc.; that is, we will need a larger and more hierarchical infrastructure to carry out the research. The smaller the study, the more likely we are to obtain more highly skilled people for each stage of the research process and to have them be able to intercommunicate for the purposes of quality control and standardization. As the staff gets bigger, quality tends to fall, and control and supervision becomes more difficult. Also, a census may take so long that the marketing phenomenon of interest may have changed. For example, questions about the awareness of a new product have meaning only at one point in time. Government censuses, such as the U.S. Census, are conducted infrequently (e.g., once a decade) and are therefore useful primarily for quantities such as populations that change in ways that can be readily modeled or predicted, and not for concepts such as attitudes and beliefs that can change from week to week.

   Like a census, a sample can involve nonsampling errors too, but typically to a lesser degree. Unlike a census, a sample also opens up the possibility of sampling error (a statistical concept discussed in detail later in this chapter). For now, we need only remember that samples are used to provide estimates of values of interest in a population. To the extent that the sample estimates

Marketing Research Focus 8.1

Consequences of Poor Sampling

Sampling is ubiquitous in marketing research. As such, sampling that is carried out poorly can entail a wide range of unintended consequences. The following represent just a few "real world" examples of problems that can result when sampling is not conducted appropriately:

- Deloitte Consulting conducted a study for the National Association of Manufacturers (NAM), an outsourcing lobbying firm, on the reasons manufacturers choose to outsource. The study found that outsourcing is largely due to a shortage of qualified U.S. workers, and is frequently cited by proponents of this view. Because only 800 of the 8000 companies contacted by Deloitte responded to the survey, self-selection bias could have skewed the results. The 10 percent that responded were, more than likely, those who had to endure the most shortages. Few of the companies that did respond followed Deloitte's recommendations of placing more emphasis on training to instill value in the workforce and better retain workers, suggesting that the firms may not have been terribly interested in retaining their U.S. employees. An alternate explanation is that the jobs of U.S. employees are being replaced with cheap labor outside the United States.
- Another longstanding debate is over the question of whether the news has a liberal or a conservative bias. Liberals say that the news is conservative because the news media are owned by wealthy interests, whereas conservatives say that the news is liberal because many reporters have liberal values. A survey by Pew Research seemed to confirm the latter view (liberal bias) with its estimate of four liberal reporters to one conservative, prompting an outcry among conservative commentators that "80 percent of reporters are self-described liberals." This result is questionable, however, due to sample selection. The sample of 547 journalists and executives reached a majority of the media outlets, but only in large cities. The average age of and education completed by the sampled reporters were not representative of those in the profession. Additionally, the sample of newspapers came from the top 100 newspapers by circulation, leaving out 1456 national dailies. Papers such as the *Houston Chronicle*, the *Arizona Republic*, and the *Detroit Free Press* were placed into the national category when they are not even distributed nationwide. From the 100 papers sampled, it appears that papers such as the *Washington Post*, the *Boston Globe*, the *New York Times*, and the *Los Angeles Times* (known to favor liberalism) were included, whereas the *Washington Times*, the *Boston Herald*, the *New York Post*, and the *Los Angeles Daily News* were not.
- In Quebec, CROP (the Centre de Recherche sur l'Opinion Publique), an accredited polling firm with 40 years experience, took a poll before and after a major election and found a strong increase in support for Canada's liberal government, along with a major decline in support for the sovereignty of Quebec. Quebec's Parti Québécois, a political party dedicated to preserving the French roots of Quebec and normally favored in elections, apparently took a beating. Based on the poll, reporters concluded that the appointment of André Boisclair as leader of the Parti Québécois was to blame for the loss of support, shaking the confidence of Quebec's political climate. However, recalculation revealed that CROP oversampled Montreal's non-Francophones, who were much less interested in preserving Quebec's French culture and were "outsiders" to Québécois culture in general. A more representative sample revealed that the level of support for Canada's liberal party had not changed since the election and that the Parti Québécois still held the top position in Quebec's federal elections.
- The National Automobile Dealer's Association (NADA) has raised a number of issues with J.D. Power and Associates regarding Power's surveys of automotive customer satisfaction. Among these issues was the selection biases related to the length of the surveys (eight pages of about 70 questions). Customers filling out the survey may be more likely to be those with complaints—potentially about the vehicle itself, and not the dealer experience. Another dealer noted what appeared to be a race-based selection bias because it was claimed to be more difficult to encourage some minority-group members to complete the surveys. Dealers say these selection biases further skew results, and argue that they are not being accurately evaluated for their particular contribution. To help alleviate this problem, manufacturers have begun switching to phone surveys, instead of written questions. Honda has found that phone interviews result in a higher response rate, fewer selection biases, conceivably less distortion from dealer influence, and more timely results.

Sources: Tolenson, Alan (2006). "The Labor Shortage Hoax." AmericanEconomicAlert.org.
Mitchell, Greg (2004), "Bias Numbers, Less than Meets the Eye?" *Editor and Publisher*. http://www.editorandpublisher.com/eandp/article_brief/eandp/1/1000586533
Black, Peter, "The Block Faces a New Foe"; Peter Black. NewsBank: *The Guelph Mercury*. Ontario, Canada. February 3, 2006.
Finlay, Steve (2003), "Those Irrepressible Satisfaction Surveys." *Ward's Dealer Business*, 1–3. June 1, 2003.

differ from the (real) population values, sampling error has occurred. Thus, a sample will be *more* accurate than a census if the *total* of sampling and nonsampling errors for the sample is smaller than nonsampling types of errors for the census.

4. *A sample is better in situations where the study itself entails contamination or even destruction of the sampled elements*. Product usage tests result in the consumption of the product, and being exposed to certain marketing inducements results in greater awareness and potential liking of the product.

In such cases, there is "contamination," in the following sense. Suppose we wish to determine whether an ad campaign increases awareness of a product. We cannot sample the same people before and after the ad campaign, asking them directly about awareness both times, because the first interview "contaminates" the respondent. If the first study had been a census, the second one would have no "uncontaminated" people to ask. Consider a more extreme situation, in which engineers wish to estimate the crash-worthiness of a new car. Each time the study is run, another car is sent careening into a wall at high speed. Clearly, the manufacturer would want to use as small a sample as possible to accurately ascertain whether the car is safe because each run literally destroys the sampled element.

element
In statistics, the unit (often individuals, but also objects or firms) under analysis, about which information is sought.

8.1b Some Crucial Sampling Concepts

With the reasons for sampling established, we now turn to the question of how a sample is selected. This task is much easier if we first master some standard terminology and basic concepts, that is, the language of sampling.

Element

An **element** is the unit about which we seek information, and it provides the basis of the (usually statistical) analysis that we will undertake. The most common elements in marketing research sampling are individual persons. In other instances, the elements can be products, stores, companies, households, and so forth. It is important to realize that the elements in any specific sample depend on the objectives of the study. If we are interested in income, for example, we could want to know how well certain professions are remunerated, and so would need individual incomes; if we were instead interested in purchasing power for homes or automobiles, we would need household incomes; and if were interested in CEO compensation, the units might be corporations. Even though the main variable of interest in all three of these studies would be "income," the elements or sampling units (which we will formally define shortly) would be entirely different.

Population

population
The total set of elements about which one can make inference, by using a sample (randomly) drawn from it.

extent
When defining a population for a study, extent refers to the geographic region demarcating the relevant population's boundaries.

A population (or *universe*, as it is sometimes called), is the aggregate of all the elements defined *before selection of the sample*. In simple language, it is "everything" that might conceivably become part of our sample and is what we would ideally like to make inferences about. A properly designated population must be defined in terms of elements, sampling units, extent, and time. Holding aside precise definitions for the moment, let us look at some examples of how a survey of consumers might specify the relevant population:

1. Element — Women, 18–50
2. Sampling units — Women, 18–50
3. Extent — Texas
4. Time — May 1–June 15

Alternatively, the population for a study designed to measure buyer reaction to a new industrial chemical might be:

1. Element — Chemical engineers
2. Sampling units — Companies purchasing more than $1 million of chemicals annually; then chemical engineers
3. Extent — Continental United States
4. Time — January 1–December 31

Or, if we wished to monitor the sales of a new consumer product, the population might be:

1. Element — Our product
2. Sampling units — Supermarkets, drugstores, wholesale clubs; then our product
3. Extent — Boston
4. Time — Week of May 5–12

It is absolutely crucial to define the population to at least this level of detail; nothing else constitutes proper sampling. Further, it allows one to judge whether *different* samples can be reasonably compared with one another when searching for meaningful changes or effects over time, geography, or population subgroups (i.e., segments).

Sampling Unit

Previously, we used the term "sampling unit" in defining a relevant population, and we now define this term precisely. **Sampling units** are the elements available for selection at some stage of the sampling process. In the simplest type of sampling—single-stage sampling—the sampling units and the elements are the same. For example, in our first population illustration, both the elements and the sampling units were women, 18–50. This indicates a direct, single-stage sampling process, in which we would select our sample directly from the entire population of women, 18–50.

sampling unit
The elements available for inclusion in a sample at some stage of the sampling process; nonoverlapping groups of elements from the population.

With more complex sampling procedures, different levels of sampling units may be utilized; in such cases, the sampling units and elements differ in all but the very last stage. Consider our second illustration. Our elements of interest are chemical engineers. However, we reach these engineers indirectly, through a two-stage process. First, we select a sample of companies purchasing more than $1 million of chemicals per year. Then, *within* these selected companies, we select a sample of chemical engineers. Note that within this two-stage sampling process, only at the final stage are the elements and sampling units identical. It is important to realize that this sort of multistage sampling process may *not* select every unit (i.e., chemical engineers working at a firm purchasing more than $1 million of chemicals per year) with equal probability. If we choose one unit from a small firm with only 5 chemical engineers and another from a large firm with 1000, having had the first stage take place at the company level leads to a relative overrepresentation of engineers from small companies.

The third illustration is also a two-stage process, with the stores constituting the first stage and "our product" the second. A sampling process may have as many stages as the researcher desires. All the researcher must do is specify the sampling unit at each stage. For example, a four-stage sample might be:

- Stage 1: Cities of more than 500,000 population
- Stage 2: City blocks
- Stage 3: Households
- Stage 4: Males aged 50 and older

The elements of interest in this study would, of course, be males aged 50 and older. The terms "primary sampling units," "secondary sampling units," "tertiary sampling units," and "final sampling units" are used to designate the successive stages, respectively, of the process in this example. We note here again that having done the primary sampling at the city level will tend to overrepresent units (males, 50 and older) from smaller cities because a city of 500,000 and one of 5 million are equally likely to be chosen. We will consider this issue in greater detail in Section 8.8.

Sampling Frame

A sampling frame is a list of all the sampling units available for selection at a stage of the sampling process. At the final stage, the actual sample is drawn from such a list. Some of the most creative thinking in a marketing research project may be related to the specification of a sampling frame. A frame may be a class list, a list of registered voters, a telephone directory, an employee list, or even a map. In the case of a map, we would be sampling by geography; a city block would be an example of this sort of sampling frame. The frame list is usually stored as a computer database and selected from using random number generators.

Once a population is specified for a specific research project, the search begins for a good sampling frame. This can be as much an art as a science, and sometimes the availability of a sampling frame comes to define the population, as no perfect fit is available between population and frame. One example (not representative of good research practice) would be to use a telephone directory to reach the population in an area, which could then be redefined as "households with telephones with listed numbers." Telephone coverage is nearly universal in developed countries, so this may not be a particularly egregious error. Doing the same with computer ownership would certainly entail a gross error for much of the world.

Each stage of a sampling process requires its own sampling frame. Thus, the four-stage sampling process presented previously would require four sampling frames, as follows:

1. a list of cities of more than 500,000 population,
2. a list of city blocks within the selected cities,

3. a list of households within the selected city blocks, and
4. a list of males aged 50 and older within the selected households.

A direct, one-stage sampling selection procedure would require only one sampling frame, which would contain all the elements in the population. One can quickly see that coming up with a list of *all* males aged 50 and older would be considerably more daunting than doing so for only specific cities, blocks in those cities, and specific households in those blocks.

In the real world of marketing research practice, an accurate, up-to-date sampling frame may not preexist or may be very difficult to obtain. For example, lists of certain targeted consumer groups or targeted companies for marketing research are problematic. There are, for example, no lists of "allergy sufferers" or of "innovative companies." These may be important populations, but they are difficult to pin down by any strict definition, and change over time. Thus, one of the chief creative tasks facing the marketing researcher is to create a sampling approach for these elusive sorts of targeted groups. We discuss the complex sampling schemes devised for these situations in the last sections of this chapter.

Study Population

study population
The elements of a population from which a sample is actually selected (ideally the same as the population itself).

A study population is, loosely speaking, what we wish to make inferences about but for which we lack the resources (time, funds, energy) allowing for a full census. More formally, a population is usually defined as "the aggregate of elements from which the sample is drawn." Previously, we defined a population as the aggregate of the elements defined *before* the selection of the sample, and in theory this is strictly accurate. Unfortunately, practical difficulties arise that invariably lead to the *actual* sample being drawn from a somewhat—hopefully only slightly—different population from the one we defined *a priori*. Among the many possibilities, the most common is simply that elements of the population are omitted from the sampling frame. For example, a club membership list may be incomplete, some households' phone numbers are missing or unlisted, a map may not include a new subdivision street, and so on. Or, due to pure errors, some elements may appear that should not, such as a few graduate students whose names are incorrectly listed as undergraduates in a university database, or (in oft-told tales) people surprised to learn they were listed as deceased by the Social Security Administration.

For all practical purposes, then, the study population should be conceptualized as the aggregation of elements from which the sample is actually selected. It is with regard to this study population that we can make proper inferences, even though our real interest is the original population. This is not a pointless or "academic" distinction: a chief source of serious errors in marketing research involves inferences about some nebulous population very different from the one actually sampled. Although one should always have a clear image and definition about the population one *intends* to sample, it is crucial that once the results are in, they are checked thoroughly to determine which population one can reasonably make inferences about based on the data actually received, not preconceptions about them.

8.1c The Sampling Process: An Overview

The steps involved in selecting a sample are:

- Step 1: *Define the population* by specifying:
  - the elements
  - the sampling units
  - the extent
  - the time frame
- Step 2: *Identify the sampling frame* from which the sample will be selected.
- Step 3: *Decide on a sample size*, the total number of elements to include in the sample.
- Step 4: *Select a specific procedure* by which the sample will be determined.
- Step 5: *Physically select the sample* based on the procedure specified in Step 4.

Steps 3 and 4 may appear simple, but this appearance is deceptive. Deciding on sample size is sometimes referred to as a "Goldilocks" sort of problem: the sample cannot be too large (or resources are wasted) or too small (or inference will be impossible); it needs to be "just right." In practice, this can be remarkably difficult to know in advance. How many people should be asked about a new product to determine what features it should have? This depends critically on what they have to say, which the research will not know until the study is conducted. Having to determine how much information to seek before any actually comes in is a nontrivial problem in sample design. Step 4 can also be tricky: Exactly how will the decision be made about which population elements to include in the sample? How can we ensure appropriate representativeness, lack of bias, and other desirable sampling properties? We take up these issues surrounding Steps 3 and 4 at length in Section 8.4, addressing sample size calculation.

8.1d Sampling Procedures

There are many different procedures by which researchers may select their samples, but one fundamental concept must be established at the outset, the distinction between a probability sample and a nonprobability sample.

In probability sampling, each element of the population has a known chance of being selected for the sample. The sampling is done by mathematical rules for decision that leave no discretion to the researcher or field interviewer. Note that we said a "known chance" and not an "equal chance" of being selected; these are *not* the same concept. Equal chance means that each element has the same probability of being selected; probability sampling requires only that the probability of each sample selected be known. Equal-chance probability sampling is only a very special case of probability sampling, called simple random sampling. Probability sampling allows us to calculate the likely extent to which the sample value differs from the population value of interest. This difference is called *sampling error*, as introduced in Chapter 2, and we will discuss it in greater detail later in this chapter.

probability sampling
A method of sampling relying on random selection, in which each population element has a known, ordinarily equal, chance of being included in the sample.

simple random sampling
A method of probability sampling where (1) every element has an equal chance of being selected, and (2) every possible sample of size *n* has an equal chance of being drawn.

In nonprobability sampling, the selection of a population element to be part of the sample is based in some part on the judgment of the researcher or field interviewer. Because there is no *known* chance of any particular element in the population being selected, we cannot calculate the sampling error that has occurred, and thus have no idea whether or not resulting sample estimates are accurate.

nonprobability sampling
A method of choosing a sample that does not assure an equal likelihood of participation of all population elements; usually allows for some degree of personal judgment in selecting the sample.

There are a number of different sampling procedures that fall into the category of nonprobability methods and a number that are probability methods. Figure 8.1 lists them. We start by discussing the three kinds of nonprobability samples (convenience, judgment, and quota), follow with simple random sampling and the determination of sample size, and finish with the more complex probability sampling procedures, stratified and cluster sampling.

8.2 Nonprobability Sampling Procedures

8.2a Convenience Sampling

Convenience samples are selected, as the name implies, on the basis of the convenience of the researcher. Examples include:

- asking for people to volunteer to test products and surveying those who agree
- stopping people in a shopping mall to get their opinion

convenience samples
A nonprobability sample whose members are chosen because they were simpler, less costly and/or more readily available than others from the population.

Figure 8.1 Sampling Procedures

Nonprobability samples	Probability samples
1 Convenience sample	1 Simple random sample
2 Judgment sample	2 Stratified sample
3 Quota sample	3 Cluster sample a Systematic sample b Area sample

- using students or social groups to conduct an experiment
- sending out bulk e-mail requests with a link to an online survey
- having "people-in-the-street interviews" conducted by a television station.

In each instance, the sampling unit or element is self-selected, has been selected because it was easily available, or both. In all cases it is unclear what population the actual sample is drawn from. The television interviewer may state that her sample represents the community, but this is clearly wrong. Most members of the community had no chance whatever of being selected; only those who happened to be where the interviewer was at the time could possibly be included in the sample. Even if the population were taken to be those who happened to be where the interviewer was at the time, the exact chance of any particular person in that group's being selected is unknown.

Recall that the very purpose of sampling is to use the sample to calculate some quantity of interest in the entire population. When one convenience-samples, the difference between the population value of interest and the sample value can never be known, in terms of both size and direction. We cannot measure sampling error, and clearly cannot make any definite or conclusive statements about the results from such a sample. For conclusive research, then, convenience samples are inappropriate and should rarely, if ever, be used. However, convenience samples can be *helpful* in certain limited situations: for example, at the exploratory stage of research, as a basis for generating hypotheses, and—when used with great care and understanding of the risks involved—for conclusive studies in which the manager is willing to accept the possibility that the study results might have substantial inaccuracies. Convenience samples are helpful in these cases because, except for conclusive research, the purpose is not an exact measurement or definitive verification, but an exploration of or way to generate ideas about and get a feel for a situation. In such cases, sample representativeness, although desirable, is not crucial, as ideas and discussions can be insightful even if they come from the wrong market niche or demographic subgroup. Examples of the use of convenience samples are described in *Marketing Research Focus 8.2: Business Uses of Nonprobability Sampling.*

8.2b Judgment Sampling

judgment samples
A type of nonprobability sample for which respondents or sample units are deliberately chosen to serve the research purpose.

Judgment samples (or *purposive samples*, as they are also called) are selected on the basis of what *an expert believes* those particular sampling units or elements will contribute to answering the particular research question at hand. For example, in test marketing, a judgment is made as to which cities would offer the best basis for testing the marketability of a new product. In industrial marketing research, the decision to interview a purchasing agent about a given product constitutes a judgment sample; the purchasing agent must be regarded as a representative of the company by the person who draws the sample. Other examples could include an instructor's choice of someone to start a class discussion; expert witnesses to present their views in court; and the selection of stores in an area to try out a new display or promotional program.

Judgment samples are ubiquitous, and in real-world research, informed opinion always plays some role in deciding how sampling will be carried out. As with convenience sampling, the degree and direction of error are unknown, and conclusive statements cannot be viewed as meaningful. Note, however, that if the expert's judgment is valid, the sample will almost certainly be better than if a convenience sample—which is based on luck and happenstance—is used.

8.2c Quota Sampling

quota samples
A method of nonprobability sampling in which respondents or units are included until a prespecified number or proportion is attained in each group.

Quota samples are a special type of sample in which researchers take explicit steps to model a population on some prespecified "control" characteristics; these characteristics are typically demographic, which allows them to possess factually correct values (e.g., age, income) and to be checked against known population distributions (e.g., census figures). To take a simple example with but a single control, suppose an interviewer has been instructed to conduct half the interviews with people 30 years and older, and half with people younger than 30. Here, the control characteristic is the age of respondents. Specifying this particular control statement implies, of course, that the researcher knows that the population of interest is equally divided between persons 30 years and older and persons younger than 30.

More realistically, in order to be more representative of a population, we would have to "control" on a number of characteristics. Therefore, to properly select a quota sample, we must specify a list of

Marketing Research Focus 8.2

Business Uses of Nonprobability Sampling

Convenience Samples

- In a study of the predictors of salesperson effectiveness, a sales consulting firm selected 80 full-time sales agents from a large insurance company who had agreed to take part in the study. Respondents were selected from training seminars held at the company, based on their willingness to participate.
- In a study of taste preferences for brands of soft drinks, a large marketing research firm selected a sample of 200 people from a large New Jersey mall over one weekend. Respondents were those who were asked and agreed to participate.
- In a study at Le Bonheur Children's Medical Center, in Memphis, Tennessee, researchers used a convenience sample of target patients available for testing. Researchers wanted to establish the level of pain in bladder catheterization for patients younger than 2 years of age and to determine whether an anesthetic lidocaine gel would help lower the degree of pain. The convenience sample consisted of 115 patients, randomly divided into 56 in the control group and 59 in the lidocaine (experimental) group. They discovered not only that the procedure was fairly painful for the young patients but also that an anesthetic gel was not adequate in reducing the pain levels.

Judgment Samples

- For a major launch campaign for a brand of bath soap, Colgate Palmolive utilized the test cities of Marion, Indiana, and Visalia, California, to do extensive testing of its advertising and promotion. The "judgment" was that on the dimensions deemed important for the study's end goals, these cities were representative of the nation at large.
- In a study of consumers who overextended themselves on credit purchases, a sample was selected from consumers who had written or called a California self-help group. It was believed (i.e., "judged") that these consumers would be representative of all consumers with similar credit problems.

Quota Samples

- In a study of purchase intentions conducted by M/A/R/C Research, a sample of 800 respondents was selected, all of whom were female heads of households who maintained primary influence on buying decisions for the household.
- In a study of air travelers' use of credit cards, rental car companies, and hotel accommodations, a prominent marketing research firm selected a sample based on miles flown per year, nationality, and gender. One of the cells designated was "those who fly more than 100,000 miles per year, are Japanese, and are male."

After designing a yogurt drink to lower low-density lipoprotein (LDL) cholesterol, Benecol hired a survey company to determine public awareness of the health issues around cholesterol in England. The company surveyed a quota sample of 882 adults older than 25. The findings were then projected onto England's 40.8 million citizens in the same segment. As with quota samples in general, the surveyors decided which demographic characteristics (in addition to being older than 25) were important for their survey and continued polling until each segment was adequately represented. Benecol went further by weighting the data "to bring it into line with national population profiles" given by England's most recent census data. The report showed that nearly 75 percent of respondents were eager to find ways to lower their cholesterol (and then segued into a pitch from a Benecol spokesperson describing the benefits of the yogurt drink). The research was most likely used to determine how exactly to promote the products.

Sources: Vaughan, Maureen, Elizabeth A. Paton, Andrew Bush, and Jay Pershad (2005), "Does Lidocaine Gel Alleviate the Pain of Bladder Catheterization in Young Children? A Randomized, Controlled Trial"; *Pediatrics*, Vol. 116 No. 4 October 2005, pp. 917–920.
"Lack of Time Is Putting Nation's Heart Health at Risk, Reveals Survey." *PR Newswire Europe*. May 4, 2004.

relevant control characteristics and know the distribution of these characteristics across our population. For example, suppose we have two control characteristics of interest, age and ethnicity, as follows:

1.	Age	Two categories: younger than 30; 30 and older
2.	Ethnicity	Three categories: European American; African American; other

The two age and three ethnicity categories imply that there are $2 \times 3 = 6$ sampling cells of interest. What we must know is the proportion of the population in each of these six cells. This is a much more complex question than just knowing the proportion of the population in a *single* control characteristic, and in practice such cross-tabulated data can be difficult to obtain. Note that when the number of control characteristics and associated categories increase, the number of sampling cells can grow unwieldy and present exceptionally stringent population-level data requirements. Suppose we had four characteristics for control, as follows:

1. Age — Four categories: younger than 18; 18–30; 31–50; older than 50
2. Ethnicity — Three categories: European American; African American; other
3. Education — Four categories: elementary school; high school; college; graduate school
4. Incomes — Five categories: under $15,000; $15,000–$24,999; $25,000–$39,999; $40,000–$59,999; $60,000 and over

This would result in $4 \times 3 \times 4 \times 5 = 240$ sampling cells, and we could require information on the proportion of the population in *each* of these 240 cells. Although these proportions may be available for the general U.S. population from sources such as the Census, analogous proportions on our particular population of interest may be impossible to find. However, if up-to-date knowledge of the distribution of the control characteristics is available, we may determine the size of sample to select for each cell:

$$\text{Cell sample size} = [\text{Total sample size}] \times [\text{Proportion desired in the cell.}]$$

For example, if our total sample is 1200 and the proportion in cell 1 is 0.05 (5 percent), the number of people with those characteristics in our sample for cell 1 would be $1200 \times .05 = 60$, and we would then direct our interviewer to interview 60 people with these characteristics. The same procedure would be repeated for all cells. The actual selection of specific sample elements would be left to the judgment of the interviewer.

Despite their simplicity and usefulness, there are some well-known problems with quota samples:

1. The proportion of respondents assigned to each cell must be accurate and up-to-date relative to the actual state of the target population. This is often difficult to achieve.
2. The "proper" control characteristics must be selected; that is, all characteristics related to the measures of interest must be included. For example, if we want to learn people's attitudes toward classical orchestral music, it would be a mistake not to use age as a control factor because age is probably related to almost all musical attitudes. In any particular study, we may omit a relevant control characteristic and not be aware of it. Indeed, this is exceedingly easy to do because researchers seldom know all relevant geodemographic covariates or predictors of a given phenomenon. Consequently, results can be misleading if some characteristics are not appropriately controlled for.
3. The third problem concerns the practical difficulties associated with including more and more control characteristics. As noted before, we end up with too many cells for the interviewers to work with, so finding desired respondents will not be easy. In extreme cases, it may be nearly impossible to locate a reasonably large sample in some specific cells, particularly if some of the control characteristics are not independent. For example, although it would not be difficult to find "college-educated women, working full-time with at least two children," it would be extremely difficult if our lowest age category were 18 to 21, as the vast majority of people meeting the first set of criteria are much older.
4. A fourth difficulty concerns the interviewer's selection of the actual respondents to interview. In looking for people who fit the desired description, the interviewer may avoid people who look unfriendly, live in distant or difficult-to-access areas, and so on. An unknown bias is thus introduced into the study. Therefore, a quota sample and population may be exactly the same on measures for which we know the characteristics of both but may differ substantially on measures for which we have only the sample value. Indeed, it is these "sample only" measures that really interest us to begin with; they are the very reason for taking the sample in the first place. (For example, people who "look friendly" may be readily selected by an interviewer, but their appearance of friendliness could turn out to be because their lives are going well or they are on vacation, thus skewing the sample.) The sample provides estimates of the unknown population value; if we knew the population value, there would be no reason for sampling. The validity of a quota sample is often defended in terms of the match between a *known* population and sample characteristics. Beware this sort of reasoning, as the error in *other* sample measures is of unknown size and direction. That is, your sample may have the same average age and income as the general population, but if they all live in the same neighborhood, they are unlikely to be truly representative of people living elsewhere, and they share similarities with one another (like taste in housing or family size) that are overtly nonrepresentative of the population.

Quota samples are useful in preliminary stages of research, and if done with great care, they can provide clear, accurate and useful information, even if they are likely to be less valid than a probability sample.

8.3 Probability Sampling Procedures

In probability sampling, the chance that a population element will be included in the sample is known, and the sample elements are selected by means of formal, usually computer-mediated, decision rules. No discretion is left to the researcher or field interviewer in selecting sample elements. Whereas with quota samples, the researcher must seek out respondents fitting a specific profile, this is all done in advance in probability sampling (a process to be described shortly), and a list of potential respondents is generated. Although there is every belief that the results obtained with a probability sample will be more accurate than those obtained with a nonprobability sample, this is by no means guaranteed; the main advantage offered by the former is the ability to estimate the degree of sampling error likely to occur in the resulting sample. With nonprobability sampling, no such measure of this important quantity exists, and the researcher is left with only a hope that sampling error has been adequately controlled. Due to its importance in marketing research, probability sampling concepts are developed in great detail throughout this chapter.

Having presented concepts essential for understanding sampling in marketing research and having drawn the fundamental distinction between probability and nonprobability sampling procedures, we can proceed to a detailed description of the most basic type of probability sampling: simple random sampling. Throughout, care is taken to present a step-by-step approach, as the principles developed for simple random sampling have direct application to the frequently used, more complex sampling procedures discussed at the end of the chapter. We will also consider the critical issue of how to determine sample size. Examples of how probability samples have been used in a variety of firms appear in *Marketing Research Focus 8.3*.

8.3a Simple Random Sampling

We hope to demonstrate that basic probability sampling concepts are fundamental to the practice of marketing research. Indeed, simple random sampling, the simplest of the probability-based procedures, is utilized in the majority of marketing research projects involving sampling, far more so than any nonprobability sampling procedure. To fully grasp the ideas and techniques of sampling, some fluency with statistical concepts is desirable. The remainder of our discussion here, and much of the rest of this text, presumes that the reader has had at least one introductory course in statistics, including properties of random samples, the normal distribution, basic hypothesis tests, and the elements of regression analysis. However, our experience in teaching this course tells us that even very capable students have found at least some aspects of statistical reasoning or technique challenging and welcome a review, if only to refamiliarize themselves with notation, distributions, and other basics. We have also discovered that the *usefulness* of statistics often gets lost in the shuffle of conveying so much new material in a typical first course. And, make no mistake, statistics is extraordinarily useful; we hope the ensuing chapters will convey some of the many ways in which statistics literally makes rigorous marketing research, and social science in general, possible.

In that spirit, we will focus throughout our presentation on usefulness, practical applications, and clear communication. At times, this will mean glossing over purely technical elements that a conscientious statistics text would provide. This material, including the fundamental statistical theory that all marketing researchers should know, is provided instead in a technical appendix at the end of the chapter. Because some readers will find this depth of presentation daunting, and others will have already mastered the underlying material, at appropriate points we will refer you to the technical appendix, in case (given your background and interests) you find it helpful. If at any point in the following discussions you find that it is moving too fast or assuming too much, we recommend reading parts A and B of the appendix before continuing. We encourage all readers to ensure that they are familiar with this material, as it is not only important to the practicing marketing researcher, but is also mathematically elegant, even beautiful, taken on its own terms.

Note that understanding the *derivations* of the formulas and theorems requires familiarity with some fairly complex mathematics. Without this background, their origins may seem a bit mysterious. Understanding their usage and applicability to statistical analysis is sufficient to follow the text of this book, and even to perform statistical analyses on a regular basis. The underlying theory is *not* a mystery,

Marketing Research Focus 8.3

Choosing Representative Probability Samples

The ability of representative (probability) samples to provide accurate measures of marketing for both profit and nonprofit organizations is well documented, as the following profiles illustrate.

- Rincón & Associates conducts an annual syndicated study, called the Dallas/Ft. Worth Latino Trendline, which surveys a probability sample of 600 Hispanic households. The sample is selected from Spanish-surnamed listings in telephone directories, supplemented by random-digit dialing to identify Hispanic households that do not have listed telephone numbers or Spanish surnames. The 2005 Trendline study discovered sharp distinctions between the attitudes of foreign-born and native-born U.S. Latinos. Eighty percent of foreign-born Latinos preferred use of the Spanish language and trusted advertising in Spanish more than in English; but 80 percent of native-born Latinos preferred to use English with their friends, reserving Spanish mainly for family members, and preferred English for their TV and written media. This contradicted prevailing marketing theories about Spanish-language marketing to Latinos. Among other results of the survey, Latinos showed strong loyalty to specific brands, placed a strong value on education for their children (preferring college 12 to 1 to the military for their children), and had a great need for health insurance (43 percent of foreign-born and 22 percent of native-born Latinos lacked insurance).
- Dell Computer needed to act when it found that its image was increasingly tarnished by the infiltration of spyware on customers' computers. Spyware not only collects information on computer usage but also slows down the other programs. Dell's poll of a representative sample of 742 Internet users showed that most consumers knew little about spyware or its risks, revealing an opportunity to decrease reliance on customer support calls as well as increase customer satisfaction and revenues. Based on these findings, Dell initiated a "PC Security Awareness Campaign," including a new Web site dedicated to online security education and resources, and improved both its sales of security subscriptions and its reputation with its customers.
- A large Japanese financial institution conducted a lifestyle study of "rich" Japanese households (those with incomes more than ¥ 1 million), using a probability sample of 1000 households. From this study, the researchers were able to accurately describe five different lifestyle segments among this well-off group, the uses they made of their income, their consumption of foreign goods, and their attitudes toward changes in Japanese society. They were also able to identify areas where there were great opportunities for providing new products to these segments.
- In June 2003, Impulse Research conducted a national online survey for Rust-Oleum, using a probability sample of more than a thousand homeowners living in the continental United States. The survey found that one in four homeowners was sufficiently dissatisfied with the state of their garages to be embarrassed to leave their garage doors open, more than half wished they had a garage that their neighbors could envy, and eight in ten considered the garage a factor in their buying decisions regarding houses. Armed with this information, Rust-Oleum launched an "America's Ultimate Garage" contest, in which contestants sent in a photograph of their garage and a description of what would make it perfect in order to win a $10,000 professional makeover of their garage.

Sources: "DFW Latino Trendline 2005: Top-Line Summary"; Rincón & Associates. http://www.rinconassoc.com/dfw05.html
"Dell Highlights Consumer Awareness, Security Tools as Key in Battle Against Spyware"; *Business Wire*. June 7, 2005.
"Want to Turn Those Neighbors Green with Garage Envy? Rust-Oleum Begins Search for a Space to Turn into an 'Ultimate' Garage." Rust-Oleum. August 1, 2003. http://www.rustoleum.com/product.asp?frm_product_id=371&SBL=1

central limit theorem
The most important result in all of statistics. States that when drawing a "large" random sample from some population, the sample mean will have a normal distribution, with certain special properties. Has widespread applications throughout statistics, economics, and the physical sciences.

however. The **central limit theorem**, for example, is a deep and profound fact about nature, not something arbitrarily invented or arrived at by guesswork; it can be rigorously proved. The *sum-of-squares measure* used throughout statistics is based on the Pythagorean theorem, a jewel of ancient Greek mathematics. Unfortunately, providing airtight proofs for many of these theorems requires mathematical tools well outside the scope of this book. Students interested in understanding the underlying theory would do well to explore the book by Larsen and Marx in the Further Reading.

8.3b Terminology and Symbols

To begin our discussion of simple random sampling, we must again define a few terms.

parameter
Any population-level quantity in a statistical model that will be estimated using sample data.

Parameter

A **parameter** is some quantity of interest in a specific population. This is the *true value* we would obtain if we undertook a census that did not contain any nonsampling errors. "The average annual income of married women in the United States" and "the average price for a new television" are parameters. So is the variance of either of those quantities because they can also be calculated from the population data. Note that for the marketing researcher, although parameters are "real"—they have precise, actual values, which can in theory be known via a census—they are essentially always beyond our reach. In fact, they are what we wish to estimate by sampling. (There is a related meaning for "parameter" as a quantity in a statistical model, and we will adopt that meaning when we study statistical models for marketing research, such as regression, in later chapters.)

variance
A common measure of *dispersion* around the central tendency (the mean); equal to the square of the standard deviation (i.e., the average of the sum-of-squared deviations from the sample or population mean).

Statistic

A statistic is any quantity deriving from a sample. In practice, the purpose of a sample statistic is to estimate a population parameter. Thus, average annual income of married women and the average price for a new television would also be statistics if calculated from samples of the relevant populations. Statistics are *not* "theoretical" quantities, but actual, tangible numbers we will calculate from sample data. (Note that it is common to refer to quantities calculated from statistical models as "parameters," which can be confusing. The reason for this is that sample statistics are *estimates* of population parameters, and often the all-important qualifier "estimates" is presumed understood, as it is less cumbersome to say "parameters" than "parameter estimates." We will maintain this distinction throughout this chapter.)

statistic
Any quantity estimated from data.

Some Symbols to Commit to Memory Forever

There are certain conventions that are used in sampling and statistics. The symbols and associated meanings in Table 8.1 will be used in this book. Basically, Greek letters are used for population parameters, and Roman (e.g., English) letters for sample statistics. The one major exception to this concerns sample size, which is designated with the lowercase Roman *n* for the sample, and with the uppercase Roman *N* for the target population.

Table 8.1 Important Statistical Measures for Marketing Research Applications, Their Symbols, Names, and Meanings

Measure or Concept	Symbol	Name	Meaning
Population mean	μ	mu	Average of all population units
Sample mean	$\bar{X}$	x-bar	Average of all sample units
Population standard deviation	σ	sigma	Degree of variation (from μ) in the population
Sample standard deviation	s	s	Degree of variation (from $\bar{X}$) in a specific sample
Standard error of the (sample) mean	$s_{\bar{X}}$	s sub x-bar	Estimated variation in $\bar{X}$ based on a sample
Population variance	σ^2	sigma squared	The population standard deviation, squared
Sample variance	s^2	s squared	The sample standard deviation, squared
Population proportion	π	pi	Proportion of "1" or "yes" population binary responses
Sample proportion	p	p	Proportion of "1" or "yes" sample binary responses
Population size	N	big N	Number of population units
Sample size	n	small n	Number of sample units
Sum of squares	SS	sum of squares	Used in many statistical calculations
Degrees of freedom	df	degrees of freedom	Used in many statistical calculations
Confidence interval	CI	confidence interval	Allows a known degree of certainty of some quantity
Level of confidence	α	alpha	Degree of certainty required by the researcher
z-Value	z	z value	Points on normal distribution, (e.g., $z_{.025}$ = 2.5% of area lies beyond)
t-Value	t	t value	Points on a *t* distribution

8.3c A Population to Examine

Table 8.2 presents a population that we will use to illustrate sampling concepts. This population consists of students who are taking an introductory marketing course. The professor of the course has collected three pieces of information from each student, as follows:

1. The student's ID number (column 1)
2. The student's age in years (column 2)
3. Whether the student intends to take a course in marketing research before graduation, coded as follows: 1 = yes, 0 = no (column 3)

Table 8.2 Age and Election of Marketing Research Course for 50 Students

Student Number (1)	Age (X_1) (2)	Election of Marketing Research Course 1 = yes 0 = no (X_2) (3)	Mean Difference ($X_1 - \mu$) (4)	Squared Difference $(X_1 - \mu)^2$ (5)
1	25	1	1.32	1.74
2	27	0	3.32	11.02
3	29	1	5.32	28.30
4	30	1	6.32	39.94
5	25	0	1.32	1.74
6	29	0	5.32	28.30
7	27	0	3.32	11.02
8	24	0	0.32	0.10
9	27	1	3.32	11.02
10	28	1	4.32	18.66
11	33	0	9.32	86.86
12	29	1	5.32	28.30
13	26	0	2.32	5.38
14	28	0	4.32	18.66
15	28	1	4.32	18.66
16	26	0	2.32	5.38
17	26	1	2.32	5.38
18	36	1	12.32	151.78
19	29	0	5.32	28.30
20	26	0	2.32	5.38
21	21	0	−2.68	7.18
22	19	0	−4.68	21.90
23	24	0	0.32	0.10
24	22	0	−1.68	2.82
25	20	1	−3.68	13.54
26	22	0	−1.68	2.82
27	19	1	−4.68	21.90
28	20	0	−3.68	13.54
29	19	0	−4.68	21.90
30	24	0	0.32	0.10

Student Number (1)	Age (X_1) (2)	Election of Marketing Research Course 1 = yes 0 = no (X_2) (3)	Mean Difference ($X_1 - \mu$) (4)	Squared Difference $(X_1 - \mu)^2$ (5)
31	25	0	1.32	1.74
32	22	1	−1.68	2.82
33	20	0	−3.68	13.54
34	21	1	−2.68	7.18
35	21	0	−2.68	7.18
36	23	1	−0.68	0.46
37	21	0	−2.68	7.18
38	23	0	−0.68	0.46
39	18	0	−5.68	32.26
40	21	1	−2.68	7.18
41	19	0	−4.68	21.90
42	23	0	−0.68	0.46
43	22	1	−1.68	2.82
44	19	0	−4.68	21.90
45	20	0	−3.68	13.54
46	20	0	−3.68	13.54
47	21	0	−2.68	7.18
48	20	1	−3.68	13.54
49	19	0	−4.68	21.90
50	18	0	−5.68	32.26
Population Summary Values				
SUM	1184	17	0	840.9
MEAN	23.68	0.34	0	16.8
VARIANCE	16.82	0.22		
STD DEV	4.10	0.47		
MEDIAN	23.00	0		
MODE	21.00	0		

We assume that statistical or spreadsheet software will always be used in calculations such as we present here; all such calculations are carried out in the spreadsheets accompanying this text, and we do them "by hand" here to illustrate concepts, *not* to suggest that managers resort to hand calculation. Here we include two additional columns (4 and 5) helpful in later calculations, and the student ID number (column 1) will be used only to identify each population element; only the other two variables (columns 2 and 3) interest us from a measurement point of view.

It is always helpful to specify what *types* of variables we are working with. The student ID number is nominal, as it is merely a label useful in identifying students for future analysis. We must be careful in describing age. As a construct, age is continuously variable: People and objects age from moment to moment, and the only decision we have to make as researchers is how *finely* we wish to record the variable. In this case, age is listed in years, but there is no question that age (in years, from birth) is a ratio-scaled variable, which means that all statistical measures—in particular, those related to regression, such as mean and variation—are valid measures. So, despite age's being *listed* in years, we will treat it as a continuous variable and manipulate it accordingly. "Election of marketing research" can take on only two values, and thus is called either a dichotomous or a binary variable. It is obviously not continuous. However, interpreted correctly, an average has meaning as the proportion of "Yes" responses.

dichotomous/binary variable
A variable having only two possible states, for example, 1 or 0, yes or no, Male or Female, Domestic or Foreign, etc.

We can now assign symbols to both variables:

$$\text{Age} = X_1$$
$$\text{Election of marketing research} = X_2$$

The population average and the standard deviation for age and election of marketing research are seen to be (using the formulas in Table 8.2, or a statistical program):

Variables	Mean	Standard Deviation
Age	23.7	4.1
Election of marketing research	0.34	0.474

Note that these values refer to the entire *population* of the class and have nothing to do with making inferences based on a sample of that class. They tell us that the mean (average) age in this (admittedly small, $N = 50$) population is 23.7 and that people in this population deviate about 4.1 years from this mean. They also tell us that 34 percent of the students intend to take marketing research (the standard deviation for binary data is typically very large—here it is 0.474—as all the data points are 0 or 1, and never "close" to the mean value; we will discuss how to use these values later in this chapter).

8.3d Calculation of Sample Statistics for Continuous Variables

Part A of the appendix to this chapter (Appendix 8) shows how to calculate parameters that describe a known population; these values are readily calculated using any statistical or spreadsheet program. Let us now proceed to sample from this population. Our interest will be to calculate statistics that describe the *sample* and to use those statistics to make inferences about population *parameters*. (In statistics courses, these are often referred to as descriptive and inferential statistics, respectively.)

descriptive statistics Any quantities used to describe features of a specific data set (i.e., the sample data).

inferential statistics A form of statistical analysis that relies on a sample to reach conclusions about a larger group (e.g., the population from which the sample was drawn).

Our method of sampling will be simple random sampling. We reiterate that these calculations are presented purely as guiding pedagogical examples: In the real world, we will not have data from the entire population made available to us; the population will, generally speaking, be much larger than 50 in size; and we will try to draw a substantially larger sample than the very small one ($n = 5$) to be used momentarily in our illustrative example. However, the methods used are identical for any population and sample drawn from it, so long as that sample is truly randomly selected. We also note before starting that our population has been constructed to be very nearly normal; that is, the variable we are sampling from has what is close to a normal distribution (i.e., what is sometimes referred to as "a bell curve"). This is crucial when trying to make inferences based on "small" samples, those less than about 25 in size. However, due to the extremely powerful law of nature embodied in the central limit theorem (about which we will hear more throughout the remainder of the book), when our sample has approximately 25 or more elements, sampling theory allows precise results for *any* population, not just for those we know to be approximately normally distributed.

There are two conditions that define the notion of simple random sampling. They are:

1. Each element has an equal chance of being selected.
2. Each *combination* of the n sample elements has an equal chance of being selected.

Previously we noted only the first condition as defining simple random sampling; this was done to keep the discussion simple. Now we must note that there are other probability sampling procedures in which the elements have an equal chance of selection. However, in all other sampling procedures, constraints are put on the possible combinations of sampling elements such that each combination of elements is not equally likely. Mechanically, selection proceeds via a random number generator, which is built into all statistical and spreadsheet programs. In the population of our example, each student is identified by a two-digit ID number ranging from 01 to 50, and we allow the computer to randomly select among them. Doing so for $n = 5$ might yield a sample similar to the following:

Element	Age	Elective
32	22	1
17	26	1
05	25	0
37	21	0
41	19	0

We have selected a sample of size $n = 5$ from a population of size $N = 50$. Thus we have selected n/N, or 5/50, or 10 percent, or 0.1 of the population elements, and we say that the *sampling fraction* is 0.1.

The **mean, or average** (these terms are interchangeable, although statisticians always use "mean"), of the sample is simply the sum of the values divided by the sample size. Thus,

$$\bar{X} = \frac{\sum_{i=1}^{n} X_i}{n} = \frac{22 + 26 + 25 + 21 + 19}{5} = 22.6$$

Our mean sample statistic value for age is 22.6. We note that this is slightly lower than our true population mean age of 23.7. Of course, in real research settings we would not know the true population mean age—it is what we are literally trying to estimate—and so would use the sample mean as our *best estimate* of the true value. Note that a different sample will very likely yield a different sample mean age; but the population mean will always remain the same, no matter what sample we choose.

We are all familiar with the mean (average) from years of test taking, news reports, and the like. Aside from the mean, there is another measure that proves crucial in statistical applications, and this is the *sample variance*. The concept of the variance is fairly simple: It measures the **dispersion** of the data around the (sample) mean. If much of the data are far from the sample mean, the variance will tend to be large. So that both positive and negative deviations count equally, we square these and add them up. However, instead of dividing by the sample size, n, as we did for the average, we use something called **degrees of freedom** instead. A general rule in statistics is that we adjust for the number of quantities calculated from the same data. For example, in the formula for calculating the sample variance, we subtract the sample mean from each piece of data; but the sample mean was calculated from the same data. This means that the degrees of freedom in this case are $n - 1$. Put generally, degrees of freedom (*df*) equal the number of *independent* observations (on the variable of interest) minus the number of statistics calculated (from that same data) used in any particular formula:

$$df = \text{sample size} - \text{number of statistics calculated.}$$

For the variance, we have "used up" one degree of freedom for the sample mean ($\bar{X}$), so we say that $df = n - 1$. Thus:

$$s^2 = \frac{\sum_{i=1}^{n} (X_i - \bar{X})^2}{n - 1}$$

For our data sample, we then have that:

$$s^2 = \frac{(22 - 22.6)^2 + (26 - 22.6)^2 + (25 - 22.6)^2 + (21 - 22.6)^2 + (19 - 22.6)^2}{5 - 1}$$
$$= \frac{(-.6)^2 + (3.4)^2 + (2.4)^2 + (-1.6)^2 + (-3.6)^2}{4}$$
$$= 8.3$$

Our population variance was 16.9, so our sample has understated it somewhat. Note that if we had (incorrectly) divided by n instead of $n - 1$, the variance would have been even smaller. If we look at our sample compared with the original population data, we will see that just by chance, our sample lacks values very far from the mean, so our sample variance had underestimated the true population variance. It is a good exercise to select a variety of samples (of size $n = 5$, or even of different sizes) to see whether this happens in general; if you try, you will see that it does *not*, and this particular sample, just by poor luck, is less accurate than most in estimating the population variance.

The **standard deviation** is always the square root of the variance, and so is:

$$s = \sqrt{8.3} = 2.88$$

We have now calculated descriptive statistics for our continuous variable, and we will use them shortly to calculate quantities useful in marketing research applications. Before doing so, there are a number of properties and connections that help in understanding how these various statistics are applied. Let us look at the numerator of our variance equation. It is

$$\sum_{i=1}^{n} (X_i - \bar{X})^2$$

In words, it is the "sum of squared deviations about the sample mean." Or, more simply, the **sum of squares**, or *SS* (sometimes, to make it clear which variable we are working with, it is denoted SS_{XX}, but

mean/average
The most common measure of central tendency, in which one adds up all a variable's values and divides by the number of values.

dispersion
One of a number of statistical measures for the degree to which values of a variable are spread around some measure of central tendency (e.g., mean, median or mode). The most common measures of dispersion are the standard deviation, variance, range, and interquartile range (difference between the 25th and 75th percentile values in the data).

degrees of freedom
An important concept in statistical models that quantifies how many *independent* pieces of data go into model calculations; usually equal to the sample size minus the number of parameters that are calculated in the model itself.

standard deviation
A very common measure of *dispersion* around the central tendency (the mean). Equal to the square root of the variance (i.e., the square root of the average of the sum-of-squared deviations from the sample or population mean).

sum of squares
In statistics, a common measure of dispersion, formed by squaring each of a set of quantities and adding them up; the mean of the quantities is ordinarily subtracted from each beforehand.

we leave off the subscripts otherwise). This terminology is standard throughout all of statistics, management, and social science, and we will use it throughout the book. We note, then, that the sample variance is given simply by the following, which should be committed to memory:

$$s^2 = \frac{SS}{df}$$

It is useful to note the following simplified formula for calculating variance (and thus the standard deviation) for a continuous variable, often called a "computational formula," as it always gives the same answer but requires fewer arithmetic operations:

$$s^2 = \frac{\sum X^2 - [(\sum X)^2/n]}{n-1}$$

Let us verify that this yields the same value as before:

$$\sum X^2 = (22)^2 + (26)^2 + (25)^2 + (21)^2 + (19)^2 = 2587$$
$$\left(\sum X\right)^2 = (22 + 26 + 25 + 21 + 19)^2 = (113)^2 = 12,769.$$

And, thus, the value for *s* is unchanged:

$$s^2 = \frac{2587 - (12,769)/5}{4} = 8.3$$

Of course, we would seldom apply these formulas by hand, using a program to calculate them. Still, the student should be familiar with how these values are calculated and, more important, what concepts are captured by the formulas.

8.3e Calculation of Sample Statistics for Dichotomous Variables

sample proportion
The number of successes (i.e., ones, positive outcomes, yeses, etc.) in a sample divided by the sample size; usually denoted by *p*.

Calculation of means, variances, and standard deviations is identical for both continuous and dichotomous (binary) variables; for example, using "election of marketing research," we can calculate the following for the **sample proportion**, typically denoted by p (note as well that the "complementary" proportion, $(1 - p)$, is usually denoted by q):

$$p = \frac{\sum_{i=1}^{n} X_i}{n} = \frac{1+1+0+0+0}{5} = .4$$

So, $p = 0.4$ and $q = (1 - p) = 0.6$. The sample variance is calculated as before:

$$\begin{aligned} s^2 &= \frac{\sum_{i=1}^{n} (X_i - p)^2}{df} \\ &= \frac{(1-.4)^2 + (1-.4)^2 + (0-.4)^2 + (0-.4)^2 + (0-.4)^2}{5-1} \\ &= .3 \end{aligned}$$

The standard deviation is, as always, the square root of the variance:

$$s = \sqrt{.3} = .548$$

We note that there is one mildly confusing element specific to dichotomous variables and the variance. For the *population*, we have that the population variance, $\sigma^2 = \pi(1 - \pi)$; which means that if we know the true population proportion, π, we can automatically calculate the population variance from it very easily. This is still true for the *sample* variance, but we also have to account for the sample size because degrees of freedom come into play, as follows:

$$\begin{aligned} s^2 &= pq\left(\frac{n}{n-1}\right) \\ &= (.4)(.6)\left(\frac{5}{4}\right) = .3 \end{aligned}$$

We have now calculated (sample) statistics for our dichotomous variable, and as always, these are estimates of the population parameters. As our sample was small, with $n = 5$, we should not expect them to be especially accurate estimates, but their *intent* is certainly to offer some measure of the associated population parameters. The actual usefulness of these statistical estimates is based on the concept of the **sampling distribution** of the mean and the theory of statistical inference. An overview of this theory is presented in Part B of the appendix to this chapter. In the following sections, we assume that the basics of this theory have been digested and well understood. If this material seems novel or hazy, it would be a good idea to review the appendix before proceeding.

sampling distribution
The distribution one would achieve if one took a very large (or infinite) number of samples of the same size from the population and calculated the value of some statistic (e.g., the mean) for each.

8.3f Drawing Inferences about Population Parameters from Sample Statistics for Continuous Variables

Using the Theory

As discussed earlier, for this particular example we knew that our population ($N = 50$) was approximately normal, and because of that, even the mean of small samples can be viewed as normal; therefore, all that we know about confidence intervals and hypothesis tests is applicable (see Appendix B for more detail). In "real world" research, knowing this about the population is rare. However, when samples are "large," at least $n = 25$ or so, we do not need to know that the population is anywhere close to normal to apply the techniques we are about to lay out. So, all the statistical tests we shall present are valid if either (1) the population is normal and our sample is any size at all or (2) the population has unknown distribution and our sample is at least of size $n = 25$. Assuming one of these conditions holds, we can always estimate

1. the mean of the *sampling distribution*, $\bar{X}$, calculated in the usual manner
2. the **standard error** of the sampling distribution* as $s_{\bar{X}} = \frac{s}{\sqrt{n}}$.

standard errors
How much an estimator or any statistic would vary if it were repeatedly calculated from samples drawn in an identical manner from the population; tends to decrease with sample size because larger samples tend to display less variability from one to the other.

In our example, $\bar{X} = 22.6$ and $s = 2.88$; thus

$$s_{\bar{X}} = \frac{2.88}{\sqrt{5}} = 1.3$$

Now let us calculate the size of the intervals—called **confidence intervals** (CI)—at ±1, ±2, and ±3 standard errors from the mean. At ±1 standard error, the interval is

$$22.6 \pm 1.3 = [21.3, 23.9].$$

confidence intervals
A region that contains a population parameter of interest with a certain stated probability, often 95 percent or 99 percent, but more generally $100(1 - \alpha)$ percent.

Statistical theory, specifically the central limit theorem, tells us that we can be 68 percent certain that the true population mean lies in this interval of one standard error from the sample mean, as illustrated in Figure 8.2.

It is useful to stress what this curious phrase really means: if we were to take many *different* samples of size $n = 5$ from this *same* population, and we were to calculate confidence intervals centered on the sample statistic $\bar{X}$ such as the one we calculated again and again, then 68 percent of the confidence intervals would contain the *true* population mean, μ. In other words, we have a 68 percent chance that the interval we just calculated contains the real population mean, which itself is a fixed (i.e., not a variable), but unknown, quantity. (Recall that in this illustrative case, because we know all the elements in the population, we happen to know that $\mu = 23.7$.)

The confidence interval, always stated as the sample mean ± some number of standard errors, is also referred to as a certain "percent confidence interval" (% CI), based on the chance of the real population mean falling within that interval. For example, a confidence interval of the sample mean ± one standard

*It is very easy to confuse standard deviations and standard errors, and sometimes they can refer to the same quantity. Conceptually, however, they are distinct: "standard error" (in this case, $s_{\bar{X}}$) is a measure of how much a *statistic* ($\bar{X}$) varies from one sample (of size n) to another, while "standard deviation" refers to variation of a *single observation* (X), either within a sample (i.e., the sample standard deviation, s or s_X) or in the population (i.e., the population standard deviation, σ or σ_X). The underlying statistical theory and the calculations of confidence intervals are the same, whether using "standard deviations" or "standard errors," so long as the correct quantity is used.

Technical purists will note that with a population as small as this one, we should apply a correction factor to the formula. However, in practice most populations are quite large, and the correction factor is not needed. So, to aid in student understanding, we are ignoring the point for now. We will address it later in the chapter.

Figure 8.2 **Estimating the Population Mean: Area Within One Standard Error of the Sample Mean for a Normal Distribution**

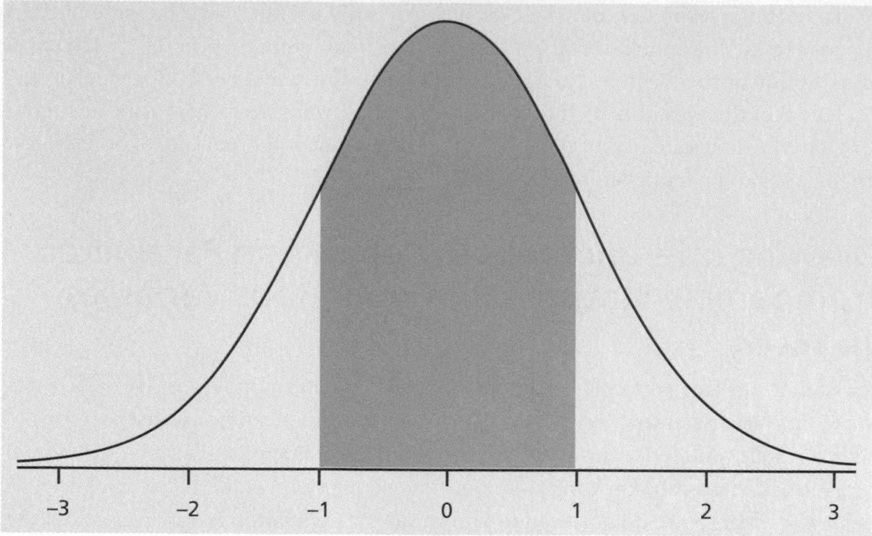

error is a 68 percent confidence interval, of the sample mean ± two standard errors is a 95 percent confidence interval, and of the sample mean ± three standard errors is a 99.7 percent confidence interval (more precise values are 68.27, 95.45, and 99.73 percent, respectively). These are fixed percentages determined by the central limit theorem.

In our example, at ±2 and ±3 standard errors, the intervals are

$$22.6 \pm 2(1.3) = 22.6 \pm 2.6 = [20.0, 25.2]$$
$$22.6 \pm 3(1.3) = 22.6 \pm 3.9 = [18.7, 26.5].$$

Again, this gives us 95 percent and 99.7 percent confidence, respectively, in locating the true population mean, μ. A way to think about confidence intervals is that with ±1, ±2, and ±3 standard errors, respectively, they will contain the true mean all but 1 time in 3, 1 time in 20, and 3 times in 1000. Although the number of standard errors we "go out" on the curve increases linearly, the probability of the resulting interval's containing the true population mean, μ, decreases dramatically. For example, going out six standard errors would yield an interval containing the true mean all but one time in more than 5 *billion*, that is, a virtual certainty. (This is in fact where the term "six sigma" comes from; being six sigma (population standard deviation) values from the mean clearly denotes an astounding level of certainty.)

Even people relatively comfortable with statistical concepts often make an error in interpreting confidence intervals, and it is helpful to say what they are *not*. A confidence level (say, 95 percent) is *not* a probability about the population mean's being in a particular interval; the population mean is a fixed number, and it is either within a specific interval or it is not. There is no "probability" about it, no more so than asking for "the probability that 7 is between 5 and 10." The *only* thing probabilistic about confidence intervals is the fact that as we draw different *samples* from a fixed *population*, we will get *different* intervals. So, when we say we have calculated a 95 percent CI, it means that 95 percent of the samples (of that same size) drawn from the population would yield intervals containing the true mean. It is the intervals that change from sample to sample, *not* the population mean.

The 95 percent confidence interval we calculated was 22.6 ± 2.6, or 20.0 to 25.2. Under repeated sampling, we would expect the true population mean to fall within such intervals in 95 samples out of 100. In our example we note that the population mean of 23.7 does fall within the 95 percent confidence interval we calculated from our sample of 5; and, again, there is nothing probabilistic about noticing this. We can also say—completely equivalently—that our estimate has a precision of ±2.6 years at a 95 percent level of confidence. Note that the size of the precision has meaning only at a designated level of confidence; at 99.7 percent, the precision of our estimate is ±3.9 years. The distance to either side we go out from the mean (here, 2.6 or 3.9 standard errors) is often called the half-width of the confidence interval and is a useful quantity in calculating sample size requirements.

precision
Half the width of a (symmetric) confidence interval.

half-width
One half of a symmetric confidence interval, usually for the mean.

The calculation of a confidence interval provides us with the measure of *sampling error* we sought earlier. We must stress again that it is *only* the use of probability-based sample selection procedures that allows us to properly calculate the confidence interval. We know nothing about the sampling distribution of means for *non*probability sampling, and in such cases we cannot calculate a meaningful confidence interval. We should note that it is not uncommon in practice for confidence intervals to be calculated from nonprobability samples; the manager who uses these intervals, however, is implicitly assuming that the nonprobability sampling procedure has yielded a simple random sample.

8.3g The Effect of Sample Size on Precision

As stated previously, the formula for the standard error of the sample mean is

$$s_{\bar{X}} = \frac{s}{\sqrt{n}},$$

where s is the standard deviation of the distribution of the variable of interest. We note that $s_{\bar{X}}$ will vary inversely with the square root of the sample size we select. That is, as the sample size increases, the distribution of $\bar{X}$ will become "tighter" (i.e., will have less variance). Another way of saying this is that the confidence interval around $\bar{X}$ will get smaller as $s_{\bar{X}}$ gets smaller and that if we want to halve the width of our interval, we will typically need *four* times the sample size, because of the square root in the denominator. This can have extreme consequences. If we are told that we need "one more decimal point" of precision, this means we will need *one hundred* times the sample size. There is no clever way around this; it is literally built into the mathematics of sampling. Thus, nature imposes a rather severe penalty on those who seek more precision than absolutely necessary, and the researcher must take great care to balance the true research requirements for precise measurement against the costs of doing so, which increase with the *square* of precision.

The other component of the calculation that affects the size of $s_{\bar{X}}$, and thus the width of our confidence interval, is the standard deviation of the distribution of the variable itself, s. It is the numerator of $s_{\bar{X}}$, and so we would like our estimate of $\bar{X}$ to have as small a variance (and therefore standard deviation) as possible. Although it is possible to know the sample size before a study is conducted, it is rare to have any sense of how large the variation in that sample will be, making it difficult to estimate the width of a confidence interval when a study is first being planned.

8.3h Drawing Inferences about Population Parameters from Sample Statistics for Dichotomous Variables

All the theory and procedures we applied to continuous variables also apply to dichotomous variables, so long as the sample size is not "too small." An immediate question is how large the sample size must be before we can invoke the central limit theorem in order to construct confidence intervals using the normality of the mean statistic. The answer here is a bit more complex than for continuous variables and depends not only on the sample size, but on the population proportion, π. A very conservative rule (meaning it is often even stronger than one needs) is that we can calculate valid confidence intervals for proportions whenever $n\pi(1 - \pi)$ is at least 5 (this is a guideline that statisticians have found to work well in practice, not a law of nature such as the central limit theorem). When π is 0.5 (i.e., half the population is a "yes" or a "1"), this means that n should be at least 20; values of π farther from 0.5 will require ever larger samples to ensure that confidence intervals calculated in the manner done for continuous variables are valid. In practice, of course, we do not know π; if we did, we would not be trying to estimate it! So, once we obtain the sample proportion, p, we calculate $np(1 - p)$ and see whether that quantity is greater than 5. If so, we can assume that the central limit theorem applies and that we can use it to calculate confidence intervals.

The sample mean of the proportion of students electing marketing research in our sample of $n = 5$ was $p = 0.4$. Because $np(1 - p) = 5(0.4)(0.6) = 1.2$, which is much less than 5, the central limit theorem does not apply and we would have to use a statistical program to calculate our confidence interval using complex statistical methods well beyond our scope here. This is a general problem with small samples: They lack sufficient information to make useful inferences.

Rather than throw up our hands, let us instead pretend, just for this example, that our population of size 50 was itself just a sample from a much, much larger population (which we can actually assume is infinite, as we do when, for example, considering the "population" of possible coin flips). Recall that the proportion observed was 0.34 and, when we calculate 50(.34)(1 − 0.34), we obtain a value of 11.22, large enough (i.e., greater than 5) to use the central limit theorem to construct valid confidence intervals. Let us construct one with two standard errors (an approximately 95 percent CI) to each side of the mean, as follows:

$$\begin{aligned} .34 \pm 2\sqrt{\frac{(.34)(1-.34)}{50}} &= .34 \pm 2\sqrt{.004488} \\ &= .34 \pm 2(.067) = .34 \pm .134 \\ &= [.206,\ .474] \end{aligned}$$

This is a fairly wide interval because we have used only 50 values (not very many) and 0.34 is close to the center of the [0, 1] scale. (Recall again that for this one example we have pretended that the original population of size 50 is itself a sample from a much larger population.) It is worth noting again that if we wanted an interval half as wide, we would need about four times as many data points, one hundred times as many for an interval one-tenth as wide, and so on. This **inverse square law** for sample size holds throughout sampling and is a very powerful rule of thumb when considering whether to collect more data.

inverse square law
Any situation where an effect's strength drops off with the square of some quantity. For example, in statistics, if one wishes to halve the width of an interval given for some estimate (based on a random sample), one needs four times the sample size.

Note that for any given sample size (n), the value of s_p, which is always $\sqrt{p(1-p)/n}$, is largest when $p = 0.5$. This is a very useful fact for dichotomous measures where the true population proportion, π, is unknown, as we will *overestimate* the width of our confidence intervals by using $p = 0.5$. Using $p = 0.5$ will allow us to be *at least as* confident as the claimed level (95 percent, 99 percent, or anything else) and is therefore a conservative, "safe" value to use. The practical implication is that marketing researchers *can* plan sample size in the absence of any data at all, because $p = 0.5$ is truly a "worst-case scenario"; no such statement can be made about continuous variables, whose variance can be arbitrarily large (that is, it can keep going up as more data are collected; this will happen for certain theoretical statistical processes, such as the Cauchy distribution, even if this is very rare in practice).

8.3i The Question of Population Size

The discussion thus far has made no mention of the size of the population as being relevant to our calculations. Many people find this surprising, on the commonsense notion that larger populations should be more difficult to pin down than smaller ones. And, as it turns out, this is true: Technically, population size should indeed be taken into account in all statistical calculations. We say "technically" because most marketing-related populations are large enough so that there is no important or even practical ramification to assuming we are dealing with a limitless (i.e., infinite) population. This may appear counterintuitive, but in practice the size of the *sample* is dramatically more important than the size of the *population* in almost all statistical calculations; we always take account of the former, but rarely the latter.

To be fully correct, for finite populations we must change the formula we use in calculating the standard error of the sampling distribution of the mean. What we do is apply the **finite population correction** or "finite correction factor" to our previous formula, so that:

finite population correction
A mathematical fix applied to standard formulas when one attempts to make inference for a population of known size, as opposed to a population presumed to be essentially limitless.

$$\sigma_{\bar{X}} = \frac{\sigma_X}{\sqrt{n}}\sqrt{\frac{N-n}{N-1}} \quad \text{and} \quad s_{\bar{X}} = \frac{s_x}{\sqrt{n}}\sqrt{\frac{N-n}{N-1}}$$

$$\sigma_p = \sqrt{\frac{\pi(1-\pi)}{n}}\sqrt{\frac{N-n}{N-1}} \quad \text{and} \quad s_p = \sqrt{\frac{pq}{n}}\sqrt{\frac{N-n}{N-1}}$$

The value $\sqrt{\frac{N-n}{N-1}}$ is the finite correction factor. For large values of N relative to n, the correction factor is approximately equal to 1 (if you are comfortable with calculus, you can see this by taking the limit; if not, try substituting actual numbers into the formula). Thus, when our samples are "small relative to the population," which they typically always tend to be, we can just use the basic formula for $\sigma_{\bar{X}}$, and $s_{\bar{X}}$ and for σ_p and s_p.

The value of the correction factor is always between 0 and 1, and it is zero when $N = n$. That is, when we take a complete census we obtain a standard error of . . . zero! This is as we should expect. Recall that the very purpose of using a sample is to calculate a corresponding value in the population. If we have sampled the entire population (i.e., taken a census), there is *no* uncertainty, and so it makes perfect sense that we have a standard error (an imprecision) of zero. Note that multiplying by the correction factor will always lower the size of the standard error (except when it equals 1). Thus, if we choose to ignore the correction factor, we *overstate* the standard error and increase the size of our confidence interval. That is, we err on the side of conservatism. As such, if we choose not to "worry" about finite populations, it will never result in our being overly bold in our predictions.

Although in most marketing applications it is safe to ignore the correction factor, as a rule of thumb some suggest applying it when the sample includes more than 5 percent of the population (so that the factor is at most 0.95). Like all rules of thumb, 5 percent is not a definite guide; others have suggested 10 percent as the magic number. Simply be sensitive to this issue when dealing with small populations.

Recall that in our example, we selected 10 percent ($n = 5$ and $N = 50$) of the population. We therefore could well have applied the correction factor in subsequent calculations.

8.3j An Important Warning about *Non*sampling Errors

The calculation of confidence intervals about an estimator gives us the feeling that we know just how much error we are dealing with. For most marketing research studies this can be very misleading. Our measurement of error was that of *sampling error only*. A confidence interval does *not* take nonsampling errors into account at all. (Please re-read that sentence until it is entirely clear and fully assimilated!) Sampling error accounts *only* for the inevitable inaccuracy of using a small sample to assess a value in a much larger population, and assumes that the sample is randomly drawn and representative. If nonsampling errors occur, a bias is introduced into our estimate of unknown degree and magnitude. Control of nonsampling errors is therefore critical. (Nonsampling errors were discussed in detail in Section 2.5b.)

8.3k The Accuracy of Probability Samples

Probability samples can be extremely accurate. In fact, the Gallup and Harris polls have successfully predicted the outcome of every presidential election in which they have applied probability sampling procedures. An immediate challenge to this is the oft-posed "What about 1948? Didn't the polls predict that Dewey would defeat Truman?" Indeed they did, but the samples were *quota* samples, as probability sampling was new at that time.

It is instructive to compare two historic presidential elections in terms of the type of sampling used and their resulting accuracy. In 1936 the *Literary Digest* conducted a poll by mail, with a sample size of more than 2 million, enormous by the standards of the day, when there were only approximately 80 million eligible voters in the entire country. They predicted a victory for Alfred M. Landon over Franklin D. Roosevelt by about 15 percent, a remarkably large margin. And, of course, they were wrong: Roosevelt won easily. In 1992, using a probability sample of less than 2000 out of more than 90 million actual voters, Gallup predicted that Bill Clinton would get 43 percent of the vote. He got 42.9 percent. How could the *Literary Digest*'s stupendously large sample produce such stupendously inaccurate results? The sampling frame used by the *Literary Digest* was more well-to-do than the true population of voters. Lower-income voters, who overwhelmingly supported Roosevelt, simply did not have a chance to respond to the poll. This tale has become famous in marketing research circles because it illustrates, to an extent few other real-world polls ever have, that increasing the size of a biased sample is like adding fuel to a fire; small, representative samples are always preferred.

The sampling procedures outlined in this chapter provide tools that enable the researcher to give accurate estimates of quantities (parameters) of interest. The major problem area lies in the nonsampling errors that arise. Later in this chapter, we shall continue our discussion of probability sampling. Specifically, we shall discuss two important types of sampling procedures: stratified sampling and cluster sampling. These procedures are more complex than simple random sampling but are used more often in practice. But before turning to sampling procedures themselves, we must first address the issue of sample size.

8.4 The Determination of Sample Size

Armed with an understanding of sampling error and nonsampling error, we turn our attention to the question of sample size determination. Both types of error bear on this question. First, let us examine sample size from the perspective of statistical theory.

8.4a The Question of Sample Size in Statistical Theory

In simple random sampling for a known sample size, we calculated the confidence interval of our estimate at a given level of confidence (usually 95 percent or 99 percent). To do this for a continuous measure, one needed the following information:

1. The sample mean, $\bar{X}$.
2. The sample standard deviation, s.
3. The sample size, n.
4. A level of confidence, α.

Using items 2 and 3, we calculated the standard error, $s_{\bar{X}}$, and then calculated the relevant confidence interval. At the 95 percent confidence level (i.e., $\alpha = 0.05$, so $100(1 - \alpha)$ percent $= 95$ percent), this is approximately:

$$\text{Confidence interval} = \bar{X} \pm 2\frac{s}{\sqrt{n}}.$$

To be precise, we should replace 2 in the formula with 1.96 when the true standard error is known (because the z-value $z_{.025} = 1.96$), or with an appropriate t-value, supplied automatically by any statistical program. Because we have calculated $\bar{X}$ and s, and know n, we calculate the precision, the total width of the confidence interval:

$$\text{Precision} = \pm 2\frac{s}{\sqrt{n}}.$$

z-value or z-statistic
Refers to a point on the *standard normal distribution*, corresponding to the number of standard deviations away from the mean some *normally distributed* statistic is observed to be. One uses a z-value when either (1) the population standard deviation is known or (2) when the sample is quite large.

t-value or t-statistic
Refers to a point on the *t* distribution (with *k* degrees of freedom) corresponding to the number of standard deviations away from the mean some statistic is observed to be. One uses a t-value when the population standard deviation is not known and is instead estimated from a sample.

Now, let us turn this procedure on its side: Suppose we want to reach a given level of precision and want to know how large a sample, n, will allow us to do so. Given the value for s, we can solve this equation for the required sample size*. Let us illustrate this for a particular example. Suppose that at the 99.7 percent level of confidence (i.e., three standard deviations) we wish to obtain an estimate of the mean age of a target segment for a new magazine that is within ±1.5 years of the *true* mean age, which, of course, we can never know for certain. In addition, we will assume that we have an estimate of $s = 6.0$. The required sample size is obtained by solving the following equation for n:

$$\text{Precision} = \pm 3\frac{s}{\sqrt{n}}$$

$$\pm 1.5 = \pm 3\ \frac{6.0}{\sqrt{n}}$$

$$n = \left(\frac{18}{1.5}\right)^2 = (12)^2 = 144$$

Thus, if $s = 6.0$, a sample size of 144 will assure us a precision of ±1.5 years. In this example we expressed the precision in units (years). We might also have expressed precision as a percentage of the mean value we calculate so that the precision in units varies depending on the size of the mean. Precision expressed in units is called **absolute precision**, whereas precision expressed in percentages is called **relative precision**. Let us calculate sample size to assure a specified relative position for a particular example. Assume that $\bar{X} = 25$, $s = 6.0$, the required precision is ±10 percent (0.1), and a 95 percent level of confidence is desired. The required equation is

absolute precision
The accuracy of any measurement based on some predetermined measurement scale, not relative to other sample statistics like the mean.

relative precision
The precision of an estimate expressed as a proportion or percentage of its mean.

$$\pm b(\bar{X}) = \pm 2\frac{s}{\sqrt{n}}$$

where b is the precision proportion. In our example, we have:

$$\pm(.1)(25) = \pm 2\left(\frac{6.0}{\sqrt{n}}\right)$$

$$n = \left(\frac{12}{2.5}\right)^2 = (4.8)^2 \approx 23$$

*If we know the true standard deviation, σ, we could use that in the place of the sample value, s. In real world applications, one rarely knows σ, which in all likelihood is a parameter we are trying to estimate. In this section, we will use values based on samples (i.e., statistics), such as ($\bar{X}$, s, p), although the corresponding population values (i.e., parameters), such as (μ, σ, π), are preferred when available.

In this case, a relative precision of 10 percent requires a sample of size $n = 23$, when as before $\bar{X} = 25$ and $s = 6.0$.

Let us pause to note one caveat based on statistical theory. Due to the central limit theorem, a sample size of 23 would be appropriate *only* if the original distribution from which the sample was selected were a normally distributed one; that is, we have a normal population. For any other type of distribution, the sampling distribution of the mean cannot be assumed to be normal unless we have a sample size of 30 or more. We must stress, however, that this is really a rule of thumb. If the population distribution is not too different from normal—for example, it is "single humped" or unimodal, and nearly symmetric—we would not need a sample as large as 30 to invoke the central limit theorem and apply all the techniques discussed here. However, for very *non*normal distributions—such as those with many humps, a very long tail, or pronounced asymmetries—we would indeed need at least 30 observations.

Returning to relative precision, we could rearrange the equation as follows (we can ignore the ± signs, as they drop out in the calculation):

$$b\bar{X} = 3\frac{s}{\sqrt{n}}$$

$$\sqrt{n} = \frac{3\ s}{b\bar{X}}$$

Rearranging the equation in this fashion demonstrates that we really do not need to know *both* $\bar{X}$ and s, but only the *ratio* of the standard deviation to the mean, $s/\bar{X}$. This ratio has a special name in statistics, the **coefficient of variation**. When dealing with positive quantities such as age, education, or income, it is often useful to calculate the coefficient of variation: Small values indicate that most of the data are "close" to the mean, and so we are dealing with a tight distribution and therefore a relatively homogeneous population.

coefficient of variation
The ratio of the standard deviation to the mean, a dimensionless quantity that helps specify the spread of a probability distribution.

Another term related to precision that is sometimes used in practice is **relative allowable error**:

$$\text{Relative allowable error} = \frac{1}{2}\left[\frac{\text{precision}}{\text{mean}}\right]$$

relative allowable error
When the error permitted in a measurement is stated relative to the mean of the quantity measured.

This defines the size of the error acceptable to the manager relative to the size of the mean. For example, in the numerical example just presented, the precision was defined as ±10 percent of the mean of 25, that is, ±0.1 [25] = ±2.5 (this yields a total precision of 5). Managers are more likely to express the error they will accept as a percentage of the mean, and to express it in terms related to half of the precision. For example, a manager might say: "I will accept an error of 2.5 years if the average age is 25." Thus the relative allowable error is 2.5/25 = 0.1. Of course, one could also say "within 10 percent in either direction" and mean the same thing.

8.4b Difficulties with the Optimal Sample Size Calculation

To calculate our "optimal" sample size, we need to know how much precision is required, our level of confidence (α), and s as an estimate of the population variation. The first two are chosen by the researcher and present no problem; the third, however, depends on knowing something about the population: its inherent variability. Well, if we knew *that*, we would probably know all about the quantity (mean value) we are hoping to estimate! So, calculating the sample size in advance of collecting any data at all is problematic. It is good to keep in mind, though, that the required sample size varies (1) inversely with the precision desired, (2) directly with s, and (3) directly with the desired confidence level.

In most studies, we want to measure many variables. To the extent that they differ in terms of precision desired, s, or confidence level, the required sample sizes will differ. There is no single sample size that is statistically optimal for any study. The only way to assure the required precision for *all* variables in the study would be to select the largest sample required by *any* of them. This is wasteful in practice, so researchers must often make trade-offs and compromises regarding the "required" level of precision. This wastefulness is exacerbated by the built-into-nature fact that the sample size rises as the *square* of the desired precision: One more decimal point requires 100 as much data! (Presuming, of course, that the sample standard deviation, s, hardly changes as more data come in.)

All is not lost, however, in the search for optimal sample size. If a researcher has experience with the problem at hand, then fairly accurate estimates of s are likely to be available at the time the sample size is being planned. For example, suppliers of store audit data have a great deal of knowledge in this area because of their experience with prior audits and the use of statistical models to anticipate promotional reactions, seasonality, and other "shocks to the system." Additionally, the scale on which the variable of interest is measured sets limits on the size of *s*. For example, a 7-point attitude rating scale is likely to have an *s* in the 1.5–2.5 range, and it is literally impossible for it to be as large as 7. (An interesting problem is to calculate the largest value of *s* that could ever possibly arise using a 7-point scale. *Hint*: Consider how the data could be "maximally dispersed" on this scale.) In contrast, a 100-point rating scale could easily have an *s* of 20–30 (try the analogous calculation of largest possible *s* for this type of scale). Thus, if the experienced researcher understands the effects that the measurement scale being used will have on *s*, then a very good estimate can be made of optimal sample size. Even with *no* prior experience, the largest possible values of *s* for such scales can be used for sample size calculation, even if it will almost surely result in conservatism and the collection of more data than are actually needed.

8.4c Optimal Sample Size for a Proportion

Let us now calculate the required sample size, *n*, for a dichotomous variable, one that takes on only two values: 0 and 1. The confidence interval for a dichotomous variable at the 95 percent level of confidence is (2 again stands in for the precise value, $z_{.025} = 1.96$),

$$p \pm 2\sqrt{\frac{pq}{n}},$$

where *p* is the proportion of 1s in the *population*, and $q = 1 - p$. Thus,

$$\text{Absolute precision} = \pm 2\sqrt{\frac{pq}{n}}.$$

Assume we have an estimate of $p = .3$ and that we want ± 0.04 as the absolute precision at the 95 percent level of confidence. Then

$$.04 = 2\sqrt{\frac{(.3)(.7)}{n}}$$

$$\sqrt{n} = \frac{2}{.04}\sqrt{(.3)(.7)}$$

$$n = (50)^2(.21) = 525.$$

The required sample size is thus 525. If we wanted three standard deviations of accuracy (a relative precision at the 99.7 percent confidence level), and 5 percent *relative* precision, we would have (where *b* is the precision relative to the mean):

$$bp = 3\sqrt{\frac{pq}{n}}$$

$$(.05)(.3) = 3\sqrt{\frac{(.3)(.7)}{n}}$$

$$n = (.3)(.7)\left(\frac{3}{.015}\right)^2 = 8,400.$$

The required sample size of 8400 reflects our use of a very high confidence level ($z_{.0015} \approx 3$) and a very tight precision (5 percent of $p = 0.3$, or ± 1.5 percent).

We note that in order to determine required sample size for a dichotomous variable, we need to know the mean value *p*. Regrettably, *p* is the value we are trying to determine in the first place. So be wary of claims of having determined the statistically optimal sample size for such a study. Most likely, this sort of claim is based on the "worst-case scenario" of performing all calculations as if *p* were 0.5, where we have the greatest possible variation about the mean. This will lead to conservatism and to using more data than are necessary. Although conservatism—stating less confidence than one really has—is preferable to overconfidence, it can still lead to costly blunders and bloated data requirements. When trying to calculate sample sizes in general, a good approach is simply to try out different values for $\bar{X}$, *s*, *p* (and so on) and see what sample sizes are required. Often, such an informal procedure can offer the researcher a very good feel for the range of useful sample sizes.

We stress that statistical calculations are just one sort of factor affecting the determination of sample size for the study. Other factors include the study objectives, the cost involved, the time requirements, the type of data analysis planned, and the existence of nonsampling errors. Any of these can have dramatic impacts, especially time and budgetary constraints.

The sample size calculations we made here were for simple random samples only. In the sampling procedures discussed later in this chapter, the formulas involved become more complicated and are often best left to statistical programs, which perform such calculations easily. However, the underlying principle is exactly the same: The researcher must specify a level of confidence, a degree of precision, and *s* as an estimate for population variability; the sample size flows from a formula specific to the type of sampling procedure undertaken.

8.4d Sample Size and Nonsampling Error

As mentioned previously, one should never blindly accept a sample size generated by a statistical formula alone. One reason for not doing so is the existence of nonsampling errors. A fundamental error sometimes made even by experienced researchers lies in the belief that large samples imply less error and therefore better results. Although this is true for sampling errors, it is most certainly *not* true for nonsampling errors. Some nonsampling errors can get *larger* as the sample size increases—for example, nonresponse errors, interviewer errors, data processing errors, and data analysis errors, among other more elusive types. Thus, a reduction in sampling error often occurs at the expense of an increase in nonsampling error. A carefully done study with $n = 200$ may have a smaller *total* error than a study of $n = 2000$; in simple language, it can be better to ask the right 200 people than the wrong 2000 people, in terms of getting a handle on an entire population.

A ubiquitous problem is that many researchers, managers, and media people like to refer to the statistical precision of estimates, often compounding the situation through inaccurate, misleading statements such as, "This poll has a 3 percent margin of error" (which would mean that we are *certain* to be within

Figure 8.3 Three Common Uses of "Random," One of Them Appropriate

3 percent of the right answer: an impossibility). Rarely are other possible errors mentioned, or even considered. A good researcher always looks beyond statistical formulas to the details of how the study was done, whether the sample was truly representative. The general public also seems to believe that larger samples are necessarily better than smaller ones; it just seems more credible to say, "Based on a study of 25,000 people . . . " than, "Based on a study of 250 people . . ." Researchers should never be similarly fooled, and honest marketers will not attempt to deceive clients or the public on the basis of sheer sample size. Indeed, in the Internet age, obtaining a huge, thoroughly inappropriate sample is a simple matter; it is a temptation researchers need to learn to resist. Finally, in many marketing research applications, a very small sample may offer statistical precision at a level suitable to the needs of decision makers, particularly at the preliminary "back of the envelope" stage of planning.

8.4e Sample Size and Other Factors

A marketing research study is always a compromise between technical elegance and practical constraints faced by researchers and managers. These constraints affect sample size decisions, and we consider each in turn.

Study Objectives

The use that management intends to make of the information provided by a study affects the sample size. A decision that does not require precise informational inputs can make do with a very small sample size. A company may be content to measure interest in its new product (i.e., sales) to within 15–20 percent, merely to get a sense of production planning or warehouse costs. In contrast, a political pollster can be off by less than 1 percent and fail to predict an election outcome. The latter obviously needs a larger sample than the former.

Time Constraints

Often research results are needed "yesterday." Of course, some time for presenting results is agreed on. The time period may be too short for anything but a small sample to be used. The larger the study, the more time needed, if resources cannot expand to accommodate it.

Cost Constraints

A limit on the amount of money available for a study obviously could limit the sample size. In almost all research situations, information requires funds: Respondents must be remunerated, researchers and data analysts have salaries, data storage and processing are not free, etc. Alternatively, the allotment of a lot of money to a study should not be the sole motivation for a large sample size! Available dollars can, and usually do, provide an upper bound constraint on sample size; it should never be the reason for increasing the sample size beyond that needed to meet the study objectives.

Audience Acceptability and Politics

The results of marketing research are subject to judgments by the audience to whom the findings are communicated. The politics surrounding a marketing decision may not allow a study with a small, but statistically optimal, sample size to have the influence of a larger sample size. Consider the example of a sample size of 23 that we previously calculated as suitable to the study's needs. This small sample size would likely be attacked by anyone who opposed the study's conclusions. All too often the results of a marketing research study must be "sold" to management and the public, and sample size is often an issue. This is especially true for political polling, where one often hears, "How can you predict how *hundreds of millions* of people will vote with only a few thousand in your study?" Appeals to statistical theory are unlikely to be persuasive.

Data Analysis Procedures

Data analysis procedures can have an effect on the sample size as well. The most basic type of analysis that can be performed deals with only one variable at a time. This is called *univariate analysis* (see Chapter 9). The relationship between sample size and various aspects of one variable (precision, variability, confidence) is exactly what we have been discussing thus far. When we examine the relationship of two variables at a time, the sample size issue becomes more complex. This is called *bivariate analysis* (see

Chapters 9 and 10). Suppose we want to examine the relationship between usage of a product and income, and further suppose that each variable (usage, income) is composed of five categories. Therefore, the cross-tabulation of usage by income results in a table of 25 cells. If we had a sample of 250 people and they were spread evenly across the cross-tabular ("crosstab") table (the 25 "conditions"), there would be only 10 respondents per cell. And this is the *best* situation, statistically speaking, as an even distribution across cells is not likely; some cells will almost certainly have fewer than 10 respondents. The precision of estimates within such "sparse" cells will be lower than those obtained in a univariate analysis, where we consider only one variable at a time. Thus, the types of bivariate analysis planned and the precision required within cells will affect the choice of sample size. A study involving only univariate analysis may require only 200 respondents, whereas a similar study involving bivariate analysis may require more than 1000 respondents. A rule of thumb often invoked in academic research using such two-way and higher breakdowns across variables is to ensure at least 15 cases per cell. Sometimes, this suggests an enormous and therefore prohibitive number of participants, causing a change in the analysis plan or research design itself.

We might want to examine the relationships among more than two variables at a time. This is called *multivariate analysis* (see Chapters 10 to 12). Different multivariate techniques require different sample sizes to allow the researcher to make valid estimates of population parameters. Generally speaking, the more parameters we are estimating, the larger the sample size must be. Beyond this statement it is difficult to offer simple generalizations. Some multivariate techniques can be used legitimately with small sample sizes. These include factor analysis, cluster analysis, multidimensional scaling, and relatively uncomplicated regression and analysis-of-variance models. At the other extreme, some techniques were designed for very large samples. The AID (automatic interaction detector) model is one example. (The details of these analysis models and their sample size requirements are discussed in detail later in the book.) In summary, the researcher must think ahead to the plan of data analysis in determining sample size.

It should now be clear that the choice of a sample size is situation specific. It depends on statistical precision requirements, concern for nonsampling error, study objectives, time available, cost, and the data analysis plan. There is no single correct answer for the choice of sample size for a study, and no substitute for foresight and planning.

8.5 Stratified Sampling

The next sections continue our discussion of probability sampling procedures, starting with the important topic of stratified sampling and working toward two types of cluster sampling: systematic sampling and area sampling. These three sampling procedures are more complex than simple random sampling, but they are also more frequently used in practice (being usually easier to both enact and monitor) and can offer researchers a good trade-off between up-front study design costs and eventual statistical power.

area sampling
A sampling method in which the population is separated into *areas* or *clusters*, which are then selected randomly. If all elements in each selected cluster are then sampled, it is *one-stage* area sampling; if the areas are then subsampled, it is *two-stage* area sampling. Area sampling is especially helpful for widely geographically dispersed populations.

8.5a Purpose

One property that we want in our estimators is efficiency—that is, we want to have as small a standard error as possible. Stratified sampling, if used well, can result in a *decrease in the standard error of the estimator*. Thus the confidence interval we calculate will be smaller, we will have more statistical power, and/or we can accomplish the same degree of confidence with a smaller sample, saving time, funds, and energy.

efficiency
When the standard error (or variance) of some statistic is as small as possible (sometimes relative to a given set of potential estimators). Efficient estimators need not be unbiased; an estimator can be off on average (biased), but still very close to the right answer most of the time (efficient).

How does such a two-stage procedure decrease the standard error of an estimator, thereby allowing us greater statistical power? It does so only if the designated strata are *more homogeneous* (less varying) on the variable (or variables) for which we are calculating our statistics. The key issue is this: If the strata are as heterogeneous on this variable as the (unstratified) whole population, no decrease in the standard error will occur. Stratification in sampling employs the same strategy as blocking in experimentation (discussed in Section 5.5); we form subgroups so that the variable of interest is more homogeneous within the groups than it would be across all groups. The result of this process is a smaller measure of sampling error.

8.5b Selecting the Stratified Sample

There are two steps in setting up a stratified sampling plan:

1. Divide the defined population into mutually exclusive and collectively exhaustive subgroups or strata. Strata are mutually exclusive if membership in one stratum precludes membership in any other stratum. For example, a population may be divided into two strata on the basis of gender; that

is, there will be a male stratum and a female stratum. An individual person cannot belong to both strata, and thus these strata are mutually exclusive. Strata are collectively exhaustive if all possible categories of a variable are used to define the strata. That is, the categories "male" and "female" define the complete domain of the variable "gender." Strata need not evenly cleave the population in half (of equal sizes). For example, "age" can be a stratifying variable, with categories "younger than 30," "30–49," and "50 and older." Strata can arise from multiple variables, not just one.

2. Once the strata themselves are specified, the researcher selects an independent simple random sample from each.

8.5c An Illustration

Let us illustrate the (potential) standard error–reducing property of stratified sampling, using part of the data presented in Table 8.2; just student number and age are presented in Table 8.3. A quick glance at these data suggests that the ages of students numbered 1–20 are generally higher than those of students numbered 21–50. In the original presentation of the data, a critical piece of information was omitted: Students 1–20 are graduate students and students 21–50 are undergraduate students. We would expect graduate students to be older than undergraduates, and they are. And not only that: The group of students numbered 1–20 has a more homogeneous age profile than the population as a whole, and so does the group of students numbered 21–50. By using a **stratification variable**, "graduate versus undergraduate," we have identified two strata that are each more homogeneous than the population as a whole on the variable of interest, age. This condition allows us to take advantage of stratification, as we shall see.

stratification variable
A variable used to define different strata (groups) in the population for the purposes of statistical analysis.

8.5d The Sample

Now let us draw two simple random samples: one of size 2 from the graduate stratum and one of size 3 from the undergraduate stratum. Note that the ratio of our two sample sizes is in proportion to the ratio of the number of population elements in each of the strata; that is, the sample ratio 2:3 is proportionate to the population ratio 20:30. This is called **proportionate stratified sampling**, and it occurs when the total sample elements are allocated to strata in proportion to the number of population elements therein. The researcher also has the option of assigning sample elements to the various strata (often referred to as "allocating the sample to strata") on a basis disproportionate with the population distribution among strata; we shall discuss disproportionate stratified sampling later in this chapter. Also note that all possible combinations of elements are *not* equally likely, as we are selecting some elements from each stratum; for example, it is not possible to have all sample elements come from just one of the strata because we have definitely sampled from both, although this would be possible with simple random sampling.

proportionate stratified sampling
A sampling method that allocates sample size to strata in proportion to the number of population elements in the strata.

To facilitate the discussion that follows, it helps to introduce some special notation. Although it may at first appear daunting, with many subscripts and periods, italics, capitalization, and overbars, it is not only standard, but not so hard to get used to:

$N_{st.1}$ = population size in stratum 1 $\bar{x}_{st.1}$ = sample mean of stratum 1
$N_{st.2}$ = population size in stratum 2 $\bar{x}_{st.2}$ = sample mean of stratum 2
$n_{st.1}$ = sample size in stratum 1 $s^2_{st.1}$ = sample variance of stratum 1
$n_{st.2}$ = sample size in stratum 2 $s^2_{st.2}$ = sample variance of stratum 2

Now let us draw a simple random sample of $n = 2$ from stratum 1 and $n = 3$ from stratum 2. Conveniently, the sample of $n = 5$ we drew earlier was just this kind of sample, so we do not have to select a new sample. Specifically, the sample by strata is as follows:

Student Number	Age
Stratum 1	
05	25
17	26
Stratum 2	
32	22
37	21
41	19

Table 8.3 Census of Age of Students

Graduate Students		Undergraduate Students	
Student Number	Age (X_1)	Student Number	Age (X_1)
1	25	21	21
2	27	22	19
3	29	23	24
4	30	24	22
5	25	25	20
6	29	26	22
7	27	27	19
8	24	28	20
9	27	29	19
10	28	30	24
11	33	31	25
12	29	32	22
13	26	33	20
14	28	34	21
15	28	35	21
16	26	36	23
17	26	37	21
18	36	38	23
19	29	39	18
20	26	40	21
		41	19
Population Summary Values		42	23
SUM	558	43	22
MEAN	27.90	44	19
VARIANCE	7.49	45	20
STD DEV	2.74	46	20
		47	21
		48	20
		49	19
		50	18
		Population Summary Values	
		SUM	626
		MEAN	20.87
		VARIANCE	3.25
		STD DEV	1.80

Note that, as before, these are extremely small (random) samples, and we would ordinarily choose larger ones (from a larger, not fully known population!). For example, we cannot know whether normality holds in each of these samples, something we would wish to ascertain before engaging in statistical analysis. Here, we use these samples to illustrate the principles and calculations of stratification, not to suggest appropriate sample sizes for real-world projects.

8.5e Calculation of Statistics within Strata

When we calculate the mean, variance, and standard deviation within each stratum and compare these results with those of the sample as a whole, rather interesting results pop out. (Details of these within-strata calculations are presented in Appendices C and D of this chapter and are easily carried out in any spreadsheet or statistical program.)

The results for the total sample and within-stratum mean and variance of the sample are summarized as follows:

	Mean	Variance	Standard Deviation
Without stratification	22.60	8.30	2.88
Within stratum 1	25.50	0.50	0.71
Within stratum 2	20.67	2.33	1.53

We note that the variance and the standard deviation within each stratum are much lower than the variance and standard deviation of the total sample (of size 5). This points out the chief advantage of stratified sampling: Analysis within strata entails a smaller standard error—meaning greater accuracy and power, using the *same* data—than when using the entire sample. Consequently, within-strata confidence intervals can be far tighter than those based on conjoining the strata.

We now turn to how to use these strata-based values to perform calculations, specifically for statements involving the *entire target population* (not just for each stratum separately).

8.5f Calculation of the Mean and Standard Error for the Whole Sample

A useful property of stratified sampling is that summary measures—specifically, the mean and standard deviation—for the entire sample can be readily calculated from the within-strata results. For example, the overall sample mean, $X_{st.}$, is simply a weighted average of the within-strata means. (Weighted averages are useful throughout marketing and statistics and can often save a great deal of unnecessary calculation.)

The ratio $N_{st.j}/N$ is the relative weight attached to each stratum. For future reference, let us call this ratio W_j. In our example, $W_1 = 0.4$ and $W_2 = 0.6$. Note that these weights are calculated from the *population* sizes, *not* the sample sizes. Therefore, we can calculate the overall sample mean under stratification as follows, as a weighted average of the strata means:

$$\bar{X}_{st.} = \sum_{j=1}^{A} W_j \bar{X}_{st.j},$$

where $A =$ the number of strata. In our example we have two strata; thus $A = 2$, and so,

$$\begin{aligned}\bar{X}_{st.} &= \sum_{j=1}^{2} W_j \bar{X}_{st.j} \\ &= W_1 \bar{X}_{st.1} + W_2 \bar{X}_{st.2} \\ &= (.4)(25.5) + (.6)(20.7) \\ &= 22.6.\end{aligned}$$

This is exactly the same mean we calculated without stratification. The reason for this is simple: We deliberately chose our sample proportions (2:3) to match our population proportions (20:30); this is why it is called "proportionate" stratified sampling. It is easy to verify that any ratio other than 2:3 would result in a different sample mean.

The calculation of the standard error of the mean from within-strata information is only slightly more complex. The standard error for the full sample under stratification can be obtained from this relationship:

$$s^2_{\bar{X}_{st.}} = \sum_{j=1}^{A} (W_j)^2 s^2_{\bar{X}_{st.j}}.$$

In our example, we had already calculated that the sample standard deviations were 0.71 and 1.53 for strata 1 and 2, respectively. These are not the standard *errors*, but standard deviations, which are easily confused with them (sample standard *deviation* estimates how much variation there is in the population, and we do not expect it to change much as more data come in; standard *error* measures the *accuracy* of our estimate of the mean and should get smaller as more data come in, that is, as the sample size increases). Converting standard deviation to standard error requires dividing by the square root of the (stratum) sample size, so:

$$s_{\bar{X}_{st.1}} = \frac{.71}{\sqrt{2}} = \frac{.71}{1.41} = .50; \;\; so\; s^2_{\bar{X}_{st.1}} = .25$$

$$s_{\bar{X}_{st.2}} = \frac{1.53}{\sqrt{3}} = \frac{1.53}{1.73} = .88; \;\; so\; s^2_{\bar{X}_{st.2}} = .78$$

Therefore, we have the following result:

$$s^2_{\bar{X}_{st}} amp = (.4)^2(.25) + (.6)^2(.78) = .32$$

$$s_{\bar{X}_{st}} amp = \sqrt{.32} = .57$$

Alternatively, we may calculate $s^2_{\bar{X}_{st}}$ directly without first calculating the standard *errors* within each stratum, as follows:

$$s^2_{\bar{X}_{st}} = \sum_{j=1}^{A} \frac{(W_j)^2 s^2_{st.j}}{n_{st.j}}.$$

In our example, this becomes:

$$\begin{aligned} s^2_{\bar{X}_{st}} &= \frac{(W_1)^2 s^2_{st.1}}{n_{st.1}} + \frac{(W_2)^2 s^2_{st.1}}{n_{st.2}} \\ &= \frac{(.4)^2(.5)}{2} + \frac{(.6)^2(2.35)}{3} \\ &= .32 \\ s_{\bar{X}st} &= \sqrt{.32} = .57. \end{aligned}$$

The answer is identical. The critical point is this: Using the unstratified sample ($n = 5$), the standard error of the mean was 1.3. By stratifying, the standard error has been reduced to 0.57, *using the same data*. This is a dramatic reduction by any standards, and its ramifications are discussed in the following section.

8.5g Calculation of Associated Confidence Interval

The 95 percent confidence interval for the stratified sample is 22.6 ± 2(0.57) = 22.6 ± 1.1 = 21.5 – 23.7 (here, as before, we have been informal and gone out two standard errors from the mean for 95 percent confidence; to be precise, we would have to obtain the correct number from a table of the *t* distributions, or from any statistical program). The unstratified 95 percent interval was 20.0 – 25.2. Thus the size of the interval has been reduced from 5.2 to 2.2 and the absolute precision from ±2.6 to ±1.1. Note that the population mean, 23.7, does fall in this new interval. Note also that the stratified 99.7 percent confidence interval would be smaller than the *unstratified* 95 percent interval. The 99.7 percent interval is 22.6 ± 3(0.57) = 22.6 ± 1.7 = 20.9 – 24.3. In statistical language, one says that the stratified sampling procedure is more efficient than the unstratified one, in that it entails smaller variance. As smaller variance is synonymous with greater accuracy and precision, this is a highly desirable feature.

Why do we obtain such a reduction in standard error, and thereby enhanced precision, using a stratified sampling procedure? The reason is that we use only *within*-stratum variability in calculating the overall standard error, and *across*-strata variability becomes irrelevant. It is like looking only within groups of friends (who tend to be close in age) to calculate variability, rather than considering the entire population. Although this may sound capricious, it is firmly grounded in statistical theory. The statistical theory supporting the observed reduction in standard error, allowing us to calculate confidence intervals for stratified samples, is presented in Part B of the appendix to this chapter, and reviewing this material may aid in understanding.

The bottom line is that stratified sampling allows us to increase the precision of our estimates with the same sample (size) used in an unstratified fashion. Alternatively, we could obtain the same precision as with an unstratified sample, but with a smaller sample and thus at lower cost.

8.5h Usefulness in Marketing Research

The types of variables measured in marketing research often display high variability of the sort that can be reduced by stratification. For example, suppose that we are asked to monitor the retail sales of Folgers coffee. To do this, we want to measure the unit sales level of Folgers in a sample of stores. What stratification variables should we use? First we must answer another question: "What factors contribute to the variability in the quantity we intended to measure?" In the Folgers example, these contributing factors might include:

1. *Size of store*. Big stores would have higher sales than small stores.
2. *Day of the week*. Stores sell more coffee on weekends than early in the week because overall shopping volume is higher.
3. *Time of day*. Relatively few sales are made after 9 p.m., compared with earlier in the day. We can solve this issue by using *daily* sales as our variable of interest, summing up across all times of the day, as we will do for this analysis.
4. *Region of the country*. Folgers is a more established and popular brand in some parts of the country (such as the western states) than in others, so we would find higher sales in these regions.

Other factors may also contribute to the variability in sales, and if they are important enough, they should also be included among the stratification variables. If we distinguished three sizes of stores (e.g., small, medium, and large), two types of days of the week (weekday and weekend), and four regions of the country (northeast, southeast, midwest, and west), we would obtain $3 \times 2 \times 4 = 24$ cells or strata. Note the obvious similarity to quota sampling in the way the number of cells expands; in quota sampling, however, we have no error measure. In the stratum composed of "large stores/weekends/western region," we might find case sale numbers such as 150, 170, and 205. In the stratum composed of "small stores/weekdays/eastern region," however, we might find case sale numbers such as 10, 6, and 7. The across-strata variability is much greater than that within each stratum. We would thus obtain more efficient estimates using stratification.

These stratification variables work because they are all *correlated* with the sales of Folgers. That is, they each help *predict* sales levels. In general, one adds stratification variables as long as they contribute meaningfully to the variability of the quantity being measured. Of course, one also must consider the cost of stratification when deciding on the number of stratification variables, as we would need to collect data for each cell or stratum, an expensive proposition if there are very many. Note as well that most studies are designed to measure multiple variables, and a good stratification variable for some variables may not be suitable for others. In selecting stratification variables, one should select those that will contribute most meaningfully across *all* variables of interest. In the Folgers example, a marketing research firm monitoring sales of other brands of coffee (or, in fact, of any frequently purchased supermarket good) would be in luck, as the four stratification variables would very likely be relevant. However, if they were monitoring store employee compensation, several of those variables, notably "day of week" and "time of day," would likely be far less useful, certainly so compared with "experience" and "seniority." *Marketing Research Focus* 8.4 presents several examples of how stratified sampling has been put to use in complex studies, including the U.S. Census.

8.5i Disproportionate Stratified Sampling

The overall sample size n can also be allocated to strata on a basis *disproportionate* with their population sizes. Proportionate allocation is straightforward, so why should we complicate things by allocating on some other basis? The answer lies in the differences in variability within strata: for a fixed sample size, we can reduce the *overall* standard error of the estimate by sampling more heavily in strata with higher variability. In simple terms, we should collect more data in those cells that are the most erratic or the hardest to pin down. An example helps clarify the underlying principle of **disproportionate stratified sampling**.

disproportionate stratified sampling
A method of stratified sampling in which more data (than suggested by their relative frequency in the population alone) are collected from strata with greater variability; this process helps lower the overall standard error of summary measures taken from the sample.

Suppose that we had added another stratification variable to our age example and that by doing so we obtained a population stratum with the elements 21, 21, and 21 in it. There is *no* variability in this stratum, and a sample of one is all that is needed to measure its mean perfectly. Alternatively, a stratum with great

Marketing Research Focus 8.4

Stratified Sampling

Stratified sampling is used throughout marketing research and social science to achieve more precise estimates than simpler sampling schemes can. Let us look at a few examples of stratified sampling "in action" and how it has been put to use.

- The U.S. Census Bureau samples in order to estimate U.S. retail sales, based on a subsample of the Census Bureau's full Retail and Food Services sample. A stratified random sampling method is used to select approximately 5000 retail and food service firms, whose sales are then weighted and benchmarked to represent more than 3 million retail and food service firms.
- Ipsos-Insight used regionally stratified random sampling to conduct a consumer perception survey comparing actual credit card fraud with perceptions of it. The study took place over two years, involving 1878 telephone surveys of adults older than 18, selected across the United States in a sample stratified by region. Although actual consumer experiences with credit card fraud in the United States, both online and offline, appear to be leveling off, the study found that Americans have a perception that credit card fraud is on the increase.
- For proposed pricing systems for one of its services, American Telephone & Telegraph (AT&T) needed to forecast consumer sales for the various alternatives and to test different promotions and distribution approaches. AT&T developed a purchase intention questionnaire for surveying a representative sample regarding the different prices, promotions, and distribution alternatives being examined. The study's goal was to assess the relationship between purchase intention and purchase behavior, measured by real-world sales. To isolate this key relationship, 2600 respondents were selected from 16 strata in the population, designed to control for any effects due to market segment, product price, promotion, and distribution. Thus, the sample was selected from within two segments that had been exposed to one of two product prices, one of two promotions, and one of two distribution systems ($2 \times 2 \times 2 \times 2 = 16$ groups). Within the identified 16 groups, a probability sample was selected from the AT&T customer list in two states. Using this approach, AT&T was able to accurately forecast market-level sales for the service package based on different levels of price, promotion, and distribution.

Sources: "US August Retail Sales Report"; *Market News International*. September 14, 2005.
"Fraud Increasing, Americans Believe"; Bell Globemedia Publishing Inc. February 18, 2005.
Infosino, William J. (1986), "Forecasting New Product Sales from Likelihood of Purchase Ratings." *Marketing Science*, 5(4), 372–384.

variability will require a large sample size to produce an efficient estimate of the mean because the standard *error* within a stratum requires dividing the within-stratum standard *deviation* by the square root of the stratum sample size, $n_{st,j}$. The only way to reduce a large (within-stratum) standard deviation—which, recall, is a property of the *population* that we cannot control—is by increasing (within-stratum) sample size.

An optimal allocation of a fixed sample size among strata is one that generates the minimum standard error of the *overall* estimate. To find this optimal allocation, we must know something about the variability within strata before sampling. Experience and past studies can often provide such knowledge, or at least useful guidelines. Companies doing retail store audits often sample the larger stores at a disproportionately high level because these larger stores exhibit more variability in sales than small stores (not to mention that they also contribute disproportionately to overall sales across stores). The result is a smaller standard error and a more reliable estimate.

There are well-known formulas for determining the optimal allocation of a sample to strata, but they are complex and beyond the scope of this book; they are available in major statistical programs used by marketing researchers, and in practice one seldom resorts to hand calculation for optimal strata sizes. In general, these formulas imply the principles raised earlier on intuitive grounds, that larger within-stratum samples are required for larger strata and for greater within-stratum variability.

How are the overall mean and standard error calculated with a disproportionate stratified sample? Perhaps surprisingly, exactly the same formulas are used as in proportionate stratified sampling (as provided in Section 8.5f). This is the case because $W_j = \frac{N_{st,j}}{N}$. That is, it is the within-strata *population* sizes and the total *population* size that determine the weighting factors. The *sample* sizes within strata are used only to calculate within-strata means and standard errors.

8.6 Cluster Sampling

In all the probability sampling methods we have discussed so far, the elements that form the sample are selected individually. In **cluster sampling**, a cluster or group of elements is randomly selected at

cluster sampling
A form of probability sampling in which the population is first separated into groups, or clusters, which are then selected randomly. If all elements in each selected cluster are then sampled, it is *one-stage* cluster sampling; if the areas are then subsampled, it is *two-stage* cluster sampling.

one time. Thus, before we can select a cluster sample, the population must be divided into mutually exclusive and collectively exhaustive groups. We then select a random sample from among these groups.

Let us consider a concrete example, where the population is very small, just to illustrate. Suppose we had a population of 20 elements divided into four equal-sized groups, as follows:

Group	Population Element Number
1	1, 2, 3, 4, 5
2	6, 7, 8, 9, 10
3	11, 12, 13, 14, 15
4	16, 17, 18, 19, 20

If we wanted to select a probability sample of 10 elements, we could select elements individually using simple random sampling, or we could randomly select two of the four groups and use all the elements in those two groups. The situation where we directly select groups and then use *all* the elements in these groups is called *one-stage cluster sampling*. Selecting a random sample of elements from *within* the selected groups is called *two-stage cluster sampling*. In both cluster and simple random sampling, the sampling fraction would be the same, 0.5. However, not all possible combinations of elements are equally likely in cluster sampling. In fact, most combinations are impossible.

What if the clusters we select have elements that are not representative of the population? Would not our estimates be biased? The answer is yes, and this suggests a criterion we should use in forming groups. We want them to be as close, in terms of overall heterogeneity on the variables of interest, as the population as a whole. That is, each should look rather like a simple random sample, if possible. If the groups are exactly as heterogeneous as the population, any one group we select will accurately represent the population; in practice, however, this ideal is seldom, if ever, reached. Note that in cluster sampling, the criterion used in forming groups is exactly the opposite of that used in stratified sampling! In stratified sampling we want homogeneous groups, whereas in cluster sampling we want heterogeneous groups. This is because, in stratified sampling, each group is supposed to represent a subgroup within the population, whose statistical properties (especially the mean) we can estimate well; in cluster sampling, each subgroup is supposed to look as much like the entire population itself as possible.

How does the size of the standard error generated from a cluster sample compare with that stemming from a simple random sample? The answer depends on the similarity of the heterogeneity in the formed groups compared with the population, as follows:

1. If the groups are exactly as heterogeneous as the population, both methods will yield the same standard error.
2. If the groups are less heterogeneous than the population, the standard error will be greater with cluster sampling than with simple random sampling.

We refer to this comparison of the standard errors generated by various sampling procedures as an assessment of the *statistical efficiency* of the procedures. Recall that we always prefer a smaller standard error, as this allows the sharpest predictions, the smallest samples sizes, and the most statistical power.

You may ask why we do not trouble ourselves over the case where the cluster sampling groups are *more* heterogeneous than the population. This is because, in practice, this is extremely rare; sample clusters are usually much less heterogeneous than the population, meaning that in most cases they are less statistically efficient than simple random samples. For reasons of cost, however, cluster samples are used extensively in marketing research applications, and they are often much cheaper than other procedures for a given sample size. Why this is so is illustrated by a version of cluster sampling called *area sampling* or *geographical cluster sampling*, in which clusters consist of geographical areas (this is covered in detail later in this chapter). When the population is geographically dispersed, it can be expensive to reach for a survey or face-to-face interview. If we can restrict our surveying activity to certain small geographic areas, *each of which resembles the population as a whole*, we can dramatically cut the costs associated with the logistics of surveying. One way to approach this would be to use block group (or census tract) data from the U.S. Census and select a subset of those block groups that most resemble the entire United States on variables of interest.

The next sections discuss two types of cluster sampling, the most straightforward, systematic sampling, and area sampling. An extensive application of cluster sampling is presented in *International Issues 8.1*.

International Issues 8.1

Cluster Sampling in International Situations

The main objective of cluster sampling is to reduce costs by increasing sampling efficiency, as contrasted with stratified sampling, the main objective of which is to increase precision. Cluster sampling can be especially useful in international research, where costs are typically higher, as the following examples illustrate:

- In a study investigating the connection between vision and quality of life in rural India, the Aravind Medical Research Foundation in Madurai employed a strategy of random cluster sampling to select respondents for the survey from 50 villages in rural southern India. Corrected visual acuity and burden of eye diseases were determined in a population aged 40 years and older. Researchers used a questionnaire previously validated for measuring quality of life and visual function. Charts from the Early Treatment Diabetic Retinopathy Study were used to measure visual acuity, and other medical tests were used to detect and measure cataracts, macular degeneration, and glaucoma. Age, education, occupation, presenting acuity in the better eye, and presence of a cataract, glaucoma, or refractive error were independently associated with overall quality-of-life and vision-function scores. The study identified a clear correlation between presenting vision in the better eye and quality of life in the population studied.
- During a Uganda study to assess whether the health systems were able to accurately distinguish the symptoms of acute respiratory infections (ARI) from malaria, researchers at the Karolinska Institute suspected that all childhood fevers were treated as malaria in the community, including cases of pneumonia. In the effort to distinguish the two populations (pneumonia sufferers and malaria sufferers), subjects were randomly selected through a two-stage cluster sampling process from eight districts of 3223 households with 3249 children aged younger than 2 years. The primary caretakers of the sampled children were interviewed regarding the children's most recent illness during the preceding two weeks. The authors found that "19 percent reported overlapping symptoms of fever, cough and 'difficult/rapid breathing.' Of these, 45 percent were given antimalarials alone." Because few of the villagers had access to health facilities, 42 percent of antibiotics used were obtained from drug shops or home stocks. The large overlap of symptoms between fever and ARI, combined with the widely reported practice of using primarily antimalarials, led the researchers to conclude that "home-based management" (HBM) health care may be resulting in the misdiagnosis and mistreatment of pneumonia. The researchers recommended that community drug distributors be tested as to whether they were able to recognize an increased respiratory rate and make a presumptive diagnosis of pneumonia based on that rate.
- Audience Measurement and Analytics (AMap), a market research and analytics company based in India similar to Nielsen in the United States, gathers viewer data and provides ratings for television serials aired on the Indian subcontinent. AMap uses a cluster sampling method to select and meter more than 3000 households in different towns all over the country. A GSM (global system for mobile communications) chip monitors the viewing patterns of the household, and the data collected are transmitted daily to a central server. Advertisers and TV serial producers can obtain demographics and monitor pertinent data such as changes in the audiences of particular shows and retention levels after commercials. This allows advertisers to fine-tune their strategies to maximize exposure of their products to their target audience.

Sources: "Respiratory Infections; Community Assessment of Breathing Symptoms in Sub-Saharan Africa Requires Testing"; *Health & Medicine Week*. February 13, 2006.
"aMap Maps the Couch Potatoes"; *The Statesman* (India). September 19, 2005.
"Relationship of Eye Disease to Vision-Impaired Quality of Life Investigated"; *Biotech Week* via NewsRx.com. September 14, 2005.

8.7 Systematic Sampling

8.7a The Method

In systematic sampling, the researcher selects every kth element in the frame, after a random start somewhere within the first k elements. Suppose we wanted to select a systematic sample of $n = 5$ from our student population in Tables 8.1 and 8.2. Here:

$$k = \frac{50}{5} = 10.$$

In general,

$$k = \frac{N}{n}.$$

This value, k, is the reciprocal of the sampling fraction we desire and is called the *sampling interval.* Thus, to select our systematic sample of $n = 5$, we do the following:

1. Obtain a random number between 1 and 10. This element will be our starting point and the first element of the sample.

2. Add 10 to this random number. This element will be the second element of the sample. Add another 10 to get the third element, and so on.

If the random number were 2, our sample would include the elements 2, 12, 22, 32, 42.

Once the sampling interval and random starting point have been specified, the elements that are included in the sample become automatic. They form a cluster of elements. In our population of 50, there are only 10 possible systematic samples of size $n = 5$ that can be drawn, because each cluster includes 1/10 of the population. In general, the number of possible samples is equal to k, the sampling interval. With populations that are large relative to the sample size, the value of k, and therefore the number of possible samples, increases substantially.

Because we use all the elements in the cluster generated by systematic sampling, the procedure is therefore a one-stage cluster sampling. Also, it should be clear that not all possible combinations of elements are equally likely. We have dramatically reduced the number of possible samples from more than 250 million ($50 \times 49 \times 48 \times 47 \times 46 \ldots$) with simple random sampling to just 10 with systematic sampling.

Fortunately, it can be shown that the mean estimate stemming from systematic sampling is *unbiased* (technically speaking, unbiasedness says that the expected value of the sampling distribution of means generated by repeated systematic sampling is equal to the population mean). So, we say that the mean from any one systematic sample is an unbiased estimator of the population mean. We may then calculate meaningful confidence intervals, just as we did with simple random sampling*. In fact, if the frame from which we are sampling is truly random, a systematic sample may be thought of as being identical to simple random sampling, in the sense that the systematic sample is itself a perfectly random choice from the *set* of possible random samples (e.g., the 10 in the previous example vs. the 250 million random samples possible). In most applications, in fact, the results are very nearly identical.

Recall that our systematic sample consists of elements 2, 12, 22, 32, and 42 from Table 8.3; the mean for this sample is therefore:

$$\bar{X} = \frac{27 + 29 + 19 + 22 + 23}{5} = \frac{120}{5} = 24.0$$

Therefore, we have

$$\begin{aligned} s^2 &= \frac{1}{n-1}\sum(X - \bar{X})^2 \\ &= \frac{1}{4}\left[(27-24)^2 + (29-24)^2 + (19-24)^2 + (22-24)^2 + (23-24)^2\right] \\ &= \frac{1}{4}\left[(3)^2 + (5)^2 + (-5)^2 + (-2)^2 + (1)^2\right] = \frac{1}{4}[64] = 16 \\ s &= 4. \end{aligned}$$

Note that this is the standard deviation, which estimates the degree of variation in the population. We can also calculate the standard error, which tells us about the accuracy of our mean sample estimate (here, 24.0); the standard error is just the standard deviation divided by the square root of the sample size. So, for example, if we wanted a confidence interval extending two standard errors from the sample mean:

$$\bar{X} \pm 2s/\sqrt{n} = 24.0 \pm 2(4)/\sqrt{5} = 24.0 \pm 3.58.$$

More appropriately, we could compute a 95 percent CI using any statistical or spreadsheet program or by looking up a t-value with $n - 1 = 4$ degrees of freedom and 0.025 in each tail, finding $t = 2.78$:

$$\bar{X} \pm (2.78)s/\sqrt{n} = 24.0 \pm (2.78)(4)/\sqrt{5} = 24.0 \pm 4.97.$$

The true mean happens to be contained within both these intervals. Because of the particular elements that formed the cluster we selected, the standard error is larger than in the simple random sample we selected earlier; thus, so is the confidence interval.

---

*Calculation of standard errors in this case entails some highly technical aspects that go well beyond the scope of this text. In most situations these refinements add little to real managerial understanding of sampling results. We thus proceed as if the formulas related to simple random sampling apply, and direct the reader to specialized texts on sampling theory and experimental design for more detail.

Systematic sampling is often used in practice because selecting a systematic sample is easy and inexpensive. In contrast to simple random sampling, systematic sampling does not require hopping all over the sampling frame according to some random number generator's whim, and we need not worry about checking for duplication of elements. Because systematic sampling substitutes well for simple random sampling, it can even be used to select elements within strata in stratified sampling.

Systematic sampling offers one other important benefit over simple random sampling: we do not need a complete sampling frame to draw a systematic sample. An interviewer instructed to interview every twentieth customer can do so without a list of all customers. A sample of every third house does not require that a full list of the houses be available.

8.7b The Problem of Periodicity

There is one major problem with systematic sampling, namely, that we will obtain biased estimates if the list of elements forming the frame forms a cyclical pattern that coincides with a multiple of the size of the sampling interval. This type of frame is said to have **periodicity**. We may illustrate this problem with two examples. Suppose we wanted to interview residents of a student housing complex and we selected housing units from a list of all units arranged in numerical order: 1, 2, . . . , 599, 600. Suppose our sampling interval was 10 and our random starting number 5. Our sample would contain the 60 housing units numbered 5, 15, 25, . . . , 585, 595. Now suppose that the complex was built such that the units ending in 5, 25, 45, 65, and 85 are corner units, which have an additional bedroom and better views, and consequently command higher rent. Further, they are allocated to students on the basis of seniority (number of years in the complex) and whether there are at least two children living in the unit. So, half of our sample would consist of people with at least two children, who have been in the complex a number of years and are willing to pay a higher rent! Our sample, despite having been chosen via a systematic sample, would not be representative.

periodicity
A problem in systematic sampling, often causing bias, that can occur when cyclical patterns in a population coincide with a multiple of the sampling frame.

Note that, in this particular example, the cyclical pattern is twice the size of the sampling interval, but the pattern could be any multiple of the sampling interval and cause bias in our estimates. Obviously, researchers must be sensitive to periodicity. When it exists, it must be removed from the frame by rearranging the elements, or some other sampling procedure must be adopted.

8.7c Implicit Stratification with Systematic Sampling

Ordered frames are not always bad news for systematic sampling. If the frame is ordered on what might be used as a stratification variable, selection of a systematic sample will automatically provide a stratified sample. In this situation, a systematic sample will produce a *more* statistically efficient result than will simple random sampling.

Consider the systematic sample of students we selected. We know that the list of students is ordered by whether they are graduates or undergraduates, in the ratio 20:30. With a sampling interval of 10, we know that the first two sample elements must come from the graduate stratum and the last three from the undergraduate stratum. Thus, we automatically selected a *proportionate stratified sample* of students with our systematic sample.

If the researcher is aware of the implicit stratification that has occurred—and this knowledge is the key criterion—it is possible to use stratified formulas to calculate the sample mean and standard error, and this will result in greater accuracy (i.e., a smaller confidence interval). In our student age sample, the ages of the students within strata would be:

Stratum 1	27, 29
Stratum 2	19, 22, 23

We encourage you to do the necessary calculations to verify the reduction in standard error. It should now be apparent by just looking at the age values arranged in strata, which are naturally clustered much more tightly about their stratum-specific means.

In summary, systematic sampling offers potential advantages in ease of sample selection, lowered cost, no need for a complete frame, and implicit stratification of properly ordered frames. Difficulties, however, are related to the problem of possible periodicity and the potential for larger standard errors than a similarly sized random sample.

8.8 Area Sampling

8.8a The Basics

With simple random sampling, stratified sampling, and most applications of systematic sampling discussed so far, a complete and accurate listing of the elements of the population is required. Unfortunately, for a great many marketing research applications, such lists are difficult or impossible to generate at a reasonable cost. Lists are often well defined and even compiled by certain organizations (e.g., private firms, the Census, local government) but are not always made readily available for research applications. It is very difficult to access accurate, up-to-date and affordable lists for such populations as all the adults in the United States, all the inhabitants of a state or city, or all university students or church members; and it is essentially impossible to obtain a list of all users of a specific product or service, or all people who hold a particular opinion. Even when it is possible to obtain such lists, their costs can be prohibitive, and inaccuracies common.

Sampling practitioners have developed an ingenious solution to this problem. They reasoned that because people reside within a specific area, why not sample the *areas* and interview those who reside there? An *area sample* is actually a sampling of areas, as opposed to its residents, who are then chosen in some way once a specific region is selected.

Let us illustrate this concept by outlining what a one-stage area sample might look like. Suppose we want to run an in-home usage test of a new brand of shampoo and have decided to run it in Atlanta, Georgia. A low-cost, accurate listing of all households in the city is unavailable, as the phone directory omits unlisted households, and the city government database is proprietary. So, we can select an area sample using the following simple method:

1. List all city blocks in Atlanta, N_B.
2. Choose a simple random or systematic sample of n_B city blocks from the population of N_B city blocks.
3. Attempt to place the product in all households in the chosen blocks, n_B.

This is a probability sampling procedure because the probability of any household's being selected is equal to the sampling fraction n_B/N_B. If Atlanta had 10,000 blocks and we selected a sample of 20, the probability of any household's being selected would be 20/10,000 = 0.002, or 0.2 percent. The reason this probability equals the sampling fraction for the blocks is that we have used *all* households in the selected blocks as part of the sample. This need not be the case, as the following section shows.

8.8b Multistage Area Samples

An area sample can have as many stages as a researcher sees fit to include to fulfill the project's information requirements. Area samples typically have more than one stage, as selection of all elements in a particular geographic area is seldom desirable or practical. If we wished to do a two-stage area sample for the in-home shampoo test in Atlanta, the steps would be similar to a one-stage design, but with some new elements in the later ones:

1. List all city blocks in Atlanta, N_B.
2. Choose a simple random sample or systematic sample of n_B city blocks.
3. List the households located in the selected city blocks, N_H.
4. Select a simple random or systematic sample of n_H households from the selected n_B city blocks.

Note that the first two steps in two-stage area sampling are the same as in one-stage area sampling. With the latter, however, we were required to make one list (of blocks), and we used probability sampling procedures only once, to select the blocks themselves. In two-stage area sampling, we are required to make two lists (blocks, and then households), and we use probability sampling procedures twice (to select blocks, then households). In a two-stage area sample, we twice repeat the sequence "list population sampling units, then sample." Thus, in a k-stage area sample, we would go through this sequence k times; refer to Figure 8.4.

8.8c The Properties of Multistage Area Samples

Multistage area sampling is much less statistically efficient than simple random sampling. In a simple random sample, a single sampling error is calculated. A two-stage area sample is subject to two sampling errors. The selection of the clusters at the first stage is only an estimate of the population of clusters; that is,

Figure 8.4 Multistage Area Samples

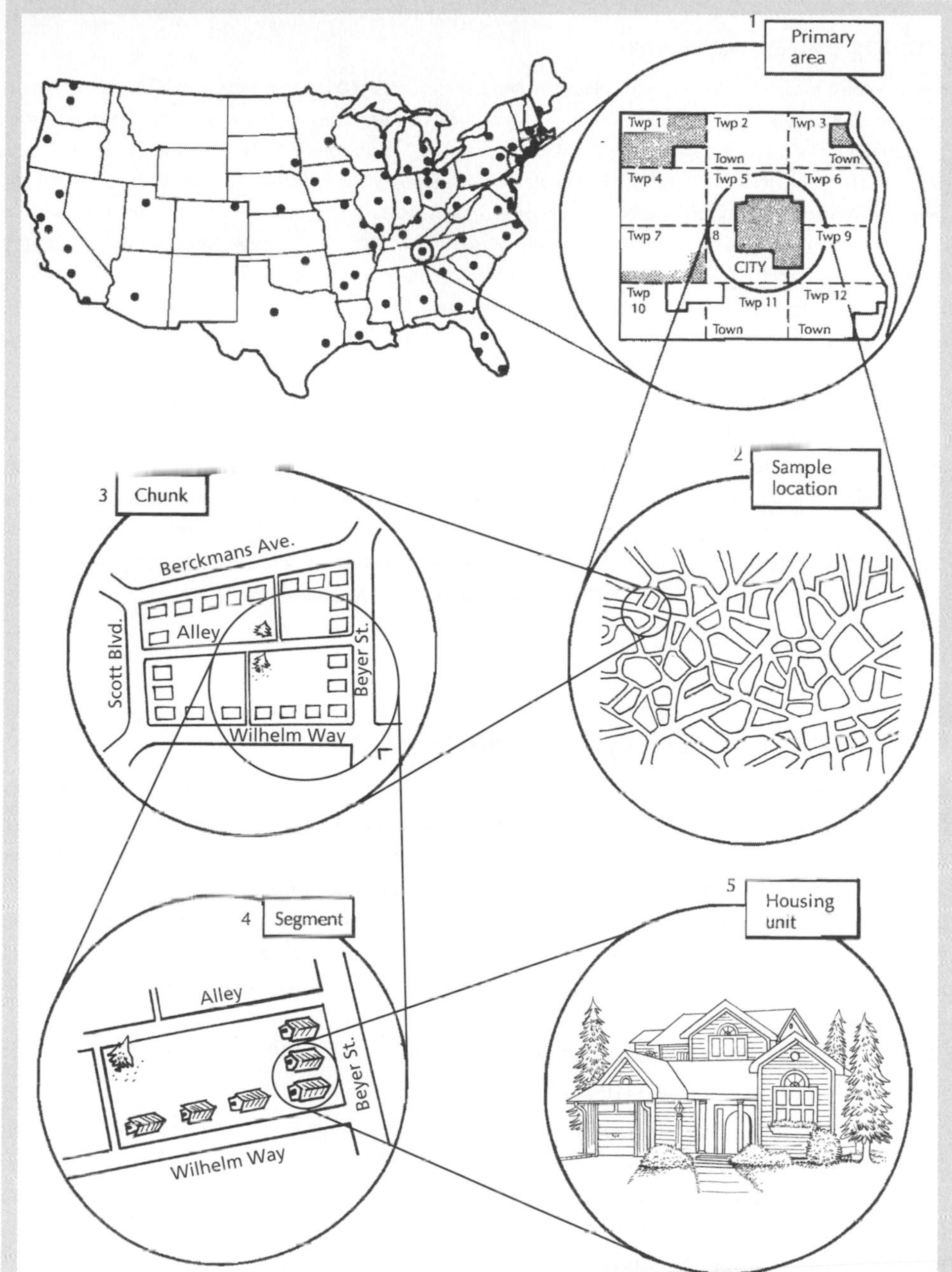

sampling error occurs. In this way, the selection of elements from *within a cluster* is only an estimate of the population of elements (within that cluster). Thus, a five-stage area sample would contain five separate sampling errors. The formulas for calculating the standard error arising from a multistage area sample are too complex to be discussed here but are natively supported in statistical programs used explicitly for that purpose. Researchers should be sensitive to this issue and prepared to consult a technical expert to ensure that calculations have been performed correctly, particularly for confidence intervals. In practice, the results obtained from the final stage are often treated as if they came from a direct probability sampling of a list of final elements. That is, the formulas used are those for simple random sampling and stratified sampling. The net effect of doing this is to *understate* the sampling error that has occurred. One needs to be particularly suspect of any method that accounts for less error than there is in actuality, as it leads to overconfidence.

Multistage area samples are popular with companies that need to make predictions over relatively large geographical areas. *Marketing Research Focus* 8.5 illustrates how Nielsen Media uses multistage area samples to estimate the size of TV audiences in the United States.

Marketing Research Focus 8.5

Multistage Area Sampling

The Nielsen People Meter, an electronic box placed on the television sets of a random sample of 5100 households in the United States, uses a multistage area sampling design to gather national estimates of TV audiences for broadcast/cable networks and different TV programs (*see also Research Innovations and Technologies 3.1*). The electronic boxes are placed on all television sets in the household and can record stations, programs, viewing times, and specific household members watching the programs. Because the age and gender of each household member is known, this information can be combined with the other household data to make projections of the total U.S. TV audience by age and gender.

Nielsen's sampling methodology uses U.S. Census Bureau counts to parse the national viewing area into more than 5000 small areas, each with the approximate population of an urban block. Households are then randomly selected within each sample area. Nielsen is thus able to quickly gather a sample used by networks and advertisers to determine the relative success of certain programming.

As an example of the successful use of this sampling method, Nielsen was able to determine not only that NBC's viewing audience was up by 150–350 percent over its normal viewing audience during the first week of the 2006 Winter Olympics, but also to evaluate this range of increase for different age groups of viewers. The 150 percent increase was in the 18–49 age group, whereas the 350 percent increase was among teens. Although these increases would seem to be cause for celebration at NBC, the numbers may actually be a source of significant concern for the network because they are down approximately 25 percent from the last Olympics held outside the United States, the 1998 Winter Olympics in Nagano, Japan. (NBC has publicly defended the ratings by citing significant drops in all major TV events.)

Source: Nielsen Media Company Web site, at www.nielsenmedia.com

8.8d Equal-Probability Area Sampling

Earlier we defined probability sampling as a technique in which each element has a known chance of being selected. In all the types of sampling discussed so far, except disproportionate statistical sampling, each element has had an equal chance of being selected. This is the easiest way to ensure that the sample selected represents the population. In this section we shall discuss how we obtain equal probabilities for each element; later in the chapter we shall discuss sampling with *un*equal probabilities for the elements.

There are two primary ways to assure equal-chance selection of elements in an area sample: equal proportion selection of elements within clusters and probability proportionate to size.

Equal-Chance Selection of Clusters: Equal-Proportion Selection of Elements within Clusters

In this method, each cluster is given an equal chance of selection regardless of size; then the same proportion of the elements is selected from within each cluster. Thus, each element has an equal chance of being selected. To illustrate, suppose we have 1000 elements divided into 50 clusters of different sizes. If we select a sample of 5 clusters, each cluster has a $\frac{5}{50}$ chance of being selected. If we then select 1/5 of the elements within each cluster, the total probability of an element being selected is $\frac{5}{50} \times \frac{1}{5} = .02$.

In this manner, larger clusters have more elements selected, correcting for the fact that both smaller and larger clusters had an equal chance of being selected. This process would require a sample size of $0.02 \times 1000 = 20$ elements. Note that for equal-probability sampling, the probability of an element being selected is equal to the sampling fraction, in this case $20/1000 = 0.02$.

More typically we would have a specified sample size and would be asked to select the number of clusters and proportion of elements within each cluster. A number of combinations of numbers of clusters and within-cluster proportions could accomplish this task. For example, the following combinations yield a probability of selection of 0.02:

$$\text{10 clusters and } \frac{1}{10} \text{ of the elements} = \frac{10}{50} \times \frac{1}{10} = .2 \times .1 = .02$$

$$\text{20 clusters and } \frac{5}{100} \text{ of the elements} = \frac{20}{50} \times \frac{5}{100} = .4 \times .05 = .02$$

We can apply this procedure to multistage designs as long as we continue to select the elements at each stage with equal proportion.

Equal-Chance Selection of Clusters: Probability Proportionate to Size

There is another method of obtaining equal element probabilities that is more statistically efficient than the equal-proportion method just discussed. In that method, a relatively small number of large clusters are selected, and thus the elements selected to represent all large clusters are selected from just a few of those small ones; this can result in some clusters not being represented at all. In response to this problem, the method of selecting first-stage clusters with **probability proportionate to size (PPS)** was developed.

probability proportionate to size (PPS)
A two-stage area sampling method that promotes equal probability of any element being selected at the second stage. For the first stage, clusters are assigned a probability of selection in proportion to the number of second-stage elements they contain. In the second stage, the same number of units is sampled from each selected cluster.

A two-stage PPS procedure would be carried out as follows: In the first stage, each cluster is assigned a chance of selection proportionate to the number of second-stage elements it contains, so that larger clusters will have a better chance of selection than smaller ones. In the second stage, the *same* number of sampling units will be selected from each selected cluster. Thus a smaller proportion of elements will be selected from larger clusters than from small ones, so that the probability of any element being selected at the second stage will be the same. To illustrate, suppose we have 10 city blocks, and their respective household populations are as follows:

Block Number	Number of Households
1	10
2	20
3	30
4	10
5	100
6	30
7	70
8	30
9	50
10	50
Total households	400

The relevant probability proportionate to size (PPS) for block *B* is:

$$PPS_B = \frac{\text{number of households in block } B}{\text{total number of households}}$$

So, to take blocks 1 and 9 as examples, we would have

$$PPS_1 = \frac{10}{400} = .025$$

$$PPS_9 = \frac{50}{400} = .125$$

We use a mechanistic procedure to select a PPS block sample, calculating the cumulative number of households and assigning random numbers in proportion to this cumulative distribution, as follows:

Block Number	Number of Households	Cumulative Number of Households	Associated Random Numbers
1	10	10	001–010
2	20	30	011–030
3	30	60	031–060
4	10	70	061–070
5	100	170	071–170
6	30	200	171–200
7	70	270	201–270
8	30	300	271–300
9	50	350	301–350
10	50	400	351–400
Total	400		

If we wanted a sample of three blocks, we would obtain three 3-digit random numbers between 001 and 400. Suppose we obtained the numbers 124, 302, and 027; our sample would be blocks 5, 9, and 2.

We would then select five households from blocks 2, 5, and 9. The probabilities of selecting elements are:

Probability of element in block B = block probability × within-block element probability:

$$\text{For elements in block 2} = \frac{20}{400} \times \frac{5}{20} = .05 \times .25 = .0125$$

$$\text{For elements in block 5} = \frac{100}{400} \times \frac{5}{100} = .25 \times .05 = .0125$$

$$\text{For elements in block 9} = \frac{50}{400} \times \frac{5}{50} = .125 \times .1 = .0125$$

The stage 1 and stage 2 probabilities balance each other to yield equal probability of selection for all elements. The same result also holds for the unselected blocks.

In a multistage area sample we can use the PPS method for the first two stages to ensure equal probabilities to that point; we can then select equal proportions from that point on to yield equal probabilities of all elements at the final stage. PPS is used to help ensure that large clusters are represented in the sample. Alternatively, this may be done by stratifying the first-stage cluster by size and sampling within clusters. PPS and stratification on size would not be used together.

8.8e Unequal-Probability Area Sampling

With the exception of disproportionate stratified sampling, each population element has had an equal chance of selection in all the probability sampling methods discussed so far. Recall that in our original definition of probability sampling, each element needed only a *known* chance of being selected to be a probability procedure. In area sampling, elements are often selected disproportionately; that is, elements have different probabilities of being selected. Unequal probabilities may arise for a number of legitimate reasons, including:

- The researcher, wanting to do detailed subgroup analysis, purposely oversamples a small subgroup to have a large enough sample to do meaningful analysis for that group. Such a subgroup might be, for example, a specific ethnic group.
- The researcher is using disproportionate stratified sampling to reduce within-stratum and overall sampling error.
- A sample yields a smaller proportion of a particular subgroup than the population proportion (assuming it to be known).
- A PPS design requires knowledge of cluster sizes. If these sizes turn out to be incorrect, the cluster will be given a disproportionately high or low probability of being selected.

Thus, we may obtain unequal probabilities for element selection from a number of deliberate or happenstance occurrences. They present no problems as long as the researcher is interested in doing only *within-subgroup* analysis. Suppose, for example, we were estimating the weekly gasoline consumption among undergraduate and graduate students in our population of 50 students. If we took a sample of 10 from each subgroup, the graduate students would have a probability of selection of $\frac{10}{20} = 0.5$, and the undergraduates $\frac{10}{30} = 0.33$. Note that the overall sampling fraction $\frac{20}{50} = .4$ does not equal the probability of each element being selected! This relationship now holds only *within* the subgroups. Suppose we estimated the average gasoline consumption of graduate students as $\frac{100}{10}$ = ten gallons per week, and of undergraduates as $\frac{50}{10}$ = five gallons per week. Those estimates are valid and can be compared with one another. However, if we combine the subgroups to fashion an overall estimate, the higher consumption of graduate students would be overrepresented, thus biasing the estimate upward. This average is

$$\bar{X}_{\text{gasoline}} = .5(10) + .5(5) = 5 + 2.5 = 7.5.$$

What we want is to have the weights reflect the subpopulation sizes. So the proper unbiased estimate is

$$\bar{X}_{\text{gasoline}} = .4(10) + .6(5) = 4 + 3 = 7.$$

You may recognize these weights as the *population* proportions arising from stratified sampling. This example was relatively simple because we knew all about the subpopulation sizes. More realistically, we are likely to know the probability of selecting an element from various subgroups. Can we use element probabilities directly to obtain proper weights? Indeed we can. The rule is that an element should be assigned a weighting factor *in proportion to the inverse of its probability of being selected.* Let us see how this might work for the gasoline example:

$$\text{Graduates: Probability of selection} = 0.5$$

$$\text{Inverse} = \frac{1}{.5} = 2.0$$

$$\text{Undergraduates: Probability of selection} = 0.33$$

$$\text{Inverse} = \frac{1}{.33} = 3.0$$

With this information there are two ways to obtain the (unbiased) overall average of seven gallons. The first is to multiply (the total gallons in each subgroup) and (the number in the sample in each subgroup) by their respective inverses, and then take the average, as follows.

$$\text{Graduates: } 100 \text{ gallons} \times 2 = 200;\ 10 \text{ students} \times 2 - 20$$

$$\text{Undergraduates: } 50 \text{ gallons} \times 3 = 150;\ 10 \text{ students} \times 3 = 30$$

$$\text{Total gallons} = 200 + 150 = 350$$

$$\text{Total students} = 20 + 30 = 50$$

$$\text{Average gallons} = \frac{350}{50} = 7$$

The value 50 here is called the *weighted sample size*. The alternative is to convert the inverses to proportions with respect to one another and then take a weighted average, as follows:

$$\text{Graduate inverse} = 2; \quad \text{Undergraduate inverse} = 3; \quad \text{Total inverse} = 5$$

$$\text{Proportion graduate} = \frac{2}{5} = 0.4 \quad \text{Proportion undergraduate} = \frac{3}{5} = 0.6$$

Once again, these are just our population weighting factors.

Many procedures built into modern data analysis software will allow the researcher to specify weighting factors, which are then automatically included as part of the analysis. When in doubt, these values should be set to their defaults, which represent equal weighting.

8.8f Note on Sample Size for Complex Sampling Procedures

The selection of a sample size in the more complex sampling procedures discussed in the preceding sections involves a trade-off among the same factors mentioned previously in the discussion for simple random sampling. There is one minor modification that must be made, however. Note that the formula for standard error differs in stratified and area sampling from that of simple random sampling. Be careful to use the correct formula, or confidence intervals and probabilities can go dramatically awry. For more detail on calculations in complex sampling schemes, please refer to any of the texts in Further Reading devoted to the topic.

8.9 Random-Digit Dialing

With regard to all the probability sampling procedures discussed thus far, there is a very important procedure for actually selecting sample elements. This procedure is *random-digit dialing*. It is in fact the dominant method when telephone interviewing has been chosen as the means of contacting respondents. An advantage of this procedure is that it allows contact with households that have unlisted numbers, that have relocated since the directory was printed, or whose number has been misrecorded in the directory, Internet listing, or database. One possible drawback is that it will tend to overcount homes with multiple phone lines, and can undercount those who tend to rely on cell phones instead of land lines.

In theory, all seven digits of a telephone number can be selected randomly. However, this is both costly and inefficient, as many unused numbers are generated. What is more common in practice is that numbers are selected from a telephone directory using a systematic sampling procedure, and then the last one or two digits are replaced with random digits. This results in a far higher percentage of in-service numbers and has the properties of a true probability sample.

This procedure can be used with any of the probability sampling methods discussed so far. We could use random-digit dialing in the context of a multistage area sample as follows:

1. proceed as far as the sample location level, yielding, say, cities and towns,
2. access telephone directories for the selected cities or towns and systematically select a sample of telephone numbers from the directories,
3. replace the last one or two digits of these selected numbers with random numbers, and
4. contact the resulting numbers.

8.10 International Sample Selection

Fundamental choices underlying sampling utilized in marketing research apply universally to both domestic and international marketing research. Indeed, the fundamentals of probability sampling are based on statistical theory, and thus apply in all contexts.

There are some major difficulties in implementing probability sampling procedures in areas with underdeveloped marketing research institutions and poor telecommunications systems. If an area has a poorly developed marketing research industry, necessary population lists are unlikely to be available, the expertise to draw samples will be reduced, and access to all but the largest urban areas may be limited. These difficulties were clearly demonstrated in a classic example, involving the Russian parliamentary election of December 1993, as noted in *International Issues* 8.2.

There are special difficulties in selecting samples in various regions of the world. This is especially true in the selection of the types of complex probability samples discussed in this chapter. The most difficult issues arise from the lack of needed census-level demographic data and of adequate lists from which to draw samples. In all but the most developed nations, census track and census block data, along with telephone directories, street housing guides, and detailed demographic data, can be difficult or impossible for the marketing researcher to obtain. For example, parts of the Middle East, South America, and Africa lack accurate street maps, and the type of GPS (global positioning system) coverage (with electronically determined location matched to geographic landmarks and routes) taken for granted in North America and Europe cannot be assumed across the globe.

International Issues 8.2

Classic Case of Poor Sampling in Russian Parliamentary Elections

Poor sampling yielded misleading poll results that surprised Russian president Boris N. Yeltsin and challenger Vladimir V. Zhirinovsky. In the December 1993 Russian parliamentary elections, Zhirinovsky's ultranationalistic Liberal Democratic Party received something approaching 25 percent of the votes cast, more than any other party. This came as a great surprise to Yeltsin and the pollsters his party had hired to monitor the electorate. The Liberal Democrats had been predicted to receive less than 5 percent of the vote. How could such a poor prediction have been made? Some posited explanations include:

- The pollsters tended to select their samples from major urban areas, where lists of households were more generally available. The rural areas voted much more heavily for the Liberal Democrats.
- In some parts of the country, quota samples were used. Those who agreed to participate in the poll tended to be more supportive of the Yeltsin government. The interviewers did not seek out or did not find a proportionate number of voters who were not Yeltsin supporters.
- Some of the polling was done by telephone. Voters who had phones were more affluent than those who did not, and were more likely to support the Yeltsin reforms. Thus, a disproportionately large percentage of Yeltsin supporters appeared in the sample.
- There was a tendency for voters in Russia not to respond to polls in a manner that ran counter to the sitting government. Thus, the Yeltsin support was overstated, and the Liberal Democratic support was understated.

It is impossible to know which, if any, of these factors was responsible, or whether some interaction among them was the culprit. Although deviations as large, and as historically important, as in this classic case are rare, it is not uncommon for sampling biases to cause substantial directional error, particularly in areas with relatively few marketing research firms.

The absence of these types of data makes the selection of probability-based area samples virtually impossible. In addition, the lack of required knowledge about population characteristics prevents both the use of stratified samples and the selection of samples with probability proportionate to size. Proper sample selection is also hampered in some countries by a spotty telephone system, with some households having many phones and others none, and a transportation system that prevents interviewers from reaching some areas of the country easily. A probability sample of the population in such circumstances is impractical. Thus, marketing researchers in such situations must rely on a combination of probability samples, where they are possible, and quota, judgment, and convenience samples. Correcting for selection biases in such samples, although difficult, must receive a great deal of dedicated attention.

SPECIAL EXPERT FEATURE

Total Survey Error

By Andy Peytchev and Norbert Schwarz

This chapter introduced the notion that maximizing a single aspect of survey design is unlikely to produce the best parameter estimates, i.e., the best estimates of population proportions, means, variances, and associations. Instead, we need to consider the interplay of different survey components. A useful framework for thinking about these issues is the concept of *total survey error*. Survey error can result from observation and from non-observation, as described below. Understanding the different sources of error is important because it informs decisions about the allocation of resources – should we spend more money on questionnaire design and interviewing quality, on increasing the sample size, or on reducing the rate of nonresponse? The answer always depends on the specific objectives of the study, but to make these decisions we need to know what each source of error is, why it occurs, how it can be measured, and how it can be reduced.

Errors of *observation* include measurement and processing errors, and errors of non-observation include sampling, coverage, and nonresponse errors. There are different ways that these error sources can be interrelated, but cost is a major constraint. So how might researchers decide to allocate resources between methods of data collection, questionnaire design, obtaining sufficient overall sample size and reducing the proportion of nonrespondents, among others?

Errors of Observation

Errors of observation come in two principal forms: measurement error and processing error. Measurement error occurs at the data collection stage, whereas processing error occurs when the data are prepared for analysis.

Measurement Error

Survey researchers speak of measurement error when an observed value for some quantity departs from the true value, e.g., when respondents report a smaller number of purchases than they actually made. Such departures from the truth can be due to the questionnaire, the respondent, the interviewer, the mode of data collection, or some combination of the four.

Vague questions, ambiguous response options or burdensome questions about very specific details of the past are some of the questionnaire factors that can induce measurement error. For example, if we asked respondents for the frequency of routine purchases, they may simply not remember them and may resort to inaccurate estimates. Using more elaborate recall procedures, or paper or electronic diaries, could increase accuracy, but at the expense of higher survey cost. How characteristics of the questionnaire can influence the question answering process is discussed in the special section on self-reports in Chapter 7.

In addition, respondents may sometimes intentionally provide untruthful answers. This is occurs when a particular question is very sensitive (e.g., how much alcohol one consumes; number of sexual partners in the past year) or evokes concerns about social desirability (e.g., library card ownership). Most methods designed to reduce this problem highlight the confidentiality or anonymity of the answers. In general, socially desirable responding is highest in face-to-face interviews and lowest when self-administered methods of data collection are used (e.g., paper questionnaires or web surveys), which can be used for the whole survey or just for sensitive parts. Telephone surveys fall in between these extremes.

For example, surveys find that men on average report two to four times as many sexual partners than women. This gender discrepancy is common, even though, considered as an average across the population, a representative sample of men should have about as many sexual partners as a representative sample of women in any society with a predominantly heterosexual population. Apparently, for this particular task, men over-report and women under-report, consistent with traditional norms. As expected, this gender difference was much larger in personal interviews than when the interviewers

continued

turned over the laptop so that respondents could complete the questions without their answers being seen. But social desirability is not the only factor that contributes to the gender discrepancy. Broadly speaking, men also tend to use estimation strategies in such reports, which can result in overreporting of behaviors in many domains. Women, by contrast, tend to use enumeration, where an attempt is made to recall every specific instance. Because it is highly reliant on memory resources, this strategy can result in underreporting.

How likely respondents are to answer in a socially desirable way is also influenced by observable characteristics of the interviewer, like age, gender, ethnicity, and overall appearance. For example, Caucasian respondents report more positive opinions about African-Americans when the interviewer is African-American (rather than Caucasian), and male respondents in a German study reported a higher income when interviewed by a woman considered attractive. In addition, interviewers can introduce other sources of measurement error through their behavior, like a fast pace of the interview or the manner in which they ask questions.

Measurement error can be estimated by comparing responses to external information. This can be done at the individual level, e.g. by comparing reports of health events or telephone use to records from the hospital or telephone company. It can also be done at the survey estimate level, for example by comparing the results with another survey or with census data. In both cases, we can attempt to obtain measures of truth to separate it from the observed response, as in the representation provided in Chapter 4 ($O = T + e_S + e_R$).

To reduce measurement error, we need to identify likely causes before data collection. For example, problems with the questionnaire can be identified through cognitive interviews, where a few respondents are asked to explain how they think about each question. Problems with interviewer behavior are best avoided through careful interviewer training and supervision. Once this preliminary work is completed, a larger pretest can be conducted – like the real survey, but on a small number of respondents.

Processing Error

An additional source of errors of observation arises in the form of *processing errors.* Put simply, survey data are not ready for analysis when the survey is over. Data need to be cleaned – we detect implausible values and often need to create data editing rules to transform such values into a category called "missing." Such edits are difficult to perform; even though some values seem impossible, it does not necessarily mean they are not legitimate. For example, we can detect an implausible value in the case of a woman who is 25 years old and has 25 children. Even though this is biologically impossible, it is logically a possibility if the woman has had several spouses with multiple children, or if numerous children were adopted. Alternatively, the value may simply be the result of a data entry error; instead of '2,' somehow '25' was entered. Identifying implausible values and deciding on how to edit them is riddled with uncertainties, resulting in processing error.

Sometimes, respondents are not provided with response options, but rather asked to provide information in their own words, e.g., to name their occupation. To facilitate analysis, such textual information is later placed into different categories by coders. However, different coders can make different judgments about how certain answers should be coded, which can again introduce processing error. This is why clear coding schemes and good training are crucial for this stage of a survey.

In addition, survey researchers use weights to reduce sampling and nonresponse errors (described below), which can again introduce processing errors. The *Survey of Income and Program Participation* (www.bls.census.gov/sipp) is a national panel survey conducted by the *U.S. Census Bureau* (www.census.gov), used for key economic indicators and policy. It was not until 2005 that errors were found and corrected in the weights for the publicly released 2001 panel data. As post-survey adjustments become exceedingly sophisticated to adjust for other sources of survey errors, ever more attention needs to be paid to processing error. Many such mistakes are caught by analysts, who acknowledge that these can occasionally occur.

Errors of Non-Observation

Errors of non-observation come in the form of sampling error, coverage error, and nonresponse error. We address each in turn.

Sampling Error

Because it is usually not feasible to collect data from the whole population of interest (i.e., a census), surveys are conducted by collecting data from a sample drawn from the population. To draw a sample from the population, the researcher needs to determine an appropriate sampling frame. In the ideal case, the researcher would have a list of all members of the population (say, the citizens of a city), which could serve as the sampling frame. If the population is heterogeneous, as is usually the case, the statistics based on the sample will vary to some extent from sample to sample. These deviations from the values of the population are called sampling error. There are two principal types of sampling error: sampling variance and sampling bias.

Sampling variance simply reflects that people differ and that each sample drawn will hence differ in random ways from other samples drawn from the same population. The larger the size of each sample, the more similar they will be; that is, sampling variance decreases with sample size. Accordingly, two large samples are more likely to include the same number of ethnic minorities or elderly than two small samples. Also, if we stratify the sample by taking proportionate samples from different parts of the country, the variability of ethnic minorities or elderly across samples will be reduced. However, survey researchers often use clusters of areas to draw their sample, which reduce costs of face-to-face interviewing. To the extent that people in the same areas are more similar, variability *across* samples is increased.

Sampling bias occurs when some people in the sampling frame are less likely to be selected. For example, if telephone numbers are randomly dialed, households with multiple telephone lines will be more likely to be selected. Sampling bias is a particular threat to nonprobability samples, which are common in marketing research. For example, if interviews are done only at malls,

continued

those who do not shop at malls and those who shop less frequently are less likely to be in the sample. Therefore, sampling error must be considered as a function of four critical design factors: a) whether probability sampling is employed; b) whether stratification is used; c) whether sample elements are drawn individually or in clusters; and d) whether a large sample is drawn.

Coverage Error

Unfortunately, a complete list of the population of interest is rarely available to serve as a sampling frame. Any mismatch between the sampling frame and the target population gives rise to *coverage error*. For example, if we use an outdated list of telephone numbers as a sampling frame and our target population is all households in the United States, we will fail to contact people who have no telephone service, have changed phone numbers or just became new telephone customers. The coverage error will be a function of the proportion all households in the United States that can be reached by phone and the extent to which they differ from those who cannot on the statistics of interest. For example, people with low income and living in rural areas are less likely to have landline telephones, and are thus excluded from telephone sampling frames at higher rates; if we are conducting a telephone survey and are interested in the percentage of people eligible for welfare benefits, our statistics will be biased, as we would fail to measure many people with low income, who are differentially likely to qualify for such benefits. This is an example of *undercoverage* of a sampling frame with respect to the target population. It is also possible that our frame contains 'foreign elements' that are not part of our target population (e.g. business telephone numbers, while we are interested in households only) and this is called *overcoverage*. It is possible for one sampling frame to exhibit both undercoverage and overcoverage problems; however, so long as the foreign elements were weeded out by the survey process itself, only the under-coverage would affect the statistics of interest.

How much undercoverage biases the statistics of interest depends on the proportion of the target population that is undercovered and the difference between the covered and the not covered. For example, if income differs between the covered and not covered parts of the population, income statistics would show a bias, whereas statistics pertaining to characteristics in which the two groups do not differ would remain unbiased.

Several techniques facilitate the reduction of coverage error. They include the use of multiple sampling frames (e.g. listed telephone numbers and random-digit-dialing that includes listed and unlisted numbers), multiplicity sampling (asking selected respondents to identify others that may have been omitted from the frame), half-open interval (interviewers check for new/missed buildings next to the selected address) and a variety of post-survey adjustments.

Nonresponse Error

Even when sampling error and coverage error are low, the obtained results may still be threatened by nonresponse, that is, by the failure to obtain responses from a large number of the sampled elements. Survey researchers distinguish between *unit nonresponse* (when a person can not be interviewed at all) and *item nonresponse* (when a respondent does not answer a particular question). There are three major types of unit-nonresponse: due to inability to contact the respondent, due to the respondent's refusal to participate, and due to the respondents' inability to participate (e.g., due to handicaps or language problems). *Nonresponse error* occurs when those who respond are different from those who fail to respond, among the selected sample. When the nonrespondents are systematically different from the respondents, nonresponse bias arises, and its degree is a function of both the response rate and any differences between respondents and nonrespondents.

Note that this implies that response rate of a survey per se is *not* a good indicator of nonresponse error. The response rate merely shows the *potential* for nonresponse error. If there is no difference between the respondents and the nonrespondents on a particular characteristic, a low response rate will not lead to an erroneous estimate of that characteristic. On the other hand, substantial nonresponse error can occur even when a high response rate is achieved. This is the case when the difference between respondents and nonrespondents is very large, in which case the missing values of a relatively small number of nonrespondents can result in an erroneous estimate. However, if the response rate is very low, say 20%, it is very likely that there is sizeable nonresponse error on many statistics – and, even worse, its magnitude will be unknown.

To minimize nonresponse error, it is critical to understand the reasons for nonresponse and their relationship with statistics of interest. When people are asked to participate in a survey on technology, those with little interest in technology may not participate, introducing nonresponse error in technology-related questions. But if those with high or low interest in technology did not differ in their political opinions, nonresponse error related to political questions might nevertheless be low. The National Household Survey on Drug Abuse focused on substance use in the U.S., yet the title of the survey could offend and drive substance users away, creating nonresponse bias. Hence, the survey was renamed in 2002 to the *National Survey on Drug Use & Health* (www.drugabusestatistics.samhsa.gov/nhsda.htm). Nonrespondents tend to share certain characteristics. For example, they tend to be either low or high in income and are more likely to live in urban areas, which can introduce nonresponse error on estimates related to these common geodemographic variables.

To protect research results from this source of error, survey designs are created to measure and reduce it. For example, the *Survey of Consumer Finances* (www.federalreserve.gov/PUBS/oss/oss2/scfindex.html) is a national face-to-face survey that draws an area probability sample of households in the U.S., but also adds a sample of high-income households from IRS records. Many surveys now use a multiphase design: at a certain point, data collection is stopped, a subsample of the nonrespondents is drawn, and interviews are attempted with an altered design, such as higher monetary incentives and a different mode of data collection. Then the respondents in the sample of initial nonrespondents

continued

can be "weighted up" to represent the rest of the nonrespondents. Apart from the sampling weights discussed earlier in the chapter, post-stratification weights can be used to adjust for nonresponse. Typically, proportions of people in the sample with given characteristics are matched to proportions in the population. More recently, more multivariate approaches (i.e., relying on many variables) to weighting for nonresponse have been used, such as response propensity weights. Such models can include rich sets of predictors of responding, including interviewer observations of the building and neighborhood, history of previous interview attempts, and so on. Other methods like imputation of responses – using a statistical model to 'fill in' unavailable data values – are more appropriate for item-missing data, so that the rest of the responses from such respondents are preserved and used in analyses. For example, income is among the variables with high rates of item-nonresponse, and a good imputation model will use all other information that the respondent has provided to suggest a replacement value suitable for further analysis.

Conclusion

Much of what we know about the sources of survey error has been learned through systematic experimentation with features of survey design. Although we speak of "survey error," it is important to emphasize that error, whether systematic (bias) or random (variance), is *not* a property of a survey as a whole. Instead, it is statistic-specific, and any source of error may affect some estimates but not others (e.g., mean age, median income, association between income and purchase frequency). The goal of survey methodologists is to minimize multiple sources of error for multiple statistics. Since reducing one source of error can lead to an increase in another error, all sources of error need to be considered concurrently. We therefore need to be aware of each error source, how to measure it, how to reduce it, and adjust for any potential substantive problems.

Andy Peytchev is a Ph.D. Candidate in Survey Methodology at the University of Michigan. His research interests include participation decisions and measurement errors in surveys.

Norbert Schwarz is Professor of Psychology at the University of Michigan, Professor of Marketing at the Ross School of Business, and Research Professor at Michigan's Institute for Social Research. His research interests focus on human cognition and judgment, including their implications for social science methodology.

Further Reading

Groves, R. M., F. J. Fowler, M. Couper, J. M. Lepkowski, E. Singer, R. Tourangeau. Survey Methodology. New York: Wiley. 2004.

Schwarz, N., Groves, R., & Schuman, H. Survey methods. In D. Gilbert, S. Fiske, & G. Lindzey (Eds.), *Handbook of social psychology* (4th edition, Vol. 1, pp. 143–179). New York: McGraw-Hill. 1998.

Courtesy of Norbert Schwartz and Andy Peytchev.

Summary

The advantages of sampling, relative to conducting a census, include saving money, saving time, obtaining more accurate information, and avoiding the destruction or contamination of all the elements in the population. The steps in the sampling process are: defining the population, identifying the sampling frame, deciding on the sample size, selecting a sampling procedure, and drawing the sample.

In probability sampling, each element of the population has a known chance of being selected; in simple random sampling, each element has an equal chance of being selected, and each combination of n sample elements has an equal chance of being selected. In nonprobability sampling, including convenience, judgment, and quota sampling, the selection of elements is based in some part on the judgment of the researcher.

The central limit theorem tells us that the mean of the sample that we select comes from a distribution of sample means that form a normal curve if $n \geq 30$, no matter what the shape of the underlying variable distribution. (And if the distribution is "unimodal"—that is, has just one hump—then even fewer than 30 elements can suffice; note that the cutoff for using the central limit theorem is often set at 25, a value we have invoked earlier in this book.) If the variable distribution is normal, then the sampling distribution of the mean is always normal, no matter what the sample size is. The theorem's implications for normal distributions allow us to calculate confidence intervals around our sample mean in the form of the mean ($\bar{X}$) $\pm$ the standard error ($s_{\bar{X}}$). Specifically, the 95 percent CI will be $\bar{X} \pm 2s_{\bar{X}}$, and the 99.7 percent CI will be $\bar{X} \pm 3s_{\bar{X}}$, where $s_{\bar{X}} = \frac{s}{\sqrt{n}}$. Precision is the absolute size of the confidence interval about the mean; e.g., at the 95 percent level of confidence, absolute precision is $\pm 2\frac{s}{\sqrt{n}}$.

A sample statistic whose expected value equals the population parameter is called an unbiased statistic. A sample statistic that has the minimum variance is the most efficient estimator. The confidence interval provides a measure of accuracy of an estimator. Calculation of sampling error does nothing to alleviate nonsampling errors. Beware of nonsampling errors.

Best practice for choosing sample size involves weighing the factors of sampling error, nonsampling error, study objectives, time constraints, cost constraints, and data analysis plans.

Stratified sampling reduces standard error by sampling separate strata in which the variable of interest is more homogeneous than in the overall target population. For a stratification variable to be useful,

Table 8.4 Managerial Summary of Sampling

	Dimensions	Census	Nonprobability Samples: Convenience	Judgment	Quota	Probability Samples: Simple Random	Stratified	Systematic	Area
1	Generation of sampling error	No	No	No	No	Yes	Yes	Yes	Yes
2	Statistical efficiency		No measurement possible			[Base level others are compared to]	High when stratification variables work	Somewhat low	Low
3	Need for population list	Yes	No	No	No	Yes	Yes	Not necessary in all applications	Only for selected clusters
4	Relative Cost	Very high	Very low	Low	Moderate	High	High	Moderate	Moderate to high

it must be correlated with the variable we are measuring. The overall mean in stratified sampling is the weighted average of the within-strata means. The overall standard error is the square root of the weighted combination of the square of the standard error within each stratum.

A proportionate stratified sample allocates sample size to strata in proportion to the number of population elements in the strata. Disproportionate stratified sampling oversamples strata with higher variability in order to reduce the standard error within those strata. In cluster sampling, we randomly select a cluster or group of sampling units, designed to be as heterogeneous as the population.

In systematic sampling, we select every *k*th element in the frame, after a random start somewhere within the first *k* elements. A systematic sample of a frame ordered on a stratification variable yields a proportionate stratified sample. A frame with a cyclical pattern that coincides with a multiple of the size of the sampling interval will yield biased results in systematic sampling.

Area sampling involves selecting pieces of geography. A multistage area sample involves the repeated process of listing sampling units and selecting a probability sample from this list. The probability of element selection equals the product of the individual proportions. With disproportionate sampling, elements should be assigned weighting factors in proportion to the inverse of their probability of being selected.

Statistical efficiency involves the comparison of the standard errors of different sampling procedures. Overall efficiency involves the comparison of the standard error per dollar spent.

Table 8.4 presents comparisons among a census and various sampling procedures on a number of relevant dimensions. The first is the possibility of generating a measure of sampling error; the second is the related concept of statistical efficiency; third is the need for a list of population elements in order to draw the sample; and fourth is the procedure's cost. A manager should consider all of these aspects when selecting a sampling procedure, regardless of project size or complexity.

Key Terms

absolute precision (p. 312)
area sampling (p. 317)
central limit theorem (p. 300)
cluster sampling (p. 323)
coefficient of variation (p. 313)
combinatorial formula (p. 345)
confidence intervals (p. 307)
convenience samples (p. 295)
degrees of freedom (p. 305)
descriptive statistics (p. 304)
dichotomous/binary variable (p. 303)
dispersion (p. 305)
disproportionate stratified sampling (p. 322)
efficiency (p. 317)
element (p. 292)
extent (p. 292)
factorial (p. 345)
finite population correction (p. 310)
half-width (p. 308)
histogram (p. 346)
inferential statistics (p. 304)
inverse square law (p. 310)
judgment samples (p. 296)
mean/average (p. 305)

nonprobability sampling (p. 295)
outliers (p. 349)
parameter (p. 300)
periodicity (p. 327)
population (p. 292)
precision (p. 308)
probability proportionate to size (PPS) (p. 331)
probability sampling (p. 295)
proportionate stratified sampling (p. 318)
quota samples (p. 296)
relative allowable error (p. 313)
relative precision (p. 312)
sample proportion (p. 306)
sampling distribution (p. 307)
sampling unit (p. 293)
simple random sampling (p. 295)
standard deviation (p. 305)
standard errors (p. 307)
statistic (p. 301)
stratification variable (p. 318)
study population (p. 294)
sum of squares (p. 305)
t-value or *t*-statistic (p. 312)
variance (p. 301)
z-value or *z*-statistic (p. 312)

Discussion Questions

1 Because nonprobability samples do not yield a measure of sampling error, why are these procedures so extensively used in commercial and academic practice?

2 Is it appropriate for the U.S. Census Bureau to agree to adjust the census count on the basis of sample results? What are the pros and cons?

3 What problems are likely to occur in implementing a field study using simple random sampling?

4 The membership director of a national fraternity wanted to do an attitude study of the fraternity's 2500 currently active members and the 12,000 alumni.
   a What sampling frame or frames would likely be available for this purpose?
   b Explain how you would select a simple random sample of current members and alumni.

5 How are whole-sample estimates made when elements have unequal selection probabilities?

6 General Motors does some evaluations of car designs and advertising themes using focus groups. These groups consist of from eight to ten potential customers who match the target segment profile for the car being evaluated. The focus group interviewees are selected by a research firm for General Motors through telephone solicitation of people who are qualified as matching the required target profile. This qualification of participants is done by a series of questions asked over the phone. The phone directories used to identify which individuals to call are from geographic areas where cars such as the one being evaluated have historically sold well.
   a What sampling procedure is being used?
   b Evaluate the sampling procedure used in terms of its appropriateness to the stated task and objectives.
   c What inferences to the whole target segment population can be drawn from this sampling approach?
   d What biases may exist due to the sample selection method?

7 Kraft Foods does some mall-intercept interviewing to evaluate new food product offerings. These samples are typically done in only a few malls for any one test. Subjects who pass by particular locations in the mall are recruited on the basis of appearing to match certain demographic characteristics: gender, age, and so on.
   a What sampling procedure is being used?
   b Evaluate the sampling procedure used in terms of its appropriateness to the stated task and objectives.
   c What inferences to the broader population can be drawn?
   d Why has mall-intercept sampling become so widely used in practice?
   e What biases may exist due to the sample selection method?

8 MINICASE
Cupertino Semiconductor supplies computer chips to the aerospace, automobile, major appliance (stoves, refrigerators, etc.), and consumer electronics industries. Cupertino sells to different-sized companies in each of these industries and to companies in all regions of the world. Historically, Cupertino's management has noted sales differences by industry type, size, and geographic region. Cupertino desires to select a quota sample to predict the sales level of a new product offering.
   a What control characteristics should be used for this quota sample?
   b What would one need to know about these control characteristics for them to be useful in this study?
   c Explain how many respondents would be specified for each cell.
   d What inferences could be drawn about Cupertino's entire customer base from such a sample?

For questions 9 through 11, prepare a sampling design. Be sure to have your design include a description of each of the following items and a statement of your reasoning.

- **a** The population
- **b** The sampling frame
- **c** The sample size
- **d** The sampling procedure (be sure to include a step-by-step description of how the sample will actually be drawn)
- **e** A method for determining the accuracy of sample results.

9 Frank Jackson was the director of student services in the business school of a major university. He wanted to conduct a survey of both BBA and MBA students to determine their attitudes toward course offerings, counseling services available, and job opportunities. There were a total of 3000 BBA students and 700 MBA students in the business school. Because a census was not possible, Frank needed to develop a sampling design.

10 Sara Ranski is a consultant to the World Church Council. One information need of the council is to develop a demographic profile of church members in the United States. Ranski has been asked to develop a sampling design to facilitate the collection of this information.

11 Roy Lena was the product manager for a new brand of cereal, named Multi-Vit, that was currently under development by a major packaged goods company located in New York City. The product offered vitamins and other nutrients not available in other cereals. Lena was in the process of designing an in-home usage test for the product. The objective of the test was to measure the reaction of adults to the product's taste. Results of this test would be used to further refine the product before it was submitted to additional in-home and market tests. The problem facing Lena was to design the sample for the in-home placement test.

Review Questions

1 Suppose you have a very large sample from some (even larger) population and gathered responses on a 7-point scale. Using the formula for sample standard deviation, what is the largest value of *s* obtainable?

- **a** 1
- **b** 3
- **c** 3.5
- **d** 7

2 What is the nature of the error generated by a nonprobability sampling procedure?

- **a** The error cannot be measured in terms of degree or direction.
- **b** The error can be sufficiently minimized when the number of control factors is maximized (e.g., at least four).
- **c** The error does not fall within the purview of the central limit theorem.
- **d** Nonprobability samples are selected by knowledgeable researchers and therefore the error is typically negligible.

3 Why is the central limit theorem critical to assessing sampling error?

- **a** It allows us to identify whether the error is within 68 percent, 95 percent, or 99 percent confidence intervals.
- **b** It tells us that the error can be corrected if the actual population is known.
- **c** It allows us to calculate confidence intervals for quantities of interest, such as the population mean.
- **d** It tells us that the error varies inversely with the sample size.

4 Which of the following pieces of information is needed to calculate a statistically optimal sample size for a continuous variable?

- **a** desired precision and sample standard deviation
- **b** sum of squares

c desired confidence level
d a and b
e a and c
f b and c

5 In practice, what information is necessary in order to calculate a statistically optimal sample size for a *dichotomous* (i.e., yes/no) variable?
a desired precision, sample standard deviation, and desired confidence level
b desired precision, population proportion, and desired confidence level
c desired precision, sample proportion, and desired confidence level
d It is not possible to identify an optimal sample size for a dichotomous variable because doing so requires information we do not have.

6 Which is a desirable property of an estimator?
a greater homogeneity
b high efficiency
c that it is mutually exclusive
d that any bias is only asymptotic

7 In an attitude study carried out for a national university honor society with more than 100,000 living members, most of the questions were on a 7-point rating scale. For a sample size of 200 current members, what is the 95 percent confidence interval for such a rating scale result where the mean answer on such a 7-point scale is 2.4 and the standard deviation is 1.1? (You may assume that because the sample size is large, we can use a *z*-value.)
a $2.4 \pm 1.1(z_{.05})$
b $2.4 \pm 1.1(z_{.05})/\sqrt{200}$
c $2.4 \pm 1.1(z_{.025})$
d $2.4 \pm 1.1(z_{.025})/\sqrt{200}$

8 One question in the attitude study referred to in Question 7 dealt with the proportion of alumni members who attend meetings of the local chapter. Historically, this proportion has been about 20 percent. The membership director reasoned that an error of ± 5 percent (that is, from 15 percent to 25 percent) was acceptable for making this estimate. What is the sample size that will yield this quality of estimate at the 95 percent confidence level, assuming that the 20 percent historical figure is a reasonable benchmark?
a $(0.2)(0.8)(z_{.025})^2/(.05)^2$
b $(0.15)(0.85)(z_{.025})^2/(.05)^2$
c $(0.25)(0.75)(z_{.025})^2/(.05)^2$
d $(0.2)(0.8)(z_{.025})^2/(.025)^2$
e $(0.15)(0.85)(z_{.025})^2/(.025)^2$
f $(0.25)(0.75)(z_{.025})^2/(.025)^2$

9 What is periodicity?
a the regular pattern of error falloff in a natural distribution, as determined by the central limit theorem
b error in systematic sampling due to the sampling pattern coinciding with a periodic pattern in the population
c error in stratified sampling when the strata being sampled exhibit a periodic pattern
d the necessity in sampling for using a periodic pattern in order to achieve a truly random sample

10 Why do researchers sometimes obtain unequal probabilities of element selection in multistage area sampling?
a because the probability of element selection varies with the inverse square root of the sample size
b because the different strata are selected according to demographic criteria, rather than a truly random sample, and therefore need to be adjusted accordingly
c because error can be reduced by sampling elements in more homogeneous groups, rather than strictly according to selection probability
d because elements in the early stage represent more or less of the population elements

Web Exercise

Log in to the Online Edition of your textbook at www.atomicdog.com to participate in this Web exercise, which can be found in your Online Study Guide for this chapter.

Further Reading

Cochran, William G. (1977), *Sampling Techniques*, 3rd edition. New York: John Wiley & Sons.

Larsen, Richard J., and Morris L. Marx (2005), *An Introduction to Mathematical Statistics and Its Applications*, 4th edition. Upper Saddle River, NJ: Prentice Hall.

Levy, Paul S., and Stanley Lemeshow (1999), *Sampling of Populations: Methods and Applications*. New York: John Wiley & Sons.

Thompson, Steven K. (2002), *Sampling*. New York: John Wiley & Sons.

Thompson, Steven K., and George A. F. Seber (1996), *Adaptive Sampling*. New York: John Wiley & Sons

APPENDIX 8: STATISTICAL CONCEPTS FOR MARKETING RESEARCH

Part A. Calculation of Population Parameters for Continuous Variables

As a way of clarifying the nature of sample statistics, we will calculate the parameters resulting from a census, which always refers to the entire population. We refer to the data from Table 8.2, a census including students' age and whether they elected to take a marketing research course. We note before starting that all measures in this section are easily obtained from any data analysis or spreadsheet program, and we encourage students to replicate these results using the program of their choice. Here we carry out calculations by hand, to emphasize the underlying concepts.

The first of these variables, age, is continuous. We can calculate measures of *central tendency* (the mean or average, μ) and *dispersion* (the variance, σ^2, or standard deviation, σ) for age as follows. The mean is simply the sum of the values divided by the number in the population. Thus,

$$\mu = \frac{\sum_{i=1}^{N} X_i}{N} = \frac{25 + 27 + \cdots + 18}{50} = \frac{1184}{50} = 23.68$$

So the average age in the class is 23.68.

The *variance* for a population is the sum of the squared deviations about the mean (the so-called "sum of squared errors") divided by the population size, N:

$$\sigma^2 = \frac{\sum_{i=1}^{N} (X_i - \mu)^2}{N}$$

These are reproduced numerically in the fourth and fifth columns of the table. Numerically, we have:

$$\begin{aligned} \sigma^2 &= \frac{(25 - 23.7)^2 + (27 - 23.7)^2 + \cdots + (18 - 23.7)^2}{50} \\ &= \frac{(1.3)^2 + (3.3)^2 + \cdots + (-5.7)^2}{50} = \frac{840.9}{50} \\ &= 16.82 \end{aligned}$$

The *standard deviation* is simply the square root of the variance, as follows:

$$\sigma = \sqrt{16.82} = 4.1$$

Calculation of Population Parameters for Dichotomous Variables

We can easily repeat these steps for the dichotomous variable, whether students elected to take a marketing research class. Yes is coded 1, and no is coded 0 (zero):

$$\pi = \frac{\sum_{i=1}^{N} X_i}{N} = \frac{1 + 0 + \cdots + 0}{50} = \frac{17}{50} = .34.$$

The proportion of the population electing marketing research is $\pi = 0.34$. The variance is:

$$\pi = \frac{\sum_{i=1}^{N} (X_i - \pi)^2}{N} = \frac{(1 - .34)^2 + (0 - .34)^2 + \cdots + (0 - .34)^2}{50}.$$

We note that $(1 - 0.34)^2$ occurs every time $X_2 = 1$, and this occurs 0.34 of the time. Also we note that $(0 - 0.34)^2$ occurs every time $X_2 = 0$, or 0.66 of the time. Thus, we can calculate the variance especially easily for dichotomous variables:

$$\sigma^2 = (1 - 0.34)^2(0.34) + (0 - 0.34)^2(0.66) = (0.66)^2(0.34) + (-.034)^2(0.66) = 0.2244$$

and

$$\sigma = \sqrt{.2244} = .473$$

Generally, we can render these as simple formulas:

$$\sigma^2 = \pi(1 - \pi) \text{ and } \sigma = \sqrt{\pi(1 - \pi)}.$$

This will be the only case in which it will not be necessary to calculate a variance! For dichotomous (i.e., binary) variables, once we know the mean, we will also know the variance; this is most certainly *not* the case when dealing with normally distributed variables, and generally speaking, we will have to calculate variances directly from the data.

Part B. The Sampling Distribution of the Mean and Statistical Inference: Basic Theory

In the text, we calculated the mean age of a sample we randomly selected from our student population. In order to evaluate the quality of an estimate of the population parameter, we must understand the theory of statistical inference.

For the sake of illustration, we set up a second student population, consisting of exactly five elements. Note that this is a very small population! We identify the students by the letters A, B, C, D, and E. Suppose we wish to select a single random sample of size $n = 2$ from this population. In this case, because there are so few population elements and the sample size is also modest, we can easily enumerate *all* possible samples, a daunting or impossible task in ordinary applications. A full list is as follows:

Sample Number	Elements in Sample
1	AB
2	AC
3	AD
4	AE
5	BC
6	BD
7	BE
8	CD
9	CE
10	DE

It may not be immediately obvious that this is a complete list, but there are exactly ten possible combinations of two elements from a population of five. Mathematically, we call this the number of all possible "combinations without replacement." The general expression for this is given by the following **combinatorial formula:**

combinatorial formula
A formula that specifies how many unique subsets of size *n* there are, taken from *N* distinct items. Formally, given by *N*!/*n*!(*N*-*n*)!, where *n*! is "n factorial." See *factorial*.

$$C_n^N = \binom{N}{n} - C(N, n)$$
$$= \frac{N!}{N!(N - n)!}$$

Here, $n!$ does not mean "*n*, emphatically," but rather something called "*n* **factorial**," all the numbers up through n multiplied together. So, in our example, $N - 5$ and $n = 2$; therefore

factorial
The product of all the integers from 1 to a given number, *n*, written *n*!.

$$C(5, 2) = \frac{5!}{2!3!} = \frac{5 \cdot 4 \cdot 3 \cdot 2 \cdot 1}{2 \cdot 1 \cdot 3 \cdot 2 \cdot 1} = \frac{20}{2} = 10$$

Each of the ten possible samples would yield an estimate of the mean of the population. Some would be better than others, that is, closer to the true population mean. The set of these ten elements constitutes what we would call the *sampling distribution*, all the values one could possibly get for an estimator (here, the sample mean) with elements drawn at random from the population. In practice, there would almost always be vastly more than ten such values, and we would turn to statistical theory to help determine the sampling distribution.

We now turn our attention back to the population of $N = 50$ students in Table 8.2. Previously we selected one sample of five from this population. The number of possible samples of this size (five) from this population is

$$\begin{aligned} C(50,5) &= \frac{50!}{5!45!} = \frac{(50 \cdot 49 \cdot \ldots \cdot 1)}{(5 \cdot 4 \cdot 3 \cdot 2 \cdot 1)(45 \cdot 44 \cdot \ldots \cdot 1)} \\ &= \frac{50 \cdot 49 \cdot 48 \cdot 47 \cdot 46}{5 \cdot 4 \cdot 3 \cdot 2 \cdot 1} = \frac{254,251,200}{120} \\ &= 2,118,760 \text{ possible samples} \end{aligned}$$

So, we have selected but one among the 2,118,760 possible samples of size $n = 5$. And this was with a population of size 50. Consider the number of possible samples from a realistic population of interest. For example, if there are 70 million voters in a presidential election and we select a sample of 1000, this sample is only one of C(70 million, 1000) possible samples.

$$C(70 \text{ million}, 1000) = \frac{70 \text{ million}}{1000!(70 \text{ million} - 1000)!} \approx 10^{5277}$$

Best guesses about the number of elementary particles in the universe hover around 10^{80}, so the number of possible samples we just calculated is literally unimaginably vast. The key point is that in any population, there are many possible samples—so many that for all intents and purposes, enumerating them explicitly is hopeless. A second crucial point is that classical statistical inference is based on what happens when we repeatedly select *different* samples from a population, or at least conceive of an experiment where one does so.

Previously, we did select one sample of $n = 5$ from our population, yielding a mean age of 22.6. Now, suppose we select another sample of $n = 5$ and calculate the mean. In this sample the mean might be 23.4 years. If we again repeat the process, we may get a third sample mean of 24.2 years. Seemingly, we have confused ourselves in that we now have three estimates of the population parameter! However, in statistical theory we would not stop at three samples; we could sample again and again, and in repeating this process we would note that certain values were more common than others. Specifically, we would note that sample means closer in value to the population mean tended to be better represented than those farther removed from the population mean. This should make intuitive sense: The average of a (randomly selected) *group* is unlikely to stray very far away from the average in the population. We could plot these values (for the sample means) using a frequency distribution graph, or **histogram**, and under very general conditions that nearly always hold in the real world, they would form the familiar bell-shaped (or normal) curve. This distribution of sample means is called, as stated earlier, the *sampling distribution of the mean*, or simply the *sampling distribution*. The sampling distribution is important for two reasons: (1) Values drawn from this distribution are distributed around the *population* mean in a known way; (2) using this distribution, we can determine how closely the sample statistics are distributed around the *population* parameter. Note that we know *nothing* about the population parameter itself! But we can still make strong, sharp, valid statements about how far away our estimate is. If this seems powerful, that is because it is; but if it seems magical, that is only because we have not rigorously derived it here. Any decent text on mathematical statistics will contain the relevant derivations and proofs, and the interested reader is invited to seek them out, as they are the crowning achievements of statistical theory and among the most beautiful of all mathematical results obtained in the two millennia since the ancient Greeks.

histogram
A bar chart of observed frequencies for some variable of interest. The heights of the bars indicate the proportion (or sometimes the raw number) of cases observed in each predetermined category or interval.

In order to capitalize on these benefits from the sampling distribution, we must formalize the nature of the sampling distribution of the mean. To do this we turn to the most important result in all of statistics, the central limit theorem, which states that for any measure of interest (such as the mean):

1. If the *population* distribution is normal, the sampling distribution of the mean will be normal for *all* sample sizes.
2. If the *population* distribution is nonnormal, the sampling distribution of the mean *approaches* normality as the sample size increases.

3. The mean of the *sampling distribution* (of the mean) is the *population* mean. Whenever the expected value of an estimator is the population quantity it hopes to estimate, the statistic is said to be *unbiased*. (Note that not all estimators are unbiased!)
4. The standard error of the sampling distribution (of the mean) is the *population* standard deviation divided by the square root of the sample size, $\sigma/\sqrt{n}$. In practice we do not know σ, so we estimate it with s, calculated from the one sample we do select. We express this as the *standard error of the sample mean*:

$$s_{\bar{X}} = \frac{s}{\sqrt{n}}$$

These four facts together tell us essentially everything we need to know about estimating means; and estimating means is by far the most common activity in statistical inference. Point (2) deserves special mention because, in essentially all real-world situations, we do not know that the population is precisely normally distributed, as would be required by (1). An analogous point can be made regarding (4), because we will, in practice, almost never know the *true* population standard deviation. Think for a moment how odd it would be for someone to say, "Can you help us estimate the population mean? We just happen to know that the population is exactly normally distributed, and we also know the population standard deviation." In practical applications, we do not know much about the overall population distribution, and we will have very little knowledge of its standard deviation.

There is one other aspect about a normal curve that will be extremely helpful in putting all this theory to work. This aspect relates to the area under various regions of the normal distribution. Recall that the area under *any* distribution, not only a normal one, is 1, exactly; other regions will therefore have areas between 0 and 1 and can be construed as probabilities. Figure 8.5 shows a normal curve with an amount of area contained within different standard deviations from the mean. Specifically, we note that

1. approximately 68 percent of cases lie within ±1 standard deviation of the mean (a more exact value is 68.27 percent)
2. approximately 95 percent percent of cases lie within ±2 standard deviations of the mean (a more exact value is 95.45 percent)
3. approximately 99.7 percent of cases lie within ±3 standard deviations from the mean (an extremely precise estimate is that 2.7 out of a thousand cases will lie outside this region).

With all these requisite pieces of theory in place, we can now evaluate how good our *sample* mean is as an estimate of the *population* mean.

Figure 8.5 Area Under the Normal Curve

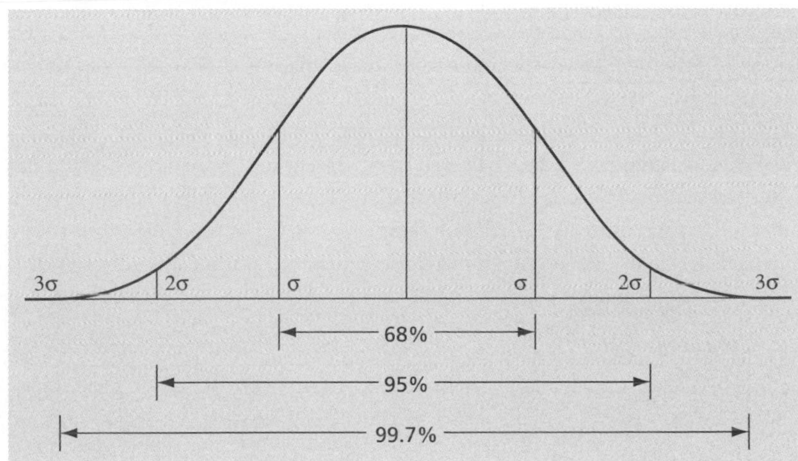

Part C. Statistical Concepts for More Complex Sampling Procedures: Calculation of Sample Statistics within Strata

In Section 8.5c through g of this chapter, we calculated the mean, the variance, and the standard deviation of the total sample without stratification. Recall that:

$$\bar{X} = 22.6 \qquad s^2 = 8.3 \qquad \text{and} \qquad s = 2.88$$

Let us perform the relevant calculations for the mean, variance, and standard deviation for each stratum. For stratum 1,

$$\bar{X}_{st.1} = \frac{\sum_{i=1}^{n_{st.1}} X_i}{n_{st.1}} = \frac{25 + 26}{2} = 25.5$$

To find $s^2_{st.1}$, we calculate

$$\sum X^2_{st.1} = (25)^2 + (26)^2 = 1301$$

and

$$\frac{(\sum X_{st.1})^2}{n_{st.1}} = \frac{(51)^2}{2} = \frac{2601}{2} = 1300.5$$

$$s^2_{st.1} = \frac{1301 - 1300.5}{n_{st.1} - 1} = .5$$

$$s_{st.1} = .71$$

Analogously, for stratum 2,

$$\bar{X}_{st.2} = \frac{22 + 21 + 19}{3} = 20.7$$

$$\sum X^2_{st.2} = (22)^2 + (21)^2 + (19)^2 = 1286$$

$$\frac{(\sum X_{st.2})^2}{n_{st.2}} = \frac{(62)^2}{3} = 1281.3$$

$$s^2_{st.2} = \frac{1286 - 1281.3}{n_{st.2} - 1} = 2.35$$

$$s_{st.2} = 1.53$$

Part D. Statistical Aspects of Stratified Samples: The Number of Possible Samples

The sampling fraction in stratum 1 was $\frac{2}{20} = 0.1$, and in stratum 2 it was $\frac{3}{30} = 0.1$. Both of these sampling fractions are identical to the sample we selected earlier in the chapter, $\frac{5}{50} = 0.1$. Under both stratified and unstratified procedures, each population element had an equal chance, 0.1, of being selected. However, with stratified sampling, *not all possible combinations of elements are equally likely*. To illustrate, we will use a population of elements identified as A, B, C, D, and E, which earlier (Appendix, Part B) had yielded ten possible simple random samples of size 2. Now, assume that elements A and B are from one stratum, and C, D, and E are from another. Again we wish to draw a sample of $n = 2$, but this time we restrict the sample to one element from each stratum. The possible sample element from stratum 1 is either A or B, and within stratum 2 it is C, D, or E. Combining possible elements from each stratum, we get the possible samples:

Sample Number	Elements in Sample
1	AC
2	AD
3	AE

Sample Number	Elements in Sample
4	BC
5	BD
6	BE

Note that there are six possible samples with stratification, but ten without. The possible samples that have been eliminated are those that could occur within one stratum before; for example, AB and CD are no longer possible as samples. Note that it is these within-strata means that are the **outliers** of our distribution of means in simple random sampling. To illustrate this result, we may assign scores to these population elements as follows:

outliers
An observation whose value is very different from others collected (or what would be expected, based on a statistical model), so much so that the researcher must decide whether to remove it to mitigate its influence

Element	Score
Stratum 1	
A	1
B	2
Stratum 2	
C	3
D	4
E	5

The mean of this distribution of scores is $15/5 = 3.0$. The possible stratified samples of size $n = 2$ are

Sample Elements	Sample Mean
AC	$(1 + 3)/2 = 2.0$
AD	$(1 + 4)/2 = 2.5$
AE	$(1 + 5)/2 = 3.0$
BC	$(2 + 3)/2 = 2.5$
BD	$(2 + 4)/2 = 3.0$
BE	$(2 + 5)/2 = 3.5$

Note that these sample means cluster reasonably tightly about the true mean of 3.0. Let us now examine the mean values generated by samples that are *not* allowed to occur in this example of stratified sampling, that is, those in which both elements are taken from the same stratum. These means are

Sample Elements	Sample Mean
Stratum 1	
AB	$(1 + 2)/2 = 1.5$
Stratum 2	
CD	$(3 + 4)/2 = 3.5$
CE	$(3 + 5)/2 = 4.0$
DE	$(4 + 5)/2 = 4.5$

These means are less well clustered about the mean of 3.0, that is, they are the outliers on the distribution of means. Although this is not always guaranteed to be the case when using stratified sampling, it will usually occur if the strata are well selected (that is, using criteria relevant to the research project).

In our example involving age, we get means such as 26 or 27 (and so on) in stratum 1, or 20 or 21 in stratum 2. These types of means are not as likely when we combine elements from different strata, as we do when we estimate the means with a stratified procedure. Removal of some outliers in stratified sampling would thus *decrease the variability* of the distribution of sample means. That is, the standard error becomes smaller. And, as we have emphasized throughout this chapter, reducing standard error allows for tighter control, stronger statements, and better predictability in all statistical applications.

That not all combinations of elements are equally likely is one aspect that distinguishes stratified sampling from simple random sampling. Note that we can easily calculate the number of possible samples with stratification, as it is the product of the number of all possible samples within each stratum. For instance, in our example, the formula with two strata is:

$$\begin{aligned}\text{Number of possible samples} &= C(N,n)_{st.1} \times C(N,n)_{st.1}\\ &= C(2,\ 1) \times C(3,\ 1)\\ &= \frac{2!}{1!\ 1!} \times \frac{3!}{1!\ 2!}\\ &= 2 \times 3 = 6.\end{aligned}$$

In our student age example, the number of possible samples with stratification is

$$\begin{aligned}C(20,2)\cdot C(30,3) &= \frac{20!}{2!18!}\cdot\frac{30!}{3!27!}\\ &= \frac{20\cdot 19}{2\cdot 1}\cdot\frac{30\cdot 29\cdot 28}{3\cdot 2\cdot 1}\\ &= 190\cdot 4{,}060\\ &= 771{,}400 \text{ possible samples.}\end{aligned}$$

Earlier in the chapter, we noted that there were more than 2 million possible simple random samples of size 5 in a population of 50; specifically, C(2, 1) = 2,118,760. The number of possible samples has decreased substantially, although it is still very large. And if the strata are well chosen, the possibilities that have been omitted are those that are most likely to be outliers. So, the standard error will be smaller than with simple random sampling, as we previously noted in our calculations. We stress yet again that the central limit theorem holds, so that the sampling distribution of the means of these samples will come very close to a normal curve. Thus, we can again calculate a legitimate confidence interval.

CASES FOR PART TWO

CASE 2.1 J.D. POWER AND ASSOCIATES AND THE CUSTOMER SATISFACTION INDEX

J.D. Power and Associates has made a name for itself in the field of surveying customer satisfaction. It conducts independent syndicated research, to assess how well industries are meeting the needs of their customers, and reports the data in the form of attributes, factors, and overall satisfaction. In general, customer satisfaction research seeks to establish benchmarks that gauge quality and customer satisfaction in an industry and to reveal where companies are doing well and where they need improvement. J.D. Power and Associates conducts such research on diverse industries, including automotive, telecommunications, real estate, and healthcare.

J.D. Power and Associates is widely considered an authoritative voice in the automotive industry; its automobile reviews and rankings involve evaluations of vehicles around the globe, according to measures of Initial Quality Study (ICS), Sales Satisfaction Index (SSI), Automotive Performance, Execution and Layout (APEAL), Consumer Financing Satisfaction Study (CFS), Tire Customer Satisfaction Study (TCS), and the most well-known—the Customer Satisfaction Index (CSI). (Note that the CSI is distinct from the American Consumer Satisfaction Index.)

J.D. Power's CSI examines customer satisfaction with vehicle quality and dealer service at 12 to 18 months of ownership. Performance factors considered in the index are problems experienced, service adviser, service performance, service timing, and facility appearance. In 2005, CSI performed a survey of more than 23,000 people published in *What Car?* magazine. Car owners completed an eight-page survey with more than 70 questions, covering their likes and dislikes about their car, any problems encountered with the car, and the cost and quality of available service from dealers. The survey covered all segments of the automobile market, including 124 models ranging from super-mini cars to four-by-four vehicles. To help mitigate sampling bias, the survey excluded any car for which fewer than 50 complete surveys were received.

The survey included a rated scale from 1 to 10, where 1 meant "unacceptable" and 10 meant "outstanding." These rankings were then used to calculate J.D. Power's Customer Satisfaction Index by incorporating the results into scores in eight categories:

1. Mechanical: Satisfaction with the reliability of the car's engine, suspension, transmission, and braking systems.
2. Interior: Satisfaction with the seats, heating, air-conditioning and ventilation, sound systems, dashboard, and interior.
3. Exterior: Satisfaction related to body panels, paint (any rust or corrosion), and exterior lights.
4. Performance: Satisfaction with the car's ride, handling, braking, engine, and transmission.
5. Interior: Satisfaction with the cabin's comfort and practicality, seats, dashboard, sound system and heating, ventilation and air conditioning.
6. Exterior: Satisfaction with the car's styling.
7. Dealer Service: Satisfaction with the performance of the franchised dealer network, from the ease of booking service to the competence of the service department at diagnosing and rectifying faults.
8. Ownership Costs: Owners' perceptions of value for money when fueling, insuring, and servicing the car.

After taking every aspect of the car into account, weighting reliability and vehicle quality most heavily, then vehicle appeal and dealer service, the car was given an overall score, in the form of a percentage and an overall rating.

Although such ratings are very influential, some automotive manufacturers and auto critics are concerned that certain quality rankings in the CSI index are not reflective of the actual vehicle quality; for example, a Mini was "dinged" for having small cup-holders. Another criticism is that a measure of satisfaction should distinguish between customer expectations of attributes and overall satisfaction, and between the actual customer experience with these attributes and perceptions of satisfaction, and should allow customers to make trade-offs among car attributes to determine which attributes were the most important to them.

Case Questions

1 What are the measurement scale characteristics of the customer satisfaction measure as described by the researchers? How could the weighting of different aspects of satisfaction potentially skew the overall rating? What precautions might help to avoid this?

2 How should the reliability and validity of this customer satisfaction measure be assessed or calculated? Do you think these can be assessed accurately?

3 What alternative methods could be used to measure customer satisfaction? Consider in particular the criticisms of potential deficiencies of the measure being used. Be specific and place your examples in the context of the present case.

4 As it stands, data on numerous questions, from thousands of respondents, are compressed into eight categories. Do these categories seem coherent? How might one go about processing this large volume of data rigorously into eight, or any of number of, dimensions or categories? Are the resulting dimensions supposedly *independent* of one another? Should they be?

5 What use should be made of the demographic and car description data that were collected? Is there a way, perhaps via statistical methods, than they can be incorporated?

6 How might trade-off data on attributes, which yield the importance of each attribute in forming overall satisfaction, be useful to automotive managers?

Sources: J.D. Power and Associates (www.jdpower.com)
WhatCar? (www.whatcar.com)

CASE 2.2 MAINLINE PACKAGE GOODS

Ken Gibbs was the recently promoted product manager for Ice-Away, a windshield de-icer marketed by Mainline Package Goods. Windshield de-icers are sprayed on car windows to instantly melt ice and frost. As brand manager, Gibbs was responsible for all marketing decisions related to Ice-Away. He was currently preparing Ice-Away's marketing plan for the next fiscal year and had to submit the finalized version to his boss in two weeks. Two major changes in package design had been test-marketed by Research Design, Inc. (RDI), and Gibbs was in the process of reviewing the results. The field experiment was designed to measure the effects of different packaging on consumer attitudes and on sales of Ice-Away.

Mainline was a thriving packaged goods firm, marketing everything from floor wax to over-the-counter drugs. Ice-Away held a strong position in its product category, windshield de-icers, with annual sales of $20 million and profits of $2.5 million. Ice-Away first entered the market in 1990, and by 1995 it was a recognized brand, mostly due to intensive advertising and retail promotion. Ice-Away's main competition came from the other major brands on the market—Snowflake, No-Frost, and Melt It! All these brands were about the same price as Ice-Away and had equivalent distribution at retail. For the past 3 years, Ice-Away had been losing market share to the competition, and Gibbs was convinced that poor packaging was the reason.

Ice-Away's package, a metal aerosol can, had not materially changed since 1990. When the competition changed to nonaerosol containers, Ice-Away retained the same packaging, and it was then that Ice-Away's market share began to decline. Mainline's R&D department had come up with two alternatives to the metal aerosol can: first, a nonaerosol plastic container that utilized a pump mechanism to expel the de-icer, and second, a nonaerosol metal can that had an aerosol-like spray. On the front of the metal version, the words "NEW NONAEROSOL FORMULA" were printed in large letters to ensure that consumers would note the difference between new and old packages. The $50,000 RDI study examined the effects of the two new package designs on sales and consumer attitudes. The research report submitted by RDI follows.

The Research Report

Objectives

1. To test the relative effectiveness of alternative package designs for Ice-Away
2. To recommend the best design

Packaging Tested

1. Metal aerosol can (control market)
2. Plastic nonaerosol pump
3. Metal nonaerosol can

The price was the same for all three alternatives.

Test Markets Used

The three cities used were selected to be as similar as possible with respect to (1) the distribution penetration of Ice-Away and its three major competitors, and (2) the economic characteristics listed in Table C2.2.1.

The metal aerosol can was tested in Newark, the metal nonaerosol can in Denver, and the plastic pump in Cleveland.

Data Collection Method

The data were collected by means of telephone interviews. Samples were chosen randomly from phone books in each of the three cities. To qualify for the questionnaire, a respondent had to be a user of windshield de-icer. The realized sample sizes were: Newark, 300; Cleveland, 297; and Denver 501. The following purchase measures were taken:

- brand of de-icer usually purchased
- brand of de-icer last purchased
- brand of de-icer the respondent intended to purchase next

Attitude measures were taken on convenience (versus scraping the windows), effectiveness in melting ice, speed in de-icing, aesthetic appeal of the package, ease in using the package, and frequency of use. Respondents were asked to rate each attribute on a seven-point scale, with a 1 indicating the lowest attitude measure and a 7 the highest.

Timing

The new package designs were introduced in December, and interviewing was done in March.

Results

Selected tables from the report appear in Tables C2.2.2 and C2.2.3.

Table C2.2.1 Economic Characteristics of Test Market Cities

	Newark	Cleveland	Denver
Population	274,000	478,000	555,000
Households	91,000	191,000	240,000
Effective buying income per household	$ 27,000	$ 26,000	$ 40,000
Retail sales index*	105	99	106

*National base of 100.

Table C2.2.2 Economic Characteristics of Test Market Cities

	Newark %	Cleveland %	Denver %
Brand usually purchased			
Ice-Away	12	10	17*
Snowflake	11	9	10
No-Frost	14	11	9
Melt It!	9	8	12*
Brand last purchased			
Ice-Away	11	11	15*
Snowflake	11	9	9
No-Frost	12	10	10
Melt It!	7	10*	13*

*Significant difference from control at $p < .05$.

Table C2.2.3 Attitude Measures

	Ice-Away			Snowflake			No-Frost			Melt It!		
Attributes	N	C	D	N	C	D	N	C	D	N	C	D
Convenience	5.4	5.6	5.5	5.5	5.8	5.6	5.8	5.1	5.4	5.5	4.9	4.6
Effectiveness melting ice	6.0	6.5*	6.0	5.9	6.0	5.8	5.7	5.8	5.6	5.2	5.0	5.7*
Speed in deicing	5.9	6.1	5.8	6.0	5.8	6.1	5.4	5.8	5.1	5.7	5.9	6.0
Package appeal	6.2	6.1	6.4	6.0	6.0	6.0	5.2	5.0	4.9	5.1	5.2	5.0
Ease in using package	4.2	5.1	4.6	4.1	4.4	4.2	4.0	3.9	4.1	3.7	3.6	4.1
Frequency of use	4.5	4.0*	5.1*	4.9	4.9	4.8	4.7	4.9	4.7	4.9	4.5	4.6

Note: N = Newark (metal aerosol)
C = Cleveland (plastic pump)
D = Denver (metal nonaerosol)

*Significant difference from control at $p < 0.05$.

Recommendations

Ken Gibbs wanted to analyze the data himself before initiating a packaging change. If his analysis of the data did not lead to the same conclusions as the RDI analysis, Gibbs planned to adopt the package he felt was best, and to this end he began to review the data.

Case Questions

1. Evaluate the experimental design used by Mainline Package Goods. Be sure to discuss the validity of the experiment.
2. Do you feel the design can be improved? If yes, indicate how you would do so. Be specific.
3. Are the statistical analyses performed appropriate? Were they carried out correctly? Should multiple tests be done on the same data set, for example, on the numerous attitude measurements, all with the .05 level of significance? (Consider, for example, if there were thousands of such tests.)
4. What conclusions can be drawn from the study? What action would you recommend if you were in Ken Gibbs's position? What follow-up studies, if any, would you plan, either to enhance the results already obtained, or to correct defects in the original study design?

Sources: 2000 U.S. Census (www.census.gov)
Area Connect (www.areaconnect.com)

CASE 2.3 COCA-COLA RECALL IN EUROPE

In 1999, after 70 years of sales of Coca-Cola in Belgium, the country banned the soft drink. This ban came about due to multiple reports of head and stomach pain experienced by Coca-Cola drinkers. Dozens of schoolchildren were hospitalized, and Coca-Cola subsequently recalled 15 million cans and bottles. The company advanced several possible explanations, including a fungicide contamination and a problem with the carbon dioxide used to give Coke its distinctive fizz.

France and Luxembourg quickly reacted by banning Coke in those countries as well. In the United Kingdom, Coke sales had not yet recovered from a scandal in which double the allowable amount of benzene was found in carbon dioxide used by Coca-Cola. The company's reputation in Europe was in serious danger. The product management team was under intense pressure to determine a course of action to resolve the quality assurance problems and save the brand's image. The team first asked for a test to demonstrate that the amount of contaminants (e.g., benzene) in the carbon dioxide used by Coke was well below the allowable levels; they wished to use the results of the test to reassure the public that Coke was safe to drink.

Case Questions

1 Prepare an experimental design that would allow management to determine the level of contaminants in Coke. Be sure to clearly identify test units, dependent variables, treatments, methods for control of extraneous variables, timing of measurements taken, selection of test units, and assignment of test units to treatments.

2 Display your design using the *R, O,* and *X* symbols of experimental design.

3 Given brand management's statement of purpose for the research, how should Coke's marketing researchers state the objective for the research?

Sources: "Belgium Bans Coca-Cola." *BBC News*, June 14, 1999.
"Latest News: Leading Soft Drinks Withdrawn." *BBC News*, June 1, 1998.
Summary of Coca-Cola Quality Assurance Procedures.

CASE 2.4 KELLOGG'S ALL-BRAN CEREAL BRAND

According to the American Heart Association, 50 percent of middle-aged Americans have cholesterol levels greater than 200 milligrams per deciliter of blood. This is the level at which the risk of heart attack begins to rise "sharply." Moreover, an average of three Americans will suffer a heart attack every minute of the day.

Dietary intake is thought to play a significant role in these conditions. Studies have shown that populations with high-fiber diets have a lower incidence of coronary heart disease and colon cancer. There are two types of fiber: water-insoluble and water-soluble. Both are found in cereals, fruits, vegetables, dried peas, and beans. Although insoluble fiber may help reduce the risk of colon cancer, research suggests that eating 10 to 15 grams of soluble fiber per day in a low-fat diet can lower elevated blood cholesterol levels. Research has identified the grain psyllium as one of the best sources of water-soluble fiber. Kellogg developed its All-Bran psyllium cereal brand high in fiber in response to these claims.

A University of Kentucky study found that men on a high-fat diet lowered their elevated cholesterol levels by 15 percent after taking a psyllium formula three times a day for 2 months. The University of Minnesota decided to investigate the effect of using psyllium as an adjunct to a low-fat diet. This study formed the basis for the previous claims. In executing the psyllium study, scientists set up the following experiment:

The study involved 75 patients (38 male and 37 female) with mild to moderate levels of high cholesterol. All participants had to meet certain requirements. They were between the ages of 24 and 68 and had cholesterol levels (adjusted for age and sex) between the 50th and 90th percentile. Candidates were further screened on the basis of a list of medical conditions, their body weight as a percentage of ideal, and the absence of certain prescription drugs in their bloodstream. All participants were required to maintain constant body weights (plus or minus 5 percent) during the study.

The experiment was a study in which subjects were randomly assigned to test groups, it was double-blind in that neither the subjects nor the doctors knew which group the subjects had been assigned to, and it had a placebo control group. The study lasted 20 weeks and was conducted in three stages. The 12 weeks before the implementation of the experimental treatment are designated as minus (−) weeks. After their initial visit, patients were given 6 weeks (weeks 12 to 7) to adapt to a step 1 diet (30 percent fat, 55 percent carbohydrates, 15 percent protein, and a maximum of 300 milligrams of dietary cholesterol). Participants were screened at the end of 6 weeks, and those who were likely to meet the entry criteria continued their diets for an additional 6 weeks (weeks 6 to 0). After 12 weeks of regulated dieting, they were screened again, and those who met the study's qualifications were randomized into two treatment groups and given their "medication."

One treatment group was given active medication, and the other group received a placebo. The active medication was orange-flavored sugar-free Metamucil, which contains psyllium. The placebo was an identical product, except that it contained an inert bulk fiber instead of psyllium. Identical doses of each product were given to each participant in matching foil packets. Participants were to take their medication in eight ounces of water before each of their three meals each day. Adherence to instructions was monitored with patient interviews and by keeping track of unopened packets returned to the clinic at each visit.

Participants were evaluated at weeks 2, 4, 6, 7, and 8. Clinic visits were scheduled in the morning, after participants had not eaten for 12 hours. Various parameters were measured each time. Body weight, blood pressure, and pulse rate were measured at every visit. A complete lipid profile and a clinical chemistry screening were conducted on predetermined visits. Patients kept food records, which were analyzed by the Nutrition Coordinating Center every 8 weeks. To further monitor dietary adherence, a registered dietician also evaluated food frequency records at five different points throughout the study.

Various analytical methods were used to determine the effects of the active medication containing psyllium. Blood samples were collected and several medical tests were run to measure the levels of various lipids and proteins, as well as the participants' cholesterol levels. Researchers used several statistical methods to further analyze the results. They calculated baseline values as the average body weight, blood pressure, and lipid values for weeks 4, 2 and 0. Posttreatment baseline values were calculated as the average for weeks 6, 7, and 8. Scientists calculated the differences from the baseline at each evaluation, and the treatment groups were compared by analysis of variance and a rank sum test. They assessed the significance from baseline by paired-*t* test and Wilcoxon signed-rank tests.

Results for the two study groups were measured and analyzed. Both groups were well-matched according to sex, age, weight, and dietary intake at baseline. Both groups also had similar baseline cholesterol levels. After 8 weeks, the group receiving the psyllium product showed a 4.8 percent reduction in total cholesterol levels relative to placebo values, and 4.2 percent reduction relative to baseline values. The psyllium treatment had no significant effect on body weight, blood pressure, serum levels of glucose and iron, or the levels of several key proteins. (Ninety-one percent of the psyllium participants and 95.4 percent of the placebo participants complied with the study's guidelines.)

Case Questions

1. Identify the test units, dependent variable(s), independent variable(s), treatments, sources of extraneous variation, methods of obtaining control, timing of measurements, selection of test units, and assignment of test units to treatments.
2. Evaluate the internal and external validity of this study. Which, if any, would give pause to medical researchers? Which might be of concern to the cereal manufacturer? To a potential consumer considering trying the product for the first time?
3. Has the study been set up in a way to allow reasonably powerful statistical analysis? Consider in particular the demographics of the participants, the measures taken on each, the overall sample size, and the time frame for the study. Which among these (or other aspects of the study) seems most in need of improvement? How might you go about doing so?
4. Is it a proper use of this research to make health claims for All-Bran cereal? Why or why not? If not, what sort of claims might be ethically reasonable, given the course of research?

Sources: Bell LP, K Hectorne, H Reynolds, TK Balm, DB Hunninghake (1989), "Cholesterol-Lowering Effects of Psyllium Hydrophilic Mucilloid." *Journal of the American Medical Association,* 3419–3423.

www.kelloggs.com

Olson, Beth, Salle M. Anderson, et al., (1997), "Psyllium-Enriched Cereals Lower Blood Total Cholesterol and LDL Cholesterol, but Not HDL Cholesterol, in Hypercholesterolemic Adults: Results of a Meta-Analysis." *The Journal of Nutrition*, 127(10), 1973–1980.

"Psyllium: Role in a Heart-Healthy Diet." Kellogg Canada, 1998.

CASE 2.5 ADVENTURES UNLIMITED CORPORATION

Barbra Lott, vice president of marketing for Adventures Unlimited Corporation, a leading manufacturer in the recreational vehicle (RV) market, was approached by Paul Ransom, Adventures Unlimited's president and chief executive officer. Ransom, sensitive to continuing developments in the RV market, was concerned whether Adventures Unlimited's strategy of concentrating on the motor home and travel trailer segments of the RV market was still sound.*

Ransom came across two studies that supported the booming prospects of the RV market. According to a University of Michigan/Recreation Vehicle Industry Association study, RV ownership has reached record levels, and was expected to outpace the overall household growth. Additionally, an industry analysis conducted by Crowe Capital Markets LLC, a Chicago-based boutique investment bank, forecasted a solid road ahead, with bullish sales increase, for the RV industry.

The RV industry has experienced a pattern of continued growth as the baby boom generation (born between 1946 and 1964) ages. With more free time and income at its disposal, baby boomers have a higher rate of ownership of recreational vehicles than any other segment of the population. Low interest rates in financing purchases have further stimulated the growth of the industry, as have the cost savings in traveling by RV (between 30 and 80 percent) relative to average vacation costs.

Considering the projected positive outlook for the RV industry, Ransom wanted to ensure that Adventures Unlimited didn't miss this opportunity to emerge as a leader in its segment. Ransom recalled that the Crowe Capital study mentioned that the trends in the RV industry were expected to mirror those in the auto industry, with larger manufacturers continuing to garner increased market share through internal expansion and acquisition. Indeed, the past 10 years have seen a wave of consolidation within the industry.

Given the company's strong cash position, Ransom told Lott that she should analyze, from a marketing perspective, whether Adventures Unlimited should expand into other RV markets and/or vertically integrate forward or backward in the RV supplier-manufacturer-distributor chain. If so, Ransom said, he knew of two companies that could be purchased. The first company, American Camper, was a respected, medium-sized manufacturer of campers. The second company, Michigan-based Spartan Motors, was a manufacturer of custom chassis for motor homes and emergency vehicles.

Lott recognized the need for marketing research as part of the process of addressing these strategic questions. She first talked with her assistant, Joel Christopherson, about the situation. Christopherson was a recent graduate of a leading business school and had solid training in the area of marketing research. After thoroughly discussing the decision situation, Lott and Christopherson formulated the following statement:

> *Management objective:* To expand Adventures Unlimited's long-term profitability by entering new market segments within the RV market and/or by integrating forward or backward in the RV business.

The RV market segments were clearly defined as those of (1) travel trailers, (2) motor homes, (3) slide-in campers, and (4) RV accessories. Given the current alternatives of purchasing American Camper and/or Spartan Motors, it was decided to concentrate initial effort on the camper segment

---

*The RV market comprises motor homes (motor vehicle combined with living unit), travel trailers (living unit pulled by car or truck), campers (living unit sits in bed of truck), and accessories (sundry items purchased for RV vehicles).

(American Camper) and backward integration to a chassis supplier (Spartan Motors). Christopherson was directed to develop a written proposal for research directed at evaluating this issue within 3 days.

Returning to his office, Christopherson decided that his first steps were to formulate clear research objectives and to specify in detail the information needed. The more he investigated the situation, the more he recognized that very little was known about the camper segment or the chassis aspect of the RV business in general.

Christopherson believed that a two-stage research program was needed. The first stage would be exploratory research designed to better understand the camper owner and importance of RV chassis. Is the reason for buying a camper different from that for buying a motor home? What are the problems with campers? What are the important considerations in purchasing a camper? Is the chassis an important feature in buying an RV? Are there opportunities for product improvement? It seemed important to find out about questions of this nature before a more formal research program could be formulated. The second stage could involve large-scale telephone or personal interviews with RV owners.

Focus group interviews appeared to be the best choice for the exploratory research phase. Of immediate concern were the many details involved in designing a focus group study. Among the most important were:

- How should the respondents be selected?
- What gender breakdown was reasonable? Should a variety of age groups participate?
- Should one concentrate on families, or include singles and childless couples as well?
- How experienced should the respondents be, in terms of their prior use of RVs and similar products?
- Should one concentrate primarily on recent purchasers or so-called "lifetime owners"?
- How many people should be in a session, how many sessions should there be, how long should the sessions run, and where should they be held?
- Who should conduct (moderate) the sessions? Should the sessions be taped?
- Should a company representative be in the room, to answer tough questions?
- What issues and specific questions need to be included on the interviewer's question guide?

Case Questions

1. Evaluate Lott's decision to concentrate efforts on the camper segment and backward integration into the chassis production in order to achieve the formulated management objective. Discuss the shortcomings and the advantages of such an approach. Does any particular alternative seem superior, either at this stage or perhaps later in the decision process? What information would you need to evaluate these alternatives relative to the ones chosen?
2. Evaluate Christopherson's assessment for a need of a two-stage research program and his proposal to use focus groups for the exploratory phase and large scale interviews for the more detailed phase. Are these methods appropriate, given Adventure Unlimited's overall goals and plans? What specific methods would you recommend for each phase and why?
3. Design the focus group study and the respective interview guide. What are the issues that Christopherson should consider when developing the focus group study's design? Are there any potential informational pitfalls or likely deficiencies?
4. How could the findings from the focus group study during the early phase of the research best be used in the second phase? Provide specific details. What additional research might be necessary to best integrate the two phases? Is there some external data that might be particularly helpful?
5. Design the interview questionnaire for the second phase of the research. Use the scales that you believe are most appropriate for each question and explain your choices.
6. What could be the potential sources of errors in the research design and implementation? What might be done to help avoid or at least mitigate these errors? Place all examples in the context of the current case.
7. There could be positive and negative consequences from entering new market segments and/or forward/backward integrating the current business. Incremental sales and a greater market share are the examples of the positive effects; cannibalization of the existing business is an example of the negative effects. How could research be used to determine all such (foreseeable) possible and negative effects, and to project their extent in case of expansion/integration? Design specific questions that would help forecast the

impact of one positive and one negative effect, as well as the statistical methods that might help with forecasting.

Sources: "Spartan Motors CEO Pilots RV on Cross Country Analyst Roadshow." PR Newswire, May 9, 2005. "Study Shows a Solid Road Ahead for the RV Industry." *RV News* 28(8), March 2003.

CASE 2.6 e-REWARDS

Founded in 1999, e-Rewards touts itself as "the revolutionary program that pays you to read e-mail," an attractive proposition since taken up by a consumer panel more than 1.6 million strong. Once enrolled, panelists receive personally relevant e-messages containing special promotional offers. Participants can earn "e-Rewards" by reading and reacting to these messages, without needing to provide any follow-up or purchase information.

Key elements of the e-Rewards business model are knowledge of consumer-level demographics and consumer behavior profiles; panelists complete a survey detailing their interests and purchase plans, and this information is used to select targeted e-messages. Responding can be lucrative, with some offers paying up to $1 in e-Rewards, redeemable for a variety of merchandise of the panelist's choosing. Even more e-Reward funds can be earned by filling out surveys, evaluating new products and services, or participating in "e-Rewards events." For example, the company offers the following payout breakdown example for one of its offers:

Action	e-Rewards
Receive e-mail from e-Rewards	$0.05
Click from e-mail to e-Offer	$0.05
Read the e-Offer	$0.25
Rate the e-Offer	$0.30
Complete the survey at the end of e-Offer	$0.35

Joining e-Rewards is free, but only by invitation, creating an aura of exclusivity, although in theory nearly anyone older than 18 and residing in the United States or its territories can participate. The company practices what is often called "incentive compatibility": the more interests panelists list, the more opportunities they have to build up e-credits in the system. Although this cache of accumulated information on individual-level longitudinal consumer demographics, interests, attitudes and actions is exceptionally valuable, e-Rewards vows never to pass along information on individual customers to third parties.

Panels and Recruitment

Via the tag line "Panels that perform," e-Rewards advertises two of the most powerful online panels available to researchers, the e-Rewards Consumer™ Panel and the e-Rewards for Business™ Panel, as well as a host of specialty panels tailored to meet specific, lower-incidence client needs. The consumer panel has more than 1.6 million consumers, a virtual cross-section of the North American population, with a higher degree of geodemographic representativeness than other industry vendors. They attribute their geodemographically diverse panel to their panel recruitment techniques: partnering with large, well-respected global companies, "invitation only" recruiting, using a controlled mix of both online (e.g., solo e-mail invitations) and offline methods (e.g., physical postcard invitations, direct mail inserts, etc.). In particular, using invitations has allowed e-Rewards to influence the demographic make-up of its panel up-front, *before* a panelist joins; invitations are made to consumer segments currently underrepresented in the panel, helping to normalize it to the population as a whole. A specific advantage of this is that the number of "professional respondents"—those who join solely to make as much as possible without inputting useful information—can be minimized.

e-Rewards learns a great deal about those panelists who choose to join. Each completes a 300+ item member profile, including information about demographics, interests, life events, health ailments, various product purchase intent data, and more. Key consumer profile dimensions include:

- Areas of personal interest
- Recent and future purchases, life events

- Medical ailments
- Political activity, affiliation, and so forth
- Home and car ownership, travel and investment activity
- Internet and phone activity (usage, frequency, and brand data)
- Online shopping activity
- Full geodemographics: Age, gender, marital status, education, number and age of children, ZIP code, income, ethnicity/race, and so forth

In addition, clients can select the following options:

- Ability to normalize sample by geography, age, gender, income, and so forth
- Health care topics, including medical conditions
- Recent purchase decisions and future intent for major purchases, including homes, automobiles, appliances, among others
- Upcoming life events, including children starting college, retirement, change of marital status, and so forth

Perhaps even more lucrative than their consumer panel is e-Rewards' business panel, which includes more than 900,000 professionals across the United States and Canada. One issue bedeviling other survey research purveyors is the notorious difficulty in getting professionals to respond, yet e-Rewards has consistently achieved a 25 percent response rate among their business panelists. Business professionals provide extensive business-related information, including their occupation, title, functional role, industry, company size, and purchase decision-making role for more than 20 product/service categories. Key business profile dimensions include:

- Job title
- Functional role
- Company size (number of employees and annual revenue)
- Industry segment
- Health care segmentation (doctors, nurses, and other health care professionals)
- Purchasing involvement, both as decision-maker and influencer (both product and service categories)
- Business type and tenure
- Number of direct and indirect reports

e-Rewards certainly offers an innovative information-rich source to its clients, one that appears to be free of many of the artifacts plaguing traditional online research vendors.

Case Questions

1. e-Rewards collects an enormous variety of individual variables, and attempts to categorize them in several concrete ways. Do you believe these are the most effective? Can you think of additional ways to "segment" these many variables into groupings meaningful to different client types?
2. A main selling point for e-Rewards' methodology is "balance": that they can exert an unusual degree of control over who joins the panel. Can one simply not use re-weighting of underrepresented segments, or other regression-based statistical methods, to achieve the same ends?
3. Another claim made by e-Rewards is that their recruitment methods greatly cut down on self-selection artifacts. Is this so? Specifically, panelists who participate have all *chosen* to do so; are they not strongly self-selected as well? How would you evaluate the claim made about freedom from "professional" respondents?
4. Do variety, balance, and representativeness along known geodemographic dimensions—which e-Rewards handles ingeniously and well—offer any protection from lack of representativeness along *unknown* (or unmeasured) dimensions? Why or why not?
5. What can you say about the sampling frame, information needs, and overall research goals for both the consumer and professional business panels? Do they differ in substantial ways? How, specifically?
6. Is it wise for e-Rewards to refuse to sell information to third parties? Would it be ethical do to so if they apprised panelists of this in advance, as they would be legally required to do? What safeguards should be

taken to prevent abuses of the sort of extremely detailed, individual-level data e-Rewards records over even a short period of time?

Source: www.e-rewards.com

CASE 2.7 MIDDLE AMERICA RESEARCH

Middle America Research (MAR) was awarded a contract to perform marketing research for National Markets, the largest supermarket chain in the Midwest.* National's market share had been steadily declining for 18 months, and the marketing department was considering a promotional effort in which stores would provide shoppers with nutritional information for most of the packaged foods carried by National. National executives hoped that a goodwill measure such as this would stimulate sales, as well as create a loyal customer base. MAR's job was to determine the extent to which nutritional information, if provided, would be used by consumers. Jose Martinez, president of MAR, was meeting with National executives to outline the specifics of the research project. He opened the meeting as follows.

"Good afternoon, ladies and gentlemen. As you know, MAR will soon be performing a major research project for National Markets. This meeting gives me the chance to clarify exactly what MAR will be doing for National. In our research proposal, two key considerations were identified: (1) consumer attitudes toward nutritional information in general and (2) which of three presentation formats would be the most useful to shoppers.

"To uncover this information, MAR has developed a list of interview questions which will be administered to shoppers sometime within the next couple of weeks. I have with me several copies of the questionnaire, which I will distribute to you for your approval."

Case Questions

1 Read Case 1.1 ("Fresh Impressions—Nutritional Labeling") to develop an understanding of the decision situation related to the questionnaire in this case. Read the questionnaire and determine how it should be modified based on the rules of questionnaire construction presented in earlier chapters. Address the following areas:
   a Proposed changes in question format, wording, content, and other such elements that, in your view, could have been stronger.
   b Proposed changes in question sequence and general structure.
   c General comments and concerns regarding the design of the questionnaire.

Questionnaire

Source: MAR utilized formats originally developed at Cornell University, Ithaca, N.Y.

Location:____________________

Date:____________________

Time:____________________

Interviewer:____________________

Respondent's name:____________________

Address:____________________

Phone number:____________________

"Hello, I'm [your name] from Middle America Research. We're doing a survey to find out how shoppers go about getting nutritional information. Would you mind giving us a few minutes of your time to answer some questions? Are you the person who buys most of the groceries for the household?"

---

*Names of the research firm, supermarket chain and managers, along with some of the financial and cost data, have been changed for confidentiality.

If respondent refuses an interview, or doesn't purchase most of the groceries for the household, thank the person for his or her time, and then call the next potential interviewee.

1 Where do you buy most of the food your family eats?

1 ( ) Large supermarket chain
2 ( ) Independent grocer
3 ( ) Farmer's market
4 ( ) Convenience store such as 7–11 or Stop-N-Go
5 ( ) Other: ____________________

2 Is this store helpful in providing nutrition information?

1 ( ) Yes
2 ( ) No

3 Do you read the labels on packaged food?

1 ( ) Yes
2 ( ) No

4 Are you hesitant or uncertain about buying foods that don't have nutrition information provided on the label?

1 ( ) Yes
2 ( ) No

5 We are interested in finding out where you get information regarding nutrition, and what type of information you find. Do you get nutrition information from:

	Yes	No	What kind of information?
Food labels	( )1	( )2	
Friends or relatives	( )1	( )2	
Advertisements	( )1	( )2	
Books	( )1	( )2	
Magazines	( )1	( )2	
Doctor	( )1	( )2	
Store clerks	( )1	( )2	

6 Which of these sources to you use "Most often"? (Read list.) "Second most often"?

	Most often	Second most often
Advertisements	( )1	( )1
Books	( )2	( )2
Doctor	( )3	( )3
Food labels	( )4	( )4
Friends or relatives	( )5	( )5
Magazines	( )6	( )6
Store clerks	( )7	( )7

7 What problems do you have finding information about the nutritional content of your food?

8 In the past, the provision of nutritional information has been primarily for those on special diets. Do you have a special diet that requires you to restrict certain foods?

1 ( ) Yes
2 ( ) No (Skip to Question 10.)

9 Do you find that there is adequate information to meet your needs?

1 ( ) Yes (Skip to Question 11.)
2 ( ) No

10 What other types of information would you like to see?

11 Most people feel that, as consumers, we deserve detailed information about the nutritional content of all the foods we eat. Do you agree?

1 ( ) Yes
2 ( ) No

12 Would you like to have more nutritional information provided to you?

1 ( ) Yes
2 ( ) No

13 Which of these foods do you regularly purchase?

1 ( ) Breakfast cereal
2 ( ) Frozen vegetables
3 ( ) Canned soup
4 ( ) Canned or bottled fruit and vegetable juice
5 ( ) Canned or bottled fruit
6 ( ) TV (frozen) dinners

14 How often do you purchase ______________?

	Don't	Every week	Every 2–3 weeks	Once a month or less
Breakfast cereal	( ) 1	( ) 2	( ) 3	( ) 4
Frozen Vegetables	( ) 1	( ) 2	( ) 3	( ) 4
Canned soup	( ) 1	( ) 2	( ) 3	( ) 4
Canned or bottled fruit and vegetable juice	( ) 1	( ) 2	( ) 3	( ) 4
Canned or bottled fruit	( ) 1	( ) 2	( ) 3	( ) 4
TV (frozen) dinners	( ) 1	( ) 2	( ) 3	( ) 4

15 Do you look for nutritional information about ______________? (Read list.)

	Yes	No
Breakfast cereal	( ) 1	( ) 2
Frozen Vegetables	( ) 1	( ) 2
Canned soup	( ) 1	( ) 2
Canned or bottled fruit and vegetable juice	( ) 1	( ) 2
Canned or bottled fruit	( ) 1	( ) 2
TV (frozen) dinners	( ) 1	( ) 2

16 How easy do you find it to obtain nutritional information about ______________? (Read name of specific item.) Is it "Very easy," "Somewhat easy," "Neutral," "Somewhat difficult," or "Very difficult"?

	Very easy	Somewhat easy	Neutral	Somewhat difficult	Very difficult
a Breakfast cereal	( ) 1	( ) 2	( ) 3	( ) 4	( ) 5
If "Difficult," ask: What makes it (somewhat/very) difficult? ______________					
b Frozen vegetables	( ) 1	( ) 2	( ) 3	( ) 4	( ) 5
If "Difficult," ask: What makes it (somewhat/very) difficult? ______________					
c Canned soup	( ) 1	( ) 2	( ) 3	( ) 4	( ) 5
If "Difficult," ask: What makes it (somewhat/very) difficult? ______________					
d Canned or bottled fruit and vegetable juice	( ) 1	( ) 2	( ) 3	( ) 4	( ) 5
If "Difficult," ask: What makes it (somewhat/very) difficult? ______________					
e Canned or bottled fruit	( ) 1	( ) 2	( ) 3	( ) 4	( ) 5
If "Difficult," ask: What makes it (somewhat/very) difficult? ______________					
f TV dinners	( ) 1	( ) 2	( ) 3	( ) 4	( ) 5
If "Difficult," ask: What makes it (somewhat/very) difficult? ______________					

17 Would readily available nutrition information influence your decision regarding which brand to buy?

1 ( ) Yes
2 ( ) No
3 ( ) Not sure

18 Would nutrition information influence you to try a new product?

1 ( ) Yes
2 ( ) No

19 Some people believe that grocery stores could help consumers by presenting nutrition information about the foods they sell in a format that is easy to read and understand. Do you think it would be helpful if, for example, a store posted the nutritional content of its products?

1 ( ) Yes
2 ( ) No (Skip to Question 21.)

20 What kinds of information would you like to see?

21 How would your opinion of a store that provided this type of information be affected? Would it be "Much higher," "Somewhat higher," "The same," "Somewhat lower," or "Much lower"?

1 ( ) Much higher
2 ( ) Somewhat higher
3 ( ) The same
4 ( ) Somewhat lower
5 ( ) Much lower

22 If a local grocer were to post these sheets for every type of food, would you be more likely to do your grocery shopping there?

1 ( ) Yes
2 ( ) No
3 ( ) Don't know

23 In general, if more nutrition information were provided, would you use it in making purchase decisions?

1 ( ) Yes
2 ( ) No

24 I'm going to hand you three formats that present some nutrition information for TV dinners. Take a few seconds to glance at these. Which do you find "Most helpful"? "Second most helpful"?

	Most helpful	Second most helpful
Matrix (format no. 1)	( ) 1	( ) 1
Summary (format no. 2)	( ) 2	( ) 2
Complete (format no. 3)	( ) 3	( ) 3

25 Why do you find format number ________ "Most helpful"?

26 Why do you find format number ________ "Second most helpful"?

27 Why do you find format number ________ "Least helpful"?

For the next part of the questionnaire, we are trying to find out what shoppers do and don't know about nutrition.

28 Do you think too much of some vitamins can be harmful?

1 ( ) Yes
2 ( ) No

29 Do you think that eating a variety of foods is ordinarily a sufficient intake of nutrients?

1 ( ) Yes
2 ( ) No

30 Do you think that fortification with seven vitamins and minerals provides all the essential nutrients?

1 ( ) Yes
2 ( ) No

31 Which of these foods do you feel is more nutritious:

a. Beef or turkey? ( ) 1 ( ) 2
b. Apple juice or tomato juice? ( ) 1 ( ) 2

Demographic Data

The following questions are for statistical purposes only. They are solely to help us analyze the data from the survey. In no way will you be identified with your answers.

32 What is your marital status?

1 ( ) Single
2 ( ) Married
3 ( ) Widowed
4 ( ) Divorced

33 Could you please tell us which age bracket you are in?

18–24	( ) 1	45–54	( ) 4
25–34	( ) 2	55–64	( ) 5
35–44	( ) 3	65 or older	( ) 6

34 What is your occupation? ____________________

35 What is the highest grade of school or college that you have completed?

1 ( ) Grade school
2 ( ) Some high school
3 ( ) High school (graduate)
4 ( ) Some college, trade, or technical school
5 ( ) College (graduate)
6 ( ) Postgraduate

36 Do you have any children?

1 ( ) Yes
2 ( ) No (Skip to Question 39.)

37 What ages?

Age range	Number
1–5	______
6–12	______
13–19	______
20 and older	______

38 How many of the children are at home?

39 Including children and all others (relatives, boarders, etc.), how many persons live in your home? ______

40 Into which income category does your total family income fall?

Under $15,000	( ) 1
$15,001–$25,000	( ) 2
$25,001–$35,000	( ) 3
$35,001–$50,000	( ) 4
$50,001–$75,000	( ) 5
$75,001–$100,000	( ) 6
More than $100,000	( ) 7

41 Thank you for your participation in our study. If you would like a copy of the survey results sent to you, please tell us now.

1 ( ) Yes
2 ( ) No

STOP—the interview has concluded. Please use the coding manual to classify respondents based on their responses to previous questions.

1 = Bachelor
2 = Newly married
3 = Full nest
4 = Full nest II
5 = Full nest III
6 = Empty nest
7 = Empty nest II
8 = Solitary survivor in labor force
9 = Solitary survivor retired

Example of the Matrix Format

TV dinners (serving size: 1 dinner)	Weight in ounces	Calories	Protein	Vitamin A	Vitamin C	Thiamin	Riboflavin	Niacin	Calcium	Iron
Beans and Franks, Banquet	10.75	591	25	40	15	20	10	15	15	20
Beef Chop Suey, Banquet	12.00	282	20	6	8	6	8	15	4	15
Beef Enchilada, Swanson	15.00	570	30	50	0	15	10	20	20	25
Beef Tenderloin, Steak House	9.50	920	70	2	30	20	20	45	4	35
Beef, Banquet	11.00	312	45	4	10	8	15	30	4	30
Beef, Chopped, Banquet	11.00	443	30	90	10	8	15	20	6	20
Beef, Chopped, Hungry-Man, Swanson	18.00	730	30	45	15	20	20	45	6	25
Beef, Hungry-Man, Swanson	17.00	540	60	2	4	20	30	30	4	20
Beef, Swanson	11.50	370	60	6	10	10	20	30	4	20
Chicken, BBQ, Hungry-Man, Swanson	16.50	760	60	110	6	30	35	60	8	30
Chicken, BBQ, Swanson	11.25	530	25	20	4	10	20	40	8	15
Chicken Crispy, Swanson	10.75	650	30	4	2	30	15	50	10	15
Chicken, Fried, Banquet	11.00	530	40	100	35	10	15	35	30	25
Chicken, Fried, Hungry-Man, Swanson	15.75	910	100	2	25	25	25	80	10	30
Chicken, Hungry-Man, Swanson	19.00	730	90	15	30	20	20	70	15	20
Chicken, Man-Pleaser, Banquet	17.00	1016	90	90	10	15	20	60	45	35
Chicken, Swanson	11.50	570	60	40	10	10	15	45	6	15
Chicken, 3-Course, Swanson	15.00	630	50	30	4	20	10	50	8	15
Chicken, Western Style, Hungry-Man, Swanson	17.75	890	70	10	0	25	35	40	10	15
Chicken, Western Style, Swanson	11.75	460	35	10	0	15	20	20	6	15
Chopped Sirloin, Steak House	9.50	760	90	2	35	20	20	50	4	35
Fish Dinner, Banquet	8.75	382	30	50	20	20	8	20	6	10
Fish N Chips, Swanson	10.25	450	50	6	10	15	8	25	4	10
Turkey, Banquet	11.00	293	35	80	35	10	10	35	8	15
Turkey, Hungry-Man, Swanson	19.00	740	100	20	40	20	15	60	10	25
Turkey, Man-Pleaser, Banquet	19.00	620	60	150	25	20	20	45	15	25
Turkey, Swanson	11.50	360	45	60	30	10	10	35	6	10
Turkey, 3-Course, Swanson	16.00	520	60	15	30	20	15	40	10	20
Veal Parmigiana, Banquet	11.00	421	30	140	20	15	15	20	20	15
Veal Parmigiana, Hungry-Man, Swanson	20.50	910	60	10	6	20	30	30	25	30

Example of the Summary Format

Nutrition quotient	TV dinners (serving size: 1 dinner)	Weight in ounces
2.2	Turkey, Banquet	11.00
1.9	Veal Parmigiana, Banquet	11.00
1.7	Turkey, Man-Pleaser, Banquet	19.00
1.7	Turkey, Swanson	11.50
1.6	Chicken, Fried, Banquet	11.00
1.5	Italian, Banquet	11.00
1.4	Sirloin, Chopped, Swanson	10.00
1.4	Salisbury Steak, Banquet	11.00
1.4	Beef, Banquet	11.00
1.3	Macaroni & Cheese, Swanson	12.50
1.3	Beef, Chopped, Swanson	11.00
1.3	Chicken, BBQ, Hungry-Man, Swanson	16.50
1.2	Beef, Swanson	11.50
1.2	Fish Dinner, Banquet	8.50
1.2	Meat Loaf, Banquet	11.00
1.2	Meat Loaf, Man-Pleaser, Banquet	19.00
1.2	Turkey, 3-Course, Swanson	16.00
0.8	Chicken, BBQ, Swanson	11.25
0.8	Spaghetti, Swanson	12.50
0.8	Chicken, Western Style, Swanson	11.75
0.7	Rib Eye, Steak House	9.00
0.7	Meat Loaf, Swanson	10.75
0.7	Salisbury Steak, Hungry-Man, Swanson	17.00
0.7	Beef Tenderloin, Steak House	9.50
0.7	Sirloin, Steak House	9.50
0.7	Salisbury Steak, Swanson	11.50
0.7	Veal Parmigiana, Hungry-Man, Swanson	20.50
0.7	Chicken, Western Style, Hungry-Man, Swanson	17.75
0.6	Noodles and Chicken, Swanson	10.50

Example of Complete Format

TV dinners (serving size: 1 dinner)	Weight in ounces	Calories	Protein	Vitamin A	Vitamin C	Thiamin	Riboflavin	Niacin	Calcium	Iron	Nutritional quotient
Beef Tenderloin, Steak House	9.50	920	70	2	30	20	20	45	4	35	.7
Beef, Banquet	11.00	312	45	4	10	8	15	30	4	30	1.4
Beef, Swanson	11.50	370	60	6	10	10	20	30	4	20	1.2
Chicken, BBQ, Hungry-Man, Swanson	16.50	760	60	110	6	30	35	60	8	30	1.3
Chicken, BBQ, Swanson	11.25	530	25	20	4	10	20	40	8	15	0.8
Chicken, Fried, Banquet	11.00	530	40	100	35	10	15	35	30	25	1.6
Chicken, Western, Hungry-Man, Swanson	17.75	890	70	10	0	25	35	40	10	15	0.7
Fish Dinner, Banquet	8.75	382	30	50	20	20	8	20	6	10	1.2
Turkey, Banquet	11.00	293	35	80	35	10	140	35	8	15	2.2
Turkey, Man-Pleaser, Banquet	19.00	620	60	150	25	20	20	45	15	25	1.7
Turkey, Swanson	11.50	360	45	60	30	10	10	35	6	10	1.7
Turkey, 3-Course, Swanson	16.00	520	60	15	30	20	15	40	10	20	1.2
Veal Parmigian, Banquet	11.00	421	30	140	20	15	15	20	20	15	1.9
Veal Parmigian, Hungry-Man, Swanson	20.50	910	60	10	6	20	30	30	25	30	0.7

CASE 2.8 ASWU AND HARRIS INTERACTIVE EUROPE ONLINE OMNIBUS SERVICE*

Ye Chang, the business unit director of ASWU, a major Chinese electronics manufacturer, was on the way to his office from an urgently assembled meeting of the firm's top executives. His thoughts were occupied by the decision that he would have to make two weeks hence, a momentous one for him and ASWU.

The main topic of the meeting concerned a product that was under the umbrella of his business unit, an MP3 player. Based on the industry projections and the internal reports available in the company, the MP3 player market was expected to experience explosive growth, especially with continuous price drops typical of the category and high-tech consumer electronics in general. The product manufactured by ASWU was already distributed across Europe, with the exception of Great Britain. The decision to enter Great Britain was clear. However, decisions regarding the mode of entry were all assigned to Ye.

ASWU made its MP3 player available in European countries through a co-branding partnership with a company whose electronics brand names enjoyed enormous awareness among European consumers, with low regional variation. The decision to co-brand was based on a survey conducted several years ago, indicating that European consumers desired the reassurance of a familiar brand name when purchasing such relatively new products as MP3 players. However, the penetration of the product category has increased dramatically since the survey had been conducted, and Ye wondered whether this change has gradually ushered in a change in consumer attitudes as well. After all, MP3 players were hardly a "new" product any longer. He kept asking himself what role brand name plays in the purchasing decision-making of today's MP3 player buyers, in Great Britain in particular. If the European MP3 player market is close to reaching the same level of commoditization that already dominates the PC industry, would it be wiser to enter Great Britain without a co-branding agreement and instead use the ASWU brand to identify its MP3 players? Doing so would certainly entail lower cost, and more channel control, consistent with market commoditization, if indeed it was occurring.

The more he thought about this matter, the more he realized the need for a new, perhaps updated consumer survey to understand the current state of consumer attitudes in Great Britain. Finding a research provider in a market he knew nothing about and completing a survey in two weeks seemed almost impossible. Ye entered his office and picked up the phone and asked his secretary to set up a meeting with the MP3 player brand management team the next morning.

The meeting produced an interesting idea, devised by an assistant brand manager, Sammy Yuke, who was hired 6 months earlier after completing his graduate studies in England. Sammy suggested that the survey be conducted via e-mail, which would save a great deal of time. After the meeting, Sammy forwarded Ye a link with the information about Harris Interactive Europe, specifically its online omnibus research service.

Searching through the Harris Interactive (HI) Europe website, Ye discovered that it is a global market research and consulting company, with headquarters in London, known for decades for its expertise in strategic business and consumer research. HI Europe's website touted its application of innovative methodologies and sophisticated technology, focusing on those that are Internet-based. Harris Interactive, among the world's 15 largest market research firms, with more than $150 million in annual revenue and based in Rochester, N.Y., was the parent company of HI Europe, and this alone added credibility to HI Europe's image in Ye's eyes. Harris Interactive's acquisition of Novatris, a Paris-based online market research firm, added 1 million Novatris panel members to Harris Interactive's current European panel of 700,000, creating a panel of 1.7 million members, believed to be the largest in Europe.

After reading about HI Europe, Ye thought that the firm could be trusted to ably carry out the assignment. Now, he had to evaluate if the firm's online omnibus service was appropriate for his needs. Among all the other information posted on the firm's website, Ye read the following with interest.

Ye was contemplating contacting HI Europe for more details. As he prepared to call the relevant personnel in HI Europe, he considered the additional information that he needed to evaluate the suitability of the survey for this objective.

---

*All information about Harris Interactive's Omnibus Services refer to Ye's observations in 2005. For up-to-date information about current Omnibus Services, please visit www.harrisinteractive.com/europe/services.asp or www.harrisinteractive.com/services/omnibus.asp.

QuickQuery™ Great Britain (GB)

Get accurate, projectable answers from 2,000 people within just 8 days.

HI Europe's QuickQuery GB is an online omnibus service that enables you to ask questions and get projectable answers from a representative sample of British adults (aged 16+). Although all respondents are Internet users, our ongoing parallel studies and extensive experience enable us to weight the sample to represent the GB adult population.

You'll get meaningful information for low-incidence populations or for specific target audiences. HI Europe's extensive online panel enables cost-effective access to hard-to-reach respondents.

Here is how QuickQuery GB works:

1. You submit and finalize your questions with our online survey consultants by midday on the second Tuesday of the month and receive results the following Wednesday.
2. Your questions are transformed into an electronic questionnaire and fielded a random subset of more than 140,000 cooperative respondents in Great Britain.
3. Eight days later, the data is tabulated and delivered to you electronically.

When should you use QuickQuery GB?

Here are a few scenarios:

- Market segmentation analyses
- Attitudes and usage studies
- Tracking studies
- Name testing
- Consumer trend analyses
- New product research
- Disaster checks
- Incidence testing
- Evaluating purchase intent
- Public opinion issues

Source:

Case Questions

1 What information should Ye Chang request from HI Europe to evaluate the potential of assigning them the research project?

2 Do you believe that the QuickQuery omnibus service is appropriate for ASWU's purpose? Explain your answer and discuss advantages and disadvantages of the service.

3 The sample size of the QuickQuery service is 2,000 people. Do you think this allows for a large enough sample for ASWU's survey objective? Is the sample representative of the population ASWU wishes to learn about? What information would Ye need to ask from HI Europe to evaluate the suitability of the sample for his needs? What statistical procedures may be employed to test whether the sample is at least approximately representative?

4 QuickQuery's sample is stratified by age, gender, and region. Discuss advantages and disadvantages of a stratified sample in general and by the aforementioned criteria in particular. Would you recommend any other way to construct the sample for ASWU's survey? How?

5 The QuickQuery online omnibus standard service offers clients the option to include up to 25 questions. Design a questionnaire that addresses the ASWU survey's objective and information needs, keeping to this relatively tight constraint.

6 The QuickQuery service provides clients answers to their questions for the (aggregated) total sample and broken-out by standard demographic variables, including

- age within gender
- household size
- marital status
- region
- social class

- income
- age and presence of children
- employment status
- education

Which demographic variables are most relevant for this survey? Are there any other variables that you would add to ASWU's questionnaire? Finally, are prespecified geodemographic categories the best way to segment this market?

Sources: "China to Lead Global MP3 Market Growth." *Macworld*, November 3, 2004.
Harris Interactive Europe (www.hieurope.com)
"Lavod's MP3 Players Boast Superior Sound Quality, Fashionable Designs." *Computex Taipei*, 2005.
MP3 player product listings: http://chinasuppliers.alibaba.com.

CASE 2.9 SKYTRAX BEST AIRLINES 2005 AWARDS

Background

Aero Airlines is a French aviation firm, headquartered in Paris, providing its customers both domestic and international flights. Several years ago, the CEO of Aero Airlines retired and, with the arrival of the new CEO, the team of top executives was replaced as well. Jaclyn Benedict was hired into a marketing manager position as part of this new organizational restructure. One of the initiatives that she brought into the organization was the QualityTrack Program, which monitored on a constant basis the service levels that the firm offered to its customers. Tracking the complaint rate and generating feedback for improvements was among the main activities undertaken by the QualityTrack Program. The Complaint Rate Report was delivered twice monthly to Jaclyn, who always thoroughly digested it and then benchmarked the most recent scores against those in previous reports.

For the past 2 months, the reports grimly indicated a steady upward trend in the complaint rate. Jaclyn sat at her desk, thinking about the last report that she just read, wondering what was generating all these additional complaints, as day-to-day company operations were unchanged. There was no evidence of decreased bookings either. Jaclyn decided to purchase the Skytrax Airline of the Year 2005 survey, which reported that Aero Airlines' ranking dropped five places since last year alone. She hoped that the Skytrax report would explain the increased complaint rate among Aero customers, saving the company the cost and time of conducting its own primary research into the matter.

As she was placing an online order for the Skytrax survey, Jaclyn wondered if the change was driven by internal flaws within Aero Airlines itself, by improved competition, or by something else entirely. She remembered the press release of a competitor firm announcing a huge investment aimed at improving its cost structure and service quality. However, Jaclyn had no data on how consumers were reacting to these changes, or even whether they did at all.

The Skytrax online survey order went through seamlessly, and Jaclyn asked herself whether it would adequately answer her questions or if she would have to conduct an additional study internally to identify the drivers of mounting customer dissatisfaction with Aero Airlines. The company had a huge customer database, albeit one that was utilized mainly for marketing activities rather than for research; and there were people in the marketing department with the necessary skills to carry out such a research project if need be, reducing outsourcing costs.

About the Skytrax Airline of the Year Survey

Skytrax Airline of the Year survey, conducted by Skytrax Research, is an annual, global barometer of passenger opinions about airlines around the world and is regarded as an important benchmarking tool for passenger airline satisfaction levels. The firm provides aviation product and service research, including customer satisfaction surveys, competitive performance, quality audits, service and product analysis, and global ranking surveys.

Skytrax Airline of the Year 2005 surveyed 12.3 million eligible respondents of 94 nationalities over an 11-month period. The survey includes both first class and economy class customers, both business and leisure travelers, among its respondents. Data sources for the survey include:

- passenger interviews
- corporate travel interviews and questionnaires
- Skytrax's panel interviews
- online surveys of passengers
- e-mail questionnaires
- telephone interviews

The 2005 survey measured the following aspects of passenger satisfaction for each airline's product and service standards, evaluating the "typical" travel experience:

GROUND / AIRPORT	ONBOARD PRODUCT	ONBOARD SERVICE
• User-friendly Internet site	• Cabin Seat comfort	• Assistance during Boarding
• Online Booking service	• Cabin Cleanliness	• Friendliness of Staff
• Ticket Counter service	• Toilet Cleanliness	• Service Attentiveness
• Waiting times at Check-in	• Cabin Lighting / Ambience	• Staff Language skills
• Quality of Check-in service	• Cabin Temperatures	• Efficiency serving Meals
• Boarding Procedures	• Selection of Reading Materials	• Availability thru Flight
• Friendliness of Ground staff	• Standard of Airline magazine	• Making PA Announcements
• Efficiency of Ground Staff	• Sound / Vision quality of Movies	• Problem solving Skills
• Transfer service	• Choice of Movie Programs	• General Staff Attitudes
• Quality of Arrival services	• Choice of Audio Programs	• Staff Grooming Standards
• Baggage Delivery times	• Quality of Meals	
• Handling of Delays	• Quantity of Food served	
	• Meal Choice Availability	
	• Selection of Drinks	

Source: Skytrax - http://www.airlinequality.com/

Skytrax used a number of methods to reduce error, such as monitoring the ISP and user information of online surveys and deleting duplicate submissions, and pattern-checking all survey responses with a proprietary "poll-breaker" program to identify nominations that followed similar rating patterns or duplicated earlier entries. The "poll-breaker" program resulted in 10.36 percent of total responses being ruled ineligible. Detailed interviews were conducted of a representative sample of survey respondents. The data were weighted to compensate for differences in airline size so that smaller regional airlines were rated according to actual quality rather than size.

Case Questions

1. In your opinion, could the Complaint Rate Report be used as a reliable indicator of customer satisfaction levels with Aero Airlines? Why or why not? What could be potential biases built into such a metric?
2. Considering the description of the Skytrax Airline of the Year survey, do you believe it will provide useful answers to Jaclyn's questions? Explain your reasoning. What, if anything, might it measure inaccurately or miss entirely?
3. Considering Skytrax survey's sample size and data collection methods, do you believe the sample is representative of the target segment(s) intrinsic to Aero's predicament? What factors should be examined in general, and in regard to each data input source, to assess sample representativeness?
4. In your opinion, were the measures taken by Skytrax to identify ineligible online responses effective? Explain your answer. If not, what additional safeguards or screens could be put into place?
5. Evaluate Skytrax's idea of adjusting for different sizes of airlines in order to ensure that the rankings are inferred based on a "quality" merit. What are the advantages and the disadvantages of weighting data in this manner? What else might have been done to achieve similar ends?
6. Discuss the suitability of a customer survey conducted *internally* to address Jaclyn's concerns. How would such a survey compare to one conducted with a broader respondent pool, both positively and negatively? What issues are critical to ensure that the resulting responses are relatively free of foreseeable biases?

7 In Jaclyn's position, how would you designate a population definition, a sampling frame, a sampling procedure, and a method for determining the accuracy of the results for the internally conducted customer survey?

Sources: "Cathay Pacific Selected as World's Best Airline." *Finfacts Ireland*, June 7, 2005.
"Cathay Pacific Voted Skytrax Airline of the Year 2005." PR Newswire, June 2, 2005.
"12.3 Million Passengers Vote for World's Best Airline." Aero Gizmo, *gizmag*, June 8, 2005.
Skytrax (www.airlinequality.com).
"World's Best: Top 10 Airlines Named." Gordon T. Anderson, *CNN Money*, June 7, 2005.

CASE 2.10 COSMOPOLITAN MAGAZINE

Surveys are often sponsored and conducted by various popular press outlets to spur interest among and create a more interactive relationship with their readers. Nowadays, surveys asking people about their consumer preferences, shopping behavior, general opinions, even their sexual habits, are commonplace, but this was not always so. A landmark survey of this kind, often characterized as such due to its enormous sample of 106,000, was conducted in 1980, by *Cosmopolitan* magazine. The tremendous response to this survey and the extended publicity that it generated caused other publications to take note; soon after, all manner of newspapers and magazines were including surveys within their pages, each geared to their particular readers' interests.

Cosmopolitan, a monthly lifestyle magazine that is targeted to a female audience, is published in more than 25 languages and sold in more than 40 countries. *Cosmopolitan* typically covers topics such as:

- relationships, careers, personal growth (e.g., personality quizzes), and female sexuality
- fashion, beauty care secrets, and tips on fitness and staying healthy
- profiles of celebrities and broad coverage of pop culture

Despite the female target audience, the magazine has a large niche of steady male readers (14.7 percent). The median age of *Cosmopolitan* readers is 31.4 years (31.8 percent in the 18–24 age group, 26.3 percent in 25–34, and 27.9 percent in 35–49). Median individual income is just more than $26,000; median household income is about $58,000, with 66.2 percent of the readership earning more than $40,000 per household. Sixty-five percent of the Cosmopolitan audience has some college education or a college or higher degree. Seventy-two percent are employed outside the home, with 54 percent employed full-time. Forty-two percent of the readers are unmarried, 40 percent married, and 19 percent divorced, widowed, or separated. The magazine also claims that its readership is more involved than that of similar publications, spending an average of 80 minutes per issue compared with 50 to 73 minutes for readers of competitors.

The decision to include a survey on sexual behaviors of American women in one of the *Cosmopolitan* issues was made in the summer of 1979. A total of 79 multiple-choice questions were created and compiled by a panel of *Cosmopolitan* editors, grouped into three sections covering personal background, sexual experience, and sexual manners and morals. The survey was run as a regular *Cosmo* article in the January 1980 issue rather than as a perforated tear-out with return postage guaranteed. In what was an unusual request for this sort of undertaking, the reader was asked to complete a fairly long questionnaire and send it at her own expense. The questionnaire was accompanied by a letter from the editor which stated the purpose of the survey and exhorted the reader to "share her sex life" with other *Cosmo* readers.

Simmons Market Research Bureau, a public-opinion research group located in Manhattan and which served many other magazines and publishers, was commissioned to coordinate the data collection and analysis. The task of interpreting the analysis compiled by Simmons was assigned to Linda Wolfe, behavior and science writer and author. Linda Wolfe was also responsible for enriching the purely statistical findings from the Simmons analysis with real-life testimonies, by reading the many messages and stories sent, without having been solicited, along with the questionnaires.

Linda Wolfe stated that she was deeply interested in the sexual changes that had taken place in America since her college days in the 1950s, but she had given up hope of ever being able to write about them until she came across the *Cosmopolitan* sex survey. When she heard that 106,000 women had responded to the survey, her interest picked up immediately. She compared this enormous sample size with those of previously conducted studies. Hite, in the *Hite Report*, had studied 3,000 women. Gay

Talese had spoken with at best a few hundred. Even Alfred Kinsey had relied on a sample of only 5,940 participants for the famous "Kinsey Report," *Sexual Behavior in the Human Female.*

However, Wolfe said that initially she was reluctant to accept the assignment of interpreting the 106,000-response survey for *Cosmo* because she believed that, although sample size was important, respondent variety and representativeness were also critical to the validity of the survey's findings. She did not want to write about the sex-related perceptions and behaviors of just the "*Cosmo* girl," a typical reader of the magazine, but to do something scientifically valid and up to accepted standards of rigor. After an appointment with Simmons executives, Wolfe was struck by how varied a sample of respondents the *Cosmo* survey had tapped. She was informed by Val Appel, research director at Simmons, that the (women) respondents were between the ages of 14 and 80, hailed from every geographical region of the country, and ranged in occupation from corporate president and college professor to motel proprietor and telephone operator. Thus, although all respondents had in common the fact that they read the *Cosmopolitan* issue in which the questionnaire appeared, their geodemographic differences conferred to the sample remarkable diversity. This diversity was the foundation of the argument that the sample represented American females and could be used to understand how the sexual revolution affected the values and behavior of American women at the dawn of the 1980s.

It was decided that the material gathered was adequate to produce an article, called "The Sexual Profile of That Cosmopolitan Girl" and published in the September 1980 issue, as well as a book, titled *The Cosmo Report,* published soon after in 1981. The two publications concerned two different groups of women. The article analyzed the sexual habits and attitudes of only a portion of the survey's respondents, some 15,000 women who most resembled the magazine's typical reader: a woman between the ages of 18 and 34, who lives in a city of more than 1 million and earns her own living. On the other hand, the book examined all 106,000 respondents, a sample comprising a much wider sector of American women. This sample composition is described as following in *The Cosmo Report* book: ". . . while 85% of the respondents are between the ages 18 and 34, some are as young as 14, and some are in their forties, fifties, sixties, and even seventies. Although a fifth of *The Cosmo Report* women come from cities of more than 1 million, another two-fifths come from smaller cities, and the remainder from suburban and rural areas. And although the women in *The Cosmo Report* are primarily women who earn their own livings, chiefly as managers, administrators, professionals, technicians and office workers, there are also some homemakers and numerous students." Later the author commented: "Having worked closely with the *Cosmo* data, I myself suspect that the sexual practices of this largely 18 to 34 year old sample is not unusually extreme, and that the *Cosmo* women may, in fact, be quite representative of young American women as a whole."

The publication of the survey results generated great publicity for the magazine. *Cosmopolitan*'s editor, Helen Gurley Brown, explained: "After all, this was the biggest response to any magazine survey in history and surely the largest sex survey ever conducted." Television programs such as the *Today* show, the *Tonight* show, and Phil Donahue, among many others, all hosted *Cosmopolitan* editors as well as the writer, Linda Wolfe, to investigate and discuss the results of the *Cosmo* sex survey.

Case Questions

1 What is the population definition of the survey? What sampling frame was used? Were these appropriate choices? If not, what would be?

2 Bearing in mind Linda Wolfe's statements about the sample size and the diversity of the respondents, do you believe the sample was representative of the *Cosmopolitan* audience? Of the American female population? Explain your answers.

3 Are there key differences between diversity and representativeness? How might the magazine have gone about (a) collecting a more representative sample of each of these groups, or (b) statistically checking and analyzing the existing data to render them more nearly representative? What statistical methods might they call on for such purposes?

4 What sampling procedure was used? List and discuss in detail its advantages and disadvantages. Would the resulting sample be adequate to extrapolate to the readership of other, similar magazines? To the population of *Cosmo* readers who chose not to respond? If you had to guess, in which directions were certain key measures biased, if they were at all?

5 Consider the description of the questionnaire design and data analysis interpretation, and identify potential problems. What would you recommend to the magazine to mitigate such problems in the future? Would any of them likely have been less severe if the magazine had remunerated respondents for their participation, or at least for additional, standardized demographic data?

6 Suppose that you were hired by the magazine to design this survey. Develop a detailed survey proposal; among other elements, include information on sample design, sample generating procedure, and type of the survey that you would propose to the magazine. Suppose that the magazine's information needs might have a *longitudinal* component; how might one handle that while ensuring respondent anonymity?

Sources: *Cosmopolitan* magazine Web site (www.cosmomediakit.com).

Hearst Corporation website (www.hearstcorp.com) > Magazines > *Cosmopolitan*.

Wolfe, Linda (1981), *The Cosmo Report*. New York: Arbor House.

Wolfe, Linda (September 1980), "The Sexual Profile of That Cosmopolitan Girl." Linda Wolfe. *Cosmopolitan*, 254–265.

CASE 2.11 THE GALLUP POLL IN IRAQ

After polling the residents of Baghdad in 2003, Gallup conducted, in Spring 2004, a nationwide survey of Iraq on attitudes toward the U.S. occupation of their country and their own prospects for the future. Gallup designed the poll to provide benchmark findings for gauging how military and diplomatic policies and cultural influences affected Iraqis' views. The poll's target population was defined as all adult citizens, ages 18 and older, residing in Iraq. Because the Central Statistical Office of Arbil did not participate in the project, Gallup was unable to poll in the governorates of Arbil and Dahuk. Of Iraq's 18 governorates, Arbil, comprising 5.1 percent of Iraq's population of 25 million, and Dahuk, 1.7 percent, are two of the three governorates with predominately Kurdish populations. The third is Sulaymaniyah, with 6.3 percent of the population. To offset this sampling problem, Gallup conducted additional interviews in Sulaymaniyah, bringing the percentage of predominantly Kurdish areas to 13 percent of the nationwide sample.

Gallup questioned 3444 Iraqis of every religion and ethnic group during in-person interviews in the respondents' homes. Interviews were conducted between March 22 and April 2, 2004, with interviews in Sulaymaniyah continuing until April 9. The lengthy questionnaire consisted of 81 questions, requiring about 70 minutes to complete. The response rate for the poll was 98 percent, unusual for such a lengthy questionnaire, even for motivated respondents.

Iraq is 70 percent urban, so two thirds of the interviews were conducted in urban areas, one third in rural areas. The structure of the Iraqi population (illustrated in Figure C2.11.1) includes 18 governorates ("mohafatha"), 93 administrative units known as qadhas, 223 districts ("nahiya"), 2,443 neighborhoods ("mahalas"), and 116,314 blocks ("majals").[1] Majals contain proximate housing units, often along the course of a given road or street (longer roads may stretch across multiple majals).

Using the probability-proportional-to-size method, Gallup selected 350 distinct locations as primary sampling units (PSUs) and conducted an average of 10 interviews, one per household, at each of these locations. All the population weights used in sample selection employed population data from the 2002 Central Statistical Office update, with adults defined as those born before 1987. The PSUs assigned to a given qadha were allocated, on a probability-based basis, to specific nahiyas, mahalas, and majals within that qadha, with no more than one majal sampled in a single mahala. When more than 10 families resided in a selected majal, families were chosen for interviewing according to a random selection table. The Kish method, a probability-based procedure used to select the respondent when more than one household member is a member of the target population, was used to select the specific adult to be interviewed. According to this research method, the age and sex of each eligible household member is recorded on a grid, and the respondent is selected according to a prescribed systematic procedure, using a look-up table. The method requires gathering additional information about members of the household eligible to be sampled, then choosing among that subset randomly, by referring to the look-up table; it helps avoid biases based on "who happens to be home," "who is considered the household spokesperson," or pervasive cultural attitudes that might interfere with the study's objectives.

[1]The number of majals reported here excludes those in Sulaymaniyah, where census data is only available to the level of mahalas.

Figure C2.11.1 Population Structure of Iraq

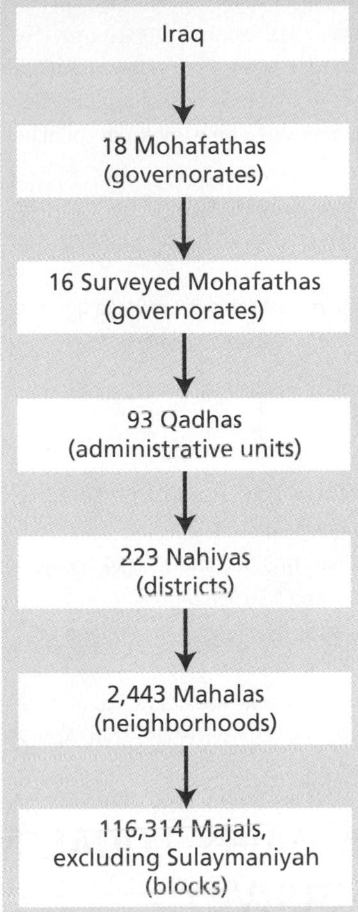

Source: Gallup.

Because the only residential listings available were those obtained from a 1997 census, and because these listings also did not distinguish the number of families living in a housing unit at a single address, Gallup had to compile updated listings that identified each independent family. The criterion used to identify independent families was whether they prepared and ate their meals independently.

Case Questions

1. What were the objective and the information needs of this survey based on the information provided about Gallup's overall goals?
2. In your opinion, what are the demographic questions that should have been included in this survey? Why do you think they would be necessary? Are there any additional question types—psychographic or behavioristic—that seem particularly prudent in a survey of this sort?
3. Evaluate Gallup's decision to conduct in-person interviews. Do you think it was appropriate or inappropriate? Explain your answer. What interview type would you recommend for a project of this type and scope? Would focus groups offer an overall advantage?
4. Do you believe the sample size was large enough, considering the total population of Iraq? What information would you need to determine the "optimal" sample size for this survey? How would you go about obtaining the needed information?
5. Based on the sample selection process as described, do you think the sample—regardless of its size—was nationally representative? What biases might have come into play? What obstacles could have prevented the sample from being representative, even though it might be in other circumstances?

6 Evaluate the Gallup's adjustment of the sample to deal with its inability to interview in Arbil and Dahuk. Discuss the advantage and disadvantages of the route taken. What other approach could have been taken to overcome this obstacle?
7 Does every element of the population have an equal probability of participating in the survey? Explain your answer.
8 Evaluate the method used to select a random sample of respondents (the Kish method) in this study. What are its advantages and disadvantages? What other methods could be used in selecting an individual within a household?
9 Evaluate the response rate of the 2004 Gallup Poll of Iraq. How does it compare to the average response rates in other countries? In the United States? What do you think are the reasons that could explain the difference or the lack of it?
10 For how long do you think the findings of this survey would be proper for use? What are the factors that should be considered to evaluate the time-based validity of the findings?

Sources: CNN/*USA Today*/Gallup Poll Nationwide Poll of Iraq, methodology and questionnaire, parts 1 and 2; www.cnn.com.
http://gallup.com
Burkholder, Richard, "Gallup Poll of Iraq: Liberated, Occupied, or in Limbo?" The Gallup Organization, *The Gallup Poll Tuesday Briefing*, April 28, 2004.
"Key Findings: Nationwide Survey of 3,500 Iraqis." *USA Today,* May 20, 2005.
Moore, Steven, "How to Poll in Iraq." Steven Moore.
"Poll: Iraqis Conflicted about War, Its Impact; Survey Done Mostly Before Recent Cycle of Violence." www.cnn.com, April 28, 2004.
Soriano, Cesar G. and Steven Komarow, "Poll: Iraqis Out of Patience." *USA Today,* April 28, 2004.
"Poll: More Iraqis Optimistic, Dislike U.S." www.cnn.com, April 29, 2004.

CASE 2.12 DELTA DAIRY LOCAL MARKET TASTE TEST SURVEY

Delta Dairy is one of four main operating companies in the Delta Group, a leading producer, retailer, and distributor of food products in Greece and selected markets in southeastern Europe (Bulgaria, Romania, Serbia, Cyprus, Croatia, Bosnia and Herzegovina, and Lebanon). Delta Dairy is among the major fully integrated dairy companies in the Greek market. It conducts the Group's business activity in the fresh dairy products (white and chocolate milk, dairy desserts, and yogurt), infant nutrition, and beverages (fresh fruit-based juices) categories.

The Greek dairy market is fairly fragmented, with five or more major players having about 70 percent market share, in addition to at least another dozen smaller producers. In the fresh milk segment, Delta Dairy has a leading position, with a 41 percent market share. This market share position is not equally distributed across Greece; Delta has a stronger lead in Athens and a weaker position in the remaining regions of Greece, particularly those in the northern part of the country.

Delta Dairy's fresh milk products were present in the northern Greek market for nearly a decade. However, the company could not achieve significant market share. The main reason for this fact was found in the particular tastes of northern Greek consumers, whose preferences and attitudes toward the fresh milk category differed significantly from those of Athenian consumers. Clearly, local marketing programs were required to "speak the language" of northern Greeks. The brand management team was doing a great job in tailoring communications and other marketing activities to northern Greek consumers' values and needs. However, there were two obstacles that had thus far prevented the team from achieving a better market position.

First, northern Greek consumers preferred a richer-tasting milk, compared with the lighter taste that dominated the preferences of other Greek regions. Second, northern Greek consumers were more regionally focused in their purchasing behavior, consciously selecting local producers of basic food and nonfood product categories. They typically rationalized their purchasing decisions as providing support for local businesses, which in turn gave back to the local community by re-investing profits locally and providing the community much-needed jobs.

Both these issues were directly linked to the fact that Delta Dairy did not have production facilities in the northern regions of Greece. The milk was produced in Athens and distributed by its distribution network through the rest of the country. Therefore, the northern Greek consumers tended to view Delta's fresh milk as "Athenian" or "nonlocal." Additionally, because the milk production was centralized in Athens, flavor was uniform and reflected the majority preference across Greece for a lighter-tasting milk.

Several years ago, the Athenian milk production plant reached its capacity and the top management made the decision to open a new plant in northern Greece. A 323,000-square-foot, state-of-the-art dairy facility was built near Thessaloniki, the capital of Macedonia and the second-largest city in Greece, after Athens. Milk from farms throughout northern Greece would be pasteurized in the new plant and distributed in Macedonia, Thrace, and Thessalia (regions in northern Greece). The plant represented an investment of 25 million euros and provided employment to 130 people in addition to the existing 1650 already employed (staff, cattle breeders, representatives, etc.) by Delta Dairy in northern Greece.

The establishment of the new production facility presented an opportunity for the white milk brand management team to re-launch Delta milk as a through-and-through *local* brand. Of course, one intended aspect of the new positioning was the richer flavor, known to appeal to the target population of northern Greek consumers; this was made possible by the new plant facility, which could balance the proportion of milk and cream to regional tastes. Given the importance of getting this newly formulated flavor just right, the brand management team responsible for the re-launch decided to conduct a taste test survey to best understand what sort of milk flavors would be most preferred by northern Greeks. They knew there were certain market realities they needed to consider when designing the taste survey:

- The primary decision-makers regarding brand purchases were adult women.
- The product users were all members in the family, with children being the heaviest users who, in addition, could sometimes influence the purchase decision.
- The most significant competitor and a leader in the northern Greek market was a local company, with production facilities in northern Greece and with distribution that was gradually achieving national levels. The company used the "local" dimension as part of its milk's positioning when targeting northern Greek consumers, and claimed that the milk's rich taste comes from the fact that the milk is exclusively gathered from the cows living on northern Greek farms, with their rich climate and unsullied natural setting.
- Other competitors in the fresh milk segment, active in the northern Greek market, were:
    - Another Athenian company, with a rather weak market share, which, nonetheless, was better than that of Delta's milk before the new plant opening.
    - Another local producer, with a much more significant market share, which, however, exhibited a negative share trend, perhaps owing to the cooperative nature of its business model and frequent quality problems of its products.
- Each company offered several types of milk; these types of milk were differentiated mainly by their fat content. Specifically,
    - The most mainstream type was the full fat milk with 3.5 percent fat content. This milk type was usually bought by families with children, and the nutritional value was the most important product benefit for them. This type of milk had more than 60 percent total market volume sales. The second largest in volume sales, 20 percent overall, was low fat milk, with 1.5 percent fat content. Mostly adults and families without children purchased this type of milk. Personal well-being was the most-sought benefit of this target group.
    - The remainder of the white milk market belonged to various niche products, "fortified" with vitamins (e.g., niacin, vitamin D) and minerals (e.g., calcium), which addressed specific customer needs.
- It is important to note that taste "richness" also differed across milk types, determined almost exclusively by fat content. That is, full fat milk offered by far the richest in taste, followed by the enriched milks and, lastly, those low in fat. When compared with the leading local producer's milk, Delta's milk types were lighter in taste within each respective type.

Finally, there were two constraints to which the survey's design needed to conform. First, due to a limited budget, only three milk samples at a time could be tested. Second, due to time pressures, only two rounds of the tests could be conducted. Both of these constraints, it was feared, could make conducting a thorough, fair test difficult.

Bearing all these factors and constraints in mind, the brand management team proceeded, holding a briefing on the survey with the selected research firm. They hoped that the survey would provide them with enough information so that Delta could formulate the best-rated milk, in terms of flavor, among northern Greek consumers. They also realized that they would have only one opportunity to do this well, and that time was running down for them to do so.

Case Questions

1 Define the population and the sampling frame for this survey project. Explain your answers in a manner that supports the proposed definitions.

2 What sampling procedure would you recommend for this taste test survey? Why? What potential deficiencies do you foresee with your suggested procedure?

3 One alternative for how to conduct the survey was to place taste tables on the most crowed streets of the "capital" of northern Greece (Thessaloniki) and select passersby who would be willing to participate in the survey. Evaluate this alternative and discuss its advantages and disadvantages. What might be a better method, from the point of representativeness, bias, and other principles of sampling?

4 Should the taste test be blind or nonblind? Why? Should explicit brand names be tested? Would it be a good idea for Delta to present information about the various milks being tasted, or even a mock-up of containers in which it will be sold? Should pricing information be tested concurrently?

5 Considering the survey's objective and the time and budget constraints, what milk samples would you include in the taste test? Would you vary them across different respondents? How? What sort of statistical methods might allow you to do this scientifically, and to analyze the results correctly? Might you allow consumers to simply try whatever milk products they like best?

6 Besides the general briefing about the survey's purpose and background to the research firm's executives, a brand manager is also responsible for providing or approving a briefing document addressed to the professionals conducting the interviews. What are the issues that should be covered in the briefing document in order to secure a homogeneous and unbiased interaction across interviewees? Place each example in the context of the described taste survey.

7 Is it important to study different regions of the country, or different regions within northern Greece? Should certain segments be deliberately overrepresented in the sample? Should any type of stratification be imposed? Finally, what sort of biases might arise from simply using a random sample—assuming one can be accessed—of the northern Greek population?

Sources: www.delta.gr
Maria Angelidou, brand manager, white milk category, Delta Dairy.

CASE 2.13 *THE BRAMPTON HERALD TRIBUNE*

The Brampton Herald Tribune (BHT) is a weekly entertainment newspaper covering music, arts, and current events. It is distributed free throughout the Brampton, Ontario, metropolitan area. Its revenue is generated largely through the sale of advertising space to local merchants. The BHT was established in 1988 to specifically address the needs of the Brampton area in much the same manner as its parent publication, *The Toronto Herald Tribune*. BHT issues include articles on a variety of subjects, music reviews, arts and theater reviews, classified ads, and a detailed current events calendar.

The management of the BHT decided to conduct a mail-in reader survey to identify and gauge its readership. Exhibit C2.13.1 presents the questionnaire used in the survey.

Case Questions

1 Prepare a coding scheme for the BHT questionnaire.

2 Critique the survey from the following perspectives, being sure to point out specific deficits and suggested improvements:

- **a** as to the overall questionnaire, in terms of its ability to fulfill the organization's information needs
- **b** as to the wording and sequence of particular questions (which should be changed, and how?)
- **c** as to the choices provided on multiple-response questions
- **d** as to whether some of the closed-response questions should be open-ended, and vice versa

3 What specific analyses would you anticipate having to perform on the resulting data? What sample size do you feel would suffice? Would some of the data types make analysis difficult? How so?

Exhibit C2.13.1: The Brampton Herald Tribune Questionnaire

1 *The Brampton Herald Tribune* comes out every Wednesday. Not including this issue, how many of the last six issues have you read or looked into?

( ) Six
( ) Five
( ) Four
( ) Three
( ) Two
( ) One
( ) This is the first.

2 Under column A, please check the features you read regularly. Under column B, check the one you enjoy the most.

A	B	
( )	( )	"Ashes & Diamonds"
( )	( )	"Toni Johnstone"
( )	( )	"Letters"
( )	( )	"Concert Confidential"
( )	( )	"In and Around Brampton"
( )	( )	"In and Around Toronto"
( )	( )	"Hot Dates"
( )	( )	"Pick of the Week"
( )	( )	"Flicks"
( )	( )	"Mondo Video"
( )	( )	"Real Astrology"
( )	( )	"The Comics Page"
( )	( )	"Toronto Live"
( )	( )	Classified ads
( )	( )	Display ads

3 Under column A, check the following *Brampton Herald Tribune* cover stories of which you read some or all. Under column B, also please check the one story you enjoyed the most.

A	B	
( )	( )	"U of T May Flunk"—a feature about the firing of three faculty members for their political views
( )	( )	"Hogtown Gothic"—an investigation into the classic architecture building in Toronto
( )	( )	"EYF"—the fashion issue
( )	( )	"The Greening of Jodi Feldman"—a profile of a Toronto mayoral candidate
( )	( )	"Rob Pulaski's Grande Days"—a music feature on his new band and a look back at the 1970s
( )	( )	"Aggressing the Retina"—a profile of Victor Vassily, optical artist
( )	( )	"A Hard Rain's Gonna Fall"—an exposition on Earth Day, environmental efforts and regional events

4 Which of the following stories did you read?

( ) "Cyberpunk Packs Literary Punch"—the fiction of Mark Townsend
( ) "Radical Makeover for Ms."—changes at *Ms.* magazine
( ) "Still Faithfull"—interview with Marianne Faithfull
( ) "Dance: Encounter with a Diary"—People Dancing show at Ontario Theater
( ) "Nicaraguan Election Surprises Brampton"
( ) "Film Fest Warms Up"—the 28th annual Brampton Film Festival
( ) "Are You Ready for 110 Decibels?"— a preview of the newest in-car speakers
( ) "Can't Play Without My Hair"—a preview of Brampton band, Wayward Chief
( ) "Activist Professor in Residence"—the proposal to establish a visiting "activist" professorship at the University of Toronto

5 What type of music would you like to see more *Brampton Herald Tribune* coverage of?

( ) Jazz
( ) Classical
( ) Blues
( ) R&B
( ) Hard rock
( ) Heavy metal
( ) Other ______________________________

6 What type of coverage do you like the best?

( ) Music
( ) Visual arts
( ) Investigative news Profiles
( ) Opinion/essay
( ) Interviews
( ) Photo stories
( ) Other ______________________________

7 Which of the following publications have you looked into or read *in the past 7 days*?

( ) *The Brampton News*
( ) *The Brampton Observer*
( ) *The Ontario Daily*
( ) *Current*
( ) *The Toronto Free Press*
( ) *The Toronto News*
( ) *Prospect Magazine*
( ) *The University Record*
( ) *Agenda*
( ) *The Ontario Review*
( ) *The New York Times*
( ) *Spotlight*
( ) *Jam Rag*

8 If you could add anything to *The Brampton Herald Tribune,* what would it be?

____
____
____

9 Your gender.

( ) Female
( ) Male

10 Including yourself, please indicate where people in your household fall in the following age categories.

( ) 5 years or younger
( ) 6–11 years
( ) 12–17 years
( ) 18–29 years
( ) 30–49 years
( ) 50 or older

11 What is your age? ______________________________

12 What is your marital status?

( ) Single
( ) Married
( ) Separated or divorced
( ) Widowed

13 Which best describes your current employment status?

( ) Full-time—30+ hours per week
( ) Part-time—1–29 hours per week
( ) Retired
( ) Homemaker
( ) Volunteer
( ) Full-time student—12+ credit hours
( ) Part-time student—1–11 credit hours
( ) Other ______________________________

14 Please check the box that describes your employment income:

( ) Less than $20,000
( ) $20,000–29,999
( ) $30,000–39,999
( ) $40,000–59,999
( ) $60,000–79,999
( ) $80,000–99,999
( ) $100,000–119,999
( ) $120,000–139,999
( ) $140,000–159,999
( ) $160,000–179,999
( ) $180,000+

15 In what kind of business, industry, or profession are you employed?

____

16 What is your highest level of education?

( ) High school
( ) College
( ) Postgraduate
( ) Advanced degree: ( ) Master's ( ) Doctorate

17 As your primary place of residence, do you:

( ) Own a private home
( ) Own a condo or co-op
( ) Rent a house
( ) Rent an apartment
( ) Live in student housing
( ) Live in cooperative housing

18 Do you plan to purchase a house, condo, or co-op in the next 12 months?

( ) Yes
( ) No

19 Do you plan to rent an apartment in the next 12 months?

( ) Yes
( ) No

20 Please indicate which of the following activities you have actively participated in, within the past 12 months.

( ) Adult education courses
( ) Antique shopping
( ) Aerobics
( ) Bicycling (outdoor)
( ) Cooking for leisure
( ) Golf
( ) Hiking or camping
( ) Jogging or distance running
( ) Outdoor gardening
( ) Photography
( ) Racquet sports
( ) Sailing
( ) Canoeing or kayaking

21 How many times have you gone to the movies in the past 30 days? ________

22 How many times have you attended a lecture or seminar open to the public in the past 60 days? ________

23 How many times have you gone to the following in the past 30 days?
_____ Art gallery
_____ Dance performance
_____ Live theater
_____ Concert (pop, rock, other)
_____ Concert (classical)
_____ Bar in which you consumed an alcoholic beverage
_____ Restaurant in which you ate lunch
_____ Restaurant in which you ate dinner

24 Please indicate how many of the following items you have purchased in the past 12 months.
_____ Compact disk
_____ Hardcover book
_____ Paperback book
_____ Record album
_____ Prerecorded cassette
_____ Prerecorded videocassette

25 Please indicate which of the following items you or other members of your household have bought in the past 12 months.

( ) Car stereo
( ) Home stereo system
( ) CD player
( ) Videocassette recorder
( ) Video camcorder

( ) Camera
( ) Personal computer
( ) MP3 Player
( ) Cell phone
( ) Small household appliance (toaster, blender, etc.)
( ) Blinds
( ) Couch, sofa, loveseat
( ) Health club membership
( ) Bicycle

26 How many passenger cars are currently owned by all the people in your household?
Please indicate make/year for each car: ______________________

______________________ Purchased new ( ) or used ( )
______________________ Purchased new ( ) or used ( )
______________________ Purchased new ( ) or used ( )
______________________ Purchased new ( ) or used ( )

27 Do you or members of your household plan to purchase a new or used car for personal use only in the next 12 months?

( ) Yes
( ) No

If yes, check the type you will purchase:
( ) New car
( ) Used car

CASE 2.14 ELYSIAN FOODS

Ice cream and frozen desserts constitute a $20 billion industry (annual sales). In recent years, premium and super-premium desserts have gained popularity, whereas the frozen yogurt market has declined. The United States is the world's leading consumer of ice cream, with 90 percent of households purchasing ice cream at least once per year and per capita consumption nearly 10 times the world average. The late 1990s saw great industry consolidation, as firms sought to leverage distribution strength.

Elysian Foods was a large, successful manufacturer of packaged foods and household products, whose markets were becoming increasingly competitive. In 1998, Elysian Foods launched Snow Queen, the first "super-premium" frozen dessert to enter national distribution. It consisted of 3.5 ounces of vanilla ice cream dipped in penuche fudge and covered with almonds. Individual bars were served on a stick and sold for just less than $3, whereas a package of four was $10.

Kim Johnson had been the product manager who launched Snow Queen. Under her watch, annual sales of Snow Queen reached $40 million, and the dessert began making a significant contribution to dessert group profits. It accounted for almost 5 percent of the market despite a price about 50 percent higher than standard frozen specialties. After 2 years of burgeoning sales, tough challenges emerged from three direct competitors, as well as several parallel concepts at various stages of test marketing. The total frozen specialties market had grown fast enough to absorb these new entrants without reducing Snow Queen sales, but revenues had been essentially flat through 2000 and 2001. Kim was currently the group manager responsible for all established dessert products.

Elysian had a new product in test markets that it hoped would complement the established Snow Queen brand frozen dessert. This new product, Chocolate Shock, consisted of sweet cream ice cream between two oversized chocolate cookies and coated with dark Belgian chocolate. Its price was comparable to Snow Queen's.

Mark Stewart, group manager responsible for all new dessert products, was the product manager for Chocolate Shock. Mark believed that Elysian Foods was vulnerable to increasing competition in its markets because of its failure to keep pace with technological change—especially the increasing sophistication of marketing research based on computer modeling, supermarket scanner data, the Internet, and targetable cable television. Though Elysian used these tools, Mark felt that top management did not embrace them with the same enthusiasm other companies did.

When Mark became product manager for Chocolate Shock, he promised himself he would do a state-of-the-art research job. The plan was to compare the performance of Chocolate Shock in two test markets in order to expose different advertising and promotion strategies. One campaign was conducted in Midland, Texas, and Pittsfield, Massachusetts, and struck an overtly self-indulgent tone: "Go Ahead, You Deserve It." It used limited price promotion to induce trial. The other campaign was conducted in Marion, Indiana, and Corvallis, Oregon, and emphasized superior quality: "Taste the Goodness." This campaign also used promotion aggressively. Sunday newspapers in the latter two cities frequently carried 50-cents-off coupons, and Chocolate Shock boxes included a 75-cent rebate voucher.

Mark used two computer-based research services—InfoScan and BehaviorScan—to evaluate Chocolate Shock's performance and long-term potential. InfoScan tracked product purchases on a national and local basis for the packaged goods industry. It collected point-of-sale information on all bar-coded products sold in a representative sample of supermarkets and drugstores. It generated weekly data on volume, price, market share, the relationship between sales and promotional offers, and merchandising conditions. Mark subscribed to InfoScan in order to monitor competitive trends in the frozen specialties segment.

BehaviorScan was used in marketing tests to measure the effect of marketing strategies on product purchases. In a typical BehaviorScan test, one group of consumer panelists was exposed to certain variables (i.e., print or television advertisements, coupons, free samples, in-store displays), and other participating consumers served as a control group. Company analysts used supermarket scanner data on both groups of consumers (who presented identification cards to store checkout clerks) to evaluate purchasing responses to marketing campaigns. A typical BehaviorScan test lasted about 1 year.

Mark Stewart's marketing research program had generated a stack of computer printouts several feet high. He had spent much of the spring trying to unravel the complex interactions between different advertising and promotion strategies for Chocolate Shock, the various promotion deals Elysian was running on Snow Queen, and the proliferation of other frozen specialties.

After 18 months of product development and test markets, the marketing committee at Elysian Foods met to decide whether it should authorize a national rollout of Chocolate Shock. After the meeting, Larry Burnam, Mark Stewart's boss, informed Mark that the committee had reached a no-launch decision, and that, based on the test results, the returns were not there. Mark disagreed.

"Not there? All they had to look at was Appendix B in my report—the data from Midland and Pittsfield. Chocolate Shock got a 3 percent share after 26 weeks! A trial rate of 15 percent. A re-purchase rate of 45 percent. If national performance were anything close to that, we'd have our launch costs back in 14 months. Who can argue with that?"

"I'm on your side here, but I had only one vote," Larry said defensively. "We both knew what Kim's position was going to be—and you know how much weight she carries around here these days. And to be honest, it was tough to take issue with her. What is the point of introducing Chocolate Shock if you end up stealing share from Snow Queen? In fact, Kim used some of your data against us. She kept waving around Appendix C, griping that 75 percent of the people who tried Chocolate Shock had bought Snow Queen in the previous four weeks. In addition, re-purchase rates were highest among Snow Queen heavy users. You know how the fourteenth floor feels about Snow Queen. Kim claimed that adjusting for lost Snow Queen sales meant Chocolate Shock would not recover its up-front costs for 3 years, and that's just too long."

Mark again disagreed. "You and I both know that things are more complicated than Kim would have people believe. There wasn't the same cannibalization effect in Marion and Corvallis. And we never did a test in Midland and Pittsfield where Kim's people were free to defend Snow Queen. We might be able to have it both ways . . ."

Larry interrupted. "The committee has made its decision. You know how this company works. We don't hold withdrawal of a new product against the manager if withdrawal is the right decision. The fact is, the committee was impressed as hell with the research you did—although to be honest, you may have overwhelmed them. A 40-page report with 30 pages of appendixes, well, even I had trouble wading through it all. But that doesn't matter. You did a great job, and the people who count know that."

Instead of playing golf over the weekend, as Larry had recommended, Mark ran more numbers on the marketing research. Kim was waiting for him in his office Monday morning. She commended his market tests, expressed her disappointment with the no-launch decision, but said the data were pretty clear and left no choice. Mark said he thought the data were clear in the opposite direction.

"Come on, Mark, you can understand the logic of the decision. The Midland and Pittsfield numbers were fine, but they were coming at the expense of Snow Queen. There wasn't so much cannibalization in Marion and Corvallis, but the Chocolate Shock numbers weren't as good either. Trial was acceptable, but re-purchase was low. We might make money, but we'd never meet the hurdle rate. Every so often a product just falls between two stools."

Mark suggested doing more tests. Kim said 18 months was long enough for tests and it was time to try new concepts. Mark expressed fear of (1) losing the valuable freezer space they had been maintaining at stores and (2) having their competitors monitor Chocolate Shock's tests and launch a clone. One such competitor, Weston & Williams, had recently rushed a new product to market on the basis of very preliminary tests and data from another competitor's test markets.

"Larry made that argument Friday," Kim said. "But you can guess how far he got. The guys upstairs have a tough enough time taking our own computer data seriously. They don't buy the idea that someone else is going to jump into the market based on our tests. Plus, that would be a huge risk."

"From what I can tell, Kim, only one issue counted: cannibalization. I understand you want to protect Snow Queen, and I understand that the company wants to protect Snow Queen. But it seems to me we're protecting a product that's getting tired." Mark further asserted that Snow Queen was maintaining market share only through heavy promotion. He called up a series of graphs on his computer. The first showed the growing percentage of Snow Queen's sales connected with promotional offers. The second graph disaggregated Snow Queen's promotion-related sales by four buyer categories Mark had created from BehaviorScan data. "Loyalists" were longtime customers who increased their purchases in response to a deal. "Trial users" bought Snow Queen for the first time because of the promotion and seemed to be turning into loyal customers. "Accelerators" were longtime customers who used coupons or rebates to stock up on a product they would have bought anyway. "Switch-on-deal" customers were nonusers who bought Snow Queen when there were promotions but demonstrated little long-term loyalty. Mark's graph showed an increasing majority of Snow Queen's coupon redeemers fell into the last two categories. His ultimate evidence was a graph that adjusted Snow Queen sales to eliminate the effect of promotions and showed that without promotions, sales of Snow Queen had been essentially flat since April 2001.

"I'm amazed you spent your weekend doing this," Kim said, "but I'm glad you did. It'll help us think through future marketing strategies for Snow Queen. But it doesn't change what the committee decided. It's time to move on."

"I'm not sure," Mark replied. "I hope you don't mind, but I think I should show these data to Larry. Maybe he can convince the committee to reconsider. After all, if Snow Queen is weakening, it's going to show up in your profit figures sooner or later."

"Data don't make decisions, Mark, people do. And the people on the marketing committee have been in the industry a lot longer than you. Their gut tells them things your analysis can't. Besides, you and I both know when you collect this much data, you can make it show just about anything. Go ahead and talk to Larry, but I'm sure he'll see things the same way I do."

Case Questions

1 Considering the purpose for which Mark's report was used by the marketing committee, did Mark identify the research's objective effectively? If not, what research objective should be recommended in its place?

2 What criteria should have been used to select the test markets, their locations, and the overall length of the test? Would those criteria lead to the choices that were in fact made? How?

3 Evaluate Chocolate Shock's cannibalization impact on Snow Queen's sales in the markets that were tested, and the difference across them. What are the factors that could explain this difference? How could Mark use the cannibalization impact difference to support his argument? Is cannibalization truly as huge an issue as management is making it out to be?

4 What techniques, statistical or otherwise, would you recommend to Mark to project the test markets' results on a nationwide-rollout basis? Discuss the advantages and the disadvantages of the recommended techniques. Are there any crucial quantities that cannot be forecasted accurately at this point in time?

5. What are the potential problems that Mark had to consider in order to secure effective projectability of the test results?
6. Given the descriptions of InfoScan and BehaviorScan, do you think these tools were appropriate for Mark's objectives? Why or why not? Are there any alternative methodologies or external data purveyor systems that would be more effective here? Which, specifically, and what would they add to what is already known based on the data available in the case?
7. Evaluate the marketing committee's no-launch decision and the rationale that Kim used to argue her opinion. Do you agree/disagree with the decision and why? Pay particular attention to the assessment of cannibalization potential and future market attrition for Snow Queen.
8. If Mark were authorized to proceed with additional tests, which do you think would be most useful—and in what sequence—to clarify the situation? Why? Design a research proposal in line with your recommendations.

CASE 2.15 BEETHOVEN BEATS BONO?

Forget Sgt. Pepper. Or so reported Britain's vaunted *The Guardian*, even though the live version of the song performed by Paul McCartney and U2 was the fastest online-selling work. As the newspaper concluded tersely, "Beethoven has routed the lot of them."

The BBC made the complete Beethoven symphonies available on its Web site for two weeks during June of 2005, during which time they were downloaded 1.4 million times. The live Sgt. Pepper track set online sales records when 20,000 downloads were sold on iTunes (at 79 pence each) in the first 2 weeks, yet this compared unfavorably with the admittedly free downloads of the Beethoven symphonies.

The controller of Radio 3, Roger Wright, said that the idea had started as "just a little extra add-on to draw attention to the fact that the BBC Philharmonic was performing their first complete Beethoven cycle for 30 years." The results surpassed all expectations. The director of Warner Classics, Matthew Cosgrove, attempted to put the success of the BBC's Beethoven symphonies in perspective by pointing out that it would take a commercial CD recording of the symphonies "upwards of 5 years" to achieve as many downloads as the BBC website did in two weeks. *The Guardian* viewed the startling level of demand for the symphonies as seeming to "defy gloomy predictions about the shrinking appetite for classical music." Wright was also quoted as saying that it was "clear that people had been coming to Beethoven for the first time" through the Beethoven downloads; he discerned this from the fact that the First and Second Symphonies had a high download rate relative to the Third, the "Eroica," a much more famous work.

Although BBC had not yet uncovered details about the downloaders' nationalities and musical habits, *The Guardian* reported that anecdotal evidence suggested an international reach, adding, "If nothing else, the figures suggest the extraordinary power of the BBC." In the words of Wright, this spate of downloads marked "an important moment, when you see how the world is changing."

Industry leaders were invited to discuss the implications of the figures. Chaz Jenkins, the head of LSO Live, the recording company set up by the London Symphony Orchestra (LSO), claimed that "downloads are the future for classical music. You can reach audiences who are intimidated by walking into a classical CD store, or who just cannot get to one. Everyone talks about the early 1980s, when catalogues were re-recorded on CD and everyone replaced their LP collection, as the big boom in the classical recording industry. This could be just as big." Russell Jones, of the Association of British Orchestras, saw downloads of classical recordings as an opportunity to build audiences for live performances. "We'd want to use it to try to drive people to the live performance. The buzz of this happening in the Bridgewater Hall can't be reproduced on a download."

Reached for comment, noted conductor Tali Makell was "pleased to hear about this, as it seems to suggest that the widely touted imminent death of classical music and of the recording industry have been largely exaggerated. However, it may indicate a blip rather than a trend." He added a cautionary note for the music industry in general, that "traditional methods of distribution must undergo critical changes, as consumers turn increasingly to new technologies as their preferred means of acquiring recorded and even live music."

In predictable contrast to all this enthusiasm was the recording industry's concerns about what it considered "unfair competition." Illegal downloads of music tracks still far outstripped online sales, despite aggressive industry lawsuits against those who upload the tracks. Cosgrove responded, "I would be worried if the BBC repeated the experiment. We would take an extremely dim view if it happened repeatedly. It's caused quite a bit of controversy—but it has also provided us with an amazing piece of free market research. I don't think anyone had any idea in their wildest dreams that there would be this level of response. Yes, the downloads were free—but if charged at a commercial rate that would have been a huge amount of revenue."

Mark Thompson, director general of the BBC, said the anxiety about the experiment with free downloads "boils down to two questions: is this the start of some new regular service from the BBC, in which, without warning and consultation, the public will be offered chunks of music free at the point of download which will inevitably distort the commercial market in music? And second, are there any limits to what the BBC might download? Could we wake up one morning to discover that half the BBC's musical archive is available on the net? The answer to these two questions is: no and no. I understand where the anxiety is coming from: the music industry is already under assault from piracy of various kinds—and the last thing it needs is the BBC unintentionally opening up some kind of second front."

This long-term conflict between legal and free downloading services started to mutate not long after this experiment. In October 2006, BitTorrent, still predominantly a source of free, illegal downloads, signed licensing agreements with a variety of media companies to sell movies and TV shows legally. This reflects the media industries' growing understanding that free downloads, such as free radio programming, can serve to increase consumer interest in their products. The media industries hope that by competing side by side with free download service providers, they can convert at least 10 percent of free users to buyers.

Predictions from research studies are that online music sales will continue to grow rapidly, though traditional music sales will still make up almost two thirds of revenues in 2011. One European study predicted a 30 percent decline in sales of physical music, with online sales filling the gap with sales of single tracks instead of whole albums.

Case Questions

1. A casual reader might conclude from this case, particularly because of statements such as "Beethoven has routed the lot of them," that Beethoven was more popular than the Beatles. What sort of evidence drawn from the text might prevent someone from drawing that immediate conclusion?
2. Cosgrove concluded that "it has also provided us with an amazing piece of free market research," and that no one "had any idea in their wildest dreams that there would be this level of response." Indeed, the research was free, but what can be said about the research design and respondent characteristics? What sort of "response" is Cosgrove talking about, and why did he believe it wouldn't be as strong as it was?
3. For each of the following assertions or conclusions drawn from the article, comment on whether it is supported by the data and, if not, what sort of research/methodology might allow one to formally study each issue:
   - A commercial CD recording of the complete Beethoven symphonies would require at least 5 years to sell as many downloads as were shifted from the BBC website in two weeks.
   - The appetite for classical music is shrinking.
   - People had been coming to Beethoven for the first time due to these downloads. Evidence for this was that downloads were greater for the less-popular First and Second Symphonies than for the famous Third.
   - The downloads seemed to indicate an international reach, and that the BBC has extraordinary power in its channel.
   - The downloads would have generated a huge amount of revenue were they not free.
   - Continued free downloading from the BBC site would distort the commercial music market.
   - Some untapped audiences are intimidated by the prospect of walking into a classical music store.
   - Downloads may present a business opportunity as big as that for CDs 25 years before.
   - Music downloads can serve to attract audiences to live performances.
4. Industry insiders and experts offer different opinions on the underlying trend one can extrapolate from this experiment. Roger Wright of the BBC thought the spate of downloads marked "an important moment, when you see how the world is changing," whereas conductor Tali Makell suggested "it may indicate a

blip rather than a trend." Clearly additional forecasting-oriented data would be required to provide support for either of these conclusions. What type of data would determine whether the BBC's inadvertent experiment is "world changing" or "a blip"? What sorts of statistical models would need to be called on once these data were in hand?

5 What sort of research might assess whether the relationship between downloading and music sales actually started to become beneficial, as the example from BitTorrent suggested? Specifically, what data could help address this? Would it be enough to simply monitor online downloads and conventional music sales over time? Why or why not?

6 Predictions were made regarding the proportion of revenue generated by traditional music sales in 2011. What type of study or data would suffice to support such a prediction? Formulate a model (statistical or otherwise) that would allow for this type of sales forecast.

7 Design a full study, melding both external sources and primary data collection, that would allow rigorous testing of which types of music represent the greatest business opportunity. Be sure to consider the secondary effects of downloading, such as increased attendance at concerts, greater artist exposure, and web-based advertising and cross-selling possibilities.

Sources: Higgins, Charlotte, "Beethoven (1.4m) Beats Bono (20,000) in Battle of the Internet Downloads." Charlotte Higgins. *The Guardian*, LondonArbor House, July 21, 2005.

"Survey Says Digital Music Will Fill The Sales Gap." *FMBQ*, March 28, 2006.

"What Comes After YouTube." *BusinessWeek online*, October 30, 2006.

PART 3

ANALYZING MARKETING RESEARCH DATA, ADVANCED TOPICS, AND FINAL REPORTS

CHAPTER NINE
DATA ANALYSIS AND STATISTICAL METHODS: UNIVARIATE AND BIVARIATE ANALYSES

"There are three kinds of lies: lies, damn lies, and statistics."

BENJAMIN DISRAELI

"If your result needs a statistician, then you should design a better experiment."

ERNEST RUTHERFORD

"Let us sit on this log at the roadside," said I, "and forget the inhumanity and ribaldry of the poets. It is in the glorious columns of ascertained facts and legalized measures that beauty is to be found. In this very log we sit up, Mrs. Sampson," says I, "is statistics more wonderful than any poem. The rings show it was sixty years old. At the depth of two thousand feet it would become coal in three thousand years. The deepest coal mine in the world is at Killingworth, near Newcastle. A box four feet long, three feet wide, and two feet eight inches deep will hold a ton of coal. If an artery is cut, compress it above the wound. A man's leg contains thirty bones. The Tower of London was burned in 1841." "Go on Mr. Pratt," says Mrs. Simpson. "Them ideas is so original and soothing. I think statistics are just as lovely as they can be."

O'HENRY, "THE HANDBOOK OF HYMEN"

9.1 The Use of Statistical Methods in Marketing Research

The preceding three quotes illustrate various popular conceptions of statistics, all of them casting the subject in an odd light. The first suggests that statistics exist to aid in deception; the second that statistics is useful only if we have not been suitably careful (or are studying something trivial); and the last, perhaps worst of all, that statistics is merely a collection of scattershot numerical facts. Although these are among the most common characterizations of statistics, they are all highly misleading, especially so for marketing researchers.

Statistical methods vary widely and have been developed over the past century for numerous ends. But, if one had to state what truly underpins them, it would be this: statistical models and methods help us understand *what is going on under all the inevitable noise in the real world*. The world of marketing—and of social science in general—is a murky, imperfect place, and we cannot expect to take a casual look and figure out the forces making it tick. For that, we have to collect suitable data and then find a rigorous way to make sense of them. And that way, invariably, is to use some form of statistical analysis.

It is difficult to convey to someone new to the discipline the extent to which the entire scientific enterprise depends on statistics. It is no exaggeration to say that all empirical human knowledge is firmly based on statistical evidence. Yet this is rarely made explicit outside of scientific literature aimed at specialists and professionals. Popular reports of a high-energy physics experiment that has finally discovered traces of an elusive particle seldom include a description of the many months of data analysis required to ensure that these sightings were "real," and not "random noise." Medical reports linking some environmental factor to a disease usually lack details of the massive statistical analyses required to rule out dozens of other plausible explanations. And reports of election polls, even when they include cryptic remarks about results being "within 3 percent," invariably ignore the careful polling design, stratification, re-weighting and regression analyses that underlie seemingly simple statements about who is likely to win, and by how much.

Statistics is literally the gold standard throughout all of the social and natural sciences, a set of methods whose praises are rarely sung, or even acknowledged. Without statistical methods, marketers, as well as economists, psychologists, physicists, and biologists, would be confronted with vast seas of numbers, with no systematic, defensible way to make sense of them. The remainder of this text is devoted to these methods, and why students of marketing research should care about them.

9.1a Overall Approach to Data Analysis

Some marketers and others mistakenly think that data analysis is the most important aspect of marketing research. Our premise is that the most sophisticated data analysis available cannot make up for shaky problem definition, bad study design, improper sampling, poor measurement, sloppy field work, or careless data processing. The phrase "garbage in, garbage out" crystallizes this idea. Although specialized data analysis techniques have been developed to "correct for" various errors of implementation, they are complex and can be used only when one knows which errors have been made. Throughout, we take the view that data analysis is just one of many activities that must be done correctly to yield relevant information for decision making. That is, it is not a goal in itself, a panacea, or a way to process poor data into informational gold.

We begin by distinguishing data analysis procedures based on the number of variables involved, making our way from univariate, through bivariate, and finally to multivariate procedures. We then spend considerable time on regression methods, distinguishing them by the form of the dependent variable one wishes to explain. Next, we cover the major statistical methods of marketing research—factor analysis, cluster and latent class analyses, multidimensional scaling and conjoint analysis—in considerable detail. Finally, we take a tour of "advanced topics," methods that are still being actively developed, about which the practicing marketing researcher should be aware. We will distinguish between methods attempting to elucidate the *structure* of a set of variables ("interdependence methods") from those attempting to help explain a separate *dependent* variable ("dependence methods"). Throughout, our emphasis will be squarely on how these methods can be used in practice to solve problems arising in marketing research.

The main technique underlying everything else we will learn about is that of regression, by far the most important method of data analysis in all of science. In the authors' experience, effort devoted to truly understanding regression is well spent, and students are encouraged to delve into the method as deeply as time allows. We will approach regression and all other methods covered here from the point of view of a practitioner, stating clearly the most vital details and describing how to convert what statistical analysis programs tell you into useful marketing information. We will *not* try to take the place of a full-scale course in statistics, and students are directed to any of the many books on business statistics or more specialized treatments for details on derivations, formulas, and applications in other domains (see Further Reading section).

But let us start, as they say, at the beginning. *Marketing Research Focus 9.1* examines univariate metrics—those that summarize one variable at a time—the simplest measures in all of marketing research and statistics.

9.2 Overview of Data Analysis Procedures

Once the data have been collected, marketing managers and researchers frequently ask, "What data analysis technique should be used?" The answer, of course, depends on the overall goal of the research, but there are several questions that can help to identify appropriate techniques:

- How many variables are to be analyzed together?
- Do we want to describe the data, or use them to make inferences?
- What level of measurement (e.g., nominal, ordinal, interval) is available in the variable or variables of interest?

Having this information in hand before attempting to come up with a full analysis plan can greatly aid in avoiding time-consuming mistakes.

9.2a Number of Variables to Analyze

The first specific aspect of the situation that must be clarified relates to the number of variables the marketer wishes to analyze together. More precisely: How many variables do we wish to *interrelate?* Let us consider a simple example that we will use throughout this and subsequent chapters. Suppose we have collected data from some sample and recorded each respondent's height, weight, age, and gender. If we were to ask questions about, say, just the weight of people in the sample, our focus would be on a single variable and would thus be a *univariate* analysis. If we were to ask whether there were some relationship between weight and height—perhaps thinking the latter could help predict the former—we would be considering two variables: a *bivariate* analysis. Finally, we might suspect that there is more to predicting weight and wish to include age in our explanation; perhaps the relationship would vary for men and women, prompting us to include gender as well. We would then be considering many variables at once: a *multivariate* analysis. As we will see, the possibilities for analysis expand rapidly with the number of

Marketing Research Focus 9.1

Estimating and Interpreting Univariate Metrics from Samples

Univariate metrics appear frequently in real-world applications, because they help summarize a complex phenomenon in just a few key figures. Projections of sales, costs, earnings, consumer satisfaction, and other managerially relevant metrics are key inputs into marketing decision making, if used with care. Despite their simplicity and clarity, they are less well suited to painting a full, subtle portrait of complex phenomena. Let us consider some examples that help illustrate why.

Because television advertising alone is a $60+ billion annual business in the United States, carefully studying ad penetration and effectiveness has blossomed into a major industry in its own right. The oft-cited Nielsen rating, established by Nielsen Media Research, is a univariate measure of television viewership constructed by sampling households to determine their media consumption patterns. Viewership is reported as a number of "ratings points," with each point representing 1 percent of households tuning in. Nielsen also collects other information, especially of a geodemographic nature, to help advertisers target key audiences, primarily through TV-watching diaries and in-set frequency measurement devices. For Nielsen ratings to be useful, they have to be timely and highly accurate, given the constraints of time for analysis and cost of sampling. Nielsen ratings are constructed using 5100-household samples that capture the viewing habits of approximately 13,000 Americans every day. Such a large sample allows reasonably confident estimates of true viewership, provided it accurately represents the population at large. This last condition can be difficult to satisfy and has led to concerns about possible ratings inaccuracies. Nielsen has attempted to refine its sampling methods to better capture information about various groups, particularly those that are considered chronically undersampled, such as certain ethnic and socioeconomic minorities, as well as hard-to-sample segments such as college dormitory residents. The widespread adoption of technologies such as digital recording devices presents an ever-advancing challenge to the accuracy of sampling methods, even for univariate metrics such as Nielsen ratings points.

Single quantities are often estimated with great accuracy but raise more questions than they answer. The *New York Times* reported that African American and Asian women with bachelor's degrees earned slightly more than similarly educated Caucasian women but that both lag Caucasian men with 4-year degrees. Using data from 2003, the Census Bureau found that a Caucasian woman with a bachelor's degree typically earned $37,800 annually, compared with $43,700 for a college-educated Asian woman and $41,100 for an African American woman, whereas women of Hispanic descent earned $37,600. However, the Census Bureau, despite having some hypotheses, could not ascertain why these differences existed. To do so would require a thorough study of the systematic differences among these different ethnic groups. But the bureau did point out that the corresponding figures for college-educated males—$66,000 for Caucasians, $52,000 for Asians, $49,000 for Hispanics, and $45,000 for African Americans—were uniformly higher. Whether this reflected differences in occupations, experience or workplace discrimination would require a multivariate analysis of the data, despite the near-perfect accuracy possible with census data.

Policy implications often lurk in univariate estimates without being settled by them. The Brookings Institution reported that, from 1970 to 2000, Metropolitan areas in the United States showed a widening gap between "the rich" and "the poor." This was most starkly portrayed by the plight of middle-income neighborhoods, those where families earn 80 to 120 percent of the local median income: researchers found that, as a percentage of all urban and suburban neighborhoods, middle-income neighborhoods in the nation's 100 largest metro areas declined over that 30-year period from 58 percent to 41 percent. Although economists speculated that this change was due to increases in economic opportunity and residential mobility among the affluent and educated, this could not be confirmed without detailed, longitudinal income and relocation data. Indeed, the Brookings study itself concluded that much more research was needed to understand why middle-income neighborhoods were vanishing faster than middle-income families. Although such univariate measurements are powerful indicators of social, economic, and managerial phenomena, they must be supplemented by other data to even begin to put together a complete or causal picture.

Sources: http://web.mit.edu/comm-forum > forums > demographic vistas, April 17, 2003
http://www.nielsenmedia.com > Inside TV ratings
The Associated Press, "Income Gaps Found Among the College-Educated"; *New York Times*. March 28, 2005.

variables at our disposal. In this chapter, we will introduce tools for univariate and bivariate analyses, moving on to the many powerful methods for multivariate analysis in subsequent chapters.

9.2b Description vs. Inference

The second question that must be answered is whether one is interested in *describing the sample* or in making *inferences about the population* from which the sample was drawn. These are very different in scope, method, and intent. "Descriptive statistics" is a branch of statistics that provides researchers with summary measures for the data *in their samples*. It provides answers to such questions as: What is the average age in the sample? What is the *dispersion* of ages in the sample? What is the *level of association* between age and weight in the sample? All these questions try to describe the data we have available, and not to go outside it in any meaningful way; when a teacher announces the average on an exam, it is a statement about all those who happened to take it, not about other people, exams, classes, or subjects.

inferential statistics
A form of statistical analysis that relies on a sample to reach conclusions about a larger group (e.g., the population from which the sample was drawn).

Inferential statistics, by contrast, uses probability theory to make statements about the *population* based on the results stemming from our limited samples. It provides answers to such questions as: Is the average age of the population 25? Are population ages more dispersed this year than last? Is the level of association between age and weight in the population greater than zero? Both descriptive and inferential statistics have important applications in marketing research, and marketers must know which type of analysis best suits their goals.

9.2c Level of Measurement

The third question that must be answered is whether the variable or variables to be analyzed have been measured at a *nominal*, *ordinal*, or *interval* scale level.* Both descriptive and inferential techniques must be chosen to match the scale level(s) inherent in the variable(s) being analyzed. This it not merely a technical or computational matter: If one asks the computer to, for example, estimate an ordinary regression on categorical (nominal) data, it will dutifully perform the analysis, but the results will be meaningless. It is difficult to overstate how critical it is to understand the nature of one's data—including all the levels of measurement involved—before attempting to set a course for its analysis.

If marketers do know the number of variables to be analyzed concurrently, whether description or inference is required, and the scale level of all the variables involved, they are in a good position to select the appropriate statistical procedure. The rest of this chapter identifies and describes the relevant techniques for the analysis of one variable (univariate) or two variables (bivariate) at a time. In presenting this material, we recognize that a computer will be doing the calculations. This does not negate the need for us to know when to use which procedure, the assumptions underlying each, or common potential pitfalls. Rather, the sheer ease of using modern statistical programs requires us to be especially diligent in understanding the domain of application of the dozens of methods at our disposal in even simple statistical programs. Throughout our presentation, we will, for illustration purposes, perform some calculations that one would always have the computer do, but we will rely on the computer entirely for complex or lengthy calculations. Again, this is no substitute for understanding what, in principle, the computer is computing for you, and why.

9.2d Overview of Univariate Data Analysis Procedures

A first step in almost all marketing research projects is to perform univariate analyses on some, or most, available variables. Statisticians are fond of the mantra "*look* at your data," and this is good advice. Before doing anything fancy—that is, looking for complex associations or patterns among variables—one should always get a feel for the variables in question, taken on their own terms. Doing so not only allows one to get a "feel" for the data, but also affords the best opportunity to weed out coding errors, outliers, and other potential problems that would be difficult to spot when embedded in complicated statistical output.

Examples of univariate analyses abound in marketing. For example, the manager might want a description of the sample's demographic characteristics, of the usage of the company's product (sales,

*There are some procedures applicable only to ratio data, but they are exceedingly rare in real marketing research problems. Any ratio data in marketing research are usually analyzed by procedures relevant to interval data, since all ratio data are also interval. We will also distinguish between data that have been measured on an explicit ordinal scale (for which we can use ordinal regression), and those that have been rank-ordered (for which more complex techniques like the rank-ordered logit model must be used; see Chapter 10 for additional detail).

Figure 9.1 Overview of Univariate Data Analysis Procedures

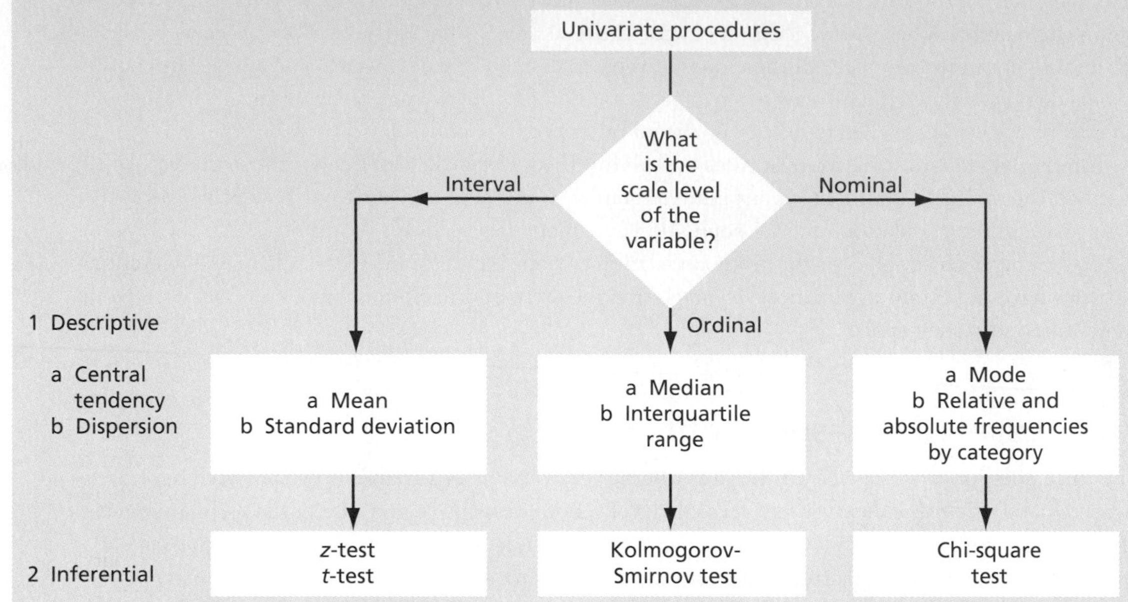

volume), or of respondent attitudes toward a competitive activity. In each situation, the researcher can gain useful information by examining statistics related to one variable at a time.

Once one has determined that one will perform univariate analyses, one should determine the scale level of the variables to be analyzed. They may be nominal, ordinal or interval, or occasionally nonstandard. Figure 9.1 presents an overview of statistical techniques appropriate for univariate data analysis. Below each of the possible answers to the scale-level question lie two boxes. The upper box presents the relevant descriptive statistics for "central tendency" and for "dispersion." The lower box lists the appropriate tests of statistical inference for each data type. Note that statistics appropriate for less structured scales can be applied to more structured scales. For example, a mode and a median can meaningfully be calculated for interval data. However, the opposite is not true; the mean is not an appropriate statistic for ordinal or nominal data.

It is not our purpose to present details of every descriptive statistic and every test of inference for every measurement level; this is what a dedicated statistics text is for. The discussion presented in these chapters will deal with only those techniques that are most relevant to marketing research practice. Thus, in this chapter we will not discuss the interquartile range statistic or the Kolmogorov-Smirnov test, for these are not in the mainstream of marketing research practice; few marketing research professionals would rely on them, or even know how to interpret them. Details on these and many other specialized tests are available in any basic statistics textbook, and through many comprehensive Web resources (see full listing in the Further Reading section of this chapter). What follows, then, is a discussion of those statistical procedures with which a practicing marketing researcher should be familiar. Some, such as ordinary regression, should be mastered in terms of both conceptual understanding and an ability to perform them on a variety of data sets; for others, such as hierarchical Bayes conjoint analysis, the practicing manager should be familiar enough to have a fruitful conversation with those who perform such analyses.

9.2e Illustration Data Set: Weight, Height, Gender, Age, LikeStat for Marketing Research Students

To make all our discussions and examples more concrete, we will refer to one "master" data set with which students can readily relate. The data stem from 448 participants in a marketing research course, collected over a period of 6 years, from three groups—undergraduates and both "regular" (full-time) and "executive" (part-time) MBA students—who provided the following information:

Variable	Description
Weight	Pounds
Age	Years
Gender	M = 1, F = 0
Height	Inches
MBA	0 = Non-MBA student, 1 = MBA student
Class	1 = undergraduate, 2 = regular MBA, 3 = evening MBA
Year	In which year data were collected: 1–6
LikeStat	"On a scale of 1–7, where 1 is 'not at all' and 7 is 'very much,' how well did you like your introductory statistics course?"

These data are intriguing for several reasons. First, we would anticipate that there would be relations among some of the variables. For example, it is easy to imagine that height and weight would show some relationship and that each of them would be related to gender; moreover, undergraduates are generally younger than executive MBA students. Second, relationships among other variables are unclear: does weight tend to rise as we age? Would we expect more women to be in the undergraduate version of the course? Which types of students seem to most appreciate their introductory statistics course? Third, these variables are of many different types: Weight, age, and height can be treated as continuous, interval-scaled variables; year is discrete but can also be treated as interval scaled; gender and MBA are binary (dichotomous); class is nominal; and LikeStat is measured on an ordinal scale. Lastly, variables such as LikeStat are often treated as interval scaled, even though, strictly speaking, they are not. Can we use statistics to see whether this makes a practical difference? Finally, and perhaps most importantly, the data set is *multivariate*. If we attempt to explain, say, weight in terms of each of age, gender, and height (etc.) by itself, will we obtain very different results when we look for a *unified explanation*, involving many of these variables in the same equation?

discrete
A quantity or variable for which a list of distinct values can be made, each of which occurs with some positive probability. Which day of the week an event will occur on is discrete; how many times one flips a coin before getting "tails" is also discrete, even though it is limitless; the set of all possible numbers between zero and one is not discrete, but rather *continuous*.

As we will see, many of the core issues in all of statistical inference have been raised by these examples and, in the course of answering them, we will cover a great deal of terrain pertaining to the proper use of regression models and other statistical methods. Throughout, we encourage students to load these data into the statistical program of their choice and attempt to replicate our results and explanations. The best way to really learn how to use statistical methods is to jump right in and start using them.

9.3 Descriptive Statistics

The objective of descriptive statistics is to provide summary measures of the data contained in all the elements of a sample. In doing so, the marketing researcher is usually concerned with measures of *central tendency* and of *dispersion*. Loosely speaking, these tell us where the bulk of the data are located, and how "spread out" the data values are around the central measure. We next formalize these intuitive notions.

9.3a Measures of Central Tendency

Three measures of central tendency are often used in marketing research and throughout statistical practice: the mean, the median, and the mode. They are fundamental, and all managers should be familiar with them.

central tendency
Any of a number of estimates of the most common of, or the center of, a variable's values; the most widely-used measures of central tendency are the mean, median, and mode.

Interval Data: The Mean

The mean is an appropriate measure of central tendency for interval data and is by far the most widely used such measure in all of statistics. The reader should already be familiar with the concept of a mean because we made extensive use of it for both a continuous variable and a proportion in the last chapter, when discussing various types of random sampling. To review, the mean is the sum of the values divided by the sample size:

$$\bar{X} = \frac{1}{n}\sum_{i=1}^{n} X_i$$

Referring to our data set of marketing research students, we see that the mean values for each of our variables is as follows:

	Age	Gender	Height	Weight	Class	MBA	Year	LikeStat
Mean	27.59	0.587	68.2	156.0	2.06	0.74	3.54	4.56

Note that these mean values do not take into account important distinctions in the data. For example, we are including both men and women in all these averages and so run the risk of much of the data for, say, height being relatively distant from the putative central tendency of approximately 68.2 inches. (When we learn about regression models, we will see that this is related to a problem called "nonnormality.")

Ordinal Data: The Median

median
A common measure of central tendency, the middle value of a variable in the sample. Exactly half the values fall above and half below the median.

If our data form an ordinal (or interval) scale, we may legitimately make use of the median as a measure of central tendency. The median is defined as the middle value when the data are arranged in order of magnitude; that is, half the values fall above the median and half fall below. (When there are an even number of data points, none is exactly "in the middle," so the median is typically calculated by taking the midpoint or average of the two middle values.)

The median is an especially important and useful measure when our data contain outliers, which are values well outside the range of most of the data. For example, if a test is given in a class of 25 students, but one student does not show up (and is given a zero), that one student can bring the average down by as much as four points, simply because a grade of zero is (hopefully!) well outside the range of scores of the students who did take the exam. If the median is used instead, the worst that can happen when adding an outlier is that its value will move to an adjacent value in the ordered data. That is, if a billionaire moves to your town, the mean income in the area could rise by many thousands, or even millions, of dollars; but the median is unlikely to change at all. This property is so important in statistics that it is given its own name, robustness; any statistic that resists large changes in the presence of a few atypical values (outliers) is said to be robust. We therefore say that the median is robust but the mean is not.

robustness
Any statistic whose value resists dramatic change in the presence of outliers.

Let us again look at our data on marketing research students:

	Age	Gender	Height	Weight	Class	MBA	Year	LikeStat
Mean	27.59	0.587	68.2	156.0	2.06	0.74	3.54	4.56
Median	28	1	68.0	150.5	2	1	4	5

These values indicate both the strengths and the weaknesses of the median, compared with the mean, as a measure of central tendency. For essentially continuous quantities, such as height and weight, the mean and median can be directly compared. For these data, median and mean height are very close to one another; but the same is not true for weight. This is because there are many more outliers for weight than height on the high side of each variable. Note that median weight is quite a bit lower than the mean weight, the result of its being robust to outliers at the upper end of the weight distribution. The median is less useful for discrete, ordered variables such as LikeStat, or those with limited range, such as year (and it is *not applicable* for nominal variables such as class, even if it *is* calculable); because it must take on a value in the actual data, it runs the risk of being uninformative when there are relatively few such values. This is taken to extremes for *binary* (dichotomous) variables, where there are only two values; the median takes on one of these. So, the median gender is 1, meaning male! In this case, the mean gender of 0.587 gives useful information: that 58.7 percent of our sample is male.

Nominal Data: The Mode

mode
A common measure of central tendency, the most frequently occurring value of a variable in the sample.

The mode is a measure of central tendency appropriate for nominal data (and of course any data with more structure, such as interval and ordinal). It is simply the category of a nominal variable that occurs most often. Let us again consider our data set of marketing research students:

	Age	Gender	Height	Weight	Class	MBA	Year	LikeStat
Mean	27.59	0.587	68.2	156.0	2.06	0.74	3.54	4.56
Median	28	1	68.0	150.5	2	1	4	5
Mode	21	1	68.0	120.0	2	1	4	7

These results make an interesting, general point about the mode: It should not be applied to ordinal or interval data unless these data have been grouped first. This can be seen for weight, where the modal value is 120 pounds. By pure chance, there were quite a few students weighing exactly 120 pounds, so the mode is quite far from the true "center" of the data, as indicated by the mean and median. And this effect is extreme for LikeStat, with mode 7; although there were many students who apparently greatly appreciated their statistics course, the median of 5 and mean of 4.56 indicate that this opinion was far from universal.

Sometimes a variable is **bimodal**. That is, two classes have similar, and relatively high, frequencies. There are some societies, for example, where wealth is concentrated in the hands of a minority, and the majority is very poor, with a small or nonexistent middle class. In such bimodal wealth distributions, measures such as mean income can be highly misleading, and wrongly suggest that the *average citizen* is doing fairly well; the median may paint a truer picture, but not a terribly accurate one. And even the mode—which would indicate poverty—would ignore that the society as a whole may have resources, even if they are inequitably distributed. Researchers need to look closely at their data to see whether bimodality is present. When it is, this should be a tip-off to the researcher to seek out some other variable that may help explain the situation. Among the marketing research students in our example, if we look at the data for age, we obtain a rather disturbing histogram (see Figure 9.2).

bimodal
Describes a variable with two distinct, relatively high rates of incidence (modes, or "humps").

Our age data are highly bimodal, indicating perhaps that they derive from two distinct populations. But we know that this is true: The left "hump" comprises the undergraduates in the sample, whose ages are much lower than those of the MBA students. Note that a normal distribution superimposed on the histogram shows a very different shape from the data themselves. Normal distributions are *unimodal*, and superimposing one with the same mean and standard deviation provides a reliable visual guide to whether multiple, distinct groups might exist for the variable in question.

9.3b Measures of Dispersion

Measures of central tendency do not provide enough information for researchers to adequately summarize the distribution of a particular variable under study. For example, the sets of numbers {14, 15, 16} and {5, 10, 30} each have a mean of 15, but the first set is symmetric and tightly centered, compared with

Figure 9.2 Histogram of Age for the Marketing Research Student Data

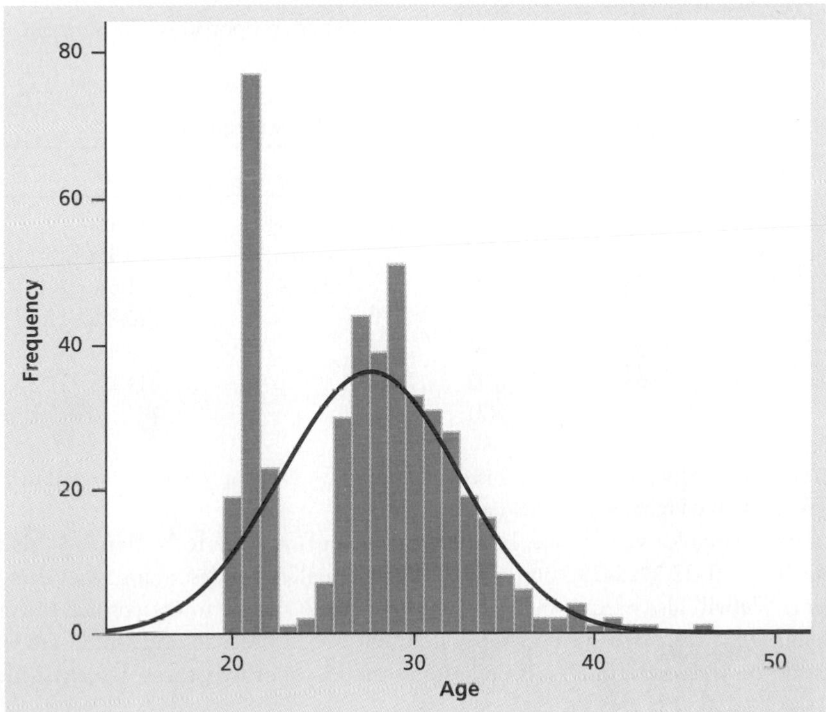

dispersion
One of a number of statistical measures for the degree to which values of a variable are spread around some measure of central tendency (e.g., mean, median or mode). The most common measures of dispersion are the standard deviation, variance, range, and interquartile range (difference between the 25th and 75th percentile values in the data).

the second. At minimum, we need a sense of the "spread" of the distribution of the variable, which can be achieved via measures of **dispersion**. As with measures of central tendency, those for dispersion will differ depending on the sort of data under examination.

Interval Data: The Standard Deviation

The appropriate measure of dispersion for interval data is the standard deviation, the measure calculated in the previous chapter for both continuous variables and proportions. Recall that the sample standard deviation is given by:

$$s = \sqrt{\frac{\sum_{i-1}^{n} (X_i - \bar{X})^2}{n-1}}$$

Let us examine these values for our data on marketing research students:

	Age	Gender	Height	Weight	Class	MBA	Year	LikeStat
Mean	27.59	0.587	68.2	156.0	2.06	0.74	3.54	4.56
Std Dev	4.92	0.493	4.0	32.2	0.76	0.44	1.67	2.13

Note that, just like the mean, the standard deviation is meaningless for MBA, because it is a nominal variable; it is also not strictly applicable to LikeStat, which is ordinal, not interval. And, because both gender and class are dichotomous, we could have calculated the standard deviation directly from the mean; for example, for gender:

$$s = \sqrt{\frac{np(1-p)}{n-1}} = \sqrt{\frac{449(.587)(1-.587)}{449-1}} = 0.493.$$

The standard deviation is, next to the mean, the most important summary measure in statistics, and should always be calculated for interval-scaled data.

Nominal Data: Relative and Absolute Frequencies

absolute frequency
The total number of times an event occurred during a study or experiment, disregarding the number of opportunities it had to occur.

relative frequency
The number of times an event occurred during a study or experiment, divided by the total number of opportunities for occurrence (or, by the total number of events that did occur).

For nominal data (or "better"), we may legitimately calculate relative and absolute frequencies as measures of dispersion. **Absolute frequencies** are the number of items in the sample in each category of the nominal variable; **relative frequencies** present these same data as proportions. Thus, in our example, we can calculate absolute frequencies as follows:

	Absolute Frequencies			Relative Frequencies		
Value	Class	Year	LikeStat	Class	Year	LikeStat
1	117	69	49	26.1%	15.4%	10.9%
2	188	82	62	42.0%	18.3%	13.8%
3	143	52	46	31.9%	11.6%	10.3%
4		93	35		20.8%	7.8%
5		89	63		19.9%	14.1%
6		63	72		14.1%	16.1%
7			121			27.0%

Frequencies are typically presented in a histogram, merely a bar graph of the relevant cell counts; for class, this would look like Figure 9.3.

Frequencies for variables such as age, height, and weight first have to be "binned," that is, placed into ranges, such as "20–22," "23–29," and so on, for age. Usually, just describing what is in the sample is not sufficient. We will also wish to make *inferences* from the sample to the *population* from which it was drawn. It is to this issue that we now turn our attention. In order to understand properly the following discussion on inference, one must understand the basics of hypothesis testing, which are presented first.

Figure 9.3 Frequency Distribution of Class for the Marketing Research Student Data

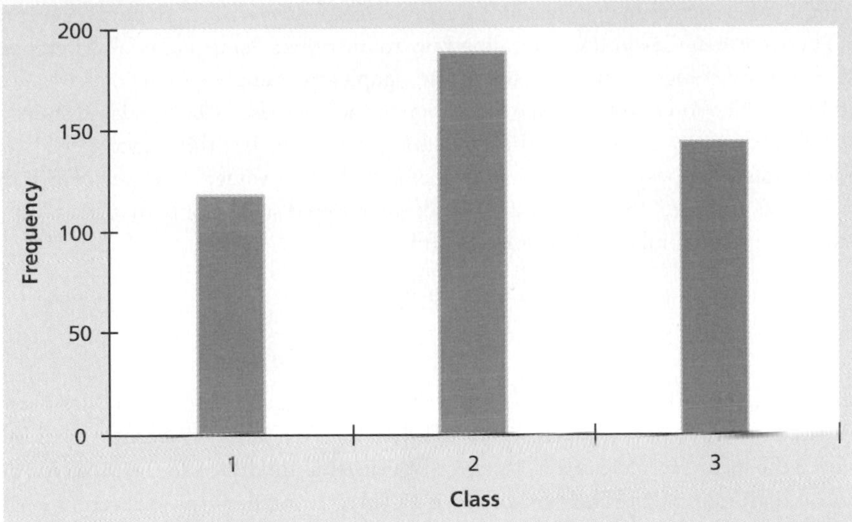

9.4 Hypothesis Testing

Hypothesis testing is a procedure familiar from any basic statistics course. Our discussion presumes that readers have had such a course, but they may nonetheless benefit from a review; if not, this section can be skipped without any loss of flow.

9.4a The Concept of a Null Hypothesis

Hypothesis testing begins with the statement of a **null hypothesis**, a forbidding term that refers to something rather simple: that a *population parameter* takes on a particular value. For example, we might wish to test to see whether the mean age of a large class (the population from which we will draw a sample) is 25 years. The null hypothesis, always written as "H_0," is therefore:

null hypothesis
A specific statement, opposed to the "alternative hypothesis," subjected to statistical test. The null hypothesis typically states that there is no effect (i.e., the effect equals zero), or that two quantities are equal to one another (i.e., their difference is zero), and this is what the researcher wishes to cast doubt on through data collection and statistical testing.

$$H_0 : \mu = 25.$$

Note that the null hypothesis should always be written as an equality, specifying some exact value for the population parameter in question. By contrast, there will be an alternative hypothesis, and this is what we are attempting to verify. If we get enough evidence, we will be able to say that "we *reject* the null hypothesis in favor of the alternative hypothesis." We will NEVER "accept" the null hypothesis, but merely fail to reject it. In such a situation, we do *not* conclude that the null hypothesis is valid. Rather, all we can say is that we do not have suitable evidence to reject it. The analogy with our legal system is exactly on the mark: When we pronounce someone not guilty, we are not making a proclamation that the person is completely innocent, only that not enough evidence has been marshaled for a conviction. In the case of hypothesis testing, even if we cannot reject H_0, it may later be rejected with the collection of new sample data (unlike in our legal system, where prosecutors get "one bite at the apple").

Note that we test the value of a population parameter using data coming from a sample. It is exceedingly rare that the sample value matches the tested population value (according to H_0) exactly, due to sampling error. For example, if we took a sample of students in the class, we would be surprised if their mean age came out to be exactly 25; and it would be foolish to claim that the hypothesis $\mu = 25$ was wrong merely because the sample value differed by a small amount. The key point is this: By examining the sampling distribution of a statistic, we can determine whether the sample value is *different enough* from the proposed null hypothesis value to have occurred just by sampling error alone. Please go back and review that last sentence until you are sure you have grasped its meaning, because it explains the logic behind all of hypothesis testing, and hypothesis testing will be with us for all of our statistical analyses.

Once we have a sample statistic (say, the mean), we can compare it with the value specified by the null hypothesis. If this difference were greater than that due to sampling error, we would *reject* the null hypothesis. If the difference were not especially large, we could *not reject* (again: never "accept") the null hypothesis. The trick here lies in understanding how to quantify a "large enough" difference, and this will depend on several things, such as the size of the sample, the sample variance, and how certain we want to be that our rejection is justified. We will examine each of these factors in detail shortly.

alternative hypothesis
A specific statement, opposed to the "null hypothesis," subjected to statistical test. The alternative hypothesis is typically what the researcher anticipates will actually happen, or the hoped-for outcome (for example, in a clinical trial of a new drug or an ad test).

Because null hypotheses always say "the population parameter has this exact value," a variety of **alternative hypotheses** are possible, including "it does *not* take that value," "it is *greater than* that value," and "it is *less than* that value." In our case, the first of these would state simply that the mean age is not 25, and we would write the null and alternative hypotheses as:

$$H_0 : \mu = 25$$

$$H_1 : \mu \neq 25.$$

In testing this null hypothesis, we would reject it if the mean age were either "significantly" (in a sense to be made precise momentarily) greater *or* less than 25. That is, either large or small values of the sample statistic (the mean) would cause us to reject. We are thus interested in the sampling distribution of mean ages on both sides of 25. This type of test is called a "two-tailed" test, because we will examine both ends ("tails") of the sampling distribution to determine the strength of our evidence against the null. "Large" deviations (from 25) on either side will help us reject the null in favor of the alternative.

Another alternative hypothesis in this situation is that the mean age is greater than 25, and we would write:

$$H_0 : \mu = 25$$

$$H_1 : \mu > 25.$$

Here, our interest is only in the upper part of the sampling distribution of means. Such a hypothesis test is called "one-tailed" because the alternative hypothesis specifies a direction; only large *positive* deviations would count against the null in favor of the alternative. A final possibility for the alternative hypothesis is that the mean age is less than 25, and this would also be a one-tailed test.

one-tailed test
A statistical test of a hypothesis that specifies a direction (e.g., that some parameter's value is specifically greater than zero.)

Whenever the alternative hypothesis is directional, a **one-tailed test** applies. This will be the case in the vast majority of marketing research applications. We are seldom interested in whether a test ad is *different* from the one already being used, but whether it is *better;* we want to see whether a promotion *increases* sales; we are concerned that our share may be *slipping;* and so forth. Take care to state the alternative hypothesis so that it is really what you wish to find evidence for, and to only "reject the null" in its favor if the evidence is strong and in the right direction. What constitutes strong evidence, and how we measure it, is what we consider next.

9.4b Possible Errors

In hypothesis testing, the decision maker either rejects or does not reject H_0. Like all decisions, either of these may be correct or incorrect. That is, the null may be true, but we reject it; or it may be false, and we do not. To be very precise, there are four possibilities, two of them correct, and two incorrect:

- H_0 is true and *is* rejected: incorrect (Type I error: α).
- H_0 is true and is *not* rejected: correct.
- H_0 is false and *is* rejected: correct.
- H_0 is false and is *not* rejected: incorrect (Type II error: β).

Note that the incorrect statements are associated with specific names for the errors involved: Type I error (α) and Type II error (β). They are sometimes referred to by the evocative phrases "convicting the innocent" (α) and "freeing the guilty" (β). In society as well as statistics, we place a far greater emphasis on not convicting the innocent, and so will try especially hard to control this source of error; that is, not rejecting the null hypothesis when it is true. Note that we can do this perfectly by *never* rejecting the null hypothesis! However, this would result in "freeing the guilty" *all* the time ($\beta = 1$), so in practice we will have to balance "tolerable" degrees of the two types of error, α and β. Table 9.1 presents a summary of

Table 9.1 Summary of Hypothesis Testing Errors

	True Condition	
Sample Conclusion	**H_0 is true**	**H_0 is false**
Do not reject H_0	Correct decision	Type II error
	Confidence level	Probability $= \beta$
	Probability $= 1 - \alpha$	
Do not reject H_0	Type I error	Correct decision
	Significance level	Power of the test
	Probability $= \alpha$	Probability $= 1 - \beta$

these considerations, including the probabilities of being correct, of making each type of error, and appropriate terminology.

9.4c Type I Error (α)

The usual starting point in hypothesis testing is to specify the *level* of Type I error (α) the researcher is willing to tolerate. Because hypotheses are always tested with data from a sample, there will always be some sampling error (recall that this is the error associated with differences from random sample to random sample, and does *not* account for any sort of researcher mistakes or biases). The further the sample statistic is from the value specified by the null hypothesis, the better our evidence that H_0 is not true. (Important note: We will never refer to the "likelihood" or "probability" that H_0 is true; H_0 is either true or it is not. The only probabilities involved are associated with values from the *sample*.) However, when H_0 is true, every now and again we will obtain unlikely values of the sample statistic, those that come from the tails of the distribution; and these values will persuade us that H_0 is *not* true. This is unavoidable, even if our sampling is done as carefully and rigorously as possible. And this is precisely the idea of a Type I error (α): mistakenly rejecting a true null hypothesis, or "convicting the innocent." To control for such unfavorable outcomes, one sets some maximally tolerable degree of error; this is referred to as the significance level, designated by α. If the researcher specifies that a Type I error can be tolerated only one time in twenty, we would state this as $\alpha = 0.05$, and say that "the test will be performed at the 0.05 (significance) level."

An equivalent way of looking at this situation is to think not of the probability of making an error (a Type I error, specifically), but the likelihood of being correct. That is, we could also consider the probability of *not* rejecting H_0 when it is true. This probability is therefore just $(1 - \alpha)$, and is referred to as the confidence level of the test. The more confidence we want in the test, the smaller we must set α. A test performed at the $\alpha = 0.05$ significance level is thus performed at the $1 - \alpha = 0.95$ confidence level. We have come across precisely the same concept of confidence before, when calculating confidence intervals in the previous chapter, based on simple random sampling. As before, this relates to the proportion of the sampling distribution (area under the curve) of a statistic that falls within a certain distance from the true population value.

Type I error (α)
The probability that the null hypothesis is (incorrectly) rejected when it is true; also known as alpha (α) error; analogous to "convicting the innocent."

significance level
Formally, the greatest probability a researcher sets of rejecting the null hypothesis, even though it happens to be true; usually denoted by α and frequently set in applied work at 0.05 or 0.01; also can refer to the *p*-value of a statistical test.

confidence level
The largest probability a researcher is willing to tolerate for concluding a null hypothesis is incorrect, even though it is. Thus, a 0.05 confidence level means there is a 1 in 20 chance that the researcher will reject a true null hypothesis, just by chance alone.

9.4d Type II Error (β)

We now examine the possible outcomes when H_0 is *false*. If we do not reject H_0 when it is false, we have made a Type II error, the probability of which is designated β. (It is important not to confuse this with the estimated coefficients in a regression, which are also typically designated as β. We will be careful in distinguishing these usages, which are both standard in statistics.) Type I error occurs when we observe an outlier (of the sampling distribution of the statistic referred to by H_0) and therefore reject the null hypothesis. By contrast, Type II error occurs when we really are looking at a value drawn from a different sampling distribution entirely (that is, a different value of the parameter than the one suggested by H_0)

Type II error (β)
The probability that one (incorrectly) fails to reject the null hypothesis when it is not true; also known as beta (β) error; analogous to "failing to convict the guilty."

and, by bad luck, it happens to be fairly likely under H_0, and we therefore *do not* reject it. The farther an observed value of a statistic is from H_0, the more likely it is that it comes from a different sampling distribution. Thus, the smaller we set α, the larger the probability of a Type II error, β. That is, it is very difficult to make both α and β small at the same time. This should make intuitive sense if we think back to our trial example. How might we come up with a procedure that would reduce the chances of "convicting the innocent" *and* "freeing the guilty" at the same time, without having to collect a great deal more data?

power of the test
Formally, the probability of rejecting the null hypothesis when it is false; usually denoted by $(1 - \beta)$ (where β is the probability of Type II error, *not* a regression coefficient, which sometimes uses the same symbol).

If H_0 is *false* and we do reject it, we have made a correct decision. We describe the probability of rejecting a false null hypothesis as the **power of the test**, given by $1 - \beta$. A powerful test means that we have great ability to detect false null hypotheses, that is, to discern when we are being lied to. Note that β (and therefore $1 - \beta$) can be calculated only when a specific alternative hypothesis is stated. Intuitively, if the null and alternative hypotheses are very similar, it will be hard to discern which is true, so our test will not have great power without an enormous sample size. For example, it is easy to distinguish a pain reliever that works in five minutes from one that works in five hours, but hard to distinguish it from one that works in six minutes. For now, it is enough to recognize that for a given sample size, β increases as α decreases.

In practice, β is often determined only after the sample has been selected or it is simply ignored. The problem with this approach in marketing is that the cost to an organization of a Type II error can be much greater than that of a Type I error. Consider this example: Suppose we have to choose the best promotional strategy for a new product introduction from among three possible strategies. The null hypothesis is that all the strategies are equally effective, and we make a Type I error, rejecting this true hypothesis. Because we would then select one of the equally effective alternatives, there is relatively little risk associated with our choice of strategies.

On the other hand, in the case where the hypothesis was false, we might fail to reject it, concluding that there is no difference in the effectiveness of the three promotional strategies, when one promotional strategy is, in fact, more effective than the others. This Type II error could be very costly, in terms of opportunity costs, if we select one of the less effective strategies.

As this example shows, in managerial settings there is some argument for not setting too small a value of α. This is most certainly not the case in, say, medical applications, where there are substantial social costs to (mistakenly) claiming that a new treatment or procedure is really better, a Type I error. Thus, the oft-posed question of "what should be our value of α?" has no universally correct reply. How small a value to set for α depends critically on context. How much of a chance would we want to take on convicting someone innocent? In legal or medical situations, we would want a much smaller value of α than in any managerial setting.

9.4e Steps in Hypothesis Testing

Hypothesis testing is a codified process, and its steps are well understood:

1. Formulate a null (H_0) and an alternative (H_1) hypothesis.
2. Select the appropriate statistical test given the type of data being analyzed.
3. Specify the significance level, α.
4. Look up the value of the test statistic, using tables or by computer, for the given α; tabulated values correspond to points on the sampling distribution of the statistic in question that occur with different Type I error (α) probabilities.
5. Perform the statistical test chosen in step 2, yielding a value of the relevant statistic.
6. Compare the value of the statistic calculated in step 5 with the value obtained in step 4. If the computed test statistic is greater than the tabulated value, we reject the null hypothesis, as it is too far out "in the tails" to be considered as coming from the sampling distribution arising via H_0. We would say informally that the test statistic is "unlikely to have come about by chance alone," so we reject H_0 at significance level α.

***p*-value**
A crucial quantity in any statistical test, distilling how strong the evidence is in favor of some quantity not being zero (in the population, based on one's sample data). All regression programs report *p*-values for each coefficient and for the entire model.

In a moment we will apply these steps and go one step further in learning to summarize all the information in the hypothesis test in a single quantity, called the ***p*-value**. But first, *Marketing Research Focus* 9.2 illustrates some of the difficulties of even defining hypotheses correctly in real-world applications, where knowing precisely what one is looking for can be half the battle in a marketing research project.

Marketing Research Focus 9.2

Defining Hypotheses Correctly in Field Work

Careful definition of the expected relationships among variables is central to all empirical work, in marketing and elsewhere. When hypotheses are defined clearly, in a manner consistent with the underlying theory, results obtained from statistical analysis are similarly unambiguous in their interpretation.

Defining a hypothesis, however, can sometimes pose a considerable challenge in itself. For example, the theory of *compensating differentials* in labor economics suggests that, all else equal, workers must be compensated for less (or more) desirable job characteristics with higher (or lower) pay. For some characteristics, such as flexibility of scheduling or "dirtiness" (say, being a trash collector), the predicted direction of the relationship is clear. Because flexibility of scheduling is preferable to inflexibility, wages for employment where scheduling is flexible should be lower than "similar" jobs with inflexible schedules. Along the same lines, because griminess is generally considered unpleasant, we would expect that compared with similar jobs that were relatively clean, dirty jobs would pay more.

However, there are some job characteristics where the direction of influence is not clear-cut. For example, some jobs require more physical exertion than others, but this is not necessarily unpleasant for everyone—many people enjoy some amount of physical exertion in their work and dislike working in a situation where they have to remain sedentary. Similarly, jobs involving work outdoors may prove harsh or distasteful to some people but quite pleasant to others. Given the variety of characteristics jobs can possess, some of these may be obviously unpleasant or pleasant, and others may vary in how potential employees react to them.

When labor economists tested the theory of compensating differentials using rigorous statistical methods, they accounted for these varying expectations in developing their hypotheses. For example, the expected effect of "dirtiness" on wages is positive, holding all else equal because it is an unpleasant element of a given job that must be compensated with higher wages; this expectation changed the definition of the alternative hypothesis to be a one-sided test.

Of course, the "all else equal" condition is particularly challenging to meet, so the investigators in this study use statistical methods more complex than simple means testing in their analysis. Such methods help account for the fact that as one aspect of a job changes, others tend to as well, not only the variable(s) one happens to be studying. Nonetheless, the measurement of how "undesirable" job characteristics affect market-rate compensation provides a telling example of how hypothesis definition can be a critical—and oftentimes challenging—element of a statistical study.

Sources: Brown, Charles (1980), "Equalizing Differences in the Labor Market." *Quarterly Journal of Economics*, (94)1, 113–134.
"Compensating Wage Differentials for Fatal and Nonfatal Injury Risk by Gender and Race" John D. Leeth and John Ruser. *Journal of Risk and Uncertainty* Volume 27, Number 3; December, 2003 Pages 257–277.
"Work-related fatality risks and neoclassical compensating wage differentials" Kevin Purse. *Cambridge Journal of Economics*, 28(4), 2004 Pages 597–617.

9.5 Inferential Statistics

As with descriptive statistics, choosing the appropriate inferential statistical test also depends on the scale level of the data to be analyzed. Here we take up suitable test procedures for interval and nominal data. Ordinal data are more complex and will be addressed in detail in Chapter 10, on regression models.

9.5a Interval Data

Two different tests, the *z*-test and the *t*-test, are appropriate for tests for the population mean based on interval data. The choice between the two depends on the researcher's knowledge of the population standard deviation, whether the underlying population is known to be normal, and the sample size. In most cases, we will not know the population standard deviation or whether the population is normal, and will need to use a *t*-test.

9.5b *z*-Test

Hypothesis testing for the mean allows researchers to compare the mean stemming from a sample ($\bar{X}$) with a mean hypothesized to exist in the population (H_0: $\mu = \mu_0$). The *z*-test allows us to decide whether the sample mean is likely to have come from a population with the hypothesized mean value (μ_0). The *z*-test is very common in practice and is appropriate for interval data in the following situations:

z-test
If a variable has a standard normal (*z*) distribution, one can test the null hypothesis of whether it is equal to zero by checking values on a standard normal table or by computer.

1. The sample is of any size, and the population standard deviation σ is known.
2. The sample size is "large," and the population standard deviation σ is unknown.

By "large," we mean large enough for the central limit theorem to apply and for which, in practice, a sample of 30 or greater suffices. In situations where $n < 30$ and σ is unknown, the *t*-test should be used (but *only* if the population is itself known to be normal). (This will be discussed shortly.)

Let us illustrate the z-test for the continuous variable for age in our data for marketing research students. Recall the following information for our sample, which is all that we will need to carry out the hypothesis test: $\bar{X} = 27.59$, $s = 4.92$, and $n = 448$. We will go through each step of the hypothesis test in turn.

Step 1. Formulate Null and Alternative Hypotheses

Let us state the following null and alternative hypotheses:

$$H_0 : \mu = 27$$

$$H_0 : \mu > 27.$$

In simple language, we wish to know whether the *sample* mean age of 27.59 will allow the conclusion that the *population* mean age is greater than 27. Note that the alternative hypothesis, H_1, is phrased so that a sample value suitably far above 27 will allow us to reject H_0. But, what is "suitably far" here? The sample mean of 27.59 certainly *seems* fairly close to the null mean of 27; but our sample size is fairly large. Note that we will be doing a one-tailed test because the alternative hypothesis is directional, and only large *positive* deviations will allow us to reject the null.

Step 2. Select the Appropriate Statistical Test

The appropriate test here is the z-test, because $n > 30$ and we are testing a hypothesis about means. This test is based on the nature of the sampling distribution of the mean (as discussed in the last chapter). We know by the central limit theorem that the sampling distribution for the (sample) mean forms a normal curve. We also know that we can determine probabilities associated with any observed value of the sample mean, assuming that the null hypothesis (H_0: $\mu = 27$) is true.

Step 3. Specify the Significance Level

A significance level, α, must always be chosen. Bear in mind that the smaller one sets α, the bigger the β (Type II error) will be for any given sample size. In our example we shall use $\alpha = 0.01$.

Step 4. Look Up the *z*-Value

We must find the z-value corresponding to $\alpha = 0.01$. To do this, we can consult a statistical program, a spreadsheet, or printed tables (such tables appear in Appendix A of this book). For example, we can use Table A-1 in Appendix A to determine values of z corresponding to several key significance levels, α. We can put together a small table for just that purpose:

α	0.1	0.05	0.025	0.01	0.005	0.0025	0.001
z	1.282	1.645	1.960	2.326	2.576	2.807	3.090

Each value of α corresponds to a one-tailed z-value; if the test is two-tailed, we would have to split α into two parts. So, if we want a total Type I error (α) of 0.1 for a one-tailed test, we would use $z = 1.282$; for that same total error in a two-tailed test, we would need to move farther out on the normal curve, to 1.645. In our particular example, we wish to have a total error of $\alpha = 0.01$, one-tailed, and so use $z = 2.326$. If our calculated test statistic is greater than this, we will "reject the null hypothesis with 99 percent confidence."

two-tailed test
A statistical test of a hypothesis that does not specify a direction (e.g., that some parameter's value is not equal to zero, where values both greater than zero or less than zero can invalidate the hypothesis).

Step 5. Perform the statistical test

If the population standard deviation (σ) is known, then:

$$z = \frac{\bar{X} - \mu}{\sigma/\sqrt{n}}.$$

In real applications, it is rare to know σ. If σ is not known, we use the sample standard deviation, s, instead:

$$z = \frac{\bar{X} - \mu}{s_{\bar{X}}} = \frac{\bar{X} - \mu}{s/\sqrt{n}}.$$

In our example, σ is not known, so we use the latter formula. What the formula does is express the difference between the observed mean $\bar{X}$ and the hypothesized mean μ (in the numerator) in terms of a number of standard errors (the denominator). The question is: Is the calculated z-value large enough to be likely to occur by sampling error alone less than $\alpha = 0.01$ of the time? In our example,

$$z = \frac{27.59 - 27}{4.92/\sqrt{448}} = 2.54.$$

Thus the difference between the sample mean of 27.59 and the hypothesized mean of 27 constitutes 2.54 standard errors.

Step 6. Compare *z*-Values

The calculated z-value (2.54) exceeds the z-value (2.326) corresponding to the $\alpha = 0.01$ significance level. Thus, we *reject* the null hypothesis. We may conclude that the average age in the population is *greater than* the hypothesized value of 27. This is sometimes phrased as "the real mean age is *significantly greater than* 27," and although this is not incorrect, it can be problematic; listeners unfamiliar with statistical terminology may construe "significant" to mean that the difference is in some way *important*. Importance has to do with implications and context; statistical significance has to do only with some quantity not being exactly zero.

The z-test may also be applied to a proportion. The appropriate test statistic is always as follows:

$$z = \frac{p - \pi}{\sqrt{p(1-p)/n}},$$

where p = sample proportion and π = hypothesized proportion. You may be wondering why there is no mention of $n > 30$, of σ_p, or of s_p. It turns out that for a proportion, the population variance is completely determined by the population mean (π), which is what we want to know! The sample variance is similarly determined by the sample mean; in fact, $s_p = \pi(1 - \pi)$. And it turns out that $n > 30$ is not always good enough for this test. Imagine something that occurs only one time in a million; in a sample of size 30, we are exceedingly unlikely to see it even once, so will typically observe a sample proportion of zero. To use the test of proportions, we must ensure that the following condition holds: $n\pi(1 - \pi) \geq 5$.*

Note that a market share can be thought of as a proportion: the proportion of the population that purchases the product. Similarly, ads can be tested by comparing the proportions of people who recall them a week later. To illustrate such a test, let us ask whether our sample of marketing research students is indicative of a population equally split between men and women, that is, whether H_0: $\pi = 0.5$ is supported. Here, deviations in *either* direction would knock down the hypothesis of gender balance, so it will be a *two-tailed* test. So, if we wish to keep the total Type I error below, say, $\alpha = 0.05$, we will need to use $z = 1.960$ (corresponding to 0.025 in each of the two tails). Let us carry out this test, recalling that the observed proportion of males in the class is $p = 0.587$. We first calculate $n\pi(1 - \pi) = 448(0.5)(1 - 0.5) = 112$; because this is much greater than 5, we can conduct the test, as follows:

$$z = \frac{.587 - .5}{\sqrt{(.5)(1 - .5)/448}} = 3.68.$$

*When $n\pi(1 - \pi)$ is less than 5, the normal approximation may be inaccurate, and the exact binomial distribution must be used. This is so atypical of real marketing research problems that we will not discuss it further.

The calculated value, $z = 3.68$, is much larger than 1.96, which corresponds to a two-tailed total Type I error of $\alpha = 0.05$. Thus, we can reject the null hypothesis with 95 percent confidence. You may be wondering whether we could reject the null with *more* than 95 percent confidence because the calculated value is quite a bit larger than the cutoff. The answer is yes; but this raises another question: Exactly how much confidence do we have, based on the calculated value of 3.68? The answer to this question is the *p*-value, which we will explore in more detail later in this chapter. If you use a statistical program or tables, however, you will find that $z = 3.68$ nearly exactly corresponds to a single-tailed area of 0.0001. Because we are doing a two-tailed test, we must double this value, so that we could reject the null even with α as small as 0.0002, or with 99.98 percent confidence! In this case, we could summarize the entirety of our evidence against the null hypothesis in a very simple statement: that $p = 0.0002$. As we will see, this is the preferred method for conveying the strength of statistical evidence.

9.5c *t*-Test

***t*-test**
A statistical test performed on sample means (or differences of them), when the population variance is unknown; commonly applied in the form of a "two sample" *t*-test, in ANOVA, and for regression coefficients.

The *t*-test is used when testing hypotheses about means when the population standard deviation, σ, is unknown; this holds for any sample size at all, not just "large" samples. The reason we use a *t*-test instead of a *z*-test is that we estimate the population standard deviation, σ, by the sample standard deviation, *s*. The *t*-test is slightly more complicated than the *z* because we must know the number of *degrees-of-freedom* (*df*) to apply it. For the testing of means, the *df* is always $n - 1$, where *n* is the sample size. (In general, the *df* value is the size of the sample, *n*, less the number of parameters estimated using the sample.)

Critical values of the *t* statistic are presented in Table A-2 in Appendix A at the end of the book. As for *z*, the critical value of *t* varies with the α level selected, the sample size, and whether a one- or two-tailed test is appropriate. When the sample size is quite large, the *t* and *z* distributions are very close to one another, as Table 9.2 shows.

Note that the last line, for *z*, would be equivalent to a *t* with infinite degrees-of-freedom. Practically speaking, once our sample has several hundred elements, one can simply use a *z*-value, as it will be indistinguishable from a *t*. Also note that this is *not* true for smaller samples; when $df = 10$, the associated *t* value for $\alpha = 0.01$ is 2.764, which is very different from the *z*-value of 2.326. With such small samples, using *s* to estimate σ introduces the possibility of much greater sampling error, so we need to go more standard errors away from the mean for the same degree of Type I error (α).

Let us quickly illustrate a *t*-test using our data for the marketing research students, this time for only the $n = 69$ undergraduate women. Their summary data are as follows:

	Age	Gender	Height	Weight	Class	MBA	Year	LikeStat
Mean	21.23	0	65.31	129.1	1	0	3.29	6.42
Std Dev	1.66	0	2.91	16.0	0	0	1.69	0.85

Suppose that we want to test the hypothesis that mean weight in the relevant population is 125 pounds against the alternative that it is really more. We would then have:

$$H_1 : \mu > 125 \text{ gallons.}$$

Table 9.2 **Critical Values of *z* and *t* for Common Values of α and $df = 10, 30, 100$ and 500**

α	$\alpha = 0.1$	$\alpha = 0.05$	$\alpha = 0.025$	$\alpha = 0.01$	$\alpha = 0.005$	$\alpha = 0.0025$	$\alpha = 0.001$
t, df = 10	1.372	1.812	2.228	2.764	3.169	3.581	4.144
t, df = 30	1.310	1.697	2.042	2.457	2.750	3.030	3.385
t, df = 100	1.290	1.660	1.984	2.364	2.626	2.871	3.174
t, df = 500	1.283	1.648	1.965	2.334	2.586	2.820	3.107
z	1.282	1.645	1.960	2.326	2.576	2.807	3.090

Our test would proceed as follows:

$$t = \frac{\bar{X} - \mu}{s/\sqrt{n}} = \frac{129.1 - 125}{16.0/\sqrt{69}} = 2.11.$$

The computer tells us that the critical value of t at $\alpha = 0.05$ for a one-tailed test at $df = 68$ is 1.668; for $\alpha = 0.01$ it is 2.382. We could therefore reject the null hypothesis with 95 percent confidence, but not 99 percent. The computer can also tell us the p-value exactly corresponding to our computed test statistic of 2.11, and this would be $p = 0.019$. Thus, we could reject the null with just over 98 percent confidence and conclude that the true mean weight for the population from which the sample was drawn is greater than 125 pounds. We encourage students to replicate these calculations and to repeat them for various tests pertaining to this data set, culminating in each case with a p-value for the test in question.

9.5d Nominal Data

One should not be left with the impression that all hypotheses are about population means, even though many, or even most, tend to be. Researchers are interested in many other quantities and summary measures of data types for which means are inapplicable. Researchers often need to make inferences about how respondents are distributed across the possible categories of a nominal variable. Demographic examples are particularly common in marketing applications: Has the consumer base changed in terms of geographic location (countries, regions, states, ZIP codes, census tracts), gender split, educational attainment, or income categories? Because nominal data are ubiquitous in marketing research, we need some way to make sense of them, both in terms of description and in terms of inference. Here, we consider univariate measures, and we will later develop more complex procedures to relate nominal variables to others using special multivariate methods.

Chi-Square Test

The **chi-square test** is a procedure for comparing a hypothesized population distribution (across nominal categories) against an observed distribution. In that way, it is just like all hypothesis tests we have seen thus far: It compares what we hypothesize in a population with what we observe in a sample. It is standard to designate the hypothesized (or *expected*) values by "E," and the *observed* values in our sample by "O." The formula for the chi-square (designated "χ^2") statistic is

chi-square test
The main test done in categorical data analysis, often to determine whether two nominal variables are independent of one another; can also be used to test whether a sample variance is significantly different from a hypothesized value.

$$\chi^2 = \sum_{i=1}^{k} \frac{(O_i - E_i)^2}{E_i},$$

where k = number of categories of the variable, O_i= observed number of respondents in category i, and E_i = expected number of respondents in category i.

Any statistical program will calculate the chi-square statistic automatically, once it is told how to compute the "expected" values (those specified by the null hypothesis). Table A-3 in Appendix A lists critical values of the chi-square distribution, which are used exactly as the z and t critical values have been: as cutoffs against which to compare the computed value. Like the t-statistic, the chi-square requires a number of degrees-of-freedom to be specified; these appear in the left-hand column of Table A-3, designated by df (or in this specific context sometimes by m, not to be confused with sample size, n). For a *univariate* chi-square test (i.e., involving just one variable), $df = k - 1$; this is because for a given sample size (n), once the number of respondents in $k - 1$ categories is known, the number in the kth category is automatically determined. The top row in Table A-3 gives the right-tail area, α; so we wish to carry out our test at $\alpha = 0.05$. We look in that column (note that some statistical tables will list the "confidence" $(1 - \alpha)$ instead of α itself, requiring subtraction from 1). Finding a critical value of chi-square is similar to using the t table. If $df = 7$ and we have specified that $\alpha = 0.05$, we look down the $\alpha = 0.05$ column until it intersects with the row representing 7 df, finding the critical chi-square value of 14.1 (rounded to one significant digit after the decimal). This could be done, of course, using any spreadsheet or statistical program as well; either would allow one to look up any level of Type I error (α) or degrees-of-freedom, not only tabled values.

Let us carry out two univariate chi-square tests for our data on the marketing research students, using the last two variables, year and LikeStat:

Value	Year	LikeStat
C = 1	69	49
C = 2	82	62
C = 3	52	46
C = 4	93	35
C = 5	89	63
C = 6	63	72
C = 7		121
SUM	448	448
Expected	74.67	64.00

The first variable, year, has six categories (designated in the left column by "C"), whereas LikeStat has seven. In each case, we wish to test the hypothesis of equal distribution across categories, so our null hypotheses would suggest 74.67 in each cell for year, and 64.00 for LikeStat. Simply "eyeballing" the data, it is difficult to tell the outcome of each of these tests. Let us calculate chi-square for each:

$$\chi^2_{Year} = \sum_{i=1}^{k} \frac{(O_i - E_i)^2}{E_i} = \frac{(69 - 74.67)^2}{69} + \ldots + \frac{(63 - 74.67)^2}{63} = 19.08$$

$$\chi^2_{LikeStat} = \sum_{i=1}^{k} \frac{(O_i - E_i)^2}{E_i} = \frac{(49 - 64.00)^2}{49} + \ldots + \frac{(121 - 64.00)^2}{121} = 63.48$$

If we carry out these tests with 95 percent confidence ($\alpha = 0.05$), we need chi-square cutoffs for $df = 5$ and 6, respectively; these values are 11.07 and 12.59. In both cases, we can *reject* the null hypothesis of equal distribution, because the calculated value of the test statistic exceeds the critical (tabled) value. It makes sense to ask just how strong our evidence against the null hypothesis is in each case, that is, for the *p*-values. For this, we appeal to a statistical program or spreadsheet, which has no trouble doing the exact computation. For year, the probability of a $\chi^2(df = 5)$ exceeding 19.08 is approximately 0.0019, or 99.81 percent confidence. For LikeStat, the probability of a $\chi^2(df = 6)$ exceeding 63.48 is stunningly small, around 10^{-11}, or one chance in 100 billion! Thus, we would conclude that we do not have an equal number of students taking the course every year (with $p = 0.0019$) and also that the distribution of answers to how well students like statistics is not equal across the seven categories (with p about 10^{-11}).

Note that other null hypotheses are possible; it need not claim that all categories have an equal number of respondents. The chi-square test is fully general and can test *any* hypothesized distribution. For most other distributions and hypotheses, we would simply have the computer do the required calculations, and any data analysis package would provide all the procedures presented in this chapter. Our purpose has been to introduce the main types of univariate analyses and guides to their use, with the presumption that the vast majority of such analyses will be carried out via statistical or spreadsheet programs. As we will now leave univariate analyses behind, we shall rely almost entirely on computer calculations.

9.6 Bivariate Procedures

In most marketing research studies, researchers and managers will want to go well beyond the sorts of univariate analyses discussed thus far in this chapter. Although the proper starting point for all data analysis is getting a strong "feel" for each variable on its own terms, we will typically be ultimately interested in *relationships* among the variables. When this involves relating one variable to one other variable, we will perform a *bivariate* analysis; if it involves many variables at the same time, a *multivariate* analysis. The remainder of this chapter is concerned with how to specify, measure, and use bivariate relationships, and the methods developed here will be extended to the complex (and wonderful) world of multivariate relationships in subsequent chapters.

Bivariate relationships can help address many common and important relationships in marketing. Typical questions for which bivariate analysis will prove useful include:

1. What is the *relationship* between use of our brand and media viewing habits?
2. Are higher levels of sales force turnover *associated with* greater sales manager age?
3. Does the season of the year help us *predict* attitudes toward our brand?

In each of these cases, we are asking whether the values of one variable offer useful information about the values of another. As we will see, questions of this nature come in many guises, and various techniques have been developed to deal with them. The most important of these is doubtless that of *linear regression*, a method we will treat in great detail. As with univariate relationships, the appropriate bivariate technique depends on the scale level of the variables involved and whether the researcher requires a descriptive or an inferential analysis.

Overview of Bivariate Procedures

Figure 9.4 presents an overview of some of the most important bivariate descriptive statistics and inferential tests. The figure applies *only* to bivariate relationships, so we must be sure that we wish to restrict our purview to two variables only. If this is the case, the scale level of the variables involved then guides us to the appropriate analytic method and associated statistics. It is important to note that not all possible combinations of bivariate relationships are presented in Figure 9.4, but only those where the two variables are of the same type (i.e., both interval, both ordinal, or both nominal). It is both possible and often desirable to analyze an interval and an ordinal variable together, or a nominal and an ordinal variable, and so on. Although we will not cover all possible such relationships in detail, we will show in Chapter 10 how regression methods can account for various interrelationships among variables of different types.

The remainder of this chapter will be devoted to the bivariate procedures that are most relevant to real marketing research problems. Specifically, from descriptive statistics for interval variables we shall discuss the linear correlation coefficient, *r*, and simple regression; from inferential statistics for interval

Figure 9.4 Bivariate Data Analysis Procedures

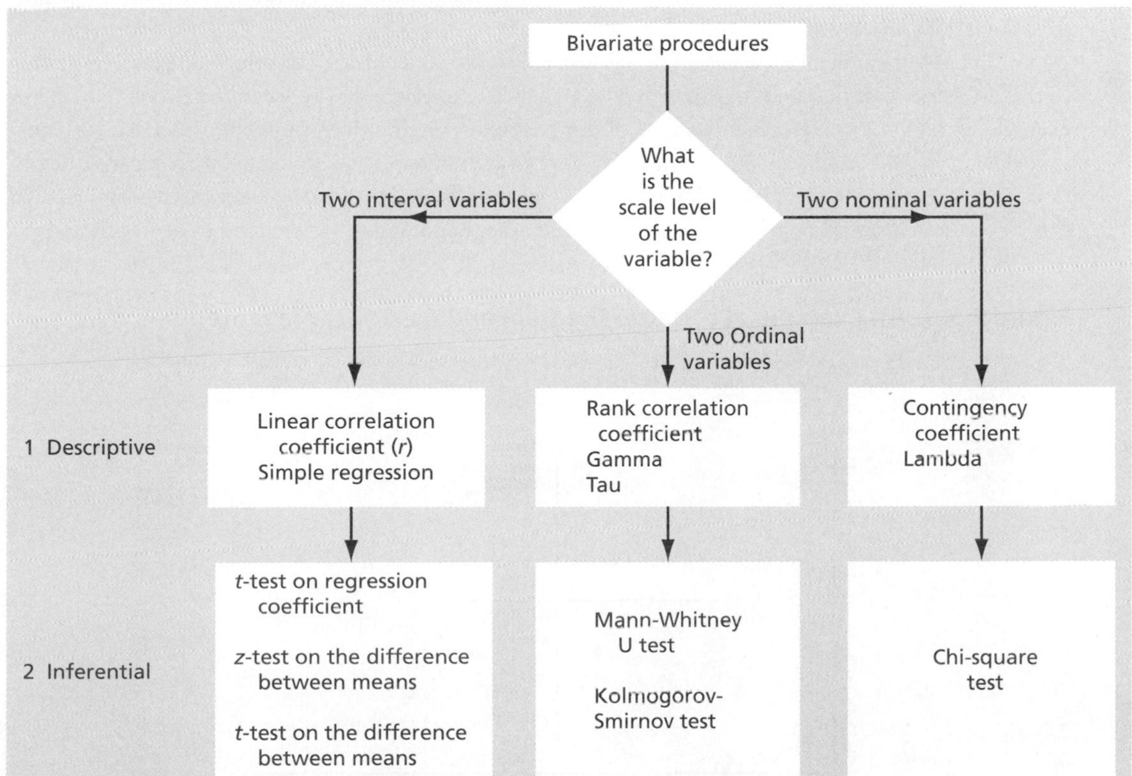

variables we shall discuss *t*-tests on regression coefficients and both the *z*- and *t*-tests on differences between means; and, finally, from inferential statistics for nominal variables, we shall discuss the chi-square test. Whatever relationships are not covered among these will be taken up later as part of our discussion of regression methods in general.

9.7 Descriptive Statistics for Bivariate Analysis

Research objectives often center on describing the nature of bivariate relationships as they exist *within a sample*, without making any inferences about the *population* from which it was drawn. This section presents the most important descriptive statistical procedure appropriate for use with two interval variables, **simple linear regression**. The main measure of association calculated in the course of running a simple linear regression is called the linear correlation coefficient, or often simply "the correlation." Because of its central importance throughout all of statistical analysis, we will explore it first.

simple linear regression
A linear regression model with only one regressor (independent variable).

9.7a Linear Correlation Coefficient

Linear correlation is a measure of the degree to which two *interval* variables are associated. For example, suppose we have data on grades in a marketing management course, X, and data on grades in a marketing research course, Y. Our interest is in determining the level and direction of a relationship between these two variables; for example, are high grades on X associated with high grades on Y, or vice versa, or is there no relationship between the two? The linear correlation coefficient, r_{XY}, is a measure of the *linear* relationship between X and Y. It does *not* measure "all possible" relationships between the two variables, nor does it make any claims about X and Y causing one another. We will return to these important points throughout our discussions.

In examining the relationship between two interval variables, a useful beginning is to plot the data on a scatter diagram. Figure 9.5 is an example of a plot for two variables, X and Y. If we draw the means of the two variables, $\bar{X}$ and $\bar{Y}$, on the scatter diagram, a first impression of possible relationships can be obtained. Including the mean values for each of the variables divides the scatter diagram into four quadrants, labeled 1, 2, 3, and 4: In quadrant 1, both the X and the Y values are above (i.e., have positive deviations from) their respective means; in quadrant 2, X values have negative deviations and Y values have positive ones; for quadrant 3, both have negative deviations; and for quadrant 4, X values have positive deviations and Y values have negative ones.

And here is the crucial observation: If the data points are concentrated mostly in diagonal quadrants (either in 1 and 3, or in 2 and 4), this would be evidence of a *relationship* between the two variables. For example, if most points were in quadrants 1 and 3, positive deviations in X would be associated with positive deviations in Y (quadrant 1), and negative deviations in X would be associated with negative deviations in Y (quadrant 3). That is, X being above its mean tells us that Y is also likely above its mean. In this case, X and Y would be *positively* related. On the other hand, if data points tend to be in quadrants 2

Figure 9.5 An Example of a Scatter Diagram and Associated Quadrants

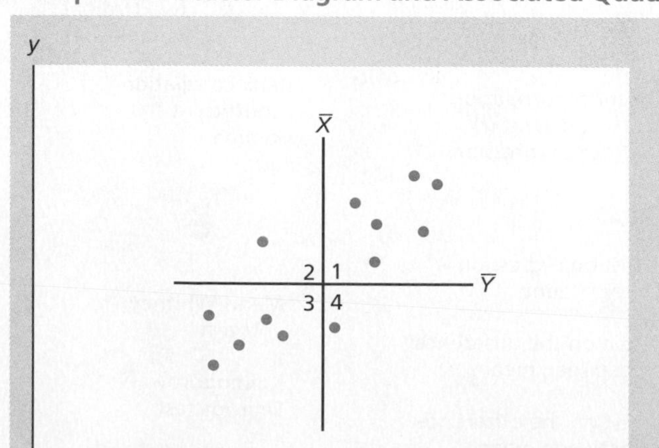

and 4, negative deviations in X are associated with positive deviations in Y (quadrant 2), and vice versa (quadrant 4). This situation would indicate a negative relationship between X and Y.

The correlation coefficient, r_{XY}, captures and precisely quantifies this relationship between two interval variables. To understand how the correlation coefficient works, we develop it from "first principles," eventually arriving at the formula for r_{XY}. We begin this process by developing a distance measure between each point's X and Y values and the means of X and Y. Let us examine the following quantity:

$$(X_i - \bar{X})(Y_i - \bar{Y}).$$

It has some very interesting properties; for example:

Quadrant 1: X_i is positive and Y_i is positive, so $(X_i - \bar{X})(Y_i - \bar{Y})$ is positive.
Quadrant 2: X_i is negative and Y_i is positive, so $(X_i - \bar{X})(Y_i - \bar{Y})$ is negative.
Quadrant 3: X_i is negative and Y_i is negative, so $(X_i - \bar{X})(Y_i - \bar{Y})$ is positive.
Quadrant 4: X_i is positive and Y_i is negative, so $(X_i - \bar{X})(Y_i - \bar{Y})$ is negative.

We see that $(X_i - \bar{X})(Y_i - \bar{Y})$ is positive in quadrants 1 and 3 and negative in 2 and 4. Recall that data points in quadrants 1 and 3 indicate a positive relationship between X and Y, and data points in quadrants 2 and 4 indicate a negative relationship between X and Y.

Therefore, the sign of $(X_i - \bar{X})(Y_i - \bar{Y})$ captures the direction of relationship between X and Y. If we simply add these values for all data points, the sign of this quantity will indicate the *overall* direction of relationship. This quantity is so important that it has its own symbol:

$$SS_{XY} = \sum_{i=1}^{n} (X_i - \bar{X})(Y_i - \bar{Y}).$$

For example, if the data come mostly from quadrants 1 and 3, positive values of $(X_i - \bar{X})(Y_i - \bar{Y})$ will outnumber negative ones, and SS_{XY} will be positive, indicating a positive relationship between X and Y. The opposite is true if the data come mostly from quadrants 2 and 4. If the data are evenly split roughly among all four quadrants, positive and negative values of $(X_i - \bar{X})(Y_i - \bar{Y})$ will tend to cancel, and SS_{XY} will be close to zero (or, put more rigorously, will not be *significantly* different from zero, as we will see later in this chapter).

The value of SS_{XY} quantifies and improves on a simple visual examination of the scatter diagram. However, it has two glaring weaknesses. First, the value of SS_{XY} is directly dependent on the number of data points, *n*: As *n* increases, and more points therefore tend to land in diagonally opposed quadrants, the value of SS_{XY} will also increase. So, comparison of relationships involving different numbers of observations would not be meaningful. Second, the value of SS_{XY} depends on the *units of measurement* being used on X and Y. For example, if X were height and Y were weight, we would obtain a different value of SS_{XY} if our units changed from inches to feet, from pounds to kilograms, and so forth.

Throughout the field of statistics, great care is taken to ensure that important measures are **scale independent**, that is, our data should not "tell a different story" just because we alter our yardstick for measuring it. If an effect is real, it should be equally real when measured in feet, inches, microns, nanometers, or parsecs. We must therefore eliminate the effects of sample size and units from our measure of association, SS_{XY}. We can eliminate the effects of sample size by "correcting" (dividing through) SS_{XY} by the degrees-of-freedom in the sample size, $n - 1$. This gives us a measure of the **covariance** of X and Y, as follows:

scale independent
When a statistic's value does not change when the scale of measurement does (e.g., from pounds to kilograms).

covariance
A measure of dispersion for some quantity, equal to the square of the standard deviation.

$$Cov(X, Y) = \frac{SS_{XY}}{n-1} = \frac{1}{n-1}\sum_{i=1}^{n} (X_i - \bar{X})(Y_i - \bar{Y}).$$

The covariance generalizes the ordinary variance measure for a single variable (either X or Y) commonly used throughout statistics:

$$Var(X) = Cov(X, X) = \frac{SS_{XX}}{n-1} = \frac{1}{n-1}\sum_{i=1}^{n} (X_i - \bar{X})^2$$

$$Var(Y) = Cov(Y, Y) = \frac{SS_{YY}}{n-1} = \frac{1}{n-1}\sum_{i=1}^{n} (Y_i - \bar{Y})^2.$$

It is called the covariance because it measures the degree to which X and Y tend to co-vary, that is, vary in the same direction from their respective means. Thus, covariance is positive if the values of X_i and Y_i tend to deviate from their respective means in the same direction, and negative if they tend to deviate in the opposite direction. If X and Y are statistically independent, $Cov(X, Y) = 0$ (importantly, the reverse is *not* true: The covariance can be zero without the variables being statistically independent).

linear correlation coefficient (r) A measure of how much of the variation in one variable is explained by a simple linear regression on a second variable.

Next, we eliminate the effect of units by dividing $Cov(X, Y)$ by the standard deviations of X and Y. The resulting quantity is the **linear correlation coefficient**, r_{XY}, and there are many equivalent, alternative formulas for it:

$$r_{XY} = \frac{Cov(X,Y)}{\sqrt{Cov(X,X)Cov(Y,Y)}} = \frac{\sum_{i=1}^{n}(X_i - \bar{X})(Y_i - \bar{Y})}{\sqrt{\left[\sum_{i=1}^{n}(X_i - \bar{X})^2\right]\left[\sum_{i=1}^{n}(Y_i - \bar{Y})^2\right]}}$$

$$= \frac{\sum_{i=1}^{n}(X_i - \bar{X})(Y_i - \bar{Y})}{(n-1)s_x s_y} = \frac{1}{(n-1)}\sum_{i=1}^{n}\left[\frac{(X_i - \bar{X})}{s_x}\right]\left[\frac{(Y_i - \bar{Y})}{s_y}\right].$$

All these will yield equivalent values for r_{XY}, which in any case is typically calculated via computer, and is usually written simply as r. We see then, especially from the last of these expressions, that correlation is just a *standardized measure of covariation*. This standardization allows two correlations to be compared regardless of the units in which observations are measured. To restate this important point, no matter what units we choose to measure two variables, their correlation will not change. The correlation coefficient may take on any value between -1 and $+1$. When $r = 1$, this indicates a perfect positive correlation, and that plotting the two variables in question will show all points exactly on a straight line (with positive slope). Analogously, $r = -1$ indicates a perfect negative correlation. If $r = 0$, there is no *linear* relationship between the variables; there may be another, more complex relationship, but the "best" line through the points will be flat (i.e., a slope of zero). Thus correlation provides a measure of the *direction* and *strength* of the relationship between two variables. However, we have yet to determine whether a correlation is *significant*, a topic taken up via regression.

coefficient of determination (r^2) A measure of how much of the variance in one (interval-scaled) variable is reduced by knowing the value of another (interval-scaled) variable; obtained by running a simple linear regression of one variable on the other.

Correlation has another important interpretation as the extent to which two variables *share variation*. The exact percentage of variation shared by two variables is calculated by squaring r. This r^2 is called the **coefficient of determination**, or more commonly simply as "the r squared" value. Students, practitioners, and even professional researchers are forever asking what constitutes a good, acceptable, or "high enough" value of r^2. We caution against even asking this question or conceptualizing along such lines. There are many reasons for this, but the most compelling is that there is no "one size fits all" use for correlation or, more generally, regression methods. In the physical sciences, where one deals with inert objects supposedly obeying natural laws, a value of r^2 below 0.99 might indicate a flaw in one's theory. In the social sciences, where one deals with the behavior of humans or large social systems, a value of r^2 as high as 0.50 might be considered remarkably powerful evidence. Even in medicine, a test that can indicate, for example, the severity of a specific disease might be considered extremely useful if it delivers an r^2 of 0.80 or less. We should recognize, however, that because r^2 measures the proportion of variation in one variable explained by another, "small" values really do indicate that far more is left *unexplained* than explained. Thus, an r^2 below, say, 0.20 really does constitute a weak relationship, and one above 0.80 a very strong one. But, we must stress that even a strong relationship can be very far from a perfect one, and a weak relationship can nevertheless be very useful in the right circumstances. In the end, we must consider *the ends* to which we are putting our correlation measure.

A Numerical Example

Let us return to our $n = 448$ marketing research students and quantify the relationship between height and weight. We would expect a strong relationship between these variables, but recognize that certain other variables, such as gender and age, should also play a role. Let us first look at a scatter plot of the data, depicted in Figure 9.6.

Figure 9.6 Scatter Plot of Weight vs. Height for the Marketing Research Student Data

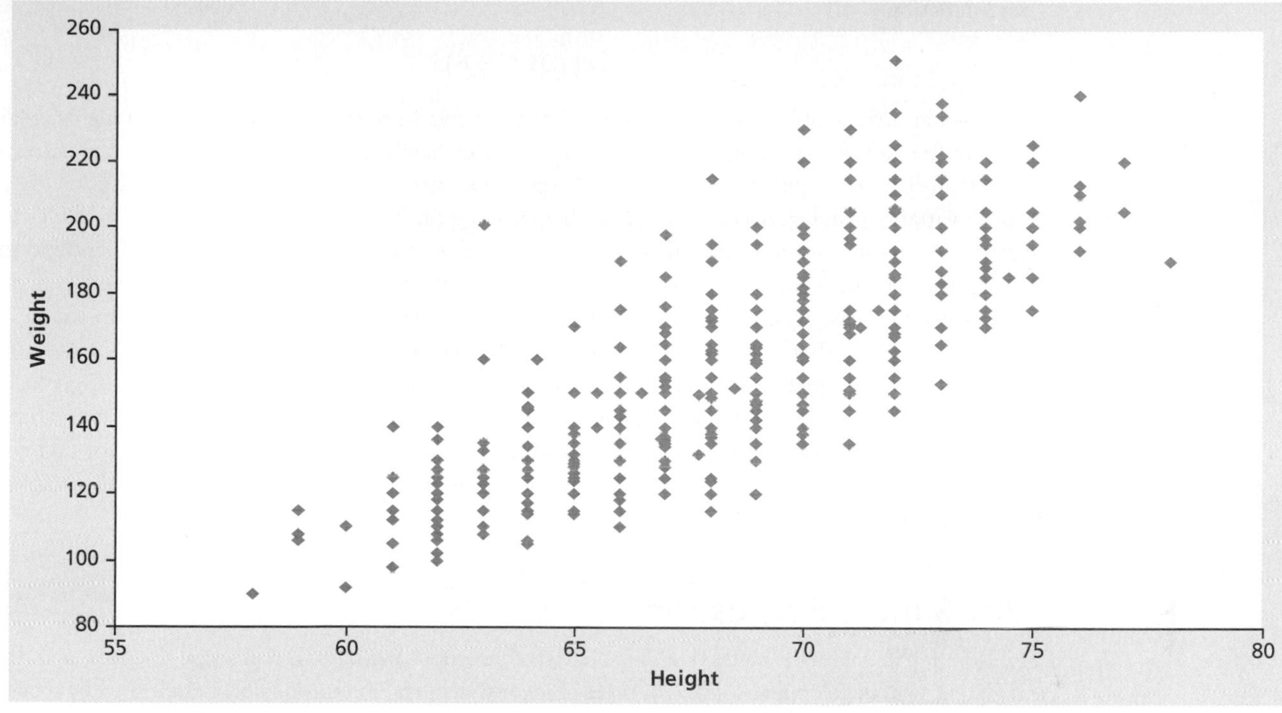

As expected, there is a clear upward trend: as one moves across the graph (height increases), the points tend to rise (weight increases). Let us have a look at some of the data in abridged form and associated calculations, assembled in Table 9.3.

It is a simple matter to calculate the means for height and weight as, respectively, 30541.9/448 = 68.2 and 69885.4/448 = 156.0. We can then use these to construct the fourth and fifth columns of Table 9.3, which list the deviations of X_i (height) and Y_i (weight) from their means; note that these *must* (and do!) sum to zero, as listed in the last row. The last three columns contain the calculations for the various *sums of squares*, $SS_{XX} = 6987.7$, $SS_{YY} = 464874.5$, and $SS_{XY} = 45788.6$, respectively.

We can now calculate the correlation coefficient, r_{XY}, between X (height) and Y (weight), as follows:

$$r_{XY} = \frac{45788.6}{\sqrt{(6987.7)(464874.5)}} = .803.$$

Table 9.3 Calculations for Simple Linear Regression of Weight on Height

i	Height X_i	Weight Y_i	Deviation$(X_i - \bar{X})$	Deviation$(Y_i - \bar{Y})$	$(X_i - \bar{X})^2$	$(Y_i - \bar{Y})^2$	$(X_i - \bar{X})(Y_i - \bar{Y})$
001	77	220.0	8.8	64.0	77.9	4096.7	564.9
002	66	125.0	−2.2	−31.0	4.7	960.6	67.4
003	69	150.0	0.8	−6.0	0.7	35.9	−5.0
...	...	...	...	...	...	...	...
447	64.0	106.0	−4.2	−50.0	17.4	2499.4	208.7
448	74.0	200.0	5.8	44.0	33.9	1936.5	256.4
SUM	**30541.9**	**69885.4**	**0**	**0**	**6987.7**	**464874.5**	**45788.6**

The proportion of variation shared by these two variables (height and weight) is given by the coefficient of determination:

$$r^2 = (.803)^2 = .645.$$

We would now be able to make the following statement: In this sample of $n = 448$ students, 64.5 percent of the variation in weight can be accounted for by height alone. If this seems like a great deal of explanatory power, that is because it is; explaining such a large proportion of variation in a "human" variable is not very common. Note that this says nothing at all about the other variables in our study! A reasonable reaction to this result might be that this is unsurprising, because men tend to be taller than women and also to weigh more. Perhaps if one redid this analysis on men and on women separately, one would find a far weaker relationship within each of those groups. In the next chapter, we will see that a far better approach to such situations is to appeal to *multiple regression*. Before we can look at many variables at the same time, we will have to develop a method to rigorously analyze two variables. When those variables are interval scaled, the dominant method of bivariate analysis is *simple regression*, which we explore next. In so doing, we will learn that the linear correlation coefficient, r, plays a central role, which will be extended and generalized for more complex regression models.

9.7b Simple Regression

Regression is the dominant method of data analysis throughout the natural and social sciences, and the next chapter will develop many different types of regression model in considerable detail. Broadly speaking, regression helps us understand how one or more *independent* variables are related to a *dependent* variable of interest, and to make predictions based on this understanding. Here, we consider the most basic form of regression, *simple regression*, appropriate for one interval-scaled dependent variable and one interval-scaled independent variable.

To make our development concrete, we will focus on the marketing research student data, and in particular on the height and weight variables (as in Table 9.3). Although it would be a simple matter to draw a line informally, by hand, through the scatter plot in Figure 9.6, this would lack rigor, precision, and quantification. We will therefore develop a mathematical procedure to linearly relate any two interval-scaled variables. After doing so, we will consider a set of assumptions and caveats valid for all regression models, as well as what makes a statistical model useful and, for lack of a better term, "good." Although our development will be valid for any subject of study, it will be squarely focused on usefulness in managerial situations.

9.7c Partitioning the Sum-of-Squares

We begin by observing that in the absence of other information, our "best guess" at the value of a variable is its mean. This not only makes intuitive sense, but is fully rigorous; if we wanted to find the single number that was "closest" to a set of data values, $\{Y_i\}$, we would ask for the number that minimizes some distance to all of them. In statistics, the principle of **least squares** suggests that we try to *minimize the sum-of-squares distances*. That is, we ask for the number, c, that minimizes the following:

least squares
A general principle used throughout statistical modeling, suggesting that one minimize the sum of squared deviations between observed values and those predicted by the model.

$$\sum_{i=1}^{n} (Y_i - c)^2.$$

The solution to this is always $c = \bar{Y}$. We therefore define the *total variation* in a set of data, called the *total sum-of-squares*, as follows:

$$SS_{YY} = \sum_{i=1}^{n} (Y_i - \bar{Y})^2.$$

This quantity (which will later be notated as SS_T) should be familiar from the previous section. It measures how much the data vary around their means or, more usefully, how much variation is "left over" if we use the mean to describe each data value. Our task in using regression will be to do better than this, to use *another* variable, X, to help explain Y and thereby reduce the variation in the data. We begin this process by formally defining three quantities:

$Y_i =$ the ith observation on the dependent variable,

$\bar{Y} =$ the mean of the $\{Y_i\}$, and

$\hat{Y}_i =$ the *predicted* value of the ith observation of the dependent variable.

The first two quantities are familiar. The third, $\hat{Y}_i$ (pronounced "Y hat"), is not, and it will be the subject of our study. Just as $\bar{Y}$ is our "best guess" at the value of Y_i if we do not use any information about the variable X, $\hat{Y}_i$ is our "best guess" for Y_i if we are allowed to take X_i into account. This is our *prediction* for Y_i, based on X_i. To take a concrete example, suppose we wished to guess at someone's weight (Y_i), knowing nothing about them. A reasonable guess, *because we know nothing about them, specifically*, would be to use $\bar{Y}$, the mean weight in an observed sample. Now, if someone told us *this particular person's height*, X_i, we could take that into account and come up with another prediction for their weight, $\hat{Y}_i$. Thus, the key issue in regression will be how to determine if, on average, our predictions $\hat{Y}_i$ are more accurate than simply using the mean, $\bar{Y}$. If you understand this point, you have grasped the main issue underlying the use of regression throughout statistical analysis: making more accurate predictions by tying in additional information.

Our goal, therefore, is to find a rigorous way to measure whether our predictions based on X_i are really any better than just using $\bar{Y}$. We start by writing any observation as a deviation from the sample mean, $\bar{Y}$:

$$\text{Total deviation for } i\text{th observation} = (Y_i - \bar{Y})$$

We now note that the total deviation can be *partitioned* as follows:

$$\begin{array}{ccccc} \text{Total deviation} & = & \text{deviation due to X} & + & \text{deviation due to "error"} \\ \downarrow & & \downarrow & & \downarrow \\ (Y_i - \bar{Y}) & = & (\hat{Y}_i - \bar{Y}) & + & (Y_i - \hat{Y}_i) \\ \downarrow & & \downarrow & & \downarrow \\ \text{Total variation} & = & \text{variation explained by regression} & + & \text{variation unexplained by regression} \end{array}$$

This partitioning is important and underlies how regression works; it is depicted graphically in Figure 9.7, and we encourage students to study it closely. Note that the "explained deviation" is the amount the "total deviation" is reduced by our knowledge of X, that is, by using the regression line value ($\hat{Y}_i$) instead of the mean ($\bar{Y}$). Note as well that even when we use the regression line value ($\hat{Y}_i$), there is some degree of "unexplained deviation"; in practical situations, we will never be able to reduce these unexplained deviations to zero, but we can often reduce them greatly compared with the total deviation, $(Y_i - \bar{Y})$.

What we wish to do is compare these total deviations across *all* observations, and as discussed several paragraphs earlier, the way to do this throughout statistics is to form a *sum of squares*. We have already discussed the total sum-of-squares, SS_{YY}, and identified it as the quantity we wish to reduce. It turns out that with a bit of algebra, we can always decompose the sum of squares for the dependent variable (which hereafter will be written SS_{Total} or SS_T, i.e., to designate total variation), as follows:

decompose
In statistical models, the variance in the dependent variable is decomposed into that attributable to the model (covariates) and that to random error. ANOVA models often feature an explicit decomposition into various sources of variation.

$$\begin{array}{ccccc} \sum_{i=1}^{n}(Y_i - \bar{Y})^2 & = & \sum_{i=1}^{n}(\hat{Y}_i - \bar{Y})^2 & + & \sum_{i=1}^{n}(Y_i - \hat{Y}_i)^2 \\ \downarrow & & \downarrow & & \downarrow \\ SS_{Total} & = & SS_{\substack{\text{Explained} \\ \text{by Regression}}} & + & SS_{\substack{\text{Unexplained} \\ \text{by Regression}}} \\ \downarrow & & \downarrow & & \downarrow \\ \text{Total Variation}(SS_T) & = & \text{Explained Variation}(SS_R) & + & \text{Unexplained Variation}(SS_E) \end{array}$$

We have decomposed the total variation (SS_T) into that attributable to (explainable by) the regression (SS_R), and everything left over is attributable to the error (SS_E). Notice that the variation explained by the regression is *always* positive (as each of the terms in the sum is squared), and so *always* serves to reduce the total variation based on the sample mean ($\bar{Y}$) alone. Our main question will be whether this degree of reduction is *significant*, meaning greater than what would be *expected by chance alone*. Before we can ask anything about significance, we must develop a procedure to fit a line to the data.

Figure 9.7 Partitioning Total Deviation in Simple Regression

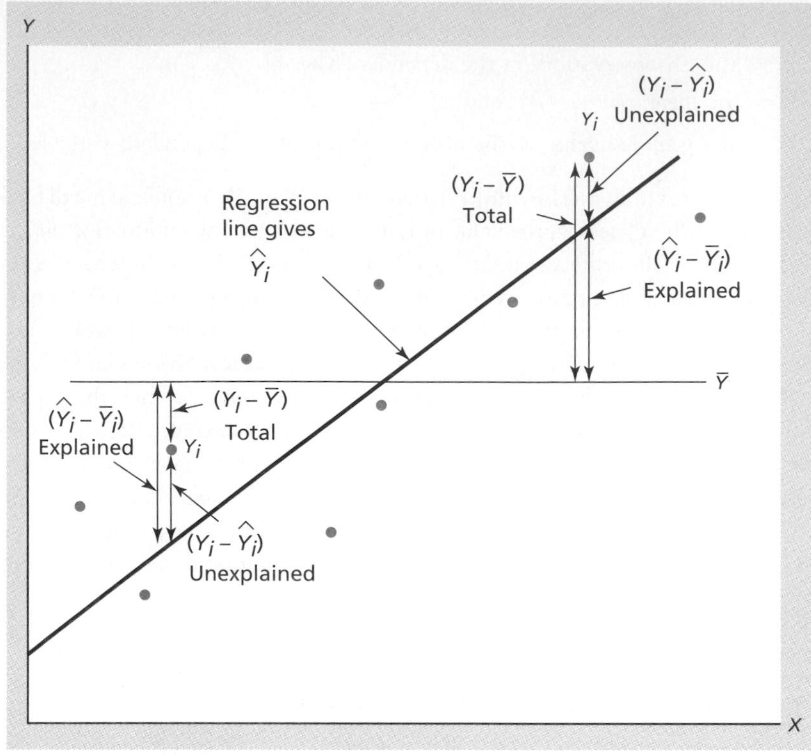

9.7d Fitting the Regression Line

regression line A straight line that represents the idealized relationship between two variables, given that they are interval scaled and related linearly to one another.

We want to be able to predict a value for the dependent variable ($\hat{Y}_i$) based on knowledge of the independent variable (X_i). To do this requires fitting, or "estimating," a **regression line**. Any line is determined exactly by two quantities: an *intercept* and a *slope*. A line's intercept is the point where it crosses the Y-axis. In regression, intercepts are often meaningless taken on their own and answer questions such as "What would be the weight of someone whose height is zero inches?" However, with very few exceptions, we will wish to allow for an intercept when estimating regression models. The *slope*, by contrast, is a very important quantity, and answers the following question: If we increase the independent variable, X, by one unit, how much do we expect the dependent variable, Y, to change? In terms of the data we have been analyzing, we might ask, "If all you knew about two people was that one was an inch taller than the other, how much more (or less) would you expect that person to weigh?" (Note that we did not ask, "What if someone grew an inch?" because then we would have to ask whether that person got older, meaning *other* variables would be changing as well; we will look at such situations more closely in the next chapter.)

In order to come up with the "best" line, we must specify its slope and intercept so that the line "comes close to the data," or "fits the data well." In statistical models, a good fit will be one that leaves as little *un*explained as possible. So, in choosing the slope and intercept, we will seek to minimize the unexplained deviation, that is, sum-of-squares errors. This least squares solution has desirable statistical properties that are dealt with extensively in texts on regression; we stress again that despite the chatty quality of our development, regression is based on a deep and powerful mathematical theory, albeit one that is beyond the scope of this text. For our purposes, an intuitive understanding suffices: a good fit means that large errors are to be avoided as much as possible. We will put this principle into practice while fitting a line of the following form:

$$\hat{Y}_i = a + bX_i,$$

where a = intercept and b = the slope of the best-fitting regression line. If we wish to maximize the variation attributable to the regression ($SS_{regression} = \sum_{i=1}^{n} (\hat{Y}_i - \bar{Y})^2$) or, equivalently, minimize that attributable to error ($SS_e = \sum_{i=1}^{n} (Y_i - \hat{Y}_i)^2$), the best values for the slope b and intercept a are always given by:

$$b = \frac{SS_{XY}}{SS_{XX}} = \frac{\sum_{i=1}^{n} (X_i - \bar{X})(Y_i - \bar{Y})}{\sum_{i=1}^{n} (X_i - \bar{X})^2}.$$

$$a = \bar{Y} - b\bar{X}$$

In practice, we would have the computer perform these calculations, but it is instructive to try them once by hand.

A Numerical Example

We can easily use the height-weight data of the marketing research students in our example, summarized in Table 9.4, to illustrate fitting the least-squares line in simple regression. We had already calculated that $SS_{XY} = 45788.6$, $SS_{XX} = 6987.7$, $\bar{X} = 68.2$, and $\bar{Y} = 156.0$. We can now use these to fit the least-squares regression line:

$$b = \frac{SS_{XY}}{SS_{XX}} = \frac{45788.6}{6987.7} = 6.55$$

$$a = \bar{Y} - b\bar{X} = 156.0 - (6.55)(68.2) = -290.73$$

We should verify that our calculations are accurate. Any statistical program will run a simple regression, and doing so for our data yields output of the form found in Table 9.4.

Note that the slope and intercept have the same values as when calculated by formula. We will allow the computer to do all our regression calculations from now on. Note also that although regression output formatting and nomenclature do vary a bit from one analysis package to another, the basic information presented is essentially identical in all. Given the importance of regression, let us go through this output to ensure that each part of it is understood. As we will see, each portion of this output will be replicated, or very nearly so, in the output from *any* regression-based statistical procedure. When in doubt about carrying out underlying calculations or mathematical theory, consult a full-featured statistics text or Web resource.

9.7e The Meaning and Significance of the Coefficients

The slope and intercept answer specific questions about our data. Recall that the slope (b) always tells us how many units the dependent variable (Y) changes when we change the independent variable (X) by one unit. So, for the data analyzed in Table 9.4, the slope tells us that each additional inch of height translates into $b = 6.55$ additional pounds of weight; note that this is true only if these are the only two

Table 9.4 Linear Regression Analysis: DepVar (Y) = Weight

Coefficients	b	Std. Error	Std. Beta	t-Test Statistic	p-Value Two-Tailed
Intercept	−290.73	15.70		−18.512	0.0000
X = height	6.55	0.23	0.803	28.493	0.0000
r	r^2	**Adj.** r^2	**Std. Error (Reg)**	***n***	
0.803	0.645	0.645	19.224	448	
Source of Variation	**Sum-of-Squares**	***df***	**Mean Squares**	***F*-Test Statistic**	***p*-Value One-Tailed**
Regression	300041.41	1	300041.41	811.84	0.0000
Error	164833.07	446	369.58		
Total	464874.47	447			

variables taken into consideration. Recall also that the intercept (a) tells us the predicted value of Y when X is zero. In our example, the intercept tells us that a person who is zero inches tall weighs $a = -290.72$ pounds. It is not difficult to tell that this is utterly meaningless because people who are zero inches tall are about as common as those with negative weights. The *only* time we would pay attention to such an intercept is if an X value of zero was *within the range of the observed data*. This happens in many settings—for example, regressing any financial quantity on stock returns, or regressing changes in sales volume on changes in price. But a height of zero, besides its physical impossibility, is well outside the range of observed data, and we would not attach any meaning to the intercept.

Any estimate in statistics is just that—an estimate—and as such needs to be accompanied by some measure of its inaccuracy. In regression models, estimated quantities are matched with *standard errors*, measures of how much uncertainty the estimate entails. For our intercept and slope of –290.72 and 6.55, respectively, the regression output lists standard errors of 15.70 and 0.23. We will always ask the following question: "How many *standard errors from zero* are our estimates?" And this question is answered by the *t*-statistics listed in the output, which are merely the estimates divided by their standard errors. Large values indicate that the estimates are many standard errors away from zero, and therefore are unlikely to have come about purely by chance. For our intercept and slope, the *t*-statistics are listed as –18.512 and 28.493, respectively. Considering that a *z*-value of 3 indicates just a 3/1000 chance, these values indicate astronomical levels of unlikelihood. Normally, to gauge the exact probability associated with a *t*-statistic, we look to the *p*-value; in our case, however, the *p*-values are both listed as 0.0000, meaning that they are less than 0.00005 and have been rounded down. (Consulting a statistical program indicates that the correct *p*-values are approximately 4×10^{-57} and 2×10^{-102}, both unimaginably small values.) We would conclude that there is extremely strong evidence that both slope and intercept were different from zero. We could also do a one-tailed test for whether the intercept was less than zero or the slope greater than zero. Given the value of the *t*-statistics in question, both of these conclusions would be strongly borne out.

9.7f Measures of Regression Fit and Quality

The next portion of our regression output lists various measures of the quality of the regression fit. Specifically, we learn the following.

r	r^2	**Adj.** r^2	**Std. Error (Reg)**	n
0.803	0.645	0.645	19.224	448

The program has verified the values for the correlation coefficient, r, and the coefficient of determination, r^2, that we calculated earlier. The next entry, called "r^2-adjusted," is new and will be important in *multiple* regression (see Chapter 10). It turns out that r^2 has one undesirable property: If we introduce additional independent (X) variables into our regression—thus making it automatically a multiple regression—then r^2 will *always* get larger. Because r^2 is often used to judge the "quality" of our overall fit, this would seem to indicate that putting more variables into our regression will always give us better results, *even when those variables are utterly meaningless* for the problem at hand. That is, if we were to put in the students' body temperatures, the longitudes of their ancestral homes, their favorite FM radio stations, and so on, these would serve to increase r^2. To help correct for this problem, statisticians have developed r^2-adjusted, which is not so "easy to fool": If you decide to put a statistically meaningless variable (i.e., one with absolutely no additional information or explanatory power) into the regression, r^2-adjusted will get *smaller*. Thus, it will not always tell us to use more variables. Note, however, that it *is* possible to add in a statistically *nonsignificant* variable and have r^2-adjusted increase; to assess significance, we will always look to the values of *t* and *p* for the newly added variable, as we will see in the next chapter on multiple regression methods.

The final new entry in this portion of the regression output is "SE(Reg)," the standard error of the regression, often denoted as s_e. This turns out to be related to none other than the total "error" left *unexplained* by the regression, $SS_e = \sum_{i=1}^{n} (Y_i - \hat{Y}_i)^2$; the precise relation will be made clear in the next section. In terms of interpretation, the standard error of the regression conveys an important quantity: the spread of the points around the regression line. In estimating a regression relationship, we have actually assumed that the points are normally distributed around the line, and s_e is our "best guess" at the standard deviation of this normal distribution. If it is "large," it means that the points are very spread out around the line, that the points are not *near* the line, and so the regression is unlikely to be a good model for the data.

The way to determine whether s_e is "large" is to compare it with the spread of the data *without* a regression line, which is simply the sample standard deviation. For these data, $s_e = 19.224$, and we had previously calculated the standard deviation of weight (Y), $s_Y = 32.2$. Certainly, s_e *looks* to be far less than s_Y; but in statistics, we simply cannot go by how quantities look. What we need is a way to *test* whether the regression has truly lessened the spread of the weight data (Y) from its initial value of 32.2. We do this in the following section, which explains how to use the model to generate predicted values for the dependent variable. Before doing so, we note one more intriguing relationship. If we wish to ask how much of a reduction s_e represents over s_Y, we can calculate the proportional reduction, as follows:

$$\frac{s_Y^2 - s_e^2}{s_Y^2} = \frac{(32.224)^2 - (19.2)^2}{(32.224)^2} = 0.645.$$

And this is exactly our value of r^2. Thus, we see that r^2 represents the degree of variation reduction in yet another, but perfectly equivalent, way. We now make this notion more rigorous by developing a way to test its significance. Note that r^2 can be fairly large without being significant—this happens all the time in small data sets, where significance is difficult to achieve due to lack of data—and that r^2 can also be very small and strongly significant, a common result in very large data sets, because even small effects are easily detected.

9.7g Using the Regression Model to Predict

We can use the regression equation to generate predicted values of Y, which as before are notated $\hat{Y}_i$ and calculated as $\hat{Y}_i = a + bX_i$. Table 9.5 presents these $\hat{Y}_i$ values, along with other pertinent calculations that we will call on, for our marketing research student data.

Let us first notice several relationships that hold not only for this data set, but for any regression at all. First, three sets of deviations always add to zero across the entire data set: $(Y_i - \hat{Y}_i)$, $(\hat{Y}_i - \bar{Y})$ and $(Y_i - \bar{Y})$. Second, our sum-of-squares equation, $SS_E + SS_R = SS_T$, is also valid: 164833.1 + 300041.4 = 464874.5. Third, these manually calculated values match those provided by the regression output.

In statistics, we will often want to calculate a "mean" of some population quantity. To do this, we will *not* divide by how many values are summed up, but by the degrees-of-freedom associated with those values. Note that the final portion of our regression output contains what is referred to as an analysis-of-variance, or ANOVA, table (see the Appendix to Chapter 11):

analysis of variance (ANOVA)
A statistical method that allows the simultaneous comparison of the means of many groups; in this way, it generalizes the two-sample *t*-test. If the groups differ on a single variable (e.g., year in college), the analysis is a *one-way* ANOVA; if on two variables (e.g., year in college and gender), a *two-way* ANOVA; and so on. ANOVA is a special case of ordinary multiple linear regression.

Table 9.5 Calculations for Making Predictions in Linear Regression

	Height	Weight	Prediction	"Error"					
i	X_i	Y_i	$\hat{Y}_i$	$Y_i - \hat{Y}_i$	$(Y_i - \hat{Y}_i)^2$	$\hat{Y}_i - \bar{Y}$	$(\hat{Y}_i - \bar{Y})^2$	$Y_i - \bar{Y}$	$(Y_i - \bar{Y})^2$
1	77	220	213.8	6.2	38.1	57.8	3344.8	64.0	4096.7
2	66	125	141.7	−16.7	280.5	−14.2	202.9	−31.0	960.6
3	69	150	161.4	−11.4	130.1	5.4	29.3	−6.0	35.9
...	...	...	...	...	...	...	...	...	...
447	64	106	128.6	−22.6	512.7	−27.4	748.1	−50.0	2499.4
448	74	200	194.2	5.8	34.0	38.2	1457.4	44.0	1936.5
					SS_E	+	**SS_R**	=	**SS_T**
SUM	**30541.9**	**69885.4**	**69885.4**	**0**	**164833.1**	**0**	**300041.4**	**0**	**464874.5**

Source of Variation	Sum-of-Squares	*df*	Mean Squares	*F*-Test Statistic	*p*-Value One-Tailed
Regression	300041.41	1	300041.41	811.84	0.0000
Error	164833.07	446	369.58		
Total	464874.47	447			

mean-squares
In statistical models, an estimate of an average squared distance, calculated by dividing a sum-of-squares by the associated degrees-of-freedom.

***F*-test**
An exceptionally common test throughout statistics, and ubiquitous in various forms of regression. Indicates whether the "entire model"—that is, all independent variables taken together—explain a significant proportion of the variation in the dependent variable.

This portion of the regression output allows us to tally sums of squares (just as we have calculated them in Table 9.5), keep track of the *df* (degrees-of-freedom) associated with each, and use them to calculate **mean squares**. In statistical models, mean squares measure variation; in regression models, the important mean square is associated with the error. Here, its value is 369.58, which is the square of 19.224 (the standard error of the regression [SE(Reg)] in our output); this is not a coincidence. The mean square error (here, 369.58) measures how much variance in each data point can be attributed to error; and the mean square regression (here, 300041.41) measures how much variance in each data point can be attributed to the regression. Note that for our data, the latter value is much larger than the former. This means that the regression is explaining far more variation than is left over for the error.

But *how much* more variance is the regression explaining? Is it *significantly* more? The answer to this is given by dividing one by the other, $300041.41/369.58 = 811.84$. This ratio is always known as the ***F*-test**. In simple regression—when there is only one independent (X) variable—this will *always* be the square of the t-value for the slope (and, indeed, $(28.493)^2 = 811.84$); but this will not be the case when there are multiple independent variables. The F-test can be challenging to look up by hand and, fortunately, the computer will calculate its associated p-value for us automatically. In simple regression, it will always match the p-value for the slope, which in our example was the exceptionally tiny 2×10^{-102}, rounded by the output to 0.0000. Note that the F-test is *always* a one-tailed test. Students often wonder why there is both an F-test and a t-test, when they give identical results in simple (one independent variable) regression. The answer is that the F-test tells you about *all* the independent variables in your model taken together, whereas the t-test tells you about *each* of the independent variables in your model considered separately; when there is just one independent variable in the model, they must agree. We will see a great deal more of both the F-test and the t-test in the next chapter, in the context of more complex regression models.

We will turn shortly to the sort of inferential statistics used to summarize important bivariate relationships. Before doing so, *Marketing Research Focus* 9.3 illustrates how bivariate analysis might be used to understand differences, if any, in how cigarettes are marketed to different ethnic communities.

9.8 Inferential Statistics for Bivariate Analysis

As with univariate analysis, researchers often wish to go beyond simply describing sample relationships to making judgments about population parameters. For example, in our regression, we have found the best estimate for how much weight increases for each inch increase in height, *for our sample*. Although this is useful information, we would typically wish to see whether we could use this information to make inferences valid for the *population* from which the sample was drawn.

It is possible to test a hypothesis about any descriptive statistic—for example, the population regression slope, intercept, or correlation coefficient. However, we will restrict our attention to a select set of bivariate inferential tests common across managerial and social science applications. Moreover, we will cover them in a special way, as special cases of regression because in the "real world," regression models are ubiquitous, as are programs for estimating them. Specifically then, for interval data, we will discuss inferential tests for regression coefficients, showing how to interpret them for different questions of interest to researchers.

9.8a Basic Inferential Test for Regression Coefficients

Researchers will often wish to test whether a regression coefficient has a specific value. For example, based on extensive medical studies, one may believe that people tend to gain weight as they age, specifically, about one pound per year. We could express this belief as "$\beta = 1$," where β signifies the value of the *population* slope in a regression of weight regressed on age. (In statistics, we generally use Greek letters for population parameters—which we will never know without collecting data on the entire

Marketing Research Focus 9.3

Bivariate Analysis

Cigarette smoking is a significant health problem in the United States and has been cited as a significant contributor to a wide variety of diseases and conditions, including various cancers and high blood pressure. Although it poses health risks to men and women of all races, it has been found that in the United States, African Americans are disproportionately impacted by the effects of smoking. Although a number of explanations for this phenomenon have been investigated, one that stands out in the context of the material for this chapter is the different strategies employed by tobacco companies in marketing different types of cigarettes to African Americans and Caucasian Americans.

Numerous studies indicate that African Americans are significantly more likely to smoke mentholated cigarettes, as opposed to their Caucasian counterparts: whereas mentholated cigarettes make up approximately 25 percent of cigarette sales, more than half of black smokers choose mentholated cigarettes. Other studies have demonstrated that consumption of mentholated cigarettes is worse in terms of a variety of health outcomes than traditional cigarettes. It should come as no surprise, then, that smoking-related disease rates are relatively high in the African American population.

Marketing has played an important role in the development of these macro-level trends: tobacco companies have long targeted mentholated cigarette advertising to the African American populace. For example, tobacco companies are more likely to advertise mentholated cigarettes in areas with higher minority populations and in magazines with high minority readership, and advertisements for mentholated cigarettes are more likely to utilize nonwhite models. Although it is impossible to conclusively determine whether or not advertising per se has caused these sorts of differential mentholated-cigarette usage patterns (and, indeed, there is likely to be a substantial reverse causality in this case), it is nonetheless troubling; after all, targeted marketing is unlikely to reduce consumption of this dangerous commodity in the population in question.

Unraveling the questions associated with this research requires the use of a number of bivariate techniques. For example, we need to understand the impact on various health outcomes of smoking either normal or mentholated cigarettes; we need to assess the choices of type of cigarette to smoke that are being made by each of the racial groups in question; we need to investigate the prevalence of marketing of each type of cigarette to each of those racial groups; and we need to understand the impact that advertising has on the decision to smoke cigarettes. Preliminary investigations of a variety of these relationships suggest that this topic deserves scrutiny and a significant ethical debate within the marketing community.

Sources: Cummings, K. Michael, Gary Giovino, and Anthony J. Mendicino, (1987). "Cigarette Advertising and Black-White Differences in Brand Preferences." *Public Health Report*, 102, 698–701.
"Harvard Researchers Gather More Evidence Implicating Menthol in Health Disparities Between White and Black Smokers." Harvard School of Public Health press release, August 18, 2005. http://www.hsph.harvard.edu/ > News/Press Releases > Search August 18, 2005.

population—and Roman letters for statistics calculated from a sample.) As in other statistical tests, then, we would have both a null and an alternative hypothesis:

$$H_0 : \beta = 1$$

$$H_0 : \beta \neq 1$$

There are many ways to carry out this test, but we would like the computer to do as much of the work for us as possible. Let us regress weight on age in the data on our marketing research students (who, we must remember, do not come from the general population). We will reproduce just the most useful part of the regression output, noting that $r = 0.217$ (CL = confidence level).

Model	b	Std. Error	Test Statistic	p-Value Two-Tailed	β Lower 95% CL	β Upper 95% CL
Constant	116.84	8.486	13.77	0.0000	100.16	133.52
Age	1.42	0.303	4.69	0.0000	0.824	2.014

In our sample, it appears that each year in age is associated with an additional $b = 1.42$ pounds in weight. The remainder of the age row tests whether $\beta = 0$ (*not* our null hypothesis that $\beta = 1$), finding very strong evidence that it does not. In fact, a 95 percent confidence interval for β is [0.824, 2.014], which does not contain 0. However, it *does* contain our hypothesized value of $\beta = 1$! We automatically know that we will not be able to reject the null hypothesis at the 95 percent confidence level, just by looking at the confidence interval and seeing whether the hypothesized value (here, $\beta = 1$) lies within it.

However, we wish to be more precise than this and to calculate an exact p-value for our hypothesis test. To do so, we will have to calculate how many standard errors away our hypothesized ($\beta = 1$) and sample ($b = 1.42$) values lie:

$$t = \frac{b - \beta}{s_b} = \frac{1.42 - 1}{0.303} = 1.386.$$

We must consult the computer to calculate the p-value associated with a t-statistic of 1.386 when $df = 446$ (a t distribution with this many degrees-of-freedom is nearly indistinguishable from a z, or standard normal, distribution). We would find that the two-tailed p-value for our test is $p = 0.166$. We would in this case *not* reject the null hypothesis, and conclude that there was not sufficient evidence to discard our belief that $\beta = 1$. One might think that the calculated sample value of $b = 1.42$ *looks* very different from 1, but this would neglect a crucial consideration in statistics: the standard error, which reflects the precision of our estimate. Here, it is 0.303, so the difference between $\beta = 1$ and $b = 1.42$ needs to be conceptualized in terms of how many of these standard errors lies between them. In statistics, that is literally all that matters. Because the "distance" between $\beta = 1$ and $b = 1.42$ is only 1.386 standard errors, we simply do not have strong enough evidence to pronounce them "significantly different." We note in closing that statistical programs will automatically test the null hypothesis that any regression coefficient (slope or intercept) is zero, that is, H_0: $\beta = 0$. For other hypothesized values, we can carry out this test by hand, but it is never more difficult than using the procedure just applied, and is *always* conceptually equivalent to asking, How many standard errors apart are the hypothesized and the calculated sample values?

9.8b Inferential Test for Difference in Population Group Means

In a first statistics course, it is common to carry out tests for differences in population means. For example, one wishes to test whether sales are the same in two regions, whether two ads have similar response levels, or whether the average exam scores in two classes are the same. It is often easier, both technically and conceptually, to carry out such tests as part of a simple regression. We can always do this very simply, by coding one group as 0 and the other as 1, then "regressing out" the group variable. Let us once again appeal to our data on marketing research students. We might ask whether it is true that men really weigh more than women. One way to assess this difference would be to gather information—means and standard deviations—from the sample of men and from the sample of women, then carry out a classical statistical test. There are several ways to do this, and they are often supported by statistical and spreadsheet programs. Here, we use regression to "correct" for weight differences between men and women. In so doing, we will see that the regression output yields a good deal of useful information in an appealing format.

If we regress Y = weight on X = gender, the most useful portion of our output is as follows (we note that $r = 0.704$):

Model	b	Std. Error	Test Statistic	p-Value Two-Tailed	β Lower 95% CL	β Upper 95% CL
Constant	128.94	1.69	76.5	0.0000	125.63	132.25
Gender	46.09	2.20	21.0	0.0000	41.77	50.41

Unlike most regressions, here the intercept ("constant") *does* have a clear meaning: It is our best guess at the average weight for women in the population from which our sample was drawn; this is because the intercept is the value taken on by Y when $X = 0$, and here X is gender (coded 0 for women). But what we are really interested in is the coefficient on gender itself, and this value is $b = 46.09$ pounds. We would say that based on this sample, men (in the relevant population) weigh about 46 pounds more than women! Of course, this does not account for differences in other variables, such as height; we will explore this in depth in the next chapter, on multiple regression methods. The first question we should ask about our value of $b = 46.09$ is whether it gives evidence that the population value, β, is really different from zero (obviously, we should ask whether it is not only different from, but *greater than*, zero). The associated test statistic, $t = 21.0$, has already been calculated; it is obviously extremely significant, considering that we ordinarily look for a t-value of at least 2. The listed p-value is 0.0000, meaning that $p < 0.00005$; the exact value turns out to be about 2×10^{-68}, well beyond any reasonable standard of evidence. We would therefore *very* confidently assert that based on this sample, men in the relevant population appear to weigh more than women. The regression output also calculates a 95 percent confidence interval for us, [41.77, 50.41], allowing us to say that we are "95 percent certain that the *true* weight difference between men and women lies between 41.77 and 50.41 pounds."

Note that all this information was provided automatically by the regression routine, making it an attractive platform for testing hypotheses for two samples. If we wanted to go further and test someone's claim that, say, the true difference was only 40 pounds, we would carry this out in the usual way, asking "how many standard errors apart" the calculated (46.09) and hypothesized (40) values were. This would be a trivial calculation: $(46.09 - 40)/(2.20) = 2.77$. If we wanted to perform a one-tailed test, the associated p-value, as calculated by the computer, would be $p = 0.0029$, allowing us to be fairly confident in *rejecting* the claim that the true weight difference in the population was only 40 pounds.

9.8c Differences in Proportions

Yet another sort of test is often carried out in marketing research: differences in *proportions*. For example, we might ask, "Did a greater proportion of people like the new ad, compared with the old one?" This test is commonly covered in introductory statistics courses, and we have included the details in the online appendices to this chapter, which can be accessed by logging in to the Online Edition of your textbook at www.atomicdog.com. We caution the reader that this test is only approximate, and in some cases—such as when the proportions involved are very near 0 or 1—can yield misleading answers. It is formally equivalent to using ordinary regression on binary (e.g., yes/no) data, which is not justified under the typical assumptions and rules of regression. A more appropriate way to approach this question is to use *binary logistic regression*, which we will explore in the next chapter. Still, if we have fairly large samples and the proportions in question are not close to 0 or to 1, we can use simple regression to test whether two population proportions are equal. Let us do this, just like in the previous case for weight and gender, for the variables MBA ("Are you currently enrolled in an MBA program?") and gender, to test whether the undergraduate student gender split is the same as for the MBA students. Again, we just regress MBA on gender, and reproduce the relevant portion of the output (here, $r = 0.213$; recall also that $n = 448$):

Model	b	Std. Error	Test Statistic	p-Value Two-Tailed	β Lower 95% CL	β Upper 95% CL
Constant	0.627	0.032	19.8	0.0000	0.565	0.690
Gender	0.190	0.041	4.6	0.0000	0.109	0.272

Our "best guess" at the difference in proportion would be 0.190, and we find this to be strongly significant, with $t = 4.6$. If we consult a table or statistical program, we learn that this implies $p = 0.000005$, a very small value indeed. So, we would conclude that the proportion of women in the MBA *population* was indeed smaller than in the undergraduate *population*. Our estimate of this difference is 19 percent, and our 95 percent CL would run from 10.9 percent to 27.2 percent. Note again that these results are approximate because the dependent variable is binary, and we should use a different type of regression (e.g., binary logistic regression) in such cases. Nevertheless, such "classical" tests of differences in proportions are used with some frequency and, with large data sets and moderate proportions, give useful and broadly valid results.

We would not want to leave the reader with the impression that marketing researchers seek to relate only interval-scaled variables to one another. As detailed at the very beginning of this chapter, many types of variables crop up in marketing applications—interval (sales, promotional discounts, investment costs), dichotomous (gender, whether a particular brand was featured), ordinal (responses on a 7-point scale), rank-ordered, multinomial (choose one from this set of items), and so on—and we would like to be able to relate them to one another. We will develop regression-based methods for exploring such relationships in the next chapter. Before doing that, we present the most common methods for analyzing (bivariate) relations between two *nominal* variables, all of which are based on the chi-square test.

9.8d Nominal Association: The Chi-Square Test

Among the most common types of bivariate analysis in marketing practice is the cross-tabulation of two nominal variables. Strictly speaking, we need not have nominal variables for cross-tabulation; interval or ordinal variables can be analyzed in this fashion if we first group them into classes or categories. In fact, some interval variables, such as age, are routinely grouped into nominal categories for the purpose of analysis. Questions arising in marketing research that are typically addressed by cross-tabulation include:

- Is there a relationship between consumer ethnicity and media consumption habits?
- Is there a relationship between region of the country and brand preference?
- Is there a relationship between lifestyle types (i.e., psychographic categories) and car ownership?

As these examples illustrate, the objective of cross-tabulation is the same as that of other bivariate methods: to identify a relationship between variables. In data from a sample, we might observe what appears to be a relationship between two *nominal* variables. The question naturally arises as to whether this observed relationship is simply the result of sampling error, and the chi-square test is designed to answer this question. The null hypothesis for a chi-square test is that the two variables are *independent* of each other. The alternative hypothesis is that they are not independent, that is, that there is a relationship between the two variables (or, more precisely, that each *depends in* some way on the value of the other).

Let us illustrate the chi-square test. Table 9.6 presents the cross-tabulation of three categories of individual income and which of three brands was purchased last. The cell entries indicate the numbers in the sample that form the various combinations of income and brand categories. For example, we note that there were 50 people earning less than $40,000 who purchased Brand 1 last. The expected number in each cell is not the same, as it was with the univariate chi-square example worked out earlier in this chapter. This is so because the category totals for each variable are not the same. For example, 650 people earn between $40,000 and $80,000, more than in the other two income categories combined, so we should certainly not expect the cell counts to be equal. What then should be the *expected* cell values? To answer this question, we turn to one of the elementary rules of probability theory, the **multiplication rule**.

multiplication rule
A fundamental rule of probability stating that the probability of two *independent* events occurring is the product of their individual probabilities.

Here, income is denoted as variable A, and income categories as A_1, A_2, and A_3. "Brand purchased last" is variable B, and the categories are B_1, B_2, and B_3. The various combinations of $\{A_iB_j\}$ are the occurrences of various events. Let us refer to the "event" A_1B_1 to illustrate how probability theory can very directly guide our computations.

If A and B are independent, we know that the probability of A_1 and B_1 occurring is the product of the probability of A_1 times the probability of B_1. This is the *multiplication rule* for independent events in elementary probability. In symbols:

$$P(A_1 \text{ and } B_1) = P(A_1)P(B_1).$$

Table 9.6 Cross-tabulation of Income and Brand Purchased Last

		B			
		Brand purchased last			
		B_1	B_2	B_3	
		Brand	Brand	Brand	
	Income	1	2	3	Total
	A_1 (Less than $40,000)	50	200	125	375
A	A_2 ($40,000–$80,000)	200	100	350	650
	A_3 (More than $80,000)	100	25	50	175
	Total	350	325	525	1200

Also we note that

$$P(A_1) = \text{relative frequency of } A_1$$
$$= \frac{A_1}{A_1 + A_2 + A_3} = \frac{375}{1200} = 0.313$$
$$P(B_1) = \text{relative frequency of } B_1$$
$$= \frac{B_1}{B_1 + B_2 + B_3} = \frac{350}{1200} = 0.292$$
$$P(A_1 \text{ and } B_1) = \frac{375}{1200} \times \frac{350}{1200} = 0.091$$

The expected number (or *cell count*) of cell A_1B_1 is then

$$n[P(A_1 \text{ and } B_1)] = 1200\left(\frac{375}{1200} \times \frac{350}{1200}\right) = 109.38.$$

In general, the formula for expected value is

$$E_{ij} = \frac{n_{Ai}n_{Bj}}{n},$$

where E_{ij} = expected number
n_{Ai} = number of elements in category A_i
n_{Bj} = number of elements in category B_j.

We can easily apply the formula to A_1B_1, to check if it matches our previous calculations:

$$E_{11} = \frac{(375)(350)}{1200} = 109.38.$$

This process is carried out for all cells in the table. Table 9.7 presents the observed and expected numbers for each cell and the calculation of the associated chi-square statistic. Recall that the formula for χ^2 is given by:

$$\chi^2 = \sum_{i=1}^{R}\sum_{j=1}^{C}\frac{(O_{ij} - E_{ij})^2}{E_{ij}}$$

where R = number of categories of the row variable
C = number of categories of the column variable
O_{ij} = observed number in cell ij
E_{ij} = expected number in cell ij.

Table 9.7 Calculation of Bivariate Chi-Square

Cell number	O_{ij}	E_{ij}	$O_{ij} - E_{ij}$	$(O_{ij} - E_{ij})^2$	$(O_{ij} - E_{ij})^2/E_{ij}$
1,1	50	109.38	−59.38	3526.0	32.2
1,2	200	101.56	98.44	9690.4	95.4
1,3	125	164.06	−39.06	1525.7	9.3
2,1	200	189.58	10.42	108.6	0.6
2,2	100	176.04	−76.04	5782.1	32.8
2,3	350	284.38	65.62	4306.0	15.1
3,1	100	51.04	48.96	2397.1	47.0
3,2	25	47.40	−22.40	501.8	10.6
3,3	50	76.56	−26.56	705.4	9.2
Total	1200	1200.00			$\chi^2 = 252.2$

The calculated chi-square is $\chi^2 = 252.2$. The number of degrees-of-freedom is $(R-1)(C-1)$ because once the number of elements in $(R-1)$ row categories and the total are known, the number in the last category is determined; an identical argument holds for column degrees-of-freedom. In our example there are $(3-1)(3-1) = 4$ degrees-of-freedom. If $\alpha = 0.01$, the critical value of chi-square with 4 *df*, written χ^2_4, is 13.28 (see Table A-3 in Appendix A or use any statistical program). Because the calculated chi-square exceeds the critical value, we *reject* the null hypothesis that income and brand purchased last are independent. For quick calculations, we note here that the expected value of a chi-square variable is its number of degrees-of-freedom, and its variance is twice the *df*. When the *df* value is fairly large (say, 25 or more), the chi-square distribution is very close to normal, specifically, $N[\mu = df, \sigma^2 = 2(df)]$. So, when the observed value of chi-square is much more than the degrees-of-freedom, we have strong evidence to reject. Here, our observed value of 252.2 is much greater than $df = 4$; in fact, the computer calculates another absurdly tiny *p*-value, in this case $p = 2 \times 10^{-53}$. Regardless, we reject the hypothesis of no association or independence between the two nominal variables—income category and brand purchased last—with a very high degree of confidence.

A Note on Using Chi-Square

In our application, we should have checked that all the expected cell sizes were 5 or greater. If this is not the case, it is generally recommended that cells be combined to give an expected frequency of at least 5, or that chi-square not be used at all, as it can yield misleading results. Fortunately, all the expected counts for our example were much larger than 5, so our test is valid.

The chi-square test may tell us that two variables are not independent. However, it does not tell anything about the true nature of the relationship. To determine this, we must take a long, hard look at the tabled data of interest. In Table 9.6, we see that as "income category" increases, "brand purchased last" shifts from Brand 2 to Brand 3 and then to Brand 1. This is much easier to discern if we form a table of "percentage deviations," where each cell denotes how much higher or lower the *observed* value is as a percentage of the *expected* value, that is, $(O_{ij} - E_{ij})/E_{ij}$:

	Percentage Deviations		
Income	B_1	B_2	B_3
A_1 (Less than \$40,000)	−54%	97%	−24%
A_2 (\$40,000–\$80,000)	5%	−43%	23%
A_3 (More than \$80,000)	96%	−47%	−35%

This shows very clearly that B_1 is overrepresented in the highest income category, B_2 in the lowest, and B_3 in the middle. However, this is merely an observation and is not only not rigorous (i.e., there is no associated statistical test), but it also does not help to quantify the strength of the suggested association. To do so, we would have to appeal to more powerful methods, such as multinomial or conditional logistic regression, as addressed in the next chapter.

Researchers often confront many cross-tabulation tables. They are, in fact, a favorite tack-on item at the end of a survey-based study, with all manner of categorical variables broken out against one another. A good strategy to use in evaluating these tables is first to check the chi-square for significance, then closely examine those tables with significant chi-square values. Fortunately, all good data analysis programs offer the chi-square test as part of a cross-tabulation output. In the online appendices to this chapter, we include some additional information on cross-tabulation, specifically regarding the use of percentages, and how to elaborate on discovered bivariate nominal relationships when additional variables are brought into play.

In any data set containing even a small number of variables, there are a great many possible cross-tabular tables. If one attempts to do "due diligence" and explore the full range of constructible tables in detail, the number of possibilities becomes astronomical. Obviously, researchers cannot just go on a "fishing trip" to find relationships, for they would be overwhelmed with computer output. They must have an *a priori* mental model of the problem, one that focuses on the interrelationships among relevant variables, to do proper cross-tabulation analysis. A clear, firm definition of the problem at hand, combined with prespecified roster information needs, can go a long way in guiding the data analysis process.

Summary

The choice of data analysis procedure depends on the number of variables to be analyzed concurrently, whether description or inference is required, and the scale level of measurement of the variable(s). Bivariate analysis involves analyzing two variables at a time.

Descriptive statistics provide summary measures of the data contained in the sample; inferential statistics allow researchers to make judgments about a population based on results from a sample.

The mean and the standard deviation are the relevant descriptive measures of central tendency and dispersion, respectively, for interval data. The median is the relevant descriptive measure of central tendency for ordinal data. The mode and relative and absolute frequencies are the relevant descriptive measures of central tendency and dispersion, respectively, for nominal data.

A null hypothesis is a statement that a population parameter takes on a specific numerical value. It may be rejected or not rejected. If it is rejected, the alternative hypothesis is accepted. A null hypothesis is never accepted.

Type I error occurs when one rejects a true null hypothesis. It occurs with probability α, where α is called the significance level of the hypothesis test. Consequently, $(1 - \alpha)$ is the probability of not rejecting a true null hypothesis, and is called the level of confidence.

Type II error occurs when we do not reject a false null hypothesis, and it occurs with a probability of β. Consequently, $(1 - \beta)$ is the probability of rejecting a false null hypothesis. It is called the power of the test.

From a managerial point of view, the cost of a Type II error may be greater than that of a Type I error, although the opposite is frequently true in other domains, such as law or medicine.

The steps in hypothesis testing are: (a) Formulate null and alternative hypotheses; (b) select the appropriate statistical test; (c) specify the significance level; (d) determine the critical value of the test statistic; (e) calculate the test statistic using the sample data; and (f) compare the critical value with the computed test value of the statistic. If (e) is greater than (d), reject the null hypothesis.

For interval data, the z-test is the appropriate inferential test for means when σ is known (for any sample size), or for situations where σ is unknown and n is very large. When σ is unknown, we instead use the sample standard deviation, s, and a t-test.

The chi-square test is the appropriate inferential test for the distribution across nominal categories.

The correlation coefficient, r, measures the degree to which two *interval* variables are *linearly* associated. It will not necessarily indicate other types of association, particularly so highly nonlinear ones.

The coefficient of determination, r^2, is the amount of variation in one variable that can be explained by knowledge of another.

Simple regression is appropriate for one interval-scaled dependent variable and one interval-scaled independent variable, and quantifies the relationship between them.

The simple regression model can be presented as

$$SS_{\text{Total}} = SS_{\substack{\text{Explained}\\ \text{by Regression}}} + SS_{\substack{\text{Unexplained}\\ \text{by Regression}}}.$$

The simple regression equation is $\hat{Y}_i = a + bX_i$, where a is the intercept and b is the slope; b estimates the unit increase in Y associated with a one-unit increase in X. A t-test on the b coefficient tests the null hypothesis that the *population* regression slope is zero.

The coefficient of determination in regression, r^2, is given by:

$$r^2 = \frac{\text{Explained variation}}{\text{Total variation}} = \frac{SS_{\substack{\text{Explained}\\ \text{by Regression}}}}{SS_{\text{Total}}}$$

The difference between two *sample* means may be tested to see whether the *population* means are really different. This may be carried out by using simple regression.

The chi-square test evaluates the null hypothesis that two nominal variables are independent.

The coefficient of determination is often adjusted so that it is less affected by nonsignificant variables. The standard error of the regression (s_e) is an estimate of the degree of error left *un*explained by the regression. The F-test tells you how much variance the regression explains for all the independent variables in your model taken together; by contrast, the t-test tells you about how much variance in the regression is explained by each independent variable considered separately.

Key Terms

absolute frequencies (p. 400)
alternative hypotheses (p. 402)
ANOVA (p. 421)
bimodal (p. 399)
central tendency (p. 397)
chi-square test (p. 409)
coefficient of determination (r^2) (p. 414)
confidence level (p. 403)
covariance (p. 413)
decompose (p. 417)
discrete (p. 397)
dispersion (p. 400)
F-test (p. 422)
inferential statistics (p. 395)
least squares (p. 416)
linear correlation coefficient (*r*) (p. 414)
mean squares (p. 422)
median (p. 398)
mode (p. 398)
multiplication rule (p. 426)
null hypothesis (p. 401)
one-tailed test (p. 402)
power of the test (p. 404)
p-value (p. 404)
regression line (p. 418)
relative frequencies (p. 400)
robustness (p. 398)
scale independent (p. 413)
significance level (p. 403)
simple linear regression (p. 412)
t-test (p. 408)
two-tailed test (p. 406)
type I error α (p. 403)
type II error β (p. 403)
z-test (p. 405)

Discussion Questions

1 Distinguish between descriptive and inferential statistics.

2 A sales manager had promised the entire sales force a special trip if average daily sales per salesperson were $8,000 or more. A sample of 10 salespersons yielded the following results: average daily sales per salesperson = $7800; standard deviation = $400. Can the sales manager conclude that the entire sales force (i.e., the population) had reached the goal? Explain your reasoning.

3 A political research firm undertook a sample of registered voters in a small community to see whether a particular candidate would win the election. The sample size was 500, and the result was that 51 percent of the sample favored this candidate. How would you set up the null and alternative hypotheses in a manner relevant to settling the question at hand? If people vote as they say they will, do the results indicate that this candidate will win the election? What assumptions must you make in order to say anything meaningful on the basis of these data?

4 MINICASE

The Lake City chief of police wanted to discover how fast the average car traveled on a particular stretch of highway. To obtain this information, he placed a hidden radar device beside the highway and clocked speeds, in miles per hour, for one hour. The following data were recorded by the device:

73	49	70	63	83	61
55	61	60	68	62	64
52	56	69	60	55	71
65	66	59	62	59	58

Calculate the appropriate statistics for central tendency and dispersion. What are the problems with this design?

5 What questions must researchers answer in order to select the appropriate bivariate statistical procedure for a given data set? Are there some data types for which no bivariate analysis is possible?

6 When can simple linear regression be used? Specifically, what sort of data must one have, and what assumptions are made about the relationship between the variables in question? When should it *not* be used?

7 A marketing manager was given the following table of frequency counts to assess the nature of the relationship between age and attendance at NFL games. What conclusion can be drawn?

	Age		
Attend NFL games	**Younger than 40**	**Older than 40**	**Total**
Yes	466	231	697
No	224	323	547
Total	690	554	1244

8 The same marketing manager also had a table of frequency counts between age and attendance at college football games. Given these new data, what conclusion can be drawn?

	Age		
Attend college football games	**Younger than 40**	**Older than 40**	**Total**
Yes	242	271	513
No	251	265	516
Total	**493**	**536**	**1029**

9 In a study of advertising effects, two waves of consumers were interviewed. Wave 1 took place before a new campaign was introduced, and Wave 2 a few months after the new campaign had started. As part of the analysis of the data, a comparison was made between the demographic characteristics of the consumers in Wave 1 and Wave 2, under the hypothesis that they had not changed. Typical of the reported results is the following:

	Gender	
	Male	**Female**
Wave 1	52%	47%
Wave 2	48%	53%

The researchers used knowledge of the sample size to calculate a chi-square of 4.16. What conclusion can be drawn from this result?

10 Mark Schwinn and Leopoldine Grier were resident advisors (RAs) assigned to the first coed hall at Bindlesmock College. A welcome party was scheduled to take place the weekend after classes started, and the RAs had the responsibility of ordering the soft drinks. They could not, however, agree on kinds of soft drinks they should order (diet cola vs. regular cola vs. other assorted flavors). Thirty to 40 cases were to be ordered, and any unopened cans could be returned. Mark wanted to order 16 cases of regular cola, 6 diet cola, 6 regular noncola, and 2 diet noncola; Leopoldine wanted to order, respectively, 11, 6, 9, and 4 cases. To avoid running out of anything, they decided to order the larger estimate of each kind, making a 35-case order (16 cases regular cola, 6 diet cola, 9 regular noncola, and 4 diet noncola). The actual consumption at the party was 12 cases of regular cola, 4 diet cola, 8 regular noncola, and 1 diet noncola. Is there a difference in preferences between regular vs. diet soft drinks? Cola vs. noncola? Is there reason to believe the two variables are in fact independent?

11 In a recent study on American travel habits, the following data were obtained.

Case	Gender	Children at Home?	Respondent Age	Vacations per Year
1	M	Y	25	1
2	M	N	52	16
3	F	N	34	8
4	F	Y	33	1
5	F	Y	51	5
6	F	Y	29	0
7	M	Y	35	2
8	F	N	27	8
9	M	Y	46	4
10	M	N	30	10
11	F	N	45	14
12	M	Y	38	3

a Is there a relationship between the presence of children at home and the gender of the respondent?

b What is the relationship between age and the presence of children at home? How might you assess this via regression?

c What is the relationship between age and number of vacations taken per year? Calculate r^2. (*Hint*: Plot the data points before doing a regression analysis. Look for the effects of another, or "extraneous," variable; and calculate your least-squares regression line or lines accordingly. Is one equation appropriate? Would two explain the data better? If so, how? If not, why not?)

d Is the relationship obtained to answer (c.) significant (i.e., was a significant proportion of the variance in the dependent variable explained by the regression)?

e Using the equation or equations you computed in the previous problem, complete the following data set by using your regression model(s) to *predict* "vacations per year" for the new cases, 13–16:

Case	Gender	Children at home?	Respondent Age	Vacations per Year
13	M	Y	40	___
14	F	N	40	___
15	M	Y	65	___
16	F	N	18	___

Review Questions

1 When describing a variable, why might a researcher want to use measures of both central tendency and dispersion?

a Two samples with the same central tendency can have very different levels of dispersion, which might lead to different conclusions about them.

b Two samples with the same level of dispersion might have very different central tendencies, which might lead to different conclusions about them.

c They are not both necessary—measures of central tendency suffice to describe a variable.

d both a and b

2 Distinguish between significance level and confidence level.

a The significance level gives the probability (α) of committing a Type I error, whereas the confidence level gives the probability (β) of committing a Type II error.

b The significance level gives the probability (α) of committing a Type I error, whereas the confidence level gives 1 – the probability (α) of committing a Type I error.

c The significance level gives the probability (β) of committing a Type II error, whereas the confidence level gives 1 – the probability (β) of committing a Type II error.

d One is simply the negative of the other.

3 What is the power of the test?

a the likelihood of correctly accepting a true null hypothesis

b the likelihood of correctly rejecting a false null hypothesis

c $1 - \alpha$

d β

4 From a sample of Nintendo users, the following frequency count was generated for the categories of the variable age in a sample of size $n = 745$.

Age	Frequency
18–24	315
25–39	205
40–54	115
55 and older	110

Does the sample data suggest that Nintendo usage spread evenly across these four population age groups?

a No

b Yes

c We cannot determine if usage is spread evenly across these four population age groups.

5 The manager of a movie theater hypothesized that twice as many of the theater's patrons were younger than 30 as were 30 and older. A sample of $n = 690$ patrons showed 450 were younger than 30, and 240 were 30 and older. What can you conclude about the theater manager's hypothesis regarding the population of patrons?

- **a** The theater manager's hypothesis is correct; we cannot reject the hypothesis of the distribution specified at even the 5 percent level.
- **b** The theater manager's hypothesis is incorrect; we can reject the hypothesis of the distribution specified at the 5 percent level.
- **c** We cannot tell whether the theater manager's hypothesis is correct or incorrect.
- **d** None of the above.

6 A company had adopted the following decision rule with respect to introducing a new product: "If average monthly consumption is 300 ounces or more, we will enter into test market." An in-home placement test of $n = 80$ yielded the following results: average monthly consumption = 290 ounces; standard deviation = 45. Given their stated decision rule, what decision should they make?

- **a** The company should enter the test market.
- **b** The company should not enter the test market.
- **c** If entering the test market is relatively cheap, the company should do it; otherwise, the company should not enter the test market.
- **d** We cannot determine, on the basis of this sample, whether or not the company should enter the test market or not.

7 How do you test to see whether a simple regression has explained a significant portion of the variation in the dependent variable?

- **a** A significant portion of the variation is explained if the coefficient on the intercept is significant.
- **b** A significant portion of the variation is explained if the coefficient on the dependent variable is significant.
- **c** A significant portion of the variation is explained if the correlation coefficient, r, is greater than some threshold value, given by the specific application.
- **d** A significant portion of the variation is explained if the r-squared value is greater than some threshold, given by the specific application.

8 For which of the following uses is the chi-square test valid?

- **a** The univariate chi-square test is used to test a hypothesized distribution over nominal categories against the results of a sample.
- **b** The bivariate chi-square test is used to test the hypothesized independence of two nominal variables.
- **c** a and b.
- **d** None of the above.

9 A study of collegiate basketball attendance related the number of home games attended in a year and the number of years the attendee has lived in the city:

Case	Number of Home Games Attended	Years Lived in City
1	8	28
2	2	6
3	1	3
4	3	12
5	8	20
6	4	23

What is the relationship, if any, between the two variables?

- **a** There does not appear to be any relationship between the two variables; even though higher number of years living in the city appears to correlate with more home games attended in a year, this relationship is not significant at the 5 percent level.
- **b** There appears to be a positive linear relationship; when a simple regression is estimated on the data, it demonstrates that living in the city for more years causes a person to attend more home games, and this relationship is significant at the 5 percent level.
- **c** We cannot determine anything about the relationship between the two variables on the basis of this sample.
- **d** There appears to be a positive linear relationship; as the number of years lived in the city increases, the number of home-games attended increases, and this relationship is significant at the 5 percent level.

10 What does the *F*-statistic in a regression with a single independent variable tell us?

- **a** The *F*-statistic conveys the likelihood that the coefficient on the intercept is zero.
- **b** The *F*-statistic conveys the likelihood that the coefficient on the single independent variable is zero.
- **c** The *F*-statistic tells us no more than the *t*-statistic for that variable's coefficient.
- **d** Both b and c.

Web Exercise

Log in to the Online Edition of your textbook at www.atomicdog.com to participate in this Web exercise, which can be found in your Online Study Guide for this chapter.

Further Reading

The Research Methods Knowledge Base, at www.socialresearchmethods.net.

Trochim, William, *The Research Methods Knowledge Base, 3rd Edition*. Cincinnati, OH: Atomic Dog/Thomson Custom Solutions. 2007.

Aczel, Amir D. *Complete Business Statistics, 5th Edition*. New York: McGraw-Hill/Irwin. 2002.

Stockburger, David. *Introductory Statistics: Concepts, Models and Applications*. Cincinnati, OH: Atomic Dog/Thomson Custom Solutions. 2001.

Lane, David. *Hyperstat*. Cincinnati, OH: Atomic Dog Publishing. 2002.

Hyperstat Online: davidmlane.com/hyperstat.

Statsoft Electronic Statistics Textbook, http://www.statsoft.com/textbook/stathome.html.

Introductory Statistics: Concepts, Models, and Applications, http://www.psychstat.missouristate.edu/sbk00.htm.

Multivariate Statistics: Concepts, Models, and Applications, http://www.psychstat.missouristate.edu/MultiBook/mlt00.htm.

The Little Handbook of Statistical Practice, http://www.tufts.edu/~gdallal/LHSP.HTM.

Rice University Virtual Stats Lab: http://www.ruf.rice.edu/~lane/rvls.html.

CHAPTER TEN
MODELING MULTIVARIATE RELATIONSHIPS: MULTIPLE REGRESSION FOR INTERVAL, BINARY, AND NOMINAL DEPENDENT VARIABLES

"The invalid assumption that correlation implies cause is probably among the two or three most serious and common errors of human reasoning."

STEPHEN JAY GOULD, "THE MISMEASURE OF MAN"

The previous chapter introduced simple linear regression and emphasized that regression is the dominant method of data analysis throughout the natural and social sciences. It is difficult to overemphasize the importance of regression methods for anyone planning a career where data play even a small role. Given the ever-expanding role of information technology throughout the world, understanding regression should be an imperative across higher education, regardless of one's course of study. For marketing research and management studies in general, a deep understanding of regression methods is essential.

One might wonder why "methods" was plural in the last sentence; isn't regression a single, unified method? Yes and no, depending on one's vantage point. In the formal theory of mathematical statistics, one can treat all types of regression as if they were really one grand method, and this is sometimes referred to by the forbidding term **"The General Linear Model."** Some advanced statistical programs even require that all regression models be viewed as special cases of this very general formulation. In this text, we take a more pragmatic view and treat various forms of regression in terms of the sort of *dependent variable* the researcher seeks to explain. Although it is not obvious that this is a reasonable way to classify regression methods, we hope that the logic of doing so will seem compelling as it is developed in this chapter.

General Linear Model
A statistical framework for taking linear combinations of (perhaps transformed) independent variables and relating them to (perhaps transformed) dependent variables, plus error (which may or may not be normally distributed). Ordinary regression models are special cases of the general linear model.

When regression is spoken of, however, it is almost never *simple* regression, with one predictor variable. The reason for this is straightforward: the world is a complex place, and rare is the application where we wish to explain a phenomenon (i.e., our dependent variable) in terms of just one predictor (i.e., our independent variable). The true power of regression is unveiled when we try to relate a variable of interest to many other variables, which may themselves be inter-correlated and consist of multiple data types. Throughout our discussions, we will assume that "regression" really means "multiple regression," and that we have several predictor (independent) variables at our disposal. As we will see, although this increases our explanatory potential, it also means we must exercise great care in examining our statistical results and turning them into appropriate, persuasive explanations.

10.1 Overview of Regression and its Uses

Before turning to the variety of regression methods covered in this chapter—specifically, for interval, binary, ordinal, nominal, rank-ordered, and count type dependent variables—we present a "big picture" overview of what regression does, how it can be used, practical strategies for its application, and explicit trouble spots that researchers need to be aware of when using it. We would ask the student to keep two things in mind when reading the forthcoming material: that regression is truly useful; and that, when understood well, it is also extremely beautiful. Between them, the authors have used regression for more than a century, and they still find its power, flexibility, and, yes, beauty, as amazing as when they first encountered it.

10.1a What Is Regression?

Although we have introduced simple linear regression in Chapter 9 and anticipate that readers have some familiarity with multiple regression, it is helpful to emphasize what the method is, how it works, and what it can—and cannot—do for marketing researchers. We begin by reviewing some of the different conceptions of what regression really "is," then discuss its various limitations and extensions.

Regression Is: A Way to Put a Line through a Group of Points

If you remember nothing else about regression, you should recall that it allows you to place the *best-fitting line* through a group of points in two dimensions (see Figure 10.1).

As detailed in the previous chapter, this line minimizes the *total sum-of-squares;* that is, the squared distance to the line, summed over all the points. When we extend this idea to *multiple* regression, we replace the line with a *surface*, but the underlying idea is the same: to make the best predictions we can.

Figure 10.1 The Best-Fitting Line: Regressing One Variable (Y) on Another (X)

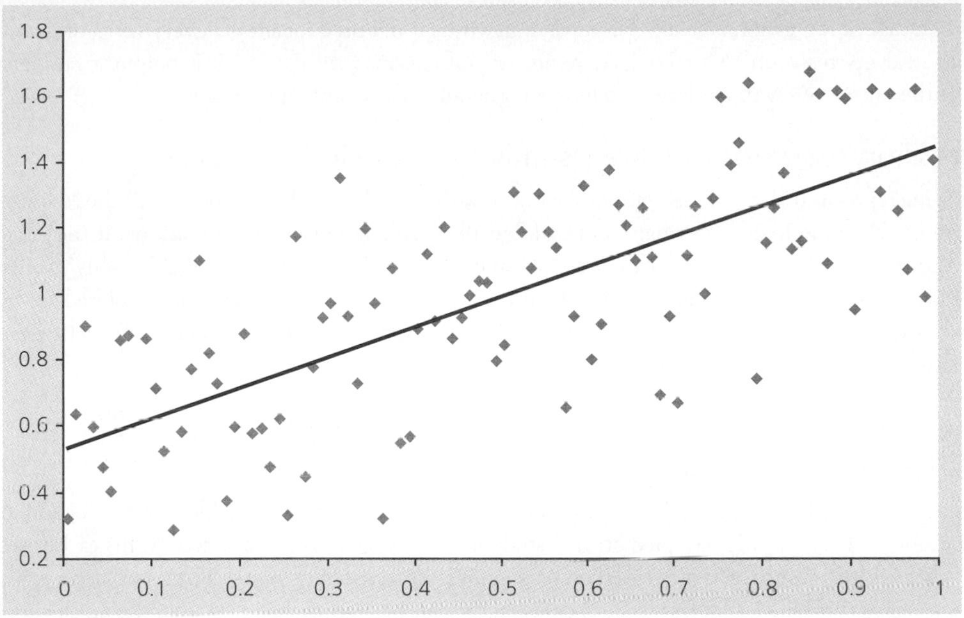

Regression Is: A Method for Testing the *Validity of Relationships*

We frequently encounter statements relating one thing to another. For example, if someone says it tends to rain on Tuesdays, he or she is saying that knowing that it is Tuesday conveys some knowledge about the likelihood it will rain. Put more compactly: there is a relationship between these two variables. Throughout the social and natural sciences, *the* method for testing the validity of such relationships is regression. In marketing research, specifically, we will often want to test whether there is a relationship between ad spending and sales, between years-in-market and market share, between depth of promotion and store volume, among many others. In concrete terms: regression can help us determine whether marketing actions *actually work*.

Regression Is: A Flexible Methodology for *Measuring* How Things Influence One Another

Marketers will always want to anticipate the likely outcome of managerial actions. "If we promote more heavily, *by how much* will profits go up?" In such situations, it is necessary not only to *verify* that promotion and profit may be related, but to *quantify* the nature of that relationship. Regression produces such estimates automatically and ensures certain desirable properties. In concrete terms: regression can help us determine *how well* marketing actions work.

Regression Is: A Scientific Approach to Forecasting and Prediction

Beyond using regression to *verify* and to *quantify*, we will also wish to use it to *predict*. That is, after the sample data set has been analyzed, what can we say about *new* data? If we have verified a strong regression-based relationship between, say, sales achieved and ad spending levels enacted, can we determine what sales *might have been* or *might be* for ad spending levels we did *not* try? Such questions are of obvious importance for marketers. In concrete terms: regression can help us determine how well *another* marketing action *may* work.

We have tried to stress why marketers should care about regression, but in a very real sense the reasons transcend marketing, business, or even the social and natural sciences. It is no exaggeration to say that there are two main methods underlying nearly all of mathematical reasoning: calculus and statistics. Broadly speaking, we use calculus (and off-shoots like differential equations) when dealing with certain quantities, and statistics when dealing with uncertain ones. And (again, speaking broadly) statistics is almost synonymous with regression, at least in terms of applications. When trying to say anything at all about the empirical world, regression is an indispensable tool for an exceptionally wide variety of applications.

10.1b Limits of Regression

One might ask: if regression is so all-encompassing, why is it not used for simply everything, and why is it not part of every researcher's toolkit? There are several reasons for this, and it is helpful to understand them at the outset. We will explore each in greater detail as the chapter progresses.

Regression Assumptions Are Usually Violated in Some Way

Underlying regression is a set of *assumptions* about how the data look, what we often call the "data generating process." These look somewhat technical, but they have important ramifications. If they are violated, the results one receives from a regression analysis may *look* fine but can yield highly misleading advice. These assumptions will actually be about the *errors* in a regression and, when violated, go by the somewhat cumbersome names of *nonnormality*, *heteroscedasticity*, and *autocorrelation*. We will examine them later in the chapter, as well as suggest possible "fixes."

Sometimes, There Are Too Many Predictor Variables, and They Are Highly Correlated

A common *data* problem is that we simply do not have enough predictor variables (our independent, or "X," variables). For example, try predicting a student's grade point average based on his or her weight and blood type or a company's sales based on how many vowels are in its name. But this is not a *regression* problem; regression may be useless in such cases, but it can be legitimately and unambiguously applied. More commonly—especially when we deal with large-scale customer databases or Internet-based data—we have enormous numbers of potential predictors, many of which are highly correlated. This is a problem known as **multicollinearity**, and it can prevent us from interpreting our regression results correctly. In the next chapter, we will learn about a method called *Factor analysis* that can help greatly with multicollinearity; in this chapter, we will discuss the problem itself, as well as how to potentially avoid it.

multicollinearity
A group of variables, each pair of which is moderately or highly correlated. There is no strict rule for how large such correlations should be, and in practice it is highly dependent on the research situation. Multicollinear data are often rectified using factor analysis.

It Is Hard to Know "What Should Predict What" (Latent Variables)

A classic study measured a large number of variables for children in the first grade and found a curious result: the children's hand size and the judged quality of their handwriting were highly correlated! All sorts of explanations were posited, ranging from nutritional to neurological to mechanical (e.g., larger hands enable greater pencil control). The real answer, of course, was more mundane: the children with larger hands were slightly older, and so were more developed and had more experience practicing their penmanship. This is known as a **latent variable** (in this case, "age"), one that gives rise to two (or more) others that are not naturally correlated. If we had regressed "handwriting quality" on "hand size," we would have gotten highly "significant" results but may have interpreted them incorrectly. Many things in the world are correlated that are not related in the way a regression might lead us to believe: the number of cars and the number of computers in the world over the past several decades are extremely strongly correlated, but we could not reduce the number of cars by restricting computer sales. Weeding out latent variables is difficult, and we will consider ways of doing so later in this chapter.

latent variable
A variable, generally not part of the research design, that correlates with two variables under study and creates the impression that the two are related, when they may not be.

Almost Nothing Is Really Linear

Linearity is an abstraction. Outside of purely definitional relationships—such as someone's weight in both pounds and kilograms—it is difficult, if not impossible, to think of two variables that are perfectly linearly related, even allowing for error (as regression always does). Fortunately, regression is a flexible method, and it allows us to estimate a wide variety of relationships, including nonlinear ones.

Regression Requires a Certain "Type" of Data, and Not All Data Are Like That

Regression, as it is often taught, is about relating one interval-scaled variable (*Y*) on another (*X*), such as weight on height, and perhaps a binary "dummy variable," such as gender. We will also see that regression allows for both independent and dependent variables that are not interval-scaled. If all regression could do was stick straight lines through points, its appeal for real-world problems would be vastly limited. We will address these issues in great detail throughout this chapter, and see that the regression method we choose is largely determined by the nature of our dependent variable.

Marketing Research Focus 10.1

Multiple Regression Analysis Reveals Predictors of Gaps in Expectation of Physician Service Quality

One of the most important of all marketing-related issues is the quality of service an organization delivers. This is especially true in the ultra-competitive world of the marketing of medical services. To develop a better understanding of the gap between patients' expectations of service quality and that perceived to be actually delivered by medical organizations, marketing researchers carried out a large-scale study of the issue, involving a survey of $n = 1128$ users of various medical services.

To understand this "expectations gap," a multiple regression analysis was conducted. The dependent variable was the size of the gap (between expectations and performance) in service quality, and the independent variables reflected the interactions of the patient with the medical practitioners and support staff. Specifically, these independent variables were:

1. the nature of the interaction with the actual physician;
2. the degree of interest the doctor showed in the patient;
3. the availability of the doctor in an emergency;
4. the professionalism of the doctor and other staff;
5. the reasonableness of fees;
6. the medical competence of the doctor;
7. the use of state-of-the-art technology;
8. the appropriate use of diagnostics;
9. the interactions with office staff and other administrative personnel; and
10. the availability of brochures and other materials related to medical issues.

All of these were measured, using widely accepted scales, for each of the study participants.

The regression fit unusually well, explaining more than 60 percent of the variance in the expectation–performance gap. All but the last two independent variables were significantly related to the size of the gap. Intriguingly, the most important independent variables were found to be interaction with the physician, professional competence of the doctor, interest by the doctor in the patient, and availability of the latest technology. These results are clearly useful to health maintenance organizations interested the key drivers of service quality perceptions.

A number of studies have shown that health care organizations are increasingly concerned about the quality of care in the face of cost-cutting, but they recognize that rigorously assessing quality is difficult. Among the reasons for this are some notorious marketing- and data-related realities: the health care market is highly focused on price; providers are unwilling to freely share data; and what data there are can be sadly outdated. These issues make regression-based, longitudinal studies of the health care industry difficult, despite the encouragingly high 60 percent explained variation in the focal study. Regardless of the depth or power of statistical analysis, a paucity of accurate, timely data continues to hinder research on medical service quality.

Sources: Stephen W. Brown and Teresa A. Swartz, "A Gap Analysis of Professional Service Quality," *Journal of Marketing*, 53, 92–98.
Susan J. Wells, "Finding the Best Medicine," *HR Magazine*, 47(1), 28–29.

Regression Can Be Overused

People who use regression for everything typify the following maxim: "To those who have only a hammer, the whole world looks like a nail."

Regression is not a "dangerous" or particularly sophisticated method, once you get the hang of it. But it *is* far more complex than, say, taking an average or making a pie chart. For simple summary methods like those, there are direct, visual "reality checks" that allow gross errors to be detected. A general rule throughout data analysis is that the more sophisticated the method, the easier it will be to make a truly colossal mistake. Because regression and methods based on it can seem a little like a "black box"—one puts in data, and the computer mysteriously churns out our estimates—there is a real chance that one can make errors that would not have come about using simpler, more familiar methods. On the other hand, regression is easy to apply: it is quick, exact, and supported in every statistical and spreadsheet program. Experience suggests that students who first learn about regression are often eager to regress everything on everything else. Although such enthusiasm is commendable, it can also lead to applying the method where it is downright wrong to do so. Throughout the remainder of the text, we will be especially conscious of suggesting when, and when not, to apply particular methods. To this end, *Marketing Research Focus 10.1* examines how a (multiple) regression helped illuminate the nature of service quality gaps, relating them to a variety of other factors.

10.1c Regression: Why, When, and How

As emphasized throughout our presentation, regression is important, something every researcher needs to know. But, practically speaking, what does it offer to the researcher that is useful? Because this is a text about marketing research and not mathematical statistics, our discussion of regression will gloss over some of the more technical aspects of the subject in favor of presenting the method so that practicing managers can use it successfully. At the same time, we will be as rigorous and complete as such a presentation allows. All our discussions from here on in will concern *multiple regression*, predicting a single dependent (Y) variable based on many independent variables (X_i). We will start with *linear* regression—relating interval-scaled variables to one another in a linear manner—then extend the method to account for many other types of variables and relationships.

Theoretical Model

Regression presumes the following *theoretical model* for the *population*:

$$Y = \beta_0 + \beta_1 X_1 + \beta_2 X_2 + \cdots + \beta_k X_k + \varepsilon$$

As usual, Greek letters signify "unknowable" population-level parameters, which we will attempt to estimate using data from a sample. In simple language, the "theoretical model" says that the dependent variable, Y, is related to the values of k independent variables, $\{X_1, X_2, \ldots, X_k\}$, but that this relation is not perfect. Rather, it is subject to *error*, in the form of variable ε. It turns out that the distribution of the error is critically important in regression models. For *linear* regression, we will make the assumption that the error is normally distributed, with zero mean, written $\varepsilon \sim N(0, \sigma^2)$. Because of this assumption, the only population parameter that we will need to estimate to understand the extent of the error is its standard deviation, σ. We therefore will need to estimate one intercept (β_0), k slopes ($\beta_1, \ldots, \beta_k$) and one error standard deviation (σ).

In exact analogy with our theoretical model, which refers to the population, we will have an *estimated model*, which refers to a *sample*:

$$\begin{aligned} Y_i &= [b_0 + b_1 X_{1i} + b_2 X_{2i} + \cdots + b_k X_{ki}] &+ \quad & e_i \\ &= \text{"Fit"}(\hat{Y}_i) &+ \quad & \text{"Error"}(e_i) \end{aligned}$$

The estimated parameters should line up in an obvious way with their "theoretical" population counterparts, with intercept b_0 estimating β_0, and slopes ($b_1, \ldots, b_k$) estimating ($\beta_1, \ldots, \beta_k$).* The one correspondence that is not obvious is that the *standard error of the regression*, s_e (which is the square root of MSE, the **mean-squared-error**) will estimate the population parameter σ.

mean-squared-error (MSE)
In regression (and related statistical models), an estimate of variance left *unexplained* by the model; often described as the "spread" of the data around a regression line.

When Is a Regression Model Useful?

We must distinguish between a *useful* model and a "correct" one; unless we wish to go out and sample the entire population, it is pointless to even talk about a "correct" model because we will never be able to identify it as such. In statistics, all we have to work with is our sample, and we must take care not to judge our results in nonsensical ways; for this reason, we will not refer to a "correct" model again. Two criteria help us determine if a model may be useful:

1. "Fit" (or prediction) should be much bigger, on average, than "error" (F-test).
2. Coefficients (the b_i's) should be clearly different from zero (t-tests).

It is crucial to understand the difference between these two types of measures, which recur in all statistical models and help distinguish the *whole* model from its *parts*. The first measure, the F-test, tells you if all the variables, *taken together*, help explain the variation in the dependent variable, Y. The second set of measures, the t-tests, help determine if *parts* of the model—that is, the different independent variables—help explain the variation in the dependent variable, Y. A good analogy here is a group that works together for a class project. If the group receives a B grade, it could be because each student is performing at B level, indicating decent, but not spectacular, performance. It could also be that one student is doing stellar work, and the others are doing nothing at all, pulling that student's group grade down.

*Note that, for multiple regression, we write the intercept as β_0 instead of a, as we had done previously for simple regression.

The overall grade of B would correspond to the F-test, which in this case would say, "This model is reasonably good." But this would tell us nothing about any of the particular students in the group; for that, we would need to consult the individual t-tests. In models with many variables, any pattern of significance among the various t- and F-tests is possible. We must examine both.

Generally speaking, the F-test is the first quantity one should check when looking over regression output. If the p-value associated with the F-test is nonsignificant, it says, in effect, that the *entire model* is not providing sufficient explanatory power. If that is the case, we must change the model, usually by attempting to remove under-performing independent variables by looking at their t-tests. Nonsignificant independent variables are then typically removed one by one until only significant variables remain.

10.1d What Must We Know about Errors?

As stated previously, the main assumptions that allow regression to "work" each concern the errors, $\{e_i\}$ (see Equation 10.1). These are all somewhat technical, but they are crucial in terms of assuring that we can believe what regression is telling us. They should always be checked. In short, errors should:

- be normally distributed (Violation: *Nonnormality*)
- have constant variance (Violation: *Heteroscedasticity*)
- not display obvious "patterns" (Violation: *Autocorrelation*)

Let us consider each of these in turn.

10.1e Nonnormality

Every regression yields estimates of what the dependent variable *should* have been, what is often called the "fit," "estimate," or "prediction," $\hat{Y}_i$. This can be compared with what actually occurred, Y_i, and the difference is error, e_i. If we create a **frequency distribution** or *histogram* of these points, they should look approximately normally distributed. Let us return to our data on marketing research students, and the regression of Y = weight on X = height. We can compute the following information for all the $n = 448$ data points, listed here for the first four:

frequency distribution
A list of individual values (or ranges of values) that a variable takes on, along with how commonly each occurs.

i	Y_i	$\hat{Y}_i$	Residual	Std. Residual
1	125	141.7	−16.7	−0.87
2	92	102.4	−10.4	−0.54
3	120	128.6	−8.6	−0.45
4	110	141.7	−31.7	−1.65

For each point, we have listed the actual value (Y_i), the predicted value ($\hat{Y}_i$), the **residual error** (e_i), and a **standardized residual**, telling us how many standard errors (s_e) away each of the residuals is from zero. Standardized residuals are useful in seeing whether there are any strong outliers; it is reasonable to examine any data point with a standardized residual greater than 3 in magnitude, unless the data set is very large. (Remember that we would *expect* deviations that large in every 3 out of 1000 normal random draws.)

residual error
In any statistical model, how far the model's predicted or estimated value falls from the true, observed value.

standardized residual
In regression, dividing the residuals by their own standard deviation, so that they have a mean of zero and a standard deviation of one. See *z-transform*.

Once we have the residuals, we can create our histogram, which is typically called a **normal probability plot**. For our regression of weight on height, such a plot appears in Figure 10.2.

Superimposed on the histogram (bar chart) is the best-fitting normal distribution. If these appear to diverge substantially, there may be a problem with **nonnormality**. There are also specific statistical tests to assess the degree of deviation from normality, such as the Kolmogorov-Smirnov, Anderson-Darling, and Shapiro-Wilk tests; many statistical programs perform them, and you should consult a statistics test or software manual for additional information on their interpretation.

normal probability plot
A histogram (i.e., frequency-based bar chart) of the residuals in a regression, superimposed against the best-fitting normal distribution; a visual aid to determine whether the regression assumption that the errors are normally distributed is violated.

Fortunately, small deviations from normality are no cause for worry, and regression can be used "as is." However, if the normal probably plot indicates extreme deviation between the histogram and superimposed normal distribution, the regression is likely to be misleading and needs to be re-done with some change in independent variables. Let us consider an idealized version of our weight vs. height regression, using simulated (e.g., made-up) data. Suppose we had a regression that looked like Figure 10.3.

nonnormality
When the graphed distribution of some variable deviates from a normal distribution. See *normal probability plot*.

We first note that there is a *very* strong regression relationship here; the upward trend as one moves rightward is extremely clear. If we were to just run a regression and carelessly check the output, we might

Figure 10.2 Standardized Residuals for a Linear Regression

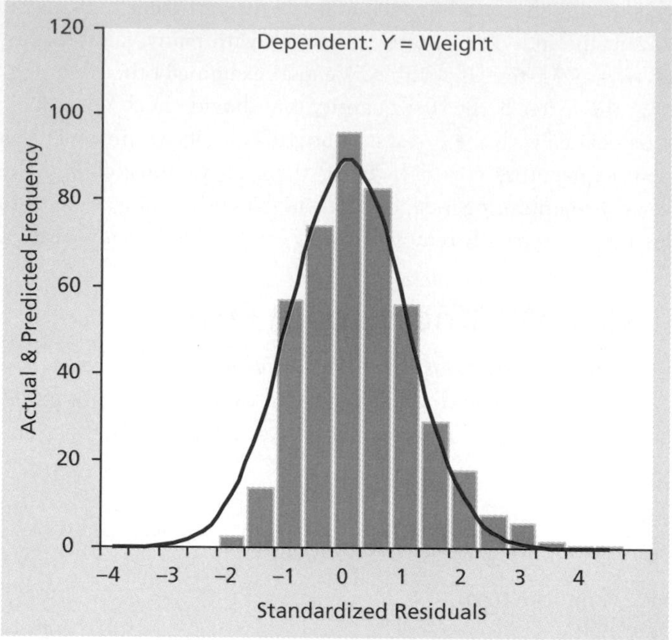

proclaim that this was a very good model. But, in fact, it is a *terrible* model. Why? Because almost none of the data points are near the regression line! These data would be highly *nonnormal* because normally distributed data lump up near the line. One might wonder what could be causing such problems, and one possible answer is that the data above the line are for *men*, and that below the line are for *women* (see Figure 10.4).

Here, we have estimated a regression of the following form:

$$\text{Weight} = b_0 + b_1 \text{ Height} + b_2 \text{ Gender}$$

We will explore this exact relationship for our student data later in this chapter. For our present purposes, one point bears special mention: b_2 measures something of importance, the difference in weight

Figure 10.3 An Example of Non-Normally Distributed Errors

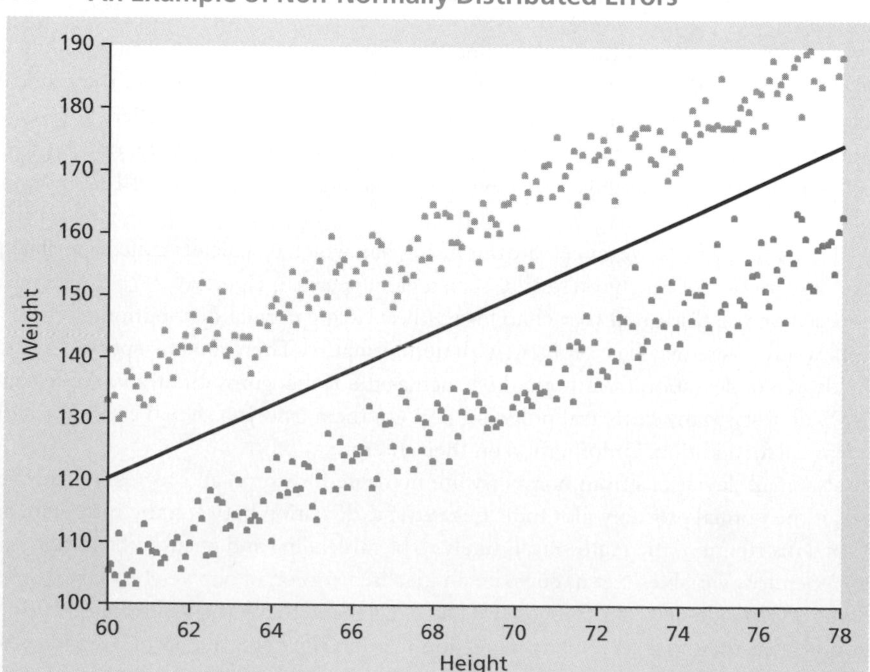

Figure 10.4 Regressing Weight on Height, Correcting for Gender

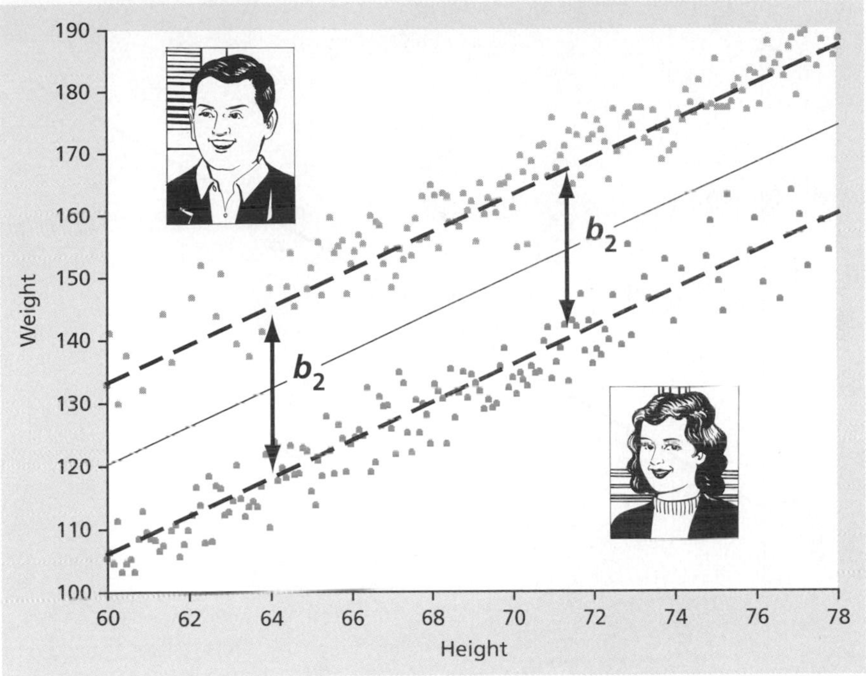

between men and women, *correcting for differences in height*. One way to think about this is as follows: if the only differences in men's and women's weights owed to their gender and height, b_2 would tell us how much a man and woman of the *same* height differed, on average. The reason this is important is that men, on average, *do* weigh much more than women. However, this comparison is not "fair" because men are, on average, taller than women, and taller people tend to weigh more (again, on average). So, we wish to *correct* for height differences in our explanatory model for weight. The (estimated) regression model relating weight to height *and* gender— Weight $= b_0 + b_1$ Height $+ b_2$ Gender—helps us do just that. Of course, there are many other variables that help explain weight besides height and gender, but the general reasoning is valid, and we will call on it throughout our presentation.

If we do encounter nonnormality, and it is pronounced, we have to fix it somehow. One way is to use a *transformation*, a topic we will take up in detail later in this chapter. Another is to check whether some critical variable was omitted, as gender was in our example.

10.1f Heteroscedasticity

Another common problem is that errors do not have constant variance. This can come about in many ways, but let us look at a "classic" pattern, again for simulated data in Figure 10.5.

Note that, although the regression line "goes right through the middle" of the data, the data are not evenly spread around the line; there is much greater spread for larger heights and weights. This should make sense: there is far greater variation in the weight of people who are 6′6″ tall (on the very right side of the graph) than those who are 5′0″ tall (on the very left). This sort of pattern—where the spread of the data varies at different levels of the independent variable—is common in real-world applications. One might wonder why this is problematic, and the answer concerns our ability to make *predictions*. We can, for each data point, ask the computer to compute a prediction interval, which is rather like a confidence interval (for a mean), but is computed instead for each data point. It will be centered around our predicted value, $\hat{Y}_i$; we can list these for the first four points in our marketing research student data, as before:

prediction interval
In a regression analysis, an interval offering a $(1 - \alpha)$ probability of containing the dependent variable, given specific values of all independent variables; used to make predictions about *single* outcomes (as opposed to confidence intervals, which make predictions about *means* of many outcomes).

i	Y_i	$\hat{Y}_i$	Lower 95% Predict	Upper 95% Predict
1	125	141.7	103.9	179.6
2	92	102.4	64.4	140.4
3	120	128.6	90.8	166.5
4	110	141.7	103.9	179.6

Figure 10.5 An Example of Heteroscedastic Errors

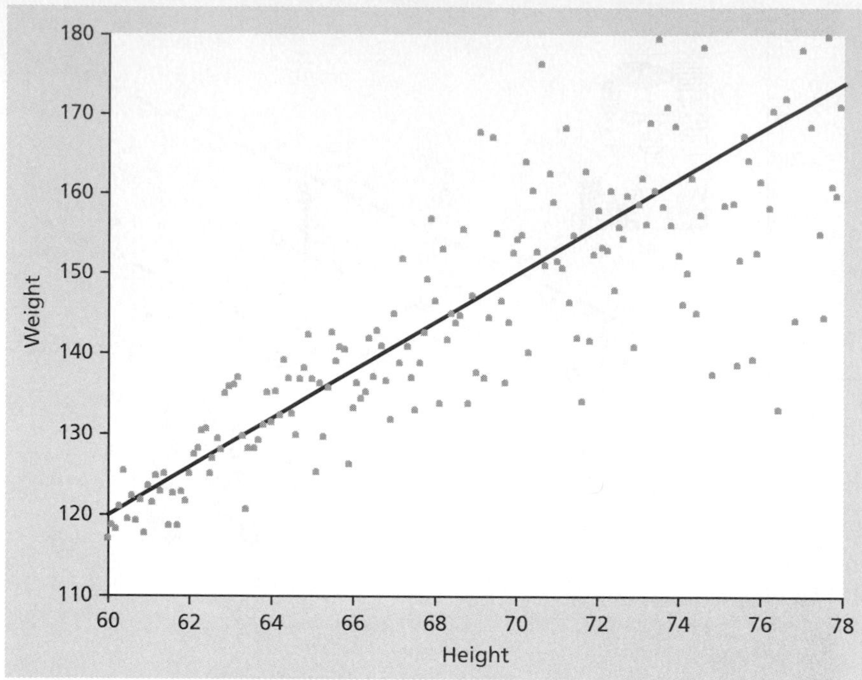

Returning to our idealized, simulated data, if we asked the computer to compute similar intervals, they would look like those of Figure 10.6.

At the lower end of the height–weight range, our "95 percent interval" actually contains *all* the points, with much room to spare; we have therefore been greatly *under*-confident in our predictions, which are much stronger than the 95 percent figure would lead us to believe. But the real problem lies at the upper end, where we have been greatly *over*-confident: nearly half of our data lies outside the supposed 95 percent limits. When our data are heteroscedastic, we run the risk of appearing far more certain about our results than we should be. We would not, for example, wish to claim that we were

Figure 10.6 Consequences of Heteroscedasticity

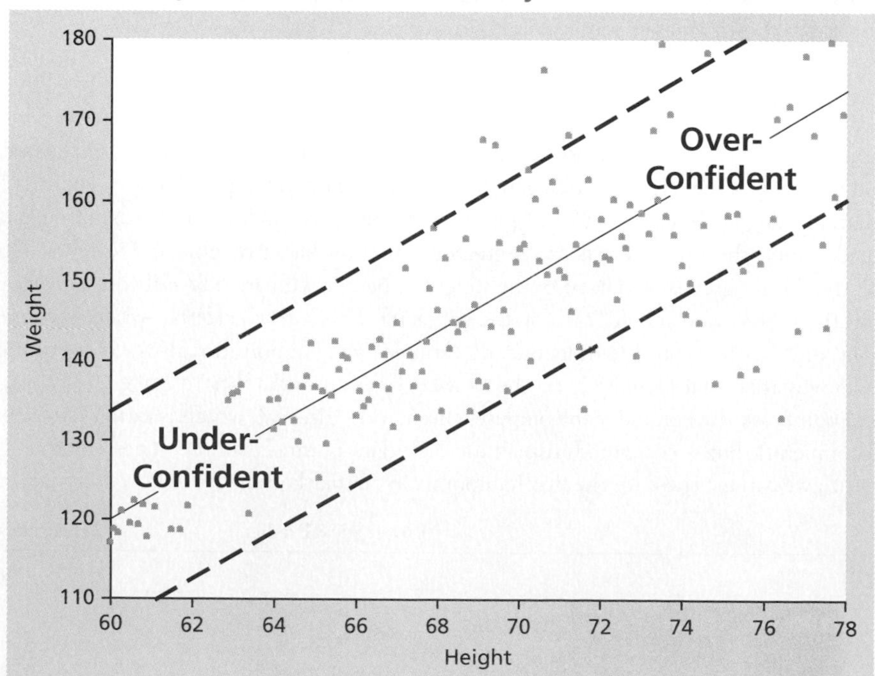

"99.99 percent" sure that sales will be in a certain range when we are only 80 percent sure, and this is precisely the sort of predicament into which **heteroscedasticity** can lead us.

The best way to see if heteroscedasticity is present is to plot the residuals against each of the independent variables and simply look at them closely. Some computer programs will perform specific tests to detect it; common examples are the **White test** and the **Breusch-Pagan test**, and you should consult your software manual for more information on which such tests are supported. If heteroscedasticity is strongly present, it should be corrected for. One way to do this is to use specific models that have been created for that purpose, like the **GARCH (Generalized AutoRegressive Conditional Heteroscedasticity)** or **WLS (Weighted Least Squares) models**; both are outside our scope, but are explained fully in texts devoted to regression, as well as many online resources. Another way to correct for heteroscedasticity is to *transform* either the independent or dependent variables. Logarithms can often work well, particularly for the dependent variable. We will examine such transformations later in this chapter.

heteroscedasticity
When the errors in a regression model do not have the same variation for all combinations of the independent variables; can often be detected by seeing the residuals "fanning out."

White test
Like the *Breusch-Pagan test*, a common and widely-supported method for assessing whether heteroscedasticity is present in a regression analysis. The White test regresses the squared residuals from a regression onto the original regressors, their squares, and their products (i.e., interactions); a significant *F*-test suggests the presence of heteroscedasticity.

Breusch-Pagan test
Like the *White test*, a common and widely-supported method for assessing whether heteroscedasticity is present in a regression analysis. The Breusch-Pagan test regresses the squared residuals from a regression onto the original regressors; a significant *F*-test indicates that heteroscedasticity may be a problem.

Generalized AutoRegressive Conditional Heteroscedasticity (GARCH) model
A type of regression model in which the variance of the error term is not constant (i.e., homoscedastic) but varies over time, in particular according to the value of the variation at previous time periods; very common in modeling financial time series.

Weighted Least Squares (WLS) model
A method of regression where certain data points are given more emphasis than others. The corresponding "weight" is typically the inverse of how much variability there is at that particular point so that lower variance observations have more influence on the parameter estimates.

10.1g Autocorrelation

A key feature of "error" is that it should be information-free, lacking meaningful patterns. If there *are* meaningful patterns, it means that we, as analysts, should come up with a model to *explain* those patterns, not chalk them up to "error." Statisticians often joke that error should be "noise" or even "garbage," and those analogies are quite useful. If we eyeball the error from any statistical model and can detect some relation or pattern, "something going on," then it is not really error in the sense that statisticians and marketing researchers mean.

One way to see whether the error is really pattern-free is to ask a simple question: will knowing the exact value of the error (e_i) for one data point tell us anything at all about the error value at another point? If the answer is yes, then our error is *not* "just noise," and a major regression assumption has been violated. Let us look at a concrete example, simulated data for sales vs. time (in weeks) as in Figure 10.7.

Looking at the superimposed regression line, there is a clear and strong upward trend, so the variable time would be "significant." But, as in our example for nonnormality, the regression line is a terrible model for these data, for two reasons: (1) a lot of the data are far away from the line; and (2) distance from the line—which is error—is *systematic*. Sales data often look like that in Figure 10.5 when there is seasonality and an overall upward trend. The regression line catches the upward sales trend but misses the seasonality entirely. The result is that the data have peaks and valleys: the regression line

Figure 10.7 An Example of Autocorrelated Errors

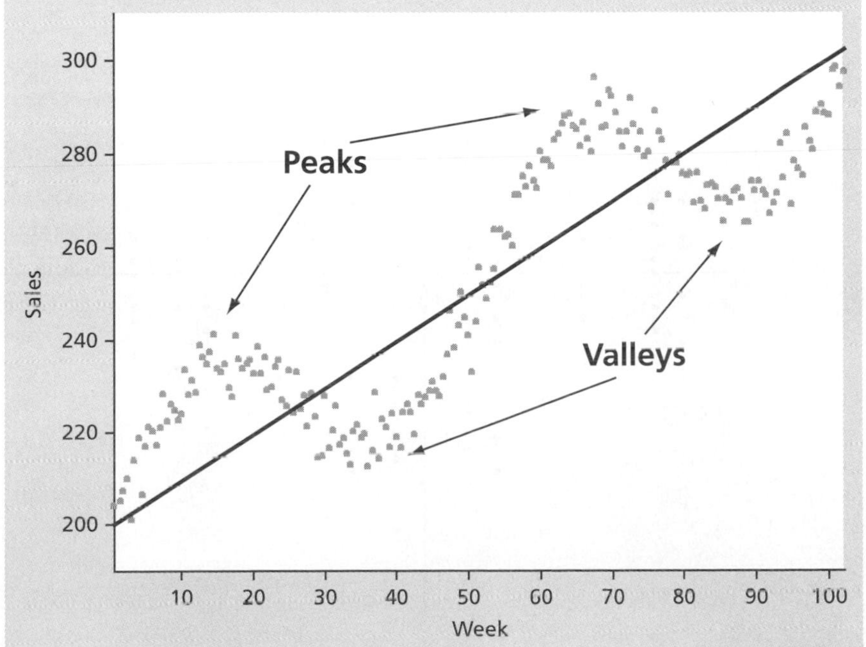

systematically underestimates the peaks and overestimates the valleys, so that there is a great deal more to explain the data than the regression line allows.

autocorrelation
When a variable's value at one point in time is correlated with its values at prior points in time; can often be a problem in regression models and must be fixed—often using lagged regressors or first-differences in the dependent variable—to obtain proper inferences.

In cases like these, we would say that there is a great deal of **autocorrelation**: that the error for one data point can help predict the value of the error for *nearby* data points. This is easy to see in Figure 10.7. If we focus on any data point in one of the peaks, it has positive error (it is well above the regression line), and so are all the points nearby. So, knowing that the error is positive for one of those points tells us that the error for nearby points is also positive. Recall, however, that knowing the error at one point should tell us *nothing* about errors anywhere else.

There are many varieties of autocorrelation, and some complex error relationships could be difficult to detect. However, a simple test does exist to detect the most common form of autocorrelation, so-called *first-order* autocorrelation. (The name refers to the fact that we are looking only at relationships between adjacent points.) This test is called the Durbin-Watson (DW), and it tests whether the residuals (errors) from a linear regression are autocorrelated. A statistical program is needed for the calculation, which will range between 0 and 4. Values near 2 indicate that autocorrelation is not a problem, and the program will generate cut-off values to help interpret the degree of autocorrelation present in the residuals.

Let us look at the residual plot for our actual $n = 448$ marketing research students, again regressing weight on height. The plot shows us the residual plotted against the model's prediction, that is, e_i vs. $\hat{Y}_i$ (see Figure 10.8).

Casual inspection indicates that autocorrelation is not a problem, but we would wish to calculate the Durbin-Watson value, which turns out to be 1.918, or very close to 2; the computer verifies that this is well within the "comfort zone" for the DW statistic, and that autocorrelation appears to be no problem at all.

When autocorrelation is present, however, it is a very serious problem—one we must rectify. It can indicate, among other things, that we simply have the wrong model, and perhaps that we should not even be attempting to put a *line* through our data, that the relationship in question is not linear at all. In such situations, once again, we would appeal to transformations, particularly logarithms, exponents, and powers. Other possibilities include using lags (using prior periods' observed values of Y or the independent variables as predictors), first-differences (e.g., predicting the *change* in Y, as opposed to Y itself), or

Figure 10.8 Predictions vs. Reality: Standardized Residuals for a Simple Linear Regression

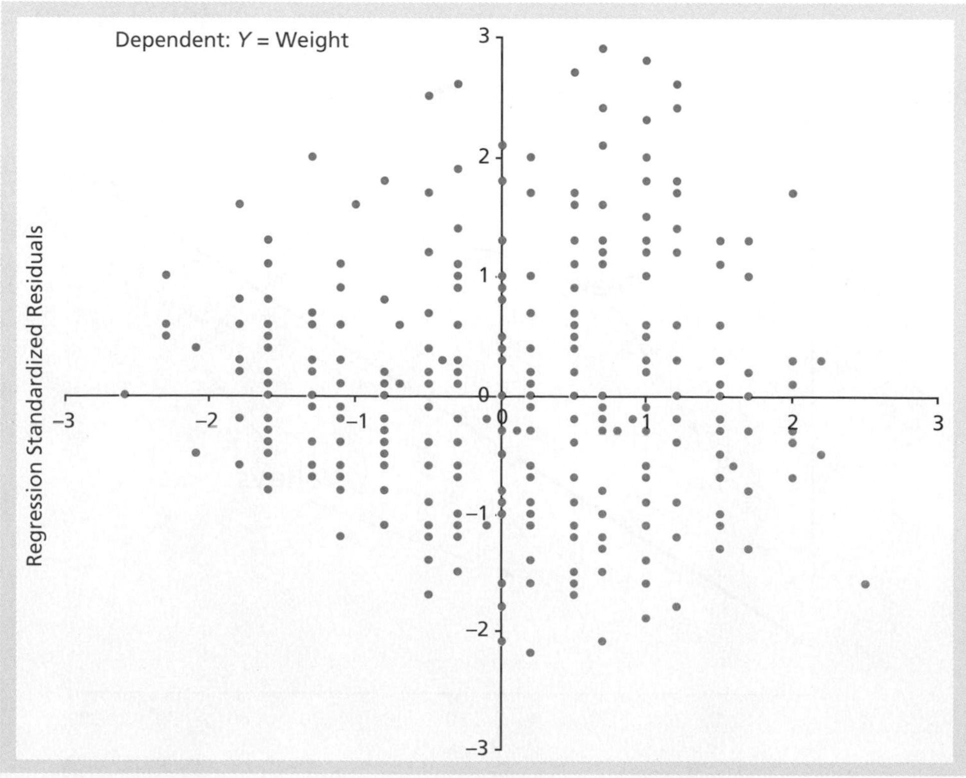

dummy variables (e.g., for seasonality). We will return to examples of many of these later in the chapter. The main point to remember is that a model with serious autocorrelation is quite simply a model that is wrong, and implications stemming from the regression are very likely to be misleading.

10.2 Multiple regression

To appropriately interpret what a regression is telling us, it is important to examine the potential problems associated with collinearity.

10.2a Multicollinearity and Interpreting Multiple Regression Coefficients

It is absolutely crucial to understand what the individual coefficients $\{\beta_1, \ldots, \beta_k\}$ in a multiple regression tell us: if a particular variable were increased by one unit, and **ALL OTHER VARIABLES STAYED THE SAME**, how much would we expect the dependent variable (Y) to change? This is easy to see from the fitted regression equation (which contains the estimated coefficients, $\{b_1, \ldots, b_k\}$), simply by increasing any of the X variables by one unit:

$$Yi = [b_0 + b_1 X_{1i} + b_2 X_{2i} + \cdots + b_k X_{ki}] + e_i$$

The reader may ask why we have emphasized this point to such an extent. The reason is simple, but one that even seasoned researchers often forget: it is sometimes difficult or impossible to change one "independent" variable without changing the others. We must remember that "independent," when applied to variables, does *not* mean unrelated or uncorrelated, just that another variable (Y) *depends* on them. In almost all real-world applications, many of our independent variables $(X_1, \ldots, X_k)$ will be *correlated* with one another, making it difficult to change one without altering the others.

Let us consider a concrete example, one common in practice. Realtors often wish to have an objective measure of the value of a home, based on data included in the Multiple Listing Service (MLS). This helps sellers feel that their homes have been appropriately priced, and buyers to believe they have made a sound investment. One way to do this is to build a multiple regression model, with Y = *Price* as our dependent variable, and many of the quantities in the MLS as independent variables; these would include the number of bedrooms, the number of bathrooms, and the square footage of the home, among other quantities. When such regressions are run, a common effect is to obtain a strongly significant *negative* value for the coefficient on the number of bedrooms in a home. A hasty—and incorrect—interpretation is that "adding a bedroom to a home decreases its value." It should be obvious that this is not true. Assuming the regression relationship explains home values reasonably well, a correct interpretation would be as follows: "adding a bedroom to a home *while holding all other aspects of it constant* decreases its value." It is not difficult to see that this makes sense. Most homes have close to an "optimal" ratio of bedrooms to bathrooms, or bedrooms to square footage; upset this balance, and home value suffers. One could even reasonably say that "adding a bedroom to a home by taking space from other rooms decreases its value."

The main point is that it is easy to forget the all-important "while holding all other independent variables constant" caveat while interpreting the results of a regression. We will take great care to highlight such potential pitfalls in our examples. However, we should point out that trying to ensure that "independent" variables are not too correlated with one another is sometimes a practical impossibility. In such cases, we will have to appeal to advanced methods, such as *Factor analysis*, presented in detail in the next chapter.

10.2b Transformations: Working with "Nonlinear" Regression Relationships

If regression allowed us only to assess purely linear relationships, it would be of limited use in the real world, because few relationships are really linear. Weight and height, for example, are not linearly related, as numerous anatomical studies have shown. If a relationship is believed not to be linear, can regression be used to assess it? In many cases, the answer is yes. Moreover, we can use regression with only minor modifications to assess these nonlinear relationships.

transformation
Any mathematical relationship (i.e., a formula) applied to a set of values or a variable. Among the most useful transformations in data analysis are log(*x*), exp(*x*), and x^k, for *k* a whole number greater than 1.

The main idea is that we will wish to use some type of **transformation**. Informally, we can say that, if Y is not really linearly related to X, we might try one of the following common transformations:

Y	vs.	Log(X)
Log(Y)	vs.	X
Log(Y)	vs.	Log(X)
Y	vs.	X^2
Y^2	vs.	X
Y	vs.	$X, X^2, X^3, \ldots, X^k$ (polynomial)

Many statistical and spreadsheet programs support these natively, making it especially simple to run them and generate visual relationships. For example, we many believe that our variables are not related linearly, but *exponentially*:

$$Y = ae^{bX}$$

exponential
A mathematical property where the rate of growth of a function at a given point is proportional to the function's value at that point; used to model population growth, compound interest, and any other phenomena.

Many natural phenomena (like the growth of bacteria in a culture) and business processes (like compound interest) operate via **exponential** relationships. Although it may seem impossible to use "linear" regression to estimate such relationships, all we need do is take logarithms:

$$\log(Y) = \log(ae^{bX}) = \log(a) + bX$$

Because a is a constant, so is $\log(a)$, meaning we have a *linear* relationship between $\log(Y)$ and X. Let us look at such a graph, along with the regression "line" that we estimate, which will appear as a *curve* when graphed along with the original points, (X_i, Y_i) (see Figure 10.9).

It is important to realize that this nonlinear relationship between Y and X has been estimated by fitting a *linear* regression between $\log(Y)$ and X. And this is precisely our strategy with transformations: using known functions—like logs, exponents, squares, square roots, and polynomials—to estimate nonlinear relationships using ordinary, linear regression.

geometric
A series in which each term is of the form ax^b, usually for *b* a positive integer (0, 1, 2, . . .); often used to smooth out or explain data taken over time.

Another important relationship is **geometric**:

$$Y = aX^b$$

Once again, taking logarithms, we find that:

$$\log(Y) = \log(aX^b) = \log(a) + b\log(X)$$

Figure 10.9 Using Regression for Exponential Relationships

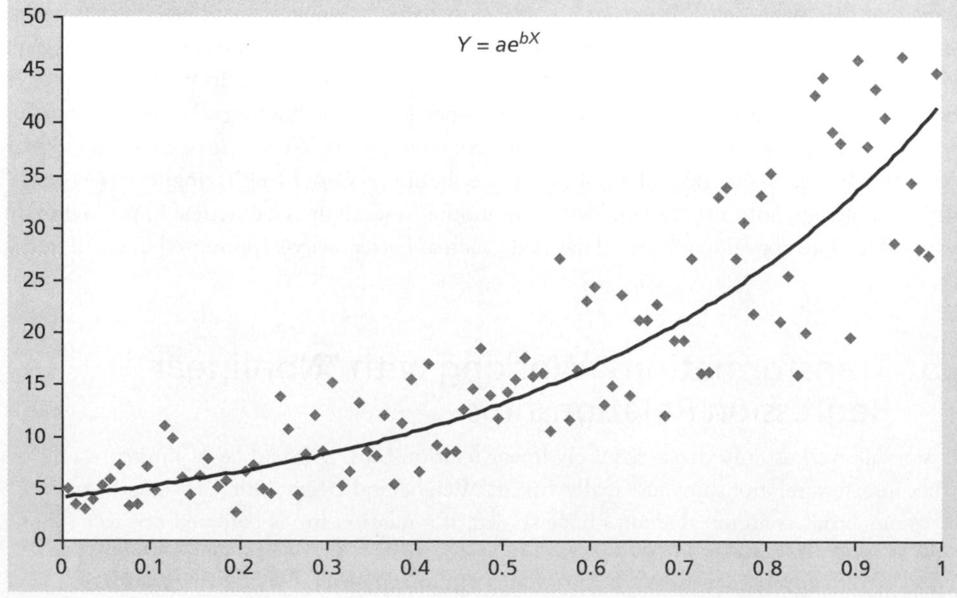

Figure 10.10 An Example of Polynomial Regression

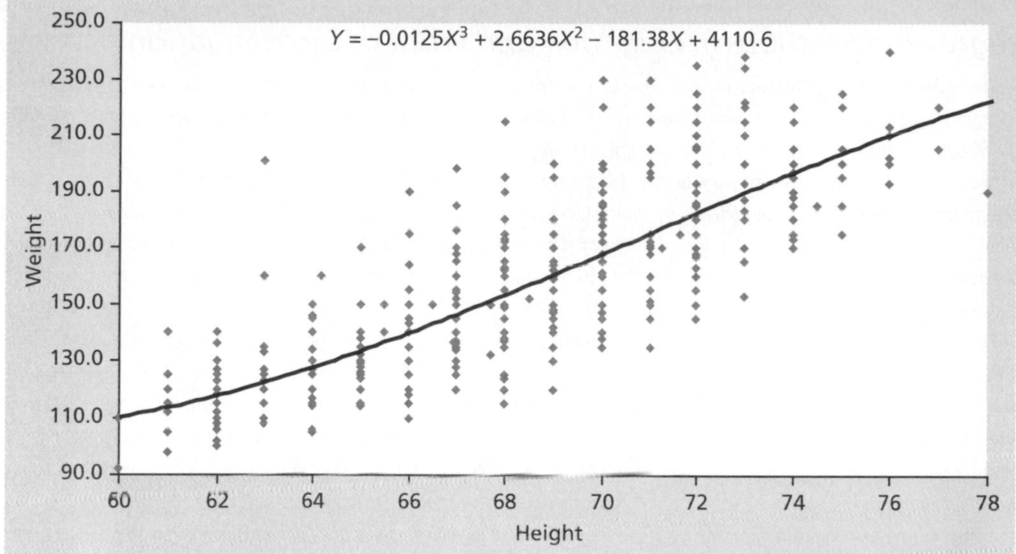

We have found that a geometric relationship between Y and X can be estimated by a linear regression of $\log(Y)$ on $\log(X)$.

When we really do not know the "order" of the relationship between Y and X, we can try to run a series of **polynomial regressions**, which regress Y on various *powers* of X: $X, X^2, X^3, \ldots, X^k$. We must be *very* careful in applying polynomial regression, because there can be very high multicollinearity in the powers of X. In simple language, it is impossible to change X by one unit without also changing X^2, X^3, and so forth. If we were to estimate a cubic (i.e., third-order) equation for our weight vs. height data, we would obtain the graph depicted in Figure 10.10.

polynomial regressions
A multiple linear regression in which some or all of the independent variables are powers of another variable; that is, they include $\{X, X^2, X^3, \ldots, X^k\}$. Interpreting the coefficients of these powers can be difficult, due to multicollinearity.

The resulting regression "line" (in this case, a cubic polynomial) deviates very mildly from an actual straight line (i.e., a first-order relationship, with no squared or cubic terms), judging by visual inspection. Although we have not yet seen how to do so, were we to run a (multiple) regression of Y on X, X^2, X^3, we would actually find all three significant; interestingly, adding the next higher power (X^4) would make *all* the variables nonsignificant! This illustrates why multicollinearity problems can make it challenging to interpret the results of polynomial regression, which should be used sparingly and then usually with only a few, low powers.

Regression is frequently applied to analyze variables that are not linearly related to others available, so that transformations must be applied first. Among the most common of these are salary, population, and other "positive" variables (i.e., they cannot take on negative values, assuming of course one is not in debt to one's employer!). *Marketing Research Focus 10.2* shows how regression was applied to a transformed variable (log of salary) to investigate claims of racial discrimination.

10.3 Using and Interpreting Multiple Linear Regression

When social scientists and marketing researchers speak of "regression," they invariably mean *multiple* regression. Rare is the situation where a phenomenon of interest (Y) is satisfactorily explicable on the basis of just one predictor variable (X) alone. In almost all applications, we will have many such predictor variables, $\{X_1, X_2, \ldots, X_k\}$. Moreover, they will be correlated with one another, making interpretation difficult. At the risk of redundancy, we repeat: it is difficult to overstate the importance of regression throughout management applications, not to mention all the social and natural sciences. We therefore need to be practically conversant with multiple regression methods and models and their useful qualities, as well as their potential pitfalls.

It is helpful to refer to a schematic of how regression works, in terms of "what goes in" and "what comes out," depicted in Figure 10.11.

Marketing Research Focus 10.2

Regression Methods in Litigation and Proof of Discrimination

Decisions arrived at using regression methods can have broad impact on society. A number of Supreme Court decisions regarding discrimination have turned on the question of whether statutes prohibiting discrimination actually prohibit "disparate impact" or merely "disparate treatment." A simple way of describing the difference is as follows: "disparate treatment" occurs when a policy directly and purposefully disadvantages some individuals because of "protected characteristics" (e.g., race, gender, or age); "disparate impact," by contrast, occurs when a policy happens to disadvantage individuals who have a certain characteristic, *regardless of whether the policy directly or purposefully attempts to do so*. Statistical analysis is important in evaluating claims of discrimination in both of these contexts, and distinctions between "disparate treatment" and "disparate impact" often hinge on exactly how regression is applied.

For example, the Age Discrimination in Employment Act of 1967 (ADEA) prohibits discrimination on the basis of age. In the landmark Supreme Court case *Hazen Paper Co. v. Biggins* (1993), this was interpreted using a "disparate treatment" standard; that is, it was viewed as prohibiting active, willful attempts to fire workers simply because they were older. By contrast, many affirmative action cases rest on a "disparate impact" standard: the under-representation of minority groups is seen *in itself* as evidence of discriminatory practices, regardless of how the under-representation came about.

Running multiple variants of a regression model is critical in assessing the impact of incorporating additional variables. The two legal standards—disparate treatment and disparate impact—entail starkly divergent interpretations of coefficient changes due to including/excluding certain key variables. Under a "disparate treatment" standard, an employer might not be judged discriminatory if including a new, important variable (e.g., whether an employee was near to "vesting" her pension benefits) makes the protected trait turn nonsignificant. Under a "disparate impact" standard, however, an employer might be judged discriminatory if *any* regression yields coefficients consistent with discrimination (e.g., a significant negative coefficient on "nonwhite ethnicity" in a regression for hourly wage), *even if additional regressions, including other relevant variables, cause the coefficient to lose significance*. A "disparate impact" standard, therefore, can allow a much wider variety of evidence to appear to support discrimination; a "disparate treatment" standard can make it exceptionally difficult to prove discrimination because seemingly airtight evidence can be nullified by even a single additional variable.

Another study of racial discrimination applied multiple regression to determine whether Major League Baseball salaries may be influenced by race. Simple averaging appeared to suggest that nonwhite players were paid substantially less than white players. The question was whether this was true once one took into account—that is, regressed out—levels of performance and other characteristics. Using data collected on the salaries of 212 players (nonpitchers) who started on opening day, the following multiple regression model was estimated:

$$Y = \beta_0 + \beta_1X_1 + \beta_2X_2 + \beta_3X_3 + \beta_4X_4 + \beta_5X_5 + \beta_6X_6 + \beta_7X_7 + \beta_8X_8 + \varepsilon$$

Y = Log of Salary
X_1 = Years of experience as a major league baseball player
X_2 = Number of home runs hit during previous season
X_3 = Batting average (i.e., ratio of hits to times-at-bat) during previous season
X_4 = 1 if the player's team made the playoffs during the previous year; 0 otherwise
X_5 = 1 if the player is an infielder or catcher; 0 otherwise
X_6 = 1 if the player is nonwhite; 0 if the player is white
X_7 = Amount ($ million) paid for broadcast rights of player's team
X_8 = 1 if the player bats left-handed or is a switch hitter; 0 if not

The results of the regression were summarized by the researchers in the following two tables:

Variable	Estimate	Std. Err.	*t*-value	*p*-value
X_1	0.037	0.004	9.25	.001
X_2	0.014	0.002	7.00	.001
X_3	2.009	0.303	6.63	.001
X_4	0.108	0.037	2.92	.010
X_5	0.078	0.029	2.69	.010
X_6	−0.046	0.028	−1.64	.100
X_7	0.042	0.034	1.24	.250
X_8	−0.027	0.027	−1.00	.350

	SS	df	MS	F	p-value
Regression	14.710	8	1.839	53.2	.001
Error	7.018	203	0.035		
Total	21.728	211			

The *p*-value calculated from the *F*-statistic suggests that the model explains a substantial proportion of variation—nearly 68 percent, according to a quick calculation of *r-squared*—in the dependent variable (log of salary). Importantly, when the other characteristics included in the regression were taken into account, the racial salary gap (as measured by the nonsignificant coefficient for variable X_6: $b_6 = -0.046$, $p \approx .10$) disappeared.

So, does this mean there is no discrimination? Not necessarily. Unless we take care to assess whether nonwhite players were allowed fewer chances to hit home runs or were assigned to less desirable positions in the field—requiring additional data and more regressions—we cannot rule out discrimination entirely. As social scientists often quip, much more research into this phenomenon is required.

Statistical arguments are central to assessing discrimination and other such claims common in legal proceedings. Consequently, the definition of what exactly constitutes discrimination is crucial to how we use regression analyses to assess its prevalence. These examples illustrate a general issue in statistical analysis: although understanding variable relationships requires running a full set of regressions, we must first clearly define what we are trying to detect, along with what constitutes ironclad evidence for its presence.

Sources: "Employee Retirement Income Security Act"; U.S. Department of Labor Web site: www.dol.gov > A to Z index > Health Plans and Benefits > Employee Retirement Income Security Act (ERISA).
"Hazen Paper v. Biggins, 507 U.S. 604 (1993)"; Cornell Law School Legal Information Institute Web site: www.law.cornell.edu > U.S. Supreme Court Opinions > Search: "Hazen Paper Co."
"Affirmative Action: What Do We Know?"; The Urban Institute Web site: www.urban.org > Search: 1000862.
Christiano, Kevin J., "Salary Discrimination in Major League Baseball: The Effect of Race," *Sociology of Sport Journal*, 3, 144–153.

So, we see that a variety of data types can easily be entered *into* regression (as predictors, or "independent variables") and also that many data types can emerge from regression (as observations, or "dependent variables"). The list in Figure 10.11 is not meant to be exhaustive, but does run the gamut of uses in marketing applications. Before covering these methods in depth, it helps to consider some common examples of the variable types used in regression:

- *Continuous*: Price, Time, Volume, Length, Distance, Sales, Market Share
- *Binary*: Gender, Promotion (Yes/No), Aisle Display, Coupon Used, College Degree
- *Ordinal*: Education Level, Age Group, Survey Scale Responses (e.g., 1 to 7)
- *Nominal*: Ethnic Group, Product Category, SKU, Payment Method
- *Rank-Ordered*: Ranking Task Survey Responses, Top 10 Lists, Athletic Medalists
- *Count*: Purchase Quantity, Children in Household, Number of TVs, Times Married

Figure 10.11 Various Components of a Regression Model

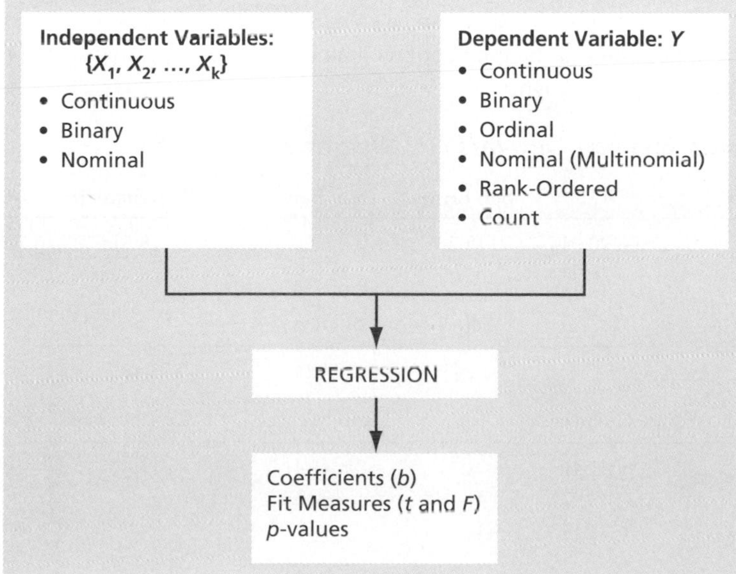

The remarkable fact about regression is that *any* of these variable types can be accommodated, with only minor modifications in interpretation. No matter what sort of variables we use in regression, the program will supply us with *coefficients* and their *significance levels* (p-values), which respectively allow us to make predictions and to judge relationship strengths. Although all regressions can be interpreted similarly, the mechanics of carrying out regression can vary dramatically based on the type of dependent variable; and, although we leave this task entirely to the computer, the analyst must know which type of regression is appropriate for which type of dependent variable. We will cover each of these in detail, but the general correspondence is as follows:

Dependent Variable	Type of Regression Analysis
Interval/continuous	Multiple linear regression
Binary	Binary regression
Ordinal	Ordinal regression
Nominal	Multinomial regression
Rank-ordered	Rank-ordered or "exploded" regression
Count	Poisson or count regression

The first four of these are used extensively in marketing applications, and consequently we will explore them in depth and work full examples. We note here that multinomial regression—for which the dependent variable is nominal—is especially important in marketing because it is used both to predict brand choice (i.e., real-world "field data") and in such widely used experimental methods as conjoint analysis (see Chapter 11).

Obviously, this description and presentation do not exhaust the topic of regression. Hundreds of texts and thousands of academic papers have been devoted to the topic, and it is still an active area of research in the statistical community. Sources for additional information are listed in Further Reading at the end of this chapter.

Throughout, our presentation will emphasize the unified nature of regression methods. We first start with a fully worked example of multiple linear regression, then show how the other types we have considered—binary, ordinal, nominal, rank-ordered, and count—build on and extend the powerful framework afforded by the linear model. In case it has not been said enough already: if there is one method you should try your best to master, linear regression is it.

10.3a Continuous or Interval-Scaled Dependent Variable: Multiple Linear Regression

We have already discussed simple linear regression—using a single predictor variable—at length in Chapter 9. It requires very little additional machinery and insight to fully understand multiple regression. Literally every element of a simple regression output is replicated in a multiple regression, and what is "new and different" in multiple regression can be seen as directly analogous to concepts already raised for simple regression. Let us recall the information obtained previously in Chapter 9 for a simple linear regression of Y = weight on X = height:

Linear Regression Analysis: DepVar (Y) = Weight, X = Height

Coefficients	b	Std. Error	Std. Beta	t-Test Statistic	p-value Two-Tailed
Intercept	−290.73	15.70		−18.512	0.0000
X = height	6.55	0.23	0.803	28.493	0.0000

r	r^2	Adj. r^2	SE(Reg)	n
0.803	0.645	0.645	19.224	448

Source of Variation	Sum of Squares	df	Mean Squares	F-Test Statistic	p-value One-Tailed
Regression	300041.41	1	300041.41	811.84	0.0000
Error	164833.07	446	369.58		
Total	464874.47	447			

And now let us contrast this with a multiple linear regression of Y = weight on X = {age, gender, height, MBA, year}:

Linear Regression Analysis: DepVar (*Y*) = Weight *X* = {Age, Gender, Height, MBA, Year}

Coefficients	*b*	Std. Error	Std. Beta	*t*-Test Statistic	*p*-value Two-Tailed
Intercept	−210.603	20.560		−10.243	0.0000
Age	0.660	0.279	0.101	2.363	0.0186
Gender	17.449	2.450	0.267	7.122	0.0000
Height	4.999	0.294	0.613	16.982	0.0000
MBA	−3.122	3.063	−0.043	−1.019	0.3087
Year	−0.111	0.507	−0.006	−0.218	0.8274

r	r^2	Adj. r^2	SE(Reg)	n
0.834	0.696	0.693	17.879	448

Source of Variation	Sum of Squares	*df*	Mean Squares	*F*-Test Statistic	*p*-value One-Tailed
Regression	323592.24	5	64718.4	202.471	0.0000
Error	141282.23	442	319.643		
Total	464874.47	447			

Let us compare these two regressions to see what has changed and how our interpretations would differ between them. First, we stress that the intercept is completely meaningless in both regressions, representing in the first the weight of someone with no height, and in the second the weight of someone also with no height, but additionally no age, of female gender, without an MBA, and in the year before we started collecting data. Next, we see that the value of r^2 has gone up, but that will *always* happen when adding additional variables, so we should not put any emphasis on this. Rather, we can look to the *adjusted* r^2, which has also gone up, in this case from 0.645 to 0.693. The adjusted r^2 measure cannot be "fooled" by adding meaningless variables, so the fact that it has gone up indicates that the second regression (with five predictors) seems to offer more explanatory power than the simple regression using height alone. Note that this is NOT a statistical test! We cannot say that this difference is *significant*. To do so would require an advanced method called a Chow Test, which some statistical programs can perform automatically (and we report for completeness that this difference *is* significant; the Chow Test shows that the multiple regression explains more variation in weight than the simple regression does with a *p*-value of about 3×10^{-12}).

We will always want to understand the effects of each "independent" predictor variable in a multiple regression. In this case, height and gender are strongly significant ($p < .00005$, rounded on the output to read .0000; the *t*-statistics of 16.98 and 7.22 indicate extreme significance). Age, by contrast, is significant, but not strongly so, with $p = 0.0186$; and both MBA and Year are nonsignificant. We might, in fact, wish to re-run the regression, first taking out the least significant variable, Year, and "seeing what happens," continuing to remove nonsignificant variables until everything remaining in the regression is significant. If we do so, we obtain the following output:

Linear Regression Analysis: DepVar (*Y*) = Weight *X* = {Age, Gender, Height}

Coefficients	*b*	Std. Error	Std. Beta	*t*-Test Statistic	*p*-value Two Tailed
Intercept	−207.74	20.21		−10.28	0.0000
Age	0.44	0.18	0.068	2.46	0.0144
Gender	17.42	2.45	0.266	7.12	0.0000
Height	5.01	0.29	0.614	17.03	0.0000

r	r^2	Adj. r^2	SE(Reg)	n
0.834	0.695	0.693	17.86	448

Source of Variation	Sum of Squares	*df*	Mean Squares	*F*-Test Statistic	*p*-value One Tailed
Regression	323,245	3	107748	337.79	0.0000
Error	141,629	444	318.98		
Total	464,874	447			

All three "independent" variables (age, gender, height) are now significant and with slightly stronger levels than in the previous regression, judging by the *t*- and *p*-values. The standardized beta values tell us how many standard deviations in the dependent variable (weight) are associated with each standard deviation in an independent variable; the value for height, 0.614, is by far the largest, again indicating a very strong relationship.

Finally, we wish to compare the actual coefficient for height in this regression with that in the simple regression allowing *only* for height. As one might expect, these are quite different: 6.55 in the simple regression, and 5.01 in the regression allowing for age and gender as well as height. Simply put, we would say that each additional inch of height translated into about 6 1/2 extra pounds of weight based on the simple regression but only about 5 pounds in the multiple regression. This is a 30 perecent difference and certainly not something to be ignored. What might be going on? The answer, typical in such applications, is that the "independent" variables are not *independent of one another;* that is, they are correlated. Specifically, if we try to explain weight *only* by height, we ignore the simple fact that men are, on average, taller than women. When we rely only on simple regression, we attribute what is really a *gender effect* to height. What the multiple regression tells us is that each additional inch in height corresponds to 5 extra pounds in weight, *and* that men weigh, on average, about 17.42 pounds more than women. The simple regression "lumped" both these effects into height, because that is all it could do. Note that this leaves out the effects of age (0.44 additional pounds for each year), but that is likely not a problem because age (for a full-grown adult) should not obviously correlate positively or negatively with gender or height.

The point of this exercise is to realize that one cannot simply run just one regression and "figure out what is going on." Rather, multiple regression is *exploratory:* one runs a sequence of regressions hoping to "converge on truth," which in practice means a useful, well-fitting model that results in accurate predictions. The only way to know this is to sequentially add and remove variables to assess their effects, which will always depend on which other variables are in the regression. Although there are some specialized techniques, such as "**stepwise regression**," to speed up this task via automation, they are no substitute for the researcher running many analyses directly and comparing them one with another to glean insight. No statistical program should ever be trusted to come up with the "best model," because that will depend critically on what the researcher is after, and not only on which model yields the best value of adjusted r^2 or some other measure.

stepwise regression
A set of techniques for automatically determining a good-fitting statistical model by successively including or removing independent variables from the estimation; often regarded with suspicion because it cannot ensure that the resulting model is substantively meaningful, only that it happens to fit the sample data well.

10.3b Binary Dependent Variable: Binary Regression

In many applications in marketing and throughout social science, we will wish to understand a *binary outcome*; that is, one that is either yes or no (or, alternatively, zero–one, on–off, heads–tails, and so forth). Common examples include predicting whether a particular action will be taken (visiting a store, accepting a job, developing a product). It can sometimes even be used to understand purchase behavior, if all we wish to model is *whether* a purchase was made, not *which* item was purchased, because the latter is a nominal variable (which we will subsequently examine via *multinomial* regression).

We must first understand that, with a dependent variable that takes on values of 0 and 1, it would be incorrect to put a line through our observations. Let us examine why this would be a bad idea by looking once again at our student data, specifically, trying to predict someone's gender ($Y = 1$ for men; $Y = 0$ for women) by his or her weight (X). A scatterplot of these data, with the associated (inappropriate!) linear regression line, looks like Figure 10.12.

Were we only to consult regression output, we might conclude that there was a strong "linear" relationship allowing us to predict gender from weight ($r^2 = 0.496$; regression output informs us of an "off the charts" *p*-value approximately 10^{-67}). However, a momentary look at the scatterplot reveals that the relationship here is *not* linear. For example, the dependent variable, gender, only takes on values of 0 and 1, but the line is continuous. It turns out that this, in itself, is much less problematic than the fact that the line predicts *out of range:* for example, it would appear that our best guess at the gender for someone with weight = 210 pounds is approximately 1.2! Is such a person 20 percent "more male" than other men? What can this possibly mean? The answer is: nothing at all. Simply put, the data are binary, and we should not put a straight line through them.

A powerful way to think of this problem is that we are trying to predict the *probability* of someone's being male, based only on weight (and perhaps other independent variables, should we wish to include them). Armed with this insight, we can see that any binary prediction makes a great deal of sense in

Figure 10.12 Example of Improper Use of Linear Regression

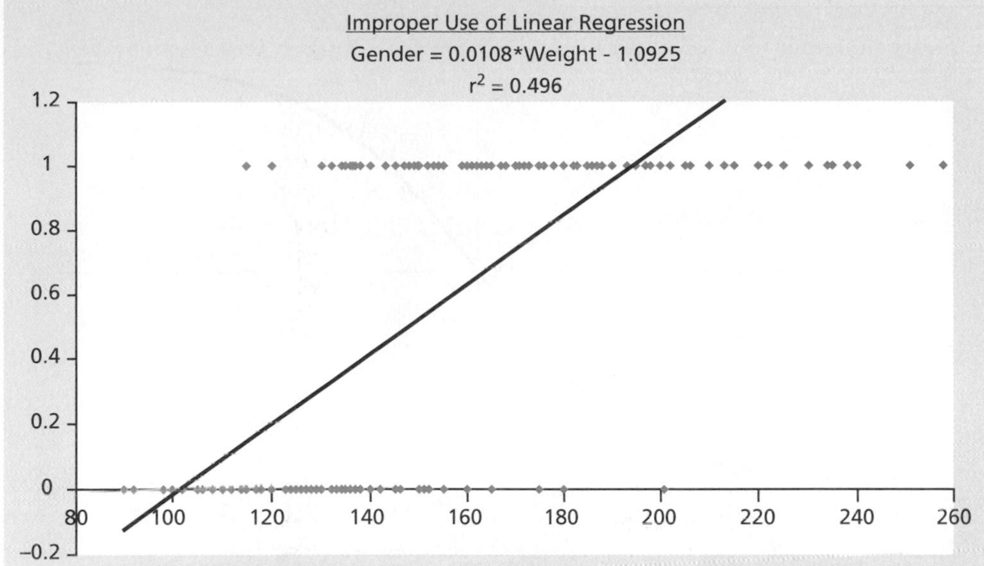

terms of probability. What is the *probability* it will rain tomorrow? What is the *probability* that the next roll of the dice will come out a "7"? "Raining tomorrow" or "coming out 7" are both binary outcomes, but we can meaningfully discuss their *probabilities* of occurrence.

Because probabilities must lie between 0 and 1, we still cannot model them with a line, because the line will necessarily extend beyond either of these boundaries. Based on a deep and beautiful mathematical theory, it is possible to model not the probability of an event's occurrence, but the **logarithm of the odds** it will occur. (Odds are quoted for gambles and bets all the time. Something that occurs one time in 10 has odds of "nine to one against"; this is, in fact, the dominant way of reporting probabilities in horse racing.) If an event has probability p of occurring, its odds can be easily calculated to be $p/(1-p)$, and its log-odds are therefore $\log[p/(1-p)]$. The remarkable and surprising thing about this *transformation* can be readily seen from the Figure 10.13, which translates the probability of an event's occurring to its log-odds. (We will always use "natural" logarithms, not those in base 10.)

logarithm of the odds (log-odds)
A way to transform probabilities, which must be between zero and one, so that they lie on the entire real line (i.e., from negative infinity to positive infinity), and so can be used as dependent variables in a regression. Formally, $\ln[p/(1-p)]$ for any probability, p.

The limited range of probability (from 0 to 1) has now been stretched to extend forever in both directions, from negative infinity to infinity. And something equally likely to occur or not occur (i.e., with probability $p = \frac{1}{2}$) can be seen to have a log-odds of zero, right in the middle of the graph. And here is the point: we can now model these probabilities with a straight line, like in ordinary regression. Our (theoretical population) equation would be as follows:

$$\log[p/(1-p)] = \beta_0 + \beta_1 X_1 + \beta_2 X_2 + \cdots + \beta_k X_k + \varepsilon$$

This is called a **logistic regression**, or *LOGIT* model, and it is supported in almost all statistical packages. It will never make predictions for probabilities outside the range of 0 to 1, and it will help predict binary outcomes in exactly the same manner that we have used linear regression for continuous outcomes.*

logistic regression (LOGIT)
A widely used probabilistic model in marketing, used for predicting individual choice behavior, often for brands. The error distribution is double exponential, which yields simple formulas for all choice probabilities, unlike the probit model, which assumes normally distributed errors.

Simple algebra immediately gives us an expression for the probability, once the statistical program has yielded the regression coefficients, $\{b_0, b_1, \ldots, b_k\}$:

$$p = 1/(1 + \exp[-(b_0 + b_1 X_1 + b_2 X_2 + \cdots + b_k X_k)])$$

This formula—which is quite famous on its own—has many applications throughout marketing and statistics in general, a topic we will discuss again at the end of this section and later in the chapter.

*To be completely accurate, the error term, ε, must be assumed to have something other than a normal distribution; rather, it must have something called a Gumbel, or double exponential, distribution. This is a technical assumption and in no way alters our interpretation. We will mention it again briefly as needed.

Figure 10.13 The Relationship between Probability and the Log-Odds Ratio

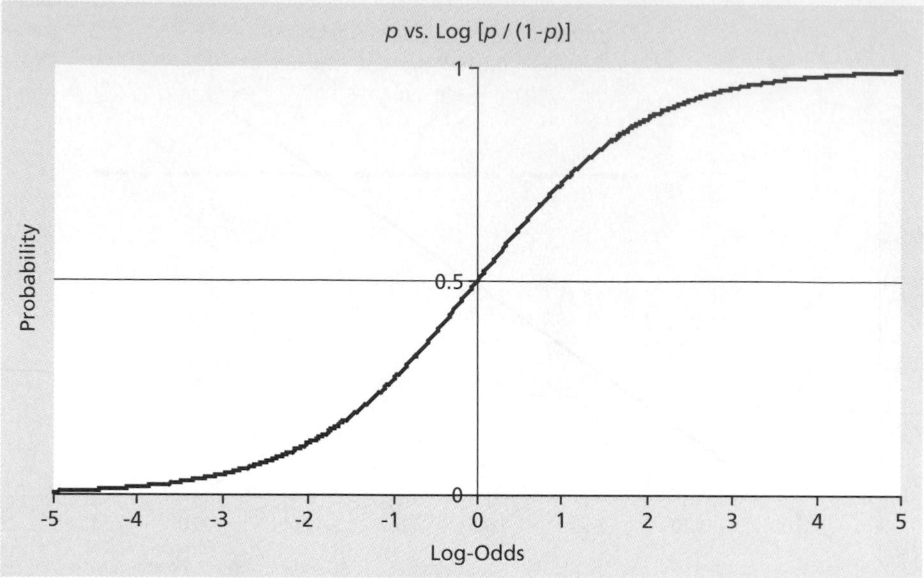

Let us apply our binary logistic regression to our previous problem of predicting Y = gender from X = weight. We would receive the following output:

Regression Results: Dependent Variable = Gender

	b	StdErr	Wald	*df*	Sig.	Exp(*b*)
Weight	0.108	0.010	111.367	1	0.0000	1.114
Constant	−15.551	1.478	110.681	1	0.0000	0.000

Classification Table: Dependent Variable = Gender

		Observed		Predicted
		Gender		Percent Correct
		0	1	
Gender	0	156	29	84.3
	1	25	238	90.5
			Overall Percentage	87.9

This output is easier to interpret than it initially looks. The first table is almost exactly like that obtained via "ordinary" linear regression. As usual, we ignore the constant, unless there is a good reason not to. We are interested in the effects of weight on gender, and this is summarized by the first line in the table of regression results. The first question one typically asks is whether it is significant, and the output suggests us that it is; the "Sig." value is listed as 0.0000, meaning that $p < 0.0001$, a very strong degree of significance. (If we ask the computer for many more decimal digits in the p-value, we obtain an answer near 10^{-25}, although one rarely requires such a degree of precision. This value is obtained from the "Wald test" listed in the output, which the computer automatically converts to a p-value. Wald is just another type of statistical test, such as z, t, or F, and we interpret the resulting p-value in the usual way.)

The next question one should ask is how to *use* this new information that $b = 0.108$. What it truly says is something about the log-odds, and that, frankly, is difficult to understand. Instead, we look to the final column, which lists exp(b), stating its value as 1.114. And this is very useful information indeed. It tells us that, for each unit (i.e., 1 pound) increase in X = weight, we would expect the probability (more accurately, the odds) of someone's being male (Y = gender) to increase by 11.4 percent. This is for a 1-pound increase! One might be skeptical of such a powerful effect. However, looking back on the scatterplot of the data (with the *incorrect* regression line) in Figure 10.12, we see that practically all the subjects with weights less than 130 pounds are women, and the majority of those with weights greater than 160 pounds are male. That is, a 30-pound difference (from 130 to 160) seems to swing our "best guess" at someone's gender from almost certainly female to almost certainly male. What our binary logistic regression has done is to *precisely quantify* the rate at which this trade-off occurs: 11.4 percent for each pound.

binary logistic regression
A special regression model where the dependent variable is binary, and the errors are assumed Gumbel or double-exponentially distributed; widely applied throughout statistics and marketing research.

The second part of the output tells us how well the binary logistic regression *predicts*. There are 185 women and 263 men. The table tells us that the model has *correctly classified* 156, or 84.3 percent of the women, and 238, or 90.5 percent of the men; and it has correctly classified 87.9 percent of the total sample (of 448 subjects). (Generally speaking, statistical models will make more accurate classifications for more common occurrences—such as being male in this data set—than for less common ones.) Note that, in the absence of *any* model, all we would be able to say is that a randomly selected person would have a 263/448 = 58.7 percent chance of being male; if all we knew about someone is that he or she was in our sample, we would have to guess that he or she was male, and we could be right only 58.7 percent of the time. Just knowing someone's weight has allowed us to make dramatically more accurate predictions, with an overall "hit rate" of 87.9 percent.

However, we have used rather little of the power (binary logistic) regression affords us, as we had but a single predictor (i.e., independent) variable. And we should rightly question whether the variable "weight" adequately captures the important differences between men and women for this data set. Men are, on average, also taller ("height"), and there may be other systematic differences as well. So, we rerun the (binary logistic) regression with an expanded set of independent variables: age, height, weight, MBA, year. The results are as follows:

Regression Results: Dependent Variable = Gender

	b	StdErr	Wald	*df*	Sig.	Exp(*b*)
Age	0.158	0.061	6.710	1	0.010	1.171
Height	0.391	0.082	22.669	1	0.000	1.478
Weight	0.071	0.012	37.339	1	0.000	1.074
MBA	0.132	0.621	0.045	1	0.832	1.141
Year	0.057	0.101	0.312	1	0.576	1.058
Constant	−41.146	5.420	57.625	1	0.000	0.000

Classification Table: Dependent Variable = Gender

Observed		Predicted		
		Gender		Percent Correct
		0	1	
Gender	0	161	24	87.0
	1	23	240	91.3
			Overall Percentage	89.5

These results can be interpreted in exactly the same manner as the prior set. First, we ignore the constant (which here predicts the log-odds of the probability that someone is male if he or she has no height, no weight, no MBA, and attended school in the year zero; it should be obvious this does not tell us much). Next, we see that only three of the five predictor variables are significant: age, height, and weight. (If we look at the Wald statistic, it is clear that the largest values are associated with those three, indicating that weight is most significant, followed by height, then age.) MBA (whether one has an MBA) and year (when one attended school) seem to lack any predictive power for gender, *over and above the other variables in the regression*. (A good exercise is to check whether that is true when we examine these two variables by themselves.)

If we look at the effects on gender (i.e., the probability of being male) for the three significant variables, we obtain values of 1.171 (age), 1.478 (height), and 1.074 (weight). In simple terms, this means that an additional year in age seems to increase the chance one is male by 17.1 percent, a 1-inch increase in height has an effect of 47.8 percent, and 1 pound in weight translates to a 7.4 percent increase. There are several points to notice here, all of them crucial:

- It would be wrong to conclude that height was most "important" because its percentage (47.8 percent) is the highest of those listed. This is entirely due to units of measurement: age in *years*, height in *inches*, weight in *pounds*. If we had used different units—say, decades, millimeters, and kilograms—

Gumbel distribution
An uncommon distribution that nonetheless plays a key role in logistic regression; often called "extreme value" or "double exponential," with cumulative density function $F(x) = \exp[-\exp(-x)]$.

logit model
A widely used probabilistic model in marketing, used for predicting individual choice behavior, often for brands. The error distribution is double exponential, which yields simple formulas for all choice probabilities, unlike the probit model, which assumes normally distributed errors.

probit model
A probabilistic model used for predicting individual choice behavior, often for brands. The error distribution is normal, which introduces computational complexity, compared with the more common *logit* model.

ordered dependent variable
A variable one wishes to predict that has some natural ordering, such as a Likert or frequency scale.

Likert-based scale
Perhaps the most common scaling method in all of survey research. Numbers represent responses arranged symmetrically about some midpoint (which may not be explicitly on the scale itself, as in a 6-point scale) and, if possible, for which the points are equally spaced in terms of the respondent's underlying reactions. The prototypical example is the "agree–disagree" scale, usually with 5, 6 or 7 points, with verbal labels like "strongly disagree," "moderately disagree," and so forth.

ordinal regression
A form of regression analysis in which the dependent variable is in some natural order, such as a 7-point scale (not to be confused with a *rank-ordered* dependent variable, for which we use a rank-ordered or exploded regression model).

ordered logit model
An ordinal regression in which errors have a double-exponential distribution.

ordered probit model
An ordinal regression in which errors are normally distributed.

the *unit percentage increase* for height would be much less than the others because it would measure the effect of being 1 millimeter taller. (In fact, the result would be about 1.55 percent per millimeter; see if you can calculate this yourself using only the output supplied for this problem. Hint: you may have to use exponents or logarithms).

- It is highly unusual that age somehow helps predict when one is male; this is *not* true for the general population, except for the elderly (who tend to be predominately female, due to their greater life spans). Closer examination of the *sample* reveals the source: the undergraduate program is approximately 40 percent male; the regular MBA program is about 60 percent male; and the executive program is about 70 percent male. Because the undergraduates are youngest, and the executive students oldest, it appears that knowing someone's age helps predict gender. And this is true for the population from which this particular sample is drawn, but *not* for other populations.
- The value associated with a 1-pound weight increase has *changed* from the first regression (where it was the only predictor) to this one (where it is one of five): 11.4 percent to 7.4 percent. The reason for this is that weight, being the only predictor, was "doing all the work," specifically for the omitted variable height, which is highly correlated with it. When height was included in the regression, it was seen to be strongly predictive of weight itself, and it therefore lessened the estimate attributed to weight alone. This is a general feature of regression models, and it will always require that we truly *think* about which variables should be included in our explanation.

We close by mentioning again that we had to assume our error term, ε, is distributed not normally but according to something called a **Gumbel distribution**. This is what gives rise to a **logit model**, and the logit model is the *only* model that yields a simple formula for probability based on the calculated coefficients. If we assume that the error is *normally* distributed, we instead wind up with something called a **probit model**. Most major statistical packages support both models. In practice, they almost always perform equally well. In fact, statisticians have determined that one would need tens of thousands of data points to detect any important differences between the logit and probit models. Their output is also interpreted identically. As such, you should feel free to use whichever model is supported in your software. Note as well that all the other models in this chapter that are called "logit" have a "probit" version as well, the only difference being the error distribution. Once again, this difference is technical, and it should not have any effect on your ability to use the models in question.

In closing, let us stress that many, many marketing variables are binary, and, as such, binary (logit or probit) regression is an important model to have in one's toolkit. We next see what happens when we have to predict not just "0 vs. 1," but a scale of the form "0 vs. 1 vs. 1 vs. . . . some larger number"; that is, an **ordered dependent variable**.

10.3c Ordinal Dependent Variable: Ordinal Regression

Among the most common types of variable in all of survey-based research is the scale. For example, respondents are asked a series of "agree–disagree" questions, using numbers from 1 to 7 to indicate their views (e.g., "1 = strongly disagree" . . . "4 = neither disagree nor agree" . . . "7 = strongly agree"). This is an example of an *ordered* or *ordinal* variable. Although in many cases researchers will treat such variables as if they were interval-scaled, this makes a strong assumption: that the "distance" between responses of "1" and "2" is the same as for "3" and "4" or any other pair of adjacent points. If we have an extremely good reason for assuming this, we may, but otherwise we should not. All we know about such a scale is that some quality or quantity increases as we move in one direction along the scale. (Note that many researchers believe that, at least in cultures whose writing systems go left to right, that positive qualities like agreement or satisfaction should increase as one moves rightward.)

Although the common **Likert-based scale**, like the 1-to-7 agree–disagree scale just discussed, can be mistaken for an interval scale, there are many other scales in marketing research that cannot. For example, frequency scales (like "never," "rarely," "sometimes," "often," "always") or adjectival scales, (like "child,", "young adult,","middle-aged," "old") clearly lack the "equal distance" property of interval scales. When we wish to understand and make predictions about responses on such a scale, we must use not ordinary multiple regression but an **ordinal regression** model. Most software packages support two of these: the **ordered logit** and **ordered probit models**. As discussed earlier in this chapter, these differ in terms of highly technical assumptions about the error and, in practice, almost always yield identical (or very close) statistical results.

What an ordinal regression model gives to the researcher is exactly the same as one would receive from a linear regression, with a few extra quantities thrown in. These extra quantities are called *cut-offs*, and they help account for the different "distances" between the scale points. For example, suppose we could put ourselves inside the heads of two different samples of people using an ordered, 1-to-5 scale, and this is what we saw:

Sample A: 1 ———— 2 ———— 3 ———— 4 ———— 5
Sample B: 1 ———————— 2 — 3 — 4 ———————— 5

Sample A's "view" of the scale is entirely consistent with interval-scaling: pairs of adjacent points are all the same distance apart. Those in Sample B, however, see the extreme points (1 and 5) as being more distant from their nearest neighbors (2 and 4) than those neighbors are to the center (3). And here is the main point: if we were to run an ordinal logit model on the data for these two samples, they would indicate that Sample A's respondents saw the scale points as evenly spaced, but those from Sample B did not. All this would be taken care of *automatically* by the statistical model; the researcher would have to make no assumptions about the data at all. In statistics, we would say that ordinal regression is *more general* than usual linear regression or that the usual regression model is *nested in* the ordinal model. Regardless of what we call it, it is the model we need to use for a large proportion of data types encountered in marketing research applications.

To make our discussion concrete, let us consider once again our marketing research class data. We have but one ordinal variable, LikeStat: "On a scale of 1–7, where 1 is "not at all" and 7 is "very much," how well did you like your introductory statistics course?" Let us try to understand this variable in terms of others in the data set; we use all variables other than "class" (which is a nominal variable; we will examine it in more detail later) and, of course, LikeStat itself. Here are the results of running an *ordinal logit* regression of Y = LikeStat on X = {age, gender, height, weight, MBA, year}:

Model Fit

Model	−2 Log Likelihood	Chi-Square	*df*	Sig.
Intercept Only	1670.235			
Final	1495.707	174.527	6	0.0000

Parameter Estimates

	Estimate	Std. Error	Wald	*df*	Sig.	95% Confidence Interval: [Lower, Upper]	
Age	−0.079	0.028	7.849	1	0.005	−0.134	−0.024
Gender	−0.915	0.267	11.763	1	0.0001	−1.437	−0.392
Height	0.021	0.039	0.292	1	0.589	−0.055	0.097
Weight	0.005	0.005	1.108	1	0.292	−0.004	0.015
MBA	−1.784	0.326	29.859	1	0.000	−2.423	−1.144
Year	0.130	0.052	6.254	1	0.012	0.028	0.232
			Cut-offs				
[LikeStat = 1]	−3.886	2.347	2.741	1	.098	−8.486	0.714
[LikeStat = 2]	−2.777	2.344	1.404	1	.236	−7.371	1.817
[LikeStat = 3]	−2.183	2.343	0.868	1	.351	−6.775	2.409
[LikeStat = 4]	−1.760	2.342	0.565	1	.452	−6.351	2.831
[LikeStat = 5]	−1.030	2.341	0.194	1	.660	−5.619	3.558
[LikeStat = 6]	−0.076	2.340	0.001	1	.974	−4.662	4.511

The output can be read much like that for ordinary linear regression, with a few small changes and additions. The first table tells us about the *entire model*, and takes the place of the F-test in linear regression. It tells us that the model with six predictors (note that *df*, degrees-of-freedom, is 6) fits significantly better than one with only an intercept; the "intercept only" model is one that just considers the overall proportion of responses in each of the seven ordered categories (for these data, the "raw" proportions in categories "1" through "7" happen to be 10.9, 13.8, 10.3, 7.8, 14.1, 16.1, and 27.0 percent). If we ask the computer to calculate an exact *p*-value, it turns out to be far smaller than the "$p < 0.00005$" we'd be able to infer from rounded-off listed value of "0.0000": about 10^{-34}. This is, by any standards, exceptionally strong statistical evidence. But that evidence tells us only that the *entire model* is strongly "significant"; it tells us nothing about *parts* of that model.

Let us next look at the second table, listing the coefficients and associated tests. Most of this table is identical to that for ordinary linear regression. For example, each of our "X" (independent) variables has an estimated value, a standard error, a significance level, and a confidence interval; these can all be interpreted as we have throughout this text. We note that age, gender, MBA, and year are each significant, but that height and weight are not. One might wonder why height and weight were so strongly significant in most of our prior analyses but not now. This is because we are not describing a different dependent variable: how well one likes a statistics course is not obviously explainable in terms of one's physical characteristics, but it is entirely possible—and in fact empirically supported by our analysis—that gender, age, MBA, and year do have some relation. In this case, we see that age, gender, and MBA have significant negative coefficients, and year a significantly positive one. This means that, in terms of the statistics course, we see stronger liking from younger students, women, undergraduates, and over time.

The only truly "new" information here involves the cut-offs. These represent demarcation points between the various categories. For example, "[LikeStat = 1]" is the dividing point between responses of "1" and "2"; there are six values listed in the output because there are six demarcation points between the seven ordered response categories. Generally speaking, the cut-offs are difficult to interpret in terms of useful information, managerial or otherwise, and we will not attempt to. Statisticians often refer to such quantities as "nuisance parameters": measurements that are important to include in the model but that are not of interest in and of themselves. We can think of cut-offs as a necessary part of understanding and modeling ordinal data, and nothing more. We should also resist the temptation to assign any importance to the "significance" levels of any of the cut-offs; all must be left in the model, regardless.

We must remember that ordinal regression *only* applies when the categorical responses are in some meaningful order. If we were predicting which state someone lived in, we could order the states alphabetically, but this would not make them an ordinal variable, unless we had some deep managerial interest in the alphabet. When we cannot say that all respondents agree on the ordering of the categories, we must use another type of regression, which we turn to next.

10.3d Nominal Dependent Variable: Multinomial Regression

One of the most important types of variable in marketing practice is nominal, where we have a set of categories, and responses consist of one of them. This variable type comes about with great frequency in three different settings:

1. Survey research, where one has to list occupation, ethnicity, geographical region, "which answer best represents your views," or any of dozens of other such responses;
2. Experimental research techniques, like conjoint analysis (see Chapter 11), where the outcome variable is which product configuration someone chooses;
3. Field data, such as the enormous number of choices made by consumers in supermarkets, department stores, and on the Web, all routinely recorded.

multinomial regression
A form of regression model in which the dependent variable is which option of a fixed set occurred.

discrete choice model
A type of statistical (regression) model where the dependent variable is a specific set of outcomes that has occurred. Most common examples are the logit (logistic regression) and probit models. One of the main applications of discrete choice models is predicting which brand will be chosen by a household on a specific purchase occasion.

All these scenarios involve analyzing *choices* made from a set of options. When our dependent variable is choice, we need to use a special kind of model, **multinomial regression**, also frequently referred to as a **discrete choice model**. It is not an overstatement to say that the introduction of this technique to marketing is the single most important modeling development in the history of the field. The first real appearance of the model was in a now-famous academic paper by Peter Guadagni and John Little,[1] where, for the first time, they showed how to make sense of UPC scanner data, which was common then and ubiquitous now. They based their research on pioneering work in the mid-1970s by Daniel McFadden, who was awarded the 2000 Nobel Prize in Economics "for his development of theory and methods for analyzing discrete choice." See *Marketing Research Focus 10.3* for more information on the Guadagni and Little model.

Given the importance of this model to marketing theory and practice, we will explore it in more depth than is customary, including its underpinnings, some flavor of its derivations, and how to use it in practice. Students uninterested in this background can skip to Section 10-3f, but we hope everyone will at least skim the discussion to get a sense of this critical and, frankly, beautiful analytic method.

We must first distinguish between two types of models for multinomial data. The first, often called the *multinomial logit model* in economics, attempts to explain choices on the basis of the characteristics of the *choosers*; for example, their ages, incomes, education levels, and other characteristics that do not

Marketing Research Focus 10.3

Guadagni and Little's Multinomial Logit Analysis of Coffee Purchase Behavior

A revolution in marketing research practice started in the early 1980s, when researchers started to apply discrete choice methods, first pioneered in economics, to the analysis of supermarket purchases. In a piece of research that has generated literally thousands of follow-up studies and launched a multibillion dollar industry, Peter Guadagni and John D.C. Little, both then at the MIT's Sloan School of Management, studied a large database of coffee purchases.

They had data from a consumer panel over a span of 78 weeks, collected in Kansas City by SAMI, for 2000 households that were at least 90 percent store loyal; store loyalty was important to ensure that almost all purchases were correctly recorded and that store-switching was kept to a minimum. They selected data from 200 of the households that made at least five purchases over the 18-month period; a multinomial logit model was estimated on those households and used to make predictions for other households and for future purposes, so-called "hold-out samples."

Data were available on five coffee brands, three of which came in both a small (1 pound) and large (3 pound) size can, so that consumers had eight separate options from which to choose, on each shopping occasion. To understand what drove consumer purchases, they used several different kinds of variables in their analysis:

Unique to each choice alternative:
Brand-specific constants

Marketing control variables for every choice alternative:
"Regular" (i.e., not promoted) price (in $/oz.)
Binary promotion variable: Was the item being promoted at all?
Depth of price cut ($/oz.): How much was the item being promoted?
Promotional lags: Was the item promoted previously?

Household Purchase Behavior:
Brand loyalty: A measure of how loyal a household was to each brand
Size loyalty: A measure of how loyal a household was to each size

Their choice of variables was ingenious. The brand-specific constants were like intercepts in an ordinary linear regression, and they measured something very important: how much is each brand liked *over and above* the effects attributable to marketing activity and household loyalty? If we were studying the soft drink market, these might be called something like "Cokeness," "Pepsihood" or "7-Up–osity," because they capture the unique traits for each brand that consumers apparently like, over and above anything marketers can do by changing prices and other inducements. They also included several marketing mix variables, among them various elements of pricing and promotional policy. By including these in the model, marketers can precisely measure the influence of their policies.

The last types of predictors are referred to as **loyalty variables**, in this case for each of the five brands and for each of the two sizes. These were calculated from the string of purchases each household made: for example, every time a brand was purchased, the "loyalty" for that brand increased a bit and decreased for all the other brands. The model automatically determined how much a "little bit" should be, and it automatically updated both brand and size loyalty variables every time a new purchase was made.

loyalty variables
In brand choice models, a variable created from a household's choices that tracks how frequently each brand is bought by that household; often calculated as a time-discounted average over all past purchase occasions.

Most of the model's findings were as seasoned managers expected, but there were a few surprises. First, brand loyalty was the single most significant variable in helping to determine brand purchasing patterns. Marketers had long claimed that the best way to predict what a household will do is to understand what it has been doing; that is, what brands it is "loyal" to. However, to the surprise of many, the second strongest predictor was size loyalty: a stronger effect than *any* of the marketing mix variables! Evidently, customers also had strong habits in terms of the size of coffee can they wished to purchase. It stands to reason that single consumers, those who drink coffee infrequently and those with limited storage space, would not find a large can of coffee attractive, even if it were deeply discounted. After the loyalty variables, the next strongest predictors were, in order, binary promotion (whether the brand was on sale), depth of price cut, "regular" price, and, finally, promotional lags, which were barely significant. Interestingly, "regular" price was a far less reliable predictor than variables measuring *changes* in price; that is, promotion. It seems that high prices *per se* did not scare customers away, nor low prices lure them; being able to get a good deal had rather more influence.

The model also made excellent predictions, closely tracking actual (hold-out) purchases. Managers, of course, consider this last criterion crucial. Strong statistical results are important, but having a model match reality is what will cause it to be used in real-world applications. As a final check, Guadagni and Little re-estimated their model without any loyalty measures, so that it only accounted for brand constants and actions taken by managers, and *not* consumers' habitual behaviors. The model fit dramatically worse, having less than half the "total information content." Evidently, managers must measure not only the effects of their own actions, but the steadfastness of consumer behavior, if they really wish to gain deep insight into what drives markets.

The power and elegance of Guadagni and Little's model caused many other researchers and companies to actively pursue discrete choice models, and to apply them far and wide. For decades, managers struggled with how they could translate the vast quantities of data they collected on marketing activity and resulting purchase behavior into clear recommendations for better marketing practice and how to make their ventures and programs more profitable. Thanks to the application of discrete choice models to purchase data, we now have good explanations for such complex phenomena as purchase timing, store-switching, purchase quantity, multicategory buying, channel dynamics, and many more. Statisticians have responded with such exotica as correlated errors, finite normal mixtures, nonlinear effects, hierarchical Bayes methods, and other arcana, all of which help marketers comprehend the choice data that streams by in ever-greater profusion. Even decades after their introduction, discrete choice models, and the multinomial logit in particular, keep finding new vistas of marketing application.

Source: Peter M. Guadagni, and John D.C. Little, "A Logit Model of Brand Choice Calibrated on Scanner Data," *Marketing Science*, 2, Summer, 1983, 203–238.
Further Reading: Peter Rossi, Greg Allenby and Robert McCulloch, "Bayesian Statistics and Marketing," Hoboken, NJ: Wiley, 2006.

change from one choice option to another (i.e., you are the same age no matter which brand of pasta you buy next time). The other, often called *(McFadden's) conditional logit model* in economics, incorporates information about the choices themselves. For example, every time you go to the store, the price and promotion level of the available brands can, and typically do, change. In marketing applications, it is critical that we include such *item-specific* information, so we will exclusively discuss this second model. Due to an unfortunate act of nomenclature, this second model is universally referred to in marketing as the "Multinomial Logit" model (MNL), and for consistency we will adopt this terminology. Note, however, that the model that often goes by that name in some statistical programs is actually the first type of model and will not accommodate item-specific information. We will not bring this issue up again, and will develop the model carefully to be applicable to marketing data and experimental techniques such as conjoint analysis.

10.3e Multinomial Logit and Modeling Consumer Choice

multinomial logit (MNL) model
A form of multinomial regression in which errors are a double-exponential distribution; exceptionally important in the analysis of scanner data and brand choice.

The **multinomial logit (MNL) model** was first used in transportation studies because city governments wanted to understand why some people drove to work, some elected to take public transportation, others walked, and so forth. Would it be possible to *model* people's choices, and thus understand the effects of, say, building a new train line or lowering bus fares? Only later did marketing researchers realize that the same model could answer critical managerial questions, such as, "What if we lowered price by 10 percent?"; "Was this sale effective?" or "Should we feature that brand in an aisle display?" That is, for the first time, we could understand the underpinnings of consumer choice, and thereby how to scientifically assess our marketing programs.

consumer utility
In economics, a measure of the level of satisfaction or usefulness a consumer receives or anticipates from a good or service. In statistics, it is a "latent" (unobserved) variable that helps provide a concrete foundation for the use of discrete choice models, such as logit and probit regression.

Underlying all such *discrete choice models* is the concept of **consumer utility**. We never get to observe this utility! To do so would require approaching shoppers as they stood in the store, and asking, "Before you pick one of those 300 cereal boxes, can I bother you to rate each of them on a 1-to-100 scale?"; and doing this every time they made a choice, for a period of years. This would not be a popular method with consumers or managers. Rather, we presume that there is something called "utility"—how much pleasure or use or other positive qualities we anticipate we will gain by purchasing any particular product—for each consumer and each brand at each purchase occasion. To be concrete, we will assume that, on some scale (which is taken care of automatically by the model), you will gain a certain number of utility points for purchasing a small box of corn flakes when you go shopping next Saturday afternoon. But also that we, as researchers, will never be able to obtain that value directly from you. As in all statistical models, we break down something we want to understand (consumer utility for each particular brand, which we index by k) into two parts: what we can explain (**deterministic**, v_k) and what we cannot (random error, ε_k)

deterministic
Any quantity that can be completely determined by other quantities, with no error. Regression models express observations as a sum of a deterministic and a stochastic component.

$$\text{Consumer Utitlity} = \text{Deterministic} + \text{Error}$$
$$u_k = v_k + \varepsilon_k$$

So far, this is exactly like all regression models, except that what is on the left side, u_k, is *not* directly observed. Also like in all regression models, the "deterministic" part will be due to "independent" variables at our disposal, usually marketing-mix variables and consumer-specific variables: price, promotion, brand loyalty, and others. Note that this can include both variables we can *control* (like price and promotion) and those that we cannot but that we can *measure* (like a consumer's loyalty level or household income). Lastly, the random error part of our equation is due to "noise" during purchase occasion (e.g., store conditions, difficulty locating product on the shelves) and "unobservables" (e.g., that a particular consumer had three boxes of cereal at home already).

As in all forms of regression we have already looked at, the deterministic portion of our model is *linear* in the independent variables:

$$v_k = b_1 x_{1k} + b_2 x_{2k} + \cdots + b_n x_{nk}$$

Here, the various "X" (independent) variables can be anything of interest to marketers. For example, x_1 might be price, x_2 promotion, x_3 whether a brand was on display, and so on. So that the equation for v_k is clear, x_{1k} might stand for the price for brand *k* on a particular occasion. Once the computer program estimated the various coefficients, $\{b_1, \ldots, b_n\}$, for us, we could calculate a deterministic value, v_k, for each brand. Those with higher values of v_k are more likely to be chosen.

Unlike standard linear regression, for the multinomial logit model to "work," we must assume that the error has a special distribution. We have mentioned this distribution, the Gumbel, before, in our discussion of the binary logit model; this distribution has other names as well, such as "Type II extreme value" and "double exponential." If you are familiar with cumulative density functions from probability theory or statistics, you will recognize this equation, which precisely specifies the shape of this distribution:

$$P[\varepsilon_k < \varepsilon] = \exp[-e^{-\varepsilon}]$$

The distribution itself looks very much like a normal, with a slight skew (see Figure 10.14).

The reason we make this assumption about the error—which, after all, we do not get to observe directly—is that it allows something almost miraculous: an *exact* formula for predicting what choices one might make. It can be proven that if we have *any* other formula for our error, this will not be possible. Once we have this formula, we can average everyone's choice probabilities to obtain something of pivotal importance to marketers, a formula for the *expected market share* for each product, based on hypothetical marketing actions.

First, let us look at this rather famous formula, which is a generalization of what we saw in the binary logit model:

$$\begin{aligned}\text{Prob[Choose Brand 1]} &= \frac{\exp(\text{deterministic for brand 1})}{\sum_{\text{all brands k}} \exp(\text{deterministic for brand k})}\\ &= \frac{\exp(v_1)}{\sum_k \exp(v_k)}\\ &= \frac{\text{“Us”}}{\text{“Us”} + \text{“Them”}}\end{aligned}$$

Figure 10.14 **The Double Exponential Error Distribution Used in Logit Models**

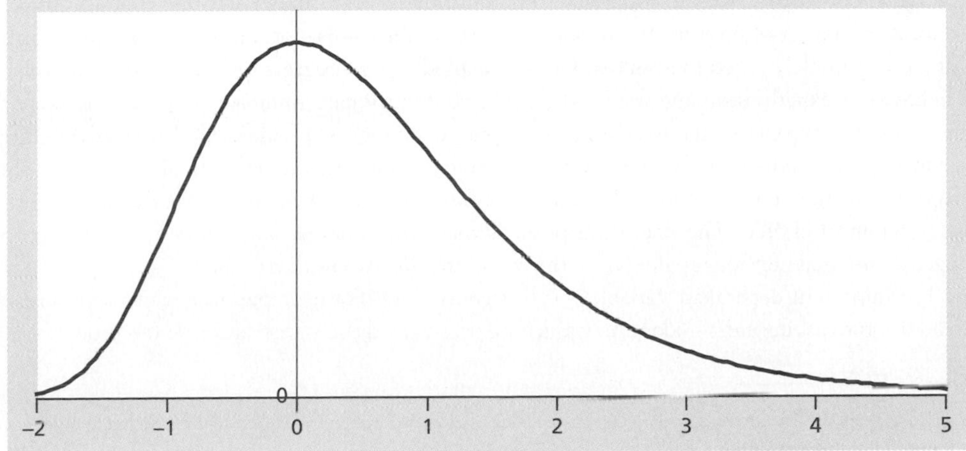

The formula is presented in three ways, each put slightly differently. The first is in words: take the exponential of the deterministic part for the focal brand (Brand 1, in this case, although we can do it for any other brand as well). Then, divide it by the sum of the exponentials for all the other brands. The second just translates these words into symbols and is the most common way the formula is written. The third puts it in a way that managers like to think of it: our "share" or probability is "our" value over the sum of "our" value and "their" values.

You should try to verify that this procedure *must* give a valid set of probabilities. No matter what values you choose for the different deterministic parts $\{v_1, \ldots, v_k\}$, the resulting probabilities will all be between 0 and 1, and all add exactly to 1. Any model with this property is called **logically consistent**, because it cannot yield bizarre probability values.

logically consistent
A model whose probabilistic predictions must all be positive and sum to one, an important property for models that predict probabilities of choice, or market share.

You might wonder what all this fuss with logit models is about. And here is the answer, one you should commit to memory:

> Logistic regression takes both binary (e.g., "Is it on sale?"; "Is there a display?") and interval (e.g., "What is the price?"; "How much is it on promotion?") data and produces *probabilities of purchase and market share projections as functions of the marketing mix.*

Managers can then ask "*What if* we had charged a different price?"; "*Should we* continue this promotion?" or any question about variables they control. That is, they can engage in scenario analysis, determine whether their past actions were wise, and attempt to optimize their marketing activities. This is what all marketing managers wish to do, and the multinomial logit model helps them do so.

If you have understood how to read the output for ordinary, binary, and ordinal regression, you already understand how to do so for the MNL model. You will obtain coefficients, standard errors, confidence intervals, and *p*-values, all with their usual interpretations. A fully worked-out example of the MNL model for a real consumer choice experiment will be presented in our discussion of conjoint analysis in Chapter 11. Here, we illustrate how the multinomial logit can be used for field data on supermarket purchases. To do so, we will look at its first and still most famous application in marketing history, in *Marketing Research Focus 10.3*. Students interested in more technical detail are directed to their clear, beautifully written, and copiously illustrated original paper, listed at the end of this chapter.

10.3f Other Types of Dependent Variables: Rank-Ordered and Count

There are many, many types of variables one encounters in marketing applications, and it is impossible to cover all possibilities, especially because survey researchers are so clever at thinking up new ways to query people about their feelings and activities. Fortunately, we were able to present a complete account of the ones encountered most frequently: the interval, the binary, the ordinal, and the multinomial. However, two others appear with some frequency: rank-ordered and count.

Rank-ordered data—not to be confused with ordinal data—consist of a set of possible options placed in order, like when we are asked to "name our top 3" (or 5, or 10) movies, cars, or soft drinks. Note that, when we name our "top 1," we can simply use the multinomial logit model, because that accounts for a single choice from a set of options. When we have a set of ranked options, however, we must turn to a different kind of model, called the **rank-ordered or exploded logit regression model**.* Fortunately, this model behaves in exactly the same way as the MNL model: we can input our variables the same way, and the computer produces literally identical output (coefficients, *p*-values, and so forth). Unfortunately, statistical programs that estimate rank-ordered regressions are uncommon, although they should be more widely available in the future. For support information, it is best to consult the documentation for your program of choice. The important point is that rank-ordered data *can* be analyzed rigorously using regression-based methods analogous to those you are already familiar with.

rank-ordered or exploded logit regression model
A type of regression model that can be applied to a rank-ordered *dependent* variable (e.g., "rank the following set of items in order of your preference").

One last important dependent variable is called **count data**. For example, in our marketing research data, in addition to asking each student how much he or she liked the statistics course (an ordinal variable

count data
A dependent variable representing how many times an event occurred; often modeled using Poisson regression.

*As with all logit type models, there is a related probit model, as introduced in Section 10.3c, which is the same in all respects, except the error is assumed to be normally distributed.

on a 1-to-7 scale), we could have asked *how many* statistics courses the student had previously taken. Although data of that type may appear ordinal, they are actually a count—answering the question "How many?" with some whole number (0, 1, 2, ...)—and require their own type of model, called **Poisson or count regression**. Once again, if you are comfortable with other types of regression, interpreting Poisson regression should be straightforward, because the output is almost exactly the same. The only difference in using count regression and ordinary linear regression is that, for counts, we would have to know not only our observation (e.g., "How many statistics courses have you taken?"), but also the number of *opportunities* (e.g., "How many semesters have you been in school"), multiplied by, say, five courses per semester. We would typically have to include the number of opportunities as one of the inputs to the count regression. Instructions on running count-based regressions, particularly the Poisson and negative binomial models, and using them for prediction (as well as sample input) appear in most full-featured statistical programs.

Poisson or count regression
A type of regression analysis where the dependent variable is the *number of times* a particular event occurred.

10.3g Using Nominal Independent Variables in Regressions

We have seen many examples of using interval-scaled and binary variables as independent variables in a regression. These are quite easy to interpret because the coefficient always represents a "one-unit increase" in the quantity in question. We have also mentioned at several junctures that it is possible to use *nominal* variables in regression, and you have likely seen such applications in an introductory statistics course. For example, one wishes to include "season" or "month" as an independent variable, and so adds, respectively, three or 11 **binary dummy variables** to account for them.

binary dummy variables
A (*binary*) *dummy variable* takes on values of either 0 or 1 and is often introduced into an analysis to represent other, nonbinary variables. For example, the four seasons of the year can be represented using three binary dummies.

Let us look one last time at our marketing research class data and, instead of using MBA as an explanatory variable, use class—undergraduate, MBA, or executive program—instead. Almost all statistical programs make this simple to do by specifying that binary and interval-scaled variables are *covariates*, whereas nominal variables are referred to as *factors* (note that these bear no relation at all to Factor analysis, which appears in Chapter 11). In this way, one need not re-code a variable like month from a single column with entries from 1 through 12 into 11 binary columns, as is common when using dummy variables. Let us simply re-run an ordinary linear regression to try to explain weight, as we did earlier, but with class instead of MBA. (Note that these are strongly related because class = 0 implies MBA = 0, and class = 1 or class = 2 implies MBA = 1; class and MBA should *not* be included in the regression simultaneously in any case.) The output for just the coefficients is:

Linear Regression Analysis: DepVar (*Y*) = Weight *X* = {Age, Gender, Height, Class (Nominal), Year}

Coefficients	*b*	Std. Error	Std. Beta	*t*-Test Statistic	*p*-value Two-Tailed
Intercept	−210.479	20.574		−10.23	0.0000
Age	0.607	0.291	0.093	2.08	0.0380
Gender	17.295	2.463	0.264	7.02	0.0000
Height	5.015	0.296	0.615	16.97	0.0000
Class = 2	−3.221	3.069	−0.049	−1.05	0.2946
Class = 3	−1.846	3.628	−0.027	−0.51	0.6111
Year	−0.102	0.508	−0.005	−0.20	0.8416

It is not difficult to see that the results are nearly identical to those obtained using MBA (a *binary* variable), as opposed to class (which is *nominal*). The only new point of interpretation is that, to account for the nominal nature of class, we must use *two* new (binary dummy) variables: "Class = 2" and "Class = 3." Each of them estimates the difference between that group and the "base" group, which we chose arbitrarily to be "Class = 1." In this case, the intercept of the model, −210.479, corresponds to "Class = 1," and the intercepts for "Class = 2" and "Class = 3" are obtained by adding: for example, (−210.479) + (−3.221) = −213.700 for "Class = 2."

Because we had three categories for class, we needed *two* additional dummy variables to account for it. If we had data on the four seasons of the year, we would need three dummies; monthly coded data would require 11 dummies, and so forth. Although this method is simple and powerful, one must be careful not to let it get out of hand: all the states in the United States would require 49 dummies, and all the major cities of the world many hundreds. Because we lose statistical power—represented by degrees of freedom—whenever we add more independent variables, we want to ensure that we add such binary dummies sparingly. So, for example, if we did not have a huge sample size and we had data coded by month, we might decide to re-code according to season of the year, which would require three dummies instead of 11 for month. Researchers must carefully weigh the pros and cons of adding additional dummy variables just because they can. Sometimes, a simpler model (one with fewer independent variables) is not only easier to understand, it may actually be more powerful and offer superior forecasts.

Summary

Regression methods allow us to test the validity of relationships, measure the extent of various influences, and make predictions. They must be used with extreme care when assumptions about the error (normality, constant variance, no autocorrelation) are violated in some way; when linearity cannot be presumed; when predictor variables are highly correlated (multicollinearity); when latent variables remain undetected; or when the data do not conform to a set of acceptable types. In each of these cases, more advanced methods can be used to supplement standard regression models.

Regression methods can be distinguished by the type of dependent variable to which they are being applied: interval, binary, ordinal, nominal, rank-ordered, or count, among others. These are examples of the general linear model, which also allows for variable transformations and nonnormal error distributions.

Regression applied to complex phenomena almost always involves many inter-correlated predictor variables (multicollinearity) and multiple data types. Each coefficient in a multiple regression measures how much the dependent variable should change if a particular independent variable were increased by one unit and all other variables stayed the same. Multicollinearity can make interpreting these coefficients difficult.

Each dependent variable data value in a regression can be decomposed into that arising from the "fit" (prediction), calculated from the regression, plus the "error." The *F*-test assesses whether the model's predictions explain a significant degree of variation in the dependent variable, and considers the quality of the entire model at once. The *t*-tests assess whether each variable's coefficient is significantly different from zero, taken on its own.

Transformations, such as log(X), X to a power, or a number to the Xth power, allow many nonlinear relationships to be handled using linear regression. A logistic regression or logit model allows the dependent variable to be binary (taking on just two values) or nominal and assumes an unusual error distribution (Gumbel); a probit model does the same but assumes the error to be normally distributed. These are examples of discrete choice models, which are widely used to analyze supermarket scanner and Web purchase data.

Key Terms

autocorrelation (p. 446)
binary dummy variables (p. 465)
binary logistic regression (p. 457)
Breusch-Pagan test (p. 445)
consumer utility (p. 462)
count data (p. 464)
deterministic (p. 462)
discrete choice model (p. 460)
exponential (p. 448)
frequency distribution (p. 441)
Generalized AutoRegressive Conditional Heteroscedasticity (GARCH) (p. 445)
General Linear Model (p. 436)
geometric (p. 448)
Gumbel distribution (p. 458)
heteroscedasticity (p. 445)
latent variable (p. 438)
Likert-based scale (p. 458)
logarithm of the odds (log-odds) (p. 455)
logically consistent (p. 464)
logistic regression (LOGIT) (p. 455)
logit model (p. 458)
loyalty variables (p. 461)
mean-squared-error (MSE) (p. 440)
multicollinearity (p. 438)
multinomial logit (MNL) model (p. 462)
multinomial regression (p. 460)
nonnormality (p. 441)
normal probability plot (p. 441)
ordered dependent variable (p. 458)
ordered logit model (p. 458)
ordered probit model (p. 458)
ordinal regression (p. 458)
Poisson or count regression (p. 465)
polynomial regressions (p. 449)
prediction interval (p. 443)
probit model (p. 458)
rank-ordered or exploded logit regression model (p. 464)
residual error (p. 441)
standardized residual (p. 441)
stepwise regression (p. 454)
transformation (p. 448)
Weighted Least Squares (WLS) model (p. 445)
White test (p. 445)

Discussion Questions

1 What are some of the main uses of linear regression analysis? Why are they important to the social sciences in general, and to marketing in particular?

2 What are some of the weaknesses and limitations of regression-based methods in general? Specifically, does regression make certain assumptions that limit its applicability in certain contexts? What are some of the ways in which researchers and statisticians have attempted to address these weaknesses?

3 What is the "theoretical model" for multiple regression? What do each of β_0, $\{\beta_1, \ldots \beta_k\}$ and ε represent? What is the importance of ε, and what assumptions does a regression model make about it?

4 Can we ever know if a regression model is correct, as opposed to its being useful? What are the basic criteria used to judge whether a regression is appropriate/accurate/useful? Can you provide some intuition for each of these criteria understandable by a nonstatistical audience?

5 How can we use the *actual sample errors*, e_i, to test the assumptions made about the population error, ε? What should we do, in regard to our posited regression model, if each of those assumptions appears to be violated?

6 What conditions should the independent variables in a multiple regression ideally satisfy? What notorious problem arises when some independent variables are correlated with one another? How can we go about fixing this problem so that regression can still be applied?

7 What are some common alternate (i.e., nonlinear) functional forms that might help relate independent to dependent variables? How do we use transformations of independent variables to investigate these possible relationship forms using ordinary linear regression models?

8 What types of data (both for independent and dependent variables) can we use for regression? What are some examples of each of these types of data? What are the names of specific forms of regression analysis appropriate when each of these types of data is involved as the *dependent* variable in the regression? How are the coefficients generated by the regression procedure interpreted in each of these cases?

9 Why should one refrain from explaining a binary dependent variable (using some set of independent variables) using a linear regression model? How do the (binary) logit and probit models address these problems? In what sense are the logit and probit models more difficult to work with and interpret than the linear regression model?

10 Why are the ordinal regression methods (ordered logit and ordered probit) important, and what sort of misinterpretations can arise if we simply use ordinary linear regression (that is, to assume an ordered variable is interval-scaled) instead? What are the conditions on categorical responses that make ordinal regression appropriate? What is an example of a categorical response type or variable for which ordinal regression would definitely be inappropriate?

11 Why is it so difficult to statistically explain which of a set of choices someone will select? Is there a difference between selecting exactly one item from a set of 10, and making a separate decision about whether you would purchase each item? What kind of models would you use for each of these situations? Can you use regression to predict *how many* boxes of cereal a household purchases on a particular shopping occasion?

12 How would you include *seasonality* in your regression model? What about month of the year and its effect on sales? Would it be reasonable to use *day of the year* as an independent variable in a regression? Why or why not?

13 Suppose you are in charge of a large-scale research project to gauge customer satisfaction, and you have thousands of customers' survey responses, each for more than 100 questions. How would you go about determining a "good" model for satisfaction? What sort of tests would you do to determine whether you had the right variables in the model, given the enormous number of possibilities? Would your model be linear? How could you tell if that was a good assumption?

14 Can you think of any managerial situations where regression could simply not be applied? Are there any types of data that would be extraordinarily difficult to work with in a regression framework?

Review Questions

1 For which of the following purposes can regression methods be used in marketing research applications?

a to test the validity of hypothesized relationships between two variables

b to test the extent to which one variable influences another

c to rigorously forecast and predict about new data, based on existing data
d for all of the above reasons

2 What is the difference in information conveyed by a regression's *F*-statistic and its individual coefficients' *t*-statistics?
  a The *F*-statistic, when compared with the *F*-distribution, gives us the probability that the *r-squared* value of the regression is greater than 0.5, indicating that the regression model explains more than 50 percent of the variation in the dependent variable; by contrast, the individual coefficients' *t*-statistics tell us whether or not those individual coefficients are significantly different from zero.
  b The *F*-statistic tells us the probability that the sum of squares of residuals is minimized, whereas the *t*-statistics for individual coefficients tell us the estimated quantifiable effect of unit changes in each of the associated independent variables on the dependent variable.
  c The *F*-statistic tells us the probability that all of the regression's coefficients are simultaneously equal to zero, whereas the *t*-statistics for individual coefficients tell us the probability that those coefficients are each equal to zero separately.
  d none of the above

3 Imagine the following idealized scenario: We wish to use a regression analysis to compare the yearly incomes of both high school graduates with no college education with the yearly incomes of college graduates, within a certain industry. Four hundred persons in each category are randomly sampled, and a wide variety of relevant covariate information (e.g. ability tests, location, prior experience, and so forth) is collected. The annual incomes of the high school graduates range from $0 to $50,000; the annual incomes of the college graduates range from $10,000 to $4.5 million. Which of the following is a likely problem for our regression analysis?
  a There is likely to be a substantial degree of autocorrelation because the college graduates will tend to have incomes above the least-squares regression line, and those with no college experience are likely to have incomes below.
  b Without more information, there is no reason to believe that there will be any conceptual or practical difficulties for this regression.
  c The fact that range of incomes is much larger for college graduates than for those with only a high school degree suggests that heteroscedasticity could be an issue; our model is likely to be over-confident in predicting the incomes of college graduates and under-confident in predicting the incomes of those with only a high school education.
  d The fact that range of incomes is much larger for college graduates than for those with only a high school degree suggests that heteroscedasticity could be an issue; our model is likely to be under-confident in predicting the incomes of college graduates and over-confident in predicting the incomes of those with only a high school education.

4 Imagine that we wish to investigate the effect of being taller than 5′8″ on annual income in a specific company, by estimating the following regression model: $Income = \beta_0 + \beta_1 * IsTaller + \beta_2 * Race + \beta_3 * Gender +$ {*several other independent variables*}$+\varepsilon$, where *IsTaller* is a binary variable (i.e., either 0 or 1) that equals 1 if the person in question is taller than 5′8″, where *Gender* is a binary variable that equals 1 when the individual in question is female, and where *Race* is a binary variable that equals 1 when the individual in question does not self-identify as Caucasian. We sample $n = 950$ individuals at the company in question: 450 are women at a number of levels of advancement, of various racial backgrounds, and ranging in height from 4′11″ to 5′8″; 500 are men, also at a number of levels of advancement, of various racial backgrounds, and ranging in height from 5′9″ to 6′2″. Which of the following is a problem with the regression we are attempting to run?
  a The data must be entered in size order for the results to be meaningful.
  b Our sample does not include enough individuals, rendering the regression results useless.
  c There is perfect multicollinearity in the sample.
  d None of these is a discernible problem with the regression as specified.

5 Imagine that we are interested in exploring a statistical relationship where we believe that a *unit percent increase* in some variable *X* yields a *fixed percent increase* in some other variable *Y*. Given data for both

variables *X* and *Y*, which transformation(s) should we perform on the data to test the posited relationship using a *linear* regression model?

- **a** None—we should simply regress *Y* on *X*.
- **b** We should regress log *Y* on *X*.
- **c** We should regress log *Y* on log *X*.
- **d** We should regress *Y* on log *X*.

6 A vacuum cleaner company has set up a certain bonus structure for its regional managers along the following lines: if the manager can be shown to be individually responsible for increasing sales in his/her region by 2 percent or more in a given year, he or she will be given a bonus; otherwise, he or she will not receive a bonus. In region X, a manager was hired at the beginning of the fiscal year and enacted a series of new policies, including completely reorganizing the sales force; sales this year, as compared with last year, were 5 percent higher, controlling for (using regression) a wide variety of relevant variables (such as changes in regional unemployment, and others). However, the central management of the company ordered an increase in advertising expenditures in region *X*, compared with the previous year; when the change in advertising expenditures is accounted for in a comprehensive and exhaustive regression analysis, the impact of the manager's policy changes is estimated at 1 percent. Using the stated criterion for rewarding bonuses, is the manager entitled to a bonus or not?

- **a** Yes, because the adoption of new policies was associated with a 5 percent increase in sales.
- **b** Yes, because the average estimated effect of the new policies, from the two regressions reported, is 3 percent, which is above the 2 percent threshold stated.
- **c** No, because the inclusion of advertising expenditures reduces the estimated impact of the manager's policy changes to less than the threshold value.
- **d** We cannot determine, on the basis of the above information, whether or not the manager is entitled to the bonus.

7 How do you determine whether adding a given variable to a regression model significantly increases its explanatory power (i.e., the amount of variation in the dependent variable explained by variation in the independent variables)?

- **a** You find the difference in *r-squared* values between the initial model and the new, augmented one. If the difference is larger than 0.05, the new regression model offers a significantly better explanation of the dependent variable than the initial regression.
- **b** You find the difference in *adjusted r-squared* values between the initial model and the new, augmented one. If the difference is larger than 0.05, the new regression model offers a significantly better explanation of the dependent variable than the initial regression.
- **c** You check to see whether or not the addition of the variable is changing the significance of the estimated coefficients on other variables.
- **d** none of the above

8 What is the major difference between the probit and logit models?

- **a** For data sets larger than 10,000 observations, they give substantially divergent coefficient estimates.
- **b** The logit model assumes that errors are distributed according to the Gumbel distribution, whereas the probit model assumes that errors are normally distributed.
- **c** The logit model only gives predictions of probabilities that are between 0 and 1, whereas the probit model predicts probabilities outside of this range.
- **d** none of the above

9 What is the assumption we make regarding the distribution of errors in the context of Multinomial Logistic (MNL) regression, and why is it important?

- **a** We assume that all errors are normally distributed; only this distribution yields an actual formula for the probability of making any of the individual discrete choices under investigation.
- **b** We assume that all errors are normally distributed; only this distribution allows us to accurately approximate the probability of making any of the individual discrete choices under investigation.
- **c** We assume that all errors are Gumbel-distributed; only this distribution yields an actual formula for the probability of making any of the individual discrete choices under investigation.

- **d** We assume that all errors are Gumbel-distributed; only this distribution allows us to accurately approximate the probability of making any of the individual discrete choices under investigation.

10 What is the appropriate way to incorporate nominal independent variables into a regression?

- **a** Give them numerical values: If, for example, we had a nominal variable with three possible values, we would transform those values into numbers (say, as 1, 2, and 3) and regress on these numerical equivalents.
- **b** You cannot incorporate nominal independent variables into regression analysis.
- **c** Because you cannot directly observe consumer utility as it pertains to nominal variables' different values, you approximate that utility by developing a comprehensive set of "deterministic" traits (such as marketing mix variables) and use them to generate the associated probabilities.
- **d** For n values of the nominal variable, you incorporate $k - 1$ binary "dummy variables."

Web Exercise

Log in to the Online Edition of your textbook at www.atomicdog.com to participate in this Web Exercise, which can be found in your Online Study Guide for this chapter.

Further Reading

Aczel, Amir D., *Complete Business Statistics*, 5th edition. 2002. Hillsdale, NJ: McGraw-Hill/Irwin.

Stockburger, David, *Introductory Statistics: Concepts, Models and Applications*, Cincinnati, OH: Atomic Dog/Thomson Custom Solutions. 2001.

Hyperstat Online: davidmlane.com/hyperstat/.

Lane, David, *Hyperstat*, Cincinnati, OH: Atomic Dog/Thomson Custom Solutions. 2002.

Hosmer, David W. Jr., and Stanley Lemeshow, *Applied Logistic Regression*, New York, NY: Wiley-Interscience. 2000.

Cohen, Jacob, Patricia Cohen, Stephen G. West, and Leona S. Aiken, *Applied Multiple Regression/Correlation Analysis for the Behavioral Sciences*, 3rd Edition. Hillsdale, NJ: Lawrence Erlbaum Associates. (2002).

Note

1 Guadagni, Peter M., and John D.C. Little (1983), "A Logit Model of Brand Choice Calibrated on Scanner Data," *Marketing Science*, 2, 203–23.

CHAPTER ELEVEN
THE MAJOR MULTIVARIATE METHODS OF MARKETING RESEARCH

"Statistical models for data are never true. The question whether a model is true is irrelevant. A more appropriate question is whether we obtain the correct scientific conclusion if we pretend that the process under study behaves according to a particular statistical model."

SCOTT ZEGER, "STATISTICAL REASONING IN EPIDEMIOLOGY"

Previous chapters have examined analytic techniques as they relate to univariate and bivariate situations, as well as the most powerful and versatile method in all of data analysis: multiple linear regression. Having mastered regression, budding researchers often feel that they are ready to take on any sort of data. Although linear regression is powerful, it is not all-powerful, and there are indeed some critical marketing applications for which specialized methods have been developed. This chapter surveys those methods: why they are important, what they tell the researcher, what sort of data requirements are involved, and how, exactly, one can go about actually using them in real marketing research.

11.1 The Uses of Multivariate Methods

Over the past decade, marketing researchers have made vastly increased use of multivariate techniques, our main reason for covering them in great depth in this text. There are a number of reasons underlying this trend. First, marketing problems are rarely, if ever, completely described by one or two variables. Sales are related to price, but not *only* to price; consumer satisfaction is driven by dozens, if not hundreds, of factors. To truly understand marketing outcomes—what we observe in the world—we need to consider many "inputs," not just one.

multivariate statistical procedure Any statistical model that helps relate a set of variables to one another. The most common such procedure is multiple regression, in which a single dependent variable is related to a group of other variables.

Second, the dizzying exponential increases in computer speed (often called "Moore's Law") and advances in statistical analysis software have made the solution of **multivariate statistical procedures** relatively quick and painless. Problems that were virtually impossible to solve by human calculation even late in the twentieth century can now be solved in milliseconds by computer, with easily comprehended output and compelling graphics. (Researchers sometimes half-jokingly lament this trend, pointing out that one no longer needs to *think* before running a statistical analysis. Of course, none of these lamenting statisticians would give up their computers for anything.)

Third, improved understanding of statistical concepts among marketing researchers and managers, who have been formally trained in marketing, operations research, and data analysis, has increased the likelihood of multivariate procedures being used to make real-world decisions.

Successful marketing researchers have adopted some common approaches to applying multivariate data analysis methods. They rarely perform multivariate analysis until they have examined their data closely, variable by variable, and further examined any hypotheses arising among pairs of those variables through cross-tabulation and perhaps simple regression, if appropriate. This keeps researchers "close to the data" and helps avoid obvious misinterpretations of multivariate results—the sort of misinterpretation that can arise from subtle errors in invoking what are complex techniques. One should always remember that it is far easier to get a spectacularly wrong answer with a sophisticated statistical technique than with a simple one; for the latter, one can at least perform "reality checks."

If the multivariate results disagree with those stemming from simple analyses, researchers then generally go back to the drawing board and start asking basic questions about the correctness of their approach. Analyses in which sophisticated techniques correctly contradict results of simpler analyses are exceedingly rare.

Researchers rely heavily on in-house statistical experts to help them interpret output and communicate complex findings in plain managerial language to management, sponsors, and other nonstatisticians, who often have no idea what correlation is, let alone multiple regression or Factor analysis (the technique illustrated in *Marketing Research Focus 11.1*).

Finally, researchers take the time to educate themselves fully about the ins and outs of standard data analysis methodologies. Even after using a technique for decades, there are always subtleties than can surprise us. Statistics, despite being a theoretical subject with high standards of rigor, is not a "spectator sport": one must use it hands-on to truly appreciate its power and utility.

11.1a Interdependence vs. Dependence Methods

dependence methods Any statistical technique that attempts to relate one set of values (the dependent variables) to another set of values (the independent variables).

We begin by distinguishing multivariate procedures that do not specify a dependent variable from those that do. In **dependence methods**, one or more variables are designated as being predicted by (dependent on) a set of independent variables. These variables have a privileged status in our analysis: we wish to

Marketing Research Focus 11.1

Factor Analysis of Banking Competition Reveals Underlying Dimensions of Competitive Success

A classic study examined the factors that contribute to the marketing strategy success of banks. The study was conducted in 50 standard metropolitan statistical areas (MSAs) in seven states, and collected data on 27 attributes (listed on the left side of Table 11.1) that were believed to define the domain of competitive activity among banks. The researchers were interested in determining the underlying strategic thrusts that defined the competition among these banks. Using the method of Factor analysis, they analyzed the responses on the 27 attributes for all banks in the sample to determine these underlying competitive dimensions. The following table shows the relationship between the attributes and the underlying competitive factors that were found. The larger (further from zero) the numeric value, the stronger the relationship. The attributes have been grouped to show those attributes that are highly related to the same factor.

Factor Analysis of Competitive Banking Attributes

	Factor					
Marketing activities	1	2	3	4	5	6
TV advertising expenditures	0.06	−0.02	0.81	0.01	0.08	0.16
Radio advertising expenditures	−0.04	0.01	0.80	−0.11	0.14	−0.09
Newspaper advertising expenditures	0.09	0.19	0.75	0.07	0.06	0.04
Expenditures on all ad media	0.09	0.09	0.93	0.06	0.04	−0.02
Contact with legislators	0.14	0.17	0.10	0.01	0.81	0.15
Contact with regulatory officials	0.13	0.03	0.14	0.07	0.68	0.17
Contact with city council members	0.13	−0.11	0.09	0.03	0.52	0.23
Survey of current customers	0.58	0.01	0.04	0.15	0.16	0.25
Focus groups with current customers	0.68	0.10	−0.01	0.09	−0.13	−0.02
Shopping competing firms for information	0.76	0.11	0.08	0.06	−0.13	−0.02
Surveying competitors' customers	0.60	0.14	0.17	0.03	0.25	0.18
Collecting traffic counts at competitor or at other locations	0.78	0.03	0.03	0.01	−0.09	−0.01
Focus groups with competitors' customers	0.73	0.09	−0.04	0.02	0.29	0.03
Re-evaluating service charges	0.02	0.15	0.04	−0.03	0.01	0.81
Reevaluating charges for extra services	0.03	0.05	−0.03	0.01	0.17	0.80
Gathering information on competitors' prices	0.19	0.21	0.06	0.04	0.18	0.50
Personality tests conducted on tellers	0.10	0.83	0.01	0.15	0.01	0.09
Aptitude tests conducted on tellers	0.04	0.80	0.09	0.06	0.01	0.05
Personality tests conducted on officers	0.11	0.85	0.06	0.05	−0.06	0.14
Aptitude tests conducted on officers	0.21	0.82	0.09	0.06	0.01	0.05
Training, including product information	0.09	0.10	−0.05	0.56	−0.15	0.05
Training in communication techniques	0.37	0.09	−0.04	0.51	−0.20	0.21
Training in company mission	0.18	0.04	−0.01	0.50	−0.25	0.23
Training to handle complaints	0.21	−0.05	0.07	0.45	−0.04	0.31
Providing officers with customer deposit history	−0.19	0.09	0.09	0.59	0.23	−0.21
Providing officers with customer business profile	−0.04	0.10	−0.04	0.61	0.10	−0.04
Providing officers with customer services profile	0.03	0.08	0.05	0.58	0.23	−0.15
Percentage variance explained	19.4	10.2	9.2	7.4	6.3	5.1

The study revealed six underlying dimensions of competition:

- Factor 1. Market scanning—the use of marketing research to stay close to the customer
- Factor 2. Screening of customer-contact employees for their fit with the job requirements
- Factor 3. Advertising activity
- Factor 4. The provision of support for customer-contact personnel
- Factor 5. Contact with political groups
- Factor 6. Activity related to pricing

This information proved very useful in planning marketing strategy for various types of banks. For example, the Factor explaining the most variation, nearly 20 percent, was the use of marketing research to "stay close to the customer," highlighting the importance of ongoing information-gathering in maintaining competitiveness. Somewhat surprisingly, of the six identified Factors, the one explaining the least variation was "activity related to pricing," tentatively suggesting a less-prominent role than pricing is ordinarily presumed to have.

Sources: McKee, Daryl O., P. Rajan Varadarajan, and William M. Pride (1989), "Strategic Adaptability and Firm Performance: A Market-Contingent Perspective," *Journal of Marketing,* 53, 21–35.
Reinartz, Werner, Manfred Krafft, and Wayne D. Hoyer (2004), "The Customer Relationship Management Process: Its Measurement and Impact on Performance," *Journal of Marketing Research*, 41(3), 293–305.

interdependence methods
Any statistical method whose goal is to *interrelate* a group of variables, without attempting to use them to make predictions about another set of variables.

understand them *in terms of* other variables. Regression, in its many forms, is an example of this type of analysis because we always have a variable designated at the outset as dependent. For example, conjoint analysis, which depends critically on regression, will try to relate product attributes (independent variables) to consumer choices (dependent variable). In **interdependence methods**, no variable or variables are designated as being predicted by others. It is the *interrelationship* among all the variables taken together that interests the researcher. Factor analysis, cluster analysis, and multidimensional scaling are examples of this type of procedure.

We have already covered regression in great detail, and note in passing that many, if not all, the methods we will soon present rely on regression in some way or another. Often, this is "hidden" in the algorithms used by the computer to perform a particular analysis, but the language, assumptions, and power of regression will all surface during our presentation. To get the most out of this chapter, readers should feel relatively comfortable with the terminology and interpretation of (linear) multiple regression, as presented in Chapter 10.

Throughout this chapter, we will be illustrating the use of the main multivariate methods of marketing research in great detail, so that you can understand their subtleties, in addition to using them yourself "out of the box." To do so, we have deliberately chosen smaller, unusually clear problems, with a modest number of variables, cases, or resulting groups. These methods scale up well to the problems faced by real firms with enormous databases of product, customers, and measured quantities. In all cases, the steps in using each method will be identical for small and large datasets, the only difference being the transparency of presenting the results.

11.1b A Word about Factor and Cluster Analyses

Factor analysis and cluster analysis are, as we shall see, both powerful methods to "compress" data in such a way that one gets a sense of its underlying structure. They are sometimes classified as "data reduction methods" because they take a great deal of data and summarize them with a much smaller set of quantities that conveys pretty much everything of interest that is going on. Our experience is that students, and even professional researchers, often confuse the two methods of analysis. This is unfortunate because they are quite distinct in both concept and operation and can be easily distinguished. In a nutshell—as a prelude to a full, rigorous development—here is what each does:

Factor analysis tells us:

> **Which VARIABLES are similar to one another and how they should be "grouped"** (approximately, in a sense to made clear later)

Cluster analysis tells us:

> **Which CASES or PEOPLE or OBJECTS are similar and how they should be "grouped" (exactly)**

This is all much clearer relative to some actual data and can be handily summarized in a spreadsheet mock-up. Here, we look at some hypothetical data for 20 students (our people, or "cases") who took 10 different exams (the "Variables"), with scores as listed below. Note that our Variables run across the top, and cases are along the side (see Figure 11.1).

The researcher would have to come to terms with 200 quantities here: the scores for 20 students on 10 different exams. This is difficult; humans cannot simply look at that much data and figure out what is going on. A researcher might question whether there is some natural way to *group* the exams, perhaps by subject, and students, perhaps by performance on those subjects. It would be far simpler to say, "There were 10 exams, but only a few *types* of exams." In fact, looking at the exams in the list, we might notice that the first four deal with, broadly speaking, "science," the next four with "humanities or languages," and the last two with "engineering." But it is hardly clear that this is the best way to group the exams *based on the students' pattern of scores*. In a very real sense, what Factor and Cluster analysis will do is to group, respectively, the exams and the students to dramatically reduce our explanatory burden. If we ran both analyses, we would obtain answers that looked something like this (note that we have not run these analyses on the earlier data; full examples will appear later in this chapter, and this example is merely illustrative):

Factor analysis says the following is a good grouping for our VARIABLES (the exams):

- FACTOR 1: Chemistry, Biology, Physics, Computer Science, Linguistics
- FACTOR 2: Literature, Psychology, History
- FACTOR 3: Geology, Electrical Engineering

Cluster analysis says the following is a good grouping for our CASES (the students and their scores):

- CLUSTER 1: Persons 2, 5, 6, 8, 11, 15, 19, 20
- CLUSTER 2: Persons 1, 3, 12, 14, 17
- CLUSTER 3: Persons 4, 10, 13, 16
- CLUSTER 4: Persons 7, 9, 18

Notice, then, that we have *reduced* our explanatory burden from 200 pieces of data down to 12: three "Factors" (that account for the original 10 Variables) and four "Clusters" (that account for the original 20 students). We could then say that there were three *types* of exams and four *types* of student score patterns, and these would be far easier to describe. In the rest of this chapter, we will explore both Factor and Cluster analyses, as well as related methods, to understand how to get a handle on what marketing research data are really telling us. Throughout, we will stress how and why the methods work, how to use them, and how to go about interpreting what a statistical analysis package might tell us.

Figure 11.1 Typical Uses of Factor and Cluster Analysis

Variables ----- Variables ----- Variables ----- Variables ----- Variables

CASES or PEOPLE

	Exam 1 Chemistry	Exam 2 Biology	Exam 3 Physics	Exam 4 Geology	Exam 5 Literature	Exam 6 Psych.	Exam 7 Linguistics	Exam 8 History	Exam 9 Elect Eng.	Exam 10 Comp. Sci.
Person 1	75	87	45	61	24	49	30	53	42	56
Person 2	75	88	49	68	24	60	30	53	42	63
Person 3	77	88	50	68	32	63	32	54	48	63
Person 4	77	89	51	74				55	48	69
Person 5	86	91	51	76				57	49	69
Person 6	87	93	53	76				62	49	69
Person 7	89			77				66	49	70
Person 8	90			78				74	52	71
Person 9	90			79	39	72	57	77	54	72
Person 10	92			85	40	72	57	77	61	78
Person 11				89	40	76	57	77	61	82
Person 12	93			92	43	83	58	77	68	86
Person 13	94			92	43	85	58	78	73	86
Person 14	94			92	43	85	59	78	73	86
Person 15	94			92	46	85	59	80	73	87
Person 16	94	99	76	92	46	85	61	83	73	87
Person 17	95	100	79	93	55	86	64	85	73	88
Person 18	97	100	80	93	55	86	64	90	74	91
Person 19	98	100	80	93	62	87	69	91	75	93
Person 20	98	100	80	93	63	90	74	91	77	95

FACTOR acts on these

CLUSTER acts on these

11.2 Factor Analysis

Suppose that someone wished to gauge your preferences for different kinds of ethnic cuisine, and you agreed to answer a short survey on that topic. All of the questions consisted of names of dishes, and you merely had to indicate how much you liked them on a 1–7 Likert-type scale, from "strongly dislike" through "neither like nor dislike" to "strongly like." The list of items started off like so:

1. "Peking Duck"
2. "Huevos Rancheros"
3. "Frijoles Negros"
4. "Arroz Con Pollo"
5. "Chiles Rellenos"
6. "Pollo Asado"

As the list is read to you, it dawns on you that, except for the first dish, which is of Chinese origin, everything else is Mexican, 50 such dishes in fact. When the survey is over, the researcher thanks you, and informs you that the data will help the project team to understand preferences among different kinds of ethnic cuisine.

Although each of the dishes on the list is certainly relevant, and many, many dishes appeared in the course of the survey, there are two glaring problems with the study as a whole:

1. Only two cuisines, Chinese and Mexican, appear at all; and
2. One of those two cuisines, Mexican, is grossly overrepresented.

You would want to say to the researcher something like, "You are *wasting* a lot of questions! You could just have asked how I liked Chinese cuisine and Mexican cuisine, instead of including 50 Mexican dishes about which I gave very similar answers. And there are so many other sorts of cuisine you did not ask about at all." That is, what the researcher may have thought to be a well-balanced, comprehensive survey instrument was, in fact, dramatically over-emphasizing some areas (Mexican cuisine), under-emphasizing others (Chinese cuisine), and leaving out many entirely.

This example is, of course, whimsical, but the problem it illustrates is all too real. Researchers are not omniscient, and they cannot come up with an ideal set of questions that each measure some perfectly independent dimension of the situation of interest. Instead, answers to the questions in a study are extremely likely to display substantial *redundancy*. And worse: some areas will be more redundant than others, and we will not even know this until our data are all collected and we discover that we have asked "one question many times," just with subtle variations. Although redundancy is not always bad—it helps gauge whether a respondent's answers are stable and reliable—a great deal of redundancy is almost always wasteful. And, when some areas, such as appreciation for Mexican cuisine, are represented fifty-fold over other areas of the study, we are likely to obtain a skewed and ultimately misleading portrait of what we wanted to understand in the first place.

Factor analysis
A form of statistical *data reduction,* aimed at examining the interrelationships between a group of variables and determining their underlying structure. Highly correlated variables will produce few underlying factors; nearly independent variables will produce many factors.

Statisticians developed **Factor analysis** to address these sorts of problems. It is one of the most powerful methods in all of statistical analysis, and, unlike many other such methods, it really has no downsides: Factor analysis clarifies the underlying structure of multivariate data in a way that makes it a perfect complement to regression analysis. It will, in fact, take a large number of intercorrelated Variables (which would not be well suited to regression) and "extract" from them a smaller number of perfectly uncorrelated **Factors**. These Factors look very much like the Variables we started with, except there are fewer of them, and, because they are uncorrelated, they can be excellent inputs (so-called "independent variables") into a regression analysis.

Factors
A set of quantities extracted by Factor analysis, meant to summarize and stand in for a set of input variables. Factors explain as much variance as possible in the original variables and are (typically) uncorrelated with one another.

One other thing Factor analysis will do for us is to help *identify the underlying constructs* in a group of Variables. This sounds forbidding, but it is not. In our earlier cuisine example, the "underlying constructs" might be "appreciation of Chinese cuisine" and "appreciation of Mexican cuisine." Factor analysis would say to us, in effect, "You asked 51 questions overall, but you only have *two* real dimensions underlying all of them." It would tell us, therefore, that we had been highly redundant, and, as we shall see, it will also indicate which questions were behind that redundancy, thereby offering a way to reduce or eliminate it. (This little example assumes, of course, that there are not vast differences in the Mexican dishes, and that some of them are not closer to the Chinese dish than to one another; both of these are possible in practice.)

Let us consider a more realistic example to get a sense of how Factor analysis could help in a real research project. Suppose that we ask a group of respondents a set of health-related questions, on a 7-point Agree–Disagree scale. (The scale itself is not important, so long as we can treat it as close to interval-scaled.)

- I frequently have trouble catching my breath.
- I often get tired from simple physical activities.
- Sometimes my joints ache seriously enough that I have to slow down.
- I cannot play sports as vigorously as I once did.
- I have trouble keeping up with my children and/or younger people.
- I'm not as vigorous as I once was.
- My heart sometimes beats quickly enough to worry me.
- Walking too quickly can really "wind me."
- I sometimes experience headaches or dizziness after exerting myself.

These statements are almost certain to yield *highly correlated* answers. After all, they all deal with the broad topic of health. But, is "health" really just one thing? Is there really more than one identifiable sort of health? How can we go about finding out? One reasonable way to approach these issues is to ask a single question: "Which of these questions *aligns* with which types of health?" If we did run a Factor analysis, we might find that three types of health are in fact represented by the sample responses to these nine questions:

- Respiratory health
- Cardiovascular health
- Skeletal/osteopathic health

That is, our nine questions were not only not independent of one another, but they really only "did the work" of three questions, in terms of the number of underlying constructs they addressed. But Factor analysis does more than this. It will also *categorize* the statements, for example:

Respiratory Health:

- I frequently have trouble catching my breath.
- I cannot play sports as vigorously as I once did.
- I have trouble keeping up with my children and/or younger people.
- I often get tired from simple physical activities.
- Walking too quickly can really "wind me."
- I'm not as vigorous as I once was.

Cardiovascular Health:

- My heart sometimes beats quickly enough to worry me.
- I sometimes experience headaches or dizziness after exerting myself.

Skeletal/Osteopathic Health:

- Sometimes my joints ache seriously enough that I have to slow down.

We would learn that, perhaps without planning to (or hoping for the opposite), we had managed to ask many questions about respiratory health, two about cardiovascular health, and just one about osteopathic health, so that the first was substantially overrepresented, relative to the last. If it were our goal to have each of the questions measure something distinct, we failed quite spectacularly. And we would have failed to be *equally* redundant, having three questions address each of the three revealed dimensions of health. Factor analysis can help us avoid precisely these sorts of errors.

Before going through a full-fledged example of how Factor analysis does its magic, it is helpful to introduce several metaphors and visual guides that will prove useful proxies for the more mathematical and data-based illustrations later on.

Suppose we asked a child to draw a picture of a plate or a platter. It may look something like the illustration shown in Figure 11.2.

In reality, all solid objects are three-dimensional, so we might wonder why the child's drawing depicts only two of those dimensions (holding aside issues of drawing skill). In fact, what the child's

Figure 11.2 How a Three-Dimensional Object Might Be Captured in Two Dimensions

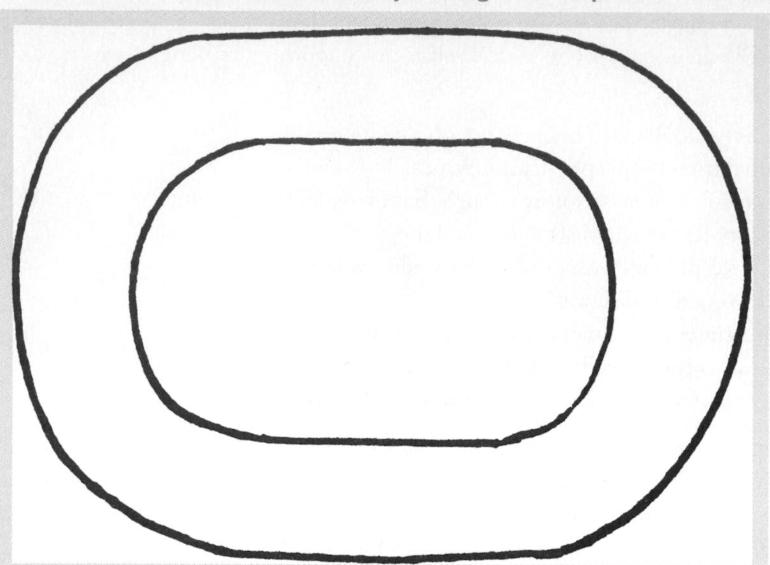

drawing has done is quite ingenious: it implicitly makes the statement, "If you have to choose the two dimensions that 'explain' the platter best, here they are, in order, and I've chosen to ignore one completely." The ignored dimension would be depth because the platter is far shallower than it is in length (the most important, or *principal*, direction) and width. In statistical language, once we have accounted for the variation explained by the platter's length and width, there really is very little left to explain. In nonstatistical language that anyone can understand: the platter is very thin and essentially flat.

This fact about platters is only obvious if we record its dimensions as, say, 2 feet in length, 1 foot in width, and 2 inches (1/6 of a foot) in depth. But data do not present themselves to us in that way. Imagine that the platter were *rotated* in space so that it looked like the illustration shown in Figure 11.3.

If we were asked to describe the platter *in that orientation*, we might say it would need to fit in a box 1¾ feet long, 1¼ feet wide, and ¾ feet deep. That is, it would *not* appear flat or two-dimensional in that orientation. And here is the point: we could only discern the *true dimensionality* of our data (platter) by

Figure 11.3 A Three-Dimensional Object Extending in Up-Down, Left-Right, and In-Out Directions

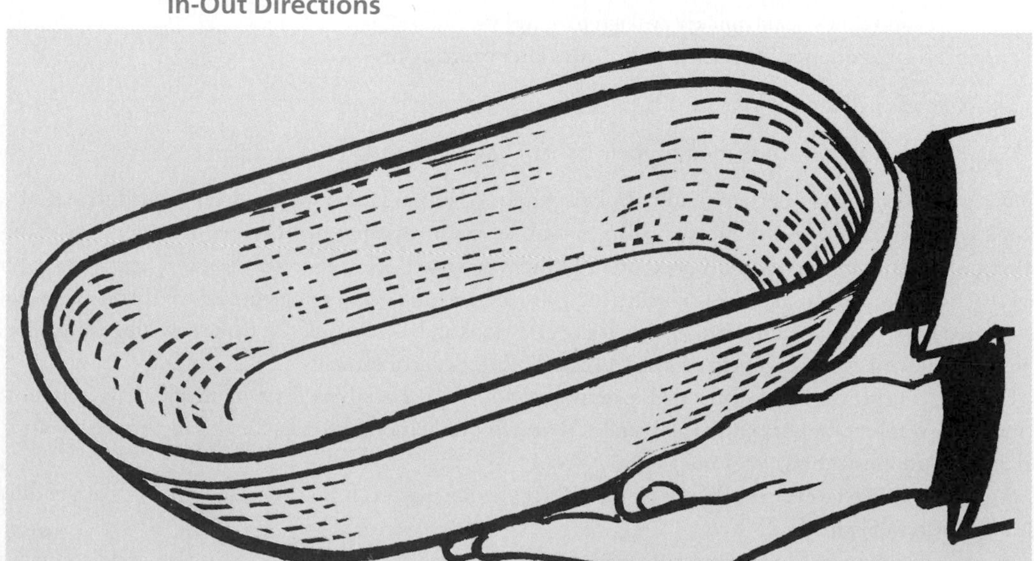

doing two things: rotating it appropriately, and deciding that one (or more) of the dimensions was dramatically less important than the others. As we will see, this is precisely what Factor analysis does. And it will do so in such a way that the new, rotated, surviving dimensions are *uncorrelated* with one another, a major benefit in statistical analysis.

11.2a Factor Analysis: What It Is, and What It Does

Factor analysis is a procedure that takes a large number of Variables and searches to see whether they have a small number of Factors in common that account for the many correlations among the Variables. For example, we might attribute the high association between grades in business administration courses (our Variables) to the Factors of general ability and diligent study; or we might attribute the association between various metrics of firm performance (Variables) to the Factors of quality of a firm's technology, remuneration of its workforce, and overall marketing effort. *Marketing Research Focus 11.1* on bank marketing strategy illustrates the power of Factor analysis in finding underlying dimensions.

Factor analysis has a number of possible applications in marketing research and, indeed, throughout social science. These include data reduction, structure identification, scaling, and data transformation. Let us take a brief look at each of these.

- *Data Reduction.* Factor analysis can be used for *reducing* a mass of data to a manageable level. For example, the researcher may have collected data on 50 attributes of a product, without a great deal of forethought as to whether this was the "optimal" information to collect. The analysis and understanding of these data may be aided by reducing the attributes (Variables) to a far smaller number of Factors that *underlie* the 50 attributes. These factors may then be used in further analysis in place of the original attributes.
- *Structure Identification.* Factor analysis can be used to discover the basic structure underlying a set of measures. For example, the previous 50 attributes (Variables) may reduce to two Factors identified by the researcher as (1) sweetness/bitterness and (2) degree of freshness. For a separate project, the researcher may wish to include additional Factors, as they are needed. In real data, it is almost always the case that at least some of the Variables collected are redundant, in the sense that they can be predicted by or reconstructed from other Variables. Factor analysis then discerns the underlying structure of this redundancy by representing the (many) original Variables in terms of the (far fewer) underlying Factors.
- *Scaling.* A researcher may wish to develop a scale on which respondents can be compared. A problem in developing any scale is in weighting the Variables being combined to form the scale, a **weighted sum**. It turns out that Factor analysis automatically solves this problem, giving the optimal weights in the sum in terms of so-called "**Factor loadings**." The higher a Variable's loading, the more important it is in understanding that particular Factor.
- *Data Transformation.* Many predictive techniques in statistics work far better when the "independent" Variables used for prediction are truly independent in the statistical sense; that is, they are uncorrelated. For instance, the coefficients in multiple regression measure the effects of unit changes in a Variable assuming *all other Variables remain constant.* Factor analysis can be used to identify and to even produce covariates that are exactly uncorrelated, and therefore make perfect inputs for dependence methods and other predictive techniques.

weighted sum or weighted average
Multiplying a set of quantities by positive numerical weights, to emphasize some over others, yields a weighted *sum;* dividing by the sum of those weights yields a weighted *average.*

Factor loadings
How well each variable in Factor analysis explains a particular Factor. A loading near −1 or 1 means the variable "loads high" on that factor and should be used to help explain its meaning; a value near 0 indicates the opposite.

The applications of Factor analysis in marketing research have been remarkably broad. All of the following application areas have made steady use of Factor analysis for decades: the development of personality scales, market segments based on psychographic data, the identification of critical product attributes, similarities among products and lines, among many others. The key issue in each of these applications is accounting for correlations among Variables and extracting their essence in the form of uncorrelated, underlying Factors.

11.2b Steps in Factor Analysis

There are essentially three steps in a Factor analysis solution. The first is to develop a set of *correlations* between all combinations of the Variables of interest. Because we are using correlations, we must be sure that it is reasonable to treat the input Variables as interval-scaled. The second step is to *extract* a set of initial Factors from the correlation matrix developed in the first step. The third step is to *rotate* the initial Factors to find a final solution. The concept of rotation will be discussed extensively later in the chapter. Before working through a real example step by step in great detail, let us examine the concepts of extraction and rotation more thoroughly, and with more mathematical detail than we have thus far; we will revisit them in many guises in our application.

Factor extraction
In Factor analysis, the process by which successive Factors are produced (automatically) by the computer.

Factor Extraction

The object of extraction is to find a set of Factors that are *linear combinations* of the Variables in the correlation matrix. To illustrate, if the Variables X_1, X_2, and X_3 were highly correlated with one another, they could be combined to form a single Factor (if they are perfectly correlated, they already *are* one Factor because they are statistically identical). A linear combination can be defined as follows:

$$z = b_1X_1 + b_2X_2 + \cdots + b_mX_m$$

principal components methodology
A type of Factor analysis procedure, typically the initial one performed, in which each successive Factor is the best that can be extracted, but without regard to how well the Factors correlate with the input variables. See *varimax rotation*.

Here, z is the linear combination, and it is called a *principal component* or a *principal factor*. The **principal components methodology** determines values for $\{b_1, b_2, \ldots, b_m\}$ in the previous equation that explain as much variance in the correlation matrix as possible. This is called the first principal factor, and it is the "best" Factor that can be extracted. The variance it explains is then mathematically subtracted from the original input Variables, after which a second Factor is extracted, then a third, and so on. We can always extract as many Factors as there are original Variables, but there is rarely any point to doing so; after the first few Factors, there is typically a precipitous decline in the quality of the remaining Factors, as we shall see in our application. It is important to note that, for this procedure, the Factors extracted are *uncorrelated* with one another. The Factors are therefore said to be **orthogonal**.

orthogonal
Any quantities that are uncorrelated, and therefore perpendicular to one another when placed in the appropriate multidimensional space. Often used in Factor analysis when factors are uncorrelated with one another, and also in experiments (e.g., conjoint analysis) that use orthogonal designs.

Factor Rotation

Because these initial Factors are usually very difficult to interpret, the initial set of extracted Factors are *rotated* in a way that helps the researcher interpret them. There are two broad classes of rotation: (1) *orthogonal rotation*, which preserves the Factors as uncorrelated with one another, and (2) *oblique rotation*, which allows the Factors to become correlated with one another. The basic idea of rotation is to yield Factors that each have some Variables that correlate well and some that correlate poorly. This avoids the problem of having our Factors correlate at best modestly with our original Variables, thus making them impossible to interpret. We will elaborate on these important concepts in our application, to which we turn next.

Factor rotation
In Factor analysis, the Factors are often rotated to aid in interpretation. See *rotated factor pattern* and *varimax rotation*.

11.2c Factor Analysis: Application and Interpretation

Here, we undertake a full-scale Factor analysis of some real data, collected by an auto manufacturer to help understand what was most important to its customers. The researcher's main goal was to try to relate psychographics, in the form of a group of "opinions, attitudes, and lifestyle" questions, to over a dozen desired attributes in car purchases, including appearance, price, prestige, safety, roominess, warranty, and others. Let us first look at the sort of questions that were used to gauge psychographics, which will be the main purpose of our Factor analysis; later, we will relate the Factors stemming from the analysis to car attributes.

The researchers asked $n = 132$ respondents a total of 35 questions based on a 1–6 agree/disagree scale. The directions were given as follows:

Listed below are a number of statements about your activities, interests, and opinions. For each statement, we would like to know whether *you personally* agree or disagree with this statement. There are no right and wrong answers, and you should reply as you see fit. After each statement, select a response on a scale of 1 to 6: the higher the number, the more you tend to agree with the statement; the lower the number, the more you tend to disagree with the statement. The numbers themselves may be described as follows:

1. I strongly disagree with the statement.
2. I moderately disagree with the statement.
3. I slightly disagree with the statement.
4. I slightly agree with the statement.
5. I moderately agree with the statement.
6. I strongly agree with the statement.

You may think many items are similar. Actually, no two items are exactly alike, so be sure to circle the most appropriate response for each statement.

01 We have more to spend on extras than most of our neighbors do.
02 Everything is changing too fast today.
03 Information from advertising helps me make better buying decisions.
04 I have more self-confidence than most of my friends.
05 TV commercials place too much emphasis on sex.
06 I have somewhat old-fashioned tastes and desires.
07 I do not like situations that are uncertain.
08 I wish I could leave my present life and do something entirely different.
09 I like my livingroom to look casual rather than formal.
10 When making an investment, maximum safety is more important than high interest rates.
11 We will probably move at least once in the next 5 years.
12 Our whole family usually eats one meal together daily.
13 I like to visit places that are totally different from my home.
14 Americans should always try to buy American products.
15 I admire a successful businessman more than I admire a successful artist or writer.
16 I do not believe a company's ad when it claims test results show its product to be better than competitive products.
17 I stick to my budget.
18 My personal associations are mostly with people like me.
19 I am more independent than most people.
20 I like to pay cash for everything I buy.
21 I am in favor of legalized abortions.
22 I consult *Consumer Reports* or similar publications before making a major purchase.
23 My friends and neighbors often come to me for advice about products and brands.
24 Magazines are more interesting than television.
25 I enjoy parties, games, shows, anything for fun.
26 I do not like to take chances.
27 I am very satisfied with the way things are going in my life these days.
28 I spend a lot of money for fashionable clothes.
29 The quality of a product is far more important than the price.
30 I would be content to live in the same town the rest of my life.
31 When making important family decisions, consideration of the children should come first.
32 I spend a lot of time visiting friends.
33 The government should restrict imports of products from Japan.
34 I often seek out the advice of my friends regarding brands and products.
35 Generally, manufacturers' warranties are not worth the paper they are printed on.

There are several things to note about these questions, scales, and the nature of the application:

- First, we have a collection of 35 Variables, and, as the researchers claimed in their directions, many of them may appear similar. For all we know, each respondent may choose the same answer for each of them, in which case we get only one piece of information per respondent. That would mean that we had been extremely redundant: each question yields the same information as all the others. This is unlikely to be the case here, but it is also unlikely that each question will yield information *independent of* (that is, uncorrelated with) all the others. The very purpose of Factor analysis will be to gauge just how much redundancy there is and to assess which questions best align with the others; that is, to group them.
- Second, each question is collected on a 1–6 scale. This scale is a Likert scale, and the phrasing of the responses should make it clear that they are *symmetric* about some middle point (which is not itself on the scale, as there is no choice claiming, "I neither agree nor disagree"; some researchers prefer this method, whereas others prefer to offer a clear midpoint). But there is no guarantee that the "distance" between 1 and 2 is the same as between, say, 3 and 4; it is hard to argue that we can know *in advance*

that the scale has the "equal interval" property. Even though this is so, we will proceed with Factor analysis, which presumes that the data are interval-scaled because such assumptions are sometimes unavoidable, and there is no test for whether the data are truly interval.

- Finally, each of these questions is of the "agree–disagree" type, which means that they are truly suited to be measured on a scale. This would *not* be the case if we were asking about behavior ("Did you do this?"), frequency ("How often did you do this?"), or many demographic categories (e.g., gender). Factor analysis does *not* presume that data are about attitudes or opinions—it is very general, and it can be applied to any source of presumably interval-scaled data—but we must take care to avoid data types that are clearly inappropriate.

11.2d Principal Components Method

We must first tell the statistical program how to proceed, and we do this by specifying the principal components method for the initial Factor analysis. A principal components analysis is ordinarily the first one performed by researchers. What it does is look for the single best "Factor" to explain *all the Variables* in the data set, then it constructs a second Factor that explains as much as what is left over as possible, and then a third, and so on. In this way, each Factor accounts for as much of the remaining variation as possible in the original set of (here, 35 in total) Variables.

There are several problems, however, with principal components. One is that the first Factor can so a superb job, "stealing" all the variance, while the subsequent Factors look impoverished by comparison; we will see evidence of this later on in our output. But a much greater problem in actual applications is that no attempt is made to make sure that the Factors *correlate* very well (i.e., near -1 or 1) with some of the Variables and not so well (i.e., near 0) with others, a necessary trait if the Factors are going to be *interpreted* later on. What we will hope to say is something like, "This Factor helps explain *this set of Variables*"; to do that, we will have to have that Factor correlate very well with those particular Variables, and very little with all the others. Principal components simply will not help with that goal, which has nothing to do with mathematical rigor and everything to do with actually putting the method to use in real problems.

Principal components is, however, a good start, because it unambiguously "extracts"—this is the exact term we will use—the best Factors it can and gives a solid idea of how quickly the Factors "degrade" in respect to the amount of variance they each can explain over and above the others. We will, in fact, see a useful graph of this degradation in Factor quality and use it to judge how many Factors we wish to select.

After running the Factor analysis routine, the computer will tell us something like the following:

$$\text{Eigenvalues of the Correlation Matrix: Total} = 35, \text{ Average} = 1$$

eigenvalues
In Factor analysis, a measure of the relative size of any Factor and the *average* Factor.

Throughout the Factor analysis procedure, reference will be made to **eigenvalues**, a term that sounds more difficult than it is. The previous statement says that the eigenvalues total 35, and that their average value is 1; recall that there are 35 Variables in the data set. A good way to think about this terminology is in relation to a pie that needs to be cut into 35 pieces. If the pie is cut perfectly, each piece is precisely 1/35 of the pie and can be said to have eigenvalue 1; that is, its size is exactly average. However, if the pie is cut imperfectly, some pieces will be larger than average (and have eigenvalue greater than one) and some smaller than average (and have eigenvalue less than one). A piece twice the average size would therefore have eigenvalue 2. The important point is that the average of these eigenvalues would have to be 1; that is, the average size of a piece of pie cannot change just because it is cut unevenly. What an eigenvalue represents in Factor analysis is how much variance a Factor explains relative to how much it would be *expected to explain by chance alone*; that is, on average. Let us look at a "pie chart" depicting this situation (see Figure 11.4).

These two pies are the same size. The only difference between them is that they are cut differently—the second evenly, the first very unevenly. (The slice sizes, in fact, exactly represent the eigenvalues for these data, as we shall see.) Regardless of how each pie is cut, they each still add up to just one pie, and the *average* slice is the same size: you cannot alter the average slice size merely by cutting it up unevenly. In the second pie, each slice has the same eigenvalue: 1. Every slice is average-sized. In the first pie, about 1/3 of the slices seem to be larger than average-sized—these would have eigenvalue greater than 1—and the rest less than 1.

Figure 11.4 Factors vs. Variables: "Equitable" vs. "Inequitable" Distribution of Variance

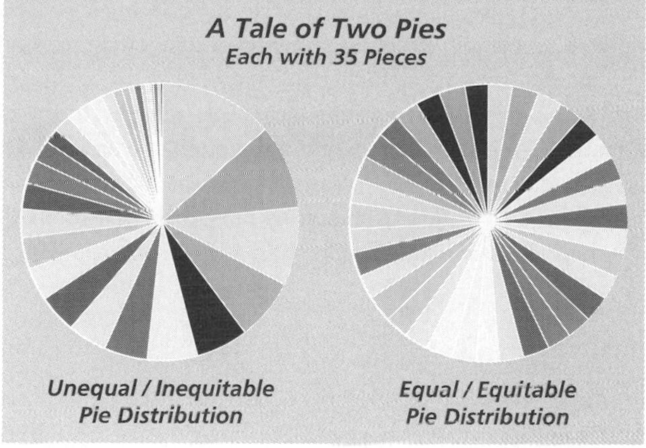

In terms of interpreting a Factor analysis, the typical approach is that Factors with eigenvalues less than 1 should be discarded; those with eigenvalues not too much greater than 1 are suspect; and those with "large" eigenvalues should be retained. The question remains as to how much greater than one an eigenvalue should be for a Factor to be deemed acceptable; the answer is subject to the experimenter's judgment and needs. Let us take a closer look at these eigenvalues in Table 11.1.

The listing in Table 11.1 continues until 35 Factors are extracted—this will capture all the variance because we will have as many Factors as original Variables—but we have truncated the table for brevity. Many computer programs impose something called the "**MinEigen criterion**," which retains *only* those Factors with eigenvalues greater than 1 (i.e., the "bigger than average" Factors). Here, the MinEigen criterion would decide that, because after the 13th Factor all eigenvalues are less than one, we can discard all but these 13 Factors. (We caution all users of Factor analysis that this is absolutely *not* a requirement of the method. If there is a compelling reason to retain more Factors, they can be retained without violating any statistical principle. Like many advanced statistical methods, Factor analysis is there to help researchers understand their data, not dictate to them how much of it they need to discard.)

MinEigen criterion
In Factor analysis, a rule suggesting one discard all factors with eigenvalues less than 1.

The "proportion" line explains how much *incremental* variance is accounted for by each successive Factor, merely the eigenvalue divided by the number of Factors; note that this gets smaller and smaller. The "cumulative" line tells us how much of the *total variance* is explained by *all the Factors taken together* up to the Factor you are considering; as the last Factor is approached, the cumulative value will get very close to 1. The first Factor alone, with an eigenvalue of 4.6237, captures more than 13 percent of the

Table 11.1 Eigenvalues for the First 15 of 35 Total Factors

Factor	1	2	3	4	5
Eigenvalue	4.6237	3.5347	3.2206	2.5224	2.1113
Proportion	0.1321	0.1010	0.0920	0.0721	0.0603
Cumulative	0.1321	0.2331	0.3251	*0.3972*	0.4575
Factor	**6**	**7**	**8**	**9**	**10**
Eigenvalue	2.0601	1.7465	1.6151	1.5247	1.3239
Proportion	0.0589	0.0499	0.0461	0.0436	0.0378
Cumulative	0.5164	0.5663	0.6124	0.6560	0.6938
Factor	**11**	**12**	**13**	**14**	**15**
Eigenvalue	1.2701	1.1380	1.0747	0.9676	0.8781
Proportion	0.0363	0.0325	0.0307	0.0276	0.0251
Cumulative	0.7301	0.7626	*0.7933*	0.8210	0.8460

total variation in the original 35 Variables. One way to think of this is as follows: the first Factor is "doing the work of" about 4.6 of the original Variables. All eigenvalues can be conceptualized this way, and so it makes sense that Factors with eigenvalues less than 1 are "doing less work than they should be," and should probably not be retained unless the researcher has a compelling reason to do so.

Notice here that just four Factors account for about 40 percent of the total variance, whereas 13 Factors account for almost 80 percent (both these values have been italicized in the table). This is remarkable: Factor analysis has managed to retain 80 percent of the original Variables' explanatory power with just about 1/3 the data (13 Factors vs. 35 Variables), and 40 percent with only about 1/10 the data (4 Factors vs. 35 Variables). This is why it is common to refer to Factor analysis as a "data reduction method," although, as we shall see, it does much more than merely compress data.

11.2e "How Many Factors Do I Need?"

An important issue in using Factor analysis concerns how many Factors one "needs." There is never a correct answer to this question that is valid for all situations: researchers need to consider the context of their study. For example, if one is trying to gauge a patient's medical history to perform surgery, one would want to consider many, many "Factors" if that surgery were elective and scheduled. If it were emergency or battlefield surgery, where speed was of utmost importance, just the most important "Factors" would suffice. Generally speaking, in business applications, researchers need to consider whether they are seeking a "quick and dirty" or a truly comprehensive understanding of their data and choose a number of Factors accordingly. We must remember that a main use of Factor analysis is *data reduction*; we want to select a sufficient number of Factors for our application and no more.

One way to select the number of Factors is to consult something called the "Scree plot," depicted in Figure 11.5.

Scree plot
In Factor analysis, an aid to help visualize how quickly the quality of the factors (i.e., their eigenvalues) are degrading. Used to help select a suitable number of Factors.

The Scree plot gives a simple, but fairly crude, visual representation of how quickly the quality of the Factors degrades, in terms of the incremental variance they explain. One looks at such a plot searching for "kinks" or places were there seems to be a sudden change in the slope of the plot, indicating a point at which additional Factors become dramatically less important. In this plot, no such point really stands out, though an argument could be made that big drop-offs occur after the third, fourth, and sixth Factor. (Do verify this on your own!) We will eventually *choose* to use four Factors for our analysis. This does not mean that four Factors is the "correct" number; we could have used 1, 3, 13, or even 35 if we thought those numbers would be more helpful. As mentioned earlier, this choice is partially based on "rational" criteria, such as checking the Scree plot, and partially based on an examination of the situation at hand and how many Factors one feels are needed to capture it.

Figure 11.5 Scree Plot of Eigenvalues for Factors

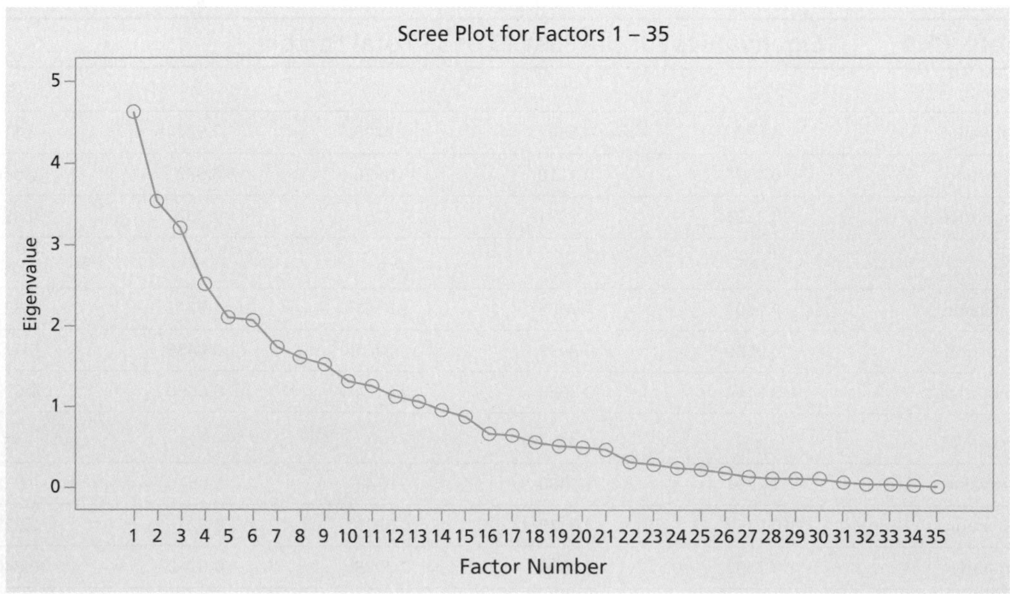

Before discarding all but four Factors, let us look at what the computer tells us about the Factors it extracted for us (remember, there are 35 of them in total, just as there are 35 total Variables). There will be two sets of numbers to reckon with here, *factor loadings* and *communalities* (see Table 11.2).

Table 11.2 is part of a listing that the computer supplies for all 13 Factors with eigenvalues greater than 1 (i.e., that explain more than the average amount of variance in the original 35 Variables); only the sub-table for the first five Factors is reproduced because the full table is very large, 35 by 35 entries. These are called "Factor loadings," and they are nothing more than the *correlations* between the original 35 Variables and each of the 35 Factors derived from them. If a correlation is high (near −1 or 1), it means that the Factor "loads high" on that Variable; that is, that Variable will be used to interpret the Factor later on. For example, note that Factor 1 loads high on Variable 7 ("I do not like situations that are uncertain"), meaning that the first Factor contains some sense of risk-aversion, and this should be part of its explanation when the Factors are studied later for a subjective interpretation of their meaning.

Beneath the Factor loadings (correlations) are listed the "communalities," another fancy term for how well two things correlate; in this case, how well all 13 Factors *taken together* explain *each* of the Variables. The listings under V01 and V02 indicate that the 13 Factors account for about 76 percent of the variance in the first Variable and more than 90 percent of the variance in the second. The total communality estimate of 27.77 should be measured against the best possible total of 35 (the number of original Variables), and it indicates that 27.77/35, or just less than 80 percent, of the total 35-Variable variance is explained by the 13 Factors. (For a bit more detail on how the various quantities in Factor analysis work their magic and are interrelated, see *A Closer Look 11.1: Interesting Details about Factor Loadings, Eigenvalues, and Communalities.*)

communalities
Measures used in Factor analysis to express how much all Factors selected by the analyst, taken together, explain each of the original input variables. A reasonable Factor solution will have communalities that do not vary dramatically across the input variables.

Table 11.2 Factor Loadings and Communalities for Variables 1–35

Factor Loadings for Variables 1–35

	Factor 1	Factor 2	Factor 3	Factor 4	Factor 5	...
V01	−0.2773	0.2910	0.3887	0.2802	0.0612	...
V02	0.4450	−0.2725	0.3406	0.0767	0.1876	...
V03	0.2686	0.3934	−0.0505	−0.0433	0.4205	...
V04	−0.5725	0.2011	0.1090	0.3327	0.0629	...
V05	0.3381	−0.3363	0.2484	0.1210	0.0332	...
V06	0.1971	−0.2674	0.4215	0.0310	0.2812	...
V07	0.6418	0.3735	0.1297	−0.1264	−0.2252	...
V08	−0.3612	0.1535	0.2029	−0.1819	−0.4528	...
.	.	.	.	.	.	
.	.	.	.	.	.	...
.	.	.	.	.	.	
V35	0.1743	−0.0921	−0.4923	0.4726	−0.2015	...

Communalities for Variables 1–35 and 13 Factors

V01	V02	V03	V04	V05	V06	V07	V08	V09	V10
0.7613	0.9035	0.8026	0.7292	0.8951	0.8283	0.8814	0.7409	0.8171	0.6839
V11	V12	V13	V14	V15	V16	V17	V18	V19	V20
0.8632	0.7751	0.7399	0.7812	0.8082	0.7142	0.8360	0.6389	0.7860	0.8903
V21	V22	V23	V24	V25	V26	V27	V28	V29	V30
0.8089	0.8071	0.8492	0.6909	0.8574	0.7351	0.8137	0.7237	0.7629	0.6942
V31	V32	V33	V34	V35					
0.8914	0.7981	0.8284	0.8210	0.8078	Final Total Communality Estimate: 27.77				

A Closer Look 11.1

Interesting Details about Factor Loadings, Eigenvalues, and Communalities

Statistics is full of sums-of-squares, and Factor analysis is no exception. The loadings are really just correlations between Variables and Factors, but they have another property that arises when we square them and add them up. When we perform this operation for a particular Factor, by summing its squared loadings on all Variables, we obtain the *eigenvalue* for that Factor. When we do this for all a Variable's loadings, summing the squared loadings across *the set of Factors in our solution*, we obtain the *communality* for that Variable (when we sum a Variable's squared loadings across *all* Factors, we obtain 1, exactly). Thus, in Factor analysis, most everything we would like to know stems directly from the Factor loadings. Later, we check these formulas for our *rotated* Factor solution.

11.2f Varimax Rotation Method

varimax rotation
A method used in Factor Analysis that allows the resulting Factors to have the greatest interpretability—while still remaining uncorrelated with one another—by getting the factor loadings to be as close to −1, 0 or 1 as possible.

The next step in the analysis is to abandon all but four Factors, as we said we would choose to do. Recall that this is based mainly on the researcher's judgment as to what is adequate in the particular situation; we could as easily have used 3, 6, or 13 Factors, had we chosen to. At this point, we also must abandon principal components as our Factor method because it does nothing to ensure that the Factor loadings are near −1, 0, or 1, the numbers that guide Factor interpretability. Instead, we resort to **varimax rotation**, a method that "reorients" the original four Factors so that their loadings are as near −1, 0, or 1 as possible. (If you have some idea how linear algebra works, what varimax rotation does is transform the sub-space spanned by the original four Factors so that the resulting basis, the new four Factors, is as nearly orthogonal or parallel to the set of 35 Variables as possible; if you do not know much linear algebra, just think of varimax as a reshuffling method to give the Factors you have chosen as much interpretability as possible.)

Once we run the Factor analysis again with varimax rotation, we have pretty much everything we will need to make sense of the Factors. The eigenvalues for these new Factors are: 4.130, 3.470, 3.409, 2.892. Note that the variance explained by each Factor has changed because of the rotation; the "best" of the four factors now has smaller eigenvalue than before, whereas the "worst" has a larger eigenvalue. The sum of the four eigenvalues, however, is the same. This is perfectly natural, and expected, and the reason we base our choice of the number of Factors on the *unrotated* eigenvalues.

rotated factor pattern
In Factor analysis, the set of Factor loadings obtained after the Factors are rotated (usually to aid in interpretation).

Let us now look at the **rotated factor pattern**, which contains the loadings on the *new* Factors, ordered by how well they correlate. We will break the full table up according to the Variables that "load high" on each of the four factors, then attempt to *interpret* the Factor based on those Variables. These interpretations will be somewhat subjective, but they are extremely helpful in understanding the structure of the full set of original Variables. An example of this interpretative process appears in Table 11.3, for Factor 1.

Table 11.3 Variables Loading High on Factor 1

	Factor 1	Factor 2	Factor 3	Factor 4	
V07	0.7488	0.1063	−0.1092	0.0130	I do not like situations that are uncertain.
V18	0.6646	0.0780	0.1274	0.0058	My personal associations are mostly with people like me.
V26	0.6027	0.1903	−0.1454	−0.1101	I do not like to take chances.
V15	0.4784	0.1322	0.3937	−0.1534	Admire successful businessman more than artist or writer.
V31	0.4569	0.3005	−0.2561	−0.2018	When making family decisions, consider children first.
V03	0.4516	−0.1638	0.0234	0.0083	Info from advertising helps me make better buying decisions.
V33	0.4150	0.2995	0.0342	−0.1279	Government should restrict imports of products from Japan.
V29	−0.5563	0.1569	0.2645	0.0070	Quality of a product is far more important than the price.
V24	−0.6145	0.0622	0.0305	0.1130	Magazines are more interesting than television.

Note that the first seven Variables in Table 11.3 are *positively correlated* with Factor 1, with correlations ranging from 0.7844 to 0.4150; the last two Variables are negatively correlated. What this means it that Factor 1 accords with people *agreeing* with the first seven statements and *disagreeing* with the last two. That is, they "do not like situations that are uncertain," their "personal associations are mostly with people like" themselves, . . . , and they believe "government should restrict imports from Japan," but also that the "quality of a product is" NOT "far more important than the price" and that "magazines are" NOT "more interesting than television." (Note as well that the loadings—that is, correlations—of these nine Variables with the *other* Factors [2–4] are all quite low, compared with their loadings for Factor 1. This is why we used varimax rotation, whose aim is to achieve this sort of loading pattern.)

Part and parcel of performing a Factor analysis is looking over the set of Variables that accord with a Factor and using them to determine what that Factor *means*. Again, this is a subjective enterprise, but a critical one. In this case, we see statements that avoid uncertainty, taking chances, encouraging protectionism, choosing low prices, and the like. As such, it would seem reasonable to call this Factor something like "Risk Aversion." We must remember that this is only a label, and it is used as a sort of shorthand to refer to the Factor later on. Let us now consider the second Factor in the same manner as we did the first, by looking over the loadings in Table 11.4.

In Table 11.4, we see many statements involving a distrust of the new or, perhaps more accurately, newfangled: not wanting to use credit, a belief that things are changing too quickly, having old-fashioned tastes, a dislike of sexual content on television, a liking for budgets, and so on. And the *negatively* correlated statements suggest an unwillingness to spend money on fashion and an opposition to abortion. Given this pattern, we might term this Factor "Old-Fashioned." Note that we should *not* call it "Old" because this is a demographic category and would require that we check against the Variable age, if it were available.

An immediate question concerns whether there is some "overlap" between our first Factor, "Risk Aversion" and our second, "Old-Fashioned." After all, things like sticking to budgets and using cash could appear to be related to both these Factors. Although it is true that individual *Variables* can correlate non-trivially with several Factors, it must be constantly stressed that the Factors themselves are *perfectly uncorrelated*. Their correlation is literally zero. So, we can say that the "underlying construct" of "Risk Aversion" and "Old-Fashioned" are (linearly) unrelated for these particular data.

The loadings in Table 11.5 indicate that Factor 3 loads high and positively on statements about self-confidence, strong friendships, being a leader, having extras, and so forth, and negatively on investment safety being important. The seven Variables here are not as obviously cohesive as was the case for Factor 1 or Factor 2. Nonetheless, it seems as if "High Social Capital" would be a reasonable description of this Factor. Again, we must remember that it is uncorrelated with all other Factors.

Our last Factor is almost unsettling, with high loadings for seeking advice from others, visiting other places, independence, wanting to leave one's present life, and a high negative loading for life satisfaction

Table 11.4 Variables Loading High on Factor 2

	Factor 1	Factor 2	Factor 3	Factor 4	
V20	−0.1797	0.6769	0.1498	0.1203	I like to pay cash for everything I buy.
V02	0.1957	0.5638	−0.1258	−0.1492	Everything is changing too fast today.
V22	−0.2700	0.5455	−0.0980	−0.2038	I consult *Consumer Reports* or similar before major purchase.
V06	0.0284	0.5367	0.0093	0.0030	I have somewhat old-fashioned tastes and desires.
V05	0.0585	0.4941	−0.1327	−0.1966	TV commercials place too much emphasis on sex.
V17	0.0604	0.4892	0.0920	0.2642	I stick to my budget.
V16	−0.2848	0.4692	−0.3974	0.0410	Do not believe competitive test results ads.
V30	0.0444	0.4497	−0.0971	0.1270	Content to live in the same town the rest of my life.
V14	0.2340	0.3628	0.0803	0.1589	Americans should always try to buy American products.
V28	0.3640	−0.4327	0.3822	0.1031	I spend a lot of money for fashionable clothes.
V21	−0.1293	−0.4779	−0.1082	0.1026	I am in favor of legalized abortions.

Table 11.5 Variables Loading High on Factor 3

	Factor 1	Factor 2	Factor 3	Factor 4	
V32	−0.0923	−0.2218	0.6500	0.3644	I spend a lot of time visiting friends.
V23	−0.1211	0.3866	0.6244	0.0857	Friends and neighbors often come to me for product advice.
V01	0.0080	0.0633	0.6198	0.0540	More to spend on extras than most of our neighbors do.
V04	−0.3124	−0.1993	0.5944	−0.0089	I have more self-confidence than most of my friends.
V11	0.1967	−0.0327	0.5121	−0.0153	We will probably move at least once in the next 5 years.
V12	−0.4975	0.0424	0.5039	−0.2525	Our whole family usually eats one meal together daily.
V10	0.2787	0.0412	−0.4555	−0.0077	Investments: safety more important than high interest rates.

(see Table 11.6). Although the Variables comprising Factor 4 are the least obviously cohesive thus far, we can append a shorthand name to the Factor, calling it "Alienation" or "Desire for Change."

Now that we have looked closely at our four Factors, we should ask whether they do a good job explaining the original 35 Variables. To do so, we ask the computer to report the communalities for this four Factor solution; results appear in Table 11.7.

The communalities show how much of the variance in each of the original Variables is explained by the four Factors taken all at once; most of these seem to be between 0.3 and 0.6. The total communality of 13.9 should be compared with a best possible value of 35, meaning that 13.9/35, or just less than 40 percent, of the variance in the original 35 questions can be explained by just four Factors. This is the same figure we saw in the (unrotated) Principal Components analysis performed at the outset; because we deemed it acceptable then, we must do so now. However, the pattern of individual Variable communalities is troubling. Most of them are about 0.4, as would be expected. However, some are quite a bit better,

Table 11.6 Variables Loading High on Factor 4

	Factor 1	Factor 2	Factor 3	Factor 4	
V34	0.2014	0.1218	0.1466	0.7255	Often seek out advice of my friends on brands and products.
V13	−0.3010	−0.0091	−0.1597	0.5410	Like to visit places totally different from my home.
V25	0.2059	−0.0770	0.4087	0.4816	I enjoy parties, games, shows, anything for fun.
V19	−0.2388	−0.0830	0.0937	0.4524	I am more independent than most people.
V08	−0.1282	−0.0600	0.2533	0.3795	Wish to leave present life, do something entirely different.
V09	−0.3036	−0.0572	−0.0945	0.3695	I like my livingroom to look casual rather than formal.
V27	0.0054	0.0970	0.2708	−0.6044	Satisfied with how things are going in my life these days.
V35	−0.0356	−0.2416	−0.1342	−0.6534	Manufacturer warranties not worth paper they are printed on.

Table 11.7 Communalities for Variables 1–35 and 4 Varimax Rotated Factors

Communalities for Variables 1–35 and Four Varimax Rotated Factors

V01	V02	V03	V04	V05	V06	V07	V08	V09	V10
0.3911	0.3942	0.2314	0.4907	0.3038	0.2890	0.5842	0.2282	0.2409	0.2869
V11	**V12**	**V13**	**V14**	**V15**	**V16**	**V17**	**V18**	**V19**	**V20**
0.3022	0.5670	0.4088	0.2180	0.4249	0.4608	0.3212	0.4640	0.2773	0.5275
V21	**V22**	**V23**	**V24**	**V25**	**V26**	**V27**	**V28**	**V29**	**V30**
0.2673	0.4216	0.5613	0.3951	0.4474	0.4327	0.4480	0.4765	0.4042	0.2298
V31	**V32**	**V33**	**V34**	**V35**					
0.4054	0.6130	0.2795	0.6031	0.5046		Final Total Communality Estimate: 13.90			

A Closer Look 11.2

Checking Eigenvalue and Communality Calculations

Let us make sure that the eigenvalues and communalities follow from the sum-of-squared Factor loadings, as advertised. Using our varimax rotated four-Factor solution, for the first few Variables in our listing, the squared loadings give us:

	Factor 1	Factor 2	Factor 3	Factor 4	SUM
V07	$(0.7488)^2$	$(0.1063)^2$	$(-0.1092)^2$	$(0.0130)^2$	0.5842
V18	$(0.6646)^2$	$(0.0780)^2$	$(0.1274)^2$	$(0.0058)^2$	0.4640
V26	$(0.6027)^2$	$(0.1903)^2$	$(-0.1454)^2$	$(0.1101)^2$	0.4327
V15	$(0.4784)^2$	$(0.1322)^2$	$(0.3937)^2$	$(-0.1534)^2$	0.4249

These match precisely the communalities listed above for those 4 Variables, and would for the other 31. If we do this summation for all 35 Variables, we get:

	Factor 1	Factor 2	Factor 3	Factor 4
V07	$(0.7488)^2$	$(0.1063)^2$	$(-0.1092)^2$	$(0.0130)^2$
V18	$(0.6646)^2$	$(0.0780)^2$	$(0.1274)^2$	$(0.0058)^2$
V26	$(0.6027)^2$	$(0.1903)^2$	$(-0.1454)^2$	$(-0.1101)^2$
.	.	.	.	.
.	.	.	.	.
.	.	.	.	.
V35	$(-0.0356)^2$	$(-0.2416)^2$	$(-0.1342)^2$	$(-0.6534)^2$
SUM	4.1301	3.4705	3.4088	2.8924

And these reproduce the eigenvalues originally obtained. Once again, the loadings tell us everything we need to know about our Factor solution.

such as 0.6130 for V32, and a few are substantially worse, such as 0.2180 for V14. If our objective is to explain the original Variables *equally well*, we have failed, based on the communalities for this four-Factor solution. In that case, we would have to abandon this solution and simply consider adding in more Factors, which will typically have the effect of "evening out" the communalities. However, it could also be that, looking back on the Variables with low communalities (here, V03, V08, V09, and V14 are all under 0.25, and many more are under 0.3), we find that some of them are unusual and not as important for our research as the bulk of the other Variables. In that case, we could proceed with the four-Factor solution, with the caveat that some of the Variables are represented far more accurately than others. Additional detail on various calculations underlying both the factor loadings and communalities appears in *A Closer Look 11.2*.

11.2g Using Factor Analysis

One could now reasonably ask, "So, what is Factor analysis good for?" There are quite a few answers to this, but two stand out. The first is conceptual and somewhat theoretical: Factor analysis helps one identify and even put names to underlying constructs in sets of at least partially redundant (intercorrelated) Variables; because researchers are often confronted with many such Variables, Factor analysis helps cut to the "heart of the issue" and reduce the number of constructs one needs to consider. A second answer is far more pragmatic and, in our view, satisfying: Factor analysis provides us with a set of quantities that, unlike the original intercorrelated Variables, can be used in a regression or other multivariate analysis technique. We must remember that regression works best, and the resulting coefficients have the clearest interpretations, when the predictors are uncorrelated. In the real world, the Variables we are given are never uncorrelated. But Factors are *always perfectly uncorrelated*. As such, they offer a great deal of statistical and explanatory power compared with the original Variables they are based on.

Let us then complete our analysis by using the Factors in a regression, to help determine the extent to which people find price, warranty, and other attributes important in buying a car. These were measured in the survey as follows:

How important would each of the following be in your car-buying decision? Please rate each on the following scale:

	Not at all important						Very important
Price	1	2	3	4	5	6	7
Warranty	1	2	3	4	5	6	7

These can now be used as dependent Variables in a regression, with the four Factors as predictors. (We avoid calling them "independent *Variables*," just to keep the distinction between Factors and Variables crystal clear.) The regression results for price are as shown in Table 11.8.

Table 11.8 **Multiple Linear Regression Analyses for Price and Warranty**

Linear Regression Analysis: DepVar (Y) = Price X = {Factor_1, Factor_2, Factor_3, Factor_4}

Coefficients	b	Std. Error	Std. Beta	t Test Statistic	p-value Two Tailed
Intercept	5.818	0.092		62.949	0.0000
Factor_1	−0.385	0.093	−0.322	−4.152	0.0001
Factor_2	0.196	0.093	0.164	2.111	0.0368
Factor_3	−0.368	0.093	−0.307	−3.961	0.0001
Factor_4	0.132	0.093	0.110	1.419	0.1583

r	r^2	Adj. r^2	SE(Reg)	n
0.487	0.237	0.213	1.062	132

Source of Variation	Sum of Squares	df	Mean Squares	F Test Statistic	p-value One Tailed
Regression	44.43	4	11.106	9.849	0.0000
Error	143.21	127	1.128		
Total	187.64	131			

And the results for Warranty are:

Linear Regression Analysis: DepVar (Y) = Warranty X = {Factor_1, Factor_2, Factor_3, Factor_4}

Coefficients	b	Std. Error	Std. Beta	t-Test Statistic	p-value Two Tailed
Intercept	5.227	0.097		54.007	0.0000
Factor_1	0.053	0.097	0.045	0.543	0.5880
Factor_2	0.059	0.097	0.051	0.611	0.5422
Factor_3	0.341	0.097	0.292	3.509	0.0006
Factor_4	0.215	0.097	0.184	2.217	0.0284

r	r^2	Adj. r^2	SE(Reg)	n
0.351	0.124	0.096	1.112	132

Source of Variation	Sum of Squares	df	Mean Squares	F-Test Statistic	p-value One Tailed
Regression	22.14	4	5.534	4.475	0.0020
Error	157.05	127	1.237		
Total	179.18	131			

So, this analysis shows that the four Factors, taken together, are adequate to account for a significant "amount" of both price variation ($F = 9.849$, $p < 0.000005$) and for warranty variation ($F = 4.475$, $p = 0.002$). This means that, for both Variables of interest, the four-Factor solution offers a greater-than-by-chance degree of explanatory power. However, r^2 for price is 23.7 percent, and for warranty only 12.4 percent. This illustrates yet again that, in regression, a result can be very strongly significant while still leaving a great deal of variation unexplained. In simple language, the four Factors explain about one quarter of the variation in price and one eighth of the variation in warranty, despite being "highly significant" for both. Researchers *must* consider not only strength of statistical evidence (as embodied by the *F*-test and associated *p*-value), but also the absolute proportion of variation explained (as embodied by r^2 and r^2-adjusted). Note that, as the sheer quantity of data increases, significance levels typically improve, whereas values like r^2 do not.

Although the Factors appear to do a reasonable job for both price and warranty when all four are taken together, we must examine them individually. And here we see that, for price, Factors 1 and 3 are very strongly significant; Factor 2 is borderline ($p \approx 0.037$); and Factor 4 is not. For Warranty, only Factor 3 is strongly significant, with Factor 4 borderline ($p \approx 0.028$). It would appear that Factor 2 ("Old-Fashioned") and Factor 4 ("Desire for Change") are really not all that helpful in describing price and warranty, and Factor 1 ("Risk Aversion") is only helpful for price. The one Factor unambiguously useful for both is Factor 3 ("High Social Capital"), and note that it is negatively correlated with price, and positively with warranty. That is, people with high scores on Factor 3 find price relatively unimportant and warranty very important, which may indicate that these people seek cars as status symbols, and so are willing to pay more for them than those who score low on "Social Capital," but that they also willing to pay more for a warranty to protect their investment. Of course, we should consult demographic information, if available, and use it in more complex regression analyses of these data.

The data set contains many other dependent Variables, and we leave these relationships—and determining whether more Factors are really needed to explain them—as exercises. We report informally that Factor 3 should not be thought of as "all powerful"; it does not (as you should verify) explain a significant portion of the variation in many of the other dependent Variables, such as safety, MPG, quiet, ride, durability, and others. We must remember that these Factors were *not* selected to explain any other Variables! Factor analysis is an *interdependence method*, and it only seeks to explain the interrelationships among the input Variables, *not* their relation to any additional quantities. For all we know, the next few Factors—which we chose to omit—may do a fantastically better job at explaining these other dependent Variables. The only way to know is to run these other analyses.

Before leaving Factor analysis, we pause to consider an "off prescription" use of the method. In real-world applications, managers are often wary of relying on Factors, which must be constructed from all the data and which are difficult to convey to those less statistically savvy. In such cases, they often resort to a quick-and-dirty method: instead of using the Factors themselves, they select the single Variable from each that has the highest (in absolute value) loading. For our four-Factor solution, these would be V07 ("I do not like situations that are uncertain," with loading 0.7488 on Factor 1), V20 ("I like to pay cash for everything I buy," with loading 0.6769 on Factor 2), V32 ("I spend a lot of time visiting friends," with loading 0.6500 on Factor 3), and V34 ("I often seek out advice of my friends on brands and products," with loading 0.7255 on Factor 4). This procedure, although not statistically wrong, is also not guaranteed to produce the best possible results; and, of course, the original Variables will not be mutually uncorrelated, as the Factors always are. At the same time, it is not a bad way to get a handle on which regression models using the original Variables might produce useful results. If you use this method, do so with caution, and be sure to test it against alternative models.

Let us close our discussion of Factor analysis with *Marketing Research Focus 11.2*, which presents a classic example of its application.

Marketing Research Focus 11.2

Using Factor Analysis to Understand Coffee Flavor

Factor analysis has been used in marketing research for a long time. Among the earliest applications was a now-classic study that attempted to understand the "qualitative" dimensions of coffee. In simple terms, the goal of the study was to compress a set of coffee attributes (Variables) to their underlying Factors. Let us look closely at the data that went into this analysis, and the various information they might yield for the researcher: Table 11.9 shows the set of 14 coffee attributes on which data were collected using a 10-point semantic differential scale; Table 11.10 presents the correlation matrix between the various combinations of attributes; Table 11.11 displays the principal Factors extracted from the correlation matrix, plus the orthogonally rotated Factors (varimax rotation).

Table 11.9 Fourteen Coffee Attributes Investigated

14 coffee attributes investigated		
	Pleasant flavor —	Unpleasant flavor
	Stagnant, muggy taste —	Sparkling, refreshing taste
	Mellow taste —	Bitter taste
	Cheap taste —	Expensive taste
	Comforting, harmonious, smooth, friendly taste —	Irritating, discordant, rough, hostile taste
	Dead, lifeless, dull taste —	Alive, lively, peppy taste
	Tastes artificial —	Tastes like real coffee
	Deep, distinct flavor —	Shallow, indistinct flavor
	Tastes warmed over —	Tastes just brewed
	Hearty, full-bodied, full flavor —	Watery, thin, empty flavor
	Pure, clear taste —	Muddy swampy taste
	Raw taste —	Roasted taste
	Fresh taste —	Stale taste
Overall preference:	Excellent quality —	Very poor quality

Note: Ten blank boxes separated each set of opposing statements. Subjects checked the position that came closest to describing how they felt toward the product.

Table 11.10 Intercorrelations among Attribute Ratings

	1	2	3	4	5	6	7	8	9	10	11	12	13	14
1 Pleasant flavor	1	0.76	0.81	0.79	0.83	0.81	0.74	0.66	0.65	0.71	0.76	0.65	0.71	0.75
2 Sparkling taste		1	0.78	0.85	0.77	0.87	0.83	0.65	0.70	0.78	0.85	0.69	0.74	0.83
3 Mellow taste			1	0.77	0.85	0.81	0.77	0.60	0.65	0.64	0.75	0.69	0.69	0.74
4 Expensive taste				1	0.78	0.87	0.83	0.76	0.69	0.81	0.81	0.64	0.71	0.87
5 Comforting taste					1	0.82	0.77	0.66	0.60	0.69	0.82	0.69	0.69	0.74
6 Alive taste						1	0.88	0.70	0.74	0.80	0.81	0.65	0.77	0.87
7 Tastes like real coffee							1	0.67	0.76	0.75	0.79	0.62	0.76	0.87
8 Deep distinct flavor								1	0.51	0.84	0.70	0.54	0.59	0.70
9 Tastes just brewed									1	0.67	0.65	0.67	0.80	0.75
10 Hearty flavor										1	0.83	0.65	0.72	0.76
11 Pure clear taste											1	0.66	0.73	0.76
12 Roasted taste												1	0.78	0.61
13 Fresh taste													1	0.73
14 Overall preference														1
Mean rating*	**4.5**	**4.3**	**4.4**	**4.6**	**4.4**	**4.2**	**4.2**	**4.3**	**4.3**	**4.2**	**4.3**	**4.4**	**4.6**	**6.9**
Standard deviation	**1.6**	**1.3**	**1.4**	**1.4**	**1.3**	**1.4**	**1.6**	**1.5**	**1.5**	**1.5**	**1.4**	**1.2**	**1.4**	**2.7**

*The 10 scale categories were assigned successive integers, beginning with 1 at the favorable side of the scale. Thus ratings could vary from 1 (very "good") to 10 (very "bad") on an attribute.

Source: This example is adapted and updated from the classic study by Bishwa Nath Mukherjee, "A Factor Analysis of Some Qualitative Attributes of Coffee," *Journal of Advertising Research*, vol. 5, pp. 35–38, March 1965. Used with permissions.

Table 11.11 Factor Loadings

	Principal factor matrix					Rotated (varimax) matrix			
	I	II	III	IV	h^2	A	B	C	D
1	0.86	−0.01	−0.20	0.04	0.78	0.63	0.38	0.36	0.34
2	0.91	−0.01	−0.01	−0.09	0.83	0.48	0.43	0.53	0.38
3	0.86	0.11	0.28	0.00	0.83	0.70	0.26	0.38	0.36
4	0.91	0.15	0.00	−0.10	0.87	0.46	0.53	0.54	0.29
5	0.87	0.00	0.31	0.10	0.87	0.74	0.38	0.30	0.32
6	0.93	0.03	−0.02	−0.16	0.90	0.49	0.43	0.59	0.35
7	0.90	−0.02	0.04	−0.21	0.86	0.42	0.38	0.64	0.37
8	0.77	0.36	0.11	0.16	0.77	0.31	0.74	0.27	0.22
9	0.79	−0.28	0.24	−0.09	0.76	0.23	0.24	0.52	0.62
10	0.87	0.25	0.22	0.17	0.89	0.28	0.75	0.33	0.39
11	0.89	0.11	0.05	0.10	0.82	0.51	0.55	0.36	0.36
12	0.76	−0.29	0.04	0.27	0.74	0.43	0.28	0.16	0.67
13	0.84	−0.27	0.19	0.12	0.83	0.33	0.32	0.36	0.70
14	0.90	0.04	0.08	−0.23	0.86	0.38	0.43	0.65	0.34
Percent common variance	90.0%	4.1%	3.3%	2.6%					
Percent total variance	74.4%	3.4%	2.7%	2.6%					

Let us first examine the unrotated principal components Factor matrix, which lists four Factors underlying the 14 attributes (Variables). Recall that choosing the *number* of Factors is subjective, and it depends on how much variation the researcher feels it necessary to capture. At this point, we will not try to "name" these Factors because rotation will help with that later on in the analysis. The elements in this matrix listed under the Factors are called *unrotated Factor loadings*. Recall that the loadings measure which Variables are involved in which Factor, to what degree, and in what direction. They can be interpreted exactly like correlation coefficients. The square of the loading equals the proportion of the variation that a Variable has in common with an unrotated Factor. Recall as well that the h^2 measures are called *communalities*, and they correspond to the proportion of a Variable's total variation that is involved in the Factors. That is, h^2 equals the sum of the squared loadings of a Variable on all Factors. For example, for attribute 1:

$$h^2 = (.86)^2+(-.01)^2+(-.20)^2+(.04)^2= 0.78$$

Communality may be interpreted as a measure of uniqueness. By subtracting h^2 from 1.0, the degree to which a Variable is *unrelated* to the others may be calculated. Here, we note that 78 percent of the variation in scores on attribute 1 can be predicted from the other Variables, leaving 22 percent uniquely related to this attribute.

To obtain the percentage of total variance in the data explained by the four Factors, we simply calculate H, where

$$H = \frac{\text{sum of all } h^2 \text{ values}}{\text{number of variables}} = \frac{11.61}{14} = 83\%$$

This value is called the *common variance* explained by the Factors.

To calculate the amount of variation in the data accounted for by a Factor, we square each loading for a Factor, add, and then divide the result by the number of Variables. For example, for Factor 1 the value is

$$(.86)^2+(.91)^2+(.86)^2+\cdots+(.90)^2= 10.42$$

This is called an *eigenvalue*. Thus, the percentage of total variance explained by Factor 1 is 10.42/14 = 74.4 percent. The percentage of common variance explained by this Factor is then 10.42/11.61 = 90 percent. Percentages of both common variance and total variance are presented in Table 11.11.

One of the main goals of Factor analysis in all marketing research applications is to name or interpret the Factors' "meaning." This is always subjective, but is guided by examining the *rotated* Factors. Table 11.12 presents one such interpretation; others are possible because we are assigning adjectives based on our own understanding. The Factors have been associated with high-loading Variables and each given a "creative" name by the author of the study: Factor A has been termed "comforting quality," and comprises the attributes "pleasant flavor," "mellow taste" and "comforting taste";

Factor B, "heartiness," includes "deep distinct flavor" and "hearty flavor"; Factor D, "freshness," loads high on "tastes just brewed," "roasted taste," and "fresh taste"; and Factor C, "genuineness," includes the other seven attributes.

Table 11.12 Interpretation of Factors

Variable	Attribute	Varimax Loading
Factor A (comforting quality)		
1	Pleasant flavor	0.625
3	Mellow taste	0.698
5	Comforting taste	0.736
Factor B (heartiness)		
8	Deep distinct flavor	0.742
10	Hearty flavor	0.745
Factor C (genuineness)		
2	Sparkling taste	0.524
4	Expensive taste	0.541
6	Alive taste	0.594
7	tastes like real coffee	0.636
8	Deep distinct flavor	0.268
10	Hearty flavor	0.332
14	Overall preference	0.653
Factor D (freshness)		
9	Tastes just brewed	0.621
12	Roasted taste	0.670
13	Fresh taste	0.698

It should be obvious that there is no unique definition of the meaning of any of these Factors; it is up to the resourcefulness and judgment of the researcher. Unfortunately, researchers can all too easily fool themselves with fanciful or deep-sounding interpretations. Worse, names can be assigned to Factors to support some pre-selected interpretation favorable to the researcher or client. As in all subjective or interpretive aspects of marketing research, great care must be taken in this regard.

Source: This example is adapted and updated from the classic study by Bishwa Nath Mukherjee (1965), "A Factor Analysis of Some Qualitative Attributes of Coffee," *Journal of Advertising Research*, 5, 35–38. Used with permission.

11.3 Cluster Analysis and Latent Class Analysis

As the introductory example using student test scores illustrated, Factor analysis and Cluster analysis, although they can appear similar, are conceptually distinct and are applied in very different ways. Factor analysis allows the researcher to study the structure of a set of *variables* in terms of how their variance is explained by a set of underlying Factors. Cluster analysis, by contrast, allows the researcher to place *objects* or *items* or *people* into subgroups. These subgroups are often called classes, segments, and other names, but the most common terms is clusters, hence the name of the technique. A crucial point is that these clusters are *not* defined *a priori* by the researcher but are formed by the cluster analysis procedure itself. Statisticians often call these clusters "latent" because they need to be discerned via analysis and are not directly observable. For example, we may try to classify businesses in a way that breaks them up into the clearest, most coherent groupings and find that the clusters appear to be well-named by labels such as "explosively successful," "in the Northwest," "primarily high-tech," and so on. We would not be able to know these groupings in advance and, moreover, would be hard-pressed to label a firm "explosively successful" without a tight, preexisting definition. Cluster analysis frees us from these tasks, fashioning the appropriate groupings for us automatically.

"Clustering" is in actuality a large set of related statistical procedures and an exceptionally rich area of current research. These procedures share some common dimensions:

- They form subgroups, assign objects ("cases") to each of them, and help determine a reasonable overall number of subgroups.
- They take as input a "matrix of associations" between cases; for example, a correlation matrix, or one involving distances or dissimilarities. (There are clustering algorithms available that take nominal, ordinal, interval, or ratio measures in this matrix of associations as input.)
- They assume that natural clusters exist within the data. Our task as analysts is to choose the right variables through which to recover these clusterings and to appropriately discern what holds them together (that is, how items in the same cluster are similar).
- The number and diversity of these algorithms make comprehensive presentation of clustering techniques possible only in book-length treatments devoted to the topic; readers are directed to Further Reading for such detailed presentations.

11.3a Visual Guides to Cluster Analysis

In our exploration of cluster analysis, we show how some of the standard—and widely supported in common statistical programs—clustering methods can be used to illuminate data encountered by marketing managers and researchers. Before doing so, it is helpful to consider several visual guides to how cluster analysis works and some of the challenges one encounters in using it. This visual emphasis is especially apt for cluster analysis among all our procedures because placing objects into clusters is something the human visual system accomplishes easily, naturally, and robustly (i.e., it does not "break down" like a statistical algorithm can). The problem is that our visual system is not terribly good at dealing with very large numbers of objects; large numbers of groupings; and, above all, more than three *dimensions* (variables) used to cluster. In situations where one has three variables or fewer through which to cluster a set of cases, it is actually expedient to simply graph them, look at them, and judge directly how to form subgroups. Our ability to do that rapidly breaks down with even a fourth variable and disappears entirely shortly thereafter. Clustering algorithms run on the computer, however, are tireless and scale well for large numbers of objects, groupings, and variables.

Consider the graph in Figure 11.6, with just six points.

Figure 11.6 Different Ways to Cluster a Small Number of Items

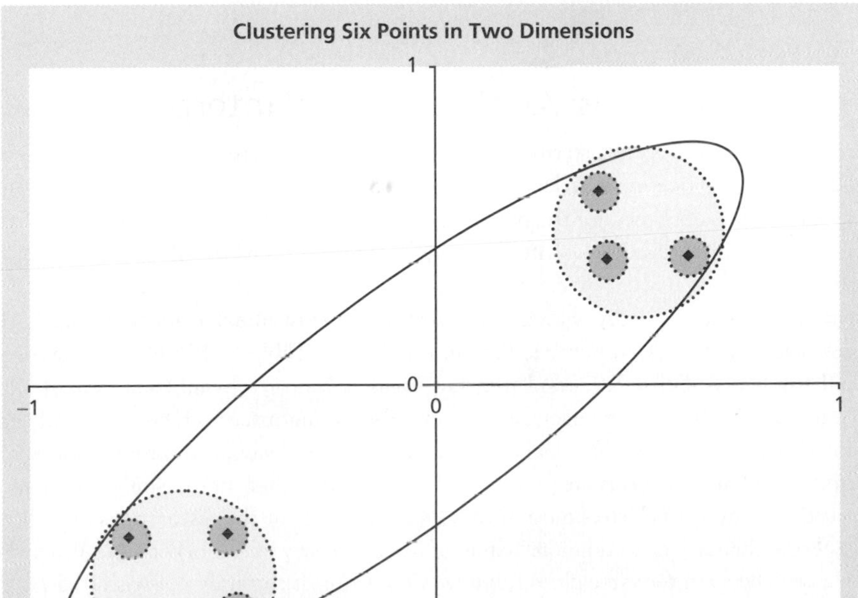

Let us now consider a deceptively simple question: How many "natural" groups do these points fall into? The obvious answer—although it is hard to explain exactly why it is obvious—is two: There's a group in the upper right, and another in the lower left. However, suppose this were a faraway image of a solar system, or a set of galaxies, with vast expanses between "points." Would it be more correct to say there were in fact *six* groups, given the distances involved? What if they were bacteria, just microns apart? Would they then be just *one* group? The correct answer is that the question itself is ill-posed: the points do not "naturally" fall into any number of groups. Rather, the researcher needs to determine what the groupings will be used for and how much "latitude" around each object is acceptable.

Because the "obvious" answer to our poor question was that there were two groups, we might question why almost everyone offers this answer first. How would we teach a computer to see what is so obvious to us? One way is to use one of the most powerful ideas in statistics: minimizing distance (recall that regression is really just a way to minimize the sum-of-squares distance between observations and predictions). With a little thought, we can see that two groups is the "obvious" answer if we pose our original question in a different way: How can we divide up the points so that those in the *same group* are "close" to one another, and those in *different groups* are "far"? What we see is that clustering involves a *trade-off* between two quantities: the distance of each point in a group to the *group center*, and the distance *between* group centers. And there will be two answers we will not like very much, because they are unhelpful and a bit boring: placing all objects in a single group (so that there is *no* distance "between groups"), and placing each object in its own group (so that there is *no* distance "within groups"). What we really want, in the language of statistics, is this: an **intermediate level of aggregation**. That is, we want to say that the number of groups is somewhere between these extremes, and to be able to defend our choice for a particular research need.

intermediate level of aggregation
In cluster analysis, finding a solution other than "all items are in a single cluster" and "each item is in its own cluster."

Clustering methods are exceptionally useful in marketing because one of the ideas that runs throughout the discipline is the vital importance of *segmentation*. When we segment a market, we are really just clustering its brands or its customer base, albeit often informally. Cluster analysis allows us to segment rigorously and to understand the basis of our allotment into clusters. It has been used extensively in marketing for applications such as developing consumer segments based on demographic and psychographic profiles, identifying test market cities, determining similar markets in various countries, finding similar groups of magazine readers or cable subscribers to aid in media selection, and so on. At the end of this section, we will introduce a powerful clustering method called *latent class analysis* that works with a wider variety of data types than the traditional cluster analysis presented next. And, in our final chapter, Advanced Topics, we will examine the types of heterogeneity that cutting-edge marketing research techniques can account for, finding they are very closely related to clustering.

11.3b Cluster Analysis: Application and Interpretation

Among the most common uses of clustering techniques in marketing are segmenting customers and segmenting products. Our application will deal with the latter and attempt to cluster a set of products in the canned beer market. The data used for the purposes of this illustrative example, as listed in Table 11.13, are attribute (caloric content, sodium content, alcohol content) and wholesale price data for 20 brands of beer.

The research goal is to determine which of these beers are most like one another: that is, to identify *clusters* of beers with *similar profiles relative to the four variables* (in Table 11.13). Depending on one's vantage point, all the beers—being beers and not, say, colas or motor oil—might appear similar and be deemed to be in a single cluster; conversely, a beer connoisseur might see each beer as totally unique and place each into a separate cluster. The goal of cluster analysis, as always, is to provide some *intermediate level of aggregation* so that some beers are pronounced similar, and others not so similar. It is important to realize that putting items into clusters must always take into account the researcher's overall purpose: if one were clustering the far larger and more heterogeneous category of "all beverages," it may be reasonable to place all the beers in the same cluster, but we would almost certainly not wish to do so if we were looking only at beers. That is, how we will cluster a set of objects will depend critically on which other objects are being clustered along with them and how much latitude we wish to allow within a cluster vs. across clusters. We will return to, and expand on, these ideas throughout our remaining discussion of Cluster Analysis.

Table 11.13 Attributes and Prices of Beer Brands for Cluster Analysis

Brand	Calories (12 oz.)	Sodium (mg./12 oz.)	Alcohol (%)	Price (Wholesale)
Budweiser	144	15	4.7	0.43
Schlitz	151	19	4.9	0.43
Lowenbrau	157	15	4.9	0.48
Kronenbourg	170	7	5.2	0.73
Heineken	152	11	5.0	0.77
Old Milwaukee	145	23	4.6	0.28
Augsberger	175	24	5.5	0.40
Stroh's Bohemian Style	149	27	4.7	0.42
Miller Lite	99	10	4.3	0.43
Budweiser Light	113	8	3.7	0.44
Coors	140	18	4.6	0.44
Coors Light	102	15	4.1	0.46
Michelob Light	135	11	4.2	0.50
Beck's	150	19	4.7	0.76
Kirin	149	6	5.0	0.79
Pabst Extra Light	68	15	2.3	0.38
Hamm's	136	19	4.4	0.43
Heileman's Old Style	144	24	4.9	0.43
Olympia Gold Light	72	6	2.9	0.46
Schlitz Light	97	7	4.2	0.47
Mean	132.4	15.0	4.4	0.50
Minimum	68	6	2.3	0.28
Maximum	175	27	5.5	0.79

11.3c Scaling and Redundancy in Cluster Analysis

Before clustering the beers, we should look closely at the input variables, remembering all along that cluster analysis is a statistical technique, not a mind-reading procedure: it does not know what the variables *mean*. Unlike in regression, where a truly meaningless independent variable will show up as unrelated to the dependent variable, cluster analysis does not *have* a dependent variable. Thus, any variables input to the procedure will be counted as equally important. For this particular data set, one might question whether sodium content is as important in segmenting beer as is price, alcohol content, or calories; by including it, we are explicitly assuming it is.

One obvious fact about the four variables is that they are measured on different scales: thermal energy (calories), milligrams (sodium), percentage (alcohol), and dollars (price). The statistical program does not know this, and it will treat all these scales the same. This is especially dangerous because the *ranges* of the variables are dramatically different, with each variable's range approximately a factor of 10 smaller than the one before it. If we used these "raw" values, calories would dominate the solution, and price would be inconsequential. If we truly believe that the variables are equally important, we must transform them first. In statistics, the usual way to do this is to use a **z-transform**: for each variable, first subtract off its mean, then divide by its sample standard deviation. This ensures that each variable is on an "equal footing" statistically, transformed to have a zero mean and standard deviation of 1. If we wish some variables to be more important than others, we can reweight them *after* standardizing. For this data set, we will only standardize, not reweight.

z-transform
When a variable is normally distributed, it can be made to (i.e., transformed to) have a standard normal (z) distribution by subtracting its mean and dividing by its standard deviation. These standard normally distributed quantities—which can have any positive or negative value—can then be converted them to probabilities (which lie between 0 and 1). (Note that this differs from Fisher's z-transform of the sample correlation r: $z = (1/2)\ln[(1+r)/(1-r)]$, and also from the z-transform common in signal processing.)

A last data-driven issue concerns the possibility of redundancy among our variables. If we calculate the correlations among these four variables, we find:

r	Calories	Sodium	Alcohol	Price
Calories	1.00			
Sodium	0.41	1.00		
Alcohol	0.92	0.32	1.00	
Price	0.32	−0.45	0.33	1.00

These correlations are modest, with one glaring exception: that between Alcohol and Calories. This is to be expected because alcohol is the main source of the calories in alcoholic beverages. A correlation of 0.92 is exceptionally high, so much so that the two variables have almost identical "information content." As such, we must bear in mind that we are, in essence, putting the same information into the cluster analysis twice, and should not be surprised if our final cluster solution reflects this redundancy. (We must not assume, however, that consumers *perceive* these two attributes similarly; some consumers may be concerned with calories and not alcohol content, or vice versa. Only detailed consumer research can address this issue, which goes well beyond mere correlation.) Still, let us proceed with these four variables—calories, sodium, alcohol, and price—for illustration purposes and see how they determine the best clustering solution for these 20 beers.

11.3d Running the Cluster Analysis

Because there are so many ways to break items into groups, statisticians have developed a wide variety of criteria one can use to determine a good clustering solution. To use cluster analysis, one must choose a **distance metric** and a **clustering criterion**. (See *A Closer Look 11.3: Different Ways to Rescale Data and Measure Distances* for more information on how these are defined and chosen.) Although in everyday life we have a clear idea what distance is, in statistics we have many choices; in regression and almost all other statistical methods, we minimize not total linear distance but sum-of-squares distance, and we may do so in cluster analysis as well. For our example, we will use "squared Euclidean distance," which is simply the sum-of-squares measure we have seen many times before. We must also choose a clustering criterion, and here there are many relevant choices. One can, for example, try to minimize the *greatest* distance between a cluster center and anything assigned to that cluster; we would be looking at a "worst-case scenario," caring only about the items that fall far from any cluster center. We will not survey all

distance metric
Any measure of dissimilarity between pairs of items. True distances are always positive and obey the triangle inequality (the distance between {A, B} is less than the sum between {A, C} and {C, B}).

clustering criterion
A rule used in cluster analysis to determine how clusters should be formed from input data.

A Closer Look 11.3

Different Ways to Rescale Data and Measure Distances

In many statistical procedures, we need to assess "how far apart things are." The usual way to start is to ensure that scaling does not matter—we do not want different answers if we measure in feet vs. inches, or dollars vs. pennies—and for this we transform the data. The most common way is to *standardize* to create z-scores, which always means the following: for a particular variable, take each value, subtract the sample mean, then divide by the sample standard deviation. But this is not the only way to put each variable on a common footing. We can linearly transform each variable to have range 0 to 1, or −1 to 1. We can simply divide each value by the maximum (this can work well if all values are positive), by the mean (so that the mean value is re-scaled to 1), or by the standard deviation, all without subtracting the mean first, as we do in standardizing. Most statistical programs allow all of these, with the "default" being to standardize. It is *extremely* important when clustering to consider some type of rescaling, or the yardstick one uses in the data will affect the research outcome.

Once all the variables have been rescaled in some way, we need to determine how to measure *distance*. The most common are the *Euclidean distance* and the *squared Euclidean distance*, both of which are familiar from high school geometry, the latter being simply the sum-of-squared deviations. The majority of statistical programs have one of these as the "default" for interval-scaled data. But there are other possibilities: the Pearson correlation (between two items' coordinates), the cosine (of the angle between two items' coordinates), Chebyshev distance (maximum *absolute* difference between two items' coordinates), City Block (sum of the *absolute* differences between two items' coordinates), among others. Users of clustering need to check carefully that distances are being measured in a manner consistent with the research being conducted, particularly if there are many "outlier" items that can greatly skew the results.

the possible distance metrics and clustering criteria that can be used, but some common examples are explained in "A Closer Look 11.3." For our example, we will use "centroid clustering," which compares the total "distance" (again, we will use sum-of-squared Euclidean distances) between cluster centers with the total "distance" from cluster centers to the points in that cluster. We note that different choices of clustering criterion can yield strikingly different final cluster solutions, so care must be taken to select the one most concordant with the researcher's needs.

11.3e "How Many Clusters Do I Need?"

This is precisely the same question we asked of Factors in Factor analysis. And the answer here is also the same: the precise number of clusters that will be appropriate is seldom known in advance, and it should be discerned from the analysis itself. Although there are situations where a researcher is asked to "split the population up into two (or three, an so on) groups," they are rare and usually not a good idea in the first place. Unfortunately, unlike in regression or Factor analysis, where there are objective measures (such as r^2) of fit, one must take a more "exploratory" approach in cluster analysis and base one's judgment on more or less pictorial evidence.

The first thing the clustering routine does is take the "raw" data, standardize it if necessary (this is almost always a good idea), and use the researcher's choice of "distance metric" to calculate distances between each pair of items. Table 11.14 provides a subset of these distances for the first ten items, which in our application we have chosen to be a sum-of-squares.

Table 11.14 shows that some pairs are much closer than others; for example, Lowenbrau (3) and Budweiser (1) are 0.38 apart, whereas Old Milwaukee (6) and Kronenbourg (4) are 17.02 apart. We would expect the first pair to be far more likely to cluster together than the second. In the language of cluster analysis, this table lists *dissimilarities* because the higher the number, the more unalike the pair is, based on the variables in question.

11.3f Hierarchical vs. Nonhierarchical Clustering

The clustering algorithm attempts to use this distance data to place the items into groups. It is at this point that the researcher must decide whether the clusters should be *hierarchical* or *nonhierarchical*. We will explore detailed examples of both types of clustering in this chapter. For now, it suffices to say that *hierarchical* clustering will help us uncover structure across *different* numbers of clusters; in *nonhierarchical* clustering, two different clustering solutions (say, into four and five groups) may look highly dissimilar, making interpretation more difficult because, in hierarchical clustering, two objects in the same cluster will never be broken apart as more clusters are added, whereas this is possible in nonhierarchical

Table 11.14 Distance (Dissimilarity) Matrix for Beer Brand Clustering Example

	Squared Euclidean Distance									
Brand	1	2	3	4	5	6	7	8	9	10
1:Budweiser	0									
2:Schlitz	0.49	0								
3:Lowenbrau	0.38	0.53	0							
4:Kronenbourg	7.00	8.23	4.84	0						
5:Heineken	6.19	7.09	4.48	0.87	0					
6:Old Milwaukee	2.59	1.65	3.73	17.02	15.27	0				
7:Augsberger	4.07	1.87	3.16	12.13	11.54	3.11	0			
8:Stroh's Bohemian	3.36	1.56	3.64	14.80	12.00	1.35	2.07	0		
9:Miller Lite	3.07	5.45	5.00	11.47	9.53	7.46	13.37	9.69	0	
10:Budweiser Light	3.92	6.87	5.82	11.54	10.07	8.96	15.80	11.50	0.94	0

clustering. An informal rule used widely in applied research is that nonhierarchical clustering works well if one needs a fixed, known number of clusters, whereas hierarchical clustering is more useful when one needs to *compare* different clustering solutions. The sometimes subtle distinction between hierarchical and nonhierarchical clustering will become clearer as examples of each technique are presented.

In the next section, we will first perform a hierarchical analysis to better understand the structure of the brands in the market; the sense of this structure will become clearer as the analysis is examined in detail. Following that, we perform several nonhierarchical (K-means) analyses to determine the "best" groupings into prespecified numbers of groups. Finally, we will apply a special type of clustering to our marketing research student data, which contain both interval-scaled and categorical variables (see Section 11-3i).

11.3g Interpreting a Hierarchical Cluster Analysis

agglomeration schedule
In hierarchical cluster analysis, a list of the order in which various smaller clusters combine for form larger ones.

Essentially, all we need to know about a hierarchical cluster analysis can be very compactly represented in the "Agglomeration Schedule," which has an overly forbidding name. It merely tells us in what order the various clusters "agglomerate," that is, join with one another. It presumes that we should first place each object in its own cluster and let the various objects join up, in a way to be explained fully later. (A less-common way to cluster is to put all the objects into one cluster, breaking that cluster apart, and then continue successively breaking; this is called "divisive," as opposed to "agglomerative," clustering. Many clustering programs support both methods, and it is good practice to try both, if available.) Let us examine the agglomeration schedule for our 20 beers, which appears in Table 11.15.

normalized centroid distance
In cluster analysis, a measure of how far apart two cluster centers are. Small values of NCD indicate items that will likely wind up in the same cluster.

The output in Table 11.15 represents the clusters derived from the attribute and price data in a rather compact form. A way to go about interpreting it is as follows. We will first be concerned with the second column, the "centroid distance"; because we have placed all the variables on the same scale before running the analysis, we will refer to this as the "normalized centroid distance" (NCD). Just think of this as

Table 11.15 Agglomeration Schedule for Centroid Hierarchical Cluster Analysis

Clusters Remaining	Centroid Distance	Clusters or Items Combined	
19	0.115	Coors (11)	Hamm's (17)
18	0.307	Miller Lite (9)	Schlitz Light (20)
17	0.309	Stroh's Bohemian (8)	Heileman's Old Style (18)
16	0.375	Budweiser (1)	Lowenbrau (3)
15	0.417	CL16	Schlitz (2)
14	0.483	CL15	CL19
13	0.606	Heineken (5)	Kirin (15)
12	0.658	CL13	Kronenbourg (4)
11	0.780	CL18	Budweiser Light (10)
10	1.038	CL11	Coors Light (12)
9	1.233	CL17	Old Milwaukee (6)
8	1.307	CL10	Michelob Light (13)
7	1.496	CL14	CL09
6	2.393	CL07	Augsberger
5	2.821	Pabst Extra Light (16)	Olympia Gold Light (19)
4	3.081	CL12	Beck's (14)
3	5.098	CL06	CL08
2	6.915	CL03	CL04
1	13.405	CL02	CL05

Figure 11.7 Hierarchical Clusters Agglomerating

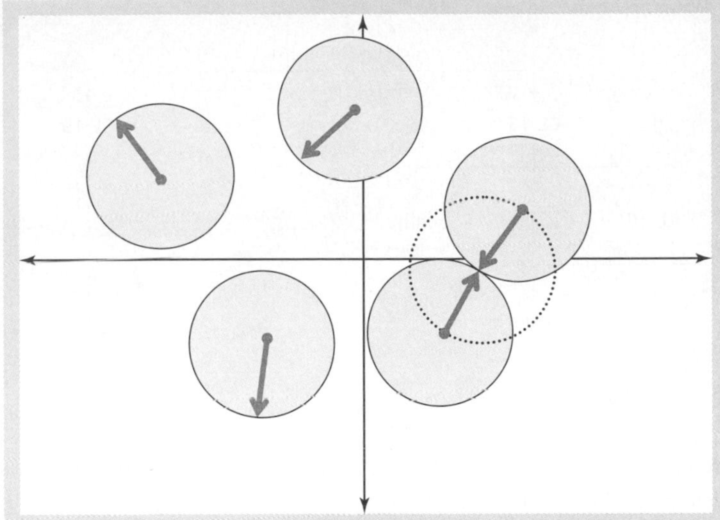

"radius of a circle/sphere that I put around each point once all four attribute dimensions are made equally important." If the NCD is small, then no two of the circle/spheres around the beers "overlap" one another, and we are forced to conclude that there are 20 separate clusters, each containing one beer. However, as the NCD gets larger, eventually some pair of beers *must* overlap. Figure 11.7 depicts this principle informally for a set of five objects.

Notice that the value of the NCD is such that two of the five objects, which are depicted at the center of each circle, have their circles exactly meet. A new circle of *exactly the same NCD* can now be drawn that takes each of them in, and its center will be at the point where the original circles meet. It is not difficult to see that we can continue this process until another pair of circles meets, and another, until all the objects are in a single circle, that is, cluster. It is important to note that this would be simple to perform visually if we were operating in just two dimensions. In our application, we have four variables, and in most real-world settings we have many more, making a visual inspection impossible.

We can now appreciate the information in the agglomeration schedule for the 20 clusters. The first row above indicates that, when the NCD (here, the sum-of-squared distances for the four prestandardized variables) gets up to around 0.115 or so, Coors (11) and Hamm's (17) are forced into the same cluster. Recall that the distinguishing feature of *hierarchical* cluster analysis (as opposed to nonhierarchical) is that once a group of objects is clustered together, *they are together for life*. Even if at a later stage it becomes evident that two large clusters should split up a smaller one between them, this is not allowed, and one of the two large clusters will have to subsume the smaller one completely. So it is that Coors and Hamm's will remain together throughout the clustering procedure. Next, Miller Lite (9) and Schlitz Light (20) form a cluster at NCD about 0.307, followed by Stroh's Bohemian (8) and Heileman's Old Style (18) at NCD = 0.309, and then Budweiser (1) and Lowenbrau (3) at NCD = 0.375. At this stage, there would be 16 clusters, 12 with a single brand, and 4 with two brands each. We can always check this by consulting the first column, "Clusters Remaining," which also, as we shall see, helps us give numerical names to the clusters formed. (Thus far, we have formed clusters CL19, CL18, CL17, and CL16, each with two objects.)

It is important to understand what happens next, near NCD = 0.417. Schlitz (2), rather than joining up with a single other brand to form a cluster of size two (as all other clusters have been formed thus far), joins up with Cluster 16 (CL16), that is, with Budweiser (1) and Lowenbrau (3), to form a cluster of size three. It should be apparent at this point that each stage in the agglomeration schedule tells when a cluster, whether it has one, two, or seventeen members, joins with another cluster; whenever this happens, the number of clusters decreases by one. Thus we see that, as NCD gets larger, we even see two clusters joining: at NCD = 0.483, CL15 and CL19 join one another, making a single cluster of five brands: Coors (11), Hamm's (17), Budweiser (1), Lowenbrau (3), and Schlitz (2). The new cluster, CL14, has *structure*, being formed of clusters than had previously formed at smaller values of NCD. It is useful to try to envision the agglomeration schedule as a structured process of clusters sequentially joining up with one

Figure 11.8 Hierarchical Cluster Analysis of Beer Brands

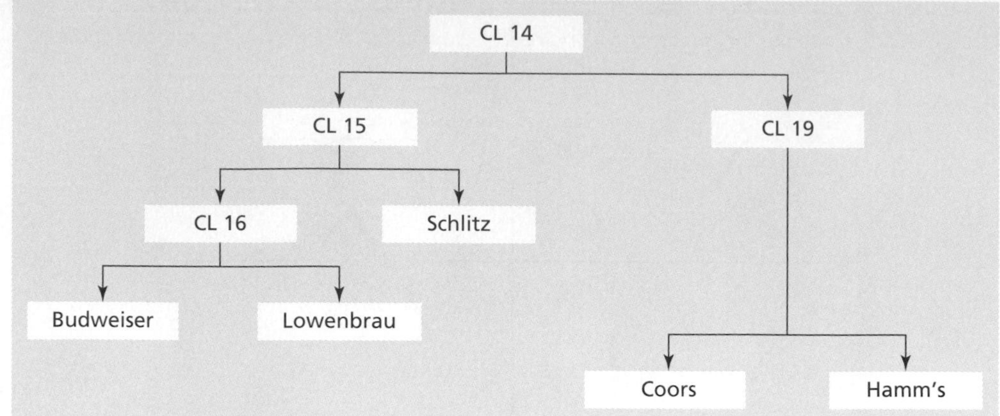

another. We can depict this graphically for CL14, as shown in Figure 11.8, to be replicated in a standard form by the statistical program later in our analysis.

Notice how each cluster is hierarchically organized into smaller clusters, and particularly how CL19 must "wait" until after CL15 and CL16 have been decomposed to yield its component brands, Coors and Hamm's. This occurs because, of all brand pairs, Coors and Hamm's are the closest, with NCD = 0.115.

Because this is a hierarchical analysis, clusters never break apart. The continual agglomeration of clusters continues until there are only clusters left, which are themselves eventually joined at NCD = 13.405; this must always happen because, if one draws exceptionally large circle/spheres around each of the brands, they will all eventually overlap. The task of the researcher is to determine, based on knowledge about the product class or situation at hand (plus several graphical aids discussed momentarily), how many clusters "make sense" in the end. Thus, cluster analysis is not a tool for passing statistical judgment on the relative merits of different numbers of clusters, merely one for determining the clusters themselves.

dendrogram
A treelike representation of the successive breakdown of the clustering solution in cluster analysis.

Because researchers will always have to decide "how many clusters there really are"—or at least how many they wish to settle on—all hierarchical clustering programs provide us with a **dendrogram** to easily visualize the structure of the clustered items.

The dendrogram in Figure 11.9 depicts the hierarchical, or "treelike," nature of the clustering solution. All the NCD values have been rescaled so that they extend from 1 to 100 (easily accomplished by

Figure 11.9 Dendrogram Using Centroid Method and Squared Euclidean Distances

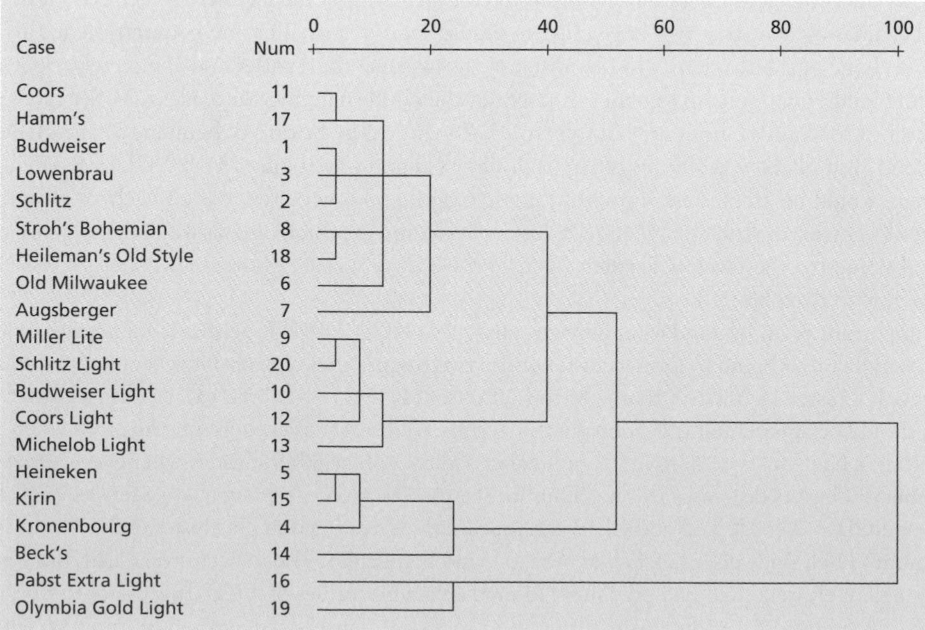

dividing all NCD values by the largest one, 13.405, and multiplying by 100), so that the biggest break in the set of items is at the rightmost side of the graph. This splits off Pabst Extra Light (16) and Olympia Gold Light (19) from the rest of the beers. Evidently, they are very different from all the others; let us examine the data for these two alone:

Brand	Number	Calories	Sodium	Alcohol	Price
Pabst Extra Light	16	68	15	2.3	0.38
Olympia Gold Light	19	72	6	2.9	0.46
Mean		132.4	15.0	4.4	0.50

Compared with mean values for the four variables, both beers are very low in calories, not high in sodium, low in alcohol, and low in price. So, their being split off from the other beers makes intuitive sense. However, they are *not* extremely similar to one another, just different from the *other* beers: if we look at the agglomeration schedule, these two beers do not "join" with one another until fairly late in the game:

Clusters Remaining	Centroid Distance	Clusters or Items Combined	
5	2.821	Pabst Extra Light (16)	Olympia Gold Light (19)

It is useful to consider the beer pairs that *are* very similar to one another, and we know these already from the agglomeration schedule, too:

Clusters Remaining	Centroid Distance	Clusters or Items Combined	
19	0.115	Coors (11)	Hamm's (17)
18	0.307	Miller Lite (9)	Schlitz Light (20)
17	0.309	Stroh's Bohemian (8)	Heileman's Old Style (18)
16	0.375	Budweiser (1)	Lowenbrau (3)

The reader should check to make sure that these pairs are joined "early on"—that is, well on the left side of the dendrogram—because the dendrogram is merely a visual distillation of the agglomeration schedule and must reproduce it perfectly.

In the end, we must decide on how many clusters are defensible, even though there is no absolutely correct answer. A tentative feel for this comes directly from the list of NCD values as depicted in the dendrogram: Do they suddenly take a big jump? It depends, of course, on what one considers "big," and we can follow the splits among the brands by starting at 100 on the right and moving leftward. Based on this visual criterion, it seems that four clusters make a good deal of sense. We can list these in Table 11.16, along with the associated data, and attempt to provide a description of the brands in each of these four clusters, bearing in mind the mean values for each of the variables (calories, 132.4; sodium, 15.0; alcohol, 4.4; price, 0.50):

It would be very helpful if we could adopt four-dimensional visual capabilities to view the clusters, but we will have to settle for a planar plot. Because calories correlates so highly with alcohol, we will just use the former; and because sodium seems less critical, we will leave it out for the time being, as shown in Figure 11.10, while noting that it *was* used in the clustering and cannot be completely ignored.

Figure 11.10 is a useful diagnostic aid in understanding the derived four-cluster solution, albeit only in relation to calories and price. Although it is undeniable that the four-cluster solution has some measure of visual appeal, it nevertheless seems that clusters 1, 2, and 4 can be perfectly discriminated by calories alone, without even considering the other variables! Recalling that calories and alcohol were both used in the analysis and were highly correlated, it is not surprising that they had a disproportionate effect on the clustering solution. It is only cluster 3 that appears to take price into account. To help solidify these insights, the dashed lines show that one can *discriminate* the clusters using simple linear functions of the variables in the analysis. These lines have a special name: **linear discriminant functions.** Although we do not delve into it here, almost all statistical programs that run cluster analysis also run another technique called discriminant analysis, the purpose of which is to yield exactly these "discriminating" lines (see Section 11-6 for a brief discussion). If we have four groups, we obtain three discriminant functions; if we have k groups, we obtain $k - 1$ discriminant functions. Note, however, that these functions include *all* the variables in the analysis, not just the two (or at most three) that humans can easily visualize.

linear discriminant functions Typically accompanies cluster analysis, and provides a linear function of variables (like in an ordinary regression) that helps best discriminate the clusters from one another.

Table 11.16 Cluster Associations and Interpretive Names for 20 Brands of Beer

Brand	Cluster	Calories	Sodium	Alcohol	Price	Description
Coors	1	140	18	4.6	0.44	"Cheap High": High on Calories, Sodium, and Alcohol; Low Price
Hamm's		136	19	4.4	0.43	
Budweiser		144	15	4.7	0.43	
Lowenbrau		157	15	4.9	0.48	
Schlitz		151	19	4.9	0.43	
Stroh's Bohemian Style		149	27	4.7	0.42	
Heileman's Old Style		144	24	4.9	0.43	
Old Milwaukee		145	23	4.6	0.28	
Augsberger		175	24	5.5	0.40	
Miller Lite	2	99	10	4.3	0.43	"Low to Moderate": Fairly Low on Calories, Sodium, Alcohol, and Price
Schlitz Light		97	7	4.2	0.47	
Budweiser Light		113	8	3.7	0.44	
Coors Light		102	15	4.1	0.46	
Michelob Light		135	11	4.2	0.50	
Heineken	3	152	11	5.0	0.77	"Super Premium": Moderate Calories and Alcohol; Low Sodium; Very High Price
Kirin		149	6	5.0	0.79	
Kronenbourg		170	7	5.2	0.73	
Beck's		150	19	4.7	0.76	
Pabst Extra Light	4	68	15	2.3	0.38	"Ultra Lite": Very Low Calories, Sodium, Alcohol, Price
Olympia Gold Light		72	6	2.9	0.46	

Figure 11.10 Calories (Y) vs. Price (X) for Four Clusters

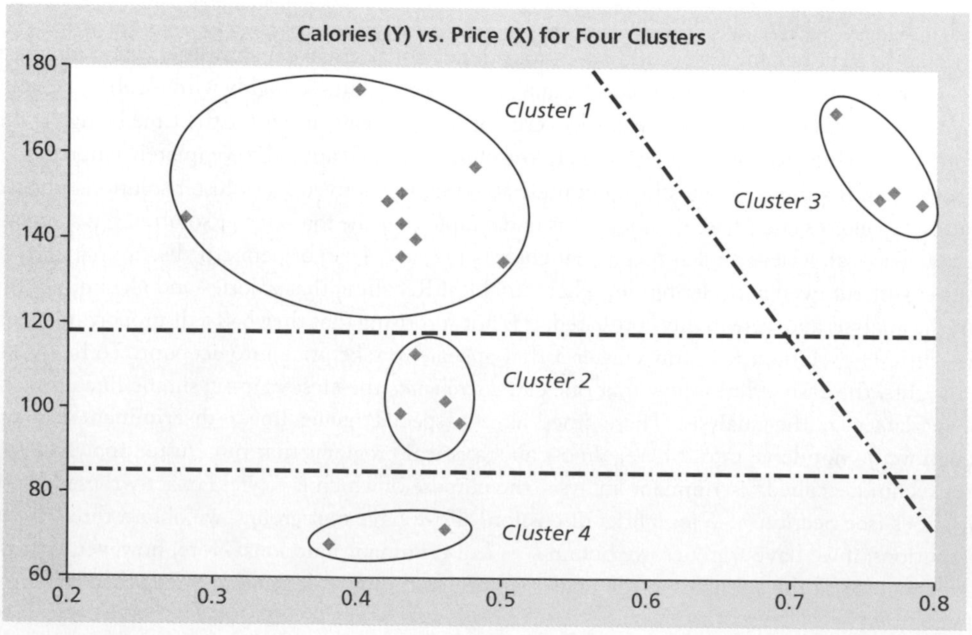

Table 11.17 Standardized Variables for the First Five (of 20) Beer Brands

Brand	Calories	Sodium	Alcohol	Price
		Standardized		
Budweiser	0.383	0.008	0.342	−0.463
Schlitz	0.615	0.615	0.605	−0.463
Lowenbrau	0.813	0.008	0.605	−0.115
Kronenbourg	1.243	−1.208	1.000	1.624
Heineken	0.648	0.600	0.737	1.903

It would be misleading at this point to claim that calories was the most important or, worse yet, the only important variable of the four, because we have considered the brands' ratings on only the two dimensions of calories and price. A next step would be to look at higher cluster (i.e., 5, 6, or more) on these same axes and see whether the price variable might account for further cluster splits. Regardless, we would have to consider the effects of the other variables, sodium and alcohol, because they had equal weight in the clustering.

Finally, we must emphasize that this hierarchical analysis was reasonable because we had a manageable number of brands to cluster. If there were thousands of objects, instead of 20, the agglomeration schedule and dendrogram would be so enormous as to obscure insight and also prohibitively time-consuming for the computer to calculate. The hierarchical analysis is important when we wish to obtain a *structural breakdown* of a set of objects—to impose a constraint that we can easily compare, say, the 4-cluster solution with the 5- and 3-cluster solutions. In many cases, this is not an important goal, and all that concerns the researcher is how to break up a group of items into the two or four or seventeen "best" clusters. If we have an enormous number of objects, or do not care about structure, we can use a powerful, non-hierarchical clustering method called *K-means*, and it is this we turn to next.

11.3h Nonhierarchical Clustering: The K-Means Method

When our research goal is to seek the best way to divide a set of items into a *known* (or hypothesized) number of clusters, K-means clustering is appropriate. Because it is nonhierarchical, there is no guarantee that comparing any two solutions will make a great deal of sense. For example, if we ask the computer to generate a 3-cluster and 4-cluster solution, we would see that objects from all three clusters would migrate between them, with some being drawn off to the new, fourth cluster. When we tried to describe the 3- and 4-cluster solutions later, we might find that the entire *basis* for clustering appeared different: one solution might have a great deal to do with price, and the other with features. Marketing researchers like to believe clusters are "real"—preexisting in the real world—and that how we break things up should not radically vary as we try different numbers of clusters.

K-means clustering
A form of cluster analysis where the items under study are broken into a fixed number of groups in an optimal way but not *hierarchically* (that is, the *k*-cluster solution will not generally form from the $(k+1)$-cluster solution by having two of the latter's clusters merge).

With these caveats, K-means clustering is a simple and powerful way to place items into groups, and it often produces more useful results than hierarchical clustering, especially when there are many items to be divided. Let us look again at our data for 20 beers, being careful to standardize each first, a critical step in a K-means analysis. For our first few beers, these data are provided in Table 11.17.

Running a K-means analysis requires simply telling the program the value for K, the number of clusters. Here, we will ask for $K = 4$ clusters, to best compare with the hierarchical analysis already performed and to later compare to $K = 3$ and $K = 5$. The output is far more readily understood than for a hierarchical analysis, and consists of cluster centers, cluster distances, and case information. We look at each in turn. Recall that, in all output, the values refer to the *standardized* variables.

Cluster Centers

	CL1	CL2	CL3	CL4
Calories	−0.77	−2.06	0.55	0.76
Sodium	−0.72	−0.68	0.83	−0.64
Alcohol	−0.45	−2.42	0.47	0.70
Price	−0.25	−0.53	−0.56	1.85
# in Cluster	5	2	9	4

	Cluster Center Distances			
	CL1	CL2	CL3	CL4
CL1	—			
CL2	2.38	—		
CL3	2.26	4.18	—	
CL4	2.84	4.84	2.84	—

The cluster distances arise directly from the cluster centers themselves by simple geometry (the square root of the sum-of-the-squares). Eyeballing them tells us that cluster 2 (CL2) is very different from the other clusters, which are about equidistant; we will examine it in detail later. The cluster centers help tell us what the clusters *mean*. Because the input variables were standardized, the values tell us how many standard deviations above or below the mean for that variable a cluster's center lies. For example, clusters 1 and 2 are both well below average on *all* four variables; but cluster 2 is very, very far below (more than 2 standard deviations, which is considered extreme) on calories and alcohol. Cluster 3 is above the mean on everything but price, whereas cluster 4 is above average on everything except sodium; it is *very* highly priced, in fact, at 1.85 standard deviations above the mean for this sample of beers.

It is not difficult to see—start by comparing the number of beers in each cluster—that our K-means solution is identical to the one obtained hierarchically. This is not a coincidence, nor is it the usual outcome: the hierarchical and nonhierarchical solutions often differ. That they are identical should help us feel confident in the assignment of beers to these four groups. Because the two solutions are identical, we will not examine the K-means clustering in detail. Instead, let us look at the assignments obtained by running the K-means analysis for $K = 2$, 3, 4, and 5 clusters in Table 11.18.

Table 11.18 Comparing 2-, 3-, 4-, and 5-Cluster K-Means Solutions for 20 Brands of Beer

		2-Cluster Solution		3-Cluster Solution		4-Cluster Solution		5-Cluster Solution	
Case	Brand	Cluster	Distance	Cluster	Distance	Cluster	Distance	Cluster	Distance
1	Budweiser	2	0.74	2	0.86	3	0.86	3	0.86
2	Schlitz	2	0.71	2	0.28	3	0.28	3	0.28
3	Lowenbrau	2	0.49	2	0.99	3	0.99	3	0.99
4	Kronenbourg	2	2.27	3	0.84	4	0.84	4	0.54
5	Heineken	2	1.98	3	0.13	4	0.13	4	0.50
6	Old Milwaukee	2	1.93	2	1.06	3	1.06	3	1.06
7	Augsberger	2	1.83	2	1.38	3	1.38	3	1.38
8	Stroh's Bohemian	2	1.68	2	1.01	3	1.01	3	1.01
9	Miller Lite	1	0.98	1	0.84	1	0.48	1	0.48
10	Budweiser Light	1	0.79	1	0.61	1	0.65	1	0.65
11	Coors	2	0.72	2	0.57	3	0.57	3	0.57
12	Coors Light	1	1.07	1	0.93	1	0.77	1	0.77
13	Michelob Light	2	1.32	1	1.46	1	0.92	1	0.92
14	Beck's	2	1.70	3	1.32	4	1.32	5	0.00
15	Kirin	2	2.52	3	0.78	4	0.78	4	0.45
16	Pabst Extra Light	1	2.05	1	2.23	2	0.84	2	0.84
17	Hamm's	2	0.99	2	0.72	3	0.72	3	0.72
18	Heileman's Old Style	2	1.26	2	0.59	3	0.59	3	0.59
19	Olympia Gold Light	1	1.29	1	1.48	2	0.84	2	0.84
20	Schlitz Light	1	0.98	1	0.87	1	0.65	1	0.65

Table 11.18 indicates an unusual degree of confluence across the $K = 2$–5 solutions. In fact, the solutions for $K = 3$–5 turn out to be hierarchical: in the 3-cluster solution, cluster 1 splits into two new clusters, and the other clusters remain intact (their number simply shifts up by 1 to relabel them for the 4-cluster solution). Similarly, the *only* thing that changes in going from $K = 4$ to $K = 5$ is that Beck's splits off into its own cluster. However, this is *not* the case in comparing the $K = 2$ and $K = 3$ solutions: many beers from the $K = 2$ cluster 2 remain in cluster 2, but Kronenbourg, Heineken, Beck's, and Kirin all shift to cluster 3, while Michelob Light shifts to cluster 1. That is, cluster 2 *redistributes* itself, rather than breaking into at most two new clusters. This is common in nonhierarchical solutions and makes interpretation difficult.

The output also includes the distance of each item to its cluster's center. Note how this tends to get smaller as we allow for more clusters. It will not *always* get smaller—Lowenbrau and Budweiser are best fit in the $K = 2$ solution—but very large values, such as that for Kirin, Kronenbourg, and a few others, tend to become far smaller as more clusters are allowed.

There is no indication here of the "best" number of clusters. Once again, we stress that this question can *only* be answered by the researcher, by balancing the project's need for accuracy (which will argue for more clusters) against the universal desire for a simple, robust explanation (which will argue for fewer).

11.3i Clustering with Different Data Types: An Application with Latent Classes

The development of powerful, affordable computers has made computationally intensive statistical methods widely available to researchers. Among these is a set of techniques called **latent class models**, which generalize the clustering methods we have studied in this chapter. A rigorous development of latent class models is outside the scope of this text—it is a vibrant and challenging area of academic and industry research—but we can make use of routines built into major statistical programs and interpret their results. We will return to the general issue of *heterogeneity* in Chapter 12, which deals with Advanced Topics; Further Readings are also listed at the end of this chapter.

latent class models
A set of statistical procedures that help break items, people, firms, products or coefficients into a fixed number of (presumed homogeneous) groups.

Let us analyze our marketing research student data to decide if there really are multiple "latent" groups (or clusters or classes; these are synonymous). Perhaps the strongest advantage of latent class methods is that they can handle many types of data simultaneously; specifically, we can input *both* interval-scaled and nominal (i.e., categorical) data and have the computer not only break our items (here, students) into groups, but to suggest, based on special measures related to the **log-likelihood function**, an appropriate number of clusters or classes. Once again, it is up to the researcher to make the final call on the number of classes, but we would do well to at least consider the program's suggestion.

log-likelihood function
In any statistical model, the logarithm of the probability of observing the sample data if the model is exactly correct.

We will treat five of the variables—age, height, weight, year, and LikeStat—as interval-scaled; and two variables, gender and class, as nominal. Because MBA simply combined categories for class, we will omit it from the analysis. The results are particularly simple to understand. The routine suggests that six clusters fit "best," so we present this 6-cluster solution in Table 11.19.

Table 11.19 Six-Cluster Latent Class Solution for Marketing Research Student Data

							Percentages for Categorical Variables				
		Means for Interval Variables					Gender		Class		
Cluster and Size		Age	Height	Weight	Year	LikeStat	Women	Men	1	2	3
1	10.7%	21.0	71.1	176.4	3.81	6.42	0%	18.3%	41.0%	0%	0%
2	25.0%	29.5	70.6	175.0	3.58	3.54	0%	42.6%	0%	59.6%	0%
3	23.0%	31.6	69.9	174.4	3.54	3.62	0%	39.2%	0%	0%	72.0%
4	15.4%	21.2	65.3	129.1	3.29	6.42	37.3%	0%	59.0%	0%	0%
5	8.9%	29.7	64.5	128.8	3.40	4.48	21.6%	0%	0%	0%	28.0%
6	17.0%	28.1	64.9	128.9	3.58	4.55	41.1%	0%	0%	40.4%	0%
Overall		27.6	68.2	156.0	3.54	4.56	100%	100%	100%	100%	100%

Table 11.20 Three-Cluster Latent Class Solution for Marketing Research Student Data

		Means for Interval Variables					Percentages for Categorical Variables				
							Gender		Class		
Cluster and Size		Age	Height	Weight	Year	LikeStat	Women	Men	1	2	3
1	26.1%	21.2	67.7	148.5	3.50	6.42	37.3%	18.3%	100%	0%	0%
2	48.0%	30.5	70.3	174.7	3.56	3.58	0%	81.7%	0%	59.6%	72.0%
3	25.9%	28.7	64.8	128.9	3.52	4.53	62.7%	0%	0%	40.4%	28.0%
Overall		27.59	68.17	155.99	3.54	4.56	100%	100%	100%	100%	100%

Note that we can summarize the interval-scaled variables with a single quantity, the mean in each cluster, but we require percentages across the various categories for the nominal variables; it is generally far more difficult to summarize nominal variables, which is one reason researchers try to avoid using them in statistical analyses.

In some sense, these results are unsurprising and unsatisfying: as the last five columns show, the groups just correspond to all possible combinations of Gender (Women, Men) and Class (1, 2, 3); the percentages of cases in each cluster (10.7 percent, 25.0 percent, 23.0 percent, 15.4 percent, 8.9 percent, 17.0 percent) bear this out as well. The nominal variables, already themselves discrete categories, "take over" the clustering solution. Simply put, it is easier to use categories to parcel items into categories.

Suppose, instead, that we knew in advance that our research required splitting the students into exactly three classes (clusters). We can specify that the solution yield precisely this number; the resulting clusters are provided in Table 11.20.

The pattern across the three clusters is not so obvious as before, although cluster 2 is composed entirely of men, cluster 3 entirely of women, and cluster 1 entirely of people in class 1 (undergraduates; note the mean age in this cluster is 21.2). It would seem that, if we had to find one set of students who looked reasonably homogeneous (alike), it would be the undergraduate students. Once someone is not an undergraduate, it seems that his or her gender offers the best way to split up members of this class.

We could easily perform this analysis with any number of clusters, as the research goals specify. As the number of clusters grows, however, the number of items in each dwindles. Once the number of items in a cluster gets very small—less than five is a usual rule of thumb—we must be very careful about accepting that cluster solution as our "final answer."

Cluster and Latent Class analyses can be exceptionally useful tools in an array of marketing projects. In practice, managers must interpret the resulting clusters or segments thoughtfully. How one firm approaches this task for a large-scale clustering application is highlighted in *International Issues 11.1*.

International Issues 11.1

International Attitude Measures Help Identify Segments

There are several attitude-based segmentation systems available to international marketers.

One such service is Global Scan. Developed originally by Backer Spielvogel & Bates Worldwide (http://www.batesusa.com), the program includes more than 15 countries and uses a 250-question survey, in which half the questions are specific to the respondents' country and half are "global" questions that measure values such as self-esteem and self-sufficiency. Six segments are consistently identified, as follows: (1) *Strivers*: youthful; living hectic, on-the-go lives; driven to achieve success; materialistic pleasure seekers. (2) *Achievers*: older than strivers, affluent, upwardly mobile, already have attained success levels the Strivers seek. (3) *Pressured*: largely female, facing constant financial and familial pressures, overwhelmed. (4) *Adopters*: older people content with their lives, yet maintaining their values. (5) *Traditionals*: "rooted to the past," resisting change, clinging to heritage and cultural values. (6) *Unassigned:* people who defy the previous classifications.

VALS™ (www.sric-bi.com/VALS) is a marketing tool that helps firms worldwide by segmenting the consumer marketplace on the basis of the personality traits that drive consumer behavior. Rather than looking at what people do and segregating people with like activities, VALS defines consumer segments on the basis of those personality traits that affect behavior in the marketplace. SRI International (www.sri.com) established the specialized Japan VALS program to determine the consumer effects of changing values and social attitudes specific to the Japanese market. Ten segments were identified, as follows: (1) *Integrators:* well-educated, modern people who enjoy the new and risky; comprise 5 percent of the population and measure highest on Innovation. As consumers, integrators are active, inquisitive, trend-leading, informed, and affluent, travel frequently, and consume a wide range of print and broadcast media, including niche and foreign. (2) *Sustainers*: are people who resist change. They score lowest on the Innovation and Self-Expression dimensions. Lacking money, youth, and high education, these consumers dislike innovation and are typically oriented to sustaining the past. (3) *Self-innovators:* young, active people who spend a lot of money on themselves. (4) *Self-adopters:* are people who pattern their buying after that of self-innovators. Self-Innovators and Self-Adopters score high on Self-Expression. As consumers, they desire personal experience; fashionable display; social activities; daring ideas; and exciting, graphic entertainment. (5) *Ryoshiki ("social intelligence") innovators:* career-oriented, highly educated middle-aged people. (6) *Ryoshiki adopters:* people who pattern their behavior after that of ryoshiki innovators. Ryoshiki Innovators and Ryoshiki Adopters score highest on the Achievement measure. They focus on education, career achievement, and professional knowledge; but home, family, and social status are their guiding concerns. (7) *Tradition innovators:* middle-aged homeowners with middle management jobs who are active in community affairs. (8) *Tradition adopters:* are affluent, young, and well-educated managers who travel frequently. Tradition Innovators and Tradition Adopters score highest on the measure of Traditional Ways. As consumers, they adhere to traditional religions and customs, prefer long-familiar home furnishings and dress, and hold conservative social opinions. (9) *High pragmatics:* the people least likely to agree with any attitude statement, unconcerned about self-improvement or preserving customs. (10) *Low pragmatics:* are attitudinally negative people with no identifiable psychological tendency who prefer inexpensive goods and established brands. High Pragmatics and Low Pragmatics do not score high on any life-orientation dimension. They are not very active and not well informed; they have few interests and seem flexible or even uncommitted in their lifestyle choices.

Figure 11.11 Japan VALS framework.

Figure 11.11 Japan VALS Segmentation System

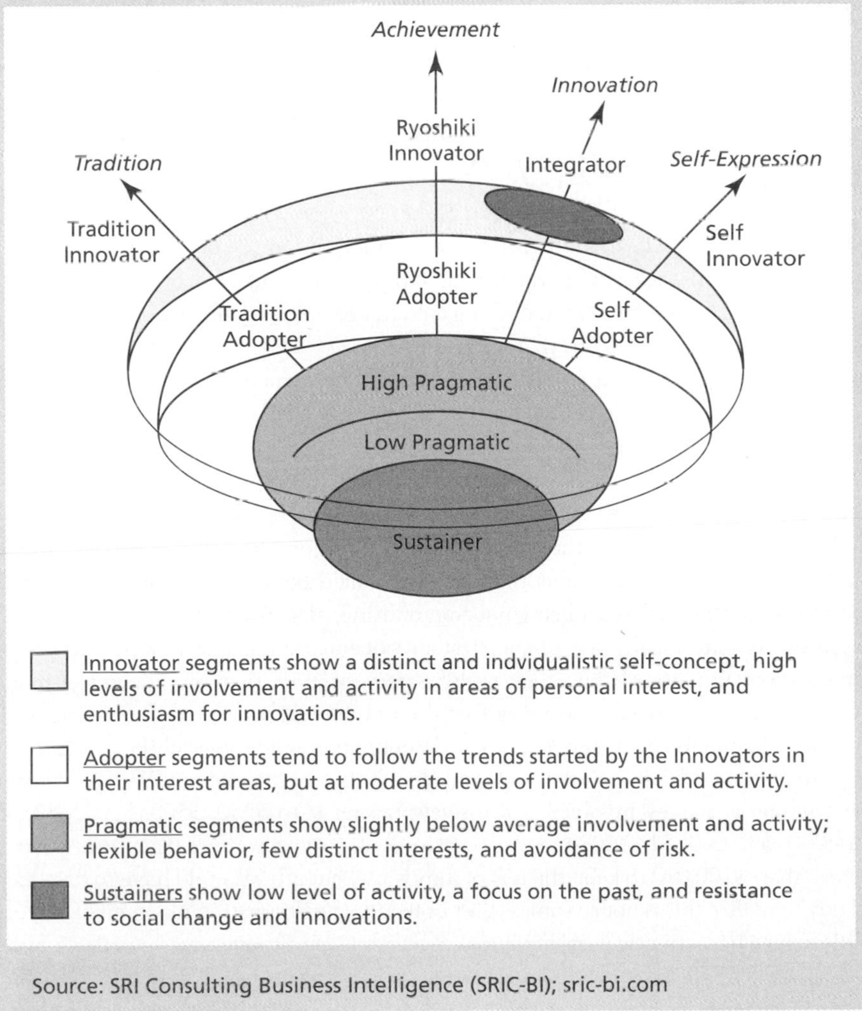

Source: SRI Consulting Business Intelligence (SRIC-BI); sric-bi.com

Young & Rubicam (www.yr.com), believing that people's goals, motivations, attitudes, and values determine consumers' choices, developed the Cross Cultural Consumer Characterization (4Cs) system (www.4cs.yr.com) of psychographic segmentation, comprising such dimensions as security, control, status, individuality, freedom, survival, and escape. The 4Cs system groups people into three major groups composed of seven segments: (1) *Resigned*: rigid, strict, authoritarian, chauvinist values, oriented to the past and to resigned roles; brand choice stresses safety, familiarity, and economy; older. (2) *Struggler*: alienated, disorganized, with few resources apart from physical/mechanical skills (e.g., auto repair); heavy consumers of alcohol, junk food, and lotteries; brand choice involves impact and sensation. (3) *Mainstreamer*: domestic, conformist, conventional, sentimental, passive, habitual; part of the mass, favoring larger, well-known value for money "family" brands; almost invariably the largest 4Cs group. (4) *Aspirer*: materialistic, acquisitive, affiliative, oriented to extrinsics (image, appearance, charisma, persona, and fashion); attractive packaging more important than quality of contents; younger, clerical/sales type occupation. (5) *Succeeder*: strong goal-orientation, confidence, work ethic, organization; support status quo, stability; brand choice based on reward, prestige, only the very best will do; also attracted to "caring" and protective brands, stress relief; top management. (6) *Explorer*: energy, autonomy, experience, challenge, new frontiers; brand choice highlights difference, sensation, adventure, indulgence, and instant effect; the first to try new brands; younger or student. (7) *Reformer*: freedom from restriction, personal growth, social awareness, value for time, independent judgment, tolerance of complexity, antimaterialistic but intolerant of bad taste; curious and inquiring, support growth of new product categories; select brands for intrinsic quality, favoring natural simplicity, small is beautiful; higher education, often graduate degree.

In these attitude-based segmentation systems, the percentage of people in each segment varies by country, and few researchers believe that a single segmentation system can be applied cross-culturally. As long as users realize the systems' limitations and are sensitive to cultural differences, these segmentation tools provide valuable starting points for international market development decisions.

Sources: Lewis C. Winters (1992), "International Psychographics." *Marketing Research,* Volume 4, Issue 3, 48–49.

Chin-Feng Lin (2002), "Segmenting Customer Brand Preference: Demographic or Psychographic." *Journal of Product & Brand Management*, 11(4)249–268.

Young and Rubicam website: http://www.yr.com.

11.4 Conjoint Analysis

Conjoint at Dinner Time
Source: STAHLER: © Columbus Dispatch/Dist. by Newspaper Enterprise Association, Inc.

"You can't always get what you want." ***The Rolling Stones***

A general principle learned early in life is that we cannot obtain the best of everything all the time. Finding the perfect dress or jacket takes time; a car with the latest luxury features will not be inexpensive; electronic gadgets that weigh next to nothing tend not to be powerful; and so on. In such situations, which confront us constantly, we learn that we must make *trade-offs*. If you think back to any purchase you made, you chose something that represented, *to you*, the best balance of cost and various valued features. On some occasions, this trade-off will lead to the lowest-priced or most powerful or lightest option; but, more often than not, we choose something nearer to the "middle of the pack."

Because marketing researchers concern themselves with why consumers make the choices they do, understanding this trade-off process is among the most intensive research areas in the discipline. The chief methods for doing so fall under the umbrella name of **conjoint analysis**. If you're going to remember nothing else about conjoint, remember that it is a set of methods to *understand and quantify trade-offs*.

conjoint analysis
A popular marketing research method to calibrate an individual's *utility* or value for different *attributes* (e.g., durability, size, price) and *levels* of each attribute. Respondents supply data on various combinations of the attributes, called profiles. Given a set of such profiles, this data can take the form of separate ratings for each, rankings of the entire set, or choosing the single best profile from the set.

Many people pride themselves on being uncompromising, always seeking out the best and greatest, or not falling short on some ideal. For example, in studies of auto purchasing, new parents will often state that "nothing is more important" than their child's safety, or even that "no amount of money" could compensate them for an increased probability that their child will be injured. But is this really so? We could study it more objectively by simply asking, "Would you double your child's chance of a serious automotive injury for $100?" Almost all would immediately say they would not. We could systematically increase the amount of money involved, successively raising it to $250, $500, $1000, $2500, $5000, $10,000, $25,000, $50,000, $100,000, and so on. No doubt, some parents may even assert that they would pay more than $100,000 to keep the risk of injury low, but all we would have to do is examine the car they did buy to realize this is not so (unless they opted for the Sherman tank or missile defense system options). This somewhat whimsical example makes a serious point: even for something exceptionally important to us, we will always be willing to make a trade-off against other important attributes if the "levels" involved become extreme. And this, as we shall see, is the key insight that allows *conjoint measurement* to work: using the trade-offs people make to precisely determine what is important to them and to measure the degree of that importance.

Before launching into an illustration of how conjoint works, let us consider a brief outline of some of its chief uses, to be supplemented later by a fuller set of real-world applications. In a sense, these four questions capture the main ideas lurking behind conjoint:

- How much are specific *attributes* of a product or service valued?
  In conjoint, "attributes" are qualities something can possess, such as safety, price, acceleration, volume, softness, stylishness, and so on. For a particular person, some attributes will be valued more highly than others.
- What *levels* of each attribute should the product or service have?
  If we are considering an ultracompact camera, two important attributes are weight and thickness, but each can have many *levels*. For weight, we might consider cameras weighing 5, 6, 8, and 12 ounces; for thickness, we might choose among ½ in., 3/4 in., and 1 in. For every attribute, we will have many levels to consider, and some of these will be strongly preferred to others. Some attributes will be *valenced:* everyone will prefer some levels of an attribute over others. Everyone, for example, will prefer a camera that is less prone to breaking, but not everyone will want the thinnest possible camera.
- How it should be priced?
  The very nature of economic transactions means that, in the end, everything is traded off against price. In an efficient market, it is more costly to create something better. Price, therefore, is almost always an element of conjoint studies. Although it is treated like any other attribute, it is often distinguished conceptually because it is not an element of the product itself but something that can be changed instantly, even by a retailer. One helpful feature of conjoint is that it quantifies how any attribute is traded against any other and therefore price as well.
- How do consumers tend to "trade off" different features (i.e., levels of attributes)?
  This, in essence, is *the* main question of all conjoint studies, and we will see how they are designed to address it.

11.4a Conjoint vs. Test Markets

One way to figure out what drives consumers to make the choices they do is to run a full-scale test market, using prototyped products. Although this is the "gold standard" in marketing research—it is just like selling the product under actual market conditions—it is phenomenally impractical. Most products do not make it to market, simply because they would not be profitable against the products already available. Test markets, particularly for durables such as cars, can run to the hundreds of millions of dollars, or even more. Compared with traditional methods of product testing, then, conjoint is far less expensive, quicker, and more flexible: unlike in a test market, where making changes to the product is difficult or impossible, a conjoint study can be adjusted on the fly if targets are not being met or the results indicate that the tested configurations need to be fixed. Thus, conjoint is often considered a *premarket testing* methodology, something to be carried out well before physical prototype products are built, an actual sales force is engaged, and real consumers are monitored pre- and postpurchase.

11.4b Conjoint Example: A New, Brighter Light Bulb

Let us consider an especially simple example to highlight implementation and interpretation issues typical of conjoint application. Suppose we wish to market a new light bulb, one that is brighter, but also costlier, than those typically on the market. Product managers have settled on three critical attributes: brightness (measured in watts of energy consumed); average bulb life (in expected hours until replacement); and, of course, price (in dollars). They are also considering just three levels of each:

Brightness	Average Bulb Life	Price
300 watts	2500 hours	$5.00
250 watts	2000 hours	$6.00
200 watts	1500 hours	$8.00

Part of the problem is that we already know what sort of bulb configuration is ideal for both the consumer and the manufacturer. For example, the consumer wants a bulb that is as bright as possible, lasts the longest, and costs the least:

Brightness	Average Bulb Life	Price
300 watts	2500 hours	$5.00

But all these qualities cost money; it is cheaper to make a bulb that is less bright and burns out more quickly and more lucrative to charge a lot for it. Thus, assuming the goal is to maximize revenue, the manufacturer's ideal bulb is:

Brightness	Average Bulb Life	Price
200 watts	1500 hours	$8.00

This raises a basic marketing issue: the ideal consumer bulb is not practical to produce, and the ideal manufacturer bulb is of no interest to consumers. The reason for this is simple: in a competitive, efficient market, a firm cannot afford to sell something that is the best in every way for the lowest price possible (the ideal consumer bulb), nor can it make any money selling something that is the worst in every way for the highest possible price (the ideal manufacturer bulb). The manufacturer and consumer will have to reach some middle ground, a *trade-off* between attribute levels and price that is reasonable for both parties. A first step for the manufacturer, then, is understanding what attributes and levels the consumer values, and how much. A traditional approach might involve simply asking the consumer to rank levels, as follows:

Rank	Brightness	Rank	Life	Rank	Price
1	300 watts	1	2500 hours	1	$5.00
2	250 watts	2	2000 hours	2	$6.00
3	200 watts	3	1500 hours	3	$8.00

This would not be a very informative exercise; we would learn that people like the best price best, the second-best price second-best, and the worst price least, and the same for the other two attributes. That is, evaluating them *individually* gives no information whatever about how respondents *trade them off*. To do that, we have to evaluate them jointly, which is what conjoint measurement is designed to do with great accuracy and efficiency. Although we will later study other methods for that evaluation, let us stay for the time being with ranking, even though it is often cumbersome.

Let us look at just the first two attributes, but this time jointly, for two hypothetical customers, Buyer A and Buyer B in Figure 11.12.

There are a number of remarkable features of these rankings, some of which are dictated by logic and consistency. First, both buyers agree on the best (1) and least (9) preferred option; *any* buyer would, because (2500 hours, 300 watts) is the best level of life with the best level of brightness, and (1500 hours, 200 watts) is the worst level of life with the worst level of brightness. (Here, we must assume that there are no *synergies* or *interactions* so that pairing the worst level on one attribute with the worst on another is somehow superior to pairing the worst with something better.) Next, if we move strictly down the chart or strictly across left to right, the rank number increases, indicating lower preference, because,

Figure 11.12 **Preference Patterns for Buyers A and B: No Observed Trade-Off Between Bulb Life and Wattage**

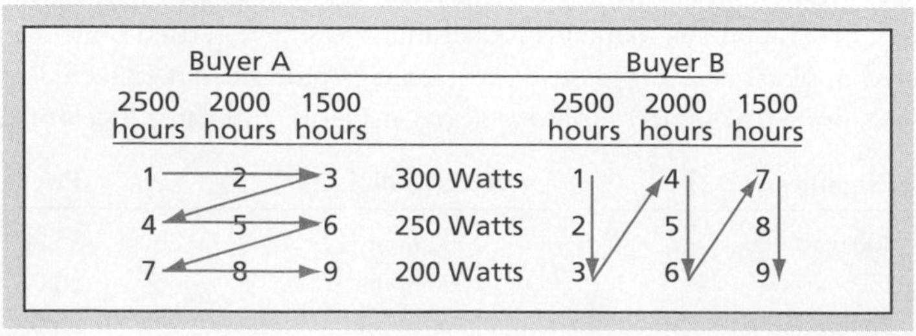

Buyer A: 2500 hours	2000 hours	1500 hours		Buyer B: 2500 hours	2000 hours	1500 hours
1	2	3	300 Watts	1	4	7
4	5	6	250 Watts	2	5	8
7	8	9	200 Watts	3	6	9

when we hold one attribute constant, but change the other in a deleterious way, we must lower overall preference.

One might think that these commonalities would mean that Buyer A and Buyer B have a similar set of preferences, but nothing could be further from the truth; all they agree on is "better is better," *not* on which attributes or levels are important. In fact, the two buyers are as different as they can be: Buyer A cares *much* more about brightness, whereas Buyer B cares *much* more about life. We can tell this by following the arrows drawn over their preference rankings. Let us start at "1" for Buyer A: given a choice between losing some bulb life (2500 hours to 2000) or some brightness (300 watts to 250), Buyer A sacrifices life. Asked again, Buyer A sacrifices some more life, moving to 1500 hours rather than sacrifice brightness. In fact, Buyer A always sacrifices life to maintain the level of brightness, within the levels included in this design. (We could not say that life is "unimportant" based on these trade-offs, but we *can* conclude that it is much less important than brightness, which is the main point.) Buyer B is literally the mirror-image opposite, *always* sacrificing brightness instead of bulb life. One can imagine that Buyer A needed to illuminate some area as intensely as possible, whereas Buyer B had to place the bulb in a difficult-to-access area and so wished to change it as infrequently as possible. When people have such uni-dimensional preferences, conjoint ranking tasks often come out like these examples.

Let us now examine the rankings of two different, and more interesting, potential customers, Buyer 1 and Buyer 2 in Figure 11.13.

Buyers 1 and 2 share a lot with Buyers A and B: they agree on the best (1) and worst (9) items; their preference always decreases top-to-bottom and left-to-right; Buyer A and Buyer 1 care much more about brightness; Buyer B and Buyer 2 care much more about life. But there is one huge, distinguishing feature about Buyers 1 and 2: they make *trade-offs*. Specifically:

> Buyer 1 prefers (250 watts, 2500 hours) to (300 watts, 1500 hours) *even though brightness is more important overall*, and Buyer 2 prefers (300 watts, 2000 hours) to (200 watts, 2500 hours) *even though life is more important overall*.

To put the general idea especially succinctly: just because something is the *most* important thing to you does not mean it is the *only* important thing. Buyer 1 and Buyer 2 were willing to compromise on the most important attributes to them when *other* attribute levels became unacceptable. This reasoning lies at the very heart of conjoint analysis and enables it to make its measurements.

The rankings collected thus far still do not tell us two crucial sets of values:

1. the relative "importances" of the various *attributes*;
2. for any particular attribute, the relative "importances" of the various *levels*.

We will call these "importances" *utilities* or, for the levels, **part worths**. These utilities are exactly the same as the "consumer utility" we read about earlier in discrete choice models such as the logit and probit. The overall goal of conjoint is to measure them using information supplied by respondents, such as ranks (in our bulb example), ratings, or choices (which we will examine later in our application). The question remains as to how, exactly, can we carry out these measurements statistically. We can ask ourselves what are the utility values that allow us to *reproduce* the rankings of Buyer 1? Table 11.21 presents a set of quantities, with the original ranks in parentheses, that allow us to do just that.

part worths
In conjoint analysis, the utilities associated with particular levels of any attribute.

Figure 11.13 Preference Patterns for Buyers 1 and 2: Some Observed Trade-Off Between Bulb Life and Wattage

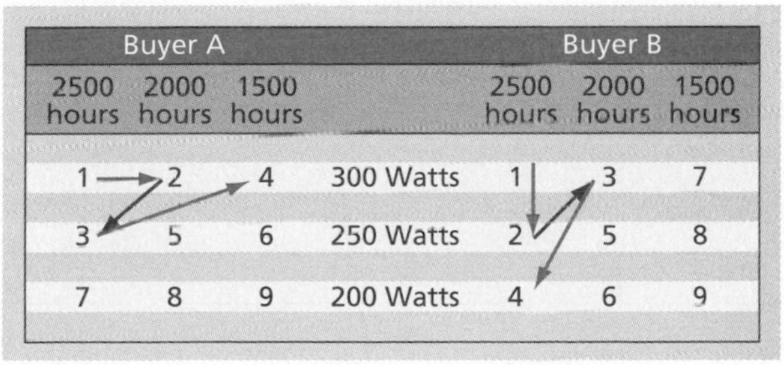

Buyer A				Buyer B		
2500 hours	2000 hours	1500 hours		2500 hours	2000 hours	1500 hours
1	2	4	300 Watts	1	3	7
3	5	6	250 Watts	2	5	8
7	8	9	200 Watts	4	6	9

Table 11.21 **Feasible Part Worth Values for Two Light Bulb Attributes (Life and Brightness) Based on Consumer Ranking Data**

	2500 hours 50	2000 hours 25	1500 hours 0
300 watts 100	(1) 150	(2) 125	(4) 100
250 watts 60	(3) 110	(5) 85	(6) 60
200 watts 0	(7) 50	(8) 25	(9) 0

When we add up the values (part worths) associated with each of the attribute levels, we obtain the numbers in Table 11.21, which do exactly reproduce the original rankings for Buyer 1. You might ask whether this is the only possible set of utility values that would give rise to the observed rankings. That is, are these utility values *unique*? The answer is . . . not even close. We have to first decide on some scale to use, and the usual convention is to find (the computer does this for us) which attribute is most important and have it span 0 to 100; this is what brightness does, with 300 watts getting 100 utility points and 200 watts 0 utility points. It is also typical to scale any other attributes from 0 to some quantity that reflects the *overall importance of that attribute*, relative to 100. So, bulb life ranges from 0 (for 1500 hours) to 50 (for 2500) hours, suggesting that life is exactly half as important (50 vs. 100) as brightness.

We will ask again whether the remaining part worth values (60 for 250 Watts; 25 for 2000 hours; and even 50 for 2500 hours, which was determined by the computer) are unique. It is easy to see that they are not. If we raised the part worth for 250 watts from 60 to 70, for example, none of the ranks in the table would change. Is this a defect in conjoint analysis? No, it is not. It is overly optimistic to think we can precisely obtain someone's utility values from just *one* set of rankings. Usually, we ask for several sets from each respondent, and we also have many respondents, allowing for great accuracy of measurement.

We now realize, somewhat distressingly, that we have only done this for two of our three attributes. What about the third, price? Because we already know how life trades off against brightness, we can just have the respondent do another ranking task for price and life, without including brightness. The ranks, and associated utility values, are provided in Table 11.22.

These results indicate that price is far less relevant than bulb life (and, by extension, brightness); in fact, it appears that *no* trade-off has taken place. Consequently, we cannot estimate utility values for price very well, but the listed values do exactly reproduce the ranks in the table. Again, we would normally request more data from this respondent and have many respondents complete the task, ensuring far greater accuracy in utility measurement than in our concise example. Let us pretend, therefore, that all the part worths thus far have been measured very accurately, so that we can use them to

Table 11.22 **Feasible Part Worth Values for Two Light Bulb Attributes (Life and Price) Based on Consumer Ranking Data**

	2500 hours 50	2000 hours 25	1500 hours 0
$5.00 20	(1) 70	(4) 45	(7) 20
$6.00 5	(2) 55	(5) 30	(8) 5
$8.00 0	(3) 50	(6) 25	(9) 0

determine what sort of bulbs to produce. To recap, our part worths, for each level of each attribute, are as follows:

Brightness		Life		Price	
300 watts	100	2500 hours	50	$5.00	20
250 watts	60	2000 hours	25	$6.00	5
200 watts	0	1500 hours	0	$8.00	0

We are now ready to apply our conjoint model. Specifically, suppose that a manufacturer can produce either of two bulbs for the same total production (and other) costs. Which might consumers, or at least this one target consumer, prefer? The two bulb configurations are as follows:

	"Super Bright" Bulb	"Long Life" Bulb
Brightness	300	250
Life	1500	2500
Price	$6.00	$8.00

The "Super Bright" bulb has the highest level of brightness, but it burns out quickly and is moderately priced. The "Long Life" bulb lasts for 2500 hours and is moderately bright, but it is very costly. Determining the better-preferred option requires only the use of addition:

	"Super Bright" Bulb		"Long-life" Bulb	
Brightness	300	100	250	60
Life	1500	0	2500	50
Price	$6.00	5	$8.00	0
TOTAL		105		110

The result is that the "Long Life" Bulb is preferred by a "small" amount, a total of five part worth points. A sense of this margin can be gained by comparing it with the range of any of the attributes, 0 to 100 for brightness, 0 to 50 for life, and 0 to 20 for price. Regardless of the size of the margin of superiority, because the manufacturer is indifferent as to which is produced (because they have identical costs), the "Long Life" bulb will fare better than the "Super Bright" bulb. This holds aside questions as to whether *both* bulbs, or any other configurations, should be produced. This is known in marketing as the *product line design problem*, and it has been studied by academic researchers for decades. To solve it requires a great deal of information over and above conjoint part worths (which are always required), in regard to production costs, retailing operations, distribution, market size, and relative demand.

11.4c Conjoint Analysis: Basic Steps, Problems, and Extensions

Our example was deliberately simplified so that we could understand the basic issues and "solution concept" behind the part worths and attribute importance values. There are in actuality many variants of conjoint, but all of them hinge on three basic steps:

- collecting trade-off data from consumers
- estimating value systems (utilities: importances and part-worths)
- making choice predictions

Conjoint methods differ primarily in the first two of these, in terms of how respondents supply information about their trade-offs, and what sort of statistical model must be used to turn them into utilities (part worths and attribute importances). To better understand the issues involved, let us look at some of the problems we would encounter if we wished to use the type of ranking data we used in our light bulb conjoint example. First, the trade-off matrix is cumbersome, time-consuming, and cognitively demanding; even with so few attributes and levels, respondents had to supply a great deal of information and compare two attributes at a time. With k attributes, we would have $k - 1$ trade-off matrices; and, with many levels, *each* of these matrices would have dozens or hundreds of entries. Second, in real-world applications, most of the trade-offs would be entirely irrelevant or nearly so: we do not want respondents asking themselves, "Is this my 42nd or 43rd most-favorite item?" Although this is preferable to ranking every possible combination (which could easily run into the millions), it is still well beyond most people's patience threshold. Third, the entire undertaking has a one-size-fits-all feel to it: stimuli are not tailored to individual respondents. If bulb brightness is relatively unimportant to you, but price is critical, researchers should not be focusing your attention and time on them equally. Rather, the conjoint task should "notice" what your responses are telling it and tailor future comparisons accordingly. Finally, the experimental task is extremely artificial: when making real purchases, people simply choose the items they like best, not stand there and rank every single thing available to them. Thus, ranking-based conjoint, particularly with every respondent seeing the same trade-offs, is a very poor use of the precious resources of respondent attention and thinking. Fortunately, conjoint researchers and practitioners have developed powerful specialized methods to address each of these problems, and three stand out as being critical for all marketing research professionals: orthogonal designs, adaptive conjoint, and choice-based conjoint. We will examine each of these more closely from the perspective of the practicing manager.

11.4d Orthogonal Designs

The number of possible product profiles in a typical conjoint design can run into the millions, if every possible attribute level is paired with every other. Conjoint itself would become a practical impossibility if respondents had to evaluate all of these. A general technique applicable throughout experimental research is that of the **orthogonal design**, which allows researchers to offer a subset of, rather than all, possible combinations. Orthogonal designs "work" because the "correlation" between attributes presented is zero (we place quotes around "correlation" because we are working with *nominal* variables; and correlations are, strictly speaking, only for interval-scaled variables, but the intuition is the same). This means that, when describing a product by its attribute levels, including a particular level of one attribute gives no information about what levels are present for other attributes.

orthogonal design
A design for which, when several quantities have to be measured in an experiment, manipulations of one quantity will not affect measurements of another; often allows a dramatic drop in the overall number of measurements that must be taken.

A great deal is known about how to construct orthogonal designs, and it is generally best left to specialized routines in our statistical programs to generate them. In practical terms, they dramatically reduce data requirements per respondent. In the movie theater example in *Marketing Research Focus 11.3*, an orthogonal design will allow us to present only 18 profiles, instead of the 108 possible; in the bathroom scale (choice-based) conjoint presented later in this chapter, more than 15,000 possible profiles can be orthogonalized into just 25 (although 50 will be used as a failsafe). For the larger conjoint designs found in real applications, even millions of possible profiles can usually be whittled down to only a few dozen. Few if any conjoint studies are planned without first generating an orthogonal design, nor should they be. *Marketing Research Focus 11.3* presents the process and results of a conjoint analysis for a movie theater that makes use of an orthogonal design to reduce the number of possible questions.

Marketing Research Focus 11.3

Designing Your Own Movie Theater Using Conjoint Analysis and an Orthogonal Design

Imagine you can design a new movie theater and are put in control of five attributes important to moviegoers in selecting a theater: ticket price, line-of-sight, seat comfort, audiovisual equipment, and concessions. Each of the attributes can take on a variety of levels. For example, suppose that you can consider ticket prices of $10, $8, or $6, and whether to install large vs. small screens. Although it is not hard to guess that most people will prefer a $6 ticket to a $10 ticket and a big screen to a small one, you have no idea how much people will *trade off* ticket price to see a movie on a larger screen. This is what conjoint analysis is designed to do: estimate trade-offs among attributes and levels.

The conjoint *design* specifies all of the attributes and levels we wish to test. For our movie theater application, these are as follows; note that we do *not* assume these are the only important attributes and levels, just those over which we have been allowed control as a manager:

Attribute	Levels
Ticket Price	$6 $8 $10
Line-of-Sight	Seats are staggered (your view is unobstructed). Seats are not staggered (your view may be obstructed).

Seat Comfort	Average-sized seats with no cup holder Average-sized seats with a cup holder Large comfortable seats with a cup holder
Audiovisual Equipment	Small screen with plain sound system Large screen with plain sound system Large screen with digital THX sound system
Concessions	Standard hot dogs and popcorn Gourmet snacks

The Conjoint Analysis Task

To test all possible "product profiles," we would need to present a respondent with 108 combinations (3 × 2 × 3 × 3 × 3) of our attribute levels. This would be prohibitive, and fortunately we can use an *orthogonal design* to greatly reduce the number of profiles required: in this case, we can use just 18 product profiles to measure all quantities of interest (the part worths for the various attributes levels). Following is a list of 18 movie theaters dictated by our orthogonal design, described by various combinations of the five attributes' levels.

The conjoint task involved *ranking* the 18 movie theater configurations from "most preferred" to "least preferred" theater:

Ticket Price	Line-of-Sight	Seat Comfort	Audiovisual Equipment	Concessions
$6	Staggered	Avg. seats; no cup holder	Small screen; plain sound	Gourmet snacks
$6	Not staggered	Avg. seats; cup holder	Large screen; plain sound	Hot dogs and popcorn
$6	Staggered	Big seats; cup holder	Large screen; digital THX	Gourmet snacks
$10	Staggered	Avg. seats; no cup holder	Large screen; plain sound	Gourmet snacks
$10	Staggered	Avg. seats; cup holder	Large screen; digital THX	Hot dogs and popcorn
$10	Not staggered	Big seats; cup holder	Small screen; plain sound	Gourmet snacks
$8	Staggered	Avg. seats; no cup holder	Large screen; digital THX	Gourmet snacks
$8	Not staggered	Avg. seats; cup holder	Small screen; plain sound	Gourmet snacks
$8	Staggered	Big seats; cup holder	Large screen; plain sound	Hot dogs and popcorn
$6	Not staggered	Avg. seats; no cup holder	Large screen; digital THX	Hot dogs and popcorn
$6	Staggered	Avg. seats; cup holder	Small screen; plain sound	Gourmet snacks
$6	Staggered	Big seats; cup holder	Large screen; plain sound	Gourmet snacks
$10	Staggered	Avg. seats; no cup holder	Small screen; plain sound	Hot dogs and popcorn
$10	Staggered	Avg. seats; cup holder	Large screen; plain sound	Gourmet snacks
$10	Not staggered	Big seats; cup holder	Large screen; digital THX	Gourmet snacks
$8	Not staggered	Avg. seats; no cup holder	Large screen; plain sound	Gourmet snacks
$8	Staggered	Avg. seats; cup holder	Large screen; digital THX	Gourmet snacks
$8	Staggered	Big seats; cup holder	Small screen; plain sound	Hot dogs and popcorn

Note that all levels for each of the attributes are represented in the design, but not all *possible* combinations of those levels. Still, with even 18 options, it can be challenging to try to rank them appropriately. You may wish to try this yourself to gain some appreciation of the sorts of trade-offs involved, and perhaps why this ranking form of conjoint is less frequently used than ratings- and choice-based conjoint tasks.

Source: Based on an award-winning simulation in Java built by Prof. Tom Novak. University of California, Riverside. Copyright © 2000, Thomas P. Novak. Used with permission.

Let us examine one such reordering, provided by a respondent in an actual conjoint study; "more desired" options appear nearer the top:

Ticket Price	Line-of-Sight	Seat Comfort	Audiovisual Equipment	Concessions
$6	Staggered	Big seats; cup holder	Large screen; digital THX	Gourmet snacks
$6	Staggered	Big seats; cup holder	Large screen; plain sound	Gourmet snacks
$6	Staggered	Avg. seats; cup holder	Small screen; plain sound	Gourmet snacks
$6	Staggered	Avg. seats; no cup holder	Small screen; plain sound	Gourmet snacks
$6	Not staggered	Avg. seats; no cup holder	Large screen; digital THX	Hot dogs and popcorn
$6	Not staggered	Avg. seats; cup holder	Large screen; plain sound	Hot dogs and popcorn
$8	Staggered	Avg. seats; cup holder	Large screen; digital THX	Gourmet snacks
$8	Staggered	Big seats; cup holder	Large screen; plain sound	Hot dogs and popcorn
$8	Staggered	Avg. seats; no cup holder	Large screen; digital THX	Gourmet snacks
$8	Staggered	Big seats; cup holder	Small screen; plain sound	Hot dogs and popcorn
$10	Staggered	Avg. seats; cup holder	Large screen; digital THX	Hot dogs and popcorn
$10	Staggered	Avg. seats; cup holder	Large screen; plain sound	Gourmet snacks
$10	Staggered	Avg. seats; no cup holder	Large screen; plain sound	Gourmet snacks
$10	Not staggered	Big seats; cup holder	Large screen; digital THX	Gourmet snacks
$8	Not staggered	Avg. seats; no cup holder	Large screen; plain sound	Gourmet snacks
$8	Not staggered	Avg. seats; cup holder	Small screen; plain sound	Gourmet snacks
$10	Staggered	Avg. seats; no cup holder	Small screen; plain sound	Hot dogs and popcorn
$10	Not staggered	Big seats; cup holder	Small screen; plain sound	Gourmet snacks

Because the Web implementation of this task is "client-side," with all code downloaded to the browser, simply hitting "calculate" instantly yields the relative importances of each of the attributes (these always sum to 100 percent) and the part worths for each attribute level. Let us examine the attributes first:

Attribute	Relative Importance
Ticket Price	53.10%
Line of Sight	21.20%
Seat Comfort	8.30%
Audio-Visual	17.40%
Concessions	0.00%
TOTAL	**100.0%**

These values paint a clear picture of this respondent's preferences: ticket price drives more than half the movie theater decision, with a score of 53.1 percent! We cannot tell whether this extends across all three levels of price, though, and we will have to wait to compare part worths to do so. After price, we have a large drop in importance to line-of-sight (21.2 percent), and audiovisual. Seat comfort (8.3 percent) is far less crucial; concessions play no role at all. One might wonder whether this could come about because concessions were placed in the last column, but audiovisual, just next to it, was definitely taken into account. Next, let us examine the part worths:

Attribute Level	Part Worths
Ticket price: $6	1.00
Ticket price: $8	0.31
Ticket price: $10	0.00

Attribute Level	Part Worths
Line-of-sight: staggered	0.57
Line-of-sight: Not staggered	0.17
Seat comfort: avg. seats; no cup holder	0.34
Seat comfort: avg. seats; cup holder	0.46
Seat comfort: big seats; cup holder	0.5
Audiovisual equipment: small screen; plain sound	0.26
Audiovisual equipment: large screen; plain sound	0.45
Audiovisual equipment: large screen; digital THX	0.59
Concessions: Hot dogs and popcorn	0.43
Concessions: gourmet snacks	0.43

These part worth values offer a much more nuanced view of which features drive this respondent's pattern of ranking choices. For price, the $8 level is preferred to $10, but not by a huge margin, 0.31 vs. 0.00. (Note that the program "sets the scale" for all part worths by assigning a range of 0 to 1 for the most important attribute, which here is ticket price.) Rather, $6 is far preferred even to $8 and has by far the largest part worth of any in the entire conjoint design.

Rather than looking through the part worths in tabular form, they really "come alive" when graphed, as in Figure 11.14. By looking at the range of each attribute and the overall slope of the graph, the researcher gets an instant feel for what is most preferred by this respondent. We can easily create an "optimal product profile" as well, simply by putting together the most-preferred levels for each attribute: $6, staggered seats, big seats with a cup holder, large screen with digital THX sound; concessions appear not to matter. In some sense, this is unsurprising, because these are each the "best" levels in their attributes. What we can now do that we could not before the conjoint is answer a hypothetical question, such as, "Is it worth paying $8 instead of $6 to be able to have staggered seating and the best audiovisual equipment?" In fact, *any* such question can now be answered, simply by summing the part worths involved.

Comparing across Attributes and Relating to Price

One question we like to answer with conjoint analysis is how much a particular attribute level is worth, in terms of dollars and cents. Before addressing this, a technical note: you cannot compare part worths for levels of *different* attributes. For example, you cannot directly compare a part worth of 0.57 for "staggered" with one of 0.59 for "large screen and digital THX" and conclude that both are nearly equally important. You *can* compare the 0.43 values for "hot dogs and Popcorn" and "gourmet snacks" in this way, because they are both for the "concessions" attribute. But it will turn out that that is not the end of the story, as discussed in just a moment.

If we want to compare the part worths for some attribute with those for price, we therefore cannot do this directly. However, one can get at this indirectly by comparing *differences* in part worths across price and a second attribute. That is, although you cannot directly compare part worths across levels of two different attributes, you *can* compare *differences in part worths* across levels of two different attributes. (You may want to read that sentence through a few times before moving on!) Let us look at an example to see how this works.

Look at the difference between the part worth for a $6 ticket (1.00) and an $8 ticket (0.31); the difference is 0.69. Now, the part worth for "staggered" is 0.57 and for "not staggered" is 0.17, so the difference is 0.40. This means that the step up from $8 to $6 (0.69) is the same as about 1.75 times the difference between "staggered" and "not staggered" (0.40). In dollar terms, you would be willing to pay about (0.40/0.69) times the $2 difference between the $8 and $6 tickets—that is, about $1.16—in order to be able to obtain "staggered" seating. This general approach works for comparing levels of any other attribute with those of price.

An interesting thing about conjoint is that it does *not* simply assume that "every dollar is the same." For example, instead of comparing a $6 ticket with an $8 ticket, you could also compare an $8 ticket with a $10 ticket. Psychologically, the $2 gaps between $6 and $8 and between $8 and $10 are not necessarily equal, even though both are $2 differences. The part worths represent the *psychological difference*, in terms of impact on this respondent's valuation and choice, corresponding to the financial difference. If we were to repeat our calculations with the $8 and $10 tickets, the difference involved is much smaller (0.31), so we would expect to have to trade off less to account for it. That is, the $2 difference added to $6 is far more important to this decision-maker than $2 added to $8. In fact, many studies of pricing find exactly these sorts of *nonlinear effects:* the more you are already paying, the less you care about another increase of a fixed

Figure 11.14 Part-Worth Graphs for Five Movie Theater Attributes

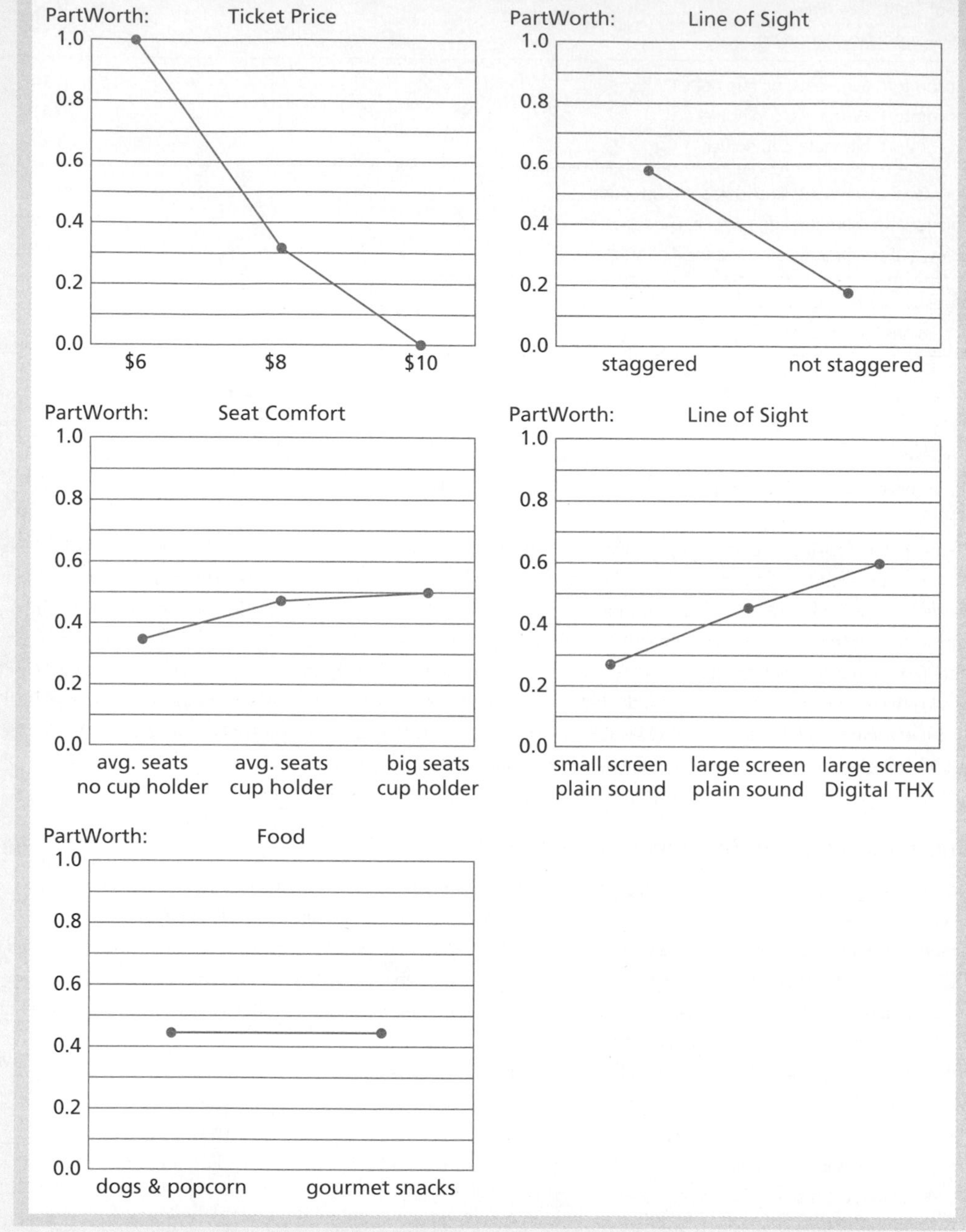

amount. It annoys us much more to pay an extra dollar for a candy bar than for an automobile. Conjoint offers a way to precisely quantify this effect.

Source: Based on an award-winning simulation in Java built by Prof. Tom Novak, eLab 2.0, University of California, Riverside. Copyright © 2000, Thomas P. Novak. Used with permission.

11.4e Adaptive Conjoint

When we have a conversation with someone we have just met, we would not persist in discussing a topic if the person seemed to lack interest or have nothing to add. A good experimental method should do the same: avoid wasting time and resources seeking unimportant information. If the first few conjoint responses strongly indicate that a person is insensitive to some aspect of a product, he or she should be questioned about trade-offs more relevant *to that person*. And this is the motivating idea behind adaptive conjoint: prior choices or responses help determine future comparisons.

To see how this might work, let us consider a *binary choice* conjoint task, where the response itself is more nuanced, and given on an *ordinal scale*:

Which of the following laptop computers would you rather purchase?

Fastest Processor		Very Fast Processor
4-hour battery life	OR	3-hour battery life
$1,999		$1,799
Strongly		Strongly
Prefer Left	1 – 2 – 3 – 4 – 5 – 6 – 7 – 8 – 9	Prefer Right

In an **adaptive conjoint**, the response to this question would be used to help generate attribute levels for all following questions. For example, a response of "1" or "9" indicates extremely strong preference but is not helpful in gauging a fine balance between the choices. Whichever of the two options was vastly preferred would have to be made less compelling—a simple way could be by raising the price—so that the response was closer to the middle of the scale.

adaptive conjoint
A type of conjoint analysis in which a respondent's answers to prior questions are used to determine subsequent questions, to help best use respondents' time and obtain superior statistical estimates.

An adaptive conjoint program will calculate part worths after each new piece of data is supplied by the respondent, then use special algorithms to better measure those part worths that are not yet determined with sufficient accuracy. The researcher can specify exactly how much accuracy is required, and respondents can continue to reply until that level of accuracy is achieved. In a nonadaptive conjoint, even when all the data are collected, there is no guarantee that we will have sufficiently accurate results. For example, if we choose all our price levels too high except one, everyone may choose the option with that low price level, and we will find out *only* that low price is very important; all other measurements will suffer and perhaps even be unusable.

Adaptive conjoint routines are highly specialized, and they must be purchased from vendors of conjoint analysis software; ordinary statistics programs lack this capability. Adaptive methods often rely on the type of scale used in the earlier question, with some fixed number of points, because it is easier to use that information to determine subsequent trade offs. There are two main advantages of the method which should be borne in mind when deciding whether to use it in a particular study: first, it allows one to quickly "zero in" on accurate utility (part worth) measurements for a particular respondent; and, second, it is especially suitable if there are many attribute levels. Against these advantages, which can be very great in practical implementations, must be balanced the costs and complexity of using specialized software, and sometimes even dedicated lab facilities to run the adaptive conjoint task.

11.4f Choice-based Conjoint

If you were standing in the aisle at the supermarket, and someone came up to you and said, "I see you just bought corn flakes, but can I ask you to tell me how many *utility points* you expect to get from them, or to rank all the other hundreds of cereals, or, if you are really busy, to simply rate them all on a 7-point scale?", you would summon the manager, the police, or an asylum. Yet this is what we do in conjoint all the time: force people to make explicit trade-offs or provide ratings in a way they never do when actually choosing products or services for themselves. Marketing researchers and economists long ago realized that a better method would be to have respondents simply make the sort of trade-offs they normally do: in their heads, reporting only the item that they would actually choose. This is the idea behind **choice-based conjoint**. All tasks present a variety of items to a respondent, who informs the researcher which he or she most prefers. No rankings, ratings, or reporting of utility points involved.

choice-based conjoint
A method of conjoint analysis in which the dependent variable is a single choice from a given set of options.

Although this seems conceptually obvious, until discrete choice models were developed (see Chapter 10 for details and development), there were no statistical methods to rigorously measure part worths based on this sort of choice data. Nowadays, discrete choice models such as logit and probit are widely available, and choice-based conjoint has come to dominate in practice.

We will present a detailed choice-based conjoint for dial-readout bathroom scales in Section 11-4h and a special section on choice-based conjoint at General Motors at the end of the chapter; for now, let us look at a typical choice-based question, again for computers:

Which of the following desktop computers would you purchase?

(1) Dell	(2) HP	(3) Sony	(4) None:
Fast Processor	Fastest Processor	Very Fast Processor	If these were my
Moderate Hard Drive	Large Hard Drive	Largest Hard Drive	only choices, I
21″ Monitor	19″ Monitor	17″ Monitor	would defer my purchase
$2,000	$1,900	$1,700	

The respondent would then indicate which of the three computer configurations he or she would choose or, importantly, that none of them is acceptable. This last possibility, called the "no choice option," is included in all choice-based studies and accounts for situations when the presented attribute level combinations are all below some threshold for purchase.

There are a number of compelling advantages to choice-based conjoint. First and foremost, it is dramatically more "real-world" than other conjoint tasks, because consumers make choices, not judge and calibrate their own preferences. Second, it is transparent and easy for respondents; because there are no scales or contrived tasks involved, respondents need only to be told to choose their favorite profile, something they do on a daily basis when shopping. Finally, because we can offer several product profiles at once—there are three in the previous example, but it is possible to include more—it can be highly efficient. At the same time, no matter how many choices are presented, we only get *one* bit of information in return—which is most preferred. Many years of experience have shown that we simply need to present respondents with a larger number of experimental tasks when using choice-based conjoint instead of ranking or rating. However, because each task is far simpler and clearer to the respondent, this increase in the number of tasks rarely inflates the complexity of the study or the quantity of time respondents must put in.

An important practical matter in using all types of conjoint is how one decides on the attributes and levels. Often, these are dictated by the study's sponsor or the explicitly stated goals of the research; if there are only three colors or five prices (for example) being considered, those are the ones we need to test. But it is relatively uncommon to have these set in stone at the outset, and marketers usually need to do some preliminary research to determine the most relevant attributes and a realistic set of levels for each.

In the earlier examples, with computers, note that *descriptors* were used, for example, "very fast processor," rather than the number of gigahertz at which it runs. This is for a good reason: many people have no idea how many gigahertz is "very fast," and some have no idea what gigahertz even means. When studying unusual or highly technical products, particularly with a heterogeneous audience, it is often a good idea to describe an attribute level, rather than include its precise technical specifications.

11.4g Conjoint Analysis: What Is It Used For and How?

Conjoint analysis is among the most widely applied techniques in all of marketing, with many thousands of studies annually across the world (see, for example, the Expert Feature "Choice-based Conjoint at General Motors" at the end of this chapter). It has proved especially helpful in a wide variety of contexts and application areas, a number of which are highlighted in Table 11.23.

Important: Conjoint Predicts Preference, *Not* Sales or Market Share

One is often asked, either before or even after running a conjoint study for a new product, "How much share will it capture?" Researchers must resist the temptation to provide an answer, no matter now great. Even if the "new" product is a "me too" brand, more or less replicating existing products in the category, predicting share is difficult; for a *really* novel product, it is essentially impossible. Why is this so? Consider that, in the real world, sales and especially share are affected by:

Distribution/Availability	In conjoint, all products appear equally available. In reality, stores do not carry every brand or SKU; people tend to shop close to home; there are stock-outs and other short-term availability effects.
Advertising	Products cannot be "advertised" in conjoint, because the effects of advertising build over time, often years. And we know advertising works well, especially for durables; there is no way to simulate these long-term effects in conjoint.
Promotion	Nothing moves a product like a price reduction, even if people do not like to think they are promotion-sensitive. Although conjoint studies can attempt to simulate a short-term price change, this is difficult, and promotional response is very often underestimated.
Awareness of product's existence	People will not purchase something until they are made aware of it. Although this sometimes happens at the point-of-purchase, in conjoint, it is impossible to "miss" anything because all products are made equally noticeable and available.

Individual consumer expertise or knowledge of relevant attributes	Consumers vary dramatically in what they know and value. They may ignore processor speed in buying a real computer but will find it hard to in conjoint when they are constantly informed about it. Worse, they may feel they *should* react to it because it is part of the study.
Purchase readiness	We buy things when we are ready to. In conjoint, we are asked to make dozens of simulated purchases in an hour, regardless of whether we have any such actual plans.

What conjoint is designed to do, and does well, is estimate what drives purchases by calibrating the sources and strengths of consumers' preferences. No one has figured out a sure-fire way to translate those into share estimates, and scrupulous researchers will avoid making such claims.

With this said, conjoint offers one great advantage over all other methods: it allows researchers to figure out the "optimal attribute mix/product design," given any set of constraints on the firm. Practically speaking, this allows managers to optimize their product designs and decisions, based on a full understanding of consumer preference. (We close our discussion of conjoint with a full analysis of a choice-based design, the data for which are included in the Online Edition of your textbook. Log in to your online edition at www.atomicdog.com.)

11.4h Conjoint Case Study: Dial Readout Scales

Professional conjoint applications are overwhelmingly choice-based, for reasons discussed in the chapter text. Here, we closely examine an actual conjoint study aimed at understanding how consumers choose

Table 11.23 Managerial Questions and Applications Areas to Which Conjoint Analysis Is Typically Applied

Managerial Question	Application Area
Product Development	
Which attributes do consumers consider most important?	In an ad campaign, which product features should be highlighted?
Which attribute levels are especially valued?	In designing a single new product, how much of each of the important features needs to be supplied?
Pricing Research	
How much would consumers pay for a specific set of attribute levels?	How can we price a preexisting product? A new version of that same product with upgraded features?
How might a set of different products compete against one another?	How should we optimize an entire *line* of products? At what price points should they be set?
Demand and Elasticity Curve estimation	Can we model and predict how demand will change if prices go up, production costs increase, and so on?
Competitive Positioning	
What effect will this new product have on an existing market?	If we already have five products in this category, what will happen if we bring in a sixth? Could overall profits drop?
What would be a good product positioning for a hypothetical new product?	How does the choice probability of this product change if we change its appearance, ad message, and such?
Market Segmentation	
Do there exist sets of consumers with markedly different tastes?	Can we *cluster* the part-worths to see whether there are natural customer segments? How can we characterize them, and reach them with ad messages?
How many products variants are needed to "cover" the market?	Given the results of a conjoint study, can we determine whether we should bring out a single product, or an entire line?
Brand Equity	
What is the value of a particular brand name (as an attribute)?	What happens to our product in a conjoint study if we re-run it with a generic name, or that of our competitor?
What are the effects of going with a new or umbrella branding strategy?	Should we go to market with an existing brand name, a new name entirely, or perhaps that of the parent corporation?

Table 11.24 Descriptions of Attributes and Levels for a Conjoint Analysis of Dial Readout Bathroom Scales

Description	Definition	Units	Levels				
Weight capacity	Weight causing a 360° dial turn	lbs	200	250	300	350	400
Aspect ratio	Platform length divided by width	–	6/8	7/8	8/8	8/7	8/6
Platform area	Platform length times width	in^2	100	110	120	130	140
Tick mark gap	Distance between 1-lb tick marks	in	2/32	3/32	4/32	5/32	6/32
Number size	Length of readout number	in	0.75	1	1.25	1.5	1.75
Price	U.S. Dollars	$	10	15	20	25	30

dial-readout bathroom scales.* A major scale manufacturer determined that there were six attributes especially relevant to consumers (other than those easily altered after production, such as color): weight capacity, aspect ratio, platform area, tick mark gap, number size, and price. These, along with the five levels used in the conjoint study for each, are described in Table 11.24.

The manufacturer wanted to know whether people really wanted their scales to go up to the traditionally maximal values of 270, 300, or even more pounds; having higher maximal weights required a larger dial, making the numbers smaller (and therefore harder to read), or having very small distances between the one-pound markings. They were also curious whether people preferred scales that were nearly square or were oblong, either more like a "portrait" (taller than wide) or "landscape" (so that their feet might more easily fit). The other attributes had similar explanatory stories, all involved with manufacturing the scale to the right dimensions and with well-made internal components. The last issue was, as always, what price people would pay for the "best" scale that could be brought to market, which the conjoint study was designed to reveal.

A choice-based conjoint design using 50 sets of three-products (plus "no choice") was implemented via the Web. A total of 184 respondents eventually completed the study; they were solicited through announcements on internet newsgroups, university courses, and flyers, and offered incentives in the form of sweepstakes for gift certificates in various amounts. The choice task corresponded to the sort found at online shopping sites: dial-readout scales were presented in terms of their underlying product attribute information in list format and pictorially, including a close-up of the dial to facilitate comparison across the last two attributes, as shown in Figure 11.15.

The researchers believed that most respondents would be unable to make sense of information such as "size 12.6 by 9.5 inches, 120 sq. in. total," so mock-ups drawn by computer-aided design (CAD) packages were provided. In case none of the scales was deemed appealing, respondents could always indicate that they "would NOT purchase any of these scales." A close-up of the dial was also provided because the scale manufacturer believed that ease of reading was a major factor in choosing a scale for many people.

All of the 50 fixed-choice sets evaluated by each subject were presented as in Figure 11.15. Table 11.25 represents the first two (of the 50 total) choice sets.

Note that the first set of items, for Choice Set 1, are exactly those depicted graphically. When respondents visited the conjoint site, they read the following description:

> Thank you for agreeing to participate in this research project. What follows is a series of questions about purchases that you might consider making, and several about yourself and your shopping habits. It should take approximately 15–20 minutes in total, but you're encouraged to work at your own pace.
>
> We are interested in a better understanding of what you, personally, look for when buying a (bathroom-type) scale. This will help with the design of scales—among other appliances—that better meet consumer needs. It is not important that you've bought one before, or whether you are considering buying one at the moment. Rather, we would ask you to imagine that you are in the market for a scale, and that your choices reflect what you might look for, but that it's not absolutely necessary to purchase one.

*Note: These data were originally collected by the Optimal Design Engineering Lab in conjunction with a major manufacturer of small appliances, and is available in the Online Edition of the textbook. Log in to the Online Edition of your text at www.atomicdog.com.

Figure 11.15 Task Design for Choice-based Conjoint on Dial Readout Bathroom Scales

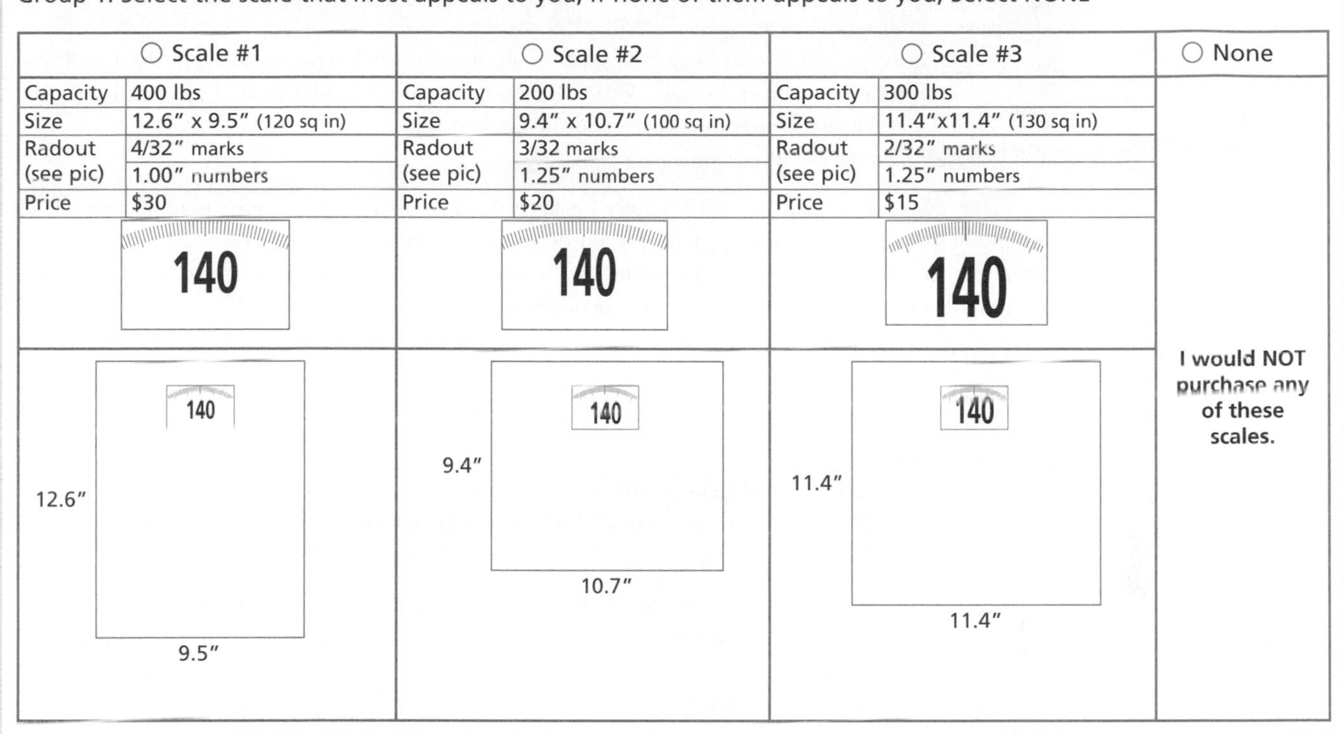

Group 1: Select the scale that most appeals to you; if none of them appeals to you, Select NONE
Scale #1
Capacity 400 lbs
Size 12.6" x 9.5" (120 sq in)
Radout (see pic) 4/32" marks 1.00" numbers
Price $30
140
12.6"
9.5"
Scale #2
Capacity 200 lbs
Size 9.4" x 10.7" (100 sq in)
Radout (see pic) 3/32 marks 1.25" numbers
Price $20
140
9.4"
10.7"
Scale #3
Capacity 300 lbs
Size 11.4"x11.4" (130 sq in)
Radout (see pic) 2/32" marks 1.25" numbers
Price $15
140
11.4"
11.4"
None
I would NOT purchase any of these scales.

The entire study consists of a total of 50 choices. On each of the (50) pages, there will be three scales from which we'd like you to choose. Please select the scale which most appeals to you; if none of them appeals to you, select the last choice on the list ("I would NOT purchase any of these scales"). Again, please assume throughout that you are in the market for a scale, but that it's not absolutely necessary to purchase one from every single group.

Each of the scale descriptions will consist of the same few elements; some may be more important to you (in a scale) than others. They are:

- Capacity (weight, pounds)
- Size (length and width, inches)
- Readout (marks and numbers, inches)
- Price ($US)

There will also be a picture of each, showing its overall dimensions, and a close-up of its readout. Each of these elements will vary from one scale to the next, and you should not assume that any scale is "necessarily better" than another: all that's important is which you believe would suit your needs and tastes most closely (if at all).

Table 11.25 First Two (of 50 Total) Choice Sets Used in Conjoint Analysis of Dial Readout Bathroom Scales

Choice Set	Weight Capacity	Aspect Ratio	Platform Area	Interval Mark Gap	Size of Number	Price
1	400 lbs.	1.33	120.0	4/32 in.	1.00 in.	$30
	250 lbs.	0.88	100.0	3/32 in.	1.25 in.	$20
	300 lbs.	1.00	130.0	2/32 in.	1.75 in.	$15
2	200 lbs.	0.75	140.0	6/32 in.	1.25 in.	$20
	350 lbs.	1.14	130.0	5/32 in.	0.75 in.	$25
	300 lbs.	1.33	120.0	3/32 in.	1.75 in.	$10

To give you a sense of how the survey works, before the 50 choices that "count," there are three strictly for practice. When you click below, you'll see these three practice pages, after which the 50 choice sets follow. Please note that you should click something on every page; if you do not care for any of the scales in a particular set, make sure to choose the "NONE" option.

At the very end of the survey are some questions about you, which will help in analyzing the data. These are purely for statistical purposes, and all data will remain completely confidential. If you at any time feel uncomfortable with this survey, please feel free to stop taking it at that point.

Again, thank you for your participation.

The "questions about you" used "purely for statistical purposes" were ones the manufacturer believed might help explain why different people chose the scales they did; these consisted mainly of demographics, as well as some information relevant to scales, such as whether the respondent tended to diet or actually purchased a scale recently. These questions were as follows:

- Gender: Male/Female
- Height: Inches
- Weight: Pounds
- Age: Years
- Question #1: Do you need vision correction to see clearly at a distance of 6 feet? (Y/N)
- Question #2: Have you tried (deliberately) to lose at least 10 pounds in the last year? (Y/N)
- Question #3: Have you purchased a scale in the past two years? (Y/N)

Armed with the 50 discrete choices from each respondent, the researchers used logistic regression (see Chapter 10) to estimate the part worths for the various attribute levels. Table 11.26 provides their findings.

Although these are interesting, they are difficult to make sense of unless they are graphed, as shown in Figure 11.16.

The graphs in Figure 11.16 clearly depict which attributes, and which levels within them, are most valued. The attribute with by far the greatest range—and therefore overall importance—is price. That it is so precipitously downward-sloping is a strong indication that the respondents took price into account in deciding which scales they most preferred.

The graphs in Figure 11.16 indicate that not all the attributes were valenced; that is, there was often a preference for the internal values among the levels. For example, it would appear that the best (i.e., highest part worth) weight capacity was around 300 pounds, as opposed to the lowest (200) or the highest (400) values available. This is rarely the case with price, and it is not here (if the conjoint study is run well, people will indicate that, *all else equal*, a lower price is preferred to a higher one; if important attributes are not included in the study, respondents may *assume* that a higher price means a higher quality on the missing attributes and actually show what seems to be a preference for higher price levels). In fact, of our six

Table 11.26 Part Worths for Six Dial Readout Scale Attributes

Weight Capacity		Platform Area		Size of Number	
200 lbs.	−0.534	100 in.^{2}	0.015	0.75 in.	−0.744
250 lbs.	0.129	110 in.^{2}	−0.098	1.00 in.	−0.198
300 lbs.	0.228	120 in.^{2}	0.049	1.25 in.	0.235
350 lbs.	0.104	130 in.^{2}	0.047	1.50 in.	0.291
400 lbs.	0.052	140 in.^{2}	−0.033	1.75 in.	0.396
Aspect Ratio		**Interval Mark Gap**		**PRICE**	
0.75	−0.058	2/32 in.	−0.366	$10	0.719
0.88	0.253	3/32 in.	−0.164	$15	0.482
1.00	0.278	4/32 in.	0.215	$20	0.054
1.14	−0.025	5/32 in.	0.194	$25	−0.368
1.33	−0.467	6/32 in.	0.100	$30	−0.908

Figure 11.16 Conjoint Part Worth Graphs for Bathroom Scale Attributes

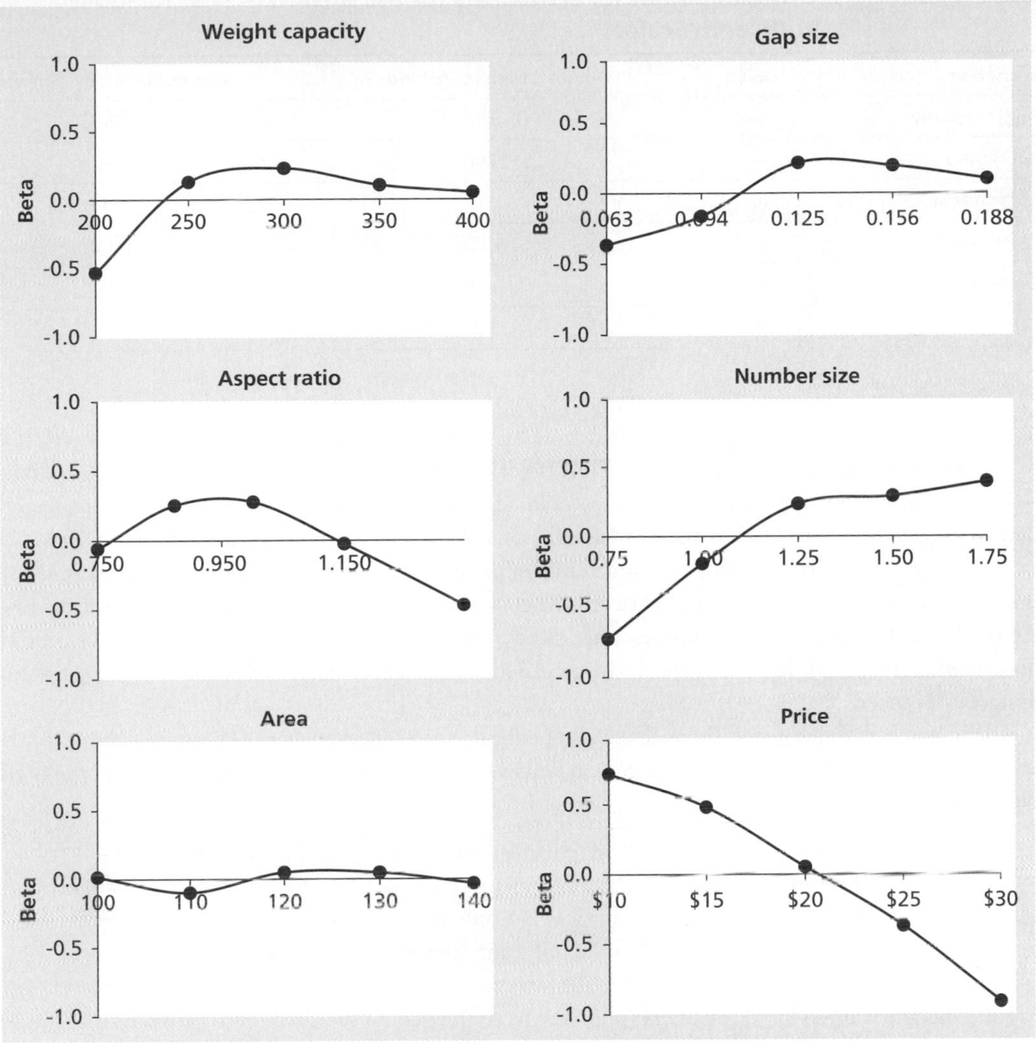

attributes here, only price and number size show monotonic (either steadily increasing or decreasing) part worth values across their ranges. For the other attributes, it appears that respondents prefer a weight capacity around 300 pounds, a gap of about 0.125, an aspect ratio of about 1 (that is, a square scale), and that they do not much care about area, with slight preference of about 120–130 square inches. When we see a graphical result like that for area, it can mean one of two things: the attribute really is unimportant, or the conjoint was not designed with the appropriate range of levels. If we had tested prices between $7.50 and $7.75, for example, we might have found very little reaction to price, because the range was so narrow; if we had tested price levels between $1000 and $1500, we also might have found little reaction because no one will pay so much for a scale to begin with. So, it is possible that people in the population *do* care about area, but that the researchers had mistakenly selected a range where they are indifferent.

The scale manufacturer wanted to know what the "optimal scale" would be, based on the conjoint part worths. There are three general approaches to this important issue. One would be to simply choose the levels with the highest part worths, right off the earlier table. Another would be to fit *continuous curves* (called "splines") through the part worths, as has been done in the graphs in Figure 11.6, and determine where they are highest. Let us look at both as provided in Table 11.27.

splines
A powerful method used in economics and statistics to draw complex curves and surfaces through sets of data points.

These two "optimal" scales are very close, and they differ only in whether we assume that we must stick with the levels actually used in the conjoint, or we should be trying to interpolate between them. Because the last two attributes, number size and price, were monotonic, there is no "internal optimum," and the two solutions agree.

We mentioned a third approach as well, and that would be to try to consider manufacturer *profit*. Profit means taking Price into account, not just in terms of what consumers would most like to pay—it is

Table 11.27 Optimal Conjoint Part Worths for the Design of Dial-Readout Bathroom Scales

Description	Unit	Optimal Levels by Part Worths	Optimal Levels by "Splines"
Weight capacity	lbs	300	283
Aspect ratio	—	1.00	0.946
Platform area	in.^{2}	120	124.2
Tick mark gap	in.	0.125	0.136
Number size	in.	1.75	1.75
Price	$	$10	$10

clear that that is "as little as possible"—but how much the manufacturer makes on each scale. It is entirely possible that the previous "optimal" configurations would involve *negative* profit; they would if the scales cost more than a $10 retail price could support. This last method would therefore require detailed knowledge of production and distribution costs. When the researchers re-ran their analysis with this new information, they found that a much higher price of about $28 was "optimal." We must always remember the key tension in conjoint between the consumer wanting "the best of everything at the lowest price" and the manufacturer wanting "the lowest production cost and the highest price." Conjoint allows marketers to find the "sweet spot" where consumers, manufacturers, and retailers can most mutually agreeably meet.

The researchers did not stop there. They also performed a detailed analysis of how the answers to the earlier questions affected how much the respondents valued different scale attributes. Among the highlights of their results were:

- Heavier people valued weight capacity significantly more than lighter people.
- Women wanted a lower weight capacity than men. When debriefed (questioned) informally after the study, many of the women reported it was not only because they did not need a scale that went above 250 pounds, but also because they did not want themselves and others to *think* they did.
- Men were somewhat more price-sensitive than women.
- Taller people wanted larger numbers (presumably, so they could see them better from further away). So did older people and those who needed vision correction.
- Those who dieted showed a higher desire for a scale in general (based on the "no choice" option, which was chosen less); those who had bought a scale in the last two years showed the opposite.

Thus, all the "personal information" variables showed an *interaction* with at least one of the attributes in the study. We must stress that these additional analyses did not only *verify* the reported relationships, but precisely measured their effects, as coefficients in the discrete choice (logit) model. As such, the manufacturer could use information on various consumer segments to predict what sort of scale configuration would most appeal to its members. We will revisit and further refine this analysis in Section 12-1c.

11.5 Multidimensional Scaling

Humans are visual creatures. Managers often claim they want "the big picture," or to have something "painted in bold strokes." What this means is that we understand information best when it is integrated into a picture, not when presented as a disembodied table of numbers. Marketers have grown fond of creating "perceptual maps" of product categories, where various brands are represented in several dimensions, nearly always two, that are given names. Let us examine a perceptual map, shown in Figure 11.17, constructed separately for 12 of the beer brands we studied in our cluster analysis.

Figure 11.17 might be very helpful in understanding the beer market, but it could also be highly misleading. It presents two dimensions, "basic vs. upscale" and "light vs. heavy," through which to understand the category. But are those the only relevant dimensions? What about "domestic vs. foreign," or any of the many attributes prized by beer aficionados? Although price may be addressed by the "basic vs. upscale" dimension, it is not necessarily synonymous with it, and we see that all three non-domestic

Figure 11.17 Perceptual Map of Beer Brands

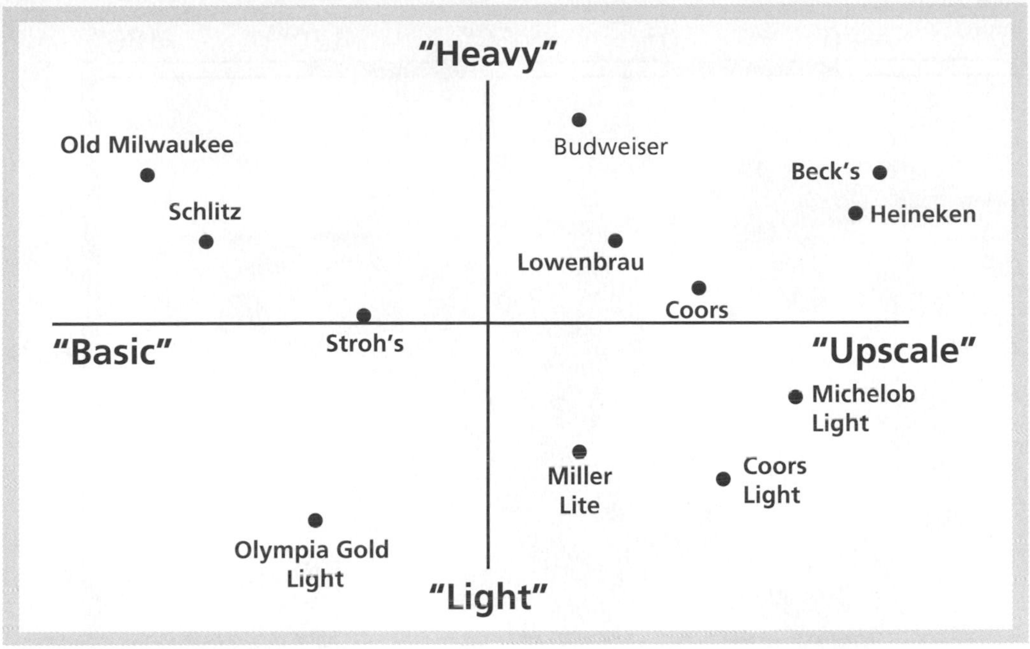

beers (Lowenbrau, Beck's and Heineken) are in the "heavy and upscale" quadrant. Can we plausibly claim that two dimensions are really orthogonal to (i.e., uncorrelated with) one another? Are they both equally important? These questions are all very difficult to answer empirically, but the perceptual map in Figure 11.17 presents them as settled: there are two dimensions, they are the only important ones; they are uncorrelated with one another; and everyone values them—and only them—identically. Clearly, there are a lot of assumptions operating in such a simple picture! (We will revisit this picture later, superimposing additional data about the beer brands.)

Marketing researchers, psychologists, and statisticians have developed a way to construct "pictures" of markets that do *not* rely on someone deciding beforehand which dimensions are important, or what data to collect in order to draw the picture. **Multidimensional scaling** summarizes data about associations between a fixed set of objects to reveal relationships between them (usually brands in a particular product class). It does this by determining two things: (1) the minimum "dimensionality" (2-D, 3-D, and so on) required to represent the objects' interrelationships well, and (2) the position of each object on each dimension (i.e., its location in the map).

multidimensional scaling
A statistical technique that takes people's perceptions of the similarities (inverse distances) of pairs of objects and uses them to make a map of those objects in multidimensional space that preserves those distances as well as possible.

Using this technique, it is possible to construct a map such as that in Figure 11.17 *without collecting any attribute-based data*. That is, we can place all those beer brands in a map—though not necessarily a two-dimensional one—without collecting any data on "light"-ness or "upscale"-hood or anything other than *which brands seem more similar to one another*. Multidimensional scaling (usually referred to as MDS) will "short circuit" the entire idea of depicting categories and brands in terms of their attributes, in favor of a much simpler and more powerful data type: item similarity. In this way, multidimensional scaling is really an extension of uni-dimensional attitude scales, such as the semantic differential (discussed in Section 4-5g), which can be used to position attitudes about brands in an *n*-dimensional "perceptual space."

Multidimensional scaling is quite simple to run, use, and interpret, once certain conceptual issues are understood. Before running through a full example based on real data (and updating the beer brand map above accordingly), let us consider two important issues when converting data on *distances* (similarities or dissimilarities) into a readily interpretable map or picture.

11.5a Multidimensional Scaling: Some Preliminaries

What is the largest nation on earth? Political boundaries keep changing, but most people reply "Russia" or "Canada" or even "China," mistaking population for land mass. Let us consult a map in Figure 11.18 to settle the issue.

Figure 11.18 Global Land Masses as Depicted by a Mercator Map

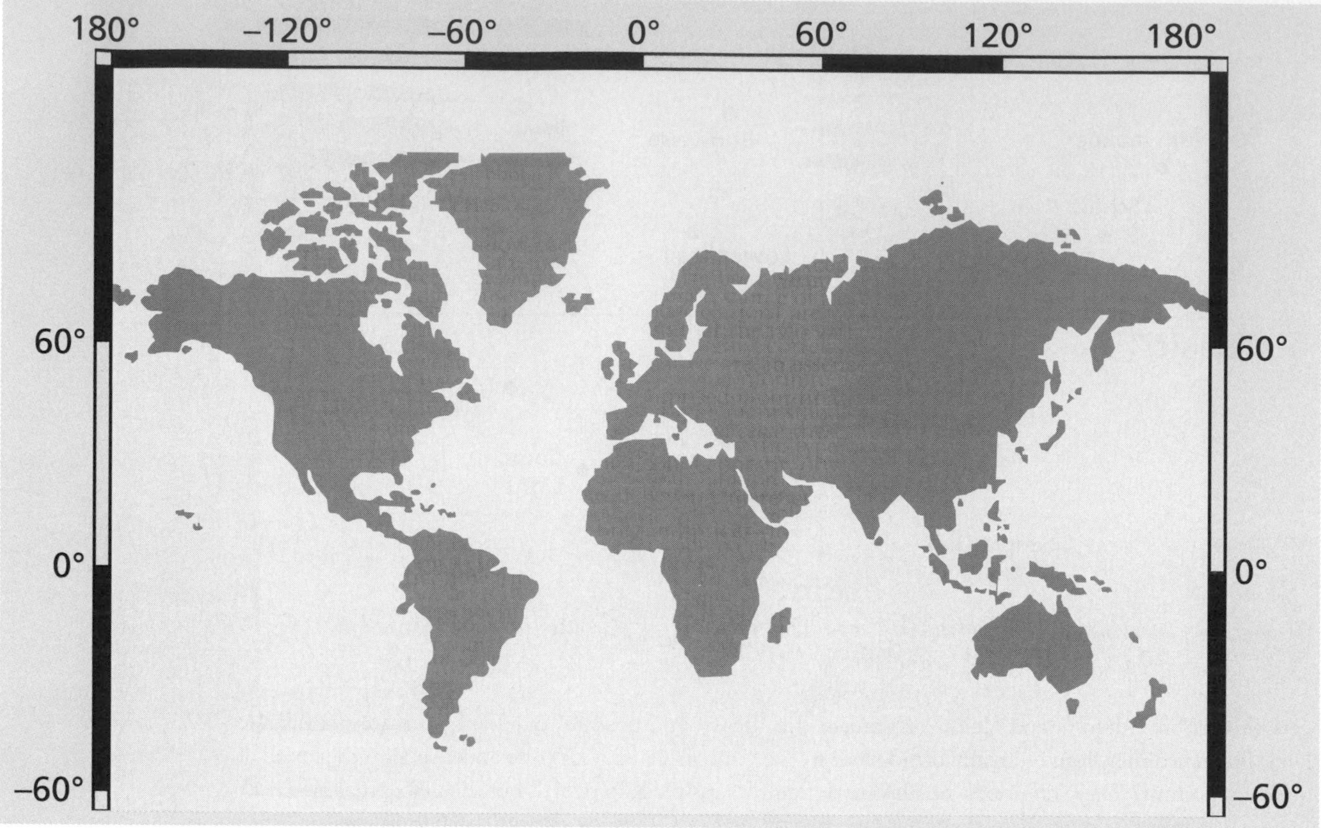

The map clearly shows that Greenland, officially part of Denmark, is larger than all of South America or Africa. Why, then, does no one call Denmark the world's largest country? Let us consult the actual land mass figures, in square kilometers:

Nation	Area (sq. km.)
Russia	17,075,200
Canada	9,976,140
United States	9,629,091
China	9,596,960
Brazil	8,511,965
Australia	7,686,850
⋮	⋮
Greenland	2,175,600

One may wonder why, if Australia is more than three times the size of Greenland, it appears less than half the size on the map. Is the map simply wrong? Of course not. This type of map, called a Mercator projection, allows all the nations of the world, which sit on the surface of a (slightly flattened) three-dimensional sphere, to be depicted in two dimensions. There is simply no way to do this without distorting some parts of the map. In this case, the further a nation is from the equator, the more it is stretched out (distorted) relative to nations near the equator. The North Pole, which is just a point, is stretched to a line a long as the equator, about 40,000 kilometers long; no wonder Greenland, which is so near the equator, is extremely distorted.

And here is the main idea: whenever you try to depict a *higher-dimensional object* in a *lower-dimensional space*, you are allowing for the possibility of distortion, sometimes severely so. In multidimensional scaling, we will be trying to represent brands (or other sorts of objects or concepts) in some relatively low dimensional space. If we push the dimensionality of our representation further down than the data

Table 11.28 Distances between Select Pairs of US Cities

Cities	1	2	3	4	5	6	7	8	9
1: Birmingham	—								
2: Boston	1052	—							
3: Buffalo	776	400	—						
4: Chicago	578	851	454	—					
5: Cleveland	618	551	173	308	—				
6: Dallas	581	1551	1198	803	1025	—			
7: Denver	1095	1769	1370	920	1227	663	—		
8: Detroit	641	613	216	238	90	999	1156	—	
9: El Paso	1152	2072	1692	1252	1525	572	557	1479	—
10: Houston	567	1605	1286	940	1114	225	879	1105	676

warrant—like onto a two-dimensional map, when three or more dimensions are really necessary—we may introduce a great degree of distortion, and therefore run the risk of poor decision-making.

A second issue arising in multidimensional scaling is how we know whether we have the "right" representation of a set of objects. This idea becomes clearer if we look at what is the classic application of MDS: reconstructing a map from distances between cities. Let us look at such an application for the U.S.; in Table 11.28, we list data for the first 10 of 28 cities, but the full data set is available in the Online Edition of this textbook. Log in to the Online Edition of your text at www.atomicdog.com.

The objective is to use these distances (here, in miles) to construct a map of the cities. Let us try to use MDS—we will cover all the details later on—to do this; see Figure 11.19A.

Figure 11.19A is a perfectly accurate rendering of the values in the distance table. The problem is that the locations of the cities seem to have been rotated and flipped from our usual map

Figure 11.19A A Valid—but Unusual-Looking—MDS Representation of Distance between Pairs of U.S. Cities

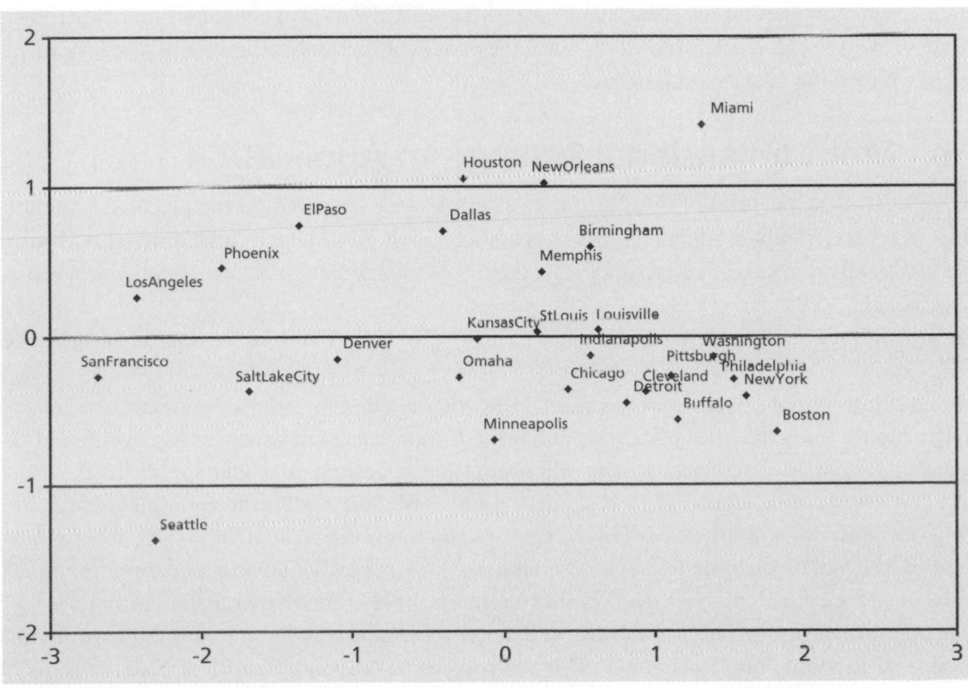

Figure 11.19B An Equally Valid—and more Usual-Looking—MDS Representation of Distance between Pairs of U.S. Cities

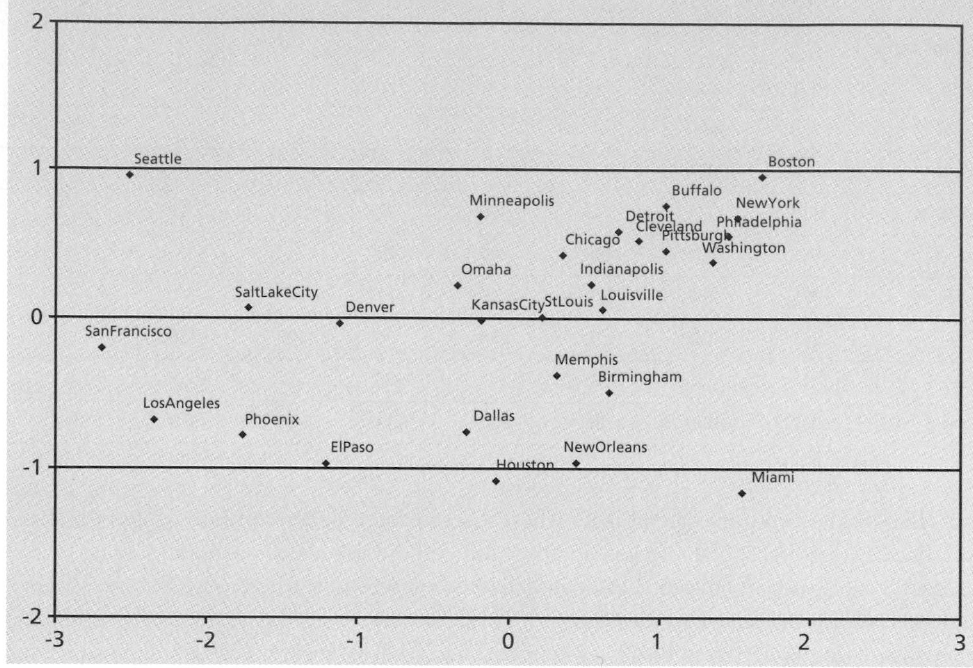

orientation. But we must remember that our usual map orientation is a *convention:* there is no "right" way to view the earth. A spaceship approaching the planet might well conceptualize these cities as they appear in Figure 11.19A, rather than a separate MDS output in Figure 11.19B that looks far more familiar.

And here is the important point: the only way we can understand the orientation of either of these graphs is to *overlay external information on them*. In this case, as soon as we overlay both the north–south and east–west directions (convince yourself that both are necessary by attempting to use just one for the first graph), we know that we have the "right" map. MDS will always provide as faithful a representation of *relative similarity or distance* as possible, but we can only attach meaning to the dimensions in the derived graph by tying in *other* kinds of data.

11.5b Multidimensional Scaling: An Application

The data used for the purposes of this illustrative example were collected on the perceived similarity of the MBA programs at nine leading U.S. business schools. Each possible pairing of nine schools with one another (36 in all) was rated by a group of respondents as to how similar they seemed on a seven-point scale (see Figure 11.20).

We will average the responses to these across all respondents, yielding the matrix of *similarities* in Table 11.29.

It is important to note that these averages (of the original question values) represent how *similar* any pair is: the higher the score, the greater the similarity. If we are trying to make a map, we should base it on *dissimilarity;* that is, distances. Be sure when entering your data that you specify to the program whether you are entering similarity or dissimilarity data. We can easily transform all these values by reversing the point order on the scale. This brings up a common issue in applying MDS: how to interpret the point on the scale indicating the greatest "closeness." It is clear that any particular item should have a zero distance *to itself*, but it is not clear whether a response of "1" (on a 1-to-7 dissimilarity scale) should count as no distance at all. This is up to the researcher to decide. It is possible to subtract one from all scale points so that anything receiving a "1" is recorded as "no distance," or to subtract off some other value. Here, we subtract all the values above from 7, so that our *distance or dissimilarity* scale is 0 to 6.

Figure 11.20 Collecting Pairwise Dissimilarity Data for Use in MDS

We are interested in your perceptions of various business schools and MBA programs. Please use the following scale to assess the given pairs as to how similar they seem to you. After each pair, there are seven numbers from 1 to 7. The higher the number, the more similar the pair of items seems to you; the lower the number, the more dissimilar the items seem:

Not at all Similar						Extremely Similar
1	2	3	4	5	6	7

MIT-Sloan	Harvard	____	MIT-Sloan	Dartmouth	____
Dartmouth	Harvard	____	Chicago	Columbia	____
Dartmouth	Columbia	____	Wharton	Northwestern	____
Wharton	Chicago	____	Columbia	Harvard	____
Harvard	Northwestern	____	Harvard	Stanford	____
Harvard	Carnegie	____	Dartmouth	Stanford	____
Stanford	Carnegie	____	Stanford	Chicago	____
Stanford	Wharton	____	Wharton	Carnegie	____
Northwestern	MIT-Sloan	____	Chicago	Carnegie	____
Chicago	MIT-Sloan	____	Northwestern	Carnegie	____
Northwestern	Dartmouth	____	Stanford	MIT-Sloan	____
Carnegie	MIT-Sloan	____	Chicago	Northwestern	____
Wharton	Dartmouth	____	Carnegie	Columbia	____
Chicago	Dartmouth	____	MIT-Sloan	Columbia	____
Columbia	Wharton	____	Harvard	Chicago	____
Columbia	Stanford	____	Wharton	MIT-Sloan	____
Harvard	Wharton	____	Carnegie	Dartmouth	____
Stanford	Northwestern	____	Northwestern	Columbia	____

Thus, if someone replied with a "7" to the original question, indicating great similarity, the answer counts as a "0" distance. These transformed values are provided in Table 11.30, and we shall compare our MDS solution with them later.

To better understand the data and discern their key features, it is helpful to highlight the most similar, and most dissimilar, pairings. These have been highlighted in the table: the most similar pair appears to be Wharton–Harvard, with a 1.79 distance, and the least similar pairs seem to be Carnegie–Harvard and Stanford–Carnegie, with a 3.21 distance. Note that the program does not need the original individual-level data, but merely their averages, to create the perceptual map (there are more complex forms of MDS that work off individual-level data, but we do not pursue those here; the basic idea is identical, however). Note that, at this point, we need know nothing at all about the various schools—their locations, tuitions, academic programs, and so forth—in order to create a map of their relative positions. This is the overriding benefit of MDS as a method, and later we will superimpose such information to help us "orient" the derived map.

As soon as we attempt to run the analysis, however, the computer offers us a warning:

> *Warning:* The total number of parameters estimated (the number of stimulus coordinates plus the number of weights, if any) is large, relative to the number of values in the data matrix. The results may not be reliable, as there may not be enough data to precisely estimate the parameter values of the parameters. You should reduce the number of parameters (e.g., request fewer dimensions) or increase the number of observations.
>
> Number of parameters is 18. Number of data values is 36.

Table 11.29 Averaged Similarity Data for All Pairs of Nine MBA Programs, 1-to-7 Scale

	MIT	Harvard	Dartmouth	Columbia	Wharton	Chicago	Northwestern	Carnegie	Stanford
MIT	—								
Harvard	4.39	—							
Dartmouth	4.11	4.68	—						
Columbia	4.16	4.37	5.16	—					
Wharton	4.87	5.21	4.87	4.45	—				
Chicago	4.03	4.24	4.26	4.42	4.87	—			
Northwestern	4.29	4.71	4.21	4.26	5.03	4.97	—		
Carnegie	4.37	3.79	4.42	4.42	4.29	4.42	3.95	—	
Stanford	4.55	4.76	4.39	4.39	4.29	4.16	4.55	3.79	—

The computer points out that only 36 numbers (average similarity ratings) have been entered to estimate the spatial positions of nine points; because each of these nine points requires two coordinates (for a two-dimensional MDS map), 36 numbers are being used to estimate 18 numbers. In statistical applications, we always want there to be many, many more (independently supplied) data values than numbers we hope to estimate from them (for example, in simple linear regression, we use just two values to describe all our points).

The program suggests that more observations (that is, schools' relative distances) be included, which may at first appear counterintuitive. Notice, however, that for n objects, data on $n(n-1)/2$ possible pairwise comparisons will be used to estimate $2n$ coordinates in two-dimensional space. Figure 11.21 illustrates why this is so.

Note that, for the first item, we require eight distances (dissimilarities) to be stated in our data because its distance to itself is zero by definition. The next item in line requires only seven distances because we already have its distance to the first item. And the next item requires six; and so on, until the last item, all of whose distances we already know. If we add up all the numbers of distances, we obtain $8 + 7 + \ldots + 2 + 1 = 36$. If we do this in general, for $n + (n-1) + \ldots + 2 + 1$, this turns out to be $n(n-1)/2$, which does yield the correct value of 36 if we "plug in" $n = 9$.

Although for nine objects the *ratio of data to parameters* is 2 (36 vs. 18), for our U.S. city map with $n = 28$, the ratio is 6.75, and for 100 objects the ratio is about 25 (4950 to 200). The point is that MDS starts being more reliable, in terms of *unambiguous interpretation of the resulting spatial dimensions*, for *large*

Table 11.30 Averaged Dissimilarity Data for All Pairs of Nine MBA Programs, 0-to-6 Scale

	MIT	Harvard	Dartmouth	Columbia	Wharton	Chicago	North western	Carnegie	Stanford
MIT	—								
Harvard	2.61	—							
Dartmouth	2.89	2.32	—						
Columbia	2.84	2.63	1.84	—					
Wharton	2.13	1.79	2.13	2.55	—				
Chicago	2.97	2.76	2.74	2.58	2.13	—			
North western	2.71	2.29	2.79	2.74	1.97	2.03	—		
Carnegie	2.63	3.21	2.58	2.58	2.71	2.58	3.05	—	
Stanford	2.45	2.24	2.61	2.61	2.71	2.84	2.45	3.21	—

Figure 11.21 All Possible Pairings of 9 Objects

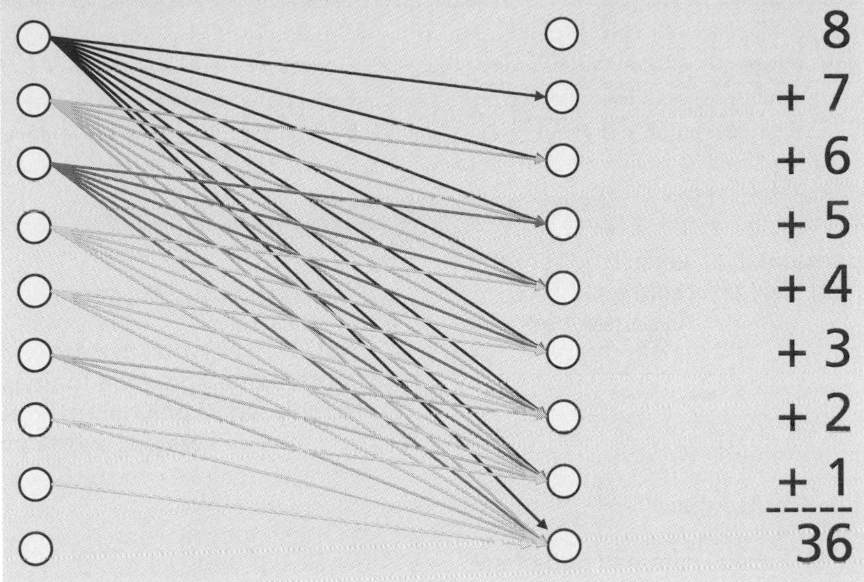

numbers of object comparisons. Of course, getting data on nearly 5000 possible comparisons for 100 objects presents problems of a different kind. And here is where the fact that we submit *averaged* distances into MDS is a strength of the method: if we need to estimate about 5000 averaged distances, we can split up the task across several hundred respondents. For example, if we asked 500 respondents to answer 50 questions (as in original task, where each had 36), we would have each of the 5000 distances estimated five times, and we would average these five values. If we wanted greater robustness (i.e., fewer potential problems with strange or outlier answers), we could simply collect more data. A study where 500 respondents answer 50 questions each is well within standard marketing research guidelines, so running an MDS analysis with even 100 items presents no real challenges.

The researcher must eventually decide on the dimensionality that best describes the data. Lower dimensions are always preferred because they allow for easy visualization, but should not be chosen if they are incapable of representing the data faithfully. One way to determine the appropriate dimensionality of the space is by calculating a goodness-of-fit measure between the input rank order and the output, called stress. As the number of dimensions increases, the stress decreases because additional dimensions afford additional flexibility. The MDS routine, unlike those for linear regression, does not operate through a set of formulas that instantly offer exactly the best fit. Rather, it is *iterative*, determining a good initial guess, calculating the stress measure, and continuing to derive better and better estimates, always attempting to lower the stress, that is, better represent the distance data.

stress
In multidimensional scaling, a measure of how well the derived MDS map actually represents the original (pairwise similarity or distance) data; this helps determine the appropriate number of dimensions for the map.

Running the MDS is quite simple, as the averaged distance data matrix is all that is necessary. The program will typically yield the following information:

Iteration History for Two-Dimensional MDS Analysis

Iteration	Stress	Improvement
1	0.3082	
2	0.2446	0.0636
3	0.2315	0.0131
4	0.2227	0.0089
5	0.2157	0.0069
6	0.213	0.0027
7	0.2122	0.0008

$R^2 = 0.719$

The output is primarily concerned with stress, the measure of how well the derived two-dimensional coordinates really represent the pairwise distance data. As indicated above, the stress of the initial configuration is 0.30823. The routine continues iterating until the improvements are less than 0.001 (the researcher can set this value, but 0.001 is a reasonable value); in this case, the final stress is 0.2122. In general, a stress level of over 0.2 is considered quite poor, indicating that there is a good deal of disparity between the derived map and the original distance data, and therefore that *a higher-dimensional solution may be called for*. As a rule of thumb, a stress of 0.1 is fair, 0.05 good, and 0.01 or less is excellent; as usual, the researcher must decide on whether a solution is adequate to the demands of the project. Finally, the r^2 value of 0.719 indicates that about 72 percent of the variance in the distance data is accounted for by the two-dimensional solution.

Two-Dimensional MDS Solution for the Spatial Locations of Nine MBA Programs

Name	Dimension 1	Dimension 2
MIT	−0.308	−1.025
Harvard	−1.422	0.482
Dartmouth	−0.585	0.999
Columbia	−0.684	1.103
Wharton	−0.087	−0.320
Chicago	−0.070	−1.045
Northwestern	1.284	−0.348
Carnegie	−2.430	−0.447
Stanford	1.460	0.603

The program has generated a two-dimensional map (Figure 11.22) consistent with the input distance data; the values on each dimension are listed above, and they correspond exactly to the derived map. We might guess that the map does a good job representing the data, as Carnegie is indeed quite far from both Harvard and Stanford, and Wharton is not far from Harvard (although it is not the closest, as it should be). But the program tells us that the map is very stressed, and the R^2 value of 0.719 is not terribly good, considering that we have "reduced" 36 pairwise distances down to 18 spatial coordinates. If we ask the computer to graph the derived distances in the map depicted in Figure 11.22 against the actual distances in our input matrix, along with a simple linear regression line, it is a sobering portrait.

There are clearly several points far from the line, indicating a poor fit and consistent with substantial stress. In short, this is not an acceptable representation, and we should discard it. Our only option is to move up one dimension, and this is what we do next. The three-dimensional solution, which uses 27 parameters to fit 36 pieces of distance data, can be expected to fit well, but one should be very careful in interpreting the resulting graphs, due to the low ratio of data to parameters.

Iteration History for Three-Dimensional MDS Analysis

Iteration	Stress	Improvement
1	0.1407	
2	0.1083	0.0324
3	0.1018	0.0065
4	0.0996	0.0022
5	0.0980	0.0016
6	0.0966	0.0014
7	0.0954	0.0012
8	0.0946	0.0008

$R^2 = 0.912$

The stress for the present three-dimensional map is lower than 0.10, less than half the value for the previous two-dimensional one, and more than 91 percent of the variance can be explained, compared with 72 percent previously. The derived three-dimensional map looks as follows:

Three-Dimensional MDS Solution for the Spatial Locations of Nine MBA Programs

Name	Dimension 1	Dimension 2	Dimension 3
MIT	0.234	2.058	−0.143
Harvard	1.485	−0.254	0.088
Dartmouth	−0.659	−0.955	1.103
Columbia	−0.748	−1.039	1.075
Wharton	0.168	0.138	−0.593
Chicago	−0.617	−0.903	−1.497
Northwest	0.905	−0.269	−1.131
Carnegie	−2.178	0.806	−0.118
Stanford	1.411	0.417	1.216

We can attempt to look at all three two-dimensional "slices" for this map, but they will be very difficult to mentally integrate; for even higher-dimensional representations, looking at dimensions two at a time will be almost pointless, in terms of gaining a mental portrait of the items. For three dimensions, though, we can imagine the items sitting in a cube, which most statistical programs will automatically generate and rotate.

A sense of whether the distances in this new representation are reasonably accurate can be gained by once again looking at a scatterplot of the original distances and those based on the derived three-dimensional ones based on the listed matrix of three-dimensional spatial positions for the nine MBA programs.

Compared with the corresponding scatterplot for the two-dimensional solution, the three-dimensional representation in Figure 11.23 has no apparent outlier problems; almost all the points are close to the regression line, as they should be.

Is this three-dimensional representation "acceptable"? As always, this will depend on the project and the researchers carrying it out. The analysis program tells us that the stress level is 0.0946, which is reasonable, but not superb, and that $R^2 = 0.912$, which is not very surprising given that there are 27 estimated quantities (spatial coordinates) being used to explain 36 pieces of distance data. Bear in mind that a four-dimensional map would entail 36 parameters, and therefore fit perfectly (or very nearly so),

Figure 11.22 Actual vs. Derived Distances for Two-Dimensional MDS Analysis of MBA Programs

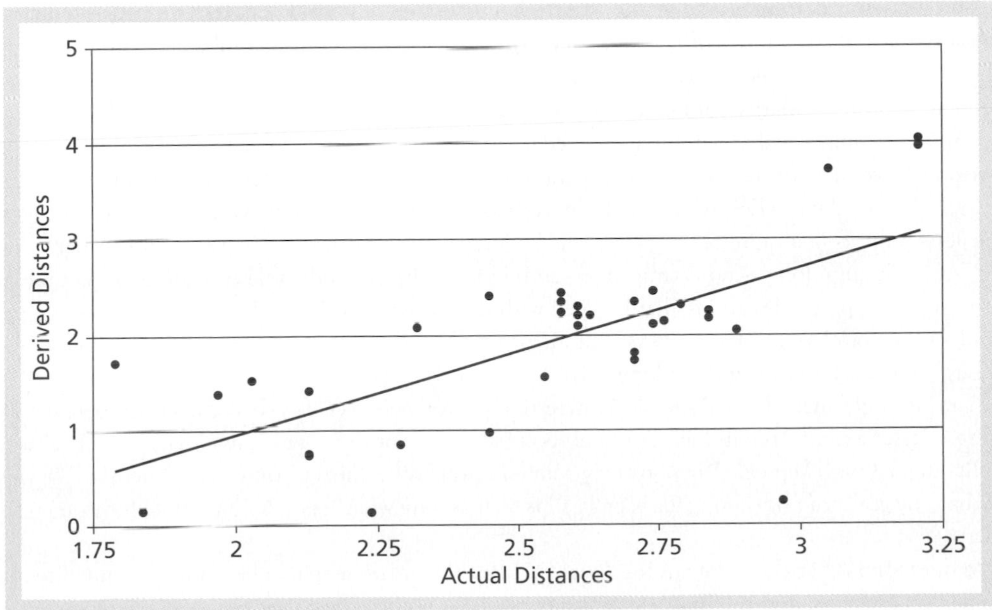

Figure 11.23 Actual vs. Derived Distances for Three-Dimensional MDS Analysis of MBA Programs

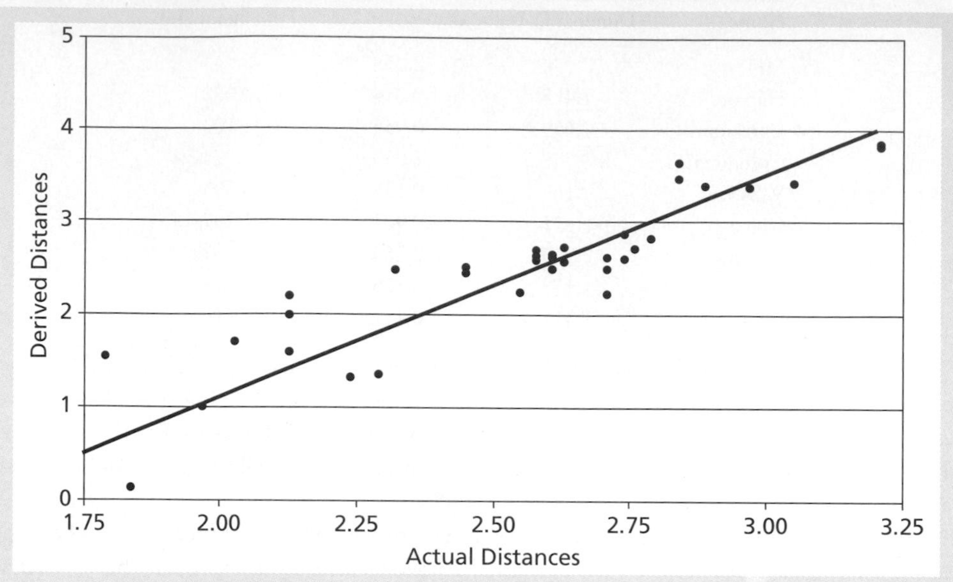

with no stress and an R^2 of 1. So, it is not really surprising that the three-dimensional solution is a dramatic improvement over the two-dimensional.

11.5c Orienting the MDS Map: Overlaying External Data

We have thus far made no attempt to "name" the dimensions, in order to orient the points within the map. This is actually fairly simple to do. If we refer back to the two-dimensional or three-dimensional tables of coordinates, each of the dimensions is merely a column of numbers. We can therefore *correlate* these numbers with any other external data. If the correlation is near zero, it means that the new information has nothing to do with *that particular dimension*. When the correlation is high (near −1 or 1), the new information is helpful in getting a sense of what that dimension means.

We can overlay as much data as we like in this manner, with the strength of relationship (correlation) automatically corresponding to the length of a superimposed arrow. Let us look back on our two-dimensional map for 12 brands of beer, and overlay information taken from a subjective survey (see Figure 11.24). Note that it is *not* necessary to collect this additional data at the same time, or from the same respondents, as the similarity (distance) data. One of the nicest aspects of using MDS is that the entire study can be commissioned and its data analyzed independently of other data being collected.

Although we did not mention it during the introduction to this chapter, the beer brand positions were indeed derived via MDS. With data from a qualitative consumer study overlaid, we can see that the dimensions were in fact quite reasonably named. Note that the arrows in Figure 11.24 for "heavy" and "light" are both quite long—indicating strong correlations with the indicated directions—and that they point in nearly opposite directions aligning well with the "heavy–light" axis. For the "basic–upscale" axis, we find strong correlations (long arrows well aligned with that axis) as well, with "value for money," "a good buy" and to a lesser extent "working class" aligned with "basic," and "celebrations," "eating out," and "premium" strongly aligned with "upscale." Interestingly, "women's beer" is also aligned with "upscale" as is, again to a lesser extent, "nonfilling." A closer look indicates that, seemingly paradoxically, "male" is *also* partially aligned with "upscale," but strongly rotated towards the "heavy" (upward) dimension. It would seem that any *gendered* positioning for beer at all is seen as somewhat "upscale," but more for women than for men.

We must stress that these are *not* the "correct" axes: the entire map can be rotated in any direction, or flipped on any axis, and the inter-item distances would remain identical. For example, if we were to

Figure 11.24 Perceptual Map of Beer Brands with Attribute Information Superimposed

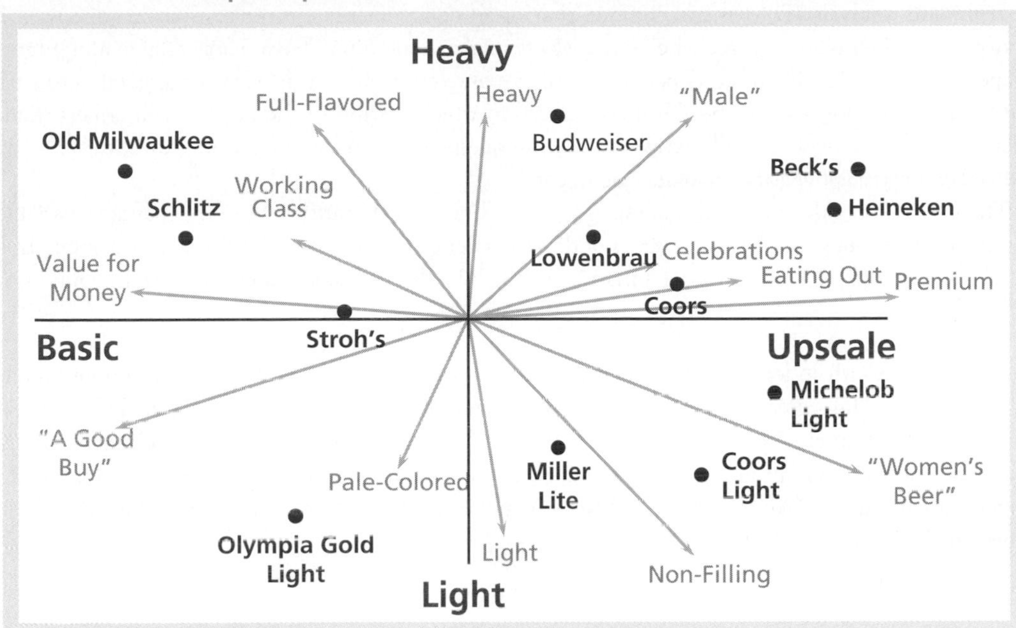

rotate the map 30 degrees clockwise, two new axes would shift into place, corresponding to something rather like "frugal–splurging" and "full-bodied less-filling." These new axes would be entirely legitimate. As such, researchers need to free themselves from the idea that the X- and Y-axes necessarily mean anything on a map: all that matters are the relative positions of the objects, and that we can overlay meaningful data. MDS is an easy-to-use and powerful method for doing so, and it can be widely applied whenever rigorous, objective, pictorial representations of markets, categories, people, or objects would prove useful.

11.5d Types and Uses of Multidimensional Scaling in Marketing Research

Our discussion has given the impression that there is only one type of multidimensional scaling, but this is not so; there are actually three general types of MDS. These types, which relate to the nature of the input and output data, have special names:

1. *Fully metric*. These methods require interval- or ratio-scaled input measures and generate a set of relationships among objects that is also interval or ratio.
2. *Fully nonmetric*. These methods take rank-ordered input measures and generate the rank order of each object on each dimension.
3. *Nonmetric*. These methods take rank-ordered input measures and generate a set of relationships among the objects that is interval. That is, the distances between objects in the perceptual space are meaningful, and can be compared like any ordinary distances.

Among the most frequent areas of marketing research application of MDS are: identifying salient product attributes perceived by buyers in a market; determining the combination of product attributes consumers most prefer; identifying products that are viewed as substitutes for (and those most differentiated from) one another; noting viable segments that exist in a market; and exposing the "holes" in a market that can support a new product venture. The method is also applicable to problems of product life-cycle analysis, market segmentation, vendor evaluation, advertising evaluation, test marketing, salesperson and store image, brand switching research, and attitude scaling, among others.

11.6 Discriminant Analysis

discriminant analysis (DA)
A statistical technique used to find the best basis for distinguishing groups (i.e., a discrete variable, from 1 to *k* groups), using a set of interval-scaled covariates; often used in conjunction with cluster analysis.

discriminant function (DF)
A function, usually linear, used in discriminant analysis.

confusion matrix
In discriminant analysis, a matrix cross-tabulating correct and incorrect predictions by for each group. Relatively large diagonal entries indicate good performance.

dummy-variable discriminant analysis (DVDA)
A special type of discriminant analysis in which nominal variables are rendered as groups of binary input variables; used infrequently in modern applications.

Discriminant analysis (DA) is a technique that often complements cluster analysis, as discussed in Section 11-3g. DA is appropriate when one seeks to analyze a nominal dependent variable and interval independent variables. Nominal dependent variables are very common in marketing: good versus bad credit risks, brand-loyal versus nonloyal consumers, in which section of the country subscribers reside, different brands' users, successful versus unsuccessful salespersons, and so on. As a result of this, DA has received extensive application in marketing research.

The basic idea of discriminant analysis is to find a linear combination of the independent variables that makes the *mean scores across categories* of the dependent variable, based on this linear combination, as different as possible. This linear combination is called the **discriminant function (DF)**. In symbols,

$$DF = v_1X_1 + v_2X_2 + \cdots + v_mX_m$$

where X_m is the mth independent variable (this formula should look exactly like an ordinary multiple regression). The objective is to find the values for the v's that yield a suitable DF, one that "maximally discriminates" among the categories of the (nominal) dependent variable. The criterion used to decide when group means are maximally different is the familiar ANOVA F-test for the differences among means (see material on ANOVA in the appendix to this chapter). Thus, the v's are derived such that

$$F = \frac{SS_{\text{between}}}{SS_{\text{within}}}$$

is maximized.

Discriminant analysis output typically includes the values of the v's, along with a **confusion matrix.** This matrix categorizes correct and incorrect predictions by cross-tabulating the dependent variable category that the discriminant function *predicts* a subject will be in with the category that the subject is *actually* in. Table 11.31 presents a confusion matrix for good and bad credit risks based on a set of demographic independent variables (e.g., age, income, years in the same residence, and so on). Note that it is the elements on the diagonal (running from top left to bottom right) that represent those subjects correctly classified by the DA. Ninety percent of subjects in this example are thus correctly classified, but it appears that the DA does a far better job categorizing good credit risks (800/840 = 95.2 percent correct) than bad ones (100/160 = 62.5 percent correct); it is in fact typical of statistical models to predict more common categories (here, "good") more accurately than less common ones. This example is for a two-category dependent variable (often called "two-group" DA), but it can easily be extended to a k-group dependent variable.

Discriminant analysis is a general method that can handle many sorts of independent variables, not only interval-scaled ones. For example, as with regression, one can convert nominal independent variables to (binary) dummy variables, and these would be proper input data for a version of DA called **dummy-variable discriminant analysis (DVDA).**

Table 11.31 Confusion Matrix for Credit Risks

	Predicted category	
Actual category	**Good**	**Bad**
Good	800	40
Bad	60	100

SPECIAL EXPERT FEATURE

Choice-Based Conjoint at General Motors

Jim Christian, Eleanor Feit, and Mark Beltramo, General Motors Corporation

General Motors has used conjoint for many years in a wide variety of competitive positioning applications. Applications include the development of OnStar®, the Bumper-Bumper® warranty, the Northstar® engine, and vehicle navigation systems, as well as many different new vehicle models. From textbook examples, it may seem that conjoint analysis is only useful for simple products with a small number of attributes, but GM has found that conjoint is very useful for the complex trade-offs involved in vehicle design. For example, GM used conjoint analysis during the early phases of the design process for a new large sport utility vehicle (SUV).

Study Planning: Deciding on Attributes and Levels

Before fielding a new conjoint study, we find it is important to get as much information as possible about the market. General Motors used a variety of secondary data sources while planning this conjoint study. This analysis of secondary data concluded that:

- There was a growing stigma attached to owning and driving a minivan and that minivan customers were switching to higher-status SUVs.
- Previous conjoint models indicated that SUVs needed to be optimized for children and that heavy towing and hauling were of lesser importance.
- GM and other manufacturers had been successful in selling other small trucks with improved fuel economy built on front-wheel-drive car chasses.
- GM had a large front-wheel-drive platform that could be used to build a large SUV.

This secondary analysis identified a large number of consumer trade-offs involved in the design of a large SUV. These trade-offs involved attributes such as exterior appearance, interior roominess, fuel economy, acceleration, and trailer towing. For example, making the SUV larger nearly always reduces fuel economy. Choice-based conjoint is ideal for understanding how consumers make trade-offs between these attributes. The resulting conjoint model can be used to quickly evaluate millions of alternative vehicle configurations without conducting any additional research. This is extremely useful in the early phases of the design process when many alternative configurations are being considered. The choice-based methodology provides relatively natural choice questions that result in conjoint models that make more accurate predictions than alternative methods.

Figure 11.25 lists the 15 attributes that the research team included in this study.

Figure 11.25 SUV Conjoint Study Attributes

Cargo Opening / Load Floor Height
Cargo Space Depth
Door Type
Engine (power / number of Cylinders)
Engine Performance (acceleration)
Exterior Size & Appearance
Fuel Economy
Interior Layout & Roominess
Make
Price
Rollover Safety
Seating Configuration
Spare Tire Type
Towing
Turning Circle
Drive Type

Choosing the right attributes and levels is generally the most challenging part of any conjoint study. This one set of attributes needs to meet a number of sometimes conflicting requirements:

- The attributes must be selected to address the research objectives identified by the cross-functional design team. Many of the design trade-offs that they are trying to resolve are complex and involve many product attributes. Sometimes, is it difficult to define a set of attributes that do not overlap with each other.
- The number of attributes and levels is limited by the ability of respondents to answer complex choice questions.
- The set of attribute levels must be able to describe both GM designs that are under consideration and the competitive vehicles that we want to compare the GM vehicle to.
- For complex products such as vehicles, it takes time and effort to describe the attributes to the consumer. The attributes must be defined in such a way that customers can understand and remember the product characteristics as they answer 20 to 30 choice questions. We often use physical prototypes to help educate consumers about new attributes, but our ability to build these prototypes may limit the attribute levels that can be included in the study.
- The attribute list needs to meet a number of additional technical research requirements that are very difficult to explain to a vehicle development team; for instance, the attribute descriptions must fit within a certain screen size.

The marketing research group worked very closely with the vehicle design team to determine which attributes and levels should be included in the study. Coming up with a set of attributes and levels that will answer the design team's questions, while still meeting the constraints of the conjoint

continued

survey, was challenging and time consuming. For instance, it was difficult to decide whether the "Engine" attribute (defined by the horsepower and number of cylinders) and the "Engine performance attribute" (defined as acceleration) should be combined or separate attributes. By leaving them independent, we were able to make share predictions for more product configurations, but respondents may have been given some product profiles that were unreasonable, such as a very large, very fast SUV with a low horsepower engine.

To create the product profiles for the conjoint survey, GM uses a commercial conjoint software package. We find the commercial software provides an optimal mix of quality, speed, and cost. Because many market research companies use this software, GM can get consistent results while using competitive bidding to award marketing research projects. Furthermore, using publicly available software insures that the majority of software problems have been identified and/or corrected. Finally, commercial software is easy to work with and reduces the time required for fieldwork and analysis. Because GM is such a large user of conjoint, several commercial software modules have been written to GM specifications, allowing us to tailor the software to our own needs.

Fielding: Collecting the Trade-off Data

GM conjoint research is generally fielded in large, central-location studies. This allows us to use physical stimuli to help the respondents understand the different attribute levels. GM uses a sample of respondents that is representative of national sales counts for particular product segment(s). Each respondent spends about three hours at the study. This includes orientation, background questionnaire, familiarization with the attributes/attribute levels, and finally the actual conjoint choice questionnaire. During the familiarization section of the interview, respondents typically review photographs or physical prototypes to help them understand the attributes that are included in the study. Then during the conjoint questionnaire they use a PC to answer 20 to 30 choice questions similar to the question pictured in Figure 11.26.

Figure 11.26 Example Conjoint Question

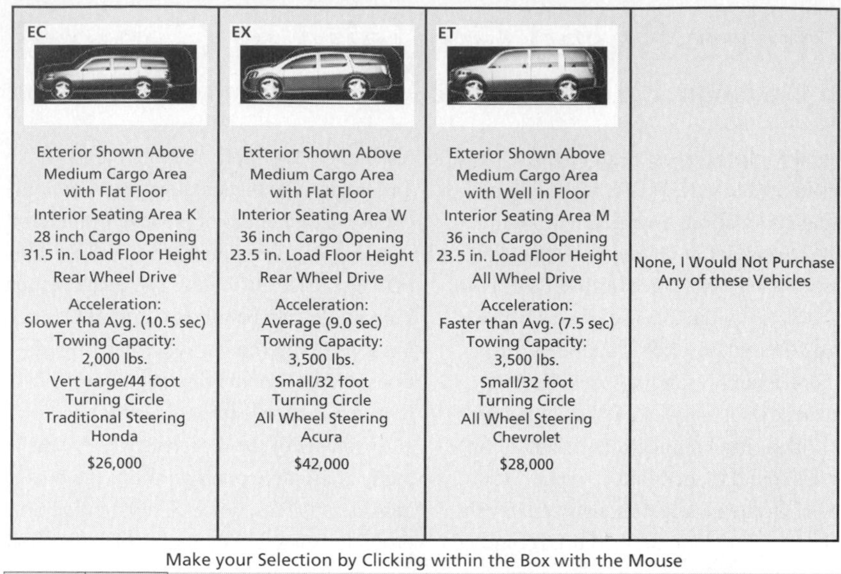

Source: Courtesy of Jim Christian, Eleanor Feit, and Mark Beltramo.

One of the most critical aspects of fielding the study is providing appropriate descriptions of the attributes. When people shop for new vehicles, they typically visit a dealership and look at full-size vehicles. If respondents do not see the same sort of stimuli as they would in the dealership, then their answers to conjoint questions may not reflect how they would choose when they really go shopping.

To the extent possible, GM tries to use attribute definitions that replicate the information available to customers during the shopping process. For example, exterior appearance is among the most important factors in new vehicle purchase. Consequently, this study used high-quality, color, full-size, projected exterior images to familiarize respondents with the styling levels. In addition to developing realistic-looking pictures to show respondents during the familiarization phase, we also included pictures in the choice questions to help the respondents remember the exterior styling levels. These pictures were chosen to be consistent with the interior spaciousness described in each of the vehicle profiles. For example, if the vehicle profile in the question had a long cargo area, the picture in the choice question reflected this characteristic. This allowed the respondents to evaluate cargo space while taking into consideration the impact that cargo space has on exterior appearance.

We familiarized respondents with the cargo space attribute by showing respondents the three full-size vehicles pictured in Figure 11.27. The levels were set at 12″ cargo depth, 24″ cargo depth, and 36″ cargo depth. We focused on the floor space

Figure 11.27 Attribute Stimuli for Cargo Space Depth

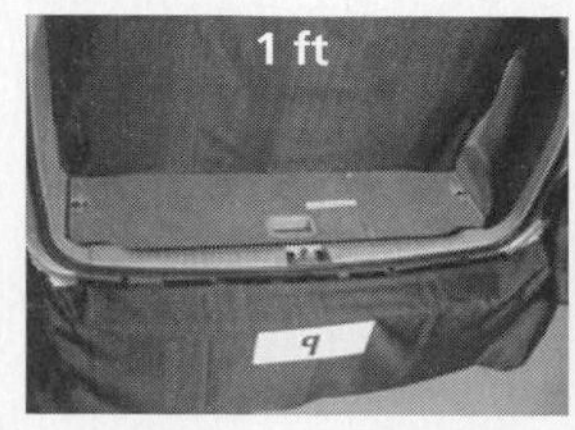

Source: Courtesy of Jim Christian, Eleanor Feit, and Mark Beltramo.

continued

because we know that customers evaluate square feet of cargo space rather than cubic feet. Respondents were able to walk up to these vehicles and touch them, giving them a very similar experience to what they would get in a dealer showroom.

Other attributes were described in words without physical stimuli. For example, towing was described in numeric towing capacities similar to dealership sales literature. Even though these stimuli are simpler than the stimuli for cargo space, they are consistent with the type of information that would be available during the shopping process. (Dealers do not typically allow customers to try out the towing capabilities during a test-drive.)

Figure 11.28 Clinic Share for GM Vehicle with Alternative Cargo Depths

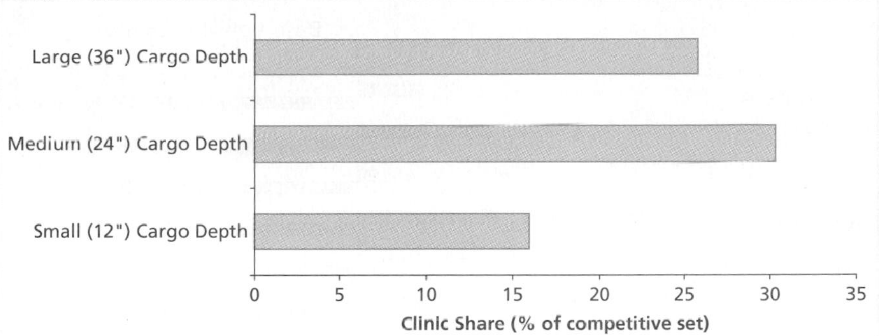

Figure 11.29 Clinic Share for GM Base Vehicle with Alternative Towing Capacity

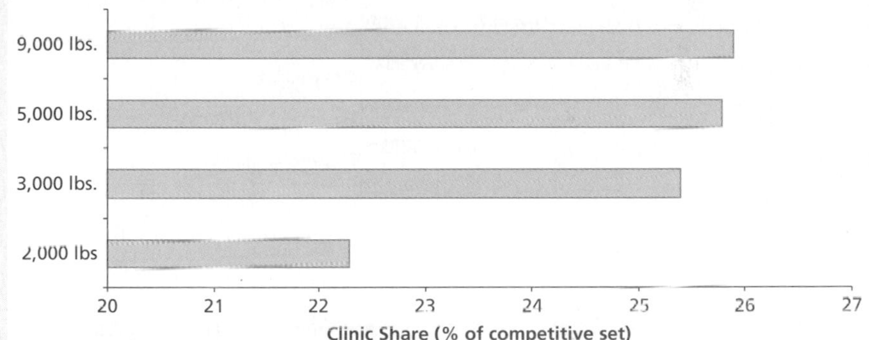

Analysis: Estimating Utilities and Making Predictions

Like most GM conjoint studies, the choices produced by the survey were analyzed using the same commercial software that was used to design the questions. Statistical analysis of the responses to the choice questions produces a model that can predict which vehicle a consumer will choose given a set of alternatives. To understand how the proposed vehicle design might fare in the market, we developed a set of approximately 20 competitive vehicles that represent the current large SUV market. We then used the conjoint model to predict the share for the new vehicle in the competitive set. We refer to this prediction as "clinic share." It is important to realize that this prediction is based both on the conjoint model and on our assumptions about the competitive vehicle set. If we were to remove a strong competitor from the set, then the clinic share for the new vehicle would increase.

To understand the impact of each attribute, we typically define a "base vehicle," which is a preliminary configuration proposed by the design team. Then we vary the attributes of this base vehicle to see the sensitivity of clinic share to changes in the attributes. A sensitivity analysis for the cargo space attribute is shown in Figure 11.28. Predicted market share was maximized at 24″, while 36″ actually reduced the predicted share. At the same research event, we asked qualitative questions about cargo space, and respondents explained that 24″ was the amount of space that they typically need. Respondents felt it is too difficult to reach cargo deep inside the 36″ area.

Figure 11.29 shows the sensitivity analysis for towing. Clinic share does not increase as you improve towing above a modest 3500-pound level. Qualitative follow-up questions revealed that few of these customers tow, and those who do tow generally described light towing applications. Understanding that towing was less important to these customers allowed GM to optimize other attributes, such as fuel economy and acceleration, that are of higher importance to customers.

We computed similar sensitivities for the other attributes in the study, and to summarize them, we created a tornado chart shown in Figure 11.30. (Because these results are proprietary, the attributes and levels have been masked in this chart.) The center line of the chart represents the clinic share for the base vehicle, which was 25.6 percent. For each attribute, we show the predicted clinic share for the best and the worst level of each attribute relative to the base vehicle's clinic share. For instance, for attribute A, clinic share could be improved to 42.5 percent if the design team were to switch to level A7 of that attribute. It could also be reduced to 20.5 percent if the attribute were switched to level A3. When we construct the tornado chart, the attributes are ordered by the amount of positive impact they could have on share, so the design team can easily see which attribute changes (over the base vehicle) would be most desirable to the respondents.

Looking at the tornado chart, we can get some idea of the relative trade-offs between these attributes. Based on this and other information, the design team created three new product profiles that they believed they could produce: Designs A, B, and C. Figure 11.31 shows the clinic share against the competitive set for these three alternatives. The results suggest that the

continued

Figure 11.30 Tornado Chart Summarizing Study Results

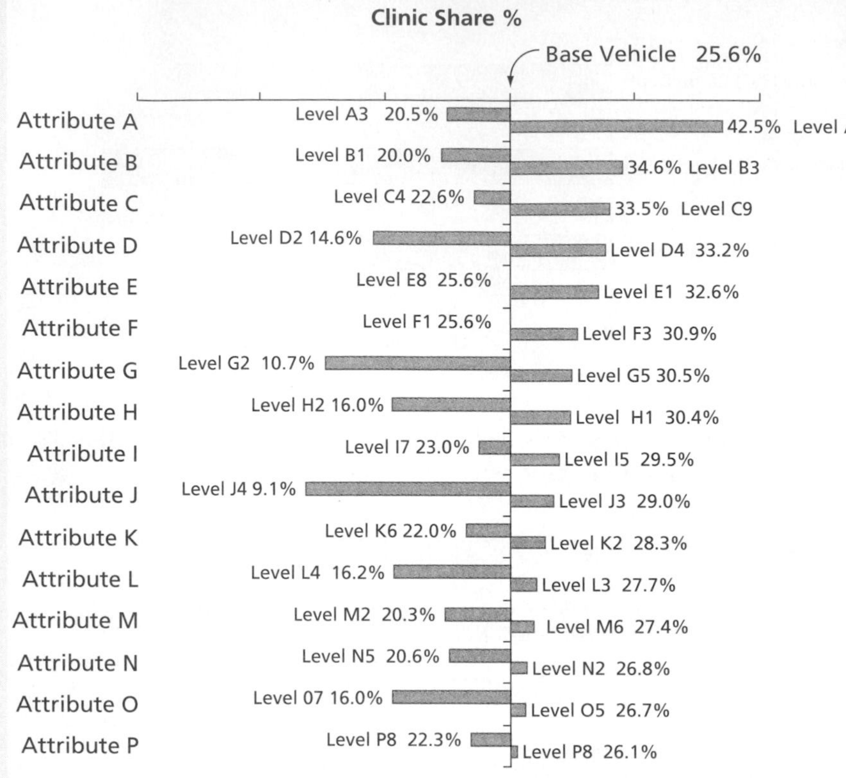

Figure 11.31 Clinic Share for Alternative GM Vehicle Designs

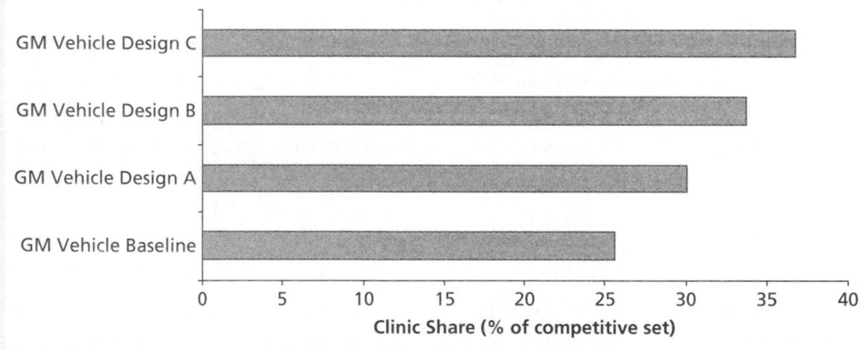

middle size SUV (Design C) provided maximum clinic acceptance through a combination of a roomy interior with reasonable fuel economy. This analysis was later extended to look at interactions with other vehicles in the GM portfolio. For example, we looked at questions such as whether the new vehicle would cannibalize (i.e., steal share from) existing GM vehicles.

After the Conjoint Study

This SUV conjoint study helped designers determine the coarse balance of features for this new vehicle early in the design process. Although conjoint models provide valuable predictions across a wide variety of alternatives, they are still only rough approximations. As sophisticated as our stimuli are, the respondents still just made decisions about lists of attributes. To follow up on the conjoint study, we used other research methods that provided the design team with in-depth evaluations of the most promising vehicle alternatives. These additional research events were used to refine the vehicle styling and to confirm the conjoint results about the other attributes.

Jim Christian is the Technical Director of Fullsize and Commercial Truck Research in GM's Global Product Research Department. He began his career at GM in 1977 in the Statistical Analysis Department of the Engineering Staff. He has been in Global Product Research for the past 15 years and has overseen many of GM's conjoint projects, including collaborations with Paul Green, Dick Smallwood, and Rich Johnson. He holds an MS from Eastern Michigan University in Organizational Behavior and Development.

Eleanor Feit worked in Advanced Vehicle Development at GM applying the results of conjoint studies to new vehicle development programs. She is currently on leave pursuing a PhD in Marketing at the University of Michigan.

Mark Beltramo is a Staff Researcher in the Vehicle Development Research Lab at the GM Research and Development Center in Warren, Michigan. His primary research interests involve using consumer data to help set priorities in product development. He holds a PhD in Management Science and Engineering from Stanford University.

Courtesy of Jim Christian, Eleanor Feit, and Mark Beltramo.

Summary

Dependence methods designate one or more variables as being predicted by a set of independent variables. Interdependence methods do not designate any variables as being predicted by others, but address the interrelationship among all the variables taken together.

Interdependence methods include Factor analysis, cluster analysis, and multidimensional scaling (MDS).

Factor analysis takes a correlation matrix of a large number of variables and evaluates whether a small number of independent Factors can account for their intercorrelations. Factor analysis outputs the *loading* of each variable on each underlying factor; this output may be rotated to aid in interpretation. A principal components analysis looks for the single best Factor to explain all the variables in the data set, then constructs a second Factor that explains as much as what is left over as possible, and so on. Applications of Factor analysis include data reduction, structure identification, scaling, and data transformation.

Cluster analysis places objects into subgroups or clusters that are defined by the procedure. The Cluster analysis input is a matrix of associations or distances between objects; the output places objects in clusters at different levels of association. Hierarchical cluster analysis results in a dendrogram depicting a branching hierarchy of clusters. K-means clustering is a nonhierarchical cluster analysis that forces items into a predetermined number of clusters. Latent class models are general statistical procedures that allow clustering using many data types, not only interval-scaled variables.

Conjoint analysis evaluates the trade-offs people make between various options to determine what drives their preferences. This enables marketing researchers to establish how much each attribute of a product or service is valued, what attribute levels are most preferred, and appropriate price points. Orthogonal designs allow researchers to present participants with a small subset of all possible attribute level combinations, yet retain statistical power. Adaptive conjoint restricts questioning of a respondent to those trade-offs most relevant to that person. Choice-based conjoint measures trade-offs purely through choices, as in the real world, instead of through rankings or ratings; this is the type of conjoint analysis most often used by marketing research professionals.

Multidimensional scaling (MDS) allows researchers to create a map of a set of products (or objects, services, and so on) using data on their (dis)similarities alone. Important dimensions can be identified by overlaying on this map external data regarding attributes and preferences.

An advantage of both cluster analysis and multidimensional scaling is that they can be used to create a visual map of statistical interrelationships useful for marketing applications.

Discriminant analysis (DA) often accompanies cluster analysis, and it helps determine which variables best separate items into given categories. It is typically used with one nominal dependent variable and a set of interval-scaled independent variables.

Key Terms

adaptive conjoint (p. 521)
agglomeration Schedule (p. 500)
choice-based conjoint (p. 521)
clustering criterion (p. 498)
communalities (p. 485)
confusion matrix (p. 540)
conjoint analysis (p. 510)
dendrogram (p. 502)
dependence methods (p. 472)
discriminant analysis (DA) (p. 540)
discriminant function (DF) (p. 540)
distance metric (p. 498)
dummy-variable discriminant analysis (DVDA) (p. 540)
eigenvalues (p. 482)
factor analysis (p. 476)
factor extraction (p. 480)
factor loadings (p. 479)
factor rotation (p. 480)
factors (p. 476)
interdependence methods (p. 474)
intermediate level of aggregation (p. 496)
K-means clustering (p. 505)
latent class models (p. 507)
linear discriminant functions (p. 503)
log-likelihood function (p. 507)
MinEigen criterion (p. 483)
multidimensional scaling (p. 529)
multivariate statistical procedure (p. 472)
normalized centroid distance (p. 500)
orthogonal (p. 480)
orthogonal design (p. 516)
part worths (p. 513)
principal components methodology (p. 480)
rotated factor pattern (p. 486)
scree plot (p. 484)
splines (p. 527)
stress (p. 535)
varimax rotation (p. 486)
weighted sum or weighted average (p. 479)
z-transform (p. 497)

Discussion Questions

1 Distinguish between dependence and interdependence methods. Can all statistical methods be so designated? Consider specifically the ones developed thus far in this text.

2 For Factor Analysis, cluster analysis, and multidimensional scaling, compare the objectives of each of these methods with the nature of their inputs and outputs. Which of them can, or should, be used in tandem? Can you think of marketing research projects that might require all three? Projects for which none of them would be suited?

3 In real-world projects, subjective interpretation of statistical results is often required. How might you "name" Factors (in Factor Analysis), clusters (in cluster analysis), and dimensions (in MDS)? Are some of the ways to do this more objective than others? How so? What type of data might you need, beyond that required by each of the methods themselves?

4 If you were vice president of marketing at a major bank, how might you use the Factor Analysis results presented in Marketing Research Focus 11-1? Which of the extracted dimensions might be most useful and why? What additional analyses might it help to perform?

5 What is a discriminant function? What criterion is used to derive its coefficients? In what sorts of marketing research applications can you imagine discriminant analysis being useful, even if cluster analysis is not performed?

6 Should conjoint analysis be used to predict market share? If so, how? If not, why not, and how might you go about coupling the conjoint measurements with share estimates from another source?

7 Managers often ask marketing researchers questions of a "how many" nature: "How many factors must we consider?", "How many segments does the cluster analysis reveal?", "How many dimensions are needed to represent our market?", "How many attributes and levels do we need in our conjoint task?", and so forth. How might you go about answering each of these in practice? For each one, think of a specific application, and what sort of evidence you would need to settle such a "how many" question.

8 What is a "latent class"? Does it differ from a cluster, or group, or segment? In what sorts of marketing applications would latent classes be particularly useful, over and above the other methods discussed in this chapter?

9 MINICASE

It is standard practice in the automobile industry to use multidimensional scaling representations of automobile brands in marketing planning. Why would this be so? How could an automobile marketing manager use the (non-metric) scaling results given in Figure 11.32 based on the data in Table 11.32? What additional data would assist in the interpretation of these scaling results?

10 MINICASE

Design a conjoint study that Marriott might use in the development and refinement of the "Courtyard by Marriott" concept (marriott.com/courtyard). Be sure to consider the relevant attributes, the appropriate

Figure 11.32 Perceptual Space Solution Based on MDS Analysis of Data in Table 11.32

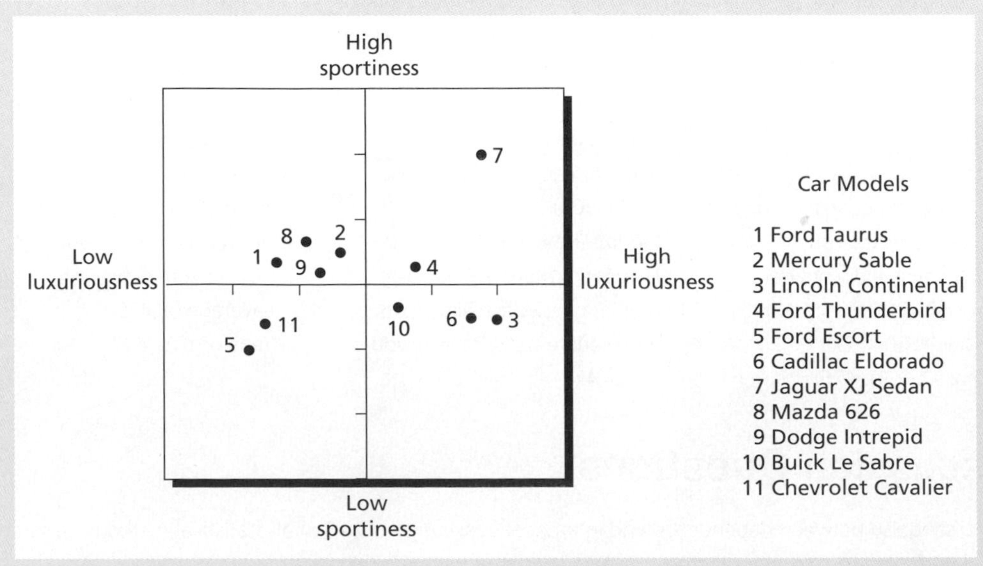

Table 11.32 Rank Order of Similarities between Pairs of Car Models

Stimuli	1	2	3	4	5	6	7	8	9	10	11
1	—	8	50	31	12	48	36	2	5	39	10
2		—	38	9	33	37	22	6	4	14	32
3			—	11	55	1	23	46	41	17	52
4				—	44	13	16	19	25	18	42
5					—	54	53	30	28	45	7
6						—	26	47	40	24	51
7							—	29	35	34	49
8								—	3	27	15
9									—	20	21
10										—	43
11											—

The rank number "1" represents the most similar pair.

levels of each attribute, and the task required of respondents in the study. How might a manager use the statistical results deriving from your study?

Review Questions

1 Why might a researcher begin a Factor Analysis using principal components instead of another method (e.g., varimax)?
  - **a** interpretation of results.
  - **b** maximize total sum of the eigenvalues.
  - **c** "Best" Factors are successively extracted.
  - **d** Resulting factors are parallel.

2 How might you accurately explain "eigenvalue" to a manager?
  - **a** It compares a Factor to "the average" Factor.
  - **b** It measures a Factor's standard deviation.
  - **c** It is a type of correlation coefficient.
  - **d** It tells you if you need to regress the Factors.

3 Why might you consult a Scree plot?
  - **a** It helps determine if the data are multicollinear.
  - **b** It tells you if Factors suddenly drop in explanatory power.
  - **c** It indicates appropriate clusterings.
  - **d** It highlights correlations in the Factors.

4 Why would a marketing researcher, faced with a large database of variables to use in a multiple regression analysis, consider Factor analyzing them first?
  - **a** Regression coefficients measure what they are intended to.
  - **b** *t*-values are more likely to be positive.
  - **c** Regression coefficients are more likely to be positive.
  - **d** R^2 is more likely to exceed R^2-adjusted.

5 What is "stress"?
  - **a** when objects do not fit well into a low-dimensional MDS map.
  - **b** how perfectly a cluster contains the original data.
  - **c** how using fewer Factors affects the overall solution.
  - **d** when conjoint attributes force the levels into a narrow range.

6 Why would a manager choose a hierarchical over a nonhierarchical Cluster Analysis?
- **a** need to list objects in a particular, known order.
- **b** need to meaningfully compare one cluster solution to another.
- **c** must prevent more than two clusters from joining at once.
- **d** only room to report the results of one or two solutions.

7 How might you go about objectively naming the axes on a map derived from MDS?
- **a** by computing the correlation of the axes themselves.
- **b** by calculating the centroid of the data relative to each axis.
- **c** by using the Scree plot.
- **d** by overlaying external information on the map.

8 Should conjoint be used to predict *market share*?
- **a** No, because share is affected by promotions and competitive actions.
- **b** No, because conjoint is based on consumer choices.
- **c** Yes, because share depends on consumer knowledge.
- **d** Yes, because it is crucial to generate a demand estimate.

9 A researcher suggests using an orthogonal design. What might be the reason for this decision?
- **a** because orthogonal designs use perpendicular Factors.
- **b** because they lead to the smallest communalities.
- **c** because they allow for many fewer queries per respondent.
- **d** because clustering will be less exact without them.

10 A researcher is confused about what sort of data one typically enters into Factor and cluster analyses in marketing research applications. Which of the following explains it most accurately?
- **a** We Factor both cases and variables.
- **b** We cluster both cases and variables.
- **c** We Factor our cases and cluster our variables.
- **d** We Factor our variables and cluster our cases.

Web Exercise

Log in to the Online Edition of your textbook at www.atomicdog.com to participate in this Web exercise, which can be found in your Online Study Guide for this chapter.

Further Reading

Borg, Ingwer, and Patrick J. F. Groenen (2005), *Modern Multidimensional Scaling: Theory and Applications.* New York: Springer Series in Statistics.

Brown, Timothy A. (2006), *Confirmatory Factor Analysis for Applied Research*. New York: The Guilford Press.

Hair, Joseph F., Bill Black, Barry Babin, and Rolph E. Anderson (2005), *Multivariate Data Analysis.* Upper Saddle River, NJ: Prentice-Hall.

Kaufman, Leonard, and Peter J. Rousseeuw (2005), *Finding Groups in Data: An Introduction to Cluster Analysis.* New York: Wiley Series in Probability and Statistics, John Wiley & Sons, Inc.

Orme, Bryan K. (2005), *Getting Started with Conjoint Analysis: Strategies for Product Design and Pricing Research.* Madison, WI: Research Publishers LLC.

The Latent Class Analysis Web Site, by John Uebersax: http://ourworld.compuserve.com/homepages/jsuebersax/

APPENDIX 11: ANALYSIS OF VARIANCE (ANOVA)

Statistical Analysis of Experiments

Analysis of variance (ANOVA) is among the main methods used in social science. Although it is, strictly speaking, a special case of regression, the techniques associated with it have become so rich that ANOVA is often treated as a special subject in itself. It is important to understand exactly what its requirements and assumptions are, so let us start there: ANOVA can be applied when the researcher is analyzing *one intervally scaled dependent variable and one or more nominally scaled independent variables*.

ANOVA is often discussed in terms of three somewhat different procedures. Before trying to make sense of them, you may wish to go back and review the material on basic statistical inference and regression in Chapters 9 and 10. These three ANOVA procedures are:

Model I: Fixed Effects. In this model, the researcher makes inferences only about differences among the *j* treatments *actually administered*, and about no other treatment that might have been included. In other words, no *interpolation* between treatments is made. For example, if the treatments were high, medium, and low advertising expenditures, no inferences are drawn about advertising expenditures between these three levels.

Model II: Random Effects. In the second model, the researcher assumes that only a *random sample* of the treatments about which he or she wants to make inferences has been used. Here, the researcher would be prepared to interpolate results between treatments, if need be.

Model III: Mixed Effects. In the third model, the researcher has some fixed and some random independent variables (treatments).

The major differences among these models relate to the formulas used to calculate sampling error and to some data assumptions. We shall show the calculations only for the fixed-effects model because the basic approach and the principles to be established are the same for the other models. Also, in marketing research, most experiments fit the fixed-effects model, as the experiments usually include all treatments that are relevant to the decision to be made. Additional detail on calculations, especially for Models II and III, can be found in any standard text on ANOVA models.

In applying the fixed-effects model, the researcher must make several assumptions about the data. Specifically:

1. For each treatment population, *j*, the experimental errors are independent and normally distributed about a mean of zero with an identical variance (this variance is determined as part of the estimation procedure).
2. The sum of all treatment effects is zero.
3. In the calculations presented here, each treatment group has the same number of observations. This assumption is not generally necessary, but it simplifies the calculations; most ANOVA programs will not require this assumption.

In experimentation, the null hypothesis is that *the treatment effects equal zero*. If τ_j represents the effect of treatment *j*, and the total number of treatments is *t*, we can write the null hypothesis as

$$\tau_1 = \tau_2 = \ldots = \tau_j = \ldots = \tau_t = 0$$

or in the equivalent notation

$$\tau_j = 0 \ (j = 1, 2, \ldots, t)$$

where j = a specific treatment. The alternative hypothesis is that

$$\tau_j \neq 0 \ (j = 1, 2, \ldots, t)$$

Note that this asserts that *at least one* of the treatments is nonzero, not that they all are. If the treatments have had no effect, we would expect the scores on the dependent variable to be the same in each group, so that the mean values would be the same in each group. So our null hypothesis is equivalent to the statement that

$$\mu_1 = \mu_2 \cdots = \mu_j = \mu$$

where 1, 2, . . ., j represent treatment groups, and μ represents the mean for the entire population, without regard to groups. So we see that ANOVA is essentially a procedure for simultaneously testing for the equality of two or more means. In this way, it extends the usual (pooled) t-test for the equality of the means of exactly two groups.

Completely Randomized Design

ANOVA applied to a *completely randomized design* (CRD) is called "one-way" ANOVA because it is being applied to categories of exactly one independent variable. Table 11A.1 presents results generated by a CRD. The measures on the dependent variable, Y, are taken on the test units. Here, there are four test units in each of three treatments, so we have $4 \times 3 = 12$ test units. The units are stores in the relevant geographic region where each of three coupon plans was applied. The dependent variable is the number of cases of cola sold the day after the different coupons were run in local newspapers. The treatments are the three categories of the independent variable, T.

T_1 Coupon plan 1
T_2 Coupon plan 2
T_3 Coupon plan 3

So, we have 3 treatments, 12 test units, and an interval-scaled measure on each test unit, ensuring that ANOVA can be applied.

In Table 11A.1, we define the mean of each treatment group as

$$\bar{Y}_{.j} = M_{.j} = \frac{\sum Y_{.j}}{n}$$

The use of the period (.) in front of the j implies that we are calculating the mean by adding all i's in the jth treatment group. Note also that $\sum Y_{i.}$ indicates the sum of all j's for given i, and $\sum Y_{..}$ indicates the sum of all i's and all j's. In our example,

$$\bar{Y}_{.1} = M_{.1} = \frac{64}{4} = 16$$

$$\bar{Y}_{.2} = M_{.2} = \frac{52}{4} = 13$$

$$\bar{Y}_{.3} = M_{.3} = \frac{36}{4} = 9$$

Table 11A.1 **Completely Randomized Design with Three Treatments (Coupon Plans)**

	Treatments (j)		
	Coupon plan 1	Coupon plan 2	Coupon plan 3
Test units (i)	20	17	14
	18	14	10
	15	13	7
	11	8	5
Treatment totals	$\sum Y_{.1} = 64$	$\sum Y_{.2} = 52$	$\sum Y_{.3} = 36$
Treatment means	$\bar{Y}_{.1} = M_{.1}$ $= \sum Y_{.1}/n_1$ $= 64/4 = 16$	$\bar{Y}_{.2} = M_{.2}$ $= \sum Y_{.2}/n_2$ $= 52/4 = 13$	$\bar{Y}_{.3} = M_{.3}$ $= \sum Y_{.3}/n_1$ $= 36/4 = 9$
		Grand total	$\sum Y_{..} = 64 + 52 + 36 = 152$
		Grand mean	$\bar{Y}_{..} = M = \sum Y_{..}/(n_1 + n_2 + n_3)$ $= 152/12 = 12.7$

Note: $n_1 = n_2 = n_3 = n_j = 4$

We also define the *grand mean* of all observations across all treatment groups as $\bar{Y}..$ or M. Here

$$M = \frac{64 + 52 + 36}{12} = 12.7$$

These various means will be used to interpret the results and calculations of an ANOVA. In an experimental context, we want to determine whether the treatments have had an effect on the dependent variable. (By "effect" we mean a functional relationship between the treatment T_j and the dependent variable Y.) That is, do different treatments give systematically different scores on the dependent variable? For example, in our coupon plan example, if the plans have had differing effects on sales, we would expect the amount of sales in the stores in treatment T_1 to differ systematically from T_2 and T_3. If in fact they did, the mean of each treatment group would also differ. In ANOVA, an *effect* is defined as a difference in treatment means from the grand mean. What we are doing in ANOVA mirrors our development throughout all regression-based statistical models: determining whether differences in treatment means are large enough to be unlikely to have occurred just by chance alone.

Some Notation and Definitions

Let Y_{ij} be the score of the *i*th test unit on the *j*th treatment. For example, in Table 11A.1,

$$Y_{11} = 20, \quad Y_{42} = 8, \quad \text{and so on.}$$

We define any individual test unit's scores as equal to

$$Y_{ij} = \text{grand mean} + \text{treatment effect} + \text{error}$$

or

$$Y_{ij} = \mu + \tau_j + \epsilon_{ij}$$

This is a simple linear, additive model with values specified in terms of population parameters. Because we are going to be using *sample* results to make inferences, we can translate this model into the language of observable, sample quantities as

$$Y_{ij} = M + T_j + E_{ij}$$

where M = the grand mean

T_i = the effect of the *j*th treatment

E_{ij} = the statistical error of the *i*th test unit in the *j*th treatment

(Note that E_{ij} plays the same role as e_{ij} in ordinary regression models. It is customary to capitalize the "*E*" in ANOVA models, so we hew to that convention, but there is no conceptual difference between E_{ij} in ANOVA and e_{ij} in regression.)

In this model, the treatment effect is defined as the difference between the treatment mean and the grand mean:

$$T_j = M_{.j} - M$$

The reason we use M as the base from which to compare the various $M_{.j}$'s is that even if we did not know from which treatment a test unit came, we could still "guess" the grand mean as their score on the dependent variable. Knowledge of treatment group memberships improves our ability to predict scores, relative to simply using the overall mean, M.

The error for an individual unit, E_{ij}, is estimated by the difference between an individual score and the treatment group mean to which the score belongs.

$$E_{ij} = Y_{ij} - M_{.j}$$

It is a measure of the difference in scores that are not explained by treatments. This is the measure of *sampling error* in the experiment, and is also referred to as *experimental error*. For example, if all scores within a treatment are close together, the individual scores will be close to the treatment mean, and the error will be small. So, this deviation is a measure of the *random variation* within each treatment in an experiment.

We can rewrite Equation 1 as

$$\begin{array}{ccccccc} Y_{ij} & = & M & + & (M_{.j} - M) & + & (Y_{ij} - M_{.j}) \\ \downarrow & & \downarrow & & \downarrow & & \downarrow \\ \text{Individual score} & = & \text{grand mean} & + & \text{treatment effect} & + & \text{error} \end{array}$$

Note that this rewritten form is an *identity:* we have just added and subtracted the same quantities—the treatment mean ($M_{.j}$) and the grand mean (M)—on the right side, so the equation is in effect saying that Y_{ij} is equal to itself; it is just helpful as a way of *decomposing* various effects. Alternatively, we can write any observation as a deviation from the grand mean. We do this by moving M to the left side of Equation 2, creating yet another identity:

$(Y_{ij} - M)$	=	$(M_{.j} - M)$	+	$(Y_{ij} - M_{.j})$	
↓		↓		↓	
Individual score deviation from grand mean	=	deviation of group mean from mean (i.e., treatment effect)	+	individual score deviation from group mean (i.e., error)	(3)

Partitioning the Sum-of-Squares

The idea of ANOVA is built around the concept of *partitioning*, which means decomposing some quantity into other quantities; these quantities will always be sums-of-squares. Specifically, ANOVA relates the sum of squared deviations from the grand mean to that from group means, in the following way. Begin by squaring the deviation from the grand mean, M, for each score in the sample, and then sum these squared deviations across all test units, *i*, in all groups, *j*. Do this by squaring Equation 3 for all individuals in all groups; this becomes

$$\sum_{i=1}^{n}\sum_{j=1}^{t}(Y_{ij} - M)^2 = \sum_{i=1}^{n}\sum_{j=1}^{t}[(M_{.j} - M) + (Y_{ij} - M_{.j})]^2 \tag{4}$$

All the $\sum_{i=1}^{n}\sum_{j=1}^{t}$ means is that we are doing this for all individuals in all treatments. Equation 4 can be expanded as follows (this is simply squaring an equation of the form "$A = B + C$" to obtain "$A^2 = B^2 + C^2 + 2BC$"):

$$\sum_{i=1}^{n}\sum_{j=1}^{t}(Y_{ij} - M)^2 = \sum_{i=1}^{n}\sum_{j=1}^{t}(M_{.j} - M)^2 + \sum_{i=1}^{n}\sum_{j=1}^{t}(Y_{ij} - M)^2 + 2\sum_{i=1}^{n}\sum_{j=1}^{t}(M_{.j} - M)(Y_{ij} - M_{.j}) \tag{5}$$

The sum of deviations (not squared deviations!) about any mean *always* equals zero.* Therefore, it is not difficult to see (and demonstrate algebraically) that the $2\sum_{i=1}^{n}\sum_{j=1}^{t}(M_{.j} - M)(Y_{ij} - M_{.j})$ portion of Equation 5 must also be zero.

Also note that

$$\sum_{i=1}^{n}\sum_{j=1}^{t}(M_{.j} - M)^2 = \sum_{j=1}^{t}n_j(M_{.j} - M)^2$$

where n_j is the number of subjects in group *j*. This is so because $M_{.j} - M$ is a *constant* (as we are dealing with means only) for each individual *i* in a particular group *j*. Equation 5 then becomes

$\sum_{i=1}^{n}\sum_{j=1}^{t}(Y_{ij} - M)^2$	=	$\sum_{j=1}^{t}n_j(M_{.j} - M)^2$	+	$\sum_{i=1}^{n}\sum_{j=1}^{t}(Y_{ij} - M_{.j})^2$
↓		↓		↓
Total sum of squared deviations from the grand mean	=	weighted sum of squared deviations of group means from grand mean	+	sum of squared deviations within groups
Total sum of squares (SS_T)	=	sum of squares between groups	+	sum of squares within groups
		treatment effect sum of squares (SS_{TR})	+	error sum of squares (SS_E)

*This basic statistical manipulation is easily illustrated: 10 + 5 + 15 = 30, and the mean is 30/3 = 10. The sum of deviations is (10 − 10) + (5 − 10) + (15 − 10) = 0 + (−5) + 5 = 0.

What we have done is divide ("partition") the total sum-of-squares into two components. These components are the sum-of-squares *within* groups and the sum-of-squares *between* groups. These are each measures of *variation*. If the treatments have had no effect, the scores in all treatment groups should be similar. If this were so, the variance of the sample calculated using all test unit scores, *without regard to treatment groups*, would equal the variance calculated *within treatment groups*. That is, the *between-group* variance would equal the *within-group* variance. If the treatments *have* had an effect, however, the scores within groups would be more similar than scores selected from the whole sample at random. That is, the variance taken *within* groups would be smaller than the variance *between* groups, and we could compare the variance between groups with the variance within groups as a way of measuring for the presence of an effect. This is precisely what the statistical procedure does, and the reader should verify this when reviewing the partitioning equations presented earlier.

But how do we get variance from the sum-of-squares terms we have in Equation 6? Because variance equals *SS/df*, all we need to do is divide each component of Equation 6 by its appropriate *df*, and we will have the necessary variance terms. To obtain the required degrees-of-freedom we apply the standard rule, as follows. For the sample as a whole, we "used up" one degree of freedom to calculate the grand mean; therefore, the relevant number of degrees of freedom for the SS_T is the total number of test units minus one. For the SS_{TR}, the number of degrees of freedom is always one less than the number of treatments, because once we have determined $t - 1$ group means and the grand mean, the last group mean can take on only one value. The degrees-of-freedom for the error term equals the number of test units minus the number of treatment groups, because we only use the *t* within-group means to calculate the error sum-of-squares. In summary:

	General formula	Our example
df for SS_T =	$tn - 1$	$(3 \times 4) - 1 = 11$
df for SS_{TR} =	$t - 1$	$3 - 1 = 2$
df for SS_E =	$tn - t$	$(3 \times 4) - 3 = 9$

Note: (*df* for SS_{TR}) + (*df* for SS_E) = (*df* for SS_T).

Knowledge of the SS_{TR} and SS_E, plus their relevant degrees-of-freedom, allows us to calculate an estimate of the associated treatment and error variances. These estimates of population variances are always called *mean squares (MS)* in experimental situations, in recognition of the fact that they are estimates of population variances.

One more piece of information is needed before we can determine the significance of any effect. Because our test involves taking the ratio of MS_{TR} to MS_E, we need to know the sampling distribution of this ratio under the null hypothesis (which always says "There is no effect"). It can be shown that this ratio is distributed as the F statistic with $t - 1$ *df* for the numerator and $tn - t$ *df* for the denominator, in accordance with the *df* listed in the previous table. (The critical values of the F distribution are given in Table A.4 in the Appendix at the end of the book.) If the treatments have had no effect, the scores in all treatments should be similar, and so the treatment and error mean squares should be almost identical. The calculated F would then equal 1, or nearly so. The larger the treatment effect, the larger the ratio MS_{TR} to MS_E will be, and the calculated F value will then be greater. F distribution values obtained via printed tables or computer correspond to various Type I error (α) levels given the null hypothesis of "no effect." What we do is compare the calculated F with the tabled value for F at a designated α. If the calculated F exceeds the table F, we reject the null hypothesis. Table 11A.2 presents the various components of the calculation of the experimental F value.

Table 11A.2 ANOVA Table for Completely Randomized Design

Source of variation	Sum of squares (*SS*)	Degrees of freedom (*df*)	Mean square (*MS*)	F ratio
Treatments between groups	SS_{TR}	$t - 1$	$MS_{TR} = \frac{SS_{TR}}{t-1}$	$\frac{MS_{TR}}{MS_E}$
Error (within groups)	SS_E	$tn - t$	$MS_E = \frac{SS_E}{tn - t}$	
Total	SS_T	$tn - 1$		

Table 11A.3 **ANOVA for Coupon Experiment with Completely Randomized Design**

Source of variation	Sum-of-squares (SS)	Degrees of freedom (*df*)	Mean square (*MS*)	*F* ratio
Treatments	98.7	2	49.4	3.3
Error	134.0	9	14.9	
Total	232.7	11		

A Calculated Example

We can now apply the developed methodology to see whether there is a significant treatment effect for the data presented in Table 11A.1.

Total Sum-of-Squares*

$$SS_T = \sum_{i=1}^{n}\sum_{j=1}^{t}(Y_{ij} - M)^2$$
$$= (20 - 12.7)^2 + (17 - 12.7)^2 + \cdots + (5 - 12.7)^2$$
$$= 232.7$$

Treatment Sum-of-Squares

$$SS_{TR} = n_j \sum_{j=1}^{t}(M_{.j} - M)^2$$
$$= 4[(16 - 12.7)^2 + (13 - 12.7)^2 + (9 - 12.7)^2]$$
$$= 98.7$$

Error Sum-of-Squares

$$SS_E = \sum_{i=1}^{n}\sum_{j=1}^{t}(Y_{ij} - M_{.j})^2$$
$$= (20 - 16)^2 + (17 - 13)^2 + \cdots + (5 - 9)^2$$
$$= 134$$

Note that once we have obtained SS_T and SS_{TR}, we can calculate SS_E by subtracting SS_{TR} from SS_T. However, we can double-check our calculations by using the formula for SS_E directly.

By applying the appropriate *df* to these *SS* values, we can obtain the mean squares necessary to calculate *F*. Table 11A.3 presents the calculations of *F* for these data, which turns out to be

$$F = \frac{49.4}{14.9} = 3.3$$

with 2 (numerator) and 9 (denominator) *df*. Now look up the critical value of *F* in Table A.4 (in the end-of-book Appendix) or using any statistical program. If using this table, degrees-of-freedom for the numerator are the column headings, and degrees-of-freedom for the denominator are the row headings. The table gives critical values at different levels of confidence $(1 - \alpha)$. The intersection of a given row and column at a given $1 - \alpha$ yields the critical values at the level of significance. In our example, the critical *F* value at $\alpha = 0.1$ (so that $1 - \alpha = 0.9$) for 2 and 9 *df* is 3.01. Our calculated *F* was 3.3, so our *F* value would occur by chance less than 10 percent of the time. If 90 percent confidence is sufficient for our purposes, we can *reject* the null hypothesis of no treatment effect.

---

*We could, of course, use the computational formula for SS that was presented in Chapters 8 and 9.

Our result would not be significant if we had set $\alpha = 0.05$, as the critical value of F is 4.26. Given $\alpha = 0.1$, however, we conclude that the choice of coupon plan *does* make a difference in sales, albeit at a fairly weak confidence level. We would then examine the data to see which plan was best; in this case, it is obviously Plan 1. Note that all an F-test does is tell us that there has been a significant effect of some sort. To gain a deeper understanding, we must dig back into the data to see *which* treatment is causing the effect. ANOVA will not pinpoint this for us, just as a significant F-test in multiple regression will not tell us *which* variable (or variables) is driving the overall result.

We have now established the procedure for determining the significance of an effect in a completely randomized design. The procedures for other designs apply exactly the same principles; the only difference relates to some extra computations.

Randomized Block Design

ANOVA for a *randomized block design (RBD)* involves only one more step than that for a CRD. Table 11A.4 presents the data for our CRD coupon experiment as if the experiment had been blocked. Note that the table is the same as Table 11A-1, except that the *i*'s now represent blocks instead of test units, and we have calculated row totals and means in addition to column totals and means. Let us assume that the blocks represent different store sizes. In essence, we are saying that we expect some variation in cola sales just due to the differences in the size of the test unit stores. Block 1 represents the largest stores, block 2 the next largest, and so on. We must also assume that treatments were randomly assigned to test units within blocks to apply the RBD.

Partitioning the Sum-of-Squares

In the RBD, we define an individual observation as

$$Y_{ij} = \text{grand mean} + \text{treatment effect} + \text{block effect} + \text{error}$$

or, in population parameter terms,

$$Y_{ij} = \mu + \tau_j + \beta_i + \epsilon_{ij}$$

As always, we will be estimating this model using sample data, so we state the model as

$$Y_{ij} = M + T_j + B_i + E_{ij} \tag{7}$$

where B_i is the effect of the *i*th block, and the other terms are defined as in the CRD. We have previously defined the M and T_j items in this model, but we must define the blocking effect and also re-define the error term. We define blocking effect in a parallel manner to the treatment effect, the only difference

Table 11A.4 Randomized Block Design with Three Treatments and Four Blocks

	Treatments (*j*)				
Blocks (*i*) Store sizes	**Coupon plan 1**	**Coupon plan 2**	**Coupon plan 3**	**Block totals**	**Block means**
1	20	17	14	$\Sigma Y_{1.} = 51$	$\bar{Y}_{1.} = M_{1.} = 51/3 = 17$
2	18	14	10	$\Sigma Y_{2.} = 42$	$\bar{Y}_{2.} = M_{3.} = 42/3 = 14$
3	15	13	7	$\Sigma Y_{3.} = 35$	$\bar{Y}_{3.} = M_{3.} = 35/3 = 11.7$
4	11	8	5	$\Sigma Y_{4.} = 24$	$\bar{Y}_{4.} = M_{3.} = 24/3 = 8$
Treatment totals	$\sum Y_{.1} = 64$	$\sum Y_{.2} = 52$	$\sum Y_{.3} = 36$		
Treatment means	$\bar{Y}_{.1} = M_{.1} = \sum Y_{.1}/n_1 = 64/4 = 16$	$\bar{Y}_{.2} = M_{.2} = \sum Y_{.2}/n_2 = 52/4 = 13$	$\bar{Y}_{.3} = M_{.3} = \sum Y_{.3}/n_3 = 36/4 = 9$		
			Grand total		$\sum Y_{1.} = 64 + 52 + 36 = 152$
			Grand mean		$\bar{Y}_{..} = M = \sum Y_{..}/(n_1 + n_2 + n_3) = 152/12 = 12.7$

being that the blocking effect is stated in terms of row means instead of column means.

$$B_i = (M_{i.} - M)$$

Here, knowledge of blocking group membership *improves our ability to predict scores as an improvement over the grand mean*. We assume that $\sum_{i=1}^{n} B_i = 0$; that is, the net block effect is zero. We can rewrite Equation 7 as

$$\begin{array}{ccccccccc} Y_{ij} & = & M & + & (M_{.j} - M) & + & (M_{i.} - M) & + & E_{ij} \\ \downarrow & & \downarrow & & \downarrow & & \downarrow & & \downarrow \\ \text{Individual score} & = & \text{grand mean} & + & \text{treatment effect} & + & \text{blocking effect} & + & \text{error} \end{array} \quad (8)$$

We can then solve this equation for E_{ij} to obtain the measurement of error effect.

$$\begin{aligned} E_{ij} &= Y_{ij} - M - (M_{.j} - M) - (M_{i.} - M) \\ &= Y_{ij} - M - M_{.j} + M - M_{i.} + M \\ &= Y_{ij} - M_{.j} - M_{i.} + M \quad \text{or} \quad Y_{ij} + (M - M_{.j} - M_{i.}) \end{aligned}$$

The error terms thus represent the difference between an individual score, Y_{ij}, and the net difference between the grand mean and the sum of the treatment and block means. If the blocking effect is significant, this error will be smaller than an error defined without blocking. As an illustration, consider score Y_{21} in Table 11A.4.This score is 18, and the error without blocking is

$$Y_{ij} - M_{.j} = 18 - 16 = 2$$

With blocking, the error is

$$Y_{ij} + M - M_{.j} - M_{i.} = 18 + 12.7 - 16 - 14 = 0.7$$

A similar pattern would be evident were this analysis performed on the other scores. The main point is this: blocking serves to reduce the size of experimental error, on average.

Note that we may rewrite Equation 8 as

$$Y_{ij} = M + (M_{.j} - M) + (M_{i.} - M) + (Y_{ij} - M_{.j} - M_{i.} + M) \quad (9)$$

If we move M to the left side of Equation 9, sum the resultant deviations across all blocks and all treatments, and square both sides, we obtain

$$\sum_{i=1}^{n}\sum_{j=1}^{t}(Y_{ij} - M)^2 = n\sum_{j=1}^{t}(M_{.j} - M)^2 + t\sum_{i=1}^{n}(M_{i.} - M)^2 + \sum_{i=1}^{n}\sum_{j=1}^{t}(Y_{ij} + M - M_{.j} - M_{i.})^2$$

You may recognize this result as

$$SS_T = SS_{TR} + SS_B + SS_E$$

It follows from the fact that all the cross-products again become zero, because each involves a sum of individual deviations about a mean. Also, we may write

$$t\sum_{i=1}^{n}(M_{i.} - M)^2 \quad \text{instead of} \quad \sum_{i=1}^{n}\sum_{j=1}^{t}(M_{i.} - M)^2$$

because we are again adding constant means over the t treatments. That is, multiplying by t is exactly the same as adding the same thing t times, and is precisely what was used in CRD.

The relevant *df* for the block is $n - 1$, because once any $(n - 1)$ block means are specified, the remaining one is automatically determined, given the grand mean value. If we subtract the treatment and block degrees-of-freedom from the total degrees-of-freedom, we obtain the error degrees-of-freedom as

$$\begin{aligned} \text{Error } df &= \text{total } df - \text{treatment } df - \text{block } df \\ &= (tn - 1) - (t - 1) - (n - 1) \\ &= tn + 1 - t - n \end{aligned}$$

In our example, the error $df = (3 \times 4) + 1 - 3 - 4 = 6$. More generally, the same result may be obtained by applying the formula

$$\text{Error } df = (t - 1)(n - 1)$$

Table 11A.5 presents the ANOVA table for an RBD.

Table 11A.5 ANOVA Table for Randomized Block Design

Source of variation	Sum of squares (*SS*)	Degrees of freedom (*df*)	Mean square (*MS*)	*F* ratio
Treatments (between columns)	SS_{TR}	$t-1$	$MS_{TR} = \frac{SS_{TR}}{t-1}$	$\frac{MS_{TR}}{MS_E}$
Blocks (between rows)	SS_B	$n-1$	$MS_B = \frac{SS_B}{n-1}$	$\frac{MS_B}{MS_E}$
Error	SS_E	$(t-1)(n-1)$	$MS_E = \frac{SS_E}{(t-1)(n-1)}$	
Total	SS_T	$tn-1$		

A Calculated Example

We shall now apply the RBD ANOVA procedure to the data in Table 11A.4.

Total Sum-of-Squares

$$\begin{aligned} SS_T &= \sum_{i=1}^{n}\sum_{j=1}^{t}(Y_{ij} - M)^2 \\ &= (20 - 12.7)^2 + (17 - 12.7)^2 + \cdots + (5 - 12.7)^2 \\ &= 232.7 \end{aligned}$$

Thus, SS_T is exactly the same here as with the CRD, as we would expect.

Treatment Sum-of-Squares

$$\begin{aligned} SS_{TR} &= n\sum_{j=1}^{t}(M_{.j} - M)^2 \\ &= 4[(16 - 12.7)^2 + (13 - 12.7)^2 + (9 - 12.7)^2] \\ &= 98.7 \end{aligned}$$

Note that the SS_{TR} is exactly the same as with the CRD.

Block Sum-of-Squares

$$\begin{aligned} SS_B &= t\sum_{i=1}^{n}(M_{i.} - M)^2 \\ &= 3[(17 - 12.7)^2 + (14 - 12.7)^2 + (11 - 12.7)^2 + (8 - 12.7)^2] \\ &= 129.8 \end{aligned}$$

Error Sum-of-Squares

$$\begin{aligned} SS_E &= SS_T - SS_{TR} - SS_B \\ &= 232.7 - 98.7 - 129.8 \\ &= 4.2 \end{aligned}$$

Table 11A.6 presents the calculated *F* values for the treatment and block effects.

Table 11A.6 ANOVA Table for Coupon Experiment with Blocking for Store Size

Source of variation	Sum-of-squares (SS)	Degrees-of-freedom (*df*)	Mean square (*MS*)	*F* ratio
Treatment	98.7	2	49.4	70.6
Block	129.8	3	43.3	61.9
Error	4.2	6	0.7	
Total	232.7	11		

For the treatment effect, the critical value of F for $\alpha = 0.1$ at 2 and 6 *df* is 3.46. For the blocking factor, the critical value of F for $\alpha = 0.1$ at 3 and 6 *df* is 3.29. Both the treatment and the block effects are statistically significant, but in this case even at $\alpha = 0.01$ the treatment effect is now significant (critical $F = 10.9$). The important point is this: by blocking, we have obtained a smaller measure of error, and thus achieved greater statistical significance for the treatment effect. Note that this does *not* mean the treatment effect has itself gotten larger; rather, we are just more certain that it is not merely a stroke of random (misleading) luck.

Finally, note that SS_B comes out of the SS_E for the CRD; that is,

$$SS_E(\text{with blocking}) = SS_E(\text{without blocking}) - SS_B$$

In our example,

$$SS_E(\text{with blocking}) = 134.0 - 129.8 = 4.2$$

Latin Square Design

If we wanted to block out and measure the effects of *two* extraneous variables, we could use the *Latin square (LS)* design. In an LS design, the number of categories of each blocking variable must equal the number of treatment categories, and each treatment must appear once—and only once—in each row and column of the design. Table 11A.7 shows selected LS designs of different sizes. The letters A, B, C, and so on, represent treatments. To generate the treatment assignment pattern for a particular study, pick the appropriately sized layout from Table 11A.7 and randomize the column order. For example, a 3 × 3 LS might yield the following treatment pattern when the columns are randomized with the (randomly-chosen) numbers 3,1,2:

C A B
A B C
B C A

Now randomize the row assignments within columns, subject to the constraint that each treatment may appear only once in each row. Among the results of this process could be the following LS:

B C A
C A B
A B C

We can now illustrate the LS design with a numerical example. Suppose we ran our coupon experiment again to see whether the results could be replicated in other areas. The only difference is that this time we want to block out and measure the effect on sales of *both* store size and day of the week. In doing so, we must anticipate substantial variation in cola sales simply because of these factors. For one reason or another, we have been unable to measure sales on the same day of the week for each test unit. Because

Table 11A.7 **Illustrative Latin Square Layout**

3 × 3

A	B	C
B	C	A
C	A	B

4 × 4

A	B	C	D
B	C	D	A
C	D	A	B
D	A	B	C

5 × 5

A	B	C	D	E
B	C	D	E	A
C	D	E	A	B
D	E	A	B	C
E	A	B	C	D

6 × 6

A	B	C	D	E	F
B	C	D	E	F	A
C	D	E	F	A	B
D	E	F	A	B	C
E	F	A	B	C	D
F	A	B	C	D	E

there are three treatments (coupon plans), we must have three categories of store size and three categories of days of the week to use the LS design. Table 11A.8 presents the data generated from this LS design experiment. The pattern of treatment assignments is the one generated previously by randomization with these three plans, as follows:

A Coupon plan 1
B Coupon plan 2
C Coupon plan 3

The treatment designation is noted next to the cola sales on Table 11A.8.

Partitioning the Sum-of-Squares

In the LS design, individual observations require three separate subscripts, and are defined as

$$Y_{ijk} = \text{grand mean} + \text{row effect } (i) + \text{column effect } (j) + \text{treatment effect } (k) + \text{error}$$

where Y_{ijk} = the measured result when the kth treatment is applied to the ith row and the jth column. Although we will never know population parameter values with certainty, the model can be expressed (using Greek symbols) in those terms as well as

$$Y_{ijk} = \mu + \alpha_i + \beta_j + \tau_k + \epsilon_{ijk}$$

Because, as always, we will be estimating this model with sample data, we state the model (using Roman symbols) as

$$Y_{ijk} = M + R_i + C_j + T_k + E_{ijk} \quad (10)$$

where R_i = the effect of the ith row block (i.e., store size)

C_j = the effect of the jth column block (i.e., day of the week)

T_k = the effect of the kth treatment (i.e., coupon plan)

E_{ijk} = the experimental error of the ijk observation

$i, j, k = 1, 2, \ldots, t$ where t = the number of treatments

The three effects of interest are:

1. Row effect (i.e., effect of store size) = $(M_{i..} - M)$, the difference between the row mean and the grand mean, adding across all j's and k's.
2. Column effect (i.e., effect of the day of the week) = $(M_{.j.} - M)$, the difference between the column mean and the grand mean, adding across all i's and k's.

Table 11A.8 Latin Square Design with Three Treatments

Rows (i)	Columns (j) 1 Mon.–Tues.	2 Wed.–Thurs.	3 Fri.–Sun.	Row totals	Row means
1 Large stores	25 (*B*)	15 (*C*)	50 (*A*)	$\Sigma Y_{1..} = 90$	$M_{1..} = 90/3 = 30.0$
2 Medium stores	5 (*C*)	25 (*A*)	25 (*B*)	$\Sigma Y_{2..} = 55$	$M_{2..} = 55/3 = 18.3$
3 Small stores	15 (*A*)	15 (*B*)	14 (*C*)	$\Sigma Y_{3..} = 44$	$M_{3..} = 44/3 = 14.7$
Column totals	$\Sigma Y_{.1.} = 45$	$\Sigma Y_{.2.} = 55$	$\Sigma Y_{.3.} = 89$	$\Sigma Y_{...} = 189$	
Column means	$M_{.1.} = 45/3 = 15.0$	$M_{.2.} = 55/3 = 18.3$	$M_{.3.} = 89/3 = 29.7$		$M = 189/9 = 21.0$
	Treatments (k)		A*	B	C
	Treatment totals		$\Sigma Y_{..1} = 90$	$\Sigma Y_{..2} = 65$	$\Sigma Y_{..3} = 34$
	Treatment means		$M_{..1} = 90/3 = 30.0$	$M_{..2} = 65/3 = 21.7$	$M_{1} = 34/3 = 11.3$

*For example $\sum Y_{..1} = 15 + 25 + 50 = 90$; i.e., we add the scores at all the places where *A* appears.

3. Treatment effect (i.e., effect of coupon plan) = $(M_{..k} - M)$, the difference between the treatment mean and the grand mean, adding across all *i*'s and *j*'s.

We assume that the net effect of each effect is zero (this is taken care of automatically by the statistical program). That is,

$$\sum_{i=1}^{t} R_i = 0 \quad \sum_{j=1}^{t} C_j = 0 \quad \text{and} \quad \sum_{k=1}^{t} T_k = 0$$

We can then rewrite Equation 10 as

$$\begin{array}{ccccccccccc} Y_{ijk} & = & M & + & (M_{i..} - M) & + & (M_{.j.} - M) & + & (M_{..k} - M) & + & E_{ijk} \\ \downarrow & & \downarrow & & \downarrow & & \downarrow & & \downarrow & & \downarrow \\ \text{Individual score} & = & \text{grand mean} & + & \text{row effect} & + & \text{column effect} & + & \text{treatment effect} & + & \text{error} \end{array}$$

We can solve this equation for E_{ijk} to obtain the measurement of error:

$$\begin{aligned} E_{ijk} &= Y_{ijk} - M - (M_{i..} - M) - (M_{.j.} - M) - (M_{..k} - M) \\ &= Y_{ijk} + 2M - M_{i..} - M_{.j.} - M_{..k} \end{aligned}$$

This is a complicated procedure, and the student may wonder whether and why it's necessary. The key point is this: if *both* blocking factors are correlated with the dependent variable, this error measure will be smaller than that obtained with a CRD or RBD that uses only *one* blocking factor. Reducing error allows for greater ability to detect the "signal" of the treatment effect, as represented by its significance level.

If we moved M to the left side, added all these deviations across all rows and columns, and squared the equation, we would obtain the required SS. The model would then be

$$SS_T = SS_R + SS_C + SS_{TR} + SS_E$$

as yet again all the cross products turn out to be zero. Table 11A.9 shows the ANOVA layout for an LS design. SS_R, SS_C, and SS_{TR} each have $t - 1$ *df*. With $(t)(t) - 1$ or $t^2 - 1$ *df* in the entire sample, this leaves $(t - 1)(t - 2)$ *df* for the error term.

A Calculated Example

We shall now apply the LS design ANOVA to the data in Table 11A.8.

Total Sum-of-Squares

$$\begin{aligned} SS_T &= \sum_{i=1}^{t} \sum_{j=1}^{t} (Y_{ijk} - M)^2 \\ &= (25 - 21)^2 + (15 - 21)^2 + \cdots + (14 - 21)^2 \\ &= 1302 \end{aligned}$$

Row Sum-of-Squares

$$\begin{aligned} SS_R &= t \sum_{i=1}^{t} (M_{i..} - M)^2 \\ &= 3[(30 - 21)^2 + (18.3 - 21)^2 + (14.7 - 21)^2] \\ &= 383.9 \end{aligned}$$

Column Sum-of-Squares

$$\begin{aligned} SS_C &= t \sum_{j=1}^{t} (M_{.j.} - M)^2 \\ &= 3[(15 - 21)^2 + (18.3 - 21)^2 + (29.7 - 21)^2] \\ &= 356.9 \end{aligned}$$

Table 11A.9 ANOVA Table for Latin Square Design

Source of variation	Sum of squares (SS)	Degrees of freedom (df)	Mean square (MS)	F ratio
Between rows	SS_R	$t-1$	$MS_R = \frac{SS_R}{t-1}$	$\frac{MS_R}{MS_E}$
Between columns	SS_C	$t-1$	$MS_C = \frac{SS_C}{t-1}$	$\frac{MS_C}{MS_E}$
Between treatments	SS_{TR}	$t-1$	$MS_{TR} = \frac{SS_{TR}}{t-1}$	$\frac{MS_{TR}}{MS_E}$
Error	SS_E	$(t-1)(t-2)$	$MS_E = \frac{SSE}{(t-1)(t-2)}$	
Total	SS_T	t^2-1		

Treatment Sum-of-Squares

$$\begin{aligned} SS_{TR} &= t\sum_{k-1}^{t}(M_{..k} - M)^2 \\ &= 3[(30-21)^2 + (21.7-21)^2 + (11.3-21)^2] \\ &= 526.7 \end{aligned}$$

Error Sum-of-Squares

$$\begin{aligned} SS_E &= SS_T - SS_R - SS_C - SS_{TR} \\ &= 1302 - 383.9 - 356.9 - 526.7 \\ &= 34.5 \end{aligned}$$

Table 11A.10 presents the calculated F values for the treatment and the two blocks. For the treatment and blocking factors, the critical value of F for $\alpha = 0.1$ at 2 and 2 df is 9.0. Therefore, both blocking factors and the treatment are significant. Note that none of these effects would have been significant at $\alpha = 0.05$, as the critical F is 19.0. If we had used a CRD or blocked with just one of our two blocking factors in an RBD, the treatment effect would not have been significant, even at $\alpha = 0.1$. This is so because the SS_R and SS_C would be added back into the LS design SS_E to give the SS_E for the CRD. As for the RBD, either SS_R or SS_C would be added back to the LS design SS_E to give the SS_E for the RBD. In either instance, the SS_R or SS_C is large enough to render the calculated F ratio nonsignificant at $\alpha = 0.1$. Here, we needed two blocking factors to find in favor of a significant treatment effect. The value of blocking in marketing experiments should be clear. Again, note that we must look closely at the data to see that treatment A is the best coupon plan; the ANOVA results alone will not make this determination for us.

Table 11A.10 ANOVA Table for Coupon Experiment with 3 × 3 Latin Square Design

Source of variation	Sum-of-squares (SS)	Degrees-of-freedom (df)	Mean square (MS)	F ratio
Row effect (store size)	383.9	2	192.0	11.1
Column effect (days of week)	356.9	2	178.5	10.3
Treatment	526.7	2	263.4	15.2
Error	34.5	2	17.3	
Total	1302.0	8		

Note: $n_{ij} = 2$ for all i's and j's.

Table 11A.11 A 2 × 3 Factorial Design with Media Plans and Coupon Plans as Independent Variables

		Coupon plans (j)				
		B_1	B_2	B_3	Media totals	Media means
Media plans (i)	A_1	20	17	14	$\sum Y_{1..} = 93$	$M_{1..} = 93/6 = 15.5$
		18	14	10		
	A_2	15	13	7	$\sum Y_{2..} = 59$	$M_{2..} = 59/6 = 9.8$
		11	8	5		
Coupon totals		$\sum Y_{.1.} = 64$	$\sum Y_{.2.} = 52$	$\sum Y_{.3.} = 36$	$\sum Y_{...} = 152$	
Coupon means		$M_{.1.} = 64/4 = 16$	$M_{.2.} = 52/4 = 13$	$M_{.3.} = 36/4 = 9$		$M = 12.7$

Treatment cell (ij)	A_1B_1	A_1B_2	A_1B_3	A_2B_1	A_2B_2	A_2B_3
Cell total	$\sum Y_{11.} = 38$	$\sum Y_{12.} = 31$	$\sum Y_{13.} = 24$	$\sum Y_{21.} = 26$	$\sum Y_{22.} = 21$	$\sum Y_{23.} = 12$
Cell mean	$M_{11.} = 38/2 = 19$	$M_{12.} = 31/2 = 15.5$	$M_{13.} = 24/2 = 12$	$M_{21.} = 26/2 = 13$	$M_{22.} = 21/2 = 10.5$	$M_{23.} = 12/2 = 6$

Note: $n_{ij} = 2$ for all i's and j's.

Factorial Design

In a *factorial design (FD)*, we measure the effects of two or more independent variables and their *interactions*. Suppose that in our coupon experiment we are interested not only in the effect of coupon plans, but also in the effect of the media plans that support the coupon plans. Table 11A.11 presents data stemming from such an experiment. You should recognize these as the data we used in Table 11A.1 for our CRD. All we have done here is regroup the data and present them as if they came from an FD.

Partitioning the Sum-of-Squares

In the FD with two independent variables, we define an individual observation as

$$Y_{ijk} = \text{grand mean} + \text{effect of treatment A} + \text{effect of treatment B} + \text{interaction effect AB} + \text{error}$$

where Y_{ijk} = the kth observation on the ith level of A and the jth level of B.

For example, here

$$Y_{111} = 20 \quad \text{and} \quad Y_{231} = 7$$

In population parameter terms, the model is

$$Y_{ijk} = \mu + \alpha_i + \beta_j + (\alpha\beta)_{ij} + \epsilon_{ijk}$$

Again, as always, we will be estimating this model with sample data, and we write

$$Y_{ijk} = M + A_i + B_j + (AB)_{ij} + E_{ijk}$$

where A_i = the effect of the ith level of A (media plan), $i = 1, \ldots, a$, where a is the number of levels in A

B_j = the effect of the ith level of B (coupon plan), $j = 1, \ldots, b$, where b is the number of levels in B

$(AB)_{ij}$ = the effect of the interaction of the ith level of A and the jth level of B

E_{ijk} = the error of the kth observation in the ith level of A and the jth level of B, that is, the ij cell

In our example $n_{ij} = 2$ for all ij cells. The four effects of interest are:

1. A_i effect (i.e., media plan) = $(M_{i..} - M)$, the difference between the row mean and the grand mean.
2. B_j effect (i.e., coupon plan) = $(M_{.j.} - M)$, the difference between the column mean and the grand mean.
3. Error = $(Y_{ijk} - M_{ij}.)$, the difference between an individual observation and the cell mean to which it belongs. That is, the only differences within a cell should be due to randomness (error).

4. Interaction effect $(AB)_{ij}$ = any remaining variation in the data after main effects and error have been removed.

We can now rewrite Equation 11 as

$$Y_{ijk} = M + (M_{i..} - M) + (M_{.j.} - M) + (AB)_{ij} + (Y_{ijk} - M_{ij.})$$

and solve for the interaction term, $(AB)_{ij}$:

$$\begin{aligned}(AB)_{ij} &= Y_{ijk} - M - (M_{i..} - M) - (M_{.j.} - M) - (Y_{ijk} - M_{ij.})\\ &= Y_{ijk} - M - M_{i..} + M - M_{.j.} + M - Y_{ijk} + M_{ij.}\\ &= M + M_{ij.} - M_{ij.} - M_{.j.}\end{aligned}$$

In our example,

$$(AB)_{11} = 12.7 + 19 - 15.5 - 16 = 0.2$$

and

$$(AB)_{23} = 12.7 + 6 - 9.8 - 9 = -0.1$$

Results like this suggest that there is little interaction in the data, although we have not yet performed any statistical tests to confirm this informal observation. We may now rewrite Equation 11 as

$$Y_{ijk} = M + (M_{i..} - M) + (M_{.j.} - M) + (M + M_{ij.} - M_{i..} - M_{.j.}) + (Y_{ijk} - M_{ij.})$$

If we moved M to the left side, added all the deviations across all scores k in all ij cells, and squared the equation, we would obtain the required *SS*. The model would then be

$$SS_T = SS_{TRA} + SS_{TRB} + SS_{INT(AB)} + SS_E$$

where

SS_{TRA} = sum-of-squares of treatment A

SS_{TRB} = sum-of-squares of treatment B

$SS_{INT(AB)}$ = sum-of-squares for interaction of A and B

This result occurs because all the cross-products are, as in our other ANOVA examples, zero. Table 11A.12 shows the ANOVA layout for a two-factor FD. Each factor has one degree-of-freedom less than its number of categories, and the interaction term has $(a - 1)(b - 1)$ *df*. With $abn - 1$ *df* in the whole sample, this leaves $ab(n - 1)$ for the error term.

A Calculated Example

Now let us apply the FD to the data in Table 11A.11.

Total Sum-of-Squares

$$\begin{aligned}SS_T &= \sum_{i=1}^{a}\sum_{j=1}^{b}\sum_{k=1}^{n}(Y_{ijk} - M)^2\\ &= (20 - 12.7)^2 + (17 - 12.7)^2 + \cdots + (5 - 12.7)^2\\ &= 232.7\end{aligned}$$

Again note that the SS_T is the same as in the CRD and RBD, as it must be.

Table 11A.12 ANOVA Table for a Two-Factor Factorial Design

Source of variation	Sum of squares (*SS*)	Degrees of freedom (*df*)	Mean square (*MS*)	*F* ratio
Treatment *A*	SS_{TRA}	$a - 1$	$MS_{TRA} = \frac{SS_{TRA}}{a-1}$	$\frac{MS_{TRA}}{MS_E}$
Treatment *B*	SS_{TRB}	$b - 1$	$MS_{TRB} = \frac{SS_{TRB}}{b-1}$	$\frac{MS_{TRB}}{MS_E}$
Interaction *AB*	$SS_{INT(AB)}$	$(a - 1)(b - 1)$	$MS_{INT(AB)} = \frac{SS_{INT(AB)}}{(a-1)(b-1)}$	$\frac{MS_{INT(AB)}}{MS_E}$
Error	SS_E	$ab(n - 1)$	$MS_E = \frac{SS_E}{ab(n-1)}$	
Total	SS_T	$abn - 1$		

Treatment A Sum-of-Squares

$$\begin{aligned} SS_{TRA} &= bn\sum_{i=1}^{a}(M_{i..} - M)^2 \\ &= (3)(2)[(15.5 - 12.7)^2 + (9.8 - 12.7)^2] \\ &= 97.5 \end{aligned}$$

Treatment B Sum-of-Squares

$$\begin{aligned} SS_{TRB} &= an\sum_{j=1}^{b}(M_{.j.} - M)^2 \\ &= (2)(2)[(16 - 12.7)^2 + (13 - 12.7)^2 + (9 - 12.7)^2] \\ &= 98.7 \end{aligned}$$

Note that this is the SS_{TR} we found for the CRD. In other words, the main effect of the coupon plan is identical under both analysis procedures, as we would expect.

Interaction Sum-of-Squares

$$\begin{aligned} SS_{INT(AB)} &= n\sum_{i=1}^{a}\sum_{j=1}^{b}(M + M_{ij.} - M_{i..} - M_{.j.})^2 \\ &= 2[(12.7 + 19 - 15.5 - 16)^2] \\ &\quad + (12.7 + 15.5 - 15.5 - 13)^2 + (12.7 + 12 - 15.5 - 9)^2 \\ &\quad + (12.7 + 13 - 9.8 - 16)^2 + (12.7 + 10.5 - 9.8 - 13)^2 \\ &\quad + (12.8 + 6 - 9.8 - 9)^2 \\ &= 0.7 \end{aligned}$$

Error Sum-of-Squares

$$\begin{aligned} SS_E &= \sum_{i=1}^{a}\sum_{j=1}^{b}\sum_{k=1}^{n}(Y_{ijk} - M_{ij.})^2 \\ &= SS_T - SS_{TRA} - SS_{TRB} - SS_{INT(AB)} \\ &= 232.7 - 97.5 - 98.7 - 0.7 \\ &= 35.8 \end{aligned}$$

Table 11A.13 presents the calculated F values for the two treatments and the interaction. For treatment A, the critical F for $\alpha = 0.05$ at 1 and 6 *df* is 5.99. Therefore, the media effect is significant. For treatment B, for $\alpha = 0.05$ at 2 and 6 *df* the critical F is 5.14. Thus, the coupon effect is also significant. Because the calculated interaction F is less than 1, we know it is not significant without even consulting the F table. We can now go back to the data to verify that it is media plan A, and coupon plan B, that yield the best results.

Table 11A.13 **ANOVA Table for Media and Coupon Experiment Using a Two-Factor 2 × 3 Factorial Design**

Source of variation	Sum-of-squares (SS)	Degrees-of-freedom (*df*)	Mean square (*MS*)	*F* ratio
Treatment *A* (media)	97.5	1	97.5	16.3
Treatment *B* (coupon)	98.7	2	49.4	8.2
Interaction (*AB*)	0.7	2	0.4	0.1
Error	35.8	6	6.0	
Total	232.7	11		

This two-factor ANOVA is usually referred to as "two-way" ANOVA. The factorial procedure can be extended to any number (*N*) of independent variables, and is often called "*N*-way" ANOVA. The calculations for an ANOVA greater than two-way are too complex to present here, although they are analogous to those carried out for the two-way ANOVA design. The analysis of such an experiment is, however, easily handled by statistical programs. In any event, the principles underlying all complex ANOVA designs are the same as those developed here.

Summary of Appendix

1. ANOVA involves the calculation and comparison of different variance estimates, SS/df.
2. The fixed-effects model allows inferences only about the different treatments actually used. It is, among the various ANOVA designs, the one most directly relevant in marketing.
3. In ANOVA, an effect is defined as a difference in treatment mean from the grand mean.
4. Experimental error is the difference between an individual score and the treatment group mean to which the score belongs.
5. ANOVA is carried out by partitioning the SS_T into SS_{TR} and SS_E and dividing each of these by their relevant degrees-of-freedom to yield an estimate of treatment and error variances, called the mean squares (MS_{TR} and MS_E). That is, the one-way ANOVA model is partitioned as follows: $SS_T = SS_{TR} + SS_E$.
6. The relevant statistic for a significance test is the F statistic, where $F = MS_{TR}/MS_E$.
7. The CRD (completely randomized design) measures the effect of one independent variable without statistical control of extraneous variation. Its basic composition is $SS_T = SS_{TR} + SS_E$.
8. The RBD (randomized block design) measures the effect of one independent variable with statistical control of one extraneous factor. Its basic composition is $SS_T = SS_{TR} + SS_B + SS_E$.
9. The LS (Latin square) design measures the effect of one independent variable with statistical control of two extraneous factors. Its basic composition is $SS_T = SS_R + SS_C + SS_{TR} + SS_E$.
10. The FD (factorial design) measures the main and interaction effects of two or more independent variables. Its basic composition for a two-way ANOVA is $SS_T = SS_{TRA} + SS_{TRB} + SS_{INT(AB)} + SS_E$.

CHAPTER TWELVE
ADVANCED TOPICS, RESEARCH FRONTIERS, AND PREPARING THE FINAL REPORT

"Quality is never an accident; it is always the result of high intention, sincere effort, intelligent direction and skillful execution; it represents the wise choice of many alternatives."

WILLIAM A. FOSTER

One might think the power and complexity of the statistical methods presented in previous chapters would suit almost any marketing research project. And one would be right: advanced methods of regression, along with factoring and clustering techniques, provide deep, useful analyses of marketing data.

Statisticians, like any scientists, are seldom content to rest on their laurels and have fashioned even more powerful methods that build upon what we have explored thus far. The models presented in this chapter represent some of the most recent triumphs of statistical modeling for marketing applications. They were created to recognize that there is often a great deal of structure in real-world data that common statistical methods—despite their generality and power—were not designed to explore. Among the most important of these recent advances is the modeling of *heterogeneity*, the fact that different people respond distinctly to the same sale, ad, or other marketing variable. Another is that objects in the real world are often arranged in a natural *hierarchy:* customers visit stores, stores are in various cities, cities lie in different geographical regions, and so on; yet many models ignore this and treat each customer or each store as interchangeable. Yet another is that we should not make use only of data that happens to be available to us in full; there is a great deal of information in values that happen to be missing, like the questions survey respondents chose *not* to answer.

Each of these common and commonsense observations about the nature of real data can be translated into the language of statistics and used to paint a clearer picture of how the world of marketing actually operates. We will explore a number of such models, relay their key ideas, and, to the extent possible without a great deal of technical development, demonstrate how they work their magic. They can seem especially magical when they are combined, and in a final case study, we will see how to use all three of the main modeling ideas presented in this chapter—heterogeneity, hierarchical Bayes modeling, and sample selection—in a single application, to the product recommendation systems used widely on the Internet.

Finally, all marketing research projects conclude with a presentation, and so it will be with this text: the final section of this chapter discusses "best practices" for making both oral and written marketing research presentations. Even the most thoughtful, faultless research will sink like a stone if conveyed poorly. Knowing how to present a project's most telling findings in a manner conducive to their being used is an art all its own, and one we shall consider at length.

Let us begin with an up-close look at a number of methodological developments available to survey researchers, in *Research Innovations and Technologies 12.1*.

12.1 Heterogeneity: A Cornerstone of Marketing Practice

You may have heard the term "heterogeneity" in casual conversation many times and had a clear conception of what it means. Marketers use this term all the time, and decades of experience has taught us that it is not only an important idea but that it may be the single most crucial concept in the discipline. If this seems like a big claim, it is, and it is incumbent upon us to explain why heterogeneity assumes the central role it does in marketing research in general, and for the statistical models used in the discipline in particular.

12.1a Heterogeneity: What Is It? And Why Is It Important?

Humans have been studying their natural environment for a long time. But casual observers, even infants, know the following:

Not Everything Is Exactly Identical

This is true not only for people but also for products, services, plants, pets, rocks, and just about any other class of concept or object, animate or inanimate. The world is teeming with variation, and it is this variation that statistical methods were designed to help us explain.

Research Innovations and Technologies 12.1

Microtargeting and Survey Panels—The Microscopes and Telescopes of Marketing Research

As marketing research continues to adopt the formal edifice of statistics, its methods are increasingly relied upon to possess the precision of a scientific instrument, even receiving funding from the National Science Foundation's Major Research Instrumentation (MRI) Program.

Jon Krosnick, a Stanford professor of communication and political science, received a $2 million MRI grant in 2006 for his 2-year project to develop a new survey methodology some believe analogous to an astronomer's telescope. Because MRI competition grants have traditionally been used to purchase large, expensive hardware, Krosnick explains this metaphor. "What is a telescope? It is a measuring device that is made available on a shared basis to lots of different researchers. That is exactly what our survey platform will be."

Krosnick's idea is to create a shared platform for collecting social science data so that government, academia, and industry can share the costs and efforts of sample recruitment. The goal is to provide representative sample surveys with fast turnaround times and high response rates at reasonable costs. To reach this goal, the project will pair Internet survey methods with in-person interviewing through a panel of survey respondents networked by computer.

Noting that surveys are the most efficient means of data-collection in social science fields, Krosnick reviewed the current obstacles and expenses of surveying:

- Telephone survey response rates have declined from a high of 70 percent in the 1970s to a maximum of 40 percent today.
- Surveys on the front pages of newspapers have response rates of less than 10 percent.
- In-person interviews can yield a response rate of 80 percent but at a cost of as much as $1000 per subject.
- Telephone interviews cost between $2.50 and $6 per minute, with a maximum length of about 20 minutes.
- Ninety percent of Internet surveys involve self-selected respondents, resulting in an unrepresentative sample.

Because government agencies, academic researchers, and businesses spend billions of dollars trying to solve this problem, Krosnick's solution to "get out of this mess" is to both share the costs of getting past those obstacles and design a means to obtain better response rates from more representative samples.

The project involves selecting a representative sample of 1000 American households from U.S. Postal Service mailing lists; randomly selecting an adult member from each household; conducting a short, in-person interview with the selected respondent; and offering the respondent a free laptop and high-speed connection in exchange for answering a 30-minute, secure Internet survey once a month. The response rate and respondent attrition will be monitored over the computer network, while a university staff researcher will supervise the fieldwork.

The long-term plan is to sell minutes on the monthly survey to researchers in all fields and industries. The 2008 U.S. presidential primaries and general election campaign pose the first test of the network, after academic researchers submit proposals for surveying the sample's views on national candidates, national issues, and the election process to the American National Election Studies (ANES, a source of data on political participation in the United States for more than 50 years).

Also in the political realm, both the Schwarzenegger and Angelides campaigns employed a method called "microtargeting" during California's 2006 gubernatorial campaign. This method, honed during George W. Bush's 2004 presidential campaign, involves a "microscopic" focus on personal buying habits to predict political preferences and thereby identify likely political supporters.

Microtargeting is an extension of marketing research methods used by companies to identify likely customers. In 2004, the Bush campaign collected information on voters' cars, magazine subscriptions, musical preferences, favorite vacation spots, and religious affiliations to zero in on likely supporters in key swing states like Ohio. The campaign then targeted these households for phone calls, mailings, and visits from volunteers who used messages designed to elicit positive responses based on issues about which the resident was likely to care.

According to the Schwarzenegger campaign, the Republican governor's reelection team had the largest microtargeting operation ever established in the country, with a vast database compiled from consumer information purchased from credit card companies, airlines, and retailers, as well as publicly available voter records. The database included millions of names, phone numbers, and addresses with all manner of consumer preferences, as well as voting histories (*when* they voted, not *how* they voted) and other demographic information.

Strategists like Josh Ginsberg, deputy political director of the Schwarzenegger campaign, believe that buying habits can reveal a voter's politics better than his or her political party affiliation or other available demographics. A caricature that illustrates the principle might suggest that a Volvo driver who subscribes to *The New Yorker* and shops at Whole Foods is likely to support Democrats, whereas a pickup driver with a gun license who subscribes to *USA Today* is likely to support Republicans. Said Ginsberg, "It's not where they live, it's how they live." Schwarzenegger's $25 million turnout operation hopes that microtargeting will also increase Republican turnout in tight Congressional races.

A coalition of unions and other progressive groups called America Votes also made use of consumer records during the 2006 campaign season to help find Democratic supporters in a number of states. The California Democratic Party gathered consumer information to aid its turnout operation for challenger Phil Angelides, although with a far more limited budget and scope than the Schwarzenegger operation. Cathy Calfo, campaign manager for Angelides, claimed that the Schwarzenegger campaign was using microtargeting as "a system to manipulate people and allow a candidate that has no specific message to tell different people different things."

Manipulative or not, microtargeting seems to be the next wave of political campaigning. As Steve Schmidt, veteran of the Bush campaign and campaign manager for Schwarzenegger, put it, "For a long time in California, the thesis has been that television advertising by itself drives voter turnout. That, in fact, is not the case. What drives voters is person-to-person contact." And the "microscope" that allows that person-to-person contact to be targeted and catered for success is the collection and analysis of consumer buying habits.

Sources: Trei, Lisa (2006, September 27). "Social Science Researcher to Overhaul Survey Methodology with $2 Million Grant." *The Stanford Report.* http://news-service.stanford.edu/news/2006/september27/krosnick-092706.html.
"Schwarzenegger Camp Uses Consumer Data." *The New York Times,* October 26, 2006.

Marketers, in particular, are quite literally obsessed with heterogeneity, because of its pivotal importance throughout the discipline. Without heterogeneity, we would make just one kind of each product, produce one ad theme to help sell it, one promotional campaign to get us to buy it "right now," and so on. And it is fair to say that, of all disciplines, it is marketing that has developed the most sophisticated methods to assess, account for, and make use of heterogeneity. Before introducing these models—and why we should care about them— it is crucial to understand what we mean when we say "heterogeneity," and also what we do *not* mean. In casual usage, "heterogeneity" can refer to many things. For example, speaking just of humans, it is clear that people differ:

- in terms of their *characteristics* (e.g., gender, age, weight, income)
- in terms of their *behavior* or *outcomes* (observables; e.g., "Did you buy it?" "How much did you bid?")
- in terms of their *sensitivity* to various stimuli (e.g., how much more likely are you to purchase something if it is on sale?)

We can understand the distinction between these three in terms of a very simple regression set-up, which (ignoring the intercept and the error for the time being) looks like:

$$Y_i = \beta X_i$$

We can easily see that the first type of heterogeneity, in *characteristics*, refers to the X variable(s) in our regression: people and objects differ in terms of information we can record about them. These characteristics can help us understand differences in *behavior* or *outcomes* (i.e., dependent variables), the Y part of our regression; heterogeneity in Y means that people or objects differ in terms of the outcomes that marketers hope to explain by using regression in the first place. The last type of heterogeneity is in β, and this is typically the most difficult to understand, because we have the least direct experience with it. When we speak of heterogeneity in coefficients (i.e., sensitivities, or β), what we mean is that different people or objects *react* differently (in Y) to the *same* changes in our X variables. [When we discuss heterogeneity theoretically or for the population, we will use the symbol β for coefficients; *estimated* values for a particular sample will be denoted *b*. The underlying concepts, however, are identical.]

If this sounds abstract, let us take a concrete example, one that labor economists and marketers have long studied: the effect of education on income. We all like to believe that more schooling will, all else equal, translate into greater remuneration. Our X heterogeneity would mean that people differ in terms of their education (among other characteristics, such as age, gender, and so on); our Y heterogeneity would mean that people differ in terms of their incomes. Both of these are uncontroversial. But, what would our β heterogeneity mean? It would explain the fact that *one additional year of education (X)* would translate into *different salary increases (Y)* for different people. For example, completing one's last year of medical school may entail an enormous increase in salary, whereas the difference between a ninth-grade and a tenth-grade education may be very small in practice; obtaining a Ph.D. in Finance may translate into a higher salary than obtaining a Ph.D. in English, all else equal; or, perhaps best among these examples, you may simply be able to make better use of the knowledge you gain from one more year of school than would a friend taking the same classes. That is, the *same* change in X (education) may lead to *different* changes in Y (income), so that β is *different for different people*.

When marketing researchers speak of heterogeneity, it is almost always this "β heterogeneity" or "coefficient heterogeneity" they are referring to. Some people *respond* to our ads; some do not. Some *react* to price changes strongly; others do not. Heterogeneity, therefore, is about people's differing responsiveness. Because evaluating the effect of marketing actions is integral to marketing research practice, understanding heterogeneity is crucial to making appropriate decisions. Unfortunately, the vast majority of statistical models used in marketing—and considered thus far in this text—yield one value for each coefficient in our model, supposedly valid for everyone. When we assessed how much someone's weight would change for an inch increase in height, we reported a *single value* for all people in our sample; we did *not* say "these people seem to put on more weight when they grow than others do." And this is what we *should have* been able to say, because that is how the world actually works.

Fortunately, statisticians and marketing researchers have formulated a powerful theory of how to measure precisely this kind of heterogeneity using typical marketing data. Here, we introduce their ideas, discuss how to go about making such measurements, and interpret results. We do not develop the methods mathematically, because they can be quite complex and rely on specialized programs; see Further Reading at the end of this chapter for a listing of such programs and texts that explain the statistical manipulations behind them.

To motivate our discussion, let us return to an example first introduced in Chapter 10, where we used multiple linear regression to explain weight in terms of height and gender (see also Figure 12.1):

$$\text{Weight} = \beta_0 + \beta_1 \text{ Height} + \beta_2 \text{ Gender} + \varepsilon$$

Before, we explained the (estimated) coefficient b_2 as "How much more men weighed than women, correcting for height," and this is accurate. An equally valid way to view this, however, is as a form (a very simple form, in fact) of heterogeneity, called **intercept heterogeneity**: men and women are equally "sensitive" to increases in height (note that the *slope* of both lines is the same), but women have lower "baseline" weight (i.e., the line for women hits the leftmost point of the chart at about 105 pounds, whereas that for men does so at about 132 pounds, and that this difference runs throughout Figure 12.1).

intercept heterogeneity
In a statistical model, like regression, when each unit (e.g., person, firm, object) is allowed to have its own intercept (i.e., the value when all regressors are zero).

We say that this is a very simple form of heterogeneity because it is really just the tip of the iceberg in terms of the relationship between height and weight. For example, consider some of these other possibilities:

Figure 12.1 Gender Differences in Weight, "Correcting for" Height

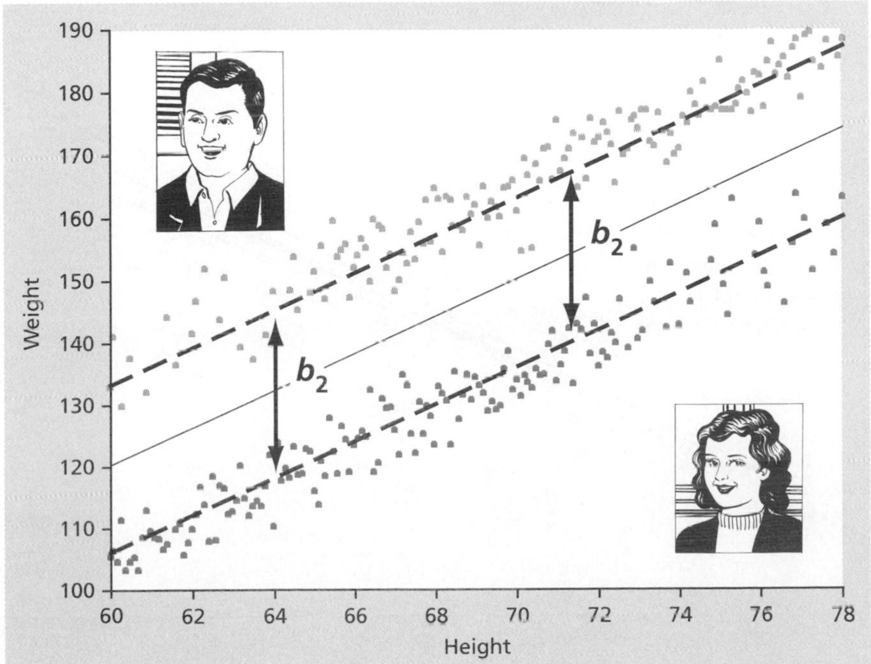

slope heterogeneity
In a statistical model, when different units (e.g., people, firms, products) are each allowed to have their own coefficients. Such models require multiple observations per unit and can be difficult to estimate quickly.

- Each inch can add more to men's weights than to women's (**"slope heterogeneity")**.
- If we want to explain weight versus height, who says the best way to categorize people is as "men" and "women"? Can there be two other *groups* or *segments* or *classes* that do better?
- Should there be *more than two groups?* Should each group have some men and some women, or should each group be broken up along lines distinct from gender?
- Perhaps not everyone *within* each group should be considered identical (i.e., within-group heterogeneity).
- Is it possible that *each individual person* can have his or her own estimated coefficient value?

All these questions are valid, and each has been addressed—and in some cases fully solved—by various heterogeneity models in marketing. The rest of this section examines these models in detail. As a prelude to doing so, we should consider the last of these questions, about "each individual." That is, why are we unable to just assign each person his or her own coefficient value? In some cases, we can. For example, if we had a situation in which each person gave us a lot of data, it might be possible to estimate *separate* regressions for each individual. In this case, our model would look like:

$$Y_i = \alpha_j + \beta_j X_i + \varepsilon_i \tag{12.1}$$

We would have to estimate a separate slope (β_j) and intercept (α_j) for each individual, j (note that *observations* are denoted in this particular equation by i, and *individuals* by j). Figure 12.2 provides an example of what this might look like.

Figure 12.2 indicates that there are 15 data points for each of six individuals (so that $j = 1, \ldots, 6$ and $i = 1, \ldots, 90$). We could estimate a single regression for all 90 points (shown here by the bold dotted line), and this would indicate a slope of about 1.5 and a healthy r-squared of approximately 0.94. However, if we were to distinguish among the six individuals, we would realize that each provided enough data for a separate regression (as pictured) and that these would yield slopes ranging from approximately 1 to 2, with r-squared values above 0.97. We might conclude that the slopes were *heterogeneous*, meaning that people differed in their degree of sensitivity (on Y with regard to X, whatever they may represent).

You may be wondering why we do not always run separate regressions, and there are many good answers to this. Foremost among them is a pragmatic concern: applications where we have many pieces

Figure 12.2 A Separate Regression for Each Person vs. One Regression for All

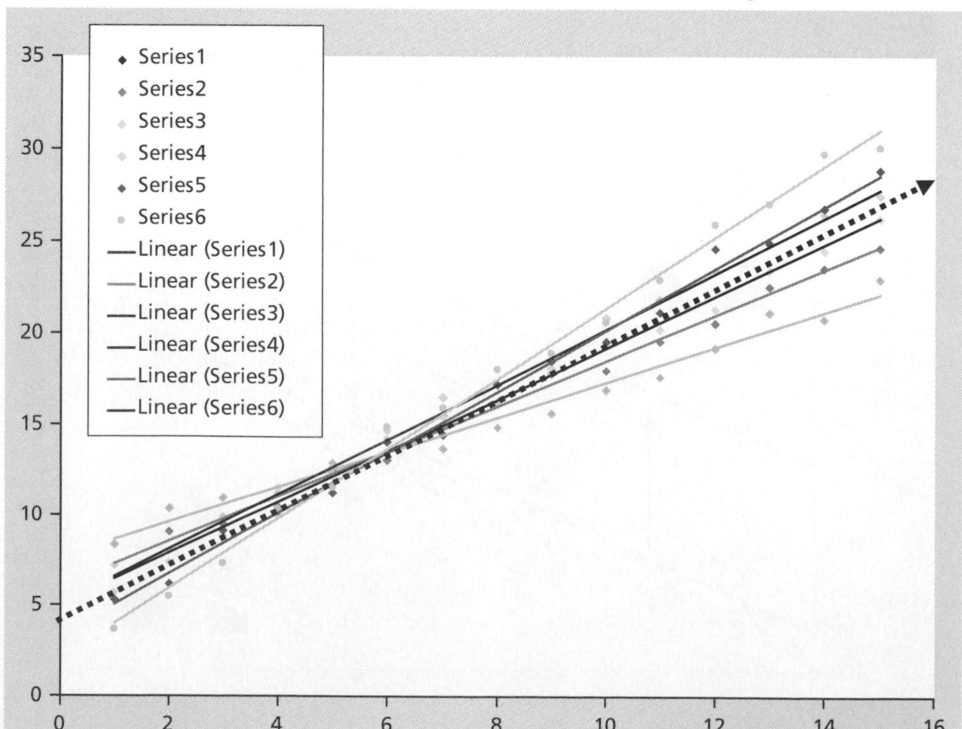

of data from each individual (or product, firm, etc.) are rare; often, we have just one point for each (as in our marketing research student data, along with many of the other data sets accompanying this text). In survey research, we get one answer for a particular question from each respondent—if the respondent indeed chose to provide an answer—and this is true in polling, most satisfaction surveys, and numerous other common marketing research applications. In fact, it is really only when we have a *panel* of respondents—who agree to offer individual- or household-level longitudinal data—that we have the luxury of many responses per subject.

A second reason that separate regressions are seldom run is that we are looking for a *unified explanation* for our phenomenon of interest: each regression is like a separate explanation—one for you, one for your friend, one for every other single person—and it is often unclear how to put these regression results together. For example, how would you convey, in simple terms, the "unified results" of Figure 12.2? How would you do it if it had the individual regressions of hundreds or thousands of respondents? Generally speaking, this is difficult, and this is what motivated statisticians and marketing researchers to create powerful methods to account for individual-level heterogeneity. In short, we know it is crucial to account for heterogeneity, and we wish to find ways to explain it simply so that managers can use it to make better decisions. Let us consider some ways to accomplish this goal.

heterogeneity model
An explicit statistical model for how consumers' sensitivity to some stimulus (e.g., marketing variable) varies across the population. For example, we might say that "willingness to pay is normally distributed" in a particular population.

12.1b Different Ways to Account for Heterogeneity in Marketing Research

discrete heterogeneity
A method of expressing the fact that different population units (e.g., consumers) have different coefficients in a statistical model, by assuming they comprise exactly *k* discrete groups.

continuous heterogeneity
A method of expressing the fact that different population units (e.g., consumers) have different coefficients in a statistical model, by assuming they can take on any values at all, with frequencies expressed by a continuous function (usually a normal distribution).

latent class model
A type of statistical model that accounts for heterogeneity by dividing units (customers, firms, etc.) into a fixed number of groups; units in each group are assumed to have the same coefficients or characteristics

finite mixture model
Assumes each individual's preferences come from one of a fixed set of groups. When those groups are themselves normally distributed, one has "finite normal mixture heterogeneity"; when the groups are each a constant value, one has a "latent class model."

In our discussion thus far, we have looked at two extreme solutions to the heterogeneity problem: the *same* value of β is assigned to everyone, or a *different* β_j is estimated for each individual, *j*. And we have already detailed reasons why each of these is unsatisfying, given the needs of real marketing research projects. The obvious middle ground is to come up with a way to assign β values according to some scheme, formula, rule, or distribution, that is, a method that describes which β values go with which individuals. It turns out that there are many ways to do this, and the best of them provide excellent solutions to our problem. (We will examine some of these in more detail in Section 12-2 on "Hierarchical Models and Bayesian Estimation.")

Generally speaking, two types of **heterogeneity models** are available to marketing researchers: **discrete heterogeneity** and **continuous heterogeneity**. Discrete heterogeneity often goes under the name **latent class model** (and sometimes **finite mixture model**, although the latter can sometimes accommodate continuous heterogeneity as well.) The very best way to get a sense of the various heterogeneity models is to look at pictures of each, to understand how they work and what they tell us. Let us start off with the simplest form of heterogeneity: none at all! This is our by-now-familiar homogeneous model, where each individual (in the population) is assumed to have the *same* value of the regression coefficient, β, as depicted in Figure 12.3.

This is rather simple to understand: everyone has the same coefficient ($\beta = 3$, for this example). We can turn to a more complex form of heterogeneity, the popular, easy-to-interpret and readily estimated form: (discrete) latent class heterogeneity, illustrated in Figure 12.4.

There appear to be three groups (classes, segments) here: 50 percent of the population has $\beta = 3$, 30 percent has $\beta = 2$, and 20 percent has $\beta = 4.5$. One of the reasons marketing researchers value this form of heterogeneity is that it provides answers that are very easily conveyed; we can say that we have determined that there are three separate segments in this market, and we can presumably choose separate strategies, products, services, and so forth, for each of them. We must caution readers that this interpretation is overly simplistic, even if it is commonly used. The number of segments found using this form of heterogeneity can depend critically on the sample; in particular, we will tend to discover more "segments"—which should, of course, represent the population from which we draw—when our sample is larger. Still, if Figure 12.4 represents something like price sensitivity or willingness-to-purchase, it is important that we distinguish among consumers in some manner, and latent classes will tend to be decidedly superior in managerial applications to a homogeneous solution.

Other forms of heterogeneity can look dramatically different from homogeneity and latent classes. For example, let us consider a form of continuous heterogeneity, called *normal heterogeneity* (for reasons that will be clear from the graph in Figure 12.5).

Here, there appears to be only one group, but there is heterogeneity *within* this group: the individuals are spread around the graph, even if they are concentrated near the center. Marketing researchers often

Figure 12.3 Distribution of Coefficients for Homogeneous Model

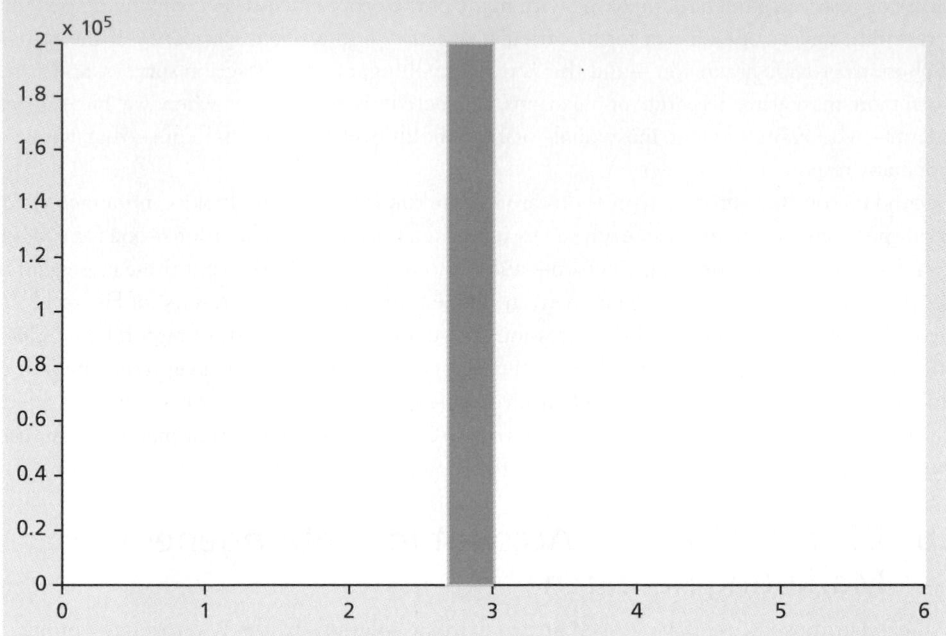

like to conceive of markets as if they "look" like this, with most consumers near some center and only a few falling far away. However, there are many markets where there are sizeable "clumps" of consumers that differ strongly from one another, and so Figure 12.5 would be inaccurate. This is certainly true for major durables purchases, such as cars and homes. In such cases, marketing researchers find it best to turn to the most general form of heterogeneity model in current use, called (hold your breath!) **finite normal mixture heterogeneity**. This model melds the best of latent classes—there are clearly distinguished consumer groups, each with its own center—and of the single hump used in the normal heterogeneity model of Figure 12.5.

finite normal mixture heterogeneity A powerful (and relatively complex) method of representing the tastes and preferences of various individuals. Assumes that each individual's parameters come from one of a fixed number of normal distributions.

Now there again appear to be three heterogeneous groups, depicted in Figure 12.6 with the same means and percentages as before: 50 percent has β centered about 3, 30 percent has β near 2, and 20

Figure 12.4 Distribution of Coefficients under Discrete Latent Class Heterogeneity

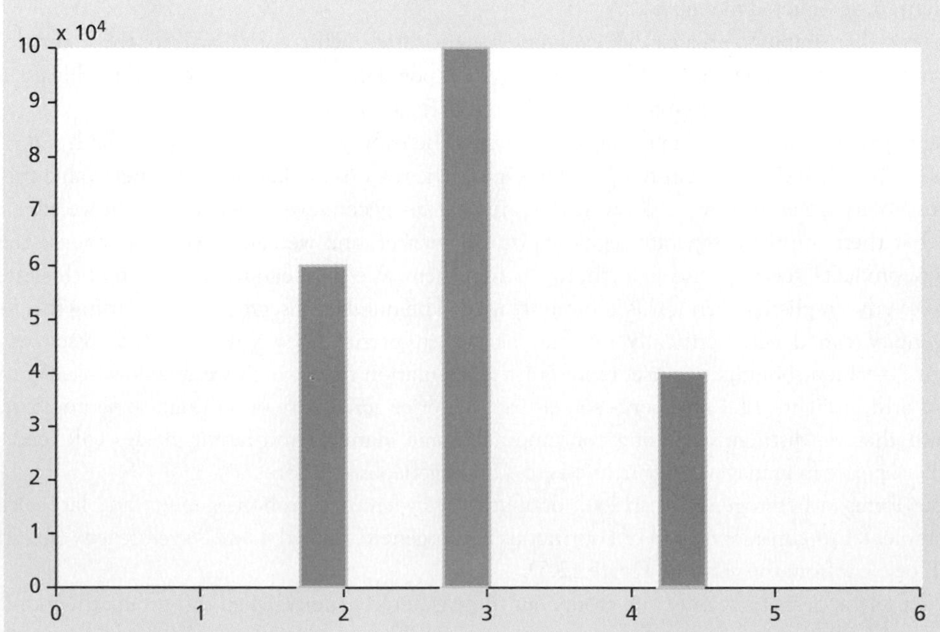

Figure 12.5 Distribution of Coefficients under Normal Heterogeneity

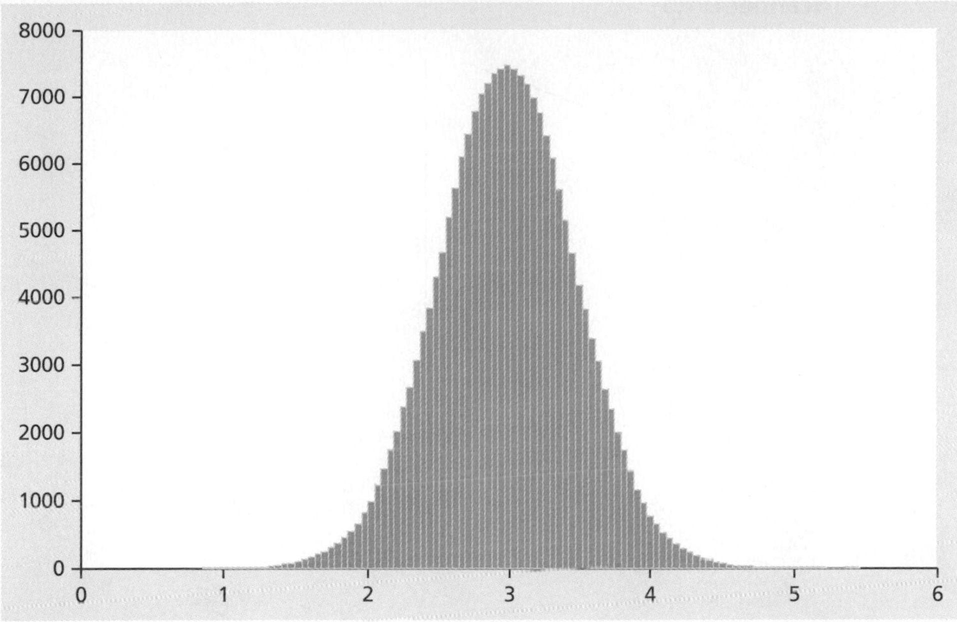

percent has β near 4.5. However, each of these groups now has *different degrees of within-group heterogeneity*. Note, for example, how the smallest group, with β near 4.5, is far more spread out than the others. To describe this form of heterogeneity, we would need to know the number of groups, what proportion of the population falls in each, and the mean and variance of each of the "humps" (which are called "mixing components," or simply segments).

Statisticians have devised methods to estimate all these forms of heterogeneity automatically, although it is often quite time-consuming for the large data sets common in marketing research. We will not delve more deeply into how one might do so, other than to refer readers to the specialized software (listed in the "Further Reading" section) and to mention that powerful Bayesian methods, which are covered later in this chapter, are typically called upon. One of the practical issues in heterogeneity

Figure 12.6 Distribution of Coefficients under Finite Normal Mixture Heterogeneity

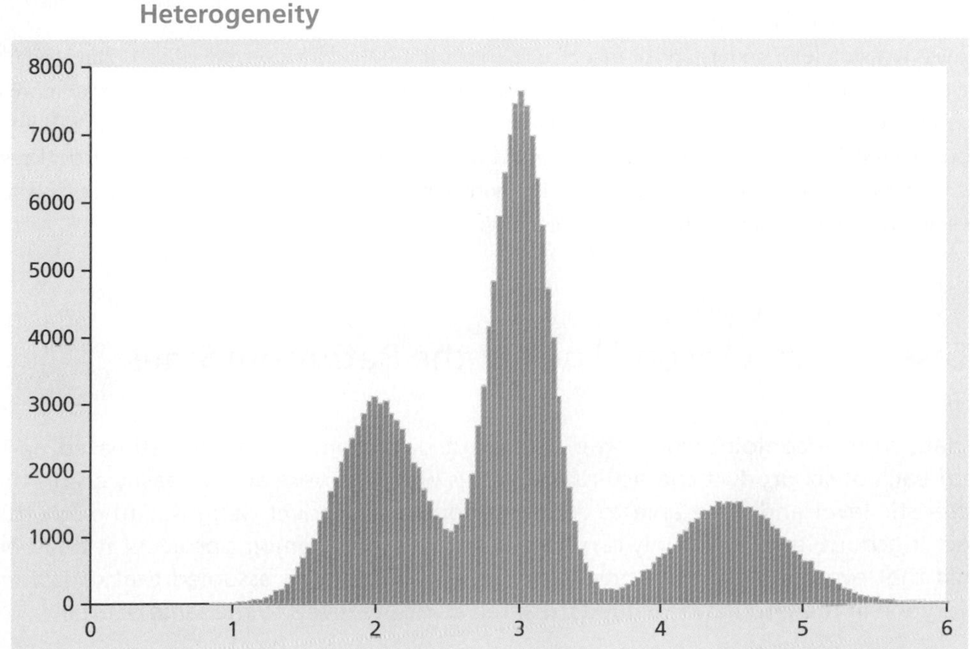

Figure 12.7 Distribution of Coefficients for Price and Display in Paper Towel Scanner Data

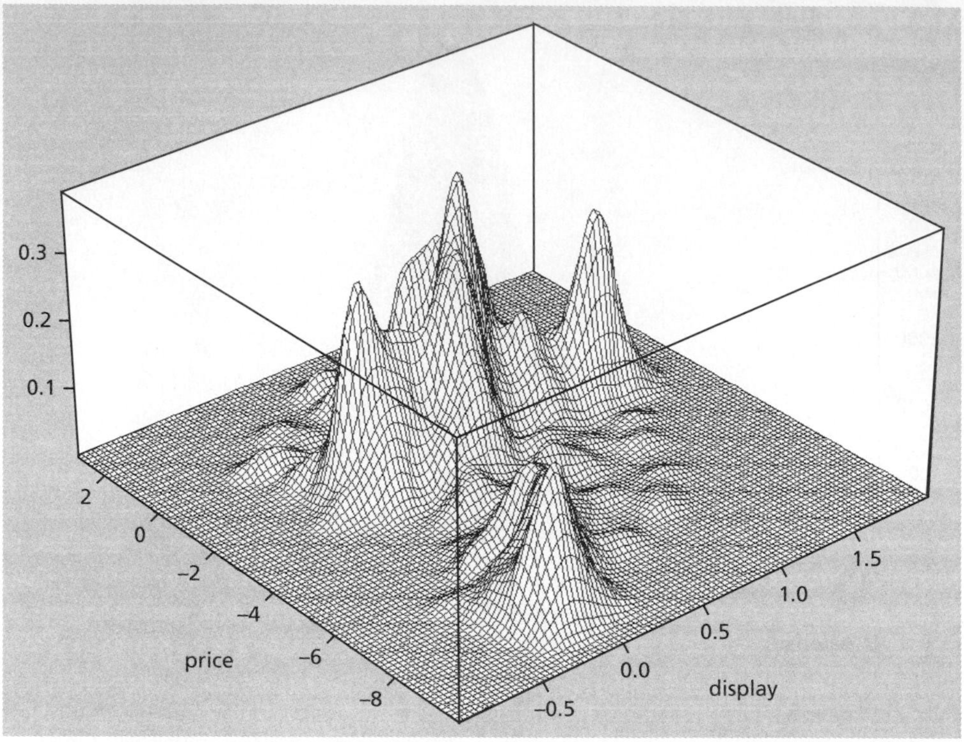

0.3
0.2
0.1
2
0
−2
−4
price
−6
−8
−0.5
0.0
0.5
1.0
1.5
display

Source: Article reprinted with permission from the publisher, The Berkeley Electronic Press, © 2004. Originally published in *The Review of Marketing Science*, available at http://www.bepress.com/romsjournal/vol2/iss1/art1.

modeling involves how many humps best represents our collected consumer data and also how many different variables' coefficients in the same regression should be modeled heterogeneously. These are seldom simple questions, and it is always best to work along with an expert in the area, to look at a lot of pictures, and to let each model make predictions so that the manager might judge which best suits the project's purpose. In real applications, it is not uncommon to have a large number of humps for each coefficient, to have many coefficients, and also to find that the coefficients may be *correlated* (e.g., people who care more about price may care less about styling). Figure 12.7 is a graph of just *two* coefficients, for the effect of price paid and for store display, on which brand of paper towel was chosen, for a real supermarket scanner panel data set.

This is not simple to understand at first glance, to put it mildly. However, we can see that it would be wrong to assume that everyone reacted the same way to price or display. Given that smaller or more negative coefficients mean, respectively, a smaller or more negative reaction, can you try to "tell a story" based on Figure 12.7? This is what managers need to do when presented with such statistical results, which help them segment the market and devise more appropriate incentives and strategies than would be possible with simpler approaches to heterogeneity.

12.1c Application Case Study: A Second Look at the Bathroom Scale Conjoint Data

In Chapter 11, we analyzed data from a conjoint study on dial-readout bathroom scales and estimated part-worths for the various levels of each of six product characteristics. In this way, we were able to easily graph the relative value of each characteristic level and were able to formulate optimal product designs. Although this analysis was statistically correct, rigorous, and commonly carried out in real-world conjoint projects, it had one major shortcoming: it assumed that everyone's part-worths were the same. That is, it assumed that consumer tastes were *homogeneous:* everyone in the population valued the same attribute levels to the same degree.

In such a world, we would have to produce only a single item (in this case, bathroom scale) to make everyone as happy as can be. This is not a world that anyone actually lives in; a trip to any appliance store indicates dozens of scale designs, each with its own special features and price point. That manufacturers create many products indicates a strong belief that consumer tastes are *not* homogeneous: some of us value funds more than how easily our scale can be read, while others need a scale with very high weight capacity, and so on. To understand these varying needs, we must reexamine our conjoint data, but this time allow for *heterogeneity* in part-worths.

As discussed earlier in this chapter, there are many ways to allow for this heterogeneity, some quite sophisticated. To illustrate the concept, however, we will present one of the most popular and easily comprehended—although usually not the most statistically powerful—forms of heterogeneity, that of (discrete) *latent classes.* This will allow a tangible benefit attractive to marketing research professionals, the ability to determine distinct, nonoverlapping market segments, each simply described by a few key numbers. For simplicity, here we will examine a heterogeneous solution with three latent classes. Note that we *cannot* claim this is the "right" or "best" number without thoroughly considering the alternatives and, for most such projects, discussing the marketing implications of different numbers of segments with the sponsoring firm (sometimes, a firm will want to know the "best way to break our market up into three groups," rather than getting bogged down in a much finer division).

To get the flavor of what the latent class solution provides, let us first look at all the part-worths, as returned by a statistical program, in Table 12.1.

The three latent classes have different *sizes,* comprising 22.7 percent, 48.1 percent, and 29.1 percent of the population (based on the sample data); clearly, the second class is by far the largest. The three classes also differ in terms of how much they *value* each of the various attribute levels. Because this is difficult to discern from the tabular presentation, let us consider graphical representations for two of the attributes, weight capacity and price, that the scale manufacturer believed to be especially important.

Table 12.1 Part-Worths for Dial-Readout Scale Conjoint, with Three Latent Classes

	Class 1	Class 2	Class 3		Class 1	Class 2	Class 3
	22.7%	48.1%	29.1%		22.7%	48.1%	29.1%
	Weight Capacity (lbs.)				**Tick Mark Gap (in.)**		
200	−0.946	−0.620	−0.283	**0.063**	−0.071	−0.534	−0.257
250	0.211	0.068	0.314	**0.094**	0.102	−0.356	0.078
300	0.233	0.146	0.546	**0.125**	0.264	0.065	0.599
350	0.267	−0.126	0.518	**0.156**	−0.140	0.066	0.641
400	0.292	−0.146	0.427	**0.188**	−0.099	0.081	0.463
	Aspect Ratio				**Number Size (in.)**		
0.750	−0.129	−0.239	0.321	**0.75**	−0.734	−1.012	−0.415
0.875	0.149	0.299	0.422	**1.00**	−0.104	−0.414	0.109
1.000	0.262	0.312	0.473	**1.25**	0.052	0.221	0.482
1.143	−0.038	0.176	0.373	**1.50**	0.380	0.199	0.643
1.333	−0.187	−0.874	−0.066	**1.75**	0.462	0.328	0.704
	Area (sq. in.)				**Price ($)**		
100	0.119	−0.113	0.308	**$10**	2.483	0.300	0.623
110	0.143	−0.144	0.219	**$15**	1.660	0.218	0.537
120	0.085	−0.137	0.417	**$20**	0.276	0.028	0.407
130	−0.008	−0.104	0.345	**$25**	−1.613	−0.301	0.225
140	0.004	−0.179	0.233	**$30**	−2.748	−0.923	−0.269

Figure 12.8 Part-Worths for Bathroom Scale Weight Capacity and Price, Based on Three Latent Classes

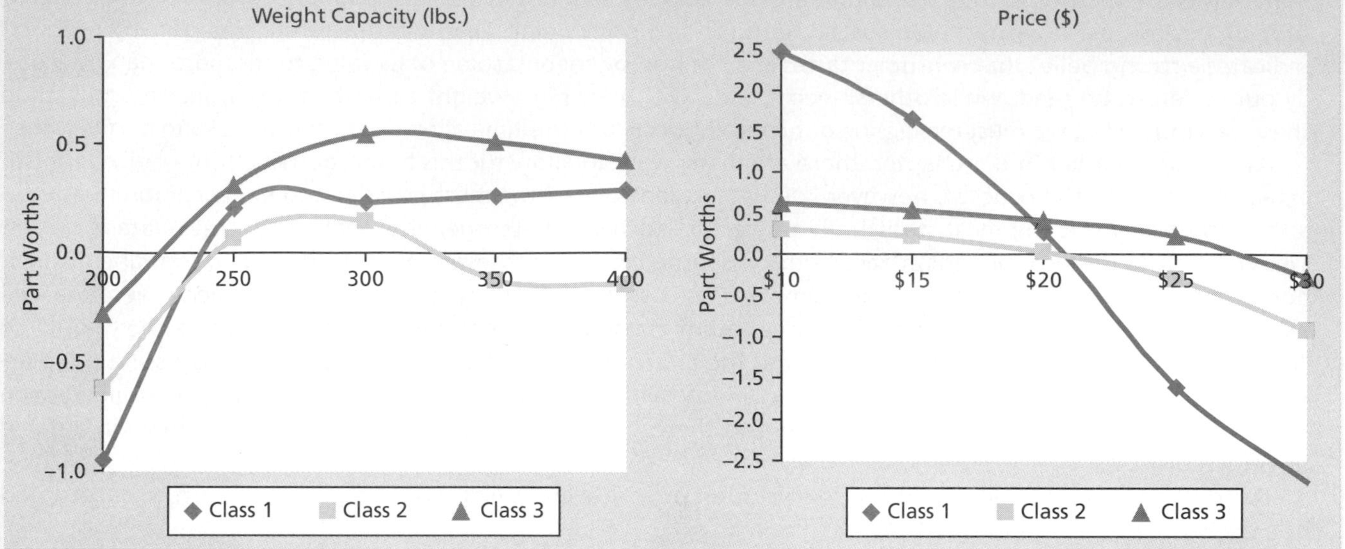

The graphs in Figure 12.8 tell subtle stories and, most importantly, *different* ones from our prior account using a homogeneous statistical model. For weight capacity, each of the three classes appears to follow a similar pattern across the five attribute levels: they all seem to believe that 200 pounds is far too low a capacity and that some moderate level would suit their needs well. Class 1 alone would prefer the highest capacity level of 400 pounds, but this degree of preference is mild. Overall, Class 3 places the greatest value on the weight capacity attribute in general (its graph is "highest"), and Class 2 places the least value on this attribute.

For pricing, as might be expected, all three classes prefer (all else equal) to pay as little as possible; we say that the price part-worth curves are strongly *downward-sloping*, as they should be. However, although the degree of falloff for Classes 2 and 3 is quite strong, for Class 1 it is fantastically so: prices of $10 and $30 are separated by more than 5 points (a lot!) on the utility scale. Checking the part-worths (Table 12.1) shows that for no other class and no other attribute do we see anything like this degree of disparity. Apparently, people in Class 1 find paying a low price extraordinarily important; we can look back at weight capacity to see that these Class 1 respondents also reacted very negatively to a (low) 200-pound capacity.

By considering the *entire pattern of part-worths* for each class, we can build up a qualitative picture of what sets people in that class apart from others who took part in the study. This can be tedious when there are many attributes, numerous levels of each, and the sponsors and researchers believe there should be a large number of classes. Unfortunately, there are no shortcuts in this endeavor, and one must truly consider the entire part-worth pattern for each class in order to place it in context and, perhaps, provide a specialized product or service suited to its needs.

It is important to realize that this entire line of analysis would be utterly impossible without accounting for heterogeneity, either by latent classes or some other method. (The Application Case Study on product recommendation systems in Section 12-3f will highlight another type of heterogeneity model.) If we truly wish to understand complex markets, and the individual needs driving them, we must come to terms with allowing for consumer heterogeneity in our statistical models.

12.2 Hierarchical Models and Bayesian Estimation

Among the most important analytical advances in marketing research in recent years has been the advent of **hierarchical models** and Bayesian estimation, especially when conjoined in the form of **hierarchical Bayes (HB) models**. These models take into account the fact that real-world items tend to appear in useful hierarchies: your class is just one in your grade, your grade is one in your school, your school is one in its district, and so forth. HB models also exploit an extremely powerful estimation technology that enables their use on the large data sets common in marketing research applications. Here, we present what is special about HB models, with an eye toward their broad deployment by marketing researchers.

There are two parts to the term "hierarchical Bayes" (HB). Their meanings are entirely distinct, and we will discuss each separately and extensively.

hierarchical models
A form of statistical model in which the units form a natural hierarchy, each level of which can be modeled. For example, students are organized into classes, classes into grades, grades into schools, and schools into a city district. Variation in student performance can be accounted for (modeled) at each of these levels.

hierarchical Bayes (HB) model
A powerful statistical platform for explaining complex marketing phenomena, essentially a hierarchical model estimated by Bayesian methods. A hallmark of HB models is that one can explain *coefficients* in terms of other explanatory variables; for example, your measured willingness to respond to a promotion is a function of, say, your income and shopping frequency. HB models almost always account for consumer preference heterogeneity as well.

12.2a What Does "Hierarchical" Mean?

The HB model is called "hierarchical" because it consists of a number of *levels* (note that these have nothing to do with the "levels" in conjoint attributes). For the sake of discussion, let us say that there are two such levels, a higher and a lower, although there can be any number in practice. The lower level of the model looks like any of the statistical models we have dealt with all along: *any* form of regression will do. For example, our "lower level" can look exactly like the model addressed in our discussion of heterogeneity (see Equation 12.1):

$$Y_i = \alpha_j + \beta_j X_i + \varepsilon_i$$

Just as before, our task would be to estimate a separate slope (β_j) and intercept (α_j) for each individual, j (note again that *observations* are denoted in this particular case by i, and *individuals* by j). The question is: Where are these individual-level slopes and intercepts supposed to come from if we have only a few observations per individual, and perhaps even only one for some individuals? This being the case, we cannot run separate regressions for everyone (refer back to Figure 12.2 to see why). The answer is that they come from the "higher" level. This is, in essence, the key insight of HB: we can write a *model* describing each person's parameters. Such a model might look like the following:

$$\beta_j = \varphi Z_j + \delta$$

This is just an *ordinary regression model* for individual j's slope (β_j), with coefficient φ and error δ (we would typically have such a model for all the regression coefficients, including the intercept, α_j). Experience suggests that this idea of writing *coefficients* as resulting from a model can be a bit forbidding at first, so let us look at a specific example. Suppose we are trying to understand how much our customers spend on their supermarket trips, and we believe this is influenced by the presence of a huge sign proclaiming "Sale!" in front of the store. Our model explaining how much they spend on each trip might look like:

$$Spending_t = \alpha_j + \beta_j Sign_t + \varepsilon_t$$

We have related the spending at time t to whether the "Sale!" sign is present; we would typically include many other marketing and environmental variables as well. But a particular person, j, may not shop often enough to estimate individual-specific coefficients, (α_j, β_j). So, we turn to our "higher" level model to help:

$$\beta_j = \varphi \times Income_j + \delta$$

What this says is that a person's *sensitivity* to a "Sale!" sign can be explained in terms of his or her income level. This makes sense: those with high incomes are probably less likely to alter their purchases based on a (typically small) grocery store sale. This would mean an anticipated *negative* value for the parameter φ (even though almost everyone's reaction to the sale itself—their personal value of β_j—was positive). We see that the hierarchical nature of this model offers three important advantages:

1. It allows us to have *different slopes* for different customers—that is, heterogeneity—without having to estimate separate regressions for each.
2. It helps *explain where the heterogeneity comes from*.
3. When there is little data for a specific individual, hierarchical methods "borrow" information for other customers to obtain better estimates (this property is often called *shrinkage*, as in "shrinking" our estimate toward an overall population mean).

The first benefit is one we have seen before in our discussion of heterogeneity in Section 12-1; indeed, hierarchical models are among the most successful modern approaches to allowing for the all-important heterogeneity intrinsic to marketing applications. The second benefit is entirely new, however. It says that we can now understand *why* there is heterogeneity, what it means, where it comes from, and perhaps how to act on it. Note that income is a demographic variable. We could add as many such variables as we want, and doing so would help us describe which sorts of consumers respond strongly to which kinds of marketing activity. The third benefit means that, even when we have a small number of observations for many people—as is typical for many survey- and Web-based applications—we can still make powerful predictions for each individual by "borrowing" information from others. All these benefits flow quite naturally in a hierarchical setting.

We have not discussed the "error" (δ) distribution in the higher-level model, but it is quite important in applications. Even if we do not put in any explanatory variables (Z_j) in our higher-level model, the hierarchical framework can still help us, because the "error" helps describe what our coefficients look like *across the population*. We can assume this has any distribution at all, and we usually assume it is normal. Once we decide what distribution this error should have, specialized software determines the individual-level β_j, which can then be used to make predictions. The predictions arising from hierarchical models have been found to be far superior to those from simple homogeneous models. And the hierarchical model, as stressed earlier, helps us understand *why* different people (or households, firms, etc.) have different sensitivities to marketing and environmental stimuli. As such, they provide direct, usable answers to questions raised in nearly all marketing research projects.

12.2b What Does "Bayesian" Mean?

The second term in "hierarchical Bayes" models refers to an entire branch of mathematics known as Bayesian statistics. Although it is impossible to cover all the nuances of this literal revolution in statistical practice in one short section, we can readily convey its flavor and main advantages for marketing research practice.

For more than a century, statistical models were estimated by trying to find the "best" values of their parameters. In a regression, for example, we have to determine the best-fitting values of each coefficient (slopes and intercept). This is not challenging for linear regression, because a known set of formulas precisely determines all coefficients, along with important quantities like their standard errors. Although these formulas can take a while to compute, there is no "searching" involved, just calculation.

But, for even slightly more sophisticated models—for example, binary, multinomial, or count regression—we must literally search for the best coefficient values; no formula can produce them exactly. Searching takes time, and it is hard to know in advance just how much; the more coefficients, the more searching one must do. Even when we are reasonably comfortable with the accuracy of our searched-for coefficient values, we then must calculate their standard errors to determine significance. For large data sets and reasonably sophisticated models, performing this search can be impractical, sometimes taking weeks, or even longer. This can lead to choosing a *parsimonious* model: one with few parameters. Although simple explanations can be very useful, they can also be simplistic, and therefore misleading. Given a choice between a simple model that can be estimated quickly or a more complete one that will take years, reasonable researchers find themselves settling for the former.

Bayesian estimation
A branch of applied statistics (or econometrics) where complex statistical models are estimated using specialized algorithms (such as Gibbs sampling or MCMC [Markov chain Monte Carlo]) for sampling from the parameters' distributions. Bayesian estimation can be difficult to perform, but it is extremely powerful and allows some models to be estimated that would be impossible using other means.

Bayesian estimation short-circuits this entire strategy. There is no search for the best parameter values. Instead, one *guesses* at the value of one parameter, guesses at the next, and keeps this guessing process going many tens of thousands of times. Magically, this produces not only the best parameter values but much useful information besides.

Markov chain Monte Carlo (MCMC)
A common algorithm used in Bayesian analysis of statistical models, it allows the researcher to efficiently estimate models with a large number of parameters.

The key is that this "guessing" is not arbitrary, but rather, it is done according to a rigorous set of guidelines and strategies that go by the acronym "MCMC," for "**Markov chain Monte Carlo.**" Although it sounds like a czar on a gambling binge, in reality it is a way to decide how to make these guesses, whether each should be "accepted" or "rejected," and then how the next guess should be generated. The subject is highly technical and requires a good deal of sophisticated mathematics, which is one reason why everyone learns "classical" statistics (like all the methods in this text) first. But modern software can take much of the heavy lifting out of using Bayesian methods, and in so doing makes it possible to solve problems that would have been unthinkable with the sort of "searching" for parameters that dominates classical statistics.

priors
In a Bayesian statistical analysis, priors represent the researchers' beliefs about model quantities (parameters) before any data are collected. After data are collected, the priors are "updated" to form *posteriors*, on which all statistical inference is based.

You may be wondering how this "guessing" proceeds in MCMC, and how it can ever give us the parameter values we seek. The general procedure operates along the following lines:

1. We make some assumptions about what our parameters look like, called "**priors.**" These can be extremely weak assumptions, such as "my parameters are somewhere between negative one million

and a million," or that they are positive. Or, we can make no assumptions at all, if we truly have no idea. We also randomly pick a set of "starting values" for all parameters.

2. We now start making guesses for each parameter *assuming that all other parameters have been correctly determined*. This may seem odd, because our starting values were random, but it is the right way to do it.
3. We then see whether our parameter guess was a good one (based on how well it explains the data). If it is better than the estimate for that parameter we already have, we keep it. If it is not, we flip a coin (not a fair coin, but the details are technical, and the computer sets up all the flips) and discard it if the coin turns up tails. (You may wonder why we do not get rid of it if it is "worse," but that happens to be the key insight of the technique!)
4. We then move on to the next parameter, assuming that the guess we just made for the last one is exactly right, and repeat this guessing procedure.
5. We cycle through all the parameters in this manner, usually at least 10,000 times each. Each time, we either accept or reject our guess. Over the many trials, we wind up with a large number of different "accepted" guesses.

After this, we are done. It can be rigorously proved that the values we obtain for each parameter in this way represents the *distribution* for that parameter; this is always called the "**posterior distribution**." And, if we want the "best" value, we just look at the highest point of the posterior distribution. Everything else about the parameter—and we mean literally everything—can be easily calculated from this distribution. Most important, it lets us know how "tightly" a parameter is estimated, simply by looking at its posterior distribution.

posterior distribution
In a Bayesian statistical analysis, the distribution of some parameter *after* data have been observed; the *prior* is updated by the data to become the *posterior*.

If this sounds complicated, it is. It can require a good deal of computer time—sometimes many hours, or even days—and both skill and patience. But, in real-world marketing applications, it allows us to estimate statistical models that would otherwise be entirely out of reach. In particular, the heterogeneous models that are now quite standard in marketing research would be unthinkable without Bayesian methods.

12.2c Hierarchical Bayes Models Revisited

To reiterate, an HB model is simply a hierarchical model that is estimated by Bayesian methods. Rarely has a marriage of two methodologies produced such satisfying results. Hierarchical models allow managers to deeply understand the "drivers" of the heterogeneity that is essential throughout marketing practice. And Bayesian methods allow us to estimate models with hundreds or even thousands of parameters, as many HB applications typically have.

In recent years, HB methods have, in fact, come to dominate all statistical modeling in marketing, finding especially fruitful application in studies of supermarket scanner data, Web-based purchases, and especially in conjoint studies. Whenever one can use regression of any sort—linear, ordinal, rank-ordered, binary, multinomial, count, and so on—to understand the structure of data, HB methods can be applied to make the resulting individual level analysis richer and more powerful. The more consumers' viewpoints and values vary across the population, the greater the gains possible by suitably modeling heterogeneity using hierarchical Bayes techniques.

We note in closing that HB can be highly demanding in terms of computational resources, and typically requires personnel with specific and extensive expertise in the method. The recent advent of "ready to wear" HB software, along with the steady exponential upswing in processor power, should dramatically fuel the method's application in the coming decade.

Our capstone application for this chapter will show how hierarchical Bayes techniques can be used to analyze a large marketing data set. It appears just after the next section and should be studied in concert with the material presented on HB methods.

12.3 Sample Selection Bias and Corrections

Statistics and marketing research texts—including this one—admonish readers to always collect a "random sample" from the population of interest. Although it is generally acknowledged that this is easier said than done, practically all statistical analysis proceeds from the premise that the sample has, in fact, been selected well, that is, at random. It is far more common in field data for the sample to display some form of *selectivity* or *selection bias*, meaning that the nonrandomness of the sample has meaningfully distorted the object of the researcher's interest. It is important to note that a sample being collected non-randomly does not necessarily constitute a bias: for example, interviewing shoppers who visit a particular store on Wednesday afternoons may yield substantively identical results to a fuller sample from all week-day afternoons; surveying people with dark brown hair is unlikely to have a great effect on collected political opinions; and so forth. But it is rare that an overt selection bias has *no* effect on a study. It is therefore crucial to understand what selection biases look like and, if possible, how to statistically correct for them. *Marketing Research Focus 12-1* presents a variety of such biases as they occurred in polling and medical research.

Marketing Research Focus 12.1

Selection Biases in the Media and Medical Research

Even surveys designed by experts can exhibit signs of selection bias, sometimes seriously enough to call the main results into question. "SLOP," an acronym for "Self-Selected Listener Opinion Polls" coined by Norman Bradburn, is a pejorative reference to research that relies on selection bias to obtain suspect samples. All of us are familiar with TV and radio polls that recruit responses from among their dedicated listeners and fail to represent anything like a cross section of mainstream opinion. A notorious example is CBS's call-in poll in the wake of one of President George H. W. Bush's "State of the Union" addresses. An impressive sample of more than 300,000 callers participated, and the obvious potential for self-selection was downplayed in the media, including by the *Washington Post.* However, a more scientific poll of more than 1200 *randomly* selected adults painted a different picture: the two polls each consisted of nine questions, but their results differed by more than 10 percent for seven of them and by more than 20 percent for two. In other words, despite a sample in the hundreds of thousands, the self-selection bias was severe. Sample size alone does nothing to correct for selection bias and can, on occasions, exacerbate it.

Among the most famous survey research in history is that of sexologist Alfred C. Kinsey. He gathered much of his data from surveys given to people who chose to attend his lectures and to prison inmates; these groups hardly ran the gamut of American demographic segments. Men, particularly Caucasian men, were also dramatically overrepresented. Among the most contentious findings were those concerning the prevalence of same-sex attraction, with subsequent researchers placing the figure at roughly one third to one fourth of the oft-quoted 10 percent attributed to Kinsey. Given the sample selection artifacts and the degree of social stigma involved, it is difficult to know what the "true" proportion might actually be, or how to go about obtaining a sample that avoids self-selection bias while obtaining accurate information from all participants.

One would imagine that medical research would exhibit the highest standards of proof, given the stakes involved: the well-being of the patient. Dr. Edzard Ernst reports on using a highly unconventional potential cancer treatment:

> Whenever I gave mistletoe injections, the results seemed encouraging. But young doctors are easily impressed, and I was no exception. What I didn't appreciate then was a relatively simple phenomenon: the hospital where I worked was well known across Germany for its approach; patients went there because they wanted this type of treatment. They were desperate and had very high expectations, and expectations can often move mountains, particularly in relation to subjective experience and symptoms. We call this 'selection bias.' It can give the impression that a therapy causes a positive health outcome even when it has no positive action of its own.

Such selection biases operate in tandem with "placebo effects," which can influence anyone, and refer to the available patient, treatment, and physician sample. The patients who came were not randomly selected from all cancer patients, their treatment was not randomly selected from a set of potential treatments, and even their doctors were selected based on their willingness to provide and believe in the efficacy of such treatment. Today, it is universally acknowledged that we do not collect information on subjective well-being only from such patients but rather conduct *randomized, double-blind trials,* where patient, treatment, and physician assignment is random and no one knows "who got what" until all the data are in and rigorously analyzed.

Sources: Carroll, Robert Todd (2005), *Becoming a Critical Thinker: A Guide for the New Millennium.* Boston, MA: Pearson (2nd edition).
Morrin, Richard. "Call-In Polls: Pseudo-Science Debases Journalism." *Sacramento Bee,* Feb. 12, 1992, p. B11.
Ernst, Edzard (2004, December 21), "Medicine Man." *The Guardian.* Available at: http://www.guardian.co.uk/g2/story/01377721,00.html.
Shermer, Michael (2004), *The Science of Good and Evil.* New York: Owl Books.

Let us first rule out the most overt forms of selection bias, where manipulations are performed to remove certain cases for dubious reasons. Researchers who exclude participants because their answers do not conform to their theory are committing fraud, even if these exclusions are based on unconscious biases. This is one reason why medical researchers are scrupulous about not informing doctors in a clinical trial whether a patient is getting the "real" treatment or a placebo: even trained physicians can unwittingly manipulate the results of a trial based on what is "supposed to" happen. These sorts of selection biases are relatively easy to prevent, as long as researchers follow well-established experimental procedures.

A more common type of selection bias occurs when, despite our best precautions, the sample made available fails to match the population in a way that affects the substantive results of the research. Researchers have identified numerous ways in which selection biases can come about. Although no such list can be exhaustive, the main culprits can be classified and summarized as follows.

12.3a Data-Based Selection Biases

Ad Hoc Rejection

Data are deemed "bad" using arbitrary criteria, often as they come in, instead of using explicitly stated or previously agreed-upon standards. ("This value looks bad, so we will leave it out.")

Endpoint Selection

Data-collection begins as soon as data fall above (or below) an acceptable threshold, after which they are likely to go in the other direction, yielding an inaccurate trend. ("These values are starting to look good, so we will begin recording them.")

Premature Termination

A trial may be terminated when its results appear to be "clear," either positively or negatively, without waiting the full prescribed period required to achieve stated statistical power. ("It is pretty clear this is working, so we will stop the project now.")

12.3b Participant-Based Selection Biases

Unequal Selection Criteria

Trial participants are prescreened based on the *outcome* variable. For example, choosing grossly overweight people for a trial of a weight loss drug, but using people of normal weight for the "control condition."

Drop-Out Bias

The data of any participants who did not complete a survey, trial, or other data-collection instrument are excised. Those who fail to complete a survey may not find the subject intriguing, and those who drop out of a trial may find the tested treatment is not working, in both cases skewing results.

Self-Selection

When respondents can decide whether or not to participate, that decision can be correlated with constructs under study. For example, car enthusiasts are far more willing to complete an auto survey and to respond enthusiastically to new, innovative products; those who simply do not care will choose not to participate.

12.3c Study-Based Selection Biases

"File Drawer Effect"

Multiple, related studies are performed, and only those that support the favored hypotheses are reported. The following ironic remark makes this clear: "I had to run that study 20 times until I got a significant result!" This is exactly what one would expect by chance alone, if the hypothesized phenomenon were false (i.e., the null hypothesis of "no effect" were true) and $\alpha = .05$.

"Data Mining" or "Fishing"

Huge numbers of analyses are performed, and the most significant results are presented as if they were the only *a priori* hypotheses. If one regresses everything on everything else, *something* will be strongly significant, by chance alone. (Not to be confused with the legitimate practice, also known as data mining, of combing large databases for useful relationships.)

Generally speaking, selection biases are most problematic when items are selected based on values of the outcome variable, that is, what we wish to study. If we want to understand what helps firms achieve profitability, we cannot study *only* profitable firms; if we wish to know what kinds of marketing expenditures lead to share growth, we cannot restrict our attention *only* to the 50 firms with greatest growth (or to the 50 with the smallest).

Let us try to envision why this should be the case, in a simple regression set-up, again using our Marketing Research Student data set. If we perform a simple linear regression of Y = weight on X = height, recall from previous chapters that we obtain the result shown in Figure 12.9, based on the full data set ($n = 448$).

The quantity of interest is how much weight increases for each unit (1 inch) increase in height, and our answer is $b = 6.55$ (pounds/inch). Suppose that instead of collecting data from everyone, we were somehow biased against subjects shorter than 71 inches. That is, we "selected on" X = height and included data only for the $n = 132$ people in our sample who were 71 inches or taller. Our result would look like Figure 12.10.

Our quantity of interest, the slope, would now be $b = 6.00$ (pounds/inch), a bit below the estimate of 6.55 based on the full sample. (Whenever we take a new sample, we should expect a different result for each *estimated* coefficient, *b*. This one is likely lower because of several outliers with large values for height and lower-than-expected values for weight. Omitting these three outliers from *both* the full ($n =$ 448) and reduced ($n = 132$) data sets changes the slope estimates to 6.62 and 6.58, respectively, that is, to nearly identical values. Outliers have more clout, often called "leverage," in smaller data sets.)

So, we see that "selecting on" the *independent* variable does not necessarily introduce any biases into what we wish to measure. Is this true if we select on the *dependent* variable? Let us choose a cutoff for Y = weight that produces a similarly sized subsample. Considering only those subjects with weight greater than 170 pounds yields a new sample of size $n = 140$. Our scatterplot and regression results come out as shown in Figure 12.11.

This is a dramatically different result! We have now estimated the quantity of interest, the change in Y = weight when X = height increases by one unit, to be $b = 2.72$, less than half its value in either of the previous regressions, even the one where we "selected on X" (and, if we remove the same outliers as we did before, the coefficient is actually further reduced, to $b = 2.31$).

Figure 12.9 **Linear Regression of *Y* = Weight on *X* = Height**

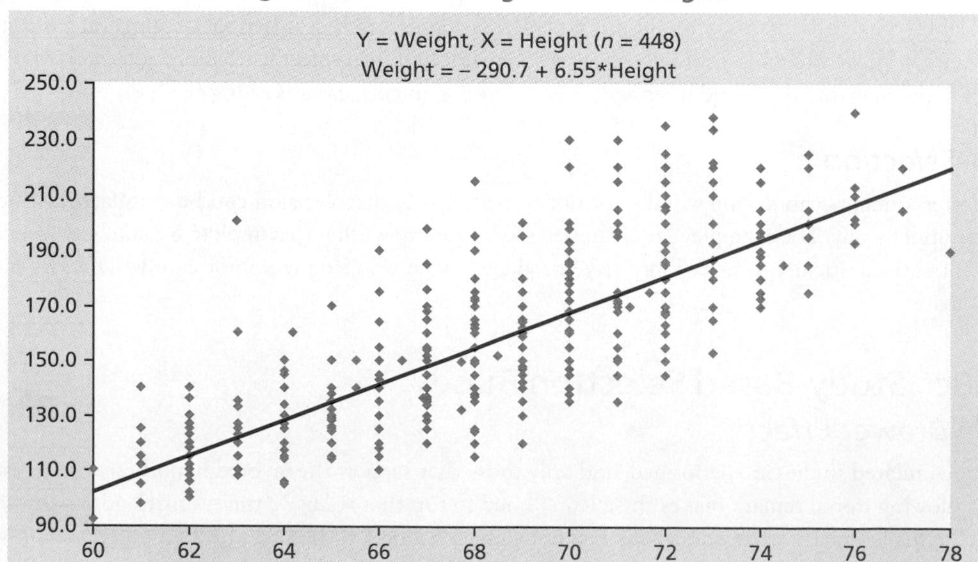

Figure 12.10 "Selecting on *X*" Has Little Effect in Regression of *Y* = Weight on *X* = Height

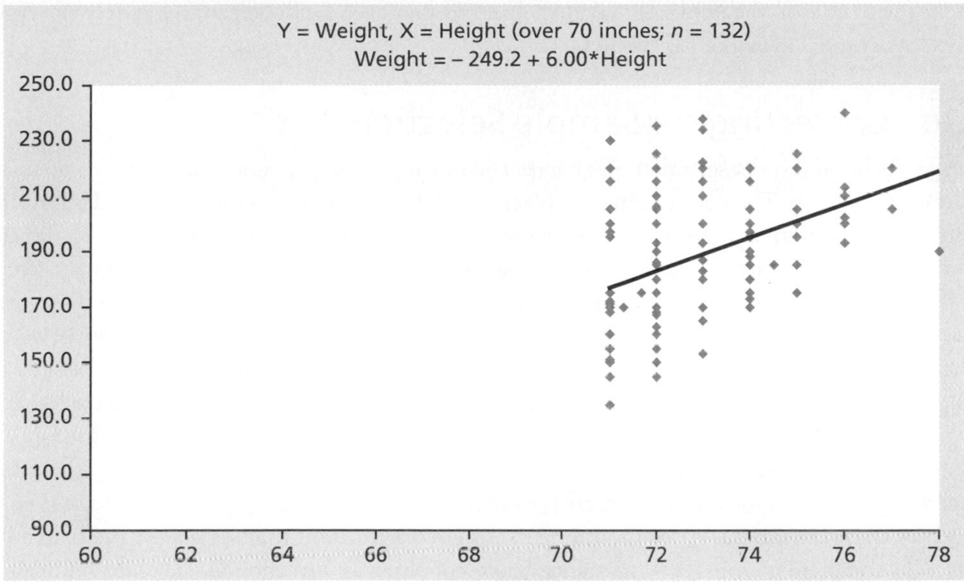

The key point is this: *never make decisions to allow or disallow items into a sample based on your study's "outcome variable," or anything clearly associated with it.* If you want to see what affects purchase, you cannot look at just heavy users; if you wish to assess effective marketing activities, you cannot analyze only firms that reacted to them; if you need to analyze sales dynamics, you should not look at your best years alone; and you should try not to base important decisions *only* on customers (or firms) that decided they would reply to your request for an interview or survey.

In the real world, selection biases are rarely this clear-cut. In many cases, we obtain our sampling frame from a database or vendor and cannot assess directly whether selection has taken place. Perhaps the vendor culled a list of e-mail addresses from an online discussion group devoted to your study topic, or the database contained names of people who had previously responded favorably to your product. Such information is seldom recorded or flagged as a bias.

Figure 12.11 "Selecting on Y" Has a Strong Effect in Regression of *Y* = Weight on *X* = Height

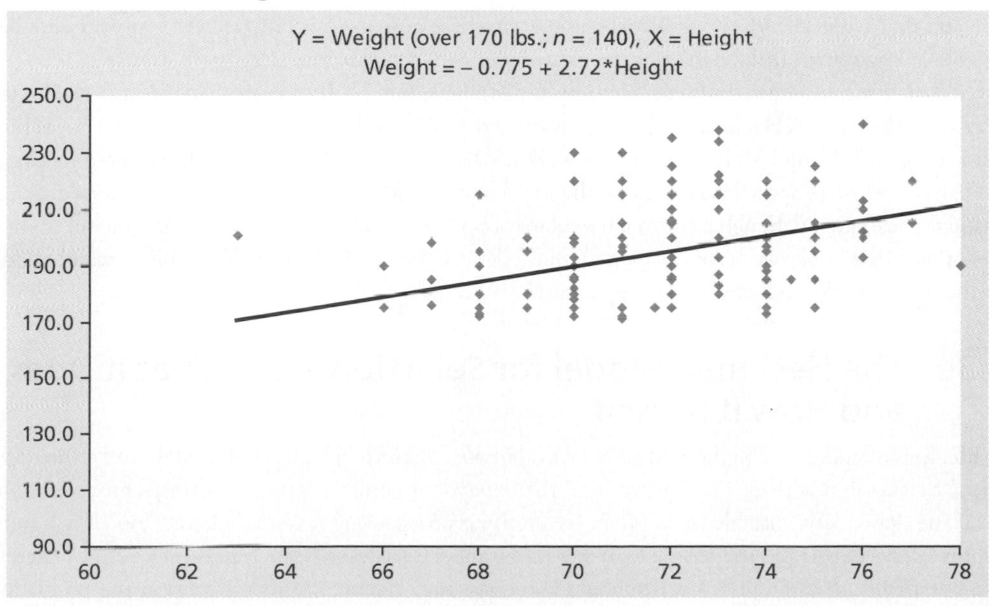

What is a researcher to do? Does this mean that we can never correct for such selection biases? Fortunately, the answer is no. In the next section, we describe a powerful set of statistical methods that can, when used with care on the right sort of data, help correct for even subtle selection biases of the type frequently encountered in marketing research practice.

12.3d Correcting for Sample Selection Bias

The most common form of selection bias comes about when the dependent variable (Y) is unavailable for part of the sample. The classic scenario comes from labor economics, which for decades has studied the effects of education on income. Labor economists long ago realized that this was far more difficult to assess for women, because in most places and times the work in which women engaged was not remunerated, so no "salary" was recorded for them. This could come about because less-educated women may be unable to command a salary that would make it worthwhile to work outside the home. That is, we would tend to observe data for women who had been "selected on" our dependent variable, salary (i.e., theirs was high enough for them to enter the labor market), and not for women whose salaries were likely to be low. (Of course, we would also record salaries for women who had no choice but to enter the labor market, if this was their sole source of income.) But the main point is that people tend to work less if they do not need the income, so some will be selected out of the market, creating a potential source of bias.

Such selection is extremely common in marketing research: firms that survive in the marketplace, people who complete a long survey, patients whose condition is dire enough to enter a clinical trial, stores that ride out a yearlong test market, families that elect to become part of a consumer or media panel, cherry-pickers and promotion-sensitive shoppers, and hundreds of other examples. In fact, *all* marketing data, simply by the fact of having been recorded (while other data were not), are subject to some form of selectivity.

Selection bias comes about when there is a process whereby individuals are divided into two (or more) groups, such as panel member/nonmember, heavy/medium/light user, and so forth, and the fundamental *nonrandomness* of this process interferes with estimating relationships of interest to the researcher. To introduce the standard statistical jargon, two distinct processes are taking place—we will call them "selection" and "prediction"—and these processes are interrelated. That is, the (statistical) errors associated with these two processes are *correlated* with one another.

This may seem a bit intimidating, but the idea of correlated errors is fundamental to selection bias, and not particularly difficult to comprehend. What it means is the following: if for some reason you are more likely (than we would predict) to *be in the sample* at all (selection), you are more likely to have a *particular outcome*. For example, if you are *unusually likely* (more so than we would predict, based on what we know about you) to complete an automotive survey, you may be *unusually likely* to appreciate a new car wax. If your family is *especially eager* to participate in a consumer panel, it may indicate yours is *less likely than similar families* to make purchases they would not want recorded. Some reflection should convince you that what selection bias is really about are these unseen correlations between your data being available to begin with (selection) and the values your data actually contains (prediction).

This was long recognized as a problem by statisticians, but a full, powerful solution proved elusive until the work of James Heckman, who was awarded the 2000 Nobel Prize in Economics for his achievement (along with Daniel McFadden, whose work on discrete choice models we encountered in Chapter 10). The model he proposed now goes by the apt name "Heckman model," and it is supported in many statistical packages. Although a thorough explanation of the mechanics of a Heckman model is outside the scope of this book, we have developed methods in Chapters 9–11 that allow us to readily convey how the model works and why marketing researchers should care.

12.3e The Heckman Model for Selection Bias: What It Does, and How It Is Used

Heckman model
A statistical model that allows researchers to overcome and correct for certain types of selection bias, like the fact that lower-performing test marketed products never make it to market to generate real sales data.

The **Heckman model** can be thought of in terms of two equations: a "selection model" and a "prediction model." Selection describes whether we "see" the dependent variable at all, meaning a binary outcome: "yes" if the dependent variable (which can be anything whatsoever) is recorded, and "no" if it is not. In Chapter 10, we developed the binary logit and probit models to describe such zero/one, yes/no outcomes; these differ only in assumptions made about the error, and Heckman models rely on the probit form, because (for technical reasons) its normally distributed error is somewhat easier to work with in this particular case. So, our "selection equation" is simply a **binary probit model**, and it can be thought of exactly as we did previously. Our binary probit model, like all regression-based models, will have some error, and we will call it ε_s, with the "*s*" for "selection."

binary probit model
A form of regression in which the *dependent* variable is binary, suitable for zero/one, yes/no outcomes.

Far simpler to understand is our prediction equation: it can be any (regression-based) model at all! So long as our error is normally distributed—the usual assumption in regression analyses—we can proceed. Regardless of the form this prediction model takes, we will make special note of its error, which we call ε_p, where the "*p*" is for "prediction."

And here is the key point: if these two models are estimated separately, their errors—ε_s and ε_p—will remain *uncorrelated* and any selection bias will remain. What a Heckman model does is estimate the selection and prediction equations *jointly* so that we can statistically measure the degree to which their errors correlate. The more correlated the errors, the more evidence that there is a selection bias. Unlike the coefficients of the separately estimated (selection and prediction) models, those of the jointly estimated model are automatically "corrected" for the bias.

Using such so-called **selection bias correction models**, of which the Heckman model is by far the most common type, can be tricky in practice. One must, for example, put the right variables into both the equation describing selection and the one for prediction. But how is a researcher to know which variables might affect whether we observe our Y (dependent) variable or not? Good bets are typically any available demographic variables; they are numerical, separately (and accurately) collected, and often can be inferred from other questions on a survey. Aside from demographics, the most common ways to guess at the appropriate variables for selection are experience and trial and error. There is no substitute for either in correcting for selection biases.

selection bias correction models
Statistical models that help compensate for the effects of a nonrandom sample caused by different types of selection bias. The most common example is the Heckman model.

Sample Selection vs. Other Sources of Bias

We caution the reader that selection bias is a distinct concept from other forms of bias frequently discussed in survey research. It should be distinguished from, for example, publication or **reporting bias**, which occurs when "uninteresting" or nonconfirmatory results go unpublished (because journals or magazines fail to find them newsworthy), and from **confirmation bias**, which comes about when researchers do not devote equal attention to both proving and disproving a theory but rather focus on demonstrating a particular pet hypothesis. Both these other types of biases are often deliberate and therefore avoidable, at least in principle. Many types of selection biases, however, are inevitable, because researchers cannot always know every demographic and control variable relevant to collecting a truly random sample from a particular population. It is only by conducting multiple studies and amassing broad experience that sample selection biases can be effectively controlled.

reporting bias
When results are selected for publication based on whether they confirm a favored hypothesis or when nonconfirmatory results are suppressed.

confirmation bias
When a researcher devotes more time, energy, or resources to supporting than to refuting a favored hypothesis, relative to alternatives.

We close our discussion with an application to Web-based product recommendation systems, one that showcases (1) a Heckman model to "correct" for massive amounts of missing data, (2) parameter heterogeneity, and (3) the use of hierarchical Bayesian estimation methods. In this application, for every piece of data with a Y recorded, there will be dozens where it was not. Although this is something of an extreme example, it amply highlights the power and usefulness of correcting for sample selection biases in business applications.

product recommendation systems
Statistical models that predict which products a target customer may like by examining the preferences and purchases of similar consumers.

12.3f Application Case Study: Understanding Product Recommendation Systems via Sample Selection and Hierarchical Bayes Models[1]

Anyone who has visited Amazon.com is familiar with its uncannily accurate product recommendations, ones that almost seem to, as some patrons put it, "read your mind." Amazon pulls off this feat by comparing your browsing and purchasing profiles with those of other customers, using them to suggest what products you may appreciate. Such **product recommendation systems** offer companies and their customers many potential benefits: to cater to

[1]Product Recommendation Application Case Study is based on Ying, Yuanping, Fred M. Feinberg, and Michel Wedel (2006). "Leveraging Missing Ratings to Improve Online Recommendation Systems." *Journal of Marketing Research*, Volume: 43, Issue: 3; August 2006; Page(s): 355–365.

individual preferences, to expand consumers' "social networks" by leveraging the tastes of like-minded others, and to save customers time by quickly locating what they might like. This last benefit can be enormous for products such as books and movies that are difficult to evaluate from descriptions alone and for which there are seemingly endless choices.

Recommendation systems usually consider all the products that customers have rated and purchased. But customers evaluate only products they have experienced; rarely is a customer familiar with even a small fraction of an e-tailer's films or books, which can number in the millions. Viewed from that perspective, each customer's ratings have a stunningly large proportion of *missing data:* all the items that have *not* been evaluated.

As discussed in the section on selection bias (Section 12-3), ignoring this missing data can be problematic, particularly when it is so prevalent. We could safely ignore it if we believed that selection (providing a rating for a product) and prediction (the actual rating itself) had nothing to do with one another. But this makes little sense; people tend to rate things for a reason. For example, if you do not think you will like something, you will not try it, and therefore also not rate it. So, there is a common belief ("I won't like it") influencing both selection and prediction; assuming they are unrelated—that is, uncorrelated—would be a mistake.

So, to understand consumer product ratings, we need to rigorously account for selection bias: one model for *whether* a product is rated (selection), another for *how* it is rated (prediction), and some correlation between their errors. (Recall that, the larger this error correlation, the greater the potential selection bias.) Our model should also allow for heterogeneity, because different people react differently to marketing inducements and have distinct product preferences.

We can illustrate these ideas using a famous data set, the "EachMovie Data," encompassing ratings of thousand of films by hundreds of thousands of consumers. (For our analysis, we will consider a random sample of $n = 2432$ customers and focus on the 78 movies rated at least once by those in our sample.) Ratings were made on 1–6 "star" scale, so a tiny snippet of the data set looks rather like Table 12.2.

Note that most of the data in Table 12.2 is missing, but this is just for illustration; in the real data set, about 93.9 percent of the ratings are missing! Clearly, this vast "missingness" is an essential feature of recommendation system data, one that marketing researchers should not simply ignore.

We need some information to help predict what our customers will like, and also some information about the customers themselves. For each of our movies (78 in the sample), we know its genre: action, animation, foreign, classic, comedy, drama, family, horror, romance, thriller. For each customer ($n = 2432$), age and gender have been recorded. To understand the products (movies) and customers, we will want our statistical models to indicate the influence of all the different genres and also of the customer characteristics available to us.

To account and correct for potential selection biases, we use a Heckman model (see Section 12-3e), consisting of a binary probit regression for "selection" and an ordinal probit regression for "prediction" (because ratings are on a 1–6 scale; Chapter 10 covers both these model types in detail). Because we must account for heterogeneity, ours is an HB model, and we estimate it using MCMC techniques. Our model therefore exemplifies the three advanced topics discussed in this chapter: heterogeneity, hierarchical Bayes, and sample selection. The estimation results are provided in Table 12.3.

Table 12.2 **Example of Consumer Ratings Data**

	Products						
Customers	**P1**	**P2**	**P3**	**P4**	**P5**	**P6**	**etc.**
C1	5	—	1	3	—	4	etc.
C2	—	—	6	2	3	—	etc.
C3	4	2	—	—	—	6	etc.
C4	1	5	3	—	6	3	etc.
C5	6	—	6	—	2	—	etc.
C6	—	—	2	5	4	—	etc.
etc.	etc.	etc.	etc.	etc.	etc.	etc.	etc.

Table 12.3 **Hierarchical Bayes Sample Selection Model for Movie Ratings Predictions**

	Selection Distribution		Prediction Distribution	
	Mean	**Std Dev**	**Mean**	**Std Dev**
Heterogeneous across Customers				
Action	0.854	0.346	0.772	0.445
Animation	0.809	0.345	2.110	0.389
Art, Foreign	−0.523	0.362	1.462	0.809
Classic	−2.070	1.118	1.375	0.666
Comedy	0.233	0.263	0.531	0.415
Drama	0.117	0.279	0.506	0.698
Family	0.585	0.088	−0.389	0.263
Horror	0.395	0.398	0.312	0.905
Romance	0.594	0.232	0.562	0.510
Thriller	−0.607	0.602	−0.053	0.188
Heterogeneous across Movies				
Age	−0.046	0.122	0.035	0.176
Gender (M = 1; F = 0)	−0.022	0.170	0.123	0.176
Error Correlation	0.105			

Note that for each variable (genres and demographics) we have a *distribution* of parameters (see Figure 12.5 for an exact depiction of this continuous, single-humped form of heterogeneity). Not only do we know the *mean* of the parameters for our sample, we also know the standard deviation, indicating the degree of heterogeneity: the larger the standard deviation, the more variation there is in sensitivity to that particular variable.

The richness of the HB model allows us to explore several types of differences systematically: (1) for genres, (2) for demographics, (3) for individuals, (4) between selection and prediction (rating) behavior. As we discuss each of these in turn, we encourage readers to match up the conclusions with the evidence for them in Table 12.3.

Differences across Genres

There are major differences in how well each movie genre is liked (rated) overall. Family-oriented movies are not well rated, nor are thrillers. By contrast, animation, art/foreign, and classic movies are far better-received, on average. However, although classic movies are *rated* very highly, they are *selected* less frequently than any other genre type, by a wide margin (as evidenced by the large negative coefficient, −2.07, for "selection"). This may indicate a core constituency who, although small in number, prize classic movies.

Differences by Demographic Groups

Because the model includes demographics—age and gender—we can explore how they affect selection and ratings. Men are slightly less likely to select a movie but are more likely to rate it highly than women. Age yielded a per-year effect of −0.046 for selection and 0.035 for ratings. Apparently, older customers are progressively less likely to rate a movie at all but, if they do, to rate it highly.

Differences across Individual Customers

By looking at the standard deviation, it is simple to spot variables with highly heterogeneous effects. In terms of selection, heterogeneity is greatest for some of the least popular (i.e., least selected) genres, including classic, thriller, and family. For ratings, the pattern is very different, with greatest variation across horror, art/foreign, drama, and classic. Certain genres, like comedy and animation, had low heterogeneity for either selection or prediction; perhaps all movies in each of these genres are perceived similarly by the respondent panel. (Recall that a standard deviation of zero would indicate that the variable had the same effect for everyone.)

Differences between Selection and Rating

Differences between whether a film is rated, and how it is rated, are stark. This is clearest for classic and art/ foreign films: neither is very popular (highly negative selection coefficients), but those customers who do rate them seem to like them a great deal. That is, two of the genres selected least are rated best. By contrast, animated films are both highly selected and highly rated, whereas comedy, drama, and horror fall near the middle of the pack on both. Clearly, selection and prediction are telling distinct stories, and both need to be considered. Although the error correlation of 0.105 is not large, it is highly significant and tells us that ignoring the missing data would have led to a selection bias.

Assessing the Model's Accuracy and Usefulness

The model definitely "tells a story"—exactly what we want a statistical model to do—but is it useful in making predictions? The answer is a resounding yes. When it is used to predict which movies a *new* set of customers will like, it outperforms similar models that neglect (1) genres, (2) demographics, (3) heterogeneity, and/or (4) sample selection. That is, everything in the model really does need to be there. Although we have not included all these comparisons, it turns out that leaving *any* of these effects out degrades the accuracy of the model's predictions by at least 10 percent, and sometimes much more. Although 10 percent may sound like a little—for example, being off by half a point on the 1–6 scale, instead of 11/20 of a point—we must remember that billions of dollars of merchandise are sold annually via recommendation systems. Even small improvements can have an enormous impact on sales and profitability, and improvements as great as 10 percent, just by adopting a more sophisticated statistical model, are uncommon.

This application case study was meant to convey how a state-of-the-art statistical model can be applied to a large, real-world marketing data set. It is important to realize that each part of the model, particularly so the regression coefficients, heterogeneity, and sample selection, offered real managerial insight into what customers appreciate and how they behave. Armed with such predictive power, managers can successfully choose among potential courses of action in competitive consumer markets.

12.4 Reporting Findings and Writing the Research Report

At the culmination of any project, marketing researchers must present their findings and prepare a report to help their sponsors put them to use. Before systematically discussing how to go about doing so, *Marketing Research Focus 12.2* illustrates some of the problems one can encounter at this stage of the research process.

The final step in the research process is the preparation and presentation of the research report. In many cases, this is the most important part of the research process. If the report is confusing or poorly written, all the time and effort spent gathering and analyzing data will have been for naught. The purpose of this section is to offer broad guidance in preparing a research report, the presentation of marketing research findings to a specific audience. We shall cover both written and oral reports, because both are usually prepared at the completion of a research project. Although there are commonalities, good researchers anticipate the differences between a compelling "live" presentation and the more staid, measured prose typifying a strong written report.

For many decision makers, the only aspects of a research project they effectively process are the oral and written reports: their evaluation of weeks or months of painstaking research often rests solely upon these presentations. Regardless of the rigor, thoroughness, and soundness of the methodology underlying the report, the research will be useless to managers and executives if the report itself befuddles or overwhelms them or if it fails to make an airtight, compelling case.

Marketing Research Focus 12.2

Marketing Research Presentation Ends in "Combat"—Film at 11:00

Lisa Barnes and Carver Thomas were the marketing research director and senior researcher of a major multidivision industrial corporation, working out of the head corporate office in Connecticut. Senior corporate management had become increasingly concerned about the decreasing market share and profitability of the firm's industrial equipment division (which made road graders, cranes, etc.). The senior management of the industrial equipment division considered themselves to be staunchly independent of the head corporate office, and they had been granted autonomy on operations questions for years. However, they had reluctantly agreed with corporate management to undertake a marketing research study in the field to determine the causes of the recent general decline.

The marketing research study consisted of field interviews with customers, distributors, and industry experts, plus the examination of a rich set of secondary data that was made available. By accepted marketing research standards, the study was competently done. During the study, the research team received cooperation from division management that could be described only as highly reluctant; one division manager had indicated, "We know what the problems are, and don't need a study to tell us the obvious."

Barnes and Thomas prepared long and hard for the presentation that they were going to make to the division management. Their primary findings were that customers perceived a lack of quality in the new product lines that had been introduced 2 years earlier and that competition from new offshore entries was giving better service support to the distributors and end customers. Their presentation was superb in terms of the written report graphics, overheads, video feeds of representative interviews, and even Web-collected survey data and blog entries.

About 10 minutes into the presentation, the general manager of the division stood up and blurted out, "You researchers don't understand our markets! I've been in this business for 25 years and know our customers too well to believe these results. We are the top-quality product and service company. I know we are." At that point the corporate vice president strongly supported the findings as being consistent with corporate management's beliefs. Chaos then ensued, with shouting by the division management and corporate representative being the main mode of interaction. Barnes and Thomas tried in vain to return the conversation to a discussion of the reasonableness of the findings by discussing the method used and seeking permission to show some of the field interview videos, all to no avail.

After 10 minutes of heated words, the general manager of the division walked out of the meeting, snorting, "Leave it to us who are close to the business to handle these problems."

Presentations as dramatic as this one are thankfully rare. However, presentations are a fact of corporate life and are crucial for the effective utilization of marketing intelligence. Marketing research professionals need to be sensitive to the entrenched viewpoints of various organizational stakeholders in order to have research findings received in a manner allowing their unimpeded deployment.

12.4a General Guidelines for Written Marketing Research Reports

Researchers who are effective in report writing have settled on methods of reportage and construction that work well for the lion's share of their projects. Although these will differ by industry, client specifications, project size, and other features, the following guidelines nonetheless constitute good general practice.

Consider the Audience

Make the report crystal clear, regardless of the supposed background of the intended audience. Use only words familiar to a broad readership, and be sure to define all technical terms, if necessary, in an appendix. To render numerical comparisons easier, make wide usage of percentages, rounded-off "ballpark" figures, ranks, or ratios; it is often a good idea to designate one scenario or set of numbers as a "baseline" or "reference" case and render all other numerical references as relative proportions. Raw, precise data can always be included in tabular or spreadsheet form, either in the text or in a dedicated appendix, turned over electronically to the client. Use graphical aids—charts, graphs, pictures, and so forth—as frequently as possible. No one, no matter how numerically literate, can scan a dense table and take away the few conclusions you hope they will draw; a simple graph conveys far more by attempting to relate fewer pieces of information. Remember that you are not being engaged to tell everything you know, but to distill just the most relevant droplets from a sea of data.

Address Promised Information Needs

Remember, above all else, that the research report is designed to communicate *information* to decision makers, information they can presumably use to arrive at superior decisions. It is not meant to showcase the cornucopia of intriguing findings discovered by the research team or the scorching power of its statistical analyses; those can be discreetly migrated to an appendix for the eyes of the interested. Management and the research team should have unambiguously laid out the information needs well before the research was contracted; make sure the research report amply fulfills this initial promise and conforms to the stated objectives of management.

Be Concise, Yet Complete

Managers' time is precious, and few will wish to pore over the details of a research project: how the sample respondents were remunerated, questions used on the survey, the software used in the analysis, and the like. Knowing what to include and what to leave out is a difficult task, but it is yours, *not* the client's. Anything relevant but tangential can be mentioned briefly in the report and provided in sufficient detail in a separate document. Clients should feel that abundant proof is available for the asking but that the heavy lifting of sorting the important from the trivial has been carried out for them, and competently so.

Be Objective

You will probably face at least one situation in which you know that the results will not be readily accepted by the client. The findings may conflict with the decision maker's experience and judgment, cause a reallocation of resources within the organization, or reflect unfavorably on the wisdom of previous decisions. In these circumstances, there is a strong temptation to slant the report, making the results seem more palatable to management. Resist this temptation. There is a world of difference between presenting conclusions diplomatically and altering their underlying nature to avoid hurt feelings. A professional researcher will know how to present research findings in an objective manner (i.e., without bias) and defend their validity if challenged. Remember that physicians serve their patients best by delivering honest assessments; the same is true for marketing researchers.

Adopt a Concise, Businesslike Writing Style

Writing style is a topic for an English or communications course, and opinions differ as to what style works best for managerial communication. Producing lean and cadenced writing that effectively communicates can take years to master; here are a few tips that will stand you in good stead in producing written marketing research reports.

- Write in brisk, businesslike English. Use short words and sentences.
- Be concise. Elaborating is easy, if called for later on.
- Consider appearance. White space (portions of the page left blank) makes a long report easier to read. Graphs and charts, used to visually illustrate statistical ideas, are dramatically preferred to tables and formulas, and also help break up a complex, wordy report.
- Avoid clichés. They convey lazy, hackneyed thinking.
- Write in the present tense. Phrase actively. Do not equivocate, unless truly tentative.
- If available, consider placing short quotes from respondents ("verbatims") throughout the report. This generates "human interest," makes the report more interesting and readable, and may spark new ideas.
- Number your pages. Number your charts. Annotate all graphical elements with brief descriptions. Banish inessentials to an appendix.
- Have someone unrelated to the project read the final report through. If numerous clarifying questions arise, rewriting is required.

12.4b Report Format

Although no single format is appropriate for all situations, the following outline constitutes a generally accepted basic format for most research projects. It can, of course, be altered to serve the needs of specific situations. Do not overlook the critical importance of the "Executive Summary" and "Conclusions and

Recommendations" sections; for some readers, these will be the first, and perhaps only, sections of the report they fully digest.

1. Title page
2. Table of contents
3. Table of tables (or figures, graphs, etc.)
4. Executive summary
    a. Objectives
    b. Results
    c. Conclusions
    d. Recommendations
5. Body
    a. Introduction
    b. Methodology
    c. Results
    d. Limitations
6. Conclusions and recommendations
7. Appendices
    a. Sampling plan
    b. Data-collection forms
    c. Supporting tables not included in the body
    d. Statistical output, cross-tabulations of variables, etc.

Title Page

The opening page should present a title that conveys the essence of the study (this often requires substantial thought!), the date of completion, the name of the organization submitting the report, and the name of the recipient organization. If the report is confidential, the individuals to receive the report should be named on the title page, with an explicit indication of the confidential nature of the contents.

Table of Contents

The table of contents provides a sequential list of the topics covered in the report, along with page references. Its purpose is to familiarize readers with the report's organization and help them find the particular sections that most concern them. See Figure 12.12 for an example of the table of contents used in reports written by the internal marketing research department at a major U.S. packaged goods firm.

Table of Tables (or Table of Figures, Illustrations, and So Forth)

This section lists the titles and page numbers of all visual aids and can be placed either on the same page with the table of contents or separately.

Figure 12.12 Sample Table of Contents

Table of Contents

Background, Purpose, and Method
Statistical Methodology [aside from standard significance testing]
Marketing Conclusions and Recommendations
Research Conclusions and Summary of Findings
Other Important Findings [list subsections if appropriate]
Statistical Results
    Index of Statistical Tables
Appendix
    Questionnaire and Field Materials Respondent Contacts
Exhibits
Methodology Summary
Abstract and Keyword Summary

Executive Summary

The executive summary is a condensed, accurate statement of the report's most crucial findings. This one- to two-page synopsis is an essential element of nearly all research reports and should be omitted only if it is against explicit guidelines. Because many managers read only the executive summary, it is crucial that this section be accurate, concise, and well written.

It is important to realize that the executive summary is *not* a miniature version of the main report. Rather, it provides decision makers those research findings likely to most directly impact the decision under consideration, enabling them to take specific action. The executive summary should include, at minimum:

1. Objectives of the research project
2. Nature of the decision problem
3. Key results
4. Conclusions (opinions and interpretations based on the research)
5. Recommendations for action

Body of Report

The details of the research project are contained in the body of the report. This section typically includes, but is not limited to, the following: (1) introduction, (2) methodology, (3) results, and (4) limitations.

Introduction

The purpose of the introduction is to provide the reader with background information needed to understand the remainder of the report. The nature of the introduction is determined by the diversity of the audience and their presumed prior familiarity with the research project. A general rule: the more diverse the audience, the more extensive the introduction. Never omit critical background details, unless there is complete certainty they are universally understood (e.g., basic anatomy for physicians, principles of accounting for financial analysts).

The introduction must clearly explain the nature of the decision problem and the research objective. Relevant background information should be provided on the product or service involved and the circumstances surrounding the decision problem. The nature of any previous research on the problem should be reviewed.

Note that implications and research conclusions should *not* be placed in the introductory section, no matter how pressing they may appear.

Methodology

The purpose of the methodology section is to describe the nature of the research design, the sampling plan, and the data-collection and analysis procedure. This can be a challenging section to write, even for seasoned researchers. Enough detail must be conveyed so that the reader can appreciate the nature of the methodology used, yet the presentation must not bore or overpower. In particular, technical jargon should be avoided beyond that necessary to convey how the research and analysis were conducted.

The methodology section should inform the reader whether the design was exploratory, conclusive, or both. The sources of data, both secondary and primary, should be explained so that potential biases are recognized and future studies can replicate or expand, as needed. The nature of the data-collection method—communication, observation, or both—should be unambiguously specified. The reader needs to know who was included in the sample (in terms of geodemographic and psychographic descriptors, not personal details that could compromise anonymity), the sample size, and the precise nature of the sampling procedure.

The methodology section is designed to summarize the technical aspects of the research project in a style that is comprehensible to the nontechnician and to instill confidence in the soundness of the procedures brought to bear. Technical details should be played down in the methodology section proper and placed in an appendix for those who desire a more detailed methodological discussion. Bear in mind that many firms have dedicated research staff, many with doctoral level statistical training, who may wish to scrutinize the more technical aspects of the research project; these procedures should be provided in some detail in a technical appendix, and in great detail upon request.

Results

The bulk of the report consists of clearly explicated research findings, which should be organized around the research objectives and information needs set forward at the outset of the project. This presentation should involve a logical unfolding of information, as if you were telling a story, because this is precisely what you are doing. The reporting of findings should have a definite point of view and fit together into a cohesive whole; it should not come off as merely an endless series of tables in search of a vantage point. Rather, it requires the organization of the data into a logical flow of information for decision-making purposes. The least effective reports are those that, in attempting to be "objective," fail to convey anything action-oriented. *Objectivity refers to lack of bias, not an unwillingness to state in clear, unequivocal terms what the research implies.*

Limitations

Every research project has weaknesses. Honest researchers will communicate these just as zealously as the strengths of the project, and with the same clarity and conciseness. The researcher should, however, avoid belaboring minor study weaknesses; the purpose of this section is not to disparage the quality of the research project but rather to enable the reader to judge the validity of the study results and determine whether further research or corrective action is required. The limitations of a marketing research project generally involve sampling and nonresponse inadequacies, along with methodological weaknesses. The writing of the conclusions and recommendations section should take these problems into account, particularly so in fashioning recommendations and plans for ongoing data-collection efforts.

Conclusions and Recommendations

The conclusions and recommendations must flow logically from the presentation of the results. The conclusions should clearly link research findings with the previously specified information needs, showing how an explicit action plan can be formulated based on this linkage.

Many executives and researchers believe that the researcher should not make recommendations. They argue that the recommendations for action must reflect a blend of the decision maker's experience and judgment with the findings from the research study. Because few researchers possess this degree of experience and judgment, the researcher's recommendations may be skewed more heavily in favor of the research findings, underweighting important situational factors—such as company history, policy, nondisclosed product development details, competitive intelligence, and so forth—that seasoned insiders would best understand how to factor in.

Alternatively, others believe that the research report should include explicit, action-oriented recommendations. They argue that as long as the decision maker recognizes the context in which recommendations are made, there are clear benefits to having them in the research report. First, the researcher has been given a mandate to focus on and solve the decision problem; he or she is free from the internal strictures, bad habits, and misplaced loyalties that can derail good advice before it is implemented or even considered. Second, the researcher, bringing to bear experience from many prior projects, can appreciate management issues in a broader sense than any single decision maker in the organization can. Finally, the researcher may identify recommendations not otherwise considered by the decision maker; indeed, it is this very possibility that prevents many organizations from acting soundly based on their own entrenched views and policies.

In the final analysis, however, the action taken is the responsibility of the decision maker, and the recommendations put forth in the research report may or may not be followed. Researchers need to develop a thick skin in this regard. Their role is to conduct a rigorous study, analyze its results, honestly present findings, and offer clear suggestions. Whether they are appreciated, much less followed, is a wholly separate issue.

Appendix

The purpose of the appendix is to provide a repository for material that is not absolutely essential to the body of the report and would otherwise detract from the "linearity" of its arguments. This material is typically more specialized and complex than that appearing in the main report, and it is designed to appeal to the specialist and the technically oriented reader. The appendix will often contain copies of any data-collection forms, details of the sampling plan, estimates of statistical error, interviewer instructions, and detailed statistical tables (e.g., cross-tabulations and actual analysis program output) associated with the data analysis process. The research team should be prepared to provide additional detail on any aspect of the analysis upon request, as it is impossible to anticipate every follow-up question the sponsoring firm might have.

12.4c Presentation of Data

Whenever numerous figures must be presented or a technical process or procedure requires extensive explanation, graphical aids can be invaluable. The two most often used in research reports are tables and graphs; all else equal, the latter are preferred, due to greater clarity of meaning and broad intelligibility. Besides making the report easier to read and comprehend, graphical aids can improve its physical appearance. This section will illustrate the various ways to present quantitative data by the judicious use of tables and graphs.

General Guidelines for Presenting Graphic Aids

Usually it is best to place illustrations in-text—as close to the related discussion as possible—if the reader will need to refer to them while reading the report. If the information is supplemental or lengthy, it is probably best dispatched to the appendix.

Always introduce the reader to an illustration before you present it; a couple of sentences will usually suffice. Highlight the extremes, averages, or other aspects of the data that are important to the report's development and eventual conclusions. Do not, however, discuss minute details of the illustration; readers will find them boring and redundant, as they are plainly available in the graphical illustrations themselves.

All graphic aids should contain the following elements:

- *Table or figure number*. This permits easy location and reference within the report.
- *Title*. The title should clearly indicate the contents of the table or figure. Do not rely on internal labeling or legends in this regard.
- *Box head and stub head*. The box head contains the captions or labels for the columns in a table. The stub head contains the analogous labels for the rows.
- *Footnotes*. Footnotes explain or qualify a particular section or item in the table or figure. When in doubt, include additional detail on the meanings of tabular elements by including a separate footnote.

Data can be presented in tabular or graphic form. The tabular form (i.e., tables) consists of numerical presentation of data with row and column headings. Spreadsheet and some matrix-based statistical analysis programs allow for the construction of multidimensional tables, which can be handy when quantities are keyed to several variables, like purchases listed by household, date, and brand.

When presenting tabular data, it is often useful to provide summary information—row and column sums, averages, minimum and maximum values, standard deviations, and so on—in nearby locations to allow for easy comparison and the construction of indices. These are standard features in spreadsheet programs, and researchers are encouraged to make broad use of them.

The graphical form (i.e., figures) involves the presentation of data in terms of visually compelling shapes. The key to successful graphical presentations is, above all, simplicity: the very purpose of graphics is to allow complex or overwhelming numerical information to be conveyed in a straightforward manner. Graphics can dress up a presentation by calling attention to important points that cannot be conveyed clearly in tables or sufficiently accurately using words alone. Humans are far, far better at perceiving relationships in pictorial than tabular form, and savvy researchers will attractively present their conclusions in a manner consistent with this capability.

Some Tips on Graphical Formats and Elements

Once your data are in hand, you must select the best graphical format to explicate their most important features. This sounds simple, but deciding which format is most appropriate can be an arduous task. Pie, bar, and line charts—each universally supported in spreadsheet and statistical analysis programs—are the graphic types used most frequently in business communication because they provide direct, universally comprehensible visual representation of complex data. Resist the temptation to create your own formats; your audience should not have to digest novel graphical conceptions along with the substantive points contained in your data set itself.

Be wary of the tendency to pack excessive information into a single pie chart. Too many divisions will make the resulting portions too small to label or even compare easily. Stick to a maximum of five or six "slices" and try to group segments representing very small percentages (usually less than 5 percent) into a collective "other" category. Pie charts also do not lend themselves to illustrating the passage of time, nor do they allow comparison of more than one group of data within a single chart. If you find yourself using many pies—say, more than four—you may wish to consider a bar chart instead.

Bar charts shine when illustrating multiple comparisons and complex relationships. To compare several distinct sets of data in one chart, use a clustered bar graph, which is supported in most spreadsheet and graphical programs. Clustered bars are similar to an outline for a report, grouping general subjects together and dividing the information into specific categories to facilitate comparisons between different but related types of data within a group or over a period of time. For simplicity, cluster bar charts should be limited to roughly four groups and four types of data within each group, and each cluster and each bar within a cluster should be clearly identified through labels or a color-coded legend.

A line chart is preferred over a bar chart in certain specific settings: when the data involve a long time period, when several series are compared on the same chart, when the emphasis is on the movement rather than actual quantities, when trends of a frequency distribution are presented, when a multiple-amount scale is used, or when estimates, forecasts, interpolation, or extrapolation need to be highlighted.

12.4d Oral Presentation

Many companies require an oral presentation of research reports, in some cases a series of them, to various entities within the firm. The oral presentation is *not* a read-out-loud version of the written report. Rather, it requires extensive planning and should be carried out by personnel with the ability to extemporize, "speak the language" of management, and understand every facet of the research.

Preparation is essential. Unlike with the written report, there are no successive drafts, and small gaffes can derail confidence in the results.

Before the presentation, it is helpful to do each of the following explicitly:

- Check all equipment (e.g., lights, microphones, projectors, Internet connections, and other visual aid equipment) thoroughly before the presentation. Have a contingency plan for equipment failure.
- Analyze your audience and anticipate their expectations. How will they react to the research findings? Will they likely be in agreement, hostile, indifferent? Gauge your opening statements accordingly. It is usually wise to begin a presentation with ideas about which there is a general consensus and broach contentious issues carefully.
- Practice the presentation many times. If possible, have someone unrelated to the project comment on its effectiveness and how to improve it.

During the presentation:

- Start the presentation with an overview: tell the audience what you are going to tell them.
- Face the audience at all times. Refer to visual materials when needed, but not as a crutch.
- Talk to the audience or decision maker, rather than reading from a script or a projection screen. Use notes *only* to make sure you do not overlook important points and to keep the presentation flowing in an organized manner. Make eye contact with many members of the audience, not just those considered most "important."
- Use visual aids effectively. Charts and tables should be simple, easily read and make sense taken out of context.
- Avoid distracting mannerisms while speaking. Constant or unnecessary motion is bothersome. Also refrain from verbal tics ("uh," "um," "OK") between words or sentences. Verbal delivery should be natural and seamless.

- Remember to ask the audience if they have questions after your report has concluded and to mention at the outset that they will have this opportunity. During the question period you should:
  a. Concentrate on the question in full. Do not formulate an answer until the speaker has completed the question.
  b. Repeat the question, paraphrasing if necessary for conciseness. If it is a tough one, mildly reformulate it to allow a useful response. This ensures that everyone in the audience has heard the question, and it gives you time to formulate an answer.
  c. Do not fake an answer. Admit that you do not know but will try to find out. After the presentation, ascertain where the questioner can be reached and make sure you follow through on your promise.
  d. Answer questions briefly. Support your answers with evidence whenever possible.

SPECIAL EXPERT FEATURE

Designing Better Products by Coordinating Marketing Research and Engineering

By Jeremy J. Michalek

Prior to the Industrial Revolution it was common for a single person or a small group to be responsible for the design, manufacturing, and marketing of a new product. As industries and markets have grown, the scale, scope, and complexity of these tasks has led to a division of labor: marketing, design, and manufacturing are typically handled in different departments, both in industry and in educational and research institutions. This compartmentalization has made the mass creation of complex products and processes possible; however, it has also created new challenges in communication between the areas. Marketing researchers, product designers, artists, and engineers often seem to speak different languages: distinct scopes, terminology, goals, representations, assumptions, and incentive structures all contribute to difficulties in maintaining a "holistic" perspective when making product decisions.

A number of practical tools have been developed to help structure the process of coordinating the unique perspectives of marketing research, design, and manufacturing in product development. For example, a method called quality function deployment examines the relationships between customer needs and technical product specifications; similarly, design for manufacturing analysis encourages early consideration of downstream impact of design decisions on manufacturing cost. Although these methods are widely used in industry, they do not explicitly coordinate the many powerful quantitative decision models developed in each discipline, such as the conjoint analysis methods described in this book. For example, marketing researchers may use conjoint to determine appropriate product attributes and levels. However, if these attribute levels are chosen without input from design and manufacturing, it is as if the decisions are "thrown over the wall" to the engineering department, with the assumption that engineering will somehow deliver products with the specified attribute levels. Although this assumption may be reasonable for well-established products with few engineering trade-offs—frequently purchased supermarket goods, for example, or even small durables—it can be problematic for products with even moderate engineering complexity. For example, automotive engineers may be able to design cars with high fuel efficiency or high performance, but providing both in the same vehicle may be prohibited by physical and technical trade-offs; a big, powerful engine will not squeeze the most mileage from a gallon of gasoline.

Clearly, it is important for marketing researchers to bear these trade-offs in mind when making positioning recommendations and to actively communicate with design and manufacturing representatives throughout the product development process. Years of experience with such "concurrent engineering" and "concurrent design" approaches have helped many product development efforts evolve from the "throw it over the wall" approach toward an iterative, integrated process of give-and-take. In the future, it will be possible for engineers and marketers (and other groups) to each post their best-performing and most relevant models—like conjoint for marketing researchers—to a common computer platform, allowing them to intercommunicate and reach decisions that are optimal for the firm. Iterative coordination of such models, as a supplement to today's costly human iterations, also has the potential to speed up the product development process and to assist communication through well-defined interfaces and objective metrics, resulting in better decisions.

The conjoint examples in this book deal with data on dial-readout bathroom scales,

continued

Figure 12.13 Internal View of Analog and Digital Bathroom Scales

Dial-readout scale with top cover removed (Note analogue indicator wheel)

Digital scale with top cover removed (Note encoder wheel and display)

Source: ©Jeremy J. Michalek.

and one might have thought that there was little else to say about that market. However, the humble bathroom scale example provides a compelling story of the potential advantages of interdisciplinary coordination. Figure 12.13 shows an analog scale and a digital scale. So far, we have considered only the first, but both designs work on the same principles, transmitting force and measuring displacement. Let us see how this actually works in more detail: the force applied to the cover is transmitted to the X-shaped levers, which transfer the force to a linear coil spring at the base of the scale. The spring resists displacement proportionally to the force applied, and a pivot arm transfers the vertical motion of the spring to the horizontal motion of a rack, which lies along the center of the scale. The rack then turns a pinion gear attached to the dial so that the output is a dial turn proportional to the force applied. In the dial-readout scale, the dial is then printed with numbers, which can be read through a window in the cover; in the digital scale, the dial is instead printed with encoder markings, and a photo-interrupter measures the number of markings that pass, which is processed and then presented on the digital display.

Reading this for the first time, most users of scales are at least somewhat surprised that two designs that seem so different to consumers can be so similar in terms of engineering design, that is, "what is inside the black box." Commonality at the engineering level saves cost—fewer designs, fewer parts, fewer production lines, and so forth—whereas differentiation at the consumer level allows marketers to target a variety of market segments and deter competitors. Achieving just the right balance between the two is important and would be impossible without substantial communication between the various disciplines involved. If conjoint and other quantitative marketing methods can be coordinated with their counterpart models in engineering design and manufacturing, this optimal balance in product variety and differentiation can be determined ever more accurately, saving both time and money for the firm, while providing a superior array of products for consumers.

Coordination of interdisciplinary perspectives can be particularly important when working with products that have significant environmental impact. With growing attention on the environment in government and among producers and consumers, the set of "environmentally relevant" products is steadily increasing. Economists have long understood that the market forces guiding production of consumer goods work differently for products that impact the environment: because benefits of the product are enjoyed privately by the consumer who purchases it while environmental costs are shared publicly by all people, the market does not automatically provide sufficient incentives to reduce environmental impact. Instead, government regulatory policies are often introduced to limit impact or alter incentives. Because such policies have complex effects on consumer preferences, cost structures, business incentives, and the space of available design alternatives, some companies devote entire departments to determining the most profitable way to satisfy policy requirements. This can be a complex undertaking, requiring extensive coordination of engineering and market knowledge. For example, in the automotive industry, separate corporate average fuel economy standards for cars and light trucks provide incentives for automakers to guide consumers away from large cars (e.g., station wagons) toward small trucks (e.g., SUVs), a practice that improves corporate averages in *both* categories; however, the net impact to society is an overall increase in fuel consumption and consequently greenhouse gas emissions. Similarly, California's attempt to achieve 10 percent sales in "zero-emission vehicles" did not succeed as planned, due to lack of consumer appeal for high-cost, poor-range electric vehicles. In order to anticipate unintended consequences and avoid policy failures, it is necessary to coordinate knowledge of consumer preferences, producer incentives, cost structures, competitive interactions, technical knowledge of the design, and regulatory policy.

Finally, one caveat: quantitative approaches in all of these disciplines are only as good as the models themselves and the appropriateness of applying them in any particular scenario. The newer and more innovative a product is, the more risk it carries in interpretation of conjoint results for attributes with which respondents may not be familiar—think about the very first time you bought a computer, digital camera, or MP3 player—as well as accuracy and validation of engineering analysis models and simulations that predict attributes of the product. Thus, marketing researchers and other modelers need sufficient knowledge of underlying assumptions and sufficient experience to determine applicability of appropriate models to the problems they hope to solve.

Quantitative models, including the many introduced in this book, offer valuable predictions, recommendations, and ability to clearly define and capture knowledge. With the exponential increase in computing power, the rise of networks, and

continued

cross-disciplinary information technology, we will see ever more coordination of these modeling approaches, as well as their increasing growth across disciplinary boundaries.

Further Reading

Kusiak, Andrew (1993), *Concurrent Engineering: Automation, Tools, and Techniques*. New York: John Wiley & Sons.

Ulrich, Karl. T., and Steven. D. Eppinger (1995), *Product Design and Development*. New York: McGraw-Hill.

Krishnan, V., and Karl. T. Ulrich (2001), "Product Development Decisions: A Review of the Literature." *Management Science*, 47(1), 1–21.

Jeremy J. Michalek is Assistant Professor of Mechanical Engineering at Carnegie Mellon University and Director of the Design Decisions Laboratory, where he studies optimization methods and the influence of market forces and policy on design decision making. He received his B.S. from Carnegie Mellon and his M.S. and Ph.D. from the University of Michigan, Ann Arbor.

Courtesy of Jeremy J. Michalek.

Summary

Among the important aspects of marketing data that common statistical methods—specifically, regression-based models—are not designed to explore are heterogeneity, natural "hierarchies," and the role played by missing data.

The concept of heterogeneity comprises the different responses of individuals, or of various groupings of individuals, to the same variables. It plays a central role in marketing research because accounting for these differences is crucial in designing a suitable array of products to satisfy the market, as well as in developing effective marketing communications and incentives. Marketing research applications typically focus on capturing "coefficient heterogeneity," which refers to differences in sensitivity to various stimuli reflected by the coefficients (β) in the usual regression relationship, $Y_i = \beta X_i$, rather than to differences in characteristics or behavior.

Various types or levels of differences between people's sensitivities (coefficients) are addressed by various heterogeneity models; the two main types are discrete (also called latent class) and continuous (e.g., normal heterogeneity). A more general formulation, incorporating features of both types, is called finite normal mixture heterogeneity.

Hierarchical models consist of levels or strata of models, from simpler to more complex. It allows individuals' coefficient (β) values to be related to other quantities (accounted for by regression relationships) that help explain this individual-level sensitivity. This more richly models where the heterogeneity originates for each individual and thereby makes individual preferences more predictable overall.

Bayesian methodology allows for the estimation of complex, general statistical models. It typically begins with a set of guesses for all parameter values, then "updates" them using a variety of techniques called Markov chain Monte Carlo, whereby new guesses at parameter values are either accepted as improvements or eliminated based on rigorous criteria. Over the course of a large number (usually 10,000 or more) of iterations, a distribution for each of the model's parameters is determined, called the posterior distribution; the mean (or mode) of this distribution is often used in marketing applications as the "best" value for each parameter. Bayesian analyses are often highly complex and time-consuming, compared with classical methods, but work well on a much wider variety of problems. A hierarchical model estimated by Bayesian methods is called a hierarchical Bayes model, a powerful statistical approach that can render analyses of individuals' behavior far richer than those possible using simpler methods.

Some of the most common forms of selection bias are data-based; these include ad hoc rejection, where data are omitted because they "look bad"; endpoint selection, where data are omitted as soon as they fall outside an acceptable range; or premature termination, where observation ceases when results appear to be "clear." Selection bias can also be participant-based; examples include unequal selection criteria, where participants are screened on the basis of the outcome variable; drop-out bias, where participants quit due to lack of interest; and self-selection, where participants have taken part based on personal enthusiasm. Finally, selection bias can be study-based, such as in the case of the "file drawer effect," where whole studies are not reported if they do not support a favored hypothesis, or "data mining," where many analyses are performed and only the most significant results are presented as hypotheses. Other types of bias include reporting bias, where nonconfirmatory results go unpublished, and confirmation bias, where researchers do not devote equal attention or effort to nonconfirmatory results.

The Heckman model provides a statistical approach to correcting for selection bias. It includes two component models: one for "selection," which models *whether* the dependent variable is observed or not (e.g., a binary probit model), and one for "prediction," which can be any type of (multiple) regression model. The Heckman methodology estimates these two component equations *jointly*, calculating the correlation between their errors; a higher error correlation constitutes greater evidence of selection bias. If the researcher has used appropriately meaningful variables in the Heckman model, the resulting coefficients are *debiased*, that is, corrected for the selection bias.

A research report is the presentation of research findings to a particular audience for a specific purpose. When writing a report or preparing a presentation, it is important to consider the audience, to be concise yet complete, and to be objective. The main elements of the written report are the title page, the table of contents, the management summary, the body of the report, the conclusions and recommendations, and the appendix. Research data can be presented in tabular form but are typically more effective presented in visual graphic forms such as pie, bar, or line charts.

Key Terms

bayesian estimation (p. 580)
binary probit model (p. 587)
confirmation bias (p. 587)
continuous heterogeneity (p. 573)
discrete heterogeneity (p. 573)
finite mixture model (p. 573)
finite normal mixture heterogeneity (p. 574)
heckman model (p. 586)
heterogeneity model (p. 573)
hierarchical Bayes (HB) models (p. 578)
hierarchical models (p. 578)
intercept heterogeneity (p. 571)
latent class model (p. 573)
Markov chain Monte Carlo (MCMC) (p. 580)
posterior distribution (p. 581)
priors (p. 580)
product recommendation systems (p. 587)
reporting bias (p. 587)
selection bias correction models (p. 587)
slope heterogeneity (p. 572)

Discussion Questions

1 Can you think of marketing research applications where it might be acceptable to consider the population homogeneous? Applications in which this would be a grave mistake? What sort of products and product characteristics might lend themselves to either of these conclusions?

2 What, exactly, do marketers mean by "heterogeneity"? Is this different from people's being different in terms of their personal characteristics? What kinds of heterogeneity is marketing research concerned with and why? What kinds of heterogeneity is it *not* concerned with? Should it be? Can you characterize a very general form of heterogeneity?

3 Why is so much of marketing research focused on accounting for heterogeneity? Can ordinary, regression-based statistical models account for heterogeneity in people's response to marketing variables? What statistical models can account for it?

4 How do hierarchical models allow marketers to better explain the views and behaviors of individual consumers? Does this require considerable collection of data from the individual, say, participation in a panel, to be effective? Why or why not? What sort of information might a hierarchical model yield that would be particular useful to marketers in general? Can hierarchical models also be used to improve customer service? If so, how?

5 What types of selection bias cannot be easily avoided by researchers? What can be done to minimize these as much as possible? Where do you think researchers need to be especially careful to guard against selection and other biases in their work? Can you think of examples of marketing findings you have seen reported where selection bias (of one form or another) seems likely?

6 What do you think is the most common type of selection bias present in pencil-and-paper surveys? In Internet-based surveys? How might one use a Heckman-type model to correct for this?

7 Why is the research report important? If the research itself is impeccable, does that research not speak for itself? What potential difficulties would you need to consider when preparing a report or presentation? How could presentation affect the future use of the research and the credibility of your research team?

8 Give some general guidelines for the preparation of written research reports. Which of these apply equally to the preparation of oral presentations? Are there any special considerations for oral presentations? What skills do you think you need to work to develop or improve in order to present better written or oral reports?

• 9 Minicase

You are presenting a marketing research report related to which of several new advertising campaigns your employer, a food products manufacturer, should run for its new low-fat snack cookies. There has been a great deal of debate among the marketing managers about whether the product should take a "health" position or a "taste" position. Your research has implications for this positioning issue, as well as the test results for the copy test of ads for each position. Discuss how you would handle the following events at the presentation.

a One manager keeps interrupting to ask questions about issues that will be presented later in your report, and several questions are entirely off-topic.

b A manager devoted to "health" positioning argues that the research seems to rely on too small a sample ($n = 300$), that the sample was collected improperly (a syndicated ad testing service mall intercept was used), and that the statistical test (the *z* test) is suspect due to the lack of an underlying normal distribution in the population. These and other similar technical arguments arose when your early results seemed to question health positioning.

c A manager devoted to "taste" positioning draws a conclusion about what the strategy and execution should be, a conclusion that interprets your results improperly.

d One manager states, "I don't care what the copy testing results are. That ad will lack true impact in the marketplace. I've been in this business too long to accept that kind of test result."

e The general manager asks what decision you would make based upon the marketing research.

Review Questions

1 Why is it so important to account for missing data in statistical models used for marketing research applications?

a The *reason* it is missing tells us a lot.

b We cannot assume that statistical relationships present in our data would hold in the missing data as well.

c It serves as a control value for error calculations and comparisons.

d It often correlates with selection bias and helps correct for it.

2 The fact that women weigh less than men (correcting for height) can be verified using dummy variable regression. It is also an example of:

a intercept heterogeneity.

b missing data.

c sample selection bias.

d multicollinearity.

3 Which of the following are potentially important biases in the collection, processing, analysis, or reporting of data in marketing research projects?

a collecting data from families as soon as they buy a new car

b running a test market until share objectives have clearly been reached

c testing a new soap on people who expressed dissatisfaction with their present one

d all of the above

4 Which of the following is a more general form of heterogeneity correction than the others?

a normal heterogeneity

b latent classes

c a finite normal mixture

d hierarchical Bayes model

5 Which of the following would be a potential use of a hierarchical model applied to a statistical model of marketing data?
- **a** relating a household's promotional sensitivity to its geodemographics
- **b** relating someone's car purchase to his or her salary
- **c** understanding how store characteristics affect sales of produce
- **d** understanding how a store's aisle display affects sales of canned tuna

6 Which of the following is an example of the sort of heterogeneity marketers hope to capture in their models?
- **a** the fact that different households have different incomes
- **b** the fact that different people buy different brands of cereal
- **c** the fact that men may purchase less produce than women
- **d** the fact that certain households respond more strongly to promotions

7 A Heckman model measures the degree of selection bias in marketing data by
- **a** using more covariates (X) in the predictive model.
- **b** estimating an additional error correlation.
- **c** applying an orthogonal design.
- **d** all of the above.

8 Suppose we are regressing $Y =$ total amount spent at the supermarket on $X =$ total family income. Which of the following restrictions would likely introduce a selection bias and strongly influence the assessment of the effect of X on Y?
- **a** Including only families with more than one working adult
- **b** Including only families who spent more than $100 during their trip
- **c** Including only families with incomes exceeding $100,000 per year
- **d** None of the above.

9 Which of the following is typically *not* a major element of a marketing research report?
- **a** executive summary setting out objectives and results
- **b** a discussion of methodology, including limitations
- **c** a main body presenting detailed data in tabular format
- **d** an appendix giving details of the analysis and sampling plan

10 Which of the following is an advantage of Bayesian estimation of statistical models, compared with other methods?
- **a** It allows the use of both nominal and interval-scaled data.
- **b** It allows quicker estimation.
- **c** It calculates means more accurately.
- **d** It is able to estimate complex models with many parameters.

Web Exercise

Log in to the Online Edition of your textbook at www.atomicdog.com to participate in this Web exercise, which can be found in your Online Study Guide for this chapter.

Further Reading

Heterogeneity

Allenby, Greg M., and Peter E. Rossi (1999). "Marketing Models of Consumer Heterogeneity." *Journal of Econometrics* 89, 57–78.

Uebersax, John S. *The Latent Class Analysis Web Site* (http://ourworld.compuserve.com/homepages/jsuebersax/), an extensive, up-to-date bibliography of Latent Class methods and software.

Hierarchical Bayes Models

Chib, S., and E. Greenberg (1995). "Understanding the Metropolis-Hastings Algorithm." *The American Statistician* 49, 327–335.

Gelman, Andrew, John B. Carlin, Hal S. Stern, and Donald B. Rubin (1995). *Bayesian Data Analysis.* London: Chapman Hall (2nd edition).

Koop, Gary (2003). *Bayesian Econometrics.* New York: John Wiley and Sons.

Rossi, Peter, Greg Allenby, and Robert McCulloch (2005). *Bayesian Statistics and Marketing.* New York: John Wiley and Sons.

WinBUGS software for Bayesian computation is freely downloadable, along with extensive documentation, from www.mrc-bsu.cam.ac.uk/bugs.

Sample Selection

Heckman, James J. (1979). "Sample Selection Bias as a Specification Error." *Econometrica* 47: 153–161.

Little, Roderick J., and Donald B. Rubin (1987). *Statistical Analysis with Missing Data.* New York: John Wiley & Sons.

Winship, Christopher, and Robert D. Mare (1992). "Models for Sample Selection Bias." *Annual Review of Sociology* 18:327–50.

Marketing Research Reports and Presentations

Moriarty, Sandra, and Tom Duncan (1995). *Creating & Delivering Winning Advertising & Marketing Presentations.* Columbus, OH: McGraw-Hill (2nd edition).

Zelazny, Gene (1999). *Say It with Presentations: How to Design and Deliver Successful Business Presentations.* Columbus, OH: McGraw-Hill.

CASES FOR PART THREE

CASE 3.1 WORCESTER SOUPS

A Boston-based research house performed a study of the new formulation of Steiner's Chowder canned soup, made by Worcester Soups of Worcester, Massachusetts, and presented the findings to Harold Steiner, president of the company, in 2005. The study had also been sent to the firm's sales manager, Kirk George, and the production manager, Edward Corey. A meeting was scheduled with the research firm and the Worcester Soups management. The purpose of the meeting was to discuss the research findings and to make decisions concerning Steiner's product offerings.

The Company

Worcester Soups was a small firm that produced and distributed a line of specialty canned soup products to both the institutional and retail markets. Approximately 62 percent of their 2004 sales volume went to the institutional market ($68,526), and 38 percent went to the retail market ($42,102).

The company was founded by Harold Steiner in 1977. Steiner's father was a successful owner of several restaurants in the Boston area that were famous for their chowder. The young Steiner convinced his father in 1976 that there was a market to sell the chowder to local institutions (restaurants, hospitals, etc.) in the New England area, and he developed a canned chowder under his father's supervision. Production facilities were acquired in the same year. After losses in the first few years, the business turned profitable in 1980. At this time, Steiner decided to enter the retail market with the Steiner's Chowder brand. Both the institutional and the retail business grew rapidly during the 1980s, as did the firm's profitability. Expanded production facilities were built in 1988, and two additional specialty soup lines were introduced in 1990. These lines experienced limited success at retail but were reasonably profitable in the institutional market.

Current Situation

The past 4 years had been a period of level and then declining sales for Steiner's Chowder (6,943 cases in 2001; 5,676 cases in 2002; 5,105 cases in 2003; and 4,900 cases in 2004). Steiner attributed this decline in sales to the market entry of two new canned chowders in 2000 and 2001 (see Appendix A). The new competitors were Fisherman's Select Chowder and Cape Cod Chowder. Both brands were produced locally and appeared very similar in formulation to Steiner's Chowder.

Both of the new competitors had entered the market with a somewhat lower selling price than the Steiner's brand. Distributors were also attracted by the slightly higher margins, plus the desire to carry a competitive alternative to Steiner's Chowder. Several large retailers had advertised the Fisherman's Select brand as a "weekly special" at 99 cents per can.

Management Objective

Steiner recognized that the firm faced a serious competitive threat from the two new brand entries. Although there were several long-term issues he was considering, his immediate concern was to develop a competitive strategy to counter the sales decline of Steiner's Chowder. Specifically, he wanted to recover the lost distribution of the brand and switch customers from competitive brands back to Steiner's. This was to be accomplished within the next 12 months. Although increased distribution outside the current market area was a possibility, Steiner's immediate objective was to improve the market position of its brand at retail within the New England area.

The Research Project

In October 2004, Steiner contacted a local research firm. After a number of meetings, the research firm recommended that a series of group interviews be conducted with current users of the two competitive chowder brands to explore reasons for product usage, reaction to the brands, and perceived product differences. Through group sessions of this nature, the research firm believed that the cause of declining sales of Steiner's Chowder could be established and potential solutions identified.

The results of the group sessions suggested that an important proportion of the competitive canned chowder users preferred a chowder that was thicker and creamier than the current Steiner's Chowder formulation. Of the former Steiner's Chowder users, the desire for a creamier formulation was the predominant reason for switching. Many of these chowder users had switched to either Fisherman's Select or Cape Cod Chowder.

Based on these findings, the research firm recommended that further research be conducted to evaluate changing Steiner's Chowder to a creamier formulation. For purposes of the test, it was recommended that two creamier formulations be developed, a "creamy" version and an "extra creamy" version. These two new formulations would be evaluated in a taste test along with Steiner's current chowder plus the two competitive brands.

After several meetings on specific aspects of the proposed research design, Steiner decided to approve the project. Appendix B presents the results of this study.

Case Questions

1 What action should Steiner take based on the research findings? Justify your answer both strategically and with relevant supporting figures.

2 Do you believe that Steiner is asking the appropriate research questions? Has the correct data been collected for the questions that were asked and for those you would suggest in addition?

3 What additional research, if any, would you recommend be carried out in the future? Be specific about the analyses you could perform were this additional research available.

APPENDIX A: Worcester Soups, Audit of Retail Food Outlets

Fifty retail food outlets for canned soups in the New England market area have been audited annually since 1985. These are deemed representative of the potential distribution outlets for Worcester Soups.

Selected Tables from the Report

Table C3.1.1 Percentage of Stores Stocking Canned Chowder Brands

Brand	2002	2003	2004
Steiner	94	86	82
Cape Cod	20	36	42
Fisherman's Select	4	18	24

Table C3.1.2 Range of Retail Prices of Canned Chowder Soup (in dollars)

Brand	2002	2003	2004
Steiner	1.12–1.22	1.11–1.27	1.08–1.24
Cape Cod	1.11–1.17	1.12–1.22	1.11–1.17
Fisherman's Select	1.06–1.15	1.08–1.17	1.08–1.12

Table C3.1.3 Number of Brands of Canned Chowder Stocked

Brand	2002	2003	2004
None	3	1	0
One	34	25	23
Two	10	20	24
Three	2	3	2
Four or more	1	1	1
Total stores	50	50	50

APPENDIX B: Research Report. Evaluation of Two New Formulations of Steiner's Canned Chowder

Research objectives. To evaluate the preference for two new chowder formulations among users of Steiner's Chowder, Cape Cod Chowder, and Fisherman's Select Chowder.

Research design and procedure. Two hundred male ($n = 100$) and female ($n = 100$) canned chowder users were selected from four geographic locations representative of the New England market area. The subjects were selected using a probability sampling procedure involving a telephone-administered qualifying questionnaire. Each subject was paid $10 for participating in the test.

The subjects came to one of four test locations (local churches). They were tested individually in 30-minute sessions. Subjects were brought into the testing room and seated at stalls. An instruction sheet explained to them that they were to evaluate several samples of chowder, that the test would consist of three parts, and that they would be required to taste a total of 15 cups of chowder. Normal taste-testing procedures were followed.

The first part involved five samples of chowder ranked from "most preferred" to "least preferred." The five chowders were Steiner's Regular, Fisherman's Select, Steiner's Creamy (version 1), Cape Cod, and Steiner's Extra Creamy (version 2). The second and third parts of the test involved tasting five samples again. The samples had different code letters, and the subjects were not told that the samples were identical to the previous five. After tasting the five samples, the subjects were again asked to rank-order them.

For each subject, the test procedures resulted in three preference orderings of the five chowder samples. The preference orderings were combined to form a composite ordering for each subject, a procedure that resulted in a more reliable measure of each subject's true preference ordering.

Results

The data set consisted of 200 preference orderings of the five chowders. Table C3.1.4 presents 20 preference orderings, which are representative of the entire data set. The difference between male and female preference orderings was not statistically significant.

The data set was analyzed by calculating the average rank order of each chowder and scaling the chowders on a five-point scale ranging from most preferred (1) to least preferred (5). Table C3.1.5 presents the results of this analysis.

Recommendation and Discussion Recommendation

Change the current Steiner's Chowder formulation to Creamy (version 1), and develop a new label that makes this change conspicuous at point of purchase.

The results in Table C3.1.4 clearly indicate that the current Steiner's Chowder formulation and the Extra Creamy formulation ranked significantly (0.05 level of significance) lower than the two competitors' brands and the Creamy formulation. (Note: this analysis was carried out by the firm; a more rigorous

Table C3.1.4 **Preference Orderings of Five Canned Chowders**

Subject	Steiner's Regular	Fisherman's Select	Steiner's Creamy	Cape Cod	Steiner's Extra Creamy
1	1	2	3	4	5
2	2	1	3	4	5
3	1	2	3	4	5
4	5	4	3	2	1
5	5	4	3	2	1
6	5	4	1	2	3
7	1	2	3	4	5
8	5	4	3	2	1
9	1	2	3	4	5
10	5	4	3	2	1
11	3	1	2	4	5
12	5	2	1	3	4
13	5	4	3	1	2
14	5	3	1	2	4
15	1	2	3	4	5
16	1	2	3	4	5
17	5	4	2	1	3
18	3	2	1	4	5
19	5	4	3	2	1
20*	4	2	1	3	5
	.	.	.	.	.
	.	.	.	.	.
	.	.	.	.	.
200	—	—	—	—	—
Total	685	550	482	588	712
n	200	200	200	200	200
Mean	3.4	2.8	2.4	2.9	3.6

*The first 20 preference orderings are representative of the total sample of 200 subjects.

Table C3.1.5 **Preference Scale ($n = 200$)**

Most preferred	1.00	
	1.25	
	1.50	
	1.75	
	2.00	
	2.25	
	2.50	← Steiner's Creamy (2.4)
	2.75	← Fisherman's Select (2.8)
	3.00	← Cape Cod (2.9)
	3.25	

	3.50	← Steiner's Regular (3.4)
	3.75	← Steiner's Extra Creamy (3.6)
	4.00	
	4.25	
	4.50	
	4.75	
Least preferred	5.00	

method to analyze *ranked* data is discussed later in this text.) These findings suggest that the market position of Steiner's Chowder can be improved by a formulation change to the Creamy version, which ranks higher than the two competitors and should recapture a significant share of sales lost to the Cape Cod and Fisherman's Select brands.

CASE 3.2 EUROPEAN ALCOHOL RESEARCH FOUNDATION

The European Alcohol Research Foundation (EARF) is a subsidiary of the European Research Advisory Board. An educational nonprofit organization, EARF is located in Brussels, Belgium, and promotes reduction of the abuse of alcohol, as well as moderation in alcohol consumption among nonabusers. It delivers its educational programs in schools and via broadcast media and conducts various forms of research on alcohol consumption.

Dr. Stanton Peele, in a pioneering article in the *Alcohol and Alcoholism Journal*, presented an array of research findings regarding the cross-cultural dynamics of alcohol consumption. One such finding was that cultural factors (e.g., religion, tendency for temperance) were statistically significant predictors of alcohol consumption in Western countries. The study supports a link between alcohol consumption and overall mortality, as well as a complex set of relationships between alcohol consumption and reduced risk for chronic heart disease (CHD), among a variety of other findings.

Michelle Lafontaine, director of EARF's consumer research, became interested in using these findings in EARF's campaign against alcohol abuse. However, she was concerned about how to assess and interpret the reliability and validity of measurements applied in the research. Selected excerpts from the original article are shown in Exhibit C3.2.1, including the results of extensive statistical analyses conducted by Dr. Peele and his colleague, Deborah McComber.

Exhibit C3.2.1: Excerpts from Stanton Peele's Article*

Predictor Variables

The current study employs the cross-cultural epidemiologic model to analyze the impact of alcohol consumption on heart disease and overall mortality independent of diet. The primary predictors examined are consumption and culture. Two variables are utilized to capture the overall character of a culture. One is religion. The other is temperance versus nontemperance cultures. In regression analyses, consumption and temperance were analyzed first; other consumption data and/or policies, such as taxation, were then considered to see if they provided a better fit.

*Source: Edited from Stanton Peele, "Utilizing Culture and Behavior in Epidemiological Models of Alcohol Consumption and Consequences for Western Nations," *Alcohol and Alcoholism Journal*, 32, 51–64, 1997. See also http://www.peele.net/lib/temperan.html

Extensive research has shown that temperance cultures are strongly concerned with alcohol abuse and maintain activist approaches to combating drinking problems, because ostentatious behavioral drinking problems are more apparent in these societies than in nontemperance cultures. Temperance cultures consume less alcohol, and a smaller proportion of their beverage alcohol is wine, than nontemperance cultures. Temperance cultures also have significantly higher rates of CHD, due to a strong inverse association between societal alcohol consumption and CHD. However, the increased incidence of accidents, cirrhosis, and cancer resulting from higher levels of alcohol consumption counterbalance the cardiovascular benefits of drinking in terms of overall mortality, which may also neutralize the benefits of higher alcohol consumption cross-nationally.

The temperance/nontemperance distinction represents, of course, just one way of operationalizing the impact of culture. Other conceptualizations have been attempted, among them efforts to identify cultural factors in drinking behavior. These variables have yet to be systematized so as to incorporate cultural analysis within a comprehensive epidemiological framework. By contrast, the temperance/nontemperance classification lends itself to epidemiological analysis. The classification of particular cultures in this model may be questioned and objections based on historical or geographical complexities may be raised. However, fine-tuning (e.g., shifting Ireland from the nontemperance to the temperance category) does not change the major findings obtained by using this model.

Dependent Variables

The current study also expands the scope of the dependent measures in the model by examining behavioral consequences (accidental deaths, suicides, murder, and membership in Alcoholics Anonymous [AA]) along with health outcomes (e.g., deaths from stroke, cirrhosis, cancer, and hypertension, as well as heart disease and total mortality). The study focuses primarily on AA membership and health measures previously related to alcohol, namely CHD and cirrhosis.

Until now, the behavioral and social problems resulting from alcohol use have not been operationalized as successfully as the health outcomes. The use of AA groups per million population in the current study for this purpose is a response to this methodological challenge. Whereas estimates of the number of individual AA members at a given place and time fluctuate and may be inflated, AA groups are a more stable measure. At a minimum, AA groups express a concern about drinking behavior. But the huge cross-cultural variations in AA groups per capita that emerge from this study appear to capture real behavioral phenomena, as represented by the amount of public drunkenness commonly observed in these societies.

The current study examines the following clusters of potential relationships between culture and drinking, health, and alcohol policy (in some cases offering tests of specific hypotheses):

- Do nontemperance cultures have less affinity for AA? Does the temperance distinction help to explain the negative association between alcohol consumption in a society and AA groups in that society?
- Do drinking patterns in nontemperance cultures enhance the health benefits of alcohol and buffer the negative consequences of drinking? Do cultural variables enhance the predictive value of alcohol consumption on health outcomes in these societies? Which sources of mortality are higher in temperance cultures and are positively associated with alcohol consumption? Do nontemperance and higher alcohol-consuming cultures have lower overall mortality? Are the same general relationships between alcohol and various non-CHD disease states discovered in within-nation epidemiologic studies evident in cross-cultural analyses?
- Are alcohol policies aimed at lowering overall consumption or at changing the balance of consumption from one type of alcohol beverage to another associated with greater or lower mortality rates for various diseases?

The current study does not examine the relationship between the institution of alcohol control policies and *changes* in health outcomes. Rather, these policies are examined for their relationship at one point in time with health outcomes.

Results

The Relationship of Religion and Alcohol Consumption

The 21 primary countries in this analysis were classified as either predominantly Protestant or Catholic (there were four countries in which neither religion was dominant) (see Table C3.2.1). Catholic countries consume significantly more alcohol than Protestant (or neither-religion-dominant) countries ($F = 6.76$, $df = 20$, $p < 0.01$). The correlation between percentage Catholic and total consumption is also highly significant ($r = .64$, $p < 0.005$). Catholic nations consume twice the percentage of their total alcoholic beverages as wine as do Protestant countries ($F = 5.78$, $df = 20$, $p < 0.05$). This difference narrowed marginally, and the percentage of wine consumed declined in Catholic countries and increased in Protestant countries over a 10-year period ($F = 5.04$, $df = 19$, $p < 0.05$; missing data for Iceland). Differences between temperance and nontemperance cultures are more significant than those based solely on religion, in terms both of total alcohol consumption ($p < 0.001$) and percentage consumed as wine ($p < 0.001$) or spirits ($p < 0.005$), but not beer.

Table C3.2.1 **Temperance Distinctions, Alcohol Consumption, and Alcoholics Anonymous (AA) Membership**

Temperance-Culture Countries				Nontemperance-Culture Countries			
Country	Consumption[a]	% Protestant[b]	AA Groups[c]	Country	Consumption[a]	% Protestant[b]	AA Groups[c]
Iceland	3.9	95 (P)	784	Netherlands	8.4	24 (N)	12
Norway	4.0	94 (P)	28	Italy	8.6	2 (C)	6
Sweden	5.5	95 (P)	33	Denmark	9.8	83 (P)	22
Canada	7.1	32 (N)	177	Belgium	9.9	3 (C)	53
Ireland	7.2	4 (C)	201	Portugal	9.9	2 (C)	1
U.S.	7.2	56 (P)	164	Spain	10.4	1 (C)	8
U.K.	7.6	49 (P)	51	Switzerland	10.8	48 (N)	22
Finland	7.8	84 (P)	110	Austria	11.5	6 (C)	92
New Zealand	7.8	47 (P)	102	Germany	12.6	44 (N)	26
Australia	8.3	51 (P)	56	France	13.2	0 (C)	7
				Luxembourg	13.6	3 (C)	—
	6.6	61	170		10.8	20	25
	+/– 1.6	+/– 31	+/– 224		+/– 1.7	+/– 27	+/– 28

[a]Liters of alcoholic beverage consumed per capita annually
[b]Dominant religious group in parentheses (P = Protestant, C = Catholic, N = Neither)
[c]AA groups per million population

AA Membership and Cultural Differences

A common drinking pattern in nontemperance cultures is one in which more alcohol is consumed and alcohol is more often consumed in the form of wine at meals and family gatherings. In temperance cultures, less alcohol is consumed, but this in the form of beer/spirits and in less socially controlled environments, usually with only men present, as in bars or at sporting events. As a result, drinking leads to more acting out and overt behavioral problems of the type recognized by AA.

Consistent with this description, AA groups are more common in temperance (170 AA groups/million population) than in nontemperance (25 groups/million) cultures (but the wide variation in temperance cultures makes significance only borderline: $t = 2.04$, $df = 9$, $p < .10$; see Table C3.2.1). National differences in AA membership are often remarkable. The country with the lowest per capita alcohol consumption in Europe (Iceland) has by far the highest density of AA groups (784 per million population). The wettest country in Europe (Luxembourg) was listed by AA as providing no data on AA groups, suggesting that there were no, or very few, AA groups in that country. The next wettest country, France, has 7 groups per million population. This cultural pattern leads to a surprising negative correlation between alcohol consumption and AA groups (Table C3.2.1). There are also highly significant correlations between number of AA groups and type of alcohol consumed: Percentage spirits consumed is most positively correlated and percentage wine consumed is most negatively correlated (the negative correlation between AA groups and proportion of wine consumed appeared but was nonsignificant).

Table C3.2.2 Temperance Countries and Alcohol Consumption

Alcohol Consumption	Temperance ($n = 10$)	Nontemperance ($n = 11$)	p
Total consumption	6.6 +/− 1.6	10.8 +/− 1.7	<0.001[a]
Percent wine	17.7 +/− 6.6	43.7 +/− 18.7	<0.001[b]
Percent beer	53.1 +/− 10.3	40.4 +/− 17.1	ns
Percent spirits	29.2 +/− 11.0	15.9 +/− 6.0	<0.005[c]

[a] $t = 5.69$, 19 *df* ($df = n - 2$ for t test)
[b] $t = 4.31$, 13 *df* (adjusted for unequal variances)
[c] $t = 3.38$, 14 *df* (adjusted for unequal variances)

Table C3.2.3 Correlations with AA Groups/Million Population

AA Correlate	Correlation	R^2	p
Percent Catholic	−.28	.08	ns
Percent Protestant	.35	.12	ns
Total consumption	−.52	.28	<0.05
Percent wine	−.64	.41	<0.005[a]
Percent spirits	−.77	.60	<0.00001

[a] Not significant for percent wine; significant ($p < 0.01$) for consumption for 27-nation analysis.

A regression model that accounts for 82 percent of the variance in AA membership has as its most highly positive predictors the percentage of alcohol consumed as beer and a national advertising policy encouraging consumption of beer/wine vs. spirits (Table C3.2.4). The temperance categorization of a country's culture is also highly significant. In multiple regression including the temperance variable, percentage Protestant and AA membership are negatively related, although they are positively correlated in a simple regression. This finding suggests that in temperance societies, the lower the percentage of majority Protestants, the more AA groups appear, as an assertion of antialcohol attitudes in the face of a present challenge from a pro-alcohol cultural perspective. This might help to explain the small percentage of AA groups in overwhelmingly Protestant Norway and Sweden and the high number in the multicultural United States. With such small sample sizes, however, such a proposed interaction can be only speculative.

Table C3.2.4 Regression on AA Groups/Million Population[a]

Variable	t	p
Percent beer	4.67	<0.0005
Percent of giving beer/wine Preference in advertising	4.26	<0.001
Temperance classification	3.77	<0.005
Percent Protestant	−3.57	<0.005

[a] Adjusted $R^2 = .82$, $F = 21.08$, 18 *df*, $p = 0.00001$ ($df = n - 1$ for ANOVA; Iceland, Luxembourg missing)

Case Questions

1 Explain the difference between temperance and nontemperance cultures. Is it valid to conduct this research by first separating countries into two such groups, in your opinion? What about the categorization of Protestant and Catholic? Are there other qualitative or statistical approaches to establishing such categories for study? If you believe that some of the groupings or clusterings are not appropriate, clearly state why and how you would perform alternative groupings, given similar research goals.

2 Evaluate the research design used in the study and discuss the bases for your evaluation. What measurement-related issues could potentially lead to Lafontaine's concerns?

3 Which of the dependent variables discussed in the report were studied sufficiently thoroughly and which, in your view, would benefit from additional study? Formulate a research design for further exploring one or more of these dependent variables.
4 Discuss the reliability and validity of temperance and nontemperance as categories—specifically, whether they can be accurately assessed and whether they are sufficient for the research task at hand. Do the same for the Protestant/Catholic and the AA/non-AA approaches.
5 What conclusions about cross-cultural dynamics of alcohol consumption can be drawn from this research project, based on the research design and subsequent statistical results?
6 How could EARF use the research findings in the European campaign against alcohol abuse?
7 Some of the covariates used in the regression analyses were not statistically significant. Based on your knowledge of the problem, the research design, and the data analyses, which of these appear(s), in your estimation, to reflect small sample size, and which lack(s) statistical power? How would you interpret the nonsignificance of percent beer in Table C3.2.2, given the variables that *were* significant there? Can you suggest a more appropriate or powerful analysis?
8 A large number of statistical analyses are presented by the study authors in the course of making their case. Which of the tests seem especially critical to the main issues at hand? Which do you believe are less critical? Why?
9 Are there any additional data you would recommend be collected to better understand temperance, AA membership, drinking patterns, and other key issues mentioned in the case? How would you incorporate such data into the existing analyses, and what additional analyses might be necessary?

Sources: Williams, Jim. "Constant Questions or Constant Meanings? Assessing Intercultural Motivations in Alcoholic Drinks"; *Marketing and Research Today*, August 1991, pp. 169–177.

Edited from Stanton Peele, "Utilizing Culture and Behavior in Epidemiological Models of Alcohol Consumption and Consequences for Western Nations", *Alcohol & Alcoholism Journal*, 32, 51–64, 1997.

CASE 3.3 ASWU AND HARRIS INTERACTIVE EUROPE ONLINE OMNIBUS SERVICE

Ye Chang, the business unit director of ASWU, a major Chinese electronics manufacturer, was on his way to his office from an urgently assembled meeting of the firm's top executives. His thoughts were occupied by the decision that he would have to make 2 weeks hence, a momentous one for him and ASWU.

The main topic of the meeting concerned a product that was under the umbrella of his business unit, an MP3 player. Based on the industry projections and the internal reports available in the company, the MP3-player market was expected to experience explosive growth, especially with continuous price drops typical of the category and high-tech consumer electronics in general. The product manufactured by ASWU was already distributed across Europe, with the exception of Great Britain. The decision to enter Great Britain had been made. However, decisions regarding the mode of entry were all assigned to Ye.

ASWU made its MP3 player available in European countries through a co-branding partnership with a company whose electronics brand names enjoyed enormous awareness among European consumers, with low regional variation. The decision to co-brand was based on a survey conducted several years ago, indicating that European consumers desired the reassurance of a familiar brand name when purchasing such relatively new products as MP3 players. However, the penetration of the product category had increased dramatically since the survey had been conducted, and Ye wondered whether this penetration had gradually ushered in a change in consumer attitudes as well. After all, MP3 players were hardly a "new" product any longer. He kept asking himself what role a brand name plays in the purchasing decision making of today's MP3-player buyers, in Great Britain in particular. If the European MP3-player market was close to reaching the same level of commoditization that already dominated the PC industry, would it be wiser to enter Great Britain without a co-branding agreement and instead use the ASWU brand to identify its own MP3 players? Doing so would certainly entail lower cost and more channel control, consistent with market commoditization, if indeed this was occurring.

The more Ye thought about the matter, the more he realized the need for a new, perhaps updated consumer survey to understand the current state of consumer attitudes in Great Britain. Finding a research provider in a market he knew nothing about and completing a survey in 2 weeks seemed almost impossible. Ye entered his office and picked up the phone to ask his secretary to set up a meeting with the MP3-player brand management team the next morning.

The meeting produced an interesting idea, devised by assistant brand manager Sammy Yuke, who had been hired 6 months earlier, after completing his graduate studies in England. Sammy suggested that the survey be conducted via e-mail, saving a great deal of time. After the meeting, Sammy forwarded Ye a link with the information about Harris Interactive (HI) Europe, specifically its online omnibus research service.

Searching through the HI-Europe Web site, Ye discovered that it was a global market research and consulting company, with headquarters in London, known for decades for its expertise in strategic business and consumer research. HI-Europe's Web site touted its application of innovative methodologies and sophisticated technology, focusing on those that were Internet-based. The parent company, HI, was among the world's 15 largest market research firms, with more than $150 million in annual revenue, based in Rochester, New York, and this alone added credibility to HI-Europe's image in Ye's eyes. HI's acquisition of Novatris, a Paris-based online market research firm, added 1 million Novatris panel members, enlarging HI's European panel from 700,000 to 1.7 million members, believed to be the largest in Europe.

After reading about HI-Europe, Ye thought that the firm could be trusted to ably carry out the assignment. Now he had to evaluate whether the firm's online omnibus service was appropriate for his needs. Among all the other information posted on the firm's Web site, Ye read the following with interest.

QuickQuery™ Great Britain (GB)
Get accurate, projectable answers from 2000 people within just 8 days.
HI-Europe's QuickQuery GB is *an online omnibus service* that enables you to ask questions and get projectable answers from a representative sample of British adults (aged 16+). Although all respondents are Internet users, our ongoing parallel studies and extensive experience enable us to weight the sample to represent the GB adult population.

You'll get meaningful information for low-incidence populations or for specific target audiences. HI-Europe's extensive online panel enables cost-effective access to hard-to-reach respondents.

Here is how QuickQuery GB works:

1. You submit and finalize your questions with our online survey consultants by midday on the second Tuesday of the month and receive results the following Wednesday.
2. Your questions are transformed into an electronic questionnaire and fielded to a random subset of more than 140,000 cooperative respondents in Great Britain.
3. Eight days later, the data are tabulated and delivered to you electronically.

When should you use QuickQuery GB?
Here are a few scenarios:

- Market segmentation analyses
- Attitudes and usage studies
- Tracking studies
- Name testing
- Consumer trend analyses
- New product research
- Disaster checks

Ye was contemplating the idea of contacting HI-Europe for more details. As he prepared to call the relevant personnel there, he considered the additional information that he needed to evaluate the suitability of the survey for this objective.

Case Questions

1 What information should Ye Chang request from HI-Europe to evaluate the potential of assigning it the research project?

2 Do you believe that the QuickQuery omnibus service is appropriate for ASWU's purpose? Explain your answer and discuss advantages and disadvantages of the service.

3 The sample size of the QuickQuery service is 2000 people. Do you think this allows for a large enough sample for ASWU's survey objective? Is the sample representative of the population ASWU wishes to learn about? What information would Ye need to ask of HI-Europe to evaluate the suitability of the sample for his needs? What statistical procedures may be employed to test whether the sample is at least approximately representative?

4 QuickQuery's sample is stratified by age, gender, and region. Discuss advantages and disadvantages of a stratified sample in general and by the aforementioned criteria in particular. Would you recommend any other way to construct the sample for ASWU's survey? How?

5 The QuickQuery online omnibus standard service offers clients the option to include up to 25 questions. Design a questionnaire that addresses ASWU's survey objective and information needs, keeping to this relatively tight constraint.

6 The QuickQuery service provides clients answers to their questions for the (aggregated) total sample, broken out by standard demographic variables, including:

   a Age within gender
   b Household size
   c Marital status
   d Region
   e Social class
   f Income
   g Age and presence of children
   h Employment status
   i Education

7 Which demographic variables are most relevant for this survey? Are there any other variables that you would add to ASWU's questionnaire? Finally, are prespecified geodemographic categories the best way to segment this market?

Sources: Harris Interactive Europe Web site, http://www.hieurope.com.
"China to Lead Global MP3 Market Growth"; *Macworld*. November 3, 2004.
"Lavod's MP3 Players Boast Superior Sound Quality, Fashionable Designs"; Computex Taipei. 2005.
Alibaba global trading, http://chinasuppliers.alibaba.com > Home Appliances > MP3 players.

CASE 3.4 HOWIE'S STUDENT CAFETERIA

James Burnett was head of Whatsamatta University's (WU) food services. WU had a student population of 25,000 and a faculty of 1800. In the fall of 2004, the WU food service had opened a 24-hour cafeteria on the central campus for WU students and faculty. "Howie's" offered breakfast from 4:30 a.m. until noon, and complete hot meals between 10 a.m. and 10 p.m. It also served salads, deli sandwiches, pizza, burgers, desserts, and beverages around the clock. The food was high quality (better than the typical dormitory fare), yet priced lower than comparable food at other restaurants. Students who had meal plans through their dormitories could get deductions from their bills when they ate at Howie's, as compensation for missed meals. In addition to food, Howie's carried morning newspapers and essential school supplies such as pens, pencils, paper, and notebooks.

One year after the opening of Howie's, the president of WU commissioned Burnett to conduct a study to find out students' opinions about the new 24-hour cafeteria. The university was in dire need of office space, and if students were not satisfied with Howie's, the president was going to have it remodeled into offices. The president was most particularly interested in (1) student awareness of Howie's, (2) student use of the 24-hour cafeteria, and (3) overall student satisfaction with Howie's. Because Burnett was fairly certain that the study results would favor keeping Howie's, he decided to include questions in the survey that would help him to improve the existing services. Burnett wanted to know what specific things the students liked and disliked about Howie's and what they felt could be added or improved on.

The questionnaire for the study was designed, pretested, and finalized by the University Research Center (URC). The version that was finally administered to students appears in Exhibit C5.2. A URC computer generated a simple random sample of 1,300 students for the purposes of the study. In January 2006, these students were mailed copies of the questionnaire. Burnett purposely chose January because it was long enough after the initial opening and far enough into the school year for an optimal number of students to have been exposed to Howie's. The questionnaire was mailed with a cover letter and a return envelope. A copy of Howie's menu and two coupons for $1 off any $5 purchase at Howie's were included as incentives. The cover letter contained a request for cooperation and assured the students of anonymity. It requested that the students complete the questionnaire and return it within 7 days. Due to time constraints, questionnaires returned after 2 weeks were not included in the study.

Forty-nine percent (637) of the questionnaires were returned within 2 weeks after the mailing. Twenty of those were not usable, leaving 47 percent suitable for analysis. This was unusually high—the last university-conducted mail survey had had only a 28 percent return rate. Burnett was extremely pleased with the success of the study. He had to give a presentation to the president in 2 days, so he sat down to begin analyzing the results. Exhibit C3.4.1 is a copy of the results as presented to Burnett by URC.

Exhibit C3.4.1: Questionnaire

1 How often do you eat out?

_________ Less than once a month
_________ One to three times a month
_________ Once a week
_________ Two to three times a week
_________ More than three times a week

2 Please rank the following characteristics in order of their importance to you when you dine out. (1 = most important)

_________ Food
_________ Service
_________ Atmosphere
_________ Price

3 What type of food do you usually eat when you dine out?

_________ Breakfast
_________ Deli sandwiches
_________ Salad bar
_________ Typical "fast food" (burgers, fries, hot dogs, etc.)
_________ Pizza
_________ Complete meals (hot entrees)
_________ Other (please specify) _________________________

4 Are you aware that the University Food Service has a 24-hour cafeteria, Howie's, located on central campus?
Yes _________ No _________

5 Have you ever eaten at Howie's? Yes _________ No _________

If you have never been to Howie's, please skip to question 9.

6 How many times since its opening in September 2004 have you eaten at Howie's?

_________ 1
_________ 2–5
_________ 6–10
_________ 11–15
_________ More than 15

7 Based on your experience with Howie's, we would like you to rank the following list of items as excellent (E), good (G), fair (F), or poor (P).

Item	*E*	*G*	*F*	*P*
Service				
Friendly	_____	_____	_____	_____
Courteous	_____	_____	_____	_____
Quick	_____	_____	_____	_____
Order taken correctly	_____	_____	_____	_____
Other __________	_____	_____	_____	_____
Overall service	_____	_____	_____	_____
Food				
Appearance	_____	_____	_____	_____
Taste	_____	_____	_____	_____
Variety	_____	_____	_____	_____
Portion size	_____	_____	_____	_____
Other ________	_____	_____	_____	_____
Overall food	_____	_____	_____	_____
Atmosphere				
Cleanliness	_____	_____	_____	_____
Noise level	_____	_____	_____	_____
Adequate seating	_____	_____	_____	_____
Other ________	_____	_____	_____	_____
Overall atmosphere	_____	_____	_____	_____
Overall experience	_____	_____	_____	_____

8 How do Howie's prices compare with the prices of similar foods at other restaurants?

	Howie's price:					
	Not sure	***Much higher***	***Somewhat higher***	***About the same***	***Somewhat lower***	***Much lower***
Food item						
Breakfast Burgers	___	___	___	___	___	___
Fries	___	___	___	___	___	___
Hot entries	___	___	___	___	___	___
Deli sandwiches	___	___	___	___	___	___
Pizza	___	___	___	___	___	___
Salad bar Desserts Beverages	___	___	___	___	___	___

Overall, Howie's prices are:

__________ Much higher
__________ Somewhat higher
__________ About the same
__________ Somewhat lower
__________ Much lower
__________ I'm not sure

9 Do you plan to eat at Howie's within the next month?
Yes ______ No ______ Don't know ______

10 Personal Information:

a. What is your age? ____________
b. Male or female?____________
c. Married or single? ____________
d. Are you a full-time or a part-time student? ____________

e. If you do not live in university housing, about how many miles are you from central campus?

_______ Less than 1/2 mile
_______ 1/2 mile up to (but not including) 1 mile
_______ 1 mile up to (but not including) 2 miles
_______ 2 miles or more

f. Do you have a meal contract through the university? ___

g. Please indicate number of years you have attended Southwest (as of May 2006).

__________ Less than 1
__________ 1
__________ 2
__________ 3
__________ 4
__________ More than 4

h. Please list the first three digits of your hometown zip code: ________

Additional comments: Please feel free to make any complaints or suggestions regarding Howie's in the space provided below.

Thank you for you cooperation in responding to this survey. Please mail your completed questionnaire within seven days. A postage-paid envelope has been provided for your convenience.

Exhibit C3.4.1 : Results

Table C3.4.1 How often do you eat out? ($n = 617$)

Less than once a month	21.1%
One to three times a month	34.5
Once a week	27.5
Two to three times a week	10.5
More than three times a week	6.3

Table C3.4.2 Importance of Restaurant Characteristics When Dining Out (1 = most important) ($n = 617$)

				Rating
Characteristic	**1**	**2**	**3**	**4**
Food	47.2%	38.2%	14.4%	0.2%
Service	5.2	9.4	36.3	49.1
Atmosphere	15.9	21.2	24.1	38.7
Price	31.8	31.1	25.1	12.0

Table C3.4.3 Are you aware of Howie's existence? ($n = 617$)

Yes	97.1%
No	2.9

Table C3.4.4 Have you eaten at Howie's? ($n = 617$)

Yes	82.2%
No	17.8

Table C3.4.5 How many times have you eaten at Howie's? ($n = 488$)

1	37.1%
2–5	24.2
6–10	19.3
11–15	15.6
More than 15	3.8

Table C3.4.6 Ratings of Service, Food, Atmosphere, and Overall Experience at Howie's ($n = 507$)

Characteristic	Average score
Overall food	3.5
Overall service	3.7
Overall atmosphere	2.4
Overall experience	3.1

Respondents rated the items on an "excellent, good, fair, poor" scale. For data analysis, this has been converted into a 4-point numeric scale, with 4 being excellent and 1 being poor. This table presents the average of the respondents' scores.

Table C3.4.7 Do you plan to eat at Howie's within the next month? ($n = 617$)

Yes	20.3%
No	23.7
Don't know	56.1

Table C3.4.8 Knowledge of Howie's by Year on Campus ($n - 617$)

	Years on Campus						
Knowledge	**Less than 1**	**1**	**2**	**3**	**4**	**More**	**Total**
Yes	0%	29.7%	24.4%	18.9%	17.4%	9.6%	100.0%
No	16.7	27.8	22.2	16.7	5.6	11.0	100.0

$p < 0.005$. (All tests are chi-square.)

Table C3.4.9 Number of Times Having Eaten at Howie's by How Often Eaten Out ($n = 488$)

	Eating-out Frequency					
Number of Times Eaten at Howie's	Less than Once a Month	3 Times a Month	Once a Week	2–3 Times a Week	More than 3 Times a Week	Total
1	32.0%	33.1%	29.3%	3.3%	2.3%	100.0%
2–5	26.3	36.4	26.3	4.2	6.8	100.0
6–10	10.6	39.4	24.5	19.1	6.4	100.0
11–15	0	38.2	28.9	22.4	10.5	100.0
More	0	5.3	26.3	26.3	42.1	100.0

$p < 0.005$.

Table C3.4.10 University Meal Contract by Number of Times Eaten at Howie's ($n = 488$)

	Times Eaten at Howie's					
Meal Contract?	1	2–5	6–10	11–15	More	Total
Yes	13.8%	32.4%	35.7%	10.0%	8.1%	100.0%
No	22.2	30.6	33.5	9.7	4.0	100.0

$p < 0.1$.

Table C3.4.11 Distance from Central Campus by Having Eaten at Howie's ($n = 545$)

	Distance from Campus				
Eaten at Howie's	In Dorm	Less than 1 Mile	1 Mile	1–2 Miles	2+ Miles
Yes	90.0%	84.5%	85.6%	65.6%	15.0%
No	10.0	15.5	14.4	34.4	85.0
Total	100.0%	100.0%	100.0%	100.0%	100.0%

$p < 0.005$

Table C3.4.12 Overall Experience by Intent to Eat at Howie's in the Next Month ($n = 507$)

	Intend to Eat at Howie's in next month (% of those who gave yes/no responses)			
Rating of Overall Experience	Yes	No	Don't Know	Total
Excellent	70.7	29.3	0	100
Good	63.2	36.8	0	100
Fair	6.4	93.6	0	100
Poor	0	100.0	0	100

$p < 0.005$.

Table C3.4.13 Having Eaten at Howie's by Gender, % ($n = 617$)

Eaten at Howie's	Male	Female
Yes	42.0	58.0
No	26.4	73.6

$p < 0.005$.

Table C3.4.14 Type of Food Usually Eaten When Dining Out by Gender, % ($n = 617$)

Food Type	Male	Female
Breakfast	14.0	4.0
Deli sandwiches	12.0	10.1
Salad bar	7.9	18.9
Typical fast food (burgers, fries, hot dogs, etc.)	19.0	13.1
Pizza	26.0	29.9
Complete meals (hot entrees)	21.1	24.0
Other (please specify)	0	0
Total	100.0	100.0

$p < 0.005$. Totals may not add to 100% due to rounding error.

Case Questions

1. Do the questions included in the questionnaire address the information needs of WU's president and Burnett? What additional questions, if any, would you recommend to be included in the questionnaire, and why? If indicated, design an updated questionnaire, or integrate the newly proposed question into the structure of the existing questionnaire.
2. Construct a codebook for the questionnaire in Exhibit C3.4.1. What is its purpose? Do any of the questions present especial challenges in terms of coding? If so, how might those questions be recoded without greatly altering their intent?
3. Twenty of the returned questionnaires were not usable. What potential reasons might have required that these questionnaires be excluded from the database? Place each example in the context of the current case. What steps could have been taken to ensure that the unusable questionnaires were readily identified? If there were a database allowing one to determine which respondents did not return their questionnaires, would it be ethical to identify them specifically? If they did give their explicit consent to be so identified, can you think of any way to use demographic information about these nonresponders to assess their impact on the survey's results?
4. Evaluate the analysis performed by Burnett to cover the objectives of the survey, and explain your answer. Were the data analysis techniques used appropriately? Examine each table, checking for statistical flaws. For each listed statistical test (usually indicated by a p-value), state what sort of test you believe was done and whether this was appropriate, given the form of the question(s) that yielded the associated data.
5. Are there any other analysis data techniques that could be useful in this survey? For which variables in particular? List your additional recommendations, if any, specifying the purpose of each.
6. In your opinion, which tables should be included in the presentation as it stands, which should not be used at all, and which require further elaboration, given the survey's objectives? Explain your recommendations in detail, with particular attention to how the tabular data help support key decisions.
7. Considering Exhibit C3.4.1, what conclusions can be drawn from each of the included tables? Based on these tables, taken together, write a management-focused summary of the study's major findings. Try to link these findings to specific quantities in the tables.
8. Do you believe there is a need for further investigation? If so, be specific about what type of follow-up studies are indicated, and sketch their information needs and preliminary designs.

CASE 3.5 THE DECLINE OF RURAL HOSPITALS AND THE RISE OF URBAN HMOS

Introduction

The advent of managed health care in the United States had raised major issues for the management of small local hospitals. There was concern that much of such hospitals' patient base would join urban-based health maintenance organizations (HMOs), bypassing their local hospitals for their primary medical care. This would have devastating financial consequences to such hospitals and limit their capacity to serve their remaining rural patients.

Marketing Research Study

A marketing research study of this issue was undertaken to determine the driving factors behind the choice of local rural versus urban hospital. A survey of 500 rural consumers of health care services was conducted by mail, and a total of 260 usable questionnaires were obtained. One key area of data in the survey was consumer

Table C3.5.1 Factor Analysis Results

	Factor 1	Factor 2	Factor 3	Factor 4
Staff courtesy (AH)	.790			
Staff compassion (AH)	.809			
Access (AH)	.771			
Building condition (AH)	.679			
Dependability (AH)	.648			
Quality of medical care (AH)	.669			−.273
Staff competency (AH)	.640			
Confidentiality (AH)	.649			
Hospital reputation (AH)	.495			−.373
Emergency care (AH)	.443			−.403
Staff compassion (LH)		.846		
Staff courtesy (LH)		.786		
Dependability (LH)		.796		
Staff competency (LH)		.733		
Hospital reputation (LH)		.666		
Emergency care (LH)		.645		
Quality of medical care (LH)		.659	.331	
Access (LH)		.682		
Building condition (LH)		.563		
Confidentiality (LH)		.494	.241	
Level of technology (LH)			.756	
Range of services (LH)			.702	
Size of hospital (LH)	.317		.333	
Level of technology (AH)				−.915
Range of services (AH)				−.888
Size of hospital (AH)				−.403
% of variance	32.10	24.40	3.30	3.10
Eigenvalue	8.34	6.35	.86	.82

LH = Local Hospital
AH = Alternative Hospital

perceptions of two potential hospitals: their local hospital and a more distant urban hospital. The comparison was based on a list of quality-related attributes believed to be related to the consumer's evaluation of overall quality. Attributes were rated on a 7-point scale with anchor points of "outstanding" and "poor."

In addition, the study collected data on the perceived out-of-pocket cost of utilizing out-of-area hospitals, as well as perceptions of travel time and distance to alternative hospitals. Consumers' current hospital utilization and future utilization intentions were also collected.

Results

One part of the data analysis of the survey involved a factor analysis of the quality-related attributes. Table C3.5.1 presents the results of this factor analysis. A special form of factor analysis was used, called oblique rotation, that allowed for the expected correlation of underlying dimensions (that is, unlike principal components and Varimax, the resulting factors are *not* uncorrelated). Four factors were extracted, with the following correlation among them: between F1 and F2, 0.144; between F1 and F4, –0.610; between F2 and F3, 0.479; between F2 and F4, 0.101; and between F3 and F4, 0.079.

Case Questions

1. What overall managerial conclusions would you draw based on the results of the factor analysis? Is factor analysis the appropriate tool for examining these data?
2. Which factors are the most important? Why do you conclude this? Have enough factors been explored? Have *too many* factors been considered? Explain your reasoning vis-à-vis the information needs of the project.
3. How would you interpret the managerial relevance of the correlation among the factors? Might you expect an orthogonal rotation (e.g., Varimax) to alter the results of the factor analysis?
4. How could these results be utilized, in conjunction with the collected data on cost perceptions and hospital choice intentions data, to provide meaningful managerial conclusions?

Sources: Smith Gooding, Sandra K. (1994), "Hospital Outshopping and Perceptions of Quality: Implication for Public Policy." *Journal of Public Policy and Marketing*, 13(2), 271–280.

Tai, Wan-Tzu Connie, Frank W. Porell, and E. Kathleen Adams (2004), "Hospital Choice of Rural Medicare Beneficiaries: Patient, Hospital Attributes, and the Patient-Physician Relationship." *Health Services Research*, 39(6), p. 1903.

Roh, Chul-Young, and M. Jae Moon (2005), "Nearby, but Not Wanted? The Bypassing of Rural Hospitals and Policy Implications for Rural Health Care Systems." *Policy Studies Journal*, 33(3), p. 377.

CASE 3.6 THE FLYING DUTCHMAN GROUP

Joel McAndrews, a strategy analyst at The Flying Dutchman Group, a conglomerate of hospitality, travel, and tourism companies, was studying changes in consumer leisure activities. The company wanted to ensure that its product portfolio was well aligned with the leisure needs of its customers. Having completed a graduate degree in psychology, Joel felt capable of turning a critical eye on the article "Analysis of the Structure of Leisure Interests," by Jo-Ida Hansen and Mark Scullard, which appeared in the *Journal of Counseling Psychology*. Indeed, the authors' use of multivariate statistical techniques to understand the results of their Leisure Interest Questionnaire (LIQ) intrigued him.

Based on responses to the LIQ (which included 250 various leisure activities), cluster analysis and principal component analysis (PCA) (a common type of factor analysis), the study first identified those leisure activities that both generated the greatest interest and received high rates of reported participation. Subsequently, standard Pearson correlations were used to help identify and group highly confluent items; this procedure resulted in the following 18 groups of activities:

1. Camping and outdoors (11 items; e.g., backpacking, canoeing)
2. Adventure sports (23 items; e.g., hang gliding, rock climbing)
3. Team sports (16 items; e.g., going to basketball games, playing softball)
4. Individual sports (8 items; e.g., golf, racquetball)
5. Hunting and fishing (11 items; e.g., ice fishing, trap shooting)
6. Cards and games (10 items; e.g., bridge, board games)
7. Computer activities (8 items; e.g., surfing the Web, playing computer games)

8. Building and restoring (11 items; e.g., refinishing furniture, electrical work)
9. Collecting (7 items; e.g., coins, baseball cards)
10. Gardening and nature (13 items; e.g., pruning bushes, bird watching)
11. Arts and crafts (13 items; e.g., jewelry making, weaving)
12. Literature and writing (9 items; e.g., mysteries, writing letters)
13. Cultural arts (20 items; e.g., art galleries, symphony concerts)
14. Dancing (9 items; e.g., tap dancing, dance clubs)
15. Culinary pursuits (9 items; e.g., gourmet cooking, reading cook books)
16. Community involvement (13 items; e.g., volunteer work, club officer)
17. Shopping and fashion (8 items; e.g., going to the mall, talking about fashion)
18. Partying (7 items; e.g., night clubs, loud noisy parties).

Two additional leisure activities, travel (10 items; e.g., traveling to foreign countries, seeing local attractions) and socializing (11 items; e.g., visiting relatives, talking on the phone), did not emerge in the PCA analysis but were deemed important for inclusion because of their high incidence of self-report in previous studies on leisure activity participation.

A multidimensional scaling (MDS) analysis was applied to these 20 scales to create a perceptual map of the psychological similarity between the variables in two dimensions. Eighty-two percent of the variance in the original data was accounted for by this method. Dimension 1 showed "instrumental" activities such as fishing, playing cards, and building to be high on the scale, and "expressive" activities such as dancing, arts, and cooking low on the scale. Dimension 2 showed "active" pursuits such as playing sports and partying to be high on the scale, and "sedentary" activities such as collecting, writing, and doing computer work low on the scale. These results are shown in Figure C3.6.1.

Figure C3.6.1 Multidimensional Scaling Map for Leisure Activities

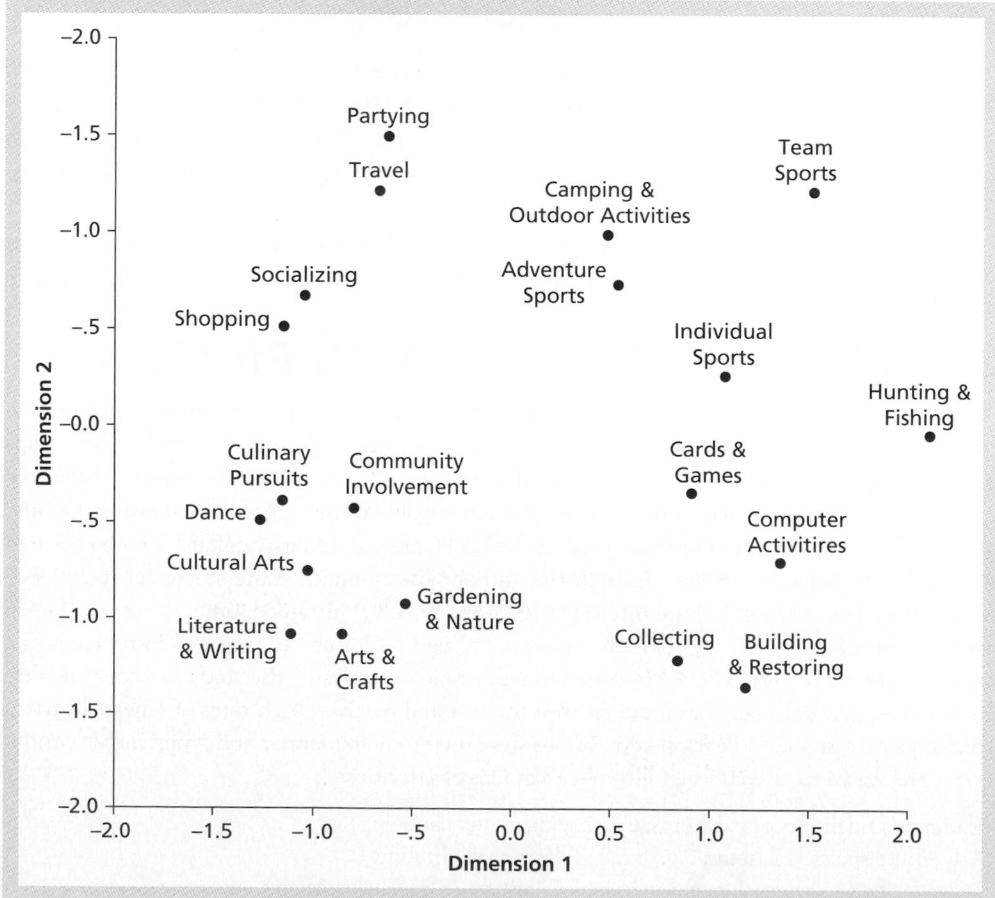

Source: Psychometric Evidence for the Leisure Excerpts from Interest Questionnaire and Analyses of the Structure of Leisure Interests; Jo-Ida C. Hansen, Mark G. Scullard. *Journal of Counseling Psychology*. July 1, 2002, Vol. 49, Issue 3. Copyright © American Psychological Association. Reprinted with permission.

Joel began by studying an MDS map of leisure activity preferences. He wanted to evaluate brand-extension opportunities to determine how The Flying Dutchman Group could command a greater dollar share of its customers' leisure expenditures by cross-selling and bundling relative activities and how the Group could attract new customers.

Case Questions

Note: For many of these questions, speculation is necessary in the absence of original, raw data or relevant summaries.

1 What interpretation would you assign to the axes of the map? Do they make intuitive sense? Would it seem as if a higher-dimensional solution—i.e., representing the 20 activity types in three- or higher-dimensional space—might help to faithfully capture the underlying structure?
2 What market segments appear to be indicated by this map? Would you need additional data of any sort to help determine this? If so, what kind(s)? What statistical methods might help determine this segmentation rigorously?
3 How could this map be used to facilitate Joel's strategic objectives? Be specific about what information from the map directly impinges on the decisions facing The Flying Dutchman Group at this point in time.
4 Considering that the revenue for The Flying Dutchman Group comes primarily from the traveling expenses of its customers, what particular expansion directions would you recommend to achieve growth? Do you believe that achieving growth is the appropriate objective? Would the activity map be better suited to other objectives the firm might reasonably adopt?
5 In your opinion, are there other data—internal or external, primary or secondary—that would be useful in pointing up new opportunities for leisure industry players? If yes, provide specific examples of those most appropriate for The Flying Dutchman Group, and explain your answer.

Source: Psychometric Evidence for the Leisure Excerpts from Interest Questionnaire and Analyses of the Structure of Leisure Interests; Jo-Ida C. Hansen, Mark G. Scullard. *Journal of Counseling Psychology*. July 1, 2002, Vol. 49, Issue 3. Copyright © American Psychological Association. Reprinted with permission.

CASE 3.7 ELWOOD FOOD COOPERATIVE

Joyce Lauchner was the general manager of the Elwood Food Cooperative (EFC). She had become concerned of late that she had lost touch with the buying patterns of the cooperative members. EFC just seemed so big now compared with the early days. She hoped to make use of some data that were available to her to increase her understanding of the members' purchasing habits to better plan the mix and quantity of goods that EFC carried.

Background of EFC

EFC was founded in 1986 by Lauchner and a small group of volunteers. Located in an old warehouse on the northwest side of the town of Elwood, it had grown from 10 original members in January 1986 to 500 members in September 2006. Elwood was a small town located in central Indiana, about 30 miles northeast of Indianapolis. EFC drew membership from a number of communities around Elwood, including Marion and Muncie.

The objective of EFC was to provide high-quality food products at prices below those available at local supermarkets. To accomplish this, EFC used shipping cartons as shelves, required shoppers to mark their own prices on goods, carried only the best-selling brands, and generally did not offer the "luxuries" associated with traditional supermarkets. To shop at EFC, one had to be a member. The membership fee was $45 per year. Any profits earned by EFC in a year were returned to the members as credits against purchases. Lauchner thought that the members bought most of their food at EFC.

Lauchner's Concerns

In the early days of EFC, Lauchner had prided herself on knowing all its members. She had spent a great deal of time in the store and felt she knew what people were buying and how much they were spending.

As the membership grew, her administrative duties kept her in her office much more. She no longer knew all the members, nor did she have a good feel for their expenditure patterns. She wanted to develop a better understanding of these aspects of her business and thought perhaps some of the data that had already been collected on the membership might provide answers.

The Available Data

In June 2006 a questionnaire had been used to collect data on the membership. During the month, all members had come into the cooperative at least once. Thus, data were available on all members. The data consisted of demographic characteristics of the members plus their weekly food expenditures.

The data were available on the cards that had been filled out by the members at the time of the interview. Lauchner had these cards in a filing cabinet in her office. A description of the contents of the cards is presented in the next section. Actual card values are tabulated in Table C5.16.

As a first step in understanding the membership, Lauchner wanted to know their average weekly expenditure on food. Because time was short, she wanted to do this without having to look at all 500 cards. However, she also wanted the average she calculated to be an accurate one. She wondered how she could make an accurate calculation.

EFC Data

Explanation of Items A–K in Table C3.7.1 (the variables)

A = household identification number (1–500)
B = weekly food expenditure, actual (e.g., $89.50)
C = number of persons in household, actual (1–9)
D = annual income of household, actual (e.g., $42,000)
E = education of head of household coded into five categories (1–5)
F = age of head of household, actual (e.g., 38)
G = weekly food expenditure, coded into seven categories (1–7)
H = any children younger than 6 years old in household, actual (1–2)
I = any children 6–18 years old in household, actual (1–2)
J = annual income of household, coded into six categories (1–6)
K = age of head of household, coded into seven categories (1–7)

Category Definitions for Variables

Variable C: Number of persons in household
1 = one person
2 = two persons
3 = three persons
4 = four persons
5 = five persons
6 = six persons
7 = seven persons
8 = eight persons
9 = nine or more persons
Variable E: Education of head of household
1 = less than grade 8
2 = grades 9–11
3 = high school graduate
4 = some college
5 = college graduate
Variable G: Weekly food expenditures
1 = less than $30
2 = $30–49.99
3 = $50–69.99
4 = $70–89.99
5 = $ 90–109.99

Category Definitions for Variables

6 = $110–129.99
7 = $130 or greater
Variable *H*: Any children younger than 6 years old in household
1 = no
2 = yes
Variable *I*: Any children 6–18 years old in household
1 = no
2 = yes
Variable *J*: Annual income of household
1 = less than $10,000
2 = $10,000–14,999
3 = $15,000–24,999
4 = $25,000–49,999
5 = $50,000–75,000
6 = $75,000 or greater
Variable *K*: Age of head of household
1 = less than 25
2 = 25–34
3 = 35–44
4 = 45–54
5 = 55–64
6 = 65–74
7 = 75 or older

Table C3.7.1 Demographic and Purchase Data for Elwood Food Cooperative Survey (ONLINE ONLY)

Log-in to the online edition of your textbook at www.atomicdog.com to access this table.

As a second step, Lauchner wanted to analyze the demographic data and determine whether there was a relationship between spending and demographics. The data presented in Table C3.7.1 was subjected to correlation and regression analysis with the following three objectives in mind:

1. Determination of the strength of association between families' food spending and demographic characteristics
2. Determination of a function by which a family's spending can be estimated from its demographic data
3. Determination of the statistical "confidence" in the earlier tests.

The variables included in this analysis were as follows:

1. Expenditures: Weekly food ($)
2. Persons: Number in household
3. Income: Annual total of household ($1000s)
4. Education: Of head of household (five levels)
5. Age: Of head of household (years)
6. Children <6: 0 or 1
7. Children 6–18: 0 or 1.

Assume for the purposes of interpreting the results of this analysis, presented in Tables C3.7.2 and C3.7.3, that the 500 households used were randomly selected from a much larger population of households.

Table C3.7.2 Correlation Results

r	Expenditures	Persons	Income	Education	Age	Children <6	Children 6–18
Expenditures	—						
Persons	0.432	—					
Income	0.374	0.162	—				
Education	0.231	0.104	0.473	—			
Age	0.068	−0.017	0.135	−0.030	—		
Children <6	0.167	0.563	−0.009	0.103	−0.325	—	
Children 6–18	0.398	0.699	0.195	0.106	0.082	0.248	—

Table C3.7.3 Regression Results. Six-Variable Regression: Weekly Food Expenditures ($)

r	r^2	Adjusted r^2	Standard Error	*n*
0.544	0.296	0.288	42.360	500

Source of Variation	Sum of Squares	*df*	Mean-Squares	*F* Test Statistic	*p*-Value One Tailed
Regression	372089.1	6	62014.8	34.561	0.0000
Residual	884630.86	493	1794.38		
Total	1256720	499			

Model	*b*	Std. Error	Std. Coeff. Beta	Test Statistic	*p*-Value Two Tailed	B Lower 95% CL	B Upper 95% CL
Constant	33.086	11.878		2.785	0.0056	9.748	56.424
Persons	8.431	1.708	0.319	4.937	0.0000	5.075	11.786
Income ($1000s)	0.527	0.088	0.265	5.994	0.0000	0.354	0.700
Education	2.657	1.815	0.063	1.464	0.1438	−0.909	6.222
Age	0.062	0.166	0.015	0.374	0.7084	−0.264	0.388
Children <6	−4.480	5.328	−0.043	−0.841	0.4009	−14.949	5.989
Children 6–18	12.699	5.515	0.126	2.303	0.0217	1.863	23.535

Case Questions

1. Did Lauchner formulate any specific hypotheses to test? If so, what were they? If not, what hypotheses might the cooperative wish to test? How would you state them in statistical language?
2. How can Lauchner validate the income and spending data that she has collected? Consider both statistical and nonstatistical types of validation.
3. What are the available alternative sampling procedures for estimating average weekly food expenditures? Explain how each of these sampling procedures would be carried out, and discuss the pros and cons of each. Are there any other variables whose averages it would be important to estimate?
4. Using the data file for all 500 households, calculate all the descriptive sample metrics that you believe might help Lauchner with the current situation. Do you believe these metrics should be considered representative of the overall EFC customer base? Explain your answer. If not, how could more representative metrics be collected?
5. Considering Lauchner's analysis objectives, what kind of analysis would you perform to address her information needs? Why? Use the full data file supplementing this case to conduct the recommended analyses. Develop a complete report (including statement of objectives, justification and description of the employed analyses, findings and conclusions) that you would submit to Lauchner. You should consider whether to

limit your report to only the information needs suggested explicitly or to include additional analyses that seem relevant.

6 Evaluate the use of the correlation and regression analysis in this case. Do you believe they provide the adequate answers to Lauchner's questions? Do you believe that the relationships here are all linear? How should the nominal variables be included? Has a nominal variable been included incorrectly and, if so, how could you correct this potential mistake? Can such nominal variables be "correlated" with the other variables?

7 For the correlation results:
   - **a** What interpretation can you give to the results shown? What can you say about "significance" here?
   - **b** What assumptions underlie your interpretations? How could these assumptions be tested?
   - **c** Is there a single "best" predictor of expenditures among the other six variables? What is it? Is this an appropriate interpretation?
   - **d** There appears to be a positive correlation between "children <6" and "children 6–18," yet one correlates positively with age, the other negatively. Has an error been made? If not, how would you interpret this finding?

8 For the regression results:
   - **a** What interpretation can you give to these results? What assumptions underlie your interpretations? How could these assumptions be tested?
   - **b** If you were to rerun this regression, what variables would you leave out, and in what order? What criterion would you use to determine whether a variable should be *permanently* omitted?
   - **c** "Children 6–18" has the largest coefficient (other than "Constant," which we always ignore) but not the largest standardized coefficient. Is that reasonable? What does it mean?
   - **d** Do you think that the R^2 is somewhat low for a managerial application such as this? Does the modest R^2 value imply that our independent variables are poor predictors of food expenditures?
   - **e** Formulate and estimate a regression model—other than the one already presented—for weekly household food expenditures (Variable B). Can you come up with a "best" such model? What would the important independent variables be? Would multicollinearity be a problem? Can you treat expenditure as an interval-scaled variable? Defend your choices based on regression theory and your estimates.
   - **f** If you wanted to model the *nominal* version of expenditure (Variable G) instead, what sort of regression model might you use?
   - **g** Are there any other important (regression) relationships that Lauchner might wish to examine? If so, provide the estimates and interpretations.

9 Convert the "education" variable (five levels) into four dummy variables and repeat the regression. What can be concluded from the obtained results?

Source: U.S. Census www.census.gov

CASE 3.8 COMFIMAX TAMPONS

Tampons were invented by Dr. Earle Cleveland Haas, a general practitioner, whose inspiration came from observations of the discomfort of his wife and of his female patients who wore bulky external pads. The idea for the tampon was patented by Haas in 1931 and commercialized by a Denver group of investors in 1934. Since then, the tampon market has experienced extraordinary growth, reaching its maturity phase in the intervening decades throughout the United States, Canada, and much of western Europe, where about 70 percent of women regularly purchase tampon products.

The tampon market itself is divided into two subproducts: tampons with and without applicators. ComfiMax S.A. is a well-established tampon manufacturer whose products, which have applicators, are branded under the ComfiMax company name. Recently, a new management team was appointed to lead the ComfiMax Tampons Business Unit. The new five-year strategic plan, approved under the new management, posed as the key goal for the ComfiMax tampon division "to achieve a leading market share in the tampon product category." Despite the brand's dominant market share in the applicator tampon segment, it was obvious that it had to expand into the nonapplicator segment to make the five-year goal possible. The task of expanding the product portfolio was assigned to Peg Buddox, the marketing manager of ComfiMax applicator tampons, and her team.

From previous studies conducted on tampon use, Buddox knew that consumers' perceptions and attitudes differed between the applicator and nonapplicator user segments. Her judgment suggested that information available from these studies was not sufficient to proceed with the nonapplicator tampon launch. Therefore, Buddox decided to commission a new study that focused on those users who preferred the nonapplicator form of the product. She requested from her team a briefing document about the project and its intended scope and information needs and planned, after reviewing it carefully, to communicate its findings to the account executive of the firm that was handling ComfiMax's research projects.

The briefing document described the study's objective as acquiring information about the nonapplicator tampon user segment that would enable ComfiMax to successfully launch a nonapplicator product and achieve 15 percent market share with a 5-year time horizon. Specifically, ComfiMax sought to answer the following questions:

- Should the nonapplicator product be launched under the ComfiMax umbrella brand name or under another, presumably new, name?
- On the one hand, ComfiMax enjoyed almost 100 percent brand awareness among tampon users overall. On the other hand, management was understandably concerned about extending this name into a new segment, for two reasons. First, there was the issue of cannibalization; perhaps using the same brand name would erode demand for its core applicator tampon product. Second, management felt that it was crucial to communicate the nonapplicator nature of the new product, and it seemed that using the same name might impede them in that goal.
- How can we best understand the decision-making process of the nonapplicator tampon segment? What spurred these users to buy in the category at all? And, once decided, how did they choose a brand?

The ComfiMax team split the decision-making process into three phases: prepurchase, point-of-purchase, and postpurchase. It was requested that the survey be performed in a manner reflecting these three distinct phases. The team asked the following questions, broken out by phase:

Prepurchase:

- What degree of category loyalty is typical among nonapplicator tampon users? Do they use other products in the feminine hygiene category (tampons with applicators, pads)?
- Which prepurchase sources help inform the decision about which brand to purchase? What is the relative importance of such sources?
- What degree of brand loyalty is typical among nonapplicator tampon users? Do some brands generate much greater loyalty than others? Can promotion help dislodge users from one brand to another?
- What factors increase the trial likelihood for a new nonapplicator tampon brand? What does it take to "convert" a loyal user?
- How do we effectively reach those who are not opposed to the idea of a new nonapplicator tampon, and, secondarily, the "aware rejectors"—those who have previously tried, but decided against, a nonapplicator tampon—and convince them to try the new ComfiMax nonapplicator brand? Can they be convinced that ComfiMax is "new and different" and persuaded to try the category once again?
- Who, what, how, and where should we target? What psychographic and geodemographic characteristics should we be on the lookout for?
- What is the correct message to drive the business for the new product? To whom should it be focused (over and above consumer segments, e.g., influencers such as gynecologists)? Through what channels?

Point-of-Purchase

- Is the brand decision made before or at the point of purchase? What is the relative proportion of those who decide in advance and those who decide when in the store? What are the typical profiles of each type of consumer?
- For the "point-of-purchase" segment, which factors affect the brand decision most effectively (e.g., packaging, "regular" price, discounts, other promotions)?
- Can cross-channel/cross-product promotions help induce trial of the new nonapplicator tampon? What sorts? Will they have to be done jointly with other manufacturers?

- When there are (inevitable) stock-outs, what do both loyal and nonloyal users do? Do they switch brands, wait, switch formats (application vs. non-), visit another store?

Postpurchase:

- Which factors most affect users' postpurchase recalled experience and satisfaction levels?
- Which factors help drive repurchase in the category, as opposed to purchases of other, competing products (e.g., pads, applicator tampons)? Which factors help drive repurchase of specific brands, ComfiMax in particular, within the nonapplicator market?
- Do satisfied users recommend their favored brands to others? Is this a positive market trait?
- What are current satisfaction levels among existing nonapplicator tampon brands? How do these brands score on the product features that affect users' repurchase decisions?

Clearly, ComfiMax wanted a great deal of information. The key issue would be how to obtain it all in a timely, cost-effective, and accurate manner.

Case Questions

1. Write a survey proposal appropriate for ComfiMax's objectives and information needs. Be specific about the details that would be needed to implement the study (e.g., sampling procedure, type of interviews).
2. Design a questionnaire that would address the information needs stated in the briefing document, and prepare a coding manual for it.
3. ComfiMax seems to want to know pretty much everything one *can* know about the nonapplicator market and user segments. Is all this information truly necessary at this stage of the decision-making process? Specifically, divide the company's wish list (the pre-, point-of-, and postpurchase questions) into those that are critical and those that can wait until after the launch. For the "critical" set, prioritize and order them explicitly. Are any likely to be especially extensive (and, by implication, costly)?
4. Do you believe that this explicit division into prepurchase, point-of-purchase, and postpurchase is an appropriate framework for understanding market and segment dynamics? Because ComfiMax's nonapplicator product has not even been introduced, are any of the stated information needs premature? Which in particular are necessary for the sort of break-even and other financial analyses typical in making early-stage, go/no-go decisions?
5. What kind of statistical analyses would you recommend to ComfiMax's marketing manager? Provide specific details about the value of each analysis that you propose.

Sources: http://www.tampax.com
http://www.stayfreemagazine.org

CASE 3.9 NETFORE, INC.

NetFore, Inc. is a Phoenix-based marketing research firm specializing in providing forecasts of economic trends, social trends, and sales levels for its clients, with expertise in the manufacturing and technology sectors. Described below are three forecasting problems the company confronted for separate clients. For each situation, the following are provided:

1. A *statement of objective*. This statement explains clients' problems and expectations in very general terms and, therefore, what the firm should take as its mandate.
2. A *description of the decision maker's line of business*.
3. A *statement of the problem*. This statement provides a detailed description of the problem that the researcher must solve using the data and assumptions as they are presented.
4. A *list of the published statistical data sources* from which case information has been taken. Note that the core problem has been rendered somewhat simpler than in a typical real-world project, as key data have been provided without having to be collected or sought in databases.
5. A *list of assumptions*. Almost all situations require assumptions that transcend available data, to allow the researcher to answer the specific questions at hand. This section provides a set of working assumptions to help guide the researcher.

6. A *data table or tables*. As described in (4.). Additional data could well be brought to bear, at the discretion of the researcher.

Case Assignment

Formulate a feasible, appropriate solution to each problem presented, using the provided data and assumptions, as needed.

A. Ready Made Containers, Inc.

Objective: To estimate the total market potential for corrugated and solid fiber boxes in a given area.
Kind of business: Manufacturer of corrugated and solid fiber boxes.
Problem: The sales manager for a manufacturer of corrugated and solid fiber boxes in one of the mountain states decided that he wanted to intensify the company's efforts in Arizona, one of the states that the firm served. For example, in the Phoenix standard metropolitan statistical area (MSA) (coextensive with Maricopa County), the firm's sales totaled $850,000 in 2000—$680,000, or 80 percent, to firms within the food and kindred products industry, and the remaining $170,000, or 20 percent, to firms manufacturing electrical equipment and supplies. The sales manager felt that this was a very poor sales record, considering the diversity of industry in the Phoenix area.

In view of this preliminary analysis, he decided to determine the market potential for fiber boxes in the Phoenix area, as the first step in establishing the firm's sales potential (or market share) and setting a realistic sales quota for the area.

Table C3.9.1 **Data on the Value of Box Shipments for the United States by Standard Industrial Classification (SIC) Major Group Code, Plus Employment by Industry Group for the United States and Maricopa County**

			Employment by Industry Group	
		Value of Box Shipments by End Use* ($1000)	Entire U.S.	Maricopa County
SIC Major Group Code	Consuming Industries	(1)	(2)	(3)
20	Food and kindred products	1,171,800	1,507,617	7,350
21	Tobacco manufacturers	29,000	28,146	—
22	Textile mill products	121,800	336,947	—
23	Apparel and other textile products	54,600	525,970	2,843
24	Lumber and wood products	42,000	585,035	1,736
25	Furniture and fixtures	147,000	642,440	7,766
26	Paper and allied products	567,000	551,560	1,278
27	Printing and publishing	58,800	830,379	12,565
28	Chemicals and allied products	260,400	889,683	4,965
29	Petroleum and coal products	33,600	101,201	100–249
30	Rubber and miscellaneous plastic products	163,800	1,088,344	6,552
31	Leather and leather products	21,000	69,356	20–99
32	Stone, clay, and glass products	365,400	202,385	3,269
33	Primary metal industries	42,000	578,025	5,070
34	Fabricated metal products	184,800	1,820,595	3,271
35	Machinery, except electrical	105,000	1,402,534	11,465
36	Electrical equipment and supplies	256,200	592,885	250–499
37	Transportation equipment	109,200	1,839,281	21,333

			Employment by Industry Group	
		Value of Box Shipments by End Use* ($1000)	Entire U.S.	Maricopa County
SIC Major Group Code	Consuming Industries	(1)	(2)	(3)
38	Instruments and related products	29,400	469,407	9,908
39	Miscellaneous manufacturing industries	403,200	747,255	3,660
99	Government	33,600	—	—
	Total	4,200,000	—	—

Data in columns 1 and 2 are for the entire United States.

*Based on data reported in Fibre Box Industry Annual Report, Fibre Box Association.
County Business Patterns, U.S. Department of Commerce, Bureau of the Census.
U.S. Industrial Outlook, Bureau of Domestic Commerce, U.S. Department of Commerce.

Source of Data:

1. *County Business Patterns*, http://censtats.census.gov/cgi-bin/cbpsic/cbp1sect.pl
2. *U.S. Industrial Outlook*, http://www.census.gov/prod/2002pubs/m00as-3.pdf
3. Fiber box statistics

B. Sputnik Radio Company

Objective: To establish national, state, and county sales quotas and a method for estimating the potential market in 2006 for satellite radios for automobiles.

Kind of business: Manufacturer of satellite radios for automobiles.

Problem: Sputnik Radio, which has been estimating sales potential and quotas for satellite radios for automobiles based on past performance, decided to develop a mathematical procedure for projecting sales of satellite radios by territory because many of the company's sales managers felt their assigned quotas did not reflect the potential of their territory.

Source of Data:

1. Highway statistics
2. *Iowa Statistical Abstract*

Assumptions:

1. The new owner is most likely to purchase a satellite radio when purchasing a car, so the primary data source is car registration information.
2. Sputnik Radio has maintained approximately an 11 percent share of total market for replacement satellite radios over the past 2 years. However, management feels that a more desirable, yet realistic, figure would be a 14 percent share of market.
3. Total automobile registrations will continue to increase at an average annual rate of 3.8 percent, as it had over the previous 10-year period.

Note: Not all the data are presented here, as the procedure is easily generalized to other geographical regions.

Table C3.9.2 **Automobile Registration for Selected States, and by Counties for Iowa**

States	Automobile Registrations* (1000s)
Alabama	1755
Arizona	1975
Arkansas	945
California	18,500
Colorado	877
Illinois	5697
Missouri	2593

States	Automobile Registrations* (1000s)
New Jersey	4402
North Carolina	3624
Ohio	6464
Counties in Iowa	
Iowa†	**2294**
Adair	6
Benton	19
Des Moines	32
Linn	753
Plymouth	19
Scott	135
Warren	30
Woodbury	81
All other counties	1219
Total United States	134,337

* *Vehicle Registration*, U.S. Department of Transportation, Federal Highway Administration, http://www.fhwa.dot.gov/policy/ohim/hs03/mv.htm
† *Vehicle Registrations*, Iowa Department of Transportation, http://www.dot.state.ia.us/mvd/ovs/regis2002.pdf

C. Ward Manufacturing Company

Objective: To disperse advertising budget for 2005 in proportion to potential markets, by states, in the South Atlantic region.

Kind of business: Manufacturer of finely crafted household furniture.

Problem: Ward was introducing a new line of furniture and wished to construct a simplified model for allocating the total introductory advertising budget, by state, so as to reach customers who were most likely to be "prime" buyers for their products.

Source of Data: Statistics of Income: Individual Income Tax Returns.

Assumptions:

1. The company decided to direct its advertising to families or individuals with an adjusted gross income of $75,000 or more, based on studies of other companies marketing similar furniture.
2. An introductory advertising budget of $150,000 was established.

Table C3.9.3 Number of Individual Income Tax Returns With an Adjusted Gross Income of $75,000 or More in 2003

South Atlantic Census Region	Number of Returns
Delaware	66,655
District of Columbia	45,769
Florida	984,304
Georgia	551,352
Maryland	545,492
North Carolina	485,330
South Carolina	207,645
Virginia	650,013
West Virginia	70,044
Total	3,606,604

Source: Statistics of Income: Individual Tax Returns, Internal Revenue Service, U.S. Department of the Treasury

Sources:

1. U.S. Census Bureau, http://www.census.gov
2. U.S. Internal Revenue Service Web site, http://www.irs.gov > Tax Stats > Individual Tax Statistics

CASE 3.10 "NO SWEAT"

San Francisco Package Goods (SFPG) is a large, rapidly expanding firm, with many new product successes over the previous decade. Its newest venture is an antiperspirant/deodorant, based on a new formulation, tentatively called "No Sweat." After a favorable employee reaction to the product, SFPG decided to conduct a concept test. Production of the new product would require considerable investment in plant and equipment, so SFPG managers planned to base much of their go/no-go decision on the results of this test. A concept test, rather than an actual product test, was undertaken because production costs were so great and the R&D crew was still trying to make minor improvements in the product.

The SFPG marketing department was considered to be one of the best in the industry. Unlike many other companies, SFPG conducted its own marketing research. Bill Freeland, who recently completed a top undergraduate business program, was asked to prepare the concept statement and to design the testing procedure for No Sweat. His concept statement and portions of his design are presented in Exhibit C3.10.1.

Exhibit C3.10.1: Study Proposal

Concept Statement for a New Antiperspirant/Deodorant

A major producer of soaps, shampoos, and other personal hygiene goods has developed a new antiperspirant/deodorant stick. The company has combined ingredients that had, in the past, been difficult to stabilize in stick form. The product has a unique appearance; its white antiperspirant center is surrounded by an outer ring of green gel deodorant. This antiperspirant/deodorant combination provides both men and women with the highest degree of protection available against odor and wetness. This new product will be available in a 2.7-ounce size for $5.00 and a 1.5-ounce size for $3.00.

Objective

Our objective is to identify the potential market for No Sweat, the new antiperspirant/deodorant created by SFPG. Given its unique appearance and its dual-action formula, we hope that No Sweat will find a niche in an already flooded market. Consumer attitudes regarding specific characteristics of the product will be investigated, as well as their overall reaction to the product concept. At the request of the new product manager, we will differentiate between spray, stick, and roll-on users in the presentation of our data.

Method

Personal interviews will be used due to the length of the survey and the quality of data that must be procured. A random sample of 50 men and 50 women will be selected from the Los Angeles phone book. Because the sample will be random, we can be assured of proportional representation of roll-on, stick, and spray antiperspirant and deodorant users. Soliciting for personal interviews will be conducted over the phone between 12 noon and 9 p.m. This will ensure that all members of the population have an equal chance of being contacted.

The Interview

Interviews will be conducted without any reference to SFPG, thus eliminating a potential source of respondent bias. All subjects will be shown the concept statement. They will then be asked to give opinions regarding specific attributes of the product. Finally, intent to purchase will be measured. The respondents will also be shown the proposed package design for No Sweat. Their feedback will be recorded and used to suggest possible changes in the design.

The study was undertaken using the methodology proposed by Freeland. Approximately 400 phone calls were made to set up the 100 interview appointments. Two of the scheduled subjects (both male) canceled their appointments before being interviewed, making the actual sample size 98. Selected results from the experiment appear in Exhibit C10.2.

Exhibit C3.10.2: Study Results

Primary Type of Antiperspirant/Deodorant Used ($n = 98$)

	Percent	Number
Roll-on	47	46
Stick	39	38
Spray	11	11
Other	3	3

Respondents were given a list of several product characteristics and then asked to use the 7-point scale appearing later to record what influence each characteristic had on purchase intent. Subjects were divided into four classes: roll-on, stick, spray, and "other" users. The table following the scale presents the average score that each characteristic received within those divisions.

Influence on purchase intent

Definitely would not influence purchase decision						Definitely would influence purchase decisions
1	2	3	4	5	6	7

Most common type of antiperspirant or deodorant used

Characteristic	Roll-on	Stick	Spray	Other
Can be used by both sexes	4.2	4.0	3.9	4.4
Effective at stopping wetness	6.2	5.9	6.1	5.8
Effective at stopping odor	6.4	6.0	6.0	6.7
Product appearance	2.5	3.1	3.6	3.0
Product (roll-on, stick, spray, other)	2.8	6.3	2.6	2.2
New formula	4.1	4.5	4.2	3.9
Package design	3.1	3.0	2.7	2.9
Package size	4.0	4.1	4.1	4.6
Package shape	3.9	3.8	3.9	3.6
Price	4.7	6.1	3.2	5.4

The following table summarizes the results into two categories: the data from respondents who said they would try the product, and the data from those who said they would not. Within each group (tryers and nontryers), the table presents the percentage of those who rated the characteristic:

- 1 or 2
- 3, 4, or 5
- 6 or 7.

Characteristic	Rating	Tryers	Nontryers	Significance
Effectiveness at stopping wetness	1–2	0	1	ns
	3–4–5	32	39	ns
	6–7	68	60	ns
	Total	100	100	
Effectiveness at stopping odor	1–2	0	0	ns
	3–4–5	28	32	ns
	6–7	72	68	ns
	Total	100	100	

Characteristic	Rating	Tryers	Nontryers	Significance
Price	1–2	20	67	($p < 0.001$)
	3–4–5	72	32	($p < 0.001$)
	6–7	8	1	ns
	Total	100	100	
Product appearance	1–2	52	74	($p < 0.1$)
	3–4–5	36	18	($p < 0.1$)
	6–7	12	8	ns
	Total	100	100	
New formula	1–2	4	11	($p < 0.1$)
	3–4–5	60	77	ns
	6–7	36	12	($p < 0.05$)
	Total	100	100	
Total number		25	73	

Note: Significance levels are for a *z* test of proportions between tryers and nontryers.

Reasons for trial: Those who said they would try the product ($n = 25$)	
Dissatisfaction with current brand	14%
Curiosity	58
Other	28

Reasons for no trial: Those who said they would not try the product ($n = 73$)	
Price	25%
Satisfaction with current brand	64
Other	11

The product package results are shown in the following table.

	Yes	No	Indifferent
Do you like the package shape?	47%	21%	31%
Do you like the package colors?	29	58	13
Do you like the lettering?	62	26	12
Do you like the package overall?	45	47	8

Case Questions

1 Evaluate the management's decision to conduct a concept test instead of an actual product test. Discuss the advantages and disadvantages of both tests for the SFPG objectives of its new venture, No Sweat.

2 Do you agree with Bill Freeland's direction to conduct a blind concept test? Why or why not?

3 Thoroughly read the concept statement of the study proposal. What are the unique attributes and the end benefits included in the statement? In your opinion, is the concept statement phrased appropriately to induce unbiased responses? Do you agree with the inclusion of the intended price points in the concept statement? Explain your reasoning.

4 Will the concept test be effective in addressing the objective stated in the study proposal? Is there any additional research you would recommend to meet SFPG's objectives and information needs? If so, provide a detailed description and explanation of your recommendations.

5 If you were asked to generate sales potential and a sales forecast analysis for the No Sweat product, how would you approach this assignment? Provide a detailed description of the necessary steps.

6 Given the sampling method described in the study proposal, assess the degree to which the generated sample is representative of the overall population and explain your answer. What other sampling approach(es) could be utilized to ensure a proportional representation of roll-on, stick, and spray antiperspirant and deodorant users? Provide specific details.

7 What are the methods that could be used to generate a relevant list of product characteristics that were used in the concept test? Place your examples in the context of the SFPG case.

8 What type of research would you recommend to SFPG to determine the optimum price points for this new product? Design a study proposal for the recommended research.

9 What would you infer from the results of the concept test presented in the case? What conclusions can be drawn for the introduction of the new product?

10 How would you go about performing the sorts of statistical tests carried out for the comparison of tryers and nontryers? What other data provided in the case can be similarly tested? Would ordinary regression-based approaches be justified?

CASE 3.11 EXECUTIVE EXPRESS AIR

Peggy McNamara is the president of Executive Express Air, a small commuter airline company based in St. Andrew. Express Air presently provides air taxi and corporate flight services to local businesses. To boost company profits, McNamara is considering offering a regular service between St. Andrew and Bayville,* major city about 340 miles from St. Andrew. There are presently no regular flights between St. Andrew and Bayville. St. Andrew–Bayville fliers must either charter a plane or leave from Eastport City Airport, which is about 50 miles from St. Andrew. Brief descriptions of the current service, the cities involved, and the potential customers follow.

- *Bayville:* Bayville is a major metropolitan area of more than six million people. It hosts the main offices of several Fortune 500 companies, so it is frequently visited by executives from Eastport and St. Andrew. Most of these business travelers arrive in the morning and leave at the end of the day. Bayville is also a cultural center; it has fine restaurants, museums, playhouses, and a world-class symphony orchestra, making it a popular weekend vacation spot.

  Bayville has two airports: Central and Lake. Central Airport is extremely busy because all major airlines land there. It is also located 25 miles from the downtown business district. Lake Airport is smaller, less busy, and closer to downtown, so business travelers generally prefer to arrive there. Both Central and Lake airports offer regular service to Eastport.
- *Eastport:* Also highly populated, Eastport has about four million inhabitants. Eastport City Airport offers hourly jet service to Bayville's Lake Airport. Flights to Central are less frequent.
- *St. Andrew:* St. Andrew is much smaller than either Bayville or Eastport, claiming slightly fewer than 100,000 residents. It is the home of St. Andrew College, which has an enrollment of 20,000 students. More than 800 businesses are located in the area, including several banks and consulting firms. Travelers flying from St. Andrew to Bayville must go via Eastport City Airport, and thus the trip takes about 2 hours; a 1-hour drive to Eastport (this includes parking and check-in) and a one-hour flight to St. Andrew.

Before establishing the new Executive Express service, however, McNamara wants to see what kind of demand there is for it. There are two additional facts that McNamara has to incorporate into her evaluation of the demand. Specifically,

1. The proposed St. Andrew–Bayville service would cut travel time in half, to one hour (including the drive to the airport).
2. The St. Andrew Airport cannot accommodate jets because its runway is too short. Because jets cannot be used, Express Air could use two alternative types of prop planes for the service. The first type, CASA, is unpressurized. This means it cannot attain the same altitudes that pressurized planes do. Because of this, CASA might not be able to fly above bad weather conditions to escape turbulence. CASA has 24 seats, and passengers are able to stand up inside the plane. Metro-liner, the other aircraft being considered, does have a pressurized cabin. Thus, it can fly higher than the CASA and probably escape bad weather conditions. But the 18-seat Metroliner is not large enough to allow passengers to stand upright inside the plane. The Metroliner and the CASA have virtually identical cruising speeds.

*The names of the three cities have been altered due to the proprietary nature of some of the case data.

McNamara had hired the Novato Group, a small specialty marketing research company, to research the demand for the new service. She had informed the research firm that based on the survey's results, she expected to make the following decisions:

1. Go/no-go decision for the new service between St. Andrew and Bayville.
2. If go, then:
   a. What airport in Bayville should be used?
   b. What plane type would be most preferred by potential customers?
   c. How many round-trip lines per day should be launched?
   d. What is the best time schedule of departures from St. Andrew and Bayville for each line?
   e. What is the optimal price that should be charged for the round trip ticket?

McNamara has just received the data and is ready to interpret the findings. The survey and questionnaire results follow. Additional cost data are presented in the Appendix.

Survey Results

Findings from a preliminary telephone survey of local travel agencies and businesses:

1. At least 50 persons per business day travel to Bayville.
2. Sixty percent of the businesses get their St. Andrew–Bayville tickets through travel agencies and internal corporate booking agents.
3. Travel agents believe that a St. Andrew–Bayville service would be popular.
4. The majority of businesses said that they would take advantage of such a service.
5. According to the chamber of commerce, "the proposed service would be substantially used by St. Andrew businesses as a more efficient and economical means of transportation to and from the Bayville area."

Questionnaire

The half-hour mail survey shown in Exhibit C6.3 was given to 50 local businesspersons who had traveled to Bayville within the past 6 months. Travel agents provided the names of potential respondents. Results follow each question. (All questions were open-ended, so the response categories were created by the researchers to analyze the data.)

For the next set of questions, respondents were asked to fill in several matrices similar to the one shown in Table C3.11.1. On a scale of 1 to 9, they were told to place a 1 in the cell they liked most and a 9 in the cell they liked least.

Exhibit C3.11.1: Questionnaire

1 When was your last trip to Bayville?

64 percent	Within the past month
12	More than 1 but less than 2 months ago
8	More than 2 but less than 3 months ago
16	More than 3 but less than 6 months ago

2 How did you get there?

92 percent	Plane
8	Car

3 What was the purpose of the trip?

74 percent	Business
20	Pleasure
4	Business/pleasure
2	Transfer planes

4 How often do you go to Bayville per year by plane? By car or train?

7.3	Average number of plane trips per year
2.8	Average number of car or train trips per year

5 At what time of day do you usually leave for Bayville?

96 percent	Before 10:00 A.M.
4	Noon

6 When do you like to leave Bayville?

68 percent	Between 5:00 P.M. and 6:00 P.M.
14	Between 6:01 P.M. and 7:00 P.M.
10	Between 7:01 P.M. and 8:00 P.M.
4	Between 8:01 P.M. and 9:00 P.M.
4	The following morning at 8:30 A.M.

7 How do you feel about the existing service from Eastport to Bayville?

Q: How is the airport?

A: Many respondents said they disliked the parking facilities.

Q: The schedule?

A: Ninety-eight percent were completely satisfied.

Q: The price?

A: For most people the price was unimportant, although 11 respondents thought it was too high for such a short distance.

Q: The service aboard?

A: Not important.

8 A small aircraft leaves from St. Andrew airport and flies to Bayville Lake Airport in 1 hour. It departs from St. Andrew at 8:30 A.M., and the return flight leaves from Bayville at 5:30 P.M. that same evening. The round-trip price is $120. Would you consider taking such a flight when you go to Bayville?

70 percent	Yes
30	No

Table C3.11.1 Conjoint Ranking Task for Price and Travel Time

	Time of Traveling (one way)		
Price (round trip)	2 hours	1 1/2 hours	1 hour
$220			
170			
120			

Data obtained from several of these matrices were analyzed using a conjoint analysis program. For each individual matrix, the program statistically estimated utility values between 0 and 1 (with 1 being highest utility) for every category of every variable in the matrix. For the earlier example, the following utilities occurred.

Price (round trip)	Utility Value	Travel Time, hours (one way)	Utility Value
$220	0.16	2	0.17
170	0.56	1 1/2	0.58
120	0.78	1	0.75

These utility values can be added to obtain utilities for various combinations of variables. The program assigns utility values so that the utilities for the cells in the matrix are in the same order as the rank order (1, 2, 3, etc.) given by the respondents. For example, a round trip with 2 hours of travel each way, costing $170, has a utility of 0.17 + 0.16 = 0.33, the lowest value in the price–travel time matrix (see Table C3.11.2). This combination was also ranked last by the respondents. The ordering of calculated utilities does not always coincide with the respondent rankings, but the program generates a set of values that come closest to accomplishing that task. (Note that these values are not unique—e.g., small changes can leave the rankings unaltered—but, statistically, they are the "best" such values in the sense of minimizing an appropriate distance-based measure).

Table C3.11.2 Estimated Utility Value Matrix for Price and Travel Time

	Time of Traveling (one way)		
Price (round trip)	2 Hours (0.17)	1 1/2 Hours (0.58)	1 Hour (0.75)
\$220 (0.16)	9 (0.33)	7 (0.74)	6 (0.91)
170 (0.56)	8 (0.73)	4 (1.14)	3 (1.31)
120 (0.78)	5 (0.95)	2 (1.36)	1 (1.53)

The relative importance of the variables has also been calculated for each matrix.

Relative importance = (range of the utility values of variable *a*)/
(range of values of variable *a* + range of values of variable *b*).

Relative importance of price and travel time:

Price: 0.52 (0.52 = 0.62/1.20),
where 0.62 = 0.78 − 0.16, the range of the price utility values
Travel time: 0.48 (0.48 = 0.58/1.20)

This means that the importance of two variables in the decision-making process is almost the same, with price having slightly more influence. In other words, a higher price is rejected slightly more than a longer travel time. The utility values and relative importance for other pairs of variables are as shown in Tables C3.11.3 to C3.11.10.

Table C3.11.3 Price and Plane Type

Price (round trip)	Utility
\$220	0.23
170	0.51
120	0.78
Plane Type	**Utility**
DC-9	0.87
Metroliner	0.60
CASA	0.23
Relative Importance	
Price	0.46
Plane	0.54

Table C3.11.4 Price and Airport of Departure

Price (round trip)	Utility
\$220	0.17
170	0.51
120	0.82
Airport	**Utility**
St. Andrew	0.72
Eastport	0.28
Relative Importance	
Price	0.60
Airport	0.40

Table C3.11.5 Price and Comfort of the Plane

Price (round trip)	Utility
$220	0.21
170	0.55
120	0.74
Comfort	**Utility**
Possible to stand upright; bathroom	0.86
Not possible to stand upright; bathroom	0.54
Possible to stand upright; no bathroom	0.50
Not possible to stand upright; no bathroom	0.10
Relative Importance	
Price	0.42
Airport	0.59

Table C3.11.6 Travel Time and Type of Plane

Travel Time, hours (one way)	Utility
1	0.74
1 1/2	0.61
2	0.15
Plane	**Utility**
DC-9 commercial jet	0.79
Metroliner pressurized prop jet (18 seats)	0.51
CASA unpressurized prop jet (24 seats)	0.20
Relative Importance	
Time	0.50
Plane	0.50

Table C3.11.7 Travel Time and Schedule

Travel Time, hours (one way)	Utility
1	0.70
1 1/2	0.62
2	0.18
Schedule	**Utility**
Leave St. Andrew or Eastport: 8:00 A.M. and 5:00 P.M.	
Leave Bayville: 9:30 A.M. and 6:30 P.M.	0.17
Leave St. Andrew or Eastport: 8:00 A.M., 1:00 P.M., 7:00 P.M.	
Leave Bayville: 9:30 A.M., 2:30 P.M., 8:30 P.M.	0.42
Leave St. Andrew or Eastport: 8:00 A.M., 1:00 P.M., 5:00 P.M.	
Leave Bayville: 9:30 A.M., 2:30 P.M., 6:30 P.M.	0.51

Schedule	Utility
Leave St. Andrew or Eastport: Hourly from 7:00 A.M. to 7:00 P.M.	
Leave Bayville: Hourly from 8:30 A.M. to 8:30 P.M.	0.90
Relative Importance	
Time	0.42
Schedule	0.58

Table C3.11.8 Type of Plane and Airport of Departure

Type of Plane	Utility
DC-9	0.84
Metroliner	0.46
CASA	0.21
Airport	**Utility**
St. Andrew	0.74
Eastport	0.26
Relative Importance	
Plane	0.57
Airport	0.43

Table C3.11.9 Type of Plane and Comfort

Type of Plane	Utility
DC-9	0.76
Metroliner	0.44
CASA	0.30
Comfort	**Utility**
Stand; bathroom	0.93
Cannot stand; bathroom	0.54
Stand; no bathroom	0.40
Cannot stand; no bathroom	0.14
Relative Importance	
Plane	0.37
Comfort	0.63

Table C3.11.10 Airport of Departure and Schedule

Airport of Departure	Utility
St. Andrew	0.66
Eastport	0.34
Schedule	
Leave St. Andrew or Eastport: 8:00 A.M. and 5:00 P.M.	
Leave Bayville: 9:30 A.M. and 6:30 P.M.	0.16

Schedule	
Leave St. Andrew or Eastport: 8:00 A.M., 1:00 P.M., 7:00 P.M.	
Leave Bayville: 9:30 A.M., 2:30 P.M., 8:30 P.M.	0.40
Leave St. Andrew or Eastport: 8:00 A.M., 1:00 P.M., 5:00 P.M.	
Leave Bayville: 9:30 A.M., 2:30 P.M., 6:30 P.M.	0.49
Leave St. Andrew or Eastport: Hourly from 7:00 A.M. to 7:00 P.M.	
Leave Bayville: Hourly from 8:30 A.M. to 8:30 P.M.	0.95
Relative Importance	
Airport	0.29
Schedule	0.71

Case Questions

1. Given the aggregate answers presented in the study results and the questionnaire, what subsequent analyses and what variables would you recommend to provide a more detailed understanding of the situation? Explain your reasoning.
2. Evaluate the appropriateness of the questionnaire used and the selected conjoint analysis to answer McNamara's questions. Are they sufficient? Specifically, does conjoint analysis make assumptions that are not warranted in this particular situation?
3. Are there any additional questions that you would add to the questionnaire in Exhibit C3.11.1? Why or why not? If yes, design the questions that you would add. Would the conjoint analysis need to be altered to accommodate these new questions and/or the underlying variables they represent? If so, how?
4. Can you recommend any other survey or data source that could replace or supplement the performed analysis to better meet McNamara's information needs? Develop a study proposal for the recommended research.
5. How could the conjoint analysis be modified or enriched to better satisfy McNamara's objectives and information needs? Be specific about the variables used, the levels of each, and the assumptions that would guide the construction of the utilities generated by the conjoint program.
6. Considering the answers received to the questionnaire in Exhibit C6.3, are there any attributes of the new service that McNamara had not considered before that would increase customers' satisfactions with the new service? How might McNamara confirm this "first reading" of the results? Provide a detailed description.
7. Based on the results provided in Tables C3.11.3 through C3.11.10, what would be your recommendations on how McNamara should best proceed with the new Executive Express Air service?

Appendix to Case 3.11

Cost data: The price for Eastport–Bayville flights varies with the time of day, the flight date, and the date of reservation. McNamara's planes are to have a flat rate for the proposed St. Andrew–Bayville service. The fares used in the questionnaire represent the highest ($220) and lowest ($120) round-trip fares charged in the last year for the Eastport–Bayville flight, and the fare at the time the questionnaire was printed ($170). The typical fare (for weekday flights) ranges from $160 to $180.

Projected Annual Cash Flows for Express Air (including $800,000 non-cash depreciation of plane purchase price)

Outflows		
	Fixed costs	$1,014,554
	Direct operating costs	$240/per round trip
Inflows		
	Depends on fare charged and the number of passengers per flight.	

Breakeven. Assume that each passenger buys one round-trip fare. At $120/round trip, breakeven occurs at 682 round trips per year (assuming 80 percent load factor). For breakeven, the "numerator" is the fixed cost of $1,014,554, which must be covered by revenues. The "denominator" comprises the $120 revenue per trip (times 18 passengers at capacity, multiplied by 80 percent capacity), less the $240 variable cost (per trip), or $120*18*80 percent – $240 = $1488 (per trip). Breakeven is therefore:

$$\frac{1{,}014{,}554 \text{ (fixed cost)}}{\$1488 \text{ (rev per trip)}} = 682 \text{ round trips}$$

At six round trips per week, or 52*6 = 312 per year, this means that we would have to make at least two round trips per day, assuming 80 percent load factor.

CASE 3.12 PC MALL, INC.

Note: This case is meant to serve as a "capstone," in that many elements of marketing research practice are illustrated, and students may offer alternative analyses based on project source data, which is provided in spreadsheet form. All information stems from an actual marketing research project, conclusions made to the sponsoring firm are unaltered, and analyses are as presented by the marketing research team. The case illustrates various elements of questionnaire design, statistical analysis, reporting, and making strategic recommendations; it should not be assumed, however, to illustrate flawless use of statistical and marketing research methodology, but rather their usage in the field by professionals.

Background

PC Mall is a publicly traded company with annual revenues more than $1 billion. The company sells a variety of merchandise, focusing primarily on computers, software, electronics, and related items. More than 100,000 different products from companies such as IBM, Microsoft, Compaq, Apple, and Hewlett-Packard, among others, are included in PC Mall's portfolio and are sold through catalogs and over the Internet. Its various catalogs include the PC Mall, MacMall, ClubMac, PC Mall Gov., and eCost.com brands. Online, the company operates Web sites for each of its catalog brands (PCMall.com, MacMall.com, ClubMac.com, PcMallGov.com, and eCost.com), as well as OnSale.com, a discount retailer and auction site. In addition, the company operates three retail showrooms that serve a dual function as "clicks and mortar" sales and awareness generators.

PC Mall serves different customer segments, among them businesses, government, educational institutions, and individual consumers. The majority of revenue comes from the MacMall and PC Mall brands. Telemarketing generates 70 percent of sales, the Internet 27 percent, and retail locations the remaining 3 percent.

Meeting customer needs in the best possible way is one of the key values that PC Mall's management believes in; it is one of the values that guide the firm's strategic decisions. For example, to achieve more rapid delivery of orders to its customers, PC Mall's distribution center was strategically located near FedEx's main hub in Memphis, Tennessee. In spite of all the efforts and activities targeted at constant improvement of the customers' satisfaction with the company, no formal systems or processes had been implemented for ongoing tracking of customer satisfaction levels.

The lack of knowledge about customer satisfaction and systems to measure it was a major topic of discussion at a recent cross-departmental meeting. Customer satisfaction was believed to affect customer loyalty, which was in turn directly related to the company's long-term profitability. The decision was made to engage a local research firm to help design such a process, to enable PC Mall's management to assess, on a quarterly basis, the state of customer satisfaction and loyalty to the company.

Project Objectives

The next day, the research firm was sent the description of the project, which, among other things, listed the following questions that the management expected to receive answers to:

1. What is the level of satisfaction among our customer base?
2. What is the relative impact of our satisfaction rating on loyalty and propensity to repurchase?

3. What are the key attributes that make up the overall satisfaction with our company? How do we perform on those attributes, and what is their relative impact on satisfaction?

Project Methodology and Results

Following the initial communication between Robert Rich, project manager, and Jack Taylor, account manager from the research firm, a meeting was scheduled to discuss several issues that would determine the scope of the project and to finalize the methodology proposed by the research firm.

One of the main issues facing the project team was heterogeneity: PC Mall had a number of distinct customer groups, such as businesses, government, educational institutions, and individual consumers, with differing needs, shopping habits, and procurement procedures. Each group could be further segmented into smaller subgroups, based on the attributes and benefits that were important to them, or other characteristics (often called "latent segmentation"). To take but one example of many, the "consumer brands" included PC Mall Consumer, MacMall, Club Mall and eCost.com—the MacMall and ClubMall brands attracted a similar customer set, but this was not the case for the PC Mall brand. Additionally, eCost, the online discount brand, seemed to attract consumers who were more willing to trade off product attributes and benefits for lower cost, compared with the typical PC Mall customer.

Because this would be an initial pilot survey, Rich and Taylor decided to explore only the "individual consumer" segment and, in particular, to focus on consumers who shopped via PC Mall and MacMall, as opposed to the other outlets, which were considered more specialized and to operate with different channel dynamics. The project team anticipated that the model developed for the "individual consumer" segment could be subsequently implemented, with suitable amendments, across other customer segments.

At a follow-up meeting of the project team with other members of PC Mall's management, Jack Taylor presented a detailed, ambitious six-step approach, calling on techniques he had learned during his MBA studies and subsequent immersion in both other projects and PC Mall's specific needs. After intensive discussions with other members of the senior management team, Robert Rich approved the proposal. The six-step methodology, exactly as proposed and implemented, was as follows:

Step 1: *Conduct interviews with PC Mall customers to determine attributes important to them.* This step involved random selection of customers from the company's database of past PC/MacMall purchasers to conduct individual and open-ended interviews. The objective of the interviews was to formulate a list of attributes that affected overall satisfaction level with the shopping experience at PC/MacMall. It was decided that interviewing 15 customers was adequate to extract the necessary insights about satisfaction-driving attributes. The interviews were conducted by phone and were transcribed to facilitate in-depth follow-up study of the provided answers.

Step 2: *Group the attributes under the benefit types that they provide to customers.* Based on the attributes and the formed benefit types, construct a survey. The 34 attributes identified from Step 1 were grouped into six benefit types: support services, product information, pricing, sales service, product, and Web convenience. The grouping was performed based on the experience of the research team and in collaboration with Robert Rich. The identified attributes and their benefit types are listed in Table C3.12.1.

The survey questionnaire was designed utilizing the information about the attributes that were found important for PC/MacMall users. The questions were constructed to evaluate the company's performance on the 34 identified attributes; also the questions were grouped to reflect the six benefits that these attributes provided to consumers. After adding questions about consumers' purchase history, their overall satisfaction, future purchase intent, and self-stated loyalty, a draft questionnaire was sent for Robert Rich's review. Because accurate inferences regarding the core "dependent variables," satisfaction and loyalty, were considered crucial, they were each measured in two different ways. Overall satisfaction was assessed by two questions: "Considering your experiences with PC Mall or MacMall, how would you rate your overall satisfaction?" and "How well does PC Mall or MacMall continually meet your expectations?" Customer loyalty was also measured by two questions: "What is the likelihood that you will purchase from PC Mall or MacMall again in the future?" and "What is the likelihood that you will recommend PC Mall or MacMall to others?"

Step 3: *Conduct test survey to finalize the questionnaire based on respondents' feedback.* Two tests were performed to perfect the draft questionnaire that was formed at Step 2. Each test involved face-to-face administration of the draft questionnaire to 10–15 respondents. After each test, corrections and clarifications in terms of phrasing, question order, elimination of redundant questions, and restructuring of

Table C3.12.1 Attributes Affecting Overall Satisfaction Levels

Benefit Type	Identified Attributes
Support services	1. Timeliness of delivery 2. Accuracy of delivery 3. Packaging of delivered product 4. Order status information
Product information	1. Product information quality 2. Catalog information 3. Product information accuracy 4. Information on compatibility of products 5. Stock information 6. Product comparisons
Pricing	1. Competitiveness of prices 2. Timeliness of rebates 3. Shipping costs 4. Package deals 5. Consistency of pricing
Sales service	1. Response to e-mail inquiry 2. Phone service availability 3. Attitude of sales staff 4. Knowledgeable salespeople 5. Ease of phone order 6. Technical support postpurchase 7. Return policy 8. Exchange policy
Product	1. Product variety 2. Product selection w/in category 3. Stock availability 4. Latest products
Web convenience	1. Web site design 2. Ease of navigation 3. Ease of checkout process on Web 4. Webpage speed 5. Ease of product search 6. Ease of rebate search 7. Readability of Webpages

unclear questions were done to finalize the questionnaire for use in the full-scale survey, which appears in Exhibit C3.12.1.

Step 4: *Conduct full-scale survey using the modified questionnaire.* The questionnaire was placed in online form, and an e-link was sent to more than 50,000 consumers who had purchased in the past from PC Mall or MacMall and whose e-mail addresses were registered in the company's database.

Nearly 5000 responses were received during the 2-week period allocated for online completion of the questionnaires, of which 3947 questionnaires were valid and could be used for the data analysis. The invalid questionnaires, which were excluded from the analysis, were excessively incomplete and/or contained contradictory answers.

The final sample size of 3947 responses contained 2,364 MacMall users, 632 PC Mall users, 719 users of both PC and MacMall, and 232 nonusers. Consumers who purchased at PC Mall and/or MacMall more than 2 years ago were classified as "nonusers" and were excluded from the analysis. It was decided that consumers with purchasing experience dated more than 2 years ago would not provide relevant and/or accurate answers. To obtain the clearest inferences, PC Mall users, MacMall users, and PC/MacMall users were treated as three separate segments in the data analysis and interpretation.

Step 5: *Analyze the collected data.* Because so much of the project hinged on the attribute grouping (into six benefits) performed during Steps 1 and 2 (Table C3.12.1), the project team felt it was essential to validate it. To do this, they turned to factor analysis (see Chapter 11), performed using standard varimax rotation to reduce ambiguity in interpreting the resulting groups. Additionally, the coefficients that belonged to the attributes within each of the six factors were used to generate the attributes' impact on the satisfaction with each factor. Specifically, each attribute's coefficient was divided by the standard deviation of that attribute's performance, to help standardize the attributes' impact across the six factors.

Factor analysis was also performed on satisfaction and loyalty questions to arrive at a single factor for each—one that represented satisfaction and another that represented loyalty. (This was important for regression analysis so that the two satisfaction questions would become one dependent variable).

Next, each attribute's performance was represented as the mean of all the answers regarding that specific attribute. The attributes' performance within each benefit, weighted by the impact of the respective attributes, was used to calculate customers' satisfaction with each benefit (or benefit performance). For example, the entire procedure can be illustrated in terms of how consumer satisfaction with support services was determined:

1. Impact and performance scores were multiplied for each of the attributes under the support services benefit. As shown in Table C3.12.1, there were four of these: timeliness of delivery, accuracy of delivery, packaging of delivered product, and order status information.
2. The quantities produced by the earlier multiplication and representing each attribute within a specific benefit (in this case four numbers) were, thereafter, simply added together to form the overall performance score of the support services benefit. This procedure was performed for each of the six benefits.

Finally, the six factors that emerged from factor analysis were used as independent variables (as proxies for the benefit scores) and regressed against the factor that was developed for satisfaction. That satisfaction factor was regressed against the loyalty factor to arrive at the impact that satisfaction had on loyalty.

The previous analysis produced satisfaction models for each of the three segments: PC Mall users, MacMall users, and users of both brands. The model for each segment differed in terms of the attributes' impact and performance, the benefits that impacted the satisfaction scores in a statistically significant way, the benefits' performance and impact scores, and the impact of the satisfaction scores on how loyal the customers were. For example, Exhibit C3.12.2 illustrates the satisfaction model that emerged for the PC Mall users. (Note how the benefit variables were formed and how the various regressions were conducted.)

The aforementioned satisfaction models enabled the PC Mall management to identify the benefits that affected the loyalty of the company's customers, to assess the current satisfaction with each of the benefits, and to recognize which attributes should be enhanced to increase satisfaction and, consequently, loyalty levels. Furthermore, the values of the impact scores made it possible to quantify the degree to which each attribute's performance should be improved to achieve a desired improvement in loyalty scores.

Table C3.12.2 **Summary of Segment Performance and Recommendations**

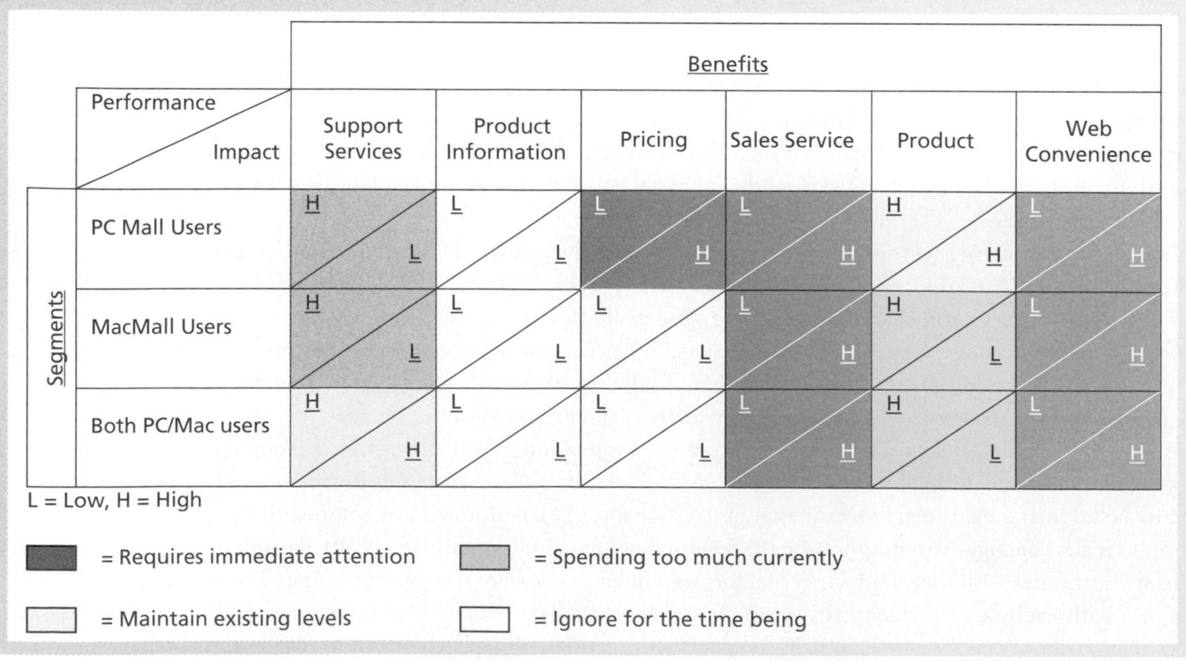

Segments (Performance / Impact)	Support Services	Product Information	Pricing	Sales Service	Product	Web Convenience
PC Mall Users	H / L	L / L	L / H	L / H	H / H	L / H
MacMall Users	H / L	L / L	L / L	L / H	H / L	L / H
Both PC/Mac users	H / H	L / L	L / L	L / H	H / L	L / H

Benefits

L = Low, H = High

= Requires immediate attention
= Spending too much currently
= Maintain existing levels
= Ignore for the time being

Step 6: *Provide recommendations.* Based on the midpoint of the overall scores produced by the analysis, the performance and the impact scores were split into "high" (H) and "low" (L) categories. This allowed the team to identify benefits/attributes that needed to be maintained at the current level, those that required immediate attention (i.e., improvement), those that could be ignored, and, lastly, those on which too many resources had been expended. Table C3.12.2 summarizes the recommendations for each customer segment.

The low impact of the product information benefit was tentatively explained by the fact that the attributes making up this benefit were standardized and undifferentiated across competitors and therefore did not affect consumers' purchasing decisions.

Conclusion

Robert Rich and the PC Mall team were impressed with the quality of the survey instrument, the many responses received, and, most of all, the thoughtfulness and sophistication of the analysis. They did have many questions, however. Data had been collected from customers in only PC Mall's database. Perhaps they were more likely to be satisfied? Would heavy users be overrepresented? Rob Rich in particular was curious whether factor analysis, even though it seemed to vindicate the initial benefit groupings, was really the best way to "compress" and clarify the data. He wondered whether there were some other ways to seek out natural segments in the data other than the ones presented by PC Mall or identified in the course of the analysis. Did demographics make a difference? Did the correlations found in the analysis really identify causal links? Rob Rich also realized that many of the variables not used in the satisfaction analysis directly were ordinal or categorical and would be difficult to incorporate into intensive statistical analyses later on because ordinary regression would not be suitable. How would they make sense of *those* patterns?

Finally, there was the pivotal issue of implementation: Some of the suggested changes would be more costly and time-consuming than others, and the team was at a loss for what to do first, despite their appreciation for the satisfaction analysis. Perhaps implementing one change would render others unnecessary, and still others even more pressing. In the end, the report from Taylor's team answered many important questions, and also raised quite a few new ones, as high-quality research often will.

Exhibit C3.12.1: Questionnaire Used in the Full-Scale PC Mall or MacMall Customer Service Survey

This survey is intended to improve the quality of the services provided by PC Mall and MacMall brands and will take approximately 10 minutes to complete. All survey responses will remain anonymous and confidential. For your efforts, you are eligible to be entered into a drawing for a new iPod Mini. If you wish to be entered into the drawing, please include your e-mail address at the end of the survey. Thank you in advance for your time and cooperation.

General Instructions

If, at any time during this survey there are any questions or sets of questions that you cannot answer, or have no opinion about, just leave them blank and go to the next question.

1. Introduction

1.1. In the past year, approximately how many electronic or computer products have you purchased online or by catalogue? (Count multiple products in one order as separate.)

- ☐ 0
- ☐ 1
- ☐ 2–4
- ☐ 5–10
- ☐ 11+

1.2. From which of the following businesses have you purchased products within the past 2 years?

- ☐ PC Mall
- ☐ MacMall
- ☐ Both PC Mall and MacMall
- ☐ I have not purchased from either of them in the past 2 years.

If 1.2 = Have not purchased from either of them in the past 2 years, then skip ahead to 9.1.

1.3. Through which of the following methods have you purchased products from PC Mall or MacMall within the past 2 years? (Choose all that apply.)

☐ Web site search followed by online order
☐ Web site search followed by phone order
☐ Catalog search followed by phone order
☐ Catalog search followed by online order

1.4. What/who influenced your decision to purchase from PC Mall or MacMall? (Check all that apply.)

☐ PC Mall or MacMall catalogs
☐ Third-party evaluation Web sites (e.g., Bizrate.com)
☐ Recommended by friend/acquaintance
☐ Price search engines (e.g., Pricescan.com)
☐ Chat rooms/message boards
☐ Banner/pop-up ads
☐ Other ________________________________

1.5. How satisfied are you with the frequency with which you receive catalogs from PC Mall or MacMall on an ongoing basis (i.e., how often you receive them)? (Check the appropriate level.)

☐	☐	☐	☐	☐	☐	☐	☐
Too few			Just right			Too many	Do not receive

1.6. How often WOULD YOU LIKE TO receive catalogs from PC Mall or MacMall? (Choose one.)

☐ Prefer not to receive
☐ Weekly
☐ Monthly
☐ Quarterly
☐ Semi-annually
☐ Annually

2. Support Services

2.1. On average, how satisfied are you with the following aspects of PC Mall or MacMall's processing of your order?

1 Very unsatisfied
2 Moderately unsatisfied
3 Slightly unsatisfied
4 Neutral
5 Slightly satisfied
6 Moderately satisfied
7 Very satisfied

1	2	3	4	5	6	7	
☐	☐	☐	☐	☐	☐	☐	Timeliness of processing your order for shipment
☐	☐	☐	☐	☐	☐	☐	Accuracy of delivered products (e.g., deliver the right product(s) to the right address)
☐	☐	☐	☐	☐	☐	☐	Condition of delivered products (i.e., was the product damaged during shipping?)
☐	☐	☐	☐	☐	☐	☐	Information about your order status (i.e., online, e-mail, U.S. Mail, phone)

2.2. What is your most preferred method of being informed of your delivery/order status? (Please check one.)

☐ E-mail
☐ Phone call
☐ Fax
☐ Online
☐ Other

3. Product Information

3.1. How satisfied are you with the following aspects of product information available on PC Mall or MacMall's Web site or catalog? (If you have not visited the Web site or viewed a catalog in the past 2 years, skip this question.)

1 Very unsatisfied
2 Moderately unsatisfied
3 Slightly unsatisfied
4 Neutral
5 Slightly satisfied
6 Moderately satisfied
7 Very satisfied

1	2	3	4	5	6	7	
☐	☐	☐	☐	☐	☐	☐	Completeness of product information on Web (Does it give you all the information you need?)
☐	☐	☐	☐	☐	☐	☐	Usefulness of the product information contained in the catalog
☐	☐	☐	☐	☐	☐	☐	Accuracy of product information
☐	☐	☐	☐	☐	☐	☐	Information about compatibility with other products
☐	☐	☐	☐	☐	☐	☐	Accuracy of in-stock/out-of-stock information on Web
☐	☐	☐	☐	☐	☐	☐	Ease of comparison among products

4. Pricing

4.1. How satisfied are you with each of the following pricing factors from PC Mall or MacMall?

1 Very unsatisfied
2 Moderately unsatisfied
3 Slightly unsatisfied
4 Neutral
5 Slightly satisfied
6 Moderately satisfied
7 Very satisfied

1	2	3	4	5	6	7	
☐	☐	☐	☐	☐	☐	☐	Competitiveness of their prices vs. other companies
☐	☐	☐	☐	☐	☐	☐	Timeliness of rebate refund
☐	☐	☐	☐	☐	☐	☐	Shipping costs
☐	☐	☐	☐	☐	☐	☐	Package deals (namely, bundled products—for example, laptop w/printer)
☐	☐	☐	☐	☐	☐	☐	Pricing consistency across time periods

4.2. Of the following factors, please check those that were not explained to you early enough in the shopping process. (Check all that apply.)

☐ Item price
☐ Sales tax
☐ Basic shipping cost
☐ Priority shipping cost
☐ Availability of shipping outside of USA
☐ Required accessories needed
☐ Optional accessories
☐ Warranty costs
☐ Other

____

5. Sales Service

5.1. How satisfied are you with each of the following quality of sales service factors from PC Mall or MacMall? (If you have not utilized a particular service, skip this question.)

1 Very unsatisfied
2 Moderately unsatisfied
3 Slightly unsatisfied
4 Neutral
5 Slightly satisfied
6 Moderately satisfied
7 Very satisfied

1	2	3	4	5	6	7	
☐	☐	☐	☐	☐	☐	☐	Responsiveness to e-mail inquiry (Did they get back to you in a timely manner?)
☐	☐	☐	☐	☐	☐	☐	Promptness of phone customer service (prepurchase)
☐	☐	☐	☐	☐	☐	☐	Courtesy of telephone sales staff
☐	☐	☐	☐	☐	☐	☐	Technical knowledge of sales staff
☐	☐	☐	☐	☐	☐	☐	Ease of phone ordering
☐	☐	☐	☐	☐	☐	☐	Postpurchase technical support
☐	☐	☐	☐	☐	☐	☐	Return policy
☐	☐	☐	☐	☐	☐	☐	Exchange policy

5.2. If you returned a product and were not satisfied with the "return" experience, please briefly tell us why.

____

____

____

____

____

5.3. If you exchanged a product and were not satisfied with the "exchange" experience, please briefly tell us why.

____

____

____

____

____

6. Product

6.1. How satisfied are you with the following product-offering factors from PC Mall or MacMall?

1 Very unsatisfied
2 Moderately unsatisfied
3 Slightly unsatisfied
4 Neutral
5 Slightly satisfied
6 Moderately satisfied
7 Very satisfied

1	2	3	4	5	6	7	
☐	☐	☐	☐	☐	☐	☐	Overall variety of products offered
☐	☐	☐	☐	☐	☐	☐	Selection of items within a product category
☐	☐	☐	☐	☐	☐	☐	Availability of products (i.e., in stock)
☐	☐	☐	☐	☐	☐	☐	Availability of newest products

6.2. If you are not satisfied with the selection within a product category, what is the reason? (Choose all that apply.)

- ☐ Too FEW products to choose from (not enough selection)
- ☐ Too MANY products to choose from (number of products were overwhelming)
- ☐ Not the RIGHT products that you were looking for
- ☐ Other

7. Web Convenience

7.1. If you have viewed their Web site(s), what kind of Internet service connection did you use most recently? (Choose one.)

- ☐ Dial-up
- ☐ Cable modem
- ☐ DSL
- ☐ Network
- ☐ Other

7.2. How would you rate PC Mall (not MacMall) on the following aspects of its Web site? (Check the appropriate level. If you have never visited PC Mall's Web site, skip this question.)

1 Very poor
2 Poor
3 Below average
4 Average
5 Above average
6 Good
7 Excellent

1	2	3	4	5	6	7	
☐	☐	☐	☐	☐	☐	☐	Overall Web site design (e.g., feeling of welcome and professionalism, etc.)
☐	☐	☐	☐	☐	☐	☐	Ease of navigation between Webpages
☐	☐	☐	☐	☐	☐	☐	Ease of checkout process
☐	☐	☐	☐	☐	☐	☐	Webpage loading speed
☐	☐	☐	☐	☐	☐	☐	Ease of product search
☐	☐	☐	☐	☐	☐	☐	Ease of finding rebate information on Web site
☐	☐	☐	☐	☐	☐	☐	Readability of Webpages (e.g., font size/type)

7.3. How would you rate MacMall (not PC Mall) on the following aspects of its Web site? (Check the appropriate level. If you have never visited MacMall's Web site, skip this question.)

1 Very poor
2 Poor
3 Below average
4 Average
5 Above average
6 Good
7 Excellent

1	2	3	4	5	6	7	
☐	☐	☐	☐	☐	☐	☐	Overall Web site design (e.g., feeling of welcome and professionalism, etc.)
☐	☐	☐	☐	☐	☐	☐	Ease of navigation between Web pages
☐	☐	☐	☐	☐	☐	☐	Ease of checkout process
☐	☐	☐	☐	☐	☐	☐	Webpage loading speed
☐	☐	☐	☐	☐	☐	☐	Ease of product search
☐	☐	☐	☐	☐	☐	☐	Ease of finding rebate information on Web site
☐	☐	☐	☐	☐	☐	☐	Readability of Webpages (e.g., font size/type)

8. Evaluation of the Company

8.1. Considering your experiences with PC Mall or MacMall, how would you rate your overall satisfaction? (Check the appropriate level.)

☐ ☐ ☐ ☐ ☐ ☐ ☐

Very dissatisfied — Neutral — Very satisfied

8.2. How well does PC Mall or MacMall continually meet your expectations? (Choose one of the following.)

☐ ☐ ☐ ☐ ☐ ☐ ☐

Not met — Met — Exceeded

8.3. What is the likelihood that you will purchase from PC Mall or MacMall again in the future? (Check the appropriate level.)

☐ ☐ ☐ ☐ ☐ ☐ ☐

Very unlikely — Neutral — Very likely

8.4. What is the likelihood that you will recommend PC Mall or MacMall to others? (Check the appropriate level.)

☐ ☐ ☐ ☐ ☐ ☐ ☐

Very unlikely — Neutral — Very likely

8.5. How important are the following in convincing you to purchase from PC Mall or MacMall in the future? (Rank the six choices from 1 to 6, where 1 is the most important and 6 is the least important. Use each number only once.)

1	2	3	4	5	6	
☐	☐	☐	☐	☐	☐	Low price guarantee
☐	☐	☐	☐	☐	☐	Loyalty program
☐	☐	☐	☐	☐	☐	Package deals (e.g., laptop with printer)
☐	☐	☐	☐	☐	☐	Free/discounted shipping
☐	☐	☐	☐	☐	☐	PC/MacMall rebates
☐	☐	☐	☐	☐	☐	Educational discounts (i.e., discounts for students and teachers)

9. Demographics

9.1. Age (please check one):

☐ 18–22
☐ 23–29
☐ 30–39
☐ 40–49
☐ 50–64
☐ 65+

9.2. Approximate pre-tax household income (please check one):

☐ Less than $20,000
☐ $20,000–$29,999
☐ $30,000–$44,999
☐ $45,000–$64,999
☐ $65,000–$89,999
☐ $90,000–$119,999
☐ $120,000 +

9.3. Highest level of education completed (please check one):

- ☐ Some schooling
- ☐ High school
- ☐ Undergraduate
- ☐ Graduate
- ☐ Postgraduate
- ☐ Other ______________________________

9.4. Occupation (please check one):

- ☐ Full-time homemaker
- ☐ Management
- ☐ Professional
- ☐ Technical
- ☐ Sales or marketing
- ☐ Tradesperson or laborer
- ☐ Student
- ☐ Retired
- ☐ Other______________________________

10. Conclusion

10.1. Is there anything else that you would like to tell us about your shopping experience with PC Mall or MacMall?

____

____

____

____

____

____

____

10.2. To be entered into the drawing for a free iPod Mini, please enter your e-mail address below. Your address will be kept separate from your answers to the survey.

____

____

____

Thank you for your time in completing the survey. Your input is valuable and appreciated.
If you are the winner of the iPod Mini, we will contact you by e-mail by Dec. 17, 2004.

Exhibit C3.12.2: Satisfaction Model for PC Mall Users**

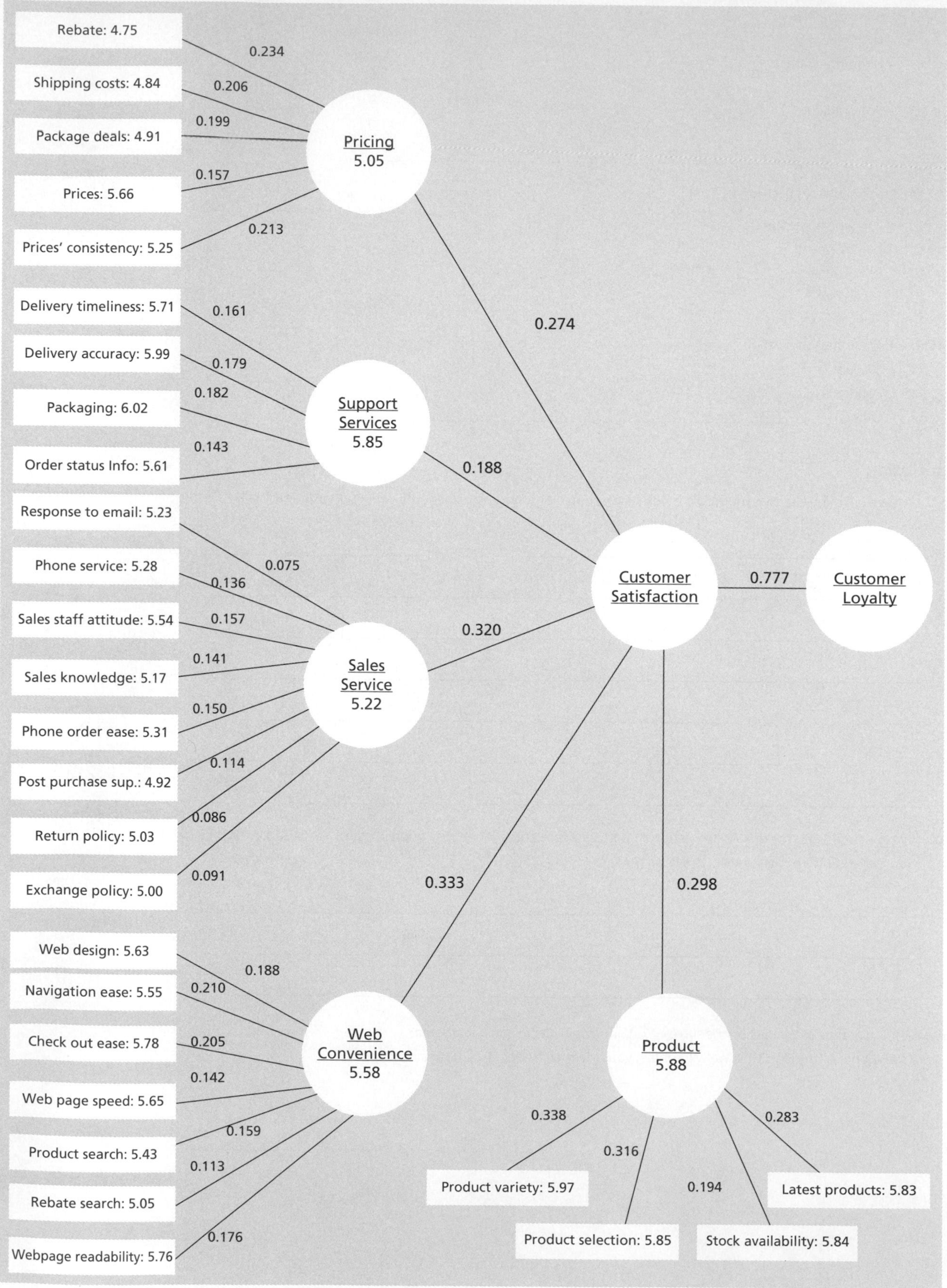

**The impact of the product information benefit was found to be statistically non-significant.

Case Questions

1. Do the constructed satisfaction models and the recommendations provided by the research firm adequately answer the questions posed at the outset by the PC Mall management? Explain in detail.
2. Consider the scope chosen for the pilot project (studying only individual consumer segments, particularly PC Mall and MacMall users). Discuss advantages and disadvantages of such an approach. Would you recommend any other way to proceed with the initial survey? Do these segments seem to capture the essence of PC Mall's business situation? To which other segments might you expand as a follow-up study?
3. Evaluate the six-step approach proposed and implemented by the research firm. Outline the shortcomings and the advantages of each step. For each identified shortcoming, propose specific corrective actions or alternative analyses. Be specific when providing your outline and recommendations.
4. The research firm used factor analysis with Varimax rotation and regression analysis to analyze the collected data. What other statistical analyses could be used to analyze the collected data and address PC Mall management's information needs? Refer to Exhibit C3.12.1 for the type of data that was collected in the survey. (Note that the analyses involving these data appear throughout the text, primarily in Chapters 10–12.)
5. Overall satisfaction and loyalty were measured with two questions each. Was this a sound research strategy? (Are two measures enough? Are they redundant?) Provide a detailed explanation of the analyses that you would select if you were assigned this task.
6. How could the model be further developed to connect customers' loyalty with revenues and profits they generate for the company? Compile a research proposal for this objective, mentioning the information needed, the statistical analyses to be used, and the detailed explanation of how these analyses would answer the question.
7. The recommendations of the research team hinge critically on their having parceled the attributes appropriately into benefits, as in Table C3.12.1. Do you think they have done so, and is this a reasonable procedure? Are certain attributes overrepresented, perhaps skewing the resulting benefits (factors)? If so, which might best be left out of future analyses, if any?
8. Robert Rich had a number of concerns at the conclusion of the case, including issues of sample selection (e.g., only prior users, and representation of heavy users), the use of factor analysis, the role of demographics, other types of segmentation, variable types difficult to analyze rigorously, and major questions of implementation. Which of these seem particularly crucial given PC Mall's predicament? Can some be safely sidestepped for the time being?

The survey is lengthy and complex, with many scale types represented. Can you identify nominal, ordinal, rank-ordered, interval, and ratio scales among the questions? For each type you can identify, attempt to perform a regression analysis of the appropriate type (based on the dependent variable you have selected), using regressors that would be sensible to explain it. Are there any variables used in the survey that simply cannot be explained by an appropriate regression analysis? Which ones, and why not? Finally, what would you do to analyze the open-ended verbal data stemming from Sections 5 and 10 of the questionnaire?

APPENDIX A

Table A.1 **Tail Areas and Critical Values for the Standard Normal Distribution (*z*)**

z distribution

Probability density function (pictured at right): $\frac{1}{\sqrt{2\pi}}e^{-x^2/2}$

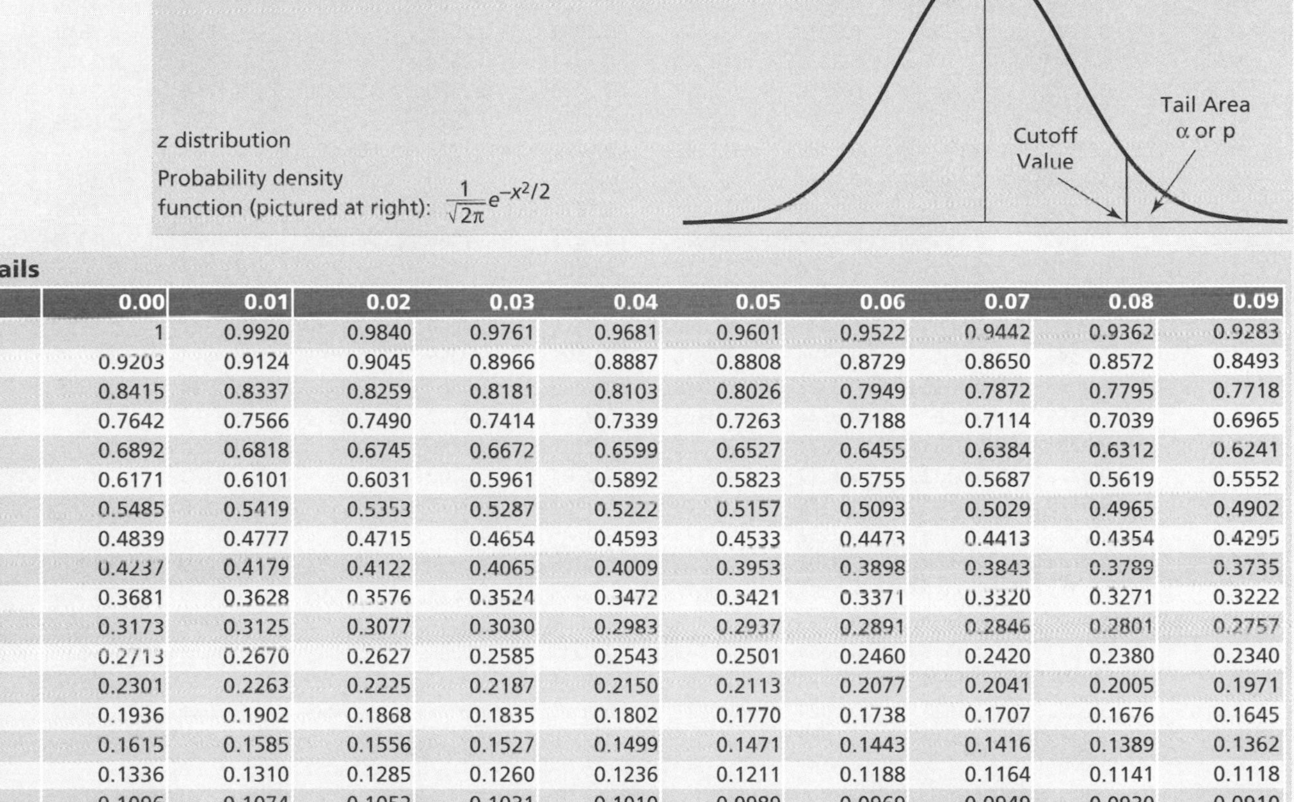

Two Tails

z	0.00	0.01	0.02	0.03	0.04	0.05	0.06	0.07	0.08	0.09
0.0	1	0.9920	0.9840	0.9761	0.9681	0.9601	0.9522	0.9442	0.9362	0.9283
0.1	0.9203	0.9124	0.9045	0.8966	0.8887	0.8808	0.8729	0.8650	0.8572	0.8493
0.2	0.8415	0.8337	0.8259	0.8181	0.8103	0.8026	0.7949	0.7872	0.7795	0.7718
0.3	0.7642	0.7566	0.7490	0.7414	0.7339	0.7263	0.7188	0.7114	0.7039	0.6965
0.4	0.6892	0.6818	0.6745	0.6672	0.6599	0.6527	0.6455	0.6384	0.6312	0.6241
0.5	0.6171	0.6101	0.6031	0.5961	0.5892	0.5823	0.5755	0.5687	0.5619	0.5552
0.6	0.5485	0.5419	0.5353	0.5287	0.5222	0.5157	0.5093	0.5029	0.4965	0.4902
0.7	0.4839	0.4777	0.4715	0.4654	0.4593	0.4533	0.4473	0.4413	0.4354	0.4295
0.8	0.4237	0.4179	0.4122	0.4065	0.4009	0.3953	0.3898	0.3843	0.3789	0.3735
0.9	0.3681	0.3628	0.3576	0.3524	0.3472	0.3421	0.3371	0.3320	0.3271	0.3222
1.0	0.3173	0.3125	0.3077	0.3030	0.2983	0.2937	0.2891	0.2846	0.2801	0.2757
1.1	0.2713	0.2670	0.2627	0.2585	0.2543	0.2501	0.2460	0.2420	0.2380	0.2340
1.2	0.2301	0.2263	0.2225	0.2187	0.2150	0.2113	0.2077	0.2041	0.2005	0.1971
1.3	0.1936	0.1902	0.1868	0.1835	0.1802	0.1770	0.1738	0.1707	0.1676	0.1645
1.4	0.1615	0.1585	0.1556	0.1527	0.1499	0.1471	0.1443	0.1416	0.1389	0.1362
1.5	0.1336	0.1310	0.1285	0.1260	0.1236	0.1211	0.1188	0.1164	0.1141	0.1118
1.6	0.1096	0.1074	0.1052	0.1031	0.1010	0.0989	0.0969	0.0949	0.0930	0.0910
1.7	0.0891	0.0873	0.0854	0.0836	0.0819	0.0801	0.0784	0.0767	0.0751	0.0735
1.8	0.0719	0.0703	0.0688	0.0672	0.0658	0.0643	0.0629	0.0615	0.0601	0.0588
1.9	0.0574	0.0561	0.0549	0.0536	0.0524	0.0512	0.0500	0.0488	0.0477	0.0466
2.0	0.0455	0.0444	0.0434	0.0424	0.0414	0.0404	0.0394	0.0385	0.0375	0.0366
2.1	0.0357	0.0349	0.0340	0.0332	0.0324	0.0316	0.0308	0.0300	0.0293	0.0285
2.2	0.0278	0.0271	0.0264	0.0257	0.0251	0.0244	0.0238	0.0232	0.0226	0.0220
2.3	0.0214	0.0209	0.0203	0.0198	0.0193	0.0188	0.0183	0.0178	0.0173	0.0168
2.4	0.0164	0.0160	0.0155	0.0151	0.0147	0.0143	0.0139	0.0135	0.0131	0.0128
2.5	0.0124	0.0121	0.0117	0.0114	0.0111	0.0108	0.0105	0.0102	0.0099	0.0096
2.6	0.0093	0.0091	0.0088	0.0085	0.0083	0.0080	0.0078	0.0076	0.0074	0.0071
2.7	0.0069	0.0067	0.0065	0.0063	0.0061	0.0060	0.0058	0.0056	0.0054	0.0053
2.8	0.0051	0.0050	0.0048	0.0047	0.0045	0.0044	0.0042	0.0041	0.0040	0.0039
2.9	0.0037	0.0036	0.0035	0.0034	0.0033	0.0032	0.0031	0.0030	0.0029	0.0028

z	0.0	0.1	0.2	0.3	0.4	0.5	0.6	0.7	0.8	0.9
3	2.70E-03	1.94E-03	1.37E-03	9.67E-04	6.74E-04	4.65E-04	3.18E-04	2.16E-04	1.45E-04	9.62E-05
4	6.33E-05	4.13E-05	2.67E-05	1.71E-05	1.08E-05	6.80E-06	4.22E-06	2.60E-06	1.59E-06	9.58E-07
5	5.73E-07	3.40E-07	1.99E-07	1.16E-07	6.66E-08	3.80E-08	2.14E-08	1.20E-08	6.63E-09	3.64E-09
6	1.97E-09	1.06E-09	5.65E-10	2.98E-10	1.55E-10	8.03E-11	4.11E-11	2.08E-11	1.05E-11	5.20E-12

continued

Table A.1 Tail Areas and Critical Values for the Standard Normal Distribution (z) (*continued*)

One Tail

z	0.00	0.01	0.02	0.03	0.04	0.05	0.06	0.07	0.08	0.09
0.0	0.5	0.4960	0.4920	0.4880	0.4840	0.4801	0.4761	0.4721	0.4681	0.4641
0.1	0.4602	0.4562	0.4522	0.4483	0.4443	0.4404	0.4364	0.4325	0.4286	0.4247
0.2	0.4207	0.4168	0.4129	0.4090	0.4052	0.4013	0.3974	0.3936	0.3897	0.3859
0.3	0.3821	0.3783	0.3745	0.3707	0.3669	0.3632	0.3594	0.3557	0.3520	0.3483
0.4	0.3446	0.3409	0.3372	0.3336	0.3300	0.3264	0.3228	0.3192	0.3156	0.3121
0.5	0.3085	0.3050	0.3015	0.2981	0.2946	0.2912	0.2877	0.2843	0.2810	0.2776
0.6	0.2743	0.2709	0.2676	0.2643	0.2611	0.2578	0.2546	0.2514	0.2483	0.2451
0.7	0.2420	0.2389	0.2358	0.2327	0.2296	0.2266	0.2236	0.2206	0.2177	0.2148
0.8	0.2119	0.2090	0.2061	0.2033	0.2005	0.1977	0.1949	0.1922	0.1894	0.1867
0.9	0.1841	0.1814	0.1788	0.1762	0.1736	0.1711	0.1685	0.1660	0.1635	0.1611
1.0	0.1587	0.1562	0.1539	0.1515	0.1492	0.1469	0.1446	0.1423	0.1401	0.1379
1.1	0.1357	0.1335	0.1314	0.1292	0.1271	0.1251	0.1230	0.1210	0.1190	0.1170
1.2	0.1151	0.1131	0.1112	0.1093	0.1075	0.1056	0.1038	0.1020	0.1003	0.0985
1.3	0.0968	0.0951	0.0934	0.0918	0.0901	0.0885	0.0869	0.0853	0.0838	0.0823
1.4	0.0808	0.0793	0.0778	0.0764	0.0749	0.0735	0.0721	0.0708	0.0694	0.0681
1.5	0.0668	0.0655	0.0643	0.0630	0.0618	0.0606	0.0594	0.0582	0.0571	0.0559
1.6	0.0548	0.0537	0.0526	0.0516	0.0505	0.0495	0.0485	0.0475	0.0465	0.0455
1.7	0.0446	0.0436	0.0427	0.0418	0.0409	0.0401	0.0392	0.0384	0.0375	0.0367
1.8	0.0359	0.0351	0.0344	0.0336	0.0329	0.0322	0.0314	0.0307	0.0301	0.0294
1.9	0.0287	0.0281	0.0274	0.0268	0.0262	0.0256	0.0250	0.0244	0.0239	0.0233
2.0	0.0228	0.0222	0.0217	0.0212	0.0207	0.0202	0.0197	0.0192	0.0188	0.0183
2.1	0.0179	0.0174	0.0170	0.0166	0.0162	0.0158	0.0154	0.0150	0.0146	0.0143
2.2	0.0139	0.0136	0.0132	0.0129	0.0125	0.0122	0.0119	0.0116	0.0113	0.0110
2.3	0.0107	0.0104	0.0102	0.0099	0.0096	0.0094	0.0091	0.0089	0.0087	0.0084
2.4	0.0082	0.0080	0.0078	0.0075	0.0073	0.0071	0.0069	0.0068	0.0066	0.0064
2.5	0.0062	0.0060	0.0059	0.0057	0.0055	0.0054	0.0052	0.0051	0.0049	0.0048
2.6	0.0047	0.0045	0.0044	0.0043	0.0041	0.0040	0.0039	0.0038	0.0037	0.0036
2.7	0.0035	0.0034	0.0033	0.0032	0.0031	0.0030	0.0029	0.0028	0.0027	0.0026
2.8	0.0026	0.0025	0.0024	0.0023	0.0023	0.0022	0.0021	0.0021	0.0020	0.0019
2.9	0.0019	0.0018	0.0018	0.0017	0.0016	0.0016	0.0015	0.0015	0.0014	0.0014

z	0.0	0.1	0.2	0.3	0.4	0.5	0.6	0.7	0.8	0.9
3	1.35E-03	9.68E-04	6.87E-04	4.83E-04	3.37E-04	2.33E-04	1.59E-04	1.08E-04	7.23E-05	4.81E-05
4	3.17E-05	2.07E-05	1.33E-05	8.54E-06	5.41E-06	3.40E-06	2.11E-06	1.30E-06	7.93E-07	4.79E-07
5	2.87E-07	1.70E-07	9.96E-08	5.79E-08	3.33E-08	1.90E-08	1.07E-08	5.99E-09	3.32E-09	1.82E-09
6	9.87E-10	5.30E-10	2.82E-10	1.49E-10	7.77E-11	4.02E-11	2.06E-11	1.04E-11	5.23E-12	2.60E-12

Table A.2 Tail Areas and Critical Values for the *t* Distribution

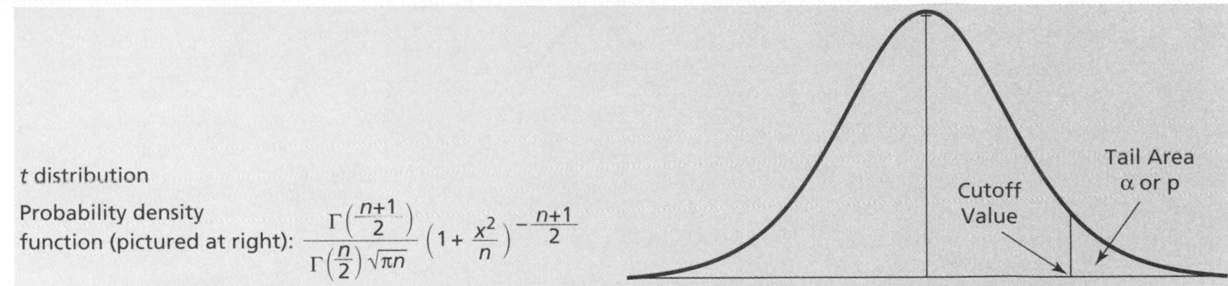

	Level of significance for two-tailed test								
df	**0.5**	**0.4**	**0.3**	**0.2**	**0.1**	**0.05**	**0.02**	**0.01**	**df**
	Level of significance for one-tailed test								
df	**0.25**	**0.2**	**0.15**	**0.1**	**0.05**	**0.025**	**0.01**	**0.005**	**df**
1	1.0000	1.3764	1.9626	3.0777	6.3138	12.7062	31.8205	63.6567	**1**
2	0.8165	1.0607	1.3862	1.8856	2.9200	4.3027	6.9646	9.9248	**2**
3	0.7649	0.9785	1.2498	1.6377	2.3534	3.1824	4.5407	5.8409	**3**
4	0.7407	0.9410	1.1896	1.5332	2.1318	2.7764	3.7469	4.6041	**4**
5	0.7267	0.9195	1.1558	1.4759	2.0150	2.5706	3.3649	4.0321	**5**
6	0.7176	0.9057	1.1342	1.4398	1.9432	2.4469	3.1427	3.7074	**6**
7	0.7111	0.8960	1.1192	1.4149	1.8946	2.3646	2.9980	3.4995	**7**
8	0.7064	0.8889	1.1081	1.3968	1.8595	2.3060	2.8965	3.3554	**8**
9	0.7027	0.8834	1.0997	1.3830	1.8331	2.2622	2.8214	3.2498	**9**
10	0.6998	0.8791	1.0931	1.3722	1.8125	2.2281	2.7638	3.1693	**10**
11	0.6974	0.8755	1.0877	1.3634	1.7959	2.2010	2.7181	3.1058	**11**
12	0.6955	0.8726	1.0832	1.3562	1.7823	2.1788	2.6810	3.0545	**12**
13	0.6938	0.8702	1.0795	1.3502	1.7709	2.1604	2.6503	3.0123	**13**
14	0.6924	0.8681	1.0763	1.3450	1.7613	2.1448	2.6245	2.9768	**14**
15	0.6912	0.8662	1.0735	1.3406	1.7531	2.1314	2.6025	2.9467	**15**
16	0.6901	0.8647	1.0711	1.3368	1.7459	2.1199	2.5835	2.9208	**16**
17	0.6892	0.8633	1.0690	1.3334	1.7396	2.1098	2.5669	2.8982	**17**
18	0.6884	0.8620	1.0672	1.3304	1.7341	2.1009	2.5524	2.8784	**18**
19	0.6876	0.8610	1.0655	1.3277	1.7291	2.0930	2.5395	2.8609	**19**
20	0.6870	0.8600	1.0640	1.3253	1.7247	2.0860	2.5280	2.8453	**20**
21	0.6864	0.8591	1.0627	1.3232	1.7207	2.0796	2.5176	2.8314	**21**
22	0.6858	0.8583	1.0614	1.3212	1.7171	2.0739	2.5083	2.8188	**22**
23	0.6853	0.8575	1.0603	1.3195	1.7139	2.0687	2.4999	2.8073	**23**
24	0.6848	0.8569	1.0593	1.3178	1.7109	2.0639	2.4922	2.7969	**24**
25	0.6844	0.8562	1.0584	1.3163	1.7081	2.0595	2.4851	2.7874	**25**
26	0.6840	0.8557	1.0575	1.3150	1.7056	2.0555	2.4786	2.7787	**26**
27	0.6837	0.8551	1.0567	1.3137	1.7033	2.0518	2.4727	2.7707	**27**
28	0.6834	0.8546	1.0560	1.3125	1.7011	2.0484	2.4671	2.7633	**28**
29	0.6830	0.8542	1.0553	1.3114	1.6991	2.0452	2.4620	2.7564	**29**
30	0.6828	0.8538	1.0547	1.3104	1.6973	2.0423	2.4573	2.7500	**30**
35	0.6816	0.8520	1.0520	1.3062	1.6896	2.0301	2.4377	2.7238	**35**
40	0.6807	0.8507	1.0500	1.3031	1.6839	2.0211	2.4233	2.7045	**40**
45	0.6800	0.8497	1.0485	1.3006	1.6794	2.0141	2.4121	2.6896	**45**
50	0.6794	0.8489	1.0473	1.2987	1.6759	2.0086	2.4033	2.6778	**50**
60	0.6786	0.8477	1.0455	1.2958	1.6706	2.0003	2.3901	2.6603	**60**
70	0.6780	0.8468	1.0442	1.2938	1.6669	1.9944	2.3808	2.6479	**70**
80	0.6776	0.8461	1.0432	1.2922	1.6641	1.9901	2.3739	2.6387	**80**
90	0.6772	0.8456	1.0424	1.2910	1.6620	1.9867	2.3685	2.6316	**90**
100	0.6770	0.8452	1.0418	1.2901	1.6602	1.9840	2.3642	2.6259	**100**
125	0.6765	0.8445	1.0408	1.2884	1.6571	1.9791	2.3565	2.6157	**125**
150	0.6761	0.8440	1.0400	1.2872	1.6551	1.9759	2.3515	2.6090	**150**
200	0.6757	0.8434	1.0391	1.2858	1.6525	1.9719	2.3451	2.6006	**200**
300	0.6753	0.8428	1.0382	1.2844	1.6499	1.9679	2.3388	2.5923	**300**
400	0.6751	0.8425	1.0378	1.2837	1.6487	1.9659	2.3357	2.5882	**400**
500	0.6750	0.8423	1.0375	1.2832	1.6479	1.9647	2.3338	2.5857	**500**
1000	0.6747	0.8420	1.0370	1.2824	1.6464	1.9623	2.3301	2.5808	**1000**
∞	0.6745	0.8416	1.0364	1.2816	1.6449	1.9600	2.3263	2.5758	∞

Table A.3 Tail Areas and Critical Values for the Chi-Square Distribution

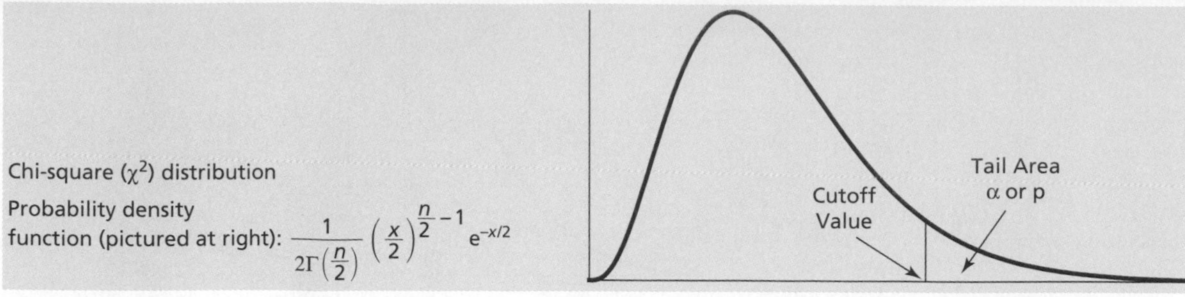

	Tail Area (α)								
df	**0.5**	**0.25**	**0.1**	**0.05**	**0.025**	**0.01**	**0.005**	**0.0025**	**0.001**
1	0.455	1.323	2.706	3.841	5.024	6.635	7.879	9.141	10.828
2	1.386	2.773	4.605	5.991	7.378	9.210	10.597	11.983	13.816
3	2.366	4.108	6.251	7.815	9.348	11.345	12.838	14.320	16.266
4	3.357	5.385	7.779	9.488	11.143	13.277	14.860	16.424	18.467
5	4.351	6.626	9.236	11.070	12.833	15.086	16.750	18.386	20.515
6	5.348	7.841	10.645	12.592	14.449	16.812	18.548	20.249	22.458
7	6.346	9.037	12.017	14.067	16.013	18.475	20.278	22.040	24.322
8	7.344	10.219	13.362	15.507	17.535	20.090	21.955	23.774	26.124
9	8.343	11.389	14.684	16.919	19.023	21.666	23.589	25.462	27.877
10	9.342	12.549	15.987	18.307	20.483	23.209	25.188	27.112	29.588
11	10.341	13.701	17.275	19.675	21.920	24.725	26.757	28.729	31.264
12	11.340	14.845	18.549	21.026	23.337	26.217	28.300	30.318	32.909
13	12.340	15.984	19.812	22.362	24.736	27.688	29.819	31.883	34.528
14	13.339	17.117	21.064	23.685	26.119	29.141	31.319	33.426	36.123
15	14.339	18.245	22.307	24.996	27.488	30.578	32.801	34.950	37.697
16	15.338	19.369	23.542	26.296	28.845	32.000	34.267	36.456	39.252
17	16.338	20.489	24.769	27.587	30.191	33.409	35.718	37.946	40.790
18	17.338	21.605	25.989	28.869	31.526	34.805	37.156	39.422	42.312
19	18.338	22.718	27.204	30.144	32.852	36.191	38.582	40.885	43.820
20	19.337	23.828	28.412	31.410	34.170	37.566	39.997	42.336	45.315
21	20.337	24.935	29.615	32.671	35.479	38.932	41.401	43.775	46.797
22	21.337	26.039	30.813	33.924	36.781	40.289	42.796	45.204	48.268
23	22.337	27.141	32.007	35.172	38.076	41.638	44.181	46.623	49.728
24	23.337	28.241	33.196	36.415	39.364	42.980	45.559	48.034	51.179
25	24.337	29.339	34.382	37.652	40.646	44.314	46.928	49.435	52.620
26	25.336	30.435	35.563	38.885	41.923	45.642	48.290	50.829	54.052
27	26.336	31.528	36.741	40.113	43.195	46.963	49.645	52.215	55.476
28	27.336	32.620	37.916	41.337	44.461	48.278	50.993	53.594	56.892
29	28.336	33.711	39.087	42.557	45.722	49.588	52.336	54.967	58.301
30	29.336	34.800	40.256	43.773	46.979	50.892	53.672	56.332	59.703
35	34.336	40.223	46.059	49.802	53.203	57.342	60.275	63.076	66.619
40	39.335	45.616	51.805	55.758	59.342	63.691	66.766	69.699	73.402
45	44.335	50.985	57.505	61.656	65.410	69.957	73.166	76.223	80.077
50	49.335	56.334	63.167	67.505	71.420	76.154	79.490	82.664	86.661
60	59.335	66.981	74.397	79.082	83.298	88.379	91.952	95.344	99.607
70	69.334	77.577	85.527	90.531	95.023	100.425	104.215	107.808	112.317
80	79.334	88.130	96.578	101.879	106.629	112.329	116.321	120.102	124.839
90	89.334	98.650	107.565	113.145	118.136	124.116	128.299	132.256	137.208
100	99.334	109.141	118.498	124.342	129.561	135.807	140.169	144.293	149.449

Table A.4 Tail Areas and Critical Values for the *F* Distribution

F distribution

Probability density function (pictured at right): $\frac{\Gamma\left(\frac{m+n}{2}\right)}{\Gamma\left(\frac{m}{2}\right)\Gamma\left(\frac{n}{2}\right)}\left(\frac{m}{n}\right)^{\frac{m}{2}}\frac{(x)^{\frac{m}{2}-1}}{\left(1+\frac{m}{n}x\right)^{\frac{m+n}{2}}}$

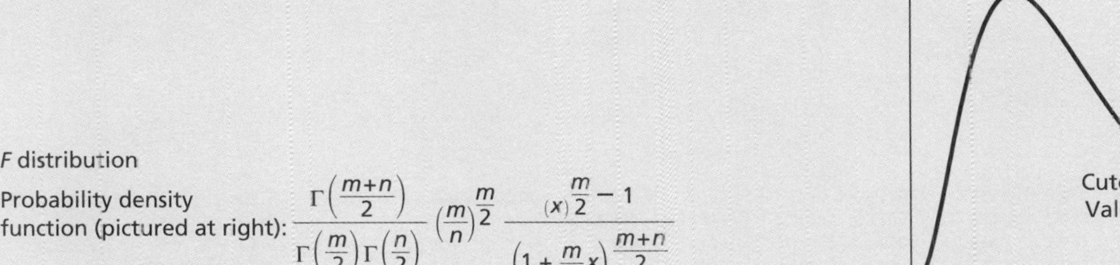

Tail Area (α)	df(denom) n	Numerator Degrees of Freedom (m)																
		1	2	3	4	5	6	7	8	9	10	12	15	20	30	60	120	∞
0.100		39.9	49.5	53.6	55.8	57.2	58.2	58.9	59.4	59.9	60.2	60.7	61.2	61.7	62.3	62.8	63.1	63.3
0.050		161.4	199.5	215.7	224.6	230.2	234.0	236.8	238.9	240.5	241.9	243.9	245.9	248.0	250.1	252.2	253.3	254.3
0.025	1	647.8	799.5	864.2	899.6	921.8	937.1	948.2	956.7	963.3	968.6	976.7	984.9	993.1	1001.4	1009.8	1014.0	1018.3
0.010		4052.2	4999.5	5403.4	5624.6	5763.6	5859.0	5928.4	5981.1	6022.5	6055.8	6106.3	6157.3	6208.7	6260.6	6313.0	6339.4	6365.9
0.005		16210.7	19999.5	21614.7	22499.6	23055.8	23437.1	23714.6	23925.4	24091.0	24224.5	24426.4	24630.2	24836.0	25043.6	25253.1	25358.6	25464.5
0.100		8.53	9.00	9.16	9.24	9.29	9.33	9.35	9.37	9.38	9.39	9.41	9.42	9.44	9.46	9.47	9.48	9.49
0.050		18.51	19.00	19.16	19.25	19.30	19.33	19.35	19.37	19.38	19.40	19.41	19.43	19.45	19.46	19.48	19.49	19.50
0.025	2	38.51	39.00	39.17	39.25	39.30	39.33	39.36	39.37	39.39	39.40	39.41	39.43	39.45	39.46	39.48	39.49	39.50
0.010		98.50	99.00	99.17	99.25	99.30	99.33	99.36	99.37	99.39	99.40	99.42	99.43	99.45	99.47	99.48	99.49	99.50
0.005		198.50	199.00	199.17	199.25	199.30	199.33	199.36	199.37	199.39	199.40	199.42	199.43	199.45	199.47	199.48	199.49	199.50
0.100		5.538	5.462	5.391	5.343	5.309	5.285	5.265	5.252	5.240	5.230	5.216	5.200	5.184	5.168	5.151	5.143	5.134
0.050		10.128	9.552	9.277	9.117	9.013	8.941	8.887	8.845	8.812	8.786	8.745	8.703	8.660	8.617	8.572	8.549	8.526
0.025	3	17.443	16.044	15.439	15.101	14.885	14.735	14.624	14.540	14.473	14.419	14.337	14.253	14.167	14.081	13.992	13.947	13.902
0.010		34.116	30.817	29.457	28.710	28.237	27.911	27.672	27.489	27.345	27.229	27.052	26.872	26.690	26.505	26.316	26.221	26.125
0.005		55.552	49.799	47.467	46.195	45.392	44.838	44.434	44.126	43.882	43.686	43.387	43.085	42.778	42.466	42.149	41.989	41.828
0.100		4.545	4.325	4.191	4.107	4.051	4.010	3.979	3.955	3.936	3.920	3.896	3.870	3.844	3.817	3.790	3.775	3.761
0.050		7.709	6.944	6.591	6.388	6.256	6.163	6.094	6.041	5.999	5.964	5.912	5.858	5.803	5.746	5.688	5.658	5.628
0.025	4	12.218	10.649	9.979	9.605	9.364	9.197	9.074	8.980	8.905	8.844	8.751	8.657	8.560	8.461	8.360	8.309	8.257
0.010		21.198	18.000	16.694	15.977	15.522	15.207	14.976	14.799	14.659	14.546	14.374	14.198	14.020	13.838	13.652	13.558	13.463
0.005		31.333	26.284	24.259	23.155	22.456	21.975	21.622	21.352	21.139	20.967	20.705	20.438	20.167	19.892	19.611	19.468	19.325
0.100		4.060	3.780	3.619	3.520	3.453	3.405	3.368	3.339	3.316	3.297	3.268	3.238	3.207	3.174	3.140	3.123	3.105
0.050		6.608	5.786	5.409	5.192	5.050	4.950	4.876	4.818	4.772	4.735	4.678	4.619	4.558	4.496	4.431	4.398	4.365
0.025	5	10.007	8.434	7.764	7.388	7.146	6.978	6.853	6.757	6.681	6.619	6.525	6.428	6.329	6.227	6.123	6.069	6.015
0.010		16.258	13.274	12.060	11.392	10.967	10.672	10.456	10.289	10.158	10.051	9.888	9.722	9.553	9.379	9.202	9.112	9.020
0.005		22.785	18.314	16.530	15.556	14.940	14.513	14.200	13.961	13.772	13.618	13.384	13.146	12.903	12.656	12.402	12.274	12.144
0.100		3.776	3.463	3.289	3.181	3.108	3.055	3.014	2.983	2.958	2.937	2.905	2.871	2.836	2.800	2.762	2.742	2.722
0.050		5.987	5.143	4.757	4.534	4.387	4.284	4.207	4.147	4.099	4.060	4.000	3.938	3.874	3.808	3.740	3.705	3.669
0.025	6	8.813	7.260	6.599	6.227	5.988	5.820	5.695	5.600	5.523	5.461	5.366	5.269	5.168	5.065	4.959	4.904	4.849
0.010		13.745	10.925	9.780	9.148	8.746	8.466	8.260	8.102	7.976	7.874	7.718	7.559	7.396	7.229	7.057	6.969	6.880
0.005		18.635	14.544	12.917	12.028	11.464	11.073	10.786	10.566	10.391	10.250	10.034	9.814	9.589	9.358	9.122	9.001	8.879
0.100		3.589	3.257	3.074	2.961	2.883	2.827	2.785	2.752	2.725	2.703	2.668	2.632	2.595	2.555	2.514	2.493	2.471
0.050		5.591	4.737	4.347	4.120	3.972	3.866	3.787	3.726	3.677	3.637	3.575	3.511	3.445	3.376	3.304	3.267	3.230
0.025	7	8.073	6.542	5.890	5.523	5.285	5.119	4.995	4.899	4.823	4.761	4.666	4.568	4.467	4.362	4.254	4.199	4.142
0.010		12.246	9.547	8.451	7.847	7.460	7.191	6.993	6.840	6.719	6.620	6.469	6.314	6.155	5.992	5.824	5.737	5.650
0.005		16.236	12.404	10.882	10.050	9.522	9.155	8.885	8.678	8.514	8.380	8.176	7.968	7.754	7.534	7.309	7.193	7.076
0.100		3.458	3.113	2.924	2.806	2.726	2.668	2.624	2.589	2.561	2.538	2.502	2.464	2.425	2.383	2.339	2.316	2.293
0.050		5.318	4.459	4.066	3.838	3.687	3.581	3.500	3.438	3.388	3.347	3.284	3.218	3.150	3.079	3.005	2.967	2.928
0.025	8	7.571	6.059	5.416	5.053	4.817	4.652	4.529	4.433	4.357	4.295	4.200	4.101	3.999	3.894	3.784	3.728	3.670
0.010		11.259	8.649	7.591	7.006	6.632	6.371	6.178	6.029	5.911	5.814	5.667	5.515	5.359	5.198	5.032	4.946	4.859
0.005		14.688	11.042	9.596	8.805	8.302	7.952	7.694	7.496	7.339	7.211	7.015	6.814	6.608	6.396	6.177	6.065	5.951

continued

Table A.4 Tail Areas and Critical Values for the *F* Distribution (*continued*)

Tail Area (α)	df(denom) *n*	Numerator Degrees of Freedom (*m*)																
		1	2	3	4	5	6	7	8	9	10	12	15	20	30	60	120	∞
0.100		3.360	3.006	2.813	2.693	2.611	2.551	2.505	2.469	2.440	2.416	2.379	2.340	2.298	2.255	2.208	2.184	2.159
0.050		5.117	4.256	3.863	3.633	3.482	3.374	3.293	3.230	3.179	3.137	3.073	3.006	2.936	2.864	2.787	2.748	2.707
0.025	**9**	7.209	5.715	5.078	4.718	4.484	4.320	4.197	4.102	4.026	3.964	3.868	3.769	3.667	3.560	3.449	3.392	3.333
0.010		10.561	8.022	6.992	6.422	6.057	5.802	5.613	5.467	5.351	5.257	5.111	4.962	4.808	4.649	4.483	4.398	4.311
0.005		13.614	10.107	8.717	7.956	7.471	7.134	6.885	6.693	6.541	6.417	6.227	6.032	5.832	5.625	5.410	5.300	5.188
0.100		3.285	2.924	2.728	2.605	2.522	2.461	2.414	2.377	2.347	2.323	2.284	2.244	2.201	2.155	2.107	2.082	2.055
0.050		4.965	4.103	3.708	3.478	3.326	3.217	3.135	3.072	3.020	2.978	2.913	2.845	2.774	2.700	2.621	2.580	2.538
0.025	**10**	6.937	5.456	4.826	4.468	4.236	4.072	3.950	3.855	3.779	3.717	3.621	3.522	3.419	3.311	3.198	3.140	3.080
0.010		10.044	7.559	6.552	5.994	5.636	5.386	5.200	5.057	4.942	4.849	4.706	4.558	4.405	4.247	4.082	3.996	3.909
0.005		12.826	9.427	8.081	7.343	6.872	6.545	6.302	6.116	5.968	5.847	5.661	5.471	5.274	5.071	4.859	4.750	4.639
0.100		3.177	2.807	2.606	2.480	2.394	2.331	2.283	2.245	2.214	2.188	2.147	2.105	2.060	2.011	1.960	1.932	1.904
0.050		4.747	3.885	3.490	3.259	3.106	2.996	2.913	2.849	2.796	2.753	2.687	2.617	2.544	2.466	2.384	2.341	2.296
0.025	**12**	6.554	5.096	4.474	4.121	3.891	3.728	3.607	3.512	3.436	3.374	3.277	3.177	3.073	2.963	2.848	2.787	2.725
0.010		9.330	6.927	5.953	5.412	5.064	4.821	4.640	4.499	4.388	4.296	4.155	4.010	3.858	3.701	3.535	3.449	3.361
0.005		11.754	8.510	7.226	6.521	6.071	5.757	5.525	5.345	5.202	5.085	4.906	4.721	4.530	4.331	4.123	4.015	3.904
0.100		3.073	2.695	2.490	2.361	2.273	2.208	2.158	2.119	2.086	2.059	2.017	1.972	1.924	1.873	1.817	1.787	1.755
0.050		4.543	3.682	3.287	3.056	2.901	2.790	2.707	2.641	2.588	2.544	2.475	2.403	2.328	2.247	2.160	2.114	2.066
0.025	**15**	6.200	4.765	4.153	3.804	3.576	3.415	3.293	3.199	3.123	3.060	2.963	2.862	2.756	2.644	2.524	2.461	2.395
0.010		8.683	6.359	5.417	4.893	4.556	4.318	4.142	4.004	3.895	3.805	3.666	3.522	3.372	3.214	3.047	2.959	2.868
0.005		10.798	7.701	6.476	5.803	5.372	5.071	4.847	4.674	4.536	4.424	4.250	4.070	3.883	3.687	3.480	3.372	3.260
0.100		2.975	2.589	2.380	2.249	2.158	2.091	2.040	1.999	1.965	1.937	1.892	1.845	1.794	1.738	1.677	1.643	1.607
0.050		4.351	3.493	3.098	2.866	2.711	2.599	2.514	2.447	2.393	2.348	2.278	2.203	2.124	2.039	1.946	1.896	1.843
0.025	**20**	5.871	4.461	3.859	3.515	3.289	3.128	3.007	2.913	2.837	2.774	2.676	2.573	2.464	2.349	2.223	2.156	2.085
0.010		8.096	5.849	4.938	4.431	4.103	3.871	3.699	3.564	3.457	3.368	3.231	3.088	2.938	2.778	2.608	2.517	2.421
0.005		9.944	6.986	5.818	5.174	4.762	4.472	4.257	4.090	3.956	3.847	3.678	3.502	3.318	3.123	2.916	2.806	2.690
0.100		2.881	2.489	2.276	2.142	2.049	1.980	1.927	1.884	1.849	1.819	1.773	1.722	1.667	1.606	1.538	1.499	1.456
0.050		4.171	3.316	2.922	2.690	2.534	2.421	2.334	2.266	2.211	2.165	2.092	2.015	1.932	1.841	1.740	1.683	1.622
0.025	**30**	5.568	4.182	3.589	3.250	3.026	2.867	2.746	2.651	2.575	2.511	2.412	2.307	2.195	2.074	1.940	1.866	1.787
0.010		7.562	5.390	4.510	4.018	3.699	3.473	3.304	3.173	3.067	2.979	2.843	2.700	2.549	2.386	2.208	2.111	2.006
0.005		9.180	6.355	5.239	4.623	4.228	3.949	3.742	3.580	3.450	3.344	3.179	3.006	2.823	2.628	2.415	2.300	2.176
0.100		2.791	2.393	2.177	2.041	1.946	1.875	1.819	1.775	1.738	1.707	1.657	1.603	1.543	1.476	1.395	1.348	1.291
0.050		4.001	3.150	2.758	2.525	2.368	2.254	2.167	2.097	2.040	1.993	1.917	1.836	1.748	1.649	1.534	1.467	1.389
0.025	**60**	5.286	3.925	3.343	3.008	2.786	2.627	2.507	2.412	2.334	2.270	2.169	2.061	1.944	1.815	1.667	1.581	1.482
0.010		7.077	4.977	4.126	3.649	3.339	3.119	2.953	2.823	2.718	2.632	2.496	2.352	2.198	2.028	1.836	1.726	1.601
0.005		8.495	5.795	4.729	4.140	3.760	3.492	3.291	3.134	3.008	2.904	2.742	2.570	2.387	2.187	1.962	1.834	1.689
0.100		2.748	2.347	2.130	1.992	1.896	1.824	1.767	1.722	1.684	1.652	1.601	1.545	1.482	1.409	1.320	1.265	1.193
0.050		3.920	3.072	2.680	2.447	2.290	2.175	2.087	2.016	1.959	1.910	1.834	1.750	1.659	1.554	1.429	1.352	1.254
0.025	**120**	5.152	3.805	3.227	2.894	2.674	2.515	2.395	2.299	2.222	2.157	2.055	1.945	1.825	1.690	1.530	1.433	1.310
0.010		6.851	4.787	3.949	3.480	3.174	2.956	2.792	2.663	2.559	2.472	2.336	2.192	2.035	1.860	1.656	1.533	1.381
0.005		8.179	5.539	4.497	3.921	3.548	3.285	3.087	2.933	2.808	2.705	2.544	2.373	2.188	1.984	1.747	1.606	1.431
0.100		2.706	2.303	2.084	1.945	1.847	1.774	1.717	1.670	1.632	1.599	1.546	1.487	1.421	1.342	1.240	1.169	---
0.050		3.841	2.996	2.605	2.372	2.214	2.099	2.010	1.938	1.880	1.831	1.752	1.666	1.571	1.459	1.318	1.221	---
0.025	**∞**	5.024	3.689	3.116	2.786	2.567	2.408	2.288	2.192	2.114	2.048	1.945	1.833	1.708	1.566	1.388	1.268	---
0.010		6.635	4.605	3.782	3.319	3.017	2.802	2.639	2.511	2.407	2.321	2.185	2.039	1.878	1.696	1.473	1.325	---
0.005		7.879	5.298	4.279	3.715	3.350	3.091	2.897	2.744	2.621	2.519	2.358	2.187	2.000	1.789	1.533	1.364	---

Table A.5 The Greek Alphabet

Capital Letter	Small Letter	Name	English Transliteration
Α	α	Alpha	a
Β	β	Beta	b
Γ	γ	Gamma	g
Δ	δ	Delta	d
Ε	ε	Epsilon	e
Ζ	ζ	Zeta	z
Η	η	Eta	e, ē
Θ	θ	Theta	th
Ι	ι	Iota	i
Κ	κ	Kappa	k
Λ	λ	Lambda	l
Μ	μ	Mu	m
Ν	ν	Nu	n
Ξ	ξ	Xi	x
Ο	ο	Omicron	o
Π	π	Pi	p
Ρ	ρ	Rho	r
Σ	σ	Sigma	s
Τ	τ	Tau	t
Υ	υ	Upsilon	u, y
Φ	φ	Phi	ph
Χ	χ	Chi	ch
Ψ	ψ	Psi	ps
Ω	ω	Omega	o, ō

GLOSSARY

A-I-O items
In lifestyle research, the respondents' activities, interests, and opinions.

absolute frequency
The total number of times an event occurred during a study or experiment, disregarding the number of opportunities it had to occur.

absolute precision
The accuracy of any measurement based on some predetermined measurement scale, not relative to other sample statistics like the mean.

abstract system
The theoretical constructs used to model marketing phenomena and to make predictions; these can then be compared with empirical data on the phenomena under study.

accuracy
Reducing both systematic (i.e., in a definite direction, a bias) and random (in any direction at all; noise) errors increases the *accuracy* of research results.

adaptive conjoint
A type of conjoint analysis in which a respondent's answers to prior questions are used to determine subsequent questions, to help best use respondents' time and obtain superior statistical estimates.

affective component
In assessing consumer attitudes toward a product, service, or brand, the component related to emotional response and subjective feelings, such as overall liking and preference.

agglomeration schedule
In hierarchical cluster analysis, a list of the order in which various smaller clusters combine to form larger ones.

aided recall test
A test of ad effectiveness that relies on "prompting" or cueing (i.e., providing some form of relevant information) when requesting that respondents recall any ad messages they remember being exposed to (seeing or hearing) during a stated time period.

alternative hypothesis
A specific statement, opposed to the "null hypothesis," subjected to statistical test. The alternative hypothesis is typically what the researcher anticipates will actually happen, or the hoped-for outcome (for example, in a clinical trial of a new drug or an ad test).

alternative-forms reliability
A method to test the reliability of a measure by giving each subject two distinct forms of the measure believed to be equivalent; the results of the measurements are then compared to determine reliability.

analysis of variance (ANOVA)
A statistical method that allows the simultaneous comparison of the means of many groups; in this way, it generalizes the two-sample *t*-test. If the groups differ on a single variable (e.g., year in college), the analysis is a *one-way* ANOVA; if on two variables (e.g., year in college and gender), a *two-way* ANOVA; and so on. ANOVA is a special case of ordinary multiple linear regression.

analyst
A marketing research position involving the general design and supervision of marketing research studies.

anonymity
A fairness criterion for decision-making systems that requires that all participants be treated equally.

area of dominant influence (ADI)
A specific geographic area surrounding a town or city; broadcasters operating within that town or city account for a larger share of viewing (television) or listening (radio) households than do other broadcasters operating nearby.

area sampling
A sampling method in which the population is separated into *areas* or *clusters*, which are then selected randomly. If all elements in each selected cluster are then sampled, it is *one-stage* area sampling; if the areas are then subsampled, it is *two-stage* area sampling. Area sampling is especially helpful for widely geographically dispersed populations.

Arrow's impossibility theorem
A theorem proven by Kenneth Arrow that demonstrates that no voting system can simultaneously meet all five of a certain set of fairness criteria (universality, citizen sovereignty, nondictatorship, monotonicity, and independence of irrelevant alternatives).

attitude scaling
Operational definitions made to help measure, using specific scales, consumers' attitudes, beliefs, intentions, and other subjective mental states.

attribute
A special term for the variables used in a conjoint analysis, or any technique where a product's features (attributes) need to be specified. Attributes are broken down into *levels;* for example, for a food processor, the attribute *capacity* might take on *levels* of 1, 2, 3, 4, or 5 liters.

audience profiles
Geodemographic and psychographic characteristics of the consumers exposed to a particular media or advertising vehicle.

audimeter
An electronic device attached to a consumer's television that monitors when it is used and the channel to which it is tuned.

autocorrelation
When a variable's value at one point in time is correlated with its values at prior points in time; can often be a problem in regression models and must be fixed—often using lagged regressors or first-differences in the dependent variable—to obtain proper inferences.

baseline
A figure that can be used to provide context for a comparison with another figure.

Bayesian estimation
A branch of applied statistics (or econometrics) where complex statistical models are estimated using specialized algorithms (such as Gibbs sampling or MCMC [Markov chain Monte Carlo]) for sampling from the parameters' distributions. Bayesian estimation can be difficult to perform, but it is extremely powerful and allows some models to be estimated that would be impossible using other means.

behavioral component
Consumers' intention to take action, particularly toward the purchase of a product or service, as well as their eventual behavior.

behavioral response
Any of a number of actions or mental states triggered by marketing actions. These can include actual purchases, intentions to purchase, feelings, attitudes, or beliefs.

bimodal
Describes a variable with two relatively high rates of incidence (modes, or "humps").

binary
A variable having only two possible states, for example, 1 or 0, yes or no, Male or Female, Domestic or Foreign, etc.

binary dummy variables
A (*binary*) *dummy variable* takes on values of either 0 or 1 and is often introduced into an analysis to represent other, nonbinary variables. For example, the four seasons of the year can be represented using three binary dummies.

binary logistic regression
A special regression model where the dependent variable is binary, and the errors are assumed Gumbel or double-exponentially distributed; widely applied throughout statistics and marketing research.

binary probit model
A form of regression in which the *dependent* variable is binary, suitable for zero/one, yes/no outcomes.

Breusch-Pagan test
Like the *White test*, a common and widely-supported method for assessing whether heteroscedasticity is present in a regression analysis. The Breusch-Pagan test regresses the squared residuals from a regression onto the original regressors; a significant *F*-test indicates that heteroscedasticity may be a problem.

categorical data analysis
A branch of statistics concerned with the analysis of nominal data that includes special forms of regression-like models, such as the logit and probit models for the analysis of discrete choices.

causal inference
A set of statistical techniques used to suggest likely cause-and-effect relationships among a set of variables.

causal model
A formal system laying out which marketing variables result in specific outcomes; the causal model can be supported or refuted by empirical data.

causal research
A formal research design whose purpose is to determine cause-and-effect relationships among a set of marketing variables.

central limit theorem
The most important result in all of statistics. States that when drawing a "large" random sample from some population, the sample mean will have a normal distribution, with certain special properties. Has widespread applications throughout statistics, economics, and the physical sciences.

central tendency
Any of a number of estimates of the most common of, or the center of, a variable's values; the most widely-used measures of central tendency are the mean, median, and mode.

centralized structure
A form of organization in which the marketing research function is brought together into a single unit, ordinarily overseen by corporate management.

chi-square test
The main test done in categorical data analysis, often to determine whether two nominal variables are independent of one another; can also be used to test whether a sample variance is significantly different from a hypothesized value.

choice-based conjoint
A method of conjoint analysis in which the dependent variable is a single choice from a given set of options.

cluster analysis
A statistical method that helps break items into relatively homogeneous groupings (called classes, segments or clusters), based on a set of supplied variables. Related to latent class analysis and mixture models, which are also general methods to achieve clustering.

cluster sampling
A form of probability sampling in which the population is first separated into groups, or clusters, which are then selected randomly. If all elements in each selected cluster are then sampled, it is *one-stage* cluster sampling; if the areas are then subsampled, it is *two-stage* cluster sampling.

clustering criterion
A rule used in cluster analysis to determine how clusters should be formed from input data.

code of ethics
A system of rules, standards, and guidelines defining ethical behavior within professional organizations and in relation to the general public.

coefficient of determination (r^2)
A measure of how much of the variance in one (interval-scaled) variable is reduced by knowing the value of another (interval-scaled) variable; obtained by running a simple linear regression of one variable on the other.

coefficient of variation
The ratio of the standard deviation to the mean, a dimensionless quantity that helps specify the spread of a probability distribution.

cognitive component
In attitude research, a person's beliefs about the object of concern; typically focuses on the elements that can be deliberately thought about, not on feelings or behaviors.

collectively exhaustive
When the response choices for a question include all possible options—for example, a listing of all the days of the week.

combinatorial formula
A formula that specifies how many unique subsets of size *n* there are, taken from *N* distinct items. Formally, given by $N!/n!(N-n)!$, where $n!$ is "n factorial." See *factorial*.

communalities
Measures used in Factor analysis to express how much all Factors selected by the analyst, taken together, explain each of the original input variables. A reasonable Factor solution will have communalities that do not vary dramatically across the input variables.

completely randomized design (CRD)
An experimental design in which treatments are assigned to test units in an entirely random manner.

conclusive research
Research aimed at evaluating and predicting the outcomes of several possible courses of action, ordinarily to select the best among them.

concurrent validity
Correlating two different measurements of the same (marketing) phenomenon administered at the same point in time, primarily to determine the validity of new measurement techniques by correlating them with established ones.

confidence intervals
A region that contains a population parameter of interest with a certain stated probability, often 95 percent or 99 percent, but more generally $100(1 - \alpha)$ percent.

confidence level
The largest probability a researcher is willing to tolerate for concluding a null hypothesis is incorrect, even though it is. Thus, a 0.05 confidence level means there is a 1 in 20 chance that the researcher will reject a true null hypothesis, just by chance alone.

confirmation bias
When a researcher devotes more time, energy, or resources to supporting than to refuting a favored hypothesis, relative to alternatives.

confounding variable (confound)
Any variable, other than those specific to the treatment, that may affect how test units respond to the treatments; confounds make it difficult to attribute effects to variables controlled or manipulated by the experimenter.

confusion matrix
In discriminant analysis, a matrix cross-tabulating correct and incorrect predictions for each group. Relatively large diagonal entries indicate good performance.

conjoint analysis
A popular marketing research method to calibrate an individual's *utility* or value for different *attributes* (e.g., durability, size, price) and *levels* of each attribute. Respondents supply data on various combinations of the attributes, called profiles. Given a set of such profiles, this data can take the form of separate ratings for each, rankings of the entire set, or choosing the single best profile from the set.

consideration set
A group of alternatives that a consumer evaluates, thinks about, or makes implicit references to when making a decision.

constitutive definition
When a construct is defined in terms of other constructs, often in the form of an equation.

construct
Any abstraction used by the researcher based on perceptions of a phenomenon, meant to serve as building blocks for more complex marketing; typical examples include sales, product positioning, demand, attitudes, and brand loyalty.

construct validity
Relating a construct of interest to other constructs in order to develop a comprehensive theoretical framework for the (marketing) phenomenon being studied; construct validity is enhanced when the correlation between the construct of interest and the related constructs increases in the predicted manner.

consumer profile
Comprehensive description of the characteristics of consumers of a particular product or service, typically including geodemographic, psychographic, and purchase data.

consumer research
Marketing research into consumer characteristics, attitudes, beliefs, opinions, and behavior.

consumer utility
In economics, a measure of the level of satisfaction or usefulness a consumer receives or anticipates from a good or service. In statistics, it is a "latent" (unobserved) variable that helps provide a concrete foundation for the use of discrete choice models, such as logit and probit regression.

content validity
Often called *face validity,* the relation of the appropriateness of the measurement to subjective judgments, typically by experts.

contingency tables
Tables containing numerical observations keyed to two or more (usually categorical) variables that are frequently analyzed using a chi-square test for independence.

continuous heterogeneity
A method of expressing the fact that different population units (e.g., consumers) have different coefficients in a statistical model, by assuming they can take on any values at all, with frequencies expressed by a continuous function (usually a normal distribution).

continuous performance measures
Measures of marketing performance (e.g., weekly sales) taken at regular intervals on an ongoing basis.

contribution margin
Sales revenue minus variable costs. When calculated for a single product (unit), often called "unit contribution," and represents the pure profit made by selling one additional unit.

contrived observation
Observations of behavior within an artificial environment where most environmental variables can be controlled.

control group
A group that is comparable to the treatment group in terms of measurable characteristics but did not receive the treatment; effects can thus be attributed to the treatment and not to between-group differences.

convenience samples
A nonprobability sample whose members are chosen because they were simpler, less costly, and/or more readily available than others from the population.

convergent validity
Measuring a construct with independent measurement techniques and demonstrating a high degree of correlation among the measures.

correlation
A measure, between −1 and 1, of the strength of the *linear* relationship between two interval-scaled variables. Values near 1 indicate a strong positive relationship; near −1, a strong negative relationship; and near 0, no relationship. Relationships among a group of variables can be assessed by assembling their correlations into a *correlation matrix*.

count data
A dependent variable representing how many times an event occurred; often modeled using Poisson regression.

counterbalancing
A means of preventing the order of questions or listed alternatives from affecting resulting responses by rotating their order among respondents; counterbalancing well can be difficult, so it is usually handled by computer, using an orthogonal design.

counterbiasing statement
A statement made by an interviewer suggesting that the behavior in question is normal or natural, to offset a respondent's reluctance to answer honestly about a sensitive topic.

course of action
One of the specific possible sets of actions to be evaluated via conclusive research.

covariance
A measure of dispersion for some quantity, equal to the square of the standard deviation.

covariates
A common name for independent variables in a statistical model.

cross-scale comparability
When answers to different questions using the same scale are comparable.

cross-sectional design
Research involving a sample of units (people, firms, products, etc.) selected from the population of interest and measured at only a single specific time.

data audit
Re-evaluating the procedures through which data are collected to determine whether they may admit various biases.

data mining
A general set of statistical techniques for determining useful relationships and generating novel insights from large data sets.

data sources
Any of a number of commercial vendors or internal repositories of information used to improve marketing research decisions. Typically include prior primary research, internal firm records, various trade publications, and both industry and government reports.

de-centralized structure
A form of organization in which the marketing research function is spread out across different corporate departments or divisions, with decision-making authority delegated accordingly.

decision criteria
A set of if-then guidelines that help managers select among predetermined courses of action; for example, that a product will be introduced nationally if its share at test market is above a certain threshold value.

decision objectives
The goals of the company (and decision-makers) that the marketing research project will help to achieve. These goals must be explicitly recognized when identifying the project's information needs.

decision support system (DSS)
A dedicated system—usually comprising both hardware (e.g., computer systems and the databases they house) and software (e.g., custom-coded programs for collecting, managing, and analyzing data)—useful for making marketing decisions and analyzing the expected outcomes of specific marketing actions (also known as "what if?" or sensitivity analyses).

decision variables
The quantities that must be determined, as in a particular marketing research project, typically including pricing, distribution, promotion levels, and sales goals.

decision variables, marketing
Those quantities under managerial control that feed into and help determine levels of sales and, therefore, profit. These typically include the "Four Ps" of Price, Product, Place

(distribution), and Promotion, as well as ad expenditure.

decision-making process
A series of steps undertaken in the course of making a marketing-related decision. These can be conceptualized as: (1) recognizing a problem or opportunity, (2) clarifying the decision, (3) identifying alternative courses of action, (4) evaluating alternatives, and (5) selecting a specific course of action.

decompose
In statistical models, the variance in the dependent variable is decomposed into that attributable to the model (covariates) and that to random error. ANOVA models often feature an explicit decomposition into various sources of variation.

degrees of freedom
An important concept in statistical models that quantifies how many *independent* pieces of data go into model calculations; usually equal to the sample size minus the number of parameters that are calculated in the model itself.

demand analysis
A formal model that will help forecast demand (either unit or volume sales) for a product. Such an analysis consists of determining the variables giving rise to demand as well as tying them in statistically to a demand forecast, usually via regression and time-series techniques.

dendrogram
A treelike representation of the successive breakdown of the clustering solution in cluster analysis.

dependence methods
Any statistical technique that attempts to relate one set of values (the dependent variables) to another set of values (the independent variables).

dependent variable
The variable whose value is related to or determined by the values of a number of independent variables; often called the "outcome variable."

depth interview
A qualitative technique in which the interviewer conducts a semistructured conversation with a respondent in an effort to accurately gauge attitudes, emotions, beliefs, and feelings.

descriptive research
Research whose emphasis is not causal, but on providing a rich descriptive portrait; for example, determining the frequency with which a marketing action or outcome occurs or the degree to which two marketing variables co-occur.

descriptive statistics
Any quantities used to describe features of a specific data set (i.e., the sample data).

deterministic
Any quantity that can be completely determined by other quantities, with no error. Regression models express observations as a sum of a deterministic and a stochastic component.

deterministic causation
The ordinary concept of causality that presumes that an effect always follows a cause; differs from the scientific concept of probabilistic causation conceptualizing effects in terms of their statistical probability.

dichotomous question
A question in which respondents are asked to choose one of two possible responses.

dichotomous/binary variable
A variable having only two possible states, for example, 1 or 0, yes or no, Male or Female, Domestic or Foreign, etc.

direct observation
A research technique in which an observer attempts to unobtrusively gather as much data as possible without taking part in the activity under study.

direct testing effect
Same as *main testing effect;* occurs when the first of two observations affects the second.

discrete
A quantity or variable for which a list of distinct values can be made, each of which occurs with some positive probability. Which day of the week an event will occur on is discrete; how many times one flips a coin before getting "tails" is also discrete, even though it is limitless; the set of all possible numbers between zero and one is not discrete, but rather *continuous*.

discrete choice models
A class of statistical models used to analyze the choices made by consumers, or any dependent variable of the "choose for exactly one from many" type.

discrete heterogeneity
A method of expressing the fact that different population units (e.g., consumers) have different coefficients in a statistical model, by assuming they comprise exactly k discrete groups.

discriminant analysis (DA)
A statistical technique used to find the best basis for distinguishing groups (i.e., a discrete variable, from 1 to k groups), using a set of interval-scaled covariates; often used in conjunction with cluster analysis.

discriminant function (DF)
A function, usually linear, used in discriminant analysis.

discriminant validity
The degree to which concepts or variables that a theory says should not be related differ in reality (often assessed by correlation, when the variables involved are interval-scaled).

disintermediated
When a respondent can interact with a test instrument without intervention by a researcher or interviewer.

dispersion
One of a number of statistical measures for the degree to which values of a variable are spread around some measure of central tendency (e.g., mean, median, or mode). The most common measures of dispersion are the standard deviation, variance, range, and interquartile range (difference between the 25th and 75th percentile values in the data).

disproportionate stratified sampling
A method of stratified sampling in which more data (than suggested by their relative frequency in the population alone) are collected from strata with greater variability; this process helps lower the overall standard error of summary measures taken from the sample.

distance metric
Any measure of dissimilarity between pairs of items. True distances are always positive and obey the triangle inequality (the distance between {A, B} is less than the sum between {A, C} and {C, B}.

distribution research
Marketing studies focused on the movement and dissemination of products, from the manufacturer to the wholesaler and retailer up through the point of purchase.

double-barreled question
A question that requires the respondent to supply two separate bits of information and that therefore has the potential to create conflict or confusion.

dummy variable
A variable that takes on binary values (0 or 1), usually used to indicate whether a condition holds or not.

dummy-variable discriminant analysis (DVDA)
A special type of discriminant analysis in which nominal variables are rendered as groups of binary input variables; used infrequently in modern applications.

efficiency
When the standard error (or variance) of some statistic is as small as possible (sometimes relative to a given set of potential estimators). Efficient estimators need not be unbiased; an estimator can be off on average (biased), but still very close to the right answer most of the time (efficient).

eigenvalues
In Factor analysis, a measure of the relative size of any Factor and the *average* Factor.

element
In statistics, the unit (often individuals, but also objects or firms) under analysis, about which information is sought.

empirical system
The set of marketing phenomena under study, often including such quantities as consumer behavior, ad expenditure, competitive tactics, and sales.

endogeneity
As opposed to an *exogenous* variable, which can be completely controlled to understand its effects on a system, an *endogenous* variable is itself at least partially affected by the system it is part of. One's decision to apply to college is affected by tuition rates, but tuition rates are also affected by the number of students applying to college. One might say, therefore, that tuition rates are determined *endogenously*.

equivalent time-sample design
An experimental design where the experimental group is used as its own control. The treatment is presented several times, measurements are repeatedly taken, and periods of treatment absence are spaced between. This design is most appropriate when the effect of the treatment is transient or reversible.

experience survey
A type of individual or depth interview with a selective cross section of respondents familiar with the problem.

experiment
A rigorous investigation in which the researcher controls several (independent) variables and measures or observes their effects on one or more dependent variables.

experimental design
A form of investigation in which the researcher can directly control one or more (independent) variables to study their effects on some other (dependent) variables.

exploratory research
Research less focused on quantification than on generating qualitative insights. Such research helps to generate hypotheses rather than systematically investigate them, and it is useful in breaking down broad, complex problems into smaller, more tractable ones.

exponential
A mathematical property where the rate of growth of a function at a given point is proportional to the function's value at that point; used to model population growth, compound interest, and any other phenomena.

extent
When defining a population for a study, extent refers to the geographic region demarcating the relevant population's boundaries.

external validity
A method of evaluating the results of experiments; formally, the degree to which conclusions would hold under other, presumably identical circumstances (e.g., for other respondents, places, and times).

extraneous variable
Any variable, other than those specific to the treatment administered to test units, that may affect the response of the test units to the treatments, including the history effect, maturation effect, testing effect, instrumentation effect, statistical regression effect, selection bias, and test unit mortality; also referred to as a *confound*.

eye-camera
Also called an eye-tracker, a device that measures the movement of the eye and helps determine the manner in which a person reads a magazine, newspaper, advertisement, product package, or other printed material.

***F*-test**
An exceptionally common test throughout statistics, and ubiquitous in various forms of regression. Indicates whether the "entire model"—that is, all independent variables taken together—explain a significant proportion of the variation in the dependent variable.

face validity
A method of validating measures, by noting its relationship to another independent measure and whether it accords with a theory's predictions.

Factor analysis
A form of statistical *data reduction,* aimed at examining the interrelationships between a group of variables and determining their underlying structure. Highly correlated variables will produce few underlying Factors; nearly independent variables will produce many Factors.

Factor extraction
In Factor analysis, the process by which successive Factors are produced (automatically) by the computer.

Factor loadings
How well each variable in Factor analysis explains a particular Factor. A loading near −1 or 1 means the variable "loads high" on that Factor and should be used to help explain its meaning; a value near 0 indicates the opposite.

Factor rotation
In Factor analysis, the Factors are often rotated to aid in interpretation. See *rotated Factor pattern* and *varimax rotation.*

factorial design
An experimental design technique used to study the effects of two or more variables at the same time, where every level of each variable is presented ("crossed") with every level of all other variables.

factorial
The product of all the integers from 1 to a given number, *n*, written *n*!.

Factors
A set of quantities extracted by Factor analysis, meant to summarize and stand in for a set of input variables. Factors explain as much variance as possible in the original variables and are (typically) uncorrelated with one another.

fairness criteria
Criteria for evaluating voting methods in terms of how accurately each allows the voting population's preferences to be represented.

field environment
As opposed to a controlled laboratory environment, an actual "real world" market setting under which an experiment is carried out.

finite mixture model
Assumes each individual's preferences come from one of a fixed set of groups. When those groups are themselves normally distributed, one has "finite normal mixture heterogeneity"; when the groups are each a constant value, one has a "latent class model."

finite normal mixture heterogeneity
A powerful (and relatively complex) method of representing the tastes and preferences of various individuals. Assumes that each individual's parameters come from one of a fixed number of normal distributions.

finite population correction
A mathematical fix applied to standard formulas when one attempts to make inference for a population of known size, as opposed to a population presumed to be essentially limitless.

focus group
An exploratory research technique consisting of a group discussion led by a moderator and used to gauge consumer attitudes, beliefs, and preferences toward a (perhaps novel) product or service. It is particularly useful in the early stages of a complex marketing research project, and it helps avoid biases intrinsic to closed-form survey questions.

frame of reference
The viewpoint of a respondent invoked by the orientation of a question.

frequency distribution
A list of individual values (or ranges of values) that a variable takes on, along with how commonly each occurs.

gaming
Subverting the fairness of a particular voting method by attempting to manipulate the likelihood of one's own preference winning; also known as "strategic voting."

General Linear Model
A statistical framework for taking linear combinations of (perhaps transformed) independent variables and relating them to (perhaps transformed) dependent variables, plus error (which may or may not be normally distributed). Ordinary regression models are special cases of the general linear model.

Generalized AutoRegressive Conditional Heteroscedasticity (GARCH) model
A type of regression model in which the variance of the error term is not constant (i.e., homoscedastic) but varies over time, in particular according to the value of the variation at previous time periods; very common in modeling financial time series.

geodemographic
A *geodemographic* variable gives information about the basic facts of someone's life, such as age, income level, education, gender, ethnic background, location, and many other such (typically categorical) variables. They are almost always collected on consumer surveys, and they allow for useful breakdowns of market behavior; for example, to men vs. women or urban vs. rural. Note that geodemographic variables do *not* include descriptions of attitudes, intentions, or behavior.

geometric
A series in which each term is of the form ax^b, usually for b a positive integer (0, 1, 2,. . .); often used to smooth out or explain data taken over time.

Gumbel distribution
An uncommon distribution that nonetheless plays a key role in logistic regression; often called "extreme value" or "double exponential," with cumulative density function $F(x) = \exp[-\exp(-x)]$.

half-width
One half of a symmetric confidence interval, usually for the mean.

Heckman model
A statistical model that allows researchers to overcome and correct for certain types of selection bias, like the fact that lower-performing test-marketed products never make it to market to generate real sales data.

heterogeneity
A general term for when a group of items, people, variables, or statistically estimated quantities differ; often applied to differences in consumers, particularly in their reactions to the same marketing stimulus.

heterogeneity model
An explicit statistical model for how consumers' sensitivity to some stimulus (e.g., marketing variable) varies across the population. For example, we might say that "willingness to pay is normally distributed" in a particular population.

heteroscedasticity
When the errors in a regression model do not have the same variation for all combinations of the independent variables; can often be detected by seeing the residuals "fanning out."

hierarchical Bayes (HB) model
A powerful statistical platform for explaining complex marketing phenomena; essentially a hierarchical model estimated by Bayesian methods. A hallmark of HB models is that one can explain *coefficients* in terms of other explanatory variables; for example, your measured willingness to respond to a promotion is a function of, say, your income and shopping frequency. HB models almost always account for consumer preference heterogeneity as well.

hierarchical models
A form of statistical model in which the units form a natural hierarchy, each level of which can be modeled. For example, students are organized into classes, classes into grades, grades into schools, and schools into a city district. Variation in student performance can be accounted for (modeled) at each of these levels.

hierarchy-of-effects model
A hypothetical model of buyer response, moving from awareness to knowledge, liking to preference, and intention-to-buy to purchase, that is often applied to assess response to advertising.

histogram
A bar chart of observed frequencies for some variable of interest. The heights of the bars indicate the proportion (or sometimes the raw number) of cases observed in each predetermined category or interval.

history effect
The occurrence of events outside of, but taking place at the same time as, the experiment that can affect the dependent variable.

hypothesis
A specific statement about a set of measurable quantities, usually assessed by collecting data.

imputation
A method for filling in missing data, referring to various methods of substitution. A simple method of imputation replaces missing values with the average of the variable(s) in question. Sophisticated methods of *multiple imputation* have been developed, usually relying on some form of regression.

independent variables
Variables that can be controlled or measured, which one hopes to relate to the dependent variable, ordinarily via a statistical model.

indirect observation
Observing some indicator of behavior, as opposed to the behavior itself.

individual effect
In statistical models, when coefficients or other such measures can be calculated for specific units, as opposed to across the entire sample.

industrial research
Marketing research aimed not at individual consumers, but at interactions between firms and their representatives; for example, in so-called "B2B" contexts.

inferential statistics
A form of statistical analysis that relies on a sample to reach conclusions about a larger group (e.g., the population from which the sample was drawn).

information
The specific data required by decision-makers to reduce uncertainty in a known decision situation.

information needs
The specific information required to attain the stated objectives of a marketing research project.

inputs
Independent variables, such as the marketing mix, that feed into marketing systems and help managers to exert some degree of control over them.

Institutional Review Boards (IRBs)
A panel charged with reviewing research proposals in regard to their potential for psychological or physical harm and to safeguard the rights of potential participants.

instrumentation effect
In statistical models, an effect that arises when instruments, observers, or scorers change over the course of an experiment.

intelligence system
An integrated computer system/database that collects and stores recurring marketing data, interprets it for managers via statistical models, and provides a user interface for accessing the resulting information.

interaction effect
In statistical models, any effect whose values must be summarized based on the levels of more than one variable.

interactive testing effect
In an experiment, the effect of the test unit's pretreatment measurement on the reaction to the treatment; same as *reactive testing effect.*

intercept heterogeneity
In a statistical model, like regression, when each unit (e.g., person, firm, object) is allowed

to have its own intercept (i.e., the value when all regressors are zero).

interdependence methods
Any statistical method whose goal is to *interrelate* a group of variables, without attempting to use them to make predictions about another set of variables.

intermediate level of aggregation
In cluster analysis, finding a solution other than "all items are in a single cluster" and "each item is in its own cluster."

internal validity
A way to evaluate experiments by verifying that changes in the dependent or criterion variable truly arose from changes in the independent or treatment variables alone.

interval scale
A measurement scale for which differences in consecutive numbers assigned correspond to constant values in the phenomenon under study; e.g., the difference in the strength of a respondent's views between 1 and 2 on a seven-point interval scale should be the same as the difference between 5 and 6.

inverse square law
Any situation where an effect's strength drops off with the square of some quantity. For example, in statistics, if one wishes to halve the width of an interval given for some estimate (based on a random sample), one needs four times the sample size.

judgment samples
A type of nonprobability sample for which respondents or sample units are deliberately chosen to serve the research purpose.

K-means clustering
A form of cluster analysis where the items under study are broken into a fixed number of groups in an optimal way but not *hierarchically* (that is, the k-cluster solution will not generally form from the $(k + 1)$-cluster solution by having two of the latter's clusters merge).

labeled response categories
A method, often used to compensate for a respondent's reluctance to answer a sensitive question, that labels response options with letters or numbers and asks the respondent to refer to one of the labels.

latent class model
A type of statistical model that accounts for heterogeneity by dividing units (customers, firms, etc.) into a fixed number of groups; units in each group are assumed to have the same coefficients or characteristics.

latent variable
A variable, generally not part of the research design, that correlates with two variables under study and creates the impression that the two are related, when they may not be.

Latin square (LS) design
A type of experimental design in which the researcher needs to control for the effects of more than one extraneous variable.

least squares
A general principle used throughout statistical modeling, suggesting that one minimize the sum of squared deviations between observed values and those predicted by the model.

level
A special term for the values of variables used in a conjoint analysis, or any technique where the specific degrees of a product's features (attributes) need to be specified. Levels are keyed to product attributes; for example, for a food processor, the attribute *capacity* might take on *levels* of 1, 2, 4, or 8 liters.

Likert scale
Perhaps the most common scaling method in all of survey research. Numbers represent responses arranged symmetrically about some mid-point (which may not be explicitly on the scale itself, as in a 6-point scale) and, if possible, for which the points are equally spaced in terms of the respondent's underlying reactions. The prototypical example is the "agree–disagree" scale, usually with 5, 6, or 7 points, with verbal labels like "strongly disagree," "moderately disagree," and so forth.

linear correlation coefficient (r)
A measure of how much of the variation in one variable is explained by a simple linear regression on a second variable.

linear discriminant functions
Typically accompanies cluster analysis and provides a linear function of variables (like in an ordinary regression) that helps best discriminate the clusters from one another.

linear regression
The most common form of statistical model, in which a dependent variable, Y, is related to a group of independent variables, $\{X_1, X_2, \ldots, X_k\}$, as follows: $Y = b_0 + b_1X_1 + b_2X_2 + \ldots + b_kX_k + \varepsilon$, where ε represents error, usually normally distributed; the coefficients, $\{b_0, b_1, b_2, \ldots, b_k\}$, are estimated based on data from a sample.

linear transformation
Any transformation that involves taking variables or a group of numbers and either multiplying them by or adding to them some constant, e.g., $y = a + bx$.

log-likelihood function
In any statistical model, the logarithm of the probability of observing the sample data if the model is exactly correct.

logarithm of the odds (log-odds)
A way to transform probabilities, which must be between zero and one, so that they lie on the entire real line (i.e., from negative infinity to positive infinity), and so can be used as dependent variables in a regression. Formally, $\ln[p/(1 - p)]$ for any probability, p.

logically consistent
A model whose probabilistic predictions must all be positive and sum to one, an important property for models that predict probabilities of choice, or market share.

logistic regression (LOGIT model)
A widely used probabilistic model in marketing, used for predicting individual choice behavior, often for brands. The error distribution is double exponential, which yields simple formulas for all choice probabilities, unlike the probit model, which assumes normally distributed errors.

longitudinal research design
Research involving a sample of units (people, firms, products, etc.) selected from the population of interest and measured at multiple points in time, yielding a time-series for each.

loyalty variables
In brand choice models, a variable created from a household's choices that tracks how frequently each brand is bought by that household; often calculated as a time-discounted average over all past purchase occasions.

main effect
In a statistical model, any effect that takes the same value for all levels of a variable, regardless of the values of other variables.

main testing effect
Same as *direct testing effect;* involves the effect of an earlier observation on the subject's response at a later observation.

market potential
An estimate of the maximum possible sales of a product or service in a specific industry over a stated time period.

market research
The collection, storage, and analysis of data for a specific marketing and/or consumer group; often contrasted with *marketing research* by its limitation to a particular market or segment.

market-share studies
Research undertaken to determine potential demand estimates as a function of the marketing mix–in particular, various pricing levels. Can be accomplished readily in test markets, but is typically approached more affordably via various pre-marketing forecasting methods, for example, ASSESSOR.

marketing concept
A focus on the role of marketing mix variables (e.g., price, distribution, promotion) and not

merely what's "inside the box" in driving the success of a product.

marketing information systems
Large-scale databases and explicit procedures for the collection, storage, and analysis of data useful in making ongoing marketing decisions.

marketing management process
A process formally relating three ongoing, interactive elements: information inputs (from marketing research and managerial judgment), the decision-making process within the marketing organization, and the marketing system itself (marketing mix, situational Factors, performance measures, and behavioral responses).

marketing mix
The set of variables that a manager or firm can use to influence a marketing outcome of interest, usually sales or market share. Marketing mix variables usually comprise the "Four Ps"—price, product (characteristics, packaging), place (distribution channels), and promotion (consumer and trade)—as well as ad expenditures.

marketing research
The systematic process of using formal research and consistent data gathering to improve the marketing function within an organization. Information from marketing research is used to identify opportunities and problems; to monitor performance; and to link marketing inputs with outputs of interest, such as awareness, satisfaction, sales, share, and profitability.

marketing research system
The series of steps involved in a research project from inception to completion, including definition of a problem or opportunity, exploratory research, design of sample, survey and data collection method, data collection, data analysis, interpretation, and presentation of results.

marketing system
A conceptual model viewing the marketing mix (what managers can control: price, product, and so forth) and situational variables (what managers cannot control: competition, legal Factors, and so forth) as independent variables ("inputs") that give rise to consumers' behavioral responses, which in turn determine performance measures ("output variables"), such as sales, share, and profit levels.

Markov chain Monte Carlo (MCMC)
A common algorithm used in Bayesian analysis of statistical models, it allows the researcher to efficiently estimate models with a large number of parameters.

maturation effect
An effect similar to the history effect except that it pertains to changes in the experimental units themselves over time (e.g., getting older, developing fatigue, gaining experience, or learning).

mean/average
The most common measure of central tendency, in which one adds up all of a variable's values and divides by the number of values.

mean-squared-error (MSE)
In regression (and related statistical models), an estimate of variance left *unexplained* by the model; often described as the "spread" of the data around a regression line.

mean-squares
In statistical models, an estimate of an average squared distance, calculated by dividing a sum-of-squares by the associated degrees-of-freedom.

measurement error
Any source of error—either systematic or random—on an observed variable. It is often defined as the difference between the measured value of the variable and its true value.

median
A common measure of central tendency, the middle value of a variable in the sample. Exactly half the values fall above and half below the median.

metric equivalence
In cross-cultural research, when researchers can verify that psychometric properties of the data exhibit the same structure across cultures (e.g., when it can be shown that people in multiple countries use a seven-point agree–disagree scale in the same way).

MinEigen criterion
In Factor analysis, a rule suggesting one discard all Factors with eigenvalues less than 1.

modal answer
The most common of a set of responses.

mode
A common measure of central tendency, the most frequently occurring value of a variable in the sample.

monotonic transformation
Any process that takes one set of numbers and produces another from them so that if values taken from the first set are increasing, then the corresponding numbers from the second set will, too; common examples include the logarithm of squaring (for positive numbers) or exponentiating (for any numbers).

multicollinearity
A group of variables, each pair of which is moderately or highly correlated. There is no strict rule for how large such correlations should be, and in practice it is highly dependent on the research situation. Multicollinear data are often rectified using Factor analysis.

multidimensional scaling
A statistical technique that takes people's perceptions of the similarities (inverse distances) of pairs of objects and uses them to make a map of those objects in multidimensional space that preserves those distances as well as possible.

multinomial logit (MNL) model
A form of multinomial regression in which errors are a double-exponential distribution; exceptionally important in the analysis of scanner data and brand choice.

multinomial regression
A form of regression model in which the dependent variable is which option of a fixed set occurred.

multiple time-series design
A form of quasi experiment utilizing a time-series design in which the researcher has put together another group of test units to serve as a control group.

multiple-response (or multiple-choice) question
A question type requiring the respondent to choose from a fixed list of pre-established answers.

multiplication rule
A fundamental rule of probability stating that the probability of two *independent* events occurring is the product of their individual probabilities.

multivariate statistical procedure
Any statistical model that helps relate a set of variables to one another. The most common such procedure is multiple regression, in which a single dependent variable is related to a group of other variables.

mutually exclusive
When a variable is such that a respondent cannot assign two values simultaneously—for example, age categories (because one cannot be two ages at once).

natural observation
Observing behavior as it takes place in its typical environment (e.g., consumers while they are shopping at the grocery store).

nominal scale
A measurement scale for which numbers are assigned to objects only as labels.

nonequivalent control group design
A quasi-experimental design involving a control group that does not have preexperimental test unit selection equivalence to the experimental group (often because the groups were convenience or self-selected, rather than random, samples); both the experimental group and the control group are given pretest and posttest measurements.

nonnormality
When the graphed distribution of some variable deviates from a normal distribution. See *normal probability plot*.

nonprobability sampling
A method of choosing a sample that does not assure an equal likelihood of participation of

all population elements; usually allows for some degree of personal judgment in selecting the sample.

non-response error
A form of "non-sampling error" that occurs when some elements meant to be included in the sample are either unavailable for measurement or choose not to reply.

non-sampling error
Any error that occurs that is not due to the vagaries of sampling itself. Non-sampling errors can introduce biases of unknown direction and magnitude, and they can arise because of faulty or incorrect problem definition, a non-representative sampling frame, non-response or measurement errors, poor questionnaire design, improper causal inferences, or even poor arithmetic.

normal probability plot
A histogram (i.e., frequency-based bar chart) of the residuals in a regression, superimposed against the best-fitting normal distribution; a visual aid to determine whether the regression assumption that the errors are normally distributed is violated.

normal viewing environment method
A form of advertising research that measures audience reactions, as in their own homes rather than in an unfamiliar environment.

normalized centroid distance (NCD)
In cluster analysis, a measure of how far apart two cluster centers are. Small values of NCD indicate items that will likely wind up in the same cluster.

null hypothesis
A specific statement, opposed to the "alternative hypothesis," subjected to statistical test. The null hypothesis typically states that there is no effect (i.e., the effect equals zero), or that two quantities are equal to one another (i.e., their difference is zero), and this is what the researcher wishes to cast doubt on through data collection and statistical testing.

objective
A key criterion of marketing research that involves careful screening of possible biases, as well as impartial application of quantifiable empirical methods during the design, implementation, interpretation, and presentation of a research project.

omnibus panel
A group of respondents whose measurements are taken repeatedly over time, such as in a longitudinal study, but with the important proviso that the *variables* on which they are measured can change from one time to the next.

one-group pretest–posttest design
A simple form of preexperimental design, equivalent to a one-shot case study design but where an additional pretest measurement is taken before the treatment.

one-shot case study design
A simple form of preexperimental design where a single group of test units is first exposed to a treatment and a measurement is then taken on the dependent variables; there is no random assignment of test units to the treatment group.

one-tailed test
A statistical test of a hypothesis that specifies a direction (e.g., that some parameter's value is specifically greater than zero).

open-ended (or free-response or free-answer) question
A question design that allows respondents to provide answers freely, in their own words, instead of choosing among various options defined by the interviewer.

operational definition
Specifies how a construct is to be measured; defines or gives meaning to a variable by spelling out what the investigator must do to measure it.

opportunities
Situations in which a company can improve its performance by adopting a new course of action, usually stated in terms of changes in its marketing mix.

ordered dependent variable
A variable one wishes to predict that has some natural ordering, such as a Likert or frequency scale.

ordered logit model
An ordinal regression in which errors have a double-exponential distribution.

ordered probit model
An ordinal regression in which errors are normally distributed.

ordinal regression
A form of regression analysis in which the dependent variable is in some natural order, such as a 7-point scale (not to be confused with a *rank-ordered* dependent variable, for which we use a rank-ordered or exploded regression model).

ordinal scale
A measurement scale for which numbers are assigned to objects based on their order (i.e., greater than or less than) or direction.

orthogonal
Any quantities that are uncorrelated, and therefore perpendicular to one another when placed in the appropriate multidimensional space. Often used in Factor analysis when Factors are uncorrelated with one another, and also in experiments (e.g., conjoint analysis) that use orthogonal designs.

orthogonal design
A design for which, when several quantities have to be measured in an experiment, manipulations of one quantity will not affect measurements of another; often allows a dramatic drop in the overall number of measurements that must be taken.

outliers
An observation whose value is very different from others collected (or what would be expected, based on a statistical model), so much so that the researcher must decide whether to remove it to mitigate its influence.

p-value
A crucial quantity in any statistical test, distilling how strong the evidence is in favor of some quantity not being zero (in the population, based on one's sample data). All regression programs report *p* values for each coefficient and for the entire model.

panel
A group of respondents who have agreed in advance to offer data to a specific researcher. Panels are common in supermarket purchases (so-called scanner panels), media assessment (e.g., Nielsen households), and online. They allow researchers to have a stable set of respondents whose core characteristics are already known, and so do not need to be measured afresh each time data are collected. They also provide individual-level response histories, allowing changes to be accurately assessed over time.

pantry audit
In consumer research, when a researcher or observer asks respondents for permission to inspect their pantries for certain types of products because such information cannot be obtained from scanner records or simply by asking.

parameter
Any population-level quantity in a statistical model that will be estimated using sample data.

part worths
In conjoint analysis, the utilities associated with particular levels of any attribute.

perceptual maps
A two- or higher-dimensional visualization of an entire market or category that can be created by working with an explicit set of attributes (e.g., durability and effectiveness) or by implicit or latent scaling techniques (e.g., multidimensional scaling).

performance measures
The output variables of the marketing system, including brand equity, consumer satisfaction or loyalty, sales, share, and profit levels.

periodicity
A problem in systematic sampling, often causing bias, that can occur when cyclical patterns in a population coincide with a multiple of the sampling frame.

Poisson or count regression
A type of regression analysis where the dependent variable is the *number of times* a particular event occurred.

polynomial regressions
A multiple linear regression in which some or all of the independent variables are powers of another variable; that is, they include $\{X, X^2, X^3, \ldots, X^k\}$. Interpreting the coefficients of these powers can be difficult, due to multicollinearity.

population
The total set of elements about which one can make inference, by using a sample (randomly) drawn from it.

population definition
Identification of the group to be studied directly by a marketing research project.

population parameter
Any quantity that could be determined (with certainty) by having data from the entire population, not merely a sample drawn from it.

population value
The value a statistic would take on if the sample were the entire population.

position bias
When a respondent's answer to some question is affected by the order of the question in the survey or the order of a set of presented answers.

posterior distribution
In a Bayesian statistical analysis, the distribution of some parameter *after* data have been observed; the *prior* is updated by the data to become the *posterior*.

posttest-only control group design
An experimental design in which randomly assigned groups receive only a posttest measurement; equivalent to the last two groups of a Solomon four-group design.

power of the test
Formally, the probability of rejecting the null hypothesis when it is false; usually denoted by $(1 - \beta)$ (where β is the probability of Type II error, *not* a regression coefficient, which sometimes uses the same symbol).

precision
Half the width of a (symmetric) confidence interval.

prediction interval
In a regression analysis, an interval offering a $(1 - \alpha)$ probability of containing the dependent variable, given specific values of all independent variables; used to make predictions about *single* outcomes (as opposed to confidence intervals, which make predictions about *means* of many outcomes).

predictive validity
A form of construct validity, also called pragmatic or criterion-related validity, that occurs when a measure can accurately predict what theory says it should.

pretest–posttest control group design
An experimental design in which all extraneous variables operate equally on both the experimental group and the control group; the only difference between the groups is the presentation of the treatment to the experimental group.

pretesting
Running a smaller experiment before the main one, so as to quickly and inexpensively perform critical measurements that may affect how the main test is conducted.

pricing research
Research undertaken to determine viable pricing levels for a product or service, especially the expected sales and share levels associated with each.

primacy bias
A survey bias that results when respondents have better memory of or preference for the response options listed earliest.

principal components methodology
A type of Factor analysis procedure, typically the initial one performed, in which each successive Factor is the best that can be extracted, but without regard to how well the Factors correlate with the input variables. See *varimax rotation*.

priors
In a Bayesian statistical analysis, priors represent the researchers' beliefs about model quantities (parameters) before any data are collected. After data are collected, the priors are "updated" to form *posteriors,* on which all statistical inference is based.

probabilistic causation
The notion, common in philosophy of science, that research can never truly prove causality, only infer it with some degree of confidence.

probability proportionate to size (PPS)
A two-stage area sampling method that promotes equal probability of any element being selected at the second stage. For the first stage, clusters are assigned a probability of selection in proportion to the number of second-stage elements they contain. In the second stage, the same number of units is sampled from each selected cluster.

probability sampling
A method of sampling relying on random selection, in which each population element has a known, ordinarily equal, chance of being included in the sample.

probit model
A probabilistic model used for predicting individual choice behavior, often for brands. The error distribution is normal, which introduces computational complexity, compared with the more common *logit* model.

problem definition
A crucial step in the marketing research process that precisely identifies the problem to be studied and solved via the acquisition and analysis of data.

problems
Conditions resulting in decreased performance (assessed by standard output measures) that may be rectified through alternate courses of action.

product recommendation systems
Statistical models that predict which products a target customer may like by examining the preferences and purchases of similar consumers.

proportionate stratified sampling
A sampling method that allocates sample size to strata in proportion to the number of population elements in the strata.

pseudo-research
Projects presented as true marketing research that are aimed toward goals unrelated to reducing uncertainty in a decision situation or to meeting the stated information needs of the research.

psychogalvanometer
A device used in experimental research to measure perspiration rate.

psychographics
In consumer research, any variables that help convey individuals' personality or lifestyle; sometimes referred to as IAO variables (interests, attitudes, opinions) variables.

pupilometer
Used often in advertising research, a device that measures a respondent's pupil dilation, thereby helping to indicate attention and interest in a visual stimulus (e.g., a print or TV ad).

quality of data
The degree to which the data are not explicitly biased by the choice of a particular communication approach (e.g., mail, phone, or Internet survey).

quasi-experimental design
A research design that appears to be true experimentation but that relies on nonrandom assignment: the researcher has control over data collection procedures but neither over the scheduling of treatments nor the assignment of respondents to treatment groups.

quota samples
A method of nonprobability sampling in which respondents or units are included until a prespecified number or proportion is attained in each group.

randomized block design (RBD)
An experimental design where test units are combined into blocks based on an external criterion, with blocks formed so that the test units' scores should vary less within a block than in the group as a whole.

randomized response technique
A survey technique in which respondents are presented with pairs of questions, one that they may be reluctant to answer (i.e., because of embarrassment or unwillingness to disclose) and one that is innocuous; which they are assigned to answer is determined randomly—for example, by a coin flip.

rank-order technique
When the respondent is asked to place various objects or items in strict order with regard to the criterion (attitudes, opinions, beliefs, etc.) in question.

rank-ordered or exploded logit regression model
A type of regression model that can be applied to a rank-ordered *dependent* variable (e.g., "rank the following set of items in order of your preference").

ratio scale
A measurement scale in which the values assigned to choices or objects possess an absolute zero point, so that both differences and quotients of scale points make sense; e.g., it makes sense to say someone is twice as old as someone else, or lives half as far away, indicating that age and distance are ratio-scaled variables.

reactive testing effect
When a test unit's pretreatment measurement affects its reaction to the treatment; same as *interactive testing effect*.

recency bias
A survey bias that results from a respondent having better memory of, or greater preference for, the response options listed most recently.

recognition
A method of stimulating a respondent's recall of an event (often, seeing an advertisement) that involves direct reference to that event, such as showing the respondent the actual ad, or some part thereof, and asking if the respondent has seen it before.

recruited audience method
A form of advertising research that measures audience reactions in a controlled environment outside their homes.

regression analysis
A powerful, general, and common form of statistical analysis that enables the researcher to model the effects of numerous independent variables on a group of dependent variables, quantifying their individual and joint effects.

regression line
A straight line that represents the idealized relationship between a set of variables, given that they are interval scaled and related linearly to one another.

relative allowable error
When the error permitted in a measurement is stated relative to the mean of the quantity measured.

relative frequency
The number of times an event occurred during a study or experiment, divided by the total number of opportunities for occurrence (or by the total number of events that did occur).

relative precision
The precision of an estimate expressed as a proportion or percentage of its mean.

reliability
The degree to which a variable is consistent in repeated measurements taken under identical conditions.

reporting bias
When results are selected for publication based on whether they confirm a favored hypothesis or when nonconfirmatory results are suppressed.

research design
The general plan guiding the data collection and analysis phases of the research; a framework that specifies the type of information to be collected, the sources of data, and all data collection procedures and analysis.

research director
A marketing research position that involves the management of a research department.

research process
The series of steps involved in a research project from inception to completion, including definition of a problem or opportunity, exploratory research, design of sample, survey and data collection method, data collection, data analysis, interpretation, and presentation of results.

research proposal
A document submitted by a marketing research firm to a potential client, detailing the problem, objectives, possible courses of action, information needs, personnel qualifications of the research team, budget, and timeline of deliverables for the research project.

research supplier
Marketing research institutions that perform research for client organizations.

residual error
In any statistical model, how far the model's predicted or estimated value falls from the true, observed value.

response bias
A tendency on the part of a respondent, either conscious or unconscious, to mis-report the quantity the researcher is attempting to measure.

response rate
The proportion of the anticipated sample (i.e., the sampling frame) for which data are actually collected.

robustness
Any statistic whose value resists dramatic change in the presence of outliers.

rotated Factor pattern
In Factor analysis, the set of Factor loadings obtained after the Factors are rotated (usually to aid in interpretation).

sales analysis
A large-scale study of a firm's sales data, across business units, products, over time, or with competitive figures.

sample
The units selected by the researcher, usually at random from some target population, to participate in the research study.

sample control
In survey-based research, the ability to reach the designated units in the sampling plan effectively and efficiently.

sample proportion
The number of successes (i.e., ones, positive outcomes, yeses, etc.) in a sample divided by the sample size; usually denoted by p.

sample value
The value of a statistic within a particular sample drawn from a target population.

sampling distribution
The distribution one would achieve if one took a very large (or infinite) number of samples of the same size from the population and calculated the value of some statistic (e.g., the mean) for each.

sampling error
The error in any measurement associated only with the randomness intrinsic to sampling itself. Often defined as the difference between the observed value of a variable and the *long-run average* of its repeated measurement.

sampling frame
The list of units from which a sample will be drawn.

sampling unit
The elements available for inclusion in a sample at some stage of the sampling process; nonoverlapping groups of elements from the population.

scalability
The ability for a project or process to be substantially expanded as required by the

researcher; some methods, such as conducting one-on-one interviews using the same interviewer, are not easily scalable, whereas others, such as Internet-based surveys, are.

scale independent
When a statistic's value does not change when the scale of measurement does (e.g., from pounds to kilograms).

scenario analysis
Assessing how results change when input quantities are assumed to take on a variety of different values (e.g., how a product's sales projections change at various price levels).

Scree plot
In Factor analysis, an aid to help visualize how quickly the quality of the Factors (i.e., their eigenvalues) are degrading. Used to help select a suitable number of Factors.

secondary data
Data collected, usually by an outside firm, for some purpose other than the study at hand (e.g., the U.S. Census). Secondary data are the appropriate starting point for almost all marketing research projects.

segmentation
The ability to break a market, consumers, or sets of objects into groups; these groups should be relatively homogeneous in terms of the criteria chosen by the researcher—e.g., demographics, behavior, prior experience—and differ substantively across the groups.

selection bias correction models
Statistical models that help compensate for the effects of a nonrandom sample caused by different types of selection bias. The most common example is the Heckman model.

selection bias
Any of a number of possible Factors that result in a non-random sample being selected from the target population, thereby causing an inaccurate measurement in a desired output.

self-reference criteria
In cross-cultural research, any references to one's own cultural values that are ordinarily taken for granted.

self-selection bias
Sample selection arises when some respondents, firms, or other entities decide not to supply data for reasons related to the study itself or to any variable germane to the research study. The resulting data will not only fail to be a random sample of the underlying population, but will typically lead to biased results.

semantic differential scale
A question type in which respondents assess an object in terms of where it falls between two opposed (bipolar) adjectives (e.g., "male–female" or "costly–inexpensive").

sensitivity analysis
An analysis performed to gauge the effects of *assumed parameter values or assumptions* on a final answer, policy, or other dependent variable. For example, if we have assumed that 10 percent of people will reply to a survey, to calculate total costs, a sensitivity analysis would ask how much costs might change for each 1 percent difference in response rates in the range 5 percent–15 percent.

sequence bias
When responses to a questionnaire are affected by the order in which questions or choices appear; often addressed by counterbalancing.

significance level
Formally, the greatest probability a researcher sets of rejecting the null hypothesis, even though it happens to be true; usually denoted by α and frequently set in applied work at 0.05 or 0.01; also can refer to the *p*-value of a statistical test.

simple linear regression
A linear regression model with only one regressor (independent variable).

simple random sampling
A method of probability sampling where (1) every element has an equal chance of being selected, and (2) every possible sample of size *n* has an equal chance of being drawn.

situation analysis
The use of present and/or historical data to determine which variables and Factors affect business performance; often aided by SWOT (strengths, weaknesses, opportunities, and treats) analysis to identify both internal and external Factors.

situational Factors
Independent variables that feed into the marketing system from the general business environment and which are therefore less affected or controlled by the choices of any single firm. These include demand; competition; the legal, political, and economic climates; technological innovations; and governmental regulation.

single source
A type of data stemming from one research provider alone, who has either collected comprehensive data directly or skillfully aggregated it from multiple sources.

slope heterogeneity
In a statistical model, when different units (e.g., people, firms, products) are each allowed to have their own coefficients. Such models require multiple observations per unit and can be difficult to estimate quickly.

Solomon four-group design
An experimental design that controls for extraneous variable effects, as well as interactive testing effects. It involves four groups, two of which receive the treatment; one treatment group and one control group receive a pretest, whereas the others do not.

splines
A powerful method used in economics and statistics to draw complex curves and surfaces through sets of data points.

split-half reliability
A method of testing reliability where a multi-item measurement device is divided into equivalent groups and the item responses are compared among the groups.

standard deviation
A very common measure of *dispersion* around the central tendency (the mean). Equal to the square root of the variance (i.e., the square root of the average of the sum-of-squared deviations from the sample or population mean).

standard error
How much an estimator or any statistic would vary if it were repeatedly calculated from samples drawn in an identical manner from the population; tends to decrease with sample size because larger samples tend to display less variability from one to the other.

standardized residual
In regression, dividing the residuals by their own standard deviation, so that they have a mean of zero and a standard deviation of one. See *z-transform*.

static-group comparison design
An experimental design in which two treatment groups, one that has been exposed to the treatment and one that has not, are observed after the treatment has been presented.

statistic
Any quantity estimated from data.

statistical-regression effects
When, in an experiment, test units are selected (for exposure to the treatment) based on an extreme pretreatment score; usually considered poor research practice.

stepwise regression
A set of techniques for automatically determining a good-fitting statistical model by successively including or removing independent variables from the estimation; often regarded with suspicion because it cannot ensure that the resulting model is substantively meaningful, only that it happens to fit the sample data well.

stratification variable
A variable used to define different strata (groups) in the population for the purposes of statistical analysis.

stratified random sampling
A sampling method that divides the target population into (relatively homogeneous)

subgroups, then takes a simple random sample from each; helps reduce overall error in estimates based on the sample.

stress
In multidimensional scaling, a measure of how well the derived MDS map actually represents the original (pairwise similarity or distance) data; this helps determine the appropriate number of dimensions for the map.

structured observation
When conducting (or analyzing) focus groups or sets of depth interviews, using predetermined protocols to determine the entire course of the interaction.

study population
The elements of a population from which a sample is actually selected (ideally the same as the population itself).

subjective estimate
When the researcher uses experience and judgment to estimate the degree of nonresponse error; requires sufficient (historical) experience with the phenomenon under study.

subsample measurement
A method for estimating the degree of nonresponse error, wherein a specially designed telephone or personal interview is used to estimate the results of the nonrespondent group; the resulting estimate is then incorporated into the data set of those who did respond.

sum of squares
In statistics, a common measure of dispersion, formed by squaring each of a set of quantities and adding them up; the mean of the quantities is ordinarily subtracted from each beforehand.

survey research design
A common marketing research design that involves a (cross-sectional) sample of various population subgroups at a particular moment in time.

symptoms
Marketing measures, often those of particular concern (e.g., decreasing sales or loyalty), which in themselves lack meaningful information for improving management decisions, but that signal that corrective action may need to be undertaken.

systematic
The requirements that a research project be planned and well-organized, the strategic and tactical aspects of the research designed in advance, the nature of the data gathered, and the mode of analysis pre-determined.

systematic error
An error in measurement attributable to a consistent bias, one not attributable merely to the randomness of the sampling process.

***t*-test**
A statistical test performed on sample means (or differences of them), when the population variance is unknown; commonly applied in the form of a "two sample" *t*-test, in ANOVA, and for regression coefficients.

***t*-value or *t*-statistic**
Refers to a point on the *t* distribution (with k degrees of freedom) corresponding to the number of standard deviations away from the mean some statistic is observed to be. One uses a *t*-value when the population standard deviation is not known and is instead estimated from a sample.

technical specialist
A marketing research position that involves providing expertise in solving a specialized aspect of marketing research, such as questionnaire design or sampling.

test unit mortality
A serious problem that occurs when test units withdraw from an experiment before their role is completed.

test units
In experimental design, the entities to whom (or to which) treatments are presented and whose response to the treatments is measured; in practice, these are typically people, products, or firms.

test–retest reliability
Repeatedly measuring the same person or group, using the same scaling device, under similar conditions, and comparing results; the greater the discrepancy, the greater the random error in the measurement process and the lower the reliability.

testing effect
An effect that can come about when the pretest itself exerts an influence on how participants perform on the posttest (e.g., when both are tests of the same skill and participants learn from the pretest).

time referent
An important element in questions referring to past behavior, specifying a time interval (e.g., "in the last year") during which the behavior took place.

time-series experiment
An experiment in which data are collected at various points in time, ordinarily for the same set of variables and multiple test units.

traditional panel
A group of respondents whose measurements are taken repeatedly over time, using the same variables.

transformation or transform
Any mathematical relationship (i.e., a formula) applied to a set of values or a variable. Among the most useful transformations in data analysis are $\log(x)$, $\exp(x)$, and x^k, for k a whole number greater than 1.

treatments
In experimental design, treatments are the manipulated alternatives or independent variables whose effects are then measured.

trend projection
A method for estimating the degree of nonresponse error. If a trend is apparent in the variables of interest in the respondent group, it can be used to estimate the characteristics of the nonrespondent group.

two-tailed test
A statistical test of a hypothesis that does not specify a direction (e.g., that some parameter's value is not equal to zero, where values both greater than zero or less than zero can invalidate the hypothesis).

Type I error (α)
The probability that the null hypothesis is (incorrectly) rejected when it is true; also known as alpha (α) error; analogous to "convicting the innocent."

Type II error (β)
The probability that one (incorrectly) fails to reject the null hypothesis when it is not true; also known as beta (β) error; analogous to "failing to convict the guilty."

unaided recall test
A test of ad effectiveness that does not allow for any form of "prompting" or cueing (i.e., no relevant information is provided that might help jog the memory) when requesting that respondents recall any ad messages they remember being exposed to (seeing or hearing) during a stated time period.

unidimensional measures
Measures of some variable that result in a single score on a predefined numerical scale.

units of analysis
The main entity being analyzed in the course of a research project; usually the "lowest level" of data available, with other comparisons based on aggregation. In marketing applications, the unit of analysis may be consumers, groups/segments, locations, salespeople, stores, or channel members.

universality
One of the fairness criteria referenced in Arrow's impossibility theorem. It requires that a voting system (1) produce a ranking of all possible choices relative to one another, (2) be capable of processing all possible voter preferences, and (3) always produce the same result for the same set of votes; sometimes called "unrestricted domain."

unrepresentative sampling
A frequent problem in panels, where those likely to take part do not represent the general population due, for example, to a greater sensitivity to inducements or a general willingness to have their purchases and behavior recorded.

unstructured observation
When conducting (or analyzing) focus groups or sets of depth interviews, using no predetermined protocols and allowing questions to be formulated naturally as the interview progresses.

valence
Property of a scale that everyone would agree is ordered in some meaningful way; e.g., everyone would agree that a lower price is more attractive than a higher one, all else being equal. However, people might differ as to whether "traditional" or "contemporary" was superior, so this would not be a valenced scale.

variable
Anything that can take on different (usually numerical) values. In marketing, age, gender, price, package size, sales, and share are commonly used variables.

variance
A very common measure of *dispersion* around the central tendency (the mean); equal to the square of the standard deviation (i.e., the average of the sum-of-squared deviations from the sample or population mean).

varimax rotation
A method used in Factor analysis that allows the resulting Factors to have the greatest interpretability—while still remaining uncorrelated with one another—by getting the Factor loadings to be as close to −1, 0, or 1 as possible.

Weighted Least Squares (WLS) model
A method of regression where certain data points are given more emphasis than others. The corresponding "weight" is typically the inverse of how much variability there is at that particular point so that lower variance observations have more influence on the parameter estimates.

weighted sum or weighted average
Multiplying a set of quantities by positive numerical weights, to emphasize some over others, yields a weighted *sum;* dividing by the sum of those weights yields a weighted *average*.

White test
Like the *Breusch-Pagan test*, a common and widely-supported method for assessing whether heteroscedasticity is present in a regression analysis. The White test regresses the squared residuals from a regression onto the original regressors, their squares, and their products (i.e., interactions); a significant *F*-test suggests the presence of heteroscedasticity.

X-O-R syntax
A special shorthand used to convey experimental designs: *X* represents the exposure of a test group to an experimental treatment; *O* refers to processes of observation or measurement of the dependent variable on the test units; *R* indicates that individuals have been assigned at random to separate treatment groups or that groups themselves have been allocated at random to separate treatments.

z-test
If a variable has a standard normal (*z*) distribution, one can test the null hypothesis of whether it is equal to zero by checking values on a standard normal table or by computer.

z-transform
When a variable is normally distributed, it can be made to have a (i.e., transformed to) standard normal (*z*) distribution by subtracting its mean and dividing by its standard deviation. These standard normally distributed quantities—which can have any positive or negative value—can then be converted to probabilities (which lie between 0 and 1). (Note that this differs from Fisher's *z*-transform of the sample correlation *r*: $z = (1/2) \ln[(1 + r) / (1 - r)]$, and also from the *z*-transform common in signal processing.)

z-value or *z*-statistic
Refers to a point on the *standard normal distribution*, corresponding to the number of standard deviations away from the mean some *normally distributed* statistic is observed to be. One uses a *z*-value when either (1) the population standard deviation is known or (2) when the sample is quite large.

Name Index

Subject Index